D1611360

A History of
Economic Reasoning

A HISTORY OF
ECONOMIC REASONING

Karl Pribram

THE JOHNS HOPKINS UNIVERSITY PRESS
Baltimore and London

This book has been brought to publication with the generous
assistance of the National Endowment for the Humanities.

The Johns Hopkins University Press, 701 West 40th Street,
Baltimore, Maryland 21211
The Johns Hopkins Press Ltd., London

The paper used in this publication meets the minimum requirements of American National
Standard for Information Sciences—Permanence of Paper for Printed Library Materials,
ANSI Z39.48-1984.

Library of Congress Cataloging in Publication Data

Pribram, Karl, 1877–1973
A history of economic reasoning

Bibliography: p. 737
Includes index.
1. Economics—History. I. Title.
HB75.P735 1983   330′.09   82–13042
ISBN 0–8018-2291-2

Contents

Publisher's Preface *xiii*
Author's Preface *xvii*
Biographical Introduction *xix*
Overview: A Summary of A History of Economic Reasoning *xlix*

BOOK ONE. The Development of Economics into an
Independent Discipline, Thirteenth through
Eighteenth Centuries *1*

Part I. *Economics As an Element of Moral Theology* *3*
Chapter 1. Thomistic Economics *3*
The logical background of Thomistic
economics *3*
The Thomistic conception of social
collectivities *7*
The conception of private property *10*
The Thomistic doctrine of value *12*
The doctrine of the just price *14*
The problem of unlawful profit *15*
The prohibition of usury *17*

Chapter 2. The Disintegration of Thomistic Reasoning *20*
The impact of nominalism *20*
Changing economic views *23*
Changes in economic institutions *25*
The School of Salamanca and the Jesuit
Scholastics *27*

Part II.   *The Development of Baconian and Cartesian*
            Economics   *31*
            Chapter 3.   The Transition Period (Fifteenth and Sixteenth
                         Centuries)   *31*
                         Changing and conflicting patterns of
                             thought   *31*
                         The "spirit of capitalism"   *38*
                         The economic views of early Mercantilists   *42*
                         The balance of trade concept   *45*
                         Colbertism   *49*
                         Changes in the conception of price, profit, and
                             interest on money   *52*

            Chapter 4.   Baconian Mercantilism   *55*
                         The territorial distribution of divergent patterns
                             of thought   *55*
                         The concept of natural law and the utilitarian
                             approach to social problems   *59*
                         Emergence of the empirical approach to
                             economics   *65*
                         Theories of value, price, money, and interest on
                             capital   *68*
                         The problem of fiduciary money   *73*
                         The problem of productive employment   *76*

            Chapter 5.   Refined Mercantilism   *79*
                         The problem of self-regulating forces   *79*
                         The last champions of mercantilism   *84*
                         Italian Mercantilists   *86*

            Chapter 6.   Cameralist Economics   *89*
                         The intellectual background of early
                             cameralism   *89*
                         Cameralism as an administrative discipline   *90*
                         Cameralism as a branch of higher learning   *93*

            Chapter 7.   Cartesian Economics   *97*
                         The reaction to Colbertism in France   *97*
                         Conflicting social philosophies in France   *99*
                         The philosophical background of Quesnay's
                             theories   *103*
                         The *tableau économique*   *104*
                         The socioeconomic doctrine of the
                             Physiocrats   *107*
                         The disintegration of the Physiocratic
                             doctrine   *113*

            Chapter 8.   The Concept of Subjective Value   *115*
                         Galiani's theory of money   *115*
                         Other adherents of the theory of subjective
                             value   *117*

Chapter 9.   The First Version of the Utilitarian Economic
             Doctrine   *120*
             The development of utilitarian reasoning   *120*
             Economics as an independent discipline: Adam
             Smith and *The Wealth of Nations*   125

BOOK TWO.   Conflicting Economic Doctrines
             (1800–1918)   *137*
   Part III. *Versions of the Utilitarian Economic Doctrine,
             1800–1870   139*
             Chapter 10. The Principles of Benthamite Economics   *139*
                          General utilitarian methodology   *139*
                          The methodological principles of Ricardian
                          economics   *143*

             Chapter 11. Ricardian Economics   *146*
                          The concept of exchange value   *146*
                          The Ricardian economic system   *150*
                          General disturbing factors: technological changes
                          and population movements   *152*
                          The laws of distribution   *154*
                          The role of money and credit   *161*
                          The theory of international trade   *164*

             Chapter 12. Early Discussions of Ricardian Economics   *166*
                          Short-run problems   *166*
                          Methodological issues   *169*
                          Utilitarian criticisms of the Ricardian
                          doctrine   *175*
                          Modifications of the Ricardian doctrine   *179*

             Chapter 13. The Spread of Smithian Economics   *190*
                          French and Italian versions of liberal
                          economics   *190*
                          Conflicting methods of theoretical analysis   *194*
                          The French Socialists   *196*
                          The German version of Smithian
                          economics   *200*
                          American discussions of Smithian
                          economics   *206*

   Part IV. *Organismic Economics   209*
             Chapter 14. The German Historical Schools   *209*
                          German ''idealistic'' philosophies   *209*
                          The emergence of historism   *212*
                          The program of the historicoethical school   *215*
                          Methodological issues   *219*

             Chapter 15. Versions of the Organismic Approach   *224*
                          Conflicting trends   *224*

The struggle for a "value-free" science   *228*
Discussion of economic theorems   *230*
Special problems   *235*
Liberal Socialists   *239*
Neoscholastic economics   *241*

Part V.   *Dialectic Economics*   *245*
           Chapter 16. The Marxian Doctrine   *245*
                        The philosophical background   *245*
                        The materialistic interpretation of history   *250*
                        The dialectic conception of the capitalist
                           economy   *253*
                        The breakdown theory   *259*
                        The class struggle   *262*

           Chapter 17. Versions of Marxism   *267*
                        The revisionist movement   *267*
                        Orthodox Marxism   *270*
                        The bolshevist version of Marxism   *272*

Part VI.   *Marginal Economics*   *277*
           Chapter 18. The Emergence of Schools of Marginal
                           Utility   *277*
                        The roots of marginal utility analysis   *277*
                        The utilitarian version of marginalism   *283*
                        The mathematical version of marginalism   *285*
                        The psychological version of marginalism   *289*

           Chapter 19. Post-Ricardian Economics   *292*
                        The intellectual climate of the Victorian
                           age   *292*
                        The methodology of Marshallian
                           economics   *298*
                        The Marshallian theory   *301*
                        Welfare economics   *306*

           Chapter 20. The Elaboration of Marginal Utility
                           Economics   *308*
                        The development of mathematical versions   *308*
                        General problems of psychological
                           marginalism   *314*
                        The rate of interest as a strategic factor   *319*

           Chapter 21. Problems of Marginal Analysis   *324*
                        Theories of distribution   *324*
                        Monetary problems   *332*
                        The quantity theory of money   *339*
                        The problem of business fluctuations   *343*

           Chapter 22. The American Approach to Marginalism   *352*

Chapter 23. Conflicting Trends   *355*
             Pragmatic economics   *355*
             Institutionalist economics   *358*
             Critical discussions of marginal utility
                 analysis   *362*

BOOK THREE.   Developments after the First World War   *369*
    Part VII.   *Organismic Economics   371*
             Chapter 24.   The Decline of the Historical School   *372*
                        Conflicting trends   *372*
                        Methodological problems of historism   *379*
                        Planning along organismic lines   *381*

             Chapter 25.   Totalitarian Economics   *385*
                        The problems of fascist economics   *385*
                        National-Socialist economics   *387*

    Part VIII.   *Dialectic Economics   393*
             Chapter 26.   Dialectic Reasoning in Western Europe   *393*

             Chapter 27.   Bolshevist Economics   *396*
                        Discussions of the transition period   *396*
                        The theoretical background of the five-year
                            plans   *399*
                        Problems of bolshevist planning   *403*
                        Changing interpretations   *407*

    Part IX.   *Hypothetical Economics   415*
             Chapter 28.   Methodological Issues   *415*
                        General observations   *415*
                        Methodological problems of marginalism   *417*
                        Institutionalist discussions   *424*
                        Methodological discussions of French
                            economists   *429*

             Chapter 29.   Further Discussion of Older Problems:
                        Production and Distribution   *435*
                        Distribution theory   *435*
                        Monopoly and competition   *443*

             Chapter 30.   Further Discussions of Older Problems: Planning
                            and Welfare   *454*
                        Discussion about Planning   *454*
                        Welfare   *461*

             Chapter 31.   Discussions about Money and Monetary
                        Reform   *467*
                        The quantity equations and the cash balance
                            approach   *467*

The income approach   *470*
Problems of monetary reform   *473*

Chapter 32.   Discussions about the Business Cycle   *475*
General observations   *475*
Simple monetary theories   *478*
Monetary double-system theories   *480*
Nonmonetary theories   *482*
Business cycle policies   *487*

Part X.   *The "New Economics"*   *489*
Chapter 33.   Discussions of the Stockholm School   *489*

Chapter 34.   Keynes's Theory of Employment, Interest, and Money   *496*

Chapter 35.   Discussions of the ''New Economics''   *503*
Interpretations of the Keynesian theory   *503*
The stagnation theorem   *509*
Summary and evaluation   *513*

Chapter 36.   Methodological Discussions of Dynamic Analysis   *515*
Dynamics versus statics   *515*
The dynamic elements of post-Keynesian economics   *519*

Chapter 37.   Dynamic Models   *521*
Models of the Keynesian type   *521*
Other dynamic models of the economy   *523*

Part XI.   *International Relations*   *531*
Chapter 38.   International Trade Theory   *531*
Appendix A. The theory of location   *542*
Appendix B. International monetary relations after the Second World War   *544*

Chapter 39.   Economic Growth and Economic Progress   *550*
Economic growth of industrialized countries   *550*
Economics growth of underdeveloped countries   *557*
Theories of economic progress   *560*

Chapter 40.   Econometric Problems   *562*

Chapter 41.   Theory of Decision Making   *572*
The theory of choice   *572*
The theory of games   *576*

Concluding Observations   *579*

Appendixes 585

Appendix A. Prolegomena to a History of Economic
Reasoning *585*
   Introduction *585*
   Baconian and Cartesian economics *587*
   Benthamite economics *591*
   Intuitional economics *594*
   Dialectic economics *596*
   Refinement of hypothetical reasoning *598*
   Modified Ricardian economics *603*
   Varying aspects of the equilibrium
     concept *605*
   Concluding observations *608*

Appendix B. Patterns of Economic Reasoning *610*
   The concept of economic equilibrium *612*
   The maximization principle *614*
   The notion of time *616*
   The concept of freedom *618*
   The concept of law *619*
   Conclusions *621*

Appendix C. Further Metaeconomic Concepts *621*
   Rationality *621*
   System *623*
   Development and evolution *626*
   Class *628*
   Value *629*

Notes *633*
Works by Karl Pribram *737*
Index *741*

Publisher's Preface

ONCE IN A WHILE there comes along the opportunity to publish a monumental work of scholarship. Such is the case with Karl Pribram's *History of Economic Reasoning,* a book that should be of interest not only to specialists in the history of economic thought but also to the members of the larger scholarly community. Pribram, who died in 1973, was one of those exceptional human beings who combined a life of scholarship with a life of public service. As we know from the following biographical note, he had been a professor of economics at the University of Frankfort before coming to the United States in 1933. Once settled in America, he applied his keen intelligence and broad learning to research and policy making, mostly in government agencies. His instrumental role in establishing the Austrian social security system made him an invaluable member of the infant U.S. Social Security Board and later a principal economist of the U.S. Tariff Commission. Yet, he never lost sight of his scholarly interests and continued to teach at local universities. F. A. Hayek has described him as "without exception the most learned person in the field."

The manuscript for *A History of Economic Reasoning,* like its author, has had an interesting history. Pribram's six previous books in German and English, on subjects ranging from the history of Austrian trade and manufacturing policies to the conflicting patterns of thought underlying Western thinking, began to reveal his mastery of the history of economic thought. In his retirement he set out to produce the history that he had sketched in "Prolegomena to a History of Economic Reasoning," published in *The Quarterly Journal of Economics* in 1951. Nine years after the appearance of this article, he submitted a draft of the book manuscript to a leading American university press, which had accepted it for publication. Being a stubborn perfectionist, Pribram continued to work on the text, which inevitably grew in length as he spun out the finer points of his discussion and added more details to the history. In 1973 the author died, leaving a text that was virtually complete except for a final editing and integrating of supplemental material. Later, when it realized that no final text was forthcoming and because of its own changing priorities, the above-mentioned publisher had to withdraw its interest in the manuscript.

This did not deter his widow, Mrs. Edith Pribram, an intellectual in her own right, from seeing her late husband's work brought to fruition. After the manuscript had remained untouched for a couple of years, she, with the assistance of a historian of economic thought, pulled much of the manuscript together. They were successful in rendering the typed pages into a complete, polished text, except for some supplemental material that was to be incorporated into book three. At this point, Mrs. Pribram sought out another publisher.

The working draft of *A History of Economic Reasoning* came to the attention of The Johns Hopkins University Press in June 1978. As the editors reviewed the material and obtained readings and comments from scholars in the field, they began to realize that they had in hand the last work of a preeminent scholar, whose contribution to scholarship was largely unknown in America (at least, in the American academe) because he had made his American career in government service instead of full-time university teaching. As Pribram's bibliography indicates, the work he published in Europe while he was still a professor at the University of Vienna and later at the University of Frankfort had been seminal for economics, economic thought, and social policy. Knowing that there was still much work to be done on the manuscript, yet also excited by its potential importance, the press set about its publication in cooperation with Mrs. Pribram.

The essential task for the editors in establishing the final manuscript was to preserve as much of the original text as possible, yet at the same time to make the text useful for potential readers. Very little of the author's style was touched in the copy editing. However, notes were corrected and an attempt was made to include as much bibliographical information as possible, information that the author perhaps intended to add before the book's publication. A number of pages left by the author appeared to be an updating of material for the draft of the last third of the book. In integrating the updated material into the text, the editors found that some sections had to be moved for the sake of clarity; a few sections were compressed; and one lengthy chapter was divided into two shorter chapters for the sake of readability. Very little of the author's original words was lost in the process, and no attempt was made to recast his thoughts or to restructure his arguments and discussion. The result is—apart from that elusive element of style which only an author can give to the final draft—a text that is as close to the author's intention as we can determine.

What makes this book unique? It goes beyond the confines of the history of economic reasoning. Pribram remarked that "the book is intended to show that economic reasoning has developed as an integral part of Western thinking and that the patterns used in analyzing the history of economic thought could be used equally for the analysis of the history of the social sciences." Thus, Pribram treated the whole pattern of economic reasoning in the context of the history of Western thought. In addition, he sought to provide the student and scholar of economics with a well-documented history of economic reasoning from the Middle Ages to the middle of the twentieth century. He wanted to make the main results of a vast economic literature available in the English, French, German, and Italian languages and thus have the book serve as a reference work.

The volume is divided into three parts, or "books." The first book, "The Development of Economics into an Independent Discipline," covers the period from the establishment of Thomistic doctrine, toward the end of the Middle Ages, to the emergence of economics as an independent discipline as taught by the Mercantilists, the French Physiocrats, the Cameralists, Adam Smith, and some Italian economists, toward the end of the eighteenth century. The second book, "Conflicting Economic Doctrines," comprising the nineteenth century, begins with an analysis of Ricardian economics and ends with the termination of the First World War. Three conflicting patterns of thought vied for prominence during this period: a hypothetical pattern of reasoning adopted by the Ricardian economists, their successors, and the various marginal utility schools; an organismic pattern endorsed by the members of the German historical school; and a dialectic pattern underlying the Marxian doctrine. The third book, "Developments after the First World War," covers the period from the end of the First World War to the middle of the twentieth century, a time that saw the rise and downfall of the fascist and national-socialist doctrines of Europe. The emergent struggle between the hypothetical and the dialectic patterns holds particular interest. Both are shown to be the object of remarkable developments: the dialectic pattern had to be adjusted to the task of organizing communist economies, and hypothetical economics, intended to explain the functioning of the free-exchange economy, underwent a considerable series of far-reaching changes, most recently in part under the influence of mathematical and econometric methods.

It appears that Pribram only began to draft an introduction to his book, so no full-scale and elaborated essay outlining the basic themes and theses of the book is included here. However, among his papers was found a summary of *A History of Economic Reasoning*. It may very well be that this was to serve as the outline of the introduction he intended to write. This summary appears as "Overview: A Summary of *A History of Economic Reasoning*," which opens the book. In addition, the reader will want to consult two articles reprinted in the appendixes: "Prolegomena to a History of Economic Reasoning" and "Patterns of Economic Development." These two articles together reflect the theoretical underpinnings of this volume.

Such a large publishing project as this one could not have been realized without the encouragement and diligent work of a number of people and organizations. Laurence Moss of Babson College, with a special research interest in the history of economic thought, offered valuable suggestions and solutions to the problems posed by an unfinished manuscript. Mrs. Edith Kornei Pribram, the author's widow, provided indispensable insight and information in the drafting of the biographical introduction. The book, however, would never have become a reality without the generous support of the National Endowment for the Humanities.

Author's Preface

THE PREPARATION of this book was closely related to the story of my life and my studies. It extended over almost half a century. I was trained in economics in the tradition of the Austrian school of Marginalism, and two masters of the school, Friedrich von Wieser and Eugen Böhm-Bawerk, drew my attention to the prominent role played by methodological issues in shaping the various economic problems. At the University of Berlin, where I spent a year of postgraduate studies, I was struck by the fundamental difference between the approach to economic research adopted by the German historical school and the principles of economic analysis applied by my Austrian teachers. The adherents of the historical school rejected the use of highly abstract notions as a starting point of deductive reasoning; they were looking for specific historical laws which in their view were instrumental in determining the economic and social developments of the various nations. The struggle over methods that was waged between the two schools appeared to center on the question of whether it was possible to grasp the full reality of economic phenomena and events with the aid of concepts of relatively low abstraction, or whether the search for "hypothetical" laws, based on the use of highly abstract concepts, was the only sound scientific procedure. The logical difficulties involved in the methodology of Gustav Schmoller's disciples became apparent when Max Weber and Werner Sombart advanced the battle cry in favor of a "value-free" social science of a nonhypothetical type.

Methodological problems of another kind were raised by members of a "Neo-scholastic" group, who endeavored to adjust some modern economic theorems to the moral precepts of the Thomistic doctrine. A third, apparently quite consistent approach to economic research was adopted by the followers of Karl Marx, who claimed for their method of dialectic materialism the capacity of providing full insight into the course of evolutionary social processes and their predetermined goal. They spurned the search for hypothetical laws and qualified it as the result of misleading processes of thinking which had been developed under the influence of capitalistic class interests.

Thus, at the beginning of the thirties, when I taught economics at the University of Frankfort a considerable number of widely divergent doctrines were represented at the economic faculties of German universities: post-Ricardian economics, the Austrian school and the school of Lausanne, several versions of historism, Neoscholastic economics, orthodox Marxism, and revisionism. It was obvious that radically different teachings were covered by the expression "economic science" and that the incompatible divergencies which existed between some of these teachings had their roots in factors outside the scope of economics strictly speaking. These factors could be found only in the history of Western reasoning, which had provided a common background for the development of all social sciences. I considered it a fascinating task to examine the various patterns of thought which prevailed in Western reasoning and to organize the history of economic doctrines in the light of these patterns. The irreconcilable antagonisms between different schools of economics could thus be related to deep-seated divergencies in forming fundamental economic concepts; the methods used in defining the objectives and problems of economic research could be regarded as the primary determinants in shaping the history of economic reasoning.

Was it not highly probable that the same intellectual movements which were responsible for the development of Ricardian economics and its successors had provided the incentives to the organization of the competitive exchange economy, as contrasted with Scholastic reasoning, which had supplied the intellectual basis for the feudal social order and medieval economics? The conception of the economy adopted by the historical school appeared to be reflected in the economic policy pursued by the German national socialist government. A distorted version of dialectic materialism was used to justify and implement the operation of the bolshevist planned economy. Consistent elaboration of these ideas led to the establishment of a chain of partly conflicting patterns of thought that have determined the intellectual movements of the Western world and that have been instrumental in shaping the development of economic doctrines and of various systems of economic organization. This book is an attempt to apply these ideas to the analysis of the history of economic reasoning.

Biographical
Introduction

KARL PRIBRAM'S long and fruitful life spanned almost a hundred years. It began in the last quarter of the nineteenth century, when the bourgeoisie enjoyed its phenomenal rise to prosperity in the large and powerful empires of Europe, and ended in the early 1970s, when the political power had shifted from Europe to the United States of America, and when the former colonies of the European powers were struggling for their own independent place in the scheme of things.

Over the years, Pribram's activities and writings reflected his keen observation of the changing scene, usually tempered by a philosophical bent of mind that saw the passing events in their historical, sociological, and intellectual context. His life was inextricably bound up in the social and political events and upheavals of his time, and can best be understood against that background. Throughout his active years he was a "useful economist," to borrow a well-known phrase, who combined an eminently practical career and factual writings with philosophical articles and books in which he developed his theory of the dichotomy of nominalism, or hypothetical thinking, and realism in the scholastic sense. He pursued these thoughts throughout his life, applying them to economics, statistics, and international and national politics. They permeate almost all of his writings since the early years of the century, when he began to publish. In his book *Conflicting Patterns of Thought,* which appeared in mid-century, in 1949, he applied his theory to the sociopolitical outlook of nations. Two years later, in 1951, he developed his ideas, in some detail, for the science of economics in his article "Prolegomena for a History of Economic Reasoning," published in the *Quarterly Journal of Economics.* It forms the outline for the present book.

Karl Pribram was born in Prague on 2 December 1877, the eldest son of a prominent and prosperous lawyer. Prague, the capital of Bohemia, was the economic and cultural center of Austria's richest and most important province. Prague's population was to a very large extent German speaking. In the surrounding countryside and the smaller cities Czech was predominately spoken, though there were important and populous German enclaves.

xix

Agriculture and industry flourished throughout the region, together with Czech nationalism. Prague not only managed and directed the country's bountiful output, but also
produced some of the best German writers through several generations.

Karl Pribram had two brothers and a sister. Their mother died before the children had
reached adolescence. The household, thereafter, was efficiently run by housekeepers and
the necessary subordinate personnel, all overseen by their father. It had a distinct mas-
culine flavor, with superfluous frivolities omitted. Nevertheless, there were sporadic
parties to celebrate a special occasion or for no occasion at all. The young people were
expected to write their own plays, poems, or music for these events. Karl Pribram retained
a facility for witty verses, doggerels, and similar compositions, often in a mixture of
languages, throughout his life from this experience.

He and his brothers received the well-rounded "classical" education, usual in upper-
middle-class circles. They attended the *gymnasium* with its mandatory instruction in
Latin, Greek, and logic, as important parts of the curriculum. Czech was evidently also
learned at school; he had a good, though not perfect, knowledge of it. Other modern
languages, such as French and English, were taught at home by tutors, or in classes at
private establishments; the social graces, like music and dancing, received equal attention. Later, during his university years, his calendar was dotted with large balls and
dances at private homes. Vacations were devoted to sports, like mountaineering, skiing,
hiking, swimming, riding, and tennis. He excelled in some of these sports, without
making much of it, and kept at them fairly regularly, in a casual way, until well into his
old age.

After the gymnasium, he entered the German university of Prague for the study of
jurisprudence. This field included economics, a subject that, at that time, was not taught
independently at most Central European universities. In Austria it was regularly attached
to the legal faculty; some German universities combined it with their philosophical departments. Almost all independent faculties for economics on the European continent were
established only after the First World War. Among Pribram's most notable teachers was
Friedrich von Wieser, who held the chair for economics in Prague for many years before
being called to the University of Vienna, as the successor of the highly respected Carl
Menger.

The German University of Prague was famous and among the oldest in Central
Europe, vying with that of Vienna for historical precedence. Both were founded around
the middle of the fourteenth century. Prague also had a Czech university of recent origin,
established in 1882, under pressure from Czech nationalistic forces. The friction between
the German-speaking and the Czech-speaking populations of Prague was quite noticeable
even in Karl Pribram's childhood. It grew in intensity with the passage of time and led to
occasional sharp clashes between the students of the two universities. Karl Pribram,
beginning in his formative years, was a strong believer in the civilizing influence of the
Austrian empire, which held its multinational and multilingual country together as a
bulwark for Europe against the threats from the East: against various invaders in the dim
past; against the Ottoman empire in earlier centuries, up to the very end of the seventeenth; and against the Soviet encroachment in his own lifetime. He considered the
nationalist Czech movement a serious danger to the very fabric of the Austrian empire
and, beyond that, to all of Central Europe. Some fifteen years later, when Czech nationalism turned into separatism during the First World War, his serious misgivings were borne
out.

Karl Pribram was not quite twenty-three years old when he completed his studies at

Prague's ancient university in 1900 and received his doctor of jurisprudence. He entered his father's law firm, but the practice of law did not appeal to his restless inquisitive spirit. Two years later, in 1902, he decided to pursue his pronounced interest in economics, with the possible goal of an academic career. He went to the University of Berlin for a year of postdoctoral study in economics and "was struck," as he wrote, "by the fundamental difference between the approach to economic research adopted by the German historical school and his Austrian teachers." He himself had been trained in the abstract-analytical school of Carl Menger's theories. In almost all German universities the historical-descriptive method prevailed, a legacy of the two successive German historical schools. In 1883, less than twenty years before Karl Pribram arrived in Berlin, this difference in methods had led to a bitter and unresolved controversy between Carl Menger, the founder of the Austrian School, and Gustav Schmoller, the representative of the second, or "younger" historical school.

The battle was fought with an important book and a long pamphlet on Menger's side, while Schmoller authored an essay and an intemperate letter, which he published. Menger expounded the need for deductive analysis as the correct way to treat the basic questions of the science of economics; Schmoller defended the inductive approach, based on the collection of historical data. Their controversy was considered the intellectual battle of the century and has entered economic lore under the name of "Methodenstreit" (the contest of the methods) as the liveliest theoretical dispute in the field. In their actual work these two scholars were not quite as far apart as this struggle indicated. But the acrimonious tone of the debate and the enthusiasm of their followers emphasized and deepened the differences for many years, long after the original battle was over. At the University of Berlin Karl Pribram evidently was caught in its aftermath. This experience sharpened forever his awareness of the two modes of thinking and of the vital importance of methodological analysis. And he observed with satisfaction the growing international recognition of the Austrian school and its influence on the development of economic science.

After Berlin he moved to Vienna in 1904, for continued study and the preparation of a *Habilitationsschrift,* a book that would gain him the desired entrance into the academic world. He settled on a topic that up to then had been neglected in economic research and was at the same time ideally suited for the combination of legal and economic experience that he had acquired during his studies. Entitled *Geschichte der österreichischen Gewerbepolitik von 1740 bis 1798 (History of Austria's Commercial Policy for Trades and Manufacturing from 1740 to 1798),* the book is an analytical description of the Austrian government's legislative policy in regulating manufactures and trade during the last two-thirds of the eighteenth century. Austria had been preceded in similar endeavors by France and England, where mercantilistic methods had flourished decades earlier, for good or ill. Wars, to defend its borders and its throne, had prevented Austria from devoting much attention to its domestic commercial problems. In the early part of the eighteenth century, Austria's production and trade were still tightly regulated, reminiscent of the guild system, and closely supervised by the security police. Yet strong social, political, and economic forces demanded liberalization. The Enlightenment had swept through the cultural sphere all over Europe and the importance of expanded trade beyond country borders became obvious in the economic field. Pribram's book deals with the commercial laws and regulations gradually introduced in Austria, to bring about such changes in the incipient industrial development and in trade.

The six-hundred-page volume is divided into five sections, arranged in chronological order, and covers the long reign of empress Maria Theresia, from 1740 to 1780, that of her two sons, the progressive emperor Joseph II, his brother emperor Leopold II, and that of her grandson, emperor Franz I. During most of that time the court was advised in its efforts by two eminent cameralists, Johannes Heinrich von Justi and, for a very extended period, Joseph von Sonnenfels. Successively, both men were professors of finance and police science at the University of Vienna, a title that showed the close connection between economics and security matters in eighteenth-century Austria. Both men also are generally designated as cameralists, representing the German and Austrian version of mercantilism; but their advice and opinions were often indistinguishable from mercantilistic ideas. The book ends with the year 1798, a few years after paper money had been introduced in Austria. This financial measure would, in the course of time, effectively complete the transition from the remnants of feudalism to modern, capitalistic forms of working and trading.

The three-year research for the book, based on original papers, was done in the archives of the appropriate ministries and specialized agencies. A rich, and almost limitless, source of previously untouched material was found in the Imperial Court Library (now the Austrian National Library). He worked on unbound and hitherto unexplored documents of that period, most of them in difficult-to-read eighteenth-century handwriting and spelling, which he had to master for his purpose. He often mentioned that he literally lived in the eighteenth century during those years of research. The eighteenth-century atmosphere was further enhanced by the fact that the Court Library was housed in a splendid eighteenth-century palace. Erected in 1726, the building was skillfully restored in the 1950s, and its famous great hall remains to this day the impressive center of an otherwise much enlarged and modernized National Library.

The *Gewerbepolitik,* the result of Pribram's intensive research, was dedicated to his father, and came out in early 1907. It was easily accepted by the University of Vienna as *Habilitationsschrift* and gained him the title of "Privatdozent," the first step in an academic career, conveying the right to teach at the university, but without compensation. The *Gewerbepolitik* is readily available today in Vienna's professional libraries and, according to very recent information, is still used, consulted, and excerpted, as the best source of information in its field.

Seven years later, in 1914, Karl Pribram was named "ausserordentlicher Professor," still an unsalaried position, but with more prerogatives for teaching and examinations. In 1917 he was selected to give the main course in economic theory as deputy for Professor Friedrich von Wieser, who became minister of commerce at that time.

His academic and theoretical interests were combined with a distinguished career in the Austrian civil service, which, similar to the British example, exposed him to a wide and variegated experience in many fields. By the accident of historical events, many of his most eminent achievements, then and later, were in the sphere of practical social problems, often in a legal context. Most of his writings, however, from the very beginning, showed his main interest: the interaction of thought and reality in the evolution of social developments. From 1907 to 1921 he held successive positions with the Vienna Central Agency for Housing Reform, with the Central Commission for Statistics, with the Ministry of Trade, and, finally, with the newly founded Ministry of Social Administration, in the capacity of Ministerial Counselor for Labor Legislation and Unemployment Insurance.

From his arrival in the city in 1904 to the outbreak of the First World War in the summer of 1914, he enjoyed and participated in the last golden years of Vienna in an epoch that, for the élite, was rich in intellectual life, productive of new thoughts in all fields of endeavor, from the social sciences and philosophy to music and art, to medicine and physics, to mathematics and linguistics. The city was tolerant of the unusual and the new, even when it disputed it with a sharp and often biting wit. This was a period of seminal ideas that often would ripen into fruition only many years later, sometimes in other countries and on other continents. With the empire's many nations represented in Vienna, the city had a cosmopolitan air, without yielding its own typical character; it reflected a probing spirit and the influence of many sources. Karl Pribram liked to call Vienna the last Eastern outpost of nominalistic, or hypothetical, thinking, by which he meant a critical and analytical approach to all problems, in contrast to fixed beliefs in immutable values.

The exchange of ideas in Vienna often took place in informal groups that met at regular intervals to discuss a welter of problems, ranging over several disciplines. Econo- mists, mathematicians, and philosophers might get together to try out their thoughts and influence one another. Economists Karl Pribram and Ludwig Mises met with legal philos- opher Hans Kelsen and continued their relations throughout their lives, which brought them all to the United States, many years later. Karl Pribram developed a warm associa- tion with Eugen Böhm-Bawerk and his wife, which was cut short by the former's untimely death in 1914. He knew Joseph A. Schumpeter well, in Vienna, and later in Germany and in the United States. And there were many others.

Karl Pribram made good use of these final years of peace and enjoyable living in Vienna, as if he felt they would not last forever. After his voluminous *Gewerbepolitik* was finished, he wrote a few articles on housing and statistics, products of his then current professional experience. More important, and characteristic for the direction his intellec- tual development was to take, were three works in the field of social philosophy and economic reasoning: in 1908 he brought out a long essay, *Die Idee des Gleichgewichts in der alteren nationaloekonomischen Theorie (The Equilibrium Concept in Older Economic Theory)*; in 1914 he published a small book, *Der Individualismus in der neueren Rechts- philosophie (Individualism in the Recent Philosophy of Law)*; but the most important of the three was his book *Die Entstehung der individualistischen Sozialphilosophie (The Origins of the Individualistic Social Philosophy)*, which appeared in 1912. All three delineated his pronounced interest in the relationship of economics, law, and philosophy within the framework of the general intellectual climate of a given period. In the foreword to the *Origins of Individualistic Social Philosophy*, he clearly expressed his hope to be able, some day, to expand on these thoughts; the first indication, one might assume, of the present book, which was to be written about half a century later in the United States. The *Origins* is a slender volume of not much over a hundred pages, which traced the gradual evolution of collective thinking during the Middle Ages to the tentative individualism of natural law at the beginning of modern times, and the final victory of the principle of individualism achieved by John Locke, whom he called the founder of nominalistic philosophy. He discussed differences between the French approach to these problems and that of the British, exemplified by Rousseau and the physiocrats on one side, and Hume and Adam Smith on the other. He referred to Germany as the one country in Europe that had never fully overcome its collectivistic, nonindividualistic approach, which flourished in the Middle Ages. In the introduction he stated that his work on mercantilism, in connection with his book *Gewerbepolitik*, gave him the incentive to delve more thor- oughly into the philosophical origin and content of economic theories.

One of the many bright spots for Pribram during those peaceful years was the meeting in Vienna of the International Statistical Institute (ISI) in 1913. He was responsible for its arrangement. Pribram had a very special attachment for this organization to which he belonged at a time when its membership was limited to about two hundred all over the world and election as member carried a certain distinction. His most interesting travels, in later years, were often to the institute's meetings in the capitals of many countries, upon invitation of their governments. Founded in 1885, the institute spearheaded the difficult fight for the idea of collecting internationally comparable statistical data many decades before the great international institutions, established after the First and Second World Wars, started to compile international statistics in immeasurable quantities. In view of this explosion of international statistics by much larger organizations, the character of the institute changed considerably after the Second World War. It gave up its exclusivity, the membership was greatly enlarged, and its tasks were adjusted to current conditions. But its headquarters are still at The Hague, the location that had been decided upon at the Vienna meeting of 1913. Its journal remains the *International Statistical Review*, which is published in English and French. Karl Pribram contributed numerous articles to it, mainly during the 1920s and 1930s.

The Vienna meeting of 1913 was the last one before the outbreak of the First World War. No other session of the ISI was held for ten years. In 1973, sixty years and two World Wars later, the institute met again in Vienna, for the first time since then. It was just a few weeks after Karl Pribram's death. The president of the institute, in his opening address, paid tribute to his memory.

Vienna's stimulating and comfortable world came to an end when the First World War broke out in the summer of 1914 and "the lights went out all over Europe." It was the first major war, affecting all of Europe, since the Napoleonic wars were ended by the Congress of Vienna in 1815, a hundred years earlier. Karl Pribram's service as an officer in the Austrian army was cut short by serious illness, caught in the field. He returned to his teaching at the university before a depleted audience, because most young men were fighting in the trenches. He also resumed with vigor his civil service jobs with the Central Statistical Commission and with the Ministry of Commerce, where every experienced hand was urgently needed to turn the machinery of government from peacetime pursuits to the requirements of war. His organizational talent and skill in preparing the necessary documents and directives for the exigencies of a war economy were recognized as outstanding, and he received two high imperial decorations, personally conferred by emperor Franz Joseph.

When and how Pribram found time and concentration for scientific writing during those turbulent years is difficult to fathom, but he did publish a surprising number of articles and essays within that period. Several pieces dealt with his immediate practical concerns as a civil servant at the ministries: the movement of food prices during the war, showing an incipient inflation, which later was to escalate to incredible dimensions; the statistics on the requirements of needed raw materials and basic foodstuffs, indicating the beginning and the location of possible shortages, and similar topics.

There were also a number of thoughtful essays showing his never-ceasing interest in the deeper meaning of social events. "Über die Beziehungen zwischen der Handelspolitik und der auswärtigen Politik" ("On the Relations between Trade Policy and Foreign Policy"), published in 1916, would have been a timely paper to consult during the peace negotiations, three years later. A strictly philosophical study was his essay "Die

Weltanschauungen der Völker und ihre Politik'' (''The Philosophies of Nations and Their Politics''). This long article written in 1917 and his book of 1912, *Die Entstehung der individualistischen Sozialphilosophie (The Origins of Individualistic Social Philosophy)*, had a decisive, long-lasting influence on the intellectual discussion of these problems in the early part of the century and are still quoted today. The ''Weltanschauungen'' was completed less than a year before the war ended and had a decidedly pessimistic undertone, uncharacteristic of Pribram. At that time the hopelessness of the war must have become apparent to the better informed circles in Central Europe. Pribram deplored the fact that the bloody fight brought with it a measure of intellectual enmity among the adversaries, which had not existed since the religious wars of the seventeenth century. And he attempted to explain that this deep animosity, which had broken all restraints of reason, had its roots in the different ways the nations thought: the British in a nominalistic manner, factual and practical; the Germans in a historical way, as nationalistic ideologues; and the Russians, who were just then involved in their revolution, in an authoritarian manner, regardless of who would be at the helm. This essay foreshadows his book *Conflicting Patterns of Thought,* a restrained, analytical outline of the logical background of leading social philosophies, which was to be written in 1949, some thirty years later, in the United States.

When the war finally ended in November 1918, the six-hundred-year reign of the Habsburgs came to a close. The Peace Treaty of St. Germain divided the Austro-Hungarian Empire of fifty-four million people into small individual states, roughly according to language criteria. Most, but not all, of the German-speaking, largely alpine, provinces formed the new Austria, with about seven million inhabitants. Vienna, still a metropolis of two million, became the oversized capital of this new, barely viable, small country. Some German-speaking provinces were incorporated into Italy, Yugoslavia, and Rumania. These successor states experienced a period of fragile independence, fraught with economic problems, during the twenty years between the two World Wars. Thereafter, they were gradually absorbed into the Soviet orbit and, with the exception of Yugoslavia, are now members of the Warsaw Pact.

Conditions after the break-up of the empire were chaotic in Vienna, though the city was not physically touched during the First World War, in contrast to the Second, when it sustained grievous damage. The hostilities in the 1914–1918 war were limited to the borders of the then large country and to the outlying provinces; but it was the social fabric that was rent asunder. Corporate headquarters in Vienna found themselves cut off from their plants and branch offices in the provinces, which had suddenly become foreign countries with foreign currencies; footstuffs, which used to be delivered to Vienna from all over the large empire, were blocked at the borders and never reached the city; soldiers streamed back from the field, looking for work, sustenance, and shelter; unemployment rose to dangerous levels; severe shortages were felt in all fields and hyperinflation soon was raging.

This runaway inflation could not be brought under control for a very long time. It completely ruined some strata of the population. Finally, with an international loan under the auspices of the League of Nations, the currency was stabilized four years later, around the turn of 1922/23, and its name changed from Krone to Schilling.

Considering the circumstances, a semblance of order was restored in a relatively short time, thanks to a large part to Austria's civil service, stationed in Vienna. It continued to function in adversity, as best as it could. The new small state of Austria needed its own new constitution. Hans Kelsen, the eminent legal philosopher of the

University of Vienna and a close colleague of Pribram, wrote it and it was speedily adopted.

Karl Pribram, by now Chief of the Legislative Division for Social Policy in the Ministry for Social Administration, was charged with the creation of a new, complete, and encompassing social legislation program, comprising social security, unemployment compensation, wage laws, certain aspects of health insurance, various labor and arbitration and mediation laws. All the laws in these fields were written by Karl Pribram himself, or under his close supervision, during the years 1918 to 1921. They were invariably accepted by the Austrian Parliament, usually without any or only minor changes. Occasionally, he had to interrupt his theoretical legal work by acting as mediator himself, to pacify rebellious groups of workers or unions who felt that their wage demands never quite caught up with the wild inflation that plagued the country as a legacy of the war. As the author of Austria's social legislation he also was coopted during that time into the Commission for Labor Law, established in Berlin by the German Ministry of Labor.

The authorship of Austria's labor legislation turned out to be not only the capstone of his career in the Austrian civil service but also its conclusion. By now, his reputation was well established in Europe. Thus, it was not surprising that the newly founded International Labour Office in Geneva, Switzerland, offered him the position as Chief of its Department for Research and Statistics. He accepted, said good-bye to Vienna, after seventeen rich and eventful years, pulled up stakes, and moved to Geneva in the spring of 1921.

The arrival in Geneva in May was a pleasant experience after the hectic time in postwar Vienna, under the physical and emotional strain of a crumbling era, serious social problems, and a collapsing currency.

The International Labour Office (ILO) was created in late 1919 by the Treaty of Versailles, as an independent affiliate of the League of Nations, which was established at the same time. Its by-laws were incorporated into the Versailles treaty. The ILO outlived the League of Nations, and when the United Nations was founded, the ILO became the U.N.'s first specialized agency. The United States never joined the League of Nations and, initially, not the ILO either. In the changed political atmosphere under Franklin Delano Roosevelt the United States became a member of the ILO in August 1934. The United States has remained a most active member ever since, except for a break of more than two years over policy matters in the late 1970s.

The objective of the ILO was the improvement of labor conditions in all their ramifications, in the interest of peace and humanitarian considerations. It was the task of the secretariat and, to a large extent, that of Karl Pribram's research department, to translate as many of its idealistic goals as possible into practical proposals that could be introduced into the laws of member countries, for their feasible application. In the foreground, at that time, were health and unemployment insurance, the eight-hour day and the forty-hour week, and the minimum wage. When Pribram took over as head of the research and statistical department, the organization was still new and the very concept of such activities on an international scale had to be freshly developed from the very beginning. Pribram drew upon his own extensive experience acquired in Austria, on comparative work done in other countries and by the International Federation of Trade Unions. International comparisons of what had been done elsewhere became imperative and most useful. New research methods had to be introduced to make international comparisons possible. Among several original concepts worked out under his direction was that of the "market basket" as a basis for the comparison of living costs in different countries. This is now considered a common tool of economic research, but at that time its introduction was a trailblazing achievement. Index numbers of living costs were calculated for similar purposes. A host of other international investigations in the field of health, mortality in various occupations, safety problems, wages, labor and working conditions, and the length of the work day and the work week were also conducted by his department.

Yet, he did not forget his love for teaching. He gave occasional courses at the University of Geneva and lectured, more regularly, at the newly founded Institut des Hautes Etudes Internationales (Institute for Higher International Studies), which was and is connected with the university. The lectures were, of course, given in French, since Geneva is the center of French Switzerland. Today, English is accepted on equal terms as a teaching language at the institute, and probably supersedes French.

Pribram's literary output during his Geneva years was substantial. Understandably, much of it dealt with social questions. A long, sixty-five-page article, "Die Sozialpolitik im neuen Oesterreich" ("The Social Policy of the New Austria"), was completed before he left Vienna in May 1921, but it was published only in December of that year. In six chapters he discussed the introduction of social measures during a period of supreme political and economic difficulties and unrest, following the collapse of the Empire. After a general introduction, he tackled the questions of unemployment relief, shop stewards, labor contracts, labor administrations, trade unions, and wage policies.

Two small but most useful books appeared during those Geneva years: *Die Probleme der internationalen Arbeitsstatistik (The Problems of International Labor Statistics)*, published in 1925, handled the question of comparability of statistics, collected in different countries from different points of view, and the need for introducing unified methods on an international basis. Two years later, in 1927, he brought out *Die Probleme der Internationalen Sozialpolitik (The Problems of International Social Policy)*, a very informative two-hundred-page introduction to the problems that faced the International Labour Office in its beginning. It contains a succinct description of its organization, its major tasks, and its attempted solutions during the early years of its existence. The book was published in Leipzig.

The article "Die Vereinheitlichung der Sozialversicheiung" ("The Unification of Social Insurance") appeared in 1925 in German, French, and English in the respective issues of the *International Labour Review*. In 1928, toward the end of his stay in Geneva, he published an article on financing the costs of social insurance, entitled "Die Verteilung der finanziellen Lasten der Sozialversicherung" ("The Distribution of the Financial Burden of Social Insurance").

A long essay of seventy-eight pages entitled "Deutscher Nationalismus und Deutscher Sozialismus" ("German Nationalism and German Socialism") appeared in 1922, very early in his Geneva stay, when his thoughts may still have been preoccupied with the problems of war and postwar discussions in Germany and Austria. Or it may have been an uncanny presentiment of future developments that were to come a decade later. He examined the changes that nationalism had wrought on the concept of socialism in Germany. He dissected German socialism; discussed the concepts of class and of nation; and analyzed the German idea of the state, the logical problems of socialization, and the logic of the German proposals for socialization. He found the German thoughts in that context irreconcilable with nominalism and characterized them as pseudo-universalistic. That, as it later turned out, was not too far removed from national socialism in its intellectual form, not in its brutal physical excesses.

A few years later, in 1926, he produced a short, fourteen-page, highly abstract piece on the concept of democracy, under the title "Les Charactères Essentiels de la Démo-cratie" ("The Essential Characteristics of Democracy"). Three elements were essential, he wrote, for a democratic government: that the state existed only in the interest of the people who formed the community; that the relative value (importance) of these interests deter-mined the relative importance of the state's tasks (purposes); and that the will of all was represented by the will of the majority. This article and "Deutscher Nationalismus" were in a similar spirit as his book *Die Entstehung der individualistischen Sozialphilosophie* of 1912, and his essay "Die Weltanschauungen der Völker und ihre Politik" of 1917, and led to important later publications in a related vein.

In a different field and a different vein was his important book-length article of 133 pages, "Die weltwirtschaftliche Lage im Spiegel des Schrifttums der Weltwirtschaftskon-ferenz" ("The International Economic Situation, as reflected in the Literature of the World Economic Conference"), published in October 1927. In May of that year the League of Nations had arranged a very large International Economic Conference, the first such broad-based economic meeting ever held. Pribram discussed in detail the volu-minous documentation, prepared by the League, which covered practically all aspects of economic and related problems that occupied the thinking of policymakers. It ran the gamut from population problems, to finances, to particular industries, to cartels, to wages and employment, to agriculture and trade. The latter was treated in more detail, especially with regard to tariffs, their application, and other forms of trade restrictions, such as export subsidies and attempts at dumping. In retrospect, the conference seems to have been held just midway between an uneven recovery in Europe from the catastrophic consequences of the First World War, its subsequent territorial changes and inflationary inroads, and the onset of the Great Depression a few years later. Pribram's article offered a succinct presentation of the socioeconomic conditions at that time and, as in most of his writing, he pointed up the difference in the philosophical and intellectual approaches to problem-solving by the different nations.

During his years as international civil servant in Geneva, Karl Pribram kept in close contact with academic circles, not only through his publications, his teaching at the University of Geneva, and at the Institute des Hautes Etudes Internationales, but also through his attendance of professional meetings of learned societies in several countries of Europe, including those of the Verein fur Sozialpolitik (now called Verein fur Wirtschaftswissenschaften und Sozialpolitik). It was therefore not unexpected that, in the course of time, he would be chosen for a chair for "Wirtschaftswissenschaften" (eco-nomic sciences). The call came from the University of Frankfort, offering him a full professorship in the field, for the fall of 1928. He accepted and moved to Frankfort in late summer of that year, to start his teaching with the fall/winter semester.

Before leaving Geneva, he became engaged to be married to Edith Körnei, an economist and social scientist from Vienna, Austria, who had joined the economics department of the League of Nations about a year earlier. This engagement seems to have been the first one between members of the League of Nations and the International Labour Office and caused, therefore, a good deal of delighted surprise and excitement among their colleagues. The marriage took place the following spring.

Frankfort in 1928/1929 still had much of the air of the free and independent city it once had been. It also cherished the fact that Johann Wolfgang Goethe, Germany's foremost poet, had been born there in the eighteenth century, and it had proudly named its university after him. It was also a city of international banking houses and large businesses with international interests and, incidentally, with close connections to the university; many a capable and ambitious banker or businessman strove hard to acquire a lectureship or even the title "Privatdozent" at the university, to join learned societies, and to draw on university professors for his professional and social gatherings. In those circles, the political outlook seemed worldwide and moderately liberal. Nevertheless, there was a certain formal reserve in their social and daily life, which contrasted with the manners and mores that had prevailed in Geneva's international groups.

The coming political storm was not noticeable in Frankfort for quite a while into the future. The more rebellious opinions were rather of the Marxist persuasion than of the National-Socialist type. Such opinions, however, were generally confined to abstract and, occasionally, abstruse discussions that did not lead to physical violence. The professors and students of that persuasion gathered in the well-known Institute for Social Research, which was connected with the university. What went on underground, among the students and other social groups, was impossible to tell for the outsider. On the surface, everything was quiet, orderly, well regulated. The economic situation and employment conditions remained fair to good until the early 1930s.

Karl Pribram greatly enjoyed his teaching at the university. His newly prepared lively lectures always attracted overflow crowds who listened with interest and, occasionally, with some perplexity, when he expounded the theories of classical (post-Ricardian) economics and those of the Austrian marginal utility school. While classical economics were taught in Germany by that time, the Austrian school had been completely neglected. The influence of the German historical school was still potent, though not as predominant as it had been during the nineteenth and very early twentieth century, when Karl Pribram had spent one study year in Berlin and was startled by the striking difference between the Austrian and German way of defining economics. In the late 1920s and early 1930s Marxist teachings also were generally represented at most German universities, by at least one professor. This was definitely the case at Frankfort. For the students it was a broadening, or a very confusing, experience to find the dismal science taught from so many different viewpoints. Pribram looked calmly at the repetition of his youthful experience. By now he was prepared for the multiplicity of methods and theories, and was ready and eager to explain the philosophical reasons behind it.

In addition to his large classes and seminars at the university, he also conducted a small private discussion group at home, as a special favor for about ten or twelve carefully selected postdoctoral students and professorial assistants, generally young people with academic ambitions. They assembled at regular intervals in his large book-lined study for an exchange of ideas on current and developing theories, new and old books, past and present principles, and for a snack.

His few years in Frankfort were productive ones for his thinking and his writings. His interest in the philosophical interpretation of economic and social events developed further in Frankfort's multifaceted discussions, his study of business cycles intensified, partly stimulated by talks and conferences at the very active Frankfort Society for Business Cycle Research; and his treatment of social and statistical problems continued.

His Frankfort publications began with his public inaugural address, delivered in the fall of 1928. This was a mandatory task to be executed by newly appointed professors of the university. The press and a selected public were invited to attend these events, in addition to the university teachers and students. Karl Pribram chose as his topic "Internationale Wirtschaftpolitik und internationale Sozialpolitik, ihre Wurzeln und Anschauungsformen" ("International Economic Policy and International Social Policy,

Their Roots and Implications''). In its factual content this paper was based on his long article about the literature prepared for the World Economic Conference of 1927, which was then still fresh in the memory of the experts in the field. Much of the text dealt with the philosophical origins and interpretations of these policies and the problem of reconciling the different approaches of the various nations in the interest of a peaceful world. The psychological and practical differences separating purely economic solutions from those of a social nature were underscored.

There are at least four important essays written during the Frankfort years that deal specifically with his philosophical approach of conflicting patterns of thought. Most of his other writings, concerning problems of statistics, housing, business cycles, social policy, and so forth, also contain some allusions and indications of this perspective. Two of his philosophical articles were discussions of the ideas of Werner Sombart, then professor of economics at the University of Berlin. In politely refuting Sombart's ideas, Pribram developed his own thoughts on the subject in this 1931 article, entitled ''Nominalismus und Begriffsrealismus in der Nationalökonomie'' (''Nominalism and Realism in the Scholastic Sense, Applied to Economics''). This is in essence a philosophical discussion of the logical grouping of economic schools according to their basic concepts. It is another precursor of the ideas underlying the present book. Two years later, in a publication honoring Sombart on his seventieth birthday, Karl Pribram chose a similar topic under the title ''Die vier Begriffe der Weltwirtschaft und ihre Problematik'' (''The Four Concepts of the World Economy and Their Problems''). This too is an abstract, logical discussion of the conceptual approach to international economic problems by different schools of thought, underlying the different schools of economics.

In two articles, both written in 1932, Pribram discussed the influence of conceptual interpretations on the scope and content of social policy. ''Die Deutungen der Sozialpolitik'' (''Definitions of Social Policy'') is particularly interesting because it emphasized the transitory character of the general attitude toward social policy at the time this piece was written and predicted a development of social measures along lines that would correspond to prevailing concepts in economics. The other article, ''Das Problem der Verantwortlichkeit in der Sozialpolitik'' (''The Problem of Responsibility in Social Policy''), referred to the fact that unemployment compensation beyond the normal calculated risk was still highly controversial and indicated the need for and the probability of a future change in this matter to come about by a change in the philosophical attitude toward economic and social considerations. The respective responsibilities of the private versus the public sector for unemployment assistance were briefly discussed. This was in 1932, when many countries, including the United States, had no provisions for unemployment compensation at all.

A number of other writings in the field of social policy were produced during his Frankfort years, such as: ''Einigungs- und Zwangssysteme im Schlichtungswesen'' (''Systems of Mediation and Compulsion in Labor Arbitration'') and ''Die Verteilung der finanziellen Lasten in der Sozialversicherung'' (''The Distribution of the Financial Burden of Social Insurance''). There were also several articles on housing and its relation to the business cycle, among them: ''Die volkswirtschaftlichen Probleme der Deutschen Wohnungwirtschaft'' (''The Economic Problems of the German Housing Policy'') and ''Rapport sur l'Uniformisation Internationale des Statistiques de l'Habitation Urbaine'' (''Report on the International Uniformization of Urban Housing Statistics''). Furthermore, a few articles on business cycle questions appeared, including: ''Konjunktur-beobachtung'' (''Observation of the Business Cycle''), ''Die städtische Grundrente im

Konjunkturverlauf'' (''The Urban Groundrent in the Course of the Business Cycle''), a topic he would take up again years later in expanded form in a study for the January 1940 issue of *Econometrica*.

Karl Pribram's tenure in Frankfort led to a good deal of travel, generally to professional conferences of various kinds, in Europe and beyond. The 1930 meeting of the International Statistical Institute, in whose work he had actively participated since his Vienna days, took him on an overland journey by the Trans-Siberian Railroad through Stalin's Russia to Tokyo, the site of the meeting. This was at a time when Japan was still considered a semi-mysterious country and when its emperor was revered as a god by its population. Not long after his return from Japan, there came an invitation from the University of Chicago to participate in the symposium ''Unemployment as a World Problem,'' planned for the early summer of 1931. As it turned out these first contacts with the United States were the most important events of Pribram's Frankfort years. It was during this time that he also received occasional visits from American academic economists, among them Frank H. Knight.

The Chicago symposium, a ten-day meeting, was to be held under the auspices of the Harris Memorial Foundation and chaired by Professor Quincy Wright. Karl Pribram accepted, and undertook his first Atlantic crossing in June 1931. The other two participants were John Maynard Keynes, of King's College in Cambridge, who had already published his well-known "Treatise of Money," but not yet his epoch-making "General Theory," and E. J. Phelan, chief of the diplomatic division of the International Labour Office. The symposium was held from 22 June to 2 July 1931, and the lectures, each one stretching over several days, were followed by seminar-type discussions. The lectures themselves were published by the University of Chicago Press in late 1931, under the title *Unemployment as a World Problem*. Keynes chose as the title for his presentation ''An Economic Analysis of Unemployment''; Phelan's topic was ''International Cooperation and Unemployment''; and Karl Pribram spoke about ''World Unemployment and Its Problems.'' This paper was divided into three parts: the economic background of unemployment; unemployment in Germany, compared with that in other European countries; and the prevention and relief of unemployment.

Pribram traced the origin of the Depression and its hitherto unheard of extent of unemployment to many causes, some of them of a cyclical and technical nature, such as the introduction of labor-saving devices, but put the main burden on two major causes: the erection of trade barriers between countries, which impeded the free flow of commerce, and disorders in the international financial world, which disrupted the functioning of the international credit system. He cited specifically the Smoot-Hawley tariff of the United States, which effectively closed the U.S. border for many imports, and he reminded his listeners of the twenty thousand miles of new customs frontiers created in Europe by the peace treaties that had cut up large unified customs areas, such as the Austro-Hungarian empire, into small competing states that defended their own industries by high tariff walls. Regarding Germany, he referred to the heavy financial burden of reparations imposed by the Treaty of Versailles, which were difficult to meet even in prosperous times, but beyond the country's capacity to pay during periods of economic distress.

He devoted special attention to the national and international banking system and its role in commerce and employment, and referred specifically to the fact that the collapse of a leading bank in Austria had triggered a decisive shockwave through the international finance system, an event usually considered the beginning of the Depression.

His suggestions for remedies were numerous, both political as well as economic and financial. Most of them were implied in his presentation of the causes of the unemployment situation. He regretted that the recent (March 1931) attempt by the League of Nations to establish a "tariff truce" had failed. He emphasized the worldwide aspect of the crisis, even though its particular features varied from country to country. His specific suggestions for immediate relief had a present-day ring: public works program, the spreading of work by shortening the working day or week for the individual worker, wage subsidies for employers willing to take on or keep workers, the establishment of labor exchanges and similar devices. An important suggestion, the extension of unemployment benefits, was applicable only in countries where unemployment insurance existed. At that time, this was the case only in a few advanced, mostly European, countries in spite of the valiant work of the International Labour Office for the introduction of this important social instrument. The United States had no unemployment insurance system when the Depression hit, making its impact much harsher than it would have been otherwise. For the long run, Pribram recommended the use of countercyclical methods for the execution of public works programs, such as roads, dams, bridges, and public buildings; as far as possible, such projects should be carried out during periods of an economic downturn, to counteract the slack in employment and, incidentally, also to save on costs.

After his Chicago lectures, there were a number of other requests from the United States for his writings, foremost among them from the *Encyclopedia of the Social Sciences*. He contributed two major articles and a number of smaller ones to the 1930s edition of this important reference work. His comprehensive article "European Housing" appeared in 1932. In it he discussed the different ways in which housing and residential buildings were treated by the legislatures of the various countries in Europe, and emphasized the influence of the business cycle movements on prices for the construction sites, building costs, mortgages, and rents. His important long article "Unemployment" was published by the *Encyclopedia* a year later. It reflected his thorough knowledge of the problem, based on his authorship of the Austrian social legislation, his long years of work at the International Labour Office in Geneva, and his recent Chicago lectures. Some shorter contributions to the *Encyclopedia* consisted of an article on "Trade Unions in Eastern Europe" and three minor biographical sketches on less well-known German economists, including Christian Jacob Kraus, Karl Heinrich Rau, and Sartorius von Waltershausen.

In 1931, on his return to Frankfort from Chicago, he had stopped over in New York City and in Washington, D.C., to pay courtesy calls on several scientific organizations, among them the Brookings Institution in Washington. He was interested to see how these research institutions were organized in the United States and to meet a few of the personalities who worked there. Two years later in the summer of 1933 on his trip home from Mexico City, where he had attended another one of the biennial ISI meetings, he visited the Brookings Institution again. By that time he had established some rapport with the scholars on its staff.

Meanwhile in Germany, Hitler had been chancellor for several months under the presidency of General Paul Hindenburg. The Reichstag had inexplicably burned down and the government ruled by emergency decree. The political situation was incredibly tense, but nobody knew where it would lead to. The old general, in spite of his very advanced age and weakness, still kept a semblance of control over the worst excesses. The day-to-day machinery of government continued to function. Karl Pribram, though a keen observer of human affairs, refused to believe, as long as possible, that Germany, the country of poets and thinkers, would really embrace the political philosophy propounded by the

Nationalist-Socialist Party. Yet, when one evening he had occasion to observe a book-burning orgy by brown-shirted troops, right in the center of the city that had been proud of its intellectual life, and when on another day a courageous student of his warned him by telephone not to come to the university that morning for his regular lectures "because it may be dangerous," he gradually changed his mind. And when the situation deteriorated further, he gladly accepted the Brookings Institution's offer for a two-year appointment to its staff. Thanks to this contract and the accompanying affidavit, the departure from Germany and the immigration into the United States were without any problems of a physical or administrative nature.

He arrived in the United States in late 1933 in ample time to attend the annual meeting of the American Economic Association in Philadelphia at the end of December. This was a good introduction to his future working life and a bit breathtaking too. Although he had been to countless meetings in the past, he was overwhelmed by the size and scope of that assembly, which surpassed anything he had seen so far. After the Philadelphia session he moved to Washington, D.C., to start his new career in the United States.

Washington as a city was a surprise in early 1934. Although it was the capital of a huge country, it had the aura, the dimensions, the charm, and the manners of a medium-sized Southern town. There were lovely green expanses and trees all over; its wide arterial roads, such as Massachusetts or Connecticut avenues and Sixteenth Street, were built up to only about their middle reaches and were partially bordered by grassy hills. The number of embassies was only a tiny fraction of what they are now. There was only one permanent theater, which did not always play; the newly founded National Symphony Orchestra struggled valiantly for its existence; the National Gallery had not yet been built; the Kennedy Center was not even a dream in anybody's mind. And Georgetown had barely begun its attempts to evolve into a desirable residential section from the very modest quarter of town it had been for generations.

But in 1933, at the depth of the Depression, a new spirit brought sparks of energy into the life of the city: the Roosevelt Administration and the New Deal that were to change the character of Washington profoundly in a few years. The New Deal attracted bright minds from all over the country, especially from the universities. Social and economic experiments to alleviate the situation followed each other in rapid succession. Some of these attempts were successful, some raised only hopes, some were later cut down by the courts as unconstitutional. Yet by early 1934 when Karl Pribram arrived, the worst of the early phases of the Depression were under a modicum of control. The city bustled with people who were trying enthusiastically to bring about a true recovery from the Depression. It was an illuminating experience and a privilege for a newcomer to this country to participate in these endeavors, albeit from the cloistered atmosphere of the Brookings Institution, then located in a townhouse fronting Lafayette Park near the White House. Most probably the Brookings was the only private research institute of rank for the social sciences in Washington during that period.

Under the auspices of the institution, Pribram wrote a book on cartels, entitled *Cartel Problems: An Analysis of Collective Monopolies in Europe with American Application*. It was published by the Brookings Institution in late 1935 and served as a standard work in the field for many years. This study was undertaken as one of the Brookings Economic Institute's series relating to the National Recovery Administration. The institute's director, Edwin G. Nourse, described the work in his preface as "an analysis of the economic conditions conductive to the formation of cartels, the attitudes which dominate cartel policy, various aspects of governmental policy in relation to cartels, and the economic effects of these forms of business organization.''

This work of about three hundred pages was divided into eight chapters and an important appendix on the cartelization movement in Europe. One chapter, entitled ''Codes and Cartels,'' dealt specifically with cartel-type movements in the United States, especially under the National Recovery Act, and discussed briefly the fact that the ''codes'' under the NRA had been declared unconstitutional by the Supreme Court. Other chapters took up the following subjects: the nature of cartels, types of collective monopolies, aspects of cartel policy, varying interpretations of the cartel movement, economic effects of cartelization, and cartels and the state.

Karl Pribram stated in his introduction that ''extensive modification of the competitive system by collective combinations of business groups is one of the most striking recent developments in economic organization. . . . Previous studies of cartels have been mainly descriptive. . . . The present volume cuts through national differentiating circumstances . . . to establish certain widely applicable generalizations concerning the character of the [cartel] movement as a whole. This approach involved . . . a resort to abstract reasoning . . . to define the general conditions under which cartelization might develop, or to determine the effects on economic life from the behavior of cartelized industries. Special attention has been given to the mutual relations between cartelization and the course of business fluctuations. . . . A clear line must be drawn between ''collective monopolies,'' represented by cartels, and monopolistic combinations of the corporate type. . . . In the last two chapters some inferences are drawn from European experiences, as to the prospects of recent American monopolistic tendencies. . . . These problems are closely related to important questions of public policy.''

Special attention was indeed given in the book to the influence of the business cycle on the formation of cartels; it was Karl Pribram's central theory. Fundamental to his analysis was the thesis that collective monopolies were formed in contracting markets, during the downward movement of the cycle, while expanding markets and prosperous business conditions fostered strong single monopolies, such as mergers, trusts, companies, and so forth. This thesis was supported by a discussion of the different policies applied in the course of the business cycle by cartels, on the one hand, and single monopolies on the other. A lengthy appendix on the cartelization movement in Europe, from the 1870s to the 1930s, with special emphasis on Germany, illustrated Pribram's points with descriptive examples. This appendix especially and the basic theory of the book were enthusiastically embraced in the *New York Times Book Review* shortly after the book's publication.

Pribram's two years at the Brookings Institution were a stimulating and intellectually most satisfying period. They gave him a chance, in an informal way, to get to know and confer with some of the liveliest and most influential people who flocked to Washington at that time. In the form of the New Deal an exciting social experiment was under way and, though new in this country, he had the rare opportunity to watch it grow and develop, observe its successes and failures, and was able to analyze the reasons for the movement in his own way. He remained in touch with the Brookings Institution for many years, after he had left, and never forgot the auspicious beginnings of his life in America.

While Karl Pribram was at the Brookings Institution, the Social Security Board was established, in August 1935, one of several new agencies created under the New Deal. The specialists who assembled the staff were familiar with Pribram's relevant work in social policy in Austria and in Geneva, and with his contributions to the *Encyclopedia for the Social Sciences* and the Harris Foundation, and were interested in his expertise. Thus, when his book on cartel problems was published and his two-year contract with the Brookings Institution expired, he joined the Social Security Board as a recognized expert, though his warnings of possible financial problems for the Social Security Fund in the then distant future were not always heeded. He stayed with the board until 1942, when the foundations of the new agency had solidified and it had become a well-working body under the conditions prevailing at that time.

During the mid-1930s Pribram also spent some time on two memorable voyages to Europe, each made to attend a session of the International Statistical Institute. While celebrating the hundredth anniversary of the British Royal Statistical Society in 1934, the City of London simultaneously hosted the institute's twenty-second biennial meeting. Karl Pribram previously had accepted an invitation from John Maynard Keynes to visit him at King's College in Cambridge, and was treated with the college's full ceremony, which dated back to the Middle Ages. He dined in the company of the teaching staff, on a dias in the great hall, while students occupied the lower level; he engaged in formal discussion, a question-and-answer session, and spent a night in a room of one of the ancient buildings.

The celebrations in London for its own Royal Statistical Society's centenary and for its guest, the International Statistical Institute, were as splendid and colorful as only the British can make them. Dressed in their sumptuous robes and wigs, the aldermen of the city drove up to the glittering guildhall in multicolored carriages. Edward, then Prince of Wales, plainly attired in sober modern dress, gave a welcoming speech at another occasion; and there were sparkling festivities all around. Statistics seemed vary far from its usual gray image. But it was not neglected. The sessions were held, as planned, in three sections: demographic and mathematic statistics; economic statistics, to which Karl Pribram contributed; and social statistics. Each group with a heavy program.

On the London trip in 1934 the dark clouds of ominous events to come were scarcely noticeable; even the depressing picture of desperate unemployment was largely hidden from view. It was different, two years later, when Pribram attended the 1936 session of the International Statistical Institute, held in Athens. On entering the Mediterranean, the boat carrying among its passengers the American contingent of the participants to the ISI meeting, stopped at Gibraltar, the British fortress in southern Spain. A short walk around the harbor revealed numerous street signs in German and an occasional German uniform. What was Germany doing there, far from its own borders? The Spanish civil war was still in its very early beginnings, but the German presence in this unexpected location was foreboding.

The mood was even more unsettling in Greece itself. The country was at that time run by John Metaxas, who carried the official title of dictator and, as it turned out, was quite openly pro-Hitler Germany. German army uniforms and scattered groups of storm-trooper units could be spotted frequently on trips through the countryside, though they kept discretely in the background. All the glory of Greece and its fascinating sights could not make up for that. The official social events and receptions were impeccably correct, elegant, and uneventful; but they were always attended by an unusual number of German-speaking civilians who did not even pretend to be social scientists or statisticians, yet their presence was never questioned by the guards.

Karl Pribram scheduled his return trip from Greece by way of Vienna and combined it with a short visit to Prague. It was the last time he saw his native city and his younger brother Ewald, who lost his life during the war that was to come only a very few years later. Vienna, in 1936, was literally dancing on a volcano. Outwardly, life seemed deceptively normal and relaxed under the mild regime of Chancellor Kurt von Schuschnigg. But only two years earlier, his predecessor, Engelbert Dollfuss, had been assassinated in an uprising against his relatively moderate but hated quasi-dictatorship, and, a few years before, Vienna's imposing Palace of Justice and its irreplaceable law library had been burned to the ground by a revolting mob. During the interwar years, from the break-up of the Austro-Hungarian empire in 1918, to the outbreak of the Second World War in 1939, Austria, and especially Vienna, lived from breathing spell to breathing spell; but it usually made the most of each.

Yet Karl Pribram still found Vienna with its familiar shops and coffeehouses tastefully stocked and well attended; theaters and concert halls still playing and mostly sold out; and its intellectuals still continuing to enjoy their rarefied discussions. As he had done on previous visits, he renewed his friendly contacts with his contemporaries and with a younger group of social scientists and economists, many of whom he would encounter again a few years later, in the United States. On that occasion, he met a considerable number of them when, upon invitation, he gave a lecture, followed by discussion, at the Vienna Economic Society. The paper was subsequently published in the Society's journal.

During that early autumn of 1936, Vienna was preoccupied almost as much with the human interest story of the impending abdication of King Edward of Britain, as it was with its own precarious political situation. The city lived its normal life, even while it offered hospitality to occasional refugees who had begun to drift in from Germany. Yet, less than a year and a half later, on 11 March 1938, Austria was "peacefully" overrun by Hitler's army. Two days thereafter, on 13 March, the Ides of March, the country was incorporated into the German Reich by annexation. It was given the name of "Ostmark" (Eastern boundary country), a designation it had first held under Charlemagne, in the eighth century. Its boundaries as an independent country, and its name of "Republic of Austria," were extinguished. Only after the end of the Second World War, in May 1945, were its territory and its proper name restored again.

The Second World War broke out in Europe in September 1939, when Germany invaded Poland, more than two years before the United States entered the conflict, after Japan's attack on Pearl Harbor, on 7 December 1941.

During the eight or nine years from his arrival in the United States until Pearl Harbor Karl Pribram produced a considerable number of articles in addition to his book, *Cartel Problems*. Most of these writings were either job-related or dealt with problems of then current politico-economic content; his special interest, the philosophical interpretation of social and economic events, was relegated slightly to the background. It was a time when he had to absorb fully the onslaught of the new perspectives and ideas that confronted him in the new surroundings of the United States, so very different from the European and international atmosphere in which he had lived all his life. Nonetheless, even the concrete topics were usually permeated with his own typical explanation of the logical and philosophical reasons behind the facts.

One clear exception to his more factual writings of this period was the paper given before the Vienna Economic Society on his visit in October 1936. It was published in 1937 by that society's journal, *Zeitschrift für Nationalökonomie,* under the title "Gleichgewichtsvorstellungen in der Konjunkturtheorie" ("Equilibrium Concepts in Business Cycle Theory"). This article compressed into the short space of fifteen pages a discussion of the equilibrium concept and its transformation from the static classical interpretation to the modern dynamic one; it described the characteristics of the various business cycle theories with respect to the equilibrium concept itself, and suggested guidelines for the compilation of the type of international statistics that could assist in ascertaining international economic disturbances, so that they might be modified before attaining unmanageable proportions, and thus prevent a recurrence of the imbalances that led to the Great Depression.

The problem of business cycles dominate five other of the articles written during this period. "The Equilibrium Concept and Business Cycle Statistics" and "The Definition of Some Notions Fundamental to Business Cycle Analysis" were written for and published by the International Statistical Institute in The Hague; the first one for the 1934 meeting in London, the second one for the Athens session in 1936. "The Notion of 'Economic System' Underlying Business Cycle Analysis" appeared in 1937, in the *Review of Economic Statistics*. This strictly theoretical paper formed a coherent trio with the preceding two articles. Its sixteen long columns started from the proposition that business cycle analysis had been impaired, so far, by the failure of the community of economists to agree on the fundamental notion of "economic system." There were three different concepts of it among the classical theories: the theories of the "independent variables," those of the "intermittent variables," and those of the "disequilibrium theories." Newer theories distinguished between those of the "money exchange system" and the "real exchange system," which may be combined or divided into mixed forms.

"Residual, Differential, and Absolute Urban Groundrents and Their Cyclical Fluctuations" was presented at the Fifth Annual Research Conference on Economics and Statistics of the Cowles Commission in Colorado Springs, in July 1939, before it was published in *Econometrica* in 1940. In this sixteen-page paper, based on the groundrent concept of Friedrich von Wieser, Pribram described the different movements of the urban groundrents in the United States and in Europe, in the course of the business cycle; he attributed the differences essentially to the dissimilarity in the credit systems and the contrasting treatments of mortgages on the two continents. He strongly advocated that greater attention be paid to the movement of the urban groundrent during the economic cycle in regulating the mortgage markets and also for the housing policy in general.

Karl Pribram was a frequent contributor to and participant at the meetings of the Cowles Commission, which was headquartered in Chicago. The Cowles Commission had been founded in 1932 and was affiliated with the University of Chicago from 1939 to 1955, when it became an integral unit of the Department of Economics at Yale University and changed its name to the Cowles Foundation. Its research is concentrated on econometrics and on statistical and logical methods of analysis, and it maintains a very large specialized library in these fields.

An interesting twenty-five-page article, "The Functions of Reserves in Old Age Benefit Plans," appeared in the *Quarterly Journal of Economics* in 1938. It analyzed in considerable detail the different points of view and their possible variations as applied to the old-age insurance systems in different countries. Pribram distinguished between the insurance point of view, the budgetary approach, and the economic point of view. He discussed the role of the reserves, or of a reserve fund, as they were handled in Germany, Great Britain, France, and Czechoslovakia. He described the effect of payroll taxes in the course of the business cycles, boom, depression, and in between. And he recommended a macro-economic approach for the United States, by suggesting that the Social Security Board cooperate with the Treasury and Federal Reserve Board in fixing and redetermining the rates to be paid at different stages of the economic cycle. Such variable rates might cause some technical difficulties, but he advocated them as economically sound because they would establish a correlation between the cyclical movements of the economy and the amounts to be levied for the reserves of the benefit plans.

In addition to these five articles focusing on the business cycle, a number of others, written during the mid- and late 1930s, dealt with social and labor questions. These pieces also referred quite often to the cyclical nature of the conditions that caused the various problems, and to the difference in methods to combat them, according to the different stages of the economic cycle. These articles were: "A Unified Program for the Unemployed" (1935); "European Experience with Social Insurance" (1936); "Some Economic and Social Problems in Health Insurance: Social Security in the United States" (1936); "Some Causes of Economic Distress and Their Social Significance" (1936); "Social 'Insurance' in Europe and Social 'Security' in the United States: A Comparative Analysis" (1937); and "Labor Dispute Disqualification in Unemployment Compensation" (1941). In addition, there were extensive monographs written at the Social Security Board for internal use, a few of them in collaboration with others. Worth mentioning are: "Merit Rating and Unemployment Compensation" (1937) and "Principles, Underlying Disqualification for Benefits in Unemployment Compensation," parts one and two (1938 and 1939).

Of the published articles, "Social 'Insurance' in Europe and Social 'Security' in the United States: A Comparative Analysis" remains of current significance. It appeared in the *International Labor Review* in December 1937, and in a two-part German edition, in February and March 1938. It contrasted the European "insurance" type of assistance, which had developed over several decades, with the American "security" concept. It argued that the difference in the two systems lay in the different concept of social responsibility on the two continents.

Two articles of general economic and sociological interest also were published during that period, both in 1935. "European Experiences and New Deal Statistics" was a brief but serious conversation piece written for the American Statistical Association. Pribram contrasted Austrian and German statistical methods with those practiced in America. Early in his civil service career, before the First World War, when he was responsible for issuing the Austrian Statistical Yearbook, the Austrian approach to statistics was strictly analytical and atomistic, corresponding to the individualistic social philosophy that predominated in the country since the middle of the nineteenth century. The prevailing approach in Germany was of the "combining" type, a compromise between the needs of the state for information and the desire of the individuals to be left alone. Before the New Deal, American statistics had been atomistic to a much higher degree than any in Europe. In view of the general lack of regional and local statistics, New Deal statistics therefore were essentially directed toward obtaining reliable information on which to build regulatory measures. The newly created Central Statistical Board seemed to have coordinating functions, rather than synthetic ones. The article concluded with the observation that American social philosophy was at a crossroads when it embarked on the New Deal and that the development of American statistics would follow the general trend.

"Controlled Competition and the Organization of American Industry," published by the *Quarterly Journal of Economics* in May 1935, discussed in about twenty pages the meaning of "controlled" and "fair" competition, as it was defined under the New Deal, before the Senate inquiry into the National Recovery Act (NRA) had started. This piece is actually a by-product of his work for *Cartel Problems* and is cited in the book. The article anticipated in impressive detail, on economic and philosophical grounds, most of the arguments on which the Supreme Court later struck down the National Recovery Act legislation as too restrictive and alien to the American way of business.

In the late 1930s Karl Pribram also had an opportunity to pursue his ever-present interest in teaching. He was named adjunct professor at the American University's Graduate School in the Department of Economics, where he began teaching evening courses and continued to do so for many years; he specialized in economic theory and in housing. These courses were a new experience for him: the majority of his students were employed during the day, many in the civil service, and were generally older and more mature than the usual student population. They often brought up practical problems of their daily professional experience for discussion. He found that give-and-take quite challenging and interesting.

After the Second World War broke out in Europe, in early September 1939, the activities of the International Statistical Institute were again in abeyance. But an energetic group of ISI members, from the United States as well as from Central and South America, not only arranged a large and important statistical Congress in Washington, D.C., in May 1940, commemorating the 150th anniversary of the first United States census and the 50th anniversary of the Pan American Union, but also took that occasion to establish a long-planned Inter-American Statistical Institute as an offspring of the International Statistical Institute. Karl Pribram became one of the charter members of the new organization, which was brought into being at the Cosmos Club, in a small meeting of a few select members of the IASI. The IASI has been flourishing ever since.

By the end of 1941, after the United States had entered the conflict that had been raging in Europe since the fall of 1939, Washington's interest in domestic problems was gradually superseded by a preoccupation with foreign affairs, and the demand grew for capable people with specialized knowledge in that field. In the meantime, Karl Pribram had acquired United States citizenship, after fulfilling the necessary residence requirements; this was a prerequisite to obtain "clearance" for any sensitive position in wartime Washington. In July 1942 he left the Social Security Board and joined the U.S. Tariff Commission as a senior economist. In the course of the war, the Tariff Commission took on additional functions, which were more closely related to its present name of "International Trade Commission" than to its original responsibility for analyzing the effects of tariffs and the application of the relevant laws on the economy. Under this new direction, the commission undertook studies of the economies of foreign countries, their trade between one another and with the United States under conditions of war, and all related problems arising from war-induced production difficulties and shortages. In this connection, the commission regularly participated in numerous interagency meetings with the Departments of State, War, Commerce, and others, which were held at frequent intervals during and after the war, to discuss measures and legislation related to trade, tariffs, and similar matters. Karl Pribram attended most of these meetings, often representing the commission, and authored the relevant reports.

A most interesting period of his years with the Tariff Commission came in the spring and summer of 1950 in the form of an assignment of almost four months to Germany and Austria for special work with the HICOG (U.S. High Commissioner's Office, Germany) in Frankfort, on matters concerning tariffs, trade, and related legal questions. As a consequence of the war, Germany and Austria remained under the control of the victorious Allies exercised by High Commissioners, for almost ten years after cessation of hostilities. Each of the two countries was divided into four "Zones," each "Zone" supervised by one of their former enemies: the United States, Britain, France, and Russia. The city of Vienna was controlled by a combined Inter-Allied Command of all four powers. The High Commissioners in Germany were civilian, those in Austria military officials. The regimes of the High Commissioners from the United States, Britain, and France were benevolent and stayed discretely in the background, while trying to help the defeated countries back to normalcy. Russia, however, carted off whole plants, machines, furniture, and other valuables from its occupation zones and had trouble keeping its often brutal soldiers in check.

With another high official from the Tariff Commission and one from the Department of Commerce, Pribram took his first transatlantic flight in late March 1950, in a military plane, which required a stop-over in the Azores to make it to Frankfort. The HICOG command was headquartered in the I. G. Farben Building in Frankfort, miraculously untouched by bombs, where the three-man Washington group obtained offices for the duration of their stay. Much of the work was done in meetings, sometimes person-to-person, but mostly in larger groups, and frequently with the two other Western high commissioners and their staffs, in tripartite conferences. The trade and tariff topics discussed concerned steel, chemicals, agricultural products, and other important basic and manufactured commodities; also questions of tariffs and other forms of trade restrictions, such as quotas, quality requirements, and so forth. On a few occasions, German experts were called upon to participate in certain meetings, and Pribram's knowledge of Germany's special problems, its laws, and its language, speeded up and facilitated the negotiations.

Pribram took the opportunity of his stay in Frankfort to meet with former colleagues from the university and gave one lecture there, "Ideenrichtungen in der Nationalökonomie" ("Leading Ideas in Economics"). A lengthy assignment in Vienna, where he also renewed scientific and personal contacts, was similar in content to the one in Frankfort; shorter trips to Berlin and Munich, for related purposes, completed his appointment in Europe. Thereafter, he added a vacation in the Austrian Alps for recreation and a trip to Geneva to meet with former colleagues inside and outside the International Labor Office.

Karl Pribram stayed with the Tariff Commission until the end of November 1951, when he retired to private life and devoted most of the next nine or ten years to researching and writing the present book. His literary output during his time with the Tariff Commission covered several, mostly war-related, fields and concluded with a book on a topic of social philosophy to which he devoted much of his own time and concentration in those years.

An informative article on the International Labor Office appeared in the October 1942 issue of *Foreign Affairs*, under the title "The ILO: Present Functions and Future Tasks." It was based on the General Conference of the ILO held in New York, a year earlier, which Karl Pribram attended (this was before the United States had entered the war). The general tone at that meeting was the confident assurance of the participants that the Axis powers would be defeated; their interest was focused on the ILO's role after cessation of hostilities. The prevailing opinion at the conference was that the ILO would have to play a decisive role in reconstruction work, restoring economic activity, resettling workers from wartime to peacetime jobs, and maintaining employment. Pribram saw a few other problems in the ILO's future: when the ILO was founded in 1919, its primary mission was the establishment of international standards of labor legislation; this would emphatically not be its task after the Second World War. The international labor front, the backbone of the ILO, had been destroyed by the suppression of the trade union movement in the countries dominated by nationalistic parties and totalitarian methods. The labor movement split into national elements by the events of the war and would remain so for the indefinite future. This surprising prediction came to full realization in the postwar period.

Two articles, one on housing, the other on tariff problems, dealt with economic questions in connection with war and rearmament efforts. They were both published in the *American Economic Review,* eleven years and two different wars apart. "Housing Policy and the Defense Program" was written and published in December 1941, just before the United States entered the Second World War. Construction activity had begun to increase noticeably under the influence of an expanding economy, stimulated by the rearmament activity that marked the end of the Depression. The building cycle, which usually moves in waves of about eighteen to twenty-one years, also had reached a point where a take-off was indicated. The incipient building boom was furthered by a considerable rise in publicly financed construction and by a respectable, though much smaller, gain in private building permits. The mortgage market, in addition, had been considerably stabilized, due largely to the creation of the Federal Housing Administration, which had guaranteed almost 50 percent of all new construction in the last few years. Although these developments were most welcome after the long and hard years of a deeply depressed economy, Pribram cautioned that the incipient construction boom, supported by private and public financing, might compete with the demands of the wartime armaments industries, and might lead to shortages in material and skilled labor as well as trigger undesirable price rises. The article suggested that the Co-ordinator of Defense Housing as well as the Office of Price Administration might have to step in to regulate the situation.

In "Rearmament and a More Flexible Tariff Structure for the United States," published during the early stages of the Korean War, in the June 1952 issue of the *American Economic Review,* Pribram argued against a flexible tariff policy, even in a period of intensified rearmament efforts. Not only could most strategically important materials be imported duty-free into the United States anyway, but the role of tariffs in international trade was gradually being relegated to a subordinate position. Furthermore, alternating expansions and contractions of a flexible tariff policy would increase the inherent instability of the international exchange of goods, with all the negative consequences such instability would bring about.

Karl Pribram's main creative effort in the mid-1940s went into the writing of a book that dealt with his favorite topic: the interplay of abstract forms of thought with concrete manifestations of action in the field of social events. His *Conflicting Patterns of Thought,* which appeared in 1949, but was finished some time earlier, was a philosophical study whose origins in Karl Pribram's own intellectual history went back to a treatise he had written in 1917–18 under the title "Die Weltanschauungen der Völker und ihre Politik" ("The Philosophies of Nations and Their Politics"). Both works were conceived during wartime, trying to explain in a measured, intellectual way the insanity of armed conflicts among civilized nations. In this book, he distinguished and described in detail four different types of thought that were basic to the intellectual fabric of various nations, which led to different social structures and different conclusions in their thinking and, finally, to dissimilar decisions in their politics. These patterns of reasoning were: the nominalistic, the universalistic, the organismic or intuitional, and the dialectic.

Nominalistic reasoning produced the social structure of the Anglo-Saxon nations, mainly that of Britain, and, to a large extent, that of the United States. Democratic institutions in politics and social life corresponded to it, as did free competition in the economic sphere. The universalistic mode of thinking prevailed in the Middle Ages but survived far beyond that period in many forms and places. Its rigid system of general concepts found its political counterpart in the rigid hierarchical system of feudalism that continued to the present in various disguised forms. The organismic pattern of reasoning, occasionally identified as intuitional pattern, led to fervent nationalism in the political sphere, when applied to states or nations, and, in the field of economics, led to a rejection of the equilibrium concept and other mechanistic principles. The home of organismic-intuitional reasoning was mostly in Germany, but it found convinced adherents in southern and south-eastern Europe. It reached an extreme form of exaggeration during the era of National Socialism. Dialectic reasoning was developed by Marx and Engels, who based it partly on a distortion of the ideas of the German philosopher Hegel. Marxism, or, as Pribram preferred to call its Russian version, Bolshevism, was the prevailing form of reasoning in Soviet Russia. The idea of "economic imperialism" was one of several of its tenets, stating that wars among world powers were inescapable.

The work further analyzed the four forms of thinking in relation to religion, to social organization and social responsibility, to the concept of liberty, to the attitude toward science and the arts, to the economic problems of planning and international trade, and returned again to the question of armed conflicts and the quest for a lasting peace, which was thwarted by the Bolshevist doctrines.

Karl Pribram ended his *Conflicting Patterns* with a challenge to nominalistic thinking, as the one objective form of reasoning, to bring about compromises with and among the other forms of thinking and to organize the fight against the one irreconcilable form—Bolshevist reasoning. In his words that conclude the book, "the struggle for democratic institutions, based on the principles of individual liberty and self-responsibility, and the struggle to maintain the validity of nominalistic methods of reasoning are fundamentally struggles for the same cause."

After retirement, Karl Pribram concentrated on the present book and wrote only very little for publication: a few book reviews, an occasional contribution to professional meetings. But he attended many such conferences in Washington, elsewhere in the United States, and abroad; much of his considerable traveling was done in connection with such meetings. He also continued his relations with the Tariff Commission, after he had left, by participating in some of its social events; and he kept in particularly regular contact with its library, which, for many years, graciously provided him with the books for his work that he could not otherwise buy or borrow.

Many of his travels abroad were planned around sessions of the International Statistical Institute (ISI). The institute itself had been thoroughly reorganized after the Second World War, under the influence and leadership of its American contingent. An important meeting in Washington, D.C., in September 1947, turned the exclusive and restricted institute into a general membership organization, open to all qualified statisticians and scientists in related fields. While the institute's pioneering character in the past was acknowledged and praised, it was obvious that it could not compete with the huge international statistical organizations that had sprung up after the First and the Second World Wars, most of them within the framework of the League of Nations and the United Nations. While long-time members regretted the loss of close personal contacts and shared experiences, they acknowledged the need for change and accepted it in a rather turbulent session. There was no change, however, in the choice of far-flung locations for the institute's biennial meetings. Yet the attendance, especially of the local participants in the various locations, increased sharply, and the relatively intimate and personal character of the former meetings came to an end.

Karl Pribram attended the ISI's twenty-eighth meeting in Rome in September 1953. He preceded it in August with a visit to Geneva, a stay in the high Western mountains and at the warm southern lakes of Switzerland, and traveled to Rome with a stopover in Milan, to see its marvelous cathedral. Rome welcomed the statistical session with particular grace. Italy's president, at that time, was Luigi Einaudi, a noted economist of international reputation and a member of longstanding of the ISI; several cabinet members also belonged to the ISI. In view of these special ties, the visitors were given a splendid reception at the magnificent Quirinale, the presidential palace, which was rarely accessible to outsiders. A mass audience with the pope was arranged at his summer residence in Castel Gandolfo. The intellectual Pius XII greeted the visitors in several languages and then gave a comprehensive talk in French on statistical problems. A memorable social event was the reception of the group in the torch-lit gardens of the U.S. Embassy by then ambassador, Mrs. Claire Booth Luce.

Rome's glorious sights make any visitor long for more. On his way north, to Vienna, Karl Pribram stopped for a few days each in Assisi, Perugia, Florence, and Venice, to enjoy their beauty, though he had seen all of these places, as well as Rome, several times before, on previous trips. This time, some five days in Vienna and about twice as long in Paris, were visits of a private character, seeing old friends and colleagues, haunting bookstores and libraries, and dropping in on universities. In Vienna, he noted with satisfaction that reconstruction work had progressed, but the city was still occupied by foreign military personnel and would remain so until 1955, when a *Staats-Vertrag* (State Treaty)* finally returned Austria's independence, under a guarantee of permanent neutrality. It was not before his next visit to Vienna, in 1957, that he saw the city free again, governed by its own citizens according to its own devices.

For the next few years he worked regular, though somewhat reduced, hours on his book, mostly at home, but also occasionally at various libraries. He kept in frequent touch with Washington's perennial discussions of economics, by attending meetings and informal get-togethers in clubs, at the Brookings Institution, at the Federal Reserve Board, at the International Monetary Fund and its sister organization, the International Bank for Reconstruction and Development, and also at the Philosophical Society. A pleasant event in early 1954 was the news from the University of Frankfort that he had been named professor emeritus for economic and social sciences (*Wirtschaftswissenschaften*).

In 1957, when he was almost eighty, he decided to attend that year's meeting of the International Statistical Institute, which was scheduled in Sweden, where he had never been. Again, he built an almost two-month voyage around the nine-day conference. The first stop was Frankfort and a visit to the university, for discussions with members of the faculty, and a special meeting on the "History of Ideas" that was called in his honor. An extended weekend was spent in Bonn, the new capital of the truncated Federal Republic of Germany: a charming old university town on the Rhine River, which, at that time, neither looked nor acted like a capital city. It has developed and grown since then. A visit to

---

*According to international law, no "Peace Treaty" could be concluded with Austria, because, theoretically, it did not exist during the war, having been gobbled up by Germany in 1938, a year and a half before the war broke out. So, the learned brains invented the "legal construction" of a "State Treaty."

nearby Cologne and its imposing dome was followed by a flight to Norway's capital, Oslo, the first of the three Scandinavian countries he was to see.

He spent several enjoyable August days sailing through fjords before coming to Oslo. A dinner conversation at the lovely estate of one of Norway's well-known citizens, a colleague and member of International Statistical Institute, provided the first inkling of the deep-seated differences among the three Scandinavian countries, which speak and write such very similar languages that the educated class can read one another's books and can make themselves understood to one another when speaking. At that time, the still vivid memories of their different war experiences, though twelve years in the past, may have accentuated the differences, but they were palpably there. Norway and Denmark had been overrun by Germans; true, Norway had its own Quisling, but also an underground resistance; Denmark resisted more openly; but Sweden had remained neutral and essentially untouched. The other two took note of that.

After stops in Stockholm and Copenhagen, he continued further South to Munich, really meant only as a transfer point to his next goal in the Austrian Alps, but tempting enough for a short stay to visit its famous Pinakothek (Art Museum), whose irreplaceable pictures had safely survived the war in one of the nearby salt mines. His destination to be reached from Munich was the European Forum Alpbach of the Austrian College. Alpbach is a mountain-village located at mid-elevation in the Austrian Alps of Tyrol, about two or three hours east of Innsbruck. Starting in 1945, right after the War, the devoted and united efforts of an international group of mostly European academicians, spearheaded by an Austrian group, had turned Alpbach into a summer college of gradually growing importance, scope, and recognition. Originally focusing on the "restoration of the lost universality of academic education," it soon encompassed all sciences of the humanistic type, with a strong emphasis on philosophy, but including social problems, political questions, and reaching as far as music and art. In recent years, economics have played an increasingly important role, largely due to American influence. The somewhat forbidding general theme of the 1957 assembly was "Mythos, Utopia, and Ideology: Elements for the Understanding of the Present." Yet it covered the then acute problem of European collaboration: August 1957 was only seven months before the establishment of the European Economic Community, by the Treaty of Rome in March 1958, a topic that was discussed by the prominent German statesman Walter Hallstein. Next to several other practical topics, the questions of the "city" found much interest: this was the time when Le Corbusier's "Cité Radieuse" (The Radiant City) was a well-known concept. Karl Pribram took part in several of the seminar-type sessions and delighted his audience by his ability to understand and answer their questions in three languages.

In addition to the Austrians and Germans, there were French, Italian, and British academicians, and the beginning of an American contingent. The American participation has since grown in large measure, both among the lecturers and the students. But even in 1957 America had done more than its share: the only modern "large" hotel, of some thirty or forty rooms, had been financed with Marshall Plan money. Those who could not be housed there—and that was the vast majority—had to content themselves with accommodations in small inns or private rooms, often in outlying villages. In the quarter century since then, Alpbach's Forum has grown considerably in size and influence and has established itself as an important meeting place for serious discussion during the summer, attracting the best minds from many countries as teachers and students to its lovely alpine location.

From Tyrol he traveled to Vienna for his first visit after the city had been freed from foreign occupation. In the two years since Austria had regained its independence in 1955, Vienna had made great strides in eliminating many of the remaining vestiges of war, occupation, and foreign influence. The half-destroyed opera house had been rebuilt, outwardly in the old style, but with a completely modernized, technically advanced interior; it was playing again, usually to sold-out performances. Some of the larger hotels that had been overused, and, in the case of the Russians, vandalized, had been restored, thoroughly cleaned, and refurbished. A new impressive high fountain decorated one of the beautiful large squares off the Ring (the tree-lined beltway around the city); and while one wondered about the need for this extravaganza in a very tight economy, one realized that the tall jet of water completely obliterated the view of a statue showing a Russian soldier with a clenched fist, which had been erected during the occupation. This was quite a skillful way of dealing with a mighty and potentially dangerous big power with whom diplomatic and trade relations and other peaceful pursuits had to be carried on: leaving its insulting memento untouched, but out of view. Some of the war damage, however, was permanent. The University of Vienna lost many of its records and parts of its specialized libraries to bombs and fire; its interesting ceiling, in vivid colors and gold, representing the four faculties, and painted by the internationally known Viennese artist Gustave Klimt, was replaced by simple masonry. The most serious loss, however, was the irreplaceable stained glass windows of St. Stephen's Cathedral, Vienna's characteristic landmark. St. Stephen's, the only authentic gothic building in the city, sits right in its center and dominates the landscape with its high slender spire. The warm colors of its windows in their pointed arched frames had filtered the light for five or six centuries of war and peace, and had remained intact. This time, they should have been removed for protection to mountain caves or salt mines, as were the pictures of the museums, or as Paris had done with the glorious windows of the Sainte Chapelle. But this precaution was not applied and so they were irretrievably destroyed; they are now replaced by rather banal pastel tinted combinations of small rectangular panes of glass.

The departure of the occupying forces made travel easy again everywhere in Vienna and its surroundings including the former Russian Zone; technically it had been possible also during the occupation, but was not advisable. Karl Pribram made ample use of these new possibilities and saw friends who lived on outlying estates with large grounds. He also met with some of his former German colleagues who had come to Vienna at the time he was there. Among the special pleasures Vienna had to offer again were its political cabarets whose biting wit, of necessity subdued during the occupation, blossomed anew under the regained freedom. This visit turned out to be his last one to the city, though it had not been planned that way.

During the next few years, while working on his book, he traveled exclusively in the United States or in this hemisphere: to big cities for meetings in winter and spring, to the mountains, the seashore, and to California during the summer. His interest in the philosophical and interdisciplinary background of his science grew even stronger than it had been throughout his life. It showed in the type of conferences in which he participated and in the material he read. It showed strongly in the invited contribution he prepared for a meeting of the International Institute for Sociology, scheduled for the summer of 1960 in Mexico City. It is entitled ''The Influence of Philosophical Principles on Social Organization.'' This is an abstract philosophical piece, which touches on economic problems only occasionally, for illustrative purposes. Pribram had presented the leading ideas of this paper before, especially in his book *Conflicting Patterns of Thought*, where they were developed in great detail, but he had never done it in such a concentrated form. The impact of these ideas, however, was all the more striking in this compact version. From his discussion he concluded with the thought that the history of the Western World can be viewed as a fight between antagonistic patterns of thought. A "logical interpretation of history" might mitigate the consequences of this antagonism and lead to suitable policies for coping peacefully with such basic difficulties. This paper was published in the institute's Report ("Memoire") of the Mexico Session, its nineteenth.

In August 1960 Pribram flew to Mexico City to participate in the meeting on sociology. He had been in Mexico once before, almost thirty years earlier, and was looking forward to seeing this lively city again and to visiting some other places in the country where he had never been. This time, however, he found Mexico City's high elevation of over seven thousand feet quite overwhelming and had to limit his activities from the start. He sharply curtailed his usually thorough sightseeing and confined it, in moderation, to the major points. Although Pribram abbreviated the rest of his trip, he nevertheless continued, as planned with short stays at several places in lower elevations, such as the "silver" cities of Cuernavaca and Taxco; historic Oaxaca, at the foot of the Sierra Mountains; and some seashore resorts like Acapulco. After his return to Washington, it took months for him to recuperate from his ill-defined exhaustion, induced by the Mexican trip. During that time he carefully refrained from any definitive work of refining and polishing his manuscript, as he had intended to do.

In August of the following year, 1961, he took part again in a meeting of the International Statistical Institute (ISI), which was held in Paris. To complete his recovery, he decided to go to France in a leisurely way, by a ship that landed in Cannes, on the French Riviera. Two weeks of swimming in the warm Mediterranean Sea and excursions into the spectacular hinterland of the Riviera greatly contributed to the restoration of his former strength. A comfortable overnight train brought him from Cannes to Paris. The meeting of the International Institute for Statistics was held at the "Centre des Conférences Internationales" located near the Etoile, at the upper end of the Champs Elysées. Paris combined the meeting of the ISI with the centenary celebration of its own Parisian Statistical Society, just as London had done in 1934, when it invited the ISI for the celebration of the Royal Statistical Society's hundred years of existence.

Two years later, he again attended a session of the International Statistical Institute, which was held in Ottawa, Canada, in late August 1963. The noted liberal politician Lester B. Pearson was prime minister at that time; he gave a very thoughtful farewell address to the meeting. Ottawa was Karl Pribram's last trip out of the country for a professional meeting, but he continued to attend many of the sessions of the American Economic Association, among them in Boston, in late 1963, the same year as Ottawa, and one in San Francisco in 1966, which he combined with visits to relatives living in that area.

During the decade of the 1960s he continued, in general, with the revision of his manuscript, possibly with the idea in the back of his mind of performing some radical changes. But it never came to that: he needed more rest and relaxation than ever before and in many ways he pursued these recreational activities with the same zest he used to devote to his work. This was the time he "discovered" the Caribbean islands, which began to become more and more accessible to leisurely travel. He went to several of those islands, and also to Bermuda, a number of times, and composed some very amusing, rhymed poems about the places, their history, their people, and their visitors. Unfortunately these verses are in German and thus accessible to only a few of his friends; in translation such light verses lose most of their wit and verve, often even their meaning.

His real love for recreation, however, had always been mountains. Over the decades, he had spent countless weekends and longer stays in the Blue Ridge Mountains south of Washington and continued to do so, several times each year, from early spring into late fall. As time went on, he had to limit his long walks on the mountain trails, but he still enjoyed the view and the fresh air.

His ninetieth birthday came in December 1967. He celebrated it at home with a large gathering of friends, without explaining that it was a special occasion. The University of Frankfort sent a special bronze medallion with his name engraved, in recognition of his work in the field of economics and social sciences, and also an appropriate valuable book. The celebration was repeated with a different group, toward the end of the month when the American Economic Association held its annual meeting in Washington, and several of his out-of-town colleagues, who attended, became available. He was in good health and spirits and enjoyed, with some amusement, his guests, who were not told the reason for the parties. Gradually, over the following years, his strength and health subsided. He died on 14 July 1973, midway between his ninety-fifth and ninety-sixth year.

EDITH PRIBRAM

Overview: A Summary of *A History of Economic Reasoning*

THE STRUGGLE over the fundamental aspects of economic analysis is due to factors outside the scope of economics strictly speaking. The ultimate causes of that struggle are found in conflicting currents of thought which have determined the development of methods of reasoning in all fields of intellectual, social, political, and moral activities of the Western Hemisphere.

The history of economics starts with the Thomistic economic doctrine, a normative discipline ruled by the principles of the Scholastic philosophy. That doctrine slowly disintegrated under the influence of a pattern of "hypothetical" reasoning which was advocated mainly by Franciscan scholars in opposition to the Dominican followers of Thomism. The hypothetical pattern found a firm footing, especially in England, where it became basic to the Baconian methodology and was refined by John Locke and David Hume. It provided the background for the development of mercantilist economics, which was marked by the increasing application of the idea of causality and of mechanistic concepts, especially the equilibrium principle, to the analysis of economic relationships. Thus, in the course of the eighteenth century, economics was transformed from a moral discipline into a science the propositions of which were derived from a few abstract premises and were largely free from normative connotations. Viewed from that angle, the reasoning of the Mercantilists is to be distinguished from the Physiocratic doctrine; the latter was strongly influenced by the Cartesian methodology and the teachings of the Cameralists, which were permeated by intuitive concepts.

About the beginning of the nineteenth century, a second period in the history of economic reasoning opened with an intellectual movement that resulted in the spread of Baconian methods among French and German economists. In England, however, consistent application of rigid mechanical principles to economic analysis was strongly supported by the development of the associational psychology which had been elaborated by adherents of the utilitarian philosophy. The Ricardian doctrine was the brainchild of that epistemology, according to which the study of dynamic economic processes was superseded by the analysis of mechanical relationships between economic magnitudes. Consequent upon that approach, any considerations relating to change or development were placed beyond the pales of economic theory strictly speaking. The influence of methodological principles on the development of science can hardly be better illustrated than by the history of economics.

The transformation of the Ricardian doctrine started, on the one hand, from the adjustment of the traditional cost of production theory to the principles of marginal productivity and, on the other, from the abandonment of the Scholastic substance concept of the goods, which had provided the basis for the labor cost theory of value. The principle of marginalism as applied to utility analysis appeared in three versions: an Anglo-Saxon version, which was derived from the utilitarian philosophy; a French, mathematical version, connected with considerations of probability; and a psychological, Austrian version, based on introspective observation of psychological processes. Methodological differences were responsible for divergencies in the setting of fundamental problems. Extraordinary difficulties were involved in adjusting the mechanistic approach to the study of the fluctuating behavior of business activity and in defining the functions of money as an important factor in influencing that behavior.

But, beginning with the middle of the nineteenth century, the principles of hypothetical reasoning were confronted with the organized resistance of the adherents of two other patterns of thought which originated on German soil: intuitive reasoning and dialectic reasoning. The large majority of German economists adopted the ''historical'' approach to economic analysis, which was based on the conviction that ''truth'' could be grasped directly with the aid of some sort of intuitive processes. That conviction provided the background for the conception of the ''national economy'' as an integrated whole or organism, ruled by historical laws of its own and involved in continuous struggles over predominance with other national powers similarly constructed. But prolonged attempts to use methods of intuitive insight for the establishment of historical laws were not crowned with significant success.

The dialectical pattern that supplied the methodological basis for the Marxian doctrine was hailed by its adherents as an infallible instrument for establishing ''evolutionary'' laws which were alleged to underlie the development of the capitalist economy and to lead to its inevitable breakdown. But in due course the doctrine became the object of conflicting interpretations, which were reflected in the struggles between orthodox Marxists and Revisionists on the one hand, and Bolshevists and Mensheviks on the other.

The fight between conflicting currents of thought which had been waged during the nineteenth century came to a climax after the First World War. Intuitive methods were abundantly used to develop fascist and national-socialist philosophies. Dialectic reasoning, adapted to their purposes by the leaders of the Soviet Union, provided the justification for the organization of a vast communist empire. Since intuitional currents of thought rapidly disintegrated after the defeat of the regimes that its adherents had glorified, the development of economic doctrine proceeded, after the Second World War, along two main lines: hypothetical reasoning was pitted in an unbridgeable contrast against bolshevist reasoning.

Bolshevist economic thought has passed through a series of stages, which were mainly determined by the task of adjusting the principles of Marxian dialectics to the purpose of Soviet power politics and the exigencies of a rapidly expanding, highly industrialized economy. That process is still in flux, and an end to it is not yet in sight.

In the sphere of hypothetical reasoning the methodological differences that had accounted for the existences of different schools of marginal analysis were gradually overcome under the increasing influence of the mathematical approach, which appeared to supply a sound basis for the analysis of economic relationships. Objections raised by the adherents of the institutional approach failed to stem that tide. About the middle of the thirties, the Keynesian theory of employment appeared to open the prospect of developing a new consistent and comprehensive doctrine. But that prospect did not materialize, and in due course the attention of the economists was drawn, in rapid succession, to an increasing range of more or less isolated problems, the treatment of which required far-reaching adjustment of old and adoption of new methods of economic analysis. These problems can be characterized by the headings imperfect competition, theory of games, centralized planning, econometrics, dynamic economics, or economic growth. It is a striking fact that in the course of intensified discussions of specific issues of that type, the search for a new comprehensive unifying doctrine was practically abandoned.

It is a moot question to what degree any significant progress in the field of economic analysis is dependent upon the establishment of a unifying doctrine. But there can be no doubt that such a doctrine is an indispensable instrument for the understanding of the functioning of the exchange economy and for its defense against the attacks of its adversaries. When viewed in the light of these considerations, the study of the history of economic reasoning is not simply the fulfillment of a historian's dream or a logician's aspirations, but a contribution to the discussion of a fundamental problem of our times, which is reflected in the splitting up of the world into two hostile camps. Any other arguments that might be advanced to justify the elaboration of the history of economic doctrines pale into insignificance when compared with that aspect of such an analysis.

A History of
Economic Reasoning

BOOK ONE

The Development of Economics into an Independent Discipline

Thirteenth through Eighteenth Centuries

Part I

Economics As an Element of Moral Theology

Chapter 1
Thomistic Economics

THE LOGICAL BACKGROUND OF THOMISTIC ECONOMICS

THE QUESTION of where to start the history of economic reasoning is an intriguing one. It has been answered in various ways by different authors. The economic views advanced by philosophers of the pre-Christian era are frequently dealt with in the introductory chapters of histories of economic thought. References are also made to the economic precepts proclaimed in the Holy Scriptures, or special attention is given to the economic principles which were basic to the codification of Roman law in the sixth century. There is no doubt that noteworthy views about economic and social conditions and remarkable economic maxims can be found in these and other documents, and they might be very interesting for a history of economic and social institutions. Modern economic reasoning, however, has not been influenced by Prescholastic ideas directly, but rather as the concepts were filtered through the minds of thirteenth- and fourteenth-century Schoolmen and as they were reinterpreted by some thinkers of the Renaissance period. In fact, the economic views which prevailed in the early Middle Ages belonged to the realm of theological ratiocination rather than to economic reasoning in its own right. Hence, the discussion of prescholastic views will find its place within the context of Scholastic economics, and the purposes of this book will be best served by starting with the thirteenth century, when a more or less consistent body of economic doctrine was developed by eminent Scholastics.

The consolidation of economic views which took place in the thirteenth century was partly due to the fact that the crusaders had brought to the cities of Italy and some other European countries the knowledge of new methods of organizing industrial and commercial activities. Even more instrumental, perhaps, in promoting a new approach to economic problems was another fact: all relevant writings of the Greek philosopher Aristotle (384–322 B.C.) were gradually made available in Latin translations,[1] along with various treatises in which Arabian philosophers had interpreted Aristotle's works in the light of their own reasoning. Of particular importance for the subsequent development of Western thought was a translation into Latin of the commentaries on Aristotle's *Ethics* by the Cordoban philosopher ibn-Rushd, called Averroës (1126–1198).[2]

A new approach to the formation of fundamental concepts was suggested by the Aristotelian logic, as distinct from the principles of the Neoplatonic philosophy which had dominated Scholastic discussions for almost eight centuries. Moreover, the Aristotelian works included extensive and highly stimulating arguments concerning many juridical, moral, and political problems; they supplied logical support for certain rules of the canonical doctrine and considerations for adjusting other precepts to changing social and economic conditions. In due course, not only was Aristotle recognized as the main authority in the field of logic but his reasoning in practically all scientific fields was also held in high esteem and was widely used to interpret and elaborate on the principles derived from Biblical texts. The authority of Aristotle occupied the highest rank among the non-Biblical sources of knowledge in the summae, the theological and philosophical treatises of the thirteenth-century Schoolmen.[3]

The adjustment of Scholastic reasoning to Aristotelian methods of cognition was mainly the work of two great Dominican theologians, Albert, Count of Bollstadt, called Albertus Magnus (d. 1280), and Thomas Aquinas (1225?–1274). In his *Summa Theologica,* Saint Thomas supplied the most systematic comprehensive presentation of the theological, moral, sociological, and economic principles developed by the Schoolmen under the influence of the Aristotelian approach. He also digested the views of his Scholastic predecessors and adapted them to the requirements of his own time. For centuries to come, the "Doctor Angelicus," the "Princeps Scholasticorum," as he was called by his admirers, became the great teacher in all Scholastic disciplines.[4] The ethical and especially the social and economic maxims of the clerical authorities were patterned after his views; his works were frequently referred to in deciding upon disputed questions, and they became dominant far beyond the sphere of religious issues in the countries in which the Catholic Church succeeded in maintaining its authority. Of course, the economic teachings of Saint Thomas and his disciples were not elaborated in special tracts or treatises; such an isolated treatment of a specific field of human relations would hardly have been compatible with Scholastic principles. But it has been possible to piece together the economic views of the leading thirteenth-century Schoolmen from their writings, and the term *Thomistic economics* can be applied conveniently to the outcome of their discussions about values and prices, the nature of money, the essential aspects of exchanges of goods, the problem of distributive justice, the justification of private ownership, the organization of productive activities and markets, and the definition of illicit gains. A coherent picture can thus be given of the leading ideas which provided the background for the economic institutions of the last centuries of the Middle Ages.

In order to understand the characteristic features of the conceptual structure of Thomistic economics, it would be advisable to contrast the principles of Aristotelian logic with those of the Neoplatonic methodology which had determined medieval thinking during the preceding centuries. Both the Neoplatonic and the Aristotelian logic were ruled by a fundamental proposition, the belief in the real existence of general notions (universals) which, established by the Creator from eternity to eternity in a hierarchical order, can be grasped by the human mind and thus can provide absolutely valid knowledge. The universals were held to represent the ideal prototypes for all perishable individual things and beings which can be perceived by the senses. This principle was expressed in the often quoted statement *"Universale intelligitur, singulare sentitur."* Underlying that statement was the belief that the substance of a thing or being, the aggregate of its essential attributes, was to be distinguished from its accidental features, and that a thing was to be considered closer to perfect, the better it was equipped with all the essential attributes of the class to which it was assigned in accordance with the divine will as expressed in the act of creation. This dichotomy between the power of cognition and the function of the senses was reflected in the distinction drawn between the immortal soul and the perishable body. It was a characteristic feature of Scholastic psychology, and it was frequently connected with the view that the human will, though free, was strictly subordinated to the dictates of reason, since the will might easily be misled by the influence of the unreliable senses.

The change in the methods of thinking which was brought about by the adoption of Aristotelian logic consisted, above all, in a redefinition of the functions of reason. The medieval adherents of Neoplatonic metaphysics had availed themselves of a hierarchical order of "emanations" and "illuminations" in linking up the human mind with an indeterminate, infinite, absolute source of all general notions. However, in accordance with the Aristotelian principles of reasoning, the mind was endowed with the faculty of using methods of abstraction to derive the general notions from the "essential" features common to a group or class of comparable objects. Every series of such objects was believed to embody a supreme generic quality which comprehended all the characteristics common to these objects.[5] Subspecies at various levels could be defined by properties belonging only to specific groups or classes of such objects.[6]

The revolutionary effects of the introduction of abstraction as an instrument for forming general notions cannot be too strongly emphasized. The universals which, according to Neoplatonic philosophy, were believed to exist in reality, independently of the things of which they were the prototypes, were now found to be directly accessible to the human mind through processes of analyzing the individual things. Thus, a limited use of observation was combined with the application of deductive methods, which consisted of drawing the logical consequences from the definitions of the abstract concepts.

It is not necessary to deal in this connection with some intricate problems which the Aristotelian Schoolmen endeavored in vain to solve, especially the question of how to reconcile the conception of general notions which had no beginning or end with the belief that these ideas provided the patterns for all individual things that are generated and that perish. Similarly, extended discussions turned on the question of how to account for the transformation of general notions into individual things or beings. As distinct from their Neoplatonic predecessors, whose world was composed of "essences," the Aristotelian Scholastics attached considerable importance to the problems of "existence" and "becoming." Logical questions quite frequently assumed metaphysical aspects, and metaphysical questions were formulated in terms of logical issues.[7]

The search for substances came to have primary importance for the Aristotelian Scholastics, since the substance of a thing represented the embodiment of its essential properties. It was the substance concept which played a dominant role in determining the

Scholastic approach to some fundamental economic problems, and up to the First World War almost every important development in methods of economic reasoning was marked by a change in the meaning and significance attached to this concept.

Adjustment of the Aristotelian methods to the requirements of the medieval theology led to a clear distinction between revelation and reason as two separate sources of knowledge. Thus, the way was opened for a separation of the *"sacra doctrina"* (supernatural theology) from "natural theology," which was held to be accessible to human understanding and was included among the *"philosophicae disciplinae."*[8] Moreover, the study of the voluminous Aristotelian writings provided effective arguments for the view that there existed outside the strictly religious issues a large sphere of questions which could be treated independently of metaphysical considerations and with a certain degree of flexibility. In this field a considerable latitude could be granted to the expression of divergent views, and due regard could be paid to the opinions of the officially recognized pagan authorities. The bulk of social and economic problems was assigned to this group and was dealt with in accordance with the principles of the Aristotelian epistemology. That treatment was reflected in the typical question form of many thirteenth-century Scholastic writings. The discussion of a disputed issue commonly started with the statement of an argument in which an accepted view was questioned. The almost incredible predilection of many Scholastic authors for subtle and even abstruse distinctions found a fertile field in such disputations. Perhaps they provided a psychological counterweight to the limitations which were imposed on Scholastic reasoning in other respects.

All general notions which referred to human beings were formulated as ideals characterized by normative attributes. A hierarchical social order was established by a range of definitions which started with the standard of duties for Christians in general. The more specific tasks and duties imposed on the various classes, and the occupational and professional groups of the population, were defined in accordance with this standard.

Thus, medieval economics consisted of a body of definitions and precepts designed to regulate Christian behavior in the spheres of production, consumption, distribution, and exchange of goods. Individual behavior and its rightfulness provided the starting point for all considerations, since the life of every human being was primarily regarded as a preparation for the salvation of his soul. But, in addition, such behavior was commonly subordinated to the obligations resulting from collective responsibilities imposed on specific groups or classes of the population.

The clerical authorities assumed the mission of adjusting the conditions of the lower perishable world to the principles derived from the "universals," the abstract notions taught by reason. They claimed the right to control not only the moral and spiritual but also the vocational and social behavior of clerics and laics alike in order to prevent the spread of practices regarded as sinful.

If absolute truth could be arrived at with the aid of abstract concepts, it was evident that only one valid definition corresponded to each of these concepts. The church claimed the exclusive privilege of deciding with finality on these definitions, and of condemning as heretical any deviation from the officially proclaimed tenets and judgments. Any opposition to final cathedral utterances constituted a sinful attack upon the logical principles underlying orthodox reasoning and implicitly upon the logical foundation of the church and its existence. As long as the belief in the absolute validity of that reasoning remained undisputed, the church could easily suppress any movements directed against the maintenance of its supreme authoritative rule, and could exercise a firm control over a wide range of social and economic functions of professional, literary, and artistic activities. Practically all educational facilities were monopolized by the church. The study of higher branches of learning was accessible only through the medium of the Latin language, which supplied the appropriate terms for the eternally valid ideas and their officially adopted definitions. That language was not only an excellent vehicle for precise expression of thoughts but also an outstanding instrument for general training in logical methods.

The vernacular was considered unfit for imparting knowledge; it could be used only for the expression of sentiments and the discussion of perishable individual things or beings and their relations. But no reliable knowledge of the eternally valid ideas could be derived from sensations, the cognitive source of individual things or events. Many characteristic features of medieval social conditions, institutions, and artistic and literary performances can be accounted for when due consideration is given to the logical principles that were fundamental to the reasoning of the Schoolmen and that were applied by them in their persistent efforts to regulate practically all aspects of life.

THE THOMISTIC CONCEPTION OF SOCIAL COLLECTIVITIES

The belief in the "reality" of the "substance" which provided each individual with unity and lasting characteristics had a counterpart in the belief in the real existence of certain human collectivities which were held to owe their origin to the divine will and to be endowed with suprahuman objectives.

A regrettable confusion has been created by the Austrian economist Othmar Spann, who has used the term *universalism* as opposed to *individualism* to denote such social philosophies as have attached reality and supraindividual existence to certain social collectivities (nations, churches, states, and the like).[9] However, according to commonly accepted usage, *universalism*, as opposed to *nominalism*, connotes those doctrines which agree in attaching reality to general notions. It is in this sense that the term *universalism* and its derivatives are used in this book.

Nevertheless it is quite obvious that a logical connection can be found to exist between the universalistic approach to the problems of cognition and the tendency to attach real existence to certain collectivities conceived of as integrated wholes. A characteristic instance in point was the Scholastic construction of the concept of mankind. Burdened with the original sin through the faults of the first couple, mankind was held to be responsible as a single body to the Creator for the behavior of all its members.[10] The idea of collective responsibility could hardly have found more consistent expression than in the conceptions underlying the doctrine of the fall from grace which characterized mankind as a *corpus mysticum*, a *universitas*.[11] The principle of collective responsibility was also widely applied to social bodies which were held to be of human origin.

The outstanding social collectivity to which the Scholastics ascribed real existence was the church. That organization was believed to have been established by the Creator from eternity to eternity. The Holy Roman Empire was similarly conceived of as an integrated part of the all-embracing (Catholic) community represented by the church which claimed supreme authority in all spiritual and temporal matters. This superiority was officially asserted by Pope Boniface VIII in the bull *Unam Sanctam* (1302).

But the Aristotelian conception of the political community as an integrated whole endowed with real existence was not simply taken over by the Scholastics.[12] They accepted only the Aristotelian proposition that it was a "natural necessity" for man to live in society;[13] hence, they connected the origin of the political communities with a social instinct, an empirical fact, not with a transcendental principle, and they analyzed integrated communities with the aid of a juridical fiction.[14] They considered man's active contribution to the realization of a sound social order prerequisite to the communal life. In accordance with this reasoning, the organization of political bodies was attributed to human convention. The exercise of legislative and coercive powers by governments was justified on the ground that secular rulers were needed in order to control the behavior of the sinful human beings more immediately and effectively than could by done by the church.[15]

The juridical prototype of the political communities as conceived of by Saint Thomas was supplied by the "corporations" of Roman law, which had been organizations created by common agreement for the promotion of the welfare of their numbers.[16] The functions of the rulers were defined in accordance with the principles of the "*justitia generalis vel legalis.*"[17] The subjects of unworthy rulers were held to be authorized not only to resist the imposition of unjust orders but also to depose such rulers.[18] The Scholastic philosophy of history centered on the task of discovering by deductive reasoning the divine will as it manifested itself in the rise and downfall of the large empires. The establishment of God's kingdom on earth was considered the ultimate outcome of all history. Prompted by ideas of this kind, the medieval historians were generally quite ready to subordinate the accuracy of their reporting to the tendency to demonstrate the final adjustment of the course of events to the principles of divine justice.

Of paramount importance to the subsequent development of the philosophies of jurisprudence and economics were the careful distinctions made by the Aristotelian Scholastics between the different sources of justice and law.[19] Divine reason, held to be beyond human understanding and comprehension, was regarded as the ultimate source of justice. Hence, revelation, a gift of God's grace, supplied a safe knowledge of the absolutely binding precepts of the divine law. The rules of the "natural law" believed to be taught by sound reasoning were regarded as another source of equally binding precepts,[20] the concept of which was Aristotelian in origin.[21] Hence, reason, assisted by revelation, could be relied upon to teach what had to be approved of as good and what had to be avoided as evil. There was nothing indifferent (*adiaphoron*), outside of these alternatives. But Saint Thomas did not clearly define the scope and content of the natural law, which thus remained open to divergent interpretations.

Natural law and divine law provided the foundation for human law, which was designed to adjust the changing conditions of social life to the precepts ordained by revelation and reason. Human law, in turn, was subdivided into the *jus gentium*, the law that was common to all nations, and the *jus civile,* the specific law proclaimed for a community by its duly established authorities and adjusted to particular social and political conditions.

The concept of the *jus gentium* was a heritage of Stoic philosophy.[22] The principles underlying that law had played an important role in the jurisdiction of the Roman praetors, since these principles were held to be applicable to all inhabitants of the Roman Empire, as distinct from those applicable to Roman citizens strictly speaking. They were incorporated in the great codification of the Roman law made at the command of Emperor Justinian in the sixth century,[23] and were given new emphasis by the "glossators," the jurists of the University of Bologna who revived the study of the Roman law in the twelfth and thirteenth centuries.[24] Progress in human legislation was considered possible and desirable. But, true to his logical principles, Saint Thomas warned that any change in legislation was likely to affect the "constructive power of the law."[25]

The economic precepts which were taught and interpreted by the Aristotelian Scholastics could be derived from revelation only in exceptional cases. Some important norms incorporated in the canon law and based on the concept of justice were held to be dictated by natural law on the ground that ordered social life would be impossible without the observation of justice. Other norms, too, were assigned to the sphere of the *jus gentium,* but within the limits set by the canonic doctrine and its imperative precepts some leeway was left for the adjustment of economic norms to divergent and varying conditions.

A community was considered closer to perfection the better its self-sufficiency was assured and the less the citizens were dependent upon the activity of traders and merchants.[26] The community (*civitas*) referred to in this connection was, as a rule, the medieval city, and the economic policies of the medieval towns were quite generally adjusted to this idea.

Ample production for local consumption, buying and selling directly among producers and consumers, was considered preferable to any supply of goods from abroad. The division of labor and the differentiation of the population by occupations were ascribed to divine providence, which had secured for all the necessities of life.[27] Exchange of goods through buying and selling had thus been made basic to general welfare.[28]

Every community was subdivided into classes, each of which was endowed with specific functions, rights, and duties. The social position of every individual was determined by his birth into a class; from that class he derived his essential attributes as a member of the community. The descendants of families belonging to the nobility inherited the privileges enjoyed by the nobility within the framework of the feudal hierarchical system. The peasants were attached to the soil, and shared the fate of the soil which they were required to cultivate and which they were not permitted to leave without the consent of their lords. The services they were obligated to render were connected with their status of being *glebae adscripti.* The inhabitants of the towns, including the artisans and traders, were free, but their economic and social behavior was regulated by the officers of the guilds in which they were incorporated, and these officers were in turn supervised by the municipal magistrates. The various trades were strictly separated from each other, and the members of every economic or professional corporation enjoyed the exclusive privilege of exercising the functions corresponding to their positions within the economy. Monopolistic control of all markets by well-organized artisans, merchants, and members of the officially recognized professions was a fundamental principle of the structure of the medieval economy. The rigid classification of occupational activities showed a strong tendency to resist perceptible changes in methods of production and technique, and to prevent risks and uncertainties from interfering with the economic activities of individuals.

The members of the clerical hierarchy enjoyed exemption from the feudal order; their status, functions, and privileges were derived from principles believed to be divine in origin. Thus, the Scholastic social philosophers could freely discuss the rights and duties of the temporal rulers of the political communities and criticize their unlawful behavior.

In no other period of Western civilization was a similar uniformity reached in the various spheres of moral and intellectual life. The medieval kings and princes and the feudal lords, administrators, and municipal and other temporal authorities who had to make decisions as a rule were looking for counsel in the teachings of the Scholastic theologians and philosophers. Since training in consistent reasoning could hardly be acquired outside the schools operated by the leading religious orders, clerical advisers played a predominant role even in the management of nonreligious affairs. Their influence contributed greatly toward sanctioning traditional behavior and providing a safe background to privileged positions.[29] In doubtful cases when revelation and reason failed to supply reliable answers, mystical procedures (ordeals, oracles of many types, magical conjurations, and the like) were frequently resorted to in order to find the "truth" or to discover the course of future events. Such methods corresponded perfectly to the thinking processes of the medieval mind, in which a prominent place was occupied by fear of the unknown and unknowable and by fear of violating the principles of faith. The conviction that rightful behavior was regulated by binding norms imposed narrow limits on the right to choose from among alternatives;[30] the search for probabilities derived from experience was inconsistent with the belief in divine guidance.

Since all universal concepts were held to be immutable, there prevailed throughout the Middle Ages a strong tendency to fix all political, social, and economic institutions as far as possible in an invariable cast. The tendency to plan in terms of rigid categories permeated all medieval activities. The construction of the castles and fortresses of the feudal lords, princes, and kings was suggested by designs believed to be eternally valid; the huge cathedrals embodied the conviction that no lapse of time could affect the canons of Gothic architecture, technique, and beauty or the traditional pattern of religious ceremonies. The element of change was permitted to affect medieval reasoning only to the extent that it signified the approximation of the ideals embodied in the abstract concepts.

THE CONCEPTION OF PRIVATE PROPERTY

In their analysis of the institution of private property, the Scholastics were faced with a difficult problem. That institution was incompatible with their conception of mankind as an integrated whole, with their interpretation of the intentions of the divine creation, and with their general condemnation of the enjoyment of earthly goods. Various passages of the New Testament—especially the Sermon on the Mount—could be understood as warnings of sinful or foolish behavior which was likely to be caused by the quest for property and wealth. Hence, almost all "Patristic Fathers" of the first centuries A.D. had been unanimous in recommending to their Christian brothers common use of all possessions.[31] A primitive communism of this kind, which was the corollary of an exaggerated asceticism, had been advocated by Tertullian (Tertullianus) (160?-230?), Ambrosius, Bishop of Milan (340?-397), Chrysostom (Chrysostomus) of Constantinople (345?-407), and others. The more moderate Apologists, however, had realized its practical absurdity and had agreed on the view that common ownership of goods had become impossible after the fall from grace and the ensuing change of human nature. This doctrine was endorsed by Saint Augustine, Bishop of Hippo (354-430), who gave a final shape to the patristic doctrine for about 800 years to come. He had developed the distinction between divine and human rights and taught that everybody possesses what he possesses by human rights only. That maxim was incorporated in the *Decretum Gratiani* (1142), the first codification of the canon law.[32]

Communist tenets were rejected by the church as heretic as early as the fifth century, and this attitude toward the question of private ownership was repeatedly confirmed after the church had acquired, along with large possessions, the right to levy tithes on the annual proceeds of land and personal industry. Striking chapters in the history of the fight against communist ideas were the prosecutions of the Albigenses, the Begards, and the Apostoli.

Even more important from a dogmatic point of view than the annihilation of heretic communist sects was a violent controversy over the principles of private property which arose in the thirteenth century within the Franciscan order. A strong faction, the so-called Spirituals, insisted that in accordance with the intentions of the founder, Saint Francis of Assisi (1182–1226), their brotherhood should abstain from the acquisition and possession of any property.[33]

Saint Thomas and his followers derived their arguments in favor of the institution of private property from considerations of expediency as outlined in the Aristotelian writings. They did not admit the existence of a natural law which would prescribe community of goods, but they rejected equally the proposition that private property could be justified by invoking a natural law. Through universal, common agreements, they argued, private property had been made an institution of the *jus gentium*. Derived only from human reason, it had generally been accepted by all nations,[34] because private production provided a far greater stimulus to economic activity than common production, and assignment of specific productive functions to various individuals had been found to secure a far better social order and to prevent constant struggles over the use of goods.

On the other hand, Saint Thomas declared that although the goods belonged to individuals as far as property or ownership was concerned, all participated in their use,[35] and that the owners should be ready to communicate the goods to others as prescribed by Saint Paul (1 Tim. 6:17, 18). Saint Thomas took considerable pains to specify the content of that moral obligation. But other contemporary Scholastics insisted upon regarding private property of goods as an institution established by natural law rather that by *jus gentium*. Alexander of Hales (d. 1245), in his *Summa Theologica,* attempted to justify that view on the ground that the prohibition of theft was included among the Ten Commandments. The Franciscan John Duns Scotus (1265?–1308) contended that after the fall from grace, communism of goods had been revoked as a natural law and replaced by private ownership of goods.[36] But the Thomistic conception of property prevailed over all these conflicting views.

The idea that, in principle, land was a common property of the community found its juridical expression in the feudal institution of "eminent domain," the lordship of the sovereign power over all the territory of the commonwealth. The standards of allotting prominence and corresponding shares in the land owned by the community were held to vary among aristocratic, oligarchic, and democratic communities.[37] The right of ownership was regulated by the *jus procurandi et dispensandi,* which included the obligation to administer one's property in the common interest. The idea that the property of the community constituted an integrated whole was also reflected in the theory of distributive justice, which had been suggested by Aristotle and which called for such property to be distributed among the members of the community in accordance with their status, their functions, and their importance for communal life.[38] Distributive justice also found expression in sumptuary and other laws—especially the statutes of the guilds—which were designed to regulate the purchase and sale of goods of many kinds, including those of common consumption.

It is not quite certain whether Saint Thomas agreed with Aristotle in justifying slavery, the ownership of human beings, on the ground that a scale of valuation was applicable to people as to any other beings and that some human beings could be considered slaves by virtue of a law of nature. But Aristotle had admitted the existence of unnatural and unjust conditions of slavery, and his views were reproduced in *De Regimine principum* (II.10), though this chapter was probably written by Ptolemy de Lucca rather than by Saint Thomas.

THE THOMISTIC DOCTRINE OF VALUE

The Thomistic economic philosophy was significantly influenced by the broad distinction which Aristotle had drawn between what was right according to nature and what was right according to convention and human law. This distinction was applied above all to the modes of acquiring goods and wealth. Included among the "natural modes" were agriculture, hunting, fishing, pirating, warfare, and, finally, the exchange of goods. Aristotle contrasted these modes with the "chrematistic" forms of acquiring wealth, which required the aid of money. Since he ascribed the use of money to human agreements, his analysis of chrematistic acquisition falls within his analysis of human law and convention.[39]

In accordance with these teachings, the Aristotelian Scholastics did not attach to money any "inner value," but only a value determined by human decisions (*valor impositus*), and they regarded all monetary transactions as juridical categories belonging to the sphere of man-made law. The rules to be observed in performing such transactions were derived from the Aristotelian principle of "commutative justice." As interpreted by the Scholastics, this principle implied that equivalence of intrinsic values (*equalitas rei ad rem*) should obtain in all cases in which goods were exchanged for each other, and that the intrinsic value of the goods should be reflected in their prices.

It is not necessary to enter into a discussion of the intricate question of whether Aristotle attributed absolute, intrinsic value to the goods or whether his standard of equivalence simply implied transactions performed at competitive prices.[40] However that may be, there is no reason to assume that the Scholastics connected their concept of equivalence with prices resulting from competitive markets. Saint Thomas regarded equivalence as a requisite of any sales contract and supported this proposition with the argument that what was introduced for the common good should not be more of a burden on the one than on the other.[41] The intrinsic value of the goods, an objective characteristic, was thus included among the essential qualities of the goods, and a fundamental economic precept, that of commutative justice, was derived from the concept of equivalence.[42]

The Scholastics ignored certain observations in which Aristotle had admitted that valuation of the goods might be influenced by subjective wants and increasing demand.[43] Probably the only thirteenth-century Scholastic who referred to the concept of subjective value was the Dominican Aegidius Lessines, a pupil of Saint Thomas. In his treatise *De usuris,* Lessines drew a distinction between *valor secundum rationem substantiae* and *valor secundum rationem usus vel fructus*. He emphasized that the latter value was determined by the needs of an individual under given conditions, and that conditions, and consequently needs, can suffer change. Lessines has also been credited with the view that future goods are not valued as highly as the same goods assembled and immediately available, since they do not afford the same utility to their owners.[44]

The peremptory precept that the "just price" should conform to the "value" of the good that was purchased, together with the Scholastic concept of value as a quality marked by perdurability in time, implied that the just price itself should be perdurable, and not subject to fluctuation. Since Scholastic reasoning did not deal with individual things but rather with abstract entities—the genera of things— the value of a thing was held to be determined by its *bonitas intrinseca,* or inner goodness, a quality attributed to the class to which the thing was assigned by the divine process of creation as described in the first chapter of Genesis.

Reasoning in terms of classes, conceived of as eternally valid categories, was an outstanding characteristic of the Scholastic methodology. The classes were ranked in an ascending order, corresponding to the stages of the act of creation, the later ones being higher.

Puzzling and apparently insoluble problems—later termed the *paradox of value*—resulted from that formulation of the value problem. Like his Scholastic predecessors, Saint Thomas was faced with the fact that a pearl fetched a high price and a mouse no price, although the class or genus of the mouse had been created after that of the pearl and appeared to be entitled to a higher rank in the scale of valuation. In his discussion of that thorny question, Saint Thomas referred to a dictum of Saint Augustine which declared that the "principle of salable things was not reckoned in accordance with the rank of nature . . . but in accordance with the extent to which the things are useful to man."[45] Thus, the concept of utility as an indispensable element of valuation was introduced into economic reasoning, but the idea of usefulness referred to in this connection was associated with qualities of abstract conceptions, the classes of the goods. Even after adjusting their value doctrine to an anthropocentric interpretation of the divine intentions, the Schoolmen continued to be faced with the paradox of value; they were unable to answer the question of why a gem was valued so much more highly than a piece of bread, or any other good which is indispensable for human want satisfaction.

On the other hand, the traditional connection between the value of goods and the process of divine creation prevented the Scholastics from attributing intrinsic value to money, which in their view owed its usefulness to an agreement among people. As mentioned above, they claimed for that view the authority of Aristotle, although the latter, in a passage of his *Politics,* had given an account of the origin of money, especially of metallic currency, and had related the value of the current means of exchange to their original use value. He stated explicitly that the stamp put on a coin only served the purpose of declaring the quantity and quality of the metal contained in the coin. This Aristotelian explanation of the value of money was disregarded by the Scholastics, who relied upon some passages of Aristotle's *Ethics* to justify their belief in the purely conventional origin of the value of money.[46] They pointed to the Aristotelian proposition that no society could exist without the exchange of goods, no exchange without equivalence, no equivalence without a common measure. The conception of money as an instrument for measuring values led to the conclusion that after a change in social habits the value of money could undergo substantial changes; money could even be rendered entirely useless.[47]

Consequent upon their interpretation of the Aristotelian monetary views, the Scholastics drew a sharp distinction between the "intrinsic value" of goods and the "*valor impositus*" of money. The seller of a good was believed to receive a claim against the community as a whole, equivalent to the payment made to him.[48]

The view that money was merely a sign, a token, provided strong support for the so-called feudal theory of money, according to which the right of the public authorities to change the metallic content of the currency was implied in the monopoly of the feudal lords to define the instruments of measurement. Hence, the Scholastic monetary doctrine had quite significant practical economic consequences.

THE DOCTRINE OF THE JUST PRICE

The right of the public authorities to impose an exchange value on the monetary metals had a counterpart in their obligation to establish "just prices," which should correspond to the *bonitas intrinseca* of the commodities. The generally accepted practical formula for defining the just price was that such a price should compensate for *labores et expensae,* that is to say, for the work done by the artisan and his aides plus expenditures for raw materials, tools, and the like supplied by other producers. Costs of production commonly incurred were thus the essential elements of the prices fixed by feudal lords, municipalities, and guilds; the remuneration for labor was graded according to the social position and skill of the worker and the nature of the work. The principle that prices should be ruled by the costs of production was advocated especially by Duns Scotus, the "subtle" Oxford Franciscan, who interpreted the general notions in accordance with refined Neoplatonic principles and who was the outstanding thirteenth-century adversary of Thomistic teachings.[49]

According to the Aristotelian Schoolmen, the just price was to be determined by the common estimate of the market.[50] Simplified solutions were thus recommended for the intricate problem of how to adjust the abstract concept of commutative justice to the requirements of daily transactions.

The doctrine of just price was regarded as an integral part of the *jus gentium* since the coexistence of men was considered impossible unless mutual exchange of goods was ruled by the observance of just prices.[51] The Schoolmen argued that the seller who transferred a certain amount of value incorporated in the object of the sale to the buyer could make an unjustified gain only at the expense of the buyer.[52] Elaborating the Aristotelian maxim of commutative justice, Saint Thomas realized, however, that changes in supply and demand (*diversitas copiae et inopiae*) might affect the value of the commodities.[53] Hence, he concluded his casuistic discussion of practices in selling and buying with the observation that the just price of a thing was not fixed with mathematical precision, but that it depended on estimates, so slight additions or subtractions would not seem to destroy the equality of justice. Among the unlawful practices which were especially condemned and prosecuted were forestalling (buying up of goods before they reached the market), regrating (buying of goods in the market with the intention to resell them at a higher price), and engrossing (the monopolistic manipulation of prices). The meaning of the term *monopoly* as applied to trading practices should be clearly distinguished from the connotation of the same term as used to characterize the general organization of the medieval guild system.[54]

The principle that just prices should conform to the permanent invariable qualities held to be inherent in goods implied that any increase in the price of a good was considered unlawful unless the good had been transformed and its usefulness increased, as a rule by human labor. In view of the role attributed by the Scholastics to labor in the process of increasing the value of goods, some modern authors have qualified the Scholastic value theory as a precursor of the labor cost theory.[55] Such an interpretation is not only incompatible with the fact that all leading Scholastics—among others Albertus Magnus, Saint Thomas, and Duns Scotus—explicitly pointed to utility as the predominant element in determining the intrinsic value of a good, but it is also inconsistent with the general line of Scholastic reasoning which connected the value of the good with an essential attribute of the class to which the good was assigned. The amount of labor spent on the production or transformation of a good was an accidental characteristic. When the Schoolmen argued that a good could fetch a higher price than before, after having been transformed by labor, the emphasis was on the transformation which had increased the utility of the good and enhanced its *bonitas intrinseca*. Hence, the Scholastics could ignore the question of how to compare different kinds of labor for purposes of value determination.

The principle that the value of a good was determined by its *bonitas intrinseca* was also referred to when payment was credited or made in advance of delivery. The value of the goods was held to be independent of the lapse of time. Price increases *pro dilatione* and price reductions *pro acceleratione pretii* were both qualified as illicit "usury."[56]

But the Thomistic principles of commutative justice were not beyond dispute. Duns Scotus, the *Doctor subtilis*, permitted the parties to an exchange to deviate from those principles by mutual agreement for the sake of better want satisfaction. [57] The Franciscan Richard of Middletown (d. 1306), an adversary of Saint Thomas, even raised the question of whether it was possible for both parties to an exchange of goods to take advantage from the transaction when strict equality obtained between what was given and what was taken.[58] Such considerations showed a certain affinity to the Roman conception of the price problem, which permitted adjustment of prices to changing conditions of the market and to changes in the importance attached to individual goods.[59]

The Scholastic definition of the "just wage" followed the pattern adopted for defining just prices. Patristic fathers elaborated the idea that, consequent upon the fall from grace, a general obligation to earn one's living by hard work had been imposed upon all men.[60] Such exhortation contributed effectively toward reforming the general contempt in which manual labor had been held by Greek and Roman public opinion. The dignity of labor was accentuated by the members of various religious orders who accepted manual labor as a discipline "which helped them to walk in the way of eternal salvation."[61] According to the moral principles of the church, everybody was required to fulfill all the duties connected with his calling; idleness was outlawed. Persons who did not perform "dignified" labor, such as actors, remained outside the benefits and protection of the law.

The Schoolmen discussed the wage problem under the heading "contracts of service" (*locatio operarum*) and frequently compared selling one's services to the letting out of houses or other objects.[62] The price of labor was to be fixed *secundum communem estimationem*, in accordance with a scale of valuations which, as mentioned above, took account of the nature of the labor performed and the social position of the worker. Saint Thomas regarded it as a principle of natural law that the worker's livelihood was to be assured by the performance of his labor and that every worker was entitled to his wages.[63] The adoption of a form of "subsistence theory" of wages concerning the payment of common labor did not cause serious difficulties as long as prices and market conditions remained fairly stable and workers in almost all trades were members of a well-organized guild system.

THE PROBLEM OF UNLAWFUL PROFIT

Within the context of a moral theology which condemned any pursuit of gain for its own sake (the *cupiditas lucri*), strict limits were placed on the tendency to expand a gainful enterprise or to increase one's earnings. Saint Thomas qualified as sinful the prudence of the flesh for which the ultimate end lay in worldly things.[64]

The economic policy of the medieval municipalities, guilds, and other corporations was adjusted to these principles. The conviction that human reason was able to decide on the optimum organization of productive and distributive activities was a determining factor in establishing the statutes and rules of the guilds, which aimed at securing for their members rigid monopolistic control of well-defined markets, in which prices could be fixed and maintained over long periods. Such control appeared to provide a safe method of excluding, as far as possible, uncertainties and risks from the daily life of the medieval citizen. Hence, the number of artisans admitted to the independent exercise of a trade was closed and strict rules obtained as to the training of the apprentices and journeymen; the latter were frequently obliged to produce a "masterpiece" before being incorporated in the guild. Techniques of production, including the use and treatment of raw materials, were carefully regulated and reached a remarkable standard of performance in many cities. But even a highly skilled and able artisan, although assured of a reasonable livelihood, had only slim chances of expanding the range of his customers and of increasing his sales.

As far as possible, consumers were prevented from perceptibly changing their demands as to the quality and quantity of the commodities, since the Scholastic economic policy was based on the belief in a predetermined order of natural wants. But during the last centuries of the Middle Ages it was increasingly difficult to assure observance of this policy.

When the principles underlying the doctrine of the just price were consistently applied to the activities of traders or merchants, serious difficulties were involved in determining the licit remuneration of such intermediaries between producers and consumers who did not add anything to the "intrinsic value" of the objects of their sales. The very essence of "trade" in the Scholastic sense was selling for the sake of gain a thing "unchanged" at a price higher than that at which it had been bought.

That question had occupied the theologians for many centuries, since most patristic authors had condemned without reservation the business of traders. Frequently cited was a dictum ascribed to Saint Chrysostom that the traders should be expelled from God's temple. Saint Augustine had emphasized that it was a vice to buy cheap and sell dear.[65] But he had admitted that trading was a means of satisfying human wants and that the trader was entitled to compensation for his activity. Nevertheless, throughout the Middle Ages it was an incontestable economic principle that the sale of a good at higher than its just price was unlawful. [66]

The Aristotelian distinction between *artes pecuniativae* and *artes possessivae vel acquisitivae,* which was adopted by the thirteenth-century Scholastics, was based on a distinction between gains derived from the production or transformation of commodities.[67] The gain of a merchant or a moneychanger, it was argued, always implied another's loss and was, therefore, incompatible with the principle of commutative justice. Saint Thomas expressed a widely held view when he said that there was "something base" about trade, but he recognized the usefulness of a merchant whose activity was to the country's advantage.[68]

Other, especially Franciscan, theologians who were impressed by the increasing expansion of trade were far more lenient than Saint Thomas in their treatment of merchants. Alexander of Hales qualified as licit those price increases which represented compensation for shipment, storage, and risk.[69] Duns Scotus approved even such gains from trade as represented remuneration for services rendered if the remuneration was commensurate with the importance and social position of the traders.[70]

Although foreign merchants were welcomed to the degree that they added desirable goods to the monotonous consumption standard of the medieval household, their activities were subjected to far-reaching control to prevent them from interfering unduly with the domestic markets and from reducing the volume of the circulating means of payment.

The business of money changing (*ars campsoria*), which Saint Thomas clearly differentiated from trading in commodities, was treated in accordance with the same principles applied to general commercial transactions. To acquire money not in exchange for other things but for money of another kind was held to be contrary to human nature. Such transactions involved the danger of being performed exclusively for the sake of sinful gain.

THE PROHIBITION OF USURY

The much-discussed Scholastic proposition that taking interest on money was sinful "usury" provides one of the most striking instances to illustrate the importance which Thomistic theologians attached to purely logical issues in their approach to moral and economic questions. The condemnation of "usury" which reflected the views of Plato and Aristotle was the logical outcome of a combination of the principle of commutative justice with the theory of the *valor impositus* of money. According to the principle of commutative justice, equivalence should obtain in all exchange transactions. Interest was regarded as a price paid by the borrower for the right to use an amount of money over a given period. But since money was held to be only an instrument for measuring values, it appeared impossible to fix a just price for the use of money.

During the formative period of the Christian doctrine, lending money against payment of interest was attacked by those theologians who advocated communion of goods.[71] However, the Holy Scriptures did not provide unequivocal support for a wholesale condemnation of usury. Thus, a passage of Deuteronomy (23: 19) could be interpreted as objecting to the taking of interest on loans concluded among Jews. Moreover, the Gospel of Luke (6: 35) merely contained a general exhortation to hope for nothing when lending. In the Latin translation that passage reads "*Mutuum date nihil inde sperantes,*" and it was the object of varying interpretations. Plato, in the *Laws,* however, recommended the prohibition of lending on interest and Aristotle, in the first book of his *Politics* (I.3, Sec. 23), qualified interest on money as the most unnatural of all modes of getting wealth, since money had not been invented for the purpose of bearing interest.[72]

The fight of the clerical authorities against taking interest on money was initiated in 325 at the Council of Nicaea, but this fight was soon virtually abandoned.[73] Eight hundred years elapsed before it was resumed in 1139 at a Lateran Council; the prohibition was included in the *Dacretum Gratiani* (1142), which defined usury by stating "*Quidquid sorti accedit usura est.*" Thus, the condemnation was applied to any payment over and above the capital sum that had been lent. The prohibition was renewed at another Lateran Council (1179), the jurisdiction of the ecclesiastical courts in cases of "usury" was definitely established in 1274 at the Council of Lyons, and the final condemnation of usury was proclaimed by Pope Clement V at the Council of Vienna in 1311. Secular legislation that tolerated "usury" was declared null and void; statements that conflicted with the maxim that interest taking was sinful were qualified as heretical. The interdiction was extended to various devices resorted to for circumventing the prohibition.[74]

Several authors have referred to economic considerations in order to account for the striking fact that the church ignored the problem of "usury" during the major part of the

Middle Ages. Some German students of medieval economic history have argued that although receipt of a yield from capital at the expense of a borrowing consumer was considered unlawful, the clerical authorities could disregard such practices until the twelfth century, when they assumed alarming proportions along with expanding production, trade, banking, and credit.[75]

There is no doubt that the twelfth century was a period of far-reaching economic changes; but it is hardly probable that the renewed attempt of the clerical authorities to enforce an absolute prohibition of usury was, in fact, motivated by the desire to provide stronger protection for the indigent borrowers. The borrowers of the twelfth century who made increased use of lending were, to a large extent, merchants who requested ''productive'' credits for speculative enterprises or princes who needed money for military purposes. It is also a significant fact that the prohibition against charging interest on money was generally not applied to Jews, who were able to develop a comprehensive network of lending at high rates of interest.[76]

The renewal of the fight against usury which took place in the twelfth century can perhaps be explained on the ground that the Schoolmen had finally found in rediscovered Greek and Roman authors some sufficient arguments justifying the prohibition.[77] These arguments started from the proposition that the main function of money consisted in measuring the usefulness of the objects of exchange; hence, illicit modification of a standard of valuation was held to take place when a larger amount of money was received than that which had been given.[78] A second argument was related to the distinction drawn by Roman law between consumable goods and goods that are lasting sources of economic use. Money was regarded as a consumable good which was used by being spent. Saint Thomas elaborated the idea that the use of money could not be computed apart from the consumption (*distractio*) of the principal; hence, payment of interest was to be qualified as payment for something that did not exist or as double compensation.[79] The disparaging connotation given to the term *usura* reflected the idea that the act of lending implied transfer of ownership of the good that was lent; that the use of consumable goods was identical with their consumption and could not be made the object of a separate transaction extending over time. This principle was also applied to all consumable goods other than money, such as foodstuffs and the like. But the use of durable goods was held to be separable from their substance, and lending of such goods for a rent was regarded as perfectly lawful.

In support of the principle that a loan resulted in the transfer of ownership of money, Duns Scotus pointed to the Latin term *mutuum* (loan), which he derived etymologically from *meum* (mine) and *tuum* (thine). He also attached particular importance to the Aristotelian dictum that money was a barren thing which could not produce money. If the borrower could use the money to his advantage and pay interest from the proceeds, he argued, the latter was due to the borrower's industry.[80]

Another argument, attributed to the Stoic philosopher Seneca, pointed to the fact that payment of interest was stipulated proportionately to the time for which the loan was granted. Since time was regarded as common property given to all men as a free gift, the lender who took interest was held to commit sinful fraud. In addition, since money was believed to have been introduced in order to facilitate exchanges, a misuse of money was held to take place when it was lent for purposes of bearing fruit. Any fruit resulting from the use of the loan should accrue to the borrower, who had to assume the risks involved in the possession of the amount lent. [81]

In accordance with the Scholastic conviction that the value of a good was impervious to the lapse of time, moneylenders could derive titles to compensation only from circumstances that were extrinsic to the concept of "loan," hence from circumstances which changed the value of the money or caused costs to the lender. Claims of such types were discussed in terms of *damnum emergens* and *lucrum cessans*. Thus, a penalty could be agreed upon to make up for damage suffered by the lender in case the loan was not repaid at the stipulated time (*titulus morae*). If a loss could be proved, *damnum emergens* incurred by reason of having made the loan and was recognized as providing a valid claim to compensation. In the course of time *lucrum cessans,* or lost opportunity through making the loan, was also included among justified claims to compensation, and the presumption of having such opportunities was generally granted in favor of merchants and traders, but it was considered necessary explicitly to separate the stipulation of such compensation from the contract of lending strictly speaking.[82]

No real exceptions to the prohibition were involved in transactions in which ownership of money was not held to be transferred to another person.[83] Hence, contracts of partnership were considered perfectly legitimate and a proportionate amount of the gain resulting from such operations could lawfully be claimed. [84] In medieval Italian cities, the so-called *commenda* played an important role among contracts of the risk-sharing type. In terms of the *commenda,* agents traveling in foreign countries assumed responsibility for the shipment and sale of merchandise in return for, generally, one-fourth in the yields of the venture. Beginning in Italy in the thirteenth century, contracts of bottomry became a frequent form of combining loans and insurance on ships and cargo.

About the same time, purchases of annuities came to be used as a device for evading the prohibition of usury. In terms of such transactions, an estate was mortgaged to guarantee the repayment through annuities of the amount lent. No contract of lending was held to be concluded in such cases, since no end was set to the payment of the annuities and no repayment of the principal agreed upon. Moreover, the debt was held to be owed by the real estate and not by a person.[85]

The more one enters into a detailed discussion of the problems involved in the medieval prohibition of usury, the more it becomes evident that the main reasons for enforcing that prohibition were derived neither from the Holy Scriptures nor from economic or social considerations. Usury was rather a "logical" sin; practically all Scholastic authors who dealt with this question agreed that "usury" was forbidden by natural law and exclusively by that law.[86] Hence, it was to be condemned in order to protect the authority of the church from being undermined by the effects of erroneous thoughts.

The history of the prohibition of usury provides a classical illustration of the deep connection between the methods of Scholastic reasoning and the economic and social institutions of the Middle Ages. Only when this connection is fully appreciated is it possible to understand why the economic policies of the medieval church were defended for a considerable time afterward by practically all Thomistic theologians, and why the ecclesiastical doctrines of usury and price were reflected in relevant secular legislation until at least the middle of the sixteenth century.[87] If these doctrines had derived their main support from economic considerations, they would hardly have survived the thirteenth century. They lost their practical significance only when the Scholastic methods of reasoning were gradually superseded by other patterns of thought.

There is, perhaps, an interesting parallelism between the place occupied by the prohibition of usury within the Scholastic economic doctrine and the position of the Ptolemaic system as a foundation of the Scholastic astronomy. In both cases, the medieval views were deeply rooted in the universalistic pattern of reasoning upon which the structure of the church had been erected. In both cases, the fight against the adversaries of these doctrines turned implicitly on the maintenance of the system of logic embodied in the teachings of the church.

Chapter 2
The Disintegration of
Thomistic Reasoning

___

THE IMPACT OF NOMINALISM

ADHERENTS of the "materialistic interpretation of history" have endeavored to demonstrate that the feudal order owed its shape to the prevailing modes of production and the social conditions of the Middle Ages and that this order was subsequently "rationalized"—made intelligible and justified—by Scholastic philosophers and theologians. However, it can be far more reasonably argued that feudalism, as established in large parts of Europe under the influence of the clerical authorities, represented an adjustment of pre-Christian social conditions to the principles of Scholastic reasoning. Hence, the medieval organization of society can be conceived of as the institutional counterpart of the Scholastic hierarchical structure of ideas. That organization was maintained as long as universalistic methods of reasoning continued to exercise their hold over the leading classes of society. But the medieval order gradually lost its logical backing after the fourteenth century, when the belief in the validity of these methods was increasingly undermined in considerable parts of Western Europe, and as a consequence the organization of economic and social life had to be adjusted to other patterns of reasoning.

On closer analysis, it appears that the introduction of Aristotelian logical principles was a first step in the process which led to the breakup of the medieval feudal society. The structure of that society, which involved a rigid grouping of higher and lower classes or castes, could be protected against the influence of "heretic" ideas and tendencies as long as the exercise of human reasoning was strictly subordinated in all spheres to the dictates of faith. Consequent upon the adoption of Aristotelian methods, however, a considerable latitude was accorded to the mind to use its power of abstraction, provided that the results of such intellectual processes did not lead to conflicts with religious doctrines. Saint Thomas, who differentiated the sciences in accordance with their methods (*ratio cognoscibilis*), clearly distinguished the behavior of the philosopher from that of the theologian. The philosopher, he said, considers everything exclusively in the light of natural reason.[1] Inevitably, however, in the course of debates as to the proper interpretation of Aristotelian methods, deep-seated conflicts were bound to arise among leading theologians as to the role to be assigned to reason and the principles to be used in formulating abstract concepts.

From the outset, Thomistic methodological principles were opposed by Franciscan Scholastics, led by Duns Scotus, who adhered to a refined form of Neoplatonic teachings.

Saint Thomas placed special emphasis on the problem of existence as a characteristic of individual things. But Duns Scotus insisted that the essence of the universals, conceived of as realities, was the primary object of knowledge.

Some decades later the Thomistic doctrine and, implicitly, the authority of the church were confronted by two significant streams of nominalistic reasoning which threatened to undermine the very foundations of medieval society. One stream originated in Italian cities, which in the wake of the Crusades had established relations with the traders of the Near East and had adopted various institutions and devices which were at variance with the rigid pattern of the medieval social and economic organization. The other, far more important, stream started within the body of Scholastic theologians, who derived their intellectual armory from the works of Arabian philosophers.

The logical foundations of the universalistic philosophy had been questioned as early as the eleventh and twelfth centuries by revolutionary thinkers such as Roscellinus de Compiegne[2] and his disciple Pierre Abelard (1079–1142). From his interpretation of the Aristotelian teachings, Abelard had arrived at the conclusion that valid knowledge could be derived from the study of individual things and phenomena, and that the analysis of religious doctrines was not beyond the power of human reason; insight into these doctrines had been anticipated by the great Greek philosophers. Abelard was eventually forced to renounce his heretic propositions by Bernard of Clairvaux (1091–1153), a fanatic Neoplatonist, but throughout the second half of the twelfth century the logical problems raised by Abelard continued to play a considerable role in philosophical discussions.[3]

In the thirteenth century, important aspects of nominalistic reasoning were elaborated by the Franciscan monk Roger Bacon (1214?–1294) in his attempts to justify a new approach to the study of the physical world.[4] He emphasized observation and experience as reliable methods of scientific analysis, and regarded singular things and phenomena as integrated composites of form and matter, which were logically prior to the universal ideas. To the human mind he attributed an innate "natural" method of thinking which required the use of mathematics for the foundation of all sciences strictly speaking.

About the same time other, less radical, theologians emphasized the subjective element involved in deriving general notions from individual phenomena by methods of abstraction. They pointed to the fact that the name for a general concept was a product of the human mind.

These developments were preparatory to far more revolutionary nominalistic teachings which were propagated in the fourteenth century. The popes, residing at Avignon and threatened by hostile secular rulers, had lost the power to protect the orthodox methods of reasoning upon which the clerical authorities had based their claim to decide with finality in practically all spiritual and temporal matters. That claim could be considered justified when everybody was convinced that absolutely valid ideas were represented by the concepts used by the authorities—when the maxims and precepts proclaimed by the authorities could be relied upon to provide absolute truth.

However, a spiritual revolution was bound to occur when doubt was cast on the validity of objective concepts existing outside the human mind, and when the attempt was made to demonstrate that the general notions were nothing but creations of the human mind, mere names (*flatus vocis*). That attack on the universalistic sources of knowledge was directed against the methods of Neoplatonic reasoning as well as against the Thomistic principles of reasoning.

The thinker who advanced that attack was the Franciscan William of Ockham (1300?–1349). In his *Summa totius logicae*, Ockham undertook to separate logic as an art, an organization of thinking, from any metaphysical speculations and from any content or object of thought. Thus, he prepared the way for the acceptance of the view that the rules of reasoning, as operated by the human mind, may not coincide with those governing the behavior of outside events. Elaboration of that view provided the background for the development of hypothetical reasoning by Ockham's disciples.[5]

With impressive arguments, Ockham attempted to show that the general notions were in no way inherent in things, as was assumed by the Thomists. He insisted that they were the results of intellectual acts adjusted to the phenomena in accordance with observation and experience.[6] Whereas the Neoplatonist theologians had placed the existence of general notions before the existence of things, and whereas the Thomists had derived the general concepts by abstraction from the things, Ockham regarded these concepts as arbitrary signs formed freely by the human mind and expressed by words (*universalia post res*).[7]

Ockham even questioned the view, shared by practically all Schoolmen, that it was possible for human reason to be absolutely certain in the results of its judgments about finite things. Hence, he established a rigid separation between the treatment of religious issues and the treatment of philosophical issues, and he rejected any attempts to apply logical considerations to the formulation or justification of propositions belonging to the realm of faith. Of paramount importance to the subsequent development of scientific methods of thought was his contention that the discursive operations of the mind were unable to reveal the intrinsic structure of the things; science, he believed, deals with propositions which refer to what is *individual* in nature. Hence, he was one of the first protagonists of the analytical method, and he advised his disciples to study specific problems, one at a time.

In his polemic writings, Ockham quite consistently rejected the pope's claim to infallibility in passing decisions on nonreligious issues. He regarded the hierarchical organization of the church as a purely human institution.[8]

The fundamental propositions of nominalist logic were condemned in 1339 and 1340 by the University of Paris, but they nevertheless gained increasing support and became effective instruments for attacks on the conceptual structure of medieval religious philosophy. When the universal concepts could be characterized as nothing but *termini* of syllogistic processes, any questions concerning their "existence" in reality became irrelevant. When reasoning of that kind was pursued to its consequences, it was difficult to apply the traditional idea of "intelligible necessity" to the understanding of the world. Some of Ockham's followers questioned even the validity of the Aristotelian methodology and took the radical step of emphasizing experience as the main source of knowledge. Hence, they placed sense perceptions on the same level as abstract thinking.[9] The way was thus opened to take the treatment of specific problems outside the framework imposed by a general philosophy.

Simultaneously, reason was bound to lose the dominant position assigned to it by the universalistic philosophies. Instead, activity of the mind was emphasized and primary importance was attached to the will as the guiding principle of human action.[10] The history of the changing behavior of the Western mind and the history of Western civilization could very well be written against the background of the history of the fight for supremacy between reason and will.

When the rigid system of absolutely valid concepts could no longer be protected against the intrusion of new, freely formed notions, the Latin language was deprived of its privileged position as the exclusive instrument for the expression of ideas of higher abstraction. The increasing use of vernacular languages for literary and even scientific purposes was symptomatic of the spread of nominalistic methods. The same was true of the increasing tendency to disregard the Scholastic procedures of close and consistent reasoning and to deal with specific questions regardless of their connection with broad logical issues.

In England, where the Franciscans had established institutions of higher learning (above all, at Oxford), Ockhamism gained a firm foothold. It also found eminent advocates among French theologians.[11] Characterized as *via moderna,* the principles of nominalistic reasoning with their far-reaching implications were accepted at the universities of Oxford and Paris, as distinct from the predominantly Thomistic *via antique* which continued to prevail at the universities of almost all other parts of the Continent. Dominican theologians continued to provide the main support for the methods of Thomistic reasoning.

The logical principles advocated by the two orders were reflected in their main activities. The Dominicans, also called Predicants, concentrated much effort on preaching in defense of the dogmatic tenets of the church. The Franciscans resorted to preaching mainly for practical purposes and devoted themselves largely to the care of the souls of the common people. The history of the Western world was, to a high degree, determined by the struggle waged by the two orders over the fundamental principles of thought.

Beginning with the fourteenth century, the universities ceased to be monopolized by the clergy. In various countries, universities were founded and financed by the governments.

CHANGING ECONOMIC VIEWS

In the field of economic thought, the *via moderna* led to significant modifications of the various traditional definitions of economic concepts. Jean Buridan (Johannes Buridanus) (d. 1358), a disciple of William of Ockham and Rector of the University of Paris, emphasized experience as the primary source of knowledge and regarded human wants as the natural "measure" of the goods of exchange.[12] He argued that the measurement of values could not be performed by using a quantitative standard, as in the case of weighing, but had to be done with the aid of proportions (*per similitudinem proportionis*). This reasoning enabled Buridan to outline the principles of a predominantly subjective value theory without violating the Aristotelian principle of equivalence. He differentiated between the exchange value of goods reflecting common wants (*indigentia communis*) and the value of goods resulting from individual needs (*indigentiae particulares*). He realized quite clearly that each partner to an exchange expected to get an advantage from the transaction and that the worker attached a higher value to his wages than to his labor; he also raised the question of why rich and poor people paid the same price for their bread although their individual needs differed widely.[13] In order to appreciate the influence of nominalistic reasoning on this formulation of the value problem, it must be borne in mind that the Thomistic definition of value was dominated by the substance concept and did not permit individual needs to affect the determination of what was valuable according to rules of reason.

Another element of the Thomistic economic doctrine which Buridan attacked was the theory of *valor impositus* of money, which provided strong support for the right of princes to fix the metal content of the coins and thus to take advantage of currency devaluations.[14]

Buridan questioned the purely conventional origin of the value of money, and connected the value of the various currencies with the *bonitas intrinseca* (the inner goodness) of the metals incorporated in the coins. Consequent upon this view, the monetary functions of the rulers were limited to the task of setting up legally binding standards concerning the relation between the values of the different coins.[15]

Buridan's disciple, Nicole Oresme (Nicolas Oresmius) Bishop of Lisieux (1330?-1382), was probably the first theologian to deal in a separate treatise with a specific economic problem, the origin and nature of currencies and their debasement.[16] He listed the qualities which had made gold and silver especially serviceable for monetary purposes, and explained the relation between the values of the two metals (twenty to one at his time) as resulting from the greater rarity of gold and the difficulties involved in producing it. Like Buridan, Oresme ascribed intrinsic value to the monetary metals, and used that view to condemn as unjust the gain derived from the debasement practices of the monetary authorities.[17] He also demonstrated, long before Sir Thomas Gresham, that good coinage was driven out of circulation by bad.[18]

Thus, when the Middle Ages drew to a close, three different monetary opinions were competing with each other: the traditional theory of the *valor impositus,* which reflected universalistic thinking and which was upheld by the Thomistic theologians and favored by the advocates of the royal monetary prerogatives; the view held by Ockhamist Scholastics, which referred to the original use made of the monetary metals to justify their belief in the "intrinsic" value of money and their attacks on the debasement of currencies; and a not quite explicit third view which concentrated on reasons for changes in the value of money. This last view was suggested by Saint Antoninus of Florence (1389-1459), also an Ockhamist, who observed that when gold was hoarded and became scarce, more goods were given for the same quantity of money.[19] Hence, he pointed to quantity relations as an essential factor in determining the value of currencies, and suggested a distinction between the "intrinsic" value of money and its exchange value.

The reformulation of the value concept led to attacks on the traditional methods of price fixing as defended by such theologians as Heinrich von Langenstein (d. 1397), professor of theology at the University of Vienna,[20] and Jean de Gerson (Johannes Gerson) (1362-1428), chancellor at the University of Paris.[21] Far more liberal in his views was the professor of law at the University of Vienna, Johannes Nider of Swabia (d. 1438), who undertook to determine the precepts which merchants were requested to observe in their transactions.[22] He redefined the Aristotelian principle of equivalence and regarded bona fide mutual estimates as a reasonable basis of equivalence (*aequalitas*). He pointed to supply and demand as factors affecting that estimate, and listed several considerations which, in his view, were relevant in influencing the just price. Among licit transactions he included sales to the highest bidder in case of competition between would-be buyers.

The principles underlying the Thomistic price theory were also questioned by Saint Antoninus of Florence, in many respects one of the most advanced Ockhamists.[23] He argued that, given the "objective" utility of a good, its value was mainly determined by its scarcity (*raritas*) and its costs (*difficultas*). As an additional element in determining exchange values, he mentioned *complacibilitas,* the individual's estimate. The buyer, he said, prefers the object of the purchase to its price, and the opposite is true of the seller.[24] Thus, he alluded to a "subjective" theory of value. Without definitely abandoning the traditional view that the *communis aestimatio* was basic to the determination of the just price, Antoninus granted a considerable latitude to the parties, and concluded that no violation of the just price was involved when deviations from the common estimate were agreed upon by the parties. He also applied a corresponding reasoning to sales on credit. A similar price theory was adopted by the Franciscan Bernardino of Siena (1380–1444), who endorsed the proposition that the just price can be fixed by the parties to the transaction.[25] He emphasized the usefulness of trading and the functions of the merchants as intermediaries engaged in equalizing prices among different localities.

The very concept of a "just price" was finally abandoned by the last Ockhamist scholastic, Gabriel Biel (1425?–1495), professor at the University of Tübingen. Biel argued that no sales or purchases would be concluded unless each party expected to have a greater advantage from performing than from nonperforming the transaction.[26] Reliance upon an objective standard was thus superseded by the recognition of the influence of individual estimates on the determination of prices.

Antoninus of Florence was one of the first Scholastic authors who definitely abandoned the traditional argument that taking interest on money was unlawful because the money lent was consumed by the borrower. In his view, taking interest was permitted when the loan was granted for purposes of embarking on industrial or commercial enterprises, since money was indispensable for successful business. Saint Bernardino argued on similar lines that the value of money might be increased when it was used for productive purposes, and that this use could be the object of a legitimate sale. He also discussed thoroughly the exceptions to the prohibition of taking interest on money: *damnum emergens, lucrum cessans,* and *poena conventionalis.*

The history of these developments could be supplemented by an analysis of changes in contractual relations which were connected with the changes in economic reasoning. As an instance in point, reference may be made to the case of the hereditary annuity which had been widely used for evading the prohibition of usury. As mentioned previously, such indeterminate payment of annuities was agreed upon by lenders and borrowers in order to avoid any connection between the transfer of the principal and the yearly payments. Thus it happened that in many regions real estate was burdened with debts which imposed recurrent payments on generations of owners. But these debts could not be erased, since repayment of the capital was considered incompatible with the prohibition of usury. A papal decision to render the annuities repurchasable was finally pronounced in 1425 after long deliberations. [27] Another economic problem of far-reaching importance turned on the payment of interest on public loans issued in the course of the fourteenth century by various city republics of Italy. The issuance of such loans was defended on the ground that payment of interest represented indemnification for the loss of gain which could be earned from the amount lent, or a reward for the kind of disposition of the citizens that had assisted the city, or even a gift.[28]

Thus, in the fifteenth century, several bulwarks of the Thomistic doctrine had lost the firm position which they had secured when backed by universalist reasoning. This was true of the theories of value, of money, of the just price, and of usury. Particularly remarkable was the subtleness displayed by Italian jurists in their attempts to justify circumventions of obsolete Scholastic precepts.

CHANGES IN ECONOMIC INSTITUTIONS

The gradual disintegration of the Thomistic economic doctrine was accompanied and supported by changes in public opinion which occurred, above all in Italy, under the influence of contacts with the Near East. Popular reasoning claimed emancipation from the hierarchical structure of concepts, upon which was based the inflexible medieval classification of professional and occupational functions. New procedures developed for organizing commercial and financial activities, by combining in a single enterprise various functions which had been strictly separated under the rigid Scholastic regime. A vague concept of "capital" emerged, denoting abstract and impersonal assets and the aggregate of shares held by the same merchant or bank in various enterprises. Partnerships of capitalists were formed in which each partner was given the freedom to sell his share without affecting the operation of the common enterprise. Such transfer of abstract ownership would have been inconsistent with traditional Scholastic reasoning.

The textile industry of Italian and Flemish cities which, beginning with the thirteenth century, was adjusted to the requirements of foreign markets, showed certain features characteristic of early capitalistic organizations. One of the earliest precursors of later capitalism was the banking system established in Italian and Dutch centers of international commerce.

When increasing doubt was cast on the rigid Scholastic moral categories, the sharp distinction between justified earnings and pursuit of gain for its own sake could hardly be maintained. Pursuit of gain was rationalized when Italian merchants of the second half of the fourteenth century learned from their neighbors in the Near East the art of systematic bookkeeping in double-entry form.[29] The balance concept, a notion derived from mechanics, supplied the logical instrument for determining net losses and gains.

The methods of bookkeeping which were applicable to any industrial and commercial enterprise implied a high degree of freedom from traditional occupational and professional categories, since the bookkeeping entries were grouped according to rules entirely divorced from the immediate objectives the individual enterprises were intended to serve. Simultaneously, the business enterprise was logically transformed into an objective entity; its relations to other enterprises and to its various markets were strictly separated from the person of the entrepreneur. The importance of that process for the ensuing organization of commercial life can hardly be overestimated.[30]

The introduction of new processes of logical abstraction into commercial life can also be illustrated by the increasing practice of using bills of exchange as means of replacing a direct transfer of money. In their primitive form, which was adopted at the end of the twelfth century, the use of such bills constituted a temporary separation of the exchange values indicated in the bills from the metallic substances (gold or silver) in which these values were held to be incorporated.[31] The bills were simply a mechanical device for facilitating the transmission of monetary metals from one place to another. An entirely new functional aspect was introduced through the insertion of the "or bearer" clause, which transformed the bills into negotiable paper and definitely severed the transfer of exchange values from the commercial transactions which had motivated the issuance of the bills.

In the fifteenth century, this clause was generally used by Italian, particularly Florentine, merchants.[32] A final step in the direction of making debt instruments independent of the business with which they had originally been connected was the issuance of bank notes, which implied an indefinite separation of abstract monetary certificates from their metallic bases.

The Florentine jurist Laurentius de Rodulphis was probably the first to analyze the various types of transactions performed by moneychangers (*Campsores*).[33] He distinguished their normal business (*cambium minutum*) from their credit operations. An important instrument of these operations was the *cambium per litteras,* a written order to pay an amount in a currency other than that in which the payment had been made. Another instrument was the *cambium siccum* (dry exchange), which was frequently used for the prohibiton of usury. The amount lent was to be repaid in terms of a higher amount based on the rate of exchange between the local and a foreign currency. Hence, a bill was drawn on some strawman, who protested it on its arrival. Thus, payment of interest for the amount lent was transformed into a compensation to the lender for the pretended loss sustained on both the exchange and rechange.[34]

Bills of exchange were indispensable instruments for facilitating the international business relations which had developed in connection with the fairs held regularly in Spanish, French, and Italian cities.[35] The practice of performing payments by such written promises became one of the main methods of transmitting the treasures of the West Indies to the manufacturing and grain-producing countries of Europe.

The development of insurance as a regular business, which began in Italy in the fourteenth century, provided another instance of the increasing application of nominalistic methods to commercial life. In the Middle Ages the need for protection against risks involved in speculative and venturesome enterprises had given rise to contracts of partnership of various types. They were restricted to specific cases. Insurance contracts strictly speaking, however, are based on a logical operation which combines a number of individual cases solely from the point of view of their exposure to a defined risk. A single "accidental" characteristic of these cases is selected for including them in a group freely formed and circumscribed by the contract between the insurer and his clients. In his treatise on usury, written at the beginning of the fifteenth century, Laurentius de Rodulphis discussed various contracts of that type, particularly those providing insurance against losses from transport on land and at sea. They were regarded as perfectly legitimate. The progressive relaxation of market restrictions encouraged risk taking, which had been hemmed in by the rigid Scholastic categories. As a consequence, the concept of probability emerged along with the establishment of the principles of life insurance.

These and similar developments were symptomatic of the role which striving for profit began to play, not as a simple expression of greed condemned by the clerical authorities, but as a rational principle of organizing production and trade. Prerequisite to this transformation of the structure of the economy was the adjustment of the modes of thought used by manufacturers, traders, and moneylenders to a new logical climate filled with risks and uncertainties. When this adjustment gained momentum, an irresistible movement was created which resulted in destroying the bases on which the predominantly static structure of medieval life had been erected.

THE SCHOOL OF SALAMANCA AND THE JESUIT SCHOLASTICS

In almost all territories of Western Europe and Italy the principles of Thomistic Scholastics lost their predominance in the course of the fifteenth and sixteenth centuries. On the Iberian Peninsula, however, owing to the prolonged struggle against the Arabian intruders, the church had succeeded in preserving a commanding position in all spiritual and worldly affairs. Dominican theologians, deeply convinced of the absolute validity of the Thomistic doctrine, exercised a firm control in all religious matters and also extended their supervision to administrative, educational, cultural, and economic activities. The most important seat of the Thomistic tradition was the University of Salamanca in Spain, which in the sixteenth century attained high fame for the achievements of its teachers in the fields of theology and jurisprudence.[36]

As interpreters of the canon laws, the Dominican theologians were requested to decide upon the legality of economic practices; hence, they had to develop procedures for analyzing specific cases and for establishing general norms of lawful behavior. Of course, in their endeavor to secure strict observance of the Thomistic economic precepts, the theologians were increasingly faced with radical changes in conditions, when streams of gold and silver were brought into the peninsula by the conquerors of Mexico and Peru following the discovery of the West Indies. Violent inflationary price movements began to undermine the stability of domestic markets, and foreign trade assumed increasing and unexpected dimensions because the newly acquired treasures were largely used for the purchase of foreign commodities. Spanish fairs where these transactions took place gained rapidly in importance.[37] Such fairs became centers of international clearing, and even merchants who did not attend them were thus provided with the opportunity of setting off mutual claims and debts against one another. Simultaneously, wide discrepancies began to develop between the value of the Spanish currency, the *maravedi*, and the currencies of the exporting countries.[38] During the first decades of the sixteenth century, the relation between the value of the *maravedi* in Flanders and its value at a Spanish fair was 360 to 410 and similar relations obtained between Italy and Spain. Hence, differences in the prices of the various commodities offered opportunities for considerable profits and, at the same time, large gains could be made, independently of any trading, through monetary transactions. The way was also open for circumventing the prohibition of "usury" by lending money at one fair and being repaid at another at a much higher rate. Hence, many doubtful practices originated at the fairs, and the theologians were frequently obliged to develop subtle distinctions between what was to be considered licit and what was to be condemned as unlawful. Reinterpretations of traditional rules were often unavoidable under the pressure of changing economic conditions. The Dominicans considered it their duty to protect the merchants against danger of committing sinful acts and to offer them guidance for the salvation of their souls. Various handbooks were written, mostly by friars, with this purpose in mind. [39]

A difficult problem of fundamental importance was the definition of the "just price" in a period of heavy inflationary price movements. Labor and other expenditures which had been considered important elements in determining a just price could hardly provide a reasonable standard when prices had lost their stability.[40] Hence, the Dominicans centered their endeavors on the defense of the traditional qualification of the just price as the expression of a *communis aestimatio*. But this formula was exposed to varying interpretations.

The question of the just price was also dealt with in the treatises of some learned Spanish Jesuit jurists who were, however, less anxious to preserve the Thomistic doctrine. Luis Molina (1535-1600) and Cardinal Juan de Lugo (d. 1660) used expressions such as "natural prudence" or "prudent economic reason" to characterize a desirable approach to the determination of the just price, and defined the conditions under which account might be taken of certain cost elements in defining licit prices. But, like the Dominicans, they rejected the formula advocated by Duns Scotus, the great adversary of Saint Thomas, that payment for labor and expenses should provide the standard for defining the just price. They pointed to the dangers involved in permitting the seller to give a very broad interpretation to the term *expenses*.[41]

The commonly adopted explanation for the rise in prices was derived from the traditional view that the value of the coins had been debased by reducing the metal content of the means of payment.[42] But Martin di Azpilcueta Novarro, writing during the 1650s, observed that saleable goods and labor had been much cheaper in Spain in times when money was scarcer than after the country was flooded with gold and silver.[43] He was among the first authors to point to the real cause of inflationary price movements.

The theory of the intrinsic value of money enjoyed general recognition. In order to reconcile the fluctuations in the value of the coins with the intrinsic value ascribed to the monetary metals, a distinction was drawn between the intrinsic value and the exchange value of the metals. The exchange value was held to fluctuate in accordance with variations in demand and supply, utility, safety, and other factors affecting common estimates. In 1553, Domingo de Soto, an outstanding Dominican theologian, arrived at the conclusion that to receive a smaller sum in a place where money was scarce, in exchange for a larger where it was abundant, was as lawful as to exchange one measure of wheat delivered where its price was high for two measures where the price was low.[44] Such procedures were held to be perfectly compatible with the principle of just prices. General conditions of demand and supply were thus taken into account in interpreting the exchange value of money.

That doctrine was elaborated by Novarro, popularized by Thomas de Mercado, and endorsed by Molina. Molina argued that just as an abundance of goods makes them go down in price when the amount of money and the number of merchants remain the same, so too an abundance of money makes goods go up in price while the number of goods and merchants remains the same; this causes the very money itself to become cheap. Molina thus developed the concept of a value of money "arising from circumstances," and abandoned the traditional view which connected any devaluations of the currency with debasement practices. At least an indirect allusion to a quantity theory of money was implied in his proposition that regardless of whether money in two places might be of the same material weight and seal, and whether or not the same value had been imposed on each in comparison with other coins of the same place, all the money taken together may be worth more in one place than all the money of another place taken together may be worth in that second place.[45] Molina applied the same reasoning to differences over time of the value of money at the same place. Changes in the value of money were also explained on the ground that opportunities for trading and gaining varied according to time and place.[46]

Even more intricate for the Salamancan Dominicans than the problems connected with the observance of the principles of the just price and the legitimate value of money were the questions which resulted from the endeavor to secure compliance with the prohibition of "usury" and to prevent commercial transactions from leading to the acquisition of illicit gains. Transfer of money through bills of exchange was considered a legitimate business, and any profit made on it was construed as compensation for the labor and risks involved in sending the money abroad. Such transfers could be performed without directly violating the embargo placed in Spain on the exportation of specie; hence, they were held to be in the public interest.[47] But double transactions of exchange and rechange which were highly profitable were condemned as usurious. Equally condemned were various practices designed to circumvent the prohibition of usury.

The question of whether a gain could lawfully be derived from lending money at one fair and being repaid at another fair at a far more favorable rate was the object of an interesting decision rendered by the theologians of the University of Paris in 1530.[48] The contract was declared to be unlawful, mainly on the ground that, as distinct from usual expenditures connected with the transfer of money, the difference between the amount paid and the amount received was due to fluctuations of the market rate and did not represent reimbursement for services rendered and risks involved in the transaction.

As distinct from the Dominicans, the Jesuit jurists showed a remarkable lenience in their treatment of problems of usury. In favor of the prohibition of taking interest on money, they advanced two main arguments: (1) that, logically, the use of money could not be separated from its consumption and made the object of a compensation, and (2) that the value of money was not lessened solely through the interval of time.[49]

It is interesting to note that the Jesuit interpreters of the canonist doctrines practically ignored the Aristotelian reference to the "sterility" of money. They distinguished between "money *per se*," or money considered by and in itself, on the one hand, and money that is fruitful *per accidens,* in certain special situations.[50] They permitted taking interest as the common price for the "privation of money," if otherwise the lenders would generally experience a loss resulting from forfeited benefit or opportunity.[51] In their discussions of questions of economic policy, the Jesuit jurists favored various institutions of early capitalism, but they were not motivated by economic considerations in establishing their subtle distinctions between what was licit and what was contrary to canon laws.[52] Adherence to Scholastic categories prevailed in virtually all their arguments.

The attempts of the Dominican theologians and the Jesuit jurists to maintain some leading principles of the Thomistic economic doctrine reached deep into the time which is commonly referred to as the period of mercantilism. In the meantime, the governments of almost all countries of Western and Central Europe had restricted the jurisdiction of the clerical courts to cases involving religious issues: canon law had been widely displaced by the application of civil law, which was increasingly freed from the residues of Scholastic juridical categories. But, independently of the decisions of secular jurisdiction, religious advice on economic behavior continued to be heeded in almost all countries until far into the sixteenth century.

Part II

The Development of Baconian
and Cartesian Economics

Chapter 3
The Transition Period (Fifteenth
and Sixteenth Centuries)

___

CHANGING AND CONFLICTING PATTERNS OF THOUGHT

THE DECLINE of the power of the clerical authorities and the progressive dissolution of the Holy Roman Empire paved the way for the emergence of powerful "national states" competing with each other for supremacy.[1] That struggle went on in a world whose inner coherence was weakened as the uniform and unifying medieval methods of reasoning were progressively undermined by the influence of other patterns of thought. These methods could no longer cope effectively with the new problems resulting from revolutionary changes of political ideas and from the application of new procedures to the organization of production and trade. A considerable variety of conflicting patterns of thought emerged in the course of these developments. Hence, beginning with the fifteenth century, the various European territories can be differentiated according to the trends of reasoning which came to dominate the thinking of the educated classes of the population.

Pre-Christian civilization achieved its fullest development in Italy under the Roman emperors. During the Middle Ages, Italy again provided the central institutions for the organization of a fundamentally uniform pattern of religious and social life in the Western world. Moreover, along with the disintegration of Scholastic teachings and the attendant decline of the dominant position of the Church, new and powerful streams of thought originated on Italian soil, and the Italian Renaissance initiated an era in the history of Western civilization through an amalgamation of pre-Christian and medieval cultural trends. Paramount among the factors which brought about the extraordinary intellectual, economic, and artistic achievements of the Renaissance was the existence of a number of industrially and commercially highly advanced city states, rivaling with each other for prominence. At the same time, strong intellectual movements were stimulated by close contacts with the Near East—where the study of Greek and Roman literature had never been discontinued. The knowledge of that literature was spread in Italy especially through a stream of refugees from the Byzantine Empire after the conquest of Constantinople by the Osmanli Turks (1453).

From Italy the new spiritual movements made their way into large parts of the European continent. The printing press was a forceful instrument for transmitting new ideas, as well as the results of critical reasoning, to ever-increasing groups of educated people.

The changes which took place in the religious, moral, political, scientific, and artistic spheres of life during this period have been the object of extensive studies. They started about a hundred years ago with the publication by the Swiss historian Jakob Burckhardt of a fascinating picture of the culture of the Italian Renaissance from the middle of the fourteenth to the middle of the sixteenth century.[2] Burckhardt conceived of that period as an intellectual unity driven forward by the creative energy of its leading personalities. Later some German philosophers, especially Wilhelm Dilthey and Ernst Cassirer, developed the concept of the "Spirit of the Renaissance," an interpretation which enjoyed far-reaching acceptance.[3]

Other students of that period raised the question of whether the Renaissance time span could be defined with reasonable accuracy. They pointed out that many ideas emphasized by thinkers of the Renaissance had their roots in medieval reasoning and, moreover, that the Renaissance period was not dominated by a unified spirit but that divergent streams of thought originated in the fifteenth and sixteenth centuries and vied with each other for prominence. Different branches of science and culture were affected to varying degrees by these intellectual processes. Hence, the loosely defined period of the Renaissance should be regarded as a transition period which provided the sources for divergent intellectual developments.

We are concerned here with these problems to the degree that the medieval approach to economic questions and to the organization of economic and social life were affected by new philosophical movements. These movements had their main seats at the various Italian universities, but found additional support in the writings of educated laymen, physicians, lawyers, bankers, and merchants.

According to a currently prevailing view, three main intellectual trends in the bewildering variety of ideas and schools emerged in the course of this fervent period. First, an important role was played by various versions of a refined Aristotelianism; they provided the backbone for research and teaching at outstanding Italian universities such as Padua, Bologna, and Pavia. The second movement, vigorously opposed to Aristotelianism, was a Neoplatonic school which enjoyed the support of the Medicis and had its headquarters at the Academy of Florence, founded in 1462. Leading members of this school were engaged in the search for "universal truth" and endeavored to give mathematics a solid metaphysical foundation. The third movement, equally hostile to the Aristotelian methodology, was a predominantly literary movement called *humanism*. It derived its ideals from the study of Latin and Greek authors.

Two main versions of Aristotelianism were pitted against each other. In its Thomistic version, Aristotelianism remained the leading philosophy of the universities occupied by Dominican scholars; in its Ockhamist version, it found fertile soil at some Italian schools of higher learning. Also important from a methodological point of view was the school of "Latin Averroists," who achieved a dominant position at the University of Padua about the middle of the fifteenth century.[4] They organized their studies in accordance with the methods adopted by their fourteenth-century predecessors at the University of Paris and developed some leading ideas of the thirteenth-century Franciscan scholar Roger Bacon, who had insisted upon the use of hypotheses and empirical investigations as methods of improving the knowledge of the forces of nature.[5]

The position held at Padua by the Averroists was disputed by the Alexandrists in a prolonged dramatic struggle. The Alexandrists emphasized the materialistic features of the Aristotelian philosophy and strongly objected to the pantheistic elements of Averroism.[6] Like the Averroists, they attempted to avoid an open break with dogmatic theology by resorting to the theory of the "double truth," according to which truth of one kind was exclusively valid within the sphere of a philosophical system and truth of an entirely other kind was derived from revelation by the theological doctrine.

What was termed *humanism* was not a school backed by a clear methodology and consistent philosophical principles but rather a movement inspired by a deep enthusiasm for the study of the Greek and Latin classical authors. From Italy, where it found its first remarkable representative in Francesco Petrarch (1304–1374), it spread to France, the Netherlands, and England. The humanists could claim the merit of discovering many remarkable and previously unknown or neglected classical writings. They placed learning and the accumulation of knowledge derived from their classical sources at the center of education, which underwent radical changes under the influence of the worldly humanistic conception of life. As distinct from the Aristotelians, they rejected all specific Christian concepts and were opposed to almost all principles of the Scholastic methodology. Striving for intellectual freedom was an outstanding objective of the humanistic movement, along with a reform of social life which was to be patterned after the ideals of the Stoic philosophers. The study of human nature and human affairs was given special attention and resulted in stimulating individualistic philosophies. Other humanists emphasized the formal aspects of the classical literary sources, such as grammar, poetry, and rhetoric. Influenced by these sources they conceived of history as a continuous process, and derived the view that human nature was fundamentally identical, regardless of the diversity of conditions under which various people lived. Beginning with the fifteenth century, humanism pressed its stamp on the educational systems of most Western European and Central European countries. Some leading humanists, such as Lorenzo Valla (1406–1457) even attempted to develop a simplified form of logic, based on the study of classical rhetoric. Similar ideas were accentuated and elaborated by Pierre La Ramée (1515–1572). They finally culminated in barren attempts to replace training in logical reasoning by a "natural logic" of common sense.

Wherever these intellectual movements, especially Averroism and humanism, could gain a firm foothold the soil was soon prepared for freeing economic thought from the fetters of medieval moral theology and for promoting the adoption of a "natural" philosophy. An essential element of this philosophy was the belief in the conformity of human nature, combined with the conviction that "progress" in all spheres of life was dependent upon intensifying the study of nature and more fully utilizing nature's forces.

Ideas of that type contributed significantly toward stimulating the creative energy of artists, artisans, and manufacturers and introduced a "dynamic" element into economic and social life. In addition, these philosophers suggested that legislative and administrative regulation of this life had to be adjusted to the operation of creative forces working independently of any government interference.

The application of certain nominalistic principles to social problems made itself felt first and foremost in the sphere of political philosophy when some outstanding Italian authors proclaimed the supremacy of the will and rejected the traditional view that reason was supreme in determining the objectives of social action as well as of individual behavior. Simultaneously, increasing doubts were cast on the leadership provided by the clerical authorities in worldly affairs. Hence, the hypothetical elements involved in making decisions became an object of widespread attention, and innumerable references were made to risk and uncertainty in art, literature, and popular writings. It was commonplace to refer to "fortune" as the ruler of all things, and to the symbols of fortune.

Emphasis placed on the will as the determinant of human action found its consummate expression in the famous treatise *Il Principe,* published in 1513 by the Florentine Niccolò Machiavelli (1469–1527). Almost all allusions to the medieval hierarchical system of concepts were discarded in Machiavelli's political philosophy, which was based on a speculative theory concerning the rise and decline of states and was designed to teach the appropriate methods of making a ruler powerful and his regime permanent. From Roman antiquity, Machiavelli derived the ideal of the state as a political community independent of any outside authority, especially the church. The interests of the prince centered on worldly objectives determined by the will; reason had to provide the means for achieving these objectives. Among the ultimate ends of Machiavelli's political ideas was the unification of Italy. The fundamentally hypothetical background of that political philosophy made Machiavelli's work a landmark in the history of Western thought. One of his most important successors, Giovanni Botero (1540–1617), broadened the basis of his political considerations by reference to historical facts.[7]

In his defense of the independence of the worldly rulers, Machiavelli referred to the theory of the social contract, which was designed to replace the Scholastic belief in a "social instinct" as the fountainhead of all political life. But, as interpreted by Machiavelli, Thomas More, and other sixteenth-century political authors, the idea of the social contract differed significantly from the corresponding idea of some leading Greek individualistic philosophers.[8] Appeal was made instead to the rules of a natural law, as conceived by reason, in establishing a doctrine which enabled these sixteenth-century political authors to derive the hereditary rights of kings and princes from contracts of submission concluded between their ancestors and their subjects, conceived as a collectivity. The covenant of the Old Testament was frequently mentioned as a prototype of contracts of that kind.

Closely connected with this theory was the belief that "civil" society had been preceded by a "natural state," although the concept of that primitive state was not clearly defined and no consistent answers were given to the question of how the transition to organized social life might have taken place. An indirect effect of the discussions which turned on the characteristics of the natural state was a clear separation of the notion of society from that of the political community. Thus, the way was prepared for an analysis of social relations independent of their political aspects and the attendant normative implications.

As a political instrument, the theory of the contract of submission provided effective arguments against any claims of the church to extend its jurisdiction beyond the strictly religious sphere. On French soil, a similar role was played by the theory of the "divine right of kings," which was backed by the Scholastic methodology. It was advanced in the second half of the sixteenth century by the French political philosopher Jean Bodin (1530–1596).[9] According to this theory, the rights and duties of rulers were prescribed by divine law, and their sovereignty was directly derived from the grace of God.[10] In accordance with Aristotelian traditions, reason was relied upon to define the principles of law and justice, which rulers were requested to observe. No reference was made in this to the existence of a possible contractual relation between the sovereign rulers and their subjects; instead, the divine sanction which underlay royal prerogative was taken to provide the firm logical and juridical basis of the far-reaching rights claimed by absolute monarchs of the sixteenth and seventeenth centuries.

When suitably amplified, both political theories could be used to substantiate the belief that each of the growing national states constituted a unified body, a whole, engaged in a struggle for power with other similar political communities. A philosophical background was given to such an idea by the widely accepted proposition that the total volume of power and wealth available for all countries was a more or less fixed magnitude, so that a gain in the struggle for power and wealth of one country could be secured only at the expense of the others. Philosophers of history used this approach to explain the rise and decline of empires which had aspired at world domination.[11] It is very probable that the idea of maximizing a share out of a given or fixed volume of power and wealth contributed greatly toward shaping the policy of the national states between the middle of the sixteenth century and the middle of the eighteenth century.[12]

The importance of these views for subsequent political and economic thinking is illustrated by two phrases written about a hundred years after the publication of Machiavelli's work by authors who otherwise differed widely as to their educational backgrounds and social philosophies. According to Francis Bacon, the protagonist of English empiricism, the increase of any estate "must be upon the foreigners, for whatever is somewhere gotten is somewhere lost."[13] The same idea was expressed by the French economist Antoine de Montchrétien (d. 1615), who said that nobody loses unless another gains, and that this state of affairs can best be observed in commerce (*en matière de trafic*).

The conflict between divergent streams of reasoning, which had pressed its stamp on the development of the Renaissance period, came to a prolonged halt in Italy after the church had reasserted its authority through the Council of Trent (1545–63). The decisions passed by that assembly enabled the church to check the lively intellectual movements which, during the preceding century, had supported widespread anticlerical and even irreligious tendencies.[14] In view of the strenuous efforts made to reinforce as far as possible the observance of Thomistic methods of reasoning, freedom to use other methods was a privilege enjoyed only by select groups of scholars in the northern regions of the peninsula. The church even endeavored for a considerable time to arrest the spread of capitalist institutions in Italy.[15]

The struggle between conflicting patterns of thought which took place in England during the period of the Renaissance assumed less striking features than in Italy. In the center of the English intellectual movements were the Franciscans and their Scholastic antagonists. The Franciscans—the protagonists of nominalistic methods of reasoning—dominated the University of Oxford and established a network of monasteries until they were expelled by order of King Henry VIII between 1538 and 1539. It is probable that purely religious problems played a subordinate role in the policies which led to the establishment of the Church of England. More important were political and economic considerations, such as the chance to put an end to the oppressive system of papal taxation (the payment of annates and the like) and the prospect of confiscating vast ecclesiastical possessions.[16]

However that may be, elements of nominalistic methods had entered deeply into the thinking of large groups of the educated population. But this trend was met with fierce opposition by the adherents of Thomistic precepts. Convinced defenders of these precepts were found especially among the ministers and leaders of various denominations which arose in opposition to Catholicism. Richard Hooker (1554–1600), a leader of the Puritan movement, has been called the Anglican Aquinas because of his far-reaching use of Scholastic teachings in his theological dissertations.[17] Between 1500 and 1550, constant appeals were made to the traditional principles of Christian morality in the extensive discussions which turned on the three burning economic issues of the time: the rise in prices, the prohibition of usury, and the land question.[18] Neither the political, the cultural, or the economic history of Elizabethan England can be fully understood without taking account of the logical background of the conflicting intellectual and social movements.

In the Netherlands, where humanism found fertile soil, the break with Scholastic views was facilitated by the political independence of a prosperous bourgeoisie with far-flung commercial interests. Hence, apart from some Italian cities, England and Holland were the main regions where the discussion of social and economic problems was approached from new angles in the sixteenth and seventeenth centuries.

When viewed in the light of economic events, this period has commonly been called the period of "mercantilism," and the term *Mercantilist* has been applied to almost all authors who dealt with economic problems from the middle of the sixteenth until about the middle of the eighteenth century. But the meaning given to these terms has been far from unequivocal. The expression *mercantilist* was introduced into economic literature by Adam Smith, who followed a suggestion of the Physiocrat Marquis de Mirabeau and referred to the "commercial" or "mercantilist" system in order to characterize the protectionist policy of eighteenth-century European governments. Ricardo's followers used the term *Mercantilists* to denote all authors who defended that policy.[19]

A radically different conception of mercantilism and its leading representatives was advanced in the second half of the nineteenth century by some members of the German historical school. Led by Gustav Schmoller, they found the "essence" of mercantilism in a process which resulted in replacing local and regional policies by the centralizing power of strong national governments.[20] In his elaborate and outstanding analysis of mercantilist theory and politics, the Swedish economist Eli Filip Heckscher distinguished Schmoller's conception of mercantilism as a unifying political system from a system of "power" as defined by William Cunningham, and from a system of protectionism and monetary organization as viewed by Adam Smith. According to Heckscher, mercantilism is best understood when viewed as a system of power politics. He considered the French minister Jean Baptiste Colbert (1619–1683) a prominent representative of mercantilism and proposed the term *Colbertism* to characterize "the whole phenomenon of mercantilism."[21] Another definition of mercantilism has been advanced by Eric Roll. Influenced by the materialistic interpretation of history, Roll connected the adoption and the defense of the principles of mercantilism with the "need of commercial capital," and has described the state of the mercantilist period as a "creature of warring commercial interests."[22]

From the point of view of a history of economic reasoning, the political aspects of mercantilism are of secondary importance. What we are concerned with are the ideas of the authors commonly termed *mercantilist,* and the methods of thinking used by them. For reasons of convenience, it appears appropriate to apply this term specifically to the English, Dutch, and Italian authors of the sixteenth, seventeenth, and eighteenth centuries who availed themselves progressively of nominalistic principles in their treatment of economic problems. Motivated by a trend which prevailed in political thinking at that time, these authors as a rule centered their analysis on relations among social collectivities; references to individual behavior as a relevant economic factor only gradually entered into their considerations. Simultaneously, they manifested an increasing tendency to use mechanical conceptions, especially the equilibrium concept, to define the relations among collective economic magnitudes.

Three periods, bullionism, Baconian Mercantilism, and refined Mercantilism can readily be distinguished in analyzing the intellectual process which finally resulted, above all in England, in establishing a fairly consistent picture of relationships among pertinent economic magnitudes. During an early period which began in the sixteenth century, Scholastic concepts such as equivalence and commutative justice still played a significant role in almost all economic discussions. In England a prolonged struggle was under way between the adherents of the medieval moral philosophy and the protagonists of commercial groups who objected to the restrictions imposed on the pursuance of their profit-seeking ventures. The possession of precious metals, believed to represent "wealth of any kind," was held to be indispensable for assuring a country's power and well-being. Hence, a predominant place in the economic discussions was occupied by the question of how to increase a country's "treasure" or "monetary stock" at the cost of other countries, the governments of which pursued the same objective. The term *bullionist* has been suggested to characterize the authors who more or less explicitly identified a country's wealth with the possession of precious metals.[23]

But the logical climate which provided the background to the reasoning of the seventeenth-century authors underwent quite significant modifications when the application of mechanical concepts to the analysis of economic magnitudes was suggested by new schools of thought. This line of reasoning led to the proposition that "natural" forces were operating in the economy and that their desirable effects might be disturbed by government interference. The range and the formulation of these questions were in various respects influenced by the fact that bankers, merchants, and the representatives of large companies endeavored to demonstrate that various policies, adjusted to their commercial or financial interests, were perfectly compatible with those of the common weal.

A new approach to economic analysis was initiated about the middle of the seventeenth century—above all in England—when various attempts were made to analyze measurable economic phenomena in accordance with the methodological principles established by Francis Bacon for purposes of scientific investigations. Statistical data were drawn upon to provide the basis upon which to generalize judgments derived from experience. Simultaneously, the meaning of fundamental economic concepts such as value, price, and money was critically examined and redefined; the application of the mechanical balance principle to economic relations developed in various directions. Moreover, the sharp line drawn by Scholastic reasoning between licit and illicit behavior was blurred by the introduction of an intermediate group of morally indifferent actions, and pursuance of self-interest in the economic sphere was included in this group. The authors who actively participated in these developments might be termed *Baconian Mercantilists.*

Elaboration of these ideas provided the bridge to the development of "refined mercantilism." This movement started in the first decades of the eighteenth century, when the range of economic problems was extended far beyond its previous limits and new methods were suggested for formulating and treating old problems. Some attempts were made to define the concept of an economic system and to clarify the objectives of government interference with regard to the behavior of the economy. Dutch and Italian economists adjusted their reasoning to similar trends.

In France, the church and representatives of the feudal classes united in counteracting any movements which favored the spread of nominalistic methods. Conflicting and poorly organized patterns of thought resulted from this struggle in the seventeenth century, and French economic reasoning was lacking a well-defined logical background. The main questions dealt with in economic discussions turned on the organization and supervision of industry and trade, and on policies designed to support the government's political objectives. Jean Baptiste Colbert, the leading statesman and minister of finance under King Louis XIV, has been most closely linked to the economic policy pursued in France in the seventeenth century and during the first decades of the eighteenth century. The system of economic measures and ideas developed under him is known as *Colbertism*. The eighteenth century was already well advanced when the influence of English mercantilist reasoning made itself felt in the writings of French authors.

On the Iberian Peninsula, Scholastic reasoning preserved a predominant position until the end of the eighteenth century, and noticeably influenced the thinking of those Spanish authors who discussed mercantilist types of restrictive economic policy in the course of the seventeenth and eighteenth centuries.

In Central Europe, especially in the territories belonging to the Holy Roman Empire, modified Aristotelian methods of thought were dominant, and the economic teachings of the German and Austrian "Cameralists" centered on administrative questions, on measures designed to regulate industry and trade, and on methods of financing public expenditures. They largely ignored the theoretical approach to economic research adopted to an increasing degree by the English Mercantilists. This is true even of the Cameralists of the eighteenth century, who endeavored to transform their discipline into a branch of higher learning.

Hence, a gradual but quite noticeable process of differentiation among prevailing patterns of thought took place in Europe between the beginning of the sixteenth century and the middle of the eighteenth century. In the light of this differentiation, it appears advisable to characterize the main trends in the development of economic reasoning and the authors who dealt with economic and social questions during this period as Neo-scholastic, early mercantilist (bullionist), Baconian mercantilist, refined mercantilist, Colbertist, and cameralist.

THE "SPIRIT OF CAPITALISM"

Before we enter an analysis of mercantilist economics, it might be advisable to describe briefly the economic conditions which provided the background for the adoption of new economic philosophies and which were in turn modified by these philosophies. These economic conditions have been frequently characterized as the first stages in the development of the "capitalistic" society. In a vast literature the concept of capitalism has been the object of widely divergent definitions. As a rule, a considerable array of economic attributes has been included in these definitions, such as uninhibited pursuance of profit-making purposes, large-scale production of staple goods for indefinite markets, development of credit facilities adjusted to the needs of industrial and commercial expansion, competitive organization of economic activities, dependence upon a large labor market for the recruitment of skilled and unskilled workers, and so on. Partisans of the materialistic interpretation of history have placed main emphasis on the existence of a free labor market, an industrial "reserve army," and the "exploitation" of the manual workers by capitalist employers as the characteristic features of capitalism.

American and European scholars, looking from the vantage point of the late nineteenth and early twentieth centuries, have viewed the emergence of capitalism at the end of the Middle Ages in different ways. Influenced by the economic theories of Thorstein Veblen, American economists have ascribed to "technological innovation" the decisive part in establishing the institutions of capitalism.[24] Other students of economic history have suggested that the roots of capitalism are to be found in the adoption of a specific ethical behavior ruled by the principles of an individualistic or utilitarian doctrine.[25]

A different approach toward the definition of the concept of "capitalism" was adopted in the 19th century by various members of the German historical school who connected the transformation of medieval society into a "capitalist" society with the emergence of a new mental attitude qualified as an "objective" phenomenon and termed the *spirit of capitalism*. Werner Sombart, who made the development of capitalism the object of extensive studies, regarded "irrational striving for gain" and "rational organization of profit-seeking enterprises" as the main characteristics of the spirit of capitalism.[26] He contrasted the "acquisitive principle"—an outstanding feature of that "spirit"—with the "principle of satisfying wants," which he extolled as the motivating economic force of the productive organization of previous periods. Many members of the German historical school accepted Sombart's views, together with his attempts to demonstrate that the Jews were primarily responsible for practicing and spreading the spirit of capitalism and that their special aptitude for "acquisitive business" was to be ascribed to racial factors.[27]

Far more penetrating was Max Weber's analysis of the roots of capitalism.[28] Using his method of establishing "ideal types," Weber contrasted medieval ethical principles with the moral and social attitudes which developed in connection with the great religious movements of the Reformation.[29] Among the outstanding characteristics of that change, he especially emphasized the role played by the spread of Calvinism in introducing a new conception of economic life. He showed that under the influence of this creed, labor was transformed into a "calling," that rectitude, severity, and diligence were elevated to the rank of primary virtues, that worldly success was considered a symptom of divine blessing, and that thriftiness combined with gainful use of one's means was a duty prescribed by Christian morality. Thus, according to Weber, the behavior of bankers, tradesmen, and artisans was gradually adjusted to a new type of "economic rationality."[30]

In this respect, the Calvinist creed differed noticeably from the teachings of the Scholastics, who rejected the performance of work for the sake of work and considered the search for gain sinful.[31] Martin Luther preached fulfillment of the duties requested by one's "calling," which he defined as that state of life in which the individual has been set by heaven and against which it is impiety to rebel.[32]

Telling arguments have been advanced against Weber's proposition to make the teaching of the Puritan divines exclusively responsible for the origin and spread of the "spirit of capitalism." It could be shown that, as mentioned in another connection, capitalistic forms of production, trading, and banking existed in Catholic territories such as the cities of Venice and Florence from the fifteenth century onward, and that these capitalistic modes were independent of the religious movements of the Reformation.

Moreover, early Calvinism, not only in Geneva but also in England, was ruled by a code of strict ethics which was supervised and enforced by clerical authorities, and relative economic freedom was introduced into that code rather later. Neither the Calvinist nor the Anglican nor the Lutheran preachers appear to have been influenced by the intention of relaxing the rules of "good conscience" imposed by Scholastic theologians to control economic transactions and social relations.[33]

The search for the "spirit of capitalism"—whatever may be the meaning attached to that ambiguous term—has been motivated by the tendency of members of the historical school to distinguish contrasting categories of moral behavior and sharply differentiated social structures. This tendency was in turn suggested by the methodological principle of distinguishing "stages" in the course of continuous historical processes, and of defining the stages according to the criterion of "objective reality."

It is, however, quite obvious that composite abstract concepts, such as "the spirit of capitalism," exist only in the mind of the observer and have no correspondence in reality. It also appears advisable to avoid the distinction of "stages" in an analysis of economic history, since stage analysis tends to dissect the continuous flow of economic developments and to telescope extended processes into ill-defined periods marked by specific characteristics.

In order to account for the origin of capitalistic institutions, it can be argued that prerequisite to any change in social or economic institutions or organizations is a change of the prevailing pattern of reasoning which had provided the background to the predominant forms of social and economic life. Such a gradual change in methods of reasoning took place toward the end of the Middle Ages, especially in England but also in other parts of Western Europe, when the rigid economic precepts of medieval Scholastics were gradually undermined by the influence of nominalistic reasoning.

When the concept of "calling" as interpreted by the Scholastics was freed from its association with narrowly defined professional and vocational functions, various lines of gainful occupations could be combined by the same person, and success or failure of such more or less speculative activities could be measured only in terms of their aggregate pecuniary yield. The concept of industrial or commercial capital as an abstract pecuniary magnitude was another outcome of this change in methods of economic reasoning.

Simultaneously, the risk element came to play an increasing role in economic considerations and transformed fixed bases of economic behavior into assumptions and expectations. Calculations had to be adjusted to a variety of unknown factors and the probability of their occurrence. The development of limited companies which started in England in the fifteenth century facilitated the distribution of commercial or industrial risks among owners of capital without enforcing their active participation in the management of the enterprises.

Merchants and bankers, who were the first to be affected by the change in the logical climate, played a leading role in modifying the economic behavior of entrepreneurs who occupied strategic positions in manufacturing industries.[34] In England, the rigid regulation of these industries as practiced during the Elizabethan period was greatly relaxed in the course of the seventeenth century, especially after the Civil War, which ended in 1646. This gradual transformation of the economic order was accompanied by a rapid growth of large-scale industrial production, increased commercial relations with other countries, the introduction of a variety of technical innovations, and the widespread promotion of inventions made by imaginative minds. During the second half of the seventeenth century the air was filled with inventions and projects.[35] Such events were symptomatic of a general change in the traditional pattern of thought, and they reflected the profound alteration in the relation between will and reason which had been initiated by philosophers of nominalistic persuasion.

The disintegration of the feudal organization in England, which was a concomitant circumstance of that change, created new social and economic problems. They found their most striking expressions in the displacement of masses of peasants through the enclosure movement,[36] and in the employment of increasing numbers of workers outside the confines of the guild system. The medieval principle of combining technical and commercial functions in the person of the skilled master became less and less compatible with the organization of large-scale, export-oriented production. The main form of organizing such production, especially in the textile industry, was the "putting out" system, which was based on the coordinated activity of domestic workshops.

Expanding markets and their exploitation by manufacturers and traders were prerequisite to these changes in the structure of the economy. The development of manufacturing and trading facilities was promoted by the system of granting "royal letters patent of monopoly," which conferred upon private persons or corporations the exclusive right to produce or sell certain commodities. In the Elizabethan period these privileges were mainly granted to chartered companies, and had become an important source of royal revenue under the Stuarts. Frequently they also served the purpose of securing the financial independence of artisans and of promoting the introduction of new lines of industries such as glass manufacture, soap production, and the exploitation of salines. But often they were also used to grant favors for political or personal reasons. The Long Parliament (1640–60) responded to the changing intellectual and economic climate, and was responsible for legal changes which favored a considerable degree of economic freedom. It abolished the system of feudal tenure and entails of real estate, abrogated many prerogatives of the crown, and placed limits on royal power to grant monopolistic privileges.[37]

The monopolies of trading companies which gained prominence in the course of the sixteenth and seventeenth centuries differed fundamentally from the collective monopolies of the guild system, which were designed to assure the exploitation of closed markets by the members of the privileged corporations. But the mercantilist authors who spent much effort on the discussion of monopolies did not succeed in clarifying the economic nature of the different types of diverse "monopolies" which arose during this period in answering the question to what degree the government could rely upon "monopolistic" organizations as instruments for promoting the expansion of industrial activities and foreign trade. One outstanding monopolistic organization was that of the Merchant Adventurers, a chartered company which enjoyed the privilege of restricting the number of its members and of regulating their practices in the export trade of undyed and undressed cloth.[38] The term *export cartel* might be a more appropriate name to denote such an association. However, the privileges granted to powerful trade organizations such as the East India Company were of an entirely different type. They opened the way to indefinite opportunities of gain at considerable risk.[39] Their exploitation required close and continuous adjustment of commercial practices to unforeseen situations, and the performance of economic operations was perforce based on changing assumptions and expectations.

The developments which took place in England in the spheres of industrial activity and trading had their counterpart in similar developments in other countries, especially in the Netherlands, which were also instrumental in promoting initial stages of capitalistic organization. A far stricter and more extensive regulation of industry and trade was applied in France in accordance with the principles of Colbertism. The violent struggle for prominence in international trade which developed in the seventeenth century was waged mainly among England, France, and Holland; it contributed noticeably toward accentuating the dynamic features of the mercantilist period.

The far-reaching changes in the organization of production and marketing are likely to provide an explanation of the contrast which Eli Heckscher has found to exist between the "hunger for goods" of the medieval cities and the "fear of goods" exhibited by mercantilist authors.[40] The rights of the medieval artisans and traders to their share in the domestic markets, as prescribed by the principles of distributive justice, were not affected by the importation of rare commodities not manufactured by domestic producers. Heckscher mentions in another connection that imports of that type were welcome additions to an otherwise rather monotonous consumption scheme. In the mercantilist period, however, imports of an entirely different kind tended to compete with manufactures which were themselves produced on a large scale for indefinite markets, with the attendant risk of unsalable surpluses. Hence, the economists of that period were almost unanimous in recommending protectionist measures.[41] Such measures were also widely applied in order to promote "nascent" industries growing out of inventions or introduced from abroad by foreign artisans.

Inflationary price movements, which were caused by the inflow of precious metals during the second half of the sixteenth century and the first decades of the seventeenth century also contributed greatly toward disrupting the medieval system of fixed economic relations. The transition from the medieval organization of industry and trade to capitalistic forms was no doubt greatly facilitated and stimulated by the vastly increased monetary supply resulting from the discovery of overseas countries. In due course many mercantilist authors were greatly disturbed by the resulting price increases and the attendant upheaval in fixed economic relations. Intensified attention was given to monetary problems and prolonged discussions started about the question of whether rising or falling prices were more conducive to common welfare. Those who insisted upon enlarging a country's share in the international supply of monetary metals but were opposed to rising prices were faced with a serious dilemma.

But monetary factors were effective in supporting the development of capitalistic enterprises only in countries in which the soil was prepared for the adoption of new methods of organizing production and trade, as in Italy, England, Holland, and partly in France. In Central Europe, where Aristotelian principles continued to determine the thinking processes until the end of the eighteenth century, capitalistic enterprises developed at a very slow pace. In Spain, where the "conquistadores" had made available the treasures of Mexico and Peru to the ruling classes, gold and silver were soon spent on the importation of large quantities of foreign goods and did not significantly promote the expansion of domestic production. The feudal structure of Spanish society and the medieval organization of the economy were preserved under the influence of a dominant Scholastic pattern of thought. Prerequisite to the development of capitalistic enterprises everywhere has been the prevalence of appropriate methods of reasoning. The rise of capitalism cannot be explained simply by a "money quantity" theory.

THE ECONOMIC VIEWS OF EARLY MERCANTILISTS

In order to arrive at a full understanding of the mental processes which led from the economic reasoning of the Aristotelian scholastics to the formulation of new social and economic problems by the representatives of early mercantilism, it would be necessary to analyze the sixteenth- and seventeenth-century literature on technology, husbandry, banking, and trading practices and to show how the rigid, static, moral aspects of the medieval conceptual structure were gradually replaced by more flexible concepts frequently borrowed from diverse spheres of observation and knowledge. In the fields of banking and trading practices, Italian authors played a leading role. Books of that type which were published in England and Central Europe in the sixteenth century were frequently translations or summaries of Italian originals.

For the purposes of this analysis, it will be sufficient to observe that the authors who dealt with economic questions were more and more inclined to leave the discussion of the moral aspects of economic behavior to ministers and preachers, and to turn their attention to general policies affecting the country or interests of large classes of the population.

Hence, politically determined concepts were introduced into economic discussions, which soon centered on the international exchange of goods and the importance to be attached to foreign trade in promoting national interests. But significant differences in assessing policy goals were reflected in the treatment of this fundamental issue. The advocates of national power politics were faced with the arguments of Neoscholastic social philosophers, who elaborated on the idea that nature had distributed the products of the earth unequally among the nations and had thus established the basis for the mutual exchange of goods. Outstanding representatives of this school were the sixteenth-century Jesuits Francisco di Vitoria (1486?–1546) and Francisco Suarez (1548–1617), who conceived of all national economies as constituent parts of the universal economy and raised the question of whether a country was permitted by natural law to seclude its economy from international commerce, thus violating the principle that the universal economy should claim precedence over national interests.[42] Similar views also found adherents among contemporary English authors who did not share Scholastic convictions.[43]

On the other hand, the conception of national states as integrated wholes of a not clearly defined type received considerable support from the still prevailing feudal structure of society, which was rooted in the privileged position occupied by the aristocratic owners of large landed properties. Under the influence of ideas of that kind, the interests of the king, the feudal overlord, were frequently identified with the interests of the country; the heritable kingdom was regarded as the king's property, and national wealth as the aggregate of the goods available for the pursuance of power politics, which did not include personal consumption goods.[44] An outstanding place among the elements of national wealth was assigned to the precious metals because of their role as means of exchange.[45] "Bullionist" authors went so far as to identify the possession of such metals with the possession of stores of value, and the idea that these metals represented "universal wealth" was expressed over and over again in a great number of variations.[46]

The substance concept played a considerable role in facilitating the acceptance of Neoscholastic monetary views which ascribed "intrinsic value" or "inner goodness" to the precious metals as to any other good. Such value was distinguished from the extrinsic or exchange value of money, which was held to fluctuate in accordance with scarcity or abundance of money at different places and different times. Lawyers especially availed themselves of the doctrine of the intrinsic value of money in their fight against the debasement of currencies.[47] In order to protect claims to payments in foreign currency against arbitrary devaluation, they requested that the declared value of the coins, their *valor impositus*, be adjusted to their *bonitas intrinsica*. On the other hand, the political theory of the contract of submission was being used to defend the opposite view, namely, that the standard of measuring values depended exclusively upon the will of the prince.

Considerations of that kind caused a Genoese jurist, Sigismondo Scaccia, to advance a twofold theory concerning the value of money.[48] He separated money as a circulating means of payment from money as an object of purchases in foreign exchange transactions. In the first case, which he called *emptio activa,* the value of money was to be fixed by the authorities; in the second case, qualified as *emptio passiva,* the monetary value was to be determined in accordance with the value of the precious metals. The idea of differentiating the exchange value of a currency according to the markets in which it was used was thus given a sort of juridical justification.

Among the sixteenth-century Italian authors who were convinced adherents of the theory of the intrinsic value of money, the banker Gasparo Scaruffi may be mentioned.[49] He ascribed only a declaratory meaning to the stamp affixed to coins. Other Italian contemporary economists who shared that opinion were Antonio Serra and Bernardo Davanzati, whose economic views will be referred to in another connection.

Economic thinking, as it prevailed in England toward the middle of the sixteenth century, was well represented in an essay, written probably in 1549 but published in 1581, entitled *Discourse of the Common Weal of this Realm of England.* Belonging to a transition period, it reflected the battle of conflicting ideas in the form of a discussion among a knight, a merchant, a husbandman, a craftsman, and a doctor.[50] The doctor expressed the views of the author. The discussion turned on the "common and universal griefs" and the "causes and occasions of the same." The three main economic evils which had befallen England—high prices, unemployment, and declines in fixed revenues—were ascribed by the doctor to monetary causes, the debasement of the coin, which had violated the intrinsic value of the money. He termed money a "storehouse of any commodity one would like to have" and considered the acquisition of precious metals an indispensable means of furthering common welfare. That objective was to be promoted by restrictions imposed on foreign imports and on the exportation of domestic raw materials, especially wool. On the other hand, the well-known arguments concerning the distribution of goods among the various nations provided the doctor with effective arguments in favor of the promotion of foreign trade.

Far more striking was the doctor's reference, in his discussion of the enclosure movement, to the profit motive as the regulator of economic activity.[51] Everyman, he argues, would seek where most advantage was, and so long as there was more advantage in grazing and breeding, the pasture would encroach upon the tillage, regardless of any laws that could ever be made to the contrary. Rewards and prices were needed in order to "provoke" men to good deeds.[52] Hence, the doctor criticized the corn laws designed to keep the price of corn low, thus discouraging its production. He rejected quite definitely the traditional preference for cheapness of goods and recommended increases in the prices of agricultural as well as manufactured commodities. He even made a vague reference to the operation of natural forces when he observed that what was profitable to one may be profitable to another and so to the commonwealth.

About two decades later, a revolutionary change in the dominant monetary views was suggested by one of the most original political authors of the sixteenth century, the Frenchman Jean Bodin, who cannot be counted among the mercantilist authors but who effectively influenced their approach to monetary problems. In his political treatise, he elaborated the Neoscholastic idea that, according to the divine wisdom, the various nations were constituent parts of a "universal republic of this world" (*république universelle de ce monde*).[53] He described the functioning of the export mechanism and showed that imports contributed toward lowering the prices of scarce goods. He realized the favorable effects upon industrial activity of the influx of precious metals and created in

France a strong predilection in favor of rising prices. But his approval of the prohibition of taking interest on money showed his adherence to certain principles of Scholastic reasoning. The same was perhaps true of his belief in the existence of a vaguely defined "natural law" embodying general precepts which were applicable to the functioning of all human communities and could be grasped by the human mind.

The lasting place which Bodin acquired in the history of economic reasoning was due to his famous *Reply to the Paradoxes of M. de Malestroit*,[54] a treatise which centered on a brilliant refutation of the traditional view that the general rise in prices which had taken place in France was to be ascribed to the repeated lowering of the specie content of the coins and the resulting debasement of the currency.[55] Bodin listed, along with the effects of the debasement, a number of causes (consumption of luxury goods, monopolies, etc.) which in his view had aggravated the general rise in prices. But he showed convincingly that the alarming general price movement was primarily due to the influx of the monetary metals brought from the West Indies to Spain and Portugal that had found their way into France as payment for greatly enhanced exports, especially of salt, wine, and wheat.[56] Bodin's reasoning implied that the value of the monetary metals was ultimately determined by the quantity relation.[57] He made no reference to the traditional idea of an "intrinsic value" of money; thus, he suggested, at least indirectly, a separation of price theory from value theory and introduced the concept of an exchange value of money as a distinct category.[58] But he can hardly be credited with formulating a quantity theory of money in the strict sense of the term. His discussion of the relation between changes in the quantity of money and prices did not point to a proportionality between the supply of money and the value of the monetary metals.[59]

As mentioned before, other French authors who participated in the discussion of economic issues dealt almost exclusively with problems of economic policy, such as the means of increasing the national stock of precious metals, the promotion of domestic industries and commerce, employment of the poor, foreign trade, the treatment of the colonies, and the like.

THE BALANCE OF TRADE CONCEPT

Some of the most striking features of mercantilism, as it developed in the sixteenth and seventeenth centuries, especially in England, were due to the fact that the main authors to participate in this movement were increasingly independent of the principles of Scholastic reasoning. Hence, they felt free to discard the Scholastic approach to economic questions and to introduce new concepts into their discussions, especially concepts derived from mechanics and allied disciplines. This development can perhaps best be characterized by the tendency to substitute for the Scholastic concept of equivalence the concept of equilibrium, and this radical change in conceptual approach had significant consequences for the analysis of economic relationships. The phenomena to which the new approach was applied were collective magnitudes derived from important aspects of national power politics.

Under the rule of the Scholastic principle of commutative justice, equivalence between a country's exports and imports should be sought since, according to the prevailing convictions, any gain in trade could be made only at a corresponding loss of the partner.[60] That principle lost its force and relevance with the development of the struggle for national power, which found a striking expression in the idea that acquisition of precious metals through foreign trade represented an advancement in power over other countries which competed for the available supply of such metals. The close relation thus established between foreign policy and foreign trade was also backed by a very practical motive, the financial strain imposed on European governments by the need to maintain large mercenary armies.[61] Foreign trade was regarded as a kind of hidden warfare waged over the possession of the monetary metals,[62] and the connection between the acquisition of these metals and political considerations was reflected in various, often repeated phrases to the effect that money was the "nerves of the state," the "sinews of war," and the like.[63]

Toward the end of the sixteenth century, an anonymous English author provided a clear formulation of the idea that increases in "wealth" were dependent upon increases in exports. He argued that, having no way to increase its treasure by mines of gold and silver at home, the realm would receive "that over-plus in money" by carrying more commodities in value over the seas than it brought home.[64] About the same time, bookkeeping devices were introduced into commercial practice in England:[65] in due course a general tendency developed to compare the incoming and outgoing volumes of bullion with the income and expenditure of a private household, and to measure a nation's gain from international trade in terms of its export surplus as represented by the inflow of specie. Toward the end of the sixteenth century, the officials of the king's treasury, as well as the merchants, were convinced that foreign trade was practically the only way of enhancing the country's wealth. Consequently, domestic trade, although considered advantageous from the point of view of private interests, was held to be irrelevant as far as the interests of the community were concerned.

The principle of equivalence was applied, as before, to the transactions taking place in domestic markets, in accordance with the view that equal values were exchanged for each other in these transactions and that the gain of one person was canceled by a corresponding loss of another. Hence, the concept of "cost" was held to be applicable only to the total volume of a country's trade with other countries, and a gain could result only when this trade showed a surplus expressed by the inflow of precious metals.

The identification of public wealth with the possession of these metals had its counterpart in the monetary policy adopted in England in the sixteenth century: all transactions involving the importation or exportation of specie were subjected to the control of the king's exchange.[66] The English merchants who sold their goods abroad were required to increase the national supply of currency through the yield from their foreign sales. Foreign merchants were compelled under the "Statutes of Employment" to spend the receipts of their sales to English customers on the purchase of English goods.[67] Sumptuary laws were another constituent element of the commercial policy of "bullionism."

English exporters, however, protested against the provisions which prevented them from purchasing and reselling in foreign markets. The public officials, on the other hand, complained, like many contemporary authors, about scarcity of money and attributed that scarcity to the speculative practices of the "exchangers," the dealers in foreign bills of exchange. They argued that fluctuations of the rate of exchange violated the prescribed harmony between the intrinsic value of the coins as fixed by their denomination and the intrinsic goodness of the coined metals as defined by their weight and fineness. Thus, they insisted upon applying the Scholastic concepts of equivalence rigidly to the relations between the various currencies and ascribed deviations from the parity of exchange to the machinations of the merchants and their illegal transactions.

The conflicting views of the two parties were aired in a number of pamphlets written in the 1620s. The "bullionist" policy, involving strict supervision of all international movements of precious metals, was vigorously defended by Gerard Malynes (1586–1641), who had been a member of the commission appointed in 1600 by Queen Elizabeth to inquire into the causes of the existing scarcity of money.[68] He argued that, in flagrant violation of the intrinsic value of money, the currency was the object of two valuations in foreign exchange transactions: one valuation ordered by the prince, the other fixed by the exchangers. He made the undervaluation of the British coins—the "cancer" of the Commonwealth—responsible for the exportation of specie.[69] However, he fully realized that fluctuations of the rate of exchange had their cause not only in speculative manipulations but also in the fact that in international transactions the claims of foreign countries might be larger (or smaller) than a country's own claims. He was also aware of the connection between the fall of a country's currency below its mint par, with the consequent outflow of specie, and the fall in domestic prices as contrasted with the rise in prices abroad. He objected to the view that the exportation of monetary metals in the form of coins could be arrested by a depreciation of the currency. He thought rising prices to be beneficial, not sharing the then almost general predilection for "cheapness of goods."

Hence, Malynes centered his attacks on the view of the exporters that "exchange was a kind of merchandise, rising and falling in price, according to plenty and scarcity of money." Moreover, he violently objected to various forms of dealing in foreign exchange which enabled the parties to circumvent the restrictions placed on the level of interest rates and caused English debtors to sell their goods at exceptionally low prices abroad, thus "overthrowing the markets of others."[70] Malynes strongly urged reestablishment of the control of foreign exchange which had been practically discontinued; among other subsidiary measures of exchange control, he requested revival of the "Ordinance of the Staple," which granted to certain towns the right to force foreign traders to offer their wares for sale and to submit to other restrictions.[71]

Malynes's views have been quite generally condemned by the historians of liberal persuasion because of his insistence on a rigid control of foreign exchange transactions. On closer analysis, however, it appears that he can be credited with having shown a remarkable understanding of balance of payment problems and of the effects on prices of the international movement of the monetary metals. This aspect of Malynes's writings was emphasized by Joseph Alois Schumpeter, and John Maynard Keynes praised him because of his attitude toward rising prices. But in spite of his lucid discussion of international monetary movements, Malynes remained a convinced defender of the Scholastic principle of equivalence as applied to the exchange relations among different currencies.[72]

The Scholastic principle of equivalence was attacked by Malynes's contemporary adversary, Edward Misselden, an outstanding member of the Merchant Adventurers Company,[73] who used the slogan "free trade" to advocate free exportation of bullion, and established a sort of landmark in the history of economic reasoning through his use of the equilibrium concept to justify the commercial policy of his company.[74] He rejected Malynes's contention that the "par of exchange," the rate determined by the "inner values" of the currencies, should and could be maintained by artificial measures. The actual prices of the exchange, he argued, fluctuated above and below an ideal price "determined by the weight and fineness of the coined metal" according to the "occasions of both parties contracting for the same." The ideal price, like the price of any other commodity, he stated, was regulated by the "inner goodness" of the monetary metals. Thus, Misselden pointed to the existence of equilibrating forces operating independently of any deliberate regulations. For the merchants, he claimed the right to seek their private gain in the exercise of their calling; he referred to the experience of the Netherlands, where trade was flourishing although no restrictions were imposed on the exportation of bullion and no such restrictions were requested by public opinion.[75]

Misselden expressed his predilection for a purely mechanical approach to problems of foreign trade even more definitely in a passage in which he suggested the use of the equilibrium concept to measure the effects of trade between two kingdoms. "As scales," he said, "is an invention to show us the waight of things, whereby one may discern the heavy from the light, so is also this Balence of Trade an excellent and politique invention to show us the difference of waight in the Commerce of one Kingdom with another: that is whether the Native Commodities exported and all the forraine Commodities imported doe balance or overballance one another in the Scale of Commerce."[76]

A concept borrowed from mechanics was thus applied to the determination of the effects of economic transactions. Such a procedure would have been incompatible with Scholastic reasoning. But by the third decade of the seventeenth century, freedom in the use of abstract concepts was far enough advanced to permit such a new formulation of the relation between economic phenomena.

Various, more fundamental, issues involved in the balance of trade concept were subsequently raised by Thomas Mun (1571–1641), a member of the Committee of the East India Company.[77] In his essay, which was greatly admired by the English Mercantilists of the seventeenth and eighteenth centuries, Mun availed himself of the balance of trade concept to formulate policy recommendations designed to assure increases in the national "wealth" through enhanced export surpluses. With this end in view, he distinguished different kinds of exports and imports according to their effects on economic well-being and suggested price policies to be practiced in markets abroad.

As Malynes and Misselden had done before him, Mun took account of the relation which had been established between increases in the volume of money and the movements of prices. Since, as distinct from Malynes, he considered rising prices highly undesirable, he proposed to counteract the effects of continuous export surpluses on the domestic price level by reinvesting these surpluses in agriculture and fisheries on the one hand and in manufactures on the other. Like some other writers of his time, he favored the exportation of commodities embodying large amounts of labor,[78] regarded abundant labor supply, low wages, and cheap victuals as prerequisite to prosperity,[79] and expressed the traditional aversion to the importation of "luxury" goods.

Among the factors which were instrumental in determining the rate of exchange, Mun also included items other than the volumes of imported and exported commodities. Hence, his considerations turned, in fact, like those of Malynes and Misselden, on the broader concept of the balance of payments. It is also quite obvious why he and other advocates of the commercial policy of the East India Company did not agree with the commercial policy of the British government, which was designed to secure export surpluses in the trade with individual countries. Mun adopted the concept of an aggregate balance of trade and argued that his company could reimport more gold and silver than had been exported if it were allowed to export bullion and to use it in multilateral trading.

A really radical innovation, however, which Mun introduced into the economic reasoning of his time was his reference to a strictly causal relation between the development of foreign commerce and the inflow and outflow of the precious metals:

Let forraign princes enhance their coins or debase their standards, and let his Majesty do the like, or keep them constant as they now stand; . . . let the meer exchanger do his worst, let princes oppress, lawyers extort, usurers bite, prodigals waste, and lastly let merchants carry out what money they shall have occasion to use in traffiquing. Yet, all these actions can work no other effect in the course of trade than is declared in this discourse. For so much treasure will be brought in or carried out of the commonwealth as the forraign trade doth over or under ballance in value.[80] And this must come to pass by a necessity beyond our resistance.[81]

From these considerations Mun drew the conclusion that, regardless of the possession of mines by the various countries, their yearly share in the world's stock of precious metals was determined by their balances of trade. The idea of causal laws comparable to those governing the realm of physics was thus introduced into a sphere which had been considered a privileged domain of administrative regulations.

To apply the principle of mechanical causality in determining the relations between economic events would have been anathema to any adherent of Thomistic Scholastics. The admiration bestowed on Mun's essay by his contemporaries revealed a growing tendency to replace the traditional belief in teleological relations with the search for mechanical laws of nature. Moreover, thinking in terms of comparable aggregates of values—such as was basic to the balance of trade concept—was likely to suggest a logical separation of the sphere of measurable economic magnitudes from other spheres of social life which did not permit the application of measurement.

In Italy, the use of nominalistic methods of reasoning had not been completely suppressed by papal decrees; it continued to play a significant role not only in some northern cities but also in Naples. Thus, ideas similar to those advanced in England by Misselden and Mun had been anticipated in the second decade of the seventeenth century by the Neapolitan author Antonio Serra, who showed a remarkable understanding of the functioning of the foreign exchange mechanism and of the effects of general economic conditions upon foreign trade and the monetary supply.[82] In his discussion of the balance of trade, Serra took account of the invisible items, and when criticizing measures of exchange control as proposed by his compatriot Marc Antonio De Santis, Serra showed that balance of payment difficulties were responsible for the outflow of gold and silver from the kingdom of Naples and objected to the proposal to stop that outflow through devaluation. The main part of Serra's treatise dealt with a clear analysis of the thesis that countries with no gold or silver mines could increase their possession of wealth only by developing their manufactures and achieving an export surplus in their foreign trade. With this end in view, Serra recommended a comprehensive system of measures designed to promote industry and commerce.

But Serra's essay does not appear to have left a distinct mark on the history of economic reasoning. He addressed his advice to the Spanish viceroy from a prison cell and did not convince the authorities of the validity of his arguments.

Continued occupation with the balance of trade concept and the effects of the international movements of monetary metals soon attracted various mercantilist authors to economic problems which were more or less connected with the objectives of national power politics. But before entering upon an analysis of these developments, we shall review the contemporary French discussion of economic questions, which was shaped far more than discussion in England by political considerations.

COLBERTISM

Some students of the history of economic thought who have defined mercantilism as a system of power politics have used *Colbertism* and *mercantilism* as interchangeable items. Colbert has been extolled as the outstanding representative of mercantilist ideas and has even been found worthy to give the mercantilist system its name. In fact, Colbertism can be characterized as a network of economic and social measures dominated by the objective of ambitious national power politics.

However, the relations between Colbertism and mercantilism appear in a different light when the logical background of English mercantilism is compared with the far less articulate reasoning which provided the basis for the predominantly practical considerations of French sixteenth- and seventeenth-century economists and politicians. As distinct from the static aspects characteristic of the views of these authors, the English Mercantilists represented a gradually changing intellectual movement and were groping for some theoretical justification of their economic policies. The equilibrium concept played a conspicuous role in these endeavors; it was virtually ignored by their French contemporaries. Nor were the adherents of Colbertism influenced by the Baconian methodology and the individualistic considerations which transformed the reasoning of the early Mercantilists. The French economists were not animated by the search for a promising methodology, and this fact might help to explain the poverty of economic writings during the reign of the ''roi soleil,'' a period otherwise marked by outstanding achievements in the fields of literature and the arts.

Of course, Jean Bodin's analysis of the relations between rising prices and the influx of precious metals from the Iberian Peninsula (1568) was an outstanding contribution to the understanding of fundamental economic problems. But his views were still affected to a significant degree by Scholastic concepts, and his studies did not result in initiating the formulation and discussion of other economic questions of similar importance.

About the middle of the sixteenth century, after bitter and prolonged struggles, governmental authority in France was assured. Assisted by his chief minister, the duke of Sully (1560–1641), Henry IV (1553–1610) adopted an economic policy designed to provide a safe basis for industrial progress in a unified country. He endeavored to restore manufacturing and trade, which had been almost ruined by devastating civil wars. Guilds were made compulsory, and their activities were placed under strict administrative supervision.[83] Various industries, the products of which had been imported from Italy, were transplanted to French soil. As distinct from that in England, French foreign trade was not the object of particular attention,[84] although large amounts of precious metals were gained through the sales of agricultural products to Spain. During this period the contributions of French authors to economic questions were not especially important for a history of economic reasoning. One of the most prolific economic authors was Barthelemy de Laffemas (d. 1611), economic adviser to Henry IV. His pamphlets deal mainly with various measures designed to develop the administrative organization of industry and trade and to promote industrial production through compulsory recruitment of labor. Although he considered the possession of precious metals of primary importance for a country's well-being, in a pamphlet he wrote about the beginning of the seventeenth century, he recommended free export of gold and silver.

Similar ideas, but elaborated in a more systematic and attractive form, were advanced by Antoine de Montchrétien in his *Traicté de l'oeconomie politique* (1615), the first book to make questions of economic policy the object of a special treatise. Political economy, as he understood it, was designed to deal with those public affairs which are especially significant from the point of view of the necessities and burdens of the state.[85] He regarded a large and industrious population as the greatest asset of a country, and defined national wealth as an abundance of goods available at low prices. He attributed the division of labor and the exchange of goods to the desire of individuals to further their own interests. However, he considered an excessive abundance of goods a danger, he objected to the importation of manufactures and the exportation of bullion, and he proposed to increase as far as possible exports into enemy countries in order to deprive them of their supply of precious metals. The conception of foreign trade as an instrument of power policy could hardly find a better illustration than by this proposal.

Discussions of that type prepared the ground for the establishment of the comprehensive system of economic policies which is associated with the name of Jean Baptiste Colbert (1619–1683), minister of finance under Louis XIV from 1663 to 1683. This system reflected the conviction that the economic forces of a country were the backbone of its power policies, and that their development depended primarily upon the adoption of appropriate administrative measures, applied by a statesman who could be relied upon to organize and direct the economy.[86] The control of the manufacturing industries was tightened, and new domestic industries were developed through the creation of royal manufactures, through monopolies, and through other privileges granted to promising entrepreneurs or companies. The barriers which obstructed trading among the different regions of the country were gradually eliminated. Hence, Colbert's frequently announced slogan that "liberty is the soul of trade" was not an empty phrase.

Under Colbert, the population policy was adjusted to the purposes of the country's power policy, foreign trade was regarded as a form of warfare waged especially against Holland and England, and the acquisition of precious metals was proclaimed as the main objective of foreign trade, while the activities of the trading companies were carefully controlled with this end in view. All measures of commercial policy were ruled by the endeavor to promote the exportation and to prevent the importation of finished products. The embargo on the exportation of precious metals remained in force, and the exportation of raw materials and of machinery was prohibited. Thus, without being backed by a consistent body of theory, this policy established a pattern for government interference in practically all lines of economic activity, except agriculture.

As a method of national power politics, Colbertism had its counterpart in the doctrine of Gallicanism, which was advocated by the bishop Jacques Bénigne Bossuet (1627–1704) and his followers and which was designed to defend the French monarchy against the pope's claim to supremacy in temporal matters.[87]

Although the measures adopted by Colbert contributed conspicuously toward promoting economic progress and enhancing the political power of France, his economic policy was subjected to an increasing criticism which became articulate toward the end of the seventeenth century. The strict regulations imposed on the manufacturing industries had failed to bring about the expected general well-being; the oppressive system of taxation had spread misery among the peasant population and had caused a decline in the agricultural production. Simultaneously, changes in the prevailing philosophy opened the way for another phase in the history of French reasoning.

Nevertheless, the economic policies pursued in France in the course of the seventeenth century found many admirers in other European countries. They influenced perceptibly the views of various officials of the Spanish government, who were faced with the deteriorating state of the Spanish economy but had to adapt their proposals to the directives of the still powerful clerical authorities and their Scholastic approach to economic questions. At the beginning of the seventeenth century, the lamentable monetary and financial conditions of the country were analyzed by the Jesuit Juan de Mariana (1536–1623?), who made various proposals of reform.[88] At a later date, the problems of Spanish economic policy were dealt with in a comprehensive treatise by Geronimo Ustariz.[89] His discussions were translated into French and English and appear to have had some practical effects in influencing the Spanish economic administration.

CHANGES IN THE CONCEPTION OF PRICE, PROFIT, AND INTEREST ON MONEY

A few years after Jean Bodin had advanced his explanation of the inflationary price movements, the conception of price as the expression of general quantitative relation was defined with far greater precision by the Florentine merchant Bernardo Davanzati. Italy, said a French author about two centuries later, was always conspicuous for two reasons: the debasement of its currencies and the splendor of its monetary treatises.[90] Davanzati connected the origin of money with an agreement among people to use the precious metals as means of exchange, and definitely derived the value of the monetary units from the commodity character of the monetary metals.[91] He was probably the first economist clearly to separate the explanation of prices from the explanation of values, since he exemplified varying degrees of utility shown by the same commodities under changing circumstances while using the equilibrium concept to explain the behavior of prices.

"All these earthly things," he stated, "which satisfy man's wants, are by the consent of nations worth all the gold (and in this I include silver and copper) that is wrought." In order to account for the prices of the individual commodities, Davanzati suggested that prior to the introduction of money, the exchange relations among the various classes of goods had been fixed in accordance with their intrinsic values and that subsequently the total volume of money was equally divided among these classes. The price of each good resulted from subdividing the volume of money assigned to its class. Hence, the Scholastic grouping of the goods by classes lurked behind that definitely quantitative approach to the treatment of a fundamental economic problem. But Davanzati's views did not perceptibly influence the reasoning of the contemporary mercantilists.

On the other hand, the apparently simple relation which Bodin had established between "plenty of money" and rising prices enjoyed general recognition. To mention just one example, Thomas Mun referred to the "common saying" that plenty or scarcity of money makes all things dear or goods cheap.[92]

Realization of the stimulating effects of rising prices on trade caused some seventeenth-century Mercantilists to abandon the traditional belief that general welfare was dependent upon cheapness of goods. They even favored measures designed to support price increases. Thus, as mentioned above, Misselden advocated rising prices as a means of promoting prosperity. In order to counteract a depression which caused unemployment during the 1620s, he recommended debasement of the coins as a "reflationary" measure.[93] But no definite solution was found for the dilemma of whether rising prices should be preferred to cheapness of goods.

A monetary problem of another type confronted the lawyers who requested that loans or other deferred payments should be repaid in weights of metal equal to those in which the loans had been made. Such reasoning had enjoyed far-reaching approval when changes in the value of the currency could be ascribed to the debasement of the coins, but it did not help the creditors when the decline in the value of the currency was caused by the increased inflow of the monetary metals.

In spite of all these changes in monetary views, there still remained strong residues of

Scholastic reasoning until at least the middle of the seventeenth century. Thus, in order to justify a ratio of 12 to 1 for the relation between the values of gold and silver, Rice Vaughan referred to the argument that the "alchymists" used to call gold sun and silver moon, and that the movements of these celestial bodies "do come near upon the point of 12 to 1."[94]

Connected with monetary problems, at least indirectly, were the lively discussions which in the sixteenth century and the first half of the seventeenth century turned on the prohibition of "usury." The fight against taking interest on money was waged not only by the Catholic Church but also by many Protestant theologians whose thinking was dominated by Thomistic precepts.[95] On the other hand, a strong pressure against the continued prohibition of usury was exercised by governments as well as by the rising commercial classes, which enjoyed the expanding credit facilities offered by the banks. The position of the defenders of the prohibition was particularly weakened by the fact that the condemnation of "usury" could not be derived from revelation and could hardly be justified on grounds of "common welfare"; "usury" was considered sinful by the clerical authorities regardless of the economic situation of the debtor, the use made of borrowed money, and the rate of interest.

In the course of the sixteenth century, a number of more or less effective procedures were devised by jurists and bankers in the form of contracts in which payment of interest could be lawfully stipulated on the ground that transmission of ownership of money was not involved in these transactions. Thus, the so-called *contractus trinus* was widely used, particularly in transactions among commercial firms and banking houses of southern Germany, as an instrument of securing a return of 5 percent. Three contracts were combined in the normal *contractus trinus:* one of partnership, the second of insurance against the loss of the principal, and the third of insurance against fluctuating returns. The defenders of the contract argued that the "investor" could use his money in other ways and had, therefore, a justified title to be indemnified for *lucrum cessans.* In 1514 and 1516, on the eve of the German Reformation, Johannes Eck (1486–1543; Luther's most noteworthy opponent) tried to obtain general approval for the contract from the theological authorities, and secured the confirmation of his views from the faculty of Bologna and the theologians of the Sorbonne. The Jesuit priests were inclined to consider the contract unlawful, but by a commission of the congregation appointed in 1581, the lawfulness of the contract was finally acknowledged.[96] Throughout these theological and juridical altercations, contracts of this type enjoyed such a wide practical application that the banker Mark Fugger from Augsburg contended that its prohibition would reduce to beggary in three years not only the Fuggers but all of Germany.[97]

Another method of circumventing the prohibition of taking interest on money was the contract of "census," or annual revenues, which involved the purchase of the right to receive an annual payment from some fruit-bearing object or a person. An agreement concerning a personal debt was not considered lawful unless some circumscribed conditions were fulfilled. The establishment of repurchasable annuities, which have been discussed in another connection, became a widespread practice in the sixteenth century. Regardless of the ultimate intention of the parties, the form of the contracts was considered the main criterion in deciding whether or not a transaction was to be exempted from the prohibition of usury, and purely logical aspects prevailed over any other considerations in this respect. The aversion to the conclusion of loan contracts was so lasting in England that the great expansion of commerce during the reigns of Elizabeth and James was organized by joint stock companies in which risks and profits were shared by all the members, and not by adopting any form of agreement which medieval morality would have condemned.[98]

Closely connected with the endeavors to enforce the prohibition of taking interest on money was the fight of the Dominicans against the percentum payments levied by the Italian *monti di pieta* on money lent against pawned objects. The Franciscans defended that practice as a necessary contribution to the maintenance of these institutions. The question was eventually resolved in favor of the Franciscan view in a bull of 4 May 1575.

In the meantime, the usury controversy assumed new aspects when John Calvin (1509–1564), in an often-quoted letter to Claude de Sachins in 1545, objected to the prohibition of taking interest on money on the grounds that the Holy Scriptures did not provide any testimony still valid for the condemnation of usury, that the borrower could reap as much advantage as the lender from the use of the money, and that what was venial as an occasional expedient was reprehensible when carried on as a regular occupation.[99] But Calvin practically ignored the fundamental logical questions which had tormented the Scholastics in their defense of the prohibition of usury. By his decision, he permitted his faithful adherents to pursue gainful commercial activities without being inhibited by moral scruples.[100]

About the same time (1546), the Scholastic concept of usury was vigorously attacked by the French jurist Charles Dumoulin (Carolus Molinaeus) (1500–1566),[101] who argued that in practically each case of lending the creditor could be shown to suffer a damage or to forgo some other advantage; that the fruition of money had a utility which was suitable for the uses of man, over and above the amount or restitution of the principal; that the use of money belonged unconditionally to the lender and could therefore be sold; and that money which had to be returned after a time yielded in the meantime a considerable return through human industry. Dumoulin's treatise, which directed a frontal attack on Thomistic economics, was placed on the list of prohibited books (the "index") by the clerical authorities. But the views which it advocated enjoyed increasing recognition.

In the various European countries, the general attitude toward the prohibition of usury was symptomatic of the degree to which the methods of Scholastic reasoning were replaced by new patterns of thought in the course of the sixteenth and seventeenth centuries. In England, relatively early popular opinion found a drastic expression in the words of a typical merchant, a participant in the dialogue of Thomas Wilson's treatise.[102] Wilson, a lawyer, defended the prohibition of usury with traditional arguments derived from the Bible, the patristic fathers, the Schoolmen, the papal decretals, the councils of the church, and commentaries to the canon laws.[103] But the merchant considered it madness to deliver one's money out of one's possession for nothing. Puritan divines of the seventeenth century adopted a more lenient attitude toward the pursuit of gain and followed Calvin's advice in their treatment of usury.[104]

In the Protestant territories of the European continent, the prohibition of usury lost the support of the authorities in the first half of the seventeenth century, after the theologian Johan Gerhard had reexamined the question and arrived at the conclusion that only payment for a loan at an immoderate rate should be considered as "usury." On the grounds of equity, all loans to merchants should bear interest.[105] In England, the "prohibition of payments" for the use of money was temporarily abolished as early as 1545, and was definitely repealed in 1571. A maximum rate was fixed at 10 percent; in the course of the seventeenth century this rate was reduced to 8 and 6 percent, and in 1713 to 5 percent. With the exception of the short-term money market, the last rate remained in force until

1854. Hence, objections were raised only against "biting" usury. The prosperity of the Netherlands excited the envy of the English observers and was frequently ascribed to the low rate of interest that prevailed in that country, where the maximum rate on borrowed money was fixed at 6 percent.[106]

Even conservative authors such as Gerard Malynes admitted the necessity of mercantile borrowing and lending. He assigned to "usurie" the function of regulating trade and business, building, and other economic activities. His contemporary, Sir Thomas Culpeper, declared that it was for theologians to show that taking of interest on money should be prohibited on moral grounds; Culpeper limited his discussion to the undesirable economic effects of high rates of interest and recommended a legal reduction of the maximum rate, which was then fixed at 10 percent.[107] A similar proposal was later advanced by Josiah Child, who discussed the question of how to prevent Dutch "money" from being drawn away from England after a reduction of the legal maximum of the rate.[108] Considerations of that type were generally supplemented by the proposition that the only available method of lowering the rate of interest was to increase the volume of money through surpluses of the balance of payments. General agreement existed on the view that the rate of interest depended upon the available supply of monetary metals. Such reasoning developed against the background of a widespread economic philosophy according to which pursuance of a gainful enterprise was in itself the discharge of a duty imposed by God; thriftiness and frugality ranked high among the Puritan virtues.

The final vindication of interest on loans was achieved for the Catholic countries by the famous jurist Claude de Saumaise, who argued in his essay on usury that taking of interest was permitted by natural and human law.[109] He characterized interest as payment for the use of money, as distinct from the repayment of the principal, but added hardly any new arguments to those put forward by other adversaries of the prohibition.[110] He recommended competition among moneylenders as a means of lowering the rate of interest. A last attempt to enforce the observation of the prohibition was made by Pope Benedict XIV in 1745. In France, the prohibition remained formally in force until the revolution (1789).

Chapter 4
Baconian Mercantilism

___

THE TERRITORIAL DISTRIBUTION OF DIVERGENT PATTERNS OF THOUGHT

IN THE COURSE of the seventeenth century the development of economic analysis received a strong impetus from new streams of philosophical thought which permeated the reasoning of the educated classes in the Western countries. Under the influence of one stream originating in England, methods of empiricism were applied to an increasing degree to the analysis of economic phenomena. Moreover, the tendency to construe the relations among economic magnitudes in accordance with mechanical principles was greatly accentuated. By contrast, the trend which contemporaneously developed in France preserved significant elements of medieval Scholasticism.

The English philosopher who provided the epistemological background for the empirical approach was Francis Bacon (1561–1626). In his *Novum Organum* (1620), he undertook to establish a consistent methodology of scientific research in the light of experience. Acceptance of his teachings resulted in a definite separation of the domain of creed from those intellectual spheres which were assigned to reason. Simultaneously, the mind acquired perfect freedom to adjust the concepts to the purposes prescribed by the will. But, whereas the Schoolmen of nominalistic persuasion had requested the separation of theology from philosophy in order to protect religion against the dangers of a knowledge derived from sense perceptions, Bacon insisted upon that separation in order to prevent creed from interfering with the results of scientific reasoning. As a safeguard against the influence of speculative, metaphysical ideas, he recommended the use of concepts of lower abstraction and the use of observation and experience as instruments for achieving practical results.

In full opposition to the Scholastics, who had endeavored to understand the laws of the universe in order to obey the intentions of the Creation, he made control of the forces of Nature the ultimate objective of scientific research. Like the thirteenth-century Franciscan theologian John Duns Scotus, the great adversary of Saint Thomas, Bacon emphasized the activity of the mind as opposed to the more passive attitude of reason. In his famous discussion of the four classes of "idols" or fallacies, he especially attacked all attempts to introduce theological considerations into the analysis and explanation of the phenomena of nature; he insisted on the exclusive use of the principle of causality to define the interrelationships among phenomena of this kind,[1] and suggested the application of the same principle to the study of ethical, psychological, and social problems. In discussing social problems, he pointed to instinct and passions as the determinant factors in the structure of social life. But mathematical methods did not receive a conspicuous place among his methodological devices, and he practically ignored the fundamental importance of deductive reasoning for scientific analysis.

The decisive step of combining Baconian empiricism with the principles of deductive reasoning was taken by Isaac Newton (1642–1727), who defined with admirable consistency the fundamental methodological problems of physics and the natural sciences.[2] In his *Principles of Natural Philosophy*,[3] he explicitly eliminated any reference to the *qualitates occultae* of the Scholastics, and he attempted to explain all movements in terms of a simple, generally valid principle, that of action and reaction. With that end in view, he reduced all complex phenomena to a common denominator—the atom—and assumed that the relations among atoms, the ultimate, indivisible elements, were determined by a law of nature which was basic to the reciprocal position of the inert masses of the bodies within absolute space.

Probably for the first time in the history of human reasoning, a consummate system concept which could be expressed in mathematical terms was devised for analyzing the behavior of a large sector of the universe. Only the beginning of movement, which inert matter was obviously unable to produce, was related to an act of divine creation; any other movements were assumed to follow their course in accordance with the laws of mechanics. Newton's often-quoted dictum *hypotheses non fingo* ("I do not make fictitious assumptions") was intended to exclude any speculations concerning the causes of the mutual "attractions" of cosmic masses.[4] This dictum was perfectly compatible with the fact that Newton's reasoning started from a fundamental bold hypothesis which was implied in the concept of an "atom" and its functions; both were products of a keen imagination applied to the construction of analytical procedures.[5]

The importance of the Newtonian system concept for the development of Western reasoning, and especially of economic reasoning, can hardly be overestimated. The success achieved by the physical sciences in supplying a consistent picture of the cosmic universe provided strong incentives for the application of mechanical principles to the relations of other observable magnitudes. The conflict between traditional and emergent patterns of thought which occurred in England during the Newtonian period was accompanied by far-reaching changes in the conception of social relationships. The analytical approach to the construction of these relationships resulted in breaking up the unified picture of society into separate departments, each of which was to be made the object of a specific analysis. The equilibrium principle was considered a primary instrument of research in almost all fields of scientific investigation.

The spiritual atmosphere which developed in France in the course of the struggle over the Scholastic methods differed widely from that which prevailed at the same time in England. In France, the struggle suggested deep dissatisfaction with the capacities of the human mind, as evidenced by the spread of skepticism and an outspoken indifference to logical problems.[6] In vain were the efforts of a clerical scholar, Pierre Gassend (1592–1655), to revive the theoretical elements of the much-maligned Epicurean philosophy with their emphasis on the problems of cognition, on the hypothetical nature of all concepts, and on the importance of positive law as the source of the rules of individual actions.[7] Gassend's main merit consisted in defending the Epicurean teachings against the misrepresentations which they had experienced on the part of the medieval Scholastics.

The ideas which subsequently became dominant in French thinking received their foundation from the philosophy of René Descartes (1596–1650). He developed his methodological principles in his *Discourse on Methods* (1637), in which he placed mathematics in the center of his methodology since its theorems could be deduced from a few axiomatic propositions.[8] Hence, he undertook to establish procedures which would give to all knowledge the same certainty which can be secured through mathematics. He was convinced that, supported by a system of innate ideas and evident truths, human reason was able to develop such knowledge. Thus, for physical science he imagined a pattern according to which the effects of the laws of motion, expressed in mathematical terms, could be made determinate. He considered similar procedures applicable to other sciences.

From his adherence to the Scholastic concepts of substance and essence, Descartes derived his often-quoted dictum *Cogito, ergo sum* ("I think, therefore I am"). Thus, he introduced into his philosophy the postulate of unity of consciousness, which had a counterpart in his belief in the unity of nature and its phenomena.[9]

Fundamental principles of Augustinian metaphysics were reflected in the Cartesian distinction between the physical world and the spiritual world, and the corresponding opposition of body and soul, the soul being conceived of as a "substance" entirely independent of any physical entity. Whereas Bacon had attempted to develop methods fit for adjusting the phenomena of the outside world to an understanding by the human mind, Descartes was looking for preestablished, absolutely valid ideas implanted in the human mind (*ideae innatae*), revealing the order of the universe. He combined this approach with a belief in the freedom of will. He was convinced that whatever could be demonstrated by deductive processes had to be approved as evident—that human reason, when left to itself, would always produce perfectly clear notions unless its operations were obscured by vague impressions resulting from sense perceptions (*ideae adventiciae*). Descartes practically identified the juxtaposition of clarity and lack of clarity with that of rational cognition and knowledge through sense perceptions; he thus initiated the great spiritual movement which, under the name of "rationalism," proclaimed the autonomy of reason as the foundation of any scientific procedures.

Hence, the use of the deductive method—as contrasted with the inductive acquisition of knowledge through observation and experience—was an outstanding characteristic of the Cartesian epistemology, which practically ignored any knowledge of a probable, contingent, conjectural type such as could be derived from the use of experimental methods.

The Cartesian philosophy and some versions derived from it became dominant factors in French intellectual movements. The significant elements of Scholastic reasoning, which were thus preserved by some outstanding leaders of French social, political, and economic life, provided a strong support for the maintenance of the feudal structure of society. They prevented the adoption of democratic procedures which could hardly be justified if "reason" provided the instruments for finding the truth and for determining what was best for the individuals and best for the common weal. Reliance on the power of reason has always been prerequisite for the maintenance of Western authoritarian regimes unless they were primarily supported by military power.

The connection which can be established between the prevalence of specific types of reasoning on the one hand and intellectual, artistic economic activities on the other can hardly be better illustrated than by contrasting the developments which took place in the sixteenth and seventeenth centuries in the Netherlands with the corresponding developments in Spain. In the Netherlands (for a long part of this period a Spanish dependency), a relatively high degree of freedom of thought had been achieved when Scholastic methods of reasoning were displaced in the course of an extended process which had started during the Renaissance period. That freedom enabled the Dutch traders, bankers, and industrialists to adapt their activities to the condition of early capitalism. The Dutch east and west trading companies were particularly successful and enjoyed public support in the 1630s and 1640s despite prolonged criticisms of their privileges.[10]

The envy aroused by the remarkable expansion of Dutch trading was reflected in the writings of various English authors who complained of the backwardness, even of the decay, of the English economy as compared with the flourishing conditions of the Netherlands. Particularly noticeable were the treatises of Roger Coke, which dealt with the reasons for the superiority of the Dutch trading policies and pointed to the advantages derived from liberalizing trade.[11] Coke and some other English writers, such as Josiah Child and the author of *Britannia Languens*,[12] considered the religious tolerance practiced by the Dutch an important factor contributing to the success of their economic policy. So threatening became the economic power of Holland in the seventeenth century that both England and France attempted to weaken this competitor through military action.[13]

The contrast between the prosperity of the Netherlands and the conditions prevailing in the countries of the Iberian Peninsula was indeed striking and did not fail to attract the attention of mercantilist authors. In Spain and Portugal, where the clerical authorities continued to impose strict observance of a Scholastic pattern of reasoning, new economic concepts were prevented from being applied to the organization of industry and trade.[14] Hence, medieval forms of life were preserved and, as mentioned in another connection, streams of gold and silver passed through Spain without perceptibly stimulating the exploitation of Spanish resources in raw materials and manpower.[15]

The spread of capitalistic forms of production and trade also met with considerable obstacles in Central Europe, especially in the German countries, where nominalistic methods of reasoning did not agree with the thinking of the leading classes of the population. Philipp S. Melanchthon, Martin Luther's adviser on philosophical problems, strongly recommended observance of the principles of the Aristotelian logic. Luther condemned the importation of luxury goods from the East and attacked banking and credit practices, speculations at the exchanges, capitalistic forms of production, combination, and monopoly as sinful even more strongly than had been done by the Scholastic inter-preters of the canon law. Hence, the Protestant theologians, who followed his teachings, did not question the validity of the logical approach adopted by the medieval Schoolmen toward economic morality.

Up to the last decades of the eventful seventeenth century, no outstanding thinker arose in central Europe to suggest a social philosophy based on a new method of thought. Instead, popular thinking was strongly attracted by purely speculative teachings derived from magical metaphysics of the type advanced by the physician Theophrastus Bombastus von Hohenheim, also known as Paracelsus (d. 1541). Even more conspicuous was the influence of mystical writings published by half-educated visionaries, who relied on purely intuitive procedures and ascribed to the human mind the power to grasp through a sort of insight the order of the world as willed by its Creator. The widespread acceptance of such mystical teachings reflected an outright negative attitude toward fundamental logical problems. The bloody Thirty Years' War (1618–48), which transformed into desert large regions of Central Europe, was waged not only over issues of power politics but also over the interpretation of certain religious tenets.

The responsibility for maintaining Christian morality in much of Central Europe was eventually transferred from the ecclesiastical authorities to state governments. Thus, the governments were charged with the task of organizing economic and social life, and obedience to the commands of the ruling kings and princes was made a primary duty of their subjects.

In the vast territories which were gradually brought under the control of the Muscovite rulers, an oriental "orthodox" version of the medieval theology was protected against the infiltration of Western patterns of thought by a theocratic regime whose power was based on the maintenance of a rigid dogmatic creed. The intellectual gap which was thus created between Russia and the rest of Europe was never bridged. The Balkan countries, which had fallen under the domination of the Osmanli Turks, remained practi-cally excluded from any spiritual contact with the Western world until late in the eighteenth century. The logical principles underlying the precepts of the Koran provided strong barriers to the free formation of concepts and to the acceptance of risks connected with long-term industrial or commercial ventures.

This attempt to survey in a few pages intellectual developments extending over centuries and large regions was, of course, perfunctory. But it will fulfill its objective if it can supply convincing support to the view that the spread of capitalistic institutions and organizations was far more determined by prevailing methods of reasoning than by geo-graphical conditions and the possession of natural resources on the part of the various countries. Though well advanced by the end of the sixteenth century, the differentiation of patterns of thought sharpened in the seventeenth century and further intensified during the course of the eighteenth and nineteenth centuries.

THE CONCEPT OF NATURAL LAW AND THE UTILITARIAN APPROACH TO SOCIAL PROBLEMS

The changes in the structure of the economy which took place in Western Europe in the seventeenth century were closely allied to the development of new social philosophies which endeavored to redefine the mutual relations between individuals and the political community, the national state. Medieval theology had derived the norms of social and economic conduct from divine commandments, a source which existed outside the human mind. Great Scholastics of universalistic persuasion had attempted to show that, independently of any revelation, these commandments and their absolute validity could be grasped by human reason. The philosophy of the Greek Stoics supplied for various thinkers of the seventeenth century a bridge which led from ecclesiastical dogmatism over the Thomistic interpretation of natural law to the belief in a universal reason permeating nature. This belief provided strong incentives to search for general principles according to which social factors were linked with each other by causal relationships, since only the existence of such relationships could guarantee the inviolability of the laws of nature. But, as mentioned in another connection, the distinction between laws of a causal type and laws of a normative type was, as a rule, not strictly observed.

From the Greek Stoic philosophers, the Roman jurists had taken over the idea of "true law." This idea was characterized by the Roman orator Cicero in the last century of the pre-Christian era as right reason, which is in accordance with nature, applies to all men, and is unchangeable and eternal. It is difficult, he added, ever to restrict its operation, and it is impossible to annul it wholly. These views were elaborated in 1625 by the Dutch scholar Hugo Grotius (1583–1645), who taught in his work *De jure belli ac pacis* that the divine sanctions of the rules of the natural law were made known to mankind by the dictates of right reasoning.[16] The human mind thus participating in universal reason was considered capable of grasping the laws which nature was teaching. This conception of the relation between reason and natural law enjoyed far-reaching acceptance. It also provided the backbone for a widely read work about natural and international law (1672) by the German teacher Samuel von Pufendorf.[17]

In these studies the source of laws, which were meant to be a body of perfect law, was not sought in a superrational revelation of a divine will, nor in customs, habits, and institutions which had been adjusted to the instincts or wants of mankind. The knowledge of the principles of the "natural law" was rather ascribed to a kind of intuitive perception available to all people.[18] The will of the Creator was identified with the precepts taught by nature, and, according to a widespread belief, the principles of a natural and just social order could be discovered by analyzing the organization of imaginary early or primitive stages of social life.

But revolutionary thinkers could also avail themselves of the principles of a natural law in support of their attempts to advocate norms of behavior which were at variance with traditional institutions and which violated the rights of hereditary rulers. Thus, alleged maxims of natural law were repeatedly invoked by moralists as a background for the description of idealized images of societies modeled in accordance with plans of radical social reforms. The *Utopia* of Thomas More (Thomas Morus; 1478–1535) the former English lord chancellor, published in Latin in 1516, was the first and by far the most important book of this type.[19] It had its root in the humanistic movement of the Renaissance, in open contrast to the attitude of medieval thinkers, who considered life on earth as preparatory to the life after death and never set their minds on the establishment of a perfect earthly community.[20]

In his *Utopia*, More outlined the picture of a communist society with a stationary population, fixed consumption habits, and a scheme of production regulated by the government. The monetary use of gold and silver was restricted to the payment of the excess of imports over exports. The description of the daily life led by the Utopians provided

More with ample opportunity to criticize institutions and habits of his time and country. His book became a model for other disguised attacks on ingrained customs, privileges, and prejudices, and it was followed in the seventeenth century by similar descriptions of imaginary communities by Tommaso Campanella, Francis Bacon, and James Harrington.[21]

A practical application was given to the radical aspects of the natural law principle by the English "Levellers" in their appeals to the nation when they attempted to justify their political and social programs. With their pamphlets, issued about the middle of the seventeenth century, they initiated a new school of English political thinking. Some adherents of the doctrine of natural law referred to the social contract as the instrument which had transformed the primitive societies into political communities. Johannes Althusius[22] and Hugo Grotius[23] were outstanding representatives of this view.

The doctrine of the social contract was also readily adopted by the followers of the Baconian methodology, since they were thus able to eliminate from the analysis of political communities the teleological characteristics ascribed to them by the Aristotelian Scholastics and to connect the origin of the "civil society" with the will of its individual members. But sooner or later a logical conflict was bound to ensue between the doctrine of a natural law as a source of self-evident principles and the belief in observation and experience as the exclusive instruments for acquiring knowledge. It was obvious that the presence of ideas innate in the mind had never been demonstrated; moreover, it was equally obvious that the advocates of the doctrine of natural law had never been able to agree on the principles which were alleged to constitute the body of that law.

In pursuance of their critical, empiricist attitude, the Baconian philosophers gradually replaced the juridical concept of natural law as used in a causal sense with the Baconian methodology employed in natural sciences. With this purpose in mind, they centered their attention, as Francis Bacon had suggested, on the role played by instinct in determining individual attitudes and social relations. Thus, they placed increasing emphasis on the psychological motivation of human behavior and on mechanical reactions of the mind to outside events in order to arrive at coherent generalized pictures of social life.

The individualistic or "atomistic" social philosophy, which corresponded to the above methodology, started with the assumption that individuals and their interests constituted the ultimate elements of the network of social relationships, for observation and experience did not show the alternative existence of any supraindividual will or teleological principle which could be made responsible for the organization, objectives, and functioning of social collectivities.[24] In their effort to simplify their sociological analysis, the philosophers of Baconian persuasion commonly assumed that all individuals were fundamentally equal with respect to their social attitudes, and that even the natural gifts and talents of various individuals were uniform to a high degree.[25] These assumptions were supplemented by the belief in a general conformity of individual wills, which was considered prerequisite to the functioning of the social order. The ensuing question of how the adjustment of the individual wills to the interests of the community was to be assured was formulated by an anonymous author in a rather primitive way by about the middle of the sixteenth century in the "Discourse of the Common Weal" (mentioned above in another connection).[26] He argued that every man will naturally follow the activity where he sees the most profit, and that opportunities for gain should be so fashioned as to make self-interest coincide with common interest, but that men would defraud the law where it interfered too much with profit. In the seventeenth century, another author could support his arguments in favor of the enclosure movement by pointing to the "undeniable maxim" that everyone, by the light of nature and reason, will do that which makes for his greatest advantage, and that the advancement of private persons will be to the advantage of the public.[27]

The first political philosopher consistently to embark on the venture of applying Baconian methods of causal research to the analysis of social phenomena was Thomas Hobbes (1588–1679). His predecessors, including Jean Bodin, Johannes Althusius, and Hugo Grotius, had still observed the Aristotelian categories. Hobbes, however, denied the existence of ultimate ends of the *summum bonum*, or greatest good, spoken of in the books of the old moral philosophers.[28] In the first part of his *Leviathan* (1651), which dealt with the functioning of the human mind, he advocated an outright nominalistic method of reasoning based on some rather primitive psychological conceptions. Quite consistently, he made sense impressions produced by outside sources the primary agents to initiate all intellectual processes, and conceived of the latter as reactions to outside stimuli rather than as spontaneous activities of the mind.[29] Thus, he connected all social problems ultimately with psychological considerations.

The psychological mechanisms with which Hobbes supported his social philosophy contained as main elements the instincts of self-preservation and the desire for security, linked with the desire for power. He regarded the motives of want and fear as the primary causes of self-interest, and used the simile of a stone falling in accordance with the laws of gravity to illustrate the influence of self-interest on human behavior.[30] In his discussion of the transition from a state of savagery to that of social organization, he argued that the war of all against all (*bellum omnium contra omnes*) had been terminated through the conclusion of a social contract. Motivated by the desire to gain security, all contractually submitted their wills to the will of one, a sovereign, who was empowered to use punishment to enforce the observance of the contract. The sovereignty of the ruler had to be unlimited, indivisible, inalienable. It was the task of the state—the Leviathan—to announce as lawful and right those manifestations of self-interest which could be expected to promote common welfare and as wrong those which imperiled that welfare.[31] Hence, the concept of *summum bonum* which the Scholastics had designated as the moral objective of the community was replaced by a utilitarian objective, the quest for security; the definition of any other purposes was left to the more or less discretionary judgments of the state.

In elaborating the relation between will and reason, Hobbes characterized reason as the instrument for devising proper means for the achievement of the purposes dictated by utilitarian motives. Thus, he introduced a new concept of "rational behavior" to characterize such attitudes as were adjusted to ends dictated by the will, and defined as "laws of nature" those laws which prescribe the rules for the actions of an ideally reasonable being.[32]

Since Hobbes denied the existence of given, absolutely valid notions, he limited the functions of scientific thinking to the task of establishing consistent systems of concepts. Whereas the Scholastics had defined *truth* as identity of the results of thinking with the "real order of the phenomena," Hobbes identified truth with a thinking which is free of contradictions.

In spite of his adherence to the doctrine of the social contract and his belief in "laws of nature," Hobbes did not suggest any principles upon which a lasting order of human societies could be based. With his purely formal definition of the motive of self-interest, he denied the existence of any a priori rule underlying the directions which human desires or wants were likely to take. This proposition has aptly been termed *randomness of want*. It became a constituent element of subsequent English economic reasoning.[33]

If maximization of gains could be included among the legitimate objectives pre-scribed by the will, the term *rational behavior* could be applied to all economic activities which served that purpose. On the other hand, basic to the Hobbesian conception of an original "war of all against all" was the idea that the goods needed for want satisfaction were in scarce supply. In the light of that proposition, various economic problems had to be reformulated.[34] Such a reformulation was also suggested by the predominantly mechanistic Hobbesian psychology according to which practically all intellectual processes had to be interpreted as reactions to stimuli produced by outside sources.

John Locke (1632–1704) took the next step on the road which eventually led to the development of the principles of utilitarian economics. Like Hobbes, he had received his training at Oxford University, which had preserved the tradition of Franciscan nominalism. His great achievement in his *Essay concerning Human Understanding* (1690) consisted in formulating the question of how to define the limits of human cogni-tion. Thus, he significantly modified the approach adopted by Bacon, who had never doubted that all comprehensive knowledge was available to the human mind and who had only attempted to determine the methods available for gaining it. The procedure chosen by Locke for defining the validity of knowledge and its limits consisted in analyzing the origins of concepts.[35]

The famous comparison of the mind with a *tabula rasa* was designed to illustrate the complete absence from the mind of any innate ideas,[36] and in his strict formulation of this proposition Locke admitted only an innate capacity of the mind to have ideas.[37] With this as the starting point of his analysis, he further assumed that the mind is wholly "passive" in receiving its simple ideas "from the existence and operation of things such as sensation and reflection offers them."[38] He also regarded affective phenomena, such as passions, as the results of agglomerated impressions.

In his endeavor to apply the principles of empiricism to the understanding of the functioning of the human intellect, Locke was even more consistent than Hobbes. He distinguished two spheres of experience: inner experience or reflection, which is im-mediately given, and sensation, which is derived from outside sources through the sense perceptions. That reasoning prepared the way for the application of scientific methods to the analysis of psychological phenomena without interfering with the traditional view that a fundamental heterogeneity existed between these two kinds of experience.[39] Thus, Locke agreed with Descartes's conviction that people have knowledge of themselves; like Hobbes, however, he insisted on the proposition that no true knowledge of the things of the outside world is accessible to the human mind, that truth does not consist in the identity of conceptions with the outside phenomena but in the mutual consistency of notions. Recognition of these limitations of the intellectual faculties of the mind led to the conclusion that human conception of the outside world is determined by the rules of thinking, regardless of the rules underlying the behavior of the external phenomena.[40]

In discussing the limits of knowledge of the outside world, Locke, like the medieval nominalists, started from an analysis of the attributes of things and showed that genuine knowledge or truth could not be assured unless all properties of an object are perfectly intelligible and can be derived from its original nature. Applying that criterion to gold, he argued that genuine knowledge of gold was not possible, since people cannot start from some determination of the "essence" of gold and deduce from it the totality of its secondary properties.[41] The distinction between primary and secondary properties was intended to differentiate between qualities which can be expressed in mathematical terms (size, number, movement, etc.) and other qualities which reflect the impressions made upon human senses and which are so variable and fluctuating (colors, tastes, sounds, etc.) that ideas do not correspond exactly to anything in the objects themselves. This distinction has been the object of varying interpretations and criticisms. Locke ascribed perfect intelligibility only to intuitive judgments regarding mathematical relations. Hence, only mathematical knowledge could claim absolute validity, since it was derived from immutable mental relations between the objects concerned. To be consistent, Locke had to reject the concept of "substance" as an independent, undefined factor commonly regarded as the background of all knowable properties of the things. But he admitted the existence of "matter," although he felt that experience did not provide any proof for that assumption.

Since it was obviously impossible to establish absolutely valid moral precepts with the aid of nominalistic processes of reasoning, Locke resorted to the Epicurean maxims that good was anything that caused pleasure, that evil was equivalent with pain,[42] and that human behavior was to be qualified as morally good or bad according to its results, that is, according to whether it was apt or unfit to promote individual happiness. "Nature," he said, "has put into man a desire of happiness, and an aversion to misery; these indeed are innate practical principles which . . . do continue constantly to operate and influence all our actions without ceasing. . . . They are . . . inclinations of the appetite to good, not impressions of truth on the understanding." He defined ethics as seeking out those rules and measures of human actions which lead to happiness, and also the means to practice them.[43]

Thus, like Hobbes, Locke arrived at the conclusion that "moral good or evil is only the conformity or disagreement of our voluntary actions to some law whereby good or evil is drawn on us by the will and power of the lawmaker."[44] But, as distinct from Hobbes, he attributed to reason the faculty of recognizing a "natural" identity of the interests of the members of the community, and used that proposition to establish "natural" rights of life, liberty, and property. That concession, which he made to the doctrine of natural law, enabled him to reject any reference to an original community of goods, to ignore the predominantly coercive functions attributed to the state by Hobbes, and to include among the tasks of the government the protection of individual natural rights.[45] The common ends of the community were, in his view, attained by the division of labor and the mutual exchange of goods as a means of satisfying a wide diversity of individual wants.

In his *Two Treatises on Government,* Locke developed his social philosophy in accordance with the role he assigned to reason. The emphasis he placed on tolerance was derived from his conviction that the human mind was unable to decide with finality what was true and what was false. From the same conviction, he derived the conclusion that legislative actions were necessary to determine what was in the interest of the community and, consequently, what was to be accepted as morally sound. As drawn from the principles of advanced nominalist reasoning, that proposition had its counterpart in the advocacy of democratic procedures as the only practical methods of settling disputed political issues.[46] With his formulation of the principles of a utilitarian philosophy, Locke supplied a new logical background to economic reasoning. Equally important for the development of this reasoning was his "theory of indifference," which permitted him to discard the rigid Scholastic distinction between lawful and unlawful actions and to qualify a considerable group of actions as morally neutral.[47] When striving for gain as the stimulus to economic activity was assigned to the sphere of morally neutral behavior, the traditional close connection between ethics and economics lost the fundamental importance it had occupied within the framework of Scholastic doctrine. The theory of indifference opened the way to an entirely new construction of economic relationships, especially when it was combined with another characteristic element of Locke's teachings, the view that everybody is the best judge of his or her own interests. Subsequently, when these propositions gained widespread acceptance among the adherents of the utilitarian philosophy, no particular attention was paid to the reservations made by Locke, who pointed out that possible errors of judgment might be committed when future events had to be taken into consideration, and that pleasures and pains "at a distance" might be misinterpreted when compared with present ones.[48]

Locke did not apply the results of his methodological teachings in the analysis employed in his minor treatises dealing with some economic problems of his day. He contributed to the actual progress of theoretical economics more by reformulating some relevant problems than by solving them.

EMERGENCE OF THE EMPIRICAL APPROACH TO ECONOMICS

The first mercantilist author explicitly to express his intention to apply Baconian methods, based on observation and experience, to the analysis of social and economic phenomena was Sir William Petty (1623–1687), whose sociological views were strongly influenced by the philosophy of Hobbes. Petty's studies marked the beginning of a new period in the development of economic reasoning. They initiated the formulation of economic problems in terms of relations among measurable magnitudes.

As had been suggested by Bacon, these studies dealt with questions of practical policy:[49] they turned on topics such as taxation, the determination of the wealth of England and Ireland, population, coinage, and the like. But, ignoring Bacon's negative attitude toward the methods of deductive reasoning, Petty used such methods to explain some fundamental economic concepts. A physician by training, whose scientific standing was generally recognized,[50] he frequently pointed to analogies which he found between social communities and physical bodies. He wrote a treatise on the *Political Anatomy of Ireland* (1672) and also wrote on the anatomy of other administrative units.[51] He characterized money as the "fat of the body politick," and the like, and among his favorite quotations was the Latin adage that "nature, though driven out, will eventually recur."[52] But such analogies were only incidental and not significant for his methodology. Of course, the experimental procedures recommended by Bacon could not be used to study social phenomena. Hence, Petty regarded observable magnitudes as the most appropriate objects of social analysis, and he undertook to investigate the characteristic features of social collectivities with the aid of "numbers, weights and measures." The first investigation in which he introduced his new method, the *Treatise of Taxes and Contributions* (1662), was devoted to the analysis of public finances and the sources of public revenues. In his *Political Arithmetick,* written between the years 1671 and 1676, he embarked on the general task of expressing by figures the wealth of England, according to the value of the country's capital assets and population. Hence, he has been hailed as the father of English administrative statistics. But it has been a disputed question whether the credit of having inaugurated the use of statistics for purposes of sociological research should not go to John Graunt, author of the *Natural and Political Investigations upon the Bill of Mortality* (1662). It is very likely that Petty participated in the preparation of that study, which can be regarded as the first important demographic treatise.

Petty's methodological principles were endorsed by Charles Davenant (1656–1714), who defined political arithmetic as the "art of reasoning by figures upon things relating to the government.'' Like Petty, he used statistical material mainly to establish a sort of economic budgeting; the main object of his studies was to determine the relation between national income and national expenditures. For some of his leading ideas, he was indebted to Gregory King, the originator of the so-called Gregory King's estimate, which was the first attempt to define the effects on prices of inelastic demand. This ''estimate'' was determined by the observation that a deficiency of 10 percent in the normal harvest raised the price of corn by 30 percent, that a deficiency of 20 percent resulted in a rise by 80 percent, and so on. In King's quite logical formulation of his problem, the calculations were based on a standard assumed to correspond to conditions of normality. King's estimate was included in Charles Davenant's *Essay upon the Probable Methods of Making a People Gainers in the Balance of Trade* (1699), section 3.[53]

The predilection for arithmetic exhibited by Baconian Mercantilists had perhaps its ultimate roots in the psychological conditions created by the adoption of refined nominalistic methods of reasoning, which rendered problematic any attempts to grasp reality with the aid of general concepts and judgments. Only the establishment of mathematical relations between measurable social and economic magnitudes appeared to provide the prospect of finding some trustworthy propositions based on experience and observation.

The inductive method, as applied in these investigations, was ruled by the idea of dissolving concepts of measurable social aggregates, such as national wealth and national income, into their component parts, which, as far as possible, were reduced to a common denominator. The magnitudes which were the objects of these measurements were almost exclusively derived from political conceptions which provided fixed given patterns for economic analysis. Only much later, when greater freedom had been gained in choosing relevant economic magnitudes, was it possible to use in one investigation a given characteristic on the assumption that it was related to a constant cause, and to assume in another investigation that the same characteristic was related to a variable cause. That formulation of fundamental statistical problems permitted a grouping of the phenomena under observation in accordance with a variety of objectives, and led eventually to the application of the theory of probability to statistical research.[54]

Another conspicuous trend in the development of economic reasoning, which was possibly suggested by the amazing achievements of the physical sciences, was the tendency to center the study of economic events on such phenomena as could be interpreted in terms of a self-regulating mechanism. The overwhelming influence of the physical sciences on research of all kinds was stressed in the last decade of the seventeenth century by Sir Dudley North (1641–1691), one of the most noteworthy mercantilist authors, who was convinced that knowledge had become ''in great measure mathematical.''[55] In its ultimate effects, this tendency was bound to undermine the belief in the effectiveness of the regulative economic policy of the authorities. Thus, in various passages of his writings Petty objected to government interference with the ''Laws of Nature,'' and occasionally suggested that limitations imposed on the exportation of bullion were perhaps contrary to such laws. Belief in the ''order of things'' was expressed by Roger Coke, Josiah Child, and Charles Davenant.

During the last decades of the seventeenth century, the fight for greater freedom from government intervention was less influenced by philosophical or logical arguments than by considerations derived from the interests of specific business groups. Interference on the part of the church and the state with matters of business and property rights was increasingly resented by the commercial classes of that period.[56] A similar movement made itself felt in France, where outright freedom from such intervention was requested—according to a repeatedly told story—by the merchant Legendre in a conversation with Colbert.[57]

The protests against export restrictions raised in England by the advocates of the privileged companies became very articulate. Their adversaries, on the other hand, were equally articulate in requesting the abolition of the trading monopolies. They accused the companies of selling a little very dear instead of selling much more at moderate profits,[58] and of contributing to the impoverishment of the country through the importation of luxury goods and the exportation of bullion.[59]

The belief in the effect of the balance of payments on a country's well-being continued to occupy a dominant position in the reasoning of most mercantilist authors. The vaguely defined balance of trade concept of their predecessors was superseded (though not in name) by a clear balance of payments concept. Even authors who showed a noticeable understanding of the interdependence of economic phenomena—such as John Cary and Charles Davenant—were convinced that the power of an enemy country could effectively be weakened by "furnishing it with products and manufactures" and thus depriving it of its money supply.[60]

Among the earliest mercantilists to question the use of the balance of trade figures as a reliable criterion of economic progress was Sir Josiah Child (1630–1699), head of the East India Company, whose treatise *Brief Observations concerning Trade and Interest on Money* was first published in 1668.[61] In it, he observed that some obviously poor regions, such as Ireland and the state of Virginia, showed export surpluses in their balances.[62] Whereas Thomas Mun and other advocates of the commercial policy of the East India Company had defended the free exportation of bullion as a means of promoting export surpluses, Child rejected the idea that achievement of the largest possible imports of bullion was a desirable goal, and he argued that, in foreign trade, money should be treated like any other commodity.

Charles Davenant, another representative of the East India Company, recommended various measures of protectionist policies,[63] but in his general considerations he anticipated a familiar argument of the liberal foreign trade doctrine, the argument that, when imports are free, each country would produce those goods for which providence manifestly destined it with least labor, that is, most economically and most profitably. Trade, he argued, is in its nature free, and all laws to give it rules and directions may serve private ends, but are seldom advantageous to the public.

In his *Discourse upon Trade* (1691), Sir Dudley North even questioned one of the logical foundations of the balance of trade doctrine, namely, the proposition that one country could gain only at the expense of others. He rejected the view that the importation of specie was particularly important for economic progress.[64] The belief in the existence of an automatic mechanism regulating economic phenomena found a significant expression in his statement that the "ebbing and flowing of money accommodates itself without any aid of politicians." North objected quite consistently to any price fixing or other regulation of commerce. He was convinced that there could be no trade unprofitable to the public "for if it proves so, men leave it off; and wherever the traders thrive, the public of which they are a part, thrives also." Such references to the operation of self-adjusting forces were among the first attempts to overcome the traditional belief in the antagonism of private and public interests.

Practically all advocates of commercial liberalism belonged to the Tory political party. Their opponents, the Whigs, who defended the principles of protectionism, made abundant use of the balance of trade concept, especially in their fight for the imposition of import prohibitions on French commodities.[65] It is a moot question to what degree the foreign policy of the English government was influenced at that time by the interests of the large trading companies, since Charles II and James II were in favor of alliances with France.[66]

Since problems of foreign trade occupied the main interest of the mercantilist authors, it was common practice to use the title *Discourse of Trade* for all treatises dealing with economic problems, regardless of the fact that frequently various other questions only remotely connected with foreign trade were dealt with more or less extensively in these writings.

THEORIES OF VALUE, PRICE, MONEY, AND INTEREST ON CAPITAL

When observation and experience were accepted as primary instruments of economic analysis, some fundamental concepts of Scholastic origin proved untenable. This was, above all, true of the traditional idea of the "intrinsic value" of things that was connected with the substance concept and that had been the source of insoluble contradictions.

The force of tradition was strong enough to prevent the majority of the mercantilists from discarding that idea entirely. In his *Two Treatises on Government* (1690), John Locke explicitly referred to it, saying, "the intrinsic value of things . . . depends only on their usefulness to the life of man.'"[67] He used that concept to explain the conditions of the "state of nature," which was assumed to have existed prior to civilized society. But, perhaps influenced by the distinction drawn by the later Scholastics between the intrinsic value and the exchange value of the goods, he suggested that after the introduction of money as a general means of exchange, the intrinsic value of a good had ceased to be determined, as before, by the utility of the class to which it was assigned. According to "experience," he argued, the value of the goods appeared to be conditioned by the labor spent on their production. Thus, he connected a measurable quality of the goods with a process belonging to their past history, and asserted that ninety-nine hundredths of the value of useful things is in most cases wholly due to labor.[68] Locke distinguished the intrinsic value or quality of a commodity from its "marketable value," and associated changes in the latter with alterations in the proportion of the quantity of a commodity to want or demand. But Locke did not suggest that units of labor could be used to measure values, and he clearly separated his price theory—which was based on a crude quantity theory of money—from his value theory.

About thirty years earlier, the question of how to account for the "intrinsic value of goods" had been formulated by Sir William Petty[69] in a far more ingenious way. Motivated by the tendency to rely on observation, he abandoned the Scholastic principle of deriving the value of the goods from the classes or genera to which they were assigned. Instead, he started from the idea that equivalence was the basic principle underlying all exchanges of goods, and he raised the question of how to determine a common denominator to which all values could be reduced.

In pursuance of this reasoning, he argued that "without derogating from the excellent use of specie as a measure of value, all things ought to be valued by two natural denominations which is land and labor.'' Thus, Petty transformed the problem of determining the intrinsic values of the goods into the problem of defining the contributions made to the value of the goods by the original productive factors. And in his attempt to reduce to a common denominator the standard units defined for each factor, he simply assumed that the value of the products of land or of any products of human labor could be reduced to the amount of labor spent on their production. "Let a hundred men," he stated, "work ten years upon corn and the same number of men, the same time, upon silver. I say that the neat proceed of the silver is the price of the whole neat proceed of corn, and like parts of the one the price of like parts of the other."[70] The substance concept played a significant role in this reasoning, which also corresponded to some leading ideas of seventeenth-century scientists. These scientists were generally convinced that likeness of properties of things indicated the presence of identical forces creating the properties.[71] The search for "forces" which were supposed to create qualities of things was greatly stimulated by Bacon's axiom that what constitutes the generic common element of a group of bodies must be somehow present in them as a separable part. Following this line of reasoning, exchange value denotes a specific type of property characteristic of goods that are the object of exchanges. Hence, the "theory of specific causation" could explain the property that renders exchange value to goods.

Implied in Petty's value theory was the idea that values are qualities which are perdurable in time after having been acquired through productive processes.[72] Consequently, a distinction was to be drawn between "productive" services, which are incorporated in the goods and transformed into essential attributes of the goods, and "unproductive" services not embodied in any goods and not creating exchange values. This distinction played a significant role in all labor cost theories of value.

The majority of the English Mercantilists, who cared about determining the intrinsic value of the goods—as distinct from their prices—followed Locke's suggestion to connect that value with the volume of labor spent upon producing the goods.

Discussions of the value problem were frequently a by-product of treatises which dealt with money, interest on money, and prices.[73] Locke treated such questions in two essays, *Some Consideration of the Consequences of the Lowering of Interest and Raising the Value of Money* (1692) and *Further Considerations concerning Raising the Value of Money* (1695). His analysis centered mainly on a practical monetary issue of his time: whether it was advisable to adjust the value of the silver coins which were legal tender to the value of their silver content. Locke's treatment of this question was marked by a considerable confusion. He objected to the proposal of a treasury official to raise the mint price of silver by 20 percent, since it was undervalued at the mint, it was hoarded, and it left the country in considerable quantities. Locke erroneously qualified this proposal as "debasement," and argued that an ounce of silver could never be worth more than an ounce of silver.[74]

Locke showed the clarity of his thinking in formulating a general monetary theory in which he abandoned the substance concept as applied to monetary metals and asserted that the quantity of money in circulation, independently of the usefulness of the metals for other purposes, was sufficient to determine its "imaginary" value. Elaborating on this idea, he suggested that the exchange value of money in general was determined by the quantity of all the money in the world, in proportion to all the trade, and that the exchange value of money in any country was fixed by the present quantity of the current money in that country in proportion to the present trade. In accordance with that view, any quantity of money would be sufficient to "drive any quantity of trade." Two noticeable ideas were implied in this reasoning: reference to relationships among measurable magnitudes, and recognition of the element of scarcity as determinants of the value of money.[75]

Locke's conception of money was hardly compatible with the prevailing identification of the precious metals with the riches of a country. Nevertheless, like Petty, he defended the validity of the balance of trade concept with the argument of "bullionist" origin that gold and silver commanded the conveniences of life, and therefore in a "plenty of them consists riches."[76] Moreover, he emphasized that a country with a small stock of money, and, consequently, cheap prices, was at a disadvantage in its international trade. He showed the dangers which would result from such a situation for all sectors of the economy, and was convinced that it was preferable to acquire precious metals through export surpluses rather than through mining, since in the former case the wealth of other competing nations was correspondingly reduced. This reasoning reflects the general belief of the mercantilists in the existence of a limited fund of wealth and power available for distribution among the nations of the earth.

There is no need to dwell on the inconsistencies of Locke's economic theories.[77] They can be overlooked when his remarkable contribution to economic reasoning is taken into account, especially as regards his application of the equilibrium concept to the analysis of the international distribution of monetary metals. With this analysis, he prepared the way for the development of the quantity theory of money. Thus, following his mechanical conception of the relation between the volumes of trade of the various countries and their shares in the available stock of the precious metals, he derived the conclusion that no country's share in this stock could be much lower than its share in international trade. From this it followed that, in order "to keep trade going without loss," the price of commodities of the same kind "should be kept approximately equal among the trading countries." But his analysis of the international monetary distributive process does not indicate that he grasped the functions of the price mechanism in international trading.

Nor did Sir Dudley North, in his attacks on the balance of trade principle, establish any clear connection between the movements of the balance of trade and the international distribution of the monetary metals. He simply asserted that in the course of international trading each country was automatically provided with the "determinate of specific money required for carrying on its trade."[78]

A generation elapsed before that connection was properly specified. In a treatise dealing with the problems of international commerce, Isaac Gervaise started from the traditional view that gold and silver were the "great denominator of the real value of all things."[79] But he went on to argue that, when a nation had attracted a disproportionate part of the precious metals, more labor (in the form of manufactured commodities) would enter the country than would go out, and the difference would be paid in gold and silver until the old proportion in the international distribution of the money metals and the national proportion of rich and poor had been restored. The effects of disproportionate increases in credit added to currency were analyzed by Gervaise on similar lines. But neither Gervaise nor other Baconian Mercantilists developed a true credit theory.

The functioning of the international price mechanism as a means of regulating the distribution of the money supply was first suggested by Jacob Vanderlint, in his argument against trade restrictions.[80] Reduction of the quantity of money circulating within a country, he argued, would render labor cheap and promote exports, and thereby the exporting nation would "fetch the money back again." This reasoning foreshadowed the tendency of later Mercantilists to look for fixed proportionate relations among relevant economic magnitudes, and to search for factors which could be relied upon to reestablish such proportions whenever they had been upset.

"Frequency of payment" was repeatedly mentioned in discussions which turned on the determination of the total amount of money needed to carry on a country's trade.

William Potter appears to have been the first English Mercantilist to draw attention to the problems connected with the velocity of circulation.[81] He tried to convince his readers of the advantages to industry and trade of large amounts of money circulating rapidly.[82] Some statistical aspects of the velocity of circulation were discussed by William Petty, who otherwise limited his views on money to some general observations. In his *Treatise on Taxes and Contributions* (1662), Petty referred to the "deep ocean of all the mysteries concerning money." In his *Verbum Sapienti* (1665), which was preparatory to his measurement of the wealth of England, Petty characterized money as the "fat of the Body Politick whereof too much doth often hinder its agility, as too little makes it sick." But in his studies designed to determine the annual expenses of the British nation, he attempted to define the quantity of money needed to cover these expenditures, and found that the whole stock of money circulated in England about once in seven weeks. Thus, he suggested the concept of a flow of money within the country, but he limited his analysis to an examination of the volume of transactions commonly performed by a given supply of money and disregarded the influence on prices of changes in the velocity of circulation. Another author who paid attention to the "quickness of circulation" was Locke, who tried to determine the length of the periods during which various classes of the population held money without spending it.[83] The "cash balance approach" to monetary theory was anticipated in Locke's reasoning.

In the course of time, it became almost commonplace to emphasize the favorable effects upon industry and trade of an "enhanced frequency of payment." The functions of money as a stimulating factor were distinguished from its functions as a means of payment and a "store of wealth." Quite frequently, money was called the "life blood of trade and business, the element which keeps the wheels of the machinery in motion."[84] The expressions "sinews" or "nerves" of war, used by the earlier Mercantilists to denote money were repeated by their successors, but hoarding of precious metals by the government ceased to figure among the recommendations of English authors, since soon after the Revolution of 1688, public credit was expanding rapidly and government borrowing could be counted upon to supply the means for large-scale expenditures in times of need.

The approach to monetary theory which had been initiated in the sixteenth century by the Italian authors Bernardo Davanzati and Gasparo Scaruffi was taken up toward the end of the seventeenth century by the mathematician Geminiano Montanari.[85] But as distinct from Locke's conception of money, the Italians related the value of money to its metallic content. Perhaps influenced by Neoscholastic value theories, they connected the value of goods with their scarcity or abundance in relation to the need, esteem, or desire which men have for them. In his explanation of prices, Montanari applied the principle of quantitative commodity relationships; he used the same principle to explain the relation between the value of gold and silver. Hence, he objected to the view—defended by Bodin and Scaruffi—that this ratio should be maintained in spite of disproportionate changes in the quantities of the metals. But he made no reference to a possible proportionality between the movement of prices and changes in the volume of the means of payment.

A reformulation of the value problem in terms of estimates and scarcity relations was suggested about the same time (1690) by the English Mercantilist Nicholas Barbon.[86] Barbon proposed the use of the term *intrinsic virtue* to denote the Scholastic concept of "intrinsic value" or the quality that accounts for the usefulness of the things, but he ascribed the "market value" of things to "wants of the mind, most of them proceeding from imagination." Things, he said, may have great virtues, but be of small value or no price if they are plentiful.[87] Rejecting the belief in the intrinsic value of money, he regarded money as a product of legislation and claimed for it a value higher than the value of the metal incorporated in the coins.

Hence, there existed at the beginning of the eighteenth century at least three different conceptions of money which rivaled each other for recognition. One conception was derived from the Scholastic doctrine of the *valor impositus*. It provided the argument for justifying the right and the powers of the ruler, not only to create money but also to change the monetary standard by mere fiat. The second was Locke's theory, according to which the quantity of the means of payment, independently of the use of the precious metals for nonmonetary purposes, was sufficient to determine the "imaginary value of money." The third conception was that of money then prevailing among the Italian authors, which derived the value of monetary units from the commodity character of the monetary metals.

There were also three value theories which vied for prominence: (1) the Scholastic theory of intrinsic value; (2) the value theory of the Italians and Barbon, which referred to scarcity relations and the relative importance of wants; and (3) Locke's theory, which connected the value of the individual goods with the amount of labor spent on their production.

"Intrinsic" values of goods were quite generally distinguished from their exchange values or prices, which later were explained in terms of relations between volumes of goods and volumes of circulating means of payment. A bridge between the balance of payment concept and price theory was established by the proposition that, by tacit agreement of the various nations, the total value of marketable commodities had been made equal to the total value of the available stock of precious metals. Since only a limited volume of monetary metals was available for all nations, expansion of national production and welfare was held to be dependent upon the share in that monetary volume which a nation could secure through surpluses of its balance of payments.

The discussion of monetary problems was frequently connected with observations concerning the rate of interest on money, since interest was generally regarded as the price paid for the "use" of money. The rate of interest was believed to be determined by the volume of the circulating means of payment. Almost general agreement existed on the favorable effects of a low rate of interest, but not all mercantilist authors agreed on the advisability of imposing legal limits on that rate. Sir Thomas Culpeper, writing in 1621, was one of the first authors to recommend the fixing of a relatively low maximum rate.[88]

Petty based his treatment of interest on money on a distinction between a loan on demand—which did not justify payment of an "*agio*"—and the case of a loan which "could not be claimed back at will."[89] For loans of the latter type, he defined "natural usury" in terms of the "rent of so much land as the money lent would buy."[90] Hence, he introduced the idea of a sort of "real rate" of interest determined by the productivity or profitability of land, and he based his objections to any legal limitation of the level of the interest rate upon the consideration that a kind of insurance was involved in all cases of long-term lending. The rise in the value of land and the fall of the rate of interest were in his view caused by the considerable increases in the quantity of money "which got some way or other into the Kingdom." That view was shared by Davenant.[91]

Locke, who still adhered to the thesis that "money was a barren thing," explained the payment for the use of money by drawing an analogy between the borrower of money and the tenant of agricultural land. Both, he argued, could earn through their activity and labor returns in excess of the payment stipulated for the use of the loan.[92] Thus, he touched upon the idea that money, like land, was a productive factor which, when combined with labor, yielded a return. Less clear was his proposition to relate the rate of interest to the "natural value of money," which he defined as the proportion of the whole quantity of circulating money to the "whole trade of the Kingdom." Although he favored a low rate of interest, he regarded legal regulation of it as just as useless as "fixing of rates upon the hire of houses or ships." A reduction of the rate of interest, he believed, could affect prices only indirectly, through changes in the exportation of specie or increases in output. The view that it was useless to set limits on the rate of interest was endorsed by all contemporary Mercantilists who were looking for natural forces to be relied upon to regulate the relationships among economic magnitudes. Sir Dudley North insisted that it was not low interest that made trade, but that trade, increasing the "stock of the nation," made interest low.[93]

Finally, some skeptical minds objected to the connection which was generally believed to exist between the level of interest and the available supply of money. Thus, Josiah Child questioned the widespread view that the low rate of interest which prevailed in the Netherlands was exclusively due to abundance of money.[94]

A new approach to the explanation of the rate of interest was suggested by Nicholas Barbon, who showed his originality in his attempt to introduce a concept of "real" capital into the discussion of economic problems.[95] He considered it a mistake to "reckon interest for money" and defined interest as a rent of "wrought or artificial stock," a counterpart to rent of land which was for "unwrought or natural" stock.[96] This juxtaposition of real and money capital foreshadowed much later discussions, suggested by the view that all real economic happenings took place behind a veil produced by monetary phenomena, and had to be explained accordingly.[97] But Barbon's conception of the rate of interest was practically ignored by his contemporaries.

THE PROBLEM OF FIDUCIARY MONEY

The increasing awareness of the stimulating effects on industrial and commercial activities exercised by price increases was obviously at variance with the prevailing predilection for cheapness of goods. Hence, the advantages of rising prices and low rates of interest which facilitated borrowing were discussed by several authors, for instance, as mentioned before, Malynes and Misselden, as well as Josiah Child and various Dutch economists.[98] But these discussions did not touch upon the theoretical aspects of that problem.

Lowering the rate of interest was considered one of the most important measures conducive to economic progress. Since, according to a generally accepted view, the rate of interest was dependent upon the available supply of money, prolonged discussions in England during the last decades of the seventeenth century turned on the question of whether the English banks should follow the practice adopted by some Italian and Dutch banks and issue notes only partly covered by metallic reserves, thus creating "artificial wealth," as distinct from the "natural wealth" represented by the precious metals. Thomas Mun had already drawn the attention of his countrymen to the Italian methods of financing trade by granting very large credits.

William Petty recommended the issuance of bank notes backed by a 50 percent coverage, as suggested by the Dutch example, and he proposed to restrict the use of precious metals for purposes of foreign trade.[99] Davenant was convinced that paper money could fulfill the functions of the circulating means of payment as well as or better than gold and silver, particularly when used to stimulate trade.[100] The creation of a bank of issue as a source of credits to the government was recommended by North and Cary.[101] After much controversy, the Bank of England was finally established in 1694 and was intended to support the government in its struggle with the heavy deficits incurred after the ascension to the throne of William and Mary in 1688.

Simultaneously, the demand for capital required for investment purposes was steadily increasing. Bankers and manufacturers were impressed by the argument that a large potential productive power was available, ready to be put into operation when newly created monetary funds were placed at the disposal of producers and traders. Intensified business activity was expected to result from increased velocity of circulation. Representatives of English country banks propagated the idea that the immobilized intrinsic value of the soil could be brought into circulation by issuing bank notes the value of which was guaranteed by mortgaging real estate. One of the first authors to propose a fantastic scheme of this type was William Potter in 1650; another land bank scheme was advanced about forty years later by Nicholas Barbon.[102] John Asgill claimed for his project, propagated in 1696, that it would create "another species of money than gold and silver," that it would lead to the highest improvement of land values and eventually to the abolition of interest on money.[103]

The discussion of the issuance of fiduciary money for the purpose of promoting trade and creating prosperity assumed new aspects when it was provided with a striking theoretical background by John Law (1671–1729), a Scottish banker. The close connection of Law's financial activities with one of the most spectacular monetary ventures has provided him with a rather unfortunate place in the history of economic events. Though his scheme eventually collapsed when put to the test of practical application, he deserves a special place in the history of economic reasoning because he was the first to examine the national and international significance of the economic effects caused by the issuance of paper money.

In his treatise on *Money and Trade* (1705), Law used a discussion of the balance of trade principle to develop his main arguments in favor of a proposal to bring about general prosperity through the creation of abundant supplies of money.[104] He asserted that England had never possessed sufficient money to provide employment for the entire population, and that equilibrium needed to be established between the volume of money and the demand for goods. Hence, he proposed to create money through land banks, to reduce interest on capital through credit operations, and thus to stimulate entrepreneurial activity. Lowered costs of production could secure considerable advantages for domestic industry over foreign competition, expenditures by landowners would be greatly increased by "mobilizing" the value of their estates, and hence employment would be provided for large masses of idle workers.

Law's analysis of the world-wide effects of his proposals was based on his conception of the economy as a self-regulating mechanism. He believed that wages in England could be kept stable in spite of the rapid expansion of industry in trade, that the rate of profit would decline but total profit would increase greatly, and that an eventual rise in prices would spread over all trading countries, which would equalize the values of their currencies. The greatest advantage would accrue to the country which had started the process of increasing the quantity of its money, since "it would only bear a share of the increase in value, according to the proportion its money had to the money of Europe." Thus, he expected a gradual constant adjustment of the economic conditions of the European countries to his proposed almost limitless increase in the volume of England's means of payment.

In his theoretical discussions, Law manifested his independence of Scholastic reasoning by repudiating the interpretation of ''utility'' as a quality of the class to which a good is assigned. He compared the value of water and the value of a diamond in order to illustrate the thesis that the value of the goods was determined by the specific use to which they were applied, in accordance with the demand for them and in proportion to their quantity. To Locke's theory of the imaginary value of money he opposed the observation that the value of precious metals was ultimately derived from the original use to which they had been put, and that their additional use for exchange purposes had added to their value. Thus, he endorsed a clear commodity theory of money which provided him with arguments against debasement of the currency. He characterized this practice as a tax imposed on the poorer classes of the population.

Adoption of the commodity theory of money was obviously inconsistent with the strong case which Law made for the issuance of undefined volumes of unredeemable paper money, and it is doubtful whether these inconsistencies can be reconciled. However that may be, it appears that his far-reaching proposals were based on a conceptual transformation of money from a traditional instrument for measuring and representing values into an instrument for influencing the course of economic activities. Hence, he felt free to recommend the use of a currency which had no original use value at all.[105] With this transformation of the role of money, he anticipated the idea of a ''managed currency.''

He supplemented his arguments in favor of paper money with an analysis of the history of past economic developments and tried to convince his readers that economic progress had been mainly promoted by two outstanding events: the discovery of the West Indies, which had provided Europe with a huge influx of precious metals, and the introduction of fiduciary money. He held out the prospect of a third event of still greater importance, namely, the possibility of practically unlimited credit expansion. This bold idea to use changes in the available supply of money for the purpose of differentiating periods of general economic development was probably the first noticeable attempt of this type; much later it found a number of successors.[106]

In accordance with a suggestion made by Professor Heckscher, Law's ideas can perhaps be characterized as an attempt to find a way out of a dilemma which resulted for the Mercantilists from the contradiction between the dynamic objectives of their policies and their fundamentally static conception of the volume of values available for purposes of national and international trading.[107] Experience showed how difficult it was to devise an appropriate solution to this dilemma.

The sober-minded English Mercantilists easily resisted the temptation to stimulate business activity by issuing fiduciary nonredeemable paper money. Their balance concept as applied to the relation between the volume of precious metals and the volume of exchangeable goods prevented them from experimenting with arbitrary increases in the volume of money.[108] They considered scarcity of money a consequence of the ''balance due'' and abundance of money a symptom, not a source, of wealth.

In France, however, no widely accepted monetary theory provided a bar to Law's reasoning, which tended to transform credit from an instrument for transferring exchange values into an instrument for facilitating large-scale investments and promoting venturesome colonial enterprises. Thus, the issuance of paper money increased rapidly within the framework of the ''Mississippi scheme'' (1718–20), under which the Banque Royale was authorized to grant loans to borrowers willing to subscribe to shares of the venturesome Compagnie des Indes. The breakdown of a wild speculative boom was brought about by the catastrophic failure of the company. But it is noteworthy that even after the collapse of that scheme in 1720, John Law's ideas found eloquent French defenders, such as Melon and Dutot.[109] Throughout the eighteenth and nineteenth centuries, popular economic thinking in France was, time and again, attracted by the dynamic aspects of his proposals, and the belief in almost miraculous powers of credit expansion was never abandoned. That belief was perhaps—at least indirectly—supported by the Cartesian cosmology which required the operation of outside forces to produce and maintain movements of otherwise inert bodies. Continued increase of the circulating means of payment was regarded as an indispensable force stimulating from the outside lagging economic activities.

THE PROBLEM OF PRODUCTIVE EMPLOYMENT

The belief that a large population was prerequisite to the pursuance of effective power policies was a constituent element of seventeenth- and eighteenth-century political philosophies. This belief was shared by the large majority of Mercantilists, among them Child and Davenant. They pointed to the prospect of economic advancement connected with the intensified exploitation of natural resources through as many laboring hands as possible.[110] A large population was likely to assure the maintenance of a low wage level, which typical mercantilist reasoning considered indispensable for promoting the development of the export industries and the achievement of a favorable balance of trade.[111] But the policy of low wages was also supported by authors such as John Pollexfen and Petty, who did not share the more traditional monetary and trade views. Wage fixing as it was generally practiced in fact entailed the establishment of maximum rates.

Discussion of population problems, however, had hardly started when the Italian Giovanni Botero considered it necessary to contrast *virtus generativa,* human propagation potential, with *virtus nutritiva,* the potential increase in means of subsistence. Thus, he emphasized the limits set to increases in the population, and, moreover, he listed positive and negative checks which operate toward determining the actual size of the population.[112]

Of particular importance for the discussion of demographic problems was Petty's decision to include a calculation of the "value" of England's population in his computation of the wealth of the kingdom made in 1676.[113] His proposition that mankind had the tendency to multiply in accordance with a law of geometrical progression became a cornerstone of subsequent population theories.[114]

A radical distinction was thus established between the two main factors of production, land and labor. Whereas land was held to be available only in limited quantities, the volume of labor was believed to allow almost limitless expansion, and its supply was apparently not affected by its cost of production. This formulation of the quantitative aspects of the two productive factors was reflected in the view that a large population, unless fully employed, was a burden rather than an advantage. Pauperism, produced by the enclosure system and aggravated by recurrent "commercial crises," was already a serious problem in sixteenth-century England; it occupied the minds of almost all authors who dealt with questions of protectionist policies, such as Josiah Child, Charles Davenant, John Pollexfen, Philanglus,[115] and John Cary.[116] The Elizabethan laws of 1597 and 1601 which placed the financial burden of the relief measures on the parishes did not enjoy general approval. Toward the end of the seventeenth century the workhouse became an important instrument of relief policy.[117]

Encouragement of consumption, partly because of its stimulating effects on technical progress and inventions, was recommended by practically all authors who favored liberalization of foreign trade. John Cary expected general increases in all incomes to result from enhanced spending.[118] On the other hand, luxury and extravagance, especially spending on unnecessary imports, were frequently criticized. Thus, the wasteful redundance of "unproductive" occupations was complained of by, among others, Petty[119] and Pollexfen.[120]

Various authors, such as Petty and Cary, emphasized that productivity of labor was greatly increased by "art," that is to say, by technological improvements and inventions.[121] Sir William Temple,[122] Petty, and Davenant observed that, especially in densely populated areas, strong incentives developed to apply inventions and to increase industrial activity. Petty listed "art" as a factor of production along with land, labor, and stock. He also gave a very clear account of the increased productive efficiency which resulted from the division of labor and industrial specialization.

Such elaboration of the economic aspects of society was accompanied by a significant change in the meaning attached to the concept of "wealth of the nation." Petty's measurement of the wealth of England and Davenant's investigation into the sources of public revenues helped to discredit the idea that foreign trade, resulting from increased supplies of bullion, was the only way to enhance the wealth of a community. Petty placed great emphasis on thrift as a means of accumulating "wealth" and ascribed such importance to well-trained labor that he considered it more advisable to burn the products of the labor of a thousand men than to allow them to lose their skill by remaining unemployed.[123] The condemnation of idleness found strong support in the moral conviction of the Puritans, who had many adherents among England's commercial classes.[124]

The distinction drawn by Thomas Mun and various later authors between "natural" and "artificial" wealth was intended to emphasize the importance of manufactures which provided net additions to the country's natural resources and were regarded as the most valuable assets of the export trade. Many mercantilist writers shared the view expressed by Davenant that the difference between the value of exported manufactures and the cost of the materials used in producing them was a clear gain, and that all "foreign consumption" was a certain profit.[125]

In pursuance of such considerations, a "balance of industry" concept was frequently substituted for the balance of trade concept, although the term *balance of industry* was introduced only at a much later date.[126] It was argued by various authors that the purchase of foreign manufactures meant purchase of foreign labor and that employment and subsistence of domestic labor were promoted by the exportation of domestic manufactures, and that, consequently, a sound commercial policy should be directed toward maximizing the amount of English wages paid by the foreign countries and minimizing the amount of foreign wages incorporated in imported commodities. In the light of this balance concept, Nicholas Barbon arrived at the conclusion that neither the exportation nor the importation of gold and silver was a matter of particular importance. He proposed to value exports in accordance with the amount of labor involved in their production and imports of raw materials in accordance with the prospect of employing labor on manufactures produced from those materials.[127] Thus, imports of raw silk were considered more profitable than imports of precious metals, and the merits of the various industries were determined according to their capacity to absorb labor.

At the beginning of the eighteenth century, the author of a treatise on the East India trade insisted that it was advantageous to spend bullion on the purchase of goods produced in Asia with less labor than in the European markets where they were sold.[128] The problem of "productive employment" played a significant role about ten years later (1713) in the "penny sheet" war between the Whigs and the Tories over the conclusion of a liberalized commercial treaty with France. The principles of protectionist policy, which corresponded to the interests of English woolen and silk manufacturers, were set forth by Sir Theodore Janssen in a pamphlet included among the propagandist publications of the Whigs.[129] The list of the elements of "good trade" established by Janssen contained such items as exportation of manufactures made of raw material produced in the country, exportation of materials in large supply (superfluities), importation of foreign raw materials to be reexported after being worked up, importation of raw materials to be worked up for domestic consumption, exchange of domestic commodities for foreign commodities, and the importation of goods for the purpose of being reexported and of indispensable goods. Janssen requested protection especially for industries which were in their infancy.[130] His general contention that the English trade with France was "bad" in every respect was elaborated on by other protagonists of the protectionist cause, such as Henry Martin, James Milner, and Joshua Gee.[131]

The Tories, who endorsed the liberal cause, published their arguments in favor of the proposed treaty in a periodical which was prepared mainly by Daniel Defoe (1659?-1731), the well-known author of *Robinson Crusoe*.[132] But they were finally defeated by their opponents.

The "balance of industry" argument was supplemented by the consideration that not only labor but also domestic land rent and the profits included in the prices of exported commodities should exceed in value the corresponding amounts included in imports. Viewed from that angle, the trade with Spain, Portugal, Italy, and Turkey was considered highly advantageous because it secured inflow of specie and caused foreign consumers to pay considerable fractions of English wages, rents, and profits.

There was perhaps a logical connection between the balance of industry concept and the prevailing value theory, which regarded labor as the source of exchange value. But the idea of a "balance of industry" was logically inferior to the traditional balance of trade concept, since it was based on a very vague equilibrium concept and could not be expressed in clear quantitative terms.

The belief that wages should be kept at a low level was frequently based on the argument that high wages were likely to reduce the incentive to work. Petty,[133] as well as Child, observed that when the necessaries of life were cheap, workers did not care to increase their standard of living (that "mean condition" to which they were accustomed),[134] and that they preferred to work less in such conditions than in times of rising prices.

One of the first authors to question the advantages attributed to the maintenance of low wages was Davenant, who showed that in poor countries rates of interest were high, land was cheap, and the price of labor likewise low. Strong reasons in favor of wage increases, along with general increases in prices, were advanced by John Cary. A convinced partisan of a policy of high wages was Daniel Defoe, who argued that it was bad policy to sell goods at low prices and ruin the people.[135]

International comparisons of the wage levels led to the conclusion that migratory movements could be brought about by wage differentials. Elaborating on an idea previously expressed by John Graunt, Child argued that "greater wages, if our law gave encouragement, would procure us a supply of people without the charges of breeding them."[136] The elements of a "quantity theory of population" were perhaps implied in such considerations, which suggested that the international movement of skilled labor might be determined by factors similar to those which regulated the international movements of goods.

Chapter 5
Refined Mercantilism

THE PROBLEM OF SELF-REGULATING FORCES

IN THE PRECEDING analysis, repeated reference has been made to the increasing emphasis placed by the Baconian Mercantilists on the functioning of automatic forces which were believed to determine the relation among certain economic magnitudes. Reliance upon these forces was derived from the use of the mechanical equilibrium concept as an instrument for analyzing such relationships; the results of these considerations were reflected in various formulations of the quantity theory of money and in propositions concerning the international distribution of the monetary metals and similar ideas. Occasionally some light was thrown on the interdependence of specific economic phenomena.

Yet hardly any attempts were made to combine such scattered observations into consistent pictures of the functioning of the economy. The only economist prior to the middle of the eighteenth century who appears to have grasped the conception of an economic system of a more or less mechanical type was an Irish-born French banker, Richard Cantillon (1680–1734), who is to be regarded as an outstanding Baconian Mercantilist. His *Essai sur la nature du commerce en général,* written between 1730 and 1734, was published only in 1755.[1] In the meantime, other writers plagiarized important parts of the manuscript without mentioning the source.[2] After publication, Cantillon's ideas were taken up by a number of French economists, and were occasionally referred to even by Adam Smith.[3] But the essay fell into oblivion and was rediscovered only in 1881 by William Stanley Jevons, who drew the attention of his fellow economists to Cantillon's outstanding contribution to the development of economic thought.[4] In fact, Cantillon showed an understanding of refined nominalistic methods of economic analysis which was not reached by any other contemporary Mercantilist. He repeatedly made use of imaginary cases to demonstrate the validity of his propositions and to test the inner consistency of his main concepts. He relied as much on experience as on deductive reasoning, and he frequently tried to verify the results of the latter through examples taken from the economic and financial history of various countries.

In his analysis of fundamental economic concepts, Cantillon started from William Petty's setting of the general economic problem. He followed Petty in defining the intrinsic value of a good as the measure (*la mesure*) of the quantity of land and labor which entered into the production of the good, due regard being paid to the fertility of the soil and the quality of labor.[5] In his search for a denominator common to land and labor, Petty had reduced land to labor. Cantillon adopted the opposite procedure and reduced labor to land on the ground that the day's work of the lowliest slave (*le travail journalier du plus vil esclave*) had to be equal to at least twice the quantity of the land needed to assure a minimum of existence, since the worker could be assumed to rear at least two children. The equivalence between land and labor, he believed, could be precisely measured in monetary terms. Occasionally he transformed his value theory into a cost of production theory by including the costs of transportation and the profits of the entrepreneurs among the elements of "intrinsic value."[6] Applying the cost principle also to wages, he pointed to the costs involved in the training of the workers as an important element in determining the level of wages of the various classes of labor.

As had been suggested by Petty, Cantillon adopted the belief in the intrinsic value of money mainly on the ground that gold and silver, like any other commodities, could not be acquired except at costs which would approximately correspond to the amount of labor spent on their production. It is interesting to note that he paid special attention to the relation of the two main monetary metals and surveyed the variations which the relative values of gold and silver had experienced in the course of time. He distinguished the real or intrinsic value of the monetary metals from their market value, which, like the value of any other commodity, he believed, was subject to fluctuations according to their abundance or scarcity and according to the uses made of them. But he rejected the view that money derived an "imaginary" additional value from its use for exchange purposes.[7]

In accordance with the prevailing opinion, Cantillon separated price analysis from value theory. He paid close attention to the behavior of prices, especially under conditions of free competition, and he observed with unusual sagacity that in well-regulated societies the market prices of commodities do not vary greatly from their intrinsic value when consumption is fairly constant and uniform. It is hardly necessary to recall that, as understood by Cantillon, the "intrinsic value of a commodity" was determined by its costs. In another acute observation concerning the functioning of the competitive economy, Cantillon connected shifts in demand with the problem of resource allocation. Thus, he pointed to a causal connection between increased demand for horses and the expansion of the use of land for fodder production.

In a critical discussion of Locke's version of the quantity theory of money, he used the equilibrium concept to demonstrate how the precious metals were automatically distributed among the various nations. But he raised objections to the proposition that increases in the quantity of money would lead to proportionate price increases. He emphasized that, starting from a rising demand for consumption goods, the resulting dearness would affect the various commodities differently and that demand might often turn to new directions.

Cantillon supplemented these general considerations with an examination of the conditions under which incomes and prices rose when newly mined precious metals were distributed among various groups of the population. In an analysis which was later highly praised by Jevons, he showed that, in a process of price dispersion, those groups of the population would be favored that participated in the early stages of the process, but that the incomes of other groups would be adversely affected. He was thus one of the first economists to take account of the time element in general theoretical considerations.

Like Petty, Cantillon attached considerable importance to the velocity of the circulation of money. In an appraisal of Petty's estimate of England's money requirements, he suggested that these requirements amounted to about one-third of annual rentals. He pointed to the influence on confidence of a possible reduction of the circulating volume of money, and clearly realized that enhanced velocity of circulation had similar effects on the price level as increases in the quantity of money. In these considerations, he anticipated ideas which provided the background for the so-called income approach to monetary theory.[8]

As distinct from Locke and other Mercantilists, Cantillon connected his explanation of price movements with changes in the volume of trade, rather than with changes in the volume of money. But, like other Mercantilists, he emphasized the favorable effect of export surpluses and regarded achievement of such surpluses at full employment of the population as the primary objective of a sound economic policy. He warned, however, that no country could forever enjoy such surpluses because of the increase in prices which was bound to result from the continuous inflow of monetary metals and the attendant enhanced velocity of circulation. The prevailing view that a more or less limited volume of money was available for distribution among the nations and was changing hands in the course of time was basic to this formulation of the balance of trade doctrine.

In his demographic analysis, Cantillon used the analogy of the behavior of mice in a barn to characterize the tendency of the population to multiply. But he pointed to counterbalancing forces which resulted in adjusting the population to the demand for labor.

Cantillon placed an analysis of the economic structure of the population in the center of his essay, and thus initiated a new, model building approach to economic research. Using his theory of ''intrinsic value'' as defined in terms of land and labor, he distinguished three ''natural'' classes of the population: landlords, farmers, and laborers. He grouped all other occupations around that central core and showed how the farmers divided their products (*le produit de la terre*) into three parts (*les trois rentes*), of which one represented their outlays, the second their profits, and the third their payment to the owners of the land. Thus, he outlined the elements of a distributive process which started from the sale of the produce of the soil. Elaborating this process with the aid of some tentative assumptions, he suggested that about one-half of the yield of agricultural production was exchanged for goods supplied by merchants and ''entrepreneurs'' of the towns. The term *entrepreneurs* was thus introduced into the economic terminology to denote the businessman who combined productive factors for manufacturing purposes. The farmers, the manufacturers, and the traders appeared as those groups of the population that sold their goods at uncertain prices, and thus participated in processes of risk bearing. Because of his attempt to develop, in numerical terms, a broad picture of the distribution of incomes among the various classes of the population, and because of the central position which he assigned to the farmers and the landowners in this process, Cantillon has frequently been regarded as a direct precursor of the physiocrats.

Himself a banker, Cantillon paid special attention to the organization and operation of credit machinery. He discussed the functions of bankers as intermediaries between would-be lenders who deposited their savings with them and borrowers in need of capital. He showed that fulfillment of these functions resulted in increasing the velocity of circulation of the means of payment.

In his treatment of interest on money, Cantillon rejected the prevailing view that the level of interest was related to the quantity of money. Instead he argued that the rate of interest was determined by the demand for and the supply of loans, and he illustrated this proposition by comparing a case in which precious metals produced by a mine were spent on consumption goods with the case in which they were lent for productive purposes. In the latter case, a rise in the rate of interest could result from an increase in the demand for loans, but the same effect was not likely to be produced in the former case. Cantillon also discussed the influence exercised on the rate of interest by the profits of the entrepreneurs, and he emphasized the risk element as another determinant of that rate. Thus, he introduced new aspects into the traditional treatment of interest on capital.

As already mentioned, many ideas advanced by Cantillon found their way into the writings of his contemporaries. But his analysis of the general functioning of the economy was too sketchy to be fully appreciated, even after the *Essai sur le commerce* had appeared in print. The lasting influence which that remarkable book has exercised on the development of economic reasoning is still the object of conflicting views.

The outstanding author who can be credited with having used refined methods of nominalistic reasoning for an effective attack on the principles and practices of mercantilist economic policy was the philosopher David Hume (1711–1776). Hume did not write a comprehensive economic treatise, but, in a series of well-organized and widely read essays, he consistently showed the advantages of a mechanistic interpretation of the relations among certain fundamental economic magnitudes and the practical consequences to be drawn from that approach.

The *Political Discourses* of Hume, which included eight essays on economic questions, were published in 1752; a ninth essay appeared in 1758. Among the problems which he discussed in these essays were some burning economic issues of his time, such as the balance of trade doctrine, the international distribution of the monetary metals, the functions of money and credit, the reactions of commercial and industrial activity to changing prices, the roles of consumption and taxes in the economy, and the problems connected with the issuance of public loans.[9]

These essays show the clarity of Hume's thinking and the lucidity of his style. In support of his fundamentally mechanistic approach to economic analysis, he alluded to a theory of "moral attraction" according to which human interests and efforts were operating as strongly as the forces of universal gravity. In order to drive home the validity of his arguments, he occasionally used hypothetically constructed examples. But his methods of economic research were not perceptibly influenced by his theory of cognition, which will be discussed in a subsequent chapter.

Hume shared the almost universal contemporary belief that trade was *the* factor that initiated production and kept industry in motion. He was convinced that the profit motive of merchants, combined with their frugality, provided the main stimulus to economic prosperity, and that refinement and technical progress were especially promoted by foreign trade. From his historical studies, he drew the conclusion that in most countries foreign trade had preceded any significant expansion of domestic manufactures, and was the prime causal factor leading to increased consumption and luxury.

His mechanistic approach to the interpretation of economic relations caused him to adopt a simple version of the quantity theory of money, based on the assumption that, when due regard was given to the velocity of circulation, changes in the level of prices were causally determined by, and proportionate to, variations in the volume of the currency. This version of the quantity theory was adopted by some English and French writers.[10]

But Hume distinguished the long-run behavior of prices from the short-run effects of expansions or contractions of the volume of the currency, and he elaborated Cantillon's observation that the various groups of prices did not react uniformly to changes in the quantity of the circulating means of payment.[11] He emphasized the stimulating effects on industry and trade of disproportionate increases in prices, and pointed out the general tendency of wages to lag behind changes in prices. Hence, he favored a slow and steady reduction of the metallic content of the currency in order to keep alive the spirit of industry and to increase the "stock of labour, wherein consists all real power and riches."[12]

Like Locke, Hume was perhaps motivated by his unwillingness to apply the substance concept, when he attributed to money a purely imaginary value which he related to the services of the precious metals as a medium of exchange. From his mechanistic approach to the formation of prices, he derived strong objections to the inflationary effects of fiduciary money and ascribed similar undesirable consequences to the floating of government loans, which he regarded as a dangerous source of speculative excesses.[13]

Mechanistic considerations provided an appropriate starting point for Hume's analysis of the international distribution of the monetary metals.[14] In the course of the exchange of goods, he argued, each nation would in the long run participate in the distribution of the total supply of the monetary metals in accordance with its share in the total volume of its internationally marketable goods. He used the analogy of the behavior of water in communicating vessels with the international flow of gold and silver to demonstrate that all countries were bound to gain such metals in their trade with Spain and Portugal, which had acquired huge quantities of gold and silver from their overseas possessions. It was impossible, in his view, "to heap up more money than any fluid beyond its proper level." He also referred to a self-regulating mechanism operating through the medium of prices in order to explain the monetary balances of the various provinces of the country. From these considerations, he drew the conclusion that it was futile to resort to artificial measures to assure a favorable balance of trade. Such measures, he exclaimed, were costly folly, since they forced the domestic consumer to purchase goods which were inferior to those he could otherwise obtain.[15] Hence, Hume criticized the prohibition imposed by France on the exportation of grains; he argued that there was no safer method of increasing the production of a commodity than to enhance its exports. But he did not develop his predilection for freedom of trade into an outright doctrine. Quite generally, he recognized the validity of the arguments advanced in favor of infant industries and in favor of protecting the domestic industries of a country threatened by the loss of their foreign markets.[16]

Hume's criticism of the mercantilist protectionist policy caused him to reject export surpluses shown by the balance of trade as an index of prosperity. He resorted to the rate of interest as a more suitable standard of measuring economic progress. He opposed the belief in the existence of a direct causal relation between the volume of money and the rate of interest, with the argument that the level of interest had not been perceptibly affected by the inflow of gold and silver from American mines, whereas commodity prices had risen nearly fourfold. Hume expected a reduction of the level of interest mainly from three causes: a small demand for borrowing, great riches to supply that demand, and small profits from commerce.[17] All these circumstances, he believed, resulted from increases of industry and commerce, not of gold and silver. Thus, he developed the concept of money capital accumulated out of savings, and showed how the transfer of liquid assets from would-be lenders to borrowers was facilitated by the concentration of savings in credit institutions.

In an excursion into the field of economic history, Hume outlined a theory of economic progress according to which the advantages achieved by an industrially advanced country were partly offset by the low price of labor in others with no extensive commerce and no abundance of gold and silver. Thus, Hume shared the view of other Mercantilists that the manufactures were gradually moving from countries which they had already enriched to others to which they were allured by cheapness of provisions and labor. But he found some consolation in the idea that domestic demand might provide work for hands previously employed by export industries and thus advanced some arguments in support of "the development of luxury industries."

Hume's fundamentally liberal convictions found their clearest expression in his essay on the jealousy of commerce, published in 1758. In an often-quoted passage, he confessed that, as a British subject, he prayed for a flourishing trade of Germany, Italy, Spain, and even France, regardless of the age-long commercial rivalry which had existed between England and France. But Hume influenced economic reasoning far less in the sphere of economic analysis strictly speaking than by his contributions to social philosophy.

THE LAST CHAMPIONS OF MERCANTILISM

Convinced Mercantilists did not easily abandon the principles of a doctrine which for more than a century had provided the guiding ideas to economic policies. Adherence to the balance of trade concept was so deeply rooted in the economic views of many eighteenth-century authors that they defended and upheld this concept and some of its important implications even after it had been criticized with telling arguments. Paramount among these authors was Josiah Tucker (1712–1799), who insisted upon identifying the wealth of a nation with its possession of precious metals and considered consistent administrative regulation of economic activities indispensable for assuring harmony between private and public interests.[18] Tucker opposed Hume's view that industrial superiority was constantly shifting from one nation to another, arguing that the advantage of cheapness of labor enjoyed by a poorer country would disappear as soon as it had started to capture markets from the richer country.[19]

Another Mercantilist, Robert Wallace, minister of the Church of Scotland,[20] questioned the relationship which Hume had established between the supply of money and the price level, and regarded possession of a great quantity of money as a permanent advantage for a richer country. But since the results of the balance of trade frequently could not be ascertained for lack of reliable foreign trade statistics, various authors adopted Hume's proposal to use the rates of exchange as indexes for determining economic progress. These rates were compared with the barometer of the mariner's compass or the pulse of the human body.

In the course of the prolonged discussions of the balance of industry concept, two main reasons were advanced to explain the high rate of unemployment among the working classes: the distribution of landed property, and the relatively rapid increase of the population. A liberalized version of the balance of industry argument was suggested by Joseph Harris, who showed considerable analytical power in his attempt to introduce the quantity theory of money into a discussion of general economic conditions.[21] Like other contemporaneous authors, he recommended hoarding and conversion of bullion into plates as an antidote to rising prices.[22]

A last comprehensive and consistent effort to maintain the mercantilist position, though with many qualifications, was made in 1767 by Sir James Steuart (1712–1780). Steuart undertook to synthesize in two volumes the refined results of a reasoning which had slowly developed under the influence of the Baconian methodology,[23] but which he modified in the light of experiences undergone during a prolonged stay in several countries of continental Europe.[24] During that stay, he asserted, he had become aware of the divergencies in conditions which existed between various nations, and of differences in their "received opinions as to morals, government and manners."

As distinct from practically all previous Mercantilists, Steuart attempted to transform political economy into a comprehensive study of social life, and to provide an imaginary statesman with full information about the economic policies to be adopted for promoting the country's well-being. He developed his ideas in five books dealing, respectively, with population and agriculture, trade and industry, money and coin, credit and debts, and taxes. To the statesman he ascribed the task of deciding upon what was in the public interest; within the limits thus defined by the statesman, everybody should be allowed to follow the dictates of his own private interests, and the statesman was requested to take account of these interests as the main motivation of economic activity. But his discussion of mercantilist policies did not arouse much interest. In the nineteenth century, Steuart's work was more appreciated by German authors than by English economists.

The principles of economic policy which Steuart elaborated in his substantial volumes centered on the balance of industry idea. The "matter" exported, he said, was what a country lost; the price of labor exported was what it gained. From propositions of that kind he derived the general prescription to discourage the importation of manufactures and to promote their exportation. True to the mercantilist tradition, he characterized the precious metals as the measure of power among nations, having been "rendered a universal equivalent of everything." With Nicholas Barbon and David Hume, he shared the conviction that money received its "estimation" only from the fact that it was made the universal measure "of what is called value." Hence, he argued that the acquisition, or at least the preservation, of a proportional quantity of the precious metals "became for the most prudent an object of last importance." In his discussion of the nature of money, he rejected the commodity theory of money and derived the value of money from the general acceptance of a commodity as the universal measure of what is called value. From "money coin" he distinguished "money of accompt," defined as an arbitrary scale for measuring values. But he did not succeed in clarifying the meaning of this concept, which was designed to explain a bookkeeping device used by the large clearing banks to facilitate their dealings among the great variety of different currency systems.[25]

Although inclined to accept a mechanistic explanation of the formation of prices, Steuart questioned Hume's version of the quantity theory of money. He considered the conditions of supply and demand as the only determinants of prices and believed that increases in the volume of money beyond the quantity required to carry on the trade would cause hoarding of the surplus; the surplus would be returned to circulation through lending only after the volume of specie had been reduced "below the proportion found necessary to carry the circulation."

In the sociological portions of his work, Steuart compared the generative faculty of the population with a "spring loaded with a weight which always exerts itself in proportion to the diminution of resistance."[26] Hence, he considered it a predominant task of true statesmanship to establish equilibrium between agriculture on the one hand and industry and commerce on the other. The absorption of "all superfluous consumers" from agriculture by industry was, in his view, a main element in the continuous transformation of economic life.

In his analysis of agricultural production, Steuart emphasized that progressively smaller yields would result when cultivation was extended to poorer and poorer soil. Thus, he pointed quite distinctly to the law of decreasing returns. However, the outlook on excessive increases in the population does not appear to have affected his general sociological considerations. With growing, stable, and declining populations he associated the successive phases in the development of the political communities.

The background to these sociological considerations was provided by Steuart's theory of economic changes, which centered on the conception of an economic cycle which included for each industrialized nation phases of growth and decline. He especially emphasized the difficulties involved in adjusting domestic industries to changing conditions during the second phase of the cycle, when competitive manufactures were being set up in foreign markets. Hence, due to possible shifts in the "balance of wealth" and to rising costs of the export products, prosperous periods of foreign trade might turn out to be only a temporary phase in a country's economic history, and the statesman was requested to correct violent maladjustments which in every growing country threatened to overthrow the "balance of work and demand."[27]

ITALIAN MERCANTILISTS

In a number of Italian cities, traditional attachment to the methods of nominalistic reasoning had created favorable conditions for the development of economic research on the lines adopted by representatives of refined English Mercantilists. Simultaneously, the far-flung interests of Italian banks and industrial and commercial enterprises had prepared the soil for the acceptance of the free trade principle as an instrument for promoting general prosperity.

Thus, systematic, consistent, and extensive economic analysis, adjusted to teaching purposes, was carried out by a number of remarkable scholars in the second half of the eighteenth century, during which period chairs of political economy were set up at some Italian universities. The first chair, founded in 1754 at Naples, was occupied by Antonio Genovesi (1712-1769), who had been a professor of moral philosophy.[28] He started the publication of a series of textbooks with his *Lezioni di commercio o sia d'economia civile* (1765).[29]

Very soon, the teachers of this new academic discipline vied with each other in their efforts to develop a synthesis of economic theory and empirical knowledge which centered on the problems of a welfare state of the utilitarian type. A series of remarkable textbooks resulted from these studies, which bear witness to the high erudition of their authors and their capacity to apply the methods of advanced Baconian mercantilism to comprehensive analyses of the economies of the Italian states. They concentrated, above all, on important questions of economic policy, such as, how to organize economic life in its various fields in order to promote general well-being and how to establish a proper balance among the different sectors of the economy. The idea of a balanced economy occupied a central position in their minds. This point of view was particularly emphasized by those authors who were attached, at least temporarily, to the Austrian administration of Northern Italy at Milan. Practical experience gained in regulating economic life provided them with the material for testing the results of more or less abstract reasoning. Count Pietro Verri (1728-1797) and Marchese Cesare di Beccaria (1738-1794) were outstanding representatives of this group of authors.

In the didactic treatises of Verri and Beccaria, utilitarian considerations provided the starting point for all discussions of measures of economic policy. Verri's *Elementi del commercio* were published in 1760, and his *Meditazioni sull' economia politica* appeared in 1770. He incidentally introduced the element of "time" into his utilitarian discussions of pleasures and pains by pointing to expectations as the determinants of the exercise of self-interest. Beccaria wrote his *Elementi di economia pubblica* in 1769, but they were published only in 1804 in Custodi's collection. He owed his fame less to his contributions to economics, which were strongly influenced by Cantillon's Essay,[30] than to his elaboration of the utilitarian thesis. He was an outstanding advocate of the belief in the egotistic nature of man, and one of the first Utilitarians to advance the formula of the greatest happiness of the greatest number as the lodestar of true statesmanship.[31] His study *Dei delitti e delle pene* (1764) was of great importance for the development of criminology. Its success was due to the consistent application of utilitarian principles to the analysis of crimes and punishment.

The utilitarian motivation, which the Italian Mercantilists regarded as the rational principle of economic behavior, was supplemented in their analyses by the balance concept as a principal instrument for the coordination of economic factors. The idea of balance was basic to their price theories and also to the construction of their somewhat vaguely conceived models of the economy. In their price theories, they placed considerable emphasis on the equilibrium of supply and demand as a prerequisite to the establishment of competitive prices. Very characteristic were their attempts to suggest mathematical formulas for the definition of such prices. Verri, for example, proposed to express the price of a good in terms of the formula $v = \frac{c}{m}$ (value is equal to the number of the buyers divided by the number of sellers). The corresponding equation advanced by Genovesi was $v = \frac{r}{m}$ (value is equal to the demand—*recerca*—divided by the volume—*massa*—of consumable goods).

Genovesi expressed a view held by most contemporary Italian Mercantilists when he spoke of a general tendency of nature to establish equilibrium positions when left to pursue its own course. A virtually equal distribution of industry and money, he believed, would take place when the free movement of economic developments was not interfered with by artificial measures.[32] In another connection, Genovesi pointed to an analogy between the physical behavior of a liquid in a system of communicating tubes and the functioning of the body politic.[33] Genovesi's mechanistic conception of economic life was completely taken over by his disciple Fernando Galiani.[34]

Although Genovesi occasionally compared the spirit of commerce with the spirit of conquest, he definitely rejected the balance of trade concept and the policies connected with it. This view was shared by most other contemporary Italian economists. Verri analyzed the problems of the balance of payments as established for the "state" of Milan as if they were a mechanical proposition.[35]

Giammaria Ortes (1713-1790), author of the textbook *Della economia nazionale* (1774), derived strong arguments in favor of freedom of trade from the consideration that a balance was found to exist between the goods supplied by a country and those received by it.[36] The criticism of the balance of trade as an instrument of economic policy was elaborated by Count Giovanni Rinaldo Carli in 1770.[37] His treatise was especially designed to refute the protectionist policy which had been defended by Marchese Girolamo Belloni, who proposed foreign trade measures as a means of securing the inflow of the precious metals.[38]

As distinct from leading English Mercantilists, the Italian economists did not develop a fundamental value theory, but considered it sufficient to define exchange value in terms of general utility of the goods and scarcity. It may be mentioned, however, that Beccaria made the doubtful attempt to connect the origin of value (*valore*) with the idea of power, or the ability to fulfill an objective.

The monetary views of these authors were influenced by the traditional predilection of Italian economists for the idea of deriving the value of money from the commodity value of the monetary metals. Comprehensive studies of the origin and function of the means of payments were undertaken by Count Carli.[39] But the two English camps of conflicting monetary views had a counterpart in Italy. Ortes rejected the commodity theory of money. He considered the means of payment as nothing but instruments for facilitating the exchange of goods, and he attached a purely imaginary value to money and excluded it from the concept of wealth. His definition of money was reminiscent of Steuart's idea that money was a pledge assuring the future purchase of any desired and marketable good.

Closer analysis of the formation of prices caused Genovesi, Verri, Beccaria, and others to emphasize the influence of the velocity of circulation on the movement of prices and the ensuing behavior of business activity. Verri observed that increases in the velocity of circulation frequently coincided with expansions of the quantity of the circulating means of payment. Beccaria also proposed to use enhanced velocity of circulation as a standard for measuring the economic progress of a country. But Verri connected the stimulating effects of changes in the volume of money with a possible fall in prices, which he definitely favored as a means of promoting public welfare. Genovesi argued that price reductions brought about by the exportation of specie were likely, in the long run, to stimulate industry and commerce. Hence, new justifications were put forward to support the predilection of so many Mercantilists for cheapness of goods.

In their sociological discussions, the Italian Mercantilists combined the application of the balance principle with a search for "natural" proportions between demographic and economic factors. The idea of such a proportion was applied by Genovesi to the relation between the population of a territory and its natural resources. He suggested the concept of a *populazione giusta*, a kind of optimum population size adjusted to the economic capacities of its territory. In 1771, a contest was arranged in Mantua for the best treatise on the proper balance between the population and the commerce of a city and its territory. The prize was won by a Count d'Arco.

The Venetian Ortes envisaged the picture of a stable, well-balanced society in terms of a fixed relation between the population and the volume of goods available for consumption. His sociological considerations represented a bridge between Botero's and Cantillon's theories of population on the one hand and the Malthusian law on the other. As James Steuart had done a few years earlier, he showed that progressively lower yields resulted from equal expenditures of productive efforts when the utilization of land was extended to poorer soils, thus applying to agriculture the principle of decreasing returns.

In conclusion, the eighteenth-century Italian economists represented in many respects the most advanced type of refined mercantilist reasoning. They used the equilibrium concept to correlate the magnitudes included in their pictures of the economy, they examined the fundamental notions underlying their analysis, and they based their proposals of economic policy on utilitarian considerations, rejecting the policies derived from the balance of trade idea.

At least some of these authors derived the characteristic general background of their economic analysis from a philosophy of history which had its roots in the Renaissance; this philosophy had resisted the far-reaching changes in reasoning which had taken place since the beginning of the sixteenth century and centered as before on the belief that a given volume of power and wealth was continuously changing hands among the different nations in the course of time. Such a belief was alluded to in Genovesi's striking prediction that in times to come Italy might be transformed into a dependency of the American colonies.[40]

Chapter 6
Cameralist Economics

THE INTELLECTUAL BACKGROUND OF EARLY CAMERALISM

THE ATTENTION of the reader has repeatedly been drawn to the fact that the methods of nominalistic reasoning failed to gain acceptance in Central Europe. During the fifteenth century, when medieval Scholasticism lost its firm hold in that region, the opposition to the Catholic doctrines exhibited a significant preference for various forms of mysticism and was generally adverse to the great philosophical movements of the Italian Renaissance.[1]

When engaged in his first reformatory crusade, Martin Luther detested any philosophical speculations, and called reason a beast which should be kept under the bench. But the need for a logical foundation of the Protestant creed was clearly realized by Luther's friend and brother in arms, Philipp Melanchthon, whose predilection for Aristotelian logic prevailed over any other methodology. Thus, a hierarchical system of general notions was adopted by the German theologians who interpreted the religious and moral tenets of their doctrine. A corresponding organic conception of political communities as integrated wholes remained for a long time a characteristic feature of German political philosophies. "The genuine early Protestantism of Lutheranism and Calvinism claimed to regulate state and society, science and education, law, commerce and industry, according to the supernational standpoint of revelations and, exactly like the Middle Ages, everywhere subsumed under itself the *Lex Naturae* as being originally identical with the Law of God."[2]

The belief in a natural law of the type taught by the Scholastics probably contributed greatly to the "reception" of Roman law by the imperial courts of Germany in the sixteenth century. It was generally held that the Justinian digests—as interpreted by the Scholastic postglossators or commentators—were based on a system of juridical concepts which were derived from the principles of the *jus gentium*, of a law common to all nations. Hence, the jurists of the Holy Roman Empire regarded the decisions of the digests as a source of universally valid juridical reasoning, and considered themselves justified in applying deductive methods to the abstract statements of the Roman codifications.

Within this conceptual framework there was not much room for a discussion of such economic questions as were raised in England as early as the sixteenth century. On German soil moral considerations predominated in many economic discussions until the eighteenth century. As an exception, a group of not very significant pamphlets may be mentioned. Written about 1530, they turned on the question of whether a policy of currency depreciation should be adopted in the Saxon countries.[3] Advocates and adversaries of depreciation derived their arguments largely from the teachings of the Scholastic jurists, and agreed on the proposition that a country's wealth was to be identified with its possession of precious metals. The advocates of depreciation could hardly refute the reasoning of their adversaries that the alleged scarcity of money was inconsistent with the generally observed increase in the prices of all things. Recognition of the relations which existed between the movement of prices and the volume of the means of payment was a remarkable intellectual achievement for that time.

There is no doubt that the general spiritual development of the peoples of Central Europe was considerably slowed down by the devastating effects of the Thirty Years' War. But even after the hostilities had been concluded in 1648 by the Westphalian Treaty, Central Europe remained practically closed to the spread of nominalistic methods of thought. German scholars abstained from actively participating in the elaboration of the Newtonian atomistic theorems. It is equally noticeable that German students of the natural sciences remained convinced adherents of the rigid classification of substances established by the medieval alchemists. In the seventeenth century, when the use of freely circulating instruments of credit was rapidly expanding in the Netherlands, France, and England, the hopes of German princes to fill their treasuries still turned on the promise of "alchymists" to transform common metals into gold and silver. This promise was backed by the belief that the various metals differed from each other by varying degrees of purity and maturity of a fundamental substance, the Aristotelian "quintessence," and could, consequently, be transmuted into each other by appropriate procedures. Thus, leading Cameralists combined their economic studies with extensive alchemistic research. The German Cameralist, Johann Joachim Becher (1635-1682), who was for a time attached to the imperial court of Leopold I, published a considerable number of alchemist studies, among others a book entitled *Physica subterranea* (1669). His contemporary, Wilhelm von Schröder, appended to his cameralistic work *Furstliche Schatz - und Rent Kammer* (1686) a discussion of how to produce gold out of other metals.[4] A similar intellectual attitude was mirrored in various political writings which analyzed the foundation of the sovereign state in terms of a religious problem. Thus, Schröder derived his main arguments against the theory of the social contract from Biblical material,[5] and Becher used the doctrine of original sin to justify the subordination of subjects under the rule of the political authorities.[6]

Application of the natural law doctrine, as advocated by Samuel von Pufendorf, resulted in the formulation of sociological issues in terms of juridical problems. This was especially true of the theory of the contract of submission, which implied that the well-being of individuals could be realized only through the state.[7] Pufendorf was well aware of the logical difficulties involved in the problem of establishing a unified will by combining individual wills. He obviated this difficulty by subordinating the subjects to the will of their rulers.

To the limited extent that some attention was given to economic questions, their treatment reflected approximately the position of the seventeenth-century Scholastic authors. Thus, Pufendorf derived the intrinsic value of goods from the utility of the classes to which they belonged, and he connected the behavior of prices with the changing scarcity of goods and money. Moral arguments played a conspicuous role in his discussions of measures of economic policy, such as restrictions imposed on the importation of luxury goods, the regulation of monopolies, and the like. Like almost all Protestant jurists, Pufendorf was opposed to the prohibition of taking interest on money.

CAMERALISM AS AN ADMINISTRATIVE DISCIPLINE

In Central Europe, the treatment of economic questions during the sixteenth and part of the seventeenth century was practically monopolized by members of the fiscal administration, the "camera" of the princes. Their discussions centered on the means of increasing public revenues designed to finance the ever-expanding military and administrative machinery. Hence, the name *Cameralists*, which applied not only to this group of authors but also to all other German and Austrian writers who dealt with economic questions until the beginning of the nineteenth century.[8]

Melchior von Osse (d. 1557) and Georg Obrecht (d. 1612) may be mentioned as representatives of early cameralism. Albion W. Small has suggested the term *Fiscalists* to denote this group of officials.[9] In accordance with the political views which prevailed in the course of the sixteenth century, each German state was conceived of as an organic whole to be administered by its ruler in accordance with the principles of justice and statesmanship. Maintenance of a numerous and well-employed population was regarded as one of the main tasks of public administration, and planning of a not clearly defined type was to be applied to the regulation of economic activities, especially to the promotion of industry and trade. Hence, as early as the sixteenth century, effective measures of administrative policy were adopted by the princes of Saxony, Bavaria, and Württemberg and, with even greater consistency, by the rulers of Prussia and the Habsburg monarchs. In the course of these reforms, leading administrative positions, which previously had been occupied by feudal lords and high dignitaries of the church, were filled with full-time salaried officials taken from the ranks of the lower nobility or the commonalty. These officials were well trained in the law and public administration.

Thus, over time there developed more or less systematic collections of administrative devices grouped around fiscal themes. Examination of a broad range of economic and social questions served the purpose of establishing directives for a centralized administration of the various sectors of public and private activities. The cameralist conception of the economic aspects of a political community corresponded approximately to a picture of a "magnified family with a big farm as its property."[10] Application of mechanical principles to the analysis of economic questions was, of course, incompatible with the organismic conception of social collectivities adopted by the cameralists. Last, but not least, the rivalries among the European powers played a considerable role in the consideration of the Cameralists, and caused them to regard the expansion of exports as an important instrument of public policy.

Veit Ludwig von Seckendorff (1626–1692) was probably the first German author to propound a coordinated program of public administration, dealing with the promotion of industry and trade and measures designed to spread employment among a dense population.[11]

The merit of having initiated in Central Europe a broad approach to the discussion of economic questions goes to three authors mentioned previously in another connection. They are frequently called "Austrian Cameralists" because they were attracted to Vienna by the imperial court and spent considerable periods of their active lives in the emperor's service. They were Johann Joachim Becher, Philipp W. von Hornigk (1638–1712), and Wilhelm von Schröder.

Becher centered his recommendations on the objective of promoting the development of a large, gainfully occupied population, which he considered indispensable to the power of the state.[12] From the early English Mercantilists he took the balance of trade concept, but he ignored the mechanistic features of some of their leading propositions, and placed great emphasis on the Thomistic principle of self-sufficiency as an important condition for a country's economic well-being. He was convinced that buying from abroad brought inevitable damage. Equally characteristic of Becher's views was his adherence to the medieval principles of price fixing and of assuring to each individual a suitable subsistence in accordance with his occupation and position. He was a convinced advocate of the guild system, and showed the traditional mistrust of the activities of merchants and traders. As regards the organization of manufactures, he proposed a sort of regulated competition and directed his attacks against the three basic evils of "monopolium, polypolium, and propolium." *Monopolium* refers to monopoly, *polypolium* was Becher's term for uncontrolled competition, and *propolium* meant forestalling, or buying up goods in order to profit by enhanced price. These terms for undesirable types of trading were used in German textbooks of economics until the middle of the nineteenth century, especially by conservative authors opposed to the competitive exchange economy.

Interesting aspects of Becher's population theory were the emphasis which he placed on mass consumption as a condition of economic advancement and his reference to the income-producing functions of such expenditures. Joseph Schumpeter has suggested the use of the term *Becher's principle* to denote the establishment of causal relations between expenditures and the creation of income.[13]

Becher's main work appeared in 1667, under the title *Politische Discurs von den eigentlichen Ursachen des Auff - und Abnehmens der Städte, Länder und Republicken* [Political discourse on the real causes of growth and decline of cities, states, and republics]. Not only was Becher a notable expert for his time in finance and economics, but he was also a trained and ingenious chemist and alchemist, like many of his colleagues among the Cameralists. He has been credited with the first experimental production of lighting gas from coal, and he is the originator of the "phlogiston" theory, a theory based on specific measurable forces of heat, presumably contained in material bodies. This theory was further developed by others and played a role in the chemical literature for well over 150 years. In his later years, Becher turned away from the alchemist's dream of producing gold to fill the state's treasury, though he still believed it was technically possible. But, he said, nobody would make bread or shoes anymore if the manufacture of gold were realized.

Philipp W. von Hornigk, Becher's brother-in-law, defined the wealth and power of a country in terms of its relation to weaker and less powerful rivals. His book *Oesterreich über alles wann es nur will* (1684) was intended to describe the measures of economic policy which, when applied, would assure Austria's supremacy in the struggle of the European powers. Sixteen editions of this treatise were published up to the end of the eighteenth century.

Hornigk's reasoning started from the idea that economic self-sufficiency provided the key to a country's political strength. Of the nine chief rules of political economy which had to be observed in order to render Austria the most powerful state, four dealt with measures designed to increase the country's stock of precious metals and the other five with methods fit for securing self-sufficiency and independence of foreign manufactures. Only the most indispensable foreign goods, he believed, should be exchanged for surplus domestic products. Methods of promoting the exploitation of the country's natural resources, methods of training labor, the regulation of guilds, and the like were the main topics of Hornigk's discussions. His monetary concepts corresponded approximately to those of the English Bullionists. His price theory was based on the view held by some Italian authors that the money metals were in their worth and use equal to all commodities.

The third prominent Austrian Cameralist was Wilhelm von Schröder, who concentrated his proposals on the means of filling a ruler's treasury.[14] During a stay in England, he had adopted the leading ideas of the early Mercantilists, and he regarded the balance of trade as a bookkeeping device designed to show increases or declines of national wealth conceived as "ready means" (*bereitetes Vermögen*). Like Becher, he appreciated the income-forming effects of the circulation of money, but he qualified domestic trade as "simple commutation" and he thought cheapness of goods was the spirit of all trade. Among Schröder's proposals was the project of a bank owned by the country's ruler and designed to issue transferable bills of exchange against merchandise stored in public warehouses. The bank would be paid 6 percent on fiduciary money and would become the sovereign master of the country's productive assets.

The conception of national states as integrated wholes caused some cameralist authors of the seventeenth century to collect all the facts which they considered relevant for the purposes of administration and to publish comparative descriptive analyses of the geographical, political, economic, and cultural conditions of the European countries.[15] They were frequently regarded as precursors of the later discipline of administrative statistics, or *Staatenkunde* (science of states) as it came to be termed, which found one of its first proponents in Herman Conring.[16] Conring characterized his new discipline as *notitia rerum politicarum*, and his work became the pattern for a large number of followers. In accordance with a practice introduced by Gottfried Achenwall in the eighteenth century, the term *statistics* was applied to studies of this type. At various German universities, they became the object of more or less extensive lectures. But reasoning in terms of quantitative concepts played no significant role in these compilations of facts and figures; they served primarily political and administrative purposes.

CAMERALISM AS A BRANCH OF HIGHER LEARNING

A second stage in the development of cameralism started in the 1730s after chairs for the cameral sciences had been created at two Prussian universities, Halle and Frankfort on the Oder, in 1727.[17] The Prussian example was followed by other rulers of Central European states. Members of the academic profession took over the work of analyzing administrative practices and developing methods of economic policies, a work previously performed by government officials. But they tried to develop their teachings against a philosophical background in order to elevate their practical instructions to the rank of a dignified scientific discipline. That background was derived from the ideas of Gottfried Wilhelm Leibniz (1646–1716), as simplified and adjusted to more popular use by Christian von Wolff (1679–1754). Leibniz was the only remarkable German philosopher prior to the great upswing of German philosophy initiated by Immanuel Kant.

Leibniz's encyclopedic erudition enabled him to make outstanding contributions to many sciences, including mathematics, chemistry, mechanics, geognosy, and history, but he never developed a consistent philosophical doctrine, and his metaphysical and scientific teachings were scattered over many articles and essays.[18] His most important contribution to the theory of knowledge was a treatise entitled *Nouveaux essais sur l'entendement humain*. It was published in 1765 after the author's death and contained a critical analysis of Locke's *Treatise of Human Understanding*.

Strongly influenced by Descartes, Leibniz endorsed the Platonic view that fundamental general concepts, such as extension, form, and motion, are elements of pure understanding and can never be established completely by sense perceptions. He also followed Descartes in his belief that knowledge of truth can be derived by deductible methods from axiomatic principles taught by reason (truths of reason). Unlike Descartes, however, Leibniz did not claim certainty of and evidence for these truths, but only the logical characteristics of demonstrability. Truth was to be found in the objective relations among ideas and could be established only for the realms of mathematics and metaphysics. Leibniz challenged the students of ethics, jurisprudence, and natural theology to discover unchangeable, generally valid principles with the aid of "truths of reason."

Leibniz contrasted "truths of reason" with "truths of fact," which result from observation and experience and are arrived at by "intuitive certainty," and which could be made evident by the demonstration of causal relationships between the observed phenomena. The distinction which Leibniz drew between "self-evident" and "incidental" truths was elaborated on by later representatives of the German idealistic philosophies who regarded intuition as a reliable tool of absolutely valid knowledge.

In his "Monadology," Leibniz contributed another important principle to German epistemology. He objected to the conception of atoms as physical entities and indivisible bodies on the ground that such bodies having extension must be divisible. Hence, in opposition to the atom of mechanics, he suggested the concept of indivisible units of life; the "monads," which he characterized as "organisms," ranged in a continuous series from *dormientes* (unconscious) to *rationales* (self-conscious) units, and differentiated according to the confusion or distinctness of their perceptions. The relations among monads were determined in accordance with the idea of a preestablished harmony.

With great sagacity, Leibniz used the simile of two clocks keeping perfect time together to illustrate three different ways of explaining the organization of the universe. The Scholastics, he said, adopted the principle of mutual influence, according to which the parts are deprived of their independence. Descartes introduced the *deus ex machina*, who was supposed to interfere continuously with the movements of the universe. Finally, the idea of "preestablished harmony" implied the existence of laws regulating the behavior of the monads in such a way that all substances remained permanently in harmony with each other. Of the infinity of possible worlds, Leibniz believed God must undoubtedly have chosen the best, acting in accordance with the highest reason. The proposition that the course of all physical and spiritual events was determined by nonmaterial forces operating through monads prepared the way for the conception of political or social collectivities as organic monads of a superior order.

In his attempt to adjust Leibniz's philosophy to the requirements of the German schools of higher learning, Christian Wolff proposed a somewhat rigid pattern for the organization of the social sciences and their methodology. Disregarding "mathematical knowledge" based on quantitative relationships, he centered his scheme on the juxtaposition of philosophy and history. Absolutely valid knowledge, or "truths of reason," could be based only on fundamental, self-evident concepts. Empirical or historical knowledge should serve the purpose of ascertaining the truth by the deductive method. In accordance with this classification, every science was divided into two parts: one, the philosophical, was supposed to supply the conceptual and explanatory exposition; the other, empirical, part was required to provide the facts for verifying and amplifying the knowledge gained by deductive reasoning. As a priori sciences, ethics, politics, and economics were qualified as branches of philosophy and natural law. Technology and administrative practice were regarded as the corresponding empirical disciplines.

In his *Grundsätz des Natur- und Völkerrechts* (1754), Wolff recommended the "Euclidean" method of establishing ultimate truth in the political sciences. His political ideal was a monarch, vested with absolute political power, but enlightened—like King Frederic II of Prussia—and ruling in accordance with the principles of sound reason.

Research and teachings at practically all universities of the German states and Austria were adjusted to these methodological principles. The learned men who occupied the chairs of cameralist disciplines at these institutions in the course of the eighteenth century centered their literary activity on the preparation of textbooks for use by students and government officials. In the introductory chapters of these books, they propounded the current principles of moral and political philosophy and classified and defined the general concepts used in that analysis. However, they were not particularly concerned about connecting these principles with the main body of their practical instructions, which they commonly divided into three parts: public administration or police, economic policy, and public finance.[19] In view of the predominantly practical purposes of the textbooks, their authors felt no incentive to deal with the theoretical analysis of social or economic problems; they placed main emphasis upon discussing the administrative and economic policies of a welfare state, and they presented these policies as derivatives of the truths of reason.

Refined cameralism achieved its highest perfection in the textbooks of Johann Heinrich Gottlob von Justi (1705–1771) and Joseph von Sonnenfels (1732–1817).[20] Justi was appointed in 1750 to the first chair of cameral sciences established at the "Theresianum" in Vienna, an academy for the education of the nobility. The chair of police and cameral sciences founded in 1763 at the University of Vienna was occupied by Sonnenfels, who also served the imperial court as an adviser on questions of public administration and economic policy. The teachings of both Justi and Sonnenfels were obviously influenced by the ideas propagated by some advanced Mercantilists, as adjusted to the traditional tasks of the eighteenth-century welfare state. They provided directives for at least two generations of Central European economists and public officials.

Justi construed the state in accordance with the principles of Leibniz's monadology as an integrated organism embracing the sovereign power and the people.[21] In order to account for the integration, he resorted to a transcendent will formed by the fusion of the individual wills. "The merging of many wills into a single will," he stated, "is the first moral ground of republics." He used the term *republic* to denote political communities of the welfare state type. Although he referred to the social contract in deriving the principal power of the state from the people, he considered the rulers responsible only to God and not to the people. "Common best" and "common happiness" were, in his view, not categories of a utilitarian philosophy but concepts taught by natural law. The natural law doctrine also provided the source for his idea of "freedom," which implied observance of the laws of the state as interpreted by the officials of the public administration.

His conception of the welfare state caused Justi to identify the wealth of a country with a sufficient supply of goods to satisfy the needs and conveniences of the citizens' lives. However, true to the mercantilist tradition, he regarded possession of a sufficient quantity of precious metals as prerequisite to a country's prosperity, and he elaborated on this idea in his comprehensive textbook *Natur und Wesen der Staaten als die Grundwissenschaft der Staatskunst, der Polizei und aller Regierungswissenschaften* (1760). As distinct from the contemporary English Mercantilists, he held the government ultimately responsible for the coordination of all economic activities and for the promotion of the harmonious expansion of all lines of such activity. Thus, he endeavored to provide the public administration with carefully devised directives for the implementation of agricultural, industrial, and commercial policies. He objected to the traditional, far-reaching use of price fixing—though not as a general advocate of the principle of free competition—and recommended encouragement of the manufacturing industries as a counterweight to the monopolistic practices of the guild system. In his discussion of foreign trade policies, Justi did not question the principle of protectionism, but as a general commercial policy he favored an import tariff of moderate proportions.

The principles of cameralistic economic policy were reflected in an Austrian decree of 1763 which provided for the establishment of annual industrial operation plans covering the entire monarchy.[22] The equilibrium concept was referred to for determining the relation between the manufactures regulated under the guild system (*Polizeigewerbe*) and the "commercial" commodity trades. The latter trades were to be distributed among the various provinces: the several branches of the textile industry (linen, woolen, and cotton manufactures) were distributed over Upper and Lower Austria, Bohemia, Moravia, and Silesia; the iron and steel industry was to be promoted especially in Styria and Carinthia; and production of silken goods was to be developed in Gorizia, Gradisca, and especially in Vienna, which, in addition, was to be made the seat of paper, leather, and apparel manufactures. The cameralist pattern of the territorial distribution of industries played a determinant role in the subsequent economic development of the monarchy and was, to a significant degree, carried over into the nation states which were carved out of the Austrian territory after the end of World War I.

The writings of Sonnenfels, like those of Justi, were designed to secure some theoretical background for the extensive discussions of economic policies adjusted to the objectives of the eighteenth-century welfare state. This was true above all of the *Grundsätze der Polizey, Handlung und Finanz* (1765), which, until the late nineteenth century, remained the standard textbook of public administration and political economy at the Austrian universities.

Sonnenfels showed less predilection than Justi for the doctrine of natural law; he borrowed from Jean Jacques Rousseau's social philosophy the concept of an "aggregate will," which he used to rationalize the ideas of "unity of purpose" and "common best." Thus, he was inclined to resort to methods of intuitive reasoning to justify the measures of administrative policy he proposed.

More individualistic than Justi, Sonnenfels argued that the welfare of the whole depended upon the welfare of the parts. The largest possible gainfully occupied population was the goal to be attained by appropriate administrative measures in the fields of agriculture, industry, trade, and public finance. Sonnenfels acknowledged his indebtedness to some French authors, such as François Veron de Forbonnais, who had taken over the ideas of various leading English Mercantilists. Thus, he was convinced that the balance of power of the European states was determined by the balance of their commercial relations. But as an instrument for measuring economic progress, he preferred the "balance of industry" principle to the traditional balance of trade idea.

Baconian principles of analysis do not appear to have perceptibly influenced the reasoning of the Austrian Cameralists or those of other Central European authors of the seventeenth and eighteenth centuries. Moreover, the conception of an economy in need of extensive administrative supervision and regulation remained deeply rooted in the minds of many Central European teachers of economics throughout the nineteenth century.

Chapter 7
Cartesian Economics

———

THE REACTION TO COLBERTISM IN FRANCE

AT THE BEGINNING of the eighteenth century it became increasingly evident that the commercial and financial policies pursued by Colbert and his successors had failed to assure general prosperity and the welfare of the French population. The public finances, in particular, were in a state of desperate disorganization. Critical minds began to question the wisdom of an economic policy that concentrated its efforts upon the promotion of exports, neglected agriculture, and spread misery among the peasant population.

One of the outstanding critics of the fiscal policies pursued under Louis XIV was Marshal Sébastien Le Prestre, Marquis de Vauban (1633–1707), who occupied a prominent position in the French military administration and extended his literary activity far beyond his professional sphere. In his main economic treatise, *Projet d'une dixme royale* (1707), Vauban submitted to the king a program of radical tax reform; as indicated in the title of his book, he recommended the introduction of a 10 percent income tax as the main device for alleviating the intolerable burden placed on the peasants by the prevailing fiscal policy. His contributions to the problems of taxation have been regarded as a remarkable achievement, since he fully realized the influence exercised by methods of taxation on different elements of the economy, and, in addition, endeavored to use facts and figures to substantiate and justify his recommendations.[1] But his general economic views, which turned on the promotion of national self-sufficiency and striving for a favorable balance of trade, did not differ perceptibly from those underlying the policy of Colbertism.

The ideas advanced by Pierre Le Pesant de Boisguillebert (1646–1714), who occupied important positions in the provincial administration of the kingdom, were far more independent of traditional French thinking. In various treatises he drew the attention of the leading authorities to the decline in wealth and to the misery of the agricultural population.[2] Starting from an organic conception of the state, he compared the various classes of the population with parts of the human body, emphasizing the fundamental importance of agricultural production and objecting to the identification of wealth with the possession of gold and silver. He connected the concept of wealth (*richesse*) with the enjoyment of want satisfaction, and called land and labor the sources of wealth. He was aware of the interdependence of economic factors and especially of the role played by consumption as a prerequisite of productive activity. Among Boisguillebert's notable contributions to the economic philosophy of his time was a theoretical consideration concerning the influence exercised upon consumption expenditures by the velocity of circulation and the use of bills of exchange.

Contrasting the rich and poor classes of the population, Boisguillebert accused the former of misusing their economic power and damaging the economy by hoarding money. Hence, in order to enhance expenditures on consumption goods, he charged the government with the task of redistributing incomes in favor of the poorer classes. He also showed his opposition to the prevailing policies by recommending free importation of grains as a measure deigned to increase and stabilize the prices of these commodities. He supplemented this proposal with a plea for a more liberal trade policy, and he used the phrase "*Pourvu qu'on laisse faire la nature*" to support the idea that liberty was a principle taught by nature. In his theoretical considerations he derived the value of money exclusively from its functions as a means of exchange, and he characterized the monetary unit as a pledge or security enabling its possessor to count upon the future delivery of the goods he would like to have. But although Boisguillebert has earned an honorable place in the history of economic reasoning and was highly praised by Eugene Daire and other students of the history of French eighteenth-century economics, his influence on later economic reasoning does not seem to have been considerable.

The attacks directed against the economic policy of Colbertism multiplied during the first decades of the eighteenth century. They turned on the high import duties, the monopolies granted to overseas companies, and the traditional system of guild control which stifled the development of manufacturing industries. Some French writers, like Boisguillebert, endorsed the liberal ideas advanced by various British Mercantilists. John Law's views, in particular, gained some support. The widespread belief in the stimulating effects of the issuance of fiduciary money was not significantly affected by the financial crisis which followed upon the collapse in 1720 of John Law's Mississippi scheme. The price system was apparently not deeply affected by the issuance of large volumes of paper money.[3]

An outstanding adherent of John Law's monetary principles was Jean François Melon, whose treatise on commerce, *Essai politique sur le commerce* (1734), was widely acclaimed by French public opinion as an attempt to adjust certain teachings of the English Mercantilists to the contemporary French social philosophy.[4] He applied the balance of trade principle to his treatment of foreign trade and discussed a considerable range of measures designed to secure export surpluses. He supplemented his defense of John Law's monetary policy and its application by the French government with the proposal to devalue the currency as a device of liquidating public debts. Among the French authors who highly appreciated the treatise were Voltaire (1694–1778), Denis Diderot (1713–1784), and particularly Charles de Montesquieu (1689–1755), whose economic views followed pretty closely those of Melon's analysis. Melon's belief in the validity of the balance of trade doctrine was shared by Charles Dutot, who, like Melon, was a partisan of Law's financial ideas.[5] He was convinced that credit expansion was a primary means of stimulating business activity.

About 1940 a comprehensive French treatise on methods of mercantilist policies written in 1722–23 was rediscovered in Paris and attributed to Ernst Ludwig Carl, councillor of the princes of Brandenburg.[6] Probably influenced by the Cartesian philosophy, the author of the treatise started with the distinction between an "*ordre naturel*" and an "*ordre positif*"; he referred to the social contract and charged the enlightened prince with the tasks of establishing a certain equilibrium between the various sectors of the economy and regulating the economic activities of the population. A remarkable understanding of the interdependence of economic activities and of the role played by prices in the functioning of the economy was a characteristic feature of this study; however, it appears to have been completely ignored until its belated rediscovery.

In discussions of European power politics, the balance of trade concept was given additional importance through its use as an instrument for measuring gains in economic power and influence. In the French literature, this aspect of foreign trade was especially emphasized by François Veron de Forbonnais (1722–1800), a very successful author.[7] He asserted that a country's balance of trade was indicative of the increase of its "conventional riches," and he showed the effects of that increase on the growth of production and population. As was done by the Italian economists, he also applied the idea of a balance to a ratio between these two factors and recommended appropriate measures to attain that balance through extensive regulation of industry and trade.

The intensified participation of public officials and businessmen in the treatment of economic questions was reflected in the publication of special periodicals dealing with economic affairs. The *Journal oeconomique*, founded in 1758, was remarkable for the relatively high level of its articles. It took account of foreign, especially English, economic literature. The *Gazette du Commerce* was founded in 1763. The *Journal d'agriculture, du commerce et des finances*, which originated in 1764, was later taken over by the physiocrats.

Characteristic of the general trend of public opinion expressed in these publications was an increasing movement in favor of freedom from the traditional administrative regulation of industry and trade. An outstanding protagonist of this movement was Jacques Vincent de Gournay (1712–1759), a successful wholesale dealer and intendant of commerce, who has been credited with having coined the axiom of economic liberalism when he exclaimed: "*laissez faire, laissez passer, le monde va de lui-même.*"[8] Gournay was convinced that private interests would coincide with the public interest if domestic trade were freed from government interference and free competition were established for the manufacturing industries.[9] But he did not advocate free trading for foreign commerce.

The ideas of economic liberalism were, however, quite clearly proclaimed in a letter written in 1751 to the editor of the *Journal oeconomique* and ascribed to René Louis de Voyer, Marquis d'Argenson (1694–1757), a rich grandseigneur who repeatedly occupied posts in the French administration and was minister of foreign affairs under Louis XV between 1744 and 1747.[10] The letter was designed to refute the strong protectionist views expressed in the treatise *Del commercio* by the Italian banker Girolamo Belloni.[11] D'Argenson's criticisms of these views climaxed in a virtual plea for the establishment of a common market for all European countries. He requested as much freedom for the transfer of commodities from one country to the other as was given to air and water. Future generations, he believed, would laugh when they remembered the ill-fated attempts to apply a system of "commercial principles" and would consider the importance attributed to the idea of the European balance of power as a sign of sickness. Such far-flung ideas were published in one of the most distinguished French economic journals about the middle of the eighteenth century.

CONFLICTING SOCIAL PHILOSOPHIES IN FRANCE

The arguments advanced in favor of specific economic policies were supported either by reference to "self-evident" principles or by appeals to practical experience. Problems connected with the struggle over methods of reasoning played only a subordinate role in these discussions.

Simultaneously, however, prolonged fights were waged among the leading intellectual movements over conflicting patterns of thought, and logical issues loomed large in the heated discussions of metaphysical, religious, political, and social problems. These controversies split the French educated classes into a number of antagonistic camps and prepared the way for the events which eventually led to the French Revolution. At least six different patterns of thought can be distinguished in this turbulent picture. They can conveniently be distinguished from each other by the different roles they assigned to reason in establishing the principles of a social order.

Conservative authors availed themselves of the results of historical experience in their attempts to set up general principles of social organization. With this end in view, they tried to develop new methods of collecting and comparing data dealing with social institutions and their functioning.

Outspokenly critical of the existing organization of society, especially of the restrictions imposed on personal freedoms, were the followers of the English sensualist philosophers, who attributed to reason the subordinate task of adjusting means to the ends prescribed by the will.

These authors met with the opposition of large groups of others who firmly believed in the power of reason to teach the principles of a "natural" order of society. But the definition of this order varied widely among at least three different schools of thought as professed by the Cartesians, the adherents of the philosophy of "Enlightenment," and the partisans of other natural law doctrines. The Cartesian conception of the "natural" order will be discussed in connection with the analysis of the physiocratic teachings. The ideas of the "Enlightenment" were initiated and propagated mainly by the "Encyclopedists," who used a poorly defined concept of "reason" as an instrument for teaching the truth, and substituted an ill-defined concept of "nature" as a creative and organizing power for the Christian conception of a personal God. They attributed to the principles of mechanics the widest possible range of application and thus introduced a "mechanistic mythology," as contrasted with the "animistic mythology" of past centuries.[12] But the maxims of the natural law which they proclaimed could still be reconciled with moderate proposals of social reform. Other far more radical groups used certain doctrines of natural law, alleged to be self-evident, to justify utopian schemes of communist societies.

Finally, some violent opponents of the institution of private property and the existing social order rejected the use of the available logical procedures, appealed to sentiments, and resorted to arbitrary intuitive concepts from which they derived their proposals of radical reforms.

Each of these different approaches to social analysis had at least one outstanding representative, who pressed the stamp of his personality on his theories and exercised a more or less lasting influence on the development of political thought.

One of the most famous eighteenth-century authors, Charles L. de Montesquieu (1689–1755), set out to examine, as Bodin had done before him, the various political communities in their historical settings.[13] He emphasized the differences in the character of the nations, brought about by divergent religions, morals, and customs, and the influence exercised upon social institutions by the physical environment, the soil, the climate, and the like. In his discussion of the policies pursued by political communities he pointed out the general objectives of all legislation on the one hand, and the divergencies which resulted from the varying structures, the peculiar ambitions, and the different "spirits" of the various peoples, on the other. Thus, he initiated a new method of historical research designed to permit the establishment of empirical generalizations, or "laws of nature," underlying the origin and functioning of social communities. He defined these laws as the expression of the "necessary relations" resulting from the nature of things. However, he did not draw a clear distinction between causal laws governing the course of events independently of the human will and normative precepts, valid in the intellectual sphere but susceptible to infringement.[14]

In his attempts to arrive at such generalizations, Montesquieu made ample use of the equilibrium concept, which he applied to the relation between human propagation and the available means of subsistence. This concept, colored by a normative tinge, also provided the logical basis for his famous doctrine of the separation of powers and for his system of political checks and balances. He made effective use of these ideas in interpreting the functioning of the English political machinery.

Montesquieu dealt with economic questions mainly in the course of his discussion of the size of public revenues and the levying of taxes, as connected with the characteristics of the various forms of political organization. In his treatment of commercial and monetary issues, he was mainly interested in the adjustment of legislative measures to the specific economic conditions of the various countries. He accepted John Locke's views about the imaginary value of the means of payment and the prevailing quantitative price theory, according to which the total volume of money in circulation was equal to the total amount of the value of goods in commerce, while the individual prices were determined by an additional, not clearly defined, mathematical operation. He shared the widespread aversion to large monopolistic business enterprises and recommended freedom of international trade mainly as a means of promoting peace.

Far less conservative than Montesquieu in their treatment of social problems were the French adherents of the English sensualist philosophers, since they placed particular emphasis on the exercise of individual freedom, especially in the spheres of religious convictions and private life. They also spread the views of the English Deists, who derived their belief in a personal god from the Newtonian creator of a mechanical universe, running its course like clockwork, independently of any supernatural interference. An outstanding representative of this line of thought was Voltaire (1694–1778), who defended Newton's philosophy against Cartesian attacks and greatly contributed toward popularizing the mechanical explanation of the behavior of the stellar world. Voltaire was also highly successful in adjusting Locke's empirical foundation of knowledge to the French intellectual atmosphere.[15] In his elegant style, he explained Locke's views about sensations as the source of all concepts, about the more or less mechanical aspects of the thinking process, and about the right of the individual to personal freedom. He used his brilliant satire to ridicule traditional institutions, and he violently attacked religious persecution and other methods of compulsion.

However, Etienne Bonnot, Abbé de Condillac (1715–1780) was far more consistent than Voltaire in interpreting Locke's empiricism. He was convinced that the real inherent qualities of things were forever hidden from human knowledge.[16] Consequently, he rejected the Cartesian belief in innate ideas, and attributed to reason only the faculty of transforming sense perceptions into abstract concepts in accordance with the rules underlying the functioning of the human mind. He employed his methodological principles when discussing economic questions.[17] Another follower of the English philosophers was Claude Adrien Helvétius, who developed a system of education which was designed to adjust selfish behavior to the interests of society.[18]

The "Encyclopedists" were in the forefront of the fight against Scholastic reasoning. They pinned their faith on the operation of "natural" forces underlying the alleged harmony of the universe. They claimed that the functioning of the universe could be fully explained in terms of mechanical principles and undertook to spread the results of knowledge and experience gained in science and industry. They were the most active protagonists of the spirit of the "Enlightenment," a movement intended to revolutionize the prevailing conception of the universe and to displace the clerical authorities from the dominant position which they occupied in the intellectual life of the nation. Their materialistic philosophy caused them to reject the belief that supernatural intervention was needed for the salvation of mankind. In place of this belief the Encyclopedists put the idea of indefinite progress to be achieved on earth by continuously increased understanding of nature and by steadily improved control of the environment and improved adjustment of human behavior to the order prescribed by nature. But they did not succeed in giving a clear definition of their concept of "nature."

The first volume of the *Encyclopédie* was published in 1751. The editors were Jean d'Alembert and Denis Diderot, who assigned a prominent role to reason as an instrument for demonstrating the fallacies which had been basic to metaphysical and religious doctrines. There was a strange contrast between their "rationalist" philosophy and the skeptical attitude toward reason displayed about the same time in England by David Hume and his followers. But not all contributors to the *Encyclopédie* shared the extreme views of the editors; different shades of mechanistic philosophies were represented in the articles of this work.

The attacks of the radical reformers who appealed to the principles of a normative "natural law" were especially directed against the institution of private property. Thus, Morelly made the "desire to possess" (*le désir d'avoir pour soi*) responsible for all evils created by selfishness and outlined the organization of an ideal communist society in which the distribution of goods and individual behavior were rigidly regulated.[19]

Gabriel Bonnet, Abbé de Mably (1709-1785), a brother of the philosopher Condillac, was another advocate of a communistic economic order.[20] An even more radical social philosophy was propagated at the threshold of the French revolution by the Girondist Jacques Pierre Brissot de Warville, who coined the phrase that "property is theft."[21]

The idea that all evils which had befallen mankind were due to the corruptive influence of social institutions was most violently emphasized by Jean Jacques Rousseau (1712-1778).[22] The methodology adopted by Rousseau provides a striking example of the use of intuitive concepts in order to justify a radical analysis of social relationships. Adherence to the theory of the social contract did not prevent him from denying the capacity of reason to supply the principles for a sound organization of society. Instead, he asserted his belief in the original perfection of human "nature," in its unadulterated sentiments, and in its creative energy. From this belief he derived questionable, but highly popular, arguments for the right of individuals to freedom, equality, and revolution against the authorities and for the principle of the indivisible sovereignty of the "general will" (*la volonté générale*) of the people.

The intuitive aspects of the premises and postulates established by Rousseau were reflected in widely varying interpretations of virtually all his leading conceptions and principles:[23] his notions of reason and individual conscience, natural law, general will, and sovereignty. Equally ambiguous were his definitions of the "state of nature," of society, and of the relations of individuals to the political community. Since Rousseau virtually identified the decisions of the majority with the "general will," he obliged the minority to accept these decisions as binding and thus established the principles of effective democratic procedures. With his antirationalist attitudes, he anticipated important aspects of the Romantic movement. Finally, Rousseau's political phraseology enabled the leaders of "totalitarian democracies" to derive their claims for the exercise of autocratic powers from the "general will" of their nations. Thus, his ideas lent themselves to varying interpretations and were used over time as instruments for promoting widely divergent political developments.

In this chaotic picture of conflicting methods of reasoning, the Cartesian philosophy provided a rallying point for more conservative minds; it suggested a well-organized and clearly defined approach to the analysis of physical and social phenomena in terms of universally applicable principles. The Physiocratic doctrine was an outstanding achievement as an attempt to establish a generally valid system of social relationships in accordance with Cartesian philosophy. Since Descartes assigned to mathematical methods the highest rank among scientific procedures, the Physiocratic doctrine was dominated by the ambitious aim to develop a mathematically defined picture of the economy conceived as a composite of magnitudes reduced to a common denominator. This conception was connected with the outline of a social order backed by the principles of a natural law. The doctrine of the Physiocrats was thus the first attempt to devise a consistent model of an imaginary economy. As combined with a remarkable social philosophy, it became a landmark in the history of Western reasoning.

THE PHILOSOPHICAL BACKGROUND OF QUESNAY'S THEORIES

The Physiocratic teachings were initiated about the middle of the eighteenth century by François Quesnay (1694–1774), physician at the court of Louis XV. The term *physiocracy* points to the metaphysical foundations of Quesnay's ideas, to his intention to establish the principles of a "government by nature." Pierre Samuel Du Pont de Nemours, one of the main protagonists of these ideas, coined the term in 1767.

In the light of a history of economic reasoning, primary importance attaches to the methods which Quesnay used in his analysis of the French economy. He outlined his logical principles in several articles which he contributed to the *Encyclopédie*,[24] and referred quite clearly to the teachings of Nicolas de Malebranche (1638–1715) as the main source of his methodology.[25] Malebranche was a disciple of Descartes, but in his work *De la recherche de la vérité* (1675) he modified the Cartesian philosophy by combining it with some features of Augustinian Neoplatonism. According to his epistemology, true knowledge could be derived only from the cognizance of ideas existing in reality in the mind of the Creator, whose concept of an ideal universe has been materialized in the actual world, though in an imperfect form. Malebranche attributed to the human mind the faculty of grasping this ideal conception through a form of intuition. Convinced of these logical principles, he rejected the application of the Aristotelian methods to theology, ethics, and cosmology. In the article "Evidence," which he contributed in 1754 to the *Encyclopédie*, Quesnay, like Malebranche, asserted a firm belief in the faculty of reason to discover the truth with the aid of an active psychological factor which he called "attention." He ascribed to the sensations the function of providing the motives of reasoning and of the will to decide.[26] Like Malebranche, he minimized the active functions of the cognitive power; he defined the latter as the light (*lumière*) which illuminates the way to be followed, and attributed to "evidence" a certainty which, he believed, it was as impossible to deny as it was impossible to ignore actual sensations.[27]

The search for God's objectives and activities in nature caused Quesnay to look for a mechanism which, when given freedom of action, could be shown to lead to the achievements of these objectives. Following Malebranche, he distinguished the *ordre naturel*—the rules of moral behavior—from the *ordre de la nature*—the laws underlying the physical world and operating independently of any interference on the part of man.[28] Like Malebranche, he included human instinct among the elements of physical nature; he made infringements of the will upon reason responsible for erroneous judgments and regarded such judgments as the primary cause of immorality. Moral disorder, he asserted in his article "Evidence," was always accompanied by disorderly thinking. Hence, he was convinced that the adoption of the ideal moral standards could be assured by proper education.

Thus, Quesnay's economic research centered upon elaborating the picture of a society to be organized in accordance with the laws most advantageous for mankind. The belief in the existence of such "natural" laws was well expressed in Quesnay's maxim *"Ex natura jus, ordo et leges, ex homine arbitrium, regimen et coercitio."* Coercion and arbitrary rulings, he declared, were bound to prevail in the societies in which the laws issued by the authorities—the *ordre positif*—did not conform to the rules prescribed by the normative "natural order" (*ordre naturel*) and held to be forever valid, unchangeable, the best possible.[29] Quesnay asserted that these rules imposed themselves upon human reasoning with a precision which demonstrated itself "geometrically and arithmetically" in all details and "did not leave any loopholes to error, imposture or illicit pretension." From the Cartesian philosophy he derived the conviction that the highest degree of evidence could be claimed for laws expressed mathematically in quantitative terms.

This conviction was reflected in the mathematical character of the scheme of income distribution which he elaborated in the *Tableau économique*. On the other hand, Quesnay's idea of regarding the entire *produit net* as a free gift of nature can perhaps be shown to have been influenced by Malebranche's "occasionalist" cosmology, according to which material bodies, constituent elements of the universe, were conceived as passive agents, unfit to originate movement and only able to transmit movement among each other. All movements had to be produced by a divine force operating from outside the universe. A similar approach to economic analysis appears to have caused Quesnay to declare that the values which represented wealth and were the object of the distributive process could not be produced by human activity but were a free gift of nature brought from outside into the economy and consumed through the distributive process in the course of the period of production. The transmission of exchange values described in the *Tableau économique* showed a remarkable parallelism with the transmission of movements through inert bodies in the cosmology of Malebranche.

THE *TABLEAU ÉCONOMIQUE*

About the middle of the eighteenth century, agricultural production was still the main source of the French national income. Of a total population of about 25 million, nearly nine-tenths drew their livelihood from agriculture. But the number of landowners was small, about 500,000, and about one-fifth of the land was owned by the church. The system of crop sharing (*métayage*) was a common form of cultivating the soil.

It is thus easy to understand that the taxes levied on the agricultural population supplied the backbone of the public revenues, while the nobility and the clergy enjoyed the privilege of tax exemption. Most oppressive was the *taille*, assessed and allocated by the *fermiers généraux* in accordance with agreements made with the treasury. An object of much hatred was the *corvée royale*, the obligation of peasants to perform personal labor, usually by work on public roads.[30]

Quesnay's economic research was primarily motivated by the intention to show the fundamental errors underlying the policy of Colbertism, which had neglected agriculture and burdened the peasants with an intolerable load of taxation. He set out to demonstrate that agriculture was the only real source of national wealth, and found a philosophical support for that view in his proposition that the creation of wealth was exclusively due to the divine power of nature.

The famous *Tableau économique*, published in 1758, supplied the foundations for the doctrine of the Physiocrats. It was the graphic presentation of a process designed to show how the exchange values supplied by nature and incorporated in the products of the soil were distributed in the course of a period of production among the main classes of the population. The yields of agricultural production provided the elements of the distributive process. The *Tableau* was supplemented by explanatory observations and by a treatise entitled *Maximes générales du gouvernement économique d' un royaume agricole* (1758), an outline of the principles to be observed by the government of an agricultural country.

In pursuance of the task which he had set himself, Quesnay applied the principles of Cartesian reasoning to the elaboration of an economic science "as constant in its principles and as susceptible of demonstration as the most certain physical sciences."[31]

The *Tableau* contained three columns, each showing a succession of shares in the national dividend for one of the main classes of the population distinguished by Quesnay. These classes were the productive class, comprising the peasants and tenant farmers; the landowners; and the sterile classes, such as manufacturers, traders, professionals, or servants. The strategic position which Quesnay assigned to the landowners in the distributive process was supported by the inclusion of ownership of the soil among the "natural rights."[32]

Five principles were basic to the structure of the *Tableau*: (*a*) that the productive class doubled the exchange value of its costs of production; (*b*) that the surplus was surrendered to the landowners as a reward for the original advances made in preparing the soil for cultivation; (*c*) that the part of the *produit net* which the *Tableau* allotted to the manufacturers and traders was the exact equivalent of the manufactured commodities supplied by them to the tenant farmers and the landowners, since the sterile classes were considered unable to produce values in excess of those which they received for purposes of consumption and manufacturing; (*d*) that each class divided its expenditures equally between agricultural and manufactured commodities; and finally (*e*) that after the termination of the distributive process each class was again equipped with the same volume of values which it had owned at the beginning of the period of production.

As formulated by Quesnay, the problem, illustrated by the graphic presentation of the *Tableau*, focused on the distribution of an annual national dividend of five billion livres among the three classes. The farmers, who start with a fund of two billion, reap four billion, of which two billion represent the *produit net*. They keep two billion in order to cover their own expenditures for productive and consumptive purposes and pay the *produit net* to the landowners. One billion is in the hands of the sterile classes in the form of goods manufactured in the preceding period.

The distributive process starts with the landowners, who return one billion to the farmers in exchange for agricultural commodities and pay another billion to the sterile classes in exchange for their products. The farmers double the value of the billion which they had received, surrender one billion as rent to the landowners, and divide the other billion equally between expenditures for their own products and purchases from the sterile class. The expenditures of the sterile classes are similarly divided between manufactured goods and agricultural products.

This method of distributing the progressively diminishing *produit net* is continued until, upon the termination of the entire process, all surplus values have been absorbed and equally distributed among the three classes of the population. The annual repetition of this essentially static process is made dependent upon the recurrent supply of the *produit net* as a free gift of nature introduced from the outside into the economy. A growth of the national wealth is expected to result only from increased investments applied to agricultural production.

Quesnay and his adherents did not admit any doubt about the absolute validity of this mathematical scheme. He explicitly insisted that the total amount of revenues should enter the annual circulation and run through its entire extension. The marquis de Mirabeau, one of Quesnay's most faithful disciples, characterized the process described in the *Tableau* as a circulation which was determined by exact rules of flux and reflux preventing the exhaustion of the channels as well as their obstruction.[33] Any deviation from the assumed exchange relations was held to lead to declines in income and wealth. Among possible obstacles to the proper functioning of the distributive process, Quesnay listed bad methods of taxation, excessive luxury, and interference with the trade in raw materials.

Expressed in economic terms, Quesnay's fundamental proposition meant that every year the farming population reaped a volume of values in excess of the costs of production including wages. The existence of such surplus values derived from cultivating the soil appeared to be demonstrated by the fact that the tenant farmers were able to surrender annually a portion of their crops to the proprietors of the soil.

Hence, the starting point of Quesnay's analysis was, in fact, a concept of physical productivity. The *produit net* was originally a physical magnitude, the excess of grain or other agricultural commodities over and above the quantities of seeds and other factors used up in the productive process. But in order to reduce to a common denominator all the magnitudes to be included in his distributive scheme, Quesnay needed a unit of value as a basis for a network of transactions in which equal values were exchanged against each other. Without being aware of the intricate relation which might exist between physical productivity and productivity of exchange values, he shifted his considerations from one to the other and formulated his scheme in terms of a monetary unit, the French *livre*.

Quesnay distinguished exchange values (*valeurs vénales*), which he virtually identified with prices, from value in use (*valeur usuelle*), which he connected, according to Scholastic principles, with the usefulness of the various classes of goods. He assigned the highest rank in this scale of valuation to agricultural products, the free gifts of nature. However, no common standard of values could be derived from the use value of goods since, as Quesnay observed, most useful things were frequently almost valueless.[34] He defined wealth as the sum total of the goods which are continuously reproduced, continuously in demand, and continuously purchased, and consequently assigned a subordinate role to the precious metals, and regarded them as nothing but instruments for facilitating the exchange of goods. He defined the monetary unit, the livre, as a common measure of all exchange values, and as a uniform, stable standard with no value of its own.

The influence of Scholastic reasoning on Quesnay's economic philosophy is quite noticeable. The background of the *Tableau* was provided by the idea of distributive justice which was given a mathematical formulation. The concept of commutative justice was basic to the process of exchange transactions described in the *Tableau*. Quesnay's hostile attitude toward merchants was similarly reminiscent of early Scholastic reasoning. The idea of the "just price" was reflected in the concept of *prix fondamental* as applied to the prices of manufactured goods, though this concept was perhaps influenced by Cantillon's proposition that under free competition prices tended to be adjusted to the costs of production.

But other aspects of the *Tableau* showed a significant emancipation from Scholastic economic views. This was true, above all, of the idea of analyzing well-defined sectoral relationships of the economy. Some Mercantilists, especially Cantillon, had visualized the economy as a composite of interdependent parts, but no attempt had been made to define exactly the nature of that interdependence. Quesnay was the first to point out the interconnection of all incomes and to attempt the construction of a model of a real exchange economy conceived as a coordinated system of interconnected measurable magnitudes. The resulting conceptual sectorialization of the economy was, without doubt, a remarkable achievement of abstract reasoning.

August Oncken, who assigned to the Physiocrats a predominant place in his history of economics,[35] emphasized the conspicuous role which Quesnay attributed to the equilibrium principle in establishing his distributive scheme. This interpretation of the *Tableau économique* was adopted by other students of the history of economics. The Cartesian background of Quesnay's doctrine was frequently disregarded, but several interpreters of the *Tableau* attempted to show that it represented "a circular flow" of values,[36] a process of continuous circulation analogous to the circulation of blood in a living organism.[37] However, the related proposition that Quesnay undertook to transform economics into a "physiology" of the human society[38] is hardly compatible with the methodology of eighteenth-century economic philosophers whose epistemological principles were provided by the rationalistic cosmologies of Descartes and Malebranche. The Physiocratic conception of the economy was a mechanistic one and in no way reflected the characteristics of growth and decay commonly connected with the concept of an organism.

THE SOCIOECONOMIC DOCTRINE OF THE PHYSIOCRATS

Very soon after the publication of the *Tableau économique*, Quesnay was surrounded by a group of enthusiastic disciples who greatly admired his graphic presentation of income distribution and placed its "discovery" on a level equal to that of the most outstanding intellectual achievements of all ages and all nations. They propagated the master's ideas and endeavored, under his guidance, to transform his original analysis of economic relationships into a broad social philosophy.[39] Paramount among his disciples were Victor Riquetti, Marquis de Marabeau (1715-1789), Paul Pierre Mercier de La Rivière (1720-1794), Guillaume François Le Trosne (1728-1780), Nicholas Baudeaux (1730-1792), and Pierre Samuel Du Pont de Nemours (1739-1817). The members of this school called themselves *philosophes économistes* and published their contributions to the Physiocratic doctrine in a number of books as well as in various periodicals, such as the *Gazette du commerce*, edited by Du Pont de Nemours, the *Journal d'agriculture, du commerce et des finances*, and, at the beginning of 1765, the *Ephémerides du citoyen*. This last journal was suppressed in 1772 because of its attacks on the government.

The Marquis de Mirabeau had already manifested his interest in agricultural questions before he embraced Quesnay's doctrine. In a voluminous work, *L'Ami des hommes, ou traité de la population* (1756), he had elaborated the idea that a country's wealth consisted in a large population and that promotion of agriculture was the best economic policy in view of the tendency of the population to increase far beyond the limits set by its supply of food. Mirabeau's main contributions to the Physiocratic literature were the *Théorie de l'impôt* (1760) and the *Philosophie rurale* (1763).

The most comprehensive and authentic interpretation of the Physiocratic doctrine was supplied in Mercier de La Rivière's *L'Ordre naturel et essentiel des sociétés politiques* (1767). Du Pont de Nemours, who later became the founder of the American Dupont dynasty, contributed greatly to the spread of Quesnay's ideas.[40] He strongly objected to Montesquieu's proposition that the laws of each nation should be adjusted to specific geographical, climatic, and historical conditions,[41] and expounded the political philosophy of the Physiocrats in a treatise entitled *Physiocratie ou constitution actuelle du gouvernement le plus avantageux au genre humain* (1768). A special analysis of the *Tableau économique* was prepared by Le Trosne in *De l'ordre social* (1777). In this study, special attention was given to some problems involved in applying mathematical operations to an economic science dealing with measurable magnitudes.[42]

The sociological considerations of the Physiocrats started from a sharp distinction between society—regarded as a physical necessity—and political organization.[43] They believed that the organization of social life had been marked by the development of several stages,[44] beginning with nomadic conditions of families living on wild growing plants (*état de la recherche des productions végétales spontanées*). The highest stage of development was reached by the societies of organized nations (*sociétés regulières*), with their intensified division of functions, their structural differentiation, and their political unification (*corps politique*). According to the Physiocratic doctrine, full harmony was assured between political requirements (*besoins politiques*) and physical needs (*besoins physiques*) by the rules of the "natural order," which could also be relied upon to secure full harmony between individual and collective interests. These views were reflected in the importance which the Physiocrats attached to the differentiation of the members of society according to their social and economic functions. They were equally reflected in the definition of justice as a sovereign rule derived from self-evident maxims which determined individual property rights. Finally, these views were reflected in their espousal of the subordination of all members of society under a central authority (*autorité tutelaire*), which was charged with the task of protecting property and fending off any violations of the natural order.

Accordingly, a hereditary monarchy headed by an enlightened ruler was the best form of political organization. The specific type of such organization was, however, of minor importance compared with the tasks to be fulfilled by the government. The ruler was expected to put into effect—through declaratory legislative acts—the precepts of the natural order and to assure observance of that order.[45] Recognition of the right of the individual to political liberty and to participation in the formation of the government would have endangered the realization of that order. In the light of this approach, democratic procedures appeared to be meaningless, since the power of reason was to be relied upon to establish valid rules of social behavior. When the philosopher proclaimed the "truth" with the aid of an infallible method, the individuals could not be permitted to choose for themselves the rules to be observed in the course of their economic activities.

But in spite of their authoritarian principles, the Physiocrats insisted on far-reaching independence of the judiciary, since they regarded the courts as an indispensable instrument for controlling the legislative actions of the government in the light of the precepts of the natural order.

The proposition that the existence and well-being of society depended upon the cooperation of an outside natural force was closely associated with the idea that any arbitrary interference with the "natural" distribution of the exchange values created by nature was detrimental to the common interest. The prevailing far-reaching regulations of industry and trade provided abundant examples of such interference.

As mentioned above, various critics of French economic policy had requested that liberty of trade be granted within the country and with regard to the importation of certain commodities, but such postulates had never been made a constituent part of a specific economic or social doctrine.

The Physiocrats advocated the demand for economic freedom not on grounds of expediency but as a principle taught by nature and evidenced by sound reasoning. The creation of a permanent tendency toward the best possible state of society could be expected from the enjoyment of liberty of trade, said Mercier de La Rivière.[46] Du Pont de Nemours condemned restrictions of free competition as violations of the rights and duties ordained by the Creator. Hence, the government was charged with the task of protecting the economic freedom of the individual and of assuring personal enjoyment of the fruits of one's labor. Expressed in such general terms, this postulate implied a challenge to the many existing privileges and the monopolistic positions derived from them.

A similar conception of economic freedom was later (1776) reflected in the famous introduction to the edict which decreed the abolition of the guild system in France and declared the right to work unhampered by legal restrictions to be the first, most sacred, and most unalienable property of every individual. This edict was probably formulated by Turgot, who at that time was head of the French domestic administration.

Without analyzing the specific aspects of free competition, the Physiocrats considered economic freedom as a form of superior power which could be relied upon to regulate prices in accordance with the natural order. Le Trosne and Mercier de La Rivière asserted that exchange values were independent of the will of the buyers and sellers, and were imposed upon them by general estimate or judgment.[47] Mercier de La Rivière spoke of a despotic power that determines prices, and he appears to have ascribed to free competition the tendency to equalize employers' profits. Profits were regarded as part of the costs of production, and were categorized as a form of wages. Mercier de La Rivière minimized the importance of those profits that could not be regarded as wages, by arguing that they tended to be neutralized by losses experienced in the course of other economic transactions. There is no doubt that these views were prompted by the desire to overcome the difficulties which resulted from the definition of the sterile classes. But they appear in a more appropriate light when it is kept in mind that about the middle of the eighteenth century the business of the overwhelming majority of French manufacturers and traders was still very small and supplied little more than subsistence incomes. The substantial profits which nevertheless accrued were attributed by the Physiocrats to the existence of monopolies and similar privileged economic positions.

The profit motive was especially mentioned in connection with the discussion of trading activities, but it did not play the role of a rational principle of economic behavior. Belief in the validity of the "natural order" permitted Quesnay to ignore the fundamental utilitarian problem of how to establish a harmony between private and public interests. Only in passing—in a discussion of the manufacturing industries—did Quesnay allude to the so-called economic principle by stating that the perfection of economic conduct consisted in obtaining the greatest possible want satisfaction (*jouissance*) at the lowest possible cost, particularly in labor.[48] But neither he nor his followers explained or elaborated that proposition.

Implied in the proclamation of the principle of economic freedom was the rejection of the mercantilist balance of trade concept, with all its consequences. Quesnay argued that the interests of the merchants were always opposed to the interests of the nation. The wealth of the country, he said in the *Maximes générales,* does not depend on the possession of a larger or smaller monetary stock, and the prohibition imposed on the exportation of specie, when such exportation is desirable in the interest of commerce, is necessarily due to some unfortunate prejudice.

The community which the Physiocrats had in mind in proposing their ideal order was an agricultural society which was self-sufficient in supplying the essential requirements of its population. Quesnay regarded industrial and commercial countries as intermediaries in the traffic between agricultural communities, as members of a universal commercial republic. Mercier de La Rivière considered foreign trade a necessary evil for countries whose domestic commerce did not suffice to dispose profitably of their home production.

The concept of an essentially stationary economy which Quesnay had in mind did not open up the prospect of rapidly increasing employment opportunities. In considering such questions of a more dynamic nature, he expressed the belief that propagation of the population tended to exceed the limits set by the means of subsistence available to a country. Increases in agricultural production were obviously prerequisite to desirable increases of the population. Enhanced agricultural production was, in turn, dependent upon investment in agricultural enterprises. In analyzing these investments, Quesnay distinguished *avances foncières* (initial expenditures), *avances primitives* (expenditures on equipment), and *avances annuelles* (current expenditures).[49] His treatment of these methods for increasing the productivity of the soil was far superior to any previous similar discussions. Particularly remarkable was the emphasis which he placed on capital accumulation through savings. True to his economic principles, he objected to the use of savings for any other investment purposes and opposed the issuance of public loans, which were bound to absorb available savings in a wasteful way. Undesirable excessive outlays on consumption goods were criticized in an essay prepared by the Abbé Baudeau.[50]

Accumulation of savings by the landowners and farmers and investments in agricultural production obviously could best be promoted by the high price of grain. Hence, in opposition to the official policy, which had always favored low prices for the necessities of life, Quesnay proclaimed that effective increases in agricultural production should be brought about by raising the prices for agricultural products to the highest possible level; workers' wages, kept at the subsistence level, should be adjusted to the food prices. In pursuance of this policy, Quesnay proposed the application of free trade for the exportation of grain, since he was convinced that only the competition of foreign buyers could raise the price of grain to a high level and thus create strong incentives to increase agricultural production. He called that reasoning the alpha and omega of the science of economics.

The yield of agricultural land provided Quesnay with a measure "fixed by nature" for determining the rate of interest in agreements between lenders and borrowers. He requested recognition of that standard through legal provisions.[51] Restrictions imposed on the rate of interest were hardly compatible with the principle of freedom of trade, but Quesnay ignored the latter when its application was likely to interfere with the objectives of his agricultural policy. Victor Mirabeau even recommended enforcement of the obsolete prohibition of taking interest on money, and defended this proposal with traditional Scholastic arguments.[52] Enforcement of this prohibition was also advocated by the French jurist Robert Joseph Pothier, who regarded the stipulation of interest on money as a violation of the principle of equivalence. These views were refuted by Anne Robert

Jacques Turgot in a treatise published after the author's death.[53] The prohibition of taking interest on money was formally abolished by the law of 12 October 1789, in which the rate of interest was limited to a maximum of 5 percent.

One of the most important inferences which Quesnay drew from his conception of "surplus value" and his distributive scheme was the proposal of the *impôt unique,* the single tax, to be levied upon the landowners who received the *produit net* without supplying labor or commodities in return. The idea of a single tax was not new, but the plausible argument advanced in favor of the tax (that it should be imposed on those whose rent receipts initiated the distributive cycle, since in the last analysis all taxes had to be paid out of this income) was a new approach. Also new were the specific proposals concerning the application of the tax: after the necessary deductions had been allowed to compensate for advances made in improving the soil, the *produit net* was to be divided between the proprietors of the soil and the state, personified by the hereditary monarch, who could claim an appropriate fraction of the wealth created by nature, according to the Right of Eminent Domain. These proposals were elaborated by Mirabeau, who recommended a comprehensive program of financial reform.[54]

Considered as a measure of social reform, the single tax was intended to relieve the peasant population of an almost unbearable burden. As a financial device, the single tax could also be defended with effective arguments. When reasonably administered and combined with other appropriate measures, it could have been adjusted to the needs of the treasury and might have provided a remedy for the constant financial difficulties of the government.

A few observations may be in order on some specific aspects of the Physiocratic doctrine: Cantillon's influence on Quesnay's thinking has been repeatedly emphasized. There is hardly any doubt that Quesnay was familiar with Cantillon's essay. In the article on grains which he contributed to the *Encyclopédie,* he referred to Cantillon as a writer who had shown the importance of agriculture as a source of revenue for the state and of income for large groups of the population. It is very probable that Quesnay's definition of the three classes of the population and his conception of the agricultural surplus were suggested by the corresponding features of Cantillon's analysis. Moreover, Quesnay closely followed Cantillon's price theory when he stated that under conditions of free competition, prices were reduced to costs of production.

Yet, although Quesnay might have borrowed some of his leading ideas from Cantillon, it is doubtful whether the latter should be qualified as a "precursor of the Physiocrats," as has been done by various French interpreters of the Physiocratic doctrine. Cantillon's largely Baconian empiricist method of economic analysis hardly appealed to the thinking of the Physiocrats, since it differed radically from their Cartesian approach to economic and social problems.

The relation of the Physiocratic doctrine to the utilitarian philosophy has also been frequently discussed. The interpretation of Quesnay's views as a version of early English utilitarianism was especially emphasized by some German students of the history of economic thought,[55] and Joseph Schumpeter characterized Quesnay as one of the "founding fathers" of utilitarianism.[56] It can be assumed that the utilitarian aspects of Quesnay's philosophy had their roots in Malebranche's appeal to "enlightened self-interest" (*amour propre éclairé*) as a guide to human action.[57] Within the context of the Physiocratic doctrine, happiness appeared as the ultimate objective of human beings, and Mercier de La Rivière spoke of the desire for joy which manifests itself in all spontaneous activities of society and unwittingly drives the latter toward the realization of the ideal type of state. Le Trosne suggested that it was necessary to seize (*prendre*) men by their desires and interests and to take advantage of these motives in order to lead them to moral and civil virtues.[58] However, the psychological considerations which were basic to the individualistic utilitarian aspects of the eighteenth-century English sensationalist philosophies were practically disregarded by the Physiocrats. There was not much room for individual volition and differentiated motivation in a social order which was to be regulated by self-evident rules to be expressed in mathematical terms.

According to Karl Marx, the Physiocrats had discovered the concept of "surplus value" and had thus introduced into economic reasoning the category of "unearned increments," which in his view was fundamental to the understanding of the capitalist economy. Marx also endeavored to show that the moral order of the Physiocrats, as derived from the operation of "laws of nature," was backed by a deterministic theory.[59] The ambiguity of the term *law* used by the Physiocrats played a considerable role in the discussions of this proposition. On closer examination, it appears that the Physiocratic concept of social laws included three kinds of rules:[60] the normative rules of the "self-evident" *droit naturel* as engraved on the minds of the citizens of the newly established social order, the rules determining rational individual economic behavior, and explanatory rules concerning the course of general economic process.

Deterministic features of the Physiocratic doctrine can be found mainly in the explanatory laws which, however, occupied a borderline between prescriptions established by deductive processes and laws based, at least partly, on observation and experience. Thus, the apparently explanatory rules underlying the distribution of incomes had a distinctly normative flavor, while the treatment of prices under competitive conditions was obviously derived from observation. Particularly ambiguous was the use of the term *lois physiques* for prescriptions designed to assure adjustment of human activities to the economic principles of the Physiocratic doctrine. Since these laws can be violated, they can hardly be qualified as laws of a deterministic type.

Closely connected with the Marxian analysis of the Physiocratic doctrine was an attempt of Norman J. Ware to demonstrate that the idea of the surplus value and the attendant single tax proposal were designed to rationalize the economic interests of a new class of capitalistic landowners, who did not enjoy the privilege of tax exemption granted to the aristocracy and the church.[61] Introduction of the proposed tax, Ware argued, would have permitted these landowners to deduct before taxation not only their costs of production but also profits earned on capital investments. It may be that the ultimate effects of the tax would have promoted the interest of capitalist landowners, but the Physiocrats made no allusions to effects of this type. Enlarged volumes of surplus values brought about by continuously increased investments in all agricultural enterprises were paramount among the objectives which they expected to achieve through the realization of their proposals.

Finally, a few words might be said about the attachment of Quesnay's disciples to the master's teachings, which has repeatedly been regarded as an extraordinary event in the history of economics. It found a counterpart only much later in the similar attitude of the Marxists. But in both cases it appears advisable to speak of philosophical or sociological schools rather than of schools of economists in the strict sense of the term, and in both cases the unshakable belief in the words of a "master" was backed by an absolute belief in the validity of a method of reasoning which had enabled the master to reveal the "truth" about alleged economic laws.

THE DISINTEGRATION OF THE PHYSIOCRATIC DOCTRINE

Since the philosophy of Malebranche was widely known among the educated classes of France, all the Physiocratic ideas and propositions which were derived from that philosophy were readily understood and appreciated. The logical consistency which Quesnay exhibited in devising an abstract mathematical picture of the distributive process appealed to all minds that were educated on Cartesian principles. But a doctrine which claimed to be absolutely valid and to show how the best of all political and economic organizations could be realized was bound to meet with much opposition, especially in a social environment so deeply undermined by skepticism as was the intellectual elite of eighteenth-century Paris. Hardly less important for the final fate of the doctrine was the fact that the measures of economic policy proposed by the Physiocrats were in open conflict with many well-established principles of the French administration.

This was especially true of the foreign trade policy proposed by the Physiocrats, which became the target of effective attacks after limited freedom of exports and imports of grains had been decreed by edicts of 1763 and 1766 and a crop failure had caused a famine in 1769–70. Public opinion put the blame for the rise in the price of grain on the export policy. Particularly striking was an essay by Abbé Galiani which ridiculed the idea that land was the sole source of wealth. He used a comparative analysis of the foreign trade policies of other European countries to illustrate the propositions that economic policies had to be adjusted to local and regional conditions, that it was a hopeless undertaking to derive them from absolute principles alleged to be universally valid.[62] Hence, Galiani's biting criticisms were not only directed against the commercial and agricultural policies of the Physiocrats, but implied a general attack on the doctrinairism of the *philosophes économistes* and their methodological principles. Nature, he said, is too great a lady to bother with every insignificant twist or turn in our lives. Let us leave only the great movements to her care. (*"Concluons donc,"* he said, *"de ne pas laisser à la nature le soin de nos petites genouilles. Elle est trop grande dame pour cela. Laissons-lui les soins des grands mouvements."*)

Other effective criticisms, especially of the Physiocratic concept of national income, were advanced by Jean L. Graslin.[63] The attacks on the commercial policy of the Physiocrats were renewed by Jacques Necker, an adversary of Turgot and his successor as director general of finance in 1776.[64]

Various other contemporary critics objected to the failure of the doctrine to deal with the production and distribution of nonagricultural commodities. The applicability of the "geometrical method" to the analysis of highly complex economic and social phenomena was questioned, among others, by the Abbé Mably, who examined the logical issues involved in the attempt to derive conclusions from a few premises without carefully examining the meaning of these premises.[65] The principles of a refined mercantilism were defended against the Physiocratic ideas by François de Forbonnais.[66] After the Physiocrats had enjoyed considerable popularity in France for about twenty years, the newly emerging trends of thought worked strongly to their disadvantage.

The social philosophies which gained the upper hand were still to a certain degree influenced by the Cartesian conception of reason, but revolutionary propositions were derived from the belief in the power of reason to establish self-evident natural laws. Several disciples of Quesnay, such as Du Pont de Nemours and Le Trosne, attempted to attract new followers by modifying certain political aspects of the doctrine. But the intellectuals of the younger generation placed their hopes on far more radical political reforms. In 1781 the school of the Physiocrats had practically ceased to exist. Their teachings were drowned in the literature which initiated the revolution. Nevertheless, it is at least probable that the proclamation of the principle of economic freedom by the revolutionary regime was directly influenced by Quesnay's doctrine.

Outside of France, the Physiocrats found the support of various authors who adhered to the principles of the Cartesian philosophy. The most important advocates of Quesnay's doctrine on German soil were Johann August Schlettwein[67] and Jakob Mauvillon.[68] In Switzerland, the doctrine was expounded by Jean Herrenschwand.[69] The Physiocratic attacks on monopolies of all kinds were welcomed by many who realized the undesirable effects on economic expansion which resulted from far-reaching regulations of industry and trade. The authoritarian aspects of the Physiocratic doctrine appealed to some "enlightened" princes who enjoyed the role which they were requested to play as the agents of a superior reason. Margrave Karl Friedrich von Baden-Durlach, who later became the grand duke of Baden, wrote an *Abrégé des principes de l'économie politique,* and attempted to give practical application to the Physiocratic policy. Among the outstanding sovereigns of that period who were deeply impressed by the idea of economic freedom proclaimed by Quesnay and his followers were Leopold I, Grand Duke of Tuscany, and his brother, Emperor Joseph II. The latter repeatedly invoked Physiocratic principles in admonitions to his councillors who balked at his attempts to modify the feudal organization of agriculture and to abolish restrictive practices in the trade of agricultural products.[70] Empress Catherine of Russia and King Gustavus III of Sweden were equally influenced by the antimercantilist arguments of the physiocratic doctrines.[71]

The thesis that agricultural surplus, and nothing else, represented net national income was endorsed in England by some authors during the Napoleonic Wars, but the important elements of Cartesian reasoning implied in the Physiocratic doctrine were not compatible with the logical procedures of the British Baconian Mercantilists. It is, however, probable that some fundamental concepts used by Adam Smith were suggested by Quesnay's teachings, such as the concept of wealth as a stream of goods, the concept of the profit motive as a stimulus to economic activity, and the principle of free competition as derived from the postulate that free course be given to the operation of natural forces. Moreover, two other ideas which became basic to subsequent economic reasoning were mentioned by the Physiocrats. They advanced the proposition that under free competition prices tended to be reduced to the costs of production. They also saw a rational economic principle emerging from the tendency of all human beings to strive for the highest possible advantage at the lowest possible costs.

Adam Smith, while he rejected the Physiocrat's concept of surplus as the only source of net national income, nevertheless asserted that the Physiocratic doctrine with all its imperfections was "perhaps the nearest approximation to truth that has yet been published." But he raised strong objections to the idea of a surplus, which was basic to the Physiocratic concept of production.[72]

Chapter 8
The Concept of
Subjective Value

GALIANI'S THEORY OF MONEY

THE ITALIAN ABBÉ Fernando Galiani (1728–1787), who has been mentioned as one of the most successful critics of the Physiocratic doctrine, deserves a special place in the history of economic reasoning because of his outstanding contributions to the theories of money and of value.[1] He published his remarkable treatise on money, *Della monete* (1751), in order to convince his compatriots, the citizens of Naples, that the rise in prices which had resulted from a monetary reform was accompanied by unquestionable symptoms of prosperity and was, therefore, advantageous to the community. Both the originality of Galiani's fundamental conceptions and the methods which he used in elaborating them made his treatise an outstanding achievement of eighteenth-century economic reasoning. Since he was only twenty-three years of age when he prepared the book, the authorship of some of his leading ideas has sometimes been attributed—without sufficient proof—to his teacher, Antonio Genovesi.[2]

Galiani's general approach to economic analysis reflected the influence of utilitarian views, which he combined with a mechanistic interpretation of economic relationships. Like other contemporary authors, he compared the desire of men to satisfy passions (*passioni*) and to achieve happiness (*felicità*) with the force of gravity in physical nature. Applying the principles of mechanics to social relationships, he asserted that the "laws of commerce corresponded exactly to those manifested by the behavior of liquids."[3]

With great clarity, Galiani rejected the substance concept as applied to goods and criticized the traditional view that value was a quality inherent in things. He characterized value as a variable relationship, formed by the human mind, between the possession of one thing and the possession of another. He gave a mathematical precision to his theory as he defined exchange value as a ratio compounded of two ratios, utility and scarcity, and regarded scarcity as the proportion between the quantity of a thing and the use made of it.

Galiani applied the same approach to estimates of human talents and labor (*faticà*) and took account of differences in natural ability and of amounts of work performed yearly in analyzing the value of labor. The core of his theory was thus provided by the idea that all values—of things and of services—were determined by the demand for more or less limited quantities of goods or labor. He even pointed out that want satisfaction would be continued up to the point at which the hardships and troubles involved in the process of obtaining the satisfaction exceeded the pleasure derived from it. Thus, he anticipated a reasoning which became fundamental to some marginal utility theories of the nineteenth century; he also understood the function of prices as determinants of demand and the influence of demand on prices.

Elaborating these relationships, Galiani characterized striving for profit as the instrument which assures the interdependence (*concatenazione*) of all exchange transactions, and which Providence had devised to regulate the behavior of prices under the rule of competition. Hence, he grasped the idea of an exchange economy in which the profit motive played the role of a rational principle.

These considerations provided the background for Galiani's monetary theory. He related the value of the precious metals quite consistently to their utility and scarcity, and scoffed at the Scholastic view that the monetary use of these metals was due to a convention. Instead, he placed great emphasis on the proposition that the introduction of money, like that of other highly ingenious human institutions, had resulted from the unconscious working of the human mind. With great precision he formulated the principle underlying the "metallist" theory of money that the use of the precious metals for monetary purposes was based on an original use value attributed to them independently of the services they rendered as a medium of exchange. Like Petty before him, he compared money with the blood of the human body, of which there might be too much. His belief in the mechanical regulation of international trade relationships caused him to reject the mercantilist measures of interfering with the free flow of the precious metals. Not the quantity of the means of payment but the velocity of their circulation was, in his view, the factor which created the impression of scarcity or abundance of money.

Galiani realized that debasement (*alzamento*) of the currency resulted in profit for the prince or state, to the citizens' detriment, because of the nature of the adjustment process lagging between the increase in the quantity of money and the increase in commodity prices. He showed that rising prices ultimately favored the debtor, that they implied "violations of nature and justice," but he argued that, as a way out of desperate financial straits, they might be a lesser evil. "Representative" (fiduciary) money did not play a major role in his considerations; he simply defined it as a manifestation of debts and treated it accordingly.

One of the most original ideas which Galiani advanced was his theory of interest (*frutto della moneta*). With great sagacity he criticized the traditional belief in the generic identity of the amount of money lent and the amount returned—a reasoning which had been associated with the idea that interest on money represented payment for the use of the principal.[4] Instead, he emphasized the risk involved in lending as the main factor responsible for creating differences between the values of these two amounts. Through the development of science, he argued, risk, like other uncertain events, had been made calculable, and interest on money was the premium paid in order to insure the lender against his risk, just as the *agio*—the twin brother of interest—was a premium paid in order to equalize differences in local values of money.

Galiani added two other reasons for justifying payment of interest: the advantage secured by the borrowers and the indemnification for the anxiety (*batticuore*) connected with lending. From all these considerations he derived his arguments against any attempts to fix the rate of interest instead of permitting the risk involved in lending to determine the appropriate level. The similarity between Galiani's explanation of interest on money and Eugen Böhm-Bawerk's *agio* theory has frequently been emphasized.[5] But Galiani ignored the time element to which Böhm-Bawerk ascribed primary importance in his proposition that the value attached to future goods is always lower than that attached to goods of the same kind presently available.

Especially in Italy, Galiani's treatise enjoyed a well-deserved reputation as an outstanding contribution to economic theory and monetary policy. Galiani's relation to his teacher Giovanni Battista Vico (1668-1744),[6] who raised strong objections to the rationalist philosophy of his time, emphasized the importance of history as a source of knowledge, and attributed to the various nations a conspicuous influence on the character of their members,[7] has been repeatedly discussed. Vico's somewhat hazy ideas were not particularly appreciated in the century of rationalism, but they later found many admirers among Italian and German adherents of organismic methods of thinking.

It is very likely that Galiani's attack on the Scholastic theory of the *valor impositus* of money was influenced by Vico's idea that many institutions ascribed to the inventiveness of the human mind were, in fact, the outcome of unconscious processes. The biting criticisms which Galiani directed against the Physiocratic doctrine in the *Dialogues sur le commerce des blés* were obviously in line with Vico's condemnation of any attempts to establish general principles about social relationships.

OTHER ADHERENTS OF THE THEORY OF SUBJECTIVE VALUE[8]

Galiani's formulation of a subjective theory of value was probably the model for a similar theory, advanced by the French statesman and economist Anne Robert Jacques Turgot (1727-1781), who, though deeply impressed by François Quesnay's teachings, tried to eliminate some Cartesian elements from the Physiocratic doctrine. Educated in the logical principles of the English sensationalists, he looked to observation and experience as guides in the sphere of scientific analysis.

At the age of twenty-three Turgot delivered a noteworthy academic discourse in which he gave a clear account of the methods of nominalistic reasoning as applied to the natural sciences.[9] In his discussion of the social sciences he referred to the history of the human race as the source of experience, and suggested the use of a vaguely conceived historical approach. Without fully elaborating a theory of social progress, he distinguished three stages in the development of the human mind and the advancement of social organizations.[10] His belief in individual natural rights reflected a characteristic feature of Locke's social philosophy.

Turgot's fame as one of the outstanding economists of the eighteenth century was not achieved by a comprehensive book but by a few essays. Especially remarkable was his treatise entitled "Réflexions sur la formation et la distribution des richesses,"[11] in which some fundamental problems of production and distribution were analyzed in accordance with the methods of nominalistic reasoning. As distinct from Galiani, who emphasized scarcity relations as the source of valuation, Turgot derived the value of a good (*valeur estimative*) from a general utility of the class to which it belonged, from a comparison of present and future wants, and from an anticipation of the difficulties involved in procuring the desired object. Thus, Turgot suggested for each isolated individual the existence of a scale of subjective valuations, and expressed the value attached to a specific good in terms of a proportion between the sum the individual was able to spend in order to acquire the good and the individual's total available means. The exchange value (the price) of goods, in his view, was determined by agreements of the parties to the transactions, and was influenced by the intensity of their needs and by their purchasing power, balanced against each other.[12]

But Turgot realized the difficulties involved in explaining exchange values in terms of subjective valuations, and he criticized Galiani's casual statement that man was the common measure of all values. Since it appeared obvious that the fundamental factor of subjective valuation, the "estimated value," was no measurable magnitude, he resorted to the conclusion that the two terms *value* and *price,* although expressions for different concepts, could be substituted for each other without inconvenience in ordinary language requiring no precision.

Along with the elimination of the idea that value was a quantity inherent in goods, Turgot transformed the Scholastic concept of equivalence, as applied to goods with identical prices, into a function of individual estimates. He argued that no exchange would occur unless each party to an exchange placed a higher estimated value upon the good demanded than upon the good offered, and he assumed without further discussion that the gain—which was in estimated value only—would be equal on each side, so that each party would give equal value for equal value. In order to account for the formation of market prices, he suggested that in the market an average esteem value was established—a "*valeur appréciative*"—as a balance struck from individual valuations.

In accordance with his subjective interpretation of the origin of values, Turgot also derived the value of the monetary metals from individual estimates which were taking place independently of any explicit agreements or legal provisions.

There was, however, hardly a clear connection between Turgot's value theory and his ideas about productivity, which on the whole, were similar to those of the Physiocrats. He distinguished a class *stipendiée*, which, as he put it, sold its labor to the productive class of the population, the tillers of the soil. What the labor of the agriculturist caused the land to produce beyond his personal needs was, according to his theory, the only fund from which all other members of society received wages.[13]

Turgot connected a new concept of capital, namely, that of "accumulated movable riches" which were advanced by the entrepreneurs, with his definition of productivity. The capital was expected to yield an annual regular profit, regardless of whether it consisted of an amount of precious metal or other things. Hence, he suggested a concept of "real capital" composed of means of production other than land, and regarded the savings of capitalists (the owners of the *richesse mobilière*) as indispensable, to bridge the time between the launching of the productive process and the appearance of its yield. The Physiocratic doctrine was responsible for his view that the annual *produit net* was the main source of savings. As Hume had done before him, Turgot derived the level of interest from the relation between the demands of the borrowers and the offers of the lenders. He based his defense of the freedom to take interest on money[14] mainly on an argument advanced by Saumaise that returns could be gained from investing borrowed money in productive enterprises. Hence, he looked for some sort of productivity of capital as the source of interest on money, and combined that idea with Galiani's view that a sum of money presently available had a higher value than the same amount available at a more or less distant future.

Turgot's attempt to determine the minimum level of interest was governed by the Physiocratic proposition that net returns could always be gained from the soil as a free gift of nature. In his view, no investment was likely to be made in any enterprise unless it was possible to secure an amount of interest corresponding to the yield of a land on which a similar investment had been made. Böhm-Bawerk proposed the term *fructification theory of interest* to characterize this theory, since, as distinct from other "productivity theories," it connected the yield from lending with the opportunity of earning a return from investing capital in the purchase of rent-bearing land.[15]

Closely related to Turgot's theory of interest was his proposition that the levels of return tended to be equalized in different investments. He illustrated this tendency by using a characteristic simile, that of the behavior of liquids of different densities communicating with each other through the arms of an inverted syphon of which they occupy the branches.

Turgot's formulation of the law of decreasing returns in agriculture was another remarkable contribution to the analysis of economic processes. He showed that progressively smaller yields were earned when equal investments (*advances*) were applied successively to a piece of land. Yet—unlike James Steuart—he did not use the law of diminishing returns to explain those cases in which cultivation was extended to soils of low fertility.

A subjective approach to the theory of value was also suggested by the Abbé Etienne Bonnot de Condillac (1715-1780), who had shown great ability in adjusting the principles of nominalistic reasoning to the French eighteenth-century taste.[16] In his treatise "De commerce et le gouvernement" (1776), Condillac emphasized quite explicitly that the value of a good was not due to its costs, but that costs were spent on its production because of the value attached to it. Unlike Galiani, he based his value theory on the traditional concept of utility as applied to the class to which a good belonged and connected the value of the individual good with estimates concerning its scarcity.[17] Thus, he considered utility and scarcity the two determinants of all prices. The influence of Galiani's views is perhaps noticeable in Condillac's treatment of the difference between the values of present and future goods.

Condillac agreed with Turgot on the proposition that differences in individual estimates were prerequisite to the performance of exchange transactions. But he objected to Turgot's view that the advantages gained from an exchange by each partner were always equal, and thus he eliminated from his price theory any vestiges of the traditional Scholastic principle of equivalence. His interpretation of the exchange problem provided him with strong arguments against the Physiocratic proposition that the system of exchange values was not affected by the activities of the manufacturers and traders.[18] Applying a similar reasoning to the conditions surrounding international trade relations, Condillac showed how these relations resulted from the need to exchange goods which were of unequal utility to the trading partners.[19]

Condillac was a convinced adherent of the idea that the value of money was based on the original use value of the monetary metals, but he was aware of the increase in value acquired by these metals through the use for monetary purposes. According to his own statement, his analysis of the circulation of the means of payment was strongly influenced by Cantillon's discussion of that topic.

The decisive factor which separated the views of the adherents of the subjective value concept from the views of the Baconian Mercantilists was their negative attitude toward the principle of equivalence as applied to the exchange of goods. Condillac's treatment of the value problem was frequently referred to in the course of the nineteenth century by French economists in support of their struggle against both the value theory of the Physiocrats and the English labor cost theories.

About one hundred years elapsed after the publication of Condillac's treatise before the idea of individual valuation outlined by him, by Turgot, and by Galiani was accepted as the starting point of a general economic theory. That long delay in the development of economic reasoning was probably due to the fact that these eighteenth-century authors failed to complete their theory by relating the value problem to the marginal utilities of the units included in a stock of goods. Their theory was also fragmentary in other respects, since it was not applied to the explanation of costs of production and the distributive processes.

There was apparently no bridge which would have led from the conception of value advocated by Galiani, Turgot, and Condillac to the premises underlying the value doctrine of British economists, who tended to construe an economic system in accordance with mechanical principles; in so doing, the British economists were led to adopt a standard unit of value to which all magnitudes included in the system could be reduced. How could that requirement be reconciled with a value theory which undertook to derive the exchange values from ever-varying individual estimates? As formulated in the eighteenth century, the subjective theory of value did not provide the logical prerequisites for the establishment of a consistent economic system. As viewed by the eighteenth- and nineteenth-century economists, the construction of such a system was dependent upon the application of the equilibrium principle to the mutual relations of all its parts.

Chapter 9
The First Version of the Utilitarian Economic Doctrine

——

THE DEVELOPMENT OF UTILITARIAN REASONING

THE CARTESIAN philosophy provided the Physiocrats with logical instruments for the adjustment of all individual interests to the superior objectives of the community. They relied on "self-evident" notions in defining these objectives and their model of the economy. The English Mercantilists, however, had no faith in the power of reason to supply absolutely valid moral or political concepts. They were faced with a fundamental proposition of the utilitarian philosophy as formulated by John Locke: that human behavior was to be qualified as morally good or bad according to whether it was apt or unfit to promote individual happiness. Such happiness could best be promoted by giving free rein to the exercise of self-interest. Since the sphere of economic activities was obviously the primary and most extensive field for the operation of self-interest, it became possible to separate the study of fundamental problems of economic analysis from the discussion of other aspects of individual and social life.

Locke had failed to give a conclusive answer to the dilemma of how to reconcile undesirable human traits, such as greed, avarice, and the like, with the interests of the community. This problem was vividly illustrated by a widely read satire, *The Fable of the Bees*, published in 1714 by Bernard Mandeville (1670–1733).[1] This pamphlet—called by Bishop George Berkeley "the wickedest book that ever was"[2]—started from the traditional mercantilist propositions that the ultimate goal of economic policy consisted in achieving the greatest possible national power and that the balance of trade provided the yardstick for measuring economic progress. From an exaggerated picture of the economic effects of self-interest, Mandeville drew the conclusion that general well-being depended upon the efficiency of egoistic motives as the exclusive agents of individual economic behavior. "Men," he asserted, "have nothing to stir them up to be serviceable but their wants which it is prudence to relieve, but folly to cure." He endeavored to show that trade was incompatible with honesty, that observance of the rules of honesty led to the ruin of the community, and that without vice no sufficient employment could be secured for the large masses of the "laborious poor" who were kept at work by a policy of low wages. The gist of Mandeville's argument, which has earned his book a conspicuous place in the history of utilitarian doctrine, was the assertion that the prevailing immoral motives of individual behavior were in intent antagonistic to public interest, but public interest was, in fact, promoted by the results of this behavior. That idea was clearly expressed in the subtitle of the satire, *Private Vices, Public Benefits.*

The widespread indignation caused by Mandeville's pamphlet was mainly due to his attack on the virtue of prudence, which the English clergy had elevated to the rank of a primary ethical principle and had set up as an integral element of their doctrine of work.[3] Thrift had been included among the characteristics of praiseworthy Christian behavior, and energetic pursuance of one's calling was regarded as a paramount Christian duty. In the *Fable of the Bees,* however, thrift was shown to be prejudicial to common interest, and successful pursuance of one's calling was shown to be motivated only by greed.

Even the severest critics of Mandeville's satire were startled by the logical implications of its reasoning. They were challenged to explain how self-interest, which was commonly believed to manifest itself in "vices," such as greed and luxury, could be conceived of as an agent of general economic welfare. A moral as well as a logical issue was involved in this problem.

A popular moral doctrine provided the incentive for launching the satire. Certain British authors tried to impute the power of distinguishing between good and evil to a specific "moral sense." The idea that man is motivated in his social behavior by an "active benevolence" had been anticipated by Richard Cumberland in a critical discussion of Hobbesian philosophy.[4]

Later, Anthony Ashley Cooper, Earl of Shaftesbury (1671–1713), qualified a moral sense as a natural faculty of the human mind; he attributed the capacity to pass absolutely valid esthetic judgments to a complementary "esthetic sense." Shaftesbury impressed his readers by his sagacity, the refinement of his style, and his predominantly esthetic approach to ethical problems. His introspective method and his mechanical conception of the human mind caused him to compare the latter with a highly artificial clockwork. "We inquire," he stated, "what is according to Interest, Policy, Fashion, Vogue, but it seems wholly strange and out of the way to inquire what is according to Nature. The Balance of Europe, of Trade, of Power is strictly sought after, while few have heard of the Balance of their Passions, or thought of holding these scales even."[5]

Within the framework of Shaftesbury's philosophy, the belief in the general validity of ethical judgments was based on the view that feelings for fellow human beings are bound to develop in those who live habitually in society, and that such feelings are likely to prevail over the exercise of pure self-interest. Moreover, the satisfaction produced by benevolent actions was described as a pleasure experienced independently of the utilitarian effects of such behavior.

A similar line of thought was later adopted by Francis Hutcheson (1694–1746), who placed even greater emphasis than Shaftesbury upon mechanical principles in defining the origin of esthetic and ethical judgments.[6] Hutcheson established a close analogy between the operation of social and egoistic motives and the functioning of cohesion and gravity in the behavior of physical bodies.[7] In pursuance of that analogy, Hutcheson even applied mathematical concepts to the construction of his system of moral philosophy. He defined virtue as a "compound ratio of the quantity of goods and the number of enjoyers."[8] From these considerations he derived a consistent expression of the utilitarian principle: "that action is best which procures the greatest happiness for the greatest number, and that is worst which in like manner causes misery.'"[9]

Hutcheson thus deserves credit for formulating the principle of the common good in terms of the sum total of happiness experienced by the individual members of the community. He also provided utilitarian arguments for the defense of private property viewed as an instrument for stimulating productive activity.

Opponents of the utilitarian doctrine countered with the contention that maximization of happiness was not a suitable standard for establishing moral judgments, that happiness was rather the indirect result of behavior adjusted to absolutely valid moral precepts. Impressed by arguments of this kind, many English intellectuals of the first half of the eighteenth century returned to the Stoic belief that the primary elements of moral and esthetic judgments were "natural ingredients" of the mind, that passing historical events and processes were responsible for "artificial" and "unreasonable" views.

The concept of "moral philosophy" which developed in the course of these discussions was designed to encompass all teachings which dealt with the problems of social life. Included in these teachings were the doctrines of natural law, ethics, and public policy. The counterpart of moral philosophy was natural philosophy which dealt with the physical sciences. English eighteenth-century philosophers, though fertile in ideas, were not animated by the desire to propose and promote changes in the existing institutions.[10] Such an attitude was perhaps prompted by the widespread lack of confidence in the power of reason to teach absolutely valid principles of social action. It was in sharp contrast to the attitude which prevailed at the same time on the European continent under the influence of Descartes and his followers.

The principles of utilitarian philosophy were discussed from a logical angle by Bishop George Berkeley (1685–1753) in connection with his analysis of the formation of abstract concepts.[11] Berkeley's contributions to economics were not particularly remarkable,[12] but he developed the logical teachings of Locke into what has been termed *psychological nominalism*,[13] and he charged philosophers with the responsibility for the erroneous distinction between the "real existence" of things—which is not accessible to our experience—and their sensible properties, which Locke called "secondary qualities." Such properties, perceptible to the senses, and nothing else were, in his view, the constituent elements of a thing. Thus, Berkeley arrived at the most radical rejection of the Aristotelian substance concept as applied to material objects.[14] Moreover, if no reality attaches to the objects of our perception, any attempts to apply the principle of causality to the relations between outside events had to be definitely abandoned. Only Fernando Galiani and some other eighteenth-century Italian economists were aware of the doubtful role played by the substance concept in the prevailing definition of the concept of value, derived from the utility of the classes to which the goods were assigned. It took almost one and a half centuries before Berkeley's criticism of the substance concept was consistently applied to a value theory which enjoyed widespread recognition.

The next step in formulating the fundamental methodological issues of utilitarian philosophy was taken by David Hume (1711–1776), who reexamined Berkeley's theorem that external or internal sensations were the only sources of all abstract notions. In his *Enquiry concerning Human Understanding* (1748), he attributed to mathematics the unique quality of being exclusively conditioned by the knowledge of quantitative and spatial relations directly supplied by inner experience.[15] Hence, he regarded mathematics as the only analytical science and mathematical propositions as axioms of unquestionable validity. He contrasted such axioms with propositions dealing with "matters of fact" which had to be derived from sense impressions in order to have a meaning and, consequently, could only be probable, but never certain. In accordance with this kind of "empirical probabilism,"[16] all general propositions with a factual content have, at best, the character of probable hypotheses. This principle became the basis of all empiricist philosophies.

Whatever may have been the considerations which caused historians to call the eighteenth century the "Age of Reason," the role attributed by Hume to "reason" was a predominantly passive one. This view permeated his theory of the thinking process, which he conceived of as the result of mutual attraction and association of ideas.[17] He based his laws of association on similarity, contrast, contiguity (temporal and spatial affinity), and causal relation.

Berkeley had attempted to preserve the substance concept for the realm of spiritual teleological ideas, but Hume, who completely accepted Berkeley's criticism of that concept, characterized it as logically untenable, though psychologically necessary. He ascribed the belief in the "essential" attributes of each material or spiritual thing to the fact that the human mind regularly performs identical combinations of perceptions when faced with a given object, and that these combinations are connected with the outside object as if they corresponded to a real entity. In accordance with this reasoning, Hume rejected the concept of "self" as a substantive ego on the ground that no such entity was observable. In his view, a self was nothing but a "bundle or collection of different perceptions"; he even objected to the idea of regarding memory as the unifying principle of the self. Thus it is easy to understand that John Stuart Mill called Hume the most profound negative thinker on record.

As Berkeley had done before him, Hume questioned the validity of the concept of causality as applied to the relations between outside events. That relationship, he argued, could not be derived by analytical procedures from a finite number of experiences or based on relations of necessities.[18] But he admitted that the existence of causal relationships, although never demonstrable, could be considered probable when experience showed phenomena to succeed each other regularly in a considerable number of cases. Hence, laws of nature could be defined as statements about regular sequences of events the recurrence of which could be regarded as highly probable. Consequently, Hume attributed to scientific research the task of determining with empirical methods the degree of probability to be assigned to the recurrence of such sequences. The importance of deductive reasoning was perceptibly reduced by Hume's proposition that hypotheses, expressed in terms of higher abstraction, were nothing but generalizations derived from experience.

In pursuance of his epistemological principles, Hume repudiated all systems of ethics that could not be founded on fact and observation. Reason, he argued, could influence the will only if it could stir up some passion or affection. As motivating forces of human action, he mentioned propensities and inclinations, and he included among such propensities the spirits of avarice, industry, art, and luxury. Though he questioned the capacity of reason to distinguish between good and evil in action, he did not suggest any satisfactory answer to the problem of how to account for moral judgments. It has been said (on good grounds) that Hume's analysis of the origin of moral judgments could be interpreted in accordance with a theory of moral sentiments, a doctrine of sympathy, or an outright utilitarian approach.[19]

Without applying his methodological principles consistently to economic analysis, Hume defined the logical prerequisites for combining the poorly coordinated theories of the Baconian economists into a coherent body of thought. He determined the limited functions to be assigned to reason and emphasized the importance of the association of ideas for any consistent processes of thinking. His associationist theory provided the elements to explain the origin of the various titles to property: occupation, prescription, right of succession, heredity, or acquisition through labor. Scarcity of goods played a prominent role in the arguments he advanced in favor of private ownership; he examined significant aspects of individual behavior and realized that a strong government was needed in order to provide protection for private property and individual liberty, but he did not attach much importance to the specific form of government.

Faced with the fundamental utilitarian problem of how to harmonize private and public interests, Hume suggested three alternative ways of achieving this purpose. Harmony could result from the operation of a principle of a "natural identity of interest," from a "fusion" of interests, or from an "artificial identification" of interests.[20] This distinction pointed to a differentiation of the social sciences according to the methods applicable in their respective fields of investigations. If a natural identity of interest could be assumed to be the determinant factor in the economic sphere without playing the same role in other sectors of social life, the treatment of economic problems could logically be separated from its traditional connections with moral philosophy on the one hand and the political doctrine of state and government and the juridical doctrine of natural law on the other.

Neither the belief in the principles of a normative "natural law" nor the theory of the social contract was compatible with Hume's philosophical convictions, since neither observation nor experience provided solid foundations for the tenets underlying these widely accepted doctrines. In his analysis of the origin of religious creeds and the origin of political communities and their institutions, Hume adopted a historical approach similar to that which was suggested by Montesquieu. Although he assumed that certain constant general characteristics were common to all human beings, he emphasized the divergent developments of societies and the factors which contributed to that process; within the context of his social philosophy, progressive differentiation of human behavior was a necessary concomitant of the advancing refinement of civilization.

Considerations of that type appeared to be at variance with the fundamental thesis of the utilitarian doctrine that human nature had always been and remained the same in its principles and operations. The thesis could best be defended when it was assumed that any differentiation which had occurred had been caused by events and conditions external to individuals. History had to supply knowledge of the circumstances under which, more or less unconsciously, varying social and economic organizations and institutions had developed and had in turn led to the differentiation of individual behavior.

Paramount among the historians who insisted upon the working of the unconscious in social life was Adam Ferguson (1723–1816).[21] In an often-quoted passage, Ferguson claimed that we ascribe to a previous design what can be known only by experience, what no human wisdom could foresee, and what, without the concurring humor and disposition of his age, no authority could enable an individual to execute. Hence, he derived the various forms of social life and social institutions, which had their roots in an obscure and distant past, from human instincts, not from speculation by men.[22] In accordance with that philosophy, history was conceived of as a process in the course of which mankind arrived at an increasingly better understanding of the natural forces and was thus enabled to adjust the social institutions to the precepts implied in nature's simple plan for a harmonious social order. The social philosopher was challenged to discover that simple plan.[23]

ECONOMICS AS AN INDEPENDENT DISCIPLINE:
ADAM SMITH AND *THE WEALTH OF NATIONS*

Problems of moral philosophy. The more or less fragmentary mercantilist discussions of economic problems were finally combined in a crowning work by Adam Smith (1723–1790), whose ideas were backed by the leading principles of utilitarian philosophy. His approach to the treatment of fundamental economic issues was widely accepted, and it dominated economic thinking for more than a century to come. Though the body of his theories did not differ perceptibly from the ideas presented in the writings of some advanced Mercantilists, he elaborated these ideas in the light of utilitarian principles and connected them with virtually all economic knowledge accumulated at his time. Finally, relying on historical facts, Smith defended with forceful arguments the policy of economic liberalism designed to secure general welfare and economic progress.

Francis Hutcheson was Adam Smith's teacher and David Hume his close friend. His utilitarian views were strongly influenced by Hutcheson's moral philosophy; to Hume he owed his general methodological approach to scientific analysis. During a prolonged stay in Paris, he was in touch with the Physiocrats and, as mentioned before, took over some of their ideas.

Economic problems, however, attracted Adam Smith's attention only in a later period of his life. He occupied a chair of moral philosophy at the University of Glasgow, and at first his interests centered on the fundamental moral issues of his time. A short survey of his treatment of these issues is likely to provide a useful introduction to a discussion of his economic teachings, which were developed against a background of the moral aspects of individual behavior. In a voluminous treatise, *Theory of Moral Sentiments* (1759), Smith undertook to define the origin of moral principles, a problem which had occupied the minds of several contemporary philosophers. The starting point of his analysis was the question of how to arrive at judgments about the behavior of other people. Lack of empirical evidence caused him to deny the existence of a moral sense, strictly speaking; like Hume, he realized that moral rules changed along with changing historical conditions.[24] He also shared Hume's conviction that it was absurd to attribute to reason the power of establishing fundamental, generally valid conceptions of right and wrong. In his search for an empirical factor which could provide guidance for the approval and disapproval of actions of others, he replaced the prevailing theory of a moral sense with a theory of sentiments of sympathy. He also attributed to these sentiments the capacity of adjusting manifestations of self-interest to the interests of society.

Apart from self-love and sympathy, Adam Smith distinguished four other general motives of human behavior, namely, the desire to be free, a sense of propriety, a natural propensity to work, and a like propensity to exchange goods for those owned by others. But he failed to establish clear connections among these instincts, and his moral theory did not provide a satisfactory background for a consistent study of social institutions and social behavior.

In order to justify the position which he assigned to self-love in his moral doctrine, Smith used the generally accepted utilitarian argument that happiness of all rational creatures had been the original purpose of nature. He expressed his firm belief in "that divine Being whose benevolence and wisdom have, from all eternity, contrived and conducted the immense machinery of the Universe so as at all times to produce the greatest possible quantity of happiness." He regarded that idea as "certainly of all the objects of human contemplation by far the most sublime."

In accordance with prevailing utilitarian views, pleasure and pain were the determining factors which stimulated desire and passions; they could not be perceived by reason but only by feelings. Accepting these views, Smith included self-interest, as Locke had suggested, among the morally neutral motives; even self-love could be considered a virtuous motive unless it caused men deliberately to inflict damages on others. In the course of this discussion, Smith characterized freedom of competition as an ethically praiseworthy basis for the organization of social relationships.[25] But that idea could hardly be elaborated in a study which centered on feelings of sympathy as instruments of moral judgments.

The structure of The Wealth of Nations.   The conception of a "natural order" was only occasionally mentioned in Adam Smith's treatise on moral philosophy. However, it assumed distinct features in the great economic work which Smith published in 1776 and which became the most famous book on economic problems that has ever been written: the *Inquiry into the Nature and the Causes of the Wealth of Nations*. This book grew out of a series of lectures on public policy which were divided into four parts: justice, police, revenue, and arms.[26] The two middle parts of the lectures dealt with economic and financial questions and foreshadowed the far more developed analysis of Smith's great economic treatise. *The Wealth of Nations* is divided into five books of unequal length. It was not meant to be a textbook on economics, but rather was intended to teach legislators and statesmen such measures as would enable the people to provide plentiful revenue for themselves and to supply the commonwealth with a revenue sufficient for the public service.[27]

The Wealth of Nations starts with the famous discussion of the division of labor, which Smith considered as the main, perhaps the only, vehicle of progress. He even contended that the differentiation of individuals had been mainly brought about by the division of labor, which had caused their adjustment to their particular tasks. In discussing the limitations of the division of labor, he introduced the concept of the market and referred to an inborn human "propensity to truck and barter" as the basic factor underlying the organization of the exchange economy. In close connection with this analysis, he dealt with some of the fundamental theoretical problems of his work, the role of money and the explanation of exchange values and prices.

In the analysis which followed in the first book, Smith formulated, in a manner that would be repeated for a long time to come, the fundamental problems of distribution. He dealt extensively with the circumstances which determine the rates of wages, of profit and interest, and which regulate the rent of land.

In the second book, Smith presented his theory of capital in its various aspects; he analyzed the functions of money and developed in this connection the concept of the net national income, which he termed *net revenues of society*. In additional chapters, he tackled the problems of saving, investment, and interest on capital. His proposition that "parsimony," and not industry, was the immediate cause of the increase of capital remained a leading economic idea until the late nineteenth century.

The third book was designed to treat some factors which in the past had promoted or hindered economic progress. The economic history of European towns after the destruction of the Roman Empire served to illustrate the development of the relations among manufacture, agriculture, and foreign trade.

The often-quoted vehement attacks on the "commercial or mercantile" system are contained in the fourth book. Here Smith marshaled the arsenal of antiprotectionist arguments in order to defend the principle of free trading and the interests of the consumer against the effects of commercial policies motivated by the balance of trade doctrine. His criticism of the Physiocratic or "agricultural" system was mainly directed against the theory of the exclusive productivity of agricultural labor, but Smith conceded the superior productivity of that labor. He also sided with the Physiocrats in their treatment of the freedom of trade.

The fifth book, largely independent of the others, dealt with the theory and practice of taxation. It is here that Smith develops his four famous principles of taxation: that taxes should be levied with equality (according to the citizen's ability to pay), with certainty (avoiding arbitrariness), with convenience (in method and time for the taxpayer), and with economy (i.e., held to a minimum compatible with the needs of the state). These four maxims have dominated the discussion on taxation for generations, often in a sense quite different from the one elaborated by Smith.

The value problem.   In order to coordinate the—partly conflicting—ideas underlying Adam Smith's conception of the economy, it appears advisable to discuss the fundamental economic problems which he endeavored to solve. In the center of these problems is the definition of the concept of exchange value, since Smith considered the "intrinsic" or "natural" value of goods basic to the conditions under which the exchange of the goods takes place. Hence, he undertook to determine the "real" measure of this value. In his search for a stable standard to which all values could be reduced, Smith eliminated from the outset the monetary unit. He also rejected any reference to the utility of the goods, since he associated the concept of utility, like the Scholastics, with the genera or classes of goods, and thus was faced with the "paradox of value." He illustrated that paradox by comparing water and diamonds: whereas water, an indispensable good, had no marketable value, a diamond fetched a high price in spite of its limited usefulness. Smith realized, however, that scarcity relationships were involved in the problem, and he argued that the whole quantity of a cheap commodity brought to the market is commonly not only greater but of greater value than the whole quantity of an expensive one.

Without much hesitation Smith endorsed the mercantilist propositions that (*a*) the determination of values was not perceptibly influenced by the consumers' demand as compared with the supply of the goods, and (*b*) as suggested by Locke, labor was the productive agent which was mainly responsible for the creation of exchange values. He regarded "labor" as a more stable standard of measuring values than any of the monetary metals or grains. In support of that view, he advanced the argument that "equal quantities of labor at all times and places may be said to be of equal value to the laborer." Thus, he arrived at the conclusion that the "real" or "natural" value of a good could be measured with the greatest accuracy, both from century to century and from year to year, by the amount of labor expended on its production.[28] But in view of the fact that important elements of the distributive process, such as land rents and profit, could not be explained in terms of "embodied" labor, he limited the validity of that explanation to conditions which had existed before money was introduced as a medium of exchange and before private ownership of the means of production achieved general recognition.

Smith's often-quoted example of the exchange of beavers for deer belongs to the realm of economic mythology. In this example, beavers were exchanged for deer in primitive societies according to the amount of labor spent on hunting them. Sociological research, however, has shown that labor time spent on production has hardly ever affected the terms of barter in primitive societies. But that example has a certain theoretical interest; it can be used to indicate some important conditions which had to be fulfilled in order to substantiate the validity of the labor cost theory. Beavers could have been exchanged for deer in accordance with the respective hunting times if the labor involved in hunting was not differentiated, if this was the only factor of production, or if labor had the same disutility for all participants and was freely accessible under the rule of free competition.

Smith distinguished the conditions of exchange which he found to prevail in primitive societies from those existing in "civilized communities." In such communities, he believed the measure of values, as distinct from the source of values, was not to be looked for in the conditions of production but in the condition of exchange, in the "power of purchasing other goods." Hence, he defined the "real measure" of the value of a commodity as the quantity of labor which the seller of the commodity would be required to spend if he had to produce the goods received in exchange. "Labor," he said, "measures the value not only of that part of the price which resolves itself into labor, but of that which resolves itself into rent and of that which resolves itself into profit." Thus, rents and profits were included in the value which a good could "command" and the labor cost theory was transformed into a cost of production theory.

Smith supplemented the cost of production theory by references to disutility considerations. "What everything is really worth to the man who wants to exchange it for something else," he said, "is the toil and trouble which it can save to himself and which it can impose upon other people." Occasionally, Smith defined individual "wealth" as the quantity of other men's labor, or "what is the same thing, of the produce of other men's labor which a man's fortune enables him to purchase or command."

Thus, Smith offered the choice among the value theory of "embodied" labor, the theory of "commanded" labor, a cost of production theory, and a disutility theory. The ambivalence which he showed in these discussions was probably due to a conflict between the tendency of the utilitarian philosopher to look for a psychological motivation of values (sacrifice, disutility) and his adherence to the traditional mercantilist procedure of associating a measurable quality of the thing (their exchange value) with the force (labor) which was assumed to have created that quality.[29]

In view of these partly conflicting statements concerning the source of exchange values and the standard of measuring them, it is doubtful whether Smith seriously attempted to establish a logical connection between these two problems. He conceded that, when used to measure exchange values, labor was really an "abstract notion" which, though it can be made sufficiently intelligible, is not altogether so "natural and obvious." He appears to have realized the hypothetical element which was implied in his proposition that "labor" provided a "stable" standard for the measurement of values.

Closely connected with the discussion of the value problem is the distinction drawn by Smith between "productive" and "unproductive" labor. This distinction was a heritage from mercantilist reasoning and was probably associated with the substance concept of goods, since labor was qualified as "productive" when it added to the value of the "subject" upon which it was bestowed, when it fixed and realized itself in some "particular subject or vendible commodity" which showed a certain perdurability in time, or when the price of the commodity could afterward put into motion a "quantity of labour equal to that which had originally produced it." The question of whether these conditions were fulfilled was to be answered in terms of commanded labor. No economic progress could be expected to result from activities which did not contribute to the accumulation of capital goods fit for promoting the employment of productive labor.[30]

In the light of Smith's concept of "intrinsic" value, the theory of fluctuating prices was clearly to be separated from value theory. Richard Cantillon's observation that in advanced societies the market prices tended to adjust themselves to the costs of production provided Smith with a starting point for the theorem that under the rule of free competition market prices oscillated around the "natural" prices—the prices determined by long-run production costs measured in forms of commanded labor. In accordance with that view, effective demand for, and supply of, goods was equalized by the mechanism of the market. Without clearly defining the rule of free competition, Smith also attributed to the operation of that rule the function of allocating the productive factors among the industries in such a way that the "whole advantages and disadvantages" as well as the money earnings would be leveled off.[31] But since he centered his attention on increases in wealth, conceived of as an ever-expanding process, he did not pay much attention to the problems connected with the allocation of resources, nor did he provide a clear picture of the functioning of the economic machinery.

Wages, rents, and profits; foreign trade.   Three main features of the distributive process—wages, rents, and profits—were basic to Adam Smith's discussion of the problems involved in the distribution of the national dividend. The corresponding elements of the national revenue were total wages, total profits, and total rents, representing the "original" sources of incomes and the shares of the main classes of the population. Thus, Smith ascribed the character of "natural" economic categories to three clearly discernible forms of income, although at least two of them had their roots in social institutions. The landlords, laborers, and capitalists, he stated, form the great, original, and constituent orders; their revenues, the rent of land, the wages of labor, and the profits of "stock" together make the national income. This conception of the economic order was, at least indirectly, associated with the assumption that the receipt of a "natural" category of income was associated with a specific sphere of economic interest which differed from the interests connected with the receipt of other categories of income. Adam Smith repeatedly referred to conflicts of interest which he found to exist between different classes of the population.

As seen by Smith, the main problem of distribution consisted in explaining the contributions made by the productive factors (labor, land, and capital) to the value of the products. His definition of the value problem made it necessary to suggest specific theorems for defining the source of rents and profits, since it was doubtful whether profits could be derived from the creative power of labor and since rents appeared to have their source in factors other than labor.

Smith's treatment of these problems was, however, beset with many difficulties and was far from satisfactory. Wages were obviously the reward for labor's contribution to the exchange value of the products, and the main question to be answered was how to account for the rates of wages. From his mercantilist predecessors, Smith had inherited the conception of a subsistence wage based on the view that the level of wages was determined by the costs of producing and training the workers. But he emphasized that in contemporary England wages were evidently higher than was necessary to enable the worker to bring up a family, although reductions in the wage level might result from the tendency of labor to multiply beyond the range of employment opportunities. In accordance with his value theory of embodied labor, deductions from values created by labor became necessary in civilized societies in order to provide income for landlords and masters. It is a moot question whether a moral judgment was implied in that statement. However this may be, the statement possibly conveyed the idea that wages were a residue left after deductions had been made for the shares of land and capital. Discussions of specific conditions under which wages were earned and regulated filled many pages of *The Wealth of Nations*. Smith also alluded to the concept of a wage fund accumulated by the employers during the period of production, and distributed among the workers in the following period. A similar idea had already been suggested by Cantillon. However, in other extensive discussions of the wage problem, Smith referred to conditions of demand and supply as the determinants of the wage level. Thus, he presents three different explanations of the wage level: a residual theory, a wage fund theory, and a supply and demand theory.

Smith's conception of the rent of land was obviously influenced by the Physiocratic doctrine, since he adopted the thesis that in agriculture nature labors along with man and supplies its contribution at no cost.[32] In other passages of his work, however, he derived rent from "monopoly" prices enjoyed by the owners of the soil. In pursuing this line of thought, he argued that every improvement in the circumstances of society leading to increases in the real value of the products of land as well as to reductions in the prices of manufactures tended to increase the real wealth of the landlord, that is, his power of purchasing the labor of other people or the produce of their labor. Hence, whereas Smith regarded wages and profits as determinants of prices, he qualified high rents as the result of high prices of agricultural products.

It has been suggested that for over a century Smith created confusion by his failure to draw a distinction between land with alternative uses and farm land with no competing use. In the first case, rent was an element of costs. In the second case, the yield depended on conditions of the market.[33]

With the introduction of profits as a fundamental category of the exchange economy, Smith started a line of economic analysis which had been ignored by the Mercantilists. They had regarded the incomes of employers as gains derived from surpluses over costs or as compensation for work done in organizing productive activities. But the concept of profits as applied by Smith was far from well defined. It covered a variety of incomes accruing to the employer from different sources: it included the yield of the capital invested in the enterprise; the remuneration for entrepreneurial, managerial, and possibly technical services; reward for risk; and additional earnings resulting from the introduction of technological improvements and other cost-saving devices and from favorable market conditions, monopolistic situations, and the like. Only very limited aspects of profits were taken into account in the argument advanced by Smith that the owner of capital could not be expected to participate in productive enterprises unless he were allotted a share in the value of the products, or "unless his stock was to be replaced to him with a profit."[34] The conception of profits as a surplus was alluded to in the distinction which Adam Smith drew between "clear profits" and receipt of interest on capital invested by the employers. He regarded interest as a payment for the use of borrowed money capital and derived it from the profits which could be earned by using that capital for productive purposes. This proposition was an outcome of the fight over the prohibition of usury. As distinct from the mercantilist view that the rate of interest was determined by the quantity of money in circulation, Smith connected this rate with the supply of, and the demand for, loanable funds, and agreed with the existing legal provisions which fixed it at 5 percent, the maximum limit set for that rate. He expected that competitive forces would result in equalizing the rate of interest.

Although Smith included profits and interest on capital among the costs of production, he occasionally characterized profits as increments over and above the exchange values created by labor; in other passages he called them deductions from such exchange values. Choosing the first alternative imposed upon the advocates of the labor cost theory the task of indicating the forces which enabled capital to "create" exchange values in excess of the values produced by labor in past and present productive processes. Choosing the second alternative eliminated capital as an original source of exchange values and income, and led to the question of why the owners of capital could claim a portion of ex˜hange values created by the "productive power" of labor. The view that labor was "exploited" by the owners of capital lurked behind this question. Adam Smith did not answer these thorny problems which resulted from the attempt to adjust a hazy concept of profit to the labor cost theory of value.[35]

The lack of clarity which was a characteristic feature of the concept of "profit" had a counterpart in the confusion which surrounded the concept of "capital." As used in some passages of *The Wealth of Nations,* "capital" meant money accumulated for lending or investment purposes, or stocks yielding interest on capital. This view was reflected in the definition of capital as "that part of the whole stock that a man possesses which he expects to afford him a revenue." As used in other connections, the term *capital* denoted physical means of production created by labor; again in others it was applied to wage goods made available by employers for "productive consumption." Such consumption, as associated with the concept of "productive labor," was distinguished from the nonproductive consumption of other classes of the population. The term *circulating* was used to distinguish "wage capital" from "fixed" or "invested" capital.

Since the network of real exchange transactions was the true object of economic analysis for Smith, he attached only secondary importance to monetary problems and ignored the functions of money as a store of value, although these functions had been emphasized by some Mercantilists. "What is bought with money or with goods," he said, "is purchased by labor as much as what we require by the toil of our own body."[36] He assumed that the volume of money was dependent upon the demand for circulation and the costs of producing precious metals, and he agreed with the adversaries of the balance of trade doctrine in the view that increases in the means of payment were the effect, not the cause, of prosperity. He rejected nonconvertible paper currency on the ground that a produce, the value of which is principally "derived from its scarcity, is necessarily degraded by its abundance."

In his defense of the principles of free trade, Smith took over from his mercantilist predecessors the picture of a world composed of states intent upon pursuing their national interests. But since he considered consumption the sole end and purpose of production, he strongly objected to the mercantilist policy of making export surpluses the ultimate goal of foreign trade, instead of pursuing the goal of the optimum use of available resources. He agreed with Hume's supposition that the various countries followed one another according to a natural process in developing their manufacturing industries and participating in the international exchange of goods. He argued that the surplus part of capital stock which cannot be employed within a country "naturally disgorges itself" into the "carrying trade" and can be employed "in performing the same office to other countries." He strongly emphasized the advantages accruing to a country from the importation of all commodities which domestic manufacturers could produce only at higher costs expressed in standard units of labor. Arguments of this type eventually prevailed over the mercantilist contention that industries would migrate to countries of cheap labor unless producers who had to pay higher wages were protected by tariffs and could attract skilled labor from abroad.

The elements of the natural order.   No survey of Adam Smith's economic theories is complete without a discussion of the sociophilosophical ideas which he considered indispensable to his conception of a society ruled by a natural order. Hence, some observations may be added to indicate the roles which he assigned to self-interest, striving for want satisfaction, and free competition.

Smith was a teacher, not a fervent social reformer, and his teachings were in no way revolutionary.[37] Their utilitarian background was derived from a widely accepted social philosophy. With great facility, he succeeded in coordinating the thoughts of advanced contemporary economists and in presenting their conclusions as the elements of a benevolent natural order. He emphasized the strategic role of the profit motive as a rational principle of economic behavior; he analyzed the processes of competitive production and exchange in terms of a few general, rather simple, premises. He made extensive use of historical material to illustrate the validity of his propositions. Various books on these separate issues had appeared in the course of the two preceding generations, and the scope of the problems to be treated had been fairly well circumscribed in these discussions. But the problems had not been connected by general principles, which would have permitted their coordination and the application of the idea of causality to their mutual relations. Prerequisite to such an analysis appeared to be the assumption that the problems belonged to a sphere of social relationships which could be separated from all other spheres of social life on the ground that those relationships were governed by a specific "natural order," such as had been alluded to in the writings of Cantillon and Hume. The belief in a natural order underlying the behavior of the exchange economy, combined with the belief in a natural harmony of individual interests, provided the background for the establishment of economics as an independent discipline.

Considerable discussion has turned on the question of why Smith made no reference to benevolent sentiments in his economic treatise.[38] It may not be unreasonable to assume that he disregarded such motives because they would have interfered in an undefinable way with the logical construction of a more or less mechanical model of the economy which he tried to create.

In his *Essays on Philosophical Subjects,*[39] Adam Smith attributed to the natural sciences the task of developing the conception of the universe as a vast machine whose parts were operating together as if according to a plan. Similarly, he was convinced that nature was working through human sentiments in order to realize a harmonious social order and to assure the continuous increase of national wealth. That belief found its eloquent expression in his famous dictum that man is led by an "invisible hand" to promote an end which was no part of his intentions.[40]

Since Smith avoided the discussion of fundamental logical issues, he disregarded the question of whether his conception of a "natural" social order was compatible with the doctrine of free will so ardently defended by the Scholastic theologians. But there is no doubt that the application of the principle of causality to the relationships of economic phenomena was predicated on assumptions which no Thomist could have accepted. These assumptions implied that the arbitrary will of individuals could not affect the determinable features of economic relations, that individual behavior was governed by a uniform motive, and that reason provided the most appropriate devices for achieving the ends prescribed by the uniform motive. The subordination of reason under the dictates of will had become a constituent element of utilitarian psychological theories. Constructions of the economy as a mechanism driven by utilitarian motives were elaborated about the same time by Italian economists. But Smith's great success was largely due to the fact that

he established the pursuance of self-interest as the rational principle of all economic activities.

The functions which he ascribed to self-interest were well characterized in his criticism of François Quesnay's view that the desire of men to better their conditions would
not operate effectively unless complete liberty was granted by the government. Smith
contended that self-interest had been acting throughout the centuries and had prevailed
over any attempts to regulate economic activities. He argued that the constant and uninterrupted efforts of all individuals to better their conditions had been almost irresistible in
their effects on counteracting social and political obstructions.

With the utilitarian proposition that in the sphere of material welfare every man was
the best judge of his interests, he combined another statement which was equally characteristic of the methods of utilitarian reasoning: increases in want satisfaction were proportional to increases in the volume of the goods providing such satisfaction, if the values of
the goods were reduced to a common denominator. Hence, expansion of the production of
physical goods, representing increases in the "net revenue" of the community, could be
identified with increases in the general happiness. This idea remained an almost unques-
tioned tenet of utilitarian economics for about one hundred fifty years, although various
utilitarian philosophers protested against the identification of wealth and happiness.[41]

Faced with the crucial question of how to prevent the pursuance of individual interests from damaging others, Smith applied a vaguely formulated maximization principle to
the mutual relations of the members of the economic community: he argued that the
endeavor of each to secure for himself the largest possible share in the available limited
volume of values was continuously counteracted and kept in balance by the like behavior
of all others. Thus, the equilibrium principle which had been used mainly to determine the
relations among measurable aggregates of values was elevated to the role of securing the
harmony between conflicting individual economic interests. The functioning of his harmonious economic order was held to be independent of conscious human behavior. The
logical problems involved in this construction were clarified only at a much later date in
the history of economic reasoning.

Free competition, considered an element of the natural order, was regarded by Adam
Smith as an essential ingredient of the effectual working of the economy from the point of
view of utility maximization. The competitive order which tended to adjust prices to the
costs of production, to reduce the rate of interest to the lowest possible level, and to
eliminate excessive profits and the exploitation of monopolistic situations appeared to be
the powerful factor which could be relied upon to create plenty and to distribute wealth
most advantageously among all the layers of society.

Other contemporaneous economists had also emphasized the benefits of free competition, but they had concentrated their attacks on restrictions of production. Smith included
among the objects of his attacks any restrictions imposed on distributive processes, and he
condemned monopolies of all kinds, whether they were granted by public authorities or
secret monopolies, which he termed *conspiracies,* of businessmen directed against the
public. He did not hesitate to assert that the monopoly price was upon every occasion the
highest which could be squeezed out of buyers, as compared with the "natural" price, the
lowest which the sellers could commonly afford to take.[42] He regarded the expansion of
markets as the most effective method of increasing economic welfare, and free competition in turn as the safest method of securing that objective.

Among the most important practical consequences of this attempt to demonstrate the
overwhelming advantages of free competition was the view that government interference

with economic activities was tantamount to a disturbance of a beneficial natural order. Justice, as Smith understood it, consisted of guaranteeing the exercise of religious freedom and freedom of speech, protecting property, and safeguarding the principles of representative government. In an often-quoted passage, he referred to the "obvious and simple" system of natural liberty which would establish itself when all systems, either of preference or of restraint, were completely taken away. "No human knowledge or wisdom," he asserted, could ever be sufficient to perform the "duty of superintending the industry of private people and of directing it towards the employment most suitable to the interest of society."

About twenty years later, Edmund Burke expressed virtually the same idea when he said that "nature is wisdom without reflection." Burke agreed with Smith on the thesis that the "benign and wise disposer of all things obliges men, whether they will or not, in pursuing their own selfish interests to connect the general good with their own individual success."[43]

Exceptions to the general principle of free competition required special justification, which Smith derived from utilitarian considerations. The spheres of necessary government intervention explicitly mentioned by him were outside the scope of the exchange economy: defense against foreign aggression, the administration of justice, and the execution of certain types of public works.

Thus, readers of *The Wealth of Nations* were faced with a flow of stimulating ideas supported by a large variety of historical material and backed by an optimistic picture of the economic order, the realization of which promised to assure general welfare and economic progress. But consistent deductive reasoning was not a characteristic feature of Smith's methodology. He did not care to coordinate the conflicting results of his analysis. The vagueness of some of his basic concepts, the inconsistencies implied in some of his leading propositions, and the contradictions which affected the formulation of some of his main problems have been the object of repeated criticism. It is, however, possible that the lasting success of *The Wealth of Nations* was promoted rather than impaired by the method of advancing a variety of possible solutions for the same problem, since it left open the way for the development of different lines of theoretical consideration.

Smith was not fully aware of the changes which occurred during his lifetime in the industrial picture of his country preparatory to a new epoch in the history of economic developments. Nor did he expect that his arguments in favor of economic liberty and free competition in national and international trade would gain widespread acceptance in the course of the next decades. But the optimistic belief in the "natural identity" of individual interests which permeated *The Wealth of Nations* greatly appealed to England's educated classes; it suggested a welcome solution to the vexing problem of how to reconcile unhindered striving for gain with the objectives of common welfare. This book provided a theoretical justification for the activities of entrepreneurs and industrialists who stood at the beginning of the era of the "industrial revolution" and tried to exploit new techniques and apply new forms of organization to the highest possible degree. To the merchants it opened the prospect of a world-wide expansion of free trading. At the same time, it paid careful attention to the interests of the working classes and of the large masses of consumers. As has been said by Luigi Einaudi, the good fortune of Smith consisted in his ability to formulate those hypotheses which provided the interpretation of the economic events of his time.[44]

The acceptance in other countries of the ideas propagated by Adam Smith was closely connected with the spread of the methods of nominalistic reasoning. France was the first country where, after the political and social revolution, the principles of economic liberalism found a fertile soil among the educated classes of the population. A successful version of *The Wealth of Nations* adjusted to the French intellectual climate was presented about a quarter of a century later in Jean Baptiste Say's *Traité d'économie politique*. This book became an outstanding instrument for spreading the principles and policies advocated by Smith, and it maintained its position even after more consistent versions of the utilitarian economic doctrine had become available.

In the countries of the European continent where cameralism had gained a firm foothold, the ideas of economic liberalism were accepted and advocated only by certain intellectual groups. The utilitarian background of Adam Smith's teachings was almost generally repudiated. Refined methods of nominalistic reasoning met with strong antagonism, and after the middle of the nineteenth century the economic theory and policy advanced by Adam Smith became the object of extended hostile attacks. But even his most convinced adversaries could not escape the influence of his ideas in formulating their fundamental economic problems. *The Wealth of Nations* stands like a signpost at the crossroad of the streams of economic reasoning. All developments in the field of economic thought which had occurred prior to 1776 appeared to be preparatory to that treatise; all subsequent developments appeared to radiate from that work in various directions. Hardly any other book in the entire field of the social sciences could claim a similar position.

BOOK TWO

Conflicting Economic Doctrines, 1800-1918

A NEW PHASE in the history of economic reasoning began after economics had been established as an independent discipline. The methods of hypothetical reasoning which had provided the logical background for the conceptual isolation of economics were more carefully defined and elaborated. In the course of these developments, fundamental economic concepts had to be adjusted to changes in economic analysis. Several schools of "hypothetical" economics can be distinguished according to the methods they applied in formulating new problems and reformulating inherited views. But the hypothetical approach to the analysis of social and economic phenomena was the object of increasing attack and criticism reflecting the persistent rivalry among conflicting patterns of thought. The controversy centered on the search for economic laws of general validity and the conception of economics as an independent discipline.

Organismic and dialectic methods of thought were paramont among the patterns which, in the course of the nineteenth century, achieved prominence on the continent of Europe, especially in Germany. Both methods appeared in various versions which supplied the logical bases for the elaboration of economic doctrines. Thus, in the course of this period a number of influential, but widely divergent, doctrines vied with each other in the attempt to establish valid economic concepts, to set forth fundamental economic problems, and to explain the functioning of the economy. The adherents of each of these doctrines claimed exclusive validity for their methods, and their mutual antagonisms were intensified through extended and at times acrimonious discussions. Divergencies in methods of reasoning were, to a significant degree, reflected in differences in the institutional setup of the various countries.

Part III

Versions of the Utilitarian
Economic Doctrine,
1800-1870

Chapter 10
The Principles of
Benthamite Economics

—

GENERAL UTILITARIAN METHODOLOGY

IN HIS GREAT TREATISE, *The Wealth of Nations,* Adam Smith conceived of economics as a
branch of the science of government and administration, designed to teach how national
wealth, considered as a volume of physical goods, could best be created and increased. He
regarded the problem of capital accumulation as centrally important, and a considerable
part of his discussion dealt with institutions and social attitudes that he considered detrimental to the growth of capital and the wealth of the nation. Since he viewed the economy
as a system of exchange relationships, his main theorems turned on problems connected
with the division of labor and the relationships between goods and markets.

Smith had inherited from his mercantilist predecessors the conception of "nations"
as political communities competing with each other in the struggle for power. His extensive references to historical events and developments were designed not primarily to teach
economic history, but rather to illustrate the general validity of his proposals. The principles of economic freedom which he advocated enjoyed increasing practical application
during the last decades of the eighteenth century.

In various European countries the still-existing remnants of medieval corporations of artisans and traders were abolished. Monopolistic trading companies, such as the French East India Company and the Dutch India Company, were dissolved. France opened its colonies' ports to foreign ships, and in 1768 concluded the Treaty of Eden with England, which marked an important step on the way to the liberalization of international trade. The British colonial system was thoroughly modified after the defection of the American colonies, at a time when the rich natural resources of the newly settled overseas territories became gradually available to the nations of Europe. Rapid progress was made in the abolition of feudal systems of bondage. Liberal movements sprang up in large parts of Europe in the wake of the Napoleonic Wars. The middle classes in England and France had gained far-reaching political and economic freedom by the end of the eighteenth century.

According to the reasoning of eighteenth-century "liberal" social philosophers, individual freedom was, as a rule, not conceived of as an integral postulate, but was successively applied to various aspects of social life: the personal sphere, the religious creed, political activity, the expression of beliefs of all types, and the field of production and trade.

The economic climate in England underwent conspicuous changes because of the introduction and intensified application of mechanical devices, which resulted in a modification of the structure of practically all manufacturing industries and prepared the way for the absorption by industry of the agricultural surplus population. The spinning jenny was introduced by James Hargreaves in 1764, the spinning frame by Richard Arkwright in 1769, the spinning mule by Samuel Crompton in 1779, and mechanical weaving by Edmund Cartwright in 1784. A revolutionary change in the production of power resulted from the improvement of the steam engine by James Watt in 1784, which initiated an era of large-scale production.

New economic problems were created by the Napoleonic Wars and the attendant inflationary price movements. Even more important were the effects of these wars on the economic and social conditions of the European continent. The Continental Blockade, which collapsed in 1815, failed to cut Britain off from trade with the rest of Europe, but the counterblockade operated by England closed the overseas markets to exports from the European continent. After the final defeat of France, the supremacy of English industry was firmly established, the British fleet dominated the oceans, London became the center of the international money markets, and England became the backbone of international trading. The British policy of the balance of powers prevented the expansionist tendencies of several European states from endangering the peace of the world. The effects of hypothetical reasoning made themselves felt in all these spheres of social action.

During the forty years that followed the publication of *The Wealth of Nations,* no consistent attempt was made to elaborate or to modify the teachings of Adam Smith. The economic problems that were treated in some monographs turned on isolated questions connected with the definition of wealth, with foreign exchange, or with population movements, as related to increases in agricultural production. It is a remarkable fact that no currents of original economic thinking were aroused by the dynamic changes that transformed the economic structure of England and spread to other countries. The challenge to elaborate a new economic doctrine did not originate from the impact produced by the technological revolution, from the transformation of economic organization, or from the upheaval in the spheres of money and credit. Rather, that impulse had its source in the desire of some social philosophers to adjust economics, conceived of as an independent science, to the principles of refined utilitarian teachings.

As propounded by Jeremy Bentham (1748–1832), utilitarian teachings started from certain psychological propositions believed to be forever valid. The essence of these teachings was the maximization of happiness, as the goal of any public policy. This principle had been previously suggested by Frances Hutchison, Adam Smith's predecessor at the University of Glasgow. It had also been emphasized by the French encyclopedist Claude Adrien Helvétius, in his book *De l'esprit,* which appeared in Paris in 1758. Helvétius identified virtue and self-interest on the ground that common welfare was tantamount to the sum of the happiness of all members of society.

Bentham and his disciples elevated the utilitarian maxim to the rank of an axiom that, though not considered susceptible to any direct proof, was held to be self-evident.[1] He used the term *felicific calculus* to express this thought, not in a strictly mathematical sense but in a philosophical sense. No satisfactory answers were given to the question of whether the principle of maximizing happiness meant maximizing the individual happiness of a relatively small number of citizens or whether such maximization should be achieved for the largest possible number, even at the cost of reducing the happiness of individual members of the community. That question came to play a significant role at a much later period in time, during the discussions about the principle of welfare economics.

Over several decades, Bentham waged an incessant war against any methodological principles not fully consistent with the maxims of the utilitarian philosophy.[2] In voluminous treatises he applied his ideas to problems of morals, legislation, jurisprudence, politics, and economics. He attempted to demonstrate that a perfectly balanced rational system could be devised to secure optimum satisfaction of all interests.[3] An impressive range of far-reaching reforms in the spheres of constitutional law; central, local, and colonial government; civil liberties; administration of justice; criminology; and public health all owed their introduction to Bentham's initiative and to the activity of the "philosophical radicals," his convinced followers. Their attacks were directed not only against the doctrine of natural law but also against traditional English jurisprudence as expounded in Blackstone's *Commentaries* (1765–69) and against the political philosophies of conservative authors such as Edmund Burke, who emphasized the presumptions that existed in favor of established institutions, traditional ideas, and ancient rights, sanctified by prescription.[4]

The concept of natural rights elicited the sharpest criticism. "The idea of natural rights," proclaimed Bentham, "is simple nonsense; natural and imprescriptible rights, rhetorical nonsense—nonsense upon stilts." "Socrates and Plato," he said in his *Deontology,* "were talking nonsense under the pretense of talking wisdom and morality. Their wisdoms were the denial of matters known to every man's experience."

In support of his criticism of metaphysics and the doctrine of natural law, Bentham developed highly effective methods of reasoning. John Stuart Mill was convinced that one of Bentham's outstanding achievements was the introduction into morals and politics of those "habits of thought and modes of investigation which are essential to the idea of science," and that it was "his method that constituted the novelty and value of what he did."[5] If Bacon can be given credit for having suggested the methodological approach adopted by the English Mercantilists and Descartes is responsible for the logical structure of the Physiocratic doctrine, then the introduction of refined methods of hypothetical thinking into economic analysis must be ascribed to Jeremy Bentham. The epistemological aspects of fully developed Utilitarianism should be clearly distinguished from any other feature of that doctrine, especially from Bentham's belief that the social and economic order could be organized in accordance with a high degree of generally valid and universally applicable rationality.

The scientific principles underlying Bentham's reasoning were derived from associational psychology as initiated by eighteenth-century Utilitarians.[6] They started on various assumptions that had been suggested by "introspection," regarded as an empirical procedure. Sensations were assumed to be, directly or indirectly, the source of all ideas and to enter into mutual combinations through the operation of a few simple laws of mutual attraction. Feelings and ideas, aided by reflection, were assumed to be mutually associated in varying combinations, and to be built into complex groups of notions.

In this process a primary role was attributed to the categories of pleasure and pain, as expressed in his "felicific calculus." Pleasure and pain were held to accompany the great majority of sensations and to provide the material for an infinite variety of judgments. Measurable by degrees of intensity, duration, uniformity, and the like, pleasures and pains were believed to provide, in turn, a reliable basis for the measurement of desires and aversions. While Bentham admitted that amounts of pleasure and pain could not actually be observed, he insisted upon the possibility of estimating the degree to which such quantities vary under changing conditions. The reduction of all pleasures to measurable magnitudes eliminated the quest for qualitative distinctions and opened the way to the application of the principle of "randomness of wants." Bentham referred to that principle in his often-quoted dictum that "quantity of pleasure being equal, pushpin is as good as poetry." Moreover, two significant inferences were drawn from associational psychology: that things that are only means to desired ends can derive from the latter their specific importance, and that results, not motives, provide the decisive elements for the evaluation of human behavior.[7]

In pursuance of their logical investigations, the utilitarian philosophers drew a distinction between associations that are particular to individuals and other associations that are common to large groups of observers. Associations that could claim general recognition were believed to secure the "truth."[8] The "art of logic" was held to consist in distinguishing such associations from others not similarly qualified. Ethics was defined as the art of establishing associations that result in harmonizing the interests of individuals with the interests of the species. Mental and physiological processes were correlated, and considerable emphasis was placed on the logical dangers involved in using verbal expressions tinged with metaphysical connotations.

According to the utilitarian epistemology, inner consistency of associations of concepts was the criterion of scientific reasoning. Hence, no distinction was to be drawn between the methods considered applicable to the social sciences and those successfully applied to the natural sciences, especially to "rational mechanics" and celestial physics. The system of "mathematical morality" that Bentham developed in close analogy to "mathematical physics" was designed to assist moral philosophers and legislators in their task of comparing and influencing passions. In his treatment of economic problems,[9] Bentham established a direct relationship between wealth and happiness and connected each portion of wealth with a corresponding portion of happiness; he argued that the greatest happiness will accrue to those who possess the greatest wealth. But he realized the effects of the principle of diminishing utility, and suggested that the quantity of happiness produced by a particle of wealth would be "less and less at every successive particle," and that the excess of happiness on the part of the most wealthy would not be as great as the excess of wealth.

Eventually, in his attempt to draw practical consequences from the principles of his philosophy, Bentham was confronted with the crucial question of Utilitarianism: whether social relationships could be assumed to be ruled by a natural identity of individual interests or whether the well-being of the community was to be achieved by specific "artificial" measures designed to harmonize these interests. He had to admit that one of the main functions of government consisted in administering a system of punishment and rewards, and he considered government better fit to remove obstacles to happiness than to promote happiness through positive action. Like his utilitarian predecessors, Bentham was convinced that individuals were the best judges of their interests but that individuals exhibited a predominately passive behavior under the combined influences of pleasures and pains. He also considered that exercise of coercion on the part of the government was likely to create pain and, consequently, was undesirable. In the light of these considerations, Bentham undertook a detailed examination of the effects of government intervention practiced within the framework of democratic institutions. An artificial balance, he argued, should be maintained among the divergent interests of different social groups and should be implemented by constitutional devices.

As distinct from political activities, economic activities appeared to be governed by the operation of self-regulating forms of a specific type. Pleasures and pains, as produced by economic behavior, were obviously reflected in measurable monetary magnitudes, in pecuniary gains and losses. "Utility" was conceived by Bentham as a power that is inherent in things and enables them to create want satisfaction. Although he emphasized the risks involved in pursuing active methods of economic policy, he admitted the desirability of government interference for a considerable range of situations, and did not rely on free competition as an instrument for securing harmony between private and public economic interests.[10]

THE METHODOLOGICAL PRINCIPLES OF RICARDIAN ECONOMICS

The problem of how to adjust economic analysis to the logical principles of utilitarian philosophy was tackled some twenty years later from another angle by David Ricardo (1772–1823), who had been a highly successful financier and became a member of Parliament. In 1815 Ricardo was persuaded by Bentham's friend James Mill (1773–1836) to devote his full energy to the study of political economy.[11] Although Ricardo did not adhere to the utilitarian philosophy in the strict sense of the term, he adopted the leading principles of Benthamite reasoning, which reflected the methods of the associationist psychology. In accordance with these principles, no understanding of mutual social relationship could be reached unless these relationships were assumed to show definite regularities comparable to the "laws" of causality that had been discovered by the natural sciences. Ricardo was not trained in philosophy or history. He ignored any reference to metaphysical forces operating behind the scenes of the economic world, such as Adam Smith's invisible hand. He adopted a similar negative attitude to the connection established by the Utilitarians between pleasures and pains on the one hand and the values attached to goods on the other. Ricardo never described the methods he used in his analysis; afterward they were clarified, at least partly, by Nassau William Senior

(1790–1864), John Stuart Mill, and John Elliott Cairnes (1823–1875). Alfred Marshall said of Ricardo "that his exposition is as confused as it is profound, that he uses words in artificial senses which he does not explain and to which he does not adhere; that he changes from one hypothesis to another without giving notice."[12] Hence, Ricardo's doctrine has been the object of divergent, sometimes misleading interpretation.[13]

In accordance with associationist logic, the teaching of Reason was unable to specify ends; it could only determine appropriate means for the attainment of ends established by individual wants. Since Reason could not be relied upon to set up and to maintain a satisfactory order of economic relationships, the actual existence of such an order had to be ascribed to the operation of forces that resulted in coordinating the effects of infinite numbers of human volitions, independently of the conscious activity of human minds. Such forces could be looked for in the equilibrating tendencies of the economy, especially the tendency of prices to equal costs under conditions of free competition. In addition, free competition could also be expected to enforce the use of hypothetical procedures for securing the most advantageous utilizations of market conditions existing independently of individual wills. It is obvious that the idea of centralized economic planning was incompatible with the role ascribed to Reason by this philosophy.

For these reasons, all Ricardian economists had a fundamental aversion to monopolistic situations of any type that made prices indeterminate and prevented the equilibrium principle from being applied to the analysis of economic relationships. Ricardo himself resorted to the device of ignoring, as far as possible, the existence of such situations, and he availed himself of the assumption that in the boundless and highly complex interplay of economic wants and their consequences, the competitive forces played approximately the same role as that played in cosmic nature by mechanical forces. But prerequisite to the construction of such a relatively simple picture of an imaginary economy was the solution of a fundamental problem: the transformation of all relevant elements of that economy into magnitudes that were reduced to a common denominator. It is an unanswerable question whether Ricardo fully realized the logical structure of his imaginary economic system, its hypothetical nature, and its relationship to the actual behavior of the dynamic economy developing all around him.

The search for the paragon of such a picture was simplified by the fact that the Newtonian conception of the mutual relationships between physical bodies was practically the only relevant pattern of that kind available at the time. In the light of the utilitarian epistemology, it was not necessary explicitly to justify the application of mechanical principles to economic analysis. The assumption that the main relationships between economic phenomena were determined by the operation of equilibrating forces had already played a conspicuous role in the theories of some mercantilist authors, and, perhaps supported by the belief in a "plan" of nature's operations, Adam Smith had emphasized the idea that "systems" resemble machines and searched for a small number of mechanical devices in his attempt to explain highly complex and apparently diverse phenomena. "A philosophical system," Smith stated, "is an imaginary machinery that endeavors in fancy to connect movements already existing in reality."[14]

The Newtonian cosmology was based on the assumption that matter could be abstracted from time; matter was conceived "at an instant."[15] Hence, timelessness became a characteristic feature of the Ricardian economic system. All reactions to changes in economic phenomena (in prices, volumes of production, savings, and the like) were assumed to take place instantaneously and without friction. Moreover, fundamental to the operation of the Newtonian system was the idea that all bodies included in it could be regarded as aggregates of an elementary indivisible standard unit, the atom, and thus be expressed in terms of a uniform denominator that permitted the application of mathematical procedures to the analysis of the behavior of the system. No atom was assumed to be lost in the course of the movements of the bodies, and the relationships among atoms were assumed to be determined by the principle of action and reaction. The atom was purely a hypothetical magnitude; its definition was derived from its function in the scheme of gravitation.

In his economic system, Ricardo attributed to the unit of exchange values a role similar to that assigned to the atom in the Newtonian system. Similarly, the application of the equilibrium principle to the relations among economic magnitudes was reflected in the propositions that in the markets all transactions were governed by the mutual exchange of equal values, and that any goods created in the natural course of productive processes could normally count upon a demand corresponding to the exchange values incorporated in these goods.

The functioning of this hypothetical economic machinery was made dependent upon the fulfillment of various additional assumptions that had played a significant role in the teachings of Adam Smith but that were more explicitly formulated only later: (a) the utilitarian principle that economic behavior of all types was determined by a single "rational" motive, namely, the objective to maximize the gain to be derived from any transaction; (b) the assumption that there was perfect freedom to pursue any productive or commercial activities; and (c) the belief in the existence of a medium of exchange that assured the closest possible adjustment of the market prices of goods and services to their "natural" values, which had their source in productive processes.

This approach to economic analysis was perfectly congenial with the intellectual climate that prevailed in England in the first decades of the nineteenth century. It accepted the institutional background of the economy as a given fact that did not require any explanation or justification. Moreover, it used generally known methods of hypothetical reasoning for adjusting important elements of the utilitarian philosophy to the principles of Newtonian mechanics. Thus, Ricardo could count on a far-reaching understanding of the processes of reasoning that he used in devising a hypothetical picture of the functioning of the economy.

The "principal problem of political economy" that Ricardo set out to solve was the establishment of the laws "which regulate the distribution of the produce of all that is derived from the surface of the earth by the united application of labour, machinery and capital." That somewhat ambiguous phraseology pointed to the task of determining for each of the main productive factors its share in the value of the products. The existence of three productive factors was obviously associated with the traditional distinction of three main classes of the population, and the way was thus prepared for an analysis of the distributive process as applied to the social dividend. Each class was held to contribute a specific productive service and to earn an income of a specific type. That distributive process was to be analyzed in terms of a mechanical proposition. The task that Ricardo had set himself consisted of devising a timeless model of an economic system "grinding out definite amounts of wages, profits and rents for the three social classes, almost with the precision and inevitability of a literal physical machine."[16]

It has been suggested that Ricardo's choice of the problem of distribution as the fundamental economic problem was primarily influenced by the contemporary parliamentary discussions, which reflected the clash between the interests of the English landowners and those of the industrial classes. It is, however, far more probable that in his search for "economic laws" Ricardo turned to the sphere of distribution, which was perhaps the only sector of the economy where he could expect to find causal relationships between economic magnitudes. In addition, problems of distribution had always occupied a privileged position that had its roots in the Scholastic conception of distributive justice. The Physiocrats had practically limited their economic doctrine to an analysis of the distributive processes.[17]

Ricardo's task differed conspicuously from the objectives that Adam Smith had in mind in writing *The Wealth of Nations*. Smith never ceased to be a moral philosopher who differentiated between desirable and prejudicial economic behavior. The question of how to harmonize individual interests and those of the common weal was uppermost in his mind. His religious conscience had to be reconciled with the attempt to apply laws of causality to the functioning of the economy, and thus to question—at least indirectly—the belief in the freedom of the will. References to the "invisible hand" provided a way out of that difficulty.

Ricardo's considerations, however, did not turn on moral issues. He ignored the problems connected with the expansion or growth of an economy and with setbacks in economic activity, although such problems had played a conspicuous role in the reasoning of mercantilist authors and had been dealt with in many passages of *The Wealth of Nations*. The elimination of such issues was the price paid for the transformation of economics into an "exact science." Ricardo's intellectual troubles were not those of a trained observer of the course of social phenomena; they were those of a logician who was searching for "economic laws" and was convinced that no law could be laid down respecting quantity but that a tolerably correct one could be laid down respecting proportions.[18] Although he was not able to give a clear account of his methods, he was convinced of their absolute validity. When faced with apparently irrefutable objections to the conclusions he had drawn from his premises, Ricardo did not question the use he had made of his methods but rather the soundness of his assumptions.

Chapter 11
Ricardian Economics

THE CONCEPT OF EXCHANGE VALUE

THE RICARDIAN CONCEPTION of the value problem started from the task of determining the causes of variations in exchange relations, which were assumed to be ruled by the Scholastic principle of equivalence of what was given and what was taken. But that approach to the value problem in terms of relationships between changing magnitudes was overshadowed by the search for the measure of absolute value which David Ricardo needed for the establishment of the social dividend, the basis of the main distributive process.[1] The determination of such a concept appeared to be dependent upon the adoption of a convenient standard unit of values which was connected with a lasting quality inherent in the goods and which could be expressed in numerical terms.[2]

Adam Smith had wrestled with the same problem when he attempted to determine the "substance" of goods, their "intrinsic" or "natural" values, as distinct from their fluctuating prices. In his search for a stable standard that could be used to measure changes in national wealth, he had eliminated from the outset the monetary unit. He had equally rejected any reference to the utility of the good, since he, like the Scholastics, associated the concept of utility with the genera or classes of the goods and thus was faced with the "paradox of value." He referred to water and diamonds to illustrate that paradox. But he realized that scarcity relationships were involved in the problem, since he argued that the whole quantity of a cheap commodity brought to the market is commonly not only greater but of greater value than the whole quantity of a dear one.

Without much hesitation Smith endorsed the mercantilist propositions that the determination of values was not perceptibly influenced by the consumer's demand as compared with the supply of the goods, and that, as suggested by John Locke, labor was the productive agent mainly responsible for the creation of exchange values. Thus, he arrived at the conclusion that the "real" or "natural" value of a good could be measured with the greatest accuracy both from century to century and from year to year by the amount of labor expanded on its production.[3] He regarded labor as a more stable standard of measuring values than any of the monetary metals or grains. In support of that statement, he advanced the problematic argument that "equal quantities of labor at all times and places may be said to be of equal value to the laborer." Labor, he added, is the "real price" of all commodities; money is only their "nominal price."

But in view of the fact that important elements of the distributive process, such as land rents and profit, could not be explained in terms of "embodied" labor, Smith limited the validity of that explanation to conditions that had existed before money was introduced as a medium of exchange and private ownership of the means of production was generally achieved. Sociological studies, however, have shown that labor time spent on production has hardly ever affected the terms of barter in primitive societies. Smith's often-quoted example of the exchange of beavers for deer belongs to the realm of economic mythology. But that example has a certain theoretical interest; it can be used to indicate some important conditions that had to be fulfilled in order to substantiate the validity of the labor cost theory. Beaver could have been exchanged for deer in accordance with the respective hunting times if the labor involved in hunting was not differentiated, was the only factor of production, had the same disutility for all participants, and was freely accessible under the rule of free competition.

In "civilized communities," however, Smith believed, the measure of value—as distinct from the source of values—was not to be looked for in the conditions of production but in the condition of exchange, in the "power of purchasing other goods." Hence, he defined the "real measure" of the value of a commodity as the quantity of labor that the seller of the commodity would be required to spend if he had to produce the goods received in exchange for the commodity. Thus, rents and profits could be included in the value that a good could "command." Labor, he said, measures the value not only of that part of price which resolves itself into labor but of that which resolves itself into rent and of that which resolves itself into profit.[4]

Smith supplemented his theory with references to disutility considerations: what everything is really worth to the man who wants to exchange it for something else, he said, is the toil and trouble that it can save to himself and that it can impose upon other people. Occasionally he defined individual ''wealth'' as the quantity of other men's labor, or, ''what is the same thing, of the produce of other men's labor which a man's fortune enables him to purchase or command.''[5] In view of these partly conflicting statements concerning the source of exchange values and the standard of measuring them, it is doubtful whether Smith seriously attempted to establish a logical connection between these two problems. The ''ambivalence'' he showed in his discussion of the value problem has been said to reflect a basic conflict of the period, that between the attitude of the traditional subsistence economy and the new acquisitive work ethic.[6] I am more inclined to connect that ''ambivalence'' with a conflict between the tendency of the utilitarian philosopher to look for a psychological motivation of values (sacrifice, disutility) and his adherence to the traditional mercantilist procedure of associating a measurable quality of the things (their exchange value) with the force (labor) that was assumed to have created the quality. The widely held view that the philosophy of natural law was responsible for the introduction of the labor cost theory of value into *The Wealth of Nations* is open to various objections. Smith even felt obliged to admit that, when used for measuring exchange values, labor was really an ''abstract notion'' that, though it can be made sufficiently intelligible, ''is not altogether so natural and obvious.'' He appears to have realized the hypothetical element that was implied in his proposition that ''labor'' provided a ''stable'' standard for the measurement of values.

Closely connected with the discussion of the value problem was the distinction Smith drew between ''productive'' and ''unproductive'' labor. That distinction was a heritage from mercantilist reasoning and was probably associated with the substance concept of goods, since labor was qualified as ''productive'' when it added to the value of the ''subject'' upon which it was bestowed, when it fixed and realized itself in some ''particular subject or vendible commodity'' which lasted for some time at least after that labor was spent, or when the price of the commodity could afterward put into motion a ''quantity of labour equal to that which had originally produced it.''[7] The application of the term *unproductive* to menial services was closely associated with the view that no economic progress could be expected from activities which did not contribute to the accumulation of ''capital goods.''[8]

Jean Baptiste Say adopted an entirely different approach to the problem of exchange values when he undertook to adjust Smith's teachings to the French intellectual climate. Say endeavored to eradicate the last vestiges of the Physiocratic doctrine which had derived the value of goods from a creative act of nature. Influenced by the ideas advanced by Anne Robert Jacques Turgot and Abbé de Condillac, he placed primary emphasis on a concept of production that took account of the conditions of demand. Hence, he insisted that production was never a creation of matter but a ''creation of utility,'' and so should be measured in utility terms, and that utility was the source of exchange values. Costs of production have the effect of limiting supply, and since the value of productive services depends on their ability to create utility, Say reversed the relationship which Smith had established between the value of costs and the value of the product. That is, Say derived the value of factors from the value of their products.[9]

Together with more or less general statements of this type, Say combined a simple supply and demand theory, which he used to explain the price of services of all types and which enabled him to disregard the distinction drawn by Smith between ''productive'' and "unproductive" labor. On similar grounds, he criticized the Smithian definition of wealth, which covered only such useful things as were created by human activity.

The French economists could rest satisfied with a rather loosely defined value concept since they were not concerned with applying the equilibrium concept to the analysis of the economic system and, consequently, did not look for a uniform, constant standard unit of value. A similar approach was adopted in England by Lord Lauderdale, who ascribed the value of goods to the "intensity of desire" to possess them.[10] He explicitly rejected the concept of "real or invariable" values and pointed to supply and demand as the determinants of values. He defined "public wealth" as the aggregate of all commodities that are generally useful and necessary to people. To public wealth he opposed the problematic concept of "individual riches as that portion of wealth which exists in a degree of scarcity" and might serve private, as distinct from public, interests.

Ricardo started his discussion of the value problems with the statement that although utility was a prerequisite condition for goods to possess value, value in use could not be measured by any known standard, since it was estimated differently by different persons. He criticized Say for having confounded value and riches, riches being defined as necessaries, conveniences, and amusements.[11] He warned that many errors in political economy had arisen from considering an increase in riches and an increase of value as meaning the same thing.[12] Like Smith, Ricardo believed that in "that early and rude state of society," which preceded both the accumulation of stock and the appropriation of land, the only circumstance which could afford any rule for exchanging one object for another was the proportion between the quantities of labor necessary for acquiring them. But he rejected the concept of "commanded" labor as applied by Smith to the measurement of exchange values in "civilized" societies. That concept implied that the exchange value of the goods might be affected by changes in the distributive process, and Ricardo argued that such variations might be out of proportion with variations of the productivity of labor. Thus, having eliminated any alternative solutions of the value problem, Ricardo arrived at the conclusion that labor bestowed on the production of the goods was the foundation of their exchangeable value and the "great cause of the variation in the values of commodities." Simultaneously he accepted the distinction drawn by Smith between productive and unproductive labor. In the light of that reasoning, exchange values were measurable lasting attributes of goods, created by past productive processes. The next step consisted in adjusting that conception of values to the logical requirements of the model of an equilibrium economy.

Ricardo did not care about defining the unit of labor time or the specific type of labor to be used in determining the standard unit. Faced with the consideration that labor showed a great variety of types which could hardly be reduced to a homogeneous standard, he referred to a casual observation by Smith that the different wage rates paid for different types of labor, once established, experienced only small variation in the course of centuries, and that, consequently, this scale, being almost independent of changes in prices, could be used to reduce "labor" of various types to a common denominator.[13] Almost all interpreters of the Ricardian value theory have pointed out the futility of this procedure, which ignores the obvious fact that payment for labor, as determined by the market, depends upon conditions of supply and demand which bear no relation to the question of how to reduce to a common physical standard the immense variety of activities covered by the ill-defined term *labor*. The methodological attitude which Ricardo adopted toward this problem has been interpreted as a symptom of his hypothetical approach to the formulation of his concepts. If the standard unit of labor was a hypothetical magnitude, it was not necessary to bother about actual relationships between different forms of labor.

It was obvious that the theory of "embodied labor" could not be used to measure the exchange value of goods—such as land—which are not directly produced by labor, nor was it applicable to commodities the quantities of which could be increased because of relative scarcities of the available resources.[14] To the extent that in cases of that type the demand for products exceeded their supply, discrepancies were bound to develop between the prices of the products and their costs. In addition, the theory of embodied labor was open to the objection that even under conditions of unhampered free competition the exchange values of goods reflected variations in the length of the processes of production and marketing and differences in the quantity or quality of capital equipment.[15] Ricardo admitted that the labor cost principle, although of "universal application in the early stages of society," experienced considerable modifications through accumulation of capital which resulted in modifying the proportions of fixed and circulating capital employed in different trades, and in changing the "degrees of durability of such fixed capital." Embarrassed by the strength of the arguments raised against his value theory, he occasionally resorted to a vague cost of production theory, and eventually observed in a conversation with John R. McCulloch (1789–1864) that the quantity of labor which provided the standard for measuring exchange values was "not the quantity of labor actually worked up in the commodity, but only a measure of this value which convention has chosen for the convenience of the science."[16] That statement is probably the most explicit allusion to the methods of hypothetical reasoning that can be found in Ricardo's writings.

THE RICARDIAN ECONOMIC SYSTEM

Exchange values, which constituted the constructive elements of the Ricardian doctrine, were sharply distinguished from the actual or market prices which were held to be purely transitory, accidental phenomena. Like some Mercantilists, David Ricardo was convinced that the use of the circulating means of payment created a veil which obscured the "substance" of the goods and prevented a full understanding of the functioning of the economy. Hence, price theory had to be separated from value theory.

The equilibrium concept had been used by Richard Cantillon to advance the proposition that the market prices tended to adjust themselves to the costs of production. Adam Smith elaborated this idea and established the theorem that under the rule of free competition market prices oscillated around "natural" prices, the prices determined by the "natural" prices of the factors of production. In accordance with that view, effective demand for and supply of goods were equalized by the mechanism of the market. Without clearly defining the rule of free competition, Smith also attributed to the operation of that rule the function of allocating the productive factors among the industries in such a way that the "whole advantages and disadvantages" of employment as well as money earnings would be equalized.[17] But since he centered his attention on increases in wealth, conceived of as an ever-expanding process, he did not give a detailed analysis of the problems connected with the static allocation of resources, nor did he suggest a clear picture of the static functioning of the economic machinery in general. He was, in fact, more concerned with the dynamic adjustment processes of the economic system.

Ricardo and his school attached primary importance to the negative aspects of free competition, which they termed *free enterprise,* namely, to the absence of monopolistic market restrictions.[18] Reference to the "desire which every capitalist has of diverting his funds from a less to a more profitable employment" provided Ricardo with a generally accepted argument in favor of the proposition that market prices did not remain "for any length of time either much above or much below their natural prices."

For Ricardo, the problem of how to allocate resources was almost identical with the problem of how to reduce to a minimum the amounts of labor to be spent on production in the various lines of industrial activity.[19] He regarded labor-saving devices of a technical type as the main instruments for lowering the exchange value of goods, thus increasing "riches." Hence, as far as manufactures were concerned, he associated a strong deflationary trend with the functioning of a sound economic machinery.

Specifying the concept of natural price, Ricardo defined it as the highest cost of production which had to be spent when production was carried on at different costs and could not be expanded indefinitely.[20] In order to adjust his conception of the economy to the requirements of equilibrium analysis, Ricardo implicitly assumed the constancy of the total volume of the exchange values included in the economic system, and argued that other people's shares must necessarily be reduced in proportion as a favored individual is able to appropriate a greater quantity to himself. If, in accordance with that assumption, total demand for goods was always equal to their total supply[21] and the use of the production services could be regarded as completely flexible, any purchasing power created by productive processes represented demand for a corresponding volume of exchange values incorporated in other goods. Consequently, general excess supply of commodities leading to excess supply of productive services such as labor was held to be impossible if, under the rule of free competition, mutual adjustment of supply and demand was secured by the price mechanism.

The same kind of reasoning provided the basis for Jean Baptiste Say's "*lois des débouchés,*" or "law of markets." "Mr. Say," said Ricardo, "has most satisfactorily shown that there is no amount of capital which may not be employed in a country because demand is only limited by production. . . . Productions can always be bought by production and services. . . . Too much of a particular commodity may be produced of which there may be such a glut in the market as not to repay the capital expended on it; but that cannot be the case with respect to all commodities."

Say's belief in the validity of his law was not affected by the view, advanced by Lord Lauderdale and Thomas R. Malthus (1766–1834), that expenditures for purposes of consumption might be reduced through the accumulation of idle capital.[22] But he was rather cautious in formulating the law, and he admitted that stagnation of business activity might be caused by lack of confidence. He considered it a foremost task of a benevolent administration to make provision for the employment of idle labor in situations of that kind.[23]

Acceptance of the law of markets led to the conclusion that the equilibrium of the relationships between the relevant economic magnitudes could be disturbed only by the operation of forces which affected "from outside" the smooth functioning of the economic machinery. Wars and mismanagement of currency standards were regarded as the main possible sources of such disturbances and of ensuing erroneous assessment of market conditions on the part of large groups of investors. But, whatever might have been the origin and the scope of adverse business conditions, self-regulating forces were relied upon by Ricardo and his adherents to bring about the reestablishment of economic equilibrium.

GENERAL DISTURBING FACTORS: TECHNOLOGICAL CHANGES AND POPULATION MOVEMENTS

On closer analysis it appeared that the equilibrium of the Ricardian system of exchange values was continuously endangered by two factors which were external to the system: changes in the cost structure due to technological improvements, and population movements which threatened to upset the conditions of demand and the balance of the labor market. It was a primary task of economic analysis to show how the effects of these factors were adjusted to the general equilibrium between supply and demand.

The analysis of the general effects of technological changes could be considered simplified when it was assumed that increases in capital invested in plants and equipment were accompanied by proportionate increases in wage capital, so that the ratio between the two capital forms remained constant. But Ricardo's views concerning the effects of radical changes in the cost structure upon working conditions were considerably influenced by a study by John Barton, who pointed out the fact that, in the long run, governed by motives of profitability, employers might be caused to increase investments (fixed capital) at a more rapid pace than wage (circulating) capital.[24] Elaborating on these ideas, Ricardo admitted that additions to the net product, the total product commanding lower prices than before the introduction of new machinery, might be accompanied by a lasting diminution of the wage capital, thus making a part of the working population "redundant," and creating poverty and distress.[25]

In other passages of his work, Ricardo argued that, in the long run, the efficiency of production could be so considerably increased by technological improvements that enlarged savings, promoted by the enhancement of the purchasing power of profits and rents, would bring up the "wage fund" to its previous level.[26] That reasoning, later termed *compensation theory,* was taken over by James Mill, McCulloch, N. W. Senior, and J. S. Mill; it became a constituent part of the post-Ricardian doctrine. As a rule, the concept of "frictions" was used to qualify the difficulties connected with the transfer of displaced workers to new jobs, but these frictions were considered more or less irrelevant to the normal functioning of the exchange economy.[27]

Far more exciting, almost passionate, were the discussions which turned on the problem of how increases in the population were adjusted to the available supply of goods. Influenced by the ideas of some of his mercantilist predecessors, Adam Smith had assumed that the "state of propagation" in the different countries of the world was regulated in an almost mechanical way by the "demand for men." He had pointed out the rapid increase in population in North America, as distinct from the "slow and gradual" progress which took place in Europe and the "altogether stationary" conditions of China.[28]

Toward the end of the eighteenth century, discussion of population problems entered a new phase when it was taken up by a group of authors known as "utilitarian anarchists." They started their considerations from some principles of a "natural law," such as equality of all men, individual liberty, and fundamental identity of all interests. From these premises they derived the view that all evils which had befallen society were due to restrictions imposed on the free exercise of the natural law, and especially to the unequal distribution of goods. They expected an ideal solution of all social problems to be achieved from the creation of vaguely conceived egalitarian communities of an agrarian type.[29] But the prospect of creating harmonious societies on these lines was incompatible with the findings of a Scottish minister, Robert Wallace, who had arrived at the conclusion that any attempts to establish an ideal social order would be frustrated by the inherent tendency of the human race to propagate beyond the available means of subsistence.[30]

In a voluminous treatise published toward the end of the century, William Godwin (1756–1836) undertook to disprove that proposition and to demonstrate that equal distribution of property, especially in land, would remove the existing barrier to the full operation of competitive forces and open unlimited prospects of economic progress.[31] His arguments and his proposals reflected the belief of the eighteenth-century "Rationalists" in the unlimited perfectibility of mankind through progress in education and technology.

The advocacy of such anarchic schemes of social relationships provided the starting point for the famous *Essay on Population* published in 1798 by Reverend T. R. Malthus.[32] Malthus undertook to collect sufficient material to demonstrate the validity of the time-honored formula concerning the tendency of the population to increase at a geometrical ratio as contrasted with the increase in the food supply at an arithmetic ratio.[33] The general trend of his reasoning showed a characteristic similarity to the approach adopted by Adam Smith. Smith had centered his analysis on the effects upon industry and progress of a single motive, self-interest; Malthus examined the effects upon the development of the human race of a single instinct, the sexual desire.[34] Both factors, partly conflicting with each other, were shown to be kept within bounds by the operation of neutralizing forces. Self-interest was assumed to be controlled by the competitive struggle within the framework of an economy based on the institution of private property. The repressive checks which, according to Malthus, assured the adjustment of the population to the available food supply, were sickness and starvation, which tended relentlessly to eliminate all those whose existence was incompatible with that balance. The preventive checks which he recommended were designed to restrict progeny through prudence and moral restraint.[35]

Since the institutions of marriage and private property were thus made responsible for regulating the movement of the population, the Malthusian law provided a missing link between the competitive order and its institutional background. Moreover, it pointed out the central position which was to be assigned in economic analysis to the problems connected with the scarcity of the available means of production, and endeavored to disprove the contention that the unequal distribution of private property was responsible for the poverty of the large masses of the population. In subsequent editions of his *Essay on Population*, Malthus placed increasing emphasis on methods of moral restraint as means of controlling the movement of the population, and he showed a tendency to hold the wage earners responsible for their living conditions if the latter were not improved along with the increasing productivity of the economy. Reasoning of that type was perfectly in line with the principles of utilitarian philosophy.

The answer given to the Malthusian challenge by William Godwin[36] was not very effective. Nassau William Senior raised the objection that people's endeavors to improve their standard of living constituted an important factor in counteracting the tendency of the population to increase beyond the means of subsistence.[37] He stressed the fact that the means of subsistence are proportionately more abundant in a civilized state than in a savage state. George Julius Poulett Scrope (1797–1876) condemned the Malthusian theory as a "most pernicious dogma" and attempted to demonstrate the increasing productive power of agriculture.[38]

The Malthusian ideas were, however, strongly defended by convinced Benthamites, such as Francis Place.[39] Their apparently exact mathematical aspects appealed greatly to all students who wanted to place economics on an equal footing with the natural sciences. The empirical methods which Malthus had developed for illustrating the validity of the law provided a model for similar investigations. The law pointed to the establishment of a definite relation between two heterogeneous ratios, the ratio of increases in population and the ratio of increases in agricultural production. That relation became a cornerstone of the Ricardian equilibrium analysis when it was connected with another important element of Ricardian doctrine, the law of "diminishing returns" in agriculture.

Sir James Steuart and Anne Robert Jacques Turgot had shown that increased investments in agricultural enterprises could not be expected to yield proportionate increases in returns.[40] James Anderson (1739–1808), a Scotsman, elaborated the case described by Steuart.[41] He gave a clear account of the various conditions under which the law of decreasing returns operated, and defined rent as a contrivance for equalizing profits on lands of different fertility.[42] Anderson did not share the view that increases in the population were limited by agricultural factors. His findings about the returns to agriculture were later confirmed in various pamphlets by Edward West (1782–1828)[43] and T. R. Malthus[44] in the course of discussions which turned on the "corn bounty," an export premium granted after 1688 on each quarter of rye when the domestic price did not reach a certain figure. West distinguished cases in which fresh land was brought into cultivation from those in which land that was already in tillage was "cultivated more highly." He suggested that continued increase of the effective powers of labor in manufactures did not compensate for the continued diminution of that power in agriculture. Both West and Malthus endeavored to demonstrate that, owing to the "niggardliness" of nature, proportionately larger labor costs were needed to produce additional quantities of agricultural commodities after the optimum output of the soil had been reached. Malthus formulated very sharply the contrast between increasing returns in manufactures and diminishing returns in agricultural production.[45] The real price of manufactures, he said, the quantity of labor and capital necessary to produce a given quantity of them, is almost constantly diminishing, while the quantity of labor and capital necessary to produce the last addition that has been made to the raw produce of a rich and advancing country is almost constantly increasing.[46] As viewed from a methodological angle, that consideration drew the attention of economists to the divergent effects which resulted from varying the contributions made by productive factors to productive processes.

When combined with the law of population, the law of diminishing returns led to the proposition that enhanced demand for the products of the soil, brought about by increases in the population, was invariably accompanied by increases in the prices of such products and ensuing shifts in the distribution of the national dividend. The idea that the economy was subjected to long-range processes of change was thus made a constituent element of the otherwise static structure of the Ricardian doctrine.[47]

THE LAWS OF DISTRIBUTION

General observations. As mentioned before, Adam Smith was not primarily interested in the distributive aspects of the economy. His discussion of the problems of distribution started from exchange values and the three elements—wages, rents and profits—into which these values can be dissolved. These elements, he argued, had their counterpart in total wages, total profits, and total rents representing the original sources of incomes and the shares of the main classes of the population.[48] Clearly discernible forms of income which had their roots in social institutions were thus identified with "natural" economic categories. That identification was, at least indirectly, connected with the assumption that the receipt of a "natural" category of income created a specific sphere of economic interests which differed from the interests connected with the receipt of other categories of income. Adam Smith repeatedly referred to conflicts of interest which he found to exist between different classes of the population.

Only the concept of wages, which was applied to the compensation paid for the performance of manual work, had a well-defined meaning. The terms *rent* and *profit*, however, frequently denoted aggregates of income derived from various sources. Rent, conceived of as the landowner's income, sometimes included compensation for investments. Smith distinguished *clear profit*, a surplus, from the receipt of interest on capital, and discussed various relations between interest and profit. But he did not advance a clear concept of profit and he failed to take account of the compensation due to employers for organization and managerial services.

The lack of clarity which was a characteristic feature of the concept of "profit" had a counterpart in the confusion that surrounded the concept of "capital." As used in some passages of *The Wealth of Nations*, capital meant money accumulated for lending or investment purposes, or stocks yielding interest or profit. That view was reflected in the definition that capital is the part of the whole stock that a man possesses which he expects to afford him a revenue. In other connections, it denoted physical means of production created by labor. In still others, it was applied to wage goods made available by employers for "productive consumption."[49] The term *circulating capital* was used to distinguish "wage" capital from "fixed" or "invested" capital.

In his version of Smithian economics, J. B. Say carefully separated the discussion of productive processes from the analysis of the problems of distribution, and outlined the latter with greater consistency than had been done in *The Wealth of Nations*. Moreover, consequent upon the rejection of the labor cost theory of value, he regarded labor, land, and capital as equal partners in the process of creating the value of the product, and derived the prices paid for the contributions of the factors from the value of the product. That approach was, of course, incompatible with some fundamental theorems of the Ricardian doctrine.

Ricardo started his discussion of the "principal problem of political economy" from collective magnitudes, the social dividend and its distribution among the three main classes of the population. Since he attributed to labor the creation of the value of the product, he had to explain the shares in the national dividend of land and capital without ascribing to these factors a productivity of their own. Accepting without much modification the meaning attached by Smith to the concepts of labor, land, and capital, he manifested considerable ingenuity in adjusting the problems of distribution to his conception of the functioning of the economy. He showed that the price paid for the use of land was entirely determined by market demand, and could thus be excluded from the cost elements. He connected the price paid for labor with the relationship between the volume of the wage goods and the number of the workers, and regarded profits as a residual category, dependent as to their size on the level of wages and the productivity of the marginal land unit. He combined various partly divergent ideas in this analysis into an apparently consistent body of theory.[50] There is no doubt that he was far more interested in the functional than the social aspects of the distributive processes.

The wage theory.   The term *wages,* as used by Smith and Ricardo, denoted contractual payment for hired—skilled or unskilled—labor. Payment for independent labor was not made the object of theoretical analysis. From his mercantilist predecessors Smith had inherited the conception of a subsistence wage based on the view that the level of wages was determined by the costs of producing and training the workers. But he emphasized that in contemporary England wages were evidently higher than was necessary to enable a worker to bring up a family. Wages were bound to rise when the increase in wealth was proportionately higher than the increase in population. But Smith added that reductions in the wage level might result from the tendency of labor to multiply beyond the range of employment opportunities. In accordance with his value theory of embodied labor, deductions from values created by labor became necessary in civilized societies in order to provide income for landlords and masters. It is a moot question whether a moral judgment was implied in that statement.

Basic to the Ricardian wage theory was the distinction between the "market price" of labor and its "natural price." In an often-quoted passage of *Principles of Political Economy and Taxation,* the natural price was defined as the amount which enables the workers to subsist and to perpetuate without increase or diminution. That price, expressed in terms of food and other necessities, was held to be variable with different times and different regions. It signified a minimum below which wages were not permitted to fall under the play of supply and demand.

Circular reasoning would have been involved in any attempt to connect the natural price of labor directly with the process of producing the goods needed for the workers' existence, since the standard of measuring exchange values was supplied by a hypothetical unit of labor time. A relatively simple solution of defining the wage level was suggested by an observation by Smith that wages were advanced by employers who were obliged to accumulate the wage capital needed for that purpose.[51] In accordance with that formulation of the problem, the natural price of labor was not defined in terms of a normal payment for the standard unit of labor, but in terms of the share allotted to the individual worker of the total amount of available wage goods. There was a logical analogy between this approach to the wage problem and the use made by the Mercantilists of the quantity theory of money for purposes of price determination.

Elaborating the idea of a wage fund, Ricardo regarded the latter as a more or less fixed aggregate of wage goods, a sort of predetermined share of labor in the national dividend, made available at the beginning of the period in which the goods were consumed. This fund was the main determinant of the demand for labor; the Malthusian population theory provided the explanation for changes in the supply of labor. Increasing pressure of the population was bound to lead to declining wages. It remained, however, a moot question whether expansions of the fund and ensuing wage increases would stimulate the growth of the population. The wage rates of specific categories of workers were held to be determined by the play of supply and demand in the labor market.

A peculiar relationship between the movement of wages and changes in the prices of agricultural products was suggested by Malthus in the course of the discussion of the corn laws. In support of his protectionist views, Malthus argued that the worker was better off when corn was expensive and worse off at falling prices of corn.[52] This reasoning was based on the assumptions, apparently shared by Ricardo, that money wages followed the movements of the prices of corn but that the same was not true of the prices of other goods which belonged to the workers' current consumption. These assumptions were questioned by Robert Torrens (1780–1864)[53] and Edward West,[54] but for a considerable time to come almost general agreement existed on the belief that money wages were regulated by the price of corn.[55]

The theory of rent. The thinking of many Mercantilists had been dominated by the idea that the rent earned by landowners was a renumeration paid for the gratuitous use of the natural and indestructible productive powers of the soil. The Physiocrats had placed that view at the center of their doctrine and had regarded the surplus value (*produit net*), as represented by rent, as a characteristic feature of agricultural production. Adam Smith appears to have connected similar effects with his conception of the fertility of the soil. In his extensive and not very lucid discussions of the "rent and land" (chapter 11 of book 1 of *The Wealth of Nations*), he adopted the Physiocratic thesis that in agriculture Nature labors along with people, and supplies its contribution at no cost. Hence, in accordance with his labor cost theory, Smith regarded land rent as a monopoly price. He argued that every improvement of the circumstances of the society, leading to increases in the real value of the products of land on the one hand and to reductions in the prices of manufactures on the other, tends to increase the real wealth of the landlord or his power of purchasing the labor of other people or the produce of their labor.[56] But, referring to a different conception of rent, Smith occasionally remarked that high rents are rather the effects of high prices. It has been suggested that for over a century he created a confusion by his failure to draw a distinction between land with alternative uses and farmland with no competing use. In the first case rent was an element of costs; in the second case the yield depended on conditions of the market.

Around the turn of the century, the Physiocratic surplus theorem was advocated by several English authors in defense of the view that the annihilation of Britain's trade through the effects of the Continental Blockade would not seriously affect national welfare.[57] But in the heated controversies which turned on the corn laws the role of the landowners in the processes of production and consumption was the object of conflicting views, and the high rents paid to them were frequently attacked as symptoms of monopolistic situations. In a commentary on the 1814 edition of *The Wealth of Nations*, David Buchanan pointed to the conception of rent as an arbitrary addition to the costs of production.

These discussions, as combined with the theorem of diminishing returns in agriculture, provided the background to the Ricardian conception of land rent as a price determined by market demand. Referring to Smith's observation that the supply of land, the natural factor of production, could not be increased when the prices of agricultural products were rising, Ricardo argued that rent was not a payment which was required to call forth the contribution of a productive factor. He asserted that rent would accrue only when the price of agricultural products was in excess of their premarginal costs, that in proportion as Nature becomes niggardly in its gifts, it exacts a greater price for its work. Ricardo availed himself of the argument concerning the "niggardliness" of nature, especially in his discussions with Malthus. The latter regarded rent as a surplus which was owed to the bounty of nature and supported that view with the argument that the land can produce more than is necessary for the maintenance of the workers employed on it.

In accordance with the fully developed Ricardian rent theory, no rent accrued to land the yield of which was produced at the highest costs just covered by the prevailing price. The rents accruing to other soils were higher, the less labor and capital were expended on their products. These considerations were reflected in the Ricardian discussion of the progressive settlement of agricultural regions, beginning with the occupation of the most fertile and ending with the occupation of the least productive soil. The introduction into that analysis of the law of diminishing returns led to the conclusion that each additional investment, though equal to the preceding one, was bound to provide proportionately lower yields, after an optimum relation between investment and returns had been reached. Thus conceived, rents were determined by the differences between the values of agricultural products obtained by the employment of equal quantities of capital and labor. Such differential rents were bound to rise with each increase in population, leading to the cultivation of land of poorer quality than before, or to a more intensified cultivation of land under tillage.

Ricardo did not explicitly indicate the simplifying assumptions which he made in developing this theory.[58] He treated the use of land as a homogeneous category and labor and capital as homogeneous factors. He did not clearly state whether he interpreted the law of diminishing returns to mean that a given ratio of increase in a variable factor is associated with a smaller ratio of increase in the total product or whether, in accordance with that law, equal successive increments of a variable factor yield decreasing increments of the product. Marginal land was tacitly assumed to be always available, so that all rents could be regarded as differential in type.[59] Income resulting from lasting improvements of the soil was not well distinguished from rent in the strict sense of the term.

Although stated in the form of an explanatory proposition, this rent theory had some very important political implications. It led to the conclusion that increasing demand for agricultural products—brought about by increases in the population—was bound to result in increasing prices of these products and rising wages, accompanied by ever-mounting rents. In the struggle over the maintenance of the corn laws the landowners fought a losing battle against the manufacturers, who availed themselves of the argument that free importation of grains was necessary in order to prevent rising wages from undermining the competitive position of British exports in international markets. Radical reformers could even argue that the "unearned increment" represented by the rent could be taxed away without adversely affecting the functioning of the economy. Some inconclusive discussions turned on the question of whether the rent principle could also be applied to the yield of mining enterprises.

The theory of profit and interest on capital.   It is a remarkable fact that Ricardo lacked adequate tools for dealing with the share attributed to capital in the distributive process. The problems involved in defining that share were not even clearly formulated. Smith regarded interest as a payment for the use of borrowed money capital, and he derived it from the profits which could be earned by using that capital for productive purposes. This proposition had previously been established in the fight over the prohibition of "usury." Another step in the development of the concept of interest had been connected with the abandonment of the mercantilist view that the rate of interest was determined by the quantity of money in circulation.[60] The proposition that the "natural" rate of interest was dependent upon the "natural" rate of profit was endorsed by Ricardo, who emphasized that interest on money is not regulated by the rate at which the bank will lend but by the rate of profit which can be made by the employment of capital and "which is totally independent of the quantity or of the value of money."

But the term *profit* was an ill-defined expression for a variety of incomes accruing to the employer from different sources. It included the yield of the capital which the employer had invested in the enterprise; the remuneration for his entrepreneurial, managerial, and possible technical services; reward for risk; and additional earnings which resulted from the introduction of technological improvements and other cost-saving devices, from favorable market conditions, from monopolistic situations, and the like. Only some limited aspects of profits were taken into account in the argument advanced by Smith that the owner of capital could not be expected to participate in productive enterprises unless he were allotted a share in the value of the products or "unless his stock was to be replaced to him with a profit."[61]

Although Smith included profits and interest on capital among the costs of production, he occasionally characterized profits as increments over and above the exchange values created by labor; in other passages he referred to profits as deductions from such exchange values. When the first alternative was adopted, the advocates of the labor cost theory were faced with the task of indicating the forces which enabled capital to "create" exchange values in excess of the values produced by labor in past and present productive processes. Adoption of the second alternative eliminated capital as an original source of exchange values and income, and led to the question of why the owners of capital could claim a portion of exchange values created by the "productive power" of labor. Smith did not give an answer to these thorny problems.[62]

Ricardo agreed with Smith on the inclusion of profits among the costs of production. The return on land that does not yield a differential rent provided him with a standard for determining a minimum level of profits; his belief in the forces of competition was responsible for his view that the returns on capital were equalized in all productive uses. But almost insuperable difficulties for his conception of profits resulted from the role played by the time factor, and his discussions of these problems were open to varying interpretations. These and other difficulties were so great that Ricardo eventually abandoned the inner consistency of his doctrine when he admitted in a letter to McCulloch that the explanation of the proportions in which the whole produce was divided among landlords, capitalists, and laborers was not essentially connected with the doctrine of value.[63] It is hardly possible to apply the term *theory* to the Ricardian views concerning the return on capital investments.[64]

Ricardo inherited from Smith the conviction that landowners spend their incomes on consumption goods and that workers' wages could hardly leave a margin for significant savings. Hence, profits were assumed to be the main source of savings and capital accumulation.[65] Ricardo shared the widely accepted view that savings were insensitive to changes in the rate of interest.[66] Since he believed that savings were instantaneously transformed into loan capital or investments, he could ignore the problems resulting from the existence of idle capital. But his concept of "productivity" had no precise and unequivocal meaning. When applied to the explanation of ground rent, the term *productivity* simply conveyed the idea that the yield of agricultural land was due to the natural fertility of the soil, and ignored the differential element involved in the concept of rent. If the expression *productivity of capital goods* was simply intended to point to the fact that more products could be gained with than without the use of capital, an empirical proposition had been elevated to the rank of a theory.

Ricardo realized, at least in his analysis of the rent concept, that the problem of distribution was, in fact, a problem connected with market conditions, not with productive processes.

With his refusal to accept the labor cost theory of value and his view that the value of the productive factors was to be derived from the value of the products, J. B. Say achieved an approach to the problems of distribution which permitted him to disregard various issues which had their roots in the formulation of the concept of costs of production adopted by Adam Smith. Instead of identifying "capital" with a wage fund, Say applied the concept of "capital" to the plant and equipment used in productive processes; he placed capital and labor on a footing of equality as two productive factors and derived interest and profits from a "productive power" of capital. From "profits of capital," the reward for the services rendered by capital goods, he distinguished "profits of industry," the reward for productive services rendered by the entrepreneur in the process of organizing productive activity. Special returns resulting from various monopolistic situations were included in the "profits of industry."[67]

Say failed, however, to clarify the meaning of his "productivity theory." He did not attempt to show that the addition to the value of the goods produced with the aid of capital was greater than the value of the capital goods used up in the productive process, nor did he deal with the question of whether the value of larger volumes of goods produced with the aid of capital was greater than the value of smaller quantities produced without such assistance. But in discussion of the contributions of productive services (as opposed to capital) to the value of the product, Say referred to conditions of supply and demand, and ascribed to the entrepreneurs the function of determining the prices of these services in accordance with the market situation.[68]

Several British authors who followed Say in advocating productivity theories were better aware than he had been of the problems involved in the productivity issue. Lord Lauderdale, who held utility and scarcity responsible for the existence of values and realized the importance of capital as a productive agent, advanced the view that productivity could be ascribed to capital only to the extent that it could be shown that human labor was supplanted by capital or that the use of capital enabled its owner to perform labor of a type which was beyond the capacities of labor unassisted by capital.[69] From his considerations he derived the conclusion that the productivity of labor was always limited by the "state of knowledge in the art of supplanting and performing labor," and that, consequently, definite boundaries were set to available investment opportunities, and that the volume of savings could possibly be overexpanded.

Another version of the productivity theory was suggested by Malthus, who rejected the belief that all values were created by labor.[70] Like Lauderdale, he qualified profits as a reward for the contribution of the capitalist to the yield of productive processes,[71] and emphasized the large increases in the volume of production which could be brought about when labor was assisted by appropriate tools and machinery. He pointed to the effects of competition in order to explain the fact that only relatively small differences—represented by the rates of profit—existed between the value of the products and the value of capital and labor spent on their production.

James Mill and John McCulloch, who realized the shortcomings of the Ricardian analysis of profits, made the problematic attempt to define profits as a reward of labor stored in the capital goods.[72] They had no answer to the question of why secondary labor of that kind, when employed in productive processes, should receive a special compensation determined by the length of the production period.

The outlook on economic developments to come, which Ricardo derived from his theorems, signified in some respects the completion of the triumph of deductive reasoning over the results of observation and experience. Surrounded by industrial developments which reflected the economic effects of new inventions, of continuous improvements of technical and managerial devices, and of far-reaching changes in the structure of the population, he based that outlook exclusively on certain inferences which he drew from his leading theorems and assumptions, especially from the positive relationship which he established between the rise in the price of food and the level of wages. His often-quoted dictum that the price of corn was the regulator of the prices of all other things was a concise expression of his theoretical convictions. On the assumption that the volume of exchange values included in the national product was a more or less fixed magnitude and that the landowners' share was determined by irresistible forces of demand, wages could rise only at the cost of profits, and a "natural tendency for profits to fall" was bound to result from the fact that "in the progress of society and wealth" additional quantities of goods could be obtained only at the sacrifice of more and more labor. The rate of profits, said Ricardo, can only be increased by a fall in wages, and there can only be a permanent fall of wages as a consequence of a fall of the necessaries on which wages are expended. Convinced of the validity of that statement, Ricardo objected to Smith's view that the rate of profits might be affected by capital accumulation. He equally rejected the connection which Say established between the volume of capital available for investment and investment opportunities.[73] Technological improvements and discoveries applied to agriculture could be expected to check, at repeated intervals, this "gravitation, as it were, of profits" without being able to arrest the general tendency. Eventually a final state was likely to be reached in which profits had dwindled to the zero, or "capital subsistence" level, capital accumulation was discounted, and, under stationary conditions, almost the whole produce of the country not spent on wages accrued to the owners of the land and the receivers of tithes and taxes.[74]

THE ROLE OF MONEY AND CREDIT

Like Adam Smith and his mercantilist predecessors, David Ricardo was convinced that, hidden behind the "veil of money," there existed a "real system of exchange values incorporated in the goods." In accordance with this view, which was probably suggested by the Scholastic substance concept, the network of real exchange transactions was the true object of economic analysis,[75] the metallic currency derived its exchange value from its costs of production,[76] and the quantity theory of money provided an instrument for the explanation of the behavior of prices. Adam Smith rejected Montesquieu's view that prices were determined by the volume of money. He made the volume of money dependent upon the demands of circulation and the costs of producing precious metals. But to inconvertible paper currency he applied the idea that a produce the value of which is principally derived from its scarcity is necessarily degraded by its abundance. But the functions of money as a store of value, which had repeatedly been emphasized by mercantilist authors, were ignored by Smith and his successors.

J. B. Say connected the value of money with the concepts of "indirect utility" and scarcity. He assumed that the quantity of the means of payment could always be adjusted to the amount required to maintain the prevailing price level.[77]

Lively discussions of monetary problems were aroused in England by the disquieting gold movements and the changes in the price level which followed upon the suspension of the free convertibility of bank notes through the Restriction Act of 1797. The influence of noticeable, but not violent, price increases on the balance of payments was obscured by vast wartime expenditures made abroad during the Napoleonic Wars and the restrictions imposed on foreign trade.

In a remarkable analysis of the monetary and economic aspects of this situation, Henry Thornton, a banker and member of Parliament, elaborated the effects upon exports of an "extravagant issue" of inconvertible notes. Adopting a broad concept of money, he attributed to changes in the volume and velocity of the circulating means of payment the same influence on prices as was generally ascribed to changes in the volume of legal tender money. He realized that, even if the principles of "sound banking practice" were observed, the prevailing methods of discounting commercial bills could easily lead to monetary expansion, which might ultimately affect prices through ensuing increases in incomes. From the connection which he found to exist between the rate of profit and the rate of interest, he drew the conclusion that credit expansions could easily be promoted by the policy of fixing the loan rate below the expected profit rate.

Thornton was well aware of the compensatory effects exercised by savings in the process of credit expansion. He also emphasized, as had Bentham before him, the characteristic features of "forced savings" which were connected with the curtailment of expenditures on the part of those groups of the population whose incomes did not increase in step with rising prices.[78] In the course of these discussions, Thornton pointed out the stimulating effects on productive activity which could be exercised by credit expansion on the part of the banks; moreover, he stressed the fact that in periods of rising prices increases in profits were likely to result from the tendency of wages to lag behind prices. He showed an equal understanding of the functioning of the credit mechanism in his analysis of the evils of "overtrading" and speculative maneuvers which had been rendered possible through the use of "fictitious" capital in business enterprises. For a considerable time to come, his analysis of inflationary situations and the measures needed to promote economic stability was unsurpassed by any other author. In 1811, when Thornton defended his monetary views in two parliamentary speeches, he added an important observation that the expectation of a change of prices would be taken into account in the process of fixing the loan rate of interest.[79]

These discussions contributed to the formulation of the Bullion Report of 1810, in which the leading monetary views were effectively presented by a group of able experts. Outstanding members of the Bullion Committee were Henry Thornton, Francis Horner (1778–1817), and William Huskisson (1770–1830). Their proposals were incorporated in the Bank Bill of 1819. These views centered on the ideas that changes in the quantity of money provided the explanation for changes in prices, that the degree of currency depreciation was indicated by the change in the currency price of gold, and that under conditions of convertibility definite limits were set to the fluctuation of the exchange rate through the exchange mechanism as influenced by the balance of payments. The remedies urgently recommended in the report were those of the reduction of the volume of the circulating means of payment and the resumption of convertibility of the bank notes at the

earliest opportunity. No regard was paid to Thronton's discussion of the effects of relatively low rates of interest on credit expansion and to his analysis of the effects of credit
expansion on business activity. Short-run considerations of that kind did not attract
particular interest. Similar recommendations had been made in a *Report of a Parliamentary Committee on Monetary Conditions in Ireland* in 1804.

Ricardo's monetary views corresponded to those advanced in the Bullion Report,
especially as far as the validity of the quantity theory of money was concerned.[80] He
strongly asserted his conviction that capital could be created only by saving and that
business activity could not be stimulated by the expansion of commercial loans. The
quantity theory of money was adopted equally by the so-called Anti-Bullionists, who
defended the monetary and credit policy of the Central Bank and ascribed to the managers
of the latter a predominantly passive attitude with regard to the note issue. They connected
the depreciation of the currency with a variety of causes.[81] The outcome of these discussions of monetary issues was strongly influenced by the general belief in the automatic
operation of economic forces, which was a characteristic feature of utilitarian philosophy.
The adoption of the rules of the international gold standard would hardly have been
supported by public opinion unless it had been backed by the conviction that the best
institutional devices were those that restricted to a minimum the sphere within which
arbitrary action could be taken by monetary authorities. Similar consideration led to the
rigid separation of the functions connected with the issuance of notes from the credit
operations of the Central Bank. The regulation of these latter operations reflected the view
that, as sources of credit, the banks played merely an intermediary role in transmitting
claims to exchange values from savers to borrowers, without affecting through their
activities the normal processes of production, distribution, and consumption.

In his application of the quantity theory of money to price analysis, Ricardo drew no
distinction between metallic currency and convertible bank notes on the one hand and
unconvertible paper money on the other, as far as quantity relationships were concerned.
It is not, he stated, the convertibility of the bank notes which keeps their value equal to
that of coin, it is the limitation of their quantity.[82] On similar grounds he questioned the
view of some Mercantilists that metallic currency constituted "wealth in circulation."

The commodity theory of money as endorsed by Ricardo made the value of the
metallic currency dependent upon its costs of production. Ricardo applied that theory
especially to the explanation of the exchange relationships between the two monetary
metals, and ascribed the relative stability of the value of gold to the constancy of the costs
of production of that metal. He regarded the use of convertible bank notes as a purely
technical device that did not affect the tendency of prices to be adjusted to the exchange
ratios of commodities as established on the basis of their "natural" or real values. Under
the rule of the gold standard, redundant domestic quantities of metallic currency could be
expected to be absorbed by exports of specie.

The difficulties which resulted from the use of two mutually incompatible theorems
(the quantity theory of money and the cost of production theory) to explain the value of
money were—at least apparently—overcome by applying the cost of production theory to
the determination of the "permanent" ("normal") value of money and the quantity
theory to short-run conditions. The quantity theory of money implied, when strictly
interpreted, instantaneous adjustment of all prices to changes in the quantity of money.
That interpretation was adopted by James Mill, who objected to David Hume's analysis of
the process of gradually rising prices and the spread of their effects on commercial and

industrial activity.[83] McCulloch was more cautious in his discussion of Hume's views, which were shared by Malthus and defended by G. P. Scrope.[84] As distinct from the large majority of the contemporaneous economists, Malthus attempted to demonstrate that the pressure on sterling in the foreign exchange markets might have been partly due to nonmonetary causes, such as crop failures, payment of subsidies to continental powers, maintenance of armies on foreign soil, and the like.[85]

The disputed question of whether Ricardo and other contemporaneous authors of monetary studies were *Metallists* in the strict sense of the term is not particularly relevant from the point of view adopted in this study. What matters is that the majority of these authors, including Ricardo, did not explain the value of money in terms of a rigid substance concept.

THE THEORY OF INTERNATIONAL TRADE[86]

The high degree of abstraction which characterized the Ricardian economic system did not permit the inclusion of purely political concepts among the factors which were relevant to the functioning of the economic machinery. In this respect the Ricardian system differed significantly from that envisaged by Smith. Smith had taken over from his mercantilist predecessors the picture of a world composed of states which were intent upon pursuing their national interests. Since he considered consumption the sole end and purpose of production, he strongly objected to the mercantilist policy of making export surpluses the ultimate goal of foreign trade, instead of seeking that goal in the optimum use of available resources. From Hume he took over the idea that the various countries followed one another in developing their manufacturing industries and in their participation in the international exchange of goods; he argued that the surplus part of capital stock which cannot be employed within a country "naturally disgorges itself" into the "carrying trade" and can be employed "in performing the same office to other countries." In his defense of the free trade principle he emphasized the advantages accruing to a country from the importation of all those commodities which domestic manufacturers could produce only at higher costs expressed in standard units of labor. But reasoning of that kind could be met by the mercantilist argument that industries would migrate to countries of cheap labor, unless producers who had to pay higher wages were protected by tariffs and could attract skilled labor from abroad.

Ricardo's imaginary economic system was spatially defined as an area in which economic relationships were determined by the operation of competitive forces. Hence, he ascribed a fundamental importance to the fact that the various national economies were separated from each other by the lack of mobility of capital and labor, and that, consequently, neither rates of interest nor wage rates could be expected to be equalized through international commercial or financial activities. Viewed from the angle of the Ricardian labor cost theory of value, the workers of different countries were characterized as noncompeting groups. Prices paid in international trade did not reflect relative costs of production expressed in a uniform standard unit of labor.

Reasoning of that kind provided the background for the Ricardian theory of comparative costs which had originally been suggested by Robert Torrens.[87] Underlying this theory was the idea that, in order to determine the advantages accruing from international trade, it was not appropriate to base the comparisons on absolute values. Rather, it was necessary to define the relationships which existed in each country between the labor costs of the various products, and to use these ratios for purposes of comparison. The results of such computations could lead to the conclusion that the international exchange of certain goods was profitable even though the imported commodities could be produced domestically at less absolute costs than in the exporting country. The famous example for demonstrating the theory of comparative costs dealt with the exchange of wine produced in Portugal for cloth produced in England. If cloth made in England by the labor of one hundred workers would exchange for wine made in Portugal by the labor of eighty workers, the exchange would be advantageous to both countries even if the Portuguese could make the cloth themselves with the labor of ninety workers. In the light of that reasoning, the product of more labor could be exchanged in international trade advantageously for the product of less labor.

The theorem of comparative costs was undoubtedly an ingenious combination of the labor cost theory and the general utilitarian principle of minimizing costs of production and thus maximizing utilities to the consumer. In accordance with that theory, the advantages to be derived from exports depended upon the value of the imports received in exchange, and increases in exports meant a loss to domestic consumption unless that loss was more than compensated by the relatively greater value of the imported goods when this latter value was measured in terms of domestic production costs. On the other hand, tariffs and other measures designed to protect domestic industries against foreign competition could be characterized as methods which resulted in transferring resources from more efficient uses in export industries to domestic industries producing at relatively higher comparative costs. This analysis of international economic relationships exclusively from the point of view of exchange values—regardless of any other effects of the international exchange of goods and services—was characteristic of the "heroic abstractions" which provided the mainstay of Ricardian reasoning.

Hardly less characteristic of the methods used in establishing the theory of comparative costs was the fact that no attempt was made to indicate the specific assumptions which placed limits on its applicability. In the example which referred to the trade between England and Portugal, one homogeneous commodity was exchanged for another commodity of the same type. The exchange took place between two spatially distinct markets in which conditions of full employment and perfect competition were assumed to exist. No regard was paid to costs of transportation and their influence on demand and supply, to changes in the costs of production, to monetary factors, and so on. Although the Ricardians were convinced that their example permitted extended application to multilateral trading between a number of countries, any attempts to justify that contention were frustrated by the difficulties involved in analyzing increasingly complex hypothetical international relationships.

Among the main objections raised by the adherents of protectionist duties to the theory of comparative costs was the "infant industry argument," which was backed by the consideration that for countries with slowly developing manufactures it was less important to provide the domestic markets with cheap articles of consumption than to stimulate the expansion of growing industries.

From the application of the labor cost doctrine to international trade, Ricardo drew the additional conclusion that the amount of exchange values available in a country would not be affected by the expansion of foreign trade unless imports resulted in reducing the real value of wage goods. In the latter case the rate of profit could rise and accumulation of capital could be stimulated. Ricardo also emphasized the gains from foreign trade, which, without increasing real values, consisted in enhancing the volume of consumption goods and, consequently, the "sum of enjoyments," but he rejected the idea of regarding that sum as a measurable magnitude.

Hume's analysis of the distribution of the precious metals among the trading countries provided Ricardo with an instrument for demonstrating how that distributive process was determined by the relative demand for money of the various regions and the relative productivity of their industries. This mechanistic price-specie-flow approach implied an application of the quantity theory of money to the problems connected with international balances of payments. Any deficits arising in the process of equalizing imports and exports were assumed to be liquidated by gold shipments, with the result that the lowering of prices in the gold-exporting country tended to increase its exports and to reduce its imports, whereas the opposite process was taking place in the gold-receiving country. The functioning of the price mechanism was thus relied upon to effect the balancing procedure;[88] the total volumes of output and employment, and the allocation of productive factors, were believed to remain unaffected monetary factors as such. "Gold and silver," said Ricardo, "having been chosen for the general medium of circulation, they are, by the competition of commerce, distributed in such proportions amongst the different countries of the world, as to accommodate themselves to the natural traffic which would take place if no such metals existed, and the trade between countries were purely a trade of barter." According to this theory, the share of every country in the total available volume of monetary metals was automatically determined by its participation in international trade, and no artificial measures were available to influence the inflow of these metals for any prolonged period. Gold movements from one country to another were held to be regulated by the relative level of prices, which in turn was regarded as a function of the relative quantities of the monetary metals circulating within the countries. Hence, the importance attached to the functioning of the gold standard, which imposed upon the Central Bank the obligation to maintain a fixed rate of exchange between the domestic currency and the international monetary metal, regardless of the deflationary influences which that policy was likely to have on the domestic price level. The firm belief in the beneficial effects of that policy could hardly be more strongly expressed than in Ricardo's dictum that "happily in this case as in most others in commerce, where there is free competition, the interest of the individual and that of the community are never at variance."[89]

Chapter 12
Early Discussions of
Ricardian Economics

SHORT-RUN PROBLEMS

THE BENTHAMITE ECONOMISTS lived in an economic world in which hypothetical reasoning enjoyed increasing practical application. Hence, at least to a certain degree, their surroundings tended to adjust themselves to the behavior ascribed by them to their imaginary economy. Productive and distributive processes were ruled by fluctuating conditions of supply and demand, costs and prices, and were subjected to the rules of intensified competition. Many categories of enterprise were confronted daily with risks and uncertainties of varying degrees. But prolonged crises which spread ruin among businesses and unemployment among workers were disregarded by the economic philosophers, who knew only one reliable method of bringing order into the chaotic picture of expectations, estimates, speculations, and anticipations. They took account only of the results of all these innumerable procedures, and introduced only such assumptions as were necessary to render these results determinate and independent of any antecedent doubts and dilemmas. That purpose was achieved through the construction of a fictitious economic system in which the time element played no significant role, all prices were automatically adjusted to the costs of production, sellers and buyers were motivated in their activities by a uniform desire to maximize their profits but were unable to exercise any perceptible influence upon prices, all economic resources were fully employed, capital and labor were perfectly mobile, and money was a neutral factor.

This representation of the economy during the turbulent years of the "industrial revolution" is one of the most striking creations in the history of Western reasoning. The convinced adherents of the Benthamite methodological principles did not even admit the validity of considerations through which some light was thrown on the obvious discrepancies between the actual course of economic events and the hypothetical picture of the Ricardian economic system.

The situation is well illustrated by the discussions which took place between T. R. Malthus and David Ricardo on the question, To what degree could the results of abstract reasoning be applied to the treatment of the burning problems of the day? Ricardo pointed out "one great cause" of differences between his views and those of Malthus when he observed that Malthus always had in mind the immediate and temporary effects of particular changes, whereas he (Ricardo) fixed his whole attention on the permanent state of things which would result from them.[1] Motivated by the endeavor to "elucidate principles," Ricardo imagined "strong cases" which permitted him to show the "operation of these principles"; he "put quite aside" the immediate and temporary effects. Malthus, however, preferred the short-run approach and criticized Ricardo's "exaggerated tendency to simplify and generalize."[2] Colonel Robert Torrens, who asserted that the nature of the premises was the real issue in the controversy between Ricardo and Malthus, arrived at the conclusion that "if Mr. Ricardo generalizes too much, Mr. Malthus generalizes too little."[3]

Since Matlhus did not attempt to devise a consistent picture of the functioning of the economy, he refused to apply to economics the rigorous principles of mechanics and rejected the idea of looking for a uniform standard unit of exchange values incorporated in the goods. The standard unit which he chose was derived from the concept of commanded labor; in other words, the quantity of labor an individual would be willing to give in exchange for a commodity was to be expressed in units of disutility.[4] That definition permitted him to include land rent and profits among the cost elements. The same amount of labor, when expended on different productive processes, could be shown to yield different volumes of exchange values, while the purchasing power of the buyers, their effective demand, could be regarded as an important factor in determining such values. Malthus did not even hesitate to describe his vaguely formulated principle of supply and demand as "the first, greatest and most universal principle of political economy." He applied that principle not only to the explanation of market prices (as was done by the Ricardians) but also to long-run natural prices.[5] He realized the importance of scarcity as a fundamental factor in determining values and was aware of the purely hypothetical nature of the labor standard which he used for measuring values.

When pursued to its consequences, this way of describing the value problem led to the abandonment of Jean Baptiste Say's law of markets. Moreover, it provided the starting point for the Malthusian "theory of gluts." On the assumption that all savings were normally used to increase the output of the wage goods, Malthus argued that in the short run the increase in the number of workers might not keep pace with the additional output of such goods, and that an "inordinate passion" for accumulation was likely to lead to a supply of commodities beyond what "the structure and habits of the society" would permit to be profitably consumed. Under these circumstances only income not earned directly by labor could provide sufficient demand for the products of accumulated capital. To a large body of "unproductive consumers," above all to landowners but also to servants, soldiers, and members of the free professions, Malthus assigned the function of supplying and safeguarding the profits of the entrepreneur. He claimed the effective demand of these groups of consumers as a necessary factor in preventing the spread of "general gluts" in the market, followed by declines of commodity prices below the elementary costs of production and by contractions of business activity.

From the functions which he ascribed to landowners in the process of maintaining the balance between consumption and savings, Malthus derived theoretical arguments in favor of a protectionist tariff for agricultural products. He believed that profits from international trade were earned without corresponding declines in other forms of income and that, consequently, they increased the demand for labor and the fund out of which wages were paid,

The general economic stagnation which followed in 1815 upon the termination of the Napoleonic Wars was ascribed by Malthus to a far-reaching reduction in consumption, brought about by price increases and enforced and voluntary savings.[6] Under the prevailing conditions of the capital market, he said, to recommend saving and to direct an increased flow of income into capital accumulation was a vain and fruitless opposition to the principle of supply and demand. Malthus argued that lack of knowledge of the human character is basic to all theories founded on the assumption that people always produce and consume as much as they have the power to produce and consume. Hence, he objected to "saving from diminished expenditure," and recommended various measures designed to raise the level of "effectual demand" for capital. He regarded the execution of public works as a desirable means of combating unemployment, since it would create incomes without requiring the inclusion of profits among the cost elements.

Ricardo accepted the Malthusian assumption that accumulated capital was to be identified with circulating capital or wage goods. But he referred to the law of markets and argued that commodities would not fail to find purchasers without any fall of prices if they were suited to the wants of those who would have the power to purchase them. Interruption of capital accumulation could be only temporary until wages had been reduced and profits had been restored by increases in the population.[7] Ricardo's objection to the execution of public works as an antidepression measure culminated in the argument that capital thus employed had to be withdrawn from some other uses.[8]

Although the Ricardian doctrine was subsequently subjected to various devastating criticisms, hardly any students of the history of economics considered the teachings of Malthus superior to those of Ricardo until, at the beginning of the 1930s, J. M. Keynes suggested that the "complete domination of Ricardo's approach for a period of 100 years had been a disaster to the progress of economics." "If only Malthus," he added, "instead of Ricardo, had been the parent stem from which 19th century economics proceeded, what a much wiser and richer place the world would be today!"[9]

Utterances of that kind have caused several authors to examine the circumstances which had assured the victory of the Ricardian approach over that adopted by Malthus. This research has led to the conclusion that some of Ricardo's leading ideas were questioned soon after his death (1823) by a remarkable array of opponents which included, among others, Lord Lauderdale, Thomas Chalmers (1780–1847), Thomas Spence (1750–1814), Robert Torrens, John Craig (1512?–1600), Samuel Bailey, and Edward West.[10] Early in 1831, at a meeting of the Political Economy Club,[11] Torrens initiated a discussion of Ricardo's teachings and suggested that all the great principles of Ricardo's work had been successively abandoned and that his theories of value, rent, and profits were considered erroneous.[12] Agreement was reached on the view that Ricardo "had reasoned out his propositions, whether true or false, with great precision," but "without sufficient regard to the many modifications which are invariably found to arise in the progress of society." Special objections were raised against the inferences which Ricardo had drawn from the Malthusian law of population and against his contention that the interests of landlords were always in conflict with those of the other classes of the population. It is a moot question to what degree the condemnation of some Ricardian propositions amounted to an acceptance of Malthusian views.

But Ricardo's doctrine was defended with relentless zeal by James Mill, Thomas De Quincey, and John R. McCulloch,[13] and the discussions of the economists were practically ignored outside the narrow circles of the economic club.[14] In the eyes of the public Ricardo appeared as the true and unrivaled successor to Adam Smith. His opponents remained isolated while McCulloch succeeded in making Ricardian economics a popular science.[15]

Moreover, compared with the forceful consistency of Ricardian doctrine, the Malthusian construction of the economic machinery lacked clarity and did not supply the elements needed for the establishment of a consistent doctrine. Its logical background was of the Baconian rather than Benthamite type, and the development of English economic reasoning might have been arrested for several decades if Malthus's *Principles of Political Economy* had been accepted as the leading textbook. The spiritual climate which prevailed in England during the nineteenth century favored teachings which were derived from a few simple propositions alleged to be self-evident; it was considered less important whether all inferences drawn from these propositions were compatible with the results of everyday experiences. The Ricardian doctrine provided apparently solid support for the general adoption of the principle of laissez-faire as the guiding economic maxim. "The political philosophers could retire in favor of the businessman—for the latter could attain the philosopher's summum bonum by just pursuing his private profit."[16]

METHODOLOGICAL ISSUES

Among the most important consequences which the Ricardians drew from their belief in the self-regulating forces of the economy was the view that the functioning of the economy, conceived of as a mechanism, had to be analyzed in strict isolation from any political, moral, or sociological considerations. In addition, they were convinced that it was necessary to prevent, as far as possible, any political or moral creeds or convictions from influencing economic policies. Those adherents of the utilitarian doctrine who identified striving for happiness with moral behavior denied the possibility of a conflict between the realization of the economic principle and the observance of generally valid moral standards. Others found it advisable to separate the foundation of utilitarian economics from the belief in the principles of utilitarian morality. These principles found a practical application in the choice of the methods adopted for implementing measures of economic policy. The procedures to be observed in such cases were so devised that, as far as possible, objective criteria were chosen for providing the directives. The regulation of the monetary policy to be practiced by the Bank of England was an outstanding instance in point; the organization of the London capital market was governed by similar considerations. The human element was practically disregarded in establishing the rules that were basic to the definition of employer-employee relationships. Adjustment of economic life to methods of that type was, of course, welcomed by industrialists, traders, and bankers, since it tended to reduce the risks and uncertainties involved in their daily operations.

N. W. Senior, an outstanding representative of the second generation of Ricardian economists, was quite explicit in emphasizing the need for the elimination of political considerations from economic analysis.[17] He asserted that the subject treated by political economy was wealth, as distinct from happiness and social welfare, which were the objectives of government. Hence, the economist's conclusions, whatever might be their generality and their truth, "did not authorize him in adding a single syllabus of advice." According to Senior, economic science could state only general principles "which it is fatal to neglect, but neither advisable, nor perhaps practicable to use as the sole or even the principal guides in the actual conduct of affairs."[18]

The same methodological attitude was endorsed by another leading member of the Ricardian school, John Elliott Cairnes, who requested political economy to "reveal laws of nature," to tell what phenomena were found together and what effects would follow from what causes. Cairnes was strongly opposed to the idea that political economy should "advocate any practical plan."[19] These teachings were perfectly in line with the leading methodological principles which implied that the operation of the laws of nature was independent of the moral beliefs or the political objectives of men, and that, consequently, in his scientific studies the economist should not permit such factors to interfere with his analysis.

As a logician of the utilitarian school, Senior undertook to define, as clearly and consistently as possible, the fundamental concepts of Ricardian economics. For the scientist he claimed full freedom to form appropriate fundamental concepts, but he requested rigid definitions of these concepts in order to avoid misunderstandings and misuses.[20] He adopted the Ricardian conception of political economy as a science of wealth, of the laws of distribution of wealth[21] and of the institutions and customs by which production may be facilitated and distribution regulated so as to give the largest possible amount of wealth to each individual. His definition of wealth included all goods and services which enter into the sphere of exchange. But, to the current conception of utility as an intrinsic quality of goods he opposed the view that utility was rather an expression of the relations of goods to the pleasures and pains of mankind. With that attempt to introduce into economic analysis certain elements of a concept of subjective value, Senior combined severe criticisms of the "inextricable confusion" which had resulted from the adoption of labor as a measure of value, and declared his preference for "Aristotle's description of value as depending on demand."[22]

In his famous discussion of the four postulates which he considered fundamental to the "theoretical branch" of economics, Senior derived the certainty and universality of his propositions from observation and consciousness. The term *consciousness* corresponds to the more modern expressions *inner experience* or *introspection*. But as distinct from McCulloch and other radical Ricardians, he endeavored to emphasize the limits set to the general validity of these propositions by the unpredictability of human actions, the effects of passions, the "variations in civilized development." He thus distinguished theonectical economics from practical economics, which latter had to draw its premises from "particular facts" related to particular climates, soils, and seasons, the influence of government and knowledge, and the like.

The four propositions which provided the framework for any subsequent elaboration of Ricardian economics were: (1) the statement that everyone desires to obtain additional wealth with as little sacrifice as possible (the "economic principle" as the basis of economics of choice),[23] (2) the Malthusian population theory,[24] (3) the operation of the law of increasing returns in the manufacturing industry, and (4) the operation of the law of diminishing returns in agriculture.[25]

Senior regarded the first of these propositions as a "matter of consciousness"; it reflected the conception of economics as a deductive science which was held to derive its generally valid laws from the unverifiable assumption that "every person has some unsatisfied desire which he believes that additional wealth would gratify." Senior attributed the origins of the Malthusian population theory and of the laws of return to observation and experience.

The final definition of the logical background of Ricardian economics was contributed by J. S. Mill, who supplied a general analysis of the "principles of evidence and the methods of scientific investigation," as established in accordance with the rules of associational psychology.[26] Consequent upon these rules, all general concepts and propositions basic to deductive reasoning were held to have been derived from inductive generalizations.[27] The key to the analysis of all logical processes was held to be provided by a mechanical principle, the mutual attraction of psychological elements[28] such as thoughts and ideas, which were assumed to be combined with each other by virtue of the law of associations through resemblance, continuity, and contiguity. Although general logical principles were held to be applicable to all scientific investigations, Mill considered the use of the deductive method appropriate only in cases in which the effects of all relevant causes could be added up—when the consequences of each cause, taken separately, were not affected by the combined operation of all causes. The inductive method, however, was to be used when the effects of the combined operation of several causes could not be foreseen, but had to be determined by observation and experience. The "empirical" laws to be established by inductive processes were divided into uniformities of existence and uniformities of change.

For political economy, as well as for the other social sciences, Mill emphasized the limits placed on the search for general laws by complexities and intricacies which surround causal relationships in the social and economic sphere where—for lack of exact measurement—only long-run tendencies could be established. Hence, he objected to the widespread view that Baconian methods of induction based on observation and specific experience were safe devices for analyzing socioeconomic relationships. Later, under the influence of Auguste Comte's methodology, Mill admitted that "empirical laws of society" could be established by inductive methods when assisted by "laws of human nature" arrived at by deductive reasoning.

In the light of these methodological considerations, J. S. Mill made explicit the methods of hypothetical reasoning which had been applied by Ricardo under the guidance of James Mill. These methods centered on the introduction of appropriate assumptions providing a basis for subsequent deductions. Cairnes compared the logical procedure of isolating the relationships between two elements with the experimental methods used in laboratories. J. S. Mill showed the importance of the *ceteris paribus* clause as an instrument of deductive reasoning which enabled the student to determine separately the effects of one cause out of a number of conflicting causes. Implied in the *ceteris paribus* clause was the assumption that of several factors which could be expected to bring about a change in a given situation, all except one remained unchanged. He clarified the meaning of the imaginary picture of a "static economy" in which the "economical phenomena" of society "were assumed to exist simultaneously"—a logical procedure which resulted in transforming an unending variety of apparently unconnected phenomena and processes supplied by observation and experience into a system of strictly determined economic relationships to which the same principles of deductive reasoning could be applied as to the analysis of the Newtonian cosmic system. Adopting Comte's distinction between "statics" and "dynamics," J. S. Mill ascribed to "dynamics" an evolutionary meaning and used that term to denote the analysis of long-range changes in economic or social conditions.

The equilibrium concept, which had acquired a predominant methodological position in the two preceding centuries, was the undisputed instrument for performing these logical operations. Archbishop Whately (1787–1863), Senior's tutor and author of a textbook on logics,[29] fully realized the importance of the logical procedures which had been basic to the conception of the economy as a system of exchange values. He proposed to apply quite generally to political economy the expression "Katallactics," or the science dealing with exchanges. But that proposal was too subtle to find significant approval.

The traditional connection of economics with Benthamite utilitarian philosophy was strengthened by J. S. Mill through the introduction of the concept of "economic man," which supplied a link between the motivation of human behavior and the functioning of the imaginary economy. The economic man was defined as an individual who is "determined by the necessity of his nature to prefer a greater portion of wealth to a smaller," and moreover, is "able of judging of the comparative efficacy of means of obtaining the possession of wealth." Mill admitted, however, the existence of two "perpetually antagonizing principles to the desire for wealth": aversion to labor and the desire for present enjoyment of costly indulgences. Implied in this definition of the abstract agents who were supposed to assure the operation of an equilibrium system was not only a maximization principle—striving for a maximum share in the available exchange values—but also the assumption of perfect fulfillment of economic expectations and the additional assumption that the quantities of consumers' satisfactions—the pleasures of the utilitarian doctrine—were roughly proportional to the quantities of the products.[30]

Mill was, of course, perfectly aware of the purely hypothetical nature of his concept of "economic man." Occasionally he compared the "arbitrary definition" of that concept with the similar procedure adopted in defining a geometrical line. He warned that conclusions grounded on a hypothesis would be true without qualifications only in purely imaginary cases,[31] thus making explicit another tacit assumption of Ricardian reasoning. Mill transformed the psychological profit motive of Benthamite philosophy into a methodological device which tended to explain the functioning of the exchange economy in terms of a generally valid rational principle.[32] That rational principle was purely formal. It was derived from the utilitarian premises that the human mind is unable to establish absolutely valid principles of moral behavior, that the definition of the ends of human actions cannot be regarded as a matter of "rational considerations," and that the main function of reason consists in guaranteeing the most advantageous choice from among available means required to achieve the objectives determined by the will. In accordance with the role assigned by J. S. Mill to the concept of economic man, that concept was commonly regarded as an abstraction introduced for purposes of equilibrium analysis.[33]

In his famous essay *On Liberty* (1859), Mill applied the methodological principles of hypothetical reasoning to the definition of "liberty." He expressed the conviction that "the only purpose for which power can be rightfully exercised over any member of a civilized community against his will" is to prevent harm to others. That statement implied the recognition of "randomness of want" as a constituent element of social organization. Mill was deeply convinced that "after the means of subsistence are assured, the next in strength of the personal wants of human beings is liberty."[34]

The maximization principle which the Mercantilists had used to analyze the relationships among political communities fighting for supremacy was applied by the Ricardians to the question of how to distribute a limited volume of exchange values among the members of a "Katallactic" economy. As combined with the conception of the economy as an equilibrium mechanism, the maximization principle provided an excellent device for assuring a hypothetical coordination of all individual economic plans and activities independently of any conscious cooperation of the members of the competitive community in the achievement of that coordination.

Under conditions of perfect competition all prices were assumed to be strictly determined by their costs and to be linked up with each other through a network of interdependent relationships. Since these relationships could very well be expressed in terms of equations, the mathematical aspects of Ricardian economics were firmly established, even before they were discovered by Antoine August Cournot (1801–1877) and his successors.

J. S. Mill perfectly realized the connection which existed between the fundamental assumptions underlying the behavior of the hypothetical economy on the one hand and the determinateness of the system on the other. Only through the principle of competition, he asserted, had political economy "any pretension to the character of science." He was equally firmly convinced that "economic laws" could be established for rents, profits, wages, and prices only insofar as these magnitudes were determined by competition. In spite of his sympathy for certain egalitarian ideas, Mill deeply resented the attacks of some Socialists on free competition. He argued that monopoly was the inevitable alternative to free competition, and that monopoly, in all its forms, meant "taxation of the industrious for the support of indolence, if not plunder."

The aversion exhibited by practically all Ricardians to monopolistic situations was perhaps due partly to the fact that the determinateness of their economic system and the fate of their science were endangered when monopolistic control of markets was likely to prevail over the rule of free competition.[35] In their economic analyses they largely ignored the conspicuous role played by monopolistic situations in large areas of the economy, although Senior took account of them in a classificatory survey. Senior pointed out the many "occasional interruptions" to which the influence of free competition on costs of production was subjected. He emphasized, however, that political economy did not deal with particular facts but with general tendencies. Recognition of the fundamental importance of private ownership of the means of production for the functioning of the competitive economy enabled the Ricardians to justify that institution without resorting to a questionable "natural law." They could refer to experience, which had shown that private property was indispensable for the pursuance of rational economic behavior and general well-being.[36]

Mill expressed the general conviction of his age when he asserted that the laws of production "partake of the nature of physical truths"; that there was nothing optional or arbitrary in them, and no difference between their general validity and the validity of the laws governing the movement of physical bodies. However, Mill assigned an entirely different category to the rules underlying the distribution of wealth, which he regarded as a "matter of human institutions solely," depending on laws and customs of society. These rules, he believed, reflected the opinions and feelings of the governing groups of the countries. Having thus opened the door for a wide range of social reforms, Mill nonetheless hesitated to endanger the validity of the Ricardian theory of distribution by admitting far-reaching, politically determined modifications of the prevailing distributive processes. He added the assertion that, once rules and regulations had been established for the distribution of wealth, their consequences were as little arbitrary and had as much of the character of physical laws as the law of production.[37]

Of the four fundamental principles of political economy enumerated by Senior, two were generally regarded as hypothetical propositions: the economic principle and the law of increasing returns as applied to manufactures. The second law was not derived from the observation of specific cases but was based on the assumption that output increased more than proportionately to the increases in the factors of production.

Empirical character, however, was ascribed to the Malthusian law and the law of diminishing returns in agriculture. Both laws had been established by experience and were, therefore, considered falsifiable, but only the validity of the Malthusian law was the object of extensive statistical investigations. In Senior's formulation of the law of diminishing returns, all productive factors, with the exception of labor, were kept constant, an assumption which provided an excellent example of the use made by the Ricardians of the *ceteris paribus* clause.[38]

Since empirical laws reflected the operation of forces working under specific historical conditions, these laws could provide a basis for forecasting future effects of observable trends. The Ricardian outlook on the ultimate consequences of a constantly declining rate of profit was an instance in point. Mill, who accepted that outlook, distinguished cultural from economic progress and identified the forthcoming "stationary state" with conditions of human perfection and freedom from economic cares.

An inconclusive controversy between Senior and Mill turned mainly on the question of whether political economy, as suggested by Mill, should be treated as a hypothetical science. Senior insisted upon substituting for Mill's "assumption" that wealth and costly enjoyment are the only objects of human desire the statement that they are universal and constant objects of desire.[39] Mill's formulation implied that the general law did not completely define the relation between the desire of wealth and other conflicting motives. In Senior's view the hypothetical elements involved in that expression of the law were easily forgotten or ignored, and a strictly hypothetical law was open to the objection that its results could not be tested by observation and experience. His own formulation, he argued, included a reference to motives other than the desire for wealth. Almost general agreement was finally reached on the hypothetical formulation of general economic laws. But a closer approach to reality was considered possible when due consideration was given to secondary causes which were likely to modify the effects of general laws.

UTILITARIAN CRITICISMS OF THE RICARDIAN DOCTRINE

Objections to the analytical approach.   The disintegration of the apparently solid body of the Ricardian doctrine which set in soon after its author's death was caused by some telling criticisms of various elements of "the science of political economy." These criticisms were directed partly against the methods of Ricardian analysis, partly against certain fundamental concepts of the doctrine, and partly against certain conclusions drawn from it. But its utilitarian aspects were hardly questioned.

During the first half of the nineteenth century only very few English economists of note were in principle opposed to the deductive method used by Ricardo. The most remarkable author of this type was Richard Jones, who admitted the validity of certain empirical generalizations but rejected the hypothetical laws and regarded the existing organization of the economy as a transitory, historically conditioned order. From a comparative study of various forms of land tenure prevailing in France, Italy, and Ireland, he drew the conclusion that even under conditions of free competition differences in the size of rent did not correspond to differences in the fertility of the soil or to differences in the returns on stock and labor employed. Hence, he questioned the usefulness of the deductions derived from Ricardo's theoretical assumptions. In his discussion of the wage fund theorem Jones pointed out that increased accumulation of capital was generally attended by fluctuations in the volume of employment.[40] But the contemporary English economists were more interested in the construction of a coherent picture of the economy than in discussions of the influence of historical conditions on economic relationships.

Thomas Tooke (1774–1858) was another noticeable English economist who was on principle opposed to the Ricardian methodology. Prompted by the idea of showing the influence of nonmonetary factors on the behavior of prices, Tooke endeavored to demonstrate that commodity prices do not depend on the "amount of the circulating medium" but on the "revenues of the different orders of the state, under the head of rents, profits, salaries and wages."[41] That reasoning led to the proposition that the aggregate of money incomes spent on the consumption of goods was the determining and limiting principle of demand, while costs of production were the limiting principle of supply. With this statement Tooke anticipated some ideas which much later provided the background to the "income approach" to the theory of money.

Assisted by William Newmarch (1820–1882), who was, like Tooke, an employee of a London commercial firm, Tooke applied his methodological views to the test of practical experience in a monumental statistical investigation into the history of prices.[42] In his discussions of the main results of their findings, Newmarch attacked the "abstract" argument of the quantity theory of money and endeavored to show that a rise in prices connected with an influx of gold was not tantamount to a simple depreciation of the currency but was brought about by a growth of all incomes.[43] Newmarch viewed changes in the volume of trade as far more important in producing changes in the level of prices than variations in the volume of money. His data (analysis by commodities of the history of prices) appeared to confirm that observation. For many years Newmarch was the most outstanding English economist to emphasize the need for statistical investigations as opposed to the methods of deductive reasoning. He strongly recommended the use of index numbers without, however, interpreting their economic significance.

In this connection mention may be made of the Scottish-American writer John Rae, although the immediate object of his criticisms was not the Ricardian theory.[44] Rather, he attacked the fallacies of the system of free trade and some leading ideas of *The Wealth of Nations* and supported these attacks by original ideas derived from keen observation of economic relationships. The considerations which he advanced in favor of the ''infant industry'' argument were so forcefully presented that J. S. Mill took account of them in his discussion of tariff policies. From an analysis of the factors which he considered responsible for the productivity of the various ''instruments'' of production, Rae drew the conclusion that the volume of such instruments and, consequently, the size of national wealth were determined by four main causes, namely, the quantity and quality of the available raw materials, the ''strength of the effective desire of accumulation,'' the wage level, and the inventive faculty. Having introduced the time element into his analysis of productivity, Rae referred to it again in elaborating the proposition that the capacity of the ''instruments'' could be increased either by lengthening the period of their efficiency or by increasing their productivity per unit of time. Rae supplemented these considerations with the observation that the instruments accruing under conditions of advanced technique are marked by gradually declining productivity.

In his analysis of the strength of the ''effective desire of accumulation,'' Rae developed one of the most impressive aspects of his theory: the influence of the time element on the subjective valuation of goods. This approach to the value problem was reminiscent of the reasoning suggested by Ferdinando Galiani. Simultaneously, Rae's reference to the time factor as a constituent element of grades of productivity anticipated in some respects Eugen von Böhm-Bawerk's idea of the role played by the length of the productive periods in economic organization. In addition, Böhm-Bawerk's *agio* theory of interest was anticipated in Rae's proposition that the level of interest on capital was determined by the effects of the time element on the valuation of goods and on the calculation of the productivity of the instruments. Also characteristic of Rae's perspicacity was the connection which he established between the operation of the ''inventive principle'' and the transfer of the instruments of production into classes of ''quicker returns,'' and the corresponding connection between the operation of the ''accumulative'' principle and the transfer of the instruments into classes of lower returns. Finally, an allusion to the idea of marginal productivity was implied in his proposition that the rate of interest was determined by the profitability of the instruments with the lowest degree of productivity out of a range of possible uses. But Rae did not succeed in combining his remarkable suggestions into a consistent body of theory. His work did not affect the development of economic reasoning, but only aroused the curiosity of some students of the history of economics.

Objections to the labor cost theory of value.   Among the first rank of authors who raised objections to some fundamental concepts of the Ricardian theory was Samuel Bailey, who realized the logical difficulties involved in the search for an ''invariable measure'' of the intrinsic values of goods.[45] Bailey insisted that the concept of ''exchange value'' could reasonably be used only in a relative sense, for comparing ''the exchange ratio in which one commodity stands at each period to some other commodity.'' Moreover, he pointed out that frequently no relation could be found to exist between the wages paid to different categories of workers and the amounts of work performed by them, and that consequently, the unit of labor time did not provide a suitable standard for measuring exchange values.[46] Bailey showed the role played by scarcity of the productive resources in monopolistic situations and discussed differential rents which, resulting from scarcity conditions, could be observed outside the range of the Ricardian agricultural rents.

John Craig, who was aware of the manifold effects which any change of relative prices is bound to have on expenditures, emphasized the mutual interdependence of all prices.[47] He connected the value of goods with their utility. That connection was even more clearly elaborated by William F. Lloyd, who pointed to some elements of the concept of marginal utility when he suggested that the value of a thing corresponded to the want which remained unsatisfied when it was lost or to the trouble caused by replacing it.[48] In its ultimate sense, Lloyd stated, value signifies a feeling of the mind which shows itself always at the margin of separation between satisfied and unsatisfied wants. He considered it irrelevant that no methods were available for measuring absolute values. The existence of the utility of the goods, he argued, was as independent of its exact measurement as the existence of heat had been independent of the invention of the thermometer.

Another noteworthy adversary of the Ricardian value theory was Mountifort Longfield, who discussed the shortcomings of that theory with a full understanding of the role which it had played in the structure of Ricardian doctrine.[49] In his analysis of the productive process, Longfield connected the productivity of capital with the length of the period of production; his "productivity" theory of interest was based on a clear concept of marginal productivity applied to capital and labor. He related the returns on these productive factors to the contributions added by the last increments of the factors to the productive process, and related the rate of profits to the lowest yield of successive profitable increments of capital invested under conditions of diminishing returns. Longfield defined savings as a sacrifice of present wants in favor of the future.

Samuel Read advanced an outright abstinence theory of interest and contended that the theory which regarded labor as the standard of value had been almost universally rejected.[50] A similar theory was advocated even more effectively by George Poulett Scrope, who also made some remarkable contributions to monetary problems, and combined the maximization principle with the idea of the equilibrating forces of supply and demand in order to show how resources were allocated and how the formation of incomes took place.[51] Almost all adversaries of the Ricardian value theory rejected the relationship which Ricardo had established between the movement of wages and that of profits.

Attacks of the Ricardian socialists. The widespread recognition of the Ricardian doctrine as an almost perfect formulation of the "science of political economy" was not significantly affected by the theoretical objections raised to various fundamental Ricardian teachings. Far more important in influencing public opinion was the use made of the labor cost theory of value by a group of socialist authors called the Ricardian Socialists. From the proposition that the existence of all values was to be attributed to the creative powers of labor, these authors could easily derive demagogic inferences such as the claim of the worker to the full proceeds of his work, and the contention that the owners of the means of production gained their incomes by withholding fractions of the yields of productive processes performed by labor. The defense of such views was facilitated by the fact that no satisfactory theory had been advanced to explain the origin of interest on capital and profits.

Popular thinking was hardly open to the arguments that reasoning in terms of natural rights was incompatible with the methodological principles of the Benthamite philosophy, and that the analysis of the standard for measuring values was to be clearly distinguished from the ethical question of how the yield of the productive processes should be distributed.[52] The socialist challenge was effectively met mainly by economists who rejected the labor cost theory of value and could support such rejection with theoretical arguments.[53]

Like practically all earlier adversaries of the private ownership of the means of production, the Ricardian Socialists started their considerations from the distributive aspects of the economy. But as distinct from the "Utilitarian Anarchists," who had propagated egalitarian distributive schemes, they had to advance at least some suggestions concerning an organization of production which could be expected to guarantee to the worker the receipt of the yield of his exertion.

The most important Ricardian Socialists were William Thompson, John Francis Bray, John Gray, and Thomas Hodgkin.[54] Their treatises were published between 1824 and 1839. Among these authors, Hodgkin was practically the only one who used theoretical arguments in support of his attacks on the capitalist order.[55] He opposed the idea of "productivity of capital," arguing that such an idea was applicable only to physical capital, that is to say, stored-up labor, but by no means to the concept of capital in the sense of a property relation between means of production and their owner.[56] Hence, Hodgkin qualified interest and profits as a sort of surplus value withheld by the owners of capital from currently created exchange values. From the increasing use of machinery he expected a rapid expansion of the middle classes and equalization in the distribution of incomes. He refrained from proposing a specific scheme of social reform.

Thompson was convinced that mankind was faced with a cruel dilemma: how to reconcile equality with security, just distribution with continued production.[57] But his proposals of reform were far from being radical. Although he claimed for labor the whole product of its exertions, his recommendations dealt mainly with changes in workers' remuneration and the creation of workmen's cooperatives.

The propagandist type of radical socialism was represented by Bray, who branded the attitude of the capitalists as "legalized robbery" and requested equal remuneration for equal labor of all kinds, regardless of the inequality in the value of labor to society.[58] Bray proposed community of property for the nation and, as a transitional measure, the establishment of a kind of national joint stock scheme, composed of a number of joint stock companies. This scheme was to be financed by fiat money the value of which was to be guaranteed by the entire national property.[59]

Gray, one of the least known Ricardian Socialists, may also be mentioned.[60] His proposals centered on the exchange of commodities in accordance with their values expressed in units of labor costs, and the creation of a bank to organize and finance these exchanges. From a "Map of Civil Society" published in 1814 by Patrick Colquhoun in a *Treatise on Wealth, Power and Resources of the British Empire,* Gray derived an estimate to the effect that each member of the "productive classes" produced nearly fifty-four pounds yearly but received only about eleven pounds.

The idea that labor costs provided the natural basis for the determination of exchange values also played a leading role in the schemes of the well-known social reformer Robert Owen (1771–1858). His far-flung "Plan for Relieving Public Distress," which he developed after the end of the Napoleonic Wars in order to combat a deep depression, included the proposal to introduce a system of barter under which producers would sell their products in return for labor notes, the value of which would correspond to the hours of work spent on producing the goods.[61] But in spite of such radical inferences (which he drew from the labor cost theory), Owen was not a Socialist in the usual sense of the term, and was not opposed to the principle of private ownership of the means of production. For support of his ideas he frequently turned to the circles of influential conservative politicians. In various respects his philosophical approach to social problems was far superior to that of the Ricardian Socialists. Owen rejected the principle of individual responsibility as preached by the churches, and believed in a sort of social determination according to which the human character is molded by the environment whereas the nature of the environment can be modified by appropriate economic measures.

Earlier social reformers, such as William Godwin, had equally emphasized the influence of a person's environment upon his or her character, but the specific association which Owen established between surrounding economic conditions on the one hand and moral and social attitudes on the other could be regarded as a hazy anticipation of the materialistic interpretation of history.[62] Owen's cooperative colonies collapsed, and the Grand National Consolidated Trade Union which he organized was dissolved in due course, but Owen exercised a lasting influence on the development of the cooperative idea, on English labor legislation, on popular education, and on city planning.

MODIFICATIONS OF THE RICARDIAN DOCTRINE

The economics of N. W. Senior.   The increasing and partly impressive criticisms of the Ricardian doctrine represented a challenge for the teachers of the "science of political economy" to reexamine the logical background of their theories, the consistency of their concepts, and the validity of their analysis of the economic machinery. Among the English economists of the first half of the nineteenth century who suggested modifications of Ricardian theorems, N. W. Senior was probably the most original thinker. To the labor cost theory he opposed considerations which were similar to those advanced by Bailey. He defined value in terms of utility, limitation of supply, and transferableness of the productive factors. Senior observed that, if all the commodities used by mankind were supplied by nature in precisely the same quantities as they are now but without any intervention of human labor, there is no reason to suppose either that they would cease to be valuable or that they would exchange in any other than their present proportions. A similar idea was expressed by Senior's tutor, Archbishop Richard Whately, in *Introductory Lectures on Political Economy.* Whately argued that people are prone to confound causes and effects: pearls do not fetch a high price because people have dived for them but, on the contrary, people dive for them because they fetch a high price.

As used in this connection, utility did not denote an intrinsic quality of the goods; it was meant to "express their relations to the pains and pleasures of mankind." Senior attributed "the motives of all exchanges" to the endless diversity in the relative utility of different objects to different persons. In his discussion of the limitation of supply he gave a clear account of the principle of diminishing utility and showed that any additional supply of an abundant article will cause it to lose all or nearly all its utility. The analysis of transferability provided arguments against the exclusion of immaterial goods from the concept of wealth.

In spite of his critical attitude toward the labor cost theory, Senior did not differ from

Ricardo in his methodological approach to the value problem. He looked for a common standard unit to which all exchange values of the economic system could be reduced, and proposed to derive that standard directly from the Benthamite calculus of pleasures and pains. He regarded a unit of pain as a logically more satisfactory hypothetical standard of measuring exchange values than the Ricardian unit of labor time, which still bore the imprint of the Scholastic substance concept of goods. But the reduction of all pains to a common denominator was hardly a more realistic procedure than the reduction of all kinds of labor to a standard unit of labor.

To Ricardo's cost of production theory Senior raised the objection that it was inadequate in all cases in which increasing or diminishing returns were involved. He emphasized the large sphere occupied in the economy by five types of situations in which the productive factors were not perfectly accessible to all producers and, consequently, monopolies of varying degrees were bound to arise. To the most frequent group he reckoned such cases in which the monopolist was not the only producer but had peculiar facilities which were diminishing and ultimately disappeared as he increased the amount of his produce. These cases assumed particular importance through Senior's definition of rent as "all revenue that nature or fortune bestows either without any exertion on the part of the recipient or in addition to the average remuneration for the exercise of industry on the employment of capital." Differential as well as absolute rents were included in this concept. Senior's rent concept was shared by Whately and was endorsed, in somewhat modified form, by Cairnes in his *Political Economy.*

With this extension of the Ricardian rent concept, Senior suggested an explanation of all incomes which could not be considered necessary to call forth the contribution of a productive factor. Considerations connected with the scarcity of productive factors caused Senior quite generally to question Ricardo's radical distinction between capital and land on the ground that capital had a constant tendency to take on the characteristics of land by being invested in durable goods and thus losing its mobility. In his reformulation of the concept of "capital," Senior was influenced by some critical observations of the German economist F.B.W. Hermann. But Senior rejected Hermann's proposal to include rent among the costs of production.[63]

The application of the concept of scarcity to the explanation of exchange values caused Senior to substitute for the Ricardian analysis of the distributive process an explanation of the shares of labor and capital in terms of a single principle, directly derived from utilitarian philosophy. He defined wages as a reward for the "toil and trouble" experienced by the workers, and interpreted skill and experience as the ability to be more efficient than others without suffering increases in disutilities caused by working. In his inclusive discussion of the wage problem, Senior practically ignored the Malthusian population theory but referred to the wage fund. He ascribed the creation of capital to the combined effects of three factors: natural materials, labor, and abstinence. He defined abstinence as a "productive function," as the "conduct of a person who either abstains from the unproductive use of what he can command, or designedly prefers the production of remote to that of immediate result." This definition was reflected in the distinction which Senior drew between "frugality" and "providence." Thus, without drawing a clear distinction between interest on capital and profits, Senior regarded both types of income as compensation for the capitalist's abstinence from the immediate consumption of goods, and asserted that capital stands in the same relation to profit as labor does to wages. The attraction which this theory exercised on English economists was partly due to the fact that, as distinct from most other theories of interest, it was free from any connection with the problematic substance concepts of goods. Moreover, it took account of the time element implied in productive processes, since abstinence (later termed *waiting*) is bound to extend over prolonged periods when conceived of as an economic factor. It is a moot question whether the "abstinence theory of interest" is to be considered as an alternative to the productivity theory or as a supplement to it.[64]

Senior accepted the Ricardian proposition that the equilibrium prices of commodities produced under conditions of constant or decreasing costs had to be sufficient to afford the ordinary rates of remuneration to labor and capital. But since he explained values in terms of scarcity relationships, it can be assumed that, contrary to the approach adopted by Ricardo, he derived the shares of the productive factors in the value of the product from the value of the product itself.[65]

This independence in formulating some crucial problems of economic analysis also found expression in Senior's approach to the definition of the functions of money and to the theory of international trade. He derived the nature of money from the capacity of the precious metals to serve as a substitute for credit and from the "commercial ubiquity" or general interlocal acceptance of these metals. He emphasized that the commodity character of gold and silver had not been altered by their use as money, and referred to the costs of production of the monetary metals as a determinant of increases in their quantity. It may be mentioned that in his discussion of the demand for money Senior dealt with the velocity of circulation by pointing to the "average proportion of the value of his income which each individual habitually keeps by him in money."[66]

Consistent application of supply and demand analysis to the problems of international trade enabled Senior to disregard the Ricardian attempt to establish a fundamental distinction between domestic and foreign trade. Immobility conditions of capital and labor, Senior argued, existed as much in the home market as between the markets of different countries, and in his view the sole difference between foreign trade and interlocal domestic trade was caused by the necessity of equating the different units of measurement. Hence, he substituted for the theory of comparative costs an analysis which was based on the comparative productivity of capital and labor in producing exportable commodities. In defense of free trade he endeavored to show that—apart from rare exceptions—outflows of specie resulted in a movement causing proportionate inflows, and that a country's economy was not impaired by losing gold through its foreign trade.[67]

But Senior's contributions to economic analysis did not find a very receptive audience, perhaps because he did not develop them into a coherent body of economic theory. His discussion of the distributive processes was fragmentary. The objections which he raised to the Malthusian population theory were resented by the convinced advocates of utilitarianism; his concept of economic system lacked the apparent consistency which made the Ricardian doctrine so attractive to the Victorian age.

J. S. Mill's principles. It was not Senior but J. S. Mill who provided the nineteenth century with the generally accepted new and definite version of the Ricardian doctrine.[68] Following the pattern set by *The Wealth of Nations,* Mill's *Principles* was designed to show the practical application of the teachings of economics, adapted to the "more extended knowledge and improved ideas of an advanced age." With this end in view, Mill added a section dealing with the problems of exchange to the traditional analysis of the problems of production and distribution, and enlarged his treatment of the theoretical aspects of the economy by extensive discussions of the relationships between production on the one hand and the progress of society and the functions of government on the other.

Mill's greatest achievement was perhaps the clarification of the logical aspects of the Ricardian doctrine and the ensuing elimination of some misunderstandings to which it had been exposed. Trained by his father, James Mill, in the application of associationist logic, he made explicit the methodological foundations of Ricardian economics which Ricardo had failed to explain. Thus, J. S. Mill provided hypothetical economics with that clear and consistent structure which was perfectly adjusted to the understanding of his generation.[69]

From the outset Mill warned his readers that the smallest error on the subject of value infects with corresponding error all other conclusions, but he attached only a subordinate importance to the problem of how to define the measurement of exchange values. Samuel Bailey's objections to the concept of absolute value and the objections raised to the labor cost theory caused Mill to abandon the Ricardian formulation of the value problem. For want of a better solution, he adopted a problematic "cost of production theory" which included return on capital among the costs. His standard unit of exchange values was a sort of hypothetical magnitude which was not clearly defined. He referred to changing utilities of goods and varying difficulties experienced in obtaining them in order to demonstrate the relative nature of exchange values. Having supplemented this discussion with considerations derived from supply and demand analysis, he arrived at the conclusion that "the value of a commodity in any market will always be such that the demand shall be exactly equal to the supply." Since he regarded exchange values as ratios, he considered it impossible for all values to move in the same direction.

In his theory of production Mill substituted for Adam Smith's definition of "wealth" as a flow of annual produce the concept of wealth as a stock, a volume of capital, and defined "wealth" as the whole "accumulation" of means possessed by individuals and communities for the attainment of their ends. Thus conceived, capital[70] could be increased not only by the employment of "productive" labor but also by any reduction in "unproductive" consumption.

Consequent upon his abandonment of the labor cost theory of value, Mill could disregard the Ricardian conception of rent and profits as deductions from the value created by labor. But nevertheless, he preserved the Ricardian formulation of the problem of distribution, and found it necessary to explain the share of each factor in accordance with a specific theory. Adopting without significant modifications the Ricardian theory of rent, he ascribed to the market the function of determining the share of land. He applied the wage fund theory to the determination of the wage level and insisted on the accumulation of a stock of wage goods as a prerequisite for the employment of workers in the subsequent period of production.[71] Hence, he argued quite consistently that the demand for labor was not dependent upon the demand for commodities but rather on the behavior of savers who were abstaining from consumption and thus were contributing to the size of the fund.[72]

Senior's "abstinence theory" suggested a convenient answer to the thorny questions which surrounded the determination of the source of interest on capital. The level of interest could thus be related to the degree of sacrifice made in postponing the present enjoyment of goods in favor of the prospect of acquiring goods in times to come. Thus, Mill abandoned the close connection which Smith and Ricardo had established between the explanation of interest on capital and profit theory. An improved formulation of the problem of profits was suggested by the distinction drawn by Say between the functions of the "entrepreneur" and those of the "Capitalist." In the light of the tasks ascribed to the entrepreneur, Mill defined profits as compensation for the abstinence, risk, and exertion involved in the employment of capital stock. But he did not elaborate on the various aspects of risk bearing, and he ignored the effects upon profits of the introduction of technological improvements. Compared with the Ricardian theory of distribution, Mill's teachings showed only some limited progress. But his view that the distribution of wealth was "a matter of human institution solely" opened the way for the discussion of the social aspects of ownership conditions and wage problems.

The statement that Mill used the wage fund theory to explain the level of wages is in apparent contradiction to the well-known "recantation" of that theory made by Mill in 1869 in a review article published in the *Fortnightly Review*.[73] That article was characteristic of Mill's—largely emotional—reaction to various attacks on the wage fund theory, which had been motivated by the need to defend the wage policy of the trade unions against the charge that, as formulated by Mill, the unions, by limiting their membership, might be looked at as simply entrenching themselves against the inroads of overpopulation.[74] The defenders of the trade union policy, Francis D. Lange[75] and Thornton, shifted the approach to the determination of the wage level from an analysis of the means available to the workers to a definition of the sectors of the national dividend, out of which wage increases could be defrayed. They replaced the idea of a wage fund by the similar idea of an income fund, and argued that wage increases could be financed by imposing higher prices on consumers or by reducing employers' profits. But Thornton admitted that changes in demand resulting from price increases might inflict losses on labor in other industries.

Mill had been impressed by the suggestion that the amount of wage goods might be enlarged by changes in the consumption of other classes of the population. But since considerations of that type were a poor substitute for the theoretical propositions underlying the wage fund concept, he preserved that concept and the wage analysis connected with it in a later edition of *Principles of Political Economy* published in 1871. It appears that the wage fund theory, when cautiously formulated, was still the most adequate wage theory available within the Ricardian setting of the problems of distribution.[76]

In his analyses of the general behavior of the economy, Mill did not question the Ricardian assumption that there was never a lack of profitable investment opportunities and that all savings were immediately invested. As a general rule he advanced the proposition that things tend to exchange for one another at such values as will give all producers the same rate of profit on their outlays. In his outlook on the development of the economy, Mill equally accepted the Ricardian formulation of the problem. Continuous pressure of the population upon the means of subsistence, he believed, would lead to a gradual diminution of profit, reductions in the rate of interest, and, consequently, a decline in savings. A decline in savings would cease to supply sufficient capital for an expanding economy.[77] But, as distinct from Ricardo, Mill was convinced that the Malthusian device of moral restraint would be generally observed and the growth of the population would be adjusted to the available food supply. Like Francis Place, Mill was an adherent of birth control, which had been rejected not only by Malthus but also by Senior. In the light of various considerations advanced by John Rae, he looked forward to a stationary state, and to the spread of moderate prosperity among all classes of society. Such a forecast was backed by Mill's conviction that maximizing the general average level of happiness was preferable to a lower average happiness attained by a larger number of people. This reasoning was perfectly in line with the general principles of utilitarian philosophy. Mill's answer to the question concerning the optimum size of the population was later modified by other utilitarian economists, Henry Sidgwick and F. Y. Edgeworth.[78]

In his *Essays on Some Unsettled Questions of Political Economy*, Mill dealt with a problem of international trade which had been raised by Torrens but had been disregarded by Ricardo. That problem turned on the fact that analysis of foreign trade in accordance with the principle of comparative costs permitted only a definition of the limits of the relative prices of traded commodities. In order to fill this gap, Mill supplemented the Ricardian doctrine with an analysis in terms of supply and demand. He simplified his discussion by restricting it to the case of two commodities, and arrived at the formulation of the so-called equation of international demand, according to which the exchange ratio is determined by the reciprocal demand of countries for each other's products. He showed how prices of imported goods were relatively increased by intensified demand for them, and how the division of gain from trade was affected by such changes.[79] But although this approach, which was independent of the labor cost theory, opened the way for the abandonment of the theory of comparative cost, Mill as well as the post-Ricardian economists attributed to it a strictly supplementary character.

Realizing that the results of demand analysis might affect the validity of the free trade argument, Mill admitted that in some cases the payment of subsidies might be a reasonable measure of foreign trade policy. He also discussed the favorable effects of protective measures applied to industries which could achieve monopolistic positions in the supply of or demand for certain commodities. But the overwhelming majority of Ricardian economists were prejudiced in favor of free trade to such a degree that they consistently denied the possibility of gaining advantages from protectionist policies.

Logician though he was, Mill did not succeed in establishing a consistent body of economic theory. He abandoned even the belief in the Benthamite principle of "randomness of wants," which was basic to the Ricardian methodology, and went so far as to suggest the adoption of a hierarchical scale of nobler and less noble utilities.[80] Mill was deeply impressed by the socialist criticisms of capitalist society, but he questioned—with a good deal of skepticism—the blessings ascribed to a communist organization of the economy, and insisted that the competitive order had not yet received a fair trial. He regarded the "coarse stimuli" provided by the struggle for riches as adequate protection against conditions under which minds might rust and stagnate. He expected great progress in the future in the development of the "public spirit."

Prompted by Auguste Comte's (1798–1857) conception of "dynamics," Mill supplemented his static analysis of an imaginary economy with extended discussions of various aspects of actual economic and social conditions, and thus attempted to add a "theory of motion" to the theory of equilibrium. The theory of motion was designed to show the effects on production and distribution of population movements, technical progress, and increases of capital. But since Mill lacked the appropriate methodology for analyzing evolutionary conditions, he had to use procedures of comparative statics to implement his analysis of developmental processes.

Mill's remarkable understanding of the problems of his time enabled him to realize the dangers which were likely to result for general economic welfare from ruthless economic struggles in a society in which inequalities in the distribution of property were reflected by similar inequalities of economic opportunity. In a period in which the powerful "Manchester School" used its influence exclusively to promote the interests of industrialists and bankers, he advocated social reforms of various kinds, especially changes in the distribution of wealth, provided they did not interfere with the exercise of free initiative. Mill favored the creation of workers' cooperatives, and expected them to become more successful in the production of wealth than individual Capitalists because of their greater efficiency, their superior social aims, and the harmonious collaboration of their members. He was a convinced advocate of the trade union movement and of some radical attempts to change the legal and social conditions which surrounded the ownership of land.[81] Views of this kind contributed greatly toward forming the social attitude of the English economists who, after the appearance of Mill's *Principles*, "for a whole generation were men of one book."[82]

One of the main logical requirements basic to post-Ricardian doctrine was the assumption that owing to the operation of competitive forces, all exchange values included in the economic system were reduced to a uniform standard unit which was independent of the behavior of money. So strong was the belief in the underlying methodological considerations that confidence in this Ricardian assumption was not seriously impaired by the findings of John Elliott Cairnes which led to the conclusion that the industrial population consisted of a "series of layers superimposed on one another . . . while those occupying the several strata were for all effective competition isolated from each other."[83] In view of the obstacles which prevented the free movement of labor even within the domestic economy, there did not appear to exist any essential difference between domestic and international trade, and reciprocal demand could be considered the determinant factor in all cases in which lack of competition resulted in diversifying the wage levels between "noncompeting" groups. It was obvious that under these conditions the unit of labor time became practically meaningless as a standard unit of measuring exchange values even for a purely hypothetical economic system;[84] but at first that inference was not generally drawn.

Adoption of the principles of hypothetical reasoning had caused the utilitarian philosophers to develop their theories in terms of quantifying concepts. But they refrained from adjusting the formulation of their problems to the use of mathematical methods. William Whewell (1794–1866) suggested algebraic treatment of such problems, but that proposal did not meet with much interest.[85] Dionysius Lardner (1793–1859) applied mathematical methods to the determination of the cost and revenue functions of a firm in the railroad industry. Using some bold assumptions about the competitive conditions underlying productive processes, Lardner endeavored to establish certain relationships among supply, demand, and freight rates.[86] Henry C. Fleeming Jenkin (1833–1885), who participated in the wage fund controversy, used algebraic methods to demonstrate that the rate of investment was not perceptibly affected by changes in the wage level, that the wage fund might show increases even in the face of diminished profits, and that reductions of profit might lead to curtailments of expenditures and not, as was generally assumed, to reductions in savings.[87] Jenkin used diagrams to illustrate his calculations. But the methods which he introduced into economic analysis received closer attention only much later.

Problems of money, credit, and commercial crises. The currency controversy which had found a preliminary solution with the adoption of the principles laid down in the Bullion Report entered upon a second stage in the wake of the economic crisis of 1825. A persistent fall of prices had set in, accompanied by serious disturbances of the economic machinery. These price movements showed that the monetary system was far from guaranteeing stability of the price level even under the rule of the metallic standard, which had been reestablished in Peel's Resumption Bill of 1819. The flaws in the functioning of the economy could not be ascribed to the impact of extraordinary events such as bad harvests, wars, and the like; hence, the blame was put on the Central Bank for having mismanaged the currency, especially by raising the value of gold.

The authors who participated in these discussions represented widely varying interests and developed partly conflicting views, which can be divided into two broad categories: adversaries of the gold standard on the one hand, and adherents of the standard on the other. Authors of the latter type differed as to the definition of the concept of "means of payment" and the measures to be adopted in order to prevent mismanagement of the currency.

Some adversaries of the gold standard recommended the adoption of so-called tabular standards which were based on commodity prices.[88] Others recommended the return to inconvertible paper currency which promised the resumption of a process of rising prices.[89] But the victory of the gold standard was assured after 1840, when gold production in Russia, Australia, and California opened the prospect of a rapidly increasing supply of gold.

Among the convinced advocates of the gold standard who insisted upon the regulation of the means of payment through free movements of gold, opinions varied on the question as to what degree the fall in prices could be attributed to mismanagement of the currency, especially to the stabilization of the pound at too high a level on the return to convertibility. To the extent that theoretical considerations played a role in determining the answers to that question, the views advanced by the various economists and bankers were influenced by their definitions of the concept of money, by the relationships which they established between changes in the volume of the means of payment and price movements, and by the functions which they assigned to credit as an element of the monetary system.[90]

General agreement existed among the adherents of the gold standard on the view that the value of the circulating means of payment depended upon the limitations set to its volume. Equal agreement existed on the dangers involved in the issuance of unredeemable banknotes. But conflicting views turned on the nature of the convertible banknotes and the distinction to be made between *money* in the strict sense of the term and credit instruments used to supplement the functions of money. The practical importance of that distinction was quite evident, since it was an almost generally accepted principle of monetary policy that the note issue should be regulated but that the credit operations of banks (including those of the Central Bank) should be left free of any interference. Paramount among the considerations which influenced this discussion was the traditional connection which had been established between the value of money and the "commodity" value of the monetary metal, a connection which had a counterpart in the sharp differentiation made by law and commercial practice between legal tender money and other means of payment.

The adherents of the so-called currency principle, who endorsed the monetary views of the Bullion Report, regarded convertible banknotes as a kind of reserve money in the strict sense of the term. Hence, in accordance with the quantity theory of money, they ascribed to the issuance of such notes considerable influence on the movement of prices and the general behavior of the economy.[91] From these considerations they derived the principle that any change in the available gold reserves should be offset by an inverse change in the quantity of redeemable currency, on the assumption that the velocity of circulation of the means of payment would remain unaltered. The gold reserves of the bank, as determined by the free flow of the metal, should be added to by a fixed amount of notes which traditional practice had added to the changing metallic supply. Lord Overstone used the phrase that notes of the Bank of England "represented" gold in circulation. A practical device used for adjusting the issue of banknotes to the principles of the gold standard was the so-called Palmer's rule, which was referred to by Governor J. Horsley

Palmer in 1832 in his evidence before a parliamentary committee. According to this rule the volume of the banks' discounts, loans, and investments was to be kept fairly constant, and changes in the volume of the currency in circulation were regulated by the inflow and outflow of gold. The defenders of the currency principle drew a fundamental distinction, between the circulating means of payment thus defined and other means of payment, such as bills of exchange (commercial bills and checks). They argued that the acceptability of bills of exchange was limited to the "real" economic sphere, in which they could not influence the formation of incomes and prices but were only media for facilitating commercial transactions. Their proposals were obviously derived from the Ricardian view that money, being a veil, should exactly reflect the values of the underlying system of real exchanges which it could never affect. Hence, the determination of the volume of "money" should be kept free from any arbitrary decisions.

The members of the banking school started from the same view and were equally convinced that, unless mismanaged, the credit system could not affect the behavior of the economy. But they objected to any regulation of the issuance of convertible notes, since they regarded these notes as credit instruments like bank deposits and bills of exchange.[92] In a somewhat exaggerated presentation of the principles advocated by the members of the Banking School, Thomas Tooke asserted that the great alterations of prices originated, and mainly proceeded, from alterations "in circumstances distinctly affecting the commodities, and not in the quantity of money." In support of his views Tooke advanced a considerable array of causes to which he ascribed the fall in prices between 1813 and 1837. But his extreme proposition that no connection existed between the evils which had befallen the economy and the management of money and credit was not shared by all members of the Banking School. From *The Wealth of Nations*, Tooke derived his distinction between circulating means of payments used for the purchase of consumers' goods and means of payments used for the transfer and distribution of capital goods. Means of payment of the latter type, he argued, were not money strictly speaking, but were designed to secure the smooth functioning of the economy without affecting the price system. The loans granted by commercial banks belonged to that category. Tooke was convinced that a low rate of interest was responsible for all cases of "overbanking"; as means of preventing overexpansion of credit he recommended the strengthening of banks' gold reserves and the tightening of the discount rate.[93]

Most members of the Banking School admitted that the commercial banks could create additional means of payment by opening credits in their books.[94] But they emphasized John Fullarton's often-quoted "Law of Reflux," according to which any credit expansion caused by discounting genuine commercial bills was bound to be annihilated in due course by the repayment of the loans. That elasticity of the expansion and contraction of commercial credits constituted in their view a fundamental distinction between the means of payment originating from commercial banks and inconvertible paper money. They argued that even inconvertible notes could not be issued in excess of the requirements of the economy if increases in the volume of the currency were strictly regulated by discounting only genuine short-term commercial loans. Thomas Joplin made the discount policy of the banks responsible for the failure of the economy to adjust itself immediately to changes in equilibrium conditions, and he proposed a rigid full coverage of banknotes in order to assure that no changes in the money rate of interest should be brought about by the issuance of such notes.[95]

The principles advocated by the Currency School provided the basis for the Bank

Charter Act of 1844, which established the clear separation of the control of the currency from the credit operations of banks. Manipulation of the discount rate and open market operations were the main instruments to be used in regulating the supply of money and credit. The charter prescribed full coverage of all notes issued in excess of the amount fixed by the law, but the reserve ratio of the banking department was allowed to vary. Economic theory did not provide a clear explanation of the ultimate effects of the application of these devices.

J. S. Mill's monetary views were determined by the Ricardian formulation of the problems of money and credit. His belief that the exchange system of objective values functioned independently of the behavior of money found a striking expression in his often-quoted dictum that there cannot be intrinsically a more insignificant thing in the economy of society than money. The idea that money provided a connecting link between economic activities which follow upon each other in the course of time played no role in his theoretical considerations.

Mill attempted to solve the dualism involved in Ricardian monetary theory by elaborating Senior's proposition that in the long run the value of money was determined by the costs of producing the monetary metal in the least profitable mines, and that additions to the available money supply were thus dependent upon the costs of production.[96] He adopted the Ricardian version of the quantity theory of money, but limited the applicability of that theory to such monetary systems in which the means of payment consisted exclusively of coin and irredeemable paper.[97] Hence, he denied the validity of the theory for all practical purposes, but refused to accept the rigid distinction drawn by the Currency School between money in the strict sense and other circulating means of payment. Along with the extension of the concept of money to commercial instruments of credit, he implicitly admitted the influence of changing business conditions on the velocity of circulation. He pointed quite explicitly to the "purchasing power" of credit, but, like practically all Ricardians, he eventually denied any influence of credit expansion on the accumulation of capital and business activity. Thus, Mill's teachings did not provide students with a well-coordinated monetary theory.

A few observations may be added about the "commercial crises" of 1815, 1825, 1836, and 1847, which accompanied the period of falling prices which set in after the Napoleonic Wars. These crises were repeatedly referred to by members of the various monetary schools. In accordance with the Ricardian doctrine, the origin of heavy general contractions of business activity had to be sought in events affecting the economic system from outside and in "predisposing circumstances," as suggested by Samuel Jones Loyd, Lord Overstone (1796–1883).[98] Errors in judgment concerning the relation between supply and demand, seasonal fluctuations of production, changes in demand, administrative mismangement of the economy, political tensions, bad harvests, and the ensuing need for increased imports were made responsible for economic recessions.

The advocates of the currency principle were inclined to assume that price fluctuation contributed toward intensifying or attenuating the trends which prevailed in the markets. The management of the currency, said Lord Overstone, is a subordinate agent; it seldom leads these markets, but it may, and often does, exert a considerable influence in restraining or augmenting the violence of commercial oscillations.[99] Lord Overstone was also probably the first author to speak of a "state of trade" that apparently revolves in an "established cycle." He divided that cycle into periods of quiescence, improvement, growing confidence, prosperity, excitement, overtrading, convulsion, pressure, stagnation, and distress, ending again in quiescence. That picture of a more or less regular sequence of stages of business activity was a clear expression of the idea that an inner coherence existed among the elements of such developmental processes.

The members of the Banking School placed particular emphasis on misdirected capital and ''overbanking'' in their analysis of the characteristic aspects of crises, but they regarded credit expansions originating from the banks as effects, rather than as causes, of excesses of speculation. They regarded the deterioration of the balance of trade as being of particular importance among the factors which they considered responsible for the downturn. Tooke, who listed a great number of factors to which he attributed an influence on the fluctuating behavior of the economy, pointed especially to the behavior of the corn trade as determined by the yield of harvests. The general idea that economic slumps were reactions to preceding structural changes of the economy was advanced by James Wilson (1805–1860), who suggested that commercial crises were largely due to excessive transformation of circulating into fixed capital and to the ensuing curtailment of the funds available for the employment of labor.[100]

Mill discussed commercial crises in the fourth book of his *Principles,* where he dealt with problems of motion. He rejected the Malthusian view that general overproduction could be created by lack of effective demand. Equally incompatible with Mill's use of equilibrium analysis were the considerations of another adversary of Say's law of markets, Reverend Thomas Chalmers, who connected business recessions with limitations set on the accumulation of capital.[101] Without adopting a clear approach to the analysis of ''commercial crises,'' Mill characterized them as economic phenomena manifesting themselves in heavy reductions of mercantile and speculative credit, and in falling prices which had been raised by a spirit of speculation. Such a spirit, he argued, was periodically stimulated by chances for extraordinary profits, leading to large-scale investments in unprofitable enterprises at home and abroad. He connected the existence of stagnations with the fact that the introduction of money had resulted in separating the action of buying from that of selling so that purchases could be deferred almost indefinitely. Although Mill admitted that the operation of Say's law was suspended during periods in which general glut of markets coincided with extreme depression of prices, he accepted the belief of the Banking School that credit expansion was never the primary cause of speculative advances.

After the periodicity of crises had become a matter of common knowledge, two members of the Manchester Statistical Society, W. Langton and John Mills,[102] approached the analysis of business fluctuations from the statistical angle. They found that wavelike movements of business activity averaging ten years were superimposed upon minor quarterly or seasonal fluctuations. Convinced adherents of the classical doctrine, they looked for extraeconomic factors—such as changes in the mental attitude of businessmen—in order to account for the sequence of the phases of the cyclical movements. (Mills suggested that the factors responsible for commercial crises are too deep and subtle to be conjured out of existence by any legislative manipulation of currencies.) Thus, they ascribed the existence of the revival period to the fact that time had steadied the nerves which had been shattered by the panic; in their view, overspeculation was due to the widespread belief that the prevailing economic conditions would last forever.

Chapter 13
The Spread of Smithian Economics

—

FRENCH AND ITALIAN VERSIONS OF LIBERAL ECONOMICS

THE STRIKING DIFFERENCES in the development of economic reasoning which prevailed during the entire nineteenth century between England on the one hand and the countries of the European continent on the other can hardly be accounted for unless it is kept in mind that the economists of the latter countries were—with few exceptions—very reluctant to adopt fully the logical principles which had supplied the background for the elaboration of the Ricardian doctrine. This was true even of France and Italy, where the use of certain methods of hypothetical reasoning was widely accepted by the students of the social sciences.

After the publication, in 1803, of Jean Baptiste Say's economic treatise, the main ideas of *The Wealth of Nations* spread rapidly among the leading French economists, and became in due course integrated elements of the official economic doctrine. The doctrine of the Physiocrats, though short-lived, had prepared the ground for the acceptance of the principles of economic liberalism. And the French Revolution which wrecked the feudal structure of society opened the way for the application of the tenets of economic individualism to the organization of the economic machinery. The Ricardian setting of economic problems, however, was repudiated by Say, who explicitly insisted on the use of Baconian methods of observation as exclusive instruments of economic analysis. The Ricardian teachings, he argued, started from abstract principles which were not perfectly founded in facts, had no relevance to the actual world, and transformed economics into a verbal and argumentative discipline. To political economy as he conceived it, he assigned the tasks of establishing connections among the observed facts and finding through observation the points "where the chain of reasoning was to be attacked." But in his application of these methodological rules Say cared little about clarifying and justifying the "empirical laws" which provided the background for the formulation of the short-run problems which were the main object of his interest.[1]

That approach to economic analysis was endorsed by the overwhelming majority of nineteenth-century French economists. Representative followers of Say's teachings were Pellegrino Rossi (1787–1848), A.L.C. Destutt de Tracy (1754–1836), Charles Comte, Michael Chevalier (1806–1879), Jérôme A. Blanqui (1798–1854), Charles Ganilh, Joseph Garnier, Jean Gustav Courcelle-Seneuil, Barthélemy Charles Dunoyer, Louis Wolowski (1810–1876), and Antoine E. Cherbuliez. Their main activity covered the years 1820–60.[2] This group did not attempt to establish consistent systems of relationships among economic magnitudes reduced to a uniform standard of value, or to develop chains of causality at a relatively high level of abstraction. Influenced by the value theory which had been advanced by Abbé de Condillac in opposition to the Physiocratic doctrine, they looked to the markets to find the origin and determination of exchange values. They defined these values as the combined effects of the demand for goods—their utility—and their available supply—their scarcity. A sort of subjective theory of value was suggested by Henri Baudrillart (1821–1892) and Courcelle-Seneuil. Thus conceived, exchange values resulted from any activity for which there was a demand in the market, and the distinction drawn by Adam Smith and the Ricardians between "productive" and "unproductive" labor could easily be disregarded.

Since the French economists failed to take account of the difference between physical productivity and value productivity, they were unable to develop a satisfactory cost of production theory. They connected the value of the productive factors with their contributions to the creation of goods and regarded all primary forms of income—ground rent, interest on capital, profits, and wages—as rewards for such contributions. Although vaguely formulated and beset with logical difficulties, the idea to derive the value of the productive factors from the value of their products was in various respects superior to the Ricardian treatment of the problems of distribution with the aid of three disconnected theories. Some French economists, such as Destutt de Tracy, did, however, take over the Ricardian theory of land rent.

Closely linked with the importance which Say and his followers attached to the processes of marketing was the central role which they assigned to entrepreneurs. They ascribed to them all the capacities needed for supervising and administering the organization of production and sales, the ability to secure the funds needed to carry on their business, and the foresight to determine with tolerable accuracy the probable demand and other market conditions, that is, their costs and prices.[3] Also, Say's *loi des débouchés* was a law of the market suggested by the idea that in the final analysis all goods were exchanged for each other under the economic laws of the competitive order. Say did admit, however, the existence of temporary gluts and ensuing unemployment conditions. In support of his proposition that in the long run markets for the products are always available, Say pointed to the fact that when he wrote his treatise five or six times as many commodities were bought and sold in France than at the beginning of the fifteenth century. In their extensive discussions of questions of monetary policy, the French economists agreed with the Banking School on the conception of bank notes as credit instruments the volume of which was automatically adjusted to the requirements of trade.

The fairly general indifference of the French nineteenth-century economists to problems of economic theory has been ascribed to the fact that they felt obliged to defend the capitalist order against socialist attacks, and that the Physiocratic tradition imposed upon them the "study of institutions.[4] But there is no doubt that Say's strict adherence to vaguely defined Baconian methods prevented the elaboration of concepts of higher abstraction and the development of procedures of refined hypothetical reasoning. In those fields of economic research for which the Baconian method supplied useful instruments, excellent scholarly work was done by some French students on the functions of economic institutions of various types.[5] In the field of economic policy they ardently defended the principles of free trade and laissez-faire without adding much to the traditional arguments.[6]

It might not be amiss to emphasize in this connection the French economists' traditional belief in the power of credit as a primary motor of business activity. This belief found striking expression in some studies in which credit restrictions were held responsible for recurrent crises and depressions. The first French study to point to a causal relationship between alternating expansions and contractions of credit on the one hand and tides of business activity on the other was Charles Coquelin, *Du crédit et des banques*

(Paris, 1848). Coquelin's conception of money was similar to that of some Mercantilists who argued that consequent upon the acceptance of money, the seller of a good became a creditor of society. Coquelin was less interested in business cycle analysis than in the credit policy of the central bank and its alleged misuse of a monopolistic power. Clement Juglar's statistical investigations into business fluctuations are generally regarded as the first attempt to establish a consistent picture of the interdependence of prosperity periods and the ensuing crises, to demonstrate the periodicity of the fluctuations, and to use the method of comparing times series of economic and social magnitudes for the purpose of determining characteristic aspects of their behavior.[7] His comparative studies covered a comprehensive array of data derived largely from various reports of French, British, and U. S. banks, and revealed a remarkable correlation between changes in volumes of credit on the one hand and movements of prices, fluctuations in marriage and birth rates, public incomes, and similar numerical phenomena on the other. Juglar's objections to the quantity theory of money were connected with his narrow interpretation of the concept of money, which caused him to exclude all credit operations from the monetary sphere.[8]

A number of French economists shared Juglar's views that crises, though engendered in boom periods, were ultimately caused by the behavior of the balance of trade, its effect on gold reserves, and the discount rate.[9] They considered every cyclical fluctuation as a strictly national phenomenon closely connected with the operation of the national credit machinery. They disregarded the question of whether the price structure of other countries was affected by the discount policy of one of the leading central banks, and whether a cyclical movement occurring in one country might thus be transmitted to others through international monetary and credit relationships.

About 1860 a different interpretation of the role played by credit expansion in influencing business activity was advanced by a group of authors including Jean Gustave Courcelle-Seneuil, V. Bonnet, and Clement Joseph Garnier (1813–1882).[10] They suggested that crises were due to excessive capital investments made at the expense of the volume of circulating capital. Twenty years later that idea was elaborated by Léon Walras.[11] To the issuance of banknotes he ascribed the effects of a credit expansion leading to a flow of loans from the money markets to the capital market and to a disruption of the equilibrium between these markets. A credit crisis was bound to occur when the liquidity of the central bank was endangered by the loss of gold and fixed capital could not be withdrawn from long-term investments. But official monetary and credit policy was hardly affected by such considerations.

The influence of socialist movements on political life was far more pronounced in France than in England. Time and again such movements led to revolutionary attacks on the existing order, and the interpretation of the existing order's effects on the various classes of the population became a foremost topic of economicopolitical discussions. The arguments advanced in defense of the competitive economy were derived from the arsenal of the economic philosophy of *The Wealth of Nations* combined with various tenets of the doctrine of natural rights. As a representative of this group, Charles Dunoyer may be mentioned. In defense of interest on capital he referred to the "productivity" theory of capital, and attempted to explain ground rent as a reward for capital invested in agricultural enterprises.[12] Relying on the operation of self-regulating forces, he hailed free competition as the most efficient instrument of economic progress.

Claude Frédéric Bastiat (1801–1850), one of the most popular nineteenth-century French economic authors, undertook to demonstrate the harmony of alleged "laws of Providence" which govern human society and operate toward the equalization of all individuals in a process of infinite progress.[13] Among his individual "natural rights" Bastiat included the right to property and the "right to exchange."[14] He conceived of interest on captial as a reward for the postponement of utilizing consumption goods.[15] From the teachings of the American Henry Charles Carey (1793–1879)[16] he took over the assertion that the share of the Capitalist in the national dividend was declining along with the progressive accumulation of capital and that, of all classes of the population, the workers as consumers reaped the largest advantages from the operation of the competitive economy.

The leading ideas and the politicoeconomic attitude of the majority of the French economists did not experience any perceptible modification when the succeeding generation assumed the task of teaching economics and elaborating that science. Like their predecessors, the new economists contributed little to economic theory;[17] they considered it their main task to defend the principles of the competitive economy and to discuss some burning problems of their times in the light of these principles. These scholars include Yves Guyot (1843–1928), Pierre Paul Leroy-Beaulieu (1842–1912), Gustave de Molinari (1819–1912), Maurice Block (1816–1901), Léon Say (1826–1896), Gustave Schelle, and Louis Baudin. The works of some of them will be mentioned in other connections.[18]

In Italy the teachings of the eighteenth-century Mercantilists were preserved from falling into oblivion by the comprehensive collection of their writings published in fifty volumes between 1803 and 1816 by Pietro Custodi under the title *Scrittori Classici Italiani di economia politica*. These writers, many of whom had endorsed the gospel of the utilitarian doctrine, had well prepared the ground for the adoption of the principles of economic liberalism as expounded in *The Wealth of Nations* and adjusted to the thinking of the Latin countries by J. B. Say. But the unfortunate political conditions which existed on the Italian peninsula absorbed almost all the intellectual capacities of the most active and constructive minds. During the first half of the nineteenth century, the Italian economists mainly contributed commentaries interpreting the teachings of Adam Smith. The names of Melchiorre Gioja (1767–1829) and Giovannia D. Romagnosi (1761–1835) may be mentioned as representative of that group.[19] Some works of Francesco Fuoco were hailed as remarkable achievements by later Italian economists,[20] but the originality of Fuoco's main contributions to economic theory has been questioned.[21]

There is no doubt that in Italy, where the principles of deductive reasoning had enjoyed widespread acceptance among eighteenth-century Mercantilists, the Ricardian methods of economic analysis did not meet with the same hostility as in France. An outstanding author and teacher who adopted these methods was Francesco Ferrara, one of the most convinced and doctrinaire defenders of the principles of economic liberalism and a violent adversary of any state intervention.[22] His proposition to connect the value of goods with the future and to replace the Ricardian labor cost theory with a "cost of reproduction theory," according to which the upper limit of the price which a buyer was willing to pay was determined by the costs of reproducing the good, was much discussed.[23] But Ferrara contributed to his science less by purely theoretical considerations than by editing the *Biblioteca dell' Economista* (1850–68), a collection of translations of foreign economic treatises. He supplemented that work with a critical study of the developments of political economy in the eighteenth century and the first half of the nineteenth century.[24]

CONFLICTING METHODS OF THEORETICAL ANALYSIS

It is a noticeable fact that in the first half of the nineteenth century a few French authors who did not belong to the class of professional economists ventured to apply mathematical methods to the analysis of the relationships among economic magnitudes. The problems which they raised, and their formulation of these problems, differed so radically from the approach adopted by the contemporary authors of textbooks on economics that their studies were practically ignored until they were "rediscovered" at a much later date.

The application of mathematics to the relationships among abstract economic magnitudes—as distinct from the statistical analysis of times series of concrete magnitudes—was inaugurated by some thinkers who were convinced that it was possible to establish for the social sciences "laws of nature" having the same validity as those of the physical sciences. The economic system, composed of a world of measurable economic magnitudes (costs, prices, wages, profits, rents, and the like), appeared to present all prerequisites to the realization of such ideas. It is a moot question to what degree reasoning of that type was supported by the influence of Cartesian philosophy, which had elevated the method of mathematical deduction to the generally valid scientific method. It is equally debatable to what degree the search for mathematical expressions of "laws of nature" was promoted by the intensified use of methods of hypothetical reasoning. The adherents of such methods, whose fundamental judgments were based on assumptions, were inclined to believe that only mathematical procedures, the validity of which was guaranteed by unquestionable logical principles, could lead to the establishment of "truths."

Considerations of the latter kind caused the mathematician Augustin Cournot to embark on the search for "natural economic laws" which could be expressed in mathematical terms.[25] He assumed that the probability of such laws was directly related to their simplicity,[26] and that the economic principle provided a sufficient foundation for the application to economic analysis of the idea of a stable equilibrium. The first limited task he set himself was to formulate a general "law of demand," which was intended to establish a connection between the annual demand for a commodity and the price of the latter in the form of a continuous function. The law did not specify the determinants of particular forms of the demand curve. In accordance with the principles of static equilibrium analysis, Cournot eliminated the time element from his observations.[27] The well-defined starting point of this partial equilibrium analysis was a market with prices expressed in a stable monetary unit. The law implied that changes in demand were inversely related to changes in prices as long as the latter changes were fractions of the initial price. Of primary importance for later methodological considerations was Cournot's idea to abandon the search for causal relationships in favor of the study of functional relationships attributed to the behavior of the economic magnitudes.

It is characteristic of the originality of Cournot's thinking that he used his law of demand to analyze monopolistic situations and regarded perfect competition as a limiting rather than a prevailing case. As formulated by Cournot in terms of a maximizing proposition, the problem consisted in determining the highest proceeds—or the highest net profits—which the monopolist could derive from the sale of his product, being in a position to vary the price according to the demand function and to take account of changes in the costs of production under conditions of diminishing, constant, and increasing returns. Cournot's attempt to make a duopolistic situation determinate through "unrealistic" assumptions was the object of prolonged discussions much later.

In a treatise which dealt with the general mathematical principles of the theory of wealth, Cournot suggested the construction of an imaginary economic system in which all parts were interconnected by the price system. However, he was unable to propose a mathematical formulation for the interdependence of exchange relationships. He realized implicitly that the prices which were assumed to be given in his algebraic schemes were in fact variables determined by a variety of unspecified factors. He equally realized the importance of the free trade principle as a scientific theorem, the methodological nature of the maximization principle as applied to the behavior of demand, and the implications of the assumption that within the framework of partial equilibrium analysis all prices and incomes covered by the *ceteris paribus* clause were kept constant.

Various suggestions made by Cournot were taken up by another Frenchman, the engineer A.J.E.J. Dupuit, and applied in studies published in 1844 and 1845 dealing with practical price problems, especially with the varying advantages derived by consumers from public transport facilities and water supply. Dupuit started from a clear formulation of the concept of marginal utility and arrived at the conclusion that the consumers derived a surplus of utility (*espèce de ce bénéfice*) from all units of a supply which had higher utilities than the last increment. With this theorem he anticipated Alfred Marshall's concept of consumer's surplus.

The third Frenchman who suggested the application of new, quantitative methods to economic analysis during the first half of the nineteenth century was Auguste Walras, whose contributions to business cycle theory have already been mentioned. In his analysis of the value problem he advanced certain principles of the marginal utility theory which were later elaborated by his son, Leon Walras.[28] He also used the concept of scarcity (*rareté*), which he considered fundamental to any study of social problems, to explain the origin of property.

The methodological principles which prevented the followers of Say's teachings from appreciating the approach adopted by the mathematically minded economists were mainly rooted in the belief that no useful knowledge could be gained from studies not firmly founded on observation and experience. The spread of Auguste Comte's philosophy helped deepen that conviction.[29] In accordance with that philosophy, the scientific treatment of the various societies, conceived of as "organisms," had to be based on a theory of linear progress revealing the succession of three stages: religious, metaphysical, and scientific. To the last, the scientific stage, Comte attributed the task of applying exclusively the "positive" method based on observation and experience. Ironically, Comte's three stages were completely speculative in origin.

Comte drew a sharp distinction between the needs of the various societies and the needs of their members; he attributed to societies, as a condition of their survival, the preservation of certain moral, political, social, and even religious principles. From the operation of forces which produce structural long-run changes in social life, he distinguished the operation of certain "social instincts" producing equilibrating processes through mutual action and reaction and providing a basis for the spontaneous order of society. This distinction between "dynamic" and "static" problems of sociological analysis was taken over, as mentioned above, by J. S. Mill. But Comte raised strong objections to the Ricardian procedure of isolating economics from all other social sciences and applying to economic relationships methods of analysis which could not be used in analyzing other aspects of social life.

THE FRENCH SOCIALISTS

The French nineteenth-century socialist authors did not derive their leading ideas and proposals from a single dominant social philosophy, as did the Ricardian Socialists. Rather, they borrowed their intellectual armor from various eighteenth-century philosophers who had proclaimed the belief in a linear advancement of society.[30] But, as distinct from these philosophers, they were convinced that any real progress was dependent upon radical transformations of the existing economic and social institutions. Vague egalitarian ideas caused some of these authors to center their attacks on private ownership of the means of production. Others held the "chaotic nature" of the capitalist economy responsible for all social evils. The story of the utopian schemes advanced by some French Socialists is an interesting topic for the psychologist rather than the economist. Poorly trained in economic analysis, they grossly misinterpreted the functioning of the competitive economy and failed to realize the incompatibility of their revolutionary objectives with their ideal of economic freedom.

J. C. L. Simonde de Sismondi (1733–1842) has frequently been included among this group of French Socialists, although he did not call for the abolition of the private ownership of the means of production or propose a radical scheme of economic organization.[31] For authors with socialist leanings he was virtually the first economist to proclaim some fundamental revolutionary theorems, such as the principle of surplus value, the idea of the "class struggle," and an underconsumption theory of crises. Fascist authors were attracted by his proposals concerning a corporative organization of productive enterprises. Advocates of labor legislation pointed to his social insurance schemes, which anticipated much later developments of welfare politics. As distinct from most socialist authors, he was familiar with the Smithian methods of economic analysis and demonstrated that knowledge in a treatise written along the lines of *The Wealth of Nations*.[32] But subsequently he supplemented that discussion with another, designed to show the appalling failure of the competitive economy to achieve the objective of social welfare.[33] Denouncing economics as a hedonistic "*science de calcul*," Sismondi rejected the deductive method used in establishing economic theories and policies. He was probably the first author to hold differences in economic power responsible for the determination of social relationships. Without suggesting a well-defined method of economic analysis, he endeavored to substitute for economics as a science of principles a historical treatment of economic conditions and institutions in the light of development of the past; thus, he introduced "dynamic" elements into his analysis.[34] In his attacks on the economic policy advocated in *The Wealth of Nations*, Sismondi started from a rigid labor cost theory of value, and qualified profits as "surplus value" (*mieux valeur*) resulting from the difference between the labor costs of the products and the wages spent during the productive process. The main objects of his extended criticisms were the belief in the mobility of the factors of production and the "dangerous" theory that the equilibrium of the economy was automatically reestablished whenever it had been disturbed. He supported his attacks on Say's law of markets with a description of the devastating effects of commercial crisis and depressions, and attributed the recurrence of these fatal economic events to "overproduction'' provoked by misleading increases in prices. Equally remarkable was Sismondi's discussion of changes in employment conditions brought about by the introduction of labor-saving machinery.

Sismondi ascribed the tendency to concentrate wealth in the hands of a relatively small number of Capitalists, and the concentration of production in increasingly larger plants, to violent competitive struggle. He contrasted the growing antagonism between employers and workers, which had become apparent under the capitalist order, with the relationships between masters and their helpers which had prevailed under the guild system of feudalism. But neither his conspicuous understanding of some ''dynamic'' aspects of the economy nor his proposals of social reform aroused the attention of his contemporaries.[35]

The influence exercised by the ideas of another radical thinker, Claude Henri de Rouvroy Comte de Saint-Simon (1760–1825), who must equally be placed outside the ranks of ''socialist'' authors strictly speaking, was very far reaching. A French aristocrat who turned to social philosophy after having led a venturesome life during the French Revolution and its aftermath, Saint-Simon based his proposals of social reform on the ambitious idea of transforming the thinking processes of the leading groups of society.[36] He derived his outlook on the future history of mankind from Condorcet's conception of linear social progress, but he substituted for the eighteenth-century individualistic approach to the promotion of progress the ''theocratic'' idea of suprarational and supraindividual forces operating toward the transformation of the structure of society.

The writings of Saint-Simon contributed significantly to the spread of deterministic ideas among French students of social philosophies. He insisted that all first causes are of the mechanical type and that mathematical laws underlie the relationships among all phenomena. The distinction which he drew between ''destructive'' or ''critical'' and ''creative'' or ''organic'' periods of social development was characteristic of his conception of ''evolutionary'' social processes; it was later elaborated by various sociologists. In his extensive discussion concerning the establishment of an ideal social order, Saint-Simon started from the belief that systems of social organization cannot be artificially created and that ''ideas'' are the prime movers of social development. He elaborated these propositions in a fragmentary social philosophy according to which social organizations developed in close alliance with an ''evolutionary process'' underlying the progress of human thinking. Thus, he associated the feudal order, conceived of as a stage in that process, with a mythological or ''fictitious'' period of reasoning, and connected the liberal or capitalist order, conceived of as another stage, with ''physical'' or abstract methods. Saint-Simon regarded labor and robbery as the only possible methods of acquiring goods. With his conception of the feudal society as an age of forceful appropriation, he contributed greatly to the spread of a distorted picture of medieval political and economic institutions. Saint-Simon's aversion to the principles of hypothetical reasoning was reflected to his contempt for individual liberty and for the system of parliamentary representation, a ''mongrel system,'' as he called it, because it allowed divergent ends to compete with each other.

A new comprehensive social science was to be elaborated, designed to initiate the ''scientific'' or ''positive'' stage of knowledge, as prerequisite to the establishment of a new social organization in which maximization of productivity was pursued as a generally valid social end. The full realization of that principle—as discovered by Adam Smith and propagated by Say—had to be effected by an economic order operated by scientific leaders and well-qualified heads of productive enterprises. In such a society of producers (*"industriels"*), individual interests would be in perfect harmony with the common interest, and the common needs of the society would be met by voluntary associations of producers.[37] A socialist element was introduced into this picture of an ideal economic order by the demand for equality of opportunity. With that demand Saint-Simon combined his often-quoted slogan, "To each according to his capacity, to each capacity in proportion to its work."

It is impossible to give a clear account even of Saint-Simon's leading ideas, since, as time went on, he advanced partly conflicting views and never succeeded in developing a coordinated system of thoughts. But he attracted quite a number of enthusiastic followers who can be grouped according to their interpretation of the master's suggestions and prognostications. The most important intellectual movement initiated by Saint-Simon culminated in the elaboration of the "positivist" philosophy by Auguste Comte. Comte's monumental work was designed to prepare the attainment of Saint-Simon's "third stage of social evolution." An entirely different approach to Saint-Simon's ideas caused an extravagant group of his adherents to develop his division of historical periods, his deterministic conception of social organization, and his sociological interpretation of predatory methods into a revolutionary system.[38] Headed by Barthélemy Prosper Enfantin (1796–1854) and Saint-Amand Bazard (1791–1832), this group cooperated in elaborating a socialist "doctrine" which turned on alleged tendencies of the competitive economy to depress wages, to promote the maldistribution of resources,[39] and to create increasing antagonisms between capitalist employers and exploited workers. Enfantin attributed the crisis to the exaggerated competitive demands for productive factors on the part of poorly informed producers, and to the owners' ignorance of what idle resources are available for investment. Only income earned by labor was regarded as economically justified, and abolition of the ownership of the means of production was presented as a postulate of the "law of progress." Powerful trade organizations, said members of this group, should be established to organize production by industries, and commercial banks should assume the task of directing economic activities into the proper channels.[40] From the master's teachings they derived the conviction that "credit" was the revolutionary instrument for delivering purchasing power from the control of hereditary wealth holders and placing it at the disposal of entrepreneurs capable of using it for the benefit of society. According to Enfantin, a radical reorganization of the credit system could lead to the desired objective of reducing the rate of interest to zero.

Other, more conservative disciples applied the master's ideas to the practical purpose of organizing credit schemes designed to place the saving capacities of the middle class at the disposal of small artisans and merchants. The brothers Jacob Emile (1800–1875) and Isaac Pereire (1806–1880) were the initiators in 1852 of a widespread system of "*crédit mobilier*" which subsequently led to the establishment of a variety of similar institutions, such as *banques de compensation, banques régulatrices, banques des valeurs, agences monétaires, banques d'assurance,* and *banques rationnelles.*

The French Socialists of the outright utopian type can be grouped according to the main characteristics of their vaguely conceived proposals concerning the ideal organization of society. One group can be formed of those whose projects were based on the belief in the blessings of voluntary cooperation. An outstanding representative of that type was François Marie Charles Fourier (1772–1837),[41] whose leading ideas were rooted in an eighteenth-century mechanistic philosophy. He combined an atomistic conception of society with the elaboration of absurd social theorems which turned on the operation of twelve passions, a "law of attraction" alleged to govern human relationships, and the like.

Fourier criticized the capitalist competitive order mainly on the ground that it wasted economic resources and lacked rationality in the organization of the productive forces. His ideal organizational forms were those of small producers' associations, called "*phalanges*." Each phalanx was designed to include a variety of productive processes and to provide for the "harmonious combination" of different human characters and tempers. Labor should be made attractive by granting each member freedom to choose, and possibly to vary, his or her occupation. Five-twelfths of the value of the products was to be assigned to labor, four-twelfths to capital, and three-twelfths to management. Although unfit to provide the basis for a sound economic organization of production, Fourier's *phalanstères* were the object of a number of practical experiments. At one time there existed in the United States not less than forty associations of that type. Most remarkable was the North American Phalanx in New Jersey (1843 to 1855).

The traditional belief of the French population in the miraculous power of credit provided the backbone for utopian projects of another type.[42] An important scheme belonging to that group was propagated by Louis Blanc (1811–1882), who played an outstanding role during the 1848 revolutionary movement.[43] As distinct from almost all other French Socialists, he charged the government with the task of organizing production and trade through the creation of *ateliers nationaux,* a sort of producers' association to be supported by cheap credits granted by a public central bank. In 1848, after Blanc had been made a member of a revolutionary government which recognized a general right to work, such cooperatives were, in fact, established in Paris. But the *ateliers* were disbanded after the revolution was quelled.[44]

The belief in credit as a creative power found its most extravagant expression in the writings of Pierre J. Proudhon, who is generally regarded as the most influential French Socialist.[45] His attacks on the capitalist order were backed by a crude labor cost theory of value which led to the conclusion that all incomes not earned by labor were taxes or contributions (*aubaines*) imposed on the workers' earnings. Proudhon's theory of exploitation was derived from the thesis that the wage paid to the worker corresponded to the latter's "individual" productivity, and that the employer's profit was made possible by the much higher yield of the combined and coordinated work of labor. His analysis of alleged contradictions implied in the capitalist order was based on a distorted version of Hegelian dialectics, which he used to demonstrate that payment of interest on capital was responsible for the disruption of the equilibrium between costs and prices.[46] With dialectic procedures of a similar kind he attempted to justify the contention that free credit issued by an exchange bank to producers' associations would free the associations from the element of time adherent to loans under the capitalist order. If the associations could at any time sell their products to the exchange bank at the "real exchange value," a "perfect" static equilibrium could be established and maintained between the demand for the goods and their supply, and Say's law of markets would operate without restrictions.[47] The abolition of interest on borrowed capital would extinguish any incentive to save; any share allotted to capital in the distributive process would be eliminated and the Capitalists would be deprived of their power to exploit labor. Society would consist of free and equal producers.[48]

Since Proudhon hated the ideas connected with the communion of goods at least as much as he hated the competitive order, his proposals have frequently been qualified as anarchistic. Some glaring defects of his interpretation of the capitalist economy, especially his profound misunderstanding of the role played by the price mechanism, were effectively criticized by Karl Marx. It might be a tempting task for students of social psychology to define those aspects of Proudhon's absurd proposals which made his ideas so attractive to large sectors of the French population. Quite conspicuous was the influence of the anarchistic features of his writings on some Russian revolutionaries, such as Mikhail Bakunin (1814–1876) and Prince Pëtr A. Krapotkin (1842–1921).[49]

In spite of the wide variety which the utopian Socialists showed in their criticisms of the capitalistic order and in their conceptions of an ideal economy, they were all convinced that the power of deductive reasoning enabled them to devise generally valid schemes of effective economic organization which ignorance and ill will of the ruling groups of the population had prevented from being realized. Hence, they appealed to the intelligence and the moral convictions of the educated classes in demonstrating the importance of their schemes. Their belief in the magic power of reason was as remarkable as their lack of understanding of fundamental economic problems. The role played by technical progress and the functions to be fulfilled by large enterprises as instruments of economic growth were realized only by Saint-Simon. Almost all utopian authors pinned their main hopes on the emergence of a cooperative spirit, on the blessings which they attributed to the abolition of interest on capital, and on almost limitless credit expansion. Their distributive schemes were derived from partly conflicting ideals of social justice. Saint-Simon referred to a vague idea of "work performed," Fourier arbitrarily allotted to each productive factor a precise share in the value of the product, Blanc advocated distribution according to need, and Proudhon connected the process of distribution with the contributions made by workers to the labor costs "embodied" in the product. The idea of centralized planning was alluded to only by Saint-Simon's disciples, who expected the banks to direct productive activities.

THE GERMAN VERSION OF SMITHIAN ECONOMICS

At the beginning of the nineteenth century the economic conditions of the central European territories were still relatively backward when compared with England's rapidly advancing industrialization. After the Holy Roman Empire of the German nation had been dissolved in 1806, the last vestiges of the unifying influence exercised by the imperial court disappeared and the princes and rulers of the large and small sovereign German territories were left to their own devices in determining their foreign and domestic policies. The remarkable consolidation of the international political situation which was achieved at the Congress of Vienna (1815) was based on the application of the principle of legitimacy, which implied recognition of the hereditary rights of all secular rulers. In practically all parts of Central Europe the methods of cameralistic administrative and economic policies were preserved until the second half of the century. Agricultural production, freed from the fetters of the feudal system, was slowly adjusted to the needs of expanding markets. But the development of large-scale industrial enterprises was hampered by the lack of capital, custom barriers, differences in monetary standards, and vexatious administrative practices which prevented free intercourse among the many politically independent communities, sometimes even among the various parts of a politically united territory.

Increasing oppositions to the traditional methods of government interference with economic activities were voiced during the first decades of the century by many teachers of economics and public officials who were deeply impressed by the principles of economic policy advocated by Adam Smith.[50] They criticized the prevailing system of agricultural organization, the restrictions imposed upon manufacture and trade, the authoritative regulation of prices and distribution, and the widespread discriminatory and monopolistic practices.[51] Influential members of the bureaucracy endeavored to put these teachings to the test of practical experience.

But proclamation of the beneficial effects of free competition did not imply the acceptance of the utilitarian doctrine and Benthamite methods of highly abstract hypothetical reasoning. The German economists did not attempt to devise an imaginary picture of the economy governed by equilibrating forces, and were under no logical obligation to adjust their teachings closely to the Ricardian doctrine. In preparing their textbooks they followed the traditional arrangement introduced by the Cameralists, and distinguished a first theoretical part from a second dealing with applied economics. The analysis of fundamental concepts and general problems was, however, frequently almost disregarded in the predominantly descriptive discussions of agricultural, manufactural, and commercial activities as enlarged by recommendations of economic policies. As time went on, the standard model for the arrangement of their teachings was provided by the textbook by Karl Heinrich Rau (1792–1870); Rau added public finance as a third part to theoretical and applied economics.[52]

In their theoretical discussions the German liberal economists practically ignored the mechanical approach which had been introduced into English economic reasoning by the Mercantilists. They made rather free use of teleological conceptions and considerations. The social collectivities or communities which they had in mind were commonly of the organic type. Their epistemological views and methodological devices were strongly influenced by Immanuel Kant's theory of cognition as expounded in the *Critique of Practical Reason* (1788). According to that theory, human behavior could not be subjected to causal determination because of man's moral freedom to act. Practical reason could subordinate itself only to a general moral law—the categorical imperative—which it established itself and which it could derive directly from a priori synthetic judgments. Kant characterized striving for individual happiness as a "pragmatic," purely hypothetical imperative, like the "technical" imperative, which refers to knowledge of the means necessary to carry out given objectives. Binding moral precepts, he argued, could be established only by an imperative having "objective existence." Kant attributed such existence to the categorical imperative, expressed by the famous formula that "the maxim of one's conduct should be such as could be willed to be a universal law."[53]

Even many German economists who strongly supported the adoption of liberal principles of economic policy were prevented by their ethical convictions from including the search for causal laws among the tasks of the social sciences. They preserved the methods of reasoning adopted by the Cameralists, avoided the use of concepts of high abstraction, and did not clearly isolate the study of economic phenomena from the research into other aspects of social relationships.

In various teachings of the German economists, the Scholastic concept of value in use (occasionally called "positive value") provided the starting point for the theoretical discussions and led to classifications of goods according to their importance for human welfare. J.F.E. Lotz even suggested a classification of goods in accordance with ethical principles. The distinction between value in use and exchange value was frequently referred to, but hardly sufficiently clarified. Production was identified with the creation of physical goods, consumption with their annihilation. The Ricardian idea that the economic problems of production and distribution had to be analyzed in terms of exchange values was largely ignored, and the labor cost theory of value found very few adherents since the prevailing conception of the economy did not require a reduction of all values to a uniform standard. Gottlieb Hufeland (1760–1817), one of the first German economists of liberal persuasion, adopted Say's definition of value in terms of scarcity and utility and emphasized the influence of individual wants on the valuation of goods. Rau advanced similar ideas, as did F.B.W. von Hermann (1795–1868), who was considered the most outstanding German economist of his time.[54]

In their analysis of price problems the German economists showed a characteristic predilection for the establishment of types of price situations as derived from observation and experience. Hermann discussed the behavior of the seller who took account of the costs of production and the market condition, and described the influences exercised on would-be buyers by the use value of the desired goods, their purchasing power, and the effective demand for the goods in the market. The quantity theory of money was referred to only in explaining changes in specific prices.

The distinction among the traditional three productive factors—land, labor, and interest—was generally connected with the three types of income.[55] Say's "productivity theory" of interest on capital appealed to many German authors because of their propensity in their sociological analyses to attribute significant roles to "forces" inherent in social agents. The German economists preferred a specific version of Say's theory which was ruled by the idea of the separation of the use of capital from its "substance," with interest being regarded as payment for the use and, incidentally, as a cost element in its own right. In accordance with this view, Hermann placed special emphasis on durability and yield in his definition of capital, and defined interest as the exchange value of the use made of capital goods. In order to apply this line of reasoning to cases in which capital goods were completely absorbed in the course of the "productive" process, Hermann developed the concept of an objective use of capital to be compensated in the form of interest.[56] Under the heading of "profit," Hermann listed various compensations earned by entrepreneurs for the fulfillment of their functions, such as payment for risks, remuneration for managerial work, and the like.

Since the German economists were loath to accept the Malthusian theory of population and practically ignored the equilibrium aspects of the Ricardian doctrine, they had no use for the narrowly defined Ricardian concept of rent. Hermann demonstrated noticeable progress in economic analysis when he applied the concept of rent to all cases in which the share allotted to a productive factor was influenced by scarcity relationships, and Hans von Mangoldt extended the concept to all cases in which increased production of a good in great demand resulted in the employment of material of poorer quality.[57] Hermann included rent among cost elements, but Mangoldt criticized him for this.

The wage fund theory, which was closely connected with the Ricardian labor cost theory, was almost unanimously rejected by the leading German economists. They did not advance a wage theory strictly speaking, but resorted to a loose method of wage determination according to which the lower limit of wages was determined by the prevailing standard of living and the upper limit by a market price resulting from the play of supply and demand. But the conditions of supply and demand which existed in the various labor markets were not closely analyzed.

Only Hermann showed a certain originality in his discussion of wage problems. He connected the wage level with the demand for goods by consumers and the prices they were willing to pay, and he emphasized the fact that the wages paid to labor in the final stages of productive processes were, as a rule, higher than those paid in the preceding stages. Thus, he alluded to the existence of noncompeting groups in the domestic labor market and remarked that effective competition in that market obtained only between groups with approximately similar skills.[58]

The discussion of these economic teachings can conveniently be concluded with a reference to some noticeable idea, which Mangoldt contributed to the elaboration of Smithian economics. In some respects Mangoldt anticipated certain concepts which later became cornerstones of marginal utility analysis: he related the value of goods to the needs which they were able to satisfy and realized that the value of a unit of a stock of goods was reduced by additions to the stock. In his price analysis he used geometrical diagrams to explain the shapes of supply curves. Mangoldt realized the importance of the principle of marginal productivity as used by Johann Heinrich von Thünen, and applied it to the explanation of the shares of the productive factors in the value of the product. His rent concept was applicable to incomes derived from profits, interest, and wages. He defined "profit" as a reward for the functions of the entrepreneur. In his theory of interest on capital he drew a distinction between the actual average interest rate and the "equilibrium" rate, defining the latter as the rate indicated by the yield of the last unit of the capital employed. Economic disturbances, he argued, were likely to ensue when the actual rate was not adjusted to the lower level determined by that yield. Hence, his explanation of crises and depressions turned on misdirected investments which had been provoked by erroneous expectations.[59]

The principles of free trade, as advocated by the English "School of Manchester," were defended in Germany by some economists of extreme "liberal" persuasion, such as John Prince-Smith (1809–1874) and Max Wirth. In support of their views they relied upon the teachings of Bastiat and his ideas about the harmony of all economic interests. They limited the functions of the state to the "production of justice," proclaimed free competition as the "natural" organization of the economy, and held armament expenditures responsible for the poverty of certain groups of the population. From the Ricardian wage theory they derived the proposition that increases in wages could result only from increasing profits used to expand the wage fund. Hence, they insisted upon keeping the relations between workers and employers free from any outside interference. Annual economic congresses organized in 1858 provided a rallying point for the members of this group.

Between about 1830 and 1870 only two German economists used important elements of the Ricardian doctrine in developing original economic theories: Thünen and Johann Karl Rodbertus (1805–1875). Neither of them belonged to the academic profession.

Thünen's political and moral philosophy differed substantially from that adopted by Ricardo. Thünen's conception of the state and his approach to social problems were tinged with organismic ideas; his studies were influenced by the writings of various Cameralists.[60] But he showed a genuine understanding of the Ricardian methods of hypothetical reasoning and used them with consummate skill in his analysis of some general problems connected with the operation of agricultural enterprises. He defined the object of his studies quite clearly as a search for the rule of law in a hypothetical state of rest, that is, under equilibrium conditions.[61]

Having observed the influence of falling grain prices on land rent, Thünen undertook a careful analysis of some spatial aspects of agricultural production;[62] the methodological device which he used in that study was the construction of an "isolated state" in which a closed market represented the center of the distributive processes. Basic to his theoretical considerations was the concept of marginal productivity which had only indirectly been alluded to by Ricardo but had been more clearly formulated by Mountifort Longfield.[63] Starting from the analysis of a ring-shaped arrangement of agricultural production around a city, Thünen demonstrated that a specific type of differential rent resulted from differences in the costs of shipping the products to the central market. Suggesting a "theory of location," he showed at the same time the influence of spatial factors on the optimum use of farmland.[64]

Thünen likewise availed himself of the concept of marginal productivity in his analysis of the distributive process as applied to the determination of the wages of agricultural workers. In accordance with the Ricardian formulation of the "law of decreasing returns," he analyzed increases in agricultural production on the assumption that the contributions of land and capital remained stable while labor was applied in increasing amounts. Successive application of increments of labor, he argued, would continue up to the point at which the additional yield obtained through the "last worker" would be equal in value to the wage paid to him; under the rule of free competition that wage level would prevail for all workers performing work of the same kind.

In his discussion of the productivity of capital, Thünen stated quite consistently that the efficiency of capital is to be measured in terms of the increment to the product of labor which accrues as the result of an increase in capital. On the assumption that under competitive conditions the return on capital was equalized in all uses, the rate of interest was shown to be determined by the still profitable use of the last applied increment of capital. The Ricardian theorem concerning the tendency of the interest rate to fall appeared to receive strong support from Thünen's contention that the progress achieved in the application of efficient machinery was slowing down and was accompanied by decreasing agricultural returns.

Thünen's contributions to the theory of rent and to marginal productivity analysis have secured him a place among the most outstanding economists of the nineteenth century. A third remarkable theoretical achievement which can be credited to him was the introduction of a concept which anticipated the idea of so-called opportunity costs. This concept was implied in his statement that the price of a product had to be high enough to assure that no higher yield could be gained when capital and land used in its production were put to other uses. In pursuance of that line of thought Thünen arrived at the conclusion that, in the last analysis, costs are determined by alternative uses of the productive factors.

But Thünen's studies in economics were not primarily motivated by purely scientific interests. Paramount in his thoughts was a zeal to work for the realization of social justice and for the adoption of social reforms in favor of the working classes. With this purpose in mind he elaborated an imaginary formula of a "just wage," defined as the square root of the subsistence wage multiplied by the value of the worker's average product. That formula was designed to assure to the worker an adequate share in the increasing efficiency of the capital employed in the productive processes.[65]

The logical principles observed by Rodbertus differed radically from the refined methods of economic analysis developed by Thünen.[66] His socialist leanings caused Rodbertus to place primary emphasis on the use of the Ricardian labor cost theory as an instrument for demonstrating the proposition that all incomes not earned by labor represented "surplus values" withheld by the owners of land and capital. Rodbertus was probably responsible for the widespread belief that the ownership of the means of production had its origin in acts of usurpation and violence, and that the inequality of incomes was exclusively due to that institutional factor.[67] Consequent upon this approach to the problems of distribution, he refused to accept the theoretical distinction drawn by Ricardo between the yield derived from the soil and the return on capital. Although he proclaimed the workers' right to the full value of the fruit of their labor, he admitted that employers who employed a number of workers for production purposes had claims to adequate rewards.

Rodbertus invoked the authority of Smith and Ricardo to justify his assertions that only goods produced by labor were "economic" goods, and that the term *labor* as used by these masters of economic analysis denoted exclusively "material" operations. On the other hand, in defense of his fundamental concepts he argued that the labor cost theory of value was deeply rooted in German national convictions. Thus, he availed himself of an intuitionist philosophy derived from the teachings of the German historical schools. In his attempts to justify his theoretical considerations, Rodbertus repeatedly resorted to devious arguments. As a specimen of that kind of reasoning, his analysis of ground rent may be mentioned. In order to connect the explanation of rent with the surplus value withheld from the workers, he characterized rent as a free contribution of nature increased by the difference between the yield of the soil and the rate of profit as equalized in all lines of investment. It may be observed that the rigid labor cost theory of value advocated by Rodbertus was incompatible with the theorem concerning the equalization of the rate of profit.[68]

Like some English social reformers, such as Robert Owen, Rodbertus was fascinated by the idea of substituting for money as a means of measuring values a labor currency based on a fixed "normal" working day and expressing "just prices" which would correspond to the amounts of labor incorporated in goods. In his ideal scheme of wage determination, wages were to be adjusted to standard output, fixed for the various occupations, and revised in accordance with the rising productivity of labor. If wages were thus to be fixed in accordance with the increasing productivity of the manufacturing processes, Rodbertus expected that crises and depressions would be eliminated, since he connected the existence of these phenomena with a "law of the falling wage quota," that is, with a gradual relative decline of the purchasing power of the wage earners.[69] Along with Sismondi, Rodbertus was one of the first authors to hold "underconsumption" responsible for the recurrent accumulation in the markets of large volumes of unsaleable commodities. Anticipating the main features of the so-called doctrine of economic imperialism, he ascribed the periodic temporary revivals of business activity to the expansion of the capitalist economy into colonial territories where new markets could be found for the otherwise unsaleable products of capitalist enterprises. In the light of that reasoning, the fight over the possession of colonies was a struggle over territories the markets of which could be reserved for the producers and traders of the conquering countries.

Influenced by some leading ideas of the historical school, Rodbertus regarded the capitalist economy as a transitory link in a historical sequence of vaguely defined "evolutionary processes." As the last stage of that process he envisioned the emergence of a Christian sociopolitical community in which the economic order, based on collective ownership of land and capital, would guarantee to each worker a share in the product corresponding exactly to the value of his or her productive contribution, whereas the receipt of "unearned" incomes would be abolished. Rodbertus warned his contemporaries that, if the moral forces lacked an established system of just wage regulations, history could be relied upon to "swing the whip of revolution."[70]

In the second half of the nineteenth century the ideas of Rodbertus found fertile soil among the adherents of Christian social movements and among some German so-called Socialists of the chair. His admirers credited him with having advanced the first doctrine of "scientific socialism," and it would be rather idle to discuss the validity of that assertion. In this connection mention may be made of a contemporary of Rodbertus, Karl Georg Winkelblech, who published his socialist propositions under the name of Karl Marlo in three volumes. This work was designed to show that the operation of the capitalist economy was bound to lead to a rapid deterioration of the conditions of the working classes and those of the small entrepreneurs. Like most German Socialists, Winkelblech charged the government with the organization of the socialist economy. Large sectors of the economy (the utility services, wholesale and foreign trade, etc.) should be centrally operated; other occupations should be carried on a guildlike basis. Winkelblech's writings have left no marks in the history of ideas.[71]

AMERICAN DISCUSSIONS OF SMITHIAN ECONOMICS

Prior to the last quarter of the nineteenth century, theoretical economics had hardly any assured place in the literature or educational institutions of the United States.[72] The utilitarian social philosophy permeated all spheres of social life outside the strictly circumscribed domain of religious activities. The economic textbooks which were commonly used were adjusted to the teachings of J. B. Say. They did not stimulate consistent theoretical analysis; although meant to be realistic, they virtually ignored the dynamic economic processes which were taking place when the vast natural resources of a continent were opened up by a rapidly increasing population and unexpected opportunities continued to attract entrepreneurial initiative. Some constitutent elements of Ricardian economics such as the Malthusian theory of population were obviously inapplicable to the American conditions, and the Ricardian setting of the problems of distribution was largely ignored. A sharp contrast also existed between the free trade principles proclaimed by the English and French economists and the American protectionist policy, the leading ideas of which had been effectively outlined in the *Report on the Subject of Manufactures,* by Alexander Hamilton (1755–1804), submitted to the House of Representatives in 1791.

Elaborating the "infant industry argument" the report attempted to demonstrate the advantages which could be gained from granting strong protection to the development of manufactures, especially of those lines which used domestic raw materials, which could replace labor through mechanized processes, could produce goods of widespread use, and were important for purposes of defense.[73]

In fact, the first noticeable American economic treatise, written by Daniel Raymond, was a plea for protectionism[74] and centered on the argument that low-priced imports should be prevented from undermining the relatively high wage level which obtained in various American industries.[75] H. C. Carey was the first American author whose ideas gained widespread attention and who became the head of a so-called school.[76] But it is difficult to form a coherent picture out of the fragments of his poorly disciplined reasoning. He attempted to develop some propositions derived from the writings of Smith and Say into a sort of general social science or sociology. From the observation that economic progress was accompanied by a relative reduction of the value of accumulated capital as compared with the increase in the value of the commodities directly produced by labor, he derived a general "law" according to which, with progressive accumulation of capital, the rate of interest had a tendency to fall, whereas, owing to the increasing "productivity" of capital, the total volume of profits was constantly growing.[77] Since Carey identified the decline in the rate of interest with corresponding increases in the workers' share in the value of their products, he believed to have demonstrated that Capitalists and workers took equal advantage from the progressive accumulation of capital.

Carey supported that optimistic picture of the capitalist order by criticizing the pessimistic aspects of the Ricardian doctrine. To the Malthusian law of population and to the theory of decreasing returns in agriculture he opposed the American experience and the prospects of a limitless expansion of productivity. He defined land rent as the equivalent of the amount of labor saved by the landowners through investments made in the soil; hence, he argued, increases in land rent did not affect the distribution of the national dividend.

In his later writings Carey endorsed the cause of strong protectionism as a permanent economic policy which he defended as indispensable for the development of diversified industries. He held tariff reductions responsible for the crises of 1822–24 and 1840–43.[78]

The Ricardian theory of rent which had been so bitterly attacked by Carey was used by Henry George (1839–1897) to justify his famous "single tax" principle.[79] The background of George's social philosophy was formed by a version of the doctrine of natural rights, according to which free access to natural resources was necessary in order to secure for everyone the liberty to work and to acquire property. Total wealth, he argued, had increased faster than population in all industrial nations, whereas the working classes had remained poor. George held the landowners responsible for that poverty, since, he believed, definite limits were set to interest and wages through the productivity of capital and labor employed on the least profitable soil. As an effective remedy he proposed the imposition of a tax designed to "skim off" the "unearned" incomes derived from the differential rents.

Highly respected Ricardian economists such as J. S. Mill had advanced similar though less radical proposals, and no objections of principle could be raised to the starting point of George's reasoning if the Ricardian rent theory were assumed to be valid. Rather, critical observations were directed against the effects which George claimed for his policy, and to the possibility of separating, for taxation purposes, the net rent from the yield of investments made to improve the soil.[80] It could easily be argued that George had greatly overestimated the share of the landowner in the national dividend, that land rent fulfilled important functions in the organization of agricultural production and in the real estate market, and that the rents derived from the soil were but a fraction of unearned incomes received in innumerable cases in which a productive factor other than labor was relatively scarce. These and other objections did not prevent the adherents of the single tax movement from regarding George's proposal as a panacea which would assure an adequate distribution of the results of economic progress among the large masses of the working population. The amazing propagandist success of the single tax idea in the United States, in England, and on the European continent has sometimes been ascribed to the fact that it was launched during a depression period. George's theory of interest on capital was reminiscent of A.R.J. Turgot's suggestion that, through a process of equalization, the distributive shares allotted to the natural productive services were extended to situations in which no such services were rendered.

Teaching of economics, as practiced in the United States, reached a more scientific level only after several chairs of political economy had been established at some leading universities in the 1870s.[81] The foundation, in 1885, of the American Economic Association was due to the initiative of a group of American students of economics who had spent some years at German universities under the guidance of teachers of the historicoethical persuasion. Hence, the "historical and statistical study" of the "natural conditions of economic life" was explicitly included among the main objectives of the association. Richard T. Ely (1854–1943) was the most influential member of this "new school" of economists which voiced strong opposition to the Ricardian methods of analysis.[82]

But the attempt to convert the American economists to the principles of organismic reasoning was not very successful. These principles were hardly compatible with the methodological rules of the utilitarian philosophy which provided the background for the American approach to social and economic problems. In economics as in other lines of sciences, the methods of hypothetical thinking maintained the upper hand. Among the American economists who made noticeable contributions to Ricardian economics, F. B. Hawley may be mentioned.[83] Having started from a criticism of various features of Mill's doctrine, Hawley centered his analysis of the economy on the behavior of the entrepreneur, emphasized the latter's functions in the sphere of "risk taking," and defined profit as the reward for the assumption of risk. He combined a broad concept of rent (which included income derived from monopolies and fixed capital goods) with a theory of total output in which the supply of the productive factors was considered independent of their rates of remuneration. He practically neglected the role generally attributed to prices in the adjustment processes of the economy.

Among the American socialist authors who were not outright followers of Fourier or Robert Owen, Edward Bellamy (1850–1898) may be mentioned. His widely read utopian *Looking Backward,* published in 1887, preached complete economic equality to be realized through a system of authoritarian state socialism.

Part IV

Organismic Economics

Chapter 14
The German Historical Schools

—

GERMAN "IDEALISTIC" PHILOSOPHIES

IT IS A remarkable fact that during the first decades of the nineteenth century the methods of hypothetical reasoning secured a firm foothold in Germany in the natural sciences but that the application of these methods to social phenomena and events was repudiated by practically all German philosophers of that period. This dichotomy could claim the support of the authority of Immanuel Kant. In his *Critique of Pure Reason,* Kant objected to the use of the substance concept in the natural sciences on the ground that human understanding had lost itself in contradictions when it ventured to pass beyond the limits of possible experience and attempted to deal with "things in themselves." But in his *Critique of Practical Reason,* which analyzed the normative aspects of human thinking, Kant admitted the possibility of forming certain "synthetic judgments" of the a priori type, and insisted that the laws of causality were not applicable to the analysis of human behavior because of their incompatibility with the principle of the freedom of will. These considerations caused many leading German philosophers, historians, and sociologists to reject the application of the methods of the physical sciences to the study of social relationships. They suggested the use of processes of "intuition" for the analysis of social phenomena, on the ground that intuitive processes enable observers to grasp the nature and the functioning of integrated collective "wholes" which, although not accessible to direct perception, could be regarded as objects possessing real existence outside the human mind.

Among the German "idealistic philosophers" who exercised a considerable influence on economic reasoning, Johann G. Fichte (1762–1814) occupied a significant position.[1] Fichte's "identity philosophy" aimed at establishing a world of concepts as a realm of ends, fully identical with the real world. Man was challenged to overcome the antagonism which was said to exist between that world and his instincts; he was requested to fulfill the "autonomous" moral tasks imposed upon him as a member of a "social organism." Within the framework of that philosophy the character of "organic entities" was attributed not only to political communities but also to "nationalities," which were charged with definite functions in the progressive fulfillment of a preestablished universal order.[2] In his widely read *Addresses to the German Nation*, delivered in 1807/8, he ascribed to the German "nation" specific mental abilities and attitudes, and claimed for it the mission of saving the world through cultural and moral achievements. The specific mission of "selected" nations had commonly been derived from Acts of Revelation. The mission of the Germans as envisaged by Fichte, however, was connected with a particular logical faculty of the members of that nation: their alleged capacity to grasp intuitive concepts. Thus, Fichte became one of the first of those apostles of German nationalism who imposed on every German the moral obligation to subordinate his interests and his will to the superior national objectives.[3]

In an economic treatise entitled *The Closed Commercial State*,[4] Fichte applied his extreme nationalistic ideas to the construction of a utopian political community the members of which were completely subordinated to the authority of the government. The government was charged with the operation of a planned economy and the issuance of fiduciary notes the circulation of which had to be adjusted to domestic requirements. Foreign trade, restricted to a minimum, was to be carried on by trading monopolies, mainly in the form of barter on a bilateral basis. Although Fichte expected that causes of warfare would be considerably reduced through the proposed cultural and commercial isolation of the political communities, he claimed for the national state the right forcibly to annex neighboring territories, if such steps were required by economic considerations.

The logical approach adopted by Fichte and other "idealistic" philosophers, such as F.W.J. von Schelling (1775–1854), radically differed from that endorsed by the thinkers of the eighteenth-century "enlightenment," who had been looking for eternal truths to be discovered by analyzing the progress achieved through intellectual and social developments. The idea of linear progress was eventually attacked and condemned on logical grounds by a third post-Kantian philosopher, G.W.F. Hegel (1770–1831), who applied the concept of "evolutionary forces" to the explanation of all historical processes, and insisted that all history must show a purpose to which actions and events can be referred.[5] Hence, Hegel not only rejected any history of the descriptive type as lacking cognitive values but he equally objected to any historical analysis not designed to confirm the validity of the predetermined course which he ascribed to the sequence of the historical events.

Closely connected with his teleological conception of history was Hegel's proposition that, in each period of history, man's activities in all the various spheres of intellectual and social life were combined into an integrated "organic" whole and permeated by a common "substance" or "spirit" which he called "Volksgeist." Since the development of the English language was governed by patterns of thought which differed widely from the methods of intuitive and dialectic reasoning, no correct English translations can be given for terms formed in accordance with the latter methods. The terms *Volk* and *Geist* belong to that category. That spirit was said to guarantee the unity, uniqueness, and specificity of the "cultural order" of a nation at a given stage of its history, and the history of each nation was said to be predetermined by its "evolutionary potentialities." In view of the close coherence thus established between all lines of human activities, there was no place in the Hegelian philosophy for economics as a separate discipline.

Hegel supplemented his doctrine of the plurality of national spirits and their predetermined evolutionary development by superimposing upon them a "universal spirit" (*Weltgeist*). To that supreme spirit he ascribed the function of assuring the ultimate triumph of the German-Christian state. Hence, he provided the German economists not only with an arsenal of arguments against the utilitarian principles of the Ricardian doctrine but also with the claim to a natural superiority of their own methods of reasoning over those of any other peoples.

The majority of the German economists did not adopt the highly complex Hegelian methods of reasoning, but rather availed themselves of "intuitional" procedures for determining the fundamental concepts and propositions of their studies, and insisted upon deriving important elements of their analyses by way of abstraction from experience.

But intuitional procedures could be used more or less independently of any experience, thus allowing complete freedom of exuberant imagination. The writings of the "Romantic" authors were permeated with thinking of that type. On the other hand, it caused some serious students of social problems who belonged to that group to attach fundamental importance to the proposition advanced by Edmund Burke that "nature is wisdom without reflection." But whereas Burke—like other eighteenth-century social philosophers[6]—had placed main emphasis on the harmony-producing, beneficial effects of unintentional, cooperative human activities, some German adherents of Romanticism elaborated the elements of irrationality implied in Burke's proposition.[7] A broad interpretation of Burke's proposition permitted others to appeal to sentiments rather than to reason, and to resort to mystical conceptions of social relationships and to idealized pictures of a remote past, especially of medieval social organization. They portrayed the feudal society as an admirable embodiment of a unifying moral spirit, and complained of the disintegration of social life brought about by the philosophy of economic liberalism. Various Catholic authors were particularly attracted by the idea of the "corporative state," in which economic and social conduct was to be governed by the principles of Christian morality and production was to be carried on by guildlike producers' associations.

A characteristic representative of Romantic social philosophy was Adam Müller (1779–1829), who applied intuitive reasoning quite consistently to the analysis of economic phenomena and was inspired by a mystic longing for a social organization like that of the Middle Ages, which reflected a fully developed hierarchical order of ideas. He ascribed logical preexistence to the social community, and asserted its predominance in relation to its members; the individual had to find happiness by subordinating her or his interests to those of the collectivity. Müller's writings were completely ignored in the second half of the nineteenth century, but they were subsequently "rediscovered" by the Viennese economist Othmar Spann, who derived some elements of his "universalistic" social philosophy from Müller's writings.[8] The conceptual isolation of economics from the other social sciences was obviously incompatible with this social philosophy, which associated almost all economic concepts with spiritual values and moral forces inherited from the past. Thus, Müller substituted a vague "value in relation to society" for the concept of exchange value.

In his discussion of monetary problems Müller rejected the view that the institution of money owed its origin to exchange practices.[9] He proclaimed money as the expression of an "inner spiritual unity" of the members of a community, and attributed to money and credit the mission of removing the antagonism which he found to exist between the institution of private property and an organic society. He used that semidialectic argument to justify a system of inconvertible paper money as opposed to the international gold standard. Needless to say, Müller, like Fichte, requested economic self-sufficiency as an important means of strengthening national unity. His Romantic social philosophy never developed beyond its somewhat embryonic stage, but it was highly appreciated by some members of the historical school of economics, such as Roscher and Knies. Apart from Müller, two other authors have been considered chief representatives of the Romantic movement in the social sciences. Friedrich Gentz, an able publicist who was employed by the conservative Austrian chancellor Prince Metternich, and Carl Ludwig von Haller, the Swiss author of a voluminous work, *Restoration of the Political Science* (1816–34).

It is also worth noting that, along with the members of the Romantic movement, some defenders of the principles of cameralism (Arnold Heeren, Rehberg, and Brandes) were engaged in a desperate struggle against any quantitative analysis of economic phenomena.[10] Characteristic of their attitude was their rejection of statistical tables as instruments of demographic or economic investigations.

THE EMERGENCE OF HISTORISM

The teachings of the idealistic philosophers, as applied to the analysis of the course of social events, provided the background for the development of the methodological principles of the so-called historical school, which exercised a dominant influence on the thinking of a generation of German jurists and were endorsed by several generations of German economists. In accordance with these principles, each nation constituted an "organic whole" whose existence and development was determined by laws and objectives of its own. The subconscious operation of these laws was said to find its expression in the national social institutions. Edmund Burke's "theory of prescription" was cited to explain how institutions which had existed for long periods were adapted to the "peculiar circumstances, dispositions, moral and social habitudes of the people of the community."[11]

It was a small step from this logical foundation of "historism" to the proposition that the diversification of national spirits was the means chosen by nature for achieving full development of the human race.[12] Rivalries among nations, even wars, could be interpreted as elements of a natural process and instruments of progress. The student of political and social events was requested to conceive of "national" communities as "organisms" with objectives and evolutionary developments of their own. A sort of intuitive insight into the behavior of such organisms was considered necessary in order to enable the student to realize the "whole" as distinct from its parts, the mutual relations between the whole and its parts, and the role played by individual events within the framework of continuous processes. Since history means change, it was considered necessary to discover certain elements which remained constant in spite of the change.[13] The search for "stages" in the analysis of historical, social, and cultural developments had its roots in this methodological approach.

German jurists led by Friedrich K. von Savigny (1779–1861), Gustav F. Hugo (1769–1844), and Karl F. von Eichhorn (1781–1854) were the first scholars to apply the methods of historism to some fundamental problems of their science. Strongly opposed to the idea of establishing legal principles common to all nations, they stressed the uniqueness and individuality of the "national spirit" as the creator of specific national laws and institutions.[14] "The national spirit," said Savigny, "operates collectively in all individuals; hence the national law is not accidental to the minds of the individual, but of necessity one and the same law." As distinct from the "nation" conceived of as a part of supraindividual reality, the state was regarded as a juridical fiction, a moral personality. Since the national spirit was assumed to develop step by step and to pass through definite stages, all social institutions were held to be time conditioned, and their transfer from one nation to another was considered impossible. The advocates of juridical historism were thus radically opposed to the doctrine of the natural law and to all inferences drawn from that doctrine. Their historical interpretation of existing social and economic laws and customs provided strong support for all conservative movements in the field of social and political organization.

Similar ideas caused many contemporary German historians to emphasize the "organic" totality of the nation and the "objective" spirit to which it was held to owe its unique political and cultural development. Leopold von Ranke (1795–1886), an outstanding representative of historism, developed the "idiographic method" according to which every historical event was to be analyzed as to its particular features, especially its national aspects. The search for general laws or regularities underlying political or social relationships or developments was practically excluded by that method.

Around the middle of the century some leading economists undertook to apply the main principles of historism to the analysis of economic phenomena.[15] They rejected the use of the deductive method and the quantifying concepts and propositions of the Ricardian doctrine. They characterized Ricardian doctrine as the outcome of a "materialistic" and "chrematistic" social philosophy which they considered incompatible with the superior German moral and social principles. From the largest possible accumulation of historical material they expected to derive full understanding of extensive ranges of economic events as differentiated by national characteristics and historically determined conditions. They expected that comparative analysis of the results of such studies would enable them to discover certain general social or economic regularities, trends, or "laws."

Friedrich List has been hailed by some German authors as a precursor to the historical school, though, strictly speaking, he does not belong to it.[16] He criticized the teachings of Adam Smith as the outcome of a boundless cosmopolitanism, dead materialism, and individualism. A special object of his attacks was the use which the English economists made of the concept of exchange values in defense of the principles of free trade; that concept, he argued, reflected the point of view of the individual merchant.[17] List contrasted his conception of the "nation," with its peculiar origin and history, conceived of as an "independent whole" and endowed with a "right for an end within itself," with the emphasis Smith and his followers placed on the individual and his economic behavior. He was convinced that the efforts of individual producers, left to their own devices, were insufficient to bring about the well-being of a poor nation and to develop, unassisted by the government, the nation's "productive forces." Using the term "productive forces" in a very broad sense, List applied it not only to the potential material resources of a "nation" but also to the intellectual capacities and abilities of its members, as acquired through education, training, and cultural achievements and strengthened through moral and political institutions. The concept of "productive forces" has survived many criticisms. Almost a century after it had been used by List, it was recommended as "particularly well formulated" in a widely used German textbook on foreign trade policies.[18]

The concept of "productive forces" provided List with an effective instrument to defend the principles of protectionism. In an elaborate historical survey he distinguished five general stages in the development of a nation's productive forces, and insisted upon the need to adjust national economic policies carefully to the conditions prevailing in each stage. He especially availed himself of the "nascent industry argument" in developing the leading principles of a tariff policy adapted to the needs of countries which had not yet reached the ultimate stage of economic progress. According to List's theory of the five economic stages, agricultural production could generally be regarded as a fully developed branch of economic activity and did not need tariff protection. The ultimate stage was marked by the exchange of domestic manufactures for foreign agricultural products and raw materials. Free trade, he argued, was a commercial policy which suited only the interests of those countries which, like England, had fully developed their productive forces; in all others the development of these forces behind the shelter of protective duties was a primary task of economic policy, and its effect far outweighed the advantages which could be derived for domestic consumers from the importation of manufactures at relatively low exchange values.

The connection which List established between the developmental stages and the concept of productive forces had a certain methodological significance, since it pointed to the existence of potentialities inherent in the "national organism." The adherents of historism were convinced that the material needed to grasp the real nature of such organisms could be supplied only by the historical methods which took account of successions of changes. Gustav Schmoller said of List that, with the ingenious insight and the passion of a great statesman, he destroyed the theoretical basis of the old system, just as his countrymen Hegel and Schelling "pushed aside the old, individualistic natural law and replaced it with a more profound and nobler concept of the state." After the First World War, so great was the admiration of Germany's leading economists for List's nationalistic approach to economics that they created an exclusive association called "Friedrich List Gesellschaft."[19]

In an outline of his teachings, advanced at the beginning of the Forties, Wilhelm Roscher (1817–1894), professor of political sciences at the University of Leipzig, suggested that the ways and means of understanding and governing peoples could best be studied by starting from the anatomy and physiology of the social organism and by analyzing the economic and social institutions from the point of view of their effects upon the well-being of the nation.[20] With the aid of the "inductive" method, past and present economic conditions of the various countries should be made the object of careful comparisons, especially with regard to their growth and decay and similar "organic" developments. Roscher used the expressions *realistic, physiological,* and *historical* to denote researches of that type; he expected them to lead eventually to the establishment of "natural laws" of historical development and to provide "benchmarks" for the appraisal of economic policies. But Roscher failed to state clearly whether "insight" into the teleological aspects of evolutionary processes was needed to establish these laws, or whether the laws were of the empirical type and could be falsified in the light of subsequent experience.

In voluminous works Roscher accumulated the results of his indefatigable research into the history of economic institutions and events, and surveyed the writings of past and contemporary German economists.[21] Although hardly interested in the discussion of theoretical problems strictly speaking, Roscher defended the Ricardian methods against the attacks of his German colleagues, and recommended the use of these methods as a counterweight to the haziness of the approach adopted by adherents of the "historical-statistical" and the "practical-political" procedures.[22]

A few years after Roscher had adumbrated various methodological issues of the historical approach, Bruno Hildebrand undertook to define them with greater precision.[23] Less inclined to methodological compromises than Roscher, he strongly objected to the utilitarian use of the principle of self-interest as a sort of mechanical force operating in the economy, and to the conception of the economy as a network of exchanges. In his reasoning, hypothetical methods of economic analysis had to give way to descriptive presentations of the actual course of economic developments; ethical and cultural standards had to be scrutinized with a view to establishing appropriate measures of welfare policy.

Roscher had failed to indicate a clear principle for distinguishing successive stages or epochs in economic developments. Hildebrand derived that principle—as John Law and Pierre Proudhon had done before him—from the observable changes in monetary and credit institutions. Thus, he arrived at a relatively primitive schema which included three stages: the "natural," the monetary, and the credit economy. But the concept of credit, as understood by Hildebrand, covered only such functions of credit as were connected with the task of facilitating exchanges. No reference to evolutionary processes strictly speaking was implied in his methodology.

The third generally recognized protagonist of historicism, as applied to economics, was Karl Knies.[24] Like Hildebrand, he rejected the methods of hypothetical reasoning, the individualistic conception of society, and the quantitative approach to economic analysis. In addition, he objected to the search for laws underlying the development of economic phenomena and suggested that the study of such developments could, at best, serve to illustrate the general principle that each period had been ruled by a spirit of its own and had produced its specific social philosophy. Viewed from that angle, the teachings of the English utilitarian economists simply reflected the intellectual and moral conditions of their country and their time.

But in spite of his objections to the deductive method, Knies used it in his extensive studies on money and credit.[25] His conception of money was derived from the consideration that only a commodity with a value of its own could function as a standard of values, and he defended the gold standard as the only sound basis for an international monetary system.

THE PROGRAM OF THE HISTORICOETHICAL SCHOOL

The emphasis which the founders of the historical school of economics had placed on the blessings of "organic developments" met with considerable reaction on the part of the next generation of economic historians. Strong, aggressive, nationalist sentiments and aspirations were aroused among large sectors of the German population in 1866 by the victories of Prussia over Austria, and in 1871 by the victories of the combined German armies in the struggle with France over hegemony on the European continent. The subsequent foundation of the German Empire was hailed as the beginning of a new era in Western history, and students of the political sciences were challenged to justify with new theoretical arguments the German nation's mission in that historical setting. The prevailing "too idyllic" interpretation of historical processes was to be replaced by another which emphasized will and actions motivated by momentous decisions.[26] Political and legal conceptions, derived from the German history of a remote past and adjusted to the requirements of the new era, provided the background for the development of the political and social sciences along nationalistic lines. In his extensive studies, Otto von Gierke developed a specific political theory which strongly influenced the thinking of German politicians and students of the social sciences. This theory connected the development of German social life with the existence of free associations which for generations had united certain groups of the population but had been strictly subordinated to the state as the highest community and supreme authority.[27]

But the unity and strength of the nation were increasingly threatened by the growing labor movement and the close relations established by that movement with similar organizations in other countries. The "First International" was founded in 1864, the German Sozialdemokratische Arbeiterpartei, headed by August Bebel (1840–1913) and Wilhelm Liebknecht (1826–1900), in 1869. Greatly alarmed by that situation, a group of German economists decided to unite their efforts in the struggle for the adoption of economic principles which took account of the needs of the large masses of the working population. Such a program, formulated by Gustav Schmoller, was adopted in 1873 at the Eisenach meeting of the newly founded Verein für Sozialpolitik. That association took the place of an "economic congress" which had been a rallying point of adherents of the free-trade principle.

The name "historicoethical" school, chosen by the proponents of the program to denote their movement, indicated their intention to combine the historical approach to the study of economic phenomena with the pursuit of economic and social politics based on definite moral principles. Any cosmopolitic tendencies were incompatible with these principles—the economic attitude of "liberal" industrialists, merchants, and bankers no less than the revolutionary activities of the international working class movement. The greatest nations, epochs, or men, said Schmoller, are not those who merely increase production, but those who succeed in propagating moral ideas. They are those who in the economic field succeed in securing juster institutions. Occasionally Schmoller compared the economy with a clock which is kept in motion by egoism and quantity relationships but is to be regulated by ethics and law.[28]

Gustav Schmoller, who very soon was generally recognized as the leader of the historicoethical school, formulated not only the economicopolitical but also the scientific program of his generation of German economists. Outstanding members of the school were Adolf Held, G. Schönberg, Erwin Nasse, and H. von Scheel. Schmoller emphasized above all the need for a "realistic" approach to economic problems, as distinct from the predominantly idealistic attitude of the preceding generation of German scholars. A hunger for facts had arisen, said Schmoller in an address delivered in 1897; everywhere there was an urgent need for empirical observation and investigation. Realism raised its claim against the evils of a dying idealism.[29] Having repudiated the use of abstract concepts as tools of economic analysis, having rejected the individualism, the materialism, and the "narrow field of the classical economists," Schmoller proclaimed the "study of economic life in the concrete" as the guiding principle of the school. He emphasized the organic conception of society and insisted upon the close interdependence of all material, spiritual, and moral aspects of social life. Schmoller defined the "national economy" as a "totality," a "real entity" which in spite of perpetual changes in its constituent parts has remained the same in its specific characteristics over years and centuries, and, as far as it has shown changes, has appeared as a "developing organism." In the light of hypothetical reasoning that definition is, of course, meaningless.[30] With the leading German historians of his time, Schmoller shared the belief that the main task of history consisted in discovering the "truth," and that careful analysis of descriptive material was the method to be adopted with this end in view. A leading German historian, Leopold von Ranke, expressed this idea by requesting historical research to "find out how things had actually happened" (*Wie es eigentlich gewesen ist*). Studies in the field of economics had to be supplemented by a variety of current statistical investigations, which were expected to reveal some vaguely defined evolutionary processes. Ultimately, however, theories of all kinds were designed to lend support to the pursuance of active economic policies. The statistical offices of the Reich, the German states, and many municipalities had been organized under the influence of cameralistic ideas. The extensive work they performed was intended to serve administrative purposes. The will, said Schmoller, remains always the regent and dominates the intellect.[31]

Although Schmoller was deeply impressed by the Hegelian conception of the state as a superior entity with supraindividual objectives of its own, he did not accept the Hegelian dialectic construction of historical developments. Rather, he followed the suggestion of Herbert Spencer (1820–1903) that the ethics of the various societies showed a linear progress from more homogeneous to more heterogeneous forms.[32] Belief in the hereditary transmission of acquired faculties was an article of faith for Schmoller. From the findings of the English biologist Sir Francis Galton (1822–1911),[33] he derived the conviction that the physicopsychical differentiation of ethnically homogeneous nations was due to the development of occupational characteristics through the influence of specific activities exercised over centuries by certain groups of the population. The interpretation of the class struggle as a symptom of social progress was perfectly compatible with his sociological views, but in his theory of social differentiation he took account of a variety of factors and refused to ascribe to property relationships a significant influence on the breaking up of the original homogeneity of classless societies. In his teachings Schmoller emphasized the proposition that in the course of history the natural play of revolutionary forces was, time and again, kept in bounds through social institutions which were continuously improved and rendered more ethical.[34]

"Social psychology" was paramount among the auxiliary sciences which Schmoller relied upon to facilitate the understanding of economic and social processes. From intensified researchers into the behavior of nations and social classes he expected the establishment of psychological historical laws as a prerequisite to economic analysis. Comprehensive studies designed to lead to the development of a science of "folk" psychology (*Völkerpsychologie*) were undertaken by German philosophers. Wilhelm Wundt was probably the most outstanding representative of that school.

Arthur Spiethoff, one of Schmoller's most faithful disciples, characterized his master's method as a "visualizing" (*anschauliche*) procedure which did not separate the presentation of facts from their explanation, but rather attempted to produce "mental pictures of reality" supported by facts and data and eventually supplemented by references to historical events and criticisms of previous doctrines.[35] A tragical conflict, said another German economist, was bound to result from Schmoller's continuous efforts to reconcile the quest for concepts of higher abstraction with the postulate that all national, political, economic, and cultural collectivities in their uniqueness and individuality could be grasped through immediate intuition.[36]

That conflict also pressed its stamp on Schmoller's attempt to provide a sociological background for his economic analysis. In his voluminous textbook of political economy,[37] he accumulated a vast array of mostly descriptive material dealing with economic, sociological, and demographic phenomena and developments. In his discussion of theoretical problems he started from a psychological version of the utility theory, which he preferred to the theory of objective value because of the emphasis which it placed on human will and activity.[38] But his treatment of the value problem was rudimentary and hardly connected with his discussion of pricing processes, which he approached primarily from an ethicopolitical angle in his attempt to achieve "appropriate approximation to reality in the full stream of complex historical processes."[39] Even some of his most faithful disciples admitted that procedures of that kind were not fit to cope with theoretical problems.[40]

When consistently applied to sociological analysis, organismic reasoning led to various attempts to elaborate analogies between biological entities and social collectivities.[41] Ferdinand Tönnies's distinction between two types of social collectivities, the community (*Gemeinschaft*) and the society (*Gesellschaft*), was extensively discussed.[42] He characterized the community as the form of life which was congenial to the German mind, and defined it as a sort of "organic" unity, the members of which were bound together by the strong belief in the solidarity of their interests, and in common destiny.[43] Tönnies contrasted this ideal picture of social organization with "society," a loose aggregate of individuals lacking a common system of ends and values and using contracts as the prevailing juridical form of organizing interpersonal relationships. The aversion of the adherents of organismic reasoning to social institutions which were permeated by hypothetical thinking was clearly reflected in Tönnies's sociological dichotomy.

Some authors who elaborated organismic constructions of social collectivities availed themselves of evolutionary theories in order to account for rivalries between nations. Fights over territories could thus be presented as "natural processes" resulting from the need of young, growing nations to expand at the expense of aging and decaying peoples. Slogans of that kind played a remarkable role in the German nationalistic literature, Schmoller interpreted the power policy of the Prussian kings as the realization of an evolutionary moral process, and regarded the victory of a strong nation over its competitors as tantamount to the victory of a superior moral principle. Many members of the historical school, including Knies and Schindler, regarded wars as inevitable cultural factors, deeply rooted in human nature.

Similar views led to the conception of the "world economy" as a collectivity of mutually antagonistic economics, each of which was striving to develop its "productive forces," to exploit foreign markets to its greatest possible advantage, and to dislodge its rivals from privileged positions in such markets. The concept of the "world economy" had an outright political connotation;[44] protective duties were not simply regarded as means of assisting manufacturers, farmers, or traders in their endeavor to secure for their commodities safe outlets in domestic markets. Rather, protective duties were included among the most effective instruments of national power policies. The ultimate objective of German foreign trade policy was to establish the most effective self-sufficiency of the Reich as a warlike measure. This view found a characteristic and succinct formulation in Chancellor Bismarck's often-quoted dictum about the "compact between iron and rye"— the agreement of mutual protection concluded between the agrarian Junkers of Prussia and the industrial magnates of the Rheno-Westphalian basin. The political considerations which motivated the teachings of many German economists were well expressed in a collection of essays by Gustav Schmoller, M. Sering, and A. Wagner designed to support official plans for the creation of a powerful navy. In this connection the reader's attention may be drawn to the significant difference between protective duties as operated within a framework of hypothetical reasoning and similar duties conceived as instruments of organismic power policies.[45]

The measures of social reform which were advocated by the economists of the historicoethical school were designed to contribute to the lasting improvement of the working and living conditions of the laboring classes and to remove, as far as possible, the causes of social conflicts. Outright aversion to the organization of the capitalist economy and the rational principles underlying its operation played a conspicuous role in motivating the proposals of social reform which were advanced by various members of the academic profession, nicknamed "Socialists of the Chair." Schmoller is frequently described as one of the "Socialists of the Chair," but other prominent members of this group, such as Adolf Wagner, Wilhelm Lexis, G. Cohn, and Lujo Brentano, did not share the methodological view of the historical school. In addition, religious convictions frequently provided strong incentives for movements in favor of radical social reforms. Socialist doctrines and proposals were studied with great care and extensively discussed. But the incompatibility of centralized social production with free choice of occupation and consumers' sovereignty was generally ignored, or at least minimized.[46]

METHODOLOGICAL ISSUES

About a decade after the formal establishment of the historicoethical school of economics, the methodological problems involved in the application of organismic reasoning to economic analysis were brought out in sharp relief in the famous "struggle over methods" (*Methodenstreit*), which started with the publication by Carl Menger (1840–1921) of an investigation into the methods of the social sciences.[47] The clash of divergent patterns of reasoning had played a considerable role in the history of economics, but never before had a divergence of that type been so clearly analyzed as in his essay, which was designed to warn of the dangers likely to result for the advancement of economic theory from the methods endorsed by Schmoller and his followers.

Menger, who had developed the leading ideas of marginal utility analysis, showed that, conceived as an "exact science," economics had the task of establishing regularities in sequence and coexistence, and that this task had to be fulfilled by reducing social phenomena to their simplest quantitative elements and by measuring them in terms of appropriate standards. In accordance with these methodological principles, it was impossible to arrive at an adequate understanding of reality and to achieve control over economic conditions unless it was first possible to form general abstract pictures of typical relationships among economic magnitudes. The methods which enabled the student to deal with these problems were those which were applied by the natural sciences and had been adjusted by Ricardo to the requirements of economic analysis. They implied the use of highly abstract concepts, which had no counterpart in reality and which could be combined with each other by appropriate logical operations.

According to Menger, social sciences enjoyed a specific advantage in that their assumptions, instead of referring to unempirical forces, could be derived from the observation of empirical factors, of human beings and their activities.[48] On the other hand, Menger recognized the particular importance for the social sciences of institutions which were not produced by purposive human activities (acts of legislation, agreements, and the like) but by the spontaneous operation of a variety of social factors.

Like his Ricardian predecessors, Menger distinguished hypothetical laws, the products of logical operations which cannot be verified in the light of practical experience, from empirical laws, derived mainly through statistical procedures. The concepts used to define such regularities in the coexistence or succession of social phenomena were obviously of lower abstraction, and marked by many—partly noneconomic—characteristics. Against these well-organized instruments of theoretical analysis Menger contrasted the ill-defined descriptive procedures used by the partisans of historicism in their attempts to establish regularities through the accumulation of specific facts and events. The question of the degree to which the inferences drawn from such laws can be confronted with the results of observation later became the object of various discussions.

In his defense of the principles of historism, Schmoller did not add any substantial new arguments to his critical discussions of Ricardian economics.[49] According to these criticisms Menger shared with Ricardo the fundamental error of regarding certain conspicuous features of a passing, historically determined order as the "essence" of the economy; moreover, he made the error of separating quite arbitrarily some characteristics of the economy alleged to be essential from others considered nonessential, although no reliable standards or guiding principles existed for drawing such a distinction in a world of "indivisible totality." To the "atomistic" approach adopted by Menger, Schmoller raised the objection that it placed main emphasis on the economic phenomena connected with money, values, and prices and neglected any others which were beyond that limited sector, especially the "organic" relationships between all economic and social phenomena and the effects on them of continuous economic processes.

The more Schmoller endeavored to clarify his methodological position, the more it became apparent that he failed to realize the fundamental logical issues involved in the controversy.[50] He tried to reduce these issues to a conflict between the inductive and the deductive methods, and to settle this conflict eventually by a compromise which implied that both methods were as indispensable for economic research as the right and left legs were for walking.[51] That statement was quoted time and again by Schmoller's disciples, but it provided no pertinent answer to the problems raised by Menger. In Italy a similar methodological discussion took place at the beginning of the twentieth century between Luigi Cossa, who advocated the need for deductive reasoning, and Achille Loria, who rejected the generalizations of the Ricardian school. Various other authors participated in these methodological discussions, which, however, did not yield new noticeable results.[52]

The opposition between deductive and inductive methods was obviously of a polar type, since the premises which provided the basis for deductive analysis were, as a rule, somehow connected with the results of observation and experience. On the other hand, even purely empirical laws or regularities could hardly be established without some preliminary deductive considerations which provided signposts in the search for uniformities. Inductive methods, as taught by Bacon, had been consistently applied by the Ricardians, and Schmoller could hardly justify the contention that these methods owed their development to the historical school.

But the methodological belief cherished by Schmoller and his followers, that general laws underlying the course of actual events could be found with the aid of concepts of low abstraction loaded with organismic and normative characteristics and frequently shaped by intuitive methods,[53] was incompatible with the methods adopted by the Ricardians and their followers. Moreover, the adherents of historism were obviously unable to avail themselves of the methods of deductive reasoning strictly speaking, since they rejected the principles of hypothetical reasoning and the use of highly abstract concepts. The fundamental logical antagonism which formed the center of the dispute was outlined with remarkable understanding in an exchange of letters between the philosopher Wilhelm Dilthey and Count Paul Yorck von Wartenburg. The latter suggested that Schmoller and his followers were intellectually akin to Gierke, fighting against the prevailing "nominalism" but in need of a philosopher who would supply a "firm intellectual background to their sentiments" (1888). In the meantime, he added, they went back to the "historical realism" of German juridical and economic life.[54] Considerable additional confusion stemmed from Schmoller's conviction that, consequent upon the "conflict of opposites" as a characteristic feature of historical developmental processes, the progress of science was marked by the alternation of periods in which empiricism prevailed and periods in which "rationalism" had the upper hand. He invested the German historical school with the mission of returning to "empirical reality," and thus entering the inheritance of cameralism, in open opposition to the "rationalism" of the Ricardians.[55] From a methodological point of view it is significant that in their search for "empirical understanding of reality," Schmoller and his adherents resorted to outright metaphysical constructions of social relationships, and attached transcendental reality to social collectivities such as the nation, the state, the national economy, and the like.[56]

There was no logical bridge which would have led from such intuitionally conceived collectivities to the "hypothetical" individual which was the active factor in Ricardian and post-Ricardian economics. Some students of historical persuasion believed that the use of the hypothetical individual in abstract economics could not be upheld in the face of the argument that continuous changes were taking place in the organization of social wholes and in the behavior of members of such wholes. Others elaborated the proposition that the teachings of the English economists were the outcome of a social philosophy which was engendered by specific historical conditions. The acceptance of the mechanistic Ricardian doctrine on the part of the educated classes of England was characterized as a glorification of self-interest and a vindication of Manchesterian economic policies.[57]

Wilhelm Hasbach analyzed the philosophical background of Physiocratic and Smithian economics, and endeavored to show that these teachings bore the imprints of the doctrines of natural law and natural ethics.[58] Lujo Brentano, an economist of liberal persuasion, considered it a fundamental methodological error that any differences due to race, age, and religion were disregarded by the Ricardian economists, that they ignored the influence exercised on human activities by occupation, class, nationality, and culture, and that they took account of only two motives of human action—striving for maximum gain and sexual instinct.[59] J. S. Mill's analysis of the hypothetical nature of the Ricardian laws was, according to Brentano, a device designed to cloak their dissonance with reality.

The sociopolitical aspects of Ricardo's *Principles* were analyzed in a comprehensive study by Karl Diehl.[60] Although he did not belong to the historical school, and protested against various misleading interpretations of the Ricardian teachings, Diehl rejected the search for general laws of the hypothetical type. Practically general agreement was reached on the view that the doctrines of the English economists were not applicable outside the country of their origin. The validity of the methods used by Ricardo and his followers continued to be the object of skeptical observations; practically all members of the historical school endorsed the belief that all social and economic doctrines were strictly determined by specific cultural and social conditions.[61]

The intuitive method was applied by many adherents of historism to the elaboration of sequences of "stages" in the development of "national economics." Many authors claimed for their schemes some sort of general validity, but they failed, as a rule, to support them by consistent theoretical considerations. The evolutionary processes said to produce the succession of stages were never clearly defined.

Friedrich List's and Bruno Hildebrand's categorizations of phases in the development of national economics were obviously very rudimentary and inadequate. G. Schönberg[62] suggested a differentiation according to the degree of separation between the production of goods and their final distribution. Elaborating a similar idea, Karl Bücher (1847–1930) distinguished domestic, self-sufficient economies from the urban economies of the Middle Ages and modern national economies as the last stage.[63] This apparently evolutionary scheme was widely appreciated, but serious doubts were cast on its usefulness when Bücher's conceptions of precapitalistic economic relationships were shown to be inconsistent with the results of subsequent research.[64] The widely discussed "theory of stages" advanced by Gustav Schmoller reflected exclusively a development which had occurred in some German territories, and the scheme proposed by Bernhard Harms (1876–1939) was logically untenable.[65] Although the problem of stages was more or less extensively treated in all German economic textbooks, no clarity was achieved as to the nature of the process that was to be analyzed in terms of stages.[66] The pictures which were given of the various stages were, as a rule, static descriptions of certain segments of extended processes, and "once the leap to the last or highest scale had been achieved, the imagination could soar no higher."[67] Frequently, any economic developments which had occurred outside Europe were tacitly ignored, and the same was true of significant "regressive movements" which had taken place in the course of economic development.[68] Ill-defined categories, such as "natural economy" and "barter economy," were applied indiscriminately to economic conditions with widely divergent characteristics.[69] Eventually, after about a century of discussion, it was still an open question whether the distinguishing of stages in economic development was intended to serve purposes of theoretical analysis or was only a device for facilitating the description of changes in economic institutions.[70]

The general analyses of economic development were supplemented by a vast literature dealing with specific aspects of various phases of history, of characteristic economic institutions, industries, and trade, and of changes in the structure of the various economics. Particularly remarkable were the contributions made to the economic history of England by Lujo Brentano (1844–1931), G. Schanz, Adolf Held (1844–1880), and Gerhard von Schulze-Gävernitz. Varying emphases were placed on the effects of population movements, the distribution of landed property, and the organization of agricultural production. The thoroughgoing discussion of the Malthusian theory of population which took place in Germany in the decade prior to the First World War was primarily motivated by nationalistic considerations. Outstanding studies concerning the development of the organization of agricultural production were made by Georg Hanssen, August Meitzen (1822–1910), and Georg Friedrich Knapp. The analysis made by Knapp (1887 and 1897) of the abolition of the villainage in German territories provided the pattern for subsequent similar research by C. Grünberg and others. The working and living conditions of labor, the development and functions of employers' and workers' organizations, and the implications of measures of social policies were all extensively discussed.

The history of institutions and of legal and administrative measures occupied a conspicuous place in studies of this kind and was sometimes designed to glorify achievements of the past or to lend support to some political or social aspiration. Thus, the mercantilist period received particular attention as a time in which economic expansion was promoted by the active policies of authoritative governments. Schmoller's extensive contribution to the industrial and commercial history of Prussia were models of such investigations.

Quite remarkable efforts were also spent on the analysis of past economic doctrines and economic and social philosophies. The ideas and theorems of almost all fairly prominent economists of the past were made the object of careful studies. But the theoretical aspects of the various doctrines frequently received rather superficial treatment, as compared with the sociological and political features. Although many researches of this type were highly useful for a deepening of sociological and historical knowledge, they could not compensate for the neglect of theoretical economic analysis strictly speaking. Toward the end of the nineteenth century, Eugen von Böhm-Bawerk warned in a prophetic vein that, owing to the methodological shortcomings of the German economists of historical persuasion, several decades might be lost for the progress of their science.[71]

In England the historical approach—divested of its outright organismic features—was adopted by economists such as Cliffe Leslie, Thorold Rogers, and John Kells Ingram. In France a version of the historical method was developed by P. G. Frédéric Le Play (1806–1882) and his school. They started with the proposition that the general characteristics of the physical environment are determinant factors in influencing economic organization and the form of family life of a people. The progress which they achieved in the study of family budgets and of the socioeconomic aspects of family life was quite remarkable.[72] Important studies dealing with the history of the French working classes were prepared by Pierre Emile Levasseur (1828–1911), and Henri Sée (1864–1936) made noteworthy contributions to the history of capitalism.[73] Refined methods of descriptive analysis were applied to economic history by outstanding scholars such as Charles Seignobos (1854–1942) and Henri Hauser (1866–?1946).[74] The creation by various universities of special chairs for the teaching of the history of economic doctrines contributed greatly to the development of this line of research. The comprehensive survey of the history of economic doctrines published by Charles Gide (1847–1932) and Charles Rist (1873–1955) occupied for a considerable period the first rank among studies of that kind.[75] In Belgium, Emile de Laveleye (1822–1892) supplied outstanding contributions to the history of economic institutions.[76] But neither the French nor the Belgian adherents of the historical method expected the latter completely to supplant the deductive approach to economic analyses.

Outside Germany, such a view was defended only in Italy, by Achille Loria

(1857–1943), who endorsed the principles of the materialistic interpretation of history and undertook to demonstrate that a specific value doctrine corresponded to each period, adjusted to the economic conditions out of which it was said to have developed.[77] Similarly, Loria insisted on the strictly historical nature of all social and historical laws. Combining a version of the Ricardian value theory with the Marxian conception of income not earned by labor, he regarded agricultural rent as a monopoly profit and centered his idea of social reform on the availability of free land.[78]

Chapter 15
Versions of the
Organismic Approach

CONFLICTING TRENDS

ABOUT THE END of the nineteenth century, the deficiencies in the methodological foundations of the historical approach to economics led to the search for some philosophical approach which could be expected to establish a link between the study of economic problems and the study of other social phenomena in their historical settings. Two Neokantian schools provided teachings of that type: the so-called Baden and Marburg versions of Neokantianism.[1]

The philosophers of the University of Marburg followed Hermann Cohen (1842–1918) in developing the Kantian principle that cognition of the ''thing in itself'' is beyond the faculty of the human mind. They concentrated their attention on the logical conditions of scientific experience, and insisted that true knowledge and generally valid laws can be arrived at only with the aid of mathematical methods which can claim self-evidence in accordance with the rules of human reasoning. Cohen's most important followers were Paul Natrop and Ernst Cassirer.

Such ideas provided the background for the teachings of the jurist Rudolf Stammler (1856–1938), who made changes in the uniformity of social experience and of norms and precepts responsible for the evolution of social processes.[2] Rejecting the possibility of establishing generally valid laws of economic or social relationships, he defined normative law as the form and economy of the material substance of society.

Fritz Berolzheimer expanded this approach into a comprehensive analysis of the relationships between economic institutions and their juridical foundations.[3] In due course a group of German economists, headed by Karl Diehl, followed suit, and endorsed the proposition that all economic phenomena were primarily determined by specific forms of social relationships and legal institutions, varying with different epochs and different nations.[4] The nature and relevance of all economic categories were held to be dependent especially on the legal regulation of proprietary rights. One version of these attempts to analyze economic phenomena in the light of normative concepts was the so-called

"social-ethic" or "social-organic" approach to economics, advocated by Rudolf
Stolzmann.[5]

The development of the teachings of the Marburg School had led to the establishment
of a close connection between economics and jurisprudence; the influence of the Baden
School of Neokantianism, however, led to primary emphasis to be placed on the historical
aspects of economic and social phenomena. The founder of the Baden School, Wilhelm
Dilthey (1833–1911), regarded history as a means of arriving at an understanding of life.[6]
Starting from the view that man does not have a nature but only a history, Dilthey drew a
sharp distinction between the "natural sciences" on the one hand and the sciences of the
"mind and culture" on the other. (That view was developed in opposition to the Aristotelian distinction between "nature" and "convention" as two different sources of social
institutions.) He rejected as futile any search for generally valid social laws, and taught
that any meaning which could be attached to social relationships and the course of social
events could originate only in the activity of the knowing observer. Only in the natural
sciences, he argued, could knowledge be gained by way of deductive reasoning in terms
of causal categories (*begreifen*); in the sciences of "culture," however, insight into
meaningful relationships (*verstehen*) should be arrived at by logical processes through
which the social phenomena are conceived of as products of the activity of the human
mind. Hence, Dilthey proposed to grasp with intuitive methods the essential characteristics of the ideas which had dominated the minds of articulate groups. He undertook to
determine the "meaningful connections" between thoughts and attitudes which in his
view were more or less hidden behind human action in history.

Two other German philosophers, W. Windelband (1848–1915) and Heinrich Rickert
(1863–1936), combined these ideas with Immanuel Kant's antithesis of "applied" versus
"pure" reason. They assigned the "nomothetic" sciences to the realm of pure reason,
and ascribed to them the use of methods suitable for establishing general laws and
regularities of the causal type. To the "idiographic" sciences, however, which they
connected with the sphere of applied reason, they attributed the task of treating individual
phenomena in their uniqueness and their historical setting, with due regard to their
complexities.[7] Rickert restricted the application of the nomothetic sciences to nature,
which he defined as the aggregate of all things the existence and growth of which is left to
spontaneous forces. According to Rickert, nature is characterized by heterogeneity of its
elements and unending continuity. In order to adjust irrational heterogeneous continuity to
scientific procedures, it is to be rendered homogeneous and dissected into discrete parts.
The object of scientific analysis is thus determined by the form of dealing with the
continuity. With "nature" he contrasted "culture," the aggregate of things produced by
people in accordance with their values and objectives.[8] The use of concepts of high
abstraction was to be limited to the nomothetic sciences, as distinct from the concepts
considered fit to characterize the specific and unique aspects of historical phenomena.
Thus, Rickert defined "reality" as history when contemplated under its particular and
unique aspects.[9] He reserved the task of specifying "cultural values" for the philosophes,
whose work would enable historians and other students of the social sciences to distinguish essential characteristics of social phenomena from purely accidental ones and to
make the necessary selections from the inexhaustible material of history. The historian
Ernst Troeltsch (1865–1923) adopted a procedure of this type in his attempt to grasp by a
process of intuition the "real essence" of historical epochs.

When ideas of this kind were applied to the study of economic developments, it appeared appropriate to substitute for a sequence of "stages" a sequence of "objective" spirits, which were held to give direction and unity to the activities of the individual members of intuitively constructed social groups. For each such group a specific unique "spirit" was believed to provide the framework of cultural "totality," which could be clearly distinguished from other totalities of the same type. But the objective spirits were as isolated from each other as had been the "stages" established by the historicoethical school; no attempts were made to show the forces which could be assumed to secure a link between one spirit and its successor.[10] The "spirits" were frequently conceived of as timeless categories reflecting pictures of "ideal reality" or "complexes of meaning" (*Sinnzusammenhänge*), characterized by normative, symbolic, or esthetic features. The German term *Volksgeist* has a specific, intuitional connotation which is foreign to the corresponding English term *national spirit*. Werner Sombart occupied a conspicuous place among the German students of economic developments who adopted this kind of methodological approach. With consummate skill he used intuitive procedures in his extensive studies on the origin and the changing aspects of the capitalist economy.[11] In these studies the development of "capitalism" was conceived of as an evolutionary process advancing in three stages: an early stage, a period of full development, and a declining stage. The "spirit of capitalism" was shown to experience characteristic modifications in the course of these processes.

During his formative period Sombart was strongly influenced by the deterministic aspects of the Marxian doctrine. He was so fully convinced of the preponderance of economic forces in molding the course of historical events that he minimized the importance of political revolutions for the development of the capitalist society. He ascribed the transformation of the feudal organization into the capitalist order to historical accidents, such as the emergence of new techniques, the discovery of great gold deposits and large natural resources, and, last but not least, the appearance of businessmen of a new type. It is interesting to note that Sombart regarded "rationalism" as a feature common to capitalism and Judaism. He ascribed to the Jews the function of having given its peculiar features to the capitalistic organization and of having "endowed economic life with its modern spirit."[12]

Subsequently, however, Sombart adopted an "idealistic" interpretation of history and developed the idea that a unifying principle, derived from the fundamental aspects of human motivation, should be adopted to explain each phase of a historical process. Hence, he suggested the establishment of types of "economic configurations" to be conceived of as "meaningful units." Each unit was to be characterized by a specific combination of the elements which he considered fundamental to all economic organizations, namely, spirit, form (or order), and technique. The concept of "type" had been introduced by Aristotle in order to define, by a process of generalized abstraction, the permanent characteristics common to a group of phenomena. It was a moot question, repeatedly discussed by German economists of intuitive persuasion, to what degree "types" could be considered representative of reality.[13]

Using a method of variation, Sombart distinguished twelve types of economic configuration. His intuitive approach to social analysis was reflected in his excessive use of tripartite arrangements in establishing his categories.[14] Thus, he based his analysis on three pairs of polar opposites: production for want satisfaction, as contrasted with production for profit; the administered economy, as opposed to the competitive economy; and techniques of the empirical-traditionalistic kind, as distinct from rational-progressive methods.[15] To each historically defined period Sombart assigned a specific "objective" spirit, operating as a supraindividual agent, occasionally qualified as a sort of "social mind" said to be shaped by acquired experience and knowledge, and characterized by a specific approach to social life. But he failed to indicate how the "spirits" came into existence, how their control over the minds and activities of the individuals was being exercised, or how they were linked together in the chain of their successive appearances.

Sombart's ability to combine apparently disparate phenomena into vivid coherent pictures, and the zeal which he showed in perusing and utilizing a vast, only superficially known historical material, excited the admiration of many adherents of intuitive methods. But critical discussions turned on the problematic procedures which he used in interpreting historical documents, on his arbitrary evaluation of institutions and ideas of the past, on the usefulness of his categories, and on his more or less speculative treatment of various economic problems, such as the origin of capital accumulation, the causes of economic crises, and the like.[16]

Max Weber, one of the outstanding sociologists of his time, was far superior to Sombart in his approach to methodological problems. Weber definitely adopted Rickert's epistemology when he set himself the task of establishing a social science based on the method of "understanding" the value judgments which had been relevant for the establishment of social relationships (*verstehende Soziologie*).[17] In accordance with this sociological approach, the empirical material of the social sciences was to be organized in terms of "relevance to value" (*Wertbeziehung*); every social order had to be characterized by its specific value attitudes, derived from autonomous ideas concerning the meaning of the universe and the destiny of man. In view of the relatively limited number of known value systems which had prevailed in the past, Weber expected to arrive at a satisfactory understanding of them, which would enable him to establish a broad coherent scheme for a scientific classification of value attitudes and cultural relationships. Weber admitted that it was desirable to analyze important general economic phenomena, such as exchanges, but he requested that account be taken in these analyses of the processes through which the exchanges had gained importance, of the cultural aspects of the exchanges, and the like. In his view, general causal economic laws were less useful, the higher their degree of abstraction. In this respect the philosophy of "understanding" was almost diametrically opposed to behaviorism.

In his methodological considerations, Weber explicitly rejected "intuition" as a procedure of grasping concepts of integrated social wholes, but he indirectly introduced intuition as a methodological device in elaborating his concept of "ideal type," which he regarded as an outstanding instrument of sociological analysis. As defined by Weber, ideal types are concepts that are formed by logical processes in which the "essential characteristics," abstracted from a group of phenomena, are combined, and exaggerated importance is attached to specific aspects of these phenomena. They are designed to provide standards for ascertaining the degree to which individual historical phenomena or events correspond to "objective potentialities." As distinct from purely abstract notions, ideal types are qualified as "limiting concepts" the cognitive value of which depends upon their usefulness as means of understanding specific cultural relationships and their importance. The students of the social sciences were thus requested to establish "conceptions and judgments" which, although not providing outright pictures of empirical reality, enable the observer to organize reality in his mind in accordance with valid methods.

Consider Weber's "ideal type" of a medieval town. This was designed to provide a

standard for determining the degree to which a specific town of the twelfth or thirteenth
century showed those features which the observer regarded as relevant for the medieval
value system. The definition of the ideal type of a capitalistic enterprise served to determine the degree to which a specific concern or institution reflected the "spirit of capitalism" and its value system, to what stage in the "development of capitalism" such a
concern was to be assigned, and the like. The intuitional element implied in the act of
selecting as particularly relevant certain characteristics of abstract concepts is quite obvious. A certain confusion has been created by the fact that Weber also applied the term
ideal types to concepts denoting specific individual social collectivities, such as Christen-
dom, modern capitalism, and so on. But neither Weber nor his followers succeeded in
developing a systematic classification of "ideal types of social relationships."[18]

In his critical discussion of the principles of Ricardian economics, Weber suggested
that the concepts of commodity markets which operated under free competition in accordance with the principles of "strictly rational" economic behavior were, in fact, "ideal
types," utopian synthetic conceptions formed by attaching exaggerated importance to
certain elements derived from reality. Thus, a limiting concept of economy had been set
up, a concept which could be used as a pattern for determining the degree to which the
significant aspects of the abstract schemes were reflected by reality. In pursuance of that
reasoning, Weber qualified the laws of valuation advanced by the marginal utility schools
as rules of "correct rationality" implying precepts of economic behavior. That interpretation of the methods adopted by Ricardian and post-Ricardian economists was characteristic of his persistent refusal to permit the application of hypothetical reasoning to the
analysis of social relationships. Analysis of such relationships in quantitative terms was,
of course, incompatible with the emphasis placed by the Neokantian philosophers on the
qualitative aspects of social life.[19]

In his sociological analysis of the origin of capitalism, Weber referred to capitalism's
"objective spirit," which exercised a coercive power over the members of the capitalist
society, and he emphasized "rationalized acquisitiveness" as a primary element of the
system of values and value attitudes of that society. As did many members of the
historical school, Weber showed an outstanding aversion to the capitalist order and its
value system. Particularly noticeable was the role which he ascribed to the capitalist
bureaucracy "as a well disciplined, impersonal instrument" of profit-seeking objectives.

The importance which Weber attached to the ethics of the "ascetic" branches of
Protestantism in molding the value attitudes of the capitalist society has already been
mentioned. In his elaborate analyses of religious ethics, Weber attempted to demonstrate
that in the Far East the development of capitalist societies met with insurmountable
obstacles because of the imcompatibility of the moral principles of capitalism with those
of the prevailing oriental religious creeds. It appears, however, that preoccupied as Weber
was with the social implications of moral attitudes, he overlooked the deep differences in
the methods of reasoning which have separated the peoples of the Far East from the
Western world. The operation of the enterprises of the competitive exchange economy is
based on the use of hypothetical methods of reasoning which are alien to the thinking
processes practiced in the Far East.

THE STRUGGLE FOR A "VALUE-FREE" SCIENCE

The deep conviction of having found appropriate methods of analyzing economic and
social processes caused Max Weber to launch a vivid attack on the increasing confusion

which had resulted from the application to economic investigations of concepts and judgments derived from religious creeds, ethics, esthetics, and even metaphysics. That situation had been repeatedly criticized by various economists of liberal persuasion who had in vain protested, especially against the view of some "Socialists of the chair," that scientific procedures were available for determining the true objectives of economic and social actions, and for adjusting economic and social policies to these objectives.

At a meeting of the Verein für Sozialpolitik held in Vienna in 1909, a lively discussion turned on Weber's formulation of the problems involved in the establishment of a value-free social science. He defended with great consistency the proposition that in the social sciences scientific research should start from individual facts, events, and processes which could be analyzed in terms of objectively observable relationships, but that value judgments should be permitted to affect scientific analysis only to the degree that choices had to be made among different topics or problems of research.[20] In support of these methodological principles, Weber argued that each stage in the development of economic and social life was marked by the prevalence of specific values and precepts; that, consequently, no propositions derived from such values could claim general validity.[21] Hence, value judgments should enter into "scientific analysis" only as hypothetical starting points of investigations into the possible effects of the practical application of such judgments. Weber distinguished "reference to values" from "value judgments," and assigned to scientific research the task of critically examining the logical connections between value judgments and their ultimate axiomatic foundation. He was convinced that such judgments could be perfectly understood and correctly interpreted by the observer.

This appeal to scientific consciousness was wholeheartedly welcomed by some economists of liberal persuasion, such as Lujo Brentano, Julius Wolf (1862–1935), Alfred Weber, and L. Pohle, who criticized the Socialists of the chair for having degraded economics as a handmaiden of politics and having supplied pseudoscientific arguments in support of measures of social policy.[22] Some epistemological aspects of the controversy were elaborated by Andreas Voigt and Richard Ehrenberg (1857–1921).[23]

The call for a "value-free" science met with by no means immediate acceptance. Heinrich Herkner vindicated the right of the social scientist to pass judgment on the economic and social conditions which are the object of his analysis, to define the concept of the "welfare of the people," to determine the objectives of economic and social policies, and to describe the measures fit for attaining these objectives.[24] Ignaz Jastrow (1856–1937) held the historical school responsible for a decline in clear thinking, but argued that economic policies could be the object of scientific treatment when the effects of such policies were examined in the light of causal relationships and no judgment was passed on the desirability of the measures concerned.[25] Metaphysical and psychological considerations were introduced into the discussions by E. Spranger and later the "cultural philosopher" Theodor Litt.[26] Albert Hesse proposed a systematic classification of economic value judgments.[27]

This perfunctory survey of an extensive methodological discussion indicates how many German teachers of economics realized that the development of their science depended on the final answer given to the problems involved in "freedom from evaluation." But it was hardly possible for the majority of Gustav Schmoller's disciples to reconcile their conception of economic analysis with the principles of a "value-free science." The scientist who undertakes to eliminate from his considerations any reference to values has to simplify his problems subconsciously by "cutting out" of the picture to be constructed his own personality, the subject of cognizance.[28] That procedure is predicated upon the use of concepts of high abstraction, which are found predominantly in the realm of quantitative thinking. But practically the entire conceptual apparatus of the "historicists" was related to historically determined national economics conceived as "integrated wholes" and permeated with characteristics which were tinged with value judgments. It was hardly possible to exclude any reference to such judgments from the use of concepts such as "systems of meaning," or "meaningful complexes," which were basic to Sombart's classification of composite economic phenomena. Value judgments were bound to affect the intuitive procedures used in determining the structure of such "complexes" and the mutual relationships of their constituent elements.[29] How could freedom from moral judgments be achieved under these circumstances, when, in addition, economic phenomena were held to be beyond the range of causal and functional relationships?

An absolute standard for measuring economic achievement was proclaimed by the advocates of "social energetics," the so-called technocrats who proposed to adjust the production of goods exclusively to "maximum utilization of power" or to some other "technical optimum." They based their claim to the universal validity of such principles on the alleged operation of "physical factors," and commonly ignored any problems connected with the scarcity of resources, considerations of profitability, and the functions to be fulfilled by interest on capital in any rational organization of productive activities.[30]

The principles of technical rationality, regarded as a methodological device, were elaborated by Friedrich von Gottl-Ottlilienfeld, in an organismic doctrine which received considerable attention among radical members of the historical school.[31] Gottl-Ottlilienfeld, who started his literary career with a violent attack on marginal utility theory and its alleged lack of realism, ascribed to the social sciences the task of combining historical processes and events into "textures of rational behavior." With the aid of a poorly defined concept of "noetic reasoning," he advocated the view that the social sciences had to derive the "meaning of reality" directly from coherent experience. Gottl-Ottlilienfeld contrasted the concept of "noetic" thinking with the concept of "phenomenological" thinking, which he used to characterize the methods of the natural sciences considered as devices of combining "heterogeneous phenomena" with no "recognizable" mutual relations.[32] As a main instrument of economic analysis he developed the concept of the "economic dimension" of goods, conceived of in terms of quantitative relationships between goods, as distinct from prices, which he associated with causal factors belonging to the past. The study of "dimensions" was designed to provide a differentiation of goods according to their "essential quantitative positions" in the economy, and to enable the observer to analyze the behavior of the economy as reflected in the upward and downward movements of the "dimensions."

DISCUSSION OF ECONOMIC THEOREMS

Quite an impressive series of comprehensive textbooks of political economy were produced during the last two decades before the First World War by German economists who remained outside the historical school. Works by Adolf Wagner, Johannes Conrad, Wilhelm Lexis, and Heinrich Dietzel bore witness to the scholarship of their authors and their extensive knowledge of economic conditions. Their general approach to economic problems, however, was tinged with organismic conceptions. Of a rather different type was *Grundriss der Politischen Oekonomie* (Freiburg, 1893), by Viennese professor Eugen Philippovich (1858–1917), an outstanding textbook which combined a lucid exposition of the Austrian marginal utility doctrine with some teachings of the historical school. It may be mentioned that the animosity which had existed between many members of the German historical school and the representatives of Austrian marginalism had been bridged largely owing to the intermediary position adopted by Philippovich. The traditional method of separating the theoretical part from the other sections dealing with applied economics and questions of economic theory was, as a rule, strictly observed and the results of the theoretical considerations were frequently ignored in the discussions which dealt with problems of applied economics.[33]

Some authors drew a distinction between "purely economic" and "historicojuridical" categories. This distinction had been suggested by Johann Karl Rodbertus, who had admitted the existence of generally valid economic laws but had insisted that the various categories of income (profits, wages, rents) were exclusively due to institutional factors, and owed their existence only to law and jurisdiction. To the first group of "purely economic" categories they assigned general theoretical economic concepts, to the latter group of "historicojuridical" categories the economic phenomena which could be connected with the prevailing social order and regarded as products of institutional factors. The term *social economics*, adopted by Adolf Wagner and Heinrich Dietzel as the title of their common voluminous textbook, was designed to indicate the broad coverage of their teachings, which extended to all aspects of social life that were more or less related to economic activities.

The Kantian theory of cognition which was generally observed did not permit the application of a concept of causality to social relationships. Thus, Wilhelm Lexis, an outstanding scholar, asserted that to apply categories of mechanics to economic analysis was likely to create a confusion similar to—and the opposite of—that committed by the ancient philosophers who ascribed reality to subjective conceptions derived from their analysis of physical nature. In his extensive work of demographic research, Lexis was governed by the conviction that times series of statistical data can never provide a clue to the existence of causal connections, but can only point to probable future relationships of the observed magnitudes.[34] The role to be assigned to economic concepts of high abstraction was, in general, not clearly defined.

The use of concepts of lower abstraction for purposes of theoretical analysis involved the danger of establishing theorems which were, at best, applicable to only a limited range of situations. This danger was enhanced by the fact that a conspicuous predilection for methods of intuitional reasoning prevailed, even among German economists who remained outside the historical school. This predilection provided a strong stimulus to many German scholars to develop original theories of their own, since the use of such methods permitted the introduction of hazy concepts and did not impose the obligation to connect these concepts through well-reasoned logical chains.[35] A remarkable confusion was thus created by the simultaneous existence of a considerable number of competing economic teachings.

Intuitional reasoning also provided strong support for organic-biological interpretations of the "national economy" and the related view that such an economy was the arena of a circular flow of economic processes. Primary emphasis placed on the "qualitative" functions exercised by the individual economic units was frequently associated with the discussion of "productive forces" and their importance for the economy. At two meetings of the Verein für Sozialpolitik held in Vienna in 1909 and 1926, problems of "productivity" were the object of extended discussions, which turned largely on the question of whether promotion of productivity could be regarded as an absolutely valid end of the economy. An attempt to use the concept of productivity to provide a sort of theoretical foundation for the definition of "objective ends" of the economy was made in an essay by Frieda Wunderlich, entitled "Produktivität" (1929). These ends were conceived of as the maximum possible adjustment of the tension (*Spannung*) between demand and supply. But Wunderlich admitted that this "objective end" could be realized by increased supply of goods as well as by reduction of want satisfaction, so that in the final analysis its content was determined by acts of subjective valuation.[36]

Equally widespread was the view that pursuance of self-interest and free competition did not provide sound principles of economic and social organization. Adolf Wagner, a highly respected teacher who did not belong to the historical school, requested the state to control by means of its law-making power the whole "organic structure" of the nation, and to establish a true "Germanic" law as opposed to the predominantly individualistic Roman law, which was basic to the regulation of contractual agreements. Among the measures of economic policy which he advocated were protective tariffs, expansion of the public ownership of means of production, and public monopolies. In support of such policies he advanced a "sociological" law of increasing state control, which in his view underlay the development of the economy.[37]

Most German economists who cared about providing their discipline with a theoretical foundation related the value of goods to the costs of production. Marginal utility analysis enjoyed very few adherents, mainly because of its individualistic aspects.[38] In the course of time ever-renewed objections to the usefulness of the concept of value as an economic category were raised, not only by advocates of historism. Mention may be made of the teachings of Robert Liefmann, which attracted considerable attention: they were based on the idea that the value of goods was not instrumental in determining economic activity, that instead such activity was regulated by the yield of economic processes and monetary calculations based on comparisons of such yields.[39] From the consideration that all the final returns obtained from satisfying wants were equal in amount, Liefmann derived a theory of prices based on the "law of the equalization of marginal returns." But in prolonged discussions these theories were shown to be merely reformulations of certain aspects of marginal productivity analysis.[40]

The Ricardian principles of price determination were adopted by the majority of the German theorists. Their monetary views were strongly influenced by the teachings of the English Banking School concerning the automatic adjustment of the circulating volume of notes to the monetary requirements of the economy. Wagner elaborated the theorem that the quantity of the circulating means of payment was determined by the level of prices.[41] He followed Thomas Tooke in developing a distinction between consumers' money, which is continuously renewed through the formation of new incomes, and producers' or business money fulfilling the functions of capital. He analyzed the process of transforming money of one category into money of the other, and criticized the traditional quantity theory of money on the ground that it failed to draw that distinction. Thus, Wagner propounded an analysis of monetary problems which was later termed the *income approach*. The idea that business money was continuously transformed into consumers' money provided N. Johannsen with the elements of an organismic construction of social life based on the concept of a "circular flow" of money.[42]

The principles of the gold standard gained increasing acceptance; the statutes of the "Reichsbank," the bank of issue of the German Empire, and the regulation of the monetary system were adjusted to these principles. But various "heretic" views were defended by authors who connected the value of money not with the commodity character of monetary metals but exclusively with its function as a means of exchange. To an international monetary conference held in 1892 Julius Wolf submitted the idea of establishing an international gold reserve as a backing for the issuance of international banknotes. A proposition to replace the gold standard by a system of stabilized paper currencies was defended by Walter Hausmann.[43]

The theories of distribution were quite generally formulated in accordance with the approach adopted by the leading English economists. The theory of land rent followed the Ricardian pattern, as modified by J. H. Thünen's contributions. The striking aspects of the rent of urban land were the object of continuous discussions and many misleading interpretations. At various national and international congresses and conferences these and many related problems of residential construction and housing reform were repeatedly discussed, along with various aspects of "garden cities," communal settlements, and municipal ownership of the urban soil, building, and housing cooperatives. The slogan "family house versus tenement house" supplied ample opportunities for a clash of conflicting social philosophies.[44] Organismic conceptions provided a sort of theoretical background to the proposals of various social reformers, who propagated different versions of taxes on "unearned income" or insisted upon the transfer of the soil to public ownership. Radical proposals of that type were advanced by M. Flürscheim, Theodor Hertzka, and Adolf Damaschke. Damaschke gained a large group of enthusiastic followers for a system of taxes designed to skim off any increases in the value of the soil which were due to the influence of social factors. He organized successful propaganda in favor of the acquisition of urban land by municipal authorities and the development of municipal housing schemes.[45] Considerable discussions turned upon the question of whether, as taught by David Ricardo, the movement of real wages was opposite to the movement of rent, or whether both forms of income moved in the same direction. The first view was defended by Dietzel and P. Arndt under the title *Konträrtheorie;* the other view, the *Paralleltheorie,* found its main advocate in Karl Diehl, who questioned the validity of the method of isolation used by Dietzel and insisted that it was impossible to establish general regularities about the relationships between the movement of the prices of agricultural products and the movement of wages.[46]

The theories of interest on capital advanced or advocated by many German economists showed better than any other lines of their reasoning their adherence to the traditional Scholastic concept of "substance." The use of that concept enabled them to attribute real existence not only to the abstract notion of "capital" but also to contributions rendered by "capital" to productive processes.[47] Thus, vaguely conceived "productivity theories" of interest were adopted by many economists, among them Thünen, J. Wolf, Karl Adler, and Karl Diehl.[48] Also, the idea that the services rendered by capital could be regarded as a separate category and made the object of a special reward enjoyed a considerable number of adherents. A. Schäffle, Karl Knies, Lujo Brentano, and H. Oswalt were the most representative defenders of this view.[49] Oswalt's theory contained some elements of Böhm-Bawerk's *agio* theory. He was one of the few German economists to elaborate the principles of the theory of subjective value. Rudolf Stolzmann developed an intricate theory which held conditions of social power responsible for the distributive process and explained interest and profits as a socially necessary reward of the Capitalist for the accumulation and use of the capital.[50]

A number of German economists adopted—with some modifications—socialist theories which implied that exploitation of labor was at the root of interest on capital and profit. According to Lexis, the owners of capital and land enjoyed a sort of monopolistic market control even under stationary conditions.[51] Dietzel was another representative adherent of a similar theory.[52]

These approaches to the problem of profit may be contrasted with the comprehensive empiricostatistical studies undertaken by R. Ehrenburg, who adopted Thünen's method of collecting material from the ledgers of various enterprises for the purpose of securing exact comparisons of cost accounting and earnings. A special periodical, the *Thünen Archiv,* founded in 1905, was designed to provide a center for the publication of the results of such research, but it gained importance only much later, under the title *Archiv für exakte Wirtschaftsforschung.* It was a rallying point for some German economists who emphasized the quantitative aspects of economic analyses.

In this connection, mention may be made of the development of a special discipline, *Betriebswirtschaftslehre* (business economics). The teachers who were charged with the task of preparing students for careers in the field of business administration centered their attention on the elaboration of well-reasoned budgetary techniques, accounting procedures, and similar practical aspects of business life.[53] But they felt the need to link these instructions with some general economic theories, and frequently availed themselves of the marginal utility approach because of its individualistic aspects.

The discussion of wage problems occupied a broad space in German economic literature, but the wage fund idea, rendered provocative under the slogan "iron law of wages," was used primarily by the Socialist Ferdinand Lassalle (1825–1864) as an instrument of political propaganda.[54] Lassalle shared the view of other German Socialists that the state was obliged to adjust the economy to the interest of the laboring classes and to organize a sort of collectivized production through workers' cooperatives. He, like Rodbertus, regarded a "national spirit" as the moving force in shaping national history and national institutions. He was a typical representative of the organismic version of socialism which appealed greatly to the German workers. Even after the militant organizations founded by Lassalle had been absorbed by associations of the Marxian type, the "Gotha Program" of the German Social Democratic Workers' party adopted in 1875 showed conspicuous traces of that influence.

The nonsocialist German authors repudiated the wage fund idea almost without exception,[55] but did not agree on a consistent wage theory. The strictly theoretical aspects of the wage problem received relatively little attention, as compared with the vast literature devoted to the descriptive analysis of specific wage conditions and to the methods of improving those conditions.

Elaborating an idea advanced by F.B.W. von Hermann many decades before, Brentano pointed to consumers' incomes as the real source of wage payments, and supported the wage policy of the trade unions with the argument that such incomes could be rendered elastic through credit expansion.[56] According to his findings, no proof had been provided for the contention that wage increases in certain industries could be achieved only at the loss of workers in other sectors of the economy.[57]

Other economists, such as Dietzel and Lexis, developed a rather primitive "productivity theory" in support of wage increases.[58] They expected wage increases to enhance workers' efficiency, to restrict luxury consumption through redistribution, to expand mass production, and to prevent misdirected investments, especially in the field of capital goods. Closely connected with discussions of this type was the old question to what degree the fixing of wages through collective bargaining or through administrative fiat was compatible with "economic laws." The view prevailed that the distributive aspects of the wage problem could be separated from the analysis of the processes of production. Some adherents of the "sociojuridical" school, in particular, ignored the theoretical problems involved in such a view, problems which were discussed by Eugen von Böhm-Bawerk in one of his last contributions to economic analysis.[59] He pointed to the efficiency of capital and to the supply and demand conditions of the market as factors which limited any arbitrary interference with distributive processes. These discussions were supplemented by Joseph Schumpeter, who demonstrated that production and distribution were two aspects of a single economic process; he applied the principles of marginal productivity analysis consistently to the theory of wages.[60] But theroretical considerations of that kind failed to convert the large majority of the German economists to the use of well-defined concepts of adequate abstraction.

SPECIAL PROBLEMS

Preference for organismic conceptions was also reflected in the attitude adopted by German economists toward changes in the economic structure which could be interpreted as impending transformations of the capitalist economy. A remarkable place among the conspicuous symptoms of such changes was occupied by cartels, trusts, mergers, and other attempts to eliminate competition or to reduce its intensity. The institutional and juridical aspects of organizations of that type were the object of extensive investigations,[61] which, however, rarely touched upon the complex theoretical problems connected with the exercise of market controls, the operation of restrictions of production, and administered prices. Some economists of liberal persuasion objected to the interference with the price mechanism and the determination of production quotas practiced by producers' and traders' associations, but the large majority of the historically minded economists were convinced that such procedures resulted in desirable adjustments of supply to demand, thus contributing to the stabilization of the economy.

The organismic approach also prevailed in the treatment of the problems of international trade. Tariff policy was analyzed from the point of view of the development of the country's productive forces and as an effective means of national power policies. Characteristic of this attitude was a discussion which turned on the future development of world trade. As visualized by A. Wagner, three large imperialistic powers loomed on the horizon: the British Empire, Russia, and the United States. These powers, he predicted, would become increasingly self-sufficient and would close their frontiers to imports from abroad. Hence, he considered it necessary to organize as a counterweight an economically united Europe under German leadership.[62]

The application of organismic conceptions to crises and depressions was practically incompatible with any general theoretical analysis of the problems involved in business cycle analysis. Among German economists the tendency prevailed to look for multiple causes in explaining these phenomena and to consider every crisis as an individual event conditioned by specific circumstances. Such an approach was adopted even by scholars who did not share the methodological convictions of the historical school. In his earlier writings, Wagner adopted J. S. Mill's idea that general economic disturbances were largely connected with the tendency of the rate of interest to decline.[63] Later he combined this view with a version of the "underconsumption" theory advocated by Johann Karl

Rodbertus. Wilhelm Lexis was convinced that various attempts to demonstrate the periodicity of crises were prompted by the misguided application of the principles of mechanical causality to human affairs. He suggested a classification of crises according to their origin in the various spheres of the economy.[64] That grouping was endorsed by other economists. Heinrich Herkner, who prepared a leading article on the question, considered it impossible to explain general economic disturbances in accordance with a uniform principle.[65]

Among the economists of the historical school, Werner Sombart was practically the only one to attempt to explain the ever-recurrent expansions and contractions of production and trade in terms of a general cause.[66] According to his interpretation of economic growth, increasing use was made of unorganic materials the production of which—as distinct from the production of organic material—was not subjected to the law of decreasing returns. Connecting changes in business activity with the effects of changes in the exploitation of gold mines, he argued that the stimulating effects which had resulted from the discovery of new mines had led to expansion of productive activity in the sector with evolutionary potentialities. Crises had occurred when rapidly increasing volumes of commodities produced in the "unorganic" sector failed to find sufficient markets among the producers of goods of organic origin.

A methodologically far superior approach to the analysis of crises was adopted by Arthur Spiethoff.[67] For his method, which he termed *empirical-realistic, concrete*, or *observational*, he claimed the merit that it derived its basic data from the "real world" and that it dealt with "essential regularities" discovered by observation and isolated as "blocks of facts." He centered his studies on the relationships between the successive phases of the cyclical movements considered as integrated wholes, and related the existence of these movements to a certain "spiritual disposition" of the free market economy and its expansionist features. Although his general methodological principles were hardly compatible with equilibrium analysis, Spiethoff accepted Michael Tugan-Baranowsky's conception of the economy as a mechanism which is subjected to a series of disequilibrating processes, and Tugan-Baranowsky's distinction between consumer goods bought by incomes and investment goods bought by capital.[68] He equally accepted the general proposition that investments in capital goods–producing industries were the instrumental factor in determining economic development and the course of business fluctuations.

In his analysis of the statistical data concerning the production of primary capital goods, Spiethoff placed main emphasis on the disproportionalities in productive activity which occurred during prosperity periods. Since he ascribed the emergence and the course of each cycle to specific historical events, he ignored the problems related to the periodicity of the fluctuations. Monetary factors played only a subordinate role in his predominantly descriptive analyses. Spiethoff practically ignored the behavior of prices and assumed that the expansion of business activity during the prosperity was financed out of savings accumulated during the preceding depression.[69]

Another noteworthy attempt to develop a strictly economic theory with the aid of methods supplied by organismic reasoning was made by Alfred Weber in a study dealing with the general problems of the location of industries.[70] These problems had attracted the attention of various German students of the social sciences who remembered the importance which Immanuel Kant had attached to the two categories of time and space. It may be recalled that J. H. von Thünen had already formulated the fundamental question of how to determine the spatial conditions under which production could be expected to achieve maximum results for agricultural enterprises. And in his subsequent "realistic" studies,

Thünen had made extensive use of actual budgetary data, designed to supplement the theorems established with the aid of a general hypothetical scheme concerning the spatial distribution of the various agricultural activities.

In his broad survey of the conditions of production, Wilhelm Roscher suggested that for industries with a highly developed division of labor, the choice of location was mainly determined by the availability of productive factors, and that for other industries proximity of the markets was of paramount importance.[71] Another author who took account of spatial problems was A. Schäffle. He drew a distinction between industries whose location was influenced by costs of transportation and others which were attracted to regions where a considerable labor force was available.[72] Like Wilhelm Roscher, he used a method of comparative descriptive analysis based on the collection of a large variety of data.

A remarkable contribution to the theory of location was W. Launhardt's attempt to supply a mathematical formulation of Thünen's scheme of agricultural production. Moreover, Launhardt availed himself of methods of marginal productivity analysis in order to determine the dependence of industrial enterprises upon the costs of transportation of materials as well as finished products.[73] But he was an outsider to the economic profession and his studies did not receive much attention.

Building on this tradition, Weber centered his analysis on the problem of how to determine the optimum location for individual firms.[74] Basic to that analysis was an abstract scheme of an economy, starting from an agricultural stratum and including four additional strata which were assumed to have grown in the course of a historical evolutionary process. Under simplified assumptions, costs of production were broken down into three categories (raw materials and fuel, labor, and transportation); locational diagrams (*Standortsfiguren*) served to differentiate industries according to the varying influence exercised upon their location by the several categories of cost. To these main determinants of location, Weber added as a secondary factor the tendency toward "agglomeration," as promoted by the advantages resulting from clustering industrial enterprises in certain localities or regions. To the operation of "deglomerative" factors, Weber ascribed opposite effects. In order to define with mathematical accuracy the forces which were pulling the choice of locations in divergent directions, Weber availed himself of combinations of the weights and of the routes of shipment. He supplemented that abstract analysis by a "realistic" theory, which attempted to show how the propositions gained by deductive reasoning are modified under the influence of special social conditions, especially those prevailing under the capitalist order.

Weber's analysis enjoyed a high reputation among German economists, but it was open to the objection that he had adopted a vaguely defined "evolutionary" concept of economic system and yet developed his considerations against the background of a network of fixed prices, given demand functions and invariable techniques.[75] Moreover, the figures which he used in his mathematical presentation of divergent forces referred to technical rather than economic factors. Instead of establishing an "exact" theory of location Weber suggested only certain relationships among various relevant spatial factors within the structure of a specific imaginary economic scheme.[76] Finally, it was a moot question whether cost minimization—rather than prospects of gain—is the determinant factor in the choice of the location of industries. Weber's theory of location provides an excellent example to demonstrate the difficulties involved in using organismic concepts for purposes of theoretical analysis.

A third much-discussed attempt to apply methods of organismic reasoning to the analysis of theoretical problems was G. F. Knapp's so-called state theory of money.[77]

This theory, which was suggested by a deep aversion to the "materialistic" foundations of Ricardian monetary views, was designed to provide the German counterpart to the commodity theory of money and to analyze the functions of money independently of any reference to the problem of value. Prompted by considerations of that type, Knapp adopted a concept of money which was practically free from any reference to economic functions. He defined money as a product of a legal order, and ascribed the generally recognized value of a monetary unit to a historical concatenation of successive monetary standards rendered necessary by the existence of debts which required the establishment of definite relationships between old and new monetary units. To the monetary views of the advocates of the international gold standard—such as Karl Knies, Karl Diehl, and Walter Lotz—he opposed the proposition that the international monetary system which achieved predominance after 1871 was not that of the gold standard but that of the British Empire, which only by accident was based on gold.

The confusion created by that approach was enhanced by the fact that Knapp defined his theory as "nominalistic," because of his opposition to the "materialistic" conceptions of money. According to commonly accepted terminology, the logical opposite of "nominalistic" is "universalistic," and not, as Knapp contended, "materialistic." The opposite of "materialistic" is "idealistic." According to Knapp's terminology the monetary theory of Thomas Aquinas was to be classified as "nominalistic," the theories of outstanding Nominalists, such as Galiani and Condillac, were non-nominalistic, and so on. Moreover, he applied—without further distinction—the attribute "metallic" to all theories which connected the value of money with a factor other than government's fiat, and included among the "metallic" theories even those which derived the value of the means of payment exclusively from their exchange functions.[78] It is much to be regretted that Knapp's misleading terminology was widely accepted by German and French authors, who applied the term *nominalistic* indiscriminately to all monetary theories according to which money is regarded as a symbol that confers a kind of claim upon its owner by virtue of some delegation on the part of a social authority. No agreement has been reached on the meaning of the term *validity,* or valuableness, of money, which Knapp introduced to connect the general acceptance of a currency with the decision of a "pay community" regarded as an organic, integrated whole.[79] *Chartal money* was the term he used to denote abstract means of providing units of computation with no backing by any "material" value.

Various problematic inferences could easily be drawn from this conception of money: that the volume of the circulating monetary units did not affect the economic operations, and that the issuance of additional means of payment was merely a procedure designed to facilitate the performance of exchanges.[80] When combined with the repudiation of the gold standard, such views culminated in the glorification of national inconvertible paper currencies, without any reference to the need to delimit the volume of the circulating means of payment. Complete isolation of a country's domestic price system by means of exchange control and similar measures could be recommended as a highly advantageous economic policy.

It is doubtful whether the term *theory* can correctly be connected with Knapp's teachings, which ignored practically all questions that are fundamental to the analysis of the means of payment. The bulk of his discussions turned on genetic and administrative aspects of monetary policies and the history of monetary institutions. A few years prior to the appearance of Knapp's work the sociological aspects of money had been discussed, equally from an organismic viewpoint, by the German philosopher Georg Simmel. Simmel analyzed the evolutionary aspects of monetary standards; he attempted to demonstrate that they revealed a declining importance of money conceived as a substance and an increasing importance of the functional character of money.[81]

The "state theory of money" appealed strongly to German economists of organismic persuasion, who hated the Ricardian quantitative approach to economic analysis and identified the functioning of the gold standard with the supremacy of the London money market. They enjoyed the idea of having been provided with a genuine "German monetary theory" by one of the leading representatives of the historical school. They placed particular emphasis on the principle that money signified an abstract claim to the acquisition of goods without serving as a standard of values. Thus, one of the ardent defenders of Knapp's theory, Friedrich Bendixen, compared the symbolic character of a monetary unit with that of a security representing a share in an enterprise;[82] similar conceptions were suggested by other faithful adherents of the state theory of money.[83] The French economist Mossé credited Knapp with contributing to the undermining of the materialistic philosophy of money and to the opening of the way to manipulated currency (*monnaie dirigée*).[84] A German jurist, Arthur Nussbaum, considered it necessary to substitute for Knapp's state theory a "societary theory" in order to take account of the fact that money, although issued by the proper authority, may at times be repudiated by the public. Nussbaum elaborated the effects of the "rule of nominalism" on the treatment of domestic debts and foreign currencies in case of depreciation and devaluation.[85]

In passing, a reference may be made to the fateful role played by that theory in Germany during and after the First World War. During the war it was used in support of the view that the inflationary effects of the issuance of paper money could be avoided by substituting the use of checks for the use of bank notes. After the war it was invoked to demonstrate that the revolutionary inflationary price increases which were undermining the economy were caused exclusively by the price movements of imported commodities. Thus, Karl Helfferich (1872–1924), one of Knapp's most influential disciples, blamed the inflation on the liabilities which the peace treaty had imposed on the country, especially on the reparation policy practiced by the French government. He insisted that not "inflation" but depreciation of the currency on foreign markets was "the first link in the chain of cause and effect."[86]

LIBERAL SOCIALISTS

In the welter of social theories which competed with each other in Central Europe, a special place should be assigned to the teachings of some Socialists of organismic persuasion, occasionally termed *Liberal Socialists* because of their insistence that some sort of common ownership of the means of production could be combined with observance of the principles of individual freedom and equality. Their criticisms of the exchange economy were vitiated by serious errors in interpreting the functioning of that economy; their radical proposals of social reform were based on erroneous assumptions. But some of their stimulating ideas were quite attractive to intellectuals in search of a new social order.

Common to the theorems of all these authors was the thesis of the Ricardian Socialists that any income not earned by labor was gained at the expense of workers' rightful earnings. That thesis played a prominent role in the teachings of the German Karl Eugen Dühring (1833–1921), whose contributions to the exact sciences were generally recognized as remarkable achievements. In his approach to social problems he rejected the materialistic interpretation of history and emphasized the influence of intellectual and political movements on economic developments. Dühring ascribed the origin of the distributive process to the operation of forces of political compulsion; hence, he denied the existence of general laws of distribution. In his "societary" system of social reform, he charged the state with the task of securing for the workers an appropriate share in the results of technological improvements. Dühring's *Kritische Geschichte der Nationalökonomie und des Sozialismus* was distinguished from all previous surveys of economic thought by its analytical and critical approach to the history of economic doctrines. It may be mentioned in passing that Dühring displayed the greatest admiration for Henry Charles Carey's teachings, and hailed them as revolutionary discoveries in the field of economics.[87]

Dühring's conception of the distributive process was taken over by other Socialists. The Russian economist Michael Tugan-Baranowsky declared "social power" to be the determinant factor in the distribution of the national dividend, and insisted upon separating the problems of distribution from those of strict economic theory.[88] Another "Liberal Socialist" who connected the problems of distribution with the effects of the exercise of political and economic power was the German Franz Oppenheimer (1864–1943), who referred to the distinction drawn by John B. Clark (1847–1938) between the problems of personal distribution and those of functional distribution, and sharply criticized David Ricardo for having related the rent of the land to the unit of the soil and thus having initiated the "dismal" theory of imputation.[89] As formulated by Oppenheimer, the problem of distribution consisted in determining the "monopolistic" situations which enabled the owners of the means of production to gain incomes not derived from labor. As various other socialist authors had suggested before him, Oppenheimer held the appropriation of land by private owners responsible for the evils which he associated with the functioning of the capitalist economy.[90] He attributed the "pathological" nature of that economy mainly to the exclusion of workmen from free access to the soil (*Bodensperre*), and he created a regrettable confusion by using the term *monopoly* to characterize the alleged power of landowners to force down the share of labor—conceived of as a complementary factor—in the national dividend.[91]

The influence of some Marxian theorems on Oppenheimer's teachings was quite remarkable. He developed with great consistency a conception of the state as an institution created and maintained by a dominant group for the purpose of assuring the exploitation of a subjugated group. This conception had been basic to the studies of the Austrian sociologist L. Gumplowicz.[92] From an analysis of the migratory movement of labor, he derived the concept of an "industrial reserve army" as a temporary historicosociological category, a relic of the feudal order. He attributed to the fluctuating volumes of unemployment an important role in his business cycle theory, which showed the characteristic features of a socialist underconsumption theory. But he rejected the Marxian law of "capitalist accumulation," and expected the disintegration of the capitalist order to result from the exhaustion of the industrial reserve army. His ideal of social reform centered on the organization of agricultural production on a cooperative basis.[93] Oppenheimer was a successful teacher in a period in which a variety of socialist ideas found fertile soil among German students.

In Italy, Arturo Labriola gained considerable following for his socialist ideas and provoked extended discussions of the various aspects of the capitalist economy.[94] Though not a strict Marxist, he was one of the most ardent Italian defenders of the materialist interpretation of history and the Marxian labor cost theory. His most original, but strongly contested, contribution to socialist reasoning was his theorem concerning the close relationship between the successive appropriation of the soil and the corresponding development of social conditions.[95] He expected the final elimination of ground rent to lead to the disappearance of salaried workers as an exploited class of the population.

NEOSCHOLASTIC ECONOMICS

Moral considerations which were constituent elements of the economic conceptions of members of the historicoethical school were assigned a central position in the economic teachings of Catholic social philosophers. Their attempts to revive the observance of certain principles of Thomistic economics found considerable support in Catholic regions of Europe where substantial groups of the population had preserved a strong attachment to important elements of the medieval feudal order. In France in the first half of the nineteenth century, Jean Paul Alban de Villeneuve-Bargemont elaborated the principles of a Catholic political economy.[96] Later, P. G. Frédéric Le Play was inspired by similar ideas.[97] Count Adrien Albert de Mun (1841–1914) became the leader of a Catholic social movement. In Belgium a similar movement was promoted by the economists C. Périn, Victor Brants, and Hector Denis. They advocated proposals of social reform which were derived from the moral precepts of Thomistic doctrine.[98] In Italy Giuseppe Toniolo attempted to reconcile certain aspects of marginal utility analysis with a Neoscholastic approach.[99]

A program of social reform adjusted to the Catholic creed was inaugurated during the Sixties by Bishop Wilhelm E. von Ketteler (1811–1877) in Germany[100] and by K. von Vogelsang and Franz Hitze in Austria. The corporative organizations which they advocated were reminiscent of the medieval guilds. Tendencies of that type were strongly promoted by the highest clerical authorities. It was perhaps no mere coincidence that in 1878 the Holy See proclaimed, through the encyclical *Aeterni Patria*, the exclusive validity of the principles of Thomistic logic at about the same time that the methods of hypothetical reasoning were repudiated by influential intellectual movements of the European continent. In another encyclical, *Quod Apostolici Muneris,* Pope Leo XIII denounced the doctrines and movements of socialism, communism, and nihilism as incompatible with the dogmatic teachings of the church.

In the famous encyclical *Rerum Novarum,* issued in 1891, the pope defined the precepts of a social and economic order in accordance with the tenets of Thomistic social philosophy. "Reason itself," said the encyclical, "deduces from the nature of things and from the individual and social character of man, what is the end and object of the whole economic order assigned by God the Creator." The institution of private ownership of the means of production was defended against the attacks of socialist doctrines, and the idea of the class struggle was condemned as inconsistent with the principles of brotherly love. In fact, the Christian trade unions which were formed in considerable numbers on the European continent generally abstained from participation in work stoppages. That policy turned out to be a serious handicap to their development. But the autonomy of the economic individual and free competition as a generally valid principle of economic organization were equally rejected, and the risk factor as a fundamental element of entrepreneurship was admitted only within narrow limits. The social duties which Thomistic ethics had imposed upon the owners of private property were reestablished, and the responsibility of the government for the social and economic conditions of the citizens, especially of the working classes, was strongly emphasized. The encyclical recommended the creation of producers' cooperatives as an especially appropriate form of economic organization. Employers and workers were exhorted to observe their mutual obligations. Thus, Catholic students of economics were confronted with the task of reconciling the teachings of prevailing economic doctrines with the principles of a moral philosophy which centered on the idea of just prices and just wages, on medieval conceptions of distributive and commutative justice.[101]

The most important analysis along these lines was the voluminous work of a German Jesuit, Heinrich Pesch, who derived his teachings from a natural moral law designed to assure the attainment of human objectives in accordance with the divine will.[102] To the human intellect he ascribed the faculty to grasp the "spiritual substance" (*ideeller Sachgehalt*) of things; to national groups he attributed the faculty to determine objective values through "*an estimatio communis.*"

Pesch considered the teleological method as fundamentally important for the establishment of a generally valid economic theory, and elaborated a system of welfare economics oriented toward the satisfaction of the material needs of the members of the community. But he ascribed only a subordinate role to the economic principle, and endeavored rather to establish "objective criteria" for the definition of legitimate want satisfaction. His analysis of the problems of production and distribution reflected a combination of Ricardian principles and marginal utility considerations as influenced by moral standards. It may be mentioned that Pesch questioned the absolute validity of the law of diminishing returns as applied to agriculture, and similarly argued that industry cannot continuously count upon increasing or constant returns, especially because of the uncertainty which affects expanding markets. In view of the fundamental changes in economic organization which had occurred after the end of the Middle Ages, Pesch considered it impossible to defend the Scholastic prohibition of taking interest on money; he justified interest payment by referring to the services rendered through lending.

Although he accepted the proposition that the competitive price was to be considered the optimum price, Pesch stressed the dangers involved in exaggerated competition which was likely to lead to artificial monopolies. From the organization of consumers' cooperatives and the creation of bilateral monopolies, he expected the establishment of "equality of power" between cartelized employers and the purchasers of their products.

As an ideal background for the creation of a morally sound social organization, Pesch advocated observance of the principle of "solidarism." The "organic unity" to be formed out of the members of a political body was not meant to put an end to the individual responsibility of the economic units, but to impose on them only the general duty to adjust their objectives to the order required by the superior ends of the state. From the principles of solidarism Pesch derived important directives for the organization of the economy, but he warned against the creation of vocational groupings not animated by "proper motivation." In an interesting chapter, he dealt with the question of the degree to which certain elements of "solidarism" had received recognition in preceding economic doctrines. Among these doctrines he listed Adam Smith's conception of the division of labor, Say's theory of markets, Bastiat's "natural harmony" of interests, and Sismondi's insistence upon the community of interests of employers and workers. Otto von Gierke (1841–1921) and Adolf Wagner were two German authors whom he credited with having developed some fundamental principles of solidarism. To the French version of solidarism, as advocated mainly by Léon Bourgeois (1851–1925) and his adherents, he raised the objection that their proposals were permeated with utilitarian, positivist, and evolutionary ideas, operated according to biological analogies, and were based on untenable sociological propositions.

Neoscholastic reasoning, freed from the influence of a religious creed but imbued with strong nationalistic ideas, found its most elaborate expression in the writings of the Austrian economist Othmar Spann.[103] His efforts centered on the attempt to develop a new epistemology not affected by the "fundamental error of the individualistic social philosophy," the "vicious atomistic, mechanistic approach to economic analysis." In opposition to that approach he applied to social communities the Aristotelian principle that the whole is the first and foremost category of being and prior and superior to its parts. From the writings of some German Romantic authors he borrowed the ideal concept of an "organic" society conceived as a logically preformed reality, and he agreed with them on the glorification of medieval institutions, especially the guild system. Spann created considerable confusion by mixing in his theory of "wholeness" (*Ganzheitslehre*) purely formal (logical) categories with ill-defined concepts that were tinged with ontological attributes. The concept of "wholeness," which he identified with "totality," "unity," and "organism," was an instance in point. We already mentioned the confusion which he created by applying the term *universalism* to social philosophies of the organismic type.

Spann, who believed he had discovered the source of economic wisdom in Adam Müller's writings, refused to separate economics from its sociological foundations. He ascribed absolutely valid ends to the state and the nation, religion, the arts, and ethics; the economy had to derive its ultimate ends from those of the community, and had to take account of available resources in achieving these ends. Hence, Spann conceived of the economy as a teleological system of activities, an "integrated structure" of performances, services, and achievements. He developed a comprehensive "theory of performances" governed by the idea that every economic phenomenon had a qualitative aspect (performance of work capital, production, trade) and quantitative aspects (value and price).

Spann's analysis provided the basis for a differentiation of the functions and performances of the productive factors (land, capital, and labor), and for an extensive discussion of the problems connected with the articulation of the services rendered by the factors. His scale of performances included direct or consumption performances, indirect or capital performances, negative capital performances, and preparatory performances. His "capital of higher order" was composed of laws and regulations dealing with the economic organization of society. The functions of money were not derived from the role of money in individual transactions, but from the "requirements of the community." In Spann's value and price theories, he accentuated his hostility to marginal utility analysis and attempted to justify the Scholastic concept of just, supraindividual prices on the ground that the system of prices had to reflect "genuine and consistent relationships of performances" as integrated in the structure of the economy. Spann's theory of equiimportance (at margins) was designed to replace the equilibrium aspects of hypothetical economics by qualitative features.[104] His analysis of distributive processes was derived from the consideration that the distribution of the national dividend was predetermined by the organization of production.

In order to assure full subordination of the activities of the parts to the superior common ends of the social whole, Spann proposed the transformation of the capitalistic machinery into an economic organization which, like the feudal society, was to be composed of distinctly separated "economic estates" (*Wirtschaftsstände*) differentiated by economic functions and legal status. His concept of an ideal economic community showed a characteristic affinity with the "corporative state" of the fascist type, since he identified his integrated social whole with a national community and included striving for self-sufficiency among his economicopolitical postulates.

Spann's belief in the absolute validity of his methods and in his capacity to understand the "essence" of the social and economic phenomena enabled him to establish with absolute self-assertion his definitions, classifications, propositions, and deductions. It is an interesting psychological fact that he found enthusiastic adherents among Austrian students of economics and some disciples (such as Walter Heinrich, Wilhelm Andreae, and A. Tautscher) who applied the master's sterile procedures to the analysis of various problems.[105] It is hardly necessary to add that practically all aspects of Spann's economics were the object of severe criticism.[106]

Part V

Dialectic Economics

Chapter 16
The Marxian Doctrine

THE PHILOSOPHICAL BACKGROUND

THE APPLICATION OF the dialectic method to the analysis of economic phenomena was, like its organismic counterpart, closely connected with the attempts of German philosophers to preserve one of the fundamental principles of Scholastic reasoning: to arrive at a full understanding of reality with the aid of appropriate concepts. But, as distinct from the fixed, eternally valid Scholastic notions, the dialectic concepts were designed to reflect with exactitude evolutionary processes held to be ruled by inexorable teleological laws. Thus, the dialectic philosophers and their followers were convinced that their methods of reasoning enabled them to arrive at full insight into the "substance of things" and into those fundamental changes which occur in the course of history. In order to justify that conviction, they ascribed—frequently by implication—to certain outstanding individuals such extraordinary intellectual faculties as enabled them to discover and forcefully apply dialectic logical procedures leading to the establishment of unquestionable truth.[1] The belief that the rules of dialectic reasoning correspond exactly to the rules underlying the course of "evolutionary" historical processes was commonly associated with a deep-seated contempt and hatred for the methods of hypothetical thinking, which, it was asserted, have denied to human reason any faculty to discover the "truth" hidden behind the "shadow" of superficial and elusive impressions.

During the first decades of the nineteenth century, dialectic reasoning was developed to a high degree of perfection by the German philosopher G.W.F. Hegel, who suggested methods of demonstrating the existence of allegedly predetermined evolutionary processes occurring in the fields of philosophy, law, and history.[2] His often-quoted dictum "Whatever is, is rational" was a succinct formulation of the dialectic principle that the rules of reasoning are identical with the laws which underlie the behavior of the universe.

The dialectic methods provided convenient instruments for circumventing one of the problems of continuity. Reference to the continuous sequence of events was included among the characteristic features of dialectic concepts, since every such concept was composed of a "thesis" and its partial negation, an "antithesis." The contradictions implied in the structure of such concepts were said to assume increasing proportions; quantitative changes accumulated over prolonged periods were said to lead to qualitative modifications of the concepts, to clashes of opposites, and to revolutionary situations, resulting in the formation of "syntheses" which provided the starting points for the continued operation of evolutionary processes. Since the behavior of the dialectic concepts was held to reflect the laws which underlie the course of actual historical events, analysis of the concepts was regarded as the appropriate method of discovering those laws.

Since the Hegelian dialectic processes turned on the transformation of concepts, Hegel's doctrine found its main application in the sphere of intellectual events. Thus, he conceived of the history of the world as the development of the idea of freedom "within the consciousness of men." He tried to demonstrate that each stage of that history was dominated by a "spirit of the time" (*Zeitgeist*) which determined the thoughts and actions of the people of that period and that the contradictions inherent in the conceptual structure of each stage constituted the driving power which led to the next higher stage. In this evolutionary process a predominant role was assigned to the state, the highest political community, which was defined as the embodiment of the "self-developing absolute idea of freedom." This idea was said to realize itself mainly in the incessant struggle among the historical nation states, and warfare appeared as an indispensable element of the evolutionary processes.

But "freedom," as understood within the framework of that dialectic philosophy, was not identical with individual liberty as defined by the nominalistic philosophers of utilitarian persuasion. Freedom meant submission to inexorable historical laws, that is to say, to the laws of the state, which was regarded as the ultimate source of individual morality. In spite of the revolutionary aspects of his dialectical processes, Hegel adopted an extremely conservative approach to the political and social problems of his days. His admiration for some kings of the Hohenzollern dynasty caused him to glorify the Prussian state as the personification of the absolute idea in history.

From the state as an ideal self-developing moral organization, Hegel distinguished the "civil society" the economic relationships of which he completely subordinated to political interests. Hence, Hegelian philosophy did not provide instruments for directly analyzing and interpreting sequences of economic events. But important elements of his philosophy were used by members of the German historical school in support of their views that the study of economic phenomena could not be isolated from the study of social institutions and political events; that economic history, like general history, was the outcome of evolutionary intellectual processes and that successive stages could be distinguished in the course of these processes; and that in each stage a specific "spirit of the time" pressed its stamp on economic behavior, economic relationships, economic techniques, and social institutions. But the concept of evolution that was used by the members of the German historical school was, as a rule, not of the dialectic type; rather, it was arrived at by loosely defined intuitional procedures.

The German theory of society which originated in the 1850s in the writings of Lorenz von Stein was strongly influenced by Hegelian ideas. Society, defined as the integration of relationships among individuals, was held to exist in reality. In his analysis of French socialism and communism, published in 1842, Stein established a close connection between the development of socialist ideas and social movements; he pointed to class struggle as a predominant factor in political history.

It is well known that Karl Marx and Friedrich Engels (1820–1895) were the two leading authors who developed the revolutionary aspects of Hegelian dialectics into a doctrine which was designed to provide a scientific basis for the belief in the inevitable breakdown of the capitalist economy and its transformation into a "classless" communist society. With that purpose in mind they modified significantly certain conspicuous elements of the Hegelian logical procedure. The most fundamental and far-reaching modification consisted in attributing the self-moving evolutionary process not to the "idea" in the Hegelian sense, but to "matter," that is, to forces which, according to their doctrine of "dialectic materialism," operate in the outside world independently of any interference on the part of will. Marx and Engels defined "motion" as the "mode of existence of matter" and asserted that motion was as uncreatable and indestructible as matter.[3]

The principle that "matter" was the primary agent of all happenings had provided the starting point for a large range of philosophies. But previous conceptions of matter had been commonly of the static and atomistic type, and this was also true of the materialism of Ludwig Feuerbach, a German philosopher whose teachings aroused the admiration of Marx and Engels.[4] Feuerbach's violently antireligious book, *Das Wesen des Christentums* (1841), was designed to show that the idea of God, and along with it all main Christian dogmas, reflected a simple desire of the human heart to resolve its inner contradictions by unconsciously transforming a mental image into an external reality clothed with superhuman authority. He ascribed to conscious reason the task of destroying the dangerous and dismal illusions which create religious ideas. Marx and Engels wanted to relieve men of the bonds of similar illusions prevailing in the field of economic and social relationships. According to Marx, dangerous illusions were connected with the concepts of price, money, and capital, which, once created, had assumed the character of external irresistible forces. One of the most outstanding interpreters of the Marxian doctrine, the Socialist Arturo Labriola, said of Marx that the latter wanted to be the "Feuerbach of political economy" and to deliver mankind from the "fetishes" of economic and social creeds by revealing the "true nature" of economic relationships.[5]

But Marx and Engels went beyond Feuerbach's approach by combining the principles of materialism with Hegelian dialectic procedures. They qualified consciousness as a property of a special form of matter, and applied the Hegelian concept of evolution to matter as transposed and translated inside the human mind. In his essay on Ludwig Feuerbach (1804–1872), Engels criticized the predominantly mechanical conceptions of earlier materialistic philosophers. In their doctrines, he stated, motion turned eternally in a circle and reproduced the same results over and over again.[6] Thus, by turning the Hegelian doctrine "upside down," Marx believed to have established a method which enabled knowledge, actively applied, to apprehend "objective reality."

It is hardly possible to give a clear account of the involved reasoning which provided the background for the Marxian doctrine. Neither Marx nor Engels elaborated the methodological aspects of that doctrine. They used ambiguous metaphors and cryptic concepts

in their methodological discussions. But at least the principles underlying the structure of
that doctrine can be reasonably elucidated by contrasting them with the principles which
were basic to the thinking of the Ricardian economists. These economists were convinced
that full insight into the highly complex social phenomena was forever beyond the reach
of the human intellect, that is, it was doubtful to what degree the results of observation
and experience represented "reality." In his analysis of the Ricardian method, John
Stuart Mill showed that establishment of hypothetical, highly abstract pictures of the
relationships among outside phenomena was prerequisite to any scientific approach to
reality, and that such an approach centered on the task of coordinating these pictures in
logically consistent schemes in accordance with the rules of the human mind. Since
observation and experience had to provide the primary material for the formation of the
abstract concepts, the Ricardians started their economic analyses from immediate objects
of perception, such as individuals and their economic behavior, prices, wages, rents,
profits, and other economic magnitudes of that type. They conceived of social or economic "collectivities" as aggregates of individual entities formed by processes of summation. Hence, they arrived at an "atomistic" conception of the economic system as a
concatenation of individual exchange transactions connected by mutually interrelated
exchange values or prices. But the difficulties involved in dealing with the time factor
prevented them from extending their theoretical considerations to the analysis of economic processes.

   All these characteristic features of hypothetical reasoning were vilified and ridiculed
by Marx, who claimed for his methods the power of revealing absolute truth. He agreed
with Feuerbach on the principles that thought is conditioned by being and that the laws of
being are also the laws of thought. Marx was convinced that the contradictions which split
up our concepts reflect the accurate translation of thought into language. Inasmuch as the
laws of thought are in fact the laws of being, the contradictions which split up our
concepts reside in the phenomena of the real word, owing to the contradictory nature of
the latter's common foundation, namely, movement.[7] Viewed from that angle, the task of
science consisted in discovering the real meaning of these contradictions as constituent
elements of evolutionary processes.

   To the atomistic approach of the Ricardians Marx opposed the belief that the individual cannot be conceived of and understood independently of the social conditions
surrounding him; man's relations to things only reflect his relations to other people who
have created the things. Hence, Marx directed his most violent attacks against "indi-
vidualist" adversaries of the capitalist order, such as Kaspar Schmidt (pseudonym Max
Stirner) and Pierre Proudhon. In his *Misère de la philosophie* (published in Paris in 1847),
Marx rejected Proudhon's proposals on the ground that they aimed at abolishing inequality without destroying the exchange system. Marx related the origin of the capitalist
system to the division of labor, which, he argued, had been responsible for the unequal
distribution of property and the exploitation and serfdom of the working classes. Hence,
he expected to reveal the antagonisms which he attributed to the capitalist order by
centering his analysis on the fundamental conflict of interest which he found to exist
between the "exploiting" and the "exploited" classes of society. The radical difference
between the Marxian method and its Ricardian counterpart can hardly be better illustrated
than by confronting the Ricardian conception of society as a mechanistic combination of
exchange values with the Marxian definition of society as a "dialectic unity of opposites"
developing toward a predetermined goal in accordance with inexorable laws. The smooth
operation of the Ricardian system was held to be disturbed by various factors affecting the

system from outside; under the rule of dialectic reasoning the same disturbances were transformed into elements of a process operating within the society and tending to destroy the existing order of property relationships.

Tautologies were basic to the hypothetical general laws of the Ricardian doctrine, and, strictly speaking, no indications about the course of events to come could be derived from such laws. Predictions concerning that course—such as Ricardo's and Mill's analysis of the path toward a final stationary economy—could be based only on observed regularities, which could be disproved by the results of additional observation and were not meant to convey the "truth."

In accordance with the methods of dialectic reasoning, however, a teleological order underlay the evolutionary process, which drives the development of society toward a predetermined goal.[8] The main task of scientific research consisted in discovering the stages through which that process was bound to pass; for each stage its historically conditional law was to be defined, a law which, independently of any will, was held to determine the transformation of that stage into another nearer to the goal to be attained.

In his occasional references to the factors to which he ascribed a decisive role in molding the general history of mankind, Marx spoke of "definite and unavoidable relations" into which men enter, independently of their will, when engaged in the "social production of their means of existence." He asserted that the economic structure of society—its social system—corresponded exactly to the particular stage which had been reached in the development of the material productive forces. In his famous *Communist Manifesto* (1848), in which he announced the coming universal proletarian revolution, Marx distinguished, in accordance with his broad evolutionary scheme, four general stages in the development of society: the Asiatic, the ancient, the feudal, and the modern, capitalist stages. He stated broadly that each stage was characterized by specific modes of production, a specific class structure, and corresponding forms of social systems, and that in each stage the antagonism between the classes assumed specific forms and was ruled by evolutionary laws of its own.[9]

It is not necessary to discuss the question of how the dialectic method could be used to analyze the development of the precapitalist stages. Neither Marx nor Engels undertook that task, and the results of later attempts to explain certain salient features to precapitalistic economies in accordance with dialectic principles were not particularly encouraging. From the point of view of a history of economic reasoning, it is irrelevant whether the Marxian distinction of stages has any scientific importance. But we cannot ignore the Marxian doctrine as applied to the analysis of the capitalist economy, set forth in the three volumes of *Das Kapital*. Few books have affected the destiny of mankind to a similar degree. The discussion of the Marxian teachings and the extensive literature in which practically all aspects of these teachings were commented upon, extolled, and criticized deals with one of the most impressive and incredible chapters of the history of Western reasoning. Volume 1 deals with the development and the characteristic features of the English economy as seen in the light of dialectic materialism; it presents a forcefully reasoned and well-organized analysis. The other volumes are more fragmentary, and the relation of their discussions to volume 1 has been the object of varying interpretations. Some particular aspects of the capitalist society, especially the "process of circulation," are dealt with in volume 2. The main theme of the third volume is the "integrated process of the capitalist production." The manuscripts left unfinished by Marx show how he struggled with the logical difficulties which remained unsolved in the first volume. Some speculation has turned on the questions of whether Marx changed the general plan of his main work in the course of its preparation and why he left the two-volume manuscript in a sadly unfinished state.[10]

THE MATERIALISTIC INTERPRETATION OF HISTORY

The Ricardian method of eliminating from economic analysis the influence of all "noneconomic" factors was perfectly consistent with the hypothetical method which provided the basis for the construction of an imaginary economic system of a strictly mechanical type. Among the outside facts or "data" which the economist could take for granted without accounting for them in his theories, an important place was assigned to the effects of "empirical laws," such as the Malthusian law and the law of diminishing returns. Moreover, almost all facts that were connected with the lapse of time were held to be beyond the reach of strictly economic analysis.

The methodological procedure of isolating, for purposes of scientific investigation, a specific sector of human activities from its connection with all other aspects of social life, and of completely ignoring these latter aspects was, however, hardly compatible with the principles of dialectic materialism which, like organismic reasoning, conceived of "society," or the "social system," as an integrated whole which was subjected, in each stage of its development, to a specific evolutionary process. Marx and Engels repeatedly expressed their conviction that these processes simultaneously affected all elements of society.[11] Hence, when Marx embarked on the plan of discovering the evolutionary laws which are basic to the development of the capitalist society, he was apparently faced with the gigantic task of analyzing all aspects of human activities and social relationships which were subjected to the operation of the evolutionary forces.

Marx obviated that almost insuperable difficulty by the ingenious device of establishing a strict causal relationship between the developments occurring in the economic sphere and those taking place in the remaining spheres of human activity.[12] He distinguished the legal and political "superstructure" from the "totality of the productive relations which forms the economic structure of society," and attributed to that superstructure a definite form of "social consciousness." To the relationship between the economic structure and the superstructure he applied the "fundamental materialistic" proposition that the "mode of production in material existence conditions social, political and spiritual evolution in general." This proposition was expressed in his often-quoted dictum "It is not man's consciousness that determines his existence, but his social existence that determines his consciousness." The "economic structure" of society, he stated, is the "form in which the movement of productive forces takes place, concretely and historically." "With the change of the productive forces the opposition of form and content assumes contradictory features, until men become conscious of the conflict and fight it out."[13] Engels expressed that "materialistic interpretation of history" in an equally enigmatic passage in which he said that the ultimate causes of all social changes and political revolutions are to be sought not in the minds of men . . . but in changes in the mode of production and exchange—not in the philosophy but in the economy of the epoch concerned."[14]

In the light of that principle of "economic determinism," the will of the individual was fully subordinated to the operation of hidden forces over which he had no control. Individuals were not even able to realize the fundamental antagonism which was bound to develop between the intended objectives of their activities and the final outcome of their efforts. If all political, moral, and intellectual developments were simply derivatives of evolutionary processes which were taking place in the economic sphere, Marx could convince himself and his followers that the problems connected with the history of all "noneconomic" aspects of social life were implicitly solved when the "dialectical laws" of the evolutionary processes had been discovered. Engels compared the importance for history of the materialistic interpretation with the importance of the law of the transformation of energy for the natural sciences.

The full implications of this fundamental principle of Marxian dialectics received scant attention for about thirty years after its proclamation. A serious discussion of the meaning to be attached to the "materialistic interpretation of history" started only in the 1890s, in connection with the preparation of a program of action for the German Social Democratic party, which had endorsed the principles of the Marxian doctrine.

Considerable divergencies of view were caused by the looseness of the terms used by Marx, as well as by Engels, to denote the "material basis" of society. Engels himself declared that from a scientific point of view all definitions were of little value.[15] How was it possible to attach a clear meaning to expressions such as "totality of the productive relations which form the economic structure of society"?[16] Moreover, what was to be understood by the assertion that a causal relationship existed between the economic structure of society and the "ideological" superstructure, both conceived of as aggregates having "real existence"? Some students of Marxism, such as Werner Sombart, Paul Barth (1858–1922), Achille Loria, and Arturo Labriola, emphasized the technological connotation of the terms *forms, processes,* and *"modes of production.*[17] It could, however, easily be shown that in the course of history quite remarkable changes in the "superstructure" had taken place without having been preceded by substantial changes in technical methods of production. Instances in point were the conditions which surrounded the breaking up of the Roman Empire and apparently also those which accompanied the dissolution of the feudal order at the end of the Middle Ages. It was hardly possible to accept at face value Marx's statements that the use of the hand mill necessitated conditions of slavery, that the use of water as the driving power resulted in a feudal order, and that the use of steam created the capitalist society.

Eventually, in several letters written between 1890 and 1894,[18] Engels admitted that it would be misleading to attach too narrow a meaning to the concepts of economic conditions and economic relationships. He wanted to include among the elements of these concepts geographical and racial factors, science, the residues of preceding stages, and even "public power." In addition, he discussed the existence of mutual relations between economic conditions on the one hand and political, juridical, religious, and philosophical developments on the other. Thus, he deprived the "materialistic interpretation" of history of any definite meaning.

A similar loose interpretation was later adopted by various authors, such as the Russian Michael Tugan-Baranowsky, the German "orthodox" Marxist H. Cunow, and the American economist E.R.A. Seligman (1861–1939). They showed that, as used by Marx, the term *modes of production* included references to distributive and marketing procedures, to relationships between owners of capital and labor, and to other forms of social organization. If these important cultural factors were made constituent elements of the "economic structure," no clear borderline could be established between "modes of production" and the "ideological superstructure." The results of these discussions were confirmed by the fact that it was necessary to take account of a considerable variety of noneconomic factors in order to explain why economic developments even in neighboring industrialized regions were marked by widely divergent characteristics, and why economic progress in the so-called underdeveloped countries exhibited so many striking differences.

Even more important than the criticisms of the Marxian formulation of the materialistic interpretation of history were the objections which were raised to the logical aspects of that principle. On closer examination it was obvious that the main elements of the concept "modes of production," as well as the elements of the concept "ideological superstructure," were supplied by a range of abstractions combined into loosely circumscribed aggregates by the observer of historical processes. If that was the case, a problematic logical procedure was implied in the attempt to establish chains of causal relationships between concepts created more or less arbitrarily by aggregating a variety of ill-defined abstractions. In order to establish a causal nexus between complex notions such as "modes of production" and "spiritual superstructure," it was necessary to believe that both notions existed in changing forms in reality outside the human mind. In fact, the belief in such transcendental units became an article of creed for all adherents of Marxism. But a considerable confusion was created by the fact that the adherents of other patterns of thought, attracted by the idea of establishing associations among the material interests of leading groups in pursuance of certain policies, divested the materialistic interpretation of history of its dialectic features and transformed it into an almost meaningless slogan. An attempt to rescue the materialistic interpretation of history as a methodological device was made by Joseph Alois Schumpeter. He proposed to translate that principle into a "working hypothesis" about what determines the physical and social data which will produce a general course of events. That hypothesis implies that all cultural manifestations of society are ultimately functions of its class structure, and that the social process of production displays an "immanent evolution," in other words, a tendency to change its economic data and, consequently, its social data. Whatever may be the usefulness of such an approach to economic and sociological analysis, there is no doubt that the hypothetical elements implied in it are inconsistent with the methods of dialectical materialism which aim at revealing the "substance" behind the shadow.[19]

In the Anglo-Saxon countries, that reformulation of a fundamental Marxian principle was reflected by the tendency to speak of the "economic" instead of the "materialistic" interpretation of history. The economic interpretation, said E.R.A. Seligman, means not that the economic relations exert an exclusive influence but that they exert a preponderant influence in shaping the progress of society. Such a definition was likely to grant the student of historical processes perfect freedom in assessing the connections between economic and noneconomic factors. Similar considerations led to M. Knight's proposal to avoid the term *materialistic* because of its "clumsiness."[20] That problematic change of an adjective enables American economists and sociologists to disregard the dialectic principle of establishing teleologically determined relationships among integrated collective wholes existing in reality. Rather, the term *economic interpretation of history* was applied to causal relationships which were found to exist between specific economic events, or specific economic interests, and corresponding political or social activities. The idea of emphasizing the influence of economically powerful groups upon public policy especially appealed to many students of history, who attempted to show that schemes of territorial expansions, warlike enterprises, and other noneconomic events could be related to the economic interests of influential sectors of society.[21] Changes in political, spiritual, and institutional factors which could be associated with technological progress pointed to another aspect of the economic interpretation of history.

Whatever may be the methodological importance of such an approach to historical developments, it does not provide a bridge to the understanding of the use which Marx made of his formulation of the materialistic interpretation of history. Convinced of the absolute validity of his analysis, Marx held the "modes of production" entirely responsible for the alleged contradictory forces operating within society, since the antagonisms which he attributed to that sphere were bound to have their exact counterpart in analogous contradictions inherent in the superimposed social order and in the intellectual and moral climates of society. This conception of history eliminated virtually any noticeable influence of human will or autonomous mental activity upon the course of economic, political, or social events. Driven by the impulse of irresistible antagonistic forces, revolutionary individuals were said to emerge at the right time and to achieve through their activities the ends prescribed by the evolutionary processes.

The Scholastics had pointed to possible conflicts between reason and will and had asserted the supremacy of reason. The adherents of nominalistic methods of thought had assigned a subordinate place to reason, and had emphasized the importance of the will for well-being and progress. Armed with the methods of dialectic materialism, Marx and Engels could circumvent a definition of the fundamental relationship between reason and will as effectively as they had circumvented the problems involved in the continuity of time. Reason and will of the human agents of history were completely subordinated to the power of outside forces which were said to operate independently of any human volition, and their influence remained hidden from those who through their actions fulfilled the objectives of the evolutionary processes. So perfect was the reliance which Marx and Engels placed on the validity of their logical procedures that they claimed absolute certainty for the predictions which they derived from their "insight" into the laws underlying the behavior of the capitalist economy.

THE DIALECTIC CONCEPTION OF THE CAPITALIST ECONOMY

In his attempt to discover the true nature of the forces operating within the capitalist economy, Marx availed himself of the method of successive approximation. He started his analysis from a model of "simple reproduction," representing a stationary economy, and subsequently transformed that model into a scheme of "extended reproduction," taking account of the forces which he considered instrumental in creating disequilibrating, disrupting tendencies.

To his stationary model, Marx attributed the essential features of the Ricardian mechanical conception of an economy consisting of exchange values which were kept in equilibrium by the combined effects of the principles of free competition and maximization of profits. In that model the technical coefficients remained unchanged, the lifetime of durable equipment was limited to one period, and no inventories were accumulated. The population was divided into two classes, employers and workers, and the economy into two sectors, one engaged in the production of capital goods and the other in the production of consumption goods.[22] Moreover, the Ricardian definition of exchange values in terms of units of labor embodied, or, as Marx said, "crystallized," in the commodities produced by independent employers for "social use" was fundamental to the conception of that economy. The expression "commodity" played a significant role in the Marxian terminology; Marx asserted that "economic" values, as determined by labor costs, were associated only with the production of commodities for purposes of exchange. In his *critique of the Gotha Program* addressed in 1875 to the German Social Democratic party, he stated that in the cooperative society of the future individual labor would exist only as a component of total labor and would cease to determine values. The interpretation of that cryptic language has been the object of various discussions by bolshevist economists.

Within the framework of the Ricardian doctrine the labor cost theory had served the purpose of measuring values and establishing equivalence between the objects of exchanges. Marx, however, transformed the theory into an instrument for demonstrating the operation of antagonistic forces within the capitalist economy. Ignoring the hypothetical elements implied in the Ricardian theory, Marx emphasized the Scholastic concept of "substance" in defense of his proposition that two commodities, equal in exchange value, could have nothing in common but identical amounts of "socially necessary" embodied labor, that not a single atom of use value contributed to their equivalence. Marx acknowledged the influence of Scholastic reasoning on his labor cost theory in a passage of *Kapital* in which he alluded to the Aristotelian dictum that there could be no exchange without equation (equivalence) and no equation without commensurability. "Socially necessary labor," as understood by Marx, was a sort of abstract labor from which all differences between the many kinds of productive activity had been eliminated. "Abstract labor," he argued, had come into existence only in the highly developed commodity-producing capitalist society in which the kind of work performed by the individual worker had become irrelevant to him. The concept of "abstract" labor conceived of as the common substance of all commodities was another cryptic concept the meaning of which was discussed animatedly by late bolshevist economists.

For the sake of consistency Marx felt obliged to ascribe use value only, and no exchange value, to goods such as land which were not produced by labor. He qualified the prices of such goods as "irrational." Various other difficulties involved in the use of the labor cost theory were met by Marx with equally problematic devices. Several bookshelves could probably be filled with treatises in which the Marxian labor cost theory and the inferences drawn from it were discussed and criticized. Most effective were the attacks of adherents of the marginal utility doctrine. Vilfiedo Pareto emphasized the ambiguity of the Marxian phraseology and the contradictions between the presentation of the value theory in volume 1 of Marx's *Kapital* and the restrictions placed on the applicability of that theory in volume 3. Eugen Böhm-Bawerk demonstrated the errors involved in the reasoning which held "equivalence" prerequisite to the performance of exchanges. A recent edition of Böhm-Bawerk's essay was enlarged by the translation of a reply to Böhm-Bawerk's criticism published by the "Neomarxist" Rudolf Hilferding in 1904. Hilferding elaborated the difference between the methodological approach adopted by Böhm-Bawerk and Marxian dialectics. There was no bridge between the Marxian belief in "objective evolutionary laws" and the substance concept of goods on the one hand and Böhm-Bawerk's hypothetical approach to economic analysis on the other.[23]

In his treatment of the problem of how to reduce the infinite variety of labor of different types to a uniform standard, Marx was no more successful than Adam Smith and David Ricardo had been. He referred to a "social process" going on behind the backs of producers, and ignored the obvious fact that the "customary rules" of the market which are instrumental in adjusting to each other the wage levels of the different kinds of workers reflect conditions of demand and supply and do not provide a basis for the establishment of a uniform standard unit of "abstract labor."[24] Another problem which Marx was unable to solve turned on increases in the exchange value of commodities which result from the lapse of time or from carrying charges accrued in the course of productive processes. With doubtful dialectic procedures Marx attempted to show that commodities could be sold at prices which did not correspond to their values. Marx dealt with that problem in some notes which were published in the third volume of *Kapital*. Subsequently it was clearly formulated and discussed in three articles published in 1906 and 1907 by L. von Bortkiewicz.[25]

Adoption of the definition of exchange values in terms of "embodied labor" implied that the influence of demand on the determination of values could be neglected. Marx did take account of demand insofar as he spoke of commodities having "no value" because they had been produced in excess of the demand of the market. Also, he admitted that effective demand was a determinant factor in the formation of monopoly prices and a main force in influencing the proportion of social labor which was allocated at a given time to a given sector of production. But for commodities produced under competitive conditions embodied labor was the source of exchange value. The importance ascribed to embodied labor as the source of exchange values was in line with the fundamental proposition of Marxian dialectics: that in the history of society the modes of exchanging products are regulated by the modes of producing them and that the modes of production are determined by the relationships between the main classes of the population. As distinct from the Ricardian hypothetical concept of exchange values, the Marxian value concept was designed to reveal the inner "hidden mechanism" of the capitalist economy and to provide a powerful instrument of dialectic reasoning. With this purpose in mind Marx started his analysis of the distributive processes from the Scholastic idea that the equivalence of what was given and what was taken was basic to all exchange transactions occurring in the markets. He argued that, in accordance with the labor cost theory, the value of products represented the sum total of the exchange values of capital goods (according to the labor embodied in them) used up in the productive process plus the additional exchange values created by labor in that process. Since all values were created by labor, the existence of incomes other than workers' wages, according to Marx, could only be accounted for by the fact that substantial parts of these values were withheld by the employers. Thus, Marx arrived at a definition of the concept of "surplus value" as the difference between the values produced by labor and the payment for "labor power," the payment for the abstract socially necessary labor needed for the maintenance of the worker. He could initiate his dialectic analysis of the distributive processes by splitting up the exchange value of commodities into two distinct parts: the payment for labor power (real wages) and the surplus value (profits) withheld by the employers.

It is doubtful whether there was any room for surplus values in the Marxian scheme of "simple reproduction," since in a stationary economy of the Ricardian type free competition was likely to reduce to zero any difference between costs and prices. Nevertheless, the surplus value theorem was hailed by Engels as the most epoch-making achievement of the Marxian doctrine. In the British Museum, Marx studied with great zeal the works of English and French economists in search of theories which had availed themselves of the concept of "plus value." He regarded Sir William Petty, who had initiated the labor cost theory of value, as the founder of economics and praised David Ricardo for having "finally reduced value and surplus values to labor in the actual process of production," for having conceived of interest as a portion of profit and rent as a "surplus above the average profit."[26] In his extended discussions of the labor market of the capitalist society, Marx repeatedly emphasized the strictly historical aspects of that market and asserted that, but for the capitalist order, labor would have only use value for the workers, and no exchange value.

The theory of labor power implied that the real wages received by the workers were equivalent to the costs involved in producing and maintaining the potential labor force. Hence, in spite of his violent attacks on the capitalist "exploiters" of labor, Marx never proclaimed—as did some Ricardian Socialists—a right of the workers to the full value of their products. Recognition of a "natural individual right" would have been incompatible with his dialectic method.

Having thus transformed the concept of the exchange value of commodities into a dichotomy, Marx used the concept of surplus value to derive from the employers' profits all incomes of the capitalist economy which were not earned by labor. He defined Ricardian rent as a historical category of income which was due to surplus profits not eliminated through competitive processes because of the scarcity of land as a non-reproducible element of production. To the landowners he attributed a monopolistic position which enabled them to impose a tax on any new capital investments applied to untilled or unleased soil. Hence, like Ricardo, he regarded land rent as a market phenomenon, but he had no use for the law of diminishing returns and other ingredients of the Ricardian theory of rent.

The Ricardian conception of interest on money provided Marx with a framework for making the receipt of income of that type dependent on the existence of profits. Marx did not attach particular importance to the rate of interest; he attributed the determination of that rate to arbitrary decisions of the banking authorities. His monetary views were influenced by a rigid commodity theory of money. Redeemable banknotes fulfilled the function of placing additional circulating capital needed for "reproductive" purposes at the disposal of the employers, and he insisted that the issuance of such notes was strictly determined by the requirements of commercial transactions. He believed that the quantity of the circulating means of payment was automatically adjusted to the volume of exchange values through processes of hoarding and dishoarding. There was no room in Marxian economics for problems connected with the existence of inconvertible paper currencies.

Marx used the term *money fetishism* to indicate his deeply rooted belief that the "veil of money" transformed social relations into qualities of things. He characterized *capitalist fetishism* as the view that, in order to account for the existence of interest on money, a kind of earning capacity was ascribed to money. Occasionally Marx spoke of the life process of society, which does not strip off its "mystical veil" until the process of "material production" is regulated by freely associated people in accordance with settled plans.

The analysis of the schemata of "extended reproduction" was designed to go beyond "simple reproduction" and show the operation of antagonistic forces within the economy and the disruptive effects especially of the use made of surplus values by employers. The method of successive approximation, as used by Marx, was open to a very serious objection. The stationary economy which provided the starting point for the Marxian analysis was a Ricardian fiction, a mechanism which ceased to function when subject to disproportionate changes of its constituent parts, as was done by the schemata of extended reproduction. The inevitable breakdown of a mechanism exposed to treatment of that type was easy to demonstrate since "mechanics assumes constancy in its ultimates."[27] Hence, the validity of any conclusions which Marx drew from his analysis of the schemes of extended reproductions as to the behavior of the actual capitalist economy depended on the additional demonstration that the Ricardian fiction provided a correct interpretation of that behavior. Marx appears to have been aware of the fundamental weakness of his method of successive approximation, since his discussions (published in the two later volumes of *Kapital*) turned largely on the question of why the capitalist economy had effectively resisted the operation of the disruptive forces. Marx distinguished "constant" capital, invested in materials, tools, and other productive factors, from "variable" capital, or real wages paid to the workers, and he defined the "degree of exploitation" as the ratio of the surplus value withheld by the employer to the variable capital.[28] Marx applied the term *organic composition of capital* to the relation between constant capital and the sum total of constant and variable capital. As used in this connection, the term *capital*, regarded as a historical category, exclusively covered instruments of "economic exploitation" owned by employers. Tools owned by workers were not "capital."

The "organic composition of capital" was held to be modified by any changes which affected the relation between investments and the wage bill, above all by the introduction of labor-saving devices and their alleged effects on the productive process. From an analysis of these effects Marx derived "capitalism's own law of population," according to which continued pressure on the wage level and maintenance of wages at a subsistence standard were brought about by the displacement of workers through labor-saving devices and the existence of an "industrial reserve army" composed of idle workers. He scoffed at the Malthusian population theory, which claimed to be generally applicable and could not be transformed into a "historical" law the validity of which was restricted to the capitalist economy.

Even more important for the Marxian doctrine was the connection which Marx established between the organic composition of capital and one of the fundamental antagonisms which he attributed to the functioning of the capitalist economy: the tendency of profits to fall. Ricardo had related the existence of such a tendency to the effects of the diminishing returns of the soil, hence, to an empirical law. According to the Marxian interpretation of the labor cost theory, however, the rate of profit was bound to be reduced by any reduction of the relation of the wage bill to the total capital employed in the enterprise. According to Marx, continuous displacement of variable by constant capital was forced upon employers through relentless competition, which caused them to increase by all means the total volume of their production in order to make up through larger sales the losses experienced in the declining rate of profit. In the light of these considerations the investment policy of the employers appeared to be hopelessly irrational; investments involving technical improvements were shown to lead to declines in the rate of profits on the one hand and to reductions of the total wage bill on the other. Consequently, as a result of declining purchasing power on the part of the workers, there would be shrinkages of the very markets which were expected to absorb the products of the additional capital investments. Critics of the Marxian analysis have raised the question of whether in an economy in which all values were said to be reduced to their "labor costs" sizable profits could be made at all. Other critics have observed that additional investments were likely to lead to increases in the productivity of labor, hence—in accordance with the labor cost theory of value—to higher profits per hour of work than before. Marx used the schemata of extended reproduction to illustrate the results of these theoretical considerations. Various mathematical errors which rendered these calculations rather meaningless were criticized by L. von Bortkiewicz.[30]

Elaborating the dismal consequences of the irrational behavior of capitalist employers, Marx established another fundamental dialectic law underlying the development of the capitalist economy, the "law of increasing accumulation and concentration of capital." That law was said to find its expression in the continued displacement of weak firms by large concerns, best equipped for waging competitive struggles. For Marx, this law was responsible for the glaring contradictions which he found to exist between the "individualistic" appropriation of incomes in the distributive process and the "collectivistic" methods of production.

Marx contrasted the law of "capital accumulation" with the law of "accumulation of misery," according to which an ever-widening gap developed between the share of labor in the national dividend and the share of the property-owning classes. Inasmuch as the wage statistics of practically all industrialized countries showed continuous improvements in the standard of living of industrial workers, later Marxist authors resorted to the problematic argument that these wage increases had been achieved through increasing exploitation of labor in colonial territories. In the history of the English industrial revolution, Marx found ample material to support his contention that the size of the proletariat was continuously swelled by the progressive elimination of artisans and small peasants from participation in productive processes.

Marx admitted, as Ricardo had done, that price reductions, brought about by the application of mechanical devices, could stimulate the accumulation of new capital and thus create new employment opportunities. But he insisted that the demand for labor would increase at a lower rate than the demand for constant capital, and that, consequently, the "organic composition of capital" would tend to be intensified.[31]

The belief of convinced Marxists in the logical consistency of their doctrine was exposed to a serious test in the course of the extended discussions of the so-called "riddle of the average rate of profit." According to Marxian labor cost theory, the rate of profit was expected to vary with the "organic composition of capital" and to decline when "variable capital" (wages) were replaced by constant capital. However, it was obvious that the rates of profits were, to a high degree, equalized among enterprises of many types regardless of whether the wage bill occupied a large or small part of the costs of production. The problems of how to explain this behavior of the rate of profit in the light of Marxian doctrine attracted the interest of quite a number of authors prior to the publication, in 1894, of the third volume of *Kapital*, in which Engels published the "solution" of the riddle as envisaged by Marx himself. Among the outstanding authors who participated in these prepublication discussions were Wilhelm Lexis, Eugen Böhm-Bawerk, Achille Loria, J. Wolf, Konrad Schmidt, Paul Lafargue, and A. Graziani. That "solution" amounted to a virtual abandonment not only of the principles of the Marxian profit theory but also implicitly of the rigid labor coat theory of value, since Marx admitted that the profit of the individual employer was not determined by the "organic composition" of his own capital but by his share in the total volume of surplus values produced in the economic system as a whole, as defined by the proportion between his capital outlays and total capital outlays. Marx attributed the formation of the "average rate of profit," which entered into the "prices of production" (the "natural" prices in the sense of the Ricardian term), to the intensification of capitalist competition.[32]

The logical validity of that "solution" was, of course, open to the objection that Marx had availed himself of dialectic procedures in ascribing reality to purely mathematical magnitudes such as the sum total of investments, averages, and the like, and in ascribing to such magnitudes the capacity to influence the actual behavior of individual prices and profits.[33]

More recent attempts to justify the Marxian theory of profits did not contribute new considerations to well-established conclusions. The Marxian profit theory appears to have been included among the tenets of bolshevist economic doctrine. In a paper submitted in 1946 to the Learned Council of the Institute of Economics of the Academy of Sciences of the U.S.S.R., S. G. Strumlin argued that competition among capitalists works through prices and results in an automatic redistribution of profits, alienated from labor, in favor of the most powerful capitalists. Hence, he concluded that the products of those branches of industry which have a lower capital intensity are made cheaper at the expense of branches with more advanced techniques of production. According to Strumlin, the development of the most advanced branches of industry is thus retarded in capitalist countries.[34] Once it was admitted that, under the rule of the average rate of profit, such commodities, whose production required relatively large volumes of constant capital, are exchanged at prices above their labor costs, and goods produced with a relatively strong participation of variable capital at prices below their labor costs, the labor cost theory was deprived of any exact meaning; it was transformed into a cost production theory, which included among its costs certain elements not connected with amounts of labor directly or indirectly spent by the employer in the productive processes. According to the teachings of the bolshevist economists, only the total of the prices of all commodities must conform to the sum of their exchange values expressed in labor costs; individual prices may deviate from the labor costs.[35] Under these circumstances many Marxists were inclined to question the fundamental importance of the labor cost theory for the Marxian doctrine.

THE BREAKDOWN THEORY

According to the Marxian conception of the capitalist society, society was ruled by the "law of heterogeneity of aims"; it was a spontaneous, anarchical, contradictory collectivity of formally independent producers who were nevertheless "objectively" connected with each other. The "blind" law of value, acting through fluctuating prices, was termed the "law of motion" of that society.

On closer analysis, all fundamental conceptions of the Marxian doctrine (value, capital, class, economy, labor, and the like) can be shown to be split by dichotomic procedures. The exchange value of every commodity was divided into wages and surplus value, capital into constant and variable capital, total population into a class of employer-Capitalists and a class of workers, labor into employed hands and the industrial reserve army, the sphere of production into a sector dealing with the production of capital goods and another engaged in the production of consumer goods, the aggregate of all countries participating in international trade into a sphere of capitalist production and a "non-capitalist space," and so on. Each of these pairs of opposites was said to reflect the operation of antagonistic forces. The analysis of the combined effects of these forces was designed to demonstrate that the accumulation and concentration of capital were rapidly advancing and that the declining rates of profit tended to reach a level at which the operation of the capitalist economy was bound to be arrested.

These antagonisms appeared to find their fullest and most articulate expression in the ever-recurrent crises and depressions. Marx and Engels vied with each other in depicting with vivid colors the irrational behavior of capitalist employers during boom periods and the ensuing inevitable crash. In an often-quoted passage Engels characterized crises as phases in which methods of production revolted against methods of marketing and productive forces revolted against the methods of production which they had outgrown.[36]

But although Marx was convinced that the recurrent crises and depressions were important symptoms of the advancing disintegration of the capitalist economy, he failed to find among the elements of his doctrine the equipment needed to develop a consistent theory to account for the ever-renewed upswing following upon each depression period. That gap in Marx's doctrine cannot be explained on the ground that Marx did not deal with the analysis of short-run phenomena.[37]

Earlier critics of the capitalist order, especially J.C.L.S. Simonde de Sismondi and Johann Karl Rodbertus, had discussed the "anarchic" character of the capitalist economy in which masses of goods, far in excess of the purchasing power of the working classes, were produced by employers guided exclusively by the profit motive. They considered "overproduction" of that type responsible for the crises, and this explanation became an important armament in the arsenal of socialist authors. Marx attacked the "planless" capitalist production with a violence which could hardly be surpassed, but he was rather careful in examining the factors which could be connected with the course of business fluctuations. Underconsumption by the working classes was not among these factors.

In his extensive and penetrating analysis of the financial aspects of the capitalist economy, Marx took account of the substantial credits granted by the banks for financing the boom and suggested that these credits were largely supplied out of deposits of idle money held by industrialists and traders. In various passages of volume 2 of *Kapital,* he also discussed the effects of an increased supply of monetary metals on the expansion of production. To "artificial credit" he ascribed contributory effects on accelerated expansion of production and increased exploitation and boom, followed by a collapse of the artificial credit structure, crisis, and unemployment. But he characterized as a myth the belief in the productive power of the credit system, and regarded the expansion and contraction of credit as mere symptoms of the periodic fluctuations of industrial activity.[38]

No significant elements of dialectic reasoning were involved in these discussions, which centered on the idea that the accumulation of monetary capital proceeded under conditions which differed from those underlying the formation of physical capital, and that there did not exist any mechanism for coordinating the movements of the monetary magnitudes and the utilization of the physical factors. Furthermore, Marx only occasionally distinguished Capitalists and employers as separate economic categories, since, according to his general theory, neither exchange values nor prices could be perceptibly affected by credit operations. Considerations of this type, though helpful in explaining certain features of prosperity periods, did not account for the periodical recurrence of crises and for the upswings which signified the termination of the depression periods. Equally nondialectic were certain observations in which Marx connected the length of the depressions with the changes in the duration of fixed capital equipment. From the acceleration of the mechanization of industry, Marx expected a reduction in the life of the enterprises and a corresponding curtailment of the prosperity periods in which violent competition was temporarily arrested. As other factors which were likely to contribute to the shortening of the prosperity periods, he listed the increasing intensity of capital accumulation and the accelerated exhaustion of the available reserves of the labor force in periods of rising employment opportunities.

Some dialectic aspects of doctrine, however, were introduced into other passages of the analysis in which Marx referred to the division of the economy into two sectors: one engaged in the production of consumption goods for the large masses of the working population, the other in the production of capital goods. He connected this split with the existence of two disproportionate streams of income: one consisting of variable capital, the income of the wage earners, the other of surplus values, the income of the capitalist entrepreneurs, largely accumulated for investment purposes. Marx was obviously fascinated by his picture of the Capitalist who was driven by the forces of dialectic materialism to fulfill, with almost mechanical precision, the destructive functions, which were bound to lead to the application of labor-saving devices, a lowering of the exchange value of his products, a declining share of labor in the national dividend, and a falling rate of profits. But Marx realized too well that the so-called underconsumption theories advanced by Sismondi and Rodbertus could, at best, account for the outbreak of the first crisis of the capitalist machinery, but that the upturn had no place in such theories. In some passages of volume 2 of *Kapital* (chapter 20), Marx even admitted that rising wages and rising shares of labor in the current consumable output were characteristic symptoms of the last phases of prosperity periods.[39] Especially in his discussions with German Socialists, he emphasized that the existence of large disproportions between the volumes of production and the corresponding purchasing power of the working classes was not sufficient to explain the recurrent nature of crises and depressions.

It was obvious that Marx perfectly realized the difficulties involved in his attempts to reconcile his conception of the capitalist economy with the fluctuating behavior of business activity, especially with the characteristic aspects of the upturn at the end of the depression. Fluctuations of that type could be explained only when recourse was had to flexible factors. Such a factor appeared to be the rate of profit, the "fundamental premise and driving force of capital accumulation." Hence, in contrast to the Ricardian long-range outlook on the tendency of the rate of profit to fall, Marx emphasized the flexibility of that rate. He interpreted crises and depressions as processes in the course of which the fall in the rate of profits was suspended, and increases in that rate were supported on the one hand by depreciation of the capital invested in overexpanded enterprises and on the other hand by wage reductions imposed upon the workers under the pressure of increasing unemployment. In addition, Marx listed other factors which in his view contributed toward supporting the level of the profit rate, namely, cheapening of raw materials and other constituent elements of constant capital, relative overpopulation, foreign trade, and increases in capital stocks.[40] At this juncture the "industrial reserve army" played an important role in the Marxian analysis. It represented the instrument for transforming the Ricardian conception of technological unemployment into the element of a dialectical process by splitting up labor into employed and idle workers. The army of idle workers had to fulfill the function of reducing wages to a sort of subsistence level whenever prosperous business conditions had resulted in increasing the share of labor in the national dividend.

Broadly speaking, it can perhaps be stated that the Marxian business cycle analysis started from emphasizing the increases in productive activity which were brought about by technical and managerial improvements introduced under the pressure of violent competition; that it emphasized capital accumulation as an important factor in promoting the expansion of business activity and pointed to reductions in the rate of profits, progressive absorption of the industrial reserve army and increasing overproduction as the factors responsible for the downturn. It is very doubtful whether the downturn could be explained in the light of Marxian analysis, which pointed to reductions in the rate of capital accumulation, full employment of the labor force, and wage increases as significant features of the prosperity period. Their combined effects were likely to establish a sort of equilibrium in the demand for and the supply of wage goods, and thus to diminish the danger of overproduction. No explanation was offered for the contention that such a situation was bound to lead to a crisis.[41] Among the conditions which prepared the upturn, Marx listed restrictions of production, depreciation of the capital invested in overexpanded enterprises, and wage reductions leading to improved profit expectations.

Since a business cycle analysis of that type did not provide a reliable basis for the prediction that the capitalist machinery was faced with an inevitable breakdown, Marx ignored the cyclical movements of business activity in his imaginary schemata of extended reproduction which were designed to illustrate the effects of disproportionate expansions of capital investments applied to the different sectors of the economy. If Marx has been credited with having been the first author to follow François Quesnay in devising a mathematical model of the economy, that merit has been impaired by his questionable use of mathematical procedures.

THE CLASS STRUGGLE

The dichotomies which Marx introduced in order to show the antagonism inherent in the capitalist economy had their counterpart in the social sphere, which Marx split up into the class of capitalist employers and the class of exploited workers. The distinction between two antagonistic classes had played a role in the teachings of Saint-Simon and in the writings of some conservative historians of the French Restoration period, such as François Guizot (1787–1874), François Mignet, and Augustin Thierry (1795–1856). It had received particular emphasis in the analysis by Lorenz von Stein (1815–1890) of contemporary French social conditions.[42] But for the Marxian analysis, the class struggle had an importance which fundamentally differed from that attributed to it by other authors. It may be pointed out that Marx and Engels believed that the main task of any scientific analysis was to serve practical purposes. The political implications of the doctrine of class struggle were quite obvious. The historical mission which Marx assigned to the struggle can well be used to illustrate some characteristic features of Marxian methodology, which required that the fundamental concepts underlying dialectic reasoning be formed by abstraction from observation and experience, that they be split up into apparently antagonistic subconcepts, and that these subconcepts, conceived of as real entities, be subjected to evolutionary changes resulting from ever-intensified antagonisms.

In accordance with the Platonic principle that wherever there is change there must be something that remains constant, Marx and Engels elevated the class struggle to a sort of cosmic driving force in the evolutionary processes of history, and developed a dialectic scheme in which, under gradually changing forms, two antagonistic groups of society, termed classes, were engaged in a perennial fight marked by predetermined developments and a final inevitable solution. That fight was said to have proceeded through centuries, although unnoticed by the members of the conflicting groups. When analyzed within the framework of the materialistic interpretation of history, the ruling class, characterized by the ownership of the means of production, had endeavored to justify the existing pattern of social relationships in each of the successive stages of economic developments, each period having been terminated by revolutionary changes of the political and social conditions when the methods of distribution became incompatible with the "modes of production."

This general schema of the dialectic process underlying the course of history was outlined in the *Communist Manifesto* of 1848, and was alluded to in various passages of the writings of Marx and Engels. According to these rather hazy indications, the class struggle had been waged in successive periods, sometimes openly, sometimes under cover, between free men and slaves, patricians and plebeians, barons and serfs, guild masters and journeymen—in a word, between oppressors and oppressed. Neither the two originators of the doctrine of class struggle nor their followers provided a consistent analysis of the various phases of that fundamental conflict. Especially, the question of how the transition between the successive phases had taken place did not receive a satisfactory answer. Also, no serious attempts have been made to show that a similar interpretation of economic and social developments is applicable to the Far East and other "underdeveloped" regions. Finally, according to the methods of nominalist reasoning, "classes" are abstractions formed in the mind of an observer on the basis of freely selected (more or less arbitrary) characteristics. No reality can be attached to such conceptions, and the proposition that a struggle has been in progress between these classes over centuries and has been instrumental in transforming them is to be regarded as a highly questionable metaphysical statement. It is even doubtful whether the "struggle of classes" can provide a sound basis for sociological analysis when transformed into a hypothetical "heuristic" principle.

As was required by his dialectic method, Marx formulated all his social, economic, and political concepts as strictly historical categories associated with, and determined by, the division of society into two classes.[43] He regarded all political, social, and moral institutions as instruments of oppression, designed to safeguard the interests of the ruling propertied classes and to assure the subservience of the exploited social groups. Within the framework of Marxian philosophy, the existence of the state as a historical institution was inextricably associated with the existence of private ownership of the means of production and the division of society into classes. Engels characterized the state as an outgrowth of society which had become necessary in order to prevent irreconcilable contradictions, the classes with conflicting economic interests, from annihilating themselves in useless civil wars.[44]

As mentioned above, Marx analyzed in the three volumes of *Kapital* only those aspects of the class struggle which he attributed to capitalist society. According to his doctrine, the capitalist phase of the struggle was preparatory to the termination of the cosmic conflict and to the advent of the classless society. The meaning which could be attached to the concept of the "classless society" has been shrouded in cryptic passages. One such passage says that, consequent upon the abolition of the private ownership of the means of production, the laws of dialectic materialism would cease to operate and men would gain full freedom to control the forces of nature. Predictions of that type have provided a fertile field for the speculations of bolshevist philosophers.

In order to adjust the traditional distinction of three main classes of the population to the dialectic dichotomy, Marx assimilated the interests of the landowners to those of the capitalist exploiters of the working classes, on the ground that with advancing capitalism the economic interests of all owners of means of production had become increasingly homogeneous, while no other significant classes had developed. An unfinished Marxian manuscript published at the end of the third volume of *Kapital* broke off in a chapter dealing with the concept of classes. This concept eventually became the object of prolonged discussions.[45]

Unconscious ties, Marx asserted, had been produced by common class interests; they were the strongest that could be imagined, far stronger than any other created by religious creeds or political sentiments. Marx attributed to the subconscious mind the role of a mysterious agent operating under the pressure of dialectic forces. Employers were said to pursue objectives which were bound to lead to their own destruction. Workers were said to participate in the class struggle without being aware of it. To their untrained minds Marx ascribed the capacity of grasping the meaning of the abstruse dialectic processes which employers, blinded by their proprietary interests, were unable to understand. The question of how far the deterministic features of the materialistic interpretation of history are compatible with the belief in the freedom of the will has been discussed by Georgi Plekhanov (1857–1918) and other Marxian philosophers.[46]

From the solidarity of the proletarian class interests, Marx expected the fulfillment of his predictions, which he expressed as, "Realization of the means of production and socialization of labor reach a point at which they become incompatible with the capitalist integument. This integument bursts. The knell of capitalist private property sounds. The expropriators are expropriated."[47]

But various interpreters of the Marxian doctrine have been puzzled by the question of how to reconcile the radical revolutionary aspects of that doctrine with its deterministic features. This question has played a significant role in the prolonged discussions of the strategies to be pursued by the European trade unions and the "social democratic" parties. Within the context of the Marxian doctrine, trade unions were primarily instruments of the class struggle. They could not be credited with the power of securing increases in real wages or enforcing improvements of working conditions. Such a conception of workers' organizations was incompatible with the doctrine of the accumulation of misery among the working classes.

The advocates of revolutionary social action were faced with the argument that it was advisable to wait for the inevitable collapse of the capitalist order instead of assuming the risks involved in revolutionary upheavals. This dilatory attitude was effectively supported by the consideration that Marxian doctrine did not provide any indications of how the communist society of the future was to be organized and how the resistance on the part of many "reactionary" elements was to be met without endangering general economic welfare. It was also increasingly obvious that the "international solidarity of the proletariat" could hardly be expected to play an effective role in the fight against the capitalist order. Hence, virtually all interpretations of the class struggle petered out in inconclusive statements.

It may be mentioned in passing that a clue to an entirely different interpretation of the "class struggle" could be found in the observation of the economic historian Richard H. Tawney that for a thousand years the social problem of Europe was not the wage earner but the peasant.[48] The Ricardian theory of land rent could provide a trained dialectician with the elements of a doctrine based on the splitting up of society into the antagonistic classes of tillers of the soil and urban dwellers (manufacturers). A deep-seated conflict between the landowners and all other classes of the population resulted, according to Ricardian reasoning, from the tendency of the land rent to enforce a continuous rise of wage costs at the expense of profits. That conflict was shown to be permanent and to be intensified by the irresistible pressure of the increasing population; it could be presented as an antagonism between the forces operating in the market and those operating in the sphere of production, leading to intensified competitive struggles among industrial enterprises and to a gradual displacement of the products of the soil from many previous uses. Changes in the structure of agricultural production could be associated with far-reaching changes in the economic and social organization, and "stages" in a general evolutionary process could be distinguished accordingly. Eventually the ultimate "meaning" of the bolshevist revolution might be found in the forceful subjection of the landed interests to those of the industrial workers. Stalin characterized the divergence of interest which existed between town and country as one of the chief obstacles on the way from "socialism" to "communism."[49] The economic and political history of some satellite countries of Eastern Europe could supply additional proof of the intensity of that antagonism.

A specific aspect of the doctrine of class struggle deserves particular attention because of its methodological implications: the proposition, so strongly emphasized by Marx and Engels, that only the proletarian class can avail itself of the method of dialectic materialism, whereas those who are blinded by their interest in the preservation of the capitalist economy are disqualified for realizing the meaning and the logical power of that method. That procedure of disqualifying certain social groups for the use of a privileged method of reasoning had a counterpart in the national socialist doctrine, which emphasized the ability of the German mind to use intuitive procedures and denied, especially to the "non-Aryans" and Slav peoples, a similar faculty. The reference to a fundamental diversity in methods of thinking was used in both cases to justify a specific universal "mission" of a nation or a social group. Prior to the advent of the Marxist and national socialist philosophies, the justification of similar missions claimed for certain peoples had commonly been derived from acts of divine revelation.

Convinced Marxists were thus provided with a convenient instrument for warding off all criticism of their doctrine advanced by "bourgeois economists," who, affected by "proprietary interests," could not be expected to understand the nature of the evolutionary social processes. That attitude found an additional expression in the violent protest raised by all Marxists against any attempts to translate the fundamental dialectic concepts into terms used by the current "bourgeois" sciences and adjusted to hypothetical methods.

In fact, practically all dialectic terms such as *value, surplus value, profits, rate of profit, modes of production and distribution, superstructure, class,* and the like are subjected to a complete change of meaning when defined in terms of another pattern of thought, hence the difficulties involved in translating treatises based on dialectic reasoning into languages which have grown under the influence of other methods of reasoning and have never experienced, as did the German language, the influence of Hegelian and Marxian dialectics.[50]

The question has been raised why Marx did not write his main work, *Kapital,* in English, although he referred almost exclusively to the development of English economic conditions to illustrate the evolutionary processes underlying the origin and growth of the capitalist economy. The use of the Ricardian economic system as a starting point for his analysis might have been an additional reason for formulating his thoughts in English. But he probably realized very well that this language was adjusted to thinking in terms of assumptions and hypotheses rather than in terms of Aristotelian categories and dialectic contradictions. It was not a "historical accident," as has been suggested by Paul M. Sweezy, that Marxism failed to win a significant following in English-speaking countries. Slogans such as "class struggle" and dialectic terms such as "materialistic interpretation of history" were practically deprived of their ominous meaning when expressed by words not tinged with dialectic connotations.[51]

Ideologies was the term Marx used to denote the manner and content of trends of thought which in his view were fundamentally vitiated by specific—especially proprietary—interests. Prior to Marx, the expression *ideology,* which was French in origin, was used, equally in a disarraying sense, to denote visionary theories. Marx availed himself of that term in the biting attacks which he launched on the leading contemporary Ricardians, whom he called "vulgar economists." It is perhaps worth mentioning that Marx endeavored to justify the adoption of some fundamental propositions of the Ricardian doctrine with the argument that Ricardo wrote in England prior to 1830, during a period in which the class struggle was still latent and, consequently, political economy could "remain a science." For Marx, the group of "vulgar economists" included J. R. McCulloch, Nassau William Senior, John Stuart Mill, and Jean Baptiste Say, all of whom had abandoned the labor cost theory of value as "servants of the interests of capital." In addition, he held their subservience to these interests responsible for the fact that they ascribed to the soil and to capital significant functions in the productive process and ignored the forces which were working within the capitalist economy toward its final disintegration.

To the present day the "ideological argument" has remained a weapon brandished by convinced Marxists, including, of course, bolshevist authors, in discussions with "bourgeois" economists and philosophers. But it has remained an open question why the principle of "ideological determinateness of thinking processes" was applicable only to "bourgeois" economists and not equally to those who defended the interests of the propertyless classes. The analysis of the relationships between "ideologies" and the thinking process has provided a starting point for the so-called sociology of knowledge, especially in the work of Karl Mannheim.

A discussion of world-wide proportions, dealing with economic, sociological, and philosophical problems, has turned on Marx's works, especially the three volumes of the *Kapital.* Not only the general trend of Marxian reasoning but almost all the specific Marxian theorems have been the object of searching scrutiny carried on from the point of view of dialectic, intuitionist, and hypothetical reasoning. It is obvious that in each case the final outcome of studies of this type was decided by the choice of the methods of reasoning used in performing the studies. The glaring deficiencies of the Marxian methods, the inconsistencies and even fallacies implied in the doctrine of dialectic materialism, and the futility of the predictions derived from it were expounded especially by perspicacious authors of nominalist persuasion. In retrospect it can be stated that the establishment of "dictatorships of the proletariat" has nowhere resulted from the breakdown of a highly capitalistic economy in accordance with Marxian theory, but has invariably been brought about by revolutionary political parties representing relatively small groups of population.[52]

On the other hand, there is no doubt that many economists who refused to accept the methodological principles of dialectic materialism and the teachings of the Marxian doctrine were impressed by the conceptions implied in the evolutionary approach to economic analysis and in the formulation of the dynamic aspects of the capitalist order. The ingenious use which Marx made of the economic and sociological effects of the "accumulation" of capital, and its concentration, the connection he established between technological improvements and the changing structure of the economy, the strategic role he assigned to the rate of profit as a determinant economic factor, the broad distinction he drew between the behavior of capital-producing industries and the sector of the economy engaged in the production of consumption goods, his formulation of various aspects of the business fluctuations—these and many other important elements of his analysis pointed to many neglected problems and to the need to open up new avenues of research.

Chapter 17
Versions of Marxism

THE REVISIONIST MOVEMENT

THE RAPID SPREAD of the Marxian doctrine, especially among large groups of the intelligentsia of Central Europe, can hardly be explained unless it is kept in mind that its message strongly appealed to revolutionary groups which associated deep hatred of the capitalistic organization of the economy with an equally deep aversion to the methods of hypothetical reasoning. They were fascinated by the idea of being supplied with a "scientific" demonstration of the contradictions inherent in that economy and of the processes which were bound to lead to the economy of the future.

During the eighties, less than twenty years after the publication of the first volume of *Kapital*, political parties or movements which had accepted the principles of the Marxian doctrine already existed in a number of European countries. In France, one such party, named *Parti Ouvrier,* was headed by Mathieu Basile (pseudonym Jules Guesde (1845–1922). In Spain a similar party was led by Pablo Iglesias. In England H. M. Hyndman was leader of the Social Democratic Federation. Russian Marxism was represented by George V. Plekhanov and P. B. Axelrod. The head of the Austrian Marxists was Viktor Adler (1852–1918). Of minor importance were similar movements which had sprung up in Norway, Switzerland, Sweden, Holland, and Belgium. In Germany, more than in any other country, Marxism provided the spiritual incentives to a widespread and highly effective organization of the working classes under the leadership of W. Liebknecht and Karl Kautsky. The political program of the Social Democratic party adopted in 1891 at the Congress of Erfurt reflected some essential principles of the Marxist creed: the belief in class struggle and the accumulation of capital, and the theorem of the progressive deterioration of the conditions of the working classes. Centralized community—ownership of all means of production in a "classless" society—was hailed as the ultimate goal of the socialist movement. But no reference was made to methods of violent revolutionary upheavals, and the program included a considerable number of positive measures of labor legislation and social reform to be attained through parliamentary action.

Toward the end of the nineteenth century, however, the Marxian doctrine was faced with a danger that is likely to threaten the spread of all teachings which claim to reveal absolute and universal truth. Such teachings cannot fail to be the object of divergent interpretations, and fights between conflicting schools are bound to arise over the exact meaning to be attached to certain fundamental tenets. The interpretation of Marxism was complicated by the fact that the methods of dialectic materialism had never been clearly formulated but were shrouded by an ambiguous phraseology, and it was quite obvious that the Marxian predictions were not borne out by the actual course of events. Progressive accumulation of capital was accompanied by the spread of the ownership of large concerns among many small stockholders, no concentration of ownership appeared to have occurred in the sphere of agriculture, and small business was not losing ground, though its character changed. Above all, working conditions experienced significant improvements and real wages were rising.

Arguments of that type found a rallying point in the so-called revisionist movements, which recruited adherents especially among the leaders of the German trade unions. They refused to accept the Marxian fundamentally mechanistic conception of the economy, the dialectic features of the doctrine and the belief in the existence of contradictions inherent in the economy. They emphasized that free competition, which had been fundamental to the Marxian analysis of the capitalist machinery, had been replaced in large sectors of the economy by employers' associations (cartels and the like) which had created monopolistic situations. They pointed to the increasing importance of collective bargaining as a method of regulating wages and working conditions, and to substantial social reforms which had been achieved through political action.

The revisionist arguments were effectively presented by Eduard Bernstein. During several years of exile in London, Bernstein had been strongly influenced by the thinking of the Fabians, who convinced him that the Marxian concept of value was untenable and was to be replaced by a value concept derived from marginal utility analysis. In addition, Bernstein discarded the dialectic features of Marxism and defended the principles of socialism primarily with ethical considerations. He attributed the final advent of the socialist society to vaguely defined "evolutionary" processes. His wage theory was adjusted to the objectives of trade union policy, since he ascribed to positions of "social power" a predominant influence on the wage level.[1]

The moderate Socialists who entertained such views were not interested in the dialectical problems that were animatedly discussed in the periodicals issued by the "orthodox Marxists" nor in the problems connected with the alleged tendency of the rate of profits to fall, with the effects of capital accumulation, or with the interpretation of the Marxian schemes of extended reproduction. Rather, the discussions between the Revisionists and their Marxist adversaries turned on the question of whether Marx had adjusted his doctrine to a preconceived thesis,[2] and on the applicability to agriculture of the Marxian law of the progressive concentration of capital. The Marxist proposition, defended by Karl Kautsky, was that the monopolistic position of the owners of the soil provided the basis for the receipt of "absolute rents" and that agriculture, not less than industry, was subjected to the law of concentration of production. Among the Marxists who participated in these discussions was Vladimir Ilyich (Nikolai) Lenin.[3]

The Revisionists were obviously quite successful in providing the large masses of the German workers with an interpretation of the socialist creed which opened the prospect of a gradual transformation of the capitalist society through vaguely defined "evolutionary" processes. The dialectic features of the Marxian doctrine were gradually eliminated from the official program of the Social Democratic party and replaced by a voluntaristic philosophy which was strongly influenced by the reasoning of the German historical school. "Classes" were divested of their fundamentally antagonistic aspects and re-defined as integrated constituent elements of the "nation." The ideas covered by the slogan "evolutionary socialism" were especially applied to the relationships of the state to industry, business, and labor. Thus, the party program was adjusted to the leading principles of "state socialism" as outlined in the writing of Johann Karl Rodbertus.[4]

The methods used in analyzing the transformation of the capitalist economy were similar to those adopted by the historical school, although the terminology was reminis-cent of the Marxian phraseology. A system of planned regulation of production and markets was said to emerge owing to the policies of cartels, trusts, combines, and financial interlockings. The growing influence of organized labor on industrial manage-ment and government was regarded as an initial step toward the final establishment of an "industrial democracy," in which the representatives of the workers would be called upon to participate in the management at least of the large industrial corporations. Increas-ing government supervision of industry and trade, expansion of labor legislation, and schemes of social insurance were regarded as additional symptoms of that evolutionary process.[5] Views of that type were adopted by many leading socialist parties of Central and Southern Europe. Intensified nationalistic movements provided an effective counter-weight to the Marxian idea of the international solidarity of the proletariat.[6]

In France the socialist movement was rent by conflicting tendencies.[7] The most outstanding leader of French moderate socialism was Jean Jaurès (1859–1914). Through gradual improvement of the conditions of the working classes he and his followers expected eventually to achieve fundamental transformations of the capitalist economy. The radical counterpart of that group—which cooperated with the socialist trade unions— was the syndicalist movement, which took a good deal of its inspiration from Georges Sorel (1847–1922).[8] The advocates of syndicalist workers' organizations rejected any affiliation with political parties in order to avoid any adjustment of their radical program to changing political conditions. They believed that the objectives of "true Marxism" consisted exclusively in concentrating on class struggle as the decisive evolutionary factor, and they supplemented the deterministic features of Marxian dialectics with a voluntaristic philosophy influenced by the concept of *élan vital*, or "vital energy," propounded by Henri Bergson (1859–1941).[9] They considered strikes among the most effective instruments of inciting and maintaining the revolutionary spirit among the work-ing classes.

The social philosophy of the Revisionists required an explanation of crises and depressions which differed substantially from the role attributed to them in the Marxian scheme of economic cataclysms. A theory that met these requirements, and yet preserved some characteristic elements of the Marxian analysis, was supplied by the Russian Michael Tugan-Baranowsky, who abandoned the labor cost theory in favor of the margin-al utility approach to the value concept and eliminated from his explanation of the fluctuating behavior of business activity any reference to changes in the rate of profit.[10] But he adopted the Marxian belief in the planlessness of the capitalist economy and concentrated his analysis on processes of production, especially on the proposition that during the expansion of business activity increases in the production of capital goods tended to outrun corresponding increases in the production of goods of consumption. He connected the collapse of the boom partly with an exhaustion of the loanable funds available for investment purposes and partly with the disproportionate development of the various branches of the economy, and followed Marx in eliminating from his analysis any reference to the lack of purchasing power of the working classes. As a remedy he recommended controlling the expansion of production through administrative devices, especially large-scale monopolies. A similar analysis of crises was advanced by the Russian economist Mentor Bouniatian. In 1908 he published studies in German on the theory and history of economic crises. Like Tugan-Baranowsky, he attributed to the capitalist economy an inherent tendency to overexpand the production of capital goods.[11] The idea to connect business fluctuations with disproportionalities in the expansion of various sectors of the economy rather than underconsumption was taken over by some members of the German historical school. On the other hand, "underconsumption theories" of a rather primitive type were advocated by Konrad Schmidt and Louis B. Boudin.[12]

ORTHODOX MARXISM

The most serious attempts to maintain all the dialectic aspects of the Marxian doctrine in interpreting and developing its characteristic features were made by a group of able Austrian writers and politicians. Karl Renner (1870–1950), Max Adler, Otto Bauer (1881–1938), and Rudolf Hilferding may be mentioned as representative members of that group. Karl Renner, who played an outstanding role in various governments of the Austrian Republic, applied the methods of dialectics to the study of juridical problems; he published these studies under the name of R. Springer. Max Adler dealt extensively with the interpretation of some philosophical aspects of the Marxian doctrine. Some gifted German and Russian adherents of Marxism were equally in the orthodox camp. Strict control of the "orthodoxy" of the Marxists was exercised during the first two decades of the twentieth century by Karl Kautsky, frequently called "the high priest of Marxism."

But the results of the many extensive and penetrating studies made by these authors were rather meager. Convinced as they were that the Marxian teachings represented the deepest source of knowledge, wisdom, and aspiration, they considered it almost blasphemy substantially to modify any important elements of the doctrine; the manipulation of the abstruse concepts and procedures of materialist dialectics placed additional obstacles in the way of free development of thought. The propositions which had been basic to the Marxian analysis of the capitalist economy became increasingly untenable as time went on. Nevertheless, the duties imposed by the rules of orthodoxy required maintenance of practically all tenets of the doctrine.

In this connection, mention may be made of a problematic attempt by Otto Bauer to demonstrate the existence of a causal relation between the expansion of capitalism into less developed areas and the exploitation of labor on the one hand and the political and economic conditions of culturally less advanced nations on the other.[13] Really remarkable, however, was Hilferding's study of the problems connected with the progressive "accumulation and concentration of capital."[14] For example, he elaborated the idea that in the course of that process the large commercial banks had succeeded in gaining increasing control over the management of industrial enterprises and, moreover, that the ownership of such enterprises had frequently been spread among many investors whose main interest consisted in the receipt of dividends.[15] Strict adherence to the principles of the Marxian labor cost theory caused him to apply it even to the explanation of prices under monopolistic conditions. Hilferding attributed the overexpansion of the heavy industries to the investment of the excessive profits they earned. Like Tugan-Baranowsky, he held the disproportionality in the development of the different sectors of the economy responsible for the fluctuating behavior of business activity.

To the changes in the national economies brought about by the concentration of capital, Hilferding juxtaposed corresponding changes in the field of international relationships. He emphasized the increasing importance of international cartels and combines and the successful endeavors of organized national groups to secure definite spheres of interest in international markets. He analyzed the penetration of financial capital into underdeveloped territories and the pressure in favor of expansionist policies exercised on the governments by representatives of that capital. That approach raised various problems which previously had hardly received due attention. But it amounted to an abandonment of the strict determinateness of all phases of an evolutionary process which had been an outstanding characteristic of the Marxian doctrine; moreover, various Marxist categories, such as "capital," "employer," "monopoly," and the like, assumed new features. In spite of his Marxist convictions, Hilferding felt obliged to admit that the progressive concentration of capital in the hands of the banks, accompanied by the establishment of monopolistic control over large markets, was likely to stabilize the functioning of the capitalist economy and thus to postpone the breakdown of the capitalist economy for an indefinite time to come.

Hilferding's interpretation of the increasing control exercised by "finance capital" over productive enterprises was later transformed by Nikolai Lenin (1870–1924) into a sort of Marxist theory according to which a handful of banks had the power to direct all commercial and industrial operations of the capitalist economies.[16] In the United States, Thorstein Veblen took over some of Hilferding's leading ideas in his discussions of absentee ownership, of the conditions of imperial Germany, and such topics. But subsequent investigations such as the Macmillan Report of 1931 in England and the investigations of the Temporary National Economic Committee of 1941 in the United States, led to the conclusion that the role which Hilferding ascribed to the banks was a passing phenomenon and that outside some countries of Central Europe the influence exercised by financial groups was hardly significant.[17]

Other Marxist studies worth mentioning turned on the interpretation of the breakdown theory. In the center of these discussions was the question of whether the ultimate collapse of the capitalist economy would be brought about by the effects of the falling rate of profit or by the lack of markets for the goods produced under the pressure of rapidly accumulating capital. Hence, a theory based on changes in the "organic composition of capital" rivaled a new version of the traditional socialist underconsumption ideas.

Rosa Luxemburg (1870–1919) was one of the most ardent partisans of revolutionary socialism and one of the most convinced adversaries of any "evolutionary" interpretation of Marxism.[18] She insisted upon deriving the logical justification of militant socialism from the dialectic theorems of the accumulation of capital and the accumulation of misery. Luxemburg particularly resented the danger involved in weakening the revolutionary spirit of the workers by the spread of theories that deprived the concept of "capitalist imperialism" of its dialectic features. She regarded the expansion of capitalism into colonies and dependencies as an important contribution to the increasing productivity of capitalistic enterprises. On the arbitrary assumptions that in the sector in which capital goods were produced the rate of accumulation of capital was 50 percent and that the same rate obtained in the sector engaged in the production of consumers' goods, she arrived at the conclusion that a progressive discrepancy was bound to develop between the total value of the consumption goods brought to market and the purchasing power of the masses. As distinct from Karl Marx, who had applied a constant rate to the process of exploitation, Rosa Luxemburg argued that the real wages of the workers remained constant and that, consequently, the share of the workers in the national dividend declined as productivity advanced through technical progress.

In her discussion of the breakdown problem, Luxemburg developed a much-discussed theory of "economic imperialism," which centered on the idea that the capitalist economies had prevented their collapse only by exporting capital and large quantities of otherwise unsaleable commodities into territories not yet included in the sphere of capitalism, territories where industry was still in its infancy and cheap labor was available in large quantities. Unlike Marx, who had practically ignored the problems connected with investments made by capitalist countries in underdeveloped territories, Luxemburg made this type of direct investment the center of her theory. Within the framework of that theory, recovery was regarded as a phase of the business cycle in the course of which investments were made in colonies and dependencies, and new markets were opened in such areas. Moreover, this explanation of prosperity periods could be adjusted perfectly to the materialistic interpretation of history, since it held the struggle over markets responsible for the modern "imperialistic" wars.

But that reformulation of the Marxian business cycle analysis was not only open to the objection that its main support was derived from the problematic "underconsumption" argument; it made also ample use of questionable propositions, such as that the real wages of the workers remained unchanged, that accumulation of capital was tantamount to displacement of workers, that the behavior of the employers was utterly irrational, and the like.[19]

The fundamental weakness of the underconsumption theorem was recognized by the Austrian Marxist Otto Bauer, who turned to changes in the "organic composition of capital" to account for the impending breakdown of the capitalist economy.[20] He started from the Marxian scheme of extended reproduction, and attempted to calculate an index for measuring the displacement of circulating capital (wages) through constant capital (investment) by relating the growth of the machinery and material employed to increase the number of workers. From the progressive intensification of the organic composition of capital, he derived a picture of a steady decline of the rate of profit. Bauer not only made various arbitrary and unfounded assumptions as to the rates of increase of the various economic magnitudes that he used in his calculations, but he also identified increases in the exchange value of the capital, and he made no allowance for temporary recoveries of the rate of profits. The results of these discussions were practically meaningless.[21]

An interesting interlude in the discussion of the nature of "imperalism" as a stage in the development of capitalism was the discovery that imperialist tendencies might not be exclusively characteristic of capitalist powers, but might also affect socialist countries. Karl Renner, who advanced that view, was greatly embarrassed by the lack of international solidarity manifested at the beginning of the world war in 1914 by practically all socialist parties.[22]

THE BOLSHEVIST VERSION OF MARXISM

The vast amount of intellectual effort spent on the task of interpreting and justifying the Marxian doctrine as a theory of "scientific socialism" was hardly commensurate with the effects of these endeavors, which became increasingly hopeless when even "orthodox Marxists" realized that the "evolutionary" development of the capitalist countries failed to confirm the predictions derived from the alleged inherent antagonisms of capitalist economy.

The leaders of the Russian bolshevist movement who apparently endorsed the Marxist doctrine to its full extent were far less interested in the scientific aspects of that doctrine than in its ability to supply powerful support for their social revolutionary objectives. Hence, they did not hesitate to adjust the Marxian teachings to their program of establishing a communist regime in a country in which the development of capitalism was only beginning, but where the existence of a strongly centralized absolutism provided reasonable chances for a continued subordination of the population to the dictates of an autocratic government.

The predilection of Lenin, Trotsky, and many other Russian Socialists for the tortuous reasoning of Marxian dialectics has been the object of varying interpretations.[23] Practically all the Russian revolutionaries were brought up in an intellectual atmosphere dominated by principles of a medieval pattern of thought and permeated by a deep hatred of Western civilization. The outstanding representative of Russian anti-Western political philosophy was Konstantin Petrovich Pobedonostsev (1827–1907), chief procurator of the Holy Synod, or the lay administrative head of the Russian Orthodox Church, between 1880 and 1905. He was highly influential in advising czars Alexander II and Nicholas II on their domestic policies.[24] The Marxian doctrine, in many respects akin to medieval Scholasticism, provided revolutionaries with strong arguments against that civilization and a logical demonstration of an evolutionary process that was bound to lead to the collapse of the capitalist economy and to an impending socialist millennium.[25] But Russia obviously was not one of the countries to which the prediction of the impending collapse was applicable.[26] In order to remedy that aspect of the Marxian doctrine, Lenin, the spiritual head of the bolshevist movement, developed a version of the doctrine which made the establishment of the communist society independent of the degree of capitalist development reached by the economy and independent of the outcome of class struggle. His version started from the considerations that in the capitalist countries the class struggle was far from being waged in accordance with the Marxian ideas, that the trade unions had provided the workers with increasing bargaining power and had become partners to collective agreements, and that the social democratic parties had abandoned any revolutionary activity and adopted a conservative, deterministic philosophy which relied upon the operation of economic and social forces to bring about gradual changes of the capitalist order. Nationalistic sentiments appeared to carry far more weight among the working classes than the feeling of class solidarity to which Marx and Engels had so strongly appealed. Under these circumstances Lenin arrived at the conclusion that the revolutionary forces had to be organized outside the cadres of the proletariat by convinced adversaries of the capitalist regime who had made revolution their profession.

Ideas of that type differed perceptibly from the attitude adopted by other radical political groups such as the *Narodniki* (Populists) and the *Mensheviki*. The Narodniki, who extolled the nationalist feelings of the peasant population but never developed a consistent body of thought, based their vague schemes of economic organization on the belief that principles which were basic to the operation of a socialist economy could be derived from the pattern provided by the organization of primitive agricultural communities of the past.[27] One of the most representative leaders of that movement, Viktor Mikhailovich Chernov (1876–1952), expected that the *obschchina*, the traditional peasant community, would supply the basis for the collective cultivation of the soil, but he was unable to suggest a method of organizing industrial production on collectivist lines.

This "peasant philosophy" was rejected by Lenin and Trotsky, who insisted upon starting the revolutionist movement in the cities since the urban proletariat could be regarded as the proper agent for fulfilling the "economic law of harmonizing productive forces and productive relations."[28] That conception of the urban proletariat was shared by the Menshevikis. But since they represented a Russian counterpart of the German revisionist movement, they were opposed to the adoption of an outright revolutionary program and preferred to wait until the time was ripe for the final overthrow of the capitalist rulers. They placed their reliance on the "spontaneous" activities of the workers, and considered the class struggle with employers far more important than the political fight against the government.[29] These views were violently attacked by Lenin. In an article published in February 1902 he elaborated the idea that nothing but the strengthening of "bourgeois ideologies" among the working classes could be expected to result from the "spontaneity of the labor movement." Left to itself, that movement could at best develop trade union consciousness. Georgi Plekhanov characterized the reliance on the spontaneity of the labor movement as a theoretical fall into sin, as a "new edition of the theory of the hero and the crowd."[30] The task of the socialist party consisted in diverting the labor movement from the spontaneous trade union tendency to revolutionary action.

With this end in view, Lenin developed the political device of forming "front organizations" bearing no party label but serving the purposes of the party. This proposal was designed to counter the Menshevist idea of placing party membership on a broad basis. In defense of the role that he ascribed to the party, he argued that theory and science could find their true application only after political power had been seized by a group whose "dynamic evolutionary reasoning" enabled its members to know the stages through which human society passes until it reaches the perfect form.[31] The revolutionary party was to be regarded as the authoritarian interpreter of Marxism; there could be no truth outside the party's declarations, but only "ideologies" representing particular interests. "Dictatorship of the party" was the slogan that Lenin substituted for the Marxian slogan "dictatorship of the proletariat."

In two essays written during the First World War, Lenin developed his theories of "imperialism" and "monopoly capitalism."[32] These theories were largely borrowed from the writings of Rudolf Hilferding, Rosa Luxemburg, and other Marxist authors. In his discussion of the colonial aspects of imperialism, Lenin was influenced by the writings of John A. Hobson (1858–1940).[33] The capitalist countries had enjoyed new prosperity through the acquisition of colonies; the workers of the conquering countries had taken advantage of the exploitation of the cheap labor in the colonies and had lost the revolutionary spirit. Progressive accumulation of capital had resulted in the concentration of the control of almost all industrial and commercial operations in a few hands. The state had become an instrument of bondholders (*rentiers*), usurers, and parasitic interests. Monopolistic exploiters had captured the most important sources of raw materials, had divided up the markets, and, supported by their respective governments, had engaged in the struggle over "spheres of influence." Destructive wars among the great powers were the inevitable consequences of the fight over the possession of colonies, and would precipitate the impending collapse of the capitalist society.

From this interpretation of the Marxian doctrine, Lenin drew the conclusion that the strain of war could be expected to break capitalism "at its weakest point"; that industrially undeveloped countries, like Russia, which had no colonies, provided better chances for the overthrow of the capitalist order than those enjoying a higher degree of capitalist development. He considered it necessary to take advantage, wherever possible, of "revolutionary situations," and thus to prepare the final struggle which was to be waged against a relatively small number of "oppressor countries" by about 70 percent of the world's population. In that struggle ample use was to be made of violence, conspiracy, distortion of facts, and similar methods of warfare which might be considered suitable for undermining the structure of capitalist societies, regardless of their stage of development. He elevated the impending Russian revolution to the rank of the outstanding social event in the process leading to the annihilation of the capitalist order, and assigned to the Russian people the mission of promoting the spread of communism in capitalist and noncapitalist areas. But the fundamental question of how a viable and effective communist economy could be organized was practically ignored in these prerevolutionary discussions.[34] Lenin's theory of "economic imperialism" as the last stage of capitalism and his strategic considerations become constituent elements of the "Marxist-Leninist" creed.

Part VI

Marginal Economics

Chapter 18
The Emergence of Schools
of Marginal Utility

THE ROOTS OF MARGINAL UTILITY ANALYSIS

ADHERENCE TO THE principles of hypothetical reasoning did not prevent the Ricardian economists from preserving certain propositions which were hardly consistent with the hypothetical pattern. Paramount among these propositions was the idea that goods derived their utility and other qualities from the classes to which they were assigned. The logical background of that idea was formed by the substance concept, which holds that the inherent properties possessed by a class or group of things are perdurable. This approach led to the well-known "paradox of value" and caused the Ricardians to deny the existence of a causal relationship between utility and exchange values.

The attitude of the British nineteenth-century economists toward the value problem was well expressed by the observation that "it is almost impossible to use the term *value* without suggesting an inherent property."[1] Prompted by the search for a "natural" value of goods, which was to be distinguished from fluctuating market prices, David Ricardo and some of his disciples adopted the mercantilist view that the origin of all exchange values was to be found in human labor spent on producing the goods, and that units of labor provided the standard of measuring exchange values. It has been suggested that the labor cost theory reflected the idea of a conflict of man with nature, and that "costs" meant efforts spent on producing the goods. It was not generally realized that this approach to the value problem did not amount to a ''theory'' in the strict sense of the term, since it did not show the process involved in the formation of values. Moreover, impressed by the objections to the labor cost principle, many Ricardians replaced it by a vague ''cost of production'' idea, which did not provide any theoretical foundation for the value problem. Another—purely fictitious—standard unit for measuring exchange values was proposed by Nassau Senior: the unit of prices experienced in producing the goods or in abstaining from their immediate consumption in favor of deferred enjoyment. But that proposal, although in line with the principles of the utilitarian doctrine, did not arouse much interest.

In the eighteenth century some Italian and French social philosophers—Ferdinando Galiani, Antonio Genovesi, Abbé de Condillac, and Anne Robert Jacques Turgot—had discarded the substance concept as applied to goods and had connected exchange values with the combined effects of the utility and scarcity of commodities. This view was endorsed by Jean Baptiste Say and his followers, but, as understood by them, the term *utility* still reflected the Scholastic concept of generic usefulness and did not provide a basis for the establishment of a standard unit of exchange values. They attributed that function to the unit of the gold standard, since they did not care about applying equilibrium analysis consistently to the construction of a model of the exchange economy.

The logical instrument which eventually provided the key to a new approach to the value problem was the concept of marginal utility. In due course the term *marginal utility*, which was suggested by the Austrian economist Friedrich von Wieser, displaced other names which had been used to denote the same concept, such as final utility, specific utility, effective utility, or marginal desirability. Philip Henry Wicksteed proposed to substitute the adjective *differential* for the adjective *marginal*, but he observed that both expressions and the similar term *incremental* were beset with ambiguities, having been applied to speculations connected with the nature of rent.[2] *Marginal utility* implied that the value of each unit out of a homogeneous stock of goods is determined by the least important use that can be made of it, in other words, by the diminution in want satisfaction caused by its loss. More recently, marginal utility thus defined was termed *substitutive* or *substractive* marginal utility. With a slight change in emphasis, it could also be defined as the difference between the total utility of a stock of goods readily available and the utility achieved by adding another unit (''additive'' marginal utility).[3] Hence, the importance of each unit could be shown to be inversely related to the size of the stock. In an exchange economy, the price of a good could be assumed to measure the preference of the buyers for a commodity bought as compared with the commodities which they could buy for the same amount of money; prices could be defined as ''coefficients of choice.''[4]

The idea that the discovery of ''laws'' or regularities in the economic sphere could be greatly facilitated by analyzing ''marginal'' situations has been one of the most significant achievements of refined economic reasoning. When associated with the assumption that changes in the elements of a process can be conceived of as additions to or subtractions from constant magnitudes, it provided a forceful instrument for productivity analysis. Mountifort Longfield and Johann Heinrich von Thünen were among the first economists to emphasize the relationship which exists between, on the one hand, the increase in the amount of a productive service required to produce an extra unit of the product and, on the other hand, the pecuniary return to the factor of production resulting from that addition. It was shown that, as a rule, increases in output obtained by adding successive increments of a productive factor steadily decreased, and that, consequently, sooner or later for each price-taking enterprise a point was reached at which further additions proved unprofitable.

A uniform principle for determining the shares of the productive factors in the given prices of the products could thus be gained on the assumption that, in equilibrium, the competitively determined price paid for the unit of the productive factor tended to be adjusted to its marginal contribution to the product. The application of the principle of marginality to the analysis of productive processes was developed quite independently of the elaboration of marginal utility reasoning.

The idea of marginal utility had its roots in three different, apparently quite separate, intellectual ventures: utilitarian philosophy, the calculus of probability, and introspective psychology. The mathematical formulation of the idea can be traced back to Daniel Bernoulli (1700–1782), who solved a gambling problem (the so-called St. Petersburg paradox) on the assumptions that the value of each equal increment in wealth was inversely proportional to the amount already owned and that interpersonal comparisons of marginal utility were possible.[5] As formulated by Bernouilli, the problem consisted in evaluating increases in welfare brought about by monetary gains which can be used for the satisfaction of wants of a given sector.

A second approach to marginal utility analysis, suggested by utilitarian considerations, was adopted by Jeremy Bentham, who advanced the proposition that the incremental utility of wealth (i.e., happiness) will diminish as the quantity of wealth is increased. In his *Introduction to the Principles of Morals and Legislation,* Bentham defined utility as "that property in any object whereby it tends to produce benefits, advantage, pleasure, good or happiness . . . or . . . to prevent the happening of mischief, pain, evil or unhappiness to the party whose interest is concerned."[6] Subsequently, the French economist Jules Dupuit, although by no means an adherent of the utilitarian philosophy, explicitly used the idea of a declining utility profile pertinent to a given volume of goods in his determination of an "optimum" pricing policy.

In an entirely different scientific setting, the German psychologists Ernst H. Weber and Gustav Fechner (1801–1887) developed a system of psychological "laws," on the assumption that the interactions of the functions of body and soul could be made the objects of measurements. They advanced a fundamental law which implied that an individual's ability to perceive an increment in any stimulus to which he is subjected is proportional to the total strength of the stimulus. Fechner arrived at the conclusion that variations in satisfaction are proportionate to the logarithms of the stimuli.[7] Since this theory hinged on sensations and reactions to them rather than on sentiments and desires, it was only indirectly connected with the marginal utility principle. But Fechner was aware of the analogy which existed between his theory and Bernouilli's contribution to marginal utility analysis, since he proposed to identify a psychological stimulus with the receipt of income. It is a moot question whether and to what degree the elaboration of the psychological version of marginal utility analysis was influenced by these studies in experimental psychology. Various supporters of the psychological version of marginal utility insisted upon keeping their discussions free of any connection with specific psychological theories, and they used a sort of "introspection" to establish the fundamental concepts of their doctrine. But it is very likely that the psychophysical approach provided some effective incentives to the adoption of the marginal utility principle on the part of Austrian economists.

An interesting episode in the history of the marginal utility principle was the publication of a book on the laws of human relations (*Die Entwicklung der Gesetze des menschlichen Verkehrs*) by a former official of the Prussian Public Administration, Hermann

H. Gossen (1810–1858).[8] The hedonistic principles underlying Gossen's ''laws'' and his mechanistic conception of the mind were abhorrent to German public opinion to such a degree that the unfortunate author decided to withdraw his book from circulation. In 1879, about twenty years after Gossen's death, Jevons drew the attention of economists to the importance of Gossen's contribution to their science. Gossen's investigations of the processes of want satisfaction were not intended to supply the background for an economic theory; rather, they were motivated by the ambitious objective of laying down the principles of rational human behavior as ordained by the Divine Creator. As Bernouilli and Bentham had done before him, Gossen examined the relationships between individuals and individual goods but, rather than directing his attention to the incremental aspects of marginal utility analysis as applied to a specific commodity, he instead undertook to define the principles which determine an individual's behavior toward a number of different goods included in a given stock.

From the general utilitarian principle that every human being tends to maximize his pleasures, Gossen derived two main ''laws'' which were subsequently associated with his name: (1) the principle of diminishing utility, based on the observations that, as a rule, wants decline rapidly in intensity when met by successive satisfactions, until a saturation point has been reached;[9] and (2) the principle of maximized want satisfaction, which implies that, in order to achieve the greatest possible sum of ''enjoyment'' an individual should satisfy at a given time only a certain fraction of each of his wants with a view to equalizing their contributions to the aggregate of his want satisfaction.

Expressed in economic terms, Gossen's first law implied that the increment in satisfaction gained from a stock of available goods declines with every addition to the stock of a new unit. The second law could be identified with the proposition that ''rational economic behavior'' is predicated upon equalizing the marginal utility levels of the desired goods (including labor and money). The law of rational economic behavior could be considered observed when the marginal utilities of the goods purchased with the unit of an individual's income were equalized, or, expressed in other terms, when for all goods purchased out of a given income, equality existed as to the marginal utilities, weighted by their prices. That law provided the basis for the construction of a consistent hypothetical model of the economy on the assumption—readily made by mathematically minded economists—that human wants as well as goods and services could be subdivided into equal infinitesimally small fractions.

Unconditional application of interpersonal comparisons of want satisfaction permitted Gossen to establish—among various other moral precepts—the general proposition that, in order to maximize values for a community, all goods should be so distributed that the last atom of every good received by an individual would provide him with a want satisfaction equal to that granted to any other individual by the last atom of the same good.

With such considerations Gossen anticipated some important aspects of marginal utility analysis, which about twenty years later was authoritatively introduced into economics by the Englishman William Stanley Jevons, the Frenchman Leon Walras, and the Austrian Carl Menger. These three thinkers had developed their ideas independently of each other. Jevons started from the utilitarian calculus of pleasures and pains, adjusting his analysis as far as possible to the Ricardian setting of economic problems, and conceived of the relationships among economic magnitudes primarily in mathematical terms. Far more radical was the methodology adopted by Leon Walras, who had inherited from his father, Auguste Walras, the conviction that economics had to be conceived of as a science of applied mathematics. Hence, he undertook to reduce to a common denominator all marginal utilities included in an imaginary economic system composed of interdependent magnitudes, and to apply equilibrium analysis rigidly to the mutual interactions among these magnitudes. A system is in equilibrium when no tendency exists for the relationships among its elements to vary, except under the influence of outside factors. These relationships are, consequently, determinate. Walras and some of his followers appear to have been convinced that the equilibrium concept is a sort of innate instrument of analysis which is applicable whenever the phenomena under review are quantifiable. That view provided them with an axiomatic approach to economic analysis which was otherwise determined by the principles of hypothetical reasoning.[10]

Menger did not adhere to the utilitarian philosophy, nor was he familiar with the mathematical approach. He believed that observation and experience had to provide the basis for his value theory, and he used a sort of psychological introspection to establish the foundations of that theory, which was designed to explain the relationships among the fundamental economic categories in terms of causal connections. He made no attempt to combine aggregate economic magnitudes into a consistent system of interdependent interactions, and did not apply the equilibrium principle to the analysis of these relationships.

Hence, from the outset, a utilitarian version of marginal utility analysis could be distinguished from a mathematical version, on the one hand, and a psychological version, on the other. Some hybrid versions followed. The differentiation of schools of marginal utility analysis provides another striking example of the influence of methods on the setting of economic problems and the conception of economic systems. The history of the origin of marginal utility analysis does not supply any support for the view that the "challenge of Marxism" acted as a stimulus to the search for a more satisfactory explanation of the distributive process. That stimulus was primarily provided by methodological considerations, which dominated scientific reasoning during the last decades of the nineteenth century. It is not likely that problems connected with the distributive process were among the primary concerns of the originators of marginal utility analysis.

The term *subjective value* came to be used to characterize the idea that the value of goods was to be derived from relationships of individuals to individual goods. Consequently, exchange values were formed in the markets and not in the course of productive processes, as had been believed by the Ricardian economists. It could even be shown that in all situations in which choices had to be made between scarce means of want satisfaction, individual behavior was determined by identical rules which were observed by the parties to exchange transactions. That idea was emphasized by Wicksteed, one of the most outstanding English representatives of marginal utility analysis. He observed that all schemes of value consisted in combining factors "in the right proportion" as fixed by that distribution of resources which establishes the equilibrium of their differential significances in securing the object contemplated. Wicksteed's article dealing with the scope and method of political economy gave an excellent survey of the fundamental problems of marginal utility analysis.[11]

One of the foremost problems in the minds of founders of marginal utility analysis consisted in deriving exchange values, as arrived at in competitive markets, directly from individual valuations. A next step in that line of reasoning led to the conclusion that the value of the productive services was indirectly determined by subjective valuations and, consequently, was to be derived from the value of their products. This conclusion was already implied in the value concept of Jean Baptiste Say and his followers. Viewed in the light of the theory of choice, the value of each productive service could be considered equivalent to the next most important alternative use which could be made of it. Hence,

costs of production could be conceived as utilities sacrificed or forgone in favor of greater
utilities derived from more effective goods.

When this idea—later termed the *principle of opportunity costs* by the American
David I. Green—was consistently applied to cost of production analysis, the problems
connected with the allocation of scarce resources were placed into the center of economic
reasoning, and the supply side was defined in accordance with the same considerations
which were influential in determining the demand side.[12] In addition, since the costs
involved in performing productive or commercial processes can be regarded as income
earned by those who are supplying the services, the fundamental problems of distribution
could be identified with the problems which turned on the pricing of the productive
factors. For these reasons, the distinction drawn between the main factors of production
lost much of its former significance.[13]

The construction of economic systems of the Ricardian type was predicated on the
assumption that all exchange values could be expressed in terms of a common standard
unit of values. That standard was lost, however, when values were derived from individual estimates changing tastes and predilections. Hence, for purposes of general equilibrium analysis, some bold assumptions had to be introduced, such as that all exchange
values could be reduced to a purely fictitious uniform standard and that all consuming and
producing units adjusted their behavior to the principles of "perfect rationality," that is to
say, abstained from consuming (or producing) any goods the marginal utility of which
was lower than that of an equally available and desired good. Moreover, direct application
of the equilibrium principle to the construction of the model of an economy was dependent
on the assumption that want satisfactions as well as the goods and services could be
conceived of as divisible into infinitesimal particles, a procedure suggested by the treatment of marginality problems in the natural sciences.

The intricacies involved in this formulation of the equilibrium conditions of the
economic system were considerably increased when it was found necessary to take account of the "complementarity" of many goods, as well as their mutual substitutability
and their position within the total supply of all goods simultaneously available. (Complementary goods are those whose values are largely determined by their combination). In
the course of these considerations, the "economic man" of Ricardian doctrine, who was
supposed to maximize his share in the total volume of exchange values, was replaced by
an economic subject who exercises "subjective rationality" in making his choice among
alternative want satisfactions, and by the perfectly "rational" entrepreneur, whose behavior is governed by the principle of continuing the expansion of his production up to the
point prescribed by the marginal value productivity of his productive services.

The method of applying the principle of perfect divisibility to want satisfaction and
goods met with strong opposition from Austrian Marginalists, who insisted that according
to observation and experience all individual estimates of the importance of goods and
services were related to units out of a given stock, were not measurable, and could be
compared with each other only by processes of grading. Closely connected with that
methodological issue was another, which turned on the applicability of the concept of
causality to processes of economic motivation, as distinct from the view that, fundamentally, economic relationships could be analyzed only in terms of functional connections.[14]
The conception of the economy as a system of functional relationships was an outstanding
methodological principle of Walrasian economics, as contrasted with the search for causal
relationships which was initiated by Menger's approach to economic analysis. The contro-

versies over these issues have never been settled. The advocates of the mathematical approach to economic analysis were convinced that only thinking in quantitative terms and the use of mathematical methods were perfectly legitimate logical procedures which could be relied upon to supply well-reasoned pictures of the outside world, even at the risk of being incomplete and shadowy. Hence, they did not hesitate to resort to assumptions which were palpably inconsistent with the results of experience—if the application of mathematical methods was facilitated by the introduction of such fictions. The adherents of the psychological version of marginalism, however, placed full confidence in a sort of inner experience or "introspection," which in their view enabled them to establish the psychological principles which were basic to the valuation of goods and the formation of exchange values, and, in the last analysis, enabled them to explain the functioning of the economy in terms of causal laws.

As a rule, the educational background of the various students of economics played a decisive role in determining their choice between the two main alternative versions of marginal utility analysis. Such methodological differences were also responsible for the fact that the leading marginal utility schools pursued their research to a large degree independently of each other.

THE UTILITARIAN VERSION OF MARGINALISM

Of the three original versions of marginal utility analysis, the theory advanced by Jevons was probably the most conservative, since he attempted to preserve, as far as possible, the utilitarian foundations of economics and the Ricardian formulation of the problems of distribution. His work, *The Theory of Political Economy*, was published in London in 1871. Among the writings to which he ascribed a perceptible influence on his thinking was Richard Jennings's *The Natural Elements of Political Economy* (London, 1855). True to the utilitarian epistemology, Jennings started from David Hartley's theory of consciousness and James Mill's conception of ideas as produced by feelings. He pointed to the relationship between pleasures, valuation, and desires on the one hand and action or exchange on the other, and argued that laborious action would be continued up to the point at which the toilsome feeling connected with it would prevail over the satisfaction derived from the pecuniary reward and its positive value.[15] In his view, maximization of happiness, "by purchasing pleasure, as it were, at the lowest cost of pain," was basic to economic behavior. In his discussion of the psychological foundations of his value theory, Jevons referred to a few general, universally valid, observations: every person will choose the greater apparent good, human wants are more or less quickly satiated, and prolonged labor becomes more and more painful. He admitted that direct measurement in terms of "units of pleasure" was impracticable, but considered it sufficient to deal with relative magnitudes which, he said, determine behavior. In order to demonstrate how means to pleasure are transformed into ends, he availed himself of the "law of association" and characterized his theory as a "mechanics of utility and self-interest." He limited the scope of economics to the analysis of wants connected with physical desires and ignored two other groups of wants: those associated with the welfare of social groups and those resulting from moral obligations. He practically disregarded social relationships in his economic analysis. Like Auguste Cournot, he was convinced that all relevant economic phenomena could be expressed in terms of measurable magnitudes.

Jevons was one of the outstanding economists who made important contributions to the methodology of the sciences. He emphasized the hypothetical element of probability involved in all scientific propositions. Like other advocates of refined methods of hypothetical reasoning, he ascribed a special logical validity to mathematical procedures and regarded as particularly reliable those propositions of a science which could be expressed in mathematical terms.[16]

Fundamental to Jevons's teaching was the proposition that value depends solely on marginal utilities. Applying that principle to the analysis of the value of units of goods out of a given stock, Jevons measured these values in terms of infinitely small quantities of pleasure and pain. In order to justify the assumption of a "continuous utility function," he asserted that, although not true of an individual, the assumption would hold true of large numbers. The influence of his methodological considerations was strong enough to appease his doubts concerning the measurability of utilities. Thus, he could avail himself to Gossen's "second law" and apply the equilibrium concept directly to the establishment of an economic model based on the equalization of the marginal utilities weighted by price by all members of the economy. The equilibrium of the model resulted from the combined effects of innumerable equilibria achieved through individual estimates of pleasure and pain: pleasure derived from the enjoyment of desired goods, and pain caused by the disutility of labor spent on their production.

According to the theory of labor advanced by Jevons, the disutility of work is a function of two variables: the "intensity" of work and its duration. He assumed that the disutility of work tends to increase rapidly as it is prolonged beyond a certain point. The determinateness of the model was secured by the assumption that the relationships among the economic elements were governed by the rule of perfect competition and were determined by the "law of indifference," which implied that no producer could influence the price of his products and that at any moment not more than one price could exist for each homogeneous commodity. The equilibrium of the system was considered assured when the "fund available for his entire demand to each individual" (his income) was so distributed among his wants that the final increments of all goods acquired by him were equal in utility when weighted by market prices. That definition was questioned by the Austrian economist Fredrich von Wieser (1851–1926), who argued that the observation of economic behavior does not reveal a tendency to derive an equalized lowest marginal utility from all goods. In view of the fact that the various goods can be put to different uses, there exists rather the tendency to secure for each use the lowest possible marginal utility without sacrificing a higher utility which could be derived from a different use.[17]

In his theory of exchange, Jevons undertook to define the equilibrium conditions underlying the barter between two individuals each possessed of a stock of goods. He established the theorem that the exchange ratio of two commodities will be the reciprocal of the ratio of their final degrees of utility. The term *final degree of utility* was defined as the ratio of the increase in total utility to the increase in the quantity of the commodity at the margin. The same concept was termed *rareté* by Walras and *ophélimité élémentaire* by Pareto. That ratio was independent of the nature of the unit used to measure the quantities of the commodities concerned. No interpersonal comparisons of utilities were involved in that analysis, since each partner compared for himself the importance which he attached to the commodities. But Jevons ignored the fact that, in order to apply this procedure to the explanation of purchases and sales at money prices, a fully developed price system was necessary to render comparable the subjective estimates. Jevons was even less successful in his attempt to define the equilibrium conditions for exchanges between larger groups of buyers and sellers ("trading bodies"), since he did not take account of the competition, within the groups, between individual sellers and individual buyers.[18]

From his theory of exchange, Jevons drew the conclusion that, when no account was taken of inequalities in the distribution of wealth, perfect competition resulted in an optimum distribution of the commodities. Jevons supplemented these more or less fragmentary contributions to marginal utility analysis with various theoretical considerations which were strongly influenced by his attachment to the Ricardian setting of the problems. In his cost of production theory he recognized the dependence of the value of the productive services upon the value of their products, but he preserved the Ricardian concept of "real costs" as the determinants of the value of such factors, and ascribed to these costs an indirect influence upon the value of the products. The precise form in which Jevons expressed these relations reads: "Cost of production determines supply; supply determines final degree of utility; final degree of utility determines value."[19] Since the sacrifice involved in the performance of labor increased in intensity with the duration of the labor, Jevons considered labor a limiting factor in determining costs of production; it would be carried on up to the point at which the increment in utility resulting from its performance would balance the increment in pain and irksomeness.

In his discussion of the problems of distribution, Jevons followed the Ricardian pattern. He gave extended application to the idea of the marginal yield implied in the theory of the land rent. Like Adam Smith and David Ricardo, he defined capital as a subsistence fund, the aggregate of the means available for the maintenance of labor. In his theory of interest he combined Senior's abstinence theory with marginal productivity theory, and established a causal relationship between a lengthening of the average period of production through increased capital investments and increased yields of the productive process. Similar ideas were later elaborated by Eugen Böhm-Bawerk. Competitive processes, he argued, resulted in reducing the rate of interest to a level which corresponded to the yield of the last invested increment of capital. Since he explained wages in terms of the disutility costs of labor, he eliminated the wage fund theory from the place it had occupied for about half a century in English economic doctrine. Jevons remained convinced that increases in wages enforced by trade union activity could be made only at the expense of other groups of workers.

Although the labor cost theory of value had been almost generally abandoned by the English economists in the second half of the nineteenth century, marginal utility analysis, as suggested by Jevons, failed to meet with widespread approval. Perhaps conservative tendencies were too deeply entrenched in England during the Victorian period to permit the introduction of radical changes into economic reasoning. Prior to the First World War marginal utility analysis, with its most important implications, was fully endorsed only by a few noted English economists, such as William Smart (1853–1915), Francis Ysidro Edgeworth (1845–1926), and Philip Henry Wicksteed. Edgeworth shared with Jevons the adherence to the utilitarian calculus of pleasures and pains, and the predilection for formulating economic problems in mathematical terms.[20] Smart showed a distinct preference for the psychological version of marginalism and Wicksteed contributed to the development of the psychological as well as the mathematical version.[21]

THE MATHEMATICAL VERSION OF MARGINALISM

For the Frenchman Leon Walras, marginal utility analysis provided an indispensable instrument for the fulfillment of his main scientific objective: that of transforming economics into applied mathematics.[22] The formulation and the solution of his problems were determined by a method which centered on the establishment of a hypothetical model of the economy and found its mathematical expression in a system of simultaneous equations the number of which was equal to the number of the unknowns. The adjustment of the model to the purposes it was designed to serve was performed with the aid of a number of "heroic" assumptions. The coefficients of production were assumed to be constant; that is, the relative quantities of the productive services per unit output used in the productive processes were assumed to remain unchanged. All firms of an industry were assumed to produce in equal quantities and with identical methods a homogeneous product; the time element and problems of location were ignored. Perfectly "rational" behavior of all producers, buyers, and sellers was equally prerequisite to the construction of the Walrasian model, in which the mutual relationships of the economic magnitudes were made determinate under the rule of pure competition. Hence, unique solutions were obtained for the equilibrium values of the prices and quantities of all products and productive factors. The model was composed of four markets: markets of goods of consumption, new capital goods, factor services, and securities. Walras defined capital goods in the strict sense as produced goods which are durable and render more than one service. He called such services "revenues." From the services of capital he distinguished those of land and labor. In the securities market the equilibrium price was represented by the rate of interest.

Pure competition implied that no single participant in production and trade could appreciably influence prices, that every commodity was sold at a uniform price, that no friction was involved in transferring productive services from one use to another, and that all goods permitted unlimited divisibility. With the assumption of a perfect market, where every event becomes known instantaneously to every member, Walras introduced into his equilibrium conditions the problematic concept of the quasi-omniscient individual later criticized by the Austrian Friedrich A. Hayek.[23] Like Cournot, Walras availed himself of the idea of continuity in his construction of the demand curve. Hardly less important was another methodological device which had also been suggested by Cournot: the application of the equilibrium concept to a system of strictly interdependent economic magnitudes, which were reduced to a common hypothetical standard unit of values. The assumption that demand, supply, prices, and all other relevant economic magnitudes were interdependent provided a methodological solution to John Stuart Mill's "paradox of two things each depending on the other" (the value of and the demand for commodities). It was a device which "required the use of mathematical logic."[24]

The economic actors of the Walrasian model were conceived of as quasi-mechanical agents governed by the principle of equalizing their marginal utilities on the assumption that utilities as well as the objects of want satisfaction could be divided into infinitesimal fractions. Walras used the term *rareté* to denote marginal utility, and defined it as "*l'intensité du dernier besoin satisfait.*" He emphasized the relativity of value in exchange, as contrasted with marginal utility. Another characteristic feature of the Walrasian equilibrium analysis was a reformulation of Say's market law to the effect that, at given prices, the supply of all commodities and the supply of money offered was identically equal to the total demand for commodities and money, so that every offer of a good for sale involved demand for its equivalent either in money or in another commodity. That formulation of Say's law has been termed *Walras's law.*[25]

In order to derive equilibrium prices from the equilibria which individuals were supposed to achieve by distributing their want satisfactions over the units of the available stocks of commodities, Walras, like Jevons, resorted to the expedient of regarding marginal utilities as measurable and mutually comparable magnitudes. Walras applied the idea of marginal utility functions to individual commodities, ignoring the fact that such functions are influenced by the simultaneous or future possession of other commodities. In addition, he assumed that all marginal utility functions decreased at the same rate. The question of the degree to which the Walrasian system must be modified in order to account for the combined effects of the marginal utilities of all commodities included in the budget of a household was examined by Luigi Amoroso.[26] Like Jevons, Walras placed purchasers and sellers into fully developed systems of market prices which enabled them to express their marginal utilities in terms of a standard unit of exchange values. That hypothetical unit of account, the "*numéraire*," was assumed to be subjected to no other demand than that resulting from its properties of a commodity. Hence, the value of the *numeraire* was assumed not to be affected by its use as a medium of exchange. Functions of money as a store of values were ignored. It is a moot question as to whether, by stabilizing the demand for and the supply of the monetary commodity, Walras did not introduce by the back door the concept of "equivalence" as applied to exchanges by the Ricardian economists. Under the rule of free competition the price system was expected to assure maximum attainable want satisfaction to each buyer and seller.

The Walrasian method of maximizing want satisfaction found its expression only in terms of quantities, since under conditions of free competition neither buyers nor sellers could influence prices.[27] Walras was convinced that generalization of that proposition was the main object of economic theory; he also believed that actual agricultural, industrial, and commercial activities should be operated under perfectly competitive conditions.

In his discussion of the pricing process, Walras abandoned his purely statistical approach and attempted to show how the relative price structure for which he had supplied a mathematical solution could actually be attained in the markets under the rule of free competition. As Edgeworth expressed it, he undertook to demonstrate the path, as it were, by which the economic system works down to equilibrium.[28] That path was the often-quoted method of "groping" (*tâtonnement*) used by entrepreneurs and traders under conditions of free competition in order to achieve equilibrium of supply and demand. In subsequent references to that method its "dynamic" aspects were frequently ignored or minimized. Edgeworth raised the objection that the Walrasian methods of groping indicate *a* way, not *the* way of descent to equilibrium. He supplemented the concept of "groping" by introducing the idea of "recontracting," which implies that the offers made by those participating in the bargaining process are not binding unless the set of prices at which the offers are made turns out to be the equilibrium set.[29]

The functioning of the Walrasian price system started from the determination of the prices of consumption goods in accordance with their *utilité directe*. Demand, as a function of price, increased proportionately with price reductions, and vice versa. Supply was regarded as a passive element, since any possible changes in the structure of production were ignored. The *utilité indirecte* of the factors of production was derived from the *utilité directe* of the consumption goods, and the prices of the factors were determined in separate markets on the assumption that, under equilibrium conditions, the prices of the products were equal to their costs. The market for capital goods covered all goods which could supply a series of services without being used up and without deteriorating. Various types of capital or revenue resources were enumerated in a comprehensive list.

In his analysis of the prices of the productive factors, Walras connected the prices of "unspecified" factors with their alternative uses, and the prices of the services required only for specific processes with the value of their products. But he admitted that product prices could be modified by varying the coefficients of production.

Walras strategically placed the entrepreneur as the link between productive services and the product markets. Following the example set by Say, Walras sharply separated the functions of the entrepreneur from those of the capitalist, and qualified the entrepreneurs' remunerations as rewards for their activities in combining and utilizing productive services. With equilibrium in production they could make neither profit nor loss. That proposition implied that, strictly speaking, profits were a category of incomes which resulted from disturbances of equilibrium situations, from monopolies, and from temporary differences between prices and costs of production. Edgeworth disregarded the fictional character of the Walrasian employer when he argued that such an entrepreneur would have no motive to continue his business.[30] Among the entrepreneurs' functions was the task of transforming savings into factors of production and of adjusting the price of the services of capital goods to the rate of interest, conceived of as the price of money. As mentioned above, interest on capital was formed in a special market.

The Walrasian theory of rent was a reformulation, in mathematical terms, of the Ricardian theory. Underlying the Walrasian wage theory was the principle that labor belongs to the category of unspecialized services, and that for such services the returns from alternative uses are equalized.

Walras dropped the assumption of fixed coefficients of production from his later studies,[31] but he simplified the ensuing analysis by introducing various assumptions which were far from being consistent with reality. Using the device of "other things being equal," he divided the increased quantity of the product by the original quantity in order to determine the marginal productivity of the service the volume of which had been increased.

The paramount achievement of the Walrasian theory consisted in establishing a fully developed equilibrium system of interdependent economic magnitudes, based on analyzing the behavior of individual economic units in accordance with the marginal utility principle. The ingenuity which he showed in establishing the model of a perfectly balanced economic system without resorting to the construction of aggregates of economic magnitudes was greatly admired by his followers, but his system was frequently regarded as an exercise in mathematical logic which did not provide a promising approach to the solution of economic problems. Alfred Marshall made the pertinent observation that there prevails in models of the Walrasian type a tendency toward assigning undue weight to those economic forces which lend themselves most easily to analytic methods. This tendency was accentuated in the exended subsequent discussions which turned on the equilibrium conditions, the determinateness, and the stability of the Walrasian model.[32]

Walras himself perfectly realized the outright fictitious nature of his theoretical considerations; nevertheless, he believed that his model could be used to demonstrate how optimum allocation of resources and maximization of consumers' satisfaction was secured through free competition. The validity of that interpretation of the Walrasian model was questioned by Wicksell, Pigou, and other economists. But the claim raised by Walras provided adherents of the ideological argument with a welcome confirmation of their contention that the alleged purely hypothetical use of the principle of free competition on the part of "bourgeois" economists was, in fact, motivated by their class interests, which caused them to demonstrate the favorable effects of the competitive order.

A considerable discrepancy has been found to exist between the methodological principles adopted by Walras in his theoretical analysis of the competitive economy and the procedures which he used in his *Études d'économie appliquée.* In these studies he undertook to define the area of economic activities which should be organized and regulated by the state in order to eliminate such factors as are likely to interfere with the achievement of maximum social want satisfaction. The duties and functions which he ascribed to the state in the spheres of production and distribution were quite substantial, and he did not hesitate to appeal to principles of "distributive justice" in order to establish "equilibrium between the rights of the individual and those of the state." Walras claimed that the individual should receive such incomes as are derived from labor and personal abilities, but, adopting the demands of radical social reformers, he called for the nationalization of land and appropriation of land rent by the state.[33] He also recommended the administrative regulation of industries in which maintenance of the competitive structure was endangered by the existence of increasing returns. He expected a truly "scientific" theory of socialism clearly to provide the principles to be applied in order to equalize supply and demand for each product.

THE PSYCHOLOGICAL VERSION OF MARGINALISM

The methods adopted by Carl Menger, the third originator of marginal utility analysis, differed in various respects from those used by Jevons and Walras. On the one hand, Menger placed main emphasis on the search for causal relationships between economic phenomena; on the other hand, he objected to the use of methods of higher mathematics for purposes of economic analysis, and he made no attempt to apply the equilibrium principle to the construction of an economic system. But, since the main economic categories were of the order of magnitudes, he considered them amenable to treatment in accordance with the methods of the "exact" sciences. In his view, these methods consisted in deriving from experience and observation hypothetical concepts of high abstraction and in combining these concepts into consistent systems that could render intelligible those causal relationships. Although Menger never explicitly referred to the Kantian epistemology, he appears to have followed, with minor variations, the general trend of reasoning adopted by Kant.[34]

Hence, Menger rejected the Ricardian value theory, because its adherents failed to demonstrate the existence of a general causal relationship between the amount of labor spent on producing a good and the exchange value of the latter and because they had to resort to different principles (productive processes, scarcities, market conditions) to explain different forms of one and the same phenomenon. The ultimate roots of any valuation, he argued, must not be looked for in any qualities inherent in the things, but in the psychological motivation of human behavior as it manifests itself in the typical attitudes of individuals toward the objects of their want satisfaction and reflects the marginal utilities of the goods.

Consistent marginal utility analysis, he believed, could most effectively be pursued when striving for maximum want satisfaction was regarded as the only motive of economic behavior, and when such behavior was assumed to take place in perfect knowledge of its economic effects and free from external compulsion. In the light of the deductions drawn from these premises, Menger expected to develop the general economic categories needed to arrive at an understanding of the functioning of the exchange economy. The "individualistic" approach to economic analysis led him and his disciples to refer the behavior of a Robinson Crusoe to illustrate the principles of subjective valuation. This approach was ridiculed by authors of organismic and dialectic persuasion who insisted on the "social" character of all economic phenomena. Considerable confusion resulted from the ambiguities of the term *social* as used in this connection.[35]

In open opposition to the assumptions made by the mathematical economists, Menger insisted that, in the light of psychological experience, marginal utilities could never be conceived of as infinitesimal magnitudes and could never be directly measured and exactly compared with one another. In his view, the concept of marginal utility could be used only for denoting estimates attached to units out of a given stock of goods, such estimates declining by leaps and bounds when more units were added to the stock. The problems connected with the "scaling" or "grading" of utilities were subsequently the object of prolonged discussions.

Although Menger was well aware of the influence exercised on the development of economic and social institutions by the unconscious behavior of thousands of individuals, he refrained from any mechanical construction of economic relationships derived from the construction of aggregates of economic magnitudes. His analysis remained within the sphere of relationships among individual economic units and the complex network of exchanges which he found to exist among such units.

When viewed in the light of the intellectual atmosphere in which he developed his ideas, Menger showed perhaps more independence of thinking than Jevons or Walras. Jevons could derive some of his leading principles from the utilitarian calculus of pleasures and pains as combined with Mill's methods of scientific analysis. Walras had taken over from his father the methodological approach suggested by Cournot, and was not particularly concerned about justifying his methods. But Menger developed his conception of economics as an exact science in the course of a dispute with convinced adherents of organismic methods, such as Gustav Schmoller, who at that time exercised a predominant influence on the economic reasoning of Central Europe. The efforts which he spent on defending his methods against misunderstandings and on clarifying fundamental issues absorbed a good deal of his activities. Thus, the scope of the problems which he elaborated was in various respects more limited than the range of those treated by Jevons and Walras.

But he succeeded in formulating with great consistency a series of concepts which had a direct bearing on the explanation of some basic economic phenomena. He suggested a classification of wants according to their importance, and a grouping of goods according to their proximity to the fulfillment of needs or desires. He emphasized the economic characteristics of complementary goods which cannot serve specific purposes without being simultaneously available. In his discussion of the problems connected with the optimum distribution of given quantities of supply, he placed main emphasis on the side of demand and ignored the conception of pains and sacrifices as cost elements. His rather modest attempt to establish a theory of exchanges was limited to the analysis of isolated transactions performed under competitive conditions. On the assumption that the ratio of the marginal utilities of the goods acquired would be the same for both parties, Menger arrived at a determination of the upper and lower price limits agreed upon in accordance with the marginal utility principle.

In his analysis of the distributive processes Menger did not attach particular importance to the Ricardian distinction of the three classes of the population or to the alleged relationship between each class and a specific productive factor on the one hand and a corresponding type of income on the other. Placing primary emphasis on scarcity relationships as the determinants of values, he argued that each productive factor could be available in varying degrees of scarcity, hence rendering a tripartite division of factors of production causally meaningless. Subsequently Menger attempted to develop a theory of wants based on biological and physiological studies. The psychological aspects of marginal analysis were elaborated by Menger's disciples, above all by Friedrich von Wieser.

A characteristic feature of Menger's cost of production analysis was his attempts to approach it with a method of "imputation," in order to determine the causal relationships according to which each productive service is allotted an appropriate fraction of the values created by the combined contributions to production of several services. The term *imputation (Zurechnung)* was suggested by von Wieser. It can broadly be defined as the method of determining the contributions made by each of several cooperative factors to a common effort or result. Applying the principle of marginalism to the solution of this problem, Menger argued that the share to be assigned to each service was determined by the change in the value of the product brought about by the withdrawal of one unit of the service. Since the cost elements of the productive processes constituted at the same time elements of income, the formation of values in all processes of production and distribution could be rendered intelligible in terms of a single principle.

Elaborating his apparently simple explanation of the value of the productive factors, Menger took account of the fact that a given quantity of a good could be produced by various combinations of productive factors, and that the "law of variable proportions" was basic to the productive processes. He defined "capital" in terms of physical goods "of higher order," but also suggested an alternative concept of capital as a sum of money productively used.[36] His theory of interest on capital was based on the problematic assumption that the use of capital goods could logically be separated from the "substance" of capital, and that interest represented the payment made for that use in the course of productive processes.

In his discussion of monetary problems, Menger placed considerable emphasis on the spontaneous, unintentional social actions which were responsible for the origin and development of the functions of money. He avoided any treatment of these problems in terms of aggregates, as was done by the advocates of the quantity theory of money. Without applying marginal utility analysis directly to the explanation of the value of money, he discussed the distinction which could be drawn between the "external" and the "internal" exchange value of money, the influence of the factors which determine the demand for money and changes in its value, and, finally, the methods of measuring that value.[37]

Although Menger never realized his ambitious plan to elaborate fully the marginal utility doctrine as he conceived it, he provided his disciples with a clear outline of the problems to be attacked and the methods to be applied to their solution. As the founder of the "Austrian school," he exercised a determinant influence on the thinking of three generations of economists. But the discussion of the development of marginalism in the strict sense of the term may be postponed in favor of a survey of the development of "post-Ricardian" economics in the Anglo-Saxon countries.

Chapter 19
Post-Ricardian Economics

THE INTELLECTUAL CLIMATE OF THE VICTORIAN AGE

IT IS A striking fact that the English post-Ricardian economists' firm belief in the validity of the Ricardian methods was not perceptibly affected by a rising tide of intellectual currents which were hostile not only to the utilitarian philosophy but also to the conception of the economy which had resulted from the elaboration of the utilitarian principles. Even the challenge implied in William Stanley Jevons's reformulation of the value theory failed to arouse a significant reaction.

Under a well-developed system of free competition and free trade, a rapid expansion of the English economy had taken place, and the British Empire had taken shape. Sterling had become the generally acknowledged international currency, and London had been made the center of a system of commercial relationships which extended to the remotest corners of the earth. The organization of that market, and the functioning of the English monetary and credit machinery, reflected the conviction that the behavior of the catallactic economy was ruled by equilibrating forces. That conviction was not perceptibly disturbed by the recurrent crises which spread misery among large masses of the population and interfered with the process of economic growth. The belief in the operation of irresistible economic laws was shared by industrialists, bankers, merchants, and public officials. Everybody was expected to adjust his behavior to the sovereign commands of the "market." "The law of supply and demand attained an authority which the Ten Commandments never had. The unforgivable sin was to be caught short on a settlement date."[1]

The reasoning which provided the background to Ricardian economics found another expression in the proposition that the history of civilization, as determined by environmental factors, was marked by a steady linear progress toward peace and freedom.[2] The eighteenth-century principle of rationality was consistently applied to the interpretation of historical developments.[3] The historian John R. Seeley (1834–1895) demonstrated that the expansion of the British Empire had not been the result of a deliberate "imperialistic" policy, but had been brought about by the activity of individual merchants, trading companies, settlers, and adventurers who, after having gained a foothold in overseas colonies, requested the protection of their homeland's government.[4] In the light of that analysis, the British colonial ventures reflected the individualistic spirit of utilitarian philosophy, which tended to minimize the influence of state and government on the course of economic and social developments.

After John Stuart Mill's death, John Elliott Cairnes became England's leading economist. He elaborated the methodological principles which were basic to deductive reasoning[5] and defended them against a variety of criticisms.[6] To the attempts to transform economics into a science of applied mathematics, he raised the objection that the mental feelings which provided the premises for the deduction of economic laws could not be expressed in quantitative forms. Fully aware of the fundamentally hypothetical background of the Ricardian doctrine, he grouped around Nassau Senior's well-known four postulates some subordinate principles and facts affecting the production and distribution of wealth, such as inventions, custom, religion, and the attitude toward the future. A bridge from the abstract teachings of economics to the phenomena of the real world had to be built by combining those subordinate principles with the dominant generalizations. But this "adding up" procedure did not find many adherents.[7]

Cairnes was well aware of the dangers which resulted for the consistency of the Ricardian doctrine from certain arguments which had been developed within the framework of the doctrine. With the gradual extension of the concept of rent to situations in which prices were not determined by competitive conditions, the economic processes were likely to assume the aspect of a struggle over rents in which the laboring classes were unable to participate. It was still an open question to what degree the conditions of labor depended upon the size of a wage fund and the use made of it by employers. On the other hand, when the wage fund concept was abandoned along with the labor cost theory of value, the Ricardian economic system was dissolved into a network of markets with no clearly discernible links to interconnect them. Cairnes suggested the term *noncompeting groups* to emphasize the observation that imperfect mobility existed even within the domestic economy among groups of workers of the same occupation. Such developments, which tended to undermine the foundations of the Ricardian doctrine, received considerable support from various attempts to modify radically the meaning of traditional concepts. A characteristic attempt of that type was Henry Dunning Macleod's definition of wealth in terms of tangible and intangible goods and his extension of the concept of money to credits granted by banks.[8]

Hence, increasing skepticism as to the validity of the current doctrine was expressed by cautious authors, who characterized the doctrine as only "a most certain and useful thing of limited extent." Walter Bagehot (1826–1877), the author of a widely read descriptive analysis of the English banking system,[9] questioned even the method of including free mobility of capital and labor among the assumptions underlying the theories of value and rent.[10]

Methodological problems of a different type were analyzed by Henry Sidgwick (1838–1900), the last eminent economist of outright utilitarian persuasion.[11] As a teacher at the University of Cambridge, he exercised an influence on intellectual life which surpassed by far that of any contemporary member of his profession. Alfred Marshall was one of his outstanding disciples. Preserving the framework of Jeremy Bentham's philosophy, he rejected the idea that moral duties identical for all human beings could be derived from experience. Hence, he resorted to the concept of an innate instinct of benevolence as the source of morality and insisted on the existence of "ultimate values" which could claim general recognition and should be implemented by measures of economic policy. Particular importance was to be attached to the distributive aspects of such policies. To the traditional formula of achieving greatest "average" happiness, Sidgwick opposed another, according to which maximum happiness should be reached by multiplying the number of persons living by the amount of average happiness.[12] Although Sidgwick admitted that only rough inductive evidence could be supplied for the belief that people are the best guardians of their own welfare, he threw the *onus probandi* on those who advocated government interference with economic operations. In this connection Sidgwick held the principle of diminishing returns responsible for the undesirable effects of land rent on income distribution. He pointed to cases in which "natural liberty," instead of securing beneficial results, led to monopolistic situations, industrial combinations, and the like.

Simultaneously, the methodological principles which were basic to Ricardian economics were confronted with an increasing stream of hostile intellectual currents. One
important current had its sources in the teachings of German "idealistic" philosophers
which permeated the political theories of some outstanding British sociologists and students of law and jurisprudence. These theories reflected the belief in the existence of
"objective spirits" that are instrumental in determining social values and ends; they
reflected the conceptions of societies as moral organisms and of individuals as subordinate
members of such integrated wholes. Prominent among the authors of such political
theories were Thomas H. Green (1836–1882), F. H. Bradley (1846–1924), and Bernard
Bosanquet (1848–1923). Sir Henry Maine, author of *Ancient Law* (London, 1861), was
an eminent jurist who adopted an organismic interpretation of law. Another jurist who
endorsed similar ideas was F. H. Maitland (1850–1906).[13] Some members of that group
even adopted the Hegelian identification of nation states with concrete manifestations of
absolute reason.[14]

The leading ideas of the German historical school found a number of more or less
convinced adherents in the British Isles. T. E. Cliffe Leslie (1827–1882), an Irishman,
occupied a prominent position among the scholars who denied the existence of generally
valid economic laws and emphasized the institutional background of all economic phenomena and their dependence upon combinations of unique historical conditions.[15]
Hence, specific "laws" had to be established for each nation in accordance with its
individuality. In the light of that approach, Leslie accused the Ricardian economists of
using an assumed knowledge of ultimate causes to establish "unwarranted
generalizations."

Another adherent of the historical school, Thorold Rogers, qualified much of the
current economic teachings as a collection of "logomachics."[16] In his voluminous and
highly valuable contributions to the economic history of England, he contrasted the actual
rent imposed by landowners on their tenants under conditions of immobility of capital and
skill with the "mean rate of profit" which could be earned under normal conditions of
mobility.[17] In his extensive research into the development of wages, Rogers endeavored
to show that acts of parliaments or governments were responsible for keeping workers'
wages at the lowest possible level.[18]

A third noticeable economist who questioned the solidity of the general laws of the
Ricardian type was Arnold Toynbee (1852–1883), the author of a much-discussed analysis of the development of the English machine age.[19] He requested close examination of
the assumptions which provided the starting point for deductive reasoning, and insisted
upon testing the conclusions arrived at in the light of facts. Applying that method to the
history of the English industry, he emphasized the uncertainty of the effect of free
competition on the distributive process.

John Kells Ingram (1823–1907) attempted to provide a more philosophical background to the principles of the historical school. He delivered a programmatic declaration
in favor of the historicoethical approach to economics, in which he characterized the study
of society as a sort of biology and denounced the "abusive preponderance" which the
economists had given to deductive procedures and to the absolute validity of their theoretical and practical conclusions.[20] Their "metaphysical habit of mind," he suggested, had
frequently caused them to mistake creations of their speculative imagination—such as the
wage fund—for "objective realities." In his well-known history of economic thought,[21]
Ingram surveyed the development of economic ideas from the point of view of historism.

Ingram, like other English adversaries of Ricardian economics, was strongly influenced by the "positive" philosophy of Auguste Comte, which placed sociology, the science of society, at the end of a scheme of the sciences and was incompatible with the conception of economics as a separate discipline to be developed in accordance with specific methods. As taught by Comte, sociological laws or generalizations had to be derived from the comparative observation of historical and ethnological events; social relationships had to be analyzed from two main points of view: that of the "spontaneous order of society" brought about by the operation of social instincts, termed *statics,* and that of "evolutionary factors," as manifested in a "natural progress," termed *dynamics.* Comte's distinction caused Mill to extend his analysis into the field of "dynamics." Characteristic of Comte's conception of society as an integrated whole was his assertion that in the field of social phenomena, as in biology, the "whole of the object" is certainly much better known and more immediately accessible than its constituent parts.

The role played by "evolution" in influencing the course of economic processes was stressed by William James Ashley (1860–1927) who endeavored to develop the methodological aspects of the legal and economic versions of historism.[22] He distinguished three different meanings of the concept of "social evolution" as used by English scientists. When derived from Comte's philosophy, that concept implied a progressive development of humanity, proceeding by stages. As defined by G.W.F. Hegel, "social evolution" meant the unfolding of an autonomous national spirit through stages determined by a dialectic process. Finally, there was Herbert Spencer's much-discussed concept of "social evolution," which was based on the Darwinian principle of random adjustment through natural selection. According to Darwin's investigations into the *Origin of the Species,* all forms of life were assumed to have developed through innumerable discontinuous processes of random selection, produced by adjustments to surrounding conditions. Consequent upon that theory the harmonious world mechanism of eighteenth-century imagination had been transformed into a blind, purposeless, ruthless mechanism which oppressed the thinking of many poets and philosophers.[23]

Only Spencer's concept was compatible with the methods of hypothetical reasoning; the Hegelian concept was dialectic in origin, and Comte's concept showed certain features characteristic of institutional methods. But Spencer had perceptibly modified the Darwinian interpretation of evolutionary processes; he connected them not only with the idea of transitions from simple to more complex states but also, in the case of "compound evolution," with the idea of transitions from homogeneity to heterogeneity, from a less coherent to a more coherent structure, from indefinite to clearly demarcated states. Hence, Spencer defined evolution as "integration of matter," accompanied by "dissipation of motion" in the course of processes in which both matter and motion passed from indefinite incoherent homogeneity to defined coherent heterogeneity.[24]

Applying such considerations to the analysis of societies, Spencer characterized "social organisms" as entities lacking definite form and continuous substance, as integrated wholes designed to serve the interests of their parts but subjected to the same rhythm of integration and disintegration as any other organism. He suggested that the "test of survival" demonstrated the ability of a social organism to adapt itself to its environment. Although opposed to the identification of evolution with progress, he pointed to the gradual development of individuality, freedom, and peace brought about by the transformation of "custom-ruled" into militaristic and finally industrial societies.

From his theory Spencer derived an extreme aversion to state intervention of any type. He used the idea of "natural selection" in support of the principle of absolute economic liberalism with all its implications, but he admitted that ethical judgments played a modifying role in influencing the competitive struggle. Starting from fundamentally hedonistic principles, he developed the idea that the ability to pass moral judgments, though empirical in origin, had generally been transformed into an ethical intuitive faculty called conscience. He qualified ethical experience as one of the most fundamental conditions of social life, and thus supplied a new interpretation of the somewhat discredited utilitarian ethics.

As used by many sociologists who adhered to the methods of historicism, the term *social Darwinism* reflected the view that survival of the fittest had been the result of economic and social processes. Certain teleological aspects were introduced into that reasoning when these processes were regarded as adaptations and adjustments taking place on an upward scale of progress. Views of that type found expression in popular slogans such as "historical inevitability," "irresistible social forces," "wave of the future," and the like. Insistence on an "inevitable" course of social or economic events provided the leaders of radical movements with telling arguments in support of their prophecies and programs. The Ricardian economists lacked satisfactory instruments to enable them to introduce "dynamic" features into their analysis; hence, they had to evade the problems raised by the advocates of evolutionary views.

Mention may be made in passing of a series of highly effective attacks on Ricardian economics which were only loosely connected with strictly methodological issues, having their roots in religious, ethical, or esthetical considerations. The outstanding protagonists in that controversy, Thomas Carlyle (1795–1881), Charles Kingsley (1819–1875), J.F.D. Maurice, and John Ruskin (1819–1900), were motivated by the conviction that the doctrine of free will and the principles of Christian morality had to be defended against deterministic, mechanistic, and materialistic philosophy.[25]

Carlyle questioned the usefulness of any purely logical method. He used intuitive reasoning in his tirades against the "mammonism" of the capitalist order and the Ricardian economists. He applied the often-quoted expressions "dismal science" and "gospel of despair" to their teachings. Carlyle's political and economic ideas, which turned on phrases such as "hero worship," had hardly any methodological importance; his predominantly artistic approach to history was accentuated by the emphasis which he placed on the personal element.[26]

John Ruskin, who won his fame as an art critic, derived his condemnation of the capitalist order and the prevailing economic doctrine from a combination of esthetic and moral judgments.[27] He attributed the "ossifiant utilitarian theory of progress" to an attitude which negated the existence of a soul; he proposed to merge all social sciences with the arts into an undifferentiated whole.

Religious convictions provided the rallying point for the Christian socialist movement, which gained in importance after the collapse of the revolutionary period of chartism (1837–48). The creation of consumers' cooperatives and the organization of labor unions were the main practical objectives pursued by the leading advocates of Christian social reform.[28]

About the middle of the nineteenth century, the attacks directed by the Ricardian Socialists against capitalist society had exhausted their effectiveness, and socialist ideas were carried on mainly by Owenite groups and later by the various associations which requested nationalization of the ownership of land. In the 1880s the socialist movement split up into two factions: one group, the Social-Democratic Federation, rallied round the Marxists H. M. Hyndman and John Burns (1858–1943); the other group, the Socialist League, was led by William Morris (1834–1895), author of the well-known Utopian novel *News from Nowhere*. Morris was strongly influenced by Ruskin. He insisted on the idea that every word should permit its producer to impress his personality on his product, and proposed to use the spontaneous combination of free terms to organize productive activities.[29] These movements did not arouse much interest.

A highly effective reformist movement, however, was launched in 1883 by the Fabian Society, an association of well-educated, gifted, and increasingly influential intellectuals of socialist persuasion. Educated in the principles of nominalistic reasoning and in the tenets of the utilitarian philosophy, they shifted the emphasis from the pains caused by government interference to the social evils caused by an economic system in which a highly unequal distribution of wealth was combined with free competition and laissez-faire.[30] Like practically all Socialists with utilitarian leanings, they centered their attention on the distributive aspects of the economy and neglected the problems connected with the rational organization of a planned economy. Their main achievement consisted in devising a comprehensive eclectic program of social reform which was designed to lead to a gradual elimination of the private ownership of the means of production, especially of land. Hence, the approach adopted by the Fabians to problems of social reform differed radically from that adopted by the German "socialists of the Chair." The latter were motivated not by utilitarian (individualistic) considerations but by nationalistic (collectivistic) ones.

A policy of "gradualism" has frequently been regarded as one of the essential features of the Fabian approach, but the views of the members of the group were split on the question of whether the "socialization" of the economy was an automatic, irresistible process or whether it was necessary to organize a separate socialist political party to carry on a struggle with the country's conservative forces. The creation of the Labor party in 1906 supplied a definite answer to that question.

The ethical criteria which provided the backbone of the Fabian program were derived from the distinction between unearned increments and incomes regarded as rewards for economic contributions to the value of the product. In the light of Ricardian theory, land rent was an outstanding specimen of unearned income, and George Bernard Shaw (1856–1950), one of the leading Fabians, placed its abolition at the center of his proposals.[31] Other Fabians realized that "taxation to extinction" of the rent of land would affect only a very small fraction of England's wealth.[32] Without advancing a theory of profit or interest, they extended the vague idea of unearned income to an equally ill-defined concept of "profits," which employers earned by paying wages that were lower than the value of "labor's contribution to the value of the product."

The Fabians borrowed only certain expressions from Marx, such as "surplus product," "proletariat," and "bourgeois." They repudiated the labor cost theory, after Wicksteed convinced Shaw in 1884 of the errors implied in that theory and of the validity of the theory of subjective value as advanced by Jevons.[33] However, they failed to pursue marginal utility analysis into its more complex aspects or to develop a clear concept of economic system. The allusions made by Shaw and other members of the group (Graham Wallas (1858–1932) and Annie Besant (1847–1933)) to a socialist organization of production and distribution were derived from experiences with the operation of monopolistic enterprises by various municipalities.

Quite a few Fabians, especially Graham Wallas, Sidney Webb, and William Clarke, were in favor of substituting a historical approach for the deductive method of Ricardian economics. The impressive studies of Sidney (1859–1947) and Beatrice Webb (1858–1943) were outstanding specimens of descriptive analysis.[34] But the value of that analysis was impaired by the introduction of various problematic concepts, such as the idea of an "objective standard" for deciding on the usefulness of goods and the connected idea of "collective judgments," the distinction between wants of "society" and wants of the members of a community, and the like.[35] Some concepts of that type which were organismic in origin were later taken over by the Labor party.

The slight attention which the Ricardians paid to the writings of the Fabians has been contrasted with the prolonged and lively attacks of the Austrian Marginalists on their socialist adversaries.[36] But it should be kept in mind that the methodological principles of the Fabians did not differ perceptibly from those of the Ricardian and post-Ricardian authors and teachers. Their more or less radical proposals could be dealt with by pointing to the lack of consistency or realism exhibited by their advocates. The struggle of the Austrians with the Marxists, however, turned on fundamental methodological problems, and on the validity of a closely reasoned doctrine which claimed to reveal the truth about an inevitable course of economic and social developments. The methodological aspects of that struggle loomed much larger in the attacks of the Austrians on Marxism than—as has frequently been assumed—the intention to defend the capitalist order.

THE METHODOLOGY OF MARSHALLIAN ECONOMICS

Alfred Marshall's great achievement consisted in adjusting the crumbling structure of the Ricardian doctrine to the intellectual climate of the Victorian age. With his *Principles of Economics,* he determined the trend of English economic reasoning for more than a generation.[37]

The methods of hypothetical thinking, as developed by John Stuart Mill, were basic to Marshall's approach to economic analysis. Free competition, mobility of productive services, and the rational pursuit of economic objectives were the main assumptions used to draw a picture of the economic system. Marshall was fully aware of the characteristic behavior of businessmen when he said that they lived according to constantly shifting visions, that their imagination was employed, like that of the master chess player, in forecasting obstacles to the successful issue of their far-reaching projects.[38] Hence, better than any of his English predecessors, Marshall recognized the difficulties involved in elaborating a science of human conduct dealing with the "various and uncertain actions of men." Although he was convinced that the main Ricardian assumptions had to be preserved in order to permit a scientific analysis of economic relationships, he emphasized that the term *law,* as used in economics, could mean nothing more than a general proposition or statement of tendencies, more or less certain, more or less definite. About half a century later, closer attention was given to the techniques used by Marshall and his school to maintain the fiction that business activity is determined by "rational" economic behavior. Elements of such rationalism were found in the tendency to rely on present market conditions as a guide for the future, and on the assumption that the prevailing state of opinion, as expressed in the character of output and the behavior of prices, correctly reflected a summing up of economic prospects. Individuals' efforts to conform with the behavior of the majority and thus to contribute to the establishment of a sort of "conventional judgment" were regarded as another symptom of this rationalism.[39]

Influenced by the views of historically minded economists, Marshall even admitted that the validity of economic laws depended upon specific conditions varying in time and space, that every change in social conditions was likely to require modifications of some economic theorems.[40] Anxious to preserve close touch with reality as far as possible, he refused to introduce the highly abstract assumptions made by the advocates of "mathematical" versions of economic analysis. Thus, he tried to keep his teachings free from any aspect of finality.[41] Continuing a trend which had been inaugurated by Mill, he combined deductive analysis with extensive references to actual economic conditions, and abundantly applied the results of his theoretical findings to the discussion of economic policy. He even showed a certain predilection for an evolutionary interpretation of the course of economic events; his studies of the Hegelian philosophy were reflected in his allusions to the "organic growth" of the economy.

After his return from Germany, where he had spent the winter of 1870–71, Marshall included discussions of Hegel's philosophy of history in some of his lectures. But his intention to combine the historical approach with his analytical treatment of economic events was greatly discouraged by Cunningham's critical article.[42] Marshall's often-quoted dictum that the "Mecca of the economist lies in economic biology rather than in economic dynamics" was intended to justify his reluctance to analyze changes in the economic structure in terms of a mechanical conception of the economic system. But he did not attempt to indicate the logical requirements which the concept of an "organic" economic system would have to fulfill in order to provide a basis for the application of biological principles. Hidden behind Marshall's idea to apply organic principles to the study of an expanding or changing economy was the formidable methodological problem of whether laws of a mechanical type could be considered applicable to the short-term analysis of the economy, whereas long-term analysis would proceed in accordance with an "organismic" approach. Marshall did not raise that question. He adopted a "cautious, almost anti-theoretical attitude towards fundamentals which he buried in an overwhelming mass of qualifications and detail."[43]

Out of the wide variety of factors which could be assumed to operate toward "expansions of business activity," Marshall explicitly took account only of increases in the population and of savings, although he claimed that the central idea of his *Principles* turned on the "forces which cause movement" and that "their keynote was that of dynamics rather than statics." Dynamic aspects of the economy were referred to in Marshall's discussions of the time factor, his distinction between short-term and long-term prices, his theory of quasi-rents, and his cash-balance approach to the treatment of money.[44] That statement was hardly compatible with the fact that his analysis was predominatly based on the operation of forces which were assumed to work toward the establishment of equilibrium positions. In the Marshallian system at any given time, facts and expectations were assumed to be given in a calculable form and risks were supposed to be amenable to exact actuarial computation.[45] Hence, Marshall endeavored to solve practically all fundamental economic problems in terms of mechanical equilibrium analysis. In his studies dealing with industrial developments he was confronted with a variety of oligopolistic practices, but he treated them in a descriptive way and avoided, as far as possible, theoretical discussions of monopolistic or oligopolistic situations which did not provide the prospects of deterministic solutions.[46]

Marshall based his aversion to the construction of abstract hypothetical models of the economy upon the consideration that attempts of that type tended to deflect economists' attention from the study of the actual working of the economic machinery. But perhaps equally important in determining his attitude toward the development of "long chains of deduction" was the fact that, with the abandonment of the labor cost theory of value, the uniform standard for measuring exchange values had been lost, while Ricardian monetary theory, divorced as it was from price theory, failed to provide a method for adjusting general equilibrium analysis to fluctuations in the purchasing power of money. Hence, in his theoretical analysis Marshall minimized the importance of his dictum that "money was the center around which the science of economics clusters"; he restricted his equilibrium analysis to typical short-term situations, which permitted him to keep the purchasing power of money constant and to assume that the price level remained reasonably stable, and that market phenomena, governed by the competitive order, reflected perfectly "rational" conduct of buyers and sellers. Marshall's assumption of the constant utility of money has been characterized as "perfect competition among goods." It implied that the value of any article is so small in relation to the total income of the individual that a change in its price has no effect on the marginal utility of his total income.[47] Thus, he carefully adjusted the setting of his problems to the methods available within the framework of Ricardian economics, and avoided the discussion of problems which could not be formulated in terms of these methods.

Marshall did not explicitly define his conception of the economy as a whole.[48] That conception was based on the assumptions that the size of the "national" income was essentially determined by the available factors of production and their effective use, that all savings were absorbed by investments through the normal operations of the economic and financial machinery, and that the equilibrium rate of interest resulted from the demand for and supply of capital.[49] Regarding the time factor as the "center of the chief difficulty" of almost every economic problem, Marshall eliminated that factor from his theoretical analysis and asserted that statical treatment alone could give definiteness and precision of thought by breaking up complex questions. Thus, he excluded from his analysis the influence of all factors likely to interfere with the harmonious and undisturbed operation of the economy. Marshall intended to deal with business fluctuations in a second volume, but it was never written.

Marshall's ample use of the assumption of "other things being equal" reflected the traditional limitations which the Ricardians placed on the range of their reasoning.[50] His hypothetical laws were statements of economic tendencies which were derived from the proposition that market prices provided an instrument for the measurement of the strength of economic motives.

The analytical backbone of Marshall's doctrine was supplied by an enlarged and generalized Ricardian theory of distribution as expounded by Mill and elaborated by means of a mathematical apparatus.[51] Especially, the translation into differential equations of Ricardian theorems offered various opportunities to fill the gaps in Ricardian doctrines. But so strong was Marshall's attachment to these doctrines that he endeavored to minimize the challenge of the marginal utility schools, which regarded the importance attributed to individual goods as the ultimate determinant of exchange values and insisted upon deriving the value of productive services from the utility of the goods of final consumption.[52]

In his discussion of utilities, Marshall avoided any direct allusions to the felicific calculus which had flavored Jevons's economics. His attitude toward the principles of utilitarian philosophy has been the object of divergent views. In fact, under the impression of mounting criticisms of the principles of hedonism he replaced the common, utilitarian expressions with a new phraseology. But his terms *desire for gratification* and *desire to avoid the sacrifices involved in labor and waiting* have been characterized as replicas of the motives underlying the felicific calculus. He referred to the marginal utility principle only as an element determining demand on the assumption that each individual tended to achieve a balance of his marginal expenditures in the distribution of his purchases. From various passages of the first edition of the *Principles of Economics,* it is evident that Marshall shared with Jevons and other contemporary economists the belief that utilities and disutilities could be measured, and that even interpersonal comparisons of utilities were valid. In later editions of the *Principles,* however, Marshall withdrew the latter proposition.[53] He believed himself to be on safe ground whem he based his price analysis on the assumption that for short periods demand was the decisive factor, whereas for long periods that role was played by supply. Thus, he practically eschewed the stimulus which marginal utility analysis exercised on economic reasoning, and to that extent contributed toward petrifying English economics for more than a generation.

Without defining the standard unit of the value of costs of production, Marshall identified costs with the long-run supply price of productive factors.[54] He used the problematic simile of the two blades of a pair of scissors to illustrate the combined effects exercised on the value of the product by utility (demand) and ''real costs of production'' (supply). He assumed the relation of costs to value always to be indirect—costs influencing supply, and supply, in conjunction with demand, influencing value.[55] Following Nassau Senior, he defined ''supply price'' as the sum of the prices that have to be paid to ''call forth'' the efforts and sacrifices needed to produce a commodity. On the assumption that the productive agents had equal earnings in alternative uses, he considered real costs to be proportional to money costs. Marshall did not pay much attention to the conditions under which money costs could be assumed to be proportional to real costs.[56] Only in the market for agricultural commodities did he ascribe primary importance for the determination of prices to marginal costs; he referred to average costs as the determinant of prices under conditions of constant or increasing returns.

Whereas Marshall applied the principles of marginal utility analysis mainly to the study of consumers' behavior, he made effective use of the idea of the margin in his productivity theory, acknowledging the pioneer work that had been done by Thünen. In the introduction to the *Principles of Economics,* he explained that, led by Cournot, he was caused to attach great importance to the fact that the demand for a thing is a continuous function of which the ''marginal increment'' is, in stable equilibrium, balanced against the corresponding increment in cost. Marshall assumed each productive agent to be used up to the point at which its marginal productivity equaled its marginal costs. Combining the idea of the margin with that of substitution, Marshall made the concept of ''substitution at the margin'' a valuable instrument for analyzing processes of replacing less profitable by more profitable resources.

THE MARSHALLIAN THEORY

When the various elements of the Marshallian theory of distribution are combined into a coherent picture, it is easy to realize the changes in the English intellectual climate which occurred after the Ricardian theory was formulated. The issue of unearned increments as connected with the agricultural rent had faded into the background. The rapid development of the mechanized industries, the incessant expansion of world trade, and the creation of an international capital market which was organized by English banks had greatly modified the structure of the English economy and had placed the manufacturing classes into the center of economic interests. The relationships between employers and workers, especially in large-scale industries, had assumed new aspects. The development of the system of joint stock companies and other devices for financing industrial and commercial enterprises had served to establish a clear distinction between the capitalist and the entrepreneur.

True to the Ricardian principle of connecting each of the general types of income with a specific productive service, Marshall elevated the managerial and organizational functions of entrepreneurs to the rank of a special productive factor, and thus gave "profits" a convenient place in the distributive scheme as a reward for entrepreneurial activity. "Entrepreneurship" as understood by Marshall was a productive factor which could not be hired in the market but fixed for the firm an optimum size for the scale of its operations.[57] As defined by Marshall, the term *profit* covered the wages for routine management and supervision, returns on investments made by the entrepreneur in his own enterprise, various forms of earnings connected with noncompetitive and fluctuating aspects of the economy (such as compensation for risk), and "extraordinary" profits earned in situations in which productive agents, successfully combined in an enterprise, were more efficient and productive than without that combination. On the assumption that in the long run the entrepreneur will expect to earn profits of a more or less determined size, Marshall regarded such minimum profits as constituent elements of the long-term supply price. Marshall connected this normal rate of profit with a hypothetical concept, the somewhat nebulous "representative firm." But neither in his discussion of profits nor in other sections of his economic analysis did Marshall attach particular importance to the risk element. He related differences in the rate of gross profits to the fact that the various constituent parts of such profits are bound to differ between industries and enterprises.

In order to account for the existence of interest on capital, Marshall referred to productiveness or technical productivity on the one hand and to prospectiveness, or waiting and saving with the expectation of earning future goods, on the other. The abstinence theory provided him with a conception of interest on capital as a reward for the sacrifice involved in the deferment of want satisfaction, or waiting, and he attributed to that sacrifice the function of preventing productive processes from being extended up to the point at which they would merely repay the costs of production. Marshall used the term *waiting* in the sense attached by Senior to the term *abstinence*.[58] Starting from these premises, Marshall explained the level of interest according to the general rules of price formation. Like the Ricardians, he was convinced that a positive correlation existed between the rate of interest and the propensity to save and the volume of savings. This reasoning led to the conclusion that the rate of interest had to be high enough to cause a "marginal" group of Capitalists to contribute their share to the existing volume of savings. Thus, a "saver's or waiter's surplus" could be shown to accrue to those Capitalists whose decisions to save were less influenced by the level of the rate. Reference to the "saver's surplus" was used to meet sarcastic allusions by socialist authors to the "reward" paid to millionaires for their "abstinence."

In his wage theory, Marshall disregarded the problems connected with the existence of "noncompeting groups" of workers. For the short-term determination of wages he adopted Thünen's principle of marginal productivity, according to which for each category of workers the level of wages is defined by the value of the product added to the existing volume of production from the last still-profitably-employed worker. In his long-run considerations, however, Marshall followed Jevons by defining wages as a reward for disutilities. Thus, he drew a lower limit below which wages could not be expected to fall without stimulating counteracting forces.

Marshall did not question the Ricardian conception of rent as a residual income, created in the market and resulting from the diminishing returns of land, due to the relative scarcity of the soil and the pressure of the population. To other, temporary, returns on fixed investments which were due to differences between prices and costs and were equally price-determined in the short run he applied the term *quasi-rent*. The qualification of these rents by the attribute ''quasi-'' was designed to emphasize the temporary nature of income of that type.

Application of the marginal utility principles to the analysis of consumers' behavior caused Marshall to elaborate the idea of a ''surplus'' or benefit which an individual can derive from his opportunities or environment. The use which he made of that idea in his theory of interest has been mentioned above. In a similar vein, he argued that a consumer would be willing to pay a price higher than he actually pays for all units of a good which have a higher value than the marginal unit; hence, he ascribed to almost all purchases a tendency to create surplus satisfactions.[59] In other connections he spoke of ''worker's'' surpluses accruing in cases in which the rate of remuneration exceeded the rate which the workers would have been willing to accept. The objections raised to the measurability and interpersonal comparability of want satisfactions, utilities, and disutilities did not prevent Marshall from suggesting the idea of an aggregate of consumers' surpluses for the economy, representing the total utilities of all commodities produced minus the sum total of the efforts and sacrifices made in producing the commodities. The idea of a ''surplus'' had a normative connotation; it was associated with the notion of unearned income. As an objective magnitude—identified with an excess of price over cost of production—it had been used by the Physiocrats and adherents of the labor cost theory of value. As a subjective magnitude it signified excess of want satisfaction over sacrifice.[60]

Marshall used the idea of surplus to develop the idea of ''consumers' rent,'' which he applied to situations in which consumers derived advantages from changes in the price of a commodity. Implied in the Marshallian concept of consumers' rent were the assumptions that the price of only one commodity is made to vary and that the marginal utility of the consumer's income remains unchanged. The corresponding concept of producers' rent was applicable to cases in which producers availed themselves of means of production that were superior to those used by marginal producers. Marshall referred to the principle of diminishing marginal utility—which he almost ignored in his value analysis—to contrast the gains accruing to some individuals from the execution of productive processes with the costs inflicted through these processes on others. Considerations of that kind provided him with convenient instruments for the establishment of a theory of ''social welfare,'' in which he placed limits on the beneficial effects of free competition and recommended paying subsidies to industries with increasing returns and imposing taxes on industries with diminishing returns.

The most original and stimulating parts of Marshall's *Principles* were those in which he organized an effective approach to the study of ''partial'' or ''particular'' equilibrium situations, that is to say, to the study of small sectors of the economy (industries, firms, and individuals) on the assumption that these sectors adjusted their equilibrium positions to the impact of outside influences without exercising perceptible effects on the other elements of the economy. Important aspects of equilibrium conditions obtaining in specific industries had been analyzed by Antoine Cournot and the two Austrians Rudolf Auspitz and Richard Lieben. Noteworthy English writers who had published contributions to partial equilibrium analysis were Dionysus Lardner and Henry C. Fleeming Jenkin. Jenkin published various papers between 1868 and 1872, but at the time of their publication these essays attracted little attention. Leon Walras and Vilfredo Pareto considered studies of this type incompatible with the general interdependence of all economic magnitudes included in a system.[61]

Problems connected with the stabilization, contraction, or expansion of industries provided the main material for Marshall's discussions; he exhibited great skill in reducing to uniform patterns the almost infinite variety of relationships shown in actual life. Marshall did this by vaguely defining an industry as a multitude of firms supplying an undifferentiated product to a market. Paramount among the hypothetical features of these analyses were the elimination of the time element and the assumption that any price movements which resulted from changes in the combination of productive factors were ruled by the tendency to return to equilibrium conditions of supply and demand under which prices were equal to costs of production.

On the assumption that the influence of the costs of production on the value of the products increased with the length of the "operational period," Marshall classified market exchange values according to the short or long run.[62] Day-to-day market price was determined by demand operating on a fixed supply: in the short term, with a limited variability of output derived from a given supply of the instruments of production, the price was shown to settle between a lower limit fixed by average prime or variable cost and an upper limit dependent upon demand and the limited elasticity of the supply curve; in the long term, earnings were allowed to influence the supply of the instruments of production. In the light of such considerations, Marshall examined the conditions under which new firms were attracted to an industry and the price policies of firms with falling demands.

The distinction which Marshall drew between external and internal economies of an industry was prompted by the intention to account for decreasing average costs of firms operating under competitive conditions. He defined external economies as reductions in cost resulting from the general development of an industry and neutral with regard to the relative competitive positions of the firms producing for the same market. Under this heading Marshall discussed the influence exercised by geographic specialization, by general technical progress, and by world production. Problems connected with the relationships among different industries were outside the scope of the Marshallian analysis. In his discussion of internal economies Marshall dealt with the various factors which tend to modify competitive positions. The effects of large-scale production occupied a prominent place among these factors. But the puzzling question of how relatively small-scale enterprises could stand the competition of large concerns operating under increasing returns received adequate treatment only at a much later date.

The Marshallian analysis of the representative firm was designed to show the behavior of a hypothetical firm operating strictly under the competitive order and adjusting its selling prices to marginal costs of production. For firms of that type, Marshall examined the effects on costs and prices of "external economies," imperfections of the market, and shifts in temporary, more or less accidental advantages. Prompted by the endeavor to

achieve closer touch with reality while remaining within the sphere of theoretical reasoning, he made extensive application of the idea of substitution at the margin as combined
with the idea of elasticity of substitution in his study of the forces which modify the size of
industries composed of small individual firms. His research into the behavior of firms
expanding their output at rising, constant, and declining unit costs prepared a scientific
setting of problems which were subsequently treated under the heading of "business
economics" as a separate discipline.[63]

These extensive excursions into the field of particular equilibrium situations provided
Marshall's disciples with an excellent training ground for the exercise of logical operations. But they deflected their attention from far more important problems which turned
on the construction of a consistent economic system, the mutual relationships of its
elements, and the role played by monetary factors in the functioning of an unstable
economy.

Marshall's place in the history of economic reasoning cannot be fully appreciated
unless account is taken of the deep ethical convictions which he expressed in almost all
not strictly theoretical parts of his work. According to his own testimony, his interest in
economic problems had originally been aroused by his desire to contribute to the improvement of the conditions of the English lower classes. Hence, he organized his economics
against a background of the value judgments which were current among the English
intellectuals of the Victorian period.[64] In contrast to many of his professional contemporaries, Marshall was much affected by the inevitable mental conflict which resulted from
the fact that the methods of hypothetical reasoning—indispensable as they were for
scientific analysis—provided no moral foundation for social organization, but pointed
only to the problematic results of trial and error, or pictures of economic conditions which
were far remote from reality. His reluctance to accept—without many reservations—the
principles of marginal utility analysis was perhaps motivated by a deep-seated aversion to
an approach which emphasized want satisfaction and demand as the fundamental elements
of economic analysis. That approach was hardly compatible with his conception of the
course of economic events as a history of increasing production, of the progressive
realization of the benefits of free enterprise, and of the stimulating effects of competition
on the development of individual initiative, responsibility, efficiency, thriftiness, and
rational conduct. His belief in economic progress prevented him from accepting J. S.
Mill's outlook on a final, stationary state of the economy.

Accepting the theory of the "secular decline" of the rate of interest, Marshall
connected that phenomenon with the rapid accumulation of savings and the increasing
supply of capital; he pointed to the spread of education and managerial abilities to account
for the decline in the efficiency earnings of the entrepreneurs. As he was convinced that
these changes in the distribution of the national dividend were not offset by increases in
land rent, he expected economic growth to be accompanied by rising real wages, which in
turn would increase the efficiency of labor and enhance the productivity of the economy.

Marshall's *Principles* secured a new lease on life for the Ricardian methodological
maxims.[65] The large majority of his disciples were convinced that he had given to
economics its more or less final shape; hence, they considered it their main task to
elaborate a few problems which in their view had not yet found a definite solution.[66]
Perhaps the most conspicuous among these problems were those of "welfare economics," which turned on the advantages and disadvantages that result from the operation of

the competitive order on the assumption that the welfare of the individual can be identified with the sum total of his want satisfaction, and that the welfare of the community is equal to the sum total of the welfare of its members.

WELFARE ECONOMICS

Welfare economics, as suggested by Marshall, was elaborated on by Arthur C. Pigou to a point at which it occupied almost the center of economic theory.[67] Using bold simplifications, Pigou applied the principles of marginal productivity to the determination of optimum welfare measured in terms of an "objective standard": the national income expressed by the monetary value of the physical goods and services annually produced while capital investment remained intact. John R. Hicks argued that a measurement of economic welfare in terms of current consumption would give the same results as a measurement in terms of productivity on the assumption that prices would be equal to marginal costs under a system of perfect competition.[68] With this approach to the problems of social welfare, Pigou initiated a promising development of national income analysis.

On the sweeping but questionable assumption that the marginal utility of money was the same for all individuals, Pigou regarded the demand price of a good as a measure of the satisfaction provided by the good. Following Marshall's example, he conceived of utilities as measurable and comparable magnitudes, and adopted the proposition that economic welfare has increased in all cases in which the absolute share of the poorer classes in the national dividend were enlarged and the size of that dividend was not reduced.

Of primary importance for Pigou's analysis was the distinction which he established between the marginal private net produce and its social counterpart. He defined marginal private net produce as the increase in the output of an enterprise resulting from the addition of a unit of a productive agent and the ensuing rational adjustment of the other agents. The marginal social net product was the sum total of the corresponding private net products when account was taken of the effects of the changes on the price system and on the conditions of other enterprises. Pigou listed various types of cases such as with inventions and scientific discoveries when divergencies occur between the social net product and the sum of private net products, but he admitted that for a number of industries uncompensated benefits and burdens could not be expressed in monetary terms.

The problems connected with the allocation of resources played a central role in his investigation. Using a method of balancing the advantages and disadvantages of very small variations in output for different industries, Pigou advanced the proposition that maximum production of wealth was dependent on such a distribution of productive resources that the net social yield of a marginal unit was equalized throughout all uses. However, since expansion of production was determined by the marginal private net product rather than by the marginal social net product, Pigou concluded that the latter net product would be lower in increasing-cost industries than in industries operating under decreasing costs. Hence, following Marshall's suggestion, he recommended that a uniform tax be imposed on industries of the former type, and that bounties be granted to decreasing-cost industries in order to stimulate their expansion.

That reasoning was criticized in various articles by Allyn A. Young, J. H. Clapham, and Dennis H. Robertson. These criticisms were elaborated on by Frank H. Knight in two articles dealing with the problem of social costs. Knight argued that in the case of increasing costs, the higher prices paid for scarce factors did not affect the exploitation of the resources but resulted from the payment of rents, an indispensable element in the mechanism of resource allocation. Real economies in the use of productive factors were, however, involved in the case of decreasing costs. External decreasing costs could be related to internal decreasing costs in other industries. Pigou's concept of national income was equally exposed to various objections.[69]

In his extensive discussions of special measures of economic policy designed to secure optimum welfare, Pigou took account of disturbing factors such as frictions and lags due to immobility and indivisibility of productive resources, imperfect knowledge of market conditions, and the like. As a counterweight to the ''irrational preference for present satisfaction'' as compared with the importance of future wants, he recommended discriminating taxation in favor of savings.

In this connection mention may be made of the comprehensive works of John A. Hobson, although his treatment of the problems of social welfare was hardly based on sound methodological principles.[70] Deeply influenced by Ruskin's attacks on the capitalist economy and Arnold Toynbee's analysis of the human costs of England's industrial expansion, Hobson rejected the Ricardian treatment of economics as a system of marketable values. Using a vaguely defined ''calculus of human costs of production,'' he applied that standard to the determination of economic progress and growth. His distinction between ''productive earnings,'' making for growth, and ''unproductive surpluses'' made the latter surpluses responsible for all defects of the productive machinery, especially ''overinvestments'' and the ever-recurrent economic crises. His idea of ''surplus incomes'' was—erroneously—regarded as a new version of the Marxian concept of surplus value.[71] In the writings of T. R. Malthus and Earl Lauderdale, Hobson discovered a good deal of confirmation for his view that ''irrational surplus incomes'' such as rent, interest on capital, and profit were the source of ''oversavings,'' the root of the main social evils. Hobson's concept of ''oversavings'' implied that all savings were invested and he attributed to savings a role which was the opposite of its role in the Keynesian theory of employment. Hence, he was strongly opposed to wage reduction as a remedy of cyclical unemployment, and he regarded equalization of incomes and promotion of consumption as the only adequate anticyclical measures.[72]

That analysis of the operation of the capitalist economy formed the background for Hobson's conviction that all markets were unethical owing to differences in purchasing power, and that the market prices were vitiated by the play of selfish interests. Although he proposed the establishment of a planned economy managed by the government, he wanted to preserve private initiative in those sectors of the economy where expansion was dependent upon the exercise of inventive capacity.[73] In support of that view he referred to G. Jarde's distribution between repetition and invention as the two principal sociological forces.

With his interpretation of the effects of excessive savings, Hobson anticipated certain views which later gained widespread recognition. The same was true of his proposition that the volume of savings, as determined by income distribution, was not affected by changes in the rate of interest. The theory of ''oversavings'' as applied to the explanation of crises and depressions appealed to many businessmen, trade union leaders, and politicians, and contributed significantly to the popularity of Hobson's ideas. Keynes himself paid tribute to Hobson for the connection he made between savings and depressions.[74]

Hobson has also been credited with having advanced an idea which was later elaborated under the slogan "theory of capitalist imperalism." He argued that the excessive rate of savings which resulted from the unequal distribution of incomes could be sustained only when surplus capital was invested on an ever-increasing scale in the less developed parts of the world.[75] To the great banking houses, Hobson ascribed the main responsibility for promoting imperialistic policies, since banking profits could be greatly enhanced by investments made in colonies and dependencies. Ruthless pursuit of such policies would eventually lead to the carving up of the undeveloped regions by the large capitalist powers, which would be forced to defend their spheres of interest against aggression and hostile infiltration, and would be involved in ever-renewed warfare. Hobson derived the inevitability of the wars among the "imperialistic" powers from the search for investment opportunities, as distinct from the Marxist theories of imperialism, which pointed to the struggles over markets for goods produced in excessive quantities. A third similar theory, advanced by some national socialist authors, derived the struggle for the possession of colonies from the desire of the large industrialized countries to secure free access to indispensable raw materials.

Chapter 20
The Elaboration of
Marginal Utility Economics

———

THE DEVELOPMENT OF MATHEMATICAL VERSIONS

THE TRANSFORMATION of economics into a science of applied mathematics as initiated by Léon Walras was consistently pursued by Vilfredo Pareto, who was Walras's successor at the University of Lausanne and the founder of the so-called school of Lausanne.[1] An engineer by training, Pareto proclaimed, even more tenaciously than Walras, the mechanical conception of economic relationships as the only valid method of economic analysis, and he insisted on the necessity of analyzing all such relationships in terms of a consistent model of interdependent magnitudes.

In accordance with this approach, the construction of such a model had to be based on the assumption that all problems which dealt with economic relationships could be rendered determinate.[2] Hence, Pareto used the disparaging expression *literary economists* to describe the adherents of other marginalist schools who availed themselves of methods of "isolating abstraction" and partial equilibrium analysis, thereby disregarding the fundamental interdependence of all elements of the equilibrium system. Enrico Barone, one of Pareto's most distinguished followers, defined mathematical economics as a science which was based on the rigid observation of two principles: (*a*) strict interdependence of all magnitudes included in the system, and (*b*) establishment among these magnitudes of as many logical relationships as there are variables.

In a very instructive discussion of the methods to be applied by the social sciences, the philosopher Benedetto Croce (1866–1952) raised the question of whether a merely "accidental" attribute, the measurability of certain phenomena, provided sufficient justification for separating rigidly economic from noneconomic facts.[3] Pareto's assumptions, he argued, included the metaphysical postulate that internal facts connected with man's will and activity had to be placed on an equal footing with the phenomena of physical nature.

Describing himself as the "most nominalist of Nominalists," Pareto traced the differences of view between his opponents and himself to the famous medieval clash between the Nominalists and the Realists. As used in this connection, the term *Realists* was intended to connote adherents of the Scholastic view that reality is to be attached to abstract generic concepts. Benedetto Croce's philosophy was strongly influenced by Hegelian dialectics. That is why Pareto rejected Croce's reference to the "nature of things" as a criterion for defining the scope of a science, and refused to discuss such topics as the "nature of man's activity," and the "nature" and "essence" of value. Pareto insisted that the equations of mathematical economics showed "objective" relations among quantities, not relations among more or less precise concepts of the mind. He emphasised that the hypotheses adopted to develop the mathematical aspects of his economic theory had not been chosen for any "intrinsic" value which could be ascribed to them, but only for the purpose of yielding deductions which could be shown to be in harmony with the facts. How much of Pareto's own theorizing actually was "in harmony with facts" is a moot question. The idea of defining a science in terms of the method used could hardly be more strongly emphasized than in Pareto's attempt to justify the principles of deductive reasoning and the application of mechanical concepts to economic analysis.

Since Pareto was convinced that the premises of deductive reasoning which he advocated had to be based on observable data, he insisted that these data be supplied by analyzing the effects of individual behavior, and he objected to the application of the same methodology to more or less freely formed aggregates. Hence, the general problem which he tried to solve consisted in demonstrating the functioning of an imaginary economic system the behavior of which was governed by two general factors: tastes or wants (*gusti*) of the individuals, and obstacles (*ostacoli*) interfering with the fulfillment of desires. The strict application of a mechanical equilibrium concept to that system was secured by the assumptions that all forces which determined the behavior of the variables were counterbalanced by equivalent tendencies and that, as in the Walrasian model, the mutual relationships of all variables could be expressed by a system of simultaneous equations.

In his treatment of tastes Pareto used the concept of *ophélimité élémentaire* to define the unit satisfaction derived by the individual from a small increment in the available quantity of a good, when the latter was conceived of as a constituent part of a group of complementary goods. *Ophélimité* originally meant individual preference. Pareto substituted that expression for the Walrasian term *rareté* in order to emphasize the dependence of marginal utilities upon the simultaneous or subsequent availability of several goods. He used the term *ophélimité pondérée* to denote the utility of the last acquired unit of a good divided by its price.

An approach of that kind had been suggested by the objections raised by Francis Ysidro Edgeworth to the simplifying assumption that increases in income were followed by corresponding increases in the purchase of each desired commodity.[4] He was convinced that mathematical procedures were at least applicable, if not indispensable, whenever quantitative data were given, permitting comparisons between magnitudes. Hence, he applied such procedures to the measurement of utility and ethical values, to the algebraic or diagrammatic determination of economic equilibrium, to the measurement of belief, probability, evidence and so on.[5] Edgeworth had insisted that the utility of a good was a function of several variables,[6] that it was influenced by changeable quantities of a large variety of other goods of the substitutive or complementary types.[7] Moreover, Edgeworth had shown that individual desires frequently concentrate on combinations of several goods, while no definite preference is given to a specific combination. In the light of these considerations, he concluded that all want satisfaction which could be derived from a good or from a combination of goods was, for all intents and purposes, connected with the total network of want satisfactions available to an individual. Elaborating on that proposition, he suggested arranging combinations of utilities in the form of "indifference curves," designed to express an individual's range of indifference as to the choice among various commodities and combinations of commodities simultaneously available.

Edgeworth advanced that suggestion in the course of an attempt to develop a theory of barter by delimiting the range of possible barter terms or exchange ratios. In his *Mathematical Investigations,* Irving Fisher adopted a similar approach, having abandoned the assumption that the marginal utility of each good depends only on its quantity.

As applied by Pareto, the idea of indifference curves provided a welcome instrument for eliminating any reference to the measurability and comparability of utilities and for transforming marginal utility analysis into a pure theory of choice. Using the ophelimity indices to indicate the order in which each individual would group the various indifference curves in accordance with his scale of preferences, Pareto believed to have secured objective foundations for the determination of the magnitudes included in his system.

On the assumption that goods and utilities were divisible into infinitesimal fractions, Pareto visualized a procedure of plotting all possible indifference combinations on a system of coordinates and drawing indifference lines by connecting the points at which different combinations of goods had the same ophelimity. Similar curves used by meteorologists provided the pattern for these graphic presentations. However, Pareto had no unequivocal answer to the question of whether a choice made between combinations of goods differing by infinitesimal amounts would be the same when the individuals were confronted with the choice between combinations differing by finite amounts.[8] An intricate problem was connected with the fact that in his arrangement of indifference curves Pareto subordinated the complementarity of the goods to the principle of their mutual substitutability.[9]

Pareto's intention was that the combined presentation of an individual's indifference curves would then supply a "photographic picture" of his observable tastes; economics could be placed on an "empirical" basis if the indifference and preference lines representing individual desires were supplemented by corresponding lines representing the "obstacles" individuals had to overcome in their endeavors to achieve maximum attainable want satisfaction. Obstacles of that kind were assumed to be caused by limits on the availability of goods, competitive conditions, costs of production, restrictions imposed by political or economic organizations, and the like. From obstacles of the first order Pareto distinguished secondary obstacles, such as circumstances that result in price changes immediately before or during exchange procedures. He extended the application of indifference curves to profits and related economic categories, and to producers' choices among available resources.

Backed by these methodological devices, Pareto raised the claim of having based his framework of a mathematical theory of consumption and production on "necessarily individual relationships of interdependence.'' Referring to the interdependence of all economic magnitudes, he considered himself justified in ignoring any problems connected with the establishment of causal relationships among economic phenomena. He emphasized this attitude especially with regard to the question of whether the value of the productive services was to be derived from the value of the products. Pareto raised the objection that marginal productivity analysis took account only of cases in which the technical coefficients were variable and, moreover, that it disregarded the existence of ''limitational factors,'' such as restrictions imposed upon production functions by technical conditions.[10]

Pareto's disciples hailed his attempt to use the technique of preference and indifference curves to eliminate aggregates of economic magnitudes from economic analysis as a major contribution to scientific methodology.[11] Moreover, they believed that his techniques provided an effective instrument for avoiding any reference to psychological factors.[12] But it remained a moot question as to what degree psychological considerations provided the logical starting point for the construction of curves which were derived from the law of decreasing utilities.[13]

In his theory of distribution Pareto followed the principles established by Léon Walras, and accepted the Walrasian categories of interest, profit, rent, and wages. The entrepreneurs, occupying the center of the distributive scheme, were led to determine, in the course of market operations, the shares in the value of the products allotted to land, labor, and capital. Profit and rent were regarded as residual categories, since under static equilibrium conditions costs of production exhausted the price. Although Pareto extended his analysis to shifts from one equilibrium situation to another, his approach remained essentially static. Very characteristic of that approach was his treatment of economic crises, in which he availed himself of Clement Juglar's statistical investigations and, like Juglar, emphasized the wavelike nature of the movements and the interconnections between prosperity and depression.[14] He attributed alternations in the behavior of the economy mainly to simultaneous economic attitudes provided by identical sentiments, and spoke of ''excitable material'' in order to characterize the predisposition of businessmen to overestimate the prospective profitability of their enterprises. Finally, he raised the question of whether the ''rhythmical movement of business activity'' was not a condition of economic progress.

Since Pareto claimed general validity for his mathematical treatment of economic relationships, he considered it applicable to any economic order, regardless of the principles underlying its organization. A prolonged discussion about economic calculation under socialism has turned on Pareto's proposition that the methods to be adopted by a socialist ministry of production would have to be the same as those used by capitalist employers.[15]

Pareto defined ''optimum collective want satisfaction'' as a situation in which no individual could achieve a preferred position at the cost of others. The list established by Pareto as conditions of maximizing collective utility was quite substantial. Included in that list were perfect knowledge and perfect realization of ends-means relationships; perfect mobility of the economic resources, no dependence of wants on the processes of satisfying them, perfect competition (involving exclusion of fraud or coercion), and the existence of a stable monetary standard (*numéraire*). According to that definition, collective want satisfaction could be enhanced only if those whose incomes experienced a gain could retain a part of that gain after having compensated those whose income had been diminished. Welfare judgments which could not be justified on purely economic grounds had to be based on ethical considerations.

Pareto's imaginary economic system, strictly ruled by mechanical principles, was the object of widely varying views. Particularly open to skeptical comments were some of his bold assumptions, such as the infinitesimal divisibility of wants and utilities, the infinite mutual substitutability of the objects of want satisfaction, the problematic nature of his indifference curves, and finally the applicability of systems of simultaneous equations to various magnitudes which are elements of time series.[16] The usefulness of a static model of an imaginary economy was questioned by economists who insisted upon the introduction of the time factor into economic analysis;[17] others objected to the purely functional conception of the relationship between economic magnitudes, regarding the study of causal relationships among economic phenomena as a primary task of economic analysis.[18] One of Pareto's main contributions to income theory was his theorem of income distribution, called ''Pareto's law.'' Based on a sort of a priori axiom, it was designed to demonstrate a high degree of constancy over time in the distribution of incomes. It showed the importance of an otherwise rather neglected problem, that of invariants in the economic structure of society. But the general validity of the Paretian law of income distribution was questioned in prolonged discussions among Alberto Benduce, V. Furlan, Giorgio Mortara, Corrado Gini, and Umberto Ricci. Pareto's income curves were open to the objection that the multiplicity of economic conditions was too considerable to permit the establishment of the alleged irregularities.[19]

Although Walras was a Frenchman and Pareto's main economic works were published in French, mathematical economics were almost ignored by the leading French economists up to the beginning of the First World War. A few studies written by Pareto's disciples, W. L. Zawadski, P. Bovens, and Jacques Moret, between 1912 and 1915 did not contribute significantly to the spread or the elaboration of his ideas. In Italy the mathematical methods were defended by Luigi Amoroso; they provided Enrico Barone with the instruments for the preparation of a remarkable textbook.[20] Only after the First World War did Pareto's teachings receive increasing recognition.

In Pareto's view, the establishment of a hypothetical economic system constituted only the first chapter of a comprehensive study of society which had to proceed according to the method of successive approximation.[21] Since the ''laws'' and ''experimental uniformities'' established by theoretical economics reflected only possibilities and probabilities, any further approach to reality had to be achieved by developing additional theories which could be combined with those applicable to the economic sphere. However, it was evident from the outset that the strict determinateness of the results of human behavior which had provided the background for the economic analysis could not be assumed to prevail in the sphere of general social relationships. Consequently, mathematical methods could not be applied to the study of social phenomena in which account had to be taken of the time element and of institutional factors and their changes in addition to ''nonlogical behavior'' resulting from certain ''states of mind,'' as contrasted with actions pursued in conformity with logical procedures. As defined by Pareto, a ''state of mind'' is a hypothetical factor which can be inferred from overt acts or expressions of sentiments frequently implied in moral, religious, or other doctrines.

Pareto used the term *residues* to denote imaginary, more or less constant determinants of human actions. His residues were: The instinct of combinations; persistence of aggregates; the need to manifest one's sentiments through actions; sentiments connected with sociality; integrity of the individual; and the sex residue. He called *derivations* any reasoning of the "nonlogicoexperimental" type designed to rationalize motives and to conceal actual incentives behind a screen of apparently logical considerations. In these discussions Pareto turned all his critical energies against reasoning based on metaphors, allegories, and analogies.

Such criticisms based on purely logical considerations did not prevent Pareto from emphasizing the role played by various metaphysical doctrines as means of maintaining the equilibrium of various societies. To such doctrines he attributed the tendency to use intuition and religious experience to arrive at the recognition of "higher" entities. To the "pseudoscientific" theories he ascribed the tendency to invoke the authority of reason and to favor attitudes of skepticism. He placed the relationships between residues and derivations into the center of his research, and suggested that the relative importance attached to the various residues were more or less constant for a uniform society, but that, in this sphere, conspicuous divergencies obtained between different societies or different classes within a society.

Hence, in Pareto's sociological scheme a predominant role was played by three groups of phenomena: those belonging to the group of "interests" and assigned to the economic sphere as generalized immediate ends of national action, those termed "residues" and held to be psychological in origin, and finally "derivations," characterized as "ideological ratiocinations," guided by specific intentions and objectives. The discussion of these phenomena was preparatory to the formulation of Pareto's most conspicuous sociological thesis, the "circulation of the elites." It centered on the idea that every known society had been composed of heterogeneous groups, and that in all societies, even those of the democratic types, social power has been exercised by "elites" alternating in the accession to power. Ideas of that kind had provided the background for Pareto's analysis of socialist theories. He especially relied upon them to support his biting attacks on the Marxian concept of a "classless" socialist society. The stability of a society was shown to be dependent upon the structure of the ruling classes, their resistance to decadence, and their power to defend their positions against other emerging elites equipped with more virile attitudes. That analysis led to the conclusion that at the stage of development arrived at in the twentieth century, in practically all industrialized countries the leading classes turned to various creeds of the past and were in favor of antiindividualistic forms of government.

Pareto's analysis of the declining power of "demagogical plutocracy" caused the fascist government of Italy to proclaim him as a prophet of the corporative state.[22] The static approach adopted by Pareto in his economic analysis was also a characteristic feature of his sociological theory, which was ruled by the assumption that all social structures could be analyzed in terms of combinations of a few basic elements, the residues.[23]

Outside the antidemocratic Italian camp, Pareto's sociological ideas were the object of much criticism. His disparaging treatment of "nonlogical" concepts such as liberty and democracy and his hostility toward all socialist creeds and ideals of solidarity were constrasted with Walras's belief in the advisability of state intervention and far-reaching social reforms. Whatever may have been the reasons which caused two thinkers to endorse the same methodological principles in their theoretical studies but to cherish widely divergent social philosophies, their example appears to confirm the view that no necessary association exists between the belief in the validity of a specific methodology and the adoption of specific ethical or political convictions.

GENERAL PROBLEMS OF PSYCHOLOGICAL MARGINALISM

The far-reaching divergencies which developed between the teachings of the mathematical economists and the theories of the psychological school of marginalism were largely due to fundamental differences in their approaches to economic analysis. The thinkers of the School of Lausanne conceived of all relationships among economic magnitudes as strictly interdependent elements of an economic system ruled by a rigid equilibrium principle. To that logical requirement they adjusted any other considerations concerning the nature and behavior of these magnitudes. Hence, they assumed infinite divisibility of goods and services, attributed to each individual the function of equalizing his want satisfactions, and the like. The Austrian economists, however—above all F. von Wieser, one of Carl Menger's most outstanding disciples—were looking for causal relationships between economic phenomena, and they ignored the problems connected with the application of mathematical procedures to the construction of equilibrium models of the economy. They were convinced that the utlimate explanation of all economic phenomena had to be found by analyzing the psychological aspects of individual behavior, and for about two decades the search for psychophysiological foundations of these phenomena played a conspicuous role in their studies.[24] Von Wieser even compared the importance of the marginal utility principle for economic analysis with the importance attached to the principle of gravity in the field of mechanics. Subtle psychological problems which were only remotely connected with economic issues were the object of extensive investigations.[25]

In order to appreciate the intellectual atmosphere in which these studies were pursued, it should be kept in mind that the Austrian adherents of marginal utility analysis were faced with unrelenting attacks on their principles of reasoning and their methods of research. Many members of the German historical school, who firmly believed in the existence of "social values" created by objective national spirits, were violently opposed to the search for general laws of the hypothetical type. Marxist authors resented not only the Marginalists' criticisms of the labor cost theory of value but also their contention that the principles of marginal analysis and general economic laws were applicable to all economies, regardless of their structure and the order underlying their operation. They associated the psychological approach adopted by the Austrians with "bourgeois mentality" and with the attempt to defend the interests of the leisure class, as evidenced by the emphasis placed on the demand for goods.[26] Bukharin elaborated in the idea suggested by various other Marxists that during the advanced stages of capitalistic developments the surplus values accumulated through the exploitation of labor flowed mainly into the pockets of persons who had no relation to production. The theory of value adopted by the Austrians was said to reflect the psychology of the consumers, the "rentiers."[27]

Faced with incessant criticism of their doctrine, the Austrian economists felt obliged to strengthen, above all, the logical foundations of their analysis and to enlarge the scope of its applicability. It may be observed in this connection that Vienna, the capital of the Austrian monarchy which for centuries had stood at the crossroad of Eastern and Western political powers, was subsequently placed at the crossroad of conflicting patterns of thought. Protected by the hereditary monarchy and its feudal background, Scholastic methods of reasoning had been preserved through educational institutions which were controlled by the Catholic Church. Simultaneously, Vienna was practically the only European city east of the Rhine where nominalistic reasoning had secured a firm foothold, not only in the natural sciences but also in various social philosophies. Adherence to organismic patterns had been fostered by nationalistic movements and the spread of German "idealistic philosophies." An "orthodox" version of Marxism—the so-called Austro-Marxism—had been developed in Vienna by convinced adherents of that doctrine. Hence, the Austrian Marginalists were continuously involved in methodological struggles of varying types. In those endeavors they followed fairly closely the theoretical outline mapped out by Menger. They made ample use of the method of isolation which permitted them to eliminate disturbing influences from the analysis of causal relationships between economic phenomena, on the assumption that subsequently the typical behavior of such disturbances could be determined and account could be taken of their effects.

Lack of a common denominator to which all magnitudes of the economic system could be reduced prevented the Austrian economists from developing a group of economic aggregates adequate to devise the model of an economic system. Moreover, they were opposed to the construction of any aggregate which had roots in organismic reasoning. Hence, the range of their problems was limited and only gradually expanded. Starting from the psychological aspects of the concepts of utility and value, they applied marginal utility analysis to the study of prices and costs of production, of the distributive processes, and of the problems involved in the allocation of scarce resources. At a later date, von Wieser endeavored to determine the conditions common to the treatment of scarce resources in an isolated household and in a centrally organized planned economy ruled by a perfectly rational mind.[28] According to his findings, important features of the distributive process, such as the land rent and interest on capital, were "natural" economic categories requiring recognition under any economic order. Gradually modifying his rigid initial assumptions, von Wieser examined the impact of marginal utility considerations on the competitive economy, on economic policy, on international economic relationships, and so on.[29]

The claim of the Austrian Marginalists that their approach was exclusively based on the observation of some simple psychological facts was supplemented by their refusal to connect their analyses with the principles of utilitarian philosophy. Hence, they ignored the concept of disutility, and argued that the sacrifice implied in the performance of labor consisted, in fact, in the loss of the advantage which could have been derived from spending one's time on another occupation.

Eugen von Böhm-Bawerk, one of the most eminent Austrian Marginalists, defended the thesis that the length of productive processes was influenced by the increasing disutility of labor only in a relatively unimportant number of cases, and that the formation of exchange values was independent of the rule of equal rewards for equal pains.[30] He showed that circular reasoning was involved in the Marshallian methods of deriving the value of the products from their costs and of explaining the value of labor in accordance with the principle of marginal productivity, which in turn implied a reference to the value of the products. To Marshall's simile of the two blades of a pair of scissors, Böhm-Bawerk opposed the marginalist method of explaining all values, including those of costs of production, in terms of a single principle.

Since all exchange values were expressed in prices, the Austrians were soon faced with the same problem William Stanley Jevons had been unable to solve: how to account for prices in terms of the marginal utility of goods on the one hand and the marginal utility of money on the other. A much-discussed question turned on the determination of the value of the total available supply of a commodity. Wieser proposed to obtain that aggregate value by multiplying the marginal value of one piece out of the supply by the number of pieces. This method enjoyed the approval of some American economists such as J. B. Clark and Frank A. Fetter. Böhm-Bawerk, however, argued that the equality of marginal utility can be applied only "disjunctively," and that the aggregate value of a supply is to be determined by adding up the specific utilities attached to the elements of that supply in the order of the fulfillment of want satisfactions. This procedure was preferred by some mathematical economists, since it implied abstraction from the time element. It was obvious that the marginal utility of the monetary unit could not be determined independently of the marginal utilities of its exchange equivalents. *Subjective exchange value* was the term used by the Austrian Marginalists to denote the value of a good which was derived from the utility of its exchange equivalents.

Böhm-Bawerk started his analysis of pricing processes from a limited strictly competitive market, in which the parties offered their goods for bartering purposes at "subjective values" which were expressed in arbitrarily chosen numerals.[31] Competitive prices were arrived at by analyzing the "rational behavior" of the parties; they were determined by the valuations of "marginal pairs," while pairs with higher and lower valuations, being excluded, had no influence on the bargaining processes. One marginal pair was determined by the valuation of the last buyer still admitted to a purchase and the valuation of the would-be seller who was the first on the list of those excluded from participating in the exchange. The other marginal pair was determined by the valuation of the seller who, though admitted to the exchange, had the least chances of being admitted and the valuation of the buyer who was at the top of list of those excluded. The problems involved in the "theory of isolated exchange" were in various respects similar to those later discussed in the theory of duopolistic pricing. But that analysis was open to the objection that the numerals, which were alleged to reflect subjective estimates of would-be buyers and sellers, did not represent undiluted psychological magnitudes, as was requested by the principles of marginal utility analysis, but rather reflected the results of preceding pricing processes.

The dangers involved in circular reasoning were enhanced when price analysis was extended beyond the schedules of a primitive barter economy, since in the monetary exchange economy the factors operating on the demand side were influenced by the size of incomes, which in turn were derived from the contributions of the productive factors to the value of the products. Thus, the estimates of utilities which Wieser used in his *Social Economics* to determine the value of the goods in an exchange economy were, in fact, based on prices which had been formed in the markets.[32]

The Swedish economist Knut Wicksell, who made outstanding contributions to the Austrian theory, used the term *marginal utility function* to denote the increase in total utilities which is achieved by adding another good to the available supply.[33] He established a system of equations for representing the pricing process, but the individual valuations which he introduced were equally related to a preexisting price system.

Von Wieser's most remarkable achievement was probably his definition of costs as displaced alternative utilities.[34] This proposition, which was not connected with the existence of a price system, identified the costs of producing a good with the loss of another having a lower marginal utility. A wide range of economic processes could be explained in accordance with this "principle of alternative costs." Among the examples advanced to illustrate the principle was the case of a journey the real costs of which were said to consist in sacrificing the enjoyment of the goods which could have been purchased with the sum spent on financing the journey. From "costs," as applied to the production of specific goods, von Wieser distinguished expenditures, as related to productive processes; in order to be economically rational, expenditures had to include interest on capital.

When the principle of alternative costs was applied to a fictitious stationary economy ruled by perfect competition, it could be shown that the returns from any unit of a given resource were equalized. A general rule concerning the allocation of resources in accordance with economic rationality could be derived from these considerations. In his excellent presentation of the results of marginal utility analysis, Philip Henry Wicksteed adopted "von Wieser's law" as a keystone of his discussions.[35] The American H. J. Davenport, another distinguished adherent of the same analysis, proposed the term *principle of displacement cost* to denote the "law," which he associated with the generally valid psychological maxim of selecting the line of least resistance when choosing among alternatives. Davenport defined as marginal such cases in which the utility gained and the utility sacrificed were approximately equal.[36]

The idea of deriving costs from lost opportunities was apparently incompatible with the Ricardian cost of production theories. But in his analysis of the treatment of productive factors being used for different, competing processes, von Wieser pointed out that limitation of the quantities of such factors was bound to lead to situations in which the value of the product could not fall below the sum of the values which these factors would obtain in competing uses. Under such circumstances the value of the product was determined by the combined values of its cost elements, and the theory of "objective costs" led to a perfectly tenable proposition.

Closely connected with the idea of determining the concept of cost in accordance with the principles of marginal utility was the problem of deriving the value of the productive services from the marginal value of the goods created by their cooperation in productive processes, in other words, the "problem of imputation." The background of the problem was constituted by the complementarity of the factors. Since in each process the value of the product could be equated with the combined value of the factors used up in the process, the problem to be solved consisted in disentangling the shares in the value of the product to be allotted to the different factors. A similar problem was found to arise in all cases in which want satisfaction is dependent upon the simultaneous or successive availability of combinations of goods.[37]

Carl Menger had suggested determining these shares through a procedure which consisted in withdrawing one element of each factor and determining the effects of that operation on the yield of the productive process. Taking account of the variability of the coefficients of production, he argued that the withdrawal of a unit of a factor would lead to mutual readjustments of the other factors. The difference between the previous, more valuable yield and the new yield would show the contribution of the productive service which had been withdrawn.

Von Wieser raised the objection to Menger's procedure that unless the value of other factors had already been determined, one might sometimes be led to impute the total value of the product to one factor of production; in other cases, the combined value attributed to the factors might exceed the value of the product. Hence, von Wieser proposed to derive the value of the factors not from their removal but from their "productive contribution," characterized as a magnitude smaller than the share in the productive process which was dependent on the cooperation of the factor but larger than the possible productive effect of the factor in other combinations. Von Wieser, as well as the other Austrian economists who dealt with the problem of imputation, endeavored to avoid any confusion of the concept of "economic imputation" as connected with the utilization of productive factors with the—insoluble—question of how to determine the physical contributions of productive factors to the yields of productive processes. Nevertheless, arguments derived from the impossibility of performing "physical imputations" were used in attacks on the theory of "productive contributions."[38] As a first result of these considerations, von Wieser advanced a "law of differential imputation," applicable to all situations in which the high value of a specific scarce factor (e.g., a mineral spring) was conditioned by the high marginal utility of its product (mineral water). He could refer to the Ricardian theory of land rent as a characteristic instance in which the explanation of values formed in markets had been connected with the relative scarcity of a productive factor. The reasoning underlying this theory could obviously be extended to all situations in which the volume of one productive factor remained fixed while the yield of the productive processes was increased by augmenting the contributions of the variable services. Under such conditions the increase in the value of the yield was always attributed to the invariable factor. Von Wieser dealt with the problem of specific productive factors in his *Social Economics*. He regarded a productive factor as specific when it could be used only in a limited number of combinations and could hardly be replaced by other factors. Von Wieser's distinction between specific and nonspecific factors was the object of various criticisms.[39]

Serious difficulties, however, were involved in the attempt to apply the idea of "productive contribution" to the determination of the value of nonspecific productive factors which could be used in alternative productive processes. On the assumption that a single marginal utility could be ascribed to each productive factor, von Wieser suggested determining the value of these marginal utilities by systems of equations in which groups of productive factors appeared in different combinations of their quantities, as determined by their cooperation in productive processes. It was obvious, however, that von Wieser's assumption concerning the existence of a single marginal utility for each factor was incompatible with the conditions of an exchange economy. Moreover, the magnitudes to be used in the equations were obviously valuations based on existing price systems and did not represent genuine marginal utilities.[40]

The difficulties involved in von Wieser's formulation of the problem of imputation caused Böhm-Bawerk to recommend the adoption of Menger's procedure, which consisted in determining the value of a productive factor by the effects of its withdrawal from the combination. According to the principle of substitution, to which Böhm-Bawerk attached particular importance, the marginal utility of a product could be shown to be strongly influenced by the marginal utilities of its productive factors as derived from their uses in other combinations.[41] Analysis of actual pricing processes led to the conclusion that the prices of reproducible factors tend to be constant and that the residual part of the value of the product is allotted to the irreplaceable factors.

When the principles underlying the idea of imputation were applied to wage analysis, unskilled and semiskilled forms of labor were characterized as typical categories of nonspecific productive agents. The subjective valuation attached by the workers to their own labor was held to be secondary in importance, as it reflected only comparisons between different possibilities or chances of using or selling their services. Hence, under competitive conditions the price paid for labor was held to be determined, in accordance with the principle of marginal productivity, by the least valuable unit of the product which it was profitable to produce. Differences in the levels of wages could be traced to differences in the values of marginal products. That approach to the wage problem, which had been anticipated by Johann Heinrich von Thünen, was independent of marginal utility analysis strictly speaking.

In a treatise published after the author's death, Böhm-Bawerk analyzed a series of hypothetical situations in order to define the conditions (free competition or monopolies) under which "artificial" increases in wages were likely to result in lasting advantages for the workers concerned, though possibly as a detriment to other classes of the community.[42] In the light of these considerations, the struggle for wage increases was affected by a special limiting factor, the existence of a subsistence fund accumulated out of previous savings. In his theory of interest on capital, Böhm-Bawerk ascribed to that fund a decisive role in determining the length of the productive processes and, indirectly, the behavior of the economy. This theory has occupied a conspicuous place in the history of marginalism and requires separate treatment.

THE RATE OF INTEREST AS A STRATEGIC FACTOR

In his comprehensive research into the function of interest on capital as a determinant of economic behavior, Böhm-Bawerk undertook to solve a problem which had been the object of many misleading discussions. His careful critical survey of the theories of interest was a model of comparative analysis of economic doctrines.[43] As he formulated it, the problem of interest on real capital in the history of thought turned on the question of why the sum total of the values of the productive factors did not exhaust the value of the product. This formulation of the problem, incidentally, prepared the ground for the elaboration of Böhm-Bawerk's so-called *agio* theory of interest.[44]

With remarkable perspicacity, Böhm-Bawerk endeavored to elucidate the logical aspects of some characteristic definitions of interest on capital by pointing to the influence of the substance concept, which provided the background for the conception of interest as payment for the "use" of capital, as distinct from the repayment of its "substance."

To the productivity theories advocated by Jean Baptiste Say and his followers, Böhm-Bawerk raised the objection that capital was not an "original" source of wealth or income, and that interest was to be conceived as the difference between the value of the services rendered by the capital goods and the cost of their replacement. He compared the belief in the value-creating power of "capital" with the belief in a metaphysical force, and applied the same reasoning to the belief in the value-creating power of labor. The Marxian labor cost theory of value and the concept of "surplus value" were special objects of his devastating criticism. Some adversaries of Böhm-Bawerk's reasoning have suggested that his attacks on that theory were primarily motivated by his animosity toward the socialist movement. But he criticized productivity theories of interest with equal vigor, although they could be interpreted as instruments in defense of capitalism.

To Nassau Senior's abstinence theory, which had been adopted by Mill, Marshall, Jevons, and many others, Böhm-Bawerk attributed the merit of having emphasized the time elements involved in the maintenance and formation of capital. But he qualified as double accounting the idea of consider sacrifices of capitalists as well as of labor required for capital goods production.[45] In his view, the real sacrifice made in all such processes consisted in forgoing the advantages which would have resulted from using other (less profitable) combinations of labor, land, and capital goods.

In his own theory of interest, Böhm-Bawerk drew a sharp distinction between capital (defined as produced physical instruments of production) and the "original" factors of production, land, and labor. His setting of the problem differed significantly from the traditional conception of interest as a share in the price of the product, since he started with the question of why the productive processes were not continued to a point at which the utility of the yield was reduced to the combined utilities of the productive services. Implied in that formulation was the assumption that interest was a general economic category which had to be taken into account in any rational organization of economic processes, regardless of the rules adopted with regard to the distribution of the yield of such processes.

Hardly less significant was the role Böhm-Bawerk assigned to the time factor, in his analysis of productive processes and in his interpretation of the marginal utility of goods. Elaborating Carl Menger's observation concerning the existence of appreciable differences between the present value of a product expected in the future and the actual value of the same product at the end of the productive process, he endeavored to demonstrate the validity of his general proposition that future goods were correspondingly less valuable, the farther away was the time at which they would be available for immediate consumption. In the light of that consideration, Böhm-Bawerk ascribed the difference between the value of the yield of a productive process and the value of the services used in that process to a systematic undervaluation of future goods, and he defined interest as the *agio* required to equalize the use value of future goods with the corresponding value of identical goods presently available. The concept of time which he used to elaborate the idea of time preference was a concept of "subjective" time, as distinct from the concept of "operational" time which he used in his analysis of productive processes. Thus conceived, all productive services had the character of future goods, increasing in value simultaneously with their gradual transformation into goods of immediate consumption.

Böhm-Bawerk ascribed that process of discounting the value of future goods primarily to a psychological factor: the preference which the need to satisfy present wants commands over similar needs which will arise in a more or less distant future. Moreover, he discussed a generally observable optimistic overestimation of future resources and irrational underestimation of future wants. The role played by the time factor in the determination of values had been emphasized by various previous authors. In the eighteenth century it had been used by Ferdinando Galiani in support of a theory of interest. In the 1830s, John Rae had based a theory of profits and interests on the difference between the values of future and present goods. The accrual of profits had been ascribed to that difference by several Marginalists, such as William Stanley Jevons; Emil Sax, a disciple of Menger, and W. Launhardt, a follower of Jevons.

Although Böhm-Bawerk was convinced that psychological motivations provided a satisfactory explanation for the existence of interest on capital, he considered it necessary to add a third reason, which was derived from technological considerations and was especially intended to establish a link between the rate of interest and the "average period of production," or the "operational time" which normally elapses between the first application of inputs to a productive process and the final production of the goods. Böhm-Bawerk's concept of the average period of production reflected the results of past experience, no account being taken of changes in technique or of changes in original plans made in the course of the productive processes. Increases in the marginal productivity of the productive agents, he argued, were directly related to the expansion of intermediary stages between the beginning and the end of productive processes, since such expansions would not take place unless the returns attributed to them were ample enough to cover the difference between the present value of the productive factors and the final value of the products. Hence, he considered production to be more "capitalistic," the more extended was the time span of the productive processes, regardless of any other aspects of economic organization.

Böhm-Bawerk supplemented that theory by the considerations that the organization of the productive processes was determined not only by the increases in the yields which could be reaped by extending the prevailing periods of production but also by the size of a subsistence fund composed of wage goods and by the volume of labor available for productive purposes. A similar idea had been advanced by Jevons, who had started from the ill-defined Ricardian concept of capital, had identified capital with the volume of wage goods available for a period of production, and had emphasized the connection which existed between the command over wage-good capital and improvements in the supply of commodities that lengthen the average interval between the moment when labor is exerted and the time when its ultimate result or purpose is accomplished.[46]

In accordance with this conception of productive processes, Böhm-Bawerk defined wages as prices paid, in the form of presently available subsistence goods, for contributions to the production of future goods, which could be expected to reach their full value after the completion of the productive process. The economically adequate wage levels at which, under conditions of perfect competition, the available labor force and the entire subsistence fund were absorbed, were determined by the marginal productivity of labor in the most profitable productive processes.

Hence, Böhm-Bawerk countered the "claim of the workers to the full value of their product" with the consideration that such a claim could only mean that the workers should receive at present the discounted value of their future product since they could not wait until the termination of the productive process to receive the value reached by the products at the time of their full maturity. That reasoning, which was obviously applicable to any regulation of wages, regardless of the organization of the economic order, provided Böhm-Bawerk with an effective argument against the Marxian conception of profit and interest as "surplus values" withheld from the workers's wages.

When the theory of the preferential treatment of goods presently available was applied to the determination of the value of investments, that value was identified with the sum of the discounted future yields which could be derived from the capital tied up in the investment. Similarly, the value of a piece of land could be related to the sum of future yields the discounted value of which gradually declined to zero. This capitalization procedure, thus plausibly set forth, was obviously not applicable to labor, except under conditions of slavery.

One of the most striking features of Böhm-Bawerk's *agio* theory of interest was his "macroeconomic" interpretation of the role played by the real rate of interest in the process of determining the length of the periods of production and the corresponding investments. When the principles of marginal productivity analysis were applied to the procedures underlying the allocation of resources, it appeared that under conditions of perfect competition, at full employment of capital and labor, the "real rate of interest" was determined by the additional yield of the most extended economically still profitable roundabout method of production. The equilibrium of the system was assured when at that interest rate all savings (as represented by the subsistence fund) were absorbed by the demand for capital. Increased savings, which permitted the expansion of the average period of production, contributed toward making profitable rates of interest which were lower than those which had obtained before. Low rates, far from having the adverse effects attributed to them in the Ricardian doctrine, offered the prospect of promoting economic growth.

For a considerable time, the psychological considerations advanced in favor of the *agio* theory enjoyed widespread acceptance, and the objections which were later raised to Böhm-Bawerk's analysis of the preferential treatment generally bestowed on present goods were not very convincing.[47] But prolonged discussions turned on the question of whether increases in capital outlays could be identified with extensions of the average period of production, leading, in turn, to increases in total output. The concept of "average period" was held to be untenable in view of the interconnection of productive processes, which made it impossible clearly to define the beginning of such a period.[48] J. B. Clark pointed to the synchronous nature of closely related productive processes. Moreover, he countered Böhm-Bawerk's concept of capital as physical means of production with the concept of "pure capital," which was designed to denote a permanent fund of abstract productive power. Böhm-Bawerk's approach differed conspicuously from that adopted by J. B. Clark in the fact that he did not apply the equilibrium concept directly to the construction of an economic system. Hence, he objected to the idea of conceiving of capital as an economic magnitude expressed in exchange values. Other critics, such as E. C. van Dorp, endeavored to show that Böhm-Bawerk had transformed his *agio* theory into a "wage fund theory" when he attributed to the subsistence fund a decisive role in determining the length of the periods of production.[49]

But even critics who fully endorsed the principle of time preference as emphasized by Böhm-Bawerk characterized his reasoning as hopelessly abstract and inapplicable to reality in view of the heroic assumptions on which it was based, such as that capital and its products consisted of physically homogeneous units differing only in quantity. Others questioned whether interest on capital—apparently a monetary phenomenon—could be accounted for in terms of a "real exchange" economy in which all economic magnitudes were derived from individual estimates of utilities, instead of being conceived of as the combined results of innumerable transactions carried on in the markets and expressed in monetary terms.

Böhm-Bawerk did not develop a monetary theory, strictly speaking, but he adopted a sort of quantity theory of money which did not affect his theory of interest.

The methodological issues involved in these discussions were set forth with great clarity by Knut Wicksell, who used the procedure of successive approximation to develop the model of an economy ruled by the principles of marginal utility and marginal productivity.[50] Böhm-Bawerk's conception of the "capitalist" economy as an imaginary model in which capital goods were the direct object of lending, without the intervention of money, was Wicksell's starting point. The "normal" rate of interest was defined as the rate at which the demand for physical loan capital coincided with the supply of savings expressed in physical magnitudes. In order to overcome the logical difficulties involved in that setting of the problem, Wicksell, in his *Lectures on Political Economy*,[51] identified the concept of "natural" or "real" interest—the yield of capital in productive processes—with employers' profits, and observed that, thus conceived, real interest was likely to show considerable variations. In subsequent discussions of the imaginary concept of "average natural rate of interest," attention was drawn to the fact that, when loans were made in kind, in terms of different commodities, there would exist at any one moment as many natural rates of interest as there are commodities, but they would not be equilibrium rates.[52] He accepted Böhm-Bawerk's proposition that under strictly competitive conditions changes in the rate of interest were instrumental in determining adjustments of the periods of production to the available supply of capital. In his discussion of Böhm-Bawerk's periods of production, Wicksell substituted the concept of a "weighted average period of investment" for the simple concept of a period covering the time between a first input of productive factors and the termination of the productive process.

That modification of Böhm-Bawerk's definition of the "roundabout" ways of productive processes was designed to meet certain objections, but otherwise it had no significant effects.[53]

Wicksell emphasized that in a monetary economy, a distinction was to be drawn between expected profits, or the anticipated return on new investments, on the one hand and the "loan rate," as determined by the relationship between the demand for and the supply of loanable monetary capital, on the other. Since the supply of real capital is limited, whereas the supply of money can be regarded as fairly elastic, Wicksell concluded that there is no reason to assume that the loan rate of interest would normally agree with the "real" rate.[54]

With those considerations Wicksell introduced a line of reasoning which had been practically ignored by the Austrian economists. It pointed to the relationships between the rates of interest and the price system, and found eloquent expression in Wicksell's dictum that any theory of money worthy of the name must be able to show how and why monetary or pecuniary demand for goods exceeds or falls short of the supply of goods in given conditions.[55] This consideration implied a repudiation of Say's law of markets, since the validity of that "law" was predicated on the assumption that demand for and supply of money were equal.

Elaborating these ideas, Wicksell questioned the traditional relationship which had been established between the volume of money and the volume of exchange transactions as a means of defining the price level. In support of these doubts he pointed to the observation that the loan rate of interest had been low during periods of low prices—periods of limited capital supply—and had been high when the supply of capital was obviously abundant and prices were rising. This relationship between the behavior of prices and movements of the rate of interest had already been observed by Tooke. Hardly less significant was Wicksell's attack on the almost generally accepted "banking principle," according to which the supply of money was automatically adjusted to the requirements of the economy when the prevailing rules of short-term lending were strictly observed.

Instead of the usual quantity equations, Wicksell substituted a formula which was based on the division of national income into total savings and the demand for consumption goods (as distinct from investments and the demand for productive factors). This formulation of the problem of the price level by Wicksell anticipated ideas which were later developed by the so-called income approach to monetary theory.[56] As a result, he indicated the role played by the interest rate in effecting changes of the price system.[57] Reductions in the loan rate, following upon increases in the gold reserves, were likely to keep that rate below the rate of profits, causing increasing demand for capital goods and upward price movements. A "cumulative" process of rising prices could thus be set in motion until finally arrested by external or internal drains on the bank reserves and ensuing increases in the rate of interest.

In his analysis of such price movements, Wicksell assumed that changes in the loan rates made by the banks were always induced by outside conditions. The idea of holding differences between the loan rate and the rate of profits responsible for fluctuating movements of business activity did not enter into Wicksell's considerations. But he emphasized some dangerous effects of the banks' policy of keeping the market rate below the "real rate" in prosperity periods when he discussed the tendency of entrepreneurs to expand the average investment period beyond its economically justified duration, to transform excessive amounts of circulating capital into fixed investments, and to reduce the supply of consumption goods in favor of the misdirected production of capital goods, and thus to exercise pressure on real wages and rents.[58] He showed that opposite tendencies were evident when the loan rates were kept above the real rates and business activity was contracting.

Wicksell's analysis of some characteristic aspects of the economic mechanism definitely discarded the myth that money was a "veil" to be lifted in order to understand the functioning of the economy. The relationships between the loan rate and the real rate of interest caused him to conclude that a system of interrelated monetary magnitudes was to be distinguished from a "real exchange system," and that it was a primary task of economic theory to formulate the equilibrium conditions of the monetary system. He considered these conditions secured when the loan or market rate was "normal," that is to say, when it was equal to the marginal technical productivity of capital in roundabout processes of production, when it equated the supply of and demand for savings, and when it guaranteed a stable price level, primarily of consumption goods.[59]

In accordance with his social philosophy, Wicksell asserted that it is "the part of man to be master in a sphere of such extraordinary significance as that of monetary influence," and in the second volume of his *Lectures* elaborated the principles of a consistent monetary policy. As a method of price stabilization, he recommended the demonetization of gold and the establishment of an international clearing system. But his equilibrium conditions were questioned by D. Davidson (1906), who argued that the general price level should vary in inverse proportion to changes in productivity, that in a progressive economy the flow of money should be increased in order to secure stability of the price level, and that, consequently, the rate of interest should be kept below the rate at which the demand for loan capital is equated to the supply of savings.[60] Many years later (1925), Wicksell admitted the validity of Davidson's objections.[61]

Although Wicksell adjusted his premises to the principles of equilibrium analysis, his treatment of the monetary system initiated a new conception of the behavior of the economy, and his formulation of the relationships among rates of interest, prices, investments, and incomes provided a bridge to the problems which were later discussed in terms of the "dynamic" approach to economic analysis.

Chapter 21
Problems of Marginal Analysis

———

THEORIES OF DISTRIBUTION

General considerations. PRACTICALLY ALL adherents to the psychological version of marginalism agreed on the proposition that the main types of income in an exchange economy (wages, rent, interest on capital, and profit) had to be conceived of as shares of product prices and to be explained accordingly. Consistent application of the principle of opportunity costs provided the instrument for transforming the Ricardian problem of a tripartite distribution of the national dividend into a problem of functional allotment.

Although criticized by followers of the Marshallian cost of production theory, such as Francis Ysidro Edgeworth,[1] this analytical procedure was strongly supported by Philip Henry Wicksteed and several noted American economists.[2] Wicksteed defined costs of production as the estimated value, measured in gold, of all the alternatives that have been sacrificed in order to place a unit of the commodity in question on the market. In an essay which attracted considerable attention, he applied marginal productivity analysis to the problem of demonstrating how the value of the product was exhausted by the distributive shares allotted to the productive factors, on the assumption that constant increases in the yield of a productive process resulted from proportional increases of all productive agents.[3] Léon Walras considered Wicksteed's equation practically identical to his own price-cost equation as implied in his general theory of the interdependence of all prices and costs.[4] Knut Wicksell added an important proviso to Wicksteed's formulation of the exhaustion problem: that all enterprises had reached the limit beyond which additional increases in the scale of production would yield no profit. Wicksell assumed the use of only two productive factors, labor and land, and argued that an enterprise reached optimum production when the rate of increase of physical productivity was proportionate to the shares of the productive factors, and it was then impossible to improve the relation between the two magnitudes through expansion of production. He argued that under conditions of full competition the prices of the productive agents would show a tendency to rise, product prices would tend to fall, and the proportionality of the rates of increases would approach equality. When that equality had been reached at constant yields, the share of each productive factor would be determined by its marginal productivity and the sum of the shares would exhaust the value of the product, leaving no room for profit.[5]

Adoption of marginal productivity analysis as a method of determining costs required a reconsideration of the laws of diminishing and increasing returns. As expressed by the Ricardian economists, the law of diminishing returns meant that increases in one or several productive factors yielded less than proportionate returns. Basic to that formulation of the law were two assumptions: that the value of the product was derived from the value of the productive factors, and that all exchange values could be reduced to a common standard unit. William Stanley Jevons, who measured all utilities and disutilities in terms of a common unit, adopted the law in that form, and the same was true of Marshall, who used the monetary unit as an invariable standard in his partial equilibrium analysis.

However, Wicksteed objected to the Ricardian method of applying the law of diminishing returns exclusively to agricultural production by keeping one productive factor—land—constant and increasing the others—capital and labor.[6] Similar effects, he argued, were obtained, whichever factor was kept constant. Hence, he considered the principle of diminishing returns applicable to all forms of production in which one factor was fixed in its relation to the others. Friedrich von Wieser and Joseph Alois Schumpeter also showed this point of view.[7]

Moreover, when the principle of substitution at the margin was strictly applied, the law of diminishing returns was generalized and increasingly formulated in terms of incremental, as distinct from proportionate, returns.[8] It gave expression to the proposition that a variable productive factor became a progressively less efficient substitute for other factors, that is, successive applications of a variable factor to a given quantity of fixed factors give rise to diminishing incremental product returns. The question of whether such a situation obtained in a specific case could be answered only by experience. Thus conceived, the *historical* law of diminishing returns was displaced from the conspicuous rank it had occupied within the theory of distribution. At best it could be used to analyze the influence of increasing expenditures upon the volume of production.[9]

Wicksell, like Eugen von Böhm-Bawerk, proposed to transform the law of diminishing returns into a law of the hypothetical type, claiming general validity. In conjunction with likely historical changes in the factor mix, the law appeared to lend support to the view that the share of capital in the yield of productive processes was bound to decline if technology remained unchanged; but Wicksell also pointed out that productivity of capital could be expected to be enhanced by technological improvements.[10] The effects of changes in technology, together with increases in population and the opening up of new markets, were likely to counteract the otherwise natural downward trend of the rate of interest.[11] Wicksell also realized that under conditions of increasing returns the employers who were first in expanding their production would render any competition ineffectual; consequently, maintenance of the equilibrium of the economic system would be impossible. Under the rule of the law of diminishing returns, however, it was possible to assume that in a competitive economy optimum cost determination could be generally achieved, along with more or less constant returns of the type obtaining in agricultural production.

Although marginal productivity analysis provided a method of determining the shares of the productive services in the value of the product, it did not account for the economic rationale of the shares. However, the explanation of the typical forms of income in which these shares manifested themselves was of considerable importance to the Austrian economists, who placed great emphasis on the analysis of causal relationships among the elements of the economy. The American followers of J. B. Clark, who had abandoned the distinction between capital and land as separate factors of production, were inclined to ignore the problems connected with the Ricardian income categories. H. J. Davenport discussed the variety of the productive services and the complex relationships of substitutability and complementarity which existed among the factors.[12] But no conclusive answer was given to the question of how to establish a convenient principle of classifying the various sources of income. L. M. Fraser also suggested a grouping of the productive factors according to their degrees of substitutability. On the other hand, some socialist authors have denounced the functional distribution of the value of the products as a characteristic attempt to justify the capitalist order, since that procedure resulted in eliminating the sharp borderline that Ricardian economics had drawn between the reward for labor and the shares allotted to the other productive agents.[13] Hence, the discussions of the character of these sources of income started from the traditional classification.

Interest and profit. The explanation of interest on capital, conceived of as a fundamental economic category, constituted one of the most baffling problems of economic analysis. It was intimately connected with the question of how to define the functions of interest as an element of the productive and distributive processes, and thus was bound to occupy a central position in any economic doctrine. It is especially interesting to observe how the choice among the available theories of interest was largely determined by methodological considerations.

Three partly conflicting theories of interest were of primary importance within the framework of marginalism: the productivity theory, which reflected the scholastic substance concept of capital; the "abstinence" theory, which conceived of interest as a reward for deferred consumption and was a heritage of utilitarianism; and the *agio* theory, which was based on the idea of time preference in favor of present, as opposed to future goods. The last theory was the most refined outcome of hypothetical reasoning.[14]

The great attraction which Böhm-Bawerk's theory of interest exercised on many Marginalists, above all in Austria, Italy, and the Scandinavian countries, was due to the fact that the main arguments in its favor appeared to be confirmed by obvious daily experience. The principles of the *agio* theory were adopted in Italy by Giuseppe Ricca-Salerno, Augusto Graziani, and Enrico Barone; in Holland by Nicholas G. Pierson; and in the Scandinavian countries by Count Hamilton, David Davidson, Einarsen, Harold L. Westergaard, and L. V. Brick, apart from Knut Wicksell, who made it a consistuent element of his teachings. In France these principles, as combined with a sort of productivity theory, were elaborated by Adolphe Landry, in *L'Intérêt du capital* (Paris, 1904). In England the theory was discussed by various economists such as James Bonar, William Smart, and Francis Ysidro Edgeworth; among its most distinguished adherents was Arthur Cecil Pigou. Much later John R. Hicks confessed that nearly everyone who comes to the study of capital falls victim to Böhm-Bawerk's theory at some stage or other.[15]

The *agio* theory ascribed original productivity only to nature and labor, and defined the reward for these factors in terms of their contributions to the discounted values of their future products; it attributed the existence of interest as a general economic category to the combined effects of time preference and the productivity of investments.[16] The productivity aspects of the *agio* theory were emphasized by Knut Wicksell, who defined interest as the difference between the marginal productivity of accumulated power of labor and soil, on the one hand, and the marginal productivity of such power when presently available, on the other. Hayek, who defended the *agio* theory, admitted that in actual life the real rate of interest is exclusively determined by the expected rate of return on investment, while time preference only determines the rate of savings.[17] Wicksell also occasionally mentioned a certain affinity between the *agio* theory and Nassau Senior's theory of waiting.[18] But Böhm-Bawerk himself connected the idea of waiting less with the process of postponing present in favor of future consumption than with the delay involved in waiting for the results of roundabout productive processes.

In the United States, Irving Fisher developed the psychological and physical aspects of the rate of interest.[19] He elaborated on the time discount, or the "impatience principle," as he called it, and on the importance of "investment opportunity," or marginal rate of return over cost. The former concept corresponded to Böhm-Bawerk's time preference; the latter, reflecting profitability of investment, was very similar to Wicksell's "real or natural" rate of interest.

In his detailed analysis of the subjective factors, Fisher formulated the time preference of present over future goods in terms of income, and introduced the concept of "expectations" into his analysis of processes of discounting as elements of the formation of capital values. The idea of contrasting income as a flow of money with the concept of capital as a stock of goods available at given prices had been suggested by Simon Newcomb, who had divided the "societary circulation" into monetary and industrial circulations.[20] In the course of his discussions, Fisher suggested a differentiation of interest rates according to the risks associated with the yields of various sources of income,[21] and proposed using index numbers to translate the nominal or money rates of interest into real rates, with the proviso that account was to be taken not only of the value of money prevailing at the time of borrowing but also of the value of money at the time of repayment.[22]

One of the most convinced American adherents of the *agio* theory of interest was Frank A. Fetter, who argued that, according to history and logic, time preference was prior to the development of interest on money, and that the latter originated independently of any "productivity" ascribed to productive agents. Fetter criticized the productivity

theories of interest advanced by H. R. Seager and Harry G. Brown, and took even Irving
Fisher to task for having introduced elements of such a theory into his analysis of
interest.[23] Like Böhm-Bawerk, Fetter related the price of all durable goods—including
land—to processes of capitalization in which the values of future uses were the object of
discounting procedures. Other American authors, such as S. M. Macvane, Frank W.
Taussig, and Charles W. Macfarlane, adopted the *agio* theory with some more or less
explicit modifications of Böhm-Bawerk's formulation.

Extensive controversies between Böhm-Bawerk on the one side and L. von
Bortkiewicz and Fisher on the other turned on the question of whether the existence of a
positive rate of interest could be accounted for exclusively in terms of the greater productivity of the roundabout methods of production (Böhm-Bawerk's third ground).[24] It was
shown that Böhm-Bawerk had tacitly introduced time preference into his analysis of the
productive process.

More important than these discussions was the opposition to the *agio* theory by the
adherents of productivity theories and abstinence theories. The principle of productivity of
capital was defended by various authors whose conceptions of the economy were independent of the role attributed to interest on capital as a strategic factor in determining the
mutual relationships of productive processes. Friedrich von Wieser belonged to that
group, but he did not succeed in establishing a bridge between the physical productivity of
capital and its capacity to produce values. Von Wieser derived a secular tendency of the
rate of interest to fall from an alleged prolonged decline in the marginal yield of investments as accompanied by relative increases in the accumulation of capital.[25] The Frenchman Albert Aftalion attempted to improve von Wieser's theory by distinguishing three
concepts of productivity: global, physical, and economic. He derived individual incomes
from the economic productivity.[26]

The most conspicuous abstinence theory that rivaled Böhm-Bawerk's *agio* theory
was Alfred Marshall's theory of interest. It emphasized "prospectiveness" as a special
reason for postponing the enjoyment of presently available goods. The American Thomas
N. Carver resorted to intricate arguments in defense of the abstinence theory, which the
Italian Umberto Ricci illustrated with mathematical examples. Carver suggested that no
sacrifice was involved in the postponement of consumption when the goods to be produced were likely to provide a greater advantage than those immediately available; no
payment of interest on capital was necessary to elicit the savings needed to finance
production of that type. Payment of interest was necessary, however, to secure the
additional savings required to produce goods the marginal utility of which was lower than
that of the goods that were otherwise immediately available, although they represented a
net yield to the capital employed.[27]

The clash between divergent theories of interest on capital was reflected in a struggle
over the meaning to be given to the concept of capital. The term *capital* had been used to
denote two different economic categories: productive factors, the results of productive
processes ("real" capital); and liquid means, available mainly in the form of loanable
funds for investment in productive enterprises. The ensuing terminological difficulties had
perhaps been accentuated by Böhm-Bawerk's method of applying the expression *capital*
to the aggregate of produced means of production (real capital) without suggesting another
term for available liquid means.[28] His "real rate of interest," to which he assigned a
central role among the equilibrating economic forces, was derived from the "physical"
productivity of productive processes.

The conception of capital as a stock of physical goods was objected to by economists who adhered to the Ricardian principle of conceiving of the economy as an aggregate of values to which a general equilibrium concept was immediately applicable. Thus, J. B. Clark insisted upon defining capital as the sum total of abstract productive power incorporated in produced means of production. A version of that view was adopted by Irving Fisher. According to Fisher, capital was the whole of things owned by individuals or societies at some particular moment in time, constituting claims or purchasing power and being capable of yielding interest.[29] But in an often-quoted dictum, Böhm-Bawerk characterized as "mythology of capital" the idea that capital is a fund of values that maintains itself automatically, so that no economic problems were involved in analyzing the process of reproducing an amount of capital that once had come into existence.[30]

Consistent opposition to the concept of marginal productivity caused Gustav Cassel to abandon any clear demarcation between income and capital, and to suggest the term *capital disposal* to denote loanable funds that were fed from three sources: savings, amortized investments, and credits created by banks. Cassel spoke of *capital claims* in order to denote claims to future incomes expressed in terms of their present valuation.[31] But that proposal did not find many adherents. Hence, the conflicting views on the definition of the concept of capital reflected characteristic divergencies in the fundamental approach to economic analysis.

But regardless of these divergencies, practically common agreement existed among nonsocialist authors on the view that, under any existing economic order, interest was to be included among the costs of production. At the very least, far-reaching agreement existed on the view that the level of the loan rate of interest was determined by the interaction of the supply and demand schedules for loanable funds. The Ricardian assumption that a strong correlation existed between the level of interest and the rate of savings was hardly questioned. A certain concentration of incomes was held to be favorable to the accumulation of savings. The available money capital was believed to be sufficient to enable the majority of the firms to choose optimum combinations of the productive resources. The view that in a planned economy no account had to be taken of interest on capital was defended by socialist authors on the ground that through consistent planning the course of future economic developments could be rendered perfectly calculable.[32]

Practically all economists who preserved the traditional static approach to economic analysis experienced insuperable difficulties in their attempts to explain profit as a separate category of income. The Marshallian definition of profit as a reward for entrepreneurial activity was obviously a misleading application of the Ricardian analysis of the distributive process. Even less satisfactory were vague statements that ascribed profit to the superior bargaining position of the entrepreneurs in their relation to landowners, Capitalists, and labor.[33]

The importance of profit as a source of income, savings, and investment was realized by a number of Austrian economists. During the last decades of the nineteenth century various studies dealing with the sources of employers' profits were prepared by Austrian economists who were disciples of Carl Menger. Victor Mataja, G. Gross, and K. Kleinwächter may be mentioned as authors of such studies, which defined profit as the difference between the prices of the products and the combined costs of the productive agents. That difference was explained partly as a remuneration for managerial activities and partly as the result of speculative gains connected with technical and financial risks.

Böhm-Bawerk did not advance a theory of profit strictly speaking; he ascribed the gains that accrued to the entrepreneurs in excess of interest on capital to a combination of fortuitous circumstances or to superior ability. But a consistent theory of profit, adjusted to the principles of marginalism, was advanced only later, when Knut Wicksell's distinction between the real rate of interest and the market rate was developed to some of its consequences.

The connection which Marshall had established between profit and the functional aspects of income distribution was virtually denied by the authors who started their analyses from the construction of imaginary stationary models of the economy, and who arrived at the conclusion that profit could emerge only under "dynamic" economic conditions. Hence, they looked for processes extending over time in order to account for the sources of profit. That problem was formulated by J. B. Clark; it was subsequently taken over by Joseph Schumpeter and placed into the center of an analysis of the fluctuating behavior of business activity.

Each of these divergent theories of profit was developed according to the different views held by the various authors of the purpose of economic theory. The Marshallian theory was primarily determined by the task of accounting for the distribution of the national dividend; the Austrian Marginalists adjusted their theory to the problems connected with the allocation of resources, and Schumpeter's theory pointed to a constituent element of dynamic economic processes.

The apparent difficulties involved in connecting profit with clearly defined productive functions provided some authors with welcome arguments to denounce profit as an "unjustified" form of income. They used the term *economic Malthusianism* to characterize situations in which profit was derived from the application of restrictive measures to productive processes. They requested the introduction of far-reaching measures of public control in order to prevent the exploitation of "conjunctures" for profit-making purposes.[34]

Rent.   The Ricardian category of rent was connected with the formation of prices in the markets, and could therefore be easily adjusted to the requirements of marginal utility analysis. But the definition of that category was given a scope far beyond the relatively narrow limits that had been a characteristic feature of the Ricardian concept. Rent was shown to come into existence whenever the quantity of a productive factor was fixed or limited in relation to the quantities of the other factors. In some early discussions of entrepreneurial gains, such as that offered by Victor Mataja, profit was likened to rent. Rudolf Auspitz and Richard Lieben qualified as rent any surplus of price over cost, including interest on capital and profit. A similar extension of the rent concept to cover all returns on production exceeding costs was suggested by Pareto's disciple Guido Sensini.[35]

J. B. Clark applied the "law of rent" to the returns of capital and land, and thus eliminated any theoretical distinction between the two productive factors. That procedure was followed by a group of American authors, among others by Thomas N. Carver, E.R.A. Seligman, and Frank A. Fetter.[36] They argued that the difference between net rent and interest on capital was mainly due to methods of accounting; net rent was related to a physical unit of capital as an absolute amount, whereas interest was expressed as a ratio related to the value of the capital. Schumpeter characterized rent as an element of the price of land derived from the competition of land for uses in agriculture as well as in industry.[37]

According to another fairly widespread usage, the term *rent* was considered to cover all permanent or temporary yields of productive processes which were carried out at costs lower than those to be defrayed by the marginal producers. Similar reasoning qualified rent as a surplus or payment which, though connected with the use of specific factors, was not instrumental in determining their supply. When the surplus was measured from the margins, emphasis was placed on the differential character of the rent; when the measurement was based on the cost-price relation, importance was attached to the relative scarcity or the monopolistic nature of a productive agent.[38]

In spite of any modifications which the concept of rent had experienced under the influence of marginalist reasoning, there were some authors who insisted upon distinguishing the returns from land sharply from all other forms of income, mainly on the ground that landed property could be regarded as a productive factor of a specific type.[39] Others pointed to the Ricardian argument that the incidence of land rent was highly irregular, as distinct from an allegedly more or less uniform level of profits in industrial and commercial enterprises.[40] Maintenance of a rigid distinction between ground rent and all other types of income was, of course, practically a tenet for the advocates of single-tax schemes as proposed by H. George and his followers. They extolled the social benefits to be gained by taxing away the ''unearned increment'' derived from increases in returns on land.

An interesting chapter in the history of the land rent was initiated when analysis in terms of the rent principle was applied to the formation of the values of residential sites of urban communities.[41] Von Wieser elaborated the idea that the rent which resulted from intensified agricultural production had a counterpart in the rent earned by the owner of a multistoried house. Von Wieser combined the rent derived from the favorable location of an urban lot within residential or commercial quarters with the rent which was due to the proximity of land to the markets of its products. But whereas agricultural rents could be ascribed primarily to differences in the production costs of goods sold at uniform prices, the rent accruing to urban sites predominantly reflected divergencies in prices paid for houses or apartments produced at the same or similar costs on different sites or under different conditions. But these aspects of rent theory received relatively little attention.

Wages.   When agreement was reached on a wage theory, it consisted in connecting the level of wages with the marginal productivity of labor. Jevons and Carl Menger placed particular emphasis upon associating the marginal product of labor with the increment of want satisfaction derived by the consumer from that increment of production. This reasoning was taken over by Menger's Austrian disciples, who included labor among the nonspecific productive factors and identified the real wage rate with the marginal product of labor. Böhm-Bawerk adjusted the theorem to his *agio* theory of interest, and spoke of the ''discounted marginal product of labor.'' Moreover, he pointed to the existence of a sort of wage fund which, accumulated out of past savings, placed limits on the amount of wages to be disbursed during a given period of production. He argued that failure to observe these limits by granting economically unjustified wage increases was likely to create unemployment. In the United States, the Austrian approach to the wage problem was adopted by Frank W. Taussig[42] and, at least partly, Irving Fisher and Frank Fetter.

According to a widespread view, the worker had no estimate of the marginal utility of his own labor, but only of the disutility of that labor. Varying within certain limits, that estimate was held to influence the supply of labor. J. B. Clark's problematic concept of ''social marginal utility of labor'' was intended to secure a basis for the determination of the wage level. Clark's idea was adopted by Carver but questioned by the majority of the American economists on the ground that it was associated with the conception of society as an organism attaching utilities of varying degrees to goods and productive services. Philip Henry Wicksteed, who elaborated the Austrian wage theory, demonstrated that under conditions of perfect equilibrium no profit was involved in the employment of labor when wages were determined by the last increment in production.[43]

Workers were assumed to participate through increasing real wages in the effects of the progressively rising productivity of capital. The existence of different wage levels for work of practically the same kind was ascribed to the division of the labor market into various sectors with different degrees of marginal productivity. It remained an open question whether increased mobility was, under all circumstances, advantageous for labor.

Other theoretical discussions turned on conditions of work and wages as affected by monopolistic positions of employers, organized labor, bilateral monopolies, and the like, and on the effects of wage-fixing devices, labor-saving techniques, and the so-called system of scientific management proposed by Frederick W. Taylor to increase the efficiency of labor.[44] Increases in real wages were occasionally attributed to the relative decline in the volume of the labor force brought about by declining birth rates. Declining birth rates provided welcome arguments for the adversaries of the Malthusian "law of population." They were registered with anxiety by the advocates of nationalistic power policies.

MONETARY PROBLEMS

Economists whose memories do not reach back to the period prior to the First World War can hardly imagine the intellectual atmosphere which surrounded monetary theory at that time. Under the widely accepted rules of the gold standard, the exchange rates of the various currencies had been stabilized. In a large sector of the European continent, which was covered by the Latin Currency Union, coins and banknotes of the participating countries could be used interchangeably. In a considerable part of the world, gold coins circulated freely and could be bought at fixed rates in any quantities. In order to prevent governments from resorting to inflationary manipulations of the currency, most countries' banks of issue were placed in the ownership of private corporations, and the management of fiduciary notes was subjected to strict rules which were carefully observed. These rules reflected the view that the means of payment made available by the exploitation of mines, the issuance of bank notes, and the credits granted by the commercial banks would automatically adjust themselves under the gold standard to the economic requirements of the countries which participated in that international scheme. The belief in the beneficial operation of the freely functioning economic forces could hardly find a stronger expression than in the organization of the monetary mechanism that was the outcome of a definite method of reasoning—the same method which had supplied the framework for the formulation of Ricardian economics.

Guided by similar principles, the international trading community had developed an intricate network of monetary and financial relationships based on well-developed rules of accounting. In the day of its greatest triumph, no one realized how miraculous was the self-adjusting quality of this individualistic, competitive, free, unregulated, unplanned system, and upon what a fortuitous combination of conditions it depended.[45] The conviction that political considerations should not be permitted to interfere with commercial relationships was deeply rooted in the minds of Western statesmen, who carefully respected the conceptual isolation that had been established for the economic sector by the Ricardian doctrine. It has been reported that during the Crimean War the British government considered it incompatible with sound principles of financial policy to interfere with the practices of English bankers who granted loans to the enemy Russian government.

The money and credit machinery operated by the London banking system greatly facilitated the mutual adjustments of national price structures. That machinery provided flexibility in the international movements of capital; it secured the short-term credits needed for the smooth functioning of the system of international exchanges and the instruments for equalizing strained balances of payments.[46] British capital, which was available for long-term overseas investments, was preferably used to finance enterprises which could count upon more or less stable markets in the industrialized countries, particularly on British markets which were open to free imports from all parts of the world. That policy was successful in securing not only the financial stability of the overseas enterprises but also the transfer to the British Capitalists of the returns on their investments. Strict fulfillment of their financial obligations on the part of the borrowing countries became a constituent element of the system of international law, in spite of the heavy sacrifices imposed by the deflationary effects of the gold standard, especially on countries whose exports consisted chiefly of raw materials and who were exposed to violent fluctuations of prices and quantities.

A certain opposition to the gold standard, which had made itself felt during preceding depression periods, lost its importance after a considerable increase in gold production had started during the 1840s. This change in the monetary situation was analyzed in France as well as in England.[47] But extensive controversies, less of a theoretical than of a practical nature, were produced by the general decline in commodity prices between 1873 and 1895. Distinguished economists, such as Sir Robert Giffen, ascribed the decline in prices and the enusing fall of profits to the fact that the increase in gold production did not keep pace with the rapidly increasing demand for gold, which was intensified by the adoption of the gold standard by practically all industrialized countries.[48] According to these principles of bimetallism, stability of the price level was to be secured by measures designed to maintain an appropriate ratio between the values of the two monetary metals. These principles gained many adherents, especially in France and the United States. Bimetallism was advocated in France by L. Wolowski, J. G. Courcelle-Seneuil, de Lavergne, and E. Théry; in Belgium by Emile de Laveleye; and in Germany by John Prince-Smith and Max Wirth. In the United States bimetallism was a political issue of primary importance.[49]

The adherents of the gold standard supported their position mainly with the argument that the slow decline in prices which occurred under the rule of gold was a lesser evil than the possible inflationary effects of continued free coinage of silver. Some authors, such as Paul Leroy-Beaulieu and Wilhelm Lexis, even expressed some doubts whether inadequate output of gold was, in fact, the real cause of the general fall of prices.[50] It also remained a moot question as to how to determine the volume of gold required to assure the stability of the price level. This question was complicated by the consideration that expanding volumes of credit provided a supplementary source of means of payment. But eventually, with the upward international price movement which set in in 1896, the Bimetallists' proposals lost the support which they had enjoyed from distinguished economists. The recovery of the nineties was commonly ascribed to the discovery of gold in the Transvaal, where mines were opened in 1890.

In 1887 an official inquiry by an English commission into the circulation of gold and silver provided Alfred Marshall with the opportunity to define the relationships between the supply of money on the one hand and the level of prices and the rate of interest on the other.[51] Marshall argued that, under the existing rules, gold production exercised only an indirect influence on the behavior of prices, in that it determined the volume of the bank reserves, which in turn placed limits on the discount rate. According to Marshall, the movement of prices was directly dependent upon the movement of the discount rate, the average rate of discount was determined by the average level of interest, and the interest rate was determined exclusively by the profitability of business. In order to provoke a rise in prices, the discount rate had to be lowered below the "normal" rate as determined by the rate of savings, because the demand for capital goods could be stimulated through enhanced entrepreneurs' profits. Marshall suggested that any reduction of the discount rate that had occurred since 1873 had only amounted to an adjustment of the normal rate. His treatment of the discount rate differed from the analysis of the discount policy advanced by Wicksell insofar as the latter had discussed the influence of the rate level on short-term rather than long-term price movements.[52] Marshall's analysis, which placed the discount rate in the center of the regulation of long-term price movements, subsequently became a constituent element of English monetary policy. It provided an important directive for the operation of the international gold standard, since it discouraged the view that the price level was entirely dependent upon gold movements and opened the possibility of influencing the price level through manipulation of the discount rate. As a measure of monetary reform, Marshall recommended the establishment of a monetary unit constituting a claim to quantities of gold and silver in fixed proportions.

Another problem of monetary policy that was discussed—especially in France—against a background of theoretical considerations was the question of whether competition among several banks of issue was preferable to the monopoly of the note issue granted to the Banque de France in 1848. Competition was defended, particularly by Michel Chevalier and J. G. Courcelle-Seneuil, on the ground that adjustment of the volume of notes to the requirements of circulation could best be achieved under such a regime. But for the majority of economists it remained almost an article of faith that the issue of notes was to be controlled by a central bank. Discount policy and measures of open market policy were regarded as the main instruments for influencing the price level and regulating the credit expansion of the commercial banks. In prosperity periods the commercial banks of England permitted the ratio of their reserves to their lending to decline, thus stimulating general price increases. On the other hand, exportation of gold, due to contractions of foreign markets, led to more than proportionate credit contractions and deflationary price movements. In view of the extremely rigid regulations that were a characteristic feature of the English Bank Charter of 1844, any extraordinary increase in circulation that was necessitated by emergency conditions between 1844 and 1928 was possible only after the charter had been suspended temporarily. The Federal Reserve system in the United States was designed to concentrate the country's gold reserves. Hoarding of gold and silver by the commercial banks during the depression of 1907 had been responsible for an acute shortage of means of payment.

In passing, attention may be drawn to the role played by the gold standard as an element of the social philosophy of the Victorian age. The traditional commodity theory of money and the gold standard were defended in England by Edwin Cannan and Arthur Cecil Pigou, and in France especially by Charles Rist. Notable American economists who belonged to that group were Horace White and James Laurence Laughlin. In Italy the gold standard was unconditionally advocated by Maffeo Pantaleoni and Vilfredo Pareto. The popular belief in the "intrinsic value" of gold coins was characterized as an aspect of the eternal struggle between the individual and the state, since possession of gold was regarded as a protection against misuses of the economic power of the government.[53] On the other hand, adherents of organismic views were opposed to the international gold standard and emphasized the sovereign right of governments to manipulate the currency. All economists of the "romantic" type, such as J. G. Fichte and Adam Müller, had been adversaries of the international gold standard. Their views were endorsed by German nationalist authors. This opposition received a consistent formulation in the Neoscholastic teachings of Othmar Spann, and in the so-called state theory of money advocated by Georg Friedrich Knapp and his followers.

Belief in the "substance" concept caused the Socialists of Marxist persuasion to connect the value of money with the labor cost theory; they were unable to account for the value of means of payment to which that theory was not applicable. Other socialist authors who were less influenced by doctrinal prejudices regarded radical monetary reforms as the most effective instruments for the promotion of revolutionary changes of the existing economic order. One of the most remarkable schemes of that type was advocated by Silvio Gesell. Gesell's proposals were designed to promote the growth of "real capital"; they centered on the idea to penalize hoarding by imposing upon the holders of money an annual tax of about 5.4 percent. Money would retain its value only by being equipped each month with a stamp to be purchased at a post office. Hence, money would cease to be hoarded, and Gesell expected such increases in capital accumulation that the rate of interest would be reduced to zero and interest would be paid only as compensation for special risks involved in financing certain enterprises. Gesell's proposals were backed by so-called Freiland-Freigeld associations in Switzerland and Germany. In France they enjoyed the support of Edouard Daladier, President of the Council. In the United States Irving Fisher defended them.[54]

The adherents of marginal utility analysis were faced with considerable difficulties when they attempted to adjust their monetary theory to the general principles of their doctrine, since the means of exchange did not appear to have a utility of their own, independent of the utility of the commodities. Carl Menger, who derived the value of money from the commodity character of monetary metals, emphasized the additional value acquired by money through its functions as general means of exchange.[55] He defined the value of money as the anticipated value of goods made available through the purchasing power of the means of payments. That view was taken over by other adherents of marginal reasoning.[56]

Careful analysis of the demand caused Menger and William Stanley Jevons to take account of the functions of money which resulted from its use as a store of value and as an instrument of protection against the uncertainty of future events.[57] But they did not connect these observations with a general monetary theory.

Leon Walras, like Jevons and Menger, adopted a commodity theory of money, but he attributed the metallic foundation of most currencies to psychological considerations petrified by the force of habit.[58] In order to render marginal utility analysis applicable to the determination of the value of money, he availed himself of a bold assumption: that the value of his *"numéraire"* was exclusively determined by the use value of the monetary metal, regardless of any modifications of that value by the monetary functions. The explanatory usefulness of that analysis was questioned by various authors, such as Knut Wicksell and L. von Bortkiewicz.[59] They pointed out the fluctuations in the exchange value of money produced by the various roles which money has to play in the markets of the catallactic economy.

In his discussion of the demand for money, Walras drew a distinction between the utility of the *"numéraire,"* or the value of money as a means of exchange, and the utility of money as *"encaisse désirée,"* readily available cash.[60] He connected the need to hold cash (*fonds de roulement*) with the fact that, once market prices had been determined by the process of "grouping," payment had to be made at later fixed dates. The holdings of money to which he referred were not meant to provide reserves against future contingencies strictly speaking. The Walrasian reference to money as means of providing stocks for future payments (*service d'approvisionnement*) was elaborated on by the Austrian economist Karl Schlesinger. In his analysis of such stocks, Schlesinger distinguished between those held to make fixed future payments and others held to meet future uncertain contingencies. To holds of the latter type he applied the principles of marginal utility analysis, since problems of alternative choices entered into the determination of their uses. This significant contribution to monetary theory was largely ignored, even by the Austrian Marginalists.[61]

The monetary policy recommended by Walras was based on the idea of retaining gold as the standard monetary metal and using silver coinage as a means of controlling the price level. He also proposed measures to prevent banks from lending amounts in excess of those deposited with them.

A serious challenge to the attempts by Menger's disciples to develop a monetary theory in accordance with marginal utility principles came from Knapp's attempt to divorce monetary problems entirely from any connection with value analysis. The Austrian economists were well aware of the practical consequences of Knapp's teaching, which were likely to provide a "theoretical" justification for any arbitrary manipulation of the means of payment by public authorities. At a meeting of the Verein für Sozialpolitik in Vienna in 1909, Friedrich von Wieser, leading the opposition to Knapp's views, defended a version of the commodity theory of money that was similar to that advanced by Menger.[62] His distinction between the external and the internal values of money was designed to differentiate between changes in the value of money brought about by alterations in the supply and demand conditions of the commodity markets and changes due to factors operating on the side of money, such as variations of monetary standards, increases in the velocity and the volume of the means of payment, and the like. In a study published in 1919 the usefulness of that distinction was questioned by the Dutch economist C. M. Verrijn Stuart on the ground that changes in the general price level could be caused exclusively by factors operating on the side of money.[63]

More important than these distinctions was von Wieser's attempt to explain the value of money as the final outcome of the combined marginal utilities of units of income. According to this line of reasoning, every individual price of a commodity reflected exactly the money equivalent of the estimates attached by the relevant groups of buyers to the utility of the commodity and to the marginal utility of the units of their incomes. Carl Menger had used the term *subjective exchange value* to denote the significance attached by an individual to the unit of his money income. Hence, the marginal utility of the income unit was bound to be lowered by any expansion of the volume of the circulating

means of payment leading to increases in incomes and ensuing price increases.[64] Von
Wieser suggested that the *objective exchange value* of money be measured with the aid of
indices based on the changes in the purchasing power of incomes over fixed groups of
commodities. These groups of commodities had to be determined by analyzing the expenditures of representative households. Under such conditions, complex processes of disproportionate price movements were likely to result in a general lowering of the exchange
value of money, unless the rise in prices was counteracted by enhanced supply of widely
marketable commodities.

Ludwig von Mises followed Wieser in applying marginal utility analysis to the
development of the monetary theory.[65] As Karl Knies had done before him, he chose the
method of historical regressus to derive the exchange value of money from an original use
value of the monetary metals; he was convinced he had thus secured a safe starting point
for the application of marginal utility analysis.[66] There were no serious objections to the
attempt to establish a genetic relationship between an original value in use and a subsequent development of a value in exchange of the monetary metals. But this procedure—
apart from relating money to the "ghost of gold"—failed to explain the value of fiat
money not clearly connected with a metallic basis.[67]

It was quite obvious that supply and demand analysis did not provide a valid procedure for determining the value of money. Schumpeter declared the demand for money
to be indeterminate, whereas the supply of the means of payment was dependent on
variations in their volume and the velocity of circulation.[68] Starting his analysis from the
monetary aspects of a Walrasian economy, Schumpeter characterized the possession of a
monetary unit as a claim to society, defined monetary circulation as a primitive system of
accounting, and held defects and misuses of that system responsible for many undesirable
aspects of the capitalist order. Although he rejected the genetic explanation of the value of
money, he defended the gold standard as a brake on arbitrary, inflationary increases in the
volume of the means of payment. He distinguished money as a standard of measuring
values from money as a means of payment.[69]

Knut Wicksell had suggested the reversal of the traditional relationship between
money and credit, and that money should be conceived of as a special type of credit
granted to society or to yet unknown suppliers of goods or would-be borrowers. The term
claim theory was used to denote the view that money had only a "nominal" value which
was connected with the relative scarcity of the means of payment and circulation at par.
The value of money and the general level of prices were regarded as correlative
concepts.[70]

This theory was heartily welcomed by authors who were opposed to marginal utility
analysis and who repudiated the gold standard because of its deflationary effects on the
economy. The most conspicuous representative of that view was Gustav Cassel, whose
systems of economic equations reflected the Walrasian conception of the stationary equilibrium economy and were based on a radical separation of the monetary theory from the
other aspects of economic analysis.[71] Cassel regarded the unit of the gold standard as an
abstract unit of reckoning which had lost any relation to its weight in gold; he proclaimed
the paper standard as the purest type of monetary organization. In view of the interdependence of all prices, he assigned to monetary theory the task of establishing the "multiplicative" factor which was required to make the price system determinate. But a number
of objections were raised to his formulation of the fundamental problems of monetary
theory.[72]

Disregarding minor divergencies of view, there existed, prior to the First World War, five distinct monetary theories: (*a*) the Ricardian commodity theory, which still had many adherents, although it was linked with an untenable cost of production theory and did not provide an explanation of the exchange value of nonmetallic currencies; (*b*) its counterpart, a doubtful version of the quantity theory of money which explained individual prices or the price level in terms of relationships between the total volume of the circulating means of payment and the volume of business transactions or of active trade (the advocates of that theory frequently disregarded the fact that the real problem to be explained was the choice of the standard unit which was prerequisite to the establishment of these relations);[73] (*c*) the "state" theory of money, organismic in origin, which ascribed the existence and functioning of any monetary institutions to government fiat and contributed effectively toward discrediting the commodity theory of money on the European continent; (*d*) the "income theory," which was derived from marginal utility analysis and connected the values of money with the importance attached by individuals to the units of their incomes; and (*e*) the "claim" theory, which connected the value of money with the purchasing power of the monetary unit.

Like the income theory, the claim theory started its analysis from individual estimates and took account of the function of money to provide stocks for use in a more or less distant future. In view of the fact that marginal utility considerations were basic to the income theory as well as to the claim theory, these two theories could be regarded as two versions of a single doctrine. The state theory and the "value" version of the quantity theory supplied no explanations of the value of money, and could hardly claim to be *theories* in the true sense of the term. Hence, the number of monetary theories worthy of that name could be reduced to two: the commodity theory and the claim theory. Knapp's misleading distinction between "commodity theories" and "nominalistic theories" resulted in widespread confusion. He applied the term *commodity theory* to all theories that associated the value of money with the value of the monetary metals, regardless of whether the value of the metals was connected with the substance concepts of the metals or derived from the importance attached by individuals to the metals and their uses.[74]

The conflicting views concerning the nature of money and the sources of its exchange value were reflected in varying definitions of the scope of the concept of money. The conservative partisans of the gold standard drew a sharp distinction between metallic currency and all other means of payment, such as banknotes, promissory notes, checks changing hands during the periods of their validity; credits granted by banks in excess of the amounts deposited with them; or uncovered paper money of all kinds.[75] Many others, especially French authors, applied the term *fiduciary money* to banknotes as distinct from metallic currency. They argued that means of payment should not be called money unless they had a "value of their own" which enabled them to serve as a standard of measuring values. This view was sometimes associated with a belief in the "substance" of the monetary metals being necessary for determining their value. A similar attempt to differentiate sharply between metallic currency regarded as "money" strictly speaking and other means of payment was made by marginalist authors such as Knut Wicksell and L. von Mises, who undertook to apply marginal utility analysis at least to the explanation of the value of metallic currencies.

The adherents of the claim theory, who regarded the metallic backing of a currency as a mere historical incident, applied the term *money* indistinctly to all means of exchange. That terminology, advanced by Schumpeter and Cassel, was adopted by a group of English authors.[76] Additional terminological difficulties were created by the adherents of Knapp's "chartalist" views, who were convinced that only fiat money, freed from any metallic foundations, represented money in the strict sense of the term.[77]

THE QUANTITY THEORY OF MONEY

The change in the conception of the economy which took place during the first decade of this century can hardly be better illustrated than by surveying the history of the quantity theory of money. Based on some first tentative attempts of mercantilist authors to establish definite relationships between aggregates of economic magnitudes, that theory connected the supply of and the demand for money with factors that could be analyzed independently of any explanation of the value of money. The term *quantity theory* as used in this connection is clearly to be distinguished from the misleading use made of the same term to denote the view that the value of money can be accounted for in terms of relationships between volumes of transactions and volumes of circulating means of payment.[78] But since the theory was formulated in terms of metallic currencies, it lost in importance when it was realized that these means of payment represented only a fraction of the total purchasing power, which constituted the counterpart to the total volume of trading.

A revival of the theory was mainly due to its reformulation and reinterpretation by Irving Fisher,[79] who adjusted it to the requirements of a refined analysis of prices. His "equation of change," which had been suggested by Simon Newcomb, was intended to define for a static economy, operating at full employment of available resources, the relationships between a set of factors considered instrumental in determining the average level of prices and the reciprocal of the purchasing power of money. Newcomb's equation was designed to illustrate the proposition that increases in all incomes would be accompanied by virtually proportionate increases of prices and wages. In his discussion of the "rapidity" of circulation he pointed to changes in expectations as an important element in determining idle balances.[80] In Fisher's equation the price level (P), an abstract magnitude, was defined in terms of five economic variables: the quantity of circulating cash (M), the volume of bank deposits (M'), the velocities of circulation of the two monetary quantities (V and V'), and the volume of trade (T). Fisher based his measurement of the velocity of circulation on the average period during which money is kept idle in cash balances. The volume of trade was represented by the aggregate value of the goods and services which were the object of exchange transactions during the period under review. The equation of exchange read: $PT = MV + M'V'$. It does not appear necessary to enter into a discussion of the intricate problems connected with the definition of the main variables (M, M', and T) included in that formula. Fisher's conception of money did not reflect a specific monetary theory; as modified by various authors, the formula was adjusted to such theories.

Widely expounded in economic textbooks, the equation fulfilled two important functions. It supplied the multiplier for transforming the relative prices of equilibrium analysis into absolute prices.[81] Moreover, it was used to illustrate two theses advanced by Fisher: (*a*) that a strict proportionality existed between the level of prices and the quantities of the circulating means of payment (including the deposit currency paid out during the year), and (*b*) that the level of prices was the dependent variable which adjusted itself to changes of the other magnitudes included in the equation and that, conversely, changes in the price level due to nonmonetary causes had no influence on the volume of money, the velocity of circulation, and the volume of trade. In his interpretation of the equation, Fisher assumed that the velocity of circulation and the volume of trade remained unchanged, and that increases in the volume of money were commonly accompanied by credit expansion, thus leading to disturbances between the level of money balances and individual expenditures. Statistical investigations were required to ascertain the specific relations between the magnitudes of which the formula was composed. For a time, Fisher regularly published estimates of the items. In his analysis of monetary problems he avoided any concepts or propositions not amenable to statistical measurement.[82]

Fisher's proposition that the quantity of money was the independent variable, whereas price was a function of that quantity, was designed to provide a theoretical background to the "compensated dollar standard," which was advocated by Fisher and centered on the proposal to adjust—at regular intervals—the quantity of the metal incorporated in the monetary unit to changes in the available gold stock.[83] This reasoning was motivated by the view that the circulation of the means of payment was extrinsic to the real functioning of the exchange economy and that the "price level" could be kept constant by appropriate manipulations of the volume of money. But the concept of the price level was open to varying interpretations.[84]

Similar considerations led to various other proposals dealing with the stabilization of the purchasing power of the international metallic standard. The establishment of a stable paper standard was equally the object of various schemes.[85] However, the idea of maintaining a stable general price level—for instance, of wholesale prices—met with the objection that measures taken with that end in view might have divergent effects on different groups of prices and might be incompatible with the far more important task of stabilizing the purchasing power of a given income.[86]

Fisher's equation enjoyed widespread recognition for some time. Particularly conspicuous was Cassel's use of it. Cassel's equation of exchange was similar to that of Irving Fisher, but Cassel questioned the possibility of determining, for a dynamic economy, the effects of increases in the quantity of money upon the velocity of circulation, the expansion of deposits, and the volume of active trade. His warnings that the world was faced with the dismal consequences of a dangerous shortage of gold aroused considerable attention and were the object of prolonged discussions until they lost practical importance through the gradual displacement of the gold standard from its previous dominant international position.

The belief in the equation of exchange as a reliable instrument of price analysis was increasingly undermined by a variety of criticisms.[87] They started from the question of whether changes in the relative value of commodities were, in fact, of no influence on the general level of prices.[88] Criticisms of another type were motivated by a theoretical aversion to the establishment of causal relationships between changes in the volumes of economic magnitudes. Also, prompted by a general opposition to equilibrium analysis, Wesley C. Mitchell argued that the three main elements of Fisher's formula—the volume of payments, the volume of prices, and the volume of trade—were three stages of a process extending over time. In his view, the static assumptions underlying the formula were incompatible with the task of analyzing economic processes.[89]

Increasing doubts turned on the assumption that the magnitudes which were supposed to determine the general level of prices were mutually independent variables. Increases in the velocity of circulation were shown to coincide frequently with expansions of the quantity of money;[90] rises in the price level were shown to be counteracted frequently by the stimulating effects exercised on the volume of trade or the circulation of goods by credit expansion; the volume of the circulating means of payment was shown to be influenced by the level of prices; and fixed relations were found to exist between the circulation velocity of cash and that of deposit currency.[91] Tooke's observation that rising commodity prices were frequently attended by rising discount rates drew attention.[92]

Critical objections were also raised to some hardly justified inferences drawn from Fisher's equation, such as that the monetary mechanism did not affect relative prices and production, provided that the general level of prices remained stable, and that a rising price level was always followed by expanding production and a declining price level by corresponding contractions. The definition of the concept of "total volume of trade" and of its relation to the national income was the object of conflicting views. Discussions of the meaning implied in Fisher's *ceteris paribus* clause revealed the existence of intricate problems connected with the influence of time on the relations between prices and the quantity of money. The methods used to measure the general price level and the volume of the means of payment were the object of additional criticisms; it was argued that the equation could be rendered more substantial by expanding the range of the variables included in it.[93]

A significant modification of the equation of exchange was eventually brought about by the elaboration of the ideas which were basic to the "cash balance" approach as suggested by Walras and developed by Wicksell. Wicksell contrasted the "individualistic" system of holding cash balances which was implied in Fisher's formula with the existence of a "collective holding of balances" which had arisen out of the acceptance of deposits on the part of the banks. His description of the "cumulative process" of rising prices was designed to explain how increases in bank reserves ultimately led to an increase in prices, and how compensatory movements operated toward the reestablishment of a more stable price level. Wicksell objected to the distinction which was commonly drawn between circulating (flowing) and noncirculating money. He raised the question of whether the velocity of circulation was autonomous or only subsidiary in character, and emphasized the divergencies between the movements of prices of capital goods and prices of consumer goods. Wicksell defined "virtual" velocity of circulation as the relation between total payments and the quantity of metal money kept in cash by the bankers and the public. It has remained an open question—whether Wicksell is to be counted among the adherents of the equation of exchange or among its adversaries.[94]

The Cambridge economists who adopted the cash balance approach substituted for the traditional "transaction version" of the quantity theory a formula reading $M = K P T$. Marshall accepted the traditional equation of exchange as a useful method of determining the relation between the volume of the currency and the level of prices, everything else remaining the same. But he questioned the procedure of impounding a large range of variables by the *ceteris paribus* clause. And he suggested to the Cambridge economists the cash balance approach with his observation that "people care to keep a greater or lesser proportion of their resources in the form of currency."[95] In that equation M stood for the total supply of money, K was an index figure representing the physical complement of the public's holdings of cash and demand deposits, P was the price level of the commodities transacted, and T was the volume of planned transactions. Hence, P T referred to the total value of transactions in current output, in other words, to the national income. K was the reciprocal of V, the velocity of circulation of the Fisher-Newcomb formula. Primary importance was ascribed to that velocity in determining the price level and its changes.

It was a characteristic feature of the cash balance approach that it could be expanded by including the demand for money among the variables.[96] Moreover, as distinct from the transaction version of the equation, it took account of the motives which influence the desire to hold liquid assets: the "precautionary" motive and considerations connected with future transactions. But the English advocates of the cash balance approach, like the adherents of Fisher's equation of exchange, ignored the influence exercised by the interest rate on monetary and price relationships. They assumed that the monetary costs of production would change proportionately with any change in the volume of the means of payment, and that, consequently, the rate of profit and the long-run equilibrium rate of interest would remain unchanged. Nor did the Cambridge economists deal with the dynamic aspects of price movements, as Wicksell had done.

The cash balance approach had a counterpart in the "income approach" as a method of price determination. That method had been suggested by Thomas Tooke in opposition to the Ricardian theory.[97] It attracted the attention of Wicksell, who referred to Tooke's proposition that the aggregate of money incomes devoted to expenditure for consumption was the determining and limiting principle of demand.[98] To the Austrian Marginalists, Tooke's approach provided an instrument for analyzing prices in terms of relationships between individuals and individual goods, as distinct from the "mechanical" approach implied in Fisher's equation, which in their view ignored the "psychological" significance of the value of money, overlooked the subjective elements implied in the determination of price movements, and disregarded the plurality of functions of the means of payment.

Von Wieser taught that the determination of prices was to be based on a flow of money and goods, not on stocks.[99] He qualified as passive factors the volume of bank credits and the velocity of circulation. Albert Aftalion, who like von Wieser believed in the income theory of money, regarded the latter as a constituent element of price theory, and believed that the velocity of circulation was implied in the idea of a stream of money.[100] Von Mises emphasized the incompatibility of the equation of exchange with marginal utility analysis. He characterized the equation as a procedure for treating dynamic changes in the value of money as if they were elements of a static system.[101]

The income approach as an instrument of price analysis owed its full development to Schumpeter's elaboration of von Wieser's suggestions.[102] Schumpeter defined the circulation round as taking place when the means of payment spent by the producers in the factor market is received by those who supply the productive factors, and is eventually spent in the markets of the goods of consumption. In the light of that reasoning he established a close analogy between the functions of money and those of the counters used in various games, and demonstrated that in the equilibrium economy of the Walrasian type equality existed between the total amount of all incomes and the total volume of all means of payment, multiplied by the average velocity of circulation.

For Fisher's velocity of circulation, Schumpeter substituted an "efficiency of money" concept, which he defined as the ratio between the average stock of money and the national income. That ratio indicated the average number of times a unit of money entered into consumers' income during the production period to which the national income was related.[103]

Another characteristic feature of Schumpeter's formula was the introduction of a dynamic factor—a time period—into the determination of the magnitudes which formed the two sides of his equation: the streams of money emanating from income, and the sum of the goods of production, multiplied by their prices.[104] Thus, he transformed the equation of exchange into an instrument for analyzing dynamic features of the economy, such as the effects on prices of credit expansion and the problems of "enforced savings."

The income version of the equation of exchange was subsequently somewhat modified by Ralph G. Hawtrey, who started from consumable incomes and assumed that the price level was directly proportional to consumers' outlays but inversely proportional to the quantity of goods (including capital goods) bought per unit of time.[105] He combined the difference between consumers' incomes and outlays with outstanding bank credits into the "unspent margin" of the circulating means of payment, and attributed a decisive effect on changes in the price level to that marginal amount. His analysis of producers' and traders' balances provided a link between the income approach and the cash balance approach; his emphasis on credit expansion as a method of enlarging the unspent margin provided a bridge to business cycle analysis.

When the means of payment were thus conceived of as vehicles of purchasing power distributed through the medium of credit among productive uses and incomes, an active role of primary importance was attributed to money in determining the course of economic processes. The static approach to the determination of the price level was shown to be inadequate; the Ricardian view that money was nothing but a veil to be removed in order to grasp the real function of the economy was shown to have been a fallacy.

THE PROBLEM OF BUSINESS FLUCTUATIONS

The existence of a close relationship between economic crises and preceding periods of brisk business activity was established by various authors during the first half of the nineteenth century. But the economists who during that period undertook to explain the fluctuating behavior of the economy—such as T. R. Malthus, Simonde de Sismondi, and Johann Karl Rodbertus—had no consistent conceptions of the functioning of the economy and did not advance business cycle theories in the strict sense of the term. Other—English and French—students of the cyclical behavior of business activity who relied on "observation and experience" in setting forth business cycles were not particularly interested in theoretical analysis. Rather, they attempted to show the behavior of prices and other economic magnitudes and to connect that behavior with certain institutional factors, such as the credit policy of the banks, fluctuations in the interest rate, and the like.

At this point in my analysis, I should mention two authors who did not advance business cycle theories strictly speaking but who pointed out certain aspects of the cyclical movements which much later received considerable attention. One of them was the English banker, Henry Dunning Macleod, who criticized various fundamental propositions of Ricardian economics and elaborated two ideas: that money was the highest and most general form of credit, and that those commercial banks which granted credit in excess of their deposits contributed considerably to the expansion of the volume of the means of payment.[106] Macleod regarded "overspeculation" and speculative "overtrading" as the consequences of liberal granting of "accommodation bills"; he ascribed the collapse of the inflated credit structure to drains on the gold reserves which eventually compelled the Central Bank to raise the rate of discount to relatively high levels. Macleod endeavored to show that business of the banks consisted in purchasing debts through promises to pay—that they were not "offices for borrowing and lending money," but "manufactories of credit."[107] That interpretation of bank credits was rejected by the adherents of the traditional commodity theory of money and found relatively few advocates among Anglo-Saxon economists.[108] But Knut Wicksell referred to credit expansion practiced by the banks in his analysis of the cumulative rise of prices.

Another author who contributed some original ideas to business cycle analysis was the German-American Nicholas Johannsen, who centered his considerations on the behavior of savings in times of depressions,[109] and associated with savings quite generally the "injurious tendency" to buy less from the community than would correspond to the quantity of goods and services made available. One of the most striking aspects of Johannsen's attacks on savings was his reference to the "multiplying principle," which implied that the initial effects of decreases in consumption and investment were intensified through subsequent losses of income. Thus, he suggested some ideas which were later developed into so-called multiplier theories.[110]

But for the Ricardian economists who endorsed Say's "law of markets" as a fundamental principle of equilibrium analysis, the alternations of prosperity and depression periods presented an almost insoluble problem. The assumptions which were basic to their construction of the economic system included premises (such as that all time coefficients were equal and that prices were determined by the combined action of supply and demand in the same time span, and especially the periodicity of the fluctuations) could not be reconciled with these premises.[111] Hence, it was necessary to ascribe the recurrent disruptions of the economy to forces affecting it from outside. The view advanced by John Stuart Mill and others that in spite of the general tendency of profits to fall, investors were, time and again, seduced by deceptive prospects to embark on extended speculative ventures which were bound to collapse sooner or later, was not very convincing.

William Stanley Jevons's much-discussed "sunspot" theory was a heroic attempt to explain the periodicity of the cyclical movements without violating the equilibrium principles of the Ricardian doctrine. Jevons related these movements to the operations of a noneconomic factor whose periodic behavior was governed by cosmic forces. He suggested that meteorological conditions and, indirectly, annual crops were influenced by periodical fluctuations in the volumes of caloric energy emanating from the sun and that business activity, in turn, was determined by the outcome of the harvests. In support of his theory, Jevons pointed to an alleged coincidence of the duration of a sunspot period (10.45 years) with the average duration of a business cycle.[112] But that theory could hardly be upheld when confronted with various criticisms of the methods used to demonstrate the alleged correlations between sunspot periods and business cycle periods, and between the various phases of the sunspot periods and corresponding changes in meteorological conditions.

Under these conditions the majority of the post-Ricardian economists tended to minimize the importance of the business fluctuations for economic analysis. They regarded crises and depressions as disturbances of the economy caused by a variety of outside factors and distinguished among monetary, financial, industrial, and commercial crises according to the sectors of the economy in which the disturbances made themselves primarily felt. Like J. S. Mill, he ascribed the recurrent disturbances of the economy to credit expansion and speculative buying.[113]

It was obvious that consistent business cycle research could be initiated only by an author whose approach to the dynamic aspects of the economy was not impaired by the firm belief in equilibrium economics of a static type. There is no doubt that the study of the Marxian doctrine by various German and Russian economists contributed considerably toward directing attention to the analysis of disproportionate changes of economic magnitudes occurring over time; the analysis of disproportionalities in the development of various sectors of the economy provided a promising approach to business cycle research. Theories of that type have frequently been termed *overproduction theories* or *nonmonetary overinvestment theories*. The term *disproportionality theories* corresponds better to the general intention of the present study to emphasize, as far as possible, the logical aspects of the various doctrines.

A leading role in pursuing research of that type was played by Michael Tugan-Baranowsky, whose studies have been mentioned in another connection. Tugan-Baranowsky emphasized the divergencies which he found during prosperity periods between the expansion of the capital-producing industries and the expansion of the consumer goods industries. He also pointed to disproportionalities between various sectors of the capital-producing industries, and to discrepancies between the supply of and the demand for capital. That approach was taken over by other economists, such as Arthur Spiethoff, who spoke of "saturation" in defining the economically justified limits of industrial expansion, and who characterized the upper turning point of the cycle as an economic position at which the production of fixed capital equipment had exceeded the needs and the demand for capital had exceeded the available loanable funds. The discrepancy between the available savings and the demand for capital was emphasized as a characteristic feature of a boom in the theory of the Frenchman Jean Lescure. Lescure attributed changes in business activity primarily to fluctuations in the profit rate and connected these fluctuations with changes in costs. A rise in costs of production, he argued, was especially pronounced at the end of a period of expansion, owing to the rapid increase in demand.[114]

Some of Tugan-Baranowski's leading ideas were reflected in the theory of the Frenchamn Albert Aftalion, who nonetheless showed a remarkable originality in his treatment of the various phases of the cyclical movements.[115] Aftalion derived his arguments against the validity of Jean Baptiste Say's law of markets from the satiability of consumers' wants, and pointed out a close correlation between the length of time needed for the production of capital goods and the length of the prosperity period, which in his view was brought to an end when a perceptible decline of the prices of consumer goods occurred due to the operation of the principle of diminishing marginal utility. Thus, Aftalion emphasized the decline in prices as a primary cause of the outbreak of crises, whereas Lescure had attributed particular importance to rising costs of production. The view that shortage of capital was responsible for the termination of prosperity periods was explicitly rejected by Aftalion, who tended to minimize the influence of monetary factors on the fluctuating behavior of the economy. Aftalion's emphasis on the length of the productive processes caused him to connect the duration of depression periods with the effects upon economic activity of the growing obsolescence of the capital equipment produced during the prosperity periods.

Aftalion supplemented these considerations with an analysis of the relationships between primary demand and derived demand, and showed that the fluctuations in the expansion and contraction of the investment industries were perceptibly intensified by "acceleration," that is to say, by the fact that relatively small increases in consumers' demand were accompanied by disproportionate increases and subsequent rapid declines in the demand for capital goods. Thus, substantial parts of the capital goods industry were likely to become idle after the machinery needed to produce the additional volume of goods had been completed. The "acceleration principle" soon became a constituent element of a considerable group of business cycle theories.[116]

None of these various versions of the disproportionality approach provided a way to a consistent explanation of the periodicity of the cyclical movements. The shifts in consumers' demand which Aftalion had stressed did not show significant regularities. Moreover, the disproportionality theories were not backed by a clear concept of the economy, and they failed to substitute a consistent construction of economic relationships for equilibrium analysis.

Attempts to achieve such a consistency started from the idea of transforming a model of the Walrasian type into an equally mechanical model in which disproportional changes of certain sectors of the economy were brought about by the influence of monetary factors, while the system was ruled by the tendency to return to new equilibrium positions. Gustav Cassel expounded a theory of that kind in his textbook.[117] As distinct from the majority of other authors, he regarded cyclical fluctuations as a phenomenon characteristic of a transition period leading from primitive to highly developed forms of capitalism. He distinguished trade cycles requiring different explanations, and expected that progress in the establishment of equilibrium between the agricultural and the industrial sectors of the economy would mitigate the violence and reduce the length of the cycles. In a revised German edition of his textbook which appeared in 1931, Cassel even raised the question of whether the postwar economics still exhibited the essential features of trade cycles.

True to his conception of the economy as a system ruled by equilibrating forces, Cassel regarded cyclical movements as the effects of an interplay of actions and reactions which was mainly caused by the behavior of the interest rate and its effects on prices and wages. In his view, the reactions to exogenous causes (such as changes in the interest rates) required time to be realized. Cassel rejected the view that depressions were caused by "overproduction," and he attributed the disproportionalities which developed during prosperity periods of errors committed in overestimating the supply of savings which were available for financing fixed capital assets. Disproportionalities which had their causes in variable institutional factors could not be considered as inevitable concomitants of capitalistic processes. But Cassel's assumptions were open to many objections.

The most effective use of the disproportionality principle as an instrument of economic analysis was made by Schumpeter, one of the few nonsocialist authors who regarded business fluctuations not as phenomena superimposed upon the linear progress of an expanding economy but as constituent elements of economic growth. Hence, in order to do full justice to Schumpeter's theory, his analysis should be conceived of not as a business cycle theory in the usual sense of the term but as the explanation of a general evolutionary process which takes place in the form of alternating expansions and contractions of business activity.[118] With the aid of a carefully chosen method, Schumpeter endeavored to demonstrate how the equilibrium conditions of the Walrasian model could be adjusted to the logical requirements of these processes. That approach was in some respects similar to the one adopted by John B. Clark, who had chosen the pattern of a stationary state as a starting point for his economic theory. But Schumpeter insisted upon drawing a clear distinction between a static and a stationary state, and started from the hypothetical picture of a "static" state. Into that picture he introduced the idea of a "circular flow" of goods and exchange values, and thus prepared the ground for the transition to a process of moving equilibria. Since the static economy could undergo changes caused by outside influences, it was not necessarily "stationary."

In the static model of the Walrasian type, an unchanging process was flowing at a constant rate, reproducing itself. Only two forms of income were assumed to exist in that model: the rewards for two "natural" productive factors, labor and land. Remuneration of employers' activities was included in "wages." Profits and interest on capital were excluded from the range of "natural" economic categories, since the employers, having perfect knowledge of the conditions of a static market, were assumed to operate under the rule of perfect competition, which guaranteed instantaneous adjustment of production to demand in terms of marginal productivity calculations. Schumpeter had no use for Böhm-Bawerk's theory of interest, which was based on the existence of a "natural" preference for present over future goods. He argued that the influence of the time element was not strong enough to guarantee a value premium on capital and to counteract the tendency of competition to reduce values to the cost of production. In his view, no reason existed for a systematic undervaluation of the means of production as compared with their products in an equilibrium economy in which production moved year in and year out through familiar, well-worn channels.[119]

Hence, the introduction of profit and interest on capital into the exchange economy had to be ascribed to factors connected with changes in the relationships among the economic magnitudes, that is to say, with movements extending over time. Equilibrium analysis was to be adjusted to the behavior of an economic system not only in which continuous changes in the mutual relationships of the magnitudes were taking place but in which the continuity was interrupted by time-consuming processes.

Using the method of successive approximation, Schumpeter transformed the static type of Walrasian model into another, in which a "circular flow" of goods and values moved smoothly from one equilibrium position to another. In a third model he abandoned the assumption that all changes in economic magnitudes were continuous; he attributed the existence of discontinuities primarily to technical causes, such as "innovations" which lead to new combinations of productive services, ensuing variations of the production functions, and the emergence of profit and interest on capital, resulting from differences between prices and costs. Among the costs to be defrayed under "dynamic" conditions, Schumpeter also included premiums for risks to be determined by experience. But he did not attach much importance to the problems connected with the risk factor. Since his theory of profit was a functional theory connected with the formation of the social product, he did not care to elaborate on the distributive aspects of profit. Only in passing did he mention the question of how entrepreneurial profits might be shared with various economic or political groups.[120]

Schumpeter ascribed the function of changing the coefficients of production to "daring" or "innovating" entrepreneurs, who opened new markets and anticipated and provoked demand. He sharply contrasted their behavior with that of the large mass of "adaptive, predominantly passive" producers or traders, and thus introduced a dialectic element into his analysis of evolutionary processes. In pursuance of that analysis, he argued that extraordinary profits, quasi-rents, and temporary monopolistic and quasi-monopolistic incomes gained by the daring employers were gradually whittled down in the course of ensuing competitive struggle and were finally wiped out when the innovations had lost their exceptional character.[121] But he regarded the earnings derived from innovations as sufficient to provide means for the continued payment of interest on capital, and he was convinced that he had supplied conclusive arguments for the conception of interest as a purely monetary phenomenon, a category of income accruing to a particular group of individuals who could count upon shifting their capital from opportunity to opportunity without impairing their economic situation. According to Schumpeter, Knut Wicksell's concept of a "natural" or "real" rate of interest reflected the desire to reconcile a nonmonetary theory of interest with the actual facts observed in the sphere of money and credit.[122]

But accumulated savings could hardly be assumed to be sufficient to cover the financial requirements of rapidly expanding business activities. Hence, Schumpeter referred to the banks' credit-creating power as the source of the credit expansion, which he regarded as a characteristic feature of prosperity periods. He distinguished "normal" credits, based on voluntary savings and providing means for the replacement of capital goods, from abnormal credits, representing claims to services or goods yet to be produced. Since the amount of such credits was not regulated by the usual process of supply, their allotment to daring employers was bound to direct productive factors into the channels of economic expansion, to provoke price increases, and to impose compulsory or "forced" savings on the "adaptive" employers. Both credit expansion and forced savings could be analyzed with the aid of the income theory of money; Schumpeter regarded both as indispensable ingredients of dynamic, disproportionate developments taking place within the productive sectors of the economy. He looked for institutional devices— especially the banks' reserve requirements—to account for the limits placed on credit expansion. As distinct from the majority of other authors, who emphasized the effects of forced savings on the distribution of the national dividend, Schumpeter assigned to such savings a conspicuous place in his analysis of productive processes.[123]

Thus Schumpeter defined profits as incomes earned when competition failed to reduce prices to costs, and as incomes subsequently eliminated when competition was fully restored, as used to happen during depression periods. But he regarded interest on capital, though derived from profits, as a lasting category of the exchange economy. In striking opposition to the views of other economists, he characterized depressions not as periods of economic disturbances but as phases of the cycle in which competitive struggles resulted in reestablishing the equilibrium of the economy through processes of readjustment, new "combinations" of resources, and the spread of technical and managerial procedures which were more advantageous than the traditional ones. Hence, he connected a fundamentally progressive trend not only with the expansion of economic activity during prosperity periods, as did other economists, but also with the general effects of business contractions.[124]

Almost all critics of Schumpeter's teachings were unanimous in acknowledging his ingenuity in transforming the Walrasian model from what may be considered as the "archetype of sterility" into a living matrix of fresh creation.[125] His application of the principle of successive approximation was a remarkable methodological achievement. Many business cycle analysts agreed with the functions he ascribed to expansions and contractions of bank credit in promoting the alternating expansions and contractions of business activity. But many other aspects of his theory, especially his method of starting the explanation of interest on capital from the conditions of a purely fictional static model governed by perfect competition among imaginary employers, met with varying objections.[126] Schumpeter's insistence on that method was backed by two problematic assumptions: the negation of the existence of any systematic time preference, and the belief that in the absence of dynamic forces no room was available for increasing the productivity of economic processes.

Another constituent element of Schumpeter's theory was equally the object of repeated critical comments: the principal role which he assigned to the "daring employers" in producing the cyclical behavior of the economy. The existence of such venturesome "captains of industry" was not questioned, but their definition as a demonstrable economic category was regarded as a doubtful proposition. The same was true of Schumpeter's sweeping contention that the upswing was always initiated by the introduction of "innovations" and that such innovations—implying shifts of the marginal productivity curves—clustered during prosperity periods.[127] Defenders of the strictly econometric approach to business cycle analysis, such as Jan Tinbergen, qualified the impact of the innovations on the economic system as exogenous "shocks." They argued that Schumpeter showed an outspoken preference for the shocks as the initial movers of the cyclical fluctuations, thus belittling the importance of the "mechanism" of the economy which in accordance with Tinbergen's econometric methodology, deserved main attention.[128]

Other objections were raised to Schumpeter's definition of depression periods as phases of the cycle in which the equilibrium of the economy was reestablished. Schumpeter's concept of equilibrium implied that there was no reason for a change in economic relationships and that, consequently, all prices remained stable. No reference was made in that definition to full employment of the economic resources. Was it justified to apply the term *equilibrium of the economy* to situations in which large quantities of economic resources—labor and capital—were unemployed? Was it justified to conceive of depression periods as stages of the cycles in which technical progress and innovations were spread throughout the economy? Was the capitalist economy not characterized by continuous instability rather than by recurrent returns to equilibrium positions? Irritating questions of that type prevented the large majority of business cycle analysts from endorsing Schumpeter's theories.

Carl Menger and the first generation of his disciples paid relatively little attention to the problems connected with the fluctuating behavior of the economy. Very characteristic in this respect was Böhm-Bawerk's view that the theory of economic fluctuations was the "last chapter" to be incorporated in the body of an economic doctrine.[129] The bridge leading from the analysis of individual behavior to the analysis of the relationships among aggregates of economic magnitudes was eventually established by Böhm-Bawerk's theory of interest on capital and the predominant role which he assigned to that economic category. Wicksell elaborated on the conception of the "real rate of interest" as the strategic factor which could be relied upon to adjust the periods of production to the available supply of loan capital. As I have already indicated, he believed the stability of the economy to be dependent upon the coincidence of the real rate and the loan rate of interest, and discussed disturbances of equilibrium positions which were likely to arise when the loan rate remained unaltered at the same time that the real rate increased, through discoveries, technical innovations, population movements, and other external factors.[130] He elaborated the idea that economic disturbances could be produced by discrepancies between savings and planned investments, and regarded business expansion as a stage in which—as suggested by Tugan-Baranowsky—large volumes of accumulated liquid capital were converted into fixed investments. He associated that process of "inventory production" with a cumulative rise of prices, manifesting itself dynamically in interdependent increases in the prices of capital goods, productive services, and consumer goods. In Wicksell's view, profit expectations, based on the difference between the real and the loan rates of interest, provided a link between impulses and changes in investments. In his analysis of that process, Wicksell made some simplifying assumptions concerning entrepreneurs' expectations of future prices—a procedure that was criticized by D. Davidson.

In order to account for "jerks" in the expansion of investments, he argued that the rate of technical progress was not likely to increase as smoothly as the curve of an increasing population; he used the simile of a rocking horse hit with a club to illustrate the ensuing transformation of a "jerk" into a cyclical movement.

Wicksell listed various factors which he believed to contribute to the collapse of a boom, such as "forced savings" (which imposed restrictions on consumption), the law of diminishing marginal productivity operating under competitive conditions, ensuing declines in the real rate of interest, and considerations of liquidity (which compelled the banks to curtail commercial credits). But he did not pay much attention to the effects of successive credit expansions and contractions upon the economy, and he did not develop his analysis of the behavior of economic magnitudes into a consistent business cycle theory. Wicksell was so thoroughly convinced of the advantages which could be secured by stabilizing economic conditions that he considered a stationary population of optimum size prerequisite to a general rise in the standard of welfare. In his *Lectures* he looked forward to a period of much slower technological progress and possibly of completely stationary conditions with falling rates of interest and a small capitalist share in the value of the product.[131]

Another Marginalist who connected the functioning of the rate of interest with certain aspects of business fluctuations was Irving Fisher, who started his analysis of such fluctuations with the behavior of prices, and ascribed the recurrent disturbances of the economy to increases in the circulating means of payment not accompanied by adequate increases in the interest rate.[132] Like Wicksell, he believed that the periodical expansions of business activity were initiated by external factors which opened the prospect of high rates of return over cost and that, however, these rates tended to fall along with the saturation of the process of expansion. According to Fisher's definition, the rate of return over cost was that rate which, employed in computing the present worth of all the costs and the present worth of all the returns, will "make these two equal."[133] He illustrated these propositions with examples provided by the economic history of the United States, and held the banking authorities responsible for the failure to adjust the loan rate of interest to their dwindling credit supply in time.

Wicksell's distinction between the equilibrium rate of interest and the bank rate provided the main elements for a business cycle theory advanced by L. von Mises, one of the most convinced adherents of the belief in the beneficial operation of the free competitive economic forces.[134] Von Mises combined the Wicksellian approach with Böhm-Bawerk's theory which believed the equilibrium of the economy to be dependent upon the adjustment of the length of the roundabout processes of production to the volume of the subsistence fund available for the payment of wages. Hence, he argued that the equilibrium rate of interest corresponded to a situation in which the demand for and supply of loanable funds were equated, and that reductions of the loan rate below that level were likely to induce employers to embark on productive processes requiring longer periods for their execution than was justified by the available volume of savings.[135] Excessive expansion of the periods of production was bound to lead to reduction of the volume of goods available for immediate consumption and to wage increases. The economically unjustified expansions of productive processes were eventually accompanied by increasing scarcities of the productive resources, and the collapse of the boom was bound to occur when liquidity considerations caused the banks to set the market rate of interest above the profit rate. Von Mises held a general predilection for holding low rates of interest responsible for the traditional banking policy, and believed that the establishment of competition among several banks of issue would compel credit institutions to adjust their policy of monetary expansion to sound principles based on the relationship between the volume of available savings and the economically justified demand for capital.

Summing up the results of the preceding survey of business cycle theories, a passing reference may be made to the commonly adopted distinction between endogenous and exogenous theories. Authors who adopted endogenous theories looked for causes inherent in the organization of the capitalist economy to account for its cyclical behavior. A remarkable representative of that view was Aftalion, who connected the cycle with the nature of the productive processes. Schumpeter, another adherent of that view, held the activity of daring employers and changes in the productivity function responsible for the wavelike behavior of the economy. Mitchell, a third representative of the same approach, pointed out processes of cumulative changes. In the light of this broad conception of the economy, measures of economic policy designed to cope with crises and depressions could, at best, succeed in mitigating the violence of the fluctuations and, perhaps, in shortening the duration of the depressions.

In a sense, the prospects of smoothing the path of economic expansion were far better if the so-called exogeneous theories, according to which cyclical movements were due to disturbances of the functioning of the economy caused by "outside" factors, were correct. The range of outside factors varied according to the definition of the economic system. Thus, monetary factors were excluded from the system by the Ricardian concept of the real exchange economy. Factors not present in the initial situation (for example, technological changes) were frequently qualified as exogenous.[136] Of course, the authors of these theories had to define these factors and their specific influence on the behavior of relevant economic magnitudes. Especially promising was the chance of combatting fluctuations when their incidence was ascribed to institutional processes which could be modified without interfering with the general principles underlying the functioning of the exchange economy. Processes of that type were emphasized in various theories. An outstanding example was the theory advanced by von Mises, which held the banks' policy responsible for causing recurrent overexpansions of investment activity. In some other theories—those of Tugan-Baranowsky, Spiethoff, Cassel, and Wicksell—banking policies were referred to only as a subordinate element in promoting business fluctuations, and main emphasis was placed on "real factors," such as growth of the population, technological changes, exploitation of expanding natural resources, or the opening up of new markets. The authors who adopted that approach endeavored to demonstrate how the effects of irregular and varying impulses were transformed into wavelike movements, and how the turning points of the cycles were brought about by economic reactions to the operation of such impulses. The intricacy of these problems was fully realized only in the course of subsequent discussions. But at least business cycle theories of the exogenous type did not suggest that fluctuations were endemic to the capitalist exchange economy.

The Ricardian economists had centered their analysis on problems of distribution; in the theories of their successors, problems connected with the allocation of resources occupied a primary rank. A new stage in the development of economics was reached when the explanation of the fluctuating behavior of the economy, instead of being regarded as the "last chapter" of a doctrine, was placed into the center of theoretical analysis. The need to develop new methods of carrying on that analysis made itself felt more urgently than ever before.

Chapter 22
The American Approach
to Marginalism

———

TOWARD THE END of the nineteenth century a new and promising era of American economics was ushered in by John Bates Clark, who used an original version of marginal utility analysis to establish a consistent and comprehensive body of economic theory. Clark pointed to the concept of "effective specific utility" as a determinant of exchange values. That concept was approximately identical to that of marginal utility. Since at the time he had no knowledge of previous discussions of marginal utility analysis, he has been regarded by Eugen Böhm-Bawerk and other authors as a fourth originator of that method.[1] Like Marshall, Clark endeavored to preserve, as far as possible, the general lines of the Ricardian approach; but, as distinct from Marshall, he applied the equilibrium concept to the construction of an imaginary model of the economy.[2] More than any other American teacher of his time, Clark contributed toward maintaining the tradition of refined hypothetical reasoning against strong attempts to propagate methodological principles similar to those proclaimed by the German historical school.

At the beginning of his academic career, Clark was inclined to join that movement. Influenced by his German teachers Wilhelm Roscher and Karl Knies, and perhaps also by some English conservative adversaries of the capitalist economy, he introduced strong ethical considerations into his *Philosophy of Wealth* and based his analysis of the economy on an organismic conception of society. He conceived of society as an organism, but in terms of observable organic relations among the individuals of which it was composed rather than of mystical nationalistic entities.[3] He analyzed the wide discrepancies that he found to exist in American society between private gains and social product, as exemplified by the violent financial struggles over the exploitation of the country's vast natural resources (with the exaggerated forms of competition on the one hand and areas of monopolistic market control on the other) and the "blind struggles" that frequently disorganized the labor market. Clark concluded that free competition, having been the "great regulator of the past," had practically been displaced from important sectors of the economy since it was incapable of working justice. He looked for a "moral force" as an alternative regulator, and recommended socioeconomic devices such as profit sharing, producers' cooperatives, and arbitration. A group of American economists who had just founded the American Economic Association hailed Clark's book as a manifesto protesting against the evils of laissez-faire capitalism.

The idea of deriving exchange values from "effective specific utility" was clearly expressed in that study. However, it was vitiated by the introduction of "society" as the source of the determinants of market valuations. The interpretation of exchange values in terms of "social utilities" remained a characteristic feature of Clark's subsequent analysis of the distributive process. A number of distinguished American economists (E.R.A. Seligman was one) were attracted by the idea of connecting the origin of exchange values with estimates of "society."[4]

Clark undertook that analysis in his *Distribution of Wealth*. Applying the marginal utility principle not to commodities as such but to the marginal increments of commodities, he elaborated the idea that market prices are not determined by the utility of the commodity that is purchased but by the utility that is added by the marginal increments to the wealth of the consumer.[5] He supplemented these considerations with discussions of the changes in marginal utilities that result from varying combinations of goods, from modifications of individual incomes or properties, and the like. As William Stanley Jevons had done before, Clark regarded utilities as measurable magnitudes, and conceived of economic behavior as a continuous process of balancing against each other want satisfactions (pleasures) and sacrifices (pains) of innumerable kinds. His hedonistic interpretation of economic behavior was quite evident.

Paramount among Clark's methodological convictions was the proposition that a fictitious economy of the static type, governed by perfect competition, provided the only starting point for an analysis of the distributive processes. He did not doubt that the same economic forces that are assumed to operate in an unchanging world are also dominant under conditions of change and that, consequently, knowledge of the "normal" or "natural" laws of the static state was prerequisite to any understanding of the functioning of the actual economic machinery. Without demonstrating the validity of that bold assertion, Clark outdid the Ricardian economists in his use of this methodological device, and he criticized them for having failed to separate heroically and perfectly the analysis of an economic system functioning under static conditions from the analysis of a "dynamic" economy.

In fact, the model of a more or less stationary economy had been vaguely suggested by the Ricardian economists; but they had placed its possible realization at the end of a prolonged developmental period during which the rate of profits was assumed to have fallen so low that any further incentive to accumulate capital had been eliminated and the factors of production had reached a position of rest, while variations of labor and capital remained still possible within relatively narrow limits.[6]

Since the element of time was eliminated from the functioning of the Clarkian equilibrium economy, and perfect competition was assumed to assure optimum utilization of all resources and optimum want satisfaction for the members of the community, there was no room in that model for differences between the expected effects of economic plans and their realization. All productive factors were assumed to be perfectly mobile and fully occupied. The return of each factor was determined by the marginal productivity of its unit, and for each factor the returns of its units were equalized. The shares allotted to the productive factors in each productive process exhausted the value of its products and left nothing for profit, conceived of as a residual category.

In the course of simplifying his assumptions, Clark eliminated the distinction between capital and land as separate productive factors. That procedure was in line with an American tradition established by Henry Charles Carey and Francis A. Walker. The assimilation of land and capital as productive factors had been motivated by the consideration that in America land was not in scarce supply and was frequently an object of investments. A fundamental difference between land and capital as sources of revenue was, of course, emphasized against Clark by the partisans of Henry George's single tax proposal. Since in a static economy the volumes of capital and labor could be assumed to be constant, land lost the privileged position of being available only in limited fixed quantities; wages and interest on capital were assumed to be the only kinds of return under a regime of "natural" values.

In accordance with the marginal utility principle, any increases in production were bound to be accompanied by declining values of the products. Clark decided to apply the principle of diminishing returns to all productive activities, and formulated it as a "universal law of economic variation," of which the theory of rent was a special case.[7] Similarly, he used a single principle, the "law of final productivity," to explain the contributions of capital (including land) as well as labor to the value of the product. He regarded both contributions as types of rent resulting from the law of diminishing returns.

The assumption that, under hypothetical static conditions, labor was a perfectly mobile agent was not likely to meet with serious objections. But the same was not true of capital as invested in productive enterprises. Hence, Clark drew a distinction between perishable or transitory "capital goods" of all forms (including land) and "pure" capital in the sense of permanent, perfectly mobile abstract quantities of productive wealth. He applied the idea of marginal productivity to a concept of "social" capital that had its origin in organismic views. The main source of the concept of "social capital" was perhaps the capital theory of Karl Knies, Clark's German teacher.[8] Thus, Clark could define the rate of interest as that marginal return on capital (or land) that was obtained when additional expenditures of labor did not provide any increase in production. Subsequently Clark modified his "productivity" theory of interest in favor of Eugen Böhm-Bawerk's *agio* theory, which was based on the preference of present goods over future goods.

The concept of "social" capital had its counterpart in the concept of "social" labor. According to marginal productivity analysis, the value of the last unit of the variable agent (labor) was determined by the value of the increment in production derived from the addition of that unit, and all marginal units of the variable agent, being interchangeable, had the same value. Thus, Clark arrived at the idea of "specific productivity." It was based on the consideration that, under conditions of perfect competition and perfect mobility of the productive agents, the increment in the value of a product which was due to the addition of a marginal unit of a factor could be attributed to any unit of that factor. Consequently, each factor received a reward which corresponded exactly to the value created by its contribution. The validity of this concept and its normative, even moral, implications were the object of many critical comments. Some critics pointed to the fact that the uniform wage principle as derived from the contributions of the marginal worker does not take account of the higher contributions of other workers. Various protests were also leveled against the confusion of problems of personal distribution and those of functional distribution, which was involved in Clark's "productivity ethics."

The utilitarian aspects of Clark's doctrine were accentuated by the use which he made of the "unit of disutility" in his theory of "real" costs, which was based on the assumption that such a unit was homogeneous for all workers, and that under equilibrium conditions one unit of marginal utility was equal to one unit of marginal disutility. This device, which took the place of David Ricardo's hypothetical standard unit of labor costs, enabled Clark to make the equilibrium concept directly applicable to the economic system.[9]

Having thus established the "normal" laws underlying the functioning of the static economy, Clark undertook to analyze the behavior of an economy in which "dynamic" forces were acting in directions different from those that determined the balance of the economy over short periods. He simplified that formidable task by limiting his discussion to the influence of a relatively small group of conspicuous factors, such as increases in population and capital, improvements of methods of production, changes in the form of industrial organization, and, above all, multiplication of consumers' wants. Moreover, he assumed throughout his discussion of ''dynamic'' forces that changes due to these forces tended to neutralize one another,[10] and that the actual form of a highly developed society hovered relatively near its static mode.

Clark visualized economic progress as a process in which the economy proceeded from one equilibrium position to another, a process accompanied by more or less serious frictions. From profits as a reward for risks Clark distinguished ''pure profit,'' resulting from changes in market conditions that were due to the operation of dynamic forces. The background of that conception was formed by a sort of ''social Darwinism,'' which implied that the survival of the fittest was assured by the outcome of the economic struggles. This theory provided some arguments for justifying profits as a special reward for entrepreneurial activity.[11]

There is no doubt that J. B. Clark succeeded in providing a generation of American economists with a consistent approach to economic analysis, in which important elements of the Ricardian doctrine were combined with the effective application of the principles of marginal utility and marginal productivity. Along with the elimination of the wage fund idea, he asserted the proposition that interest on capital, profits, and wages could increase simultaneously in an advancing economy. He deprived ground rent of the privileged position it had occupied in Ricardian economics, and explained the contributions of the productive factors in terms of a single principle. He defined the characteristic features of the static economy, and used the concept of moving equilibrium to analyze changes in economic conditions. His conspicuous merit consisted in inaugurating the active participation of American economists in the elaboration of marginalist doctrines.

Chapter 23
Conflicting Trends

PRAGMATIC ECONOMICS

IT MIGHT NOT be amiss to facilitate the understanding of the specific development of American economic reasoning by introducing at this stage of my discussion a short account of an intellectual movement which hoped to arrest the prevailing trends and, in fact, perceptibly influenced the thinking of at least one generation of American economists. Like similar movements which found adherents in other countries, the reaction which arose in America against certain salient features of the capitalist economy was mixed with an outbreak of hostility toward some aspects of hypothetical reasoning.

A sort of prelude to the revolt against Ricardian and marginalist economics was initiated by the teachings of Simon N. Patten (1852–1922), who attempted to develop a sort of ''dynamic'' approach to the study of the social sciences.[1] He rejected various assumptions which were fundamental to traditional economics, and used a sort of economic interpretation of history to elaborate the idea of a deep antagonism between the "genetic" growth of a vigorous industrialism and a "cultural lag" rooted in inherited mental attitudes. He expected a solution of that conflict from a cooperative organization of the economy.

But the organismic conception of society as adopted by Patten was eclipsed by the so-called institutional approach suggested by Thorstein Bunde Veblen. The success of Veblen's writings was especially remarkable because he failed to develop a consistent economic or social doctrine.[2] The general background of his studies was provided by the American pragmatic philosophy, but he also used poorly coordinated elements of German intuitional thinking, Marxian dialectics, and Herbert Spencer's social Darwinism.

The American pragmatic philosophy, as developed in the 1860s in the writings of Charles S. Peirce (1839–1914) culminated in the idea that the universe had come into existence through "original spontaneity," and that among conditions of boundless possibilities certain uniformities of behavior had resulted from chance happenings. Hence, Peirce rejected any speculations which turned on concepts of "substance," "mind," "matter," and the like. Instead, he insisted upon adjusting people's conceptions of the various objects to the practical effects which they conceive these objects to have.[3]

These ideas were further developed by the American philosophers William James (1842–1910) and John Dewey (1859–1952) who emphasized instincts and habits and the functional aspects of the emergent and continuous processes of experience, thought, and inquiry.[4] Their methodology led to the conclusion that scientific hypotheses are justified only to the degree that they contribute toward organizing in progressive unification the isolated data supplied by sense perceptions. There remained, however, the questions of whether and how the "universal truths" of logic and mathematics are related to the world of empirical objects.

The fundamental importance attached to "rational behavior" by the economists of the Ricardian and marginal utility schools was hardly compatible with the pragmatic conception of the mind as a highly complicated psychological mechanism and the conception of reason as an instrument for selecting useful actions among available alternatives presented by changing economic and social institutions. In accordance with the pragmatic methodology, the starting point of theoretical considerations could not be supplied by assumptions derived from the idea of a uniform, changeless type of motivation. The starting point of any analysis of social phenomena had to be sought in systems of relationships among individuals in their empirical settings.

In accordance with this methodology, Veblen qualified the Ricardian and post-Ricardian doctrines as "taxonomic" disciplines which had their roots in a natural law philosophy and a hedonistic psychology, and treated men as passive creatures reacting mechanically to external stimuli.[5] Inasmuch as "taxonomic" means dealing exclusively with classification, a definite derogatory sense was attached to that term when applied to the science of economics. These doctrines, Veblen argued, had reduced all human motives to acquisitive pecuniary terms and had proclaimed the belief in an unchangeable competitive economic order, although that order represented, in fact, only a phase in a "natural" growth. Hostility to economic theorizing of any type caused Veblen to regard the logical isolation of the economic sphere as the outcome of an obsolete habit of thought. He rejected any quantifying approach to economic analysis, and scoffed at the application of the equilibrium concept to the relationships among economic magnitudes and at the construction of a consistent imaginary model of the economy.

But Veblen's own socioeconomic doctrine was hardly a satisfactory substitute for the theories which he repudiated. Starting his considerations from a study of people's conduct in their dealings with the material means of existence, he applied a theory of "cumulative social change" to the interpretation of the history of material civilization. Adopting the behaviorist approach to psychological analysis, he attempted to derive the fundamental conceptions of his theory from the proposition that instincts, as modified by the influence of surrounding conditions, were the motivating forces of human actions and attitudes.[6] But the list of instincts which supplied the framework of his sociological analysis was not derived from careful behaviorist observation; it was composed of some ill-defined congeries of human motivation so arranged that they could be used to support biting attacks on the capitalist economy. Veblen's list of instincts included the "paternal bent" (unselfish sentiments, mainly those promoting group interest), the "instinct of workmanship," the self-regarding disposition, "pugnacity," and the bent to "idle curiosity" or disposition toward "aimless inquiry." (It is beyond the scope of this study to refer to the justified objections to the poorly coordinated group of "instincts.")

Veblen assigned economics the task of analyzing the development of "institutions," as the transient results of interactions between human nature and the material environment. The term *institution,* which played a major role in Veblen's teachings, has been the object of varying interpretations. Particularly confounding has been the indiscriminate application of the term to political and economic organizations that owe their origins to deliberate human action as well as to social devices that—like money—cannot be regarded as the products of conscious planning.[7] Still, it became the generally accepted practice to use the expression *institutionalism* to characterize Veblen's teachings. In his sociological studies Veblen attempted to demonstrate that all social change implied changes in "habits of thought and customs" as crystallized in institutions.[8] But his concept of "habits of thought" was vague, as was his concept of "evolution," which he defined as the "unfolding of processes" in accordance with the Darwinian canons of "selection and survival." Influenced by the methodology adopted by the German historical school, Veblen distinguished four stages in the "evolution" of material civilization: the savage era, the barbarian era, the era of handicraft, and the era of the machine process. Like other adversaries of the capitalist economy, he ascribed to "predatory exploitation" the growth of private ownership of the means of production. Veblen's distinction of four stages in the development of economic and social organization was as arbitrary as his theory of instincts.

Veblen contrasted the Darwinian approach with the Marxian "pre-Darwinian" conception of evolution as a sequence of processes governed by a predetermined goal and kept in motion by the dialectic action of antagonistic forces. Although he rejected that conception, his reasoning was obviously influenced by the Marxian procedure of holding antagonistic forces responsible for the "irrational" behavior of the capitalist economy. From the opposition of destructive and constructive "drives" he derived a system of grouping instincts or "native proclivities" as beneficial and constructive or as deflecting and contaminating "generically human ends of life." Elaborating on this rather primitive pattern of antagonistic forces, he transformed the Ricardian profit motive into a blind quest for pecuniary gain,[9] and established a series of social opposites by contrasting "economic" values with pecuniary values, "industries" with "business," the productive mode of economic activity with the acquisitive mode, the serviceability of commodities with veniaility, individual with ultimate needs, and the world of producers (engineers and workers animated by the instinct of workmanship) with the world of entrepreneurs, promoters, and financiers (motivated by the desire for parasitic gains).[10]

In this vein, Veblen undertook to demonstrate that the capitalist economy, lacking efficiency, was the arena of widespread parasitic trades, monopolistic controls of markets, and other "predatory" forms of vested interests. In his much-discussed theory of the "leisure class," he elaborated the idea that a class which enjoyed the advantages of "absentee ownership" and appropriated incomes without performing work had become heir to the position occupied among savage peoples by warriors, chieftains, medicine men, and other predatory groups of the population. To the Marxian theory of class struggle he opposed the observation that the attitudes of the leisure class were the object of general emulation by the lower classes.

The alleged contradictions between the technological and the pecuniary aspects of the capitalist economy provided Veblen with the background for a distinction between "economic" and "pecuniary" values. Only to the economic values, as created by industry, did he ascribe "social" usefulness, and he attempted to show that the value of capital assets was persistently jeopardized by the continuous progress of technology and the "inordinate" productivity of the modern machine process which enhanced the obsolescence of equipment.[11] Thus, he held lack of coincidence between pecuniary and economic values responsible for the fundamental economic problems confronting capitalist society, especially for the ever-recurrent crises and depressions. Since Veblen placed special emphasis on the relation between current capitalization of earnings and anticipated earning capacity, he regarded depressions as those phases of business cycles in which rising costs had eliminated the expectation of high profits, and the results of capitalization were higher than was warranted by prospective profits.[12] The evils that he connected with the organization of the capitalist economy were deeply rooted on the one hand in the failure of the masses to understand "the line of argument by which property rights are upheld" and on the other hand in the failure of the owners of the means of production to comprehend the working of the machine process. He pinned his hopes on the establishment of an economic order of a "technocratic" type, in which unhindered application of technical progress could be expected to lead to the realization of maximum welfare. The "technocrats" requested an organization of the economy ruled by the principles of technical rationality. According to these principles all productive activities could ultimately be reduced to "social energies," and productive factors and capacities could be used as interchangeable units of abstract energy, regardless of considerations of economic rationality. In the course of the discussions on "planning" that took place during the Depression of the thirties, the "technocrats" requested extension of the principles of "scientific management" to the control of the entire industrial system without clearly defining the objectives and the methods of the proposed control.[13]

INSTITUTIONALIST ECONOMICS

The enthusiasm which many American students displayed for Veblen's teachings was not affected by the palpable defects in his methods.[14] He made up for these defects with the keenness and perspicacity which he showed in characterizing some weaknesses of traditional economics, and with his biting attacks on the capitalist order, which exercised a strong attraction on young radical minds. The "institutionalist" approach appealed to those who considered conflicts of interest between social groups as a convenient starting point for economic analysis. With minor modifications, they adopted Veblen's definition of "institutions" as "frozen habits, invested with juridical authority," and sought the origin of "institutions" in various moral conceptions or psychological factors. They felt that the impacts of economic events or intellectual movements were responsible for changes in institutions to accommodate generally recognized needs. In discussions of the tasks of economics as an "institutionalist" science, the semidialectical elements of Veblen's teachings were commonly ignored. They were hardly compatible with the methods of thinking adopted by the overwhelming majority of Anglo-Saxon students of the social sciences.

The striking fact that it was not the use of a common method which established the connection among Veblen's followers can hardly be better illustrated than by surveying the work of his two outstanding disciples, John R. Commons (1862–1945) and Wesley C. Mitchell. The critical aspects of Veblen's writings appear to have influenced their thinking far more than his positive contributions to sociology and economics. They initiated two divergent lines of economic analysis which differed so widely as to the setting of their problems and the conception of the economy that only reasons of convenience can be advanced to justify their treatment in one and the same chapter.

John R. Commons set himself the task of developing "institutionalism" into a well-defined discipline based on the application of David Hume's analytical methods.[15] He conceived of social processes as a series of intended and purposeful changes (managed equilibria), and emphasized the tendency of economic behavior to be adjusted to definite patterns of socially sanctioned habits. To the "bargaining transactions" which had been the object of general economic analysis, he juxtaposed "managerial" and "rationing" transactions as additional important objects of economic research into predominant manifestations of collective action. The elements of his study of economic transactions were provided by five more or less arbitrarily chosen principles of explanation: efficiency, scarcity, working rules, sovereignty, and futurity. The inclusion of "futurity" among these principles showed that Commons realized the significance of expectations as a constituent element of economic behavior. By "sovereignty," Commons understood the changing process of authorizing, prohibiting, and regulating the use of physical force in human affairs. Since he identified "institutions" with "collective action in control of individual action," he devoted large parts of his studies to the task of describing the judicial processes of the United States as specific, fundamental forms of collective control.

The "pragmatic" approach to economic analysis, as called for by Commons, was to be backed by a "volitional" psychology, concerned with action, purpose, conflict, and the human will involved in these phenomena.[16] Like John A. Hobson and some German economists of the historical school, he emphasized the importance of economic power as a social factor. His attempt to distinguish several stages in the process of economic developments was based on the idea that the principles which underlie economic transactions had experienced, in the course of time, significant changes in their importance and in their mutual relationships.

But Commons did not succeed in establishing a consistent body of economic or social theories. His definitions of capitalism as a process and of the economy as a "going concern," an "aggregate of institutions" kept together "by working rules," were too vague to provide a satisfactory basis for sociological or economic analysis. His well-reasoned description of American cultural developments and their manifestation in juridical and administrative institutions was of lasting value. Even more important was the influence which he exercised on his disciples. They became the main protagonists in the struggle for the "New Deal" and in the introduction of the principles of the welfare state into the economic policies of the United States.

Whereas many adherents of Veblen's social philosophy were attracted—like Commons—by the institutionalist features of a "pragmatic" sociology, Wesley C. Mitchell was almost exclusively influenced by the critical aspects of Veblen's teachings. He was convinced that the adoption of Jeremy Bentham's felicific calculus and the principle of maximizing happiness, utilities, welfare, and the like as the starting point of economic analyses had been a deplorable fallacy; that Ricardian economics had to be interpreted as the historical product of a philosophical radicalism; and that, as a hypothetical science, a doctrine of tendencies, it had failed to develop a "realistic" method. True to his institutionalist creed, Mitchell placed primary emphasis on the mutual relationships between the development of the economic doctrines and the contemporaneous political and social events: "It is because successive generations have faced different problems than Ricardo did, that they have worked out new ideas, new sides of the subject and given opinions which differ from those of the classical group."[17]

Mitchell also followed Veblen in treating as "implicit hedonists" all economists who adopted the principles of marginal utility analysis, and he shared with Veblen the view that the main task of economics consisted in analyzing the cumulative changes of institutions and the various, but highly standardized, social habits.[18]

Under the influence of John Dewey's pragmatic psychology, Mitchell rejected the Ricardian method of holding a single motive responsible for economic behavior. He insisted upon determining through observation the kind of behavior that is adopted in reality. Hence, he decided to discard the use of highly abstract concepts, and to concentrate his studies on economic problems which can be so formulated that the results of deductive analysis can be controlled by facts.

But, as distinct from Veblen, Mitchell cared little about "instincts" in devising the psychological foundations of his studies. Rather, he attempted to develop a "social psychology" based on "objectified" psychological analysis and on investigations into mass behavior. Thus, he arrived at the proposition that, consequent upon the development of the exchange economy, the increasingly perfected use of money, and the introduction of a refined system of accountancy, the behavior of the members of a monetary community had been cast in an apparently "rational mold."[19] Substantial features of economic activity had thus been adjusted to monetary concepts to such a degree that the Ricardian economists had identified the pecuniary motives with forces attracting and repelling men with mechanical precision.

But, engaged in the preparation of other studies, Mitchell did not find the time to elaborate these fundamental aspects of an evolutionary sociology.[20] His main efforts centered instead on the task of developing reliable methods of analyzing the wavelike movements of economic magnitudes. With this end in view, he proceeded like a "naturalist, collecting series of statistical material and examining them as to their likenesses and similarities."[21]

Prompted by the principle of "reasoning from conduct to conditioning motive and circumstance," Mitchell was struck by the fluctuating behavior of business activity, which he regarded as a normal characteristic of the capitalist economy.[22] Research into that behavior, as reflected by the alternations of prosperity and depression periods, became a lifetime task to which he devoted amazing efforts.[23] He was governed by the intention to transform business cycle analysis from an "exercise in logic" into a "tested explanation of experience" and into a theory dealing with the actual working of the economic organization.[24]

From his conception of the money economy and its characteristic features, Mitchell drew the conclusion that financial factors were mainly responsible for the fluctuating behavior of business activity, since the variations in prices and monetary revenues far exceeded any observable fluctuations in the volumes of physical magnitudes.[25] The term *business fluctuations*, which Mitchell used to denote the object of his investigations, was a characteristic expression of his view that an "organic" connection existed between the form of economic organization, which we may call business economy, and recurrent cycles of prosperity and depression.[26] His refusal to distinguish cycles of different types was motivated by his aversion to the search for general "causal" explanations of the fluctuations. He also ignored the almost generally adopted method of dividing each cycle into four phases, since that procedure was primarily suggested by an interpretation of the cycles as movements to and from equilibrium conditions. Rejecting any equilibrium analysis, Mitchell was convinced that each fluctuation represented, in many respects, a singular phenomenon, accompanied by structural changes of the economy, and that in view of the complexity of social and economic relationships it was impossible to account for any particular economic situation in terms of a few simple causal connections.

In accordance with his methodological principles, Mitchell drew up a comprehensive list of questions that should be made the object of statistical investigations as a preliminary to any theoretical explanation of the cyclical movements.[27] These questions turned on the fluctuating behavior of wage rates and of consumers' spending and its relation to the national income, and on changes in investments and inventories, in profits, in the volume of the circulating medium of exchange, and the like. He devoted special attention to the methodological problems involved in the elaboration of quantitative analyses[28] and initiated a new line of economic research that developed rapidly under his leadership. Mitchell's studies proved the pattern for a large series of statistical investigations into the various aspects of the American economy undertaken by the National Bureau of Economic Research.

But his methodological principles did not prevent Mitchell from establishing various propositions which reflected the broad orientation of his investigations. Paramount among these propositions was the thesis that business cycles are self-generating movements, the specific form in which the evolutionary process of capitalism is taking place. Hence, he endeavored to clarify certain relationships among economic magnitudes which later became constituent elements of business cycle analysis, such as the lag of consumption expenditures behind income receipts, the time span which elapses between investment decisions and their execution, and the divergencies in the movements of various sectors of the cost price structure. Arthur F. Burns was probably right in stating that a sensation would be created in the scientific world if Mitchell's "homely work of 1913" were translated into the picturesque vocabulary of "propensities, multipliers, acceleration coefficients and the like."[29] But Mitchell did not stress the theoretical aspects of his findings; he remained true to his purely empiricist methods in his later publications in

which he elaborated the results of comprehensive statistical research without fully justifying the reasons for the selection of his data and without attempting to analyze possible
causal relationships between the movements of the economic variables.[30]

Mitchell looked forward to an "empirical" science of economics, to be based upon
an analytic study of actual behavior. That science, he believed, was to be as definitely a
by-product of a later phase of the money economy as mercantilism and the speculations of
Ricardo had been by-products of earlier phases.[31] Similar ideas, less clearly expressed by
other influential members of the Veblenian group, contributed toward discrediting the
theories of the Ricardian and marginal utility type. Thus it happened that in the United
States the study of economic problems was split up into a number of branches, each with a
scope and problems of its own. Differences in methods provided the main reasons for a
progressive departmentalization of a previously highly unified discipline.

CRITICAL DISCUSSIONS OF MARGINAL UTILITY ANALYSIS

During the last decade of the nineteenth century the psychological version of marginal utility analysis enjoyed increasing acceptance in Italy and the United States. In Italy
Menger's ideas were spread and elaborated upon mainly by Maffeo Pantaleoni, in *Principi di economia pura*. Pantaleoni combined the psychological version of marginalism
with certain elements of Jevons's theory. Other noted Italian economists who adopted the
principles of marginalism were Giuseppe Ricca-Salerno, Augusto Graziani, and Camillo
Supino. The most outstanding American economists who introduced marginal utility
analysis into American economics were Simon N. Patten, Frank A. Fetter, H. J. Davenport, and Irving Fisher. The stimulating effects of this new approach to economic problems were quite remarkable in both Italy and the United States; in France, however, the
large majority of economists preserved the traditional attachment to the teachings of Jean
Baptiste Say. Marginal utility analysis of the psychological type was adopted in France by
Paul Leroy-Beaulieu, C. Gide, Albert Aftalion, A. Landry, and M. Roche-Agussol. A
widely used, remarkable textbook that was strongly influenced by psychological marginalism was Leon C. Colson's *Cours d'économie politique*.

However, time and again, the development of marginal utility analysis was retarded
by the need to clarify serious misunderstandings of the principles underlying that analysis.
Such misunderstandings were especially caused by the tendency to conceive of "utility"
not as a relationship between individuals or economic units and desired objects but as a
quality inherent in things. Prolonged discussions also turned on the misleading belief in
the existence of "social values" that were derived from estimates of the society as a
whole.[32] The usual consideration advanced in favor of the existence of "social values"
started from the argument that the importance attached by individuals to various goods
was largely determined by generally accepted judgments. Social determinants of the
formation of prices were emphasized by E.R.A. Seligman, who elaborated the proposition that in many markets the existence of various classes of the population was reflected
in the appearance of diverse groups of buyers and sellers. Eugen Böhm-Bawerk, however,
endeavored to show that it was one of the most characteristic features of the exchange
economy that extreme variations existed among the marginal utilities attached to the same
goods by different persons.[33] The belief in "social values" was countered with the
arguments that the concept of the "society as a whole" was an ill-defined notion that had

no counterpart in actual experience and that even values attached to specific objects in accordance with religious or moral convictions, tradition, or legal procedures had their ultimate roots in the minds of individual members of society and were subjected to conspicuous modifications in the course of time. Only when understood in a very broad sense could the term *social values* be used to denote the concepts that provided the background for the economic policies of the "welfare state."[34]

Discussions of a different kind turned on the close connection that some English economists, such as William Stanley Jevons and Francis Ysidro Edgeworth,[35] had established between the economic concept of utility and the felicific calculus of the utilitarian philosophy. Edgeworth had ascribed to the unit of the economic calculus two dimensions—intensity and time—and to the "moral calculus" an additional third dimension—interpersonal comparisons—as a prerequisite to the establishment of utilitarian maximizing propositions. Likewise, utilitarian considerations were basic to J. B. Clark's marginal analysis. The utilitarian philosophy had never gained a firm foothold in Central Europe.

But the Walrasian conception of utility was free from any utilitarian connotations. Pareto's construction of indifference and preference curves was even designed to eliminate the concept of utility entirely from theoretical analysis. Leading representatives of psychological marginalism, such as Carl Menger and Eugen Böhm-Bawerk, explicitly repudiated the suggestions that their concept of utility was influenced by the teachings of utilitarian philosophy. Von Wieser insisted that the method of "introspection" which he used to establish the principles of subjective valuation was independent of the teachings of any specific school of psychology or philosophy.[36] His formulation of a "law of subjective rationality" or "law of motivation" was endorsed with various modifications by most economists of the Austrian School.[37] They were practically unanimous in emphasizing the empirical foundations of that principle.[38]

Even the majority of Marshall's followers abandoned the belief in the principles of utilitarianism. The propositions which provided the basis for their deductive reasoning were formulated with great clarity by J. N. Keynes who elaborated the methodological aspects of Marshallian economics.[39] These propositions were: (*a*) the economic principle according to which maximum satisfaction was to be attained with the minimum sacrifice possible; (*b*) the law that final (marginal) utility decreases as the stock of commodities increases; and (*c*) the application of the law of diminishing returns to the returns from land. There was no reference to utilitarian concepts in that formulation of a methodological credo.

Philip Henry Wicksteed was strongly opposed to the use of utilitarian concepts; he defined the psychological laws that determined economic behavior as the "laws of life."[40] Wicksteed was a minister by profession and one of the few convinced English advocates of Jevons's marginal utility theory, which he elaborated upon in various important directions. Although he shared the socialist convictions of the Fabians, he hesitated to support measures of deliberate planning. To projects of economic planning he raised the objection that the economic machinery was moved by individuals for individual ends, and that its social effects were incidental. Various leading American economists who endorsed the psychological version of marginalism, above all Irving Fisher (1867–1947), equally refused to connect their teachings with utilitarian principles. H. J. Davenport insisted that the utility of an object should be taken as nothing more than one way of expressing the simple fact that the object is desired.[41] The term *desirability* was similarly adopted by Fisher and Frank H. Knight to characterize the importance attributed by individuals to individual goods.[42] Frank A. Fetter qualified the fundamental economic act of choosing as an impulsive or instinctive rather than a rational act, and saw the basis of value in simple acts of choice.[43]

Such considerations were accompanied by attempts to apply the concepts of disutility and sacrifice of utility to the definition of costs, and to render the concept of costs amenable to marginal utility analysis. Some American authors, such as Fisher, F. W. Taussig (1859–1940), Henry R. Seager (1870–1930), and E.R.A. Seligman, approached the problem of costs from that angle. These repeated and categorical assertions by leading economists did not prevent adversaries of the marginal utility doctrine from arguing that the doctrine implied the belief in a rational "hedonistic" consumer, the adoption of a concept of disutility, and the identification of market prices with expressions of utilities "to the community." Similar criticisms were repeated, time and again, by German students of the history of economics. They were also reflected in Gunnar Myrdal's analysis of post-Ricardian economics.[44]

Renewed endeavors were made to establish a solid foundation for price analysis in terms of the marginal utility principle. In 1925, Jacob Viner summarized the results of these discussions by stating that if a law of diminishing desire is substituted for the law of diminishing utility, and if all references to gratification, satisfaction, benefit, pleasure, pleasantness, pains, irksomeness, and unpleasantness are eliminated, there will remain sufficient to supply an immediate psychological background for the concept of the negatively inclined pecuniary demand schedule, and, therefore, for the explanation of the mode of determination of market price.[45] A considerable confusion, criticized by various Marginalists, was connected with the view that utility schedules could be identified with demand schedules and that prices could be used to measure utilities.[46] However, it was quite obvious that no suitable standard for such measurements was supplied by the marginal utility of the monetary unit, which varies widely among individuals and is itself derived from the demand for goods and their prices.

Time and again Fisher took up the insoluble problem of demonstrating how subjective estimates concerning the desirability of goods are transformed into prices. He elaborated on some ideas suggested by two Austrian authors only loosely attached to the Austrian school, Rudolf Auspitz and Richard Lieben.[47] Auspitz and Lieben started with the assumption that utilities could be regarded as measurable and comparable magnitudes and dealt mainly with partial equilibrium situations. Fisher adopted the Walrasian procedure of dividing utilities into infinitesimal fractions in order to adjust them to the requirements of mathematical integration.[48] He borrowed the concepts of complementarity and substitutability of commodities from the psychological school; in addition, he availed himself of Edgeworth's suggestion to use indifference curves in order to avoid direct interpersonal comparisons of utilities. Finally, he simplified his problems by introducing some bold assumptions, such as that the marginal utilities of increasing or decreasing quantities of desired commodities could be represented as a continuous scale and that the marginal utilities of the various commodities were independent of each other. But he was unable to reduce to manageable proportions the problems involved in measuring utility functions when account was taken of the complementarity of goods.[49]

For a considerable time, however, little importance was attached to the so-called generalized utility functions, which dealt with the interdependence of the utilities of goods; the simple "additive" function was considered a reasonable approximation to reality. In addition, interpersonal comparability of utilities appeared to be a prerequisite of the application of marginal utility analysis to the problems of welfare economics and of progressive taxation.[50] Alfred Marshall had admitted the validity of such comparability in his often-quoted dictum that "if the money measures of the happiness caused by two events are equal, there is not in general any very great difference between the amounts of the happiness in the two cases." But this view was open to serious objections. Knut Wicksell realized the difficulties involved in interpersonal comparisons of utilities and showed that not even under a system of perfect competition could maximum want satisfaction be considered assured.[51] Motivated by the endeavor to arrive at determinate solutions to their problems, the Marginalists, like their Ricardian predecessors, avoided thorough-going discussions of the questions connected with foresight, expectations, and the like. A discussion of that type was initiated only later, when the role played by risk in influencing economic behavior received due attention.[52]

In the course of the prolonged discussions of the price problem, it was definitely established that any attempt to use the concept of subjective values to explain prices was conditioned by the assumption of an existing price system.[53] The use of ratios was eventually suggested to account for the formation of exchange values. An individual's selection among different goods was held to depend upon his indifference ratios as compared with the cost ratios. A relative concept of marginal utility was suggested by Davenport. "The only characteristic," he said, "which different buyers have in common is the equality of ratio between the thing purchased and the thing forgone. To be upon the margin is merely to recognize a ratio of equality between competing and alternative utilities."[54]

Thus, a functional relationship, a constant mutual interaction, was assumed to exist between the exchange values of the products and the cost ratios. The marginal utilities of infinite chains of buyers and sellers participating in market transactions were shown to be linked with each other through ties of mutual interdependence which had a counterpart in the markets in which the prices of the productive services were determined. Therefore, if all subjective valuations were related to a price system, and if the purchasing power of the monetary unit, varying from one market to the other, was in turn determined by the existing systems of prices and income distribution, any attempts to define causal sequences between utility schedules and prices had to be regarded as hopeless.[55]

The procedures of introspection and experience as applied to the verifications of processes of valuation were questioned by Joseph Schumpeter, who characterized the principles of marginalism as "nothing more than one of possible avenues to equilibrium analysis and an excellent method for demonstrating in an easily understandable way the relations . . . that make a unified system out of the mass of economic phenomena which departmentalize so easily.[56] He attached only limited importance to the results of price analysis, but he added the observation that increases in the marginal yields of productive processes, and, consequently, expansions of such processes, could be interpreted as the effects of integrated marginal utilities of the consumers, expressed in monetary terms.[57]

The difficulties involved in connecting the formation of prices with marginal utility analysis also affected the explanation of costs of production by methods of imputation.[58] Various economists of the Marshallian School, who had never enjoyed the use of refined methods of marginal utility analysis, were convinced that the extensive discussions of price and cost determination were likely to end up in the traditional definition of costs as the amount that must be paid in order to cause the producer to play his part in organizing the productive process.[59] They regarded the theory of value as a "technique of thinking" and doubted whether conclusions drawn from it could be applied to considerations of economic policy.[60]

But, unnoticed by the Marshallian economists, their demand theory was the object of significant criticism. The Marshallian demand schedule showed the changes in the sales prices of a commodity brought about by changes in its quantity. In an article published in 1915 the Russian economist E. Slutsky argued that Marshall had also included, by the general clause "other things being equal," the unjustified assumption of fixed incomes.[61] Slutsky contended that, unless a commodity had a continuous demand elasticity equal to unity, any change of prices had two combined effects: the "income effect," resulting from changes in real incomes, and the "substitution effect," due to the tendency to rearrange purchases so as to substitute cheaper goods for more expensive ones. With the aid of Paretian indifference and preference curves, Slutsky showed characteristic modifications of economic situations that resulted from the substitution of one good for another. He defined the marginal rate of substitution as the quantity of one good that can be replaced by the increase in the consumption of another without affecting the individual's want satisfaction. More precisely, that rate indicates the ratio between the marginal utilities of two goods. The application of indifference curves to demand analysis implies that an individual can so determine his outlays on any commodity that he will be on the margin of indifference between the last small increment of that commodity and an additional alternative increment of any other commodity that might be substituted.[62]

Slutsky's reasoning had been primarily motivated by the objective of eliminating the psychological background of marginal utility analysis; he succeeded in replacing Hermann Gossen's first principle, as applied to demand analysis, by the same proposition that the consumer tends to "maximize" his or her demand functions. When pursued to its consequences, that approach led to the transformation of marginalism into a theory dealing with abstract acts of choice among available alternatives.

For a considerable time the importance of that approach was virtually ignored, and the objections raised against marginal utility analysis were so effective that even authors who adhered to the quantifying Walrasian methodology denied the value problem any legitimate place in economic theory. They insisted that economic analysis should start when the effects of valuations were expressed in measurable magnitudes or prices.[63] An especially influential representative of that view was the Swedish economist Karl Gustav Cassel (1866–1945) whose textbook on economics was widely used on the European continent.[64]

Cassel was probably influenced by the Neokantian school of philosophers, whose epistemological principles were ruled by the idea that only self-evident mathematical methods can provide the instruments for the acquisition of true knowledge. Cassel, a trained engineer familiar with higher mathematics, objected to the use of any psychological concepts for purposes of economic analysis and was convinced that all that was needed to develop a consistent body of economic theory was a unit of account to which all economic magnitudes could be reduced. Hence, he restricted the scope of economics to an analysis of the functions of an interdependent price system conceived of as an instrument for adjusting demand to a limited supply of goods on the assumptions that the technical coefficients were known and that the value of money was fixed.[65] Thus, he could use Walrasian techniques to establish an economic model in terms of simultaneous equations. Equilibrium analysis enabled him to determine the distribution of the productive factors among the productive processes and to derive the distribution of incomes from the contributions made by the productive factors to these processes. In that analysis he avoided any reference to the principle of marginal productivity and to the explanation of incomes in terms of rewards ''for services rendered.''

Critics of Cassel's economics have shown that his so-called general price theory was applicable only to an exchange economy in which the rule of perfect competition was strictly observed, all technical coefficients were fixed, producers' profits were zero, supply and demand were equalized in each market, and all available resources were allocated in accordance with their most ''rational uses.''[66] It was argued on good grounds that at least an indirect recognition of the concept of subjective value was implied in the concept of ''scarcity'' that provided the starting point for Cassel's analysis of the market phenomena. That concept was a poor substitute for the concept of marginal utility and did not permit a convenient transition to the analysis of price expectations that are important elements of the mechanics of economic change but are not susceptible to external observations.[67] Moreover, any economic phenomena that were connected with changes in price relations or in the purchasing power of money were outside the sphere of equilibrium analysis of that type. Cassel's teachings were extensively commented upon by German and Austrian authors, such as Joseph Schumpeter, W. Kromphardt, O. Conrad, E. Schams, Hans Neisser (b. 1895), Karl Diehl, Emil Lederer, Hans Mayer, A. Predöhl, and Adolf Weber.[68] Fundamental methodological issues were involved in all of the objections to Cassel's economics.

BOOK THREE

Developments after the First World War

Part VII

Organismic Economics

THE ANGLO-SAXON COUNTRIES' answer to the power policy of the German Empire had found a succinct expression in the slogan that the world had to be made safe for democracy. When account is taken of the fundamental logical aspects of democracy, the struggle for democracy amounted to a fight against the principles of organismic reasoning that were basic to German power policies. But after the termination of the hostilities, it soon became apparent that over all of Central Europe, and especially in Germany, nationalistic passions had been intensified by the war; they acted as a catalyst in determining the map of Europe, which was adjusted according to political rather than economic considerations. A number of economically weak countries were carved out of the body of the dismembered Austro-Hungarian monarchy, which had offered to its inhabitants the advantages of an old cultural heritage and an economically well-integrated large territory. In due course, organismic reasoning, with its social, political, moral, and economic implications achieved virtual ascendancy in Central and Southern Europe and, consequently, large territories became easy prey to the power policies of the Third Reich. In its extreme form, as expressed in the tenets of the National Socialist party and the slogans of fascism, this pattern of thought provided the logical justification for the complete subordination of the members of a "national" community to a leader who was believed to grasp intuitively that community's "mission" and to know the ways and means of carrying out that mission. In the regions where such patterns of thought dominated, economic reasoning was forcibly adjusted to political principles.

Another pattern of thought, a distorted version of dialectic materialism, supplied the logical background for the establishment of the communist regime in the Soviet Union, where all spheres of political, cultural, and economic life were subjected to the commands of an autocratic government. The ultimate justification for that political and economic organization was derived from the belief in the existence of "dialectical," absolutely valid, laws of socialist development, and in the intellectual power of the autocratic leaders to adjust their dictates to the principles of these laws. After the Second World War, large territories of Eastern Europe and Asia were engulfed by powers governed by that pattern of thought, with its far-reaching political and economic implications.

371

Hypothetical methods maintained the upper hand in the Western parts of the world, and reasserted themselves in Central Europe and Italy after the collapse of the national socialist and fascist regimes. These developments resulted in the splitting up of the world into two antagonistic camps, each ruled by deeply rooted convictions concerning the capacity of the human mind, the relations between reason and will, the nature of the laws which underlie social, economic, and political developments, and the ultimate objectives of human beings and their communities. The following discussion is designed to show the changes that economic reasoning underwent under the influence of these three patterns of thought.

Chapter 24
The Decline of
the Historical School

―――――

CONFLICTING TRENDS

IN GERMANY the First World War was followed by a period of hyperinflation. The discussion of "socialization" schemes which took place during that period were abortive, and about the middle of the twenties successful attempts were made to adjust the German economy to the conditions imposed by the Treaty of Versailles. But even competent foreign observers failed to realize the degree to which large masses of the German population were longing for a strong government which would lead the nation on the road to the fulfillment of vast nationalistic aspirations.

Of course, the specific version of organismic reasoning which supplied the logical background to extreme nationalism was challenged by a variety of other, conflicting patterns of thought; that struggle was faithfully reflected in the variety of economic doctrines which vied with each other for supremacy. At almost all large German universities with several chairs of economics, the student of economics was confronted with widely divergent teachings. The numerical preponderance of those teachers who had been educated in the methodological principles adopted by Gustav Schmoller's school was incontestable. They prepared the soil—for the most part unwittingly—for the subsequent acceptance of the National Socialist creed. But they were opposed by a group of (mostly older) adherents of the principles of *the Wealth of Nations* and the methods used by Adam Smith. Ricardian economics had very few adherents, and Alfred Marshall's *Principles* was virtually ignored. A few chairs were occupied by members of the Austrian school of marginalism, and the methodological principles of the School of Lausanne were adopted by a small group of younger economists with mathematical leanings. A certain acquaintance with Walrasian methods was also secured by the spread of a textbook by the Swedish economist Gustav Cassel, *Social Economics*. Other notable translations into German of foreign textbooks were Knut Wicksell's *Über Wert, Kapital und Rente nach den Neureren Nationalökonomischen Theorien* (Jena, 1893); the Dutchman C. A. Verrijn Stuart's *De*

Wetenshcap der Voklsh vishoudkunde en de Grondslagen der Volkshvishouding
(Haarlem, 1930); and the Italian Enrico Barone's *Principi di Economia Finanziaria*
(Rome, 1921), translated into German by Hans Stachle as *Grundzüge der Theoretischen
Nationalökonomie* (Bonn, 1927). However, they were recommended only by teachers
who favored marginal utility analysis. A highly eclectic postwar German textbook, first
published in 1928, was prepared by Adolf Weber. It took account of conflicting trends in
economic analysis and dealt extensively with problems of applied economics. The influence of yet another group of teachers, who endorsed the principles of neoscholastic
economics as proclaimed in the papal encyclical *Rerum Novarum*, was of little significance.

Socialistic doctrines, which were more or less permeated with elements of dialectic
reasoning and which reflected significant aspects of the Marxian conception of the capitalist economy gained in importance during this period. Along with the increasing political
influence of the Social Democratic parties, outspoken advocates of Marxism had secured
admission to the philosophical and economic faculties of various universities. Especially
at some Prussian universities, the conservative views of older professors frequently contrasted sharply with those of socialist teachers, who combined the materialistic interpretation of history with versions of the class struggle, the breakdown theory, and other
constituent elements of the Marxian doctrine. Other teachers of economics were deeply
impressed by the prospect of an idealized political struggle over the transformation of the
capitalist economy into a classless society with collectivized production and distribution.[1]

Economists such as Robert Liefmann, F. Gottl-Ottlilienfeld, and Franz Oppenheimer
occupied a special position.[2] They advanced eclectic doctrines for which they claimed
absolute validity, thus intensifying the methodological controversy and the debate over
the proper setting of almost all economic problems, as may be illustrated by a short survey
of contemporary discussions which turned on the problems of value, money, and business
cycles.

Prolonged controversies over the value problem climaxed in an occasionally passionate exchange of views which took place in September 1932 at a meeting of the scientific
committee of the Verein für Sozialpolitik.[3] In the center of the debate were two questions:
(1) whether a consistent price theory backed by a value theory was prerequisite to the
elaboration of any economic doctrine, and (2) whether and to what degree that requirement was fulfilled by the subjective value theory, especially in its psychological version.
The conflicting views were presented in a series of preparatory papers. The main problems at issue were analyzed from the point of view of the Austrian principles of marginalism in a remarkable essay by O. Morgenstern. Morgenstern endeavored to minimize the
differences among the three main types of the subjective theory of value. He questioned
the contention of the Paretian school that any reference to the value concept had been
eliminated by the indifference curve procedure.

The principal participants in the debate included: W. Kromphardt, a disciple of
Cassel, who elaborated his master's view that economic analysis could start, independently of any value theory, from a given system of prices; Gottl-Ottlilienfeld, who put forward
his idea of the "economic dimension" in opposition to marginal utility analysis; Liefmann, who summarized his theory of "marginal yield" as distinct from the theories of
marginal utility and marginal productivity; Oppenheimer, who defended his version of the
labor cost theory of value and developed a formula designed to demonstrate that in all
phases of the productive processes the static price is proportionate to the amount of labor

spent by the marginal producers: H. Zeisl, who attempted to demonstrate that the fundamental Marxian laws, especially those of distribution and capital accumulation, could be
formulated in terms of the subjective theory of value; and Othmar Spann, who expounded
the main aspects of his "universalistic" theory of value and prices.[4] Oppenheimer's value
theory started from the concept of a "normal income" earned by each "freely producing" member of an economy operating under conditions of perfect equilibrium. Making
all prices and incomes proportional to the labor time spent in producing the goods, he
arrived at the conclusion that all individual valuations of goods were "socially determined," and hence were "objective phenomena." The usual arguments against any
theory of value were summarized in a critical survey by W. Vleugels.

L. von Mises opened the discussion and gave a vivid picture of the clash of the
divergent methodological principles. He started with a plea for general acceptance of the
proposition that over the centuries the logical structure of human thinking has remained
unchanged for all peoples, regardless of their racial characteristics and their social structure. He claimed that the Austrian version of the marginal utility doctrine had solved the
most important problems of theoretical economics—the problems of exchanges and
prices, as well as those connected with money, with banking and credit, and with business
fluctuations. The achievements of the Austrian School were equally emphasized by other
speakers. P. Rosenstein-Rodan related one of the main differences between the Austrian
School and the School of Lausanne to the fact that the latter, like the Ricardians, had taken
its start from equilibrium positions of the economic system, whereas the Austrians had
endeavored to determine the processes by which such positions were reached. But various
objections were raised to the contention that the problem of deriving prices directly from
marginal utility considerations had actually been solved.

Adherents of organismic views, such as G. Mackenroth, discussed the relationships
between the subjective theory of values and psychology, and asserted that subjective value
theory was a purely "rationalistic construction" which had no basis in experience. In a
somewhat similar critical vein, G. Colm insisted upon supplementing the theoretical
analysis of the price system with data supplied by "economic sociology," while Arthur
Spiethoff attempted in vain to reconcile the general attitude of the historical school with
the principles of the subjective value theory.

The struggle between these various theories was restricted to the sphere of fundamental methodological considerations, but the corresponding controversy over the meaning
and functions of the means of exchange reached deeply into the domain of economic
policies. A hypothetical approach to monetary problems was a characteristic feature of
marginal utility analysis, as distinct from the organismic approach adopted by the adherents of Georg Friedrich Knapp's state theory of money and from Spann's monetary
theory, which showed strong elements of neoscholastic reasoning. In marked contrast,
Marxist economists attributed to the use of money an important role in the dialectic
processes leading to the breakdown of the capitalist economy. Various other monetary
theories occupied intermediate positions between these radically divergent conceptions of
the same phenomenon: the means of payment.[5]

Some leading German economists who adhered to Knapp's monetary views contributed significantly toward justifying the disastrous inflationary policy pursued by the
German government after the end of the First World War. They ascribed the rapid
depreciation of the currency which resulted from that policy to the balance of payment
deficits, and attributed these deficits in turn to the reparation payments imposed by the

Treaty of Versailles.[6] Arguments of that type constituted the official explanation of the processes which ended in 1923 with the collapse of the inflated currency.[7] These inflationary processes can be divided into two parts: a period of moderate inflation, which lasted until the spring of 1922, and a subsequent period of violent inflation. During the eight years of the first period (1914–22) the rate of exchange of the mark to the dollar rose from 4.20 to about 280; in the one and a half subsequent years it increased from 280 to over 4.2 billion marks to the dollar. During the first period the rate of exchange showed wide oscillations, as compared with the relatively steady upward movement of the domestic price level. During the second period, however, a strong parallelism developed between the two movements.

Not even the stabilization of the mark in 1924 was backed by a clear and consistent monetary theory. The official argument for the expected stability of the *Rentenmark*— advanced by Karl Helfferich, among others—was that the new monetary standard was guaranteed by mortgaging the country's agricultural estates, and that consequently the value of the currency was based on the stability of the price of rye! The opposition to the return to the gold standard was supported with arguments derived from Knapp's theory, and England's abandonment of that standard was hailed as a remarkable turning point of economic history by quite a number of authors.[8] Knapp's theory provided the background for some widely used textbooks, such as Ernst Wagemann's *Allgemeine Geldlehre* (Berlin, 1923). According to Wagemann, the value of money—like any other value—was rooted in a "collective mind." For him, as for many German economists, the concept of "social values" was an "axiomatic proposition." But he admitted that the feelings and the will of the "collectivity" belonged to the sphere of hazy (*dumpf*) thinking.[9] Knapp's thinking was also reflected in the discussion of some ill-conceived problems, such as whether the services rendered by money were exclusively connected with the circulatory functions of the means of payment (Knapp's "chartal theory") and whether a rational economic order could be operated independently of any monetary system.[10]

The theories of the German Marxists also played a significant role in support of the disastrous official monetary policy, since, according to their doctrine, the value of metallic currencies was related to the labor cost of the monetary metals, and no explanation was available for the value of paper money. During the period of violent inflation the German ministry of finance was headed by an adherent of the Marxian doctrine, Rudolf Hilferding. The fallacies advanced to justify the official policy were effectively demonstrated by L. Albert Hahn, an adherent of the claim theory of money, who made the prospect of unlimited credit expansion basic to his analysis.[11] Similar criticisms were voiced by Walter Eucken and Hans Neisser.[12] As distinct from Gustav Cassel's purchasing power parity theory, Neisser connected the readjustment of distorted exchange rates not with the general price level but with the prices of the goods which were the object of international exchanges. Noticeable improvements in the teaching of monetary theory made themselves felt only toward the end of the twenties.[13]

It is easy to understand why the overwhelming majority of German economists did not care about developing a consistent business cycle theory. They regarded every cycle and every crisis as an individual historical phenomenon caused by a variety of circumstances, and attached little importance to the problems involved in explaining the typical course of cyclical movements and their periodicity. This conception of business fluctuations was emphasized by many members of the historical school, such as Carl G. von Brinkmann, A. Muller-Armack, and H. Aubin.[14]

Adolph Lowe, who surveyed the German business cycle literature in 1925, observed
that the quantity theory of money as reflected in many monetary analyses of economic
fluctuations was generally ignored by German economists.[15] The view that purely descriptive, statistical business cycle analysis and even business forecasting could be developed independently of any theoretical foundation was defended by the head of the German
Institute for Business Cycle Analysis, Ernst Wagemann, who asserted that a business
barometer based on Arthur Spiethoff's theory had turned out to be a complete failure.[16] In
Wagemann's view it was impossible to discover "final causes" of crises and depressions;
rather, he was convinced that correlations which had apparently no theoretical significance might be indicative of tendencies, of the operation of "economic forces" and
tensions. Such analysis, he argued, was a revival of the descriptive approach adopted by
Schmoller's historical school. Wagemann's intuitive procedures were not clearly defined,
but under his direction his collaborators successfully applied them to some statistical
studies.[17]

The "antitheoretical" attitude of other economists who did not belong to the historical school was motivated by the consideration that equilibrium analysis was incompatible
with any theoretical approach to the study of business fluctuations.[18] Among these authors, the tendency to minimize the importance of monetary factors was quite general, an
attitude frequently motivated by adherence to a Ricardian model of the economy as
composed of "objective" exchange values.[19] Erich Carell, for example, characterized
business cycle theory as an empiricorealistic science, distinct from pure theory and its
logical structure. He discarded the concept of equilibrium and the implied rigid interdependence of factors, emphasized extreme diversities in forms of economic behavior, and
pointed to lags and disproportionalities as two aspects under which differences in time
coefficients may appear in real life. Economists who were explicitly or implicitly hostile
to the capitalist economy also minimized the importance of monetary factors, not least
because practically all monetary theories opened the prospect of mitigating the violence of
capitalist fluctuations.

The proposition that no generally valid explanation of business fluctuations could be
established was most consistently defended by Friedrich Lutz, who argued that statistical
experience did not supply sufficient confirmation for the periodicity or the supposed
typical course of such movements, and that the character of each phase of a cycle was
determined by a number of specific factors, such as capital formation, technical progress,
or changes in the monetary supply.[20] Lutz emphasized equally strongly the incompatibility of equilibrium analysis with the assumption that the periodic recurrence of
business fluctuations was inherent in the behavior of the economy. Other economists also
requested closer examination of the various factors which could be assumed to contribute
to the instability of the economy. The view that the postwar cyclical movements differed
radically from those of the prewar period was defended by R. Stucken and Werner
Sombart.[21] Neisser called for the pursuance of empirical studies dealing with the "circular flow" of goods within the economy, designed to differentiate among the cycles in
accordance with an appropriate typology.[22] Prolonged but inconclusive discussions
turned on the stabilizing effects frequently attributed to the policy of monopolistic employers' associations, cartels, interlocking directorates, trusts, and the like.

The principle that the analysis of facts has to be preceded by a chapter on the theory
of business cycles was strongly defended by all authors who had been trained in a Marxian
approach to economic analysis. An outstanding author of that type was Adolph Lowe,

who challenged the theory of formulating the questions to be answered by facts.[23] It is interesting to note that, commenting on that statement, Wesley C. Mitchell argued that theory and experience are not mutually exclusive, that theories cannot be conceived of as existing apart from the facts of human experience, and that people can apprehend facts only in terms of the notions with which their minds are furnished. In his view, both the theory and the facts had to be elaborated on at various stages of an investigation, and later writers could be assumed to start with a ''fact-theory blend'' improved by the new contribution.[24]

In a widely read article published in 1926, Lowe raised the general question of how to solve the contradiction which appeared to exist between the logical requirements of equilibrium analysis and the cyclical movements of prices, volumes of production, incomes, and other economic magnitudes.[25] He characterized as antitheoretical those theories which introduced ill-defined concepts such an anarchy, errors, and the like and contended that circular reasoning was involved in other theories which, like those of Albert Aftalion and Cassel, started from the apparent equilibrium conditions obtaining during a depression without accounting for the existence of these conditions. To a third group of theories, those advanced by Werner Sombart, Joseph Schumpeter, Liefmann, and by most advocates of monetary theories, he raised the objection that they erred in generalizing partial disturbances of equilibrium positions. Lowe's criticism of the monetary business cycle theories was supplemented by an article by his disciple Fritz Burchardt. Burchardt endeavored to demonstrate that these theories applied monetary factors mainly to explain the rise of prices during the upswing while other factors, in a bewildering variety, were used to explain the uniform behavior of prices and quantities, the upturn of the movements, and so on.[26]

Regarding Irving Fisher's theory, which held lags in the reaction to certain changes responsible for the cyclical movements, Lowe countered with the argument that the principle of general interdependence was abandoned when varying time spans were applied to the reactions. Hence, Lowe called for the introduction into the economic model of an independent variable which could be assumed to cause continuous disturbances of the equilibrium conditions. He credited Rosa Luxemburg's business cycle theory with having defined technological progress as an independent variable of the required type and having radically modified the concept of a closed equilibrium system by pointing to sales of redundant commodities in markets outside the capitalist areas. In Lowe's view, the expansion of bank credit during the upswing was a purely accidental factor which contributed toward intensifying the fluctuations.

Emil Lederer was equally opposed to a purely monetary approach to business cycle analysis. He connected disproportionalities in the expansion of business activity with the observation that during the upswing wages lagged behind rising prices, thus causing discrepancies between the demand for and the supply of goods.[27] But he considered credit expansion indispensable for financing the upswing. In another version of an ''underconsumption'' theory, advanced by Erich Preiser, the origin of disproportionate movements of economic magnitudes was mainly ascribed to ''heteronomous'' savings resulting from excessive profits during the prosperity period.[28] These savings were said to lead to misdirected investments, falling real wages, and restrictions in the purchasing power available for consumption purposes. Underconsumption theories of that kind were frequently welcomed by trade union leaders.

In the discussions of business cycle research, organized in 1928 by the *Verein für Sozialpolitik*, the monetary approach to business cycle analysis was defended only by adherents of the Austrian version.[29] These discussions turned mainly on two problems: (a) whether the practical studies of the institutes of business cycle research could be expected to contribute to the solution of theoretical issues, and (b) whether the fluctuations of money and capital markets provided a sound starting point for business cycle analysis. The discussion was prepared by a number of papers. The principles underlying monetary theories were defended by F. A. Hayek and criticized by A. Lowe. The antagonism of the conflicting theories was well illustrated in these discussions, and foreshadowed the political developments in Germany in the coming years.

Members of the historical school who used "organismic" concepts of the economy placed particular emphasis on "structural" characteristics of the economies.[30] They connected "structural" changes of economies with the operation of "dynamic" factors, and contrasted them with changes produced by cyclical fluctuations.[31] Ideas of that kind caused H. Weigemann to suggest the establishment of "elementary markets," characterized by the least degree of elasticity, as a starting point for the study of endogenous changes of the spatial structures as distinct from "global" movements, which he assigned to business cycle analysis.[32]

In an ambitious organismic scheme, Ernst Wagemann availed himself of "determinant" structural features of various economies to analyze the rhythmical international flow of goods and services.[33] This grouping of the various economies according to their "economic intensity" was based on a method of combining population density measurements with measurements of relative land capital intensity. Wagemann ascribed the "gradients" characteristic of the behavior of the "world economy" to these differences in the structure of the various economies, and he ascribed the prolonged duration of many crises and depressions to "unorganic" structural conditions exhibited by the economies.

Investigations into the "organic" structure of the German economy were stimulated by the desire to justify various frequently used political watchwords coined in support of nationalistic aspirations: "a people without space" (Volk ohne Raum), "vital space" (Lebensraum) and "natural and historical frontiers" were slogans implying aggressive intentions.[34] A tempting imperialistic vision had been advanced during the war by Friedrich Naumann, an outstanding "democratic" member of the German parliament. Naumann's ideal ws the creation of a federated "superstate" covering the entire territory of Central Europe, economically integrated, surrounded by a tariff wall, and dominated by Germany.[35] Such schemes were supplemented by "geopolitical" considerations advanced by R. Kjellén, Karl Haushofer, and other political geographers who pointed to the need to assure the economic and political domination of vast territories by the German Reich as a prerequisite to the establishment of a world empire.[36] As viewed from the economic angle, the post-Marxian theory of "economic imperialism," which explained the struggle over colonies and dominions in terms of a fight over markets, was superseded by an organismic theory according to which the control of indispensable sources of agricultural products and raw materials was to be secured by military conquest. Thus, effective arguments were supplied to the leaders of German national socialism in support of their ambitious political programs.

Other extended discussions were designed to define the prospects of world-wide economic developments to come.[37] Gloomy predictions concerning Germany's economic future were derived by Sombart from the so-called law of the declining export quota[38] and by others from the expected loss of markets in overseas agricultural territories, from the fact that the rate of increase in industrial productivity was declining from the spread of cartelization among industries and trades, from the creation of autarkic blocs outside the economic sphere of Central Europe,[39] and ultimately from the falling birth rate and the ensuing stagnation of the national energies.[40] The principles underlying the functioning of the capitalist economy were attacked from all sides, and the view that the days of the capitalist order were numbered was elaborated not only by authors who derived their arguments from the arsenal of Marxian dialectics but also by economists and sociologists who adhered to other intellectual movements.[41]

METHODOLOGICAL PROBLEMS OF HISTORISM

After the war, the German economists of organismic persuasion who resumed the discussion of their unsolved methodological problems felt, more intensively than ever before, the need to give safe logical foundations to their conception of the national economy and to their belief in the existence of "historical laws" adjusted to the nature and the objectives of the national economy.[42] As before, they were faced with the age-old questions of whether the principle of causality was applicable to economic analysis and whether economics could be conceived of as an essentially normative discipline.[43]

As before, the moral aspects of economic behavior were strongly emphasized by representatives of Neo-scholastic methods who modified their teachings in accordance with the ethical principles established by the Catholic Church.[44] The maxim of "equivalence" provided them with a guiding principle in their discussions of the problems of prices, wages, profits and interest and in their approach to the class conflict. The moral aspects of economics were equally emphasized by Protestant authors, who rejected the principle of free competition.[45]

Othmar Spann's organismic theories, though widely criticized, enjoyed increasing adherence among the younger generation of Austrian and German economists.[46] Another economic philosopher who attracted a considerable number of disciples was Gottl-Ottlilienfeld, who was violently opposed to the method of isolating economics from all other social sciences. To the "primitive and naive" idea of developing economic analysis around "comparisons of costs and yields," he opposed his conception of the economy as a "living organism" and claimed general validity for "ontological value judgments" on which to base the "structural" (gestalthafte) guarantee of permanent harmony between demand and supply. Gottl-Ottlilienfeld's analysis was designed to visualize the "meaningful structure" (Sinnstruktur) of the economy as a category free of any specific historical characteristics. Thus, he hoped to arrive at an understanding of the "essential" social relationships underlying the economy as a "reality"; he expected to determine for each economy the conditions of the "fundamental principles of its existence." His teachings could easily be adjusted to the nationalistic ideals of the National Socialist party and provided welcome instruments to justify the totalitarian organization of the German economy. Some of Gottl-Ottlilienfeld's leading ideas were elaborated by his disciples Joseph Back, Erich Egner, and Georg Weippert.[47]

The methodological discussions of the problems of the historical school received a strong impetus from the publication of a comprehensive study in which Sombart attempted to settle once and for all the logical problems of "interpretative" economics (verstehende Nationalökonomie), and thus to provide definite directives for the development of the "visualizing" approach to economic analysis.[48] In pursuance of that approach the economist was expected to reach a profound understanding of economic phenomena and their historically conditioned relationships, and to conceive of these relationships as expressions of "objective systems" defined by three characteristic features: economic order, economic way of thinking (*Wirtschaftsgesinnung*), and economic technique. The unity of each economic system was said to be assured by an "objective spirit," which was credited with the power of determining the laws which are basic to the relationships among the individual phenomena. In his analysis of "laws" of various types (quantitative, structural, and fictional) Sombart requested the search for "structural" laws suitable for arriving at an "insight" into the necessary connections among the elements of the integrated wholes. The title of Sombart's 1930 book—*Die drei Nationalökonomien*—pointed to an alleged fundamental division of economic doctrines into those which were based on metaphysical principles, others which adopted the methodology of the natural sciences, and still others which were determined by the methodology of the sciences of the mind. True to his organismic convictions, Sombart claimed exclusive validity for the theories of the last type. The objects of this arbitrary grouping, which was not based on a clear principle of classification, were discussed in detail in my "Nominalismus und Begriffsrealismus in der Nationalökonomie."[49]

In the ensuing discussion of Sombart's methodology, Arthur Spiethoff characterized Sombart's "economic systems" as "ideal types" devised by attaching exaggerated importance to certain particularly relevant features of cultural entities and to more or less utopian mixtures of history and theory.[50] Less adverse than Sombart to "pure" theory, Spiethoff raised no objections to the study of isolated phenomena and their mutual relations, regardless of their location in a "total situation." He even admitted the possibility of devising purely hypothetical economic models. In opposition to Sombart's construction of timeless types of collectivities conceived of as logically coherent unities, he proposed the use of "visualizing" procedures designed to include among the characteristics of a given "economic reality" entire complexes of causally related phenomena, and the construction of "economic styles" abstracted from reality and conceived of as "real types" not requiring logical consistency. Spiethoff illustrated the distinction between his conception of "styles" and "utopian" constructions by contrasting his own business cycle analysis with Schumpeter's theory of economic development. The latter, he argued, started from the "unrealistic" conception of economic equilibrium, whereas his own research had been made in closest approximation to historical experience, and was based on an interaction of empirical and analytical methods which resulted in establishing a model describing in general terms the stages of the typical business cycle of fully developed capitalism.[51]

In order to give broad identification to such main "styles," Spiethoff used the concepts of self-sufficient economy, household economy, regional economy, and capitalist economy, and, following the traditional principles of the historical school, called for theories appropriate to the conditions of the various styles. In view of the ever-possible emergence of new styles, economic theory could never assume a definite form.[52]

Other authors who insisted that cognizance of "essences" and "meanings" was the supreme task of the sciences of the mind emphasized three aspects of economic life—a mechanical, an organizatory, and an organic aspect—but insisted that these be visualized together in a single concept of the essence of the economy.[53] After the distinction of "stages" in the development of economic life had been discredited by the results of careful historical research, a new science, called "economic sociology," was suggested for analyzing the biological, sociological, and ethical elements of the various economic and cultural patterns.[54] The methodological problems involved in defining the scope and objects of such analyses were discussed in connection with renewed attempts to differentiate characteristic periods in the economic development of various nations.[55]

PLANNING ALONG ORGANISMIC LINES

Economic planning on organismic lines occupies a position about midway between the organization of the exchange economy and that of a socialist economy based on the principle of centralized planning. Together with the advocates of the exchange economy and the closely related institution of private ownership of the means of production, many partisans of organismic planning shared the view that individual initiative, as associated with the elements of chance and risk taking, is more or less indispensable for securing progress in considerable sectors of the economy. But, like the adherents of centralized planning, they were convinced that the profit motive as the driving agent of economic activity is incompatible with the conception of the economy as an "organism" in which all members of the community should be obliged to adjust their economic behavior to the superior objectives of a common will.[56] Hence, many adherents of organismic ideas practically subordinated economic considerations to normative principles which were frequently derived from nationalistic or socialistic convictions. They supported their reasoning with the contention that the productivity of a planned economy is bound to be far greater than that of the "wasteful" competitive order.

Planning on organismic lines has frequently been marked by the intention to combine two contradictory principles: one based on the belief in "laws" which underlie the functioning of the economy, the other reflecting the conviction that the minds of a few centrally placed individuals are able to decide upon the ultimate objectives of the economy and to determine the ways and means of achieving these objectives. Friedrich A. Hayek has pointed to the intellectual somersault committed by many adherents of collectivistic planning, who pass from the assertion that society is in some sense "more" than merely the aggregate of all individuals to the thesis that this larger entity must be subjected to conscious control, i.e., to the control of what in the last resort must be an individual mind, a sort of mastermind.[57] Hence, organismic schemes have frequently remained in the blueprint stage. To the extent that they were put to the test of practical experience, their operation was dependent upon the authority of a strong government which was in a position to enforce the observance of its orders and directives and eventually to transfer considerable sectors of the economy into public ownership. The exercise of such authority could be most easily assured when the main objectives of the economy were defined in terms of some overriding value principles derived from aggressive power policies.

The adherents of organismic planning can be divided into two groups according to whether they regard the nation or the working class as the supreme integrated collective whole. But the borderline between the two groups was blurred by the fact that the interests of the nation were frequently identified with those of the working class, and vice versa.

Wartime experience had shown how effectively the German economy could be adjusted to requirements not derived from the demands of individual economic units, how easily consumption could be regulated and production could be directed, and how resources could be allocated in accordance with the orders of a strong central authority if these orders were willingly executed by the large majority of producers and traders. The idea of "total war," which amounted to the subordination of almost all economic activity to the requirements of warfare, was frequently ascribed to the character of the new armaments, the mass production of which was said to be dependent upon intensified coordinated planning.[58] However, it is more likely that the adjustment of the economy to the principles of "total war" was not enforced by technological changes, that it reflected rather the consistent application of methods of organismic reasoning to the direction of economic activities. It is well known that the establishment of the German economy during the First World War was carried out in accordance with the proposals of Walther Rathenau, a leading protagonist of an organismic construction of economic and social life.[59] The existing well-organized cartels and other employers' associations provided the agencies for the distribution of government orders and for the collection and allocation of scarce resources; traders' organizations were charged with the task of controlling the flow of goods: the administrative offices of the Reich and the states supervised the distribution of the rationed commodities and prevented violation of the system of price and wage fixing. There is no doubt that the effective coordination of the available economic forces contributed greatly to the efficiency of the armed forces and enabled the government to prolong the duration of the war.

The socialist governments which were formed after the First World War in some countries of Central and Eastern Europe, especially in Germany and Austria, appeared to be in a position to realize the ultimate objectives of social democratic programs and to substitute the much-discussed "socialization" of the means of production for the competitive system of the capitalist exchange economy. The expression "socialization of production" was derived from the usual Marxian terminology, and was designed to assure the workers that the ownership of the means of production was to be transferred to "society" as distinct from the state. The use of that terminology was characteristic of the ill-defined approach to the problems of planning. But at this juncture it became evident that no plans had ever been prepared for the organization of a "socialized" economy. As Paul Lensch put it, the leaders of the social democratic parties behaved like the foolish virgins of the Bible who had no oil for their lamps when the bridegroom came.[60]

The confusion which existed in the ranks of the "evolutionary" Socialists was well illustrated by the discussion of the problems of socialization which took place at the Regensburg meeting of the Verein für Sozialpolitik in 1919.[61] The main argument advanced by Lederer, the leading advocate of socialization, was that the political events and the difficulties involved in reestablishing the peacetime economy had led to such a disorganization of the productive machinery that it was necessary to revive the morale and the energy of the working classes by measures which would give them new confidence in the future. But he rejected the belief of some convinced Marxists in the superior productivity of the socialized economy; to R. Wilbrandt's argument that the operation of a socialist economy could be expected to reduce Germany's dependence on imports from abroad he opposed the view that "socialism" was designed to organize the economic forces of the world economy, not simply those of a specific country.[62] This attempt to justify revolutionary changes in the economic order with considerations of expediency or principles of morality found little support, and the fundamental problems of how to organize a planned economy were hardly mentioned in these discussions.

Subsequent attempts to establish the principles of a planned economy started from Walther Rathenau's proposal to adjust the warlike organization of the economy to peacetime conditions, to create for each industry an autonomous "corporation," and to charge the corporations with the task of adjusting their economic policies to the interests of the "national economy.[63] A plan of that type provided certain directives to the Commission for Socialization, composed of politicians and economists, which was appointed in 1919 by the German parliament.[64]

The studies of the Commission, which were published in several volumes, were governed by the idea of transforming the existing voluntary employers' organizations into compulsory corporations. The adjustment of the behavior of these corporations to a kind of collective will or common spirit was to be achieved by their governing bodies, in which the various economic interests (employers, workers, clerical employees, consumers, the government) would receive appropriate representation. Questions of general economic policy were to be handled by superior bodies formed in accordance with the same principle. But these plans remained in the blueprint stage when economic life returned to more normal channels and the difficulties involved in operating the proposed organizational machinery were generally realized. A policy-making body organized in accordance with these proposals was set up only for the coal-mining industry, which included many enterprises operated by the government. The same was true of a comprehensive scheme dealing with the "socialization" of residential construction. A radical economic program adopted in September 1921 by the Social Democratic party at Görlitz remained equally a dead issue. The attempts of the Austrian Social Democratic party to "socialize" the big industries were frustrated by the Italian government.

Under these conditions many convinced apostles of socialization resorted to the traditional belief in the operation of "evolutionary" forces which were said to be working toward the absorption of the competitive sectors of the economy by monopolistic organizations of all types.[65] An outstanding advocate of that view was Sombart, who spoke of "capitalism in chains" and advanced the proposition that social reform and socialism were shading into each other at their borderlines.[66]

An interesting light was shed on the problems of socialism by the studies of the Belgian Hendrik de Man.[67] He elaborated the observation that the large majority of continental European workers were suffering from an "inferiority complex" produced by the feeling of being unfree, exploited, and unable to find satisfaction in their work. Thus, they were torn between the wish to see at least their children move up into the ranks of the bourgeois class on the one hand and on the other the lure of socialism, which promised the establishment of a superior moral order and the pursuance of superpersonal objectives. De Man contrasted the results of that analysis with the mechanistic and rationalistic aspects of Marxism, and expected that large masses of workers would prefer a sort of religious socialism.

Some of the fundamental economic problems involved in operating a socialist economy were formulated by L. von Mises.[68] He demonstrated that competitive price determination was prerequisite to the economically justified allocation of scarce resources; that collective ownership of the means of production with the attendant monopolistic control of these goods rendered the prices of the cost elements indeterminate and thus destroyed the indices which, in the competitive economy, were instrumental in directing the productive factors into the appropriate channels. He stressed that economic rationality was not to be confounded with technological rationality, and that the concept of rationality was deprived of any reasonable meaning when mixed commissions, composed of representatives of divergent interests, were charged with the task of operating economic enterprises.

Considerations of that type caused some more moderate socialist economists to analyze carefully the conditions under which a planned economy could reasonably be expected to function.[69] But they failed to answer the question of how to ensure, in a socialist economy, the rational allocation of resources, and they were unable to formulate operational socialist principles of capital formation and investment policy. These difficulties did not prevent many Western advocates of socialization from agreeing—at least tacitly—on a vague program which practically ignored the objections to the functioning of a "democratic" socialist economy.[70] The program included the establishment of collective ownership of the means of production, control of the economy by a central administrative body, preservation of a monetary system, operation of a free market of consumer goods, maintenance of free choice of occupation, remuneration of services rendered in accordance with their importance, and the protection of the socialist economy against possible interference from outside economic forces. Strong emphasis was placed on the intensification of the technical achievements of the capitalist economy and on the expansion of productive equipment, mass production, and the like.

To the extent that collectivist planning was advocated in England, it was tainted with romanticism as prompted by the writings of John Ruskin, Thomas Carlyle, and William Morris. These authors had turned to medieval ideals of economic life to find an organization of production not governed by the profit motive. Christian socialist authors such as Gilbert K. Chesterton and Hilary Belloc had elaborated the picture of the "distributive state." The National Guild League, founded in 1915, was intended to promote the establishment of "self-governing associations of mutually dependent people, organized for a responsible discharge of a particular function of society in the spheres of industrial, civic, and distributive activities."[71] According to the ideals of the guild movements, local and regional corporations, managed by workers' delegates and enjoying monopolistic positions in their respective markets, were designed to displace privately owned enterprises. National councils composed of representatives of the local guilds had to provide for a coordination of local and regional activities. The principle of reducing, as far as possible, the influence of the national government on the operation of the guild system was especially emphasized by G.D.H. Cole, one of the most active advocates of the guild movement.[72]

Since the chances of mobilizing the political parties in favor of such ideas were insignificant, the adherents of guild socialism recommended the methods of "collective contract" or "encroaching control"; employers should be prevailed upon to turn over to a trade union or a workers' committee a lump sum to be distributed as wages among their workers in any manner decided upon by the workers themselves. But that procedure turned out to be impractical, and the few guilds which started operations in the building trades were unable to compete successfully with other enterprises.

The principles of Fabian socialism provided the basis for a program of radical social reform advanced by Sidney and Beatrice Webb.[73] Richard H. Tawney attacked the existing capitalist society[74] on the grounds that it granted rights to the receipt of earnings independently of the performance of economic functions, and that the competitive order had been fundamentally modified by combinations of industrial enterprises. Tawney outlined the ideal of a functional society in which control of production was to be exercised by those who rendered productive services.[75]

The progressive trustification and cartellization of European industries appeared to confirm the view of the advocates of "economic democracy" that the "planned" sector of the economy was increasing in size and importance. The reasoning of the managers of cartels and combines, trusts, patent agreements, and interlocking directorates appeared to be governed by the organismic ideas that the monopolistic organizations which they headed could claim the right of covering the demand of well-defined markets under conditions of strictly limited competition. They were convinced that their price and production policies perceptibly contributed toward stabilizing the economy, and they enjoyed the support of governments which interpreted the concept of "public interest" in accordance with the principles of cartel philosophy.[76] Measures of tariff policy and other devices which were adjusted to that philosophy also facilitated the control of international markets through international cartels, patent agreements, and similar understandings.[77]

The tendency to promote schemes of planning, applied to limited sectors of the various economies, spread over the entire European continent and was greatly intensified under the impact of the depression of the thirties. The view that the capitalist organization of the economy had become obsolete found significant expressions in a variety of slogans in which the advent of socialism was ascribed to "irresistible historical forces," "inevitable trends," and the like. Karl Mannheim suggested that, along with the advancing "age of planning," the recommendations concerning philosophy, morality, and other lines of spiritual life would take the shape of a "consistent system similar to the Summa of St. Thomas."[78] Deterministic philosophies of that type had a counterpart in the propagandist literature of strongly organized nationalist parties, which claimed for the national state the unlimited right to transform the economy into an instrument of its power policy, and to subject private property and the exercise of economic activity to any restriction which might be deemed appropriate in pursuance of such a policy.

Chapter 25
Totalitarian Economics

THE PROBLEMS OF FASCIST ECONOMICS

ITALIAN FASCISM asserted itself a few years after the end of the First World War in opposition to an almost anarchic communist movement. Benito Mussolini emphasized the intuitionist background of fascism in the outline of his leading ideas which he contributed to the *Enciclopedia Italiana*. He declared that fascism affirms the state as the "true reality" of the individual and as a totality, as a "unity and as a synthesis of all values." A characteristic political feature of fascism was the attempt to revive the medieval concept of "status," to organize the economic and social structure accordingly on a corporate basis, and to assign each individual to a definite group or class in an economic and professional hierarchy. This longing for the return of a unifying spirit which would permeate political, social, and economic life was combined with an intense voluntaristic attitude which found its expression in strong efforts to increase the nation's productive efficiency and to create the basis for a forceful aggressive foreign policy.[1]

Mussolini derived some of his ideas from the French revolutionary author Georges Sorel, who looked for the operation of a blind will in order to account for the development of nature and society.[2] Sorel ascribed the existence of capitalism to the working of a "cunning force" which evolved higher forms of society independently of any human intention and will. Like other Socialists who held "irrational" factors responsible for the course of the evolutionary processes, he relied on the driving power and the will of the proletariat as the instruments for the realization of revolutionary social changes. He attributed to "intuition" the creation of the "political myth," which he defined as a body of images capable of instinctively evoking sentiments and of giving cohesion to a social group.[3]

Mussolini's belief in the function of a rising, well-organized new elite, which was called upon to replace the ruling, disintegrating party, received apparent theoretical support from Vilfredo Pareto's sociological theories. But Mussolini had no use for Pareto's economic teachings. The "corporation," the instrument for securing the "organic and totalitarian" coordination of the nation's productive forces, was basic to the fascist organization of the economy. Industries were grouped, as far as possible, in accordance with their relation to "productive cycles," which covered all processes from the production of raw materials to the marketing of the finished products. The corporations established for the various industries were operated by boards composed of representatives of employers and labor, the government, and the Fascist party. Paramount among the functions of the corporations were adjustment of production to the conditions of demand and supply, adjustment of prices to the interests of the community, promotion of technical innovations and cost-saving devices, and participation in the execution of the export policy. In order to assure unity of purpose within each major occupational group, organizations of employers and workers were combined in "syndicates" endowed with the privilege of regulating labor conditions through compulsory collective agreements.[4] Strikes and other labor disputes were outlawed.

In actual practice, that ambitious plan of creating an "organic" totalitarian economy led to the establishment of a network of monopolistic markets in which prices and investments were controlled by the government and losses were largely "socialized."[5] It is a moot question to what degree the interests of specific classes of the population were promoted by fascism.

Italian economists endeavored to back up this interventionist organization with sociological arguments and theoretical considerations.[6] They started from the proposition that the heavy burden of fixed overhead costs and the increasing rigidity of the entire economic machinery had been responsible for the intensified cartelization and trustification of the various industries and had greatly modified the structure of the capitalist economy.[7] They argued that the policy of interfering with the establishment of collective monopolies had to be abandoned when it was realized that the spread of monopolistic tendencies was a concomitant of the decline of capitalism.[8] In accordance with an "organic vision" of society, the state had been entrusted with the task of organizing the economy and of guiding it consciously to the fulfillment of the ideals of social justice.[9]

The defenders of fascist economics opposed the advocates of socialist schemes by arguing that the great advantages connected with the exercise of individual initiative could very well be preserved by establishing a system of controls under which those responsible for the management of the productive and marketing processes would play the main role but would be obliged to exercise self-discipline in their capacity as organs of the national economy. The formation and operation of voluntary cartels was regulated by a law of June 1932; the same law provided for the formation of compulsory cartels when such a step was proposed by a qualified majority of the members of an industry and justified by the competitive conditions that existed in the latter. Viewed from that angle, government control of employers' associations was held to imply effective support of autonomous equilibrating economic forces, and the concept of "regulated competition" was believed to be free of contradictions.

On closer examination it was recognized that delicate problems were involved in the task of controlling the application of the marginal cost principle to the price policy of monopolistic organizations and of regulating the prices of raw materials and capital goods, that it was difficult to prevent the misuse of economic power of vertical concentrations and interlocking directorates on the part of the managers, and that outsiders could not effectively be protected against coercion.[10] Various discussions turned on the chameleonlike nature of monopolies and their changing forms, the methods of exercising monopolistic power, and the effects of these methods. It was emphasized that these effects can, at best, be traced within a narrow field, directly subjected to monopolistic operations. The more remote, but perhaps most important, effects were, as a rule, beyond the reach of available evidence. It may be mentioned that in 1933, under the impact of the Depression, the erection of new plants and the enlargement of existing ones were made dependent on governmental authorization in almost all important lines of industry.

Thomistic economics were occasionally resorted to in determining the idea of the *summum bonum*.[11] Other authors attempted to reconcile the corporate organization of the economy with the principles of post-Ricardian theories.[12] But the attempt to demonstrate that Pareto had endeavored to transcend the mechanical limits set to economics by the Ricardians was effectively refuted.[13] In passing, mention may be made of the construction of a hypothetical "corporative" man, who was assumed to adjust his behavior to the dynamics of the corporative state,[14] and of studies dealing with the adaptation of Walrasian and Paretian equations to the monopolistic features of the corporative economy.[15] But the fascist economic literature does not appear to have made significant contributions to economic theory.[16]

NATIONAL-SOCIALIST ECONOMICS

National-Socialism owed its logical background to the intuitive method of reasoning which had been widely used by leading representatives of the German "idealistic" philosophy and had been applied by the historical schools to practically all "sciences of the mind," especially to sociology, psychology, jurisprudence, the science of government, and economics. Adolf Hitler, regarded as the embodiment of the "national spirit," was credited with the ability of operating that method to the highest perfection. Confident of his power of "charismatic leadership," he assumed the task of defining the "mission" of the "German nation": the establishment of the Thousand Years' Reich, the domination of Europe, and, finally, the domination of the world.[17]

Beginning with J. G. Fichte, German authors and politicans had attributed to the Germans a special moral and cultural vocation, based primarily on the idea of materializing the "principles of justice" as contrasted with the prescriptions of a formal law. During and after the First World War that mission was frequently identified with the task of preparing the way for the creation of a socialist society.[18] Oswald Spengler, the well-known author of *Decline of the West,* endeavored to show that "socialism" in its purest form had found its expression in the political, economic, and social convictions of the Prussian kings.[19] The belief in the universal socialist mission of the German people was supported by the sociologist Max Scheler.[20]

Political philosophers drew a distinction between nations united by cultural ties

(*Kulturnationen*) and those united under a common government (*Staatsnationen*). They characterized a nation as a ''spiritual community'' that has become conscious of its will, that feels, by itself or through its leaders, a powerful individuality, a great historical unit, and that requests self-determination, the right of the fully developed personality.[21]

These sociopolitical ideas were combined with the view that, as asserted by Fichte and other German philosophers, the German mind was endowed with the specific faculty of using ''insight'' as an instrument for understanding ''reality.'' That conviction amounted to a claim to a natural intellectual superiority for the members of a specific race or ethnic group, whereas all other races were classified according to their intellectual and moral faculties. Mystical slogans such as ''blood and soil'' pointed to an insoluble connection between the ''indigenous'' inhabitants of German territories (and their progeny) and the soil of their fatherland.[22] Essential characteristics of the German people were said to have been preserved over the centuries and to justify its claim to racial superiority, especially in its application to moral and logical faculties. That claim provided a convenient instrument for depriving undesirable citizens (especially those of Jewish origin) of their rights and properties by disqualifying them from any participation in the German national heritage. The ''vision'' of the ''Führer'' as interpreted by the philosophers of the party called for a ''conservative revolution'' to be performed by the national spirit, independently of any evolutionary processes.[23]

The National-Socialist party assumed the role of executive organ of the ''national will to power'' in strict obedience to the orders and intentions of the Führer. A new social ''elite'' was formed by the functionaries of the party machine; their primary task was to establish the ''organic'' connection between the state and the nation.[24] The control that they exercised was designed to assure not only strict coordination of the administrative, military, and economic sectors but also to subordinate all literary, scientific, artistic, and educational activities to the supreme national objectives. The term *Gleichschaltung* was used to denote the strict coordination of thought and action in all spheres of life.[25]

The logical isolation of the economy, as performed by hypothetical reasoning, and the conception of the economy as an instrument for the satisfaction of individual wants, were both incompatible with National-Socialism. In the early programs of the movement, various socialist ideas played a conspicuous role, especially the fight against interest on capital, which was waged under the slogan ''abolition of the tyranny of interest.'' G. Feder defined the tyranny of interest on capital as the subordination of state and nation to independent financial forces. That subordination was to be eliminated by new methods of financing large public orders through debentures bearing no interest, by subsidizing residential construction through free credits, and by similar measures.[26] But these socialist demands were dropped when the party asserted its hold over the economy and succeeded in subordinating the activities of individual enterprises to the requirements of nationalistic power politics. It would serve no reasonable purpose, said Fritz Nonnenbruch, a leading national-socialist economist, to treat the capitalist economy with the sledge hammer; it is necessary to create a new, dynamic economy. When the economy is made an instrument of politics, it is made the object of a valuation that differs widely from the valuation that was characteristic of traditional capitalism.[27]

The main instruments of economic control were the strong industrial organizations, the cartels, trusts, concerns, and other centers of economic power. They became the elements of the warlike construction of the economy in the course of which increasing sectors of productive activity were made dependent on government orders. Financial

participation of the government and the ruling party in industrial and commercial enterprises took place on an expanding scale, as determined by considerations of expediency.
The credit system was subjected to strict control. Surplus income not absorbed by taxes
was directed into channels that made it available to the requirements of the treasury.

The fascist principle of organizing the economy on a corporative basis was rejected
by the National-Socialists, who were unwilling to grant to industrial organizations even a
limited autonomy. Adopting the principle of "leadership," they applied the pattern
provided by the organization of the armed forces not only to public administration but also
to the operation of all plants and concerns and large and small industrial and agricultural
enterprises. All those working in the same establishment should thus be united under the
undisputed command of their leader and should cooperate in the spirit of a complete
harmony of their interests. The suppression of all workers' organization and the establishment of a sort of feudal relationship between the owners of the plants and their workers
was, of course, welcomed by the large majority of the employers.

The National-Socialist agrarian reforms were ruled by the organismic idea of creating
a hereditary attachment of the farmer to the soil and of establishing a sort of family
ownership of agricultural land, as had prevailed under the feudal order. Large increases in
agricultural production were achieved through an elaborate system of managerial and
technical devices.

Economic planning of the National-Socialist type did not follow a consistent set of
principles. The task of adjusting production and distribution to varying political objectives
had to be entrusted to experts who had not fully absorbed the party doctrine and were
lacking an economic theory to implement that doctrine. But wartime experience had
taught them how to apply the administrative machinery of an autocratic government to the
task of husbanding scarce resources, how to control the operation of monopolistic industries, how to prevent inflationary price movements from upsetting the economy, how to
regulate foreign trade, and how to manipulate the foreign exchange value of the currency.
Since the government enjoyed the support of the large masses of the population, it could
count upon far-reaching compliance with its orders. Employers and workers, farmers and
traders were ready to accept heavy restrictions of their freedom in exchange for the
prospect of having their national aspirations fulfilled by a victorious Führer.

Later, when large territories were conquered and subjected to the authority of the
German government, planning in terms of the national economy was extended to planning
in terms of geopolitical considerations. Ambitious schemes were developed for preparing
the economic integration of vast areas that were expected to be attached permanently to
the German economic orbit. It is difficult to determine the degree of efficiency to which
the management of that highly complex administrative and industrial machinery might
have developed, had it not been overstrained by the effects of a devastating war. Critics of
the national socialist organization of the economy, such as Nicholas Kaldor, have pointed
to defects in the administration of controls over rivalries between functionaries of the state
and those of the party, and to the problematic effects of the principle of leadership on the
exercise of genuine responsibility.[28]

Economic theory of the traditional type was considered useless and obsolete by the
fervent adherents of the National-Socialist creed. They contrasted the idea of a "dynamic" economy subordinated to the objectives of national power politics with the economies
of the "acquisitive type." The theories dealing with the latter were held to be unworthy of
a "heroic" generation which had no use for individualistic and liberal teachings. The

ranks of the economic profession were rapidly depleted when the racial laws were strictly applied and when many adversaries of National Socialism preferred emigration to life under the new regime. Outright socialist, especially Marxist, teachings were outlawed and their adherents were prosecuted as enemies of the nation. Marginal utility analysis was the object of renewed attacks.

The economic philosopher whose conception of the economy could best be used for interpreting the vague phraseology of National-Socialist authors was Gottl-Ottlilienfeld, whose theory of "structural economic unities" centered on the subordination of individuals under a superior integrated social whole, and whose concept of a "spirit of community" provided the background for an analysis of the "economic conditions of social coexistence" as manifested through processes of price and wage determination, through productive and distributive activities, and the like.[29]

Far-reaching compromises with the principles of National-Socialism were made by some adherents of the historical school who separated the analysis of "social processes of circulation and distribution" from the "surface phenomena of the quantitative type."[30] They argued that the true meaning of the economy could be realized by adjusting it to the value judgments of a specific social philosophy.[31] The logical framework of that reasoning could be construed from Max Weber's category of "ideal types" and Arthur Spiethoff's conception of "economic styles." Few economists adopted the extreme attitude of Werner Sombart, who combined his endorsement of National-Socialist tenets with violent attacks on the "work of the devil," which had forced the profit motive on the individual by the "economic ratio."[32]

But the scientific principles of the historical school were obviously incompatible with the antiintellectual attitude exhibited by representatives of the ruling party. Thus, O. Dietrich, the chief of the German press, asserted in 1935 that the National Socialist party had proceeded according to the principle of first adjusting practical life to the Führer's philosophy, and afterward of performing the "scientific" implementation of that philosophy.[33] Other difficulties arose from a split in the ranks of the school over the question of the degree to which political as well as scientific reasoning were strictly determined by historical conditions. Some members of the historical school hailed the national socialist movement as a new confirmation of the temporal, spatial, and national limitations placed on any creations of the human mind.[34] Others requested close adjustment of specific economic theories to the "essences" of the varying economic structures.[35]

It was obvious that these developments threatened to discredit the work of more than two generations of German historians, philosophers, jurists, sociologists, and economists; hence, some prominent adherents of historism availed themselves of the opportunity provided by the hundredth anniversary of Gustav Schmoller's birthday to defend their master's teachings against various criticisms and misinterpretations.[36] Particularly significant was an essay entitled "Historism," in which the philosopher Erich Rothaker undertook to justify the inclusion of generalized propositions among the tasks of sociological research. He protested against the tendency to emphasize the relativistic aspects of the historical approach and the formulation of social problems in terms of political and volitional motivation. It is very likely that the subservience of the German teachers of psychology, history, law, and economics to the dictates of the national socialist government was greatly facilitated by their adherence to a relativistic methodology. When requested to adjust their teachings and writings to the official party doctrine, they could defend compliance with that order on the ground that all verities, ethical principles, and ultimate objectives were conditioned by historical situations.

Rothaker's essay was also designed to ward off a specific interpretation of historism, which was suggested by Walter Eucken in a number of articles.[37] In a survey of the development of the historical methodology, Eucken had connected the relativistic aspects of that methodology with the influence of the Marxian doctrine, with Wilhelm Dilthey's neo-Kantian philosophy[38] and the speculations of Friedrich Nietzsche and O. Spengler, and with the "sociology of knowledge." According to Eucken, economics, along with jurisprudence and psychology, thus had been deprived of any solid scientific foundation, and the search for general problems of economic theory had become meaningless. Eucken went on to attack this relativistic approach as applied to the social sciences, raising the well-known objection that a fundamental inconsistency was implied in setting up relativism as an unconditional proposition. Moreover, he rejected the belief that in the course of historical developments human reasoning had undergone significant changes.

Motivated by their opposition to the relativism of the historical school, a group of jurists and economists undertook to establish leading principles for an economic order in which an adequate degree of individual responsibility was to be granted to the owners and managers of economic enterprises. These ideas were elaborated in a series of publications edited by F. Böhm, Walter Eucken, and H. Grossman-Doerth in 1937. Böhm's book, which opened the series, pleaded for the maintenance of the competitive order, but emphasized the need for public control of private business and even for large-scale government participation in economic enterprises in order to safeguard the interests of the community, especially where monopolistic tendencies were supported by technological conditions.[39] This group of scholars also called for a return to theoretical analysis—which had to achieve the closest possible approach to reality—and proposed a renewal of the search for fundamental and lasting elements of historical processes.

Eucken attempted to provide the movement with a solid theoretical foundation by solving what he called the "Great Antinomy," the deep-seated conflict between the methods adopted by the historical school and those used for theoretical purposes.[40] He proposed to overcome that antinomy by establishing a number of "pure forms" of economic order, based on the polar opposition of the centrally planned economy on one end of the range and the exchange economy on the other. In his analysis of the exchange economy he used a scheme of twenty-five market forms derived from H. Stackelberg's discussion of monopolistic situations as supplemented by different forms of monetary organization. And in his analysis of the planned economy, he proposed the establishment of forms of organization specifying different methods of central planning.[41] Economic theory was to undertake the task of analyzing basic economic relationships and processes of change within the framework established by his "pure forms" of economic order. In his view, economic reality could subsequently be described and explained in the light of such analysis.

The struggle against the relativism of the historical school was resumed with renewed vigor after the collapse of the National-Socialist regime. The "neoliberalistic"[42] movement led by Eucken and his group found a center in the so-called Ordo circle and was strengthened by the return to Europe of a number of economists who had spent the war years abroad. Their ideas were supported by the powers who occupied the western zones of Germany and who were opposed to the intensified industrial cartelization and the concentration of financial capital that had taken place under the totalitarian order.

Part VIII

Dialectic Economics

Chapter 26
Dialectic Reasoning
in Western Europe

AFTER THE FIRST World War the "scientific" character of Marxism was officially recognized by the governments of some countries of Central Europe (Germany, Austria, Poland) in which Social-Democratic parties succeeded in securing large political followings and participated in the formation of governments; their adherents obtained important political and administrative positions. At a number of schools of higher learning, chairs of economics and political science were filled by convinced Marxists. This radical change in the official attitude toward the Marxian doctrine was hailed by some educators as a crowning achievement of full freedom of teaching. But it introduced into academic life intolerant adherents of an economic creed who used their lectures for purposes of political propaganda. Many students who were frustrated by the outcome of the war and the meager economic prospects awaiting them after graduation were impressed by the so-called scientific demonstration of the impending breakdown of the existing economic order and the promise of an ensuing millennium of abundance, democratic equality, and social justice. Since dialectic procedures were backed by the belief in the "identity of thinking and being," Marxist philosophers and prophets could claim infallible insight into the evolutionary course of historical events, and the tenets of Marxism became the object of a blind quasi-religious conviction.

On the other hand, relatively narrow limits were set to the spread of "orthodox" Marxism by the petrification which that doctrine had experienced. Its adherents waited for the fulfillment of the Marxian predictions concerning the processes of capital accumula-

tion and the impoverishment of the proletariat.[1] But these predictions failed to materialize, and it was hardly possible to reconcile the obvious results of observation and experience with the Marxian theorems concerning the falling rate of profits, the accumulation
and concentration of capital, the increasing misery of the working classes, the effects of
crises and depressions, and the like. Hence, no significant progress was achieved in
adjusting the doctrine to the conditions of postwar capitalism. In addition, the position of
orthodox Marxists was weakened by the fact that even in Russia, where dialectic materialism had become the official doctrine, various notable attempts were made to dilute the
teachings of Marx's *Kapital* by combining them with various ideas advanced by the
historical school, and even with certain elements of the marginalist approach. A remarkable attempt of that type had been made by Michael Tugan-Baranowski, the author of a
much-discussed business cycle theory. Considerable concessions to the views of "bourgeois" economists were made in a textbook of Marxian economics by W. Gelesnoff.[2]
Although insisting on a formulation of the value theory in terms of relationships between
antagonistic social groups, Gelesnoff criticized Marx for having regarded the problems of
distribution as economic problems and for connecting them with the value theory.

The most important discussions of "orthodox" Marxists turned on the interpretation
of the "breakdown theory" and the explanation of the fact that, in spite of its "inherent
contradictions," the capitalist economy had continued to survive and had shown a remarkable elasticity in sustaining its burden during the war, and subsequently in recovering
from its devastating effects. But these discussions did not result in any new contribution to
the dialectic analysis of the economy.

Otto Bauer's "disproportionality theory" (mentioned in a previous chapter) was
elaborated on by Henryk Grossman, who emphasized the existence of a certain analogy
between monopolistic policies pursued by colonial powers in unprotected markets and the
monopolistic policies of the cartelized industries.[3] It was to these practices that Grossman
ascribed the delay in the inevitable breakdown of the capitalist economy, and he illustrated the process leading to such a catastrophe with the aid of arbitrary calculations of
progressive changes in the "organic" composition of capital.[4]

Less compatible with the rigorous reasoning of the Marxian doctrine was the so-
called "theory of economic imperialism," according to which the impending collapse of
capitalism had been prevented by the exportation of otherwise unsaleable commodities
into noncapitalist areas. In the view of orthodox Marxists, that reasoning was inconsistent
with the theorem that in international trade, as in any other trade, equal values were
exchanged for each other, and that, consequently, the exportation of unusable commodities depended upon the existence of domestic purchasing power for the absorption of
the imports. How was that purchasing power to be secured in view of the continuous
"overproduction" of surplus values? That problematic theory, which had been suggested
by Rosa Luxemburg and expounded by Nikolai Lenin, was elaborated by Fritz Sternberg,
who attributed the improvement of the standard of industrial workers to the exploitation of
cheap labor made available in underdeveloped regions.[5] For the Marxists who regarded
economic imperialism as the last stage of capitalism, it became almost a tenet that
continued wars for the domination of "noncapitalistic" territories could be avoided only
by world-wide revolutionary introduction of the socialist economic order. About twenty-
five years later, Sternberg abandoned the theory of economic imperialism. He admitted
that colonial imperialism and imperialistic expansion had been arrested everywhere.
Although he expressed the conviction that the capitalist order would not survive the

twentieth century, his extensive analysis of the political and economic conditions of the "world of today" showed little, if any, influence of Marxist reasoning.[6]

The sterility that resulted from adherence to the methods of dialectic materialism can hardly be better illustrated than by the fact that the orthodox Marxists were unable to suggest workable schemes for the organization of "socialist economics." Faced with problems of planning, even the outstanding representatives of Marxism had no better devices to offer than general proposals concerning some administrative and managerial aspects of "socialized" industries. Their proposals were commonly ruled by the idea that a sort of "social value" could be established by boards composed of representatives of workers and consumers and assisted by the advice of scientific and technological experts.[7] According to Otto Bauer's proposals, which dealt almost exclusively with administrative questions, each industry was to be controlled by a board of directors. One-third of the directors were to be elected by the trade unions of the industry, another third by the consumers, and one-third were to be appointed by the government from a list of candidates recommended by the teaching staffs of the technical universities and the technical managers of the respective industries.[8] Cartels and similar monopolistic organizations obviously provided the models for socialist planning of this type, with the proviso that the profit motive that had supplied the incentive for the creation of industrial associations was expected to play no role in the economic policy of the socialized industries. The fundamental economic problems involved in operating a planned economy were virtually ignored in these discussions.

The outright revolutionary aspects of the Marxist doctrine were rejected by all political leaders of the Social-Democratic parties of Central Europe. These leaders were opposed to the idea of a "dictatorship of the proletariat," and they relied upon the working of evolutionary forces to bring about a gradual transformation of the capitalist economy. But closer analysis of these forces was undertaken only by some economists of dialectic persuasion who were free from the fetters of the Marxian doctrine. Eduard Heimann's *Social Theory of Capitalism*, which was based on the expectation that a gradual transformation of the capitalist economy would take place under the combined effects of labor legislation, trade union activity, and other constituent elements of social politics, may serve as one example.[9] Rejecting the idea of the class struggle, Heimann argued that labor had ceased to be a "commodity" and that a perceptible advancement toward "social freedom" was taking place, but that the workers still lacked the effective power to enforce the socialization of the means of production and to organize a planned economy. Philosophical, religious, and economic considerations provided the background for sociological discussions of this type, which were closely adjusted to the specific conditions of postwar Germany. But these discussions were abruptly silenced by the advent of the National-Socialist regime.

Lack of an effective indigenous socialist doctrine was probably responsible for the fact that during and after the thirties a number of English and American adversaries of the capitalist economy turned to Marxism as a source of inspiration. Ignoring the dialectical aspects of that doctrine, they created considerable confusion by interpreting Marxian theorems in the light of Keynesian economics.

Chapter 27
Bolshevist Economics

DISCUSSIONS OF THE TRANSITION PERIOD

THE OUTCOME OF the Russian revolution and the establishment of the "dictatorship of the proletariat" signified the final victory of the bolshevist movement over the Mensheviki and the Narodniki. The bolshevist leaders, who modified the Marxian methods of dialectic materialism according to the logical principles of a medieval religious philosophy, endeavored to spread among their followers the conviction that their revolutionary activity was governed by the inexorable laws of an evolutionary process. Lenin, adopting Friedrich Engels's distinction between idealism and materialism, identified the opposition between these two lines of philosophical reasoning with the antagonism of the classes. He identified idealism, according to which no final knowledge of phenomena is possible, with the philosophy of the bourgeois classes; dialectic materialism, however, the "proletarian" philosophy, he asserted, was able to arrive at a "scientific" explanation of the objective existence of the material world.[1] In accordance with a somewhat mystical theory concerning the relationship between the masses and their leaders, the members of the party "elite" assumed the roles of prophets acting in the name of an infallible proletariat.[2]

Karl Marx had alluded to the establishment of a dictatorship of the proletariat for a transition period leading from capitalism to communism in his criticism of the Gotha Program of the German Socialists, written in 1875. That program had been influenced by Ferdinand Lasalle's views concerning the peaceful development of socialism through productive associations supported by the state. Marx argued that an ideal organization of society including the distribution of goods according to need would be accomplished only in the "higher stages" of the communist society, after the individuals had been freed from the fetters imposed by the division of labor, the existing differences between the exercise of physical and mental labor had been eliminated, and the springs of cooperative wealth had started to flow freely.[3] The idea of individual freedom was qualified as a bourgeois prejudice.

Regardless of whether or not Lenin was right in ascribing to his compatriots a special capacity for the practical application of communist ideas, it was no doubt far easier in Russia than in any Western country to adjust the economic machinery to the dictates of an authoritarian government. In Russia the government had always played a major role in directing and regulating economic processes, especially in the sphere of industrial expansion.[4] Moreover, blind subordination of large masses of the population to the orders of a centralized administration had been a traditional feature of Russian political and social life. But for a considerable period the factors which favored the establishment of a communist economy were outweighed by the fact that the leaders of the revolution lacked a clear understanding of the problems involved in organizing and coordinating the production of the nationalized industries and in scaling agricultural production to the requirements of a planned expansion of industrial activity. From a Marxian dictum they derived the conviction that the logical categories of dialectics could be used only to analyze the conditions of the precommunist society, and that their economy was no longer subject to economic laws.[5] N. I. Bukharin, C. E. Preobazhensky, and other theoreticians of the bolshevist movement agreed that the functioning of a planned socialist economy provided no basis for the development of economic theories. Expressions such as "social engineering" were used to define the tasks of the managers of the Soviet economy.[6] In his essay *The Next Tasks of the Soviets*, published in August 1918, Lenin regarded accounting and control as the most important conditions for the functioning of the communist society.[7] He compared such a society to a single office and a single factory where work and wages were equalized.[8] He placed the greatest emphasis on the development of the mechanical and electrical powers of the country, and rejected Bukharin's proposal to rely on the cooperative movement as the instrument for organizing agricultural production.

In the sphere of agricultural production, chaotic conditions resulted from the parceling out of the large estates; in the industrial sphere the efficiency of labor was seriously impaired by the mismanagement of the monopolistic enterprises, the introduction of a system of equal pay for work of any kind, and increasing scarcity even of commodities of primary necessity.[9] Under these conditions the economic situation deteriorated so rapidly that in 1921 the government decided to limit the control of production and distribution to the nationalized, large-scale enterprises and to abandon the other sectors of the economy to the traditional methods of the competitive order.[10] A monetary reform, designed to put an end to the chaotic inflationary price movements of the revolutionary era, was connected with an attempt to return to a sort of gold standard. An institute for economic research was charged with the analysis of business fluctuations. The textbook by W. Gelesnoff, which was prepared during that period, reflected an extremely moderate version of Marxism, combined with noticeable elements of other economic doctrines.[11] In another textbook of economics a summary of the Marxist-Leninist interpretation of the behavior of the capitalist economy was supplemented by a cautious discussion of the "laws" of the Soviet economy.[12] The "law of value," as used by the government, was said to provide an instrument for strengthening the socialist elements.

This period of the so-called NEP (New Economic Policy) came to an end after Lenin's death in 1924. A violent clash of conflicting views developed over the question of how to deal with the agricultural crisis, which threatened to set narrow limits to industrial expansion. It was obvious that rapid industrialization, as contemplated by the country's rulers, was incompatible with an agricultural structure in which subsistence farming prevailed and surplus production for the urban population was largely dependent upon the activity of rich peasants, the *Kulaks*, who succeeded in reestablishing the traditional methods of capitalist production and marketing.

The struggle over agricultural policy was intensified by an even more passionate conflict over the principles of foreign policy to be pursued by the Soviet Union. Some outstanding protagonists of the Bolshevist party, led by Leon Trotsky, Grigori Zinoviev, and Lev Kamenev, believed that the antagonism between the proletarian minority and the peasant majority was insoluble unless settled on a world-wide scale. Hence, they insisted that primary attention be given to the mission of the Russian people to prepare and to foment the world revolution. Such ideas played a significant role in the program adopted by the Communist International in 1928.[13] Joseph Stalin and his adherents, however, realized the utopian character of such views and were convinced that, at least during a transition period, the Soviet economy should be developed side by side with capitalist countries. In his *Foundations of Leninism*, published in 1924, Stalin argued that in accordance with the "law of uneven development" any country could become ripe for socialism, and that Trotsky's insistence on the "permanent revolution" was symptomatic of his lack of faith in the power of the dictatorship of the proletariat to save Russia. It has been observed that in his fight against Trotsky and his adherents, Stalin developed the psychological devices that later became his standard method of attacking adversaries. That technique—which he took over from Marxist politicians—consisted in pointing to the "hidden significance" of perfectly obvious and self-explanatory events and statements.[14] At the Fourteenth Party Conference, held in April 1925, the policy of "socialism in one country" was adopted. Beginning in 1928, the Soviet Union participated in the activities of the League of Nations in order to gain a breathing space for a peaceful reorganization of the economy.

Of course, the belief of the bolshevist interpreters of Marxism that disrupting forces were operating within the capitalist economy was not affected by these political maneuvers. They continued to demonstrate to their satisfaction that the progressive disintegration of the capitalist society was evidenced by the "crisis" of the bourgeois sciences.[15] They contrasted that "crisis" with the conditions of the sciences under the bolshevist regime, where the "Marxian scientific investigator" participated in a "single and inseparable complex of theoretical and practical activity of a class" that was to be regarded as the agent and motivating force of historical progress.[16] With Marxism, philosophy was said to have reached for the first time its "sociological self-knowledge."[17]

Sharply conflicting and mutually incompatible views created an ominous split among the leading interpreters of the official doctrine and produced a struggle that was eventually settled in terms of power politics. It was fought against the background of a mounting resistance of the peasant population to the enforced delivery of their products. A conservative group, led by Bukharin, recommended continuation of the policy that had been pursued under Lenin. That policy was designed to reestablish the traditional relations between industry and agriculture. The prices of the agricultural products were to be permitted to rise, and the method of wholesale requisitioning was to be replaced by the imposition of a limited tax in kind.[18] Capitalist methods were to be applied in the sphere of small-scale production, and the "monopolistic parasitism of the nationalized industries" was to be prevented from expanding production independently of increases in the demand for final products. That warning was directed against policy recommendations made by Michael Tugan-Baranowski. Bukharin's conservative views were shared by Aleksei Rykov and Mikhail Tomski.

Bukharin's ideas were violently attacked by left-wing economists led by Preobazhensky.[19] These left-wingers argued that mutually antagonistic forces were operating in the economy: the "socialist sector" was developing under the "law of planned organization," whereas in the competitive sector, in which self-regulating tendencies prevailed, the "laws of value" were the determining factor. They were opposed to the "psychology of the restoration period" and to the application of past experience, and proposed to concentrate all efforts on the rapid expansion of industrial production, the modernization of obsolete equipment, the exploitation of neglected national resources, the absorption of the agricultural surplus population, and the improvement of the power system and of transport facilities. Pursuance of that policy was to be rendered possible by imposing a high rate of compulsory savings on the agricultural sector and the small-scale producers; the demand for goods of consumption was to be discouraged by effective measures of price control.[20]

These proposals met with the objection that they were likely to enhance the social tensions they were designed to alleviate. Stalin, fighting for leadership, at first sided with the conservative group and admitted that Russian industry was dependent on the peasant markets. But, after eliminating his left-wing rivals and gaining undisputed domination of the Politbureau, he endorsed the economic policy advocated by his adversaries. Faced with an increasingly critical food situation and intensified resistance by the peasant population to his relatively moderate program of "collectivization," he insisted upon the enforced introduction of collective farming. (It is a moot question whether Stalin's attitude toward collectivization was determined by considerations of expediency rather than by dogmatic principles.)[21] To justify that radical measure he referred to the Marxian view that large-scale enterprise was more productive than small-scale operation. Moreover, he proclaimed the maxim that, without having antagonistic effects, the laws of dialectics continued to be valid in the classless society until that society ceased to be exposed to the hostility of capitalist classes from within or from abroad. That proposition was probably based on the consideration that dialectic reasoning, believed to reflect exactly the operation of "real" antagonistic forces, could be regarded applicable to social and economic conditions until all such forces had been eliminated.

A resolution, passed in January 1930 by the Central Committee of the Communist party, abrogated the Marxist-Leninist theory that law and state would "wither away" in a classless society. In an address to the Sixteenth Party Congress, held in June 1930, Stalin emphasized the contradiction between the need to strengthen the power of the bolshevist state and the Marxian formula concerning the withering away of the state. In his view, whoever failed to understand the characteristic features of that contradiction was "dead to Marxism." An interesting chapter of the history of dialectic reasoning could be filled with an analysis of the discussions that have turned on the meaning of the enigmatic phrase "withering away of the state."

Stalin countered Bukharin's conservative program of economic reform with the argument that it was prompted by a "vulgar concept of abstract moving equilibrium." The concept of a "moving equilibrium" appears to have been particularly obnoxious to the defenders of the official Stalinist economic doctrine. It was condemned as "counter-revolutionary" when it was revived in a theory of "national economy balances" advanced in 1936 by the academician S. G. Strumilin, a prominent economist. In fact, the concept of "moving equilibrium" reflects the nominalistic attempt to deal with continuous movements as if they were composed of discontinuous shifts of equilibrium positions.[22]

To Bukharin's theory of the "equilibrium of the sectors," Stalin opposed the ill-defined doctrine of a "dialectically dynamic equilibrium," derived from the Marxian scheme of extended reproduction and from the postulate that internal congruence was to be established between the component parts of the economy.[23] Without the conscious creation of an initial disequilibrium, he argued, the foundations of a new type of "ordered dynamics" could never be laid. During the execution of the First Five-Year Plan, these dynamics were designed to remove the lag of industry behind the requirements of the national economy and the lag of agricultural production behind the expansion of industry. Thus, by the end of 1929 a first phase in the process of "dogmatizing" the bolshevist doctrine had been virtually terminated.[24] General acceptance and observance of that doctrine was assured through the liquidation of its adversaries.

THE THEORETICAL BACKGROUND OF THE FIVE-YEAR PLANS

It is very doubtful whether Stalin's superiority over his ill-fated opponents was due to the strength of his arguments. Yet he felt obliged to justify his policies as the fulfillment of propositions derived from the laws of dialectic materialism. He could thus present them as the fruits of a sublime reasoning that enabled him to adjust his decisions to a course of events prescribed by inevitable evolutionary processes.

The official reinterpretation of the Marxian doctrine that was reached after the establishment of Stalin's undisputed leadership was termed the *Marxist-Leninist-Stalinist doctrine of socialism*.[25] (It has been observed on good grounds that in Soviet Russia much of what goes under the name of "established doctrine" has in reality little or nothing to do with Marxism.) In due course, Andrej Vishinsky, who at that time occupied the position of procurator general, undertook the task of justifying the existence of a dictatorial regime endowed with the broadest possible power of coercion in all spheres of political, economic, and intellectual life.[26] In violent attacks he criticized the views of some Russian jurists who had minimized the importance of law and government for the communist state; in his view, a strong government was indispensable until the danger of capitalist encirclement had been eliminated, until all citizens had learned how to operate social production and habitually observed the basic rules of society. Vishinsky contrasted the Soviet state, which he hailed as the most "democratic" authority and the full realization of the "general will," with the "instrument of exploitation and suppression" as represented by the bourgeois state.

From the thesis that human nature was susceptible to far-reaching changes through mutual interaction with its environment, Vishinsky derived the conclusion that the destruction of capitalism had opened unlimited opportunities to every citizen and had assured the conformity of individual interests with the interests of society. Having thus identified the policy of the communist dictatorship with the objectives of a "welfare state," Vishinsky endeavored to show that the written law of the Soviet Union had been adjusted to the "law of revolution" and that "freedom" was achieved through subservience to the dictates of the government. This juridical definition of the functions of the Soviet dictatorship was combined with more or less mystical ideas concerning the mission of the Russian people to assure the final world-wide victory of communism and the complete annihilation of all capitalist regimes.[27]

The interpretation of the dictatorship as the embodiment of a general will was facilitated by the abandonment of the Marxian dialectic maxim that all historical events, including the emergence of the communist society, were exclusively the products of impersonal forces operating independently of the human will. Instead, official recognition was given to the theorem that "creative changes" in political and economic developments could be brought about by outstanding personalities such as Lenin and Stalin. According to an official declaration, this modification of the doctrine of dialectic materialism was derived from an unpublished manuscript written by Friedrich Engels between 1878 and 1882, which was later brought out in Moscow under the title "Dialectics of Nature."[28] In a resolution passed in January 1930 by the Central Committee of the Communist party, the problems of the "Marxist-Leninist philosophy" were outlined in accordance with that theorem. The way was thus opened for the prolonged propagandist movement which clothed Stalin with the paraphernalia of the providential leader of the Russian people.

After achieving complete command of the legislative and executive machinery of the Soviet Union, Stalin and his aides embarked on the task of adjusting the Russian economy to the objectives of the five-year plans, conceived of as successive steps in a gigantic process of economic expansion. No outsider knows the considerations which prevailed in determining the rates of growth for the economy as a whole, its sectors and its subdivisions down to individual enterprises and plants. Regardless of any protestations to the contrary, it is probable that these rates were more or less arbitrarily adjusted to changing circumstances. Investments in primary industries and in armament production (in the broadest sense of the term) received paramount consideration, at the expense of agricultural production, residential construction, and the manufacture of consumption goods. According to reasonable estimates, total personal incomes increased by only two-thirds from 1928 to 1955, whereas funds withheld by the state and used primarily for investment and defense were expanded fifteenfold. About 45 percent of the investment funds appears to have been directed into heavy industry during that period.[29] But the Soviet economy remained free of crises and depressions, since the expansion of capital goods–producing industries proceeded independently of corresponding increases in incomes and demand for consumption goods.[30] Enforced savings were imposed upon the population through inflationary price movements, which were frequently brought about by events which affected the scarcity relationships between productive factors, such as misdirected investments, bad harvests, and the like.[31]

The collectivization of agriculture, carried out with incredible ruthlessness, resulted in breaking the resistance of the peasants and in subordinating their interests completely to the purpose of industrial expansion. *Kolkhozes* (collective farms), state farms, machine-tractor stations, and cooperative stores were the main instruments used to implement that process. It was supported by the establishment of rural Soviets and youth organizations. The psychology of the peasants was to be adjusted to the spirit of "proletarian socialism."[32]

Along with the proclamation of the "principle of dynamic equilibrium" as a mainstay of the official bolshevist doctrine, Stalin announced that the operation of the "law of value," which Marx had established in order to account for the ratio at which commodities are exchanged in the capitalist economy, continued to operate in the socialist economy. The law was considered applicable to "commodity production" performed in the not fully nationalized sectors of the economy. But when consciously applied in a planned economy it was held to have none of the destructive effects ascribed to it in the analysis of the capitalist economy. Another radical change of the Leninist interpretation of the Marxist doctrine consisted in repudiating the view that equality of incomes was a leading principle of the Marxist social philosophy. This decision was adopted at the Seventeenth Party Congress, held in 1931.[33]

In due course, wage fixing was largely modified in accordance with the principles of piecework systems practised in capitalistic enterprises. The efficiency of individual workers was to be stimulated by the distribution of special bonuses among "Stakhanov workers" whose achievements surpassed the norms established by average productivity. The results of that policy were soon reflected in a differentiation of incomes, the scale of which exceeded by far any dispersion of incomes observed in capitalist countries.

Identification of the economic policy of the Soviet government with the fulfillment of the "dialectic laws of the socialist economy" was an outstanding characteristic of these developments.[34] Soviet economists were required to teach that, under conditions of the socialist method of production, "objective necessity" operates as an economic law "which is known to and is working through the consciousness and will of men," as represented by the leading forces of the society—the Soviet state and the Communist party.[35] In the "Short History of the Communist Party of the Soviet Union" the Party was said to be able to find, through the power of the Marxist doctrine, the right orientation in any situation, to understand the inner connection of current events, to foresee their course, and to perceive not only how and in what direction they were developing but how and in what direction they are bound to develop in the future.[36] No stronger logical argument could have been invoked to justify the decisions of a government vested with dictatorial powers. Stalin's reinterpretation of the laws of the socialist economy was hailed as a new stage in the advancement of the science of Marxist-Leninist economics. To deny the existence of economic laws under socialism was termed the "most vulgar voluntarism."

At the beginning of the forties the interpretation of the "economic laws" operating in the Soviet society was subjected to renewed scrutiny.[37] Logical difficulties resulted from the obligation of the teachers of economics to use the labor cost theory and the concept of surplus value to explain the fact that the price of a particular commodity need not coincide with its "value," while the sum of the prices of all commodities was to be regarded as the equivalent of the sum of their values.[38] Numerous discussions turned on the official procedure of wage and price determination and its relation to the labor cost theory of value, according to which divergencies between the values of the labor power of different workers had to be related to differences in the labor time necessary to produce the means for securing the workers' education and subsistence. The background of these discussions was provided by the official view that "socially necessary labor," as defined by Marx, remained a heterogeneous category during the stage of undeveloped communism, since the skilled worker was still able to produce a larger amount of value in a unit of time than the unskilled worker, while the money calculus was to be preserved in order to reduce dissimilar, heterogeneous forms of labor to a common denominator.

Within the framework of bolshevist reasoning, the labor cost theory appears to have played a role similar to that assigned to the theory of the "just price" in Thomistic economics. Abandonment of the theory would have dealt a mortal blow to the logical structure of the official doctrine.[39] Similar reasoning was used to explain why incomes in the "socialist" economy could not be distributed on a basis of equality or according to need, but had to be adjusted to efficiency, ability, and effort. The term *socialism* was officially used to denote the transitional economic order leading to a future communist organization in which abundance of goods would permit their distribution according to need. Certain elements of marginal utility analysis were perhaps involved in the proposal of the economist L. A. Leontief to determine the value of various kinds of labor indirectly, by means of calculating and comparing the values of the products.

General agreement existed on the view that some categories characteristic of the functioning of the capitalist economy, such as money, credit, prices, costs of production, etc., were equally indispensible elements of the socialist economy, but these categories, instead of acting as disrupting forces, as under the capitalist order, were characterized as "expressions of harmony" when used by the planning authority of the socialist state.[40] Capital accumulation, which Marx had rendered responsible for the market anarchy and the industrial crises of the capitalist economy, was said to have beneficial effects under conditions of public ownership of the means of production and planned organization of the economy. The operation of the Marxian law of the equalization of the rate of profit was held to be applicable only under competitive conditions, whereas under socialism different rates of profit could prevail in various sectors of the economy.[41] But such general apologetic assertions had a counterpart in repeated discussions of the Learned Council of the Institute of Economics of how to adjust the official theorems to the requirements of the planning authorities. The difficulties involved in meeting these requirements were ascribed to the unsatisfactory state of economic research, the insufficient application to that research of a "practical active spirit," the lack of scientific keenness, the erroneous introduction of problems pertinent only to the capitalist economy, and the failure to coordinate central and peripheral economic institutions. The mathematical approach to economic problems was rejected as an attempt to divorce theory from practice.[42]

PROBLEMS OF BOLSHEVIST PLANNING

Labeling the Soviet economy as a type of fully centralized state capitalism is incompatible with the bolshevist doctrine, since according to bolshevist terminology the expression *capitalism* is applicable only to economic and social conditions under which the working classes are exploited by private owners of the means of production. Such a definition of capitalism was proclaimed in Stalin's report to the Fourteenth Party Congress in 1928. The use of the expression *capitalism* to characterize a planned economy is also misleading, insofar as it appears advisable to associate that expression with economies the organization of which is permeated with strong elements of hypothetical reasoning, such as assumptions, expectations, and anticipations. The inconsistency of hypothetical methods with the principles of bolshevist reasoning was strongly emphasized by the economist S. G. Strumilin in his standard work, *"Problems of Planning in the U.S.S.R."*[43] Soviet planning was not primarily designed to secure maximum yield of productive assets, nor the optimum distribution of that yield, nor an "economically sound" allocation of the available resources. Rather, it was governed by the objective of promoting, to the highest possible degree, the mechanization and growth of the economy, as expressed in productive capacity. A characteristic feature of bolshevist planning was the often-repeated claim that the socioeconomic optimum of the growth of the communist economy is far superior to the technical maximum attainable under the rules of the capitalist "laws of value." In fact, up to the end of the Second World War the growth of the Soviet economy attained unusual proportions only between 1934 and 1936. But during the recovery period of 1946 to 1950 the rates of growth were remarkable and continued to be high from 1951 to 1956. The increase of industrial output between 1950 and 1955 has been estimated at about 65 percent. In the history of economic development, that growth has been paralleled only in Japan during the first decades of this century.[44] The communist planners scoffed at the view, attributed especially to the British Labor government, that efficient planning can be based on the study of trends and the formulation of progress with different variants of development, on the selection of an optional variant and its attempted materialization through persuasion and agreement of all those participating in productive processes.

Their real or pretended belief in the infallibility of their dialectic procedures enabled the bolshevist planners to establish the successive Five-Year Plans in terms of rigid definitions of the functions of all productive and distributive agencies and their subdivisions, down to individual plants; to impose targets of performance on state farms and *Kolkhozes*, on industries, and on factories; to allocate, from above, all economic resources, including labor; to assign to each productive unit its sources of supply and its outlets; and to apply price- and wage-fixing procedures to the entire socialized sector of the economy. That system of planning has a counterpart in a vast organization of administrative statistics with two branches: (1) continuous recording and reporting of production and consumption, fulfillment of plans, and social, political, demographic, vital, legal, and similar data; and (2) continuous bookkeeping and accounting based on financial data.[45] These planning procedures were supplemented by measures of rigid control of the execution of the plans. As little leeway as possible was to be left to chance or to uncontrolled decisions of individuals, such as consumers' demand, voluntary savings, and the like. Direct savings, which were repeatedly imposed upon the population, were not designed to provide funds for investment purposes but to absorb redundant purchasing power and to regulate the quantity of circulating means of payment.[46] Yet in spite of strict limitations on the functions of the managers of the various enterprises, these managers were frequently admonished to mobilize additional resources in the interest of extended production, to enhance productivity, and to avoid indulgence in the "opportunity theory of equilibrium." Western analysts of the managerial aspects of Soviet industrial enterprises have pointed out the bewildering variety of partly conflicting goals, controls, penalties, and incentives that face such managements. The difficulties involved in establishing a theory of the behavior of the Soviet "firm" are enhanced by the fact that each of the three leading officials of a Soviet enterprise—the chief bookkeeper, the plant director, and the representative of the Party—might be interested in the fulfillment of specific aspects of the targets. Although reduction of the costs of production is regarded as a primary obligation of all those responsible for the yields of factories and plants, conflicting criteria were often used in deciding on the success or failure of plant management.[47]

The fetters imposed by the labor cost theory on bolshevist reasoning prevented Russian planners from clearly formulating the principles of a sound investment policy. At the beginning of the First Five-Year Plan (1927–30), Soviet economists embarked on a lively discussion of the problems connected with industrial expansion and its highest possible rate. An abstract Soviet model of economic growth was construed in 1928 by G. A. Feldmann, a member of the Soviet State Planning Commission. It was based on the Marxian division of total output into producers' goods and consumers' goods, and on the use of the categories of constant capital, variable capital, and surplus value, to determine the distribution of the exchange values. But proposals of that type remained in the blueprint stage.[48] The methods of determining "effectiveness of capital investment" were analyzed in the light of conflicting interpretations of the Marxian doctrine.[49] But the discussion came to a sudden end after the purge of the economists who had sided with Stalin's adversaries.

Allotment of any remuneration for services rendered by capital was declared to be incompatible with the principles of the Marxist-Leninist doctrine; credits needed for the establishment and the operation of the state-owned enterprises were granted free of charge, and interest on capital was excluded from the cost elements of Soviet production.[50] Interest charges were held to delay the increase of fixed capital and to interfere with the effectiveness of the utilization of natural resources.[51]

But managers of plants, engineers, and especially technicians engaged in the construction of large-scale productive units (power stations, railroads, and the like) soon realized that scarcity relationships of resources were ignored when no account was taken of interest on capital. In their professional papers they pointed to the problems of cost-accounting and cautiously referred to the need to include among the cost elements some charges related to capital investments. They argued that in the absence of such a procedure preference was likely to be given to projects that, requiring enormous capital outlays, were economically unjustified in view of the prevailing scarcity of capital. In order to avoid a conflict with the official doctrine, the introduction of charges on capital was often justified as a means through which capital accumulation could be promoted. In fact, the engineers and technicians agreed on using, under different names, "rates of accumulation'' as a substitute for interest on capital. A rate of 6 percent per annum was used in the projects of hydroelectric power stations, higher rates in later projects.[52]

Only about the middle of the forties, after the end of the Second World War, did several economists dare to join the engineers in the discussion of the problems of cost accounting. They used the term *economic accounting* to differentiate their methods from those of *commercial accounting* as practiced by the capitalist enterprises.[53] Although no agreement was reached on the questions of whether or not charges on capital were justified and how they should be applied, such charges were commonly taken into account; they were related to a rate of return on capital, frequently to a rate derived from other uses. Thus, the principle of opportunity costs received implicit recognition when scarce resources had to be allocated to specific projects, though in their discussions of the problems connected with the allocation of productive factors, some Soviet economists resorted to highly tortuous interpretations of some Marxian concepts.[54]

Several experts recommended the establishment of ''uniform rates of profitability'' or ''capital accumulation'' either for the entire economy or at least for an entire industry, such as railroad construction. Additional confusion was introduced into the problems of cost accounting by the belief of the planning authorities, proclaimed in 1930, that depreciation of fixed capital was a category of the capitalist economy and could be ignored in the Soviet economy. Hence, in his search for an investment criterion compatible with the principles of bolshevist cost accounting, Strumilin developed the concept of ''rate of devaluation of fixed capital,'' which took account of the increase in labor productivity and the ensuing fall in the value of the yield of the investment.[55] Thus, he regarded depreciation not as a direct function of time and use but as a function of the time rate of technological change. Depreciation of that type was to be added to the rate of amortization and the costs of keeping the capital intact when a choice had to be made among alternative investment possibilities. Indices of ''efficiency'' were to be established in order to express, per unit of current labor, the increments in national income achieved by different plans.[56] For these thoughts, Strumilin was accused of applying the criterion of ''profitability'' to the entire program of planning and of using the ''antiscientific'' principle of achieving maximum effects with minimum costs. Strumilin's proposals thus shared the fate of other similar ideas: they were rejected on the ground that they deviated from the official interpretation of Marxian doctrine.[57]

Robert W. Campbell, in an article published in 1956, analyzed the problem of depreciation in the Soviet economy. After surveying the changes in the rules concerning the valuation of fixed assets and the determination of depreciation rates, he concluded that heterogeneity and understatements in the valuation of fixed assets had been compounded with such errors in the rates of depreciation that the resulting amount, charged off as depreciation, constituted practically an arbitrary levy. But he considered it an open question whether or not the consequent distortions of cost calculations were substantial enough to lead to mistakes in economic decision making.[58]

The first attempts to analyze the structure of the Soviet economy in the form of balance sheets were made for the year 1923/24 and published in 1926.[59] During the fight over Stalin's program of economic reforms the Central Statistical Administration was abolished and replaced (in May 1931) by the Central Administration of Economic Record Keeping, with the State Planning Commission (Gosplan).[60] That decision was motivated by the consideration that there was no place for statistics in a centrally administered planned economy with no stochastic environment. The treatment of statistics as a handmaiden of bookkeeping prevailed until after the end of the Second World War, in spite of objections by a group of distinguished authors such as Strumilin and V. S. Nemchinov. The reestablishment of the Central Statistical Administration as a semiindependent agency, no longer subordinated to planning authorities, was decreed in August 1946 in connection with a reorganization of the State Planning Commission.

The balances, established in order to define the elements of the Five-Year Plans and to account for their results, were of two kinds: material balances for groups of products admitting of homogeneous physical measurement, and "synthetic," or value, balances expressed in roubles and designed to coordinate the economic processes defined by the plans. Later, when it was found necessary to throw a veil of secrecy over all important aspects of the Russian economy, it became common practice to publish, for the various lines of production, only the percentage figures of planned increases and to observe the same method in tables indicating the fulfillment of the targets. These figures were the object of widely varying interpretations by Western observers who endeavored to estimate the growth of the Russian economy.

Under the rigid rules of Stalinism only one method of organizing production and markets was considered compatible with the "laws of socialist development of society." That method was ruthlessly imposed on the satellite countries of Eastern Europe (Czechoslovakia, Poland, Rumania, Hungary, Bulgaria, and East Germany). Since Stalinist methods of planning were officially regarded as a perfect realization of socialist objectives, any defects connected with their practical application were attributed to remnants of capitalist ideologies and to intrigues of enemies of socialism.[61] The nationalization of industries was almost completed in these countries (with the exception of East Germany) by the end of the 1940s, but the process of adjusting agricultural production to the principles of collective and state ownership met with prolonged difficulties. The population, especially in those regions that had been part of the Austro-Hungarian monarchy or of Germany, had reached far higher standards of living and of cultural development than they were permitted to experience under the authoritarian Soviet rule. They deeply resented the hardship imposed upon them by Moscow and reacted with much skepticism to the theorems of dialectic materialism. The farming population in particular adopted a hostile attitude toward the enforced collectivization of agricultural production.

Prompted by the objective of adjusting the productive capacities of these regions to the economic and political requirements and aims of the Soviet Union, Soviet authorities applied a variety of methods designed to ensure Russian participation in the exploitation of vital resources and the control of important lines of industrial production. Rapid overexpansion of the heavy industries was enforced at the expense of consumer goods industries.[62] Time and again, attempts were made to coordinate the economic plans of the satellite states and to transform the territories included in the Soviet bloc into a huge economic machine functioning in accordance with strictly centralized directives. Their economic cooperation was to be promoted by the Council for Economic Mutual Assistance, set up in 1949. These attempts failed. It became increasingly evident that the methods of Soviet planning could reasonably be applied only in vast, economically unified territories in which large natural resources were available and practically no account had to be taken of the material and cultural interests of the population. From 1953 on there was a growing awareness that Soviet economic growth would not easily be duplicated by the satellite countries, that in Eastern Europe autarchic tendencies placed strict limits on the establishment of an economically unified communist bloc. But under the pressure of the Soviet dictatorship the political leaders of these countries had virtually no other choice than to continue to rationalize, to the best of their ability, the situation in terms of the Marxian scheme of "reproduction." Any attempt to deviate from the rules imposed by the Soviet government was ruthlessly suppressed by armed force.

Only Yugoslavia, favored by particular political, military, and economic conditions, could dare to defy the dictates of Moscow and to modify the bolshevist pattern of planning in favor of conspicuous aspects of the exchange economy.[63] As viewed from the angle of the official Marxist-Leninist-Stalinist doctrine, such modifications constituted heretical aberrations from an exclusively valid communist creed and had to be persecuted with all available means.

CHANGING INTERPRETATIONS

Eventually, it was acknowledged that the dialectic laws of Marxism were applicable to the analysis of the Soviet economy. This recognition was made acceptable by separating the doctrine into two concepts: *dialectic materialism* was conceived of as a method, or theory, of knowledge, while *historical materialism* was defined as the method, or technique, for the interpretation of evolutionary processes. That distinction permitted the bolshevist interpreters of Marxism to argue that antagonistic contradictions were a characteristic feature only of societies split by divergent class interests and had to be solved by revolutionary explosions. But the contradictions which were found to obtain in classless or socialist societies were qualified as "nonantagonistic"; they were declared to be open to gradual solution through "scientific" social and political control. The central plan was hailed as the instrument for constantly and consciously adjusting the "production relations" to the growth of the productive forces.[64]

On the other hand, since the workers of the main capitalist countries were obviously indifferent to social revolutionary ideas, Lenin's theory of "monopoly capitalism" was brought into play to explain the forces alleged to work toward the inevitable disintegration of the capitalist economy. Toward the end of the 1940's the tenets of dialectic materialism found renewed support in an intellectual and political movement organized by Andrei Zhdanov and directed against the increasing influence of Western thinking on Russian philosophy, science, and art.[65] Absolute observance of the official views proclaimed by the Party was to be secured in all lines of cultural activity. All writers were requested to support in their literary works the fulfillment of the plans of construction and rehabilitation, and to extol the achievements of the socialist economy.[66] Since Marxism, as interpreted by Lenin and Stalin, was regarded as the instrument for "transforming the unknown into truth," any views which did not strictly conform to the official Party doctrine were condemned as being influenced by erroneous "ideologies." *Partiinost* was the term used to denote strict adherence to the official doctrine.

Zhdanov revived the messianic ideas which had been propagated between 1935 and 1938 by the Comintern, the international organization of all communist parties under the leadership of Moscow. Constituent elements of that creed were the tenets that the united communist parties represented the proletariat of the world, the only "creative" social class; that they expressed, through an elite, the general will of that class, as based on a solidarity of interests of the leaders and the guided masses; that they derived absolutely valid knowledge from the use of the methods of dialectical and historical materialism; and

that they were called upon to deliver the world from the worst evil, the capitalist society.[67] The Comintern was disbanded and reestablished according to consideration of
political expediency.

In the sphere of economics, the influence of the "Zhdanovist" movement made
itself felt in the condemnation of Professor E. Varga's extensive analysis of the structural
changes which had occurred in the capitalist countries.[68] Varga's interpretation of the
future of capitalism was discussed in May 1947 under the chairmanship of K. V. Ostrovitianov. Violent objections were raised to his assertion that the capitalist states had ceased
to be dominated exclusively by the interests of the "monopolists" and that after the war
English workers had secured a perceptible influence on public policy. Equally incompatible with the official doctrine of "economic imperialism" was Varga's proposition that
wars between the capitalist powers could no longer be considered inevitable. Lengthy
discussions turned on the question of whether a capitalist country could engage in
"planning."

Consequent upon his deviation from the orthodox doctrine, Varga was disqualified
from his position as head of the Institute of World Economics and World Politics.
(Ostrovitianov became Varga's successor, and the institute was merged with the Institute
of Economics of the Academy of Science.) In May 1949, after a long, remarkably valiant
defense of his views, Varga was forced to recant practically all his heretic assertions. The
condemnation of the work which had been performed under Varga's direction listed all
mortal sins which could be committed by Soviet social scientists: adoption of a non-
Marxist methodology, distortion of Leninist-Stalinist teachings on imperialism, defection
from the official theory concerning the general crisis of capitalism, virtual refusal to take
account of the struggle of the two antagonistic economies, a "technoeconomic approach," lack of partisanship, "objectivism," and adulation for bourgeois science and
technique.[69]

The preparation of an official textbook of political economy that was decided upon in
1951 provided Stalin with an opportunity to clarify *ex cathedra* some issues of the official
doctrine. His declarations were designed to correct some "erroneous" views expressed
by Soviet economists at conferences that were held preparatory to the elaboration of the
textbook in November 1951. In an editorial in the bolshevist paper *Pravda* (3 October
1953), these declarations were hailed as the "most significant event in the intellectual life
of the Party and the Soviet people" and as "the highest stage in the development of
Marxist-Leninist economics."[70] Stalin confirmed his repeatedly expressed conviction
that in accordance with Marxism the "laws of science" are the reflection of objective
processes that take place independently of the will of man, but he insisted on the restricted, historical character of economic laws. He reemphasized the principle that, as
distinct from the inexorable operation of these laws under the capitalist order, consistent
utilization of the laws in the interest of society was possible under socialist and communist
planning. With biting observations Stalin rejected the attempt by some planners to draw a
broad distinction between economic laws that work through the consciousness and will of
men, and others that operate independently of these factors. He defined the "basic
economic law of socialism" as the task of securing maximum satisfaction of the constantly rising material and cultural requirements of the whole of society through continuous expansion and perfection of socialist techniques. He contrasted that "law" with the
"law of surplus value," the determinant characteristic of capitalist production, the cause
of all the evils ascribed to the capitalist order. This primitive version of the Marxist

doctrine, in which the term *law* was ambiguously used in an analytical as well as normative sense, was hailed by obedient bolshevist economists as being of profound theoretical
significance, as the discovery of the basic economic law of contemporary capitalism, the
"clarification of the nature of economic laws under socialist conditions and the formulation of the most important economic laws of a socialist system of production."[71]

In his discussion of the operation of the socialist economy, Stalin asserted that
planning, as applied to the Soviet economy, has been carried out in accordance with "the
objective law of balanced proportionate development of the national economy." He
limited his discussions of "planning" to a few general observations and ignored the
fundamental problems connected with the proportionate development of complementary
lines of productive activity, with the rational allocation of resources, the economic utilization of technological improvements, and the like. He admitted that in the Soviet economy
certain contradictions existed between the productive forces and the productive relations,
but he was convinced that these contradictions could always be reduced to conformity,
and he repudiated the view of some "half-baked" Marxists "that commodity production,
as practiced in some sectors of the economy, was bound to lead to capitalism." He
attributed such a view to the erroneous belief that the economic categories that were
characteristic of capitalism played the same roles in socialist production. He emphasized
that, as far as prices were influenced by scarcity relationships, they did not fulfil the same
regulatory functions as in the capitalist economy, and he pointed to the very limited field
of application assigned to the Marxian law of value in the socialist economy in which the
means of production were allocated by the central authorities and used in accordance with
preestablished plans. But account had to be taken of the law of value in the sphere of
consumer goods, which were designed to compensate the labor power expended in productive processes. In foreign trade, commodity character was to be attributed even to
productive factors. With some critical comments on the prevailing price policy Stalin took
the "business executive and planners" to task for being poorly acquainted with the
operations of the law of value, and thus being unable to consider them in their
computations.

In defense of the preference given to heavy industry in the Five-Year Plans, Stalin
strongly objected to the view that the degree of profitability provided an acceptable
standard for planning purposes. The determination of the profitability of individual enterprises was, however, to be maintained as a significant indicator of economic efficiency.
According to bolshevist terminology, *profit* is the difference between the yield of a public
enterprise as realized at the prices fixed by the authorities and the costs of production.
Thus, as determined by the volumes of sales and reductions of costs, profits were used to
estimate the efficiency of enterprises. Until 1949 that criterion was seriously vitiated by
the tendency to leave the costs of productive factors unchanged over lengthy periods.

Minimizing the importance of the antagonism between town and country which
obviously existed in the socialist economy, Stalin declared that, according to the "law of
the necessary conformity of the productive relations with the character of the forces of
production," the property of the collective farms had to be gradually elevated to the level
of public property, and that, consequently, it was imperative to eliminate any institution
that interfered with the complete nationalization of all agricultural enterprises. In accordance with the principles of that policy, the ownership of the *Kolkhozes* (the collective
farms) was restricted to buildings, light tools, and livestock. The farms had to rent their
heavy equipment from the machine-tractor stations owned by the state. During 1951–52
large units (averaging 5,000 acres) were formed out of existing farms and unsuccessful

attempts were made to create centralized settlements, so-called *agrotowns*, for the rural population. In his *Economic Problems* Stalin minced no words in criticizing the proposal of two economists to transfer the ownership of land and machinery to the *Kolkhozes*. He used the expressions "reversion to old backwardness" and "attempts to turn back the wheel of history" to disqualify the suggested abandonment of state ownership of the means of agricultural production. In order to raise collective farm property to the "level of national property," he proposed a system according to which the state would contract in advance to barter industrial goods for the entire remaining output of the collective farms after their own requirements had been covered.

In Stalin's view, the establishment of a single, all-embracing production center was prerequisite to the advent of the "second phase of communist society," in which the distribution of labor would be regulated by the "requirements of society" and the amounts of labor spent on the production of goods would be measured—not in a round-about way, through value and its forms, but directly and immediately—by the "amount of time, the number of hours expended on the production of goods." Stalin supplemented this outlook on the future of communist society with the assertion that the disintegration of the all-embracing world market and the close economic cooperation of the Soviet Union with the "People's Democracies" would inevitably intensify the general crisis of capitalistic economies.

The voluminous textbook that was eventually prepared along the lines of Marxist-Leninist-Stalinist economics clearly reflected the principles of bolshevist reasoning. It was published in 1954 under the title *Political Economy* (a German translation prepared in East Germany appeared in 1955).[72] About half the book was filled with a discussion of the evolutionary stages that, according to the Marxian doctrine, led to the era of capitalism, and with an analysis of the capitalist economy patterned after the Marxian prototype. This analysis was supplemented by a description of the conditions of "economic imperialism" or "monopoly capitalism" characterized as the ultimate phase on the way to the inevitable breakdown of the capitalist order. But no attempts were made to replace the obsolete features of the Marxian breakdown proposition with new dialectic constructions, and no convincing arguments in favor of the breakdown proposition were derived from the distorted analysis of Western capitalism. A coexistence of socialist and capitalist economies for an indefinite duration was readily admitted, and no predictions were offered as to the probable life span of the capitalist society.

This interpretation of economic history in the light of the bolshevist doctrine was followed by a "survey of the economic teachings of the era of capitalism," which was just as closely adapted to the purposes of bolshevist "indoctrination." The discussion of socialist writings occupied a foremost place, but sharp attacks were directed against the views of "Revisionists" such as Edward Bernstein, Petr Struve, and Michael Tugan-Baranowski and against the "opportunists of the Second International," such as Karl Kautsky and Rudolf Hilferding. The Menshevists, Trotskyists, Bukharin, and his ad-herents were designated as enemies of socialism. The discussion of "modern bourgeois economics" was designed to demonstrate that the economists of the Western countries were mainly engaged in refuting the Marxian doctrine, but that the disintegration of non-Marxist social and economic sciences was advancing rapidly. It may not be amiss to observe that in their critical analysis of Western doctrines the authors of the textbooks failed to display any skill in handling dialectic procedures. Thus, their objections to the marginal utility theory were based on the irrelevant argument that the price paid for a piece of bread was the same for all purchasers, regardless of the size of their income. The Keynesian theory of interest was objected to on the ground that lacking demand for consumption goods was not due to a "mystical propensity to save" but to the increasing misery of labor. As measures proposed by Keynes for promotion employment, the textbook listed increased expenditures on armaments and other unproductive purposes.

The constructive parts of the textbook started with a discussion of the conditions that had prevailed in Russia during the transition from the capitalist order to the organization of the socialist economy, that is, its progressive industrialization, and the collectivization and mechanization of agriculture. The explanation of the "fundamental economic laws of socialism" was adjusted to the principles proclaimed by Stalin. The same was true of the analysis of commodity production and the functions to be attributed to the law of values in determining the prices of products sold in consumers' markets. Other chapters dealt with the problems of economic accounting, the organization of agricultural production and trade, national income, budgetary problems, monetary circulation, and capital accumulation. Special attention was given to the tasks involved in performing the transition to an imaginary "communist" society in which the essential distinctions between city and country would be removed, the difference between manual and intellectual labor would be eliminated, and goods would be distributed according to need. Some concluding chapters dealt with the economic organization of the European satellites and China, and with the economic cooperation of the socialist countries.

The publication of the textbook after Stalin's death occurred at a time when the Stalinist economic policies were the object of prolonged critical discussions. During the short-lived premiership of Georgi M. Malenkov, some attempts were made to establish a better balance between investment in the heavy industries on the one hand and in agriculture and consumer goods industries on the other. In practically all satellite countries, particularly in Hungary and Poland, leading members of the government acknowledged that the rate of industrialization had been out of proportion with the development of economic forces and national income. As was pointedly said in October 1953 by the premier of Poland, Boleslaw Bierut, "the problem where to place the emphasis in determining future economic developments had appeared with equal force and timeliness in all countries of the Soviet camp."[73] But the economic dislocations caused by the pressure of Stalin's policies were not solely responsible for the strikes of the Polish workers and the revolutionary upheaval in Hungary in 1956.

Also symptomatic of a general dissatisfaction with the principles of the official investment policy were the conclusions reached at a conference of Soviet economists held in 1954, intended to establish standards for determining the choice among investment alternatives. Profitability of individual enterprises was to be ignored by deciding upon the allocation of resources. Five indices were proposed for estimating the effects of labor-saving devices. Allocation of investments for individual plants was to be based on calculations of the period during which additional capital outlay could be justified by savings on current costs (recoupment period). But the concept of "economic rationality" could not be clearly defined in accordance with bolshevist reasoning. No conclusive answer was given to the problem of how to choose among processes requiring different amounts of capital, nor was it considered possible perceptibly to improve the methods of cost accounting and price determination. It is a moot question whether and to what degree large-scale misinvestments can be avoided under these conditions in preparing and carrying out the plans.[74] In a paper on capital investments in the U.S.S.R. submitted to the 1957 meeting of the American Economic Association, the Russian economist J. S. Khatchaturov, a corresponding member of the Academy of Sciences of the U.S.S.R., stated that about one-quarter of the national income was currently devoted to capital formation, but he failed to indicate how he arrived at that accumulation-consumption ratio. Instead, he discussed some general problems connected with the allocation of capital productivity and capital effectiveness, and the methods of comparing alternative projects.[75]

The advocates of the Stalinist investment policy gained the upper hand in 1955 after Nikita S. Khrushchev had secured a dominant position in the Soviet government. Malenkov had to confess that he was responsible for the deficiencies of agricultural production and that the planned increase in the production of consumption goods at the expense of the heavy industries was inconsistent with the true Party doctrine. A similar investment policy was also imposed on the satellite countries, although with varying success. In a second edition of the textbook, renewed emphasis was placed on the progress of industrialization, but the attacks on capitalism and bourgeois economics lost some of their previous acidity.

However, shortly after his coming to power, Khrushchev further constructed his position by attacking the Stalinists. A far-reaching modification of the official economic doctrine was bound to be produced by Khrushchev's violent criticisms on the authoritative position that had been assigned to Stalin and his cathedratic proclamations. At the Twentieth Party Congress, held at the beginning of 1956, at which the Stalinist legend was effectively undermined, the Soviet economists were severely criticized because of their "blind adherence to the old quotations, formulas and principles." They were also accused of misinterpreting the actual stage of capitalistic development and of being guilty of grave deficiencies in their treatment of the problems of socialist political economy. They were challenged to adopt a "creative approach" to Marxist-Leninist theory. Among the main speakers who advanced such criticisms were A. J. Mikoyan, Deputy Chairman of the Council of Ministers, and M. A. Suslov, Chairman of the Foreign Affairs Commission.

In the course of the far-reaching economic reforms initiated by Khrushchev, the agricultural policy pursued by Stalin experienced a radical modification that can perhaps best be explained by the fact that Khrushchev did not share Stalin's belief in a deep-seated antisocialist attitude of the peasantry. Although the officials of the machine-tractor stations had fulfilled important functions in controlling the political behavior of the members of the collective farms, these stations were dissolved in the spring of 1958 and the *Kolkhozes* were permitted to purchase their own equipment. Khrushchev and his followers expected a relaxation of the tensions that existed between town and country through the assignment to the collective farms of the former officials of the tractor stations.[76]

Another break with Stalinist economic policy was prompted by the determination to prevent the immobilization of industrial production by an oversized bureaucratic apparatus centralized in Moscow. Considerable discussions turned on the question of whether the existence of bottlenecks in industrial production was to be ascribed to defective planning or to inefficiencies in allocations and use of materials.[77] But the administrative reform that was introduced in May 1957 was not designed to start a process of decentralization. The dissolution of a considerable number of central economic agencies and the creation of 105 regional councils of the national economy appear to show elements of such intentions. But the decision to charge regional bodies with the supervision of the managers of the plants was accompanied by a reorganization of the Council of Ministers and the State

Planning Commission with a view to strengthening their control over production and allocation of resources. A system of checks and safeguards was established to keep the economic councils responsive to the central direction.[78]

Other more or less far-reaching modifications of Soviet economic policy that are likely to follow cannot yet be foreseen, and it is a moot question to what degree the prevailing doctrinaire approach to fundamental problems of economic organization will be modified when certain irrational features of Soviet planning are increasingly emphasized by Soviet economists, such as the distorted methods of cost accounting, the arbitrary investment policy, and the insistence on "economic growth" as the ultimate objective of planning. Representatives of a strengthened administrative and technical bureaucracy can be expected to play a leading role in the struggle over problems of "economic rationality" and its application to the organization of production and distribution.

At first, the decisions of the government which took over Stalin's dictatorship were backed by repeated assertions that they reflected full insight into the laws underlying the development of the "socialist economy." Yet the belief in such statements was shattered when the mistakes and crimes committed by Stalin were revealed in official discussions. Even the theorem of the impending breakdown of the capitalist economies—one of the pillars of Stalin's political and economic philosophy—was not maintained in its traditional rigidity, since Stalin's apparent confidence in his interpretation of the laws of dialectic materialism was not inherited by his successors. In 1958 the only members of the Soviet "Presidium" who could be called "intellectuals" were M. A. Suslov and Pyotr Pospelov, former head of the Marx-Engels Institute.[79] Hence, the development of the bolshevist economic doctrine appears to have arrived at a critical turning point, and endless inconclusive discussions about the "orthodox" interpretation of the Marxist-Leninist economic philosophy are likely to be in store. As before, the struggle between conflicting theories will probably be decided in terms of power politics.

The influence of divergent patterns of thought on economic organization can hardly be better illustrated than by contrasting the " socialist economy" of the Soviet Union with the economies of the Western democracies. Genuine or pretended belief in the sovereign power of the dialectic methods has enabled the Soviet rulers to impose a centralized scheme of planned production on the entire territory subjected to their domination, and to enforce the execution of similar schemes by the governments of the European satellites. If it had not been backed by such a belief in the power of dialectic reasoning, centralized planning would have been exposed to unending doubts and criticisms and might have proved unworkable. A similar confidence in the power of their reasoning has permitted Soviet politicians and historians to ascribe to the Russian people the role of the protagonist in a merciless fight against the capitalist order, and to charge them with the mission of bringing the blessings of communism to all parts of the world.

The use of the methods of dialectic reasoning has rendered its adherents incapable of understanding the functioning of an economic system based on individual initiative and individual planning in terms of assumptions and expectations. On the other side of the fence, Western minds are bewildered by the absurdity of dialectic reasoning, which claims to be guided by full insight into the course of evolutionary social processes. They are frightened by the development of a vast hostile economic organization based on the ruthless suppression of any individual freedom and governed by the principles of dictatorial power politics. There is no bridge to span the abyss between two irreconcilable methods of thinking.

Part IX

Hypothetical Economics

Chapter 28
Methodological Issues

GENERAL OBSERVATIONS

DURING THE FIRST decade of the interwar period, the changes in economic reasoning which took place in the Western countries affected the general approach to economic policy problems rather than the fundamental aspects of the predominant hypothetical doctrines. The traditional methods of Marshallian analysis were evidently not suited to coping with problems of large-scale economic maladjustment, especially with the devastating effects of violent inflations. Following the First World War, even superficial examinations of these effects appeared to demonstrate the futility of the attempts to arrive at an understanding of the economy without taking account of the fluctuations of the monetary and credit supply.

The logical connection thus established between alternating changes in the money supply and the behavior of the economy was reflected in a number of business cycle theories which were advanced and actively discussed during the twenties. Most noteworthy, perhaps, were various studies by the Swedish disciples of Knut Wicksell, who elaborated some of their master's suggestions; they paid special attention to the importance of the difference between expectations and their fulfillment in the field of investments and other economic transactions. Moreover, they considered it advisable to replace the prevailing conception of the economy as a system of interdependent prices with that of a system of interdependent incomes; thus they initiated a new approach to the problems connected with the stability of the economy.

Up to the middle of the thirties, theoretical pursuits of the economists centered on problems which had been inherited from the past. New problems which subsequently

415

emerged, though mainly suggested by practical considerations of economic policy, were also supported by the growing conviction that the "microeconomic" approach to equilibrium analysis, based on the behavior of individual units, had to be replaced by reasoning in terms of aggregates of economic magnitudes regarded as constitutent elements of the economic system. The laissez-faire doctrine came to an end during the world-wide Great Depression of the 1930s. In the United States, it struck like lightning out of a blue sky of prosperity. For a time, some writers claimed that the economics of the highly industrialized countries had experienced deep-seated structural modifications and had lost the elasticity required for securing uninterrupted adequate growth. Unemployment was regarded as a more or less permanent attribute of a stagnant economy, as an inevitable concomitant of a declining "propensity to consume." Hence, commercial orders by public authorities were considered necessary to maintain appropriate expansions of investment activities. At the same time, the intensified study of the problems of centralized economic planning and of "welfare economics" contributed greatly toward promoting critical examinations of almost all aspects of the exchange economy in comparison with imaginary systems of planned organization of production and distribution.

The obvious difficulties involved in devising reliable foundations for a consistent theoretical analysis of the exchange economy provided the adversaries of deductive reasoning with effective arguments in favor of the inductive realistic approach and the introduction into economic analysis of sociological concepts of relatively low degrees of abstraction. But it remained an open question whether appropriate methods could be developed for the application of inductive reasoning to economic analysis. Such attempts, however, are to be clearly distinguished from the inductive approach of the German historical school, which is couched in terms of organismic conceptions of social collectivities.

A new stage in the history of deductive economics was reached when it was quite generally realized that any further progress of economic theorizing was dependent upon the inclusion of the element of *time* among the factors that determine economic relationships. When account was taken of the "dynamic" aspects of the economy, problems connected with expectations and anticipations and their influence on economic behavior could be ignored no longer. Moreover, extensive discussions turned on the definition of the conditions of economic growth in highly industrialized as well as in underdeveloped countries.

At the same time, an increasing predilection from the application of mathematical procedures led to various attempts to construct "models" designed to explain the characteristic features of more or less unstable economies in accordance with mechanical principles. Comprehensive investigations into the development of national incomes and of productive and distributive processes served to provide material for the analysis of the behavior of specific economic aggregates. Mathematically minded economists applied statistical methods to the verification of various theorems dealing with the fluctuating behavior of the economy. The transformation of economics into a science of applied mathematics was hailed as a most promising achievement, especially by many American economists.

Under the impact of these intellectual movements, the psychological version of the marginal utility doctrine lost importance. The rigid equilibrium approach of its mathematical counterpart became increasingly untenable. Eventually, the importance attached to the mathematical formulation of economic problems resulted in a reduction of the methodological differences which had prevented the amalgamation of the various schools of marginalism. That development was facilitated by the fact that the need for a consistent economic doctrine was emphasized only by some staunch adherents of the Austrian and Wicksellian schools. In the Anglo-Saxon countries, especially in the United States, the search for such a doctrine was superseded by the search for methods suitable for dealing with specific problems. The unified approach to economic analysis which had been aimed at by preceding generations gave way to the isolated treatment of theoretical and practical questions. That approach was succinctly characterized by Prof. H. S. Ellis in the preface to a "Survey of Contemporary Economics," published in 1949. "The day of the exhaustive economic treatise," he wrote, "might have passed; its place might be taken by compendia consisting of essays on specific topics, each contributed by a specialist in his field"—"less personal, less literary and less unified, perhaps, but it is to be hoped—less intuitive, less prescinded, and no less inspiring."

METHODOLOGICAL PROBLEMS OF MARGINALISM

The adherents of the marginal utility analysis emphasized the flexibility of exchange values and derived the value of the productive factors from those of the products they helped produce. This approach was in distinct contrast to the Ricardian assumptions, which were based on the cost of production theory values. But the conception of the economy as a static network of exchange values was maintained, along with the premise that the market economy is ruled by competitive forces and that individual producers maximize profit. Thus, the Marginalists secured a firm foothold for the proposition that rational utilization of the available resources is assured by the undisturbed operation of the market economy.

After the First World War the adherents of post-Ricardian and marginalist doctrines were faced with a number of new problems, especially the task of explaining the effects of violent inflationary price movements on the real exchange economy. Moreover, the competitive order had experienced perceptible alterations. John Maynard Keynes, a keen observer of social and economic conditions, characterized these changes as the "end of laissez-faire."[1] In the writings of Hobbes, Locke, Hume, Rousseau, Paley, Smith, Bentham, and Martineau, he found the roots of the belief in the blessings of free trade and democracy. He credited economics with having supplied a sort of scientific basis for the idea of a harmony between private advantage and the public good: "To the philosophical doctrine that Government has no right to interfere, and to the divine miracle that it has no need to interfere, there is added a scientific proof that the interference is inexpedient."[2] Keynes pointed to the support lent by Darwinism to the reliance on economic laissez-faire, since, as emphasized by Herbert Spencer, the principle of the survival of the fittest could be considered a vast generalization of the Ricardian doctrine.

Pursuing his analysis of the origins and foundations of the laissez-faire doctrine, Keynes criticized some problematic assumptions which were basic to this doctrine and listed a variety of factors likely to create disproportionate developments of some sectors of the economy. He connected the end of laissez-faire with the revolutionary social movements that pervaded large parts of the European continent, and he regarded these movements as reactions to the traditional policy of encouraging and protecting the money motives of individuals. Under these conditions he recommended large-scale interference of the state and of other bodies with the functioning of the economy, especially with the manipulation of currency and credit, and with the utilization of savings.

The laissez-faire doctrine received a final death blow when the world was plunged into the devastating Great Depression of the thirties. The antidepression policies pursued in the various countries reflected only in exceptional cases the results of consistent lines of theoretical considerations. But the general abandonment of the rigid gold standard and of the deflationary policy that had been associated with it opened the way for the adoption of flexible monetary and credit policies, which proved to be effective instruments for diminishing the intensity of business fluctuations.

As Keynes explained in the thirties, traditional methods of Marshallian analysis were apparently unfit for coping with problems of large-scale economic maladjustment, especially with the devastating effects of violent inflations. Even superficial examinations of these effects appeared to demonstrate the futility of the attempts to arrive at an understanding of the economy without taking account of the fluctuations of the monetary and credit supply. By the end of the Second World War, Sir H. D. Henderson voiced a conviction shared by many Anglo-Saxon economists when he declared in a presidential address that the necessary equilibrium of aggregate demand and aggregate supply simply cannot be ensured by trusting the autonomous responses of a laissez-faire economy.[3]

The remarkable changes in the formulation of economic policy problems that occurred during the interwar period were accompanied by lively discussions of methodological issues. These discussions were initiated by representatives of the Austrian school of marginalism. Many members of that school insisted on clarifying the logical background of their doctrine, on demonstrating the inner consistency of their theorems, and on defending them against other interpretations of marginal utility analysis. An impressive survey of the achievements of the Austrian school, entitled *Wirtschaftstheorie der Gegenwart*, was published in four volumes between 1928 and 1932 in Vienna.[4] The keynote to the survey was provided by a comprehensive critical analysis of the "functional price theories" of the mathematical school. Hans Mayer, the author of this study, was professor of economics at the University of Vienna. He centered his attacks on the "unrealistic assumptions" made by Antoine Cournot, Léon Walras, Vilfredo Pareto, and Karl Gustav Cassel that utilities could be the object of direct measurements and could be subjected to the procedures of the infinitesimal calculus.[5] He questioned the Walrasian "law of the equalization of marginal utilities" and pointed to the fact that, in accordance with common experience, changes in the size of an income did not lead to the proportional distribution of the increases or declines among the same expenditures as before, but to significant modifications of the demand functions. He listed the fictions which provided the basis for the Lausanne type of equilibrium models, such as infinite divisibility and mutual substitutability of goods, perfect mobility of all economic factors, reversibility of the variable relationships assumed to exist among the economic magnitudes, and lack of distinction between dependent and independent variables. He questioned the explanatory value of these models which represented only static pictures of imaginary relationships between the elements of a system devised in accordance with outright mechanical principles. In opposition to the functional approach to economic analysis adopted by the mathematical school of Lausanne, Mayer emphasized the need to establish causal relationships between the economic factors and to analyze a wide variety of causally determined processes. Special importance was to be assigned to the element of time and to the "dynamic setting" of economic problems. In another connection Mayer ridiculed the conception of cyclical fluctuations of business activity as "disturbances" of the economy.[6]

The introduction of the time element into economic analysis implied a fundamental modification of the traditional Walrasian assumptions that the mutual effects of changes in prices, demand, and supply operate simultaneously and in the same direction.[7] It was obvious that the marginal utility of a changing volume of goods related to several periods of want satisfaction differs conspicuously from the marginal utility of the same volume related to a single period.[8] Time coefficients varying in length were taken into account by some disciples of Alfred Marshall who studied partial equilibrium situations of specific markets. They considered the movement toward new equilibrium positions assured on the assumption that demand developed at exactly the same rate as supply.[9]

The search for causal relationships between the elements of the economy was incompatible with the strict interdependence attributed by the mathematical economists to the constituent elements of their models. They insisted upon using exclusively "pure hypothesis not subject to change" and qualified as "intuitional" any attempts of "synthetic" economics to take account of assumptions conditioned by the "analysis of interpolated trends, ex-ante collective propensities to save and to invest, discounted profit rates," and the like.[10]

In defense of this methodology, Pareto argued that a system of practically complete divisibility of goods and of virtually uninterrupted scales of utility functions could be established, provided that detailed statistical data could be made available for very large numbers of economic units.[11] But even when it was conceded that, at least theoretically, finite want satisfactions could be transformed into infinitely small ones, there remained the objection that mathematical procedures could not take account of qualitative differences between psychical magnitudes of different intensities. In order to clarify these problems, the Austrian economists drew a distinction between the "logical rationality" of the indirect measurement of marginal utilities and the "empirical rationality" of measurement.[12] But there was no logical bridge from one type of rationality to the other.

The sterility of the rigid mathematical approach to economic analysis was due, at least in part, to the strict observance of the principle that the construction of systems of interdependent variables is incompatible with any attempt to isolate, for purposes of economic analysis, the relationship between specific variables included in the equilibrium model. Alfred Marshall had considered such isolating procedures justifiable, when the effects of variations on the system as a whole were indirect, of relatively small intensity, and remote in time. (A similar view was expressed by Schumpeter in his analysis of disturbances of equilibrium conditions in *Wesen und Hauptinhalt.*) But other economists of mathematical persuasion, such as Francis Ysidro Edgeworth and Enrico Barone, did not object to the procedure of isolating certain relationships.[13] Henry Schultz argued that in practice only a small advantage was gained when account was taken of more than the first few variables which were clearly associated with a demand function.[14] The Polish economist Oskar Lange proposed to select a "criterion of relevancy" as a first step in developing the methods of isolation.[15] This criterion was to be based on a definition, in quantitative terms, of the border line between irrelevant variations and variations assumed to be relevant. But this problem does not appear to have found a satisfactory solution.

In his controversy with Pareto, the Italian philosopher Benedetto Croce raised fundamental objections to the assumption that economic relations, resulting from purposive actions, could be reduced to mechanical processes[16] and could be treated by the same methods applicable to the movements of physical bodies. The establishment of a system of economic magnitudes that could be made determinate by simplifying assumptions and could be adjusted to the requirements of equilibrium analysis was basic to the mechanical approach to economic analysis. Paramount among such assumptions was the concept of "economic man" equipped with perfect knowledge of the market conditions. But this conception was shown to be untenable, since the general exercise of such foresight was bound to result in indeindeterminate solutions.[17] In discussing the application of purely mechanical principles to the analysis of conscious or reflective human actions, Friedrich A. Hayek characterized such methodology as "scientism."[18]

Hayek contended, moreover, that the application of the equilibrium concept to economic analysis was based on the assumption that the equilibrating tendencies were produced by combined human actions, the motives of which were entirely independent of each other. From this premise he concluded that the traditional equilibrium concept was predicated on the establishment of a balance between the results of mutually independent economic actions, based on the mutual compatibility of individual economic plans, and, furthermore, on the condition that no alterations of these plans would occur in the course of their execution.[19] These assumptions, however, were incompatible with the fact that in the course of economic processes, anticipations are continuously adjusted to changing market conditions. Hence, he stated, equilibrium positions could be expected to exist only during very short periods.[20] In the light of these deliberations the fictional nature of the traditional equilibrium analysis became quite apparent.

The Austrian economists were themselves faced with the task of defending their epistemological principles against a considerable array of adverse criticism, especially against the view that their theories were ultimately derived from the preconceptions of the utilitarian philosophy and that the very concept of value was indicative of the "normative ambitions of the economists."[21] Moreover, adherents of the materialistic interpretation of history raised the question of whether the theories of choice and of equalizing marginal utilities really led into the center of economic activity under any social conditions what-soever.[22] Finally, some critics objected to the Austrian school's relatively extensive use of the *ceteris paribus* clause.

The logical problems involved in establishing the Austrian doctrine were carefully analyzed by Alfred Amonn as early as 1911, and again in 1927, in a revised edition of his treatise on economic theory.[23] Amonn drew a distinction between the object of cognition, conceived of as the abstract product of isolating mental processes which are to be adapted to the purposes of scientific analysis. The fundamental problem of the degree to which the laws of human reasoning correspond to the laws underlying the behavior of the phe-nomena loomed in the background of this discussion. It was also alluded to by the Austrian economist Richard Strigl, who undertook to define the logical aspects of the "economic categories," those hypothetical concepts from which the theoretical laws can be derived by deductive reasoning.[24] The "economic data" that Strigl distinguished from the categories were characterized as economic magnitudes or other factors that are related to historical, social, psychological, and political conditions and are assumed to be given. To the degree that relations between certain of the data can be assumed to be invariable, the functioning of the economy can be made the object of exact analysis; hence the importance attached to the existence of such invariable relations.

These studies were supplemented by an essay by Lionel Robbins, of the London School of Economics, which aroused considerable attention.[25] Endeavoring to eliminate from economic analysis the last vestiges of the substance concept of goods and any reference to normative ideas, Robbins protested against all attempts to claim "scientific" validity for procedures which cannot be justified or refuted by appeal to "laboratory methods."[26] He rejected any reference to the materialistic interpretation of history as "sheer metaphysics," and he proclaimed as the leading principle of economic analysis the proposition that economic problems in the strict sense arise only when the attainment of one set of ends involves the sacrifice of others. He conceived of economics along Austrian lines, as a series of deductions from the fundamental concept of scarcity of time and material, and restricted the scope of economic theory to the analysis of the relationships between ends and scarce means as expressed in the forms of exchange.[27] Thus, he excluded from the scope of his theory the search for the psychological explanation of economic behavior, and the investigations into the causes of material welfare and into techniques of production, quoting Mayer's dictum that problems of technique are given when there is one end and a multiplicity of means, and that economic problems arise when both ends and means are multiple.[28]

Robbins agreed with the leading representatives of the Austrian school that measurability and interpersonal comparability of utilities are incompatible with the results of experience and that the existence of a price system expressed in monetary terms is prerequisite to the measurement of economic magnitudes. For the traditional division of economics into a theory of production and a theory of distribution he substituted a distinction between a theory of equilibrium and a theory of variations. He assigned to the equilibrium theory the task of defining the conditions under which the interdependent but conceptually discrete relationships between men and goods are constant, and the related task of dealing with the changes in the distribution of goods resulting from the operation of equilibrating forces. To the theory of variations he allotted the problems connected with changes in a given economic structure and corresponding changes in equilibrium positions. Continuous improvement and extension of the available analytical apparatus could be expected from procedures designed to "try out pure theory on concrete situations" and to refer residual difficulties back to pure theory. Since Robbins was convinced that generally valid theoretical propositions could be arrived at only by deductive procedures based on clearly defined, highly abstract concepts, he objected to the search for empirical "quantitative laws." Such laws, he argued, were merely derived from the correlation of trends, the combined results of a great diversity of phenomena occurring under the influence of many heterogeneous factors.[29]

Robbins's attempt to clarify the logical foundations of economics as a "pure science" was heartily welcomed by many members of the Austrian school who adhered to the rigid principles of nominalistic reasoning and believed that his definition of the scope and methods of economics could be accepted by all economists, regardless of their political convictions. The conception of economics defined by Robbins as a system of exchange values was endorsed by Amonn and shared by Gaëtan Pitou.[30]

Critics of marginal utility analysis, however, objected to some fundamental concepts introduced by the Austrian school, such as "individual rationality," "exogenous changes," "plurality of unspecified ends," and the like.[31] Moreover, they protested against the definition of economics as a science the scope of which was restricted to the analysis of ends-means relationships. Advocates of Marshallian teachings argued that the economist could exercise no advisory functions unless his studies were governed by certain normative principles concerning the distribution of productive resources. Ray F. Harrod did not question the validity of the marginal utility principle, but he believed that too much importance had been attached to the general theory of value and too little to the maxim that productive resources should be so distributed as to yield equimaximal social net products. He proposed to divide economics into two parts: one dealing with value and distribution and the other dealing with the application of that maxim.[32] Howard S. Ellis suggested that one end must be stipulated by economics itself, namely, the "freedom of the individual to make the best of his situation."[33]

Nor was agreement reached on the fundamental problem of how to define the nature of the "economic laws." In accordance with the methodological principles of Carl Menger, Robbins insisted that general laws of a hypothetical type had to be derived from assumptions based on simple and indisputable facts of experience.[34] But the picture of the economy that resulted from such assumptions was in no way intended to correspond to reality and could not be verified in the light of actual experience. This position was strongly supported by various representatives of the Austrian school, especially by Hayek and Ludwig von Mises.[35] In a later study, Mises drew a distinction between "praxeology," or the science of human action, and "catallactics," the science dealing with the phenomena of the market. Underlying his analysis was the methodological principle that the ultimate yardstick of an economic theorem's correctness or incorrectness is solely reason, unaided by experience. Accordingly, Mises insisted that certain propositions of praxeology are self-evident and universally true, implied in the very existence of human action, a priori in nature, like the propositions of mathematics and logic, hence "conveying exact and precise knowledge." He expressed with equal vigor his conviction that the functioning of the catallactic economy is ruled by the principle of "rational calculation" when the competitive forces are permitted to operate freely in the markets.[36] The main argument advanced in support of the axiomatic character of these principles was the proposition that those who deny their validity qualify human behavior as inconsistent or instinctive or strictly traditional, lacking rational characteristics. This argument was modified by Oskar Lange. Motivated by socialist tendencies, Lange proposed a distinction between "private" and "social" rationality.[37] Social rationality opened the door to state planning and the attenuation of certain forms of private decision making.

The Austrian argument about the logical premise of economic laws was, of course, irreconcilable with the empirical approach to economic analysis. T. W. Hutchinson, a convinced adherent of the empirical approach, elaborated the view that in the course of time nearly every deductive proposition of economic theory had been shown to be a tautology and that such propositions, by themselves, have no prognostic value or causal significance and cannot provide scientific knowledge since they can never conceivably be shown to be true or false.[38] The authors who insisted upon the hypothetical nature of economic laws had to defend the results of their deductive reasoning against the argument that their theories could not be tested in the light of experience and could not be used for purposes of prediction.

An attitude closer to that of the Austrians was adopted by Frank H. Knight, who argued that Hutchinson's methodology drew an artificial distinction between propositions that can be tested in the light of experience and "vague conceptions of common sense."[39] Knight flatly rejected the proposition that there could be a real contrast between the fundamental laws of nature and those of the human mind. In his view, economics in the usual meaning, as a science of principles, was not primarily a descriptive science in the empirical sense at all. Hence, he proposed to derive the principles of economics from certain assumptions that, describing an ideal, are unverifiable by any empirical procedure but are so devised that their "hypothetical validity" can be confirmed by a "community of discourse" composed of competent and trustworthy "observers of facts which are common to the experience of reasonable men." Among these "rational basic" assumptions Knight included the basic notion of marginalism about the "ideal apportionment which under given conditions would achieve the general end in a maximum degree."[40] In another connection Knight pointed to the existence of ideas that are not only "real to the individual" but "sufficiently uniform and objective to form a useful standard of comparison for a given country at a given time."[41]

The definition of the logical nature of the marginal utility principle was closely connected with the outcome of the epistemological discussions. Any attempts to use utilitarian arguments to justify this principle were repudiated by practically all adherents of the Austrian school. The psychological approach to marginalism, adopted by Friedrich von Wieser, requested the student of economics to rely on "introspection" as a method, providing an empirical basis for the postulate of "intrinsic rationality," that is, for a principle that connects means and ends and enables the individual to maximize his utility. This formulation of the marginal utility principle was endorsed not only by many members of the Austrian school but also by English economists such as Robbins and Harrod. Harrod suggested that the law of diminishing returns was based on an experience broad enough to be taken as an axiom of the highest possible degree of empirical probability.[42] An apparently effective argument in favor of that interpretation of the postulate was the consideration that, unless it was adopted, human behavior lost its rational characteristics and was to be qualified as inconsistent, instinctive, or strictly traditional.[43]

It was obvious that the principle of intrinsic rationality was falsifiable when observation was relied upon to justify its validity and when choices from among economic alternatives were found to be suggested by "irrational motives such as habit, temptation, ignorance, self-abnegation, auto-suggestion, reasoning in terms of symbols and the like."[44] Knight asserted categorically that it was not possible by any observation to tell whether or in what degree any act was "economic," that is, consistent with the general rules of allocating scarce means among alternatives uses.[45]

Under these conditions some adherents of Menger's methodology decided to renounce any attempt to provide an empirical basis of "rational behavior." They identified "rational behavior" with the choices *actually made* among alternative economic actions. This proposition implied that economic conduct of any kind was declared by definition to be rational and sensible. It was endorsed by Ludwig von Mises, Hano Bernardelli, and Friedrich A. Hayek, who spoke of the "pure logic of choice."[46] The English economist John R. Hicks asserted that marginal utility analysis had been reduced to a general theory of choice which is applicable whenever the choice is between alternatives that are capable of quantitative expression.[47] However, when the search for an empirical basis of the principle of economic rationality was abandoned, the Austrian Marginalists were faced with the argument that one of the main premises of their deductive science was nothing but an analytical hypothetical generalization. Economists of empiricist persuasion qualified as a "pointless tautology" the so-called law of motivation according to which people are assumed to dispose of their resources in the most rational way.[48]

The "law of motivation" could also be formulated as a sort of economic imperative, a precept to adjust economic behavior to rational principles. Thus, according to the American economist John M. Clark, one has to assume that the individual has a scale of values or preferences, that his various economic acts are the expression of this one scale of values, and that the values in his personal economy reach an equilibrium. In interpreting this proposition Clark argued that it can be expressed either as an actual tendency or as an ideal of good management and can have sufficient truth to justify its place in a static economy, being itself a static assumption.[49]

Joseph Schumpeter resorted to the expedient of declaring the principles of marginal

utility analysis useful instruments of deductive reasoning. Felix Kaufmann, who examined the issues involved in the controversy, concluded that it was inappropriate on the one
hand to claim a priori validity for the so-called law of motivation and on the other to make
its validity dependent on the existence of certain conditions. He proposed to regard the
principle of marginal utility as an "heuristic" postulate and spoke of "rules of procedure" which remain accepted as long as they have "heuristic value."[50]

The discussion of the "postulational structure of economic theories" was continued
by the American economist Milton Friedman, who requested that theoretical generalizations be so devised as to fit as fully and comprehensively as possible a set of related facts
about the real world.[51] But that requirement was faced with the argument that it is rarely
possible to use for economic analysis the simple method of moving directly back and forth
between reality and theory; strict observance of the requirement would permit the economist to analyze only past situations or developments, leaving to the economic politician
the task of deciding how relevant the description might be to other situations.[52]

J. G. Koopmans dealt with these fundamental methodological problems in an essay
in which he criticized Friedman's theorem that the "realism" of the assumptions underlying a theory is entirely irrelevant, that the validity of a theory is to be tested solely by its
predictions with respect to a given class of phenomena.[53] Koopmans insisted that the
postulates of an economic theory are not self-evident and that the implications of various
sets of postulates cannot be readily tested by observation. But he was convinced that the
knowledge supplied by deductions from some economic postulates is the best we have.

A similar position was defended by Fritz Machlup.[54] He advocated the use of
deductive methods even though their results cannot be verified and even though it is not
possible to check the fulfillment of all the conditions stipulated in the postulational
system. Even events that are recurrent features of economic life rarely recur under the
same conditions. In other words, the phenomena to which hypothetical laws refer can be
observed only in the full context of unique events from which they cannot be isolated.[55]
The results of these and similar discussions can be summed up in the statement that the
leading propositions of pure theory were interpreted alternatively as basic postulates of
economic conduct, as fundamental assumptions of evident empirical validity, as axiomatic truths inherent in the rationality of human thinking, and as logical inferences from
useful tools of analysis.

Empirical laws, established by observing and collecting facts, are considered verifiable to the extent that they were not formulated in terms of the *ceteris paribus* clause.
Attempts to devise some verifiable economic laws, strictly limited as to time and space,
have been facilitated by elaborating statistical methods applied to the study of sequences
and coexistence of real phenomena.[56] The study of such "sequences and coexistence" of
the real phenomena depicted in the statistical records was pointed to as a promising
method of establishing verifiable laws, especially "historical propositions, strictly limited
as to time and space." With the development of econometric methods and the increasing
emphasis placed on the use of "operational" concepts after the Second World War, the
debate over the interpretation of the postulates of "pure theory" lost much of its
importance.

INSTITUTIONALIST DISCUSSIONS

The logical problems which perturbed the minds of the adversaries of post-Ricardian
economics can hardly be better illustrated than by surveying the views of a number of

young American authors who, after the end of the First World War, stood up in arms against the predominant economic doctrines of their day. They represented a movement of dissent, and had a certain atmosphere of "sectarianism" which is concomitant of such movements. Thorstein Veblen's fragmentary and poorly coordinated sociological ideas provided them with some of their main slogans.[57] His interpretation of the existing capitalist society as the evanescent phase of an evolutionary process greatly appealed to their iconoclastic minds. They were equally impressed by the deterministic features of his social philosophy, which gave to his teachings the aspects of a consistent approach to economic analysis. They enjoyed his criticism of equilibrium analysis; their aversion to the psychological foundations of marginal utility analysis was intensified by their belief in the principles of the behaviorist philosophy. Indeed, their opposition to marginalism had "about it the general cast of a theological controversy."[58]

In accordance with the teachings of "pragmatism," these opponents of post-Ricardian economics derived the criteria for the validity of a general proposition from observation and experience and rejected the formulation of such propositions in terms of highly abstract concepts.[59] United more by the negative aspects of Veblen's teachings than by his economic philosophy, they nevertheless accepted the term *Institutionalism* to assert their adherence to a vaguely conceived scientific movement. This term was designed to point to the need to connect the study of economic relationships and developments with that of "institutions," which were defined by Veblen as "any habit of action and thought widely current in an economic group." But no agreement was reached on a clear meaning of the concept of "institutions." Some adherents of Institutionalism followed Veblen in emphasizing the "ceremonial character" as a specific characteristic of "institutions." Others stressed the sociological aspects of their approach to economic analysis and adopted John R. Commons's definition, which implied control of individual action by "collective action."[60]

The methodological problems which occupied the leading members of the group were discussed with intense interest in a number of "symposiums" published during the twenties. In a collection of essays he edited in 1924, R. G. Tugwell complained of the "bad metaphysical odor of economics that only a rebuilding from the ground could dissipate."[61] Violent protests were very common against the use of high abstractions, the psychological foundations of marginalism, the subtleties of the value theory, and the static approach adopted by equilibrium analysis. But an amazing difference of views existed on the question of the degree to which the pragmatic philosophy and a behaviorist psychology were likely to supply adequate bases for economic analysis. Under the influence of Veblen's sociological teachings some Institutionalists emphasized instincts as the motivating forces of human behavior, in contrast to the Ricardians who had attached importance to the principle of rationality and to free competition as the "natural form of economic organization." The capitalist order was characterized as a "tangled thing" which contemporary schoolmen had intellectualized into a purposive and self-regulating instrument of general welfare.[62] Other adherents of the movement elaborated the idea that "cultural lags" or actual changes in behavior were poorly coordinated with evolutionary changes in institutions.[63] Considerations of this kind were combined with the idea that it was necessary to apply appropriate measures of social control based on "sociological principles."[64]

An extreme wing of the group was formed by authors who strongly objected to the identification of science with the use of quantifying methods. They centered their proposals on the elaboration of welfare economics backed by a "scientific" behaviorist psychology and "objectively scientific norms."[65] Tugwell believed that the economy was unable to digest the full effects of the accumulating technological improvements, and that the organization of business activity was unfit for securing continuous demand schedules of adequate size. Hence, he proposed to develop a theory of "mature capitalism" and a program of "social management" based on "constructive administration" and "national economic planning."[66] Sumner H. Slichter supported Tugwell's idea of concentrating economic research on the problems connected with the efficiency of free enterprise to fulfill its functions.[67]

Other, more conservative, authors conceded the need for quantitative research and requested the inclusion of data "derived from experience" among the assumptions made basic to the construction of economic models.[68] John M. Clark started his essay "Socializing of Theoretical Economics" from the sociological elements of Veblen's teachings and pointed to the limitation of the canons of scientific adequacy by the available material and the methods of research. Surveying the wide variety of economic axioms and theorems, he suggested that the origin of economic conceptions be connected with specific economic situations. In an essay published a few years later, Clark advanced the idea of substituting a framework dealing with processes which do not visibly tend to reach any complete and definable static equilibrium for equilibrium models of the economy.[69]

F. C. Mills and Wesley C. Mitchell advocated statistical analysis as the only appropriate method of economic research. Elaborating some suggestions of Joseph Royce, Mills contrasted "statistical" knowledge with "historical" and "mechanical" knowledge, and qualified the concepts of average, approximation, and probability as indispensable elements of statistical analysis. To these concepts he opposed the notions of invariant mechanical laws, of causal relationships, and of complete certainty, which, in his view, had their origin in the necessities of our thinking rather than in results of our perception.[70]

Pursuing this line of thought, Mills proposed to substitute the distinction between "rational" and "statistical" laws for the juxtaposition of hypothetical and empirical laws. He characterized the *ceteris paribus* clause as a subterfuge which had been used to cover up the fact that the relations between economic phenomena are not constant but rather are relations of partial dependence in which the element of probability bulks large. Yet he conceded that an initial "a priori probability" in favor of a given conclusion is prerequisite to the application of statistical methods in economic research. The question of whether the term *tendency* has an essentially statistical connotation was left unanswered.[71]

In his contribution to *The Trend of Economics*, W. C. Mitchell wholeheartedly supported the Veblenian attacks on the Ricardian assumptions concerning the motives of economic behavior.[72] He requested economists to adjust these assumptions to the result of studies starting from the "original nature of man" and its subsequent modifications. In his view, problems surrounding the theory of production were the primary object of quantitative analysis.

Last but not least, Knight's closely reasoned paper "Limitations of Scientific Methods in Economics" may be mentioned. Knight did not share the enthusiasm displayed by other "Institutionalists" for behaviorist psychology and the theories of instincts, since he considered consciousness an indispensable element of psychological analysis. In another connection, he qualified the "vogue of behaviorism" as a dogmatic repudiation of everything properly to be called psychology; the ultimate result of the application of behaviorism to economics, he argued, would be to confine this science to commodity statistics. Knight criticized as utterly inadequate the traditional use of the price mechanism for analyzing economic interaction and coordination. He insisted upon replacing this method with a study of the "laws of motion," the "kinetics" of economic changes, and with a study of wants conceived of as dependent variables that are caused and formed by economic activity.[73]

The attempts of the institutionalist economists to develop a new methodological approach to economic analysis were sarcastically described by John M. Clark. In an essay that he contributed to a symposium in 1927, he outlined the diversity of methods applied to the analysis of economics.[74] Some of these authors, Clark argued, expect their science to be genetic, evolutionary, Darwinian, fit for tracing laws of cumulative change in human institutions; others want their science to be mathematical in language, but are opposed by those who reject any measurement of welfare in terms of prices and request the adjustment of economic analysis to normative principles established independently of considerations of economic rationality. Finally, he said, authors who insist on the observation of facts as the starting point of economic research are guided by the illusory hope of developing a "sound inductive" theory.[75]

A vaguely formulated "economic interpretation of history"—supported by slogans such as "wave of the future" and by illusions such as the concept of "cultural lag"—was used by some adherents of Veblenism to demonstrate that dangerous social frictions resulted from the contrast between a rapidly changing industrial technology and a slowly changing sociopolitical order, and that the country was faced with the inevitable transformation of the economy into a planned economic mechanism.[76] A search for social tensions and their possible economic causes was a characteristic feature of the reasoning of almost all the Institutionalists.

The Great Depression of the thirties appeared to corroborate the view of those who were convinced that the expansion of the American economy—perhaps even the expansion of the world economy—had reached frontiers which put an end to the prospect of any lasting recovery. They dwelt upon the restrictions of competition which appeared to permeate the American industry, and emphasized the effects of corporate market control on employment and allocation of resources. Many members of the institutionalist movement participated in the official investigations organized by the Temporary National Economic Committees. Several of the measures they proposed were made constituent parts of the New Deal Policy pursued by the Roosevelt Administration. They were hardly aware of the fact that their enthusiasm for government control of the industry sharply contrasted with Veblen's convictions.[77]

Some well-trained adherents of the movement, such as Gardiner C. Means and members of the National Planning Association suggested a "theory of the developing system of the American economy."[78] A comprehensive, rather conservative program of "democratic gradualism," advanced by J. M. Clark, was designed to adjust the expansion of the capital goods industries as far as possible to changes in consumers' demands.[79] But some radical apostles of Institutionalism proposed an extension of public control to all key industries in which monopolistic situations were found to exist and suggested vague programs of "collective economic management" and "economic planning." They supported such proposals with the argument that in the modern economy only two functions were important enough to require remuneration, namely, working and risk taking, but that the functions of risk taking could be considerably reduced by public regulation of productive activities and ensuing stabilization of economic life.[80]

A special position was occupied by the disciples of John R. Commons who interpreted the functioning of the economy in terms of an interplay of advancing technology and a more or less rigid legal framework of the social institutions. According to Commons, a main task of economics consisted in determining the "reasonableness of the working rules" underlying the general economic order in an age in which citizens, corporations, and labor unions have economic power.[81] Hence, his followers centered their studies on the partly conflicting, partly cooperative forces which they regarded as the constituent elements of the economic organization. The conditions of the labor market provided a large field for studies of this type which were perhaps prompted by the "unrecognized premise" to regard coercion, not competition, as the predominant factor in economic life.[82]

One distinguished American scholar has spoken of four academic generations of economists "lost" between 1924 and 1936 because their interests were directed to the study of current institutional practices and their sociological appraisal of economic institutions was misled by egalitarian tendencies.[83]

The search for general economic laws was completely displaced by inductive analyses of specific institutional aspects of the American economy, such as "monopoly capitalism" conceived of as the outcome of material and technological advancement.[84]

Toward the end of the thirties the institutionalist movement lost the attraction it had exercised for almost twenty years on several generations of American economists. Many members of the movement, disappointed by the apparent sterility of the inductive methods, seized the opportunity provided by the teachings of Keynes to endorse a promising new approach to economic analysis, an approach hailed as a radical departure from post-Ricardian economics, which had no use for the theorems of marginalism and supplied strong support for far-reaching intervention in the functioning of the economy. As viewed from the institutionalist angle, the Keynesian theory of employment implied that the "growth of the heritage of improvement was impeded by a feudally conditioned propensity to consume." This situation was to be remedied by altering the flow of income and by "planning" the realization of the social heritage.[85] At the same time, econometric studies, making increasing use of statistical material, were regarded as attempts to take account of the full complexity of economic reality.[86]

Veblenian ideas were kept alive by some teachers of economics who were motivated by the prospect of establishing a unified theory of human behavior, social structure, and cultural developments. They introduced principles of Darwinian evolution into their analyses, combined this method with sociological research,[87] assigned to technological problems a conspicuous place in their conception of a new science of economics, and emphasized their responsibility "to look beyond methodological convenience to the larger issues which unfortunately as yet defy precise scientific handling."[88]

As applied to the study of evolutionary social processes, the reasoning of this school led to the elaboration of a sociological scheme according to which the American society was outgrowing a phase in which the quest for the mastery by the individual of his environment had provided the prevailing goal.[89] These goals were said to be gradually displaced by the recognition of the "group's expectations" as the predominant principle. A far-reaching transformation of the capitalist economy in all its sectors was held to be associated with this radical change of the traditional value attitudes.

The view that the treatment of economic problems is incomplete unless account is taken of their sociological setting was also advocated by various American economists who were not influenced by the institutionalist movements.[90] These economists emphasized the connection between specific value attitudes and the ultimate ends pursued in a given society; they studied the measures adopted for achieving these ends. Discarding the thesis of the "randomness of wants," endorsed by the Utilitarian economists, they insisted that the effective functioning of an economic and social organization is conditioned by pursuing ends compatible with harmonious value orientation and with the available resources. The consideration that existence and functioning of a social collectivity is dependent upon the prevalence of a common system of ends was held to provide sufficient arguments for regarding such a collectivity as a "unity" and "reality sui generis." Some elements of organismic reasoning were thus introduced into this type of sociological analysis.

In addition, significant associations between economic and sociological problems were elaborated in studies dealing with the emergence of specific societies and the conditions of their stability, in investigations dealing with the development of technology, capital accumulation, social and "antisocial" forms of acquisition, and the like. The quest for individual security and stability and the desire for "status" and power, as determined by specific value attitudes, were analyzed with regard to their economic repercussions and their connection with the problems treated by welfare economics. Research of this type received additional incentives through the emergence of the complex problems connected with the promotion of economic growth in territories where the prevailing value systems conspicuously differ from those which dominate the economic reasoning of Western industrialized countries.

METHODOLOGICAL DISCUSSIONS OF FRENCH ECONOMISTS

A survey of methodological principles adopted by leading French economists after the First World War reveals a great variety of conflicting views which can perhaps conveniently be grouped around the traditional juxtaposition of deductive and inductive methods of economic analysis. The Ricardian conception of the economy as a mechanism governed by equilibrating tendencies of the economic forces and the practical consequences derived from this conception were defended by a very limited number of French economists. Neomarginalism found some outstanding adherents, and the same was true of the *school of Lausanne*. However, mathematical economics were rejected by a considerable group of leading French economists, convinced advocates of inductive methods. An important school was formed by followers of the sociologist Emile Durkheim; they applied the master's "positive" methodological principles. The need to introduce sociological considerations into economic analysis was emphasized by authors of socioeconomic studies who derived their arguments against high abstractions and deductive reasoning from Auguste Comte. These authors made use of Comte's epistemology, his insistence on the use of procedures, and his conception of economics as an integrated part of sociology. A separate place was occupied by various Marxists, convinced partisans of dialectic reasoning.

The most remarkable contribution to the neo-Ricardian approach to economics was Jacques Rueff's impressive volume dealing with the social order.[91] Starting from a discussion of the behavior of prices, Rueff applied the principles of equilibrium analysis to the construction of a real exchange system, on the assumption that the institution of the private ownership of the means of production is prerequisite to the functioning of economic laws of the mechanical type. He supplemented his analysis of the real exchange system with an elaborate discussion of the dynamic effects of expansions and contractions of the means of payment and endeavored to demonstrate that "true rights" are guaranteed to the members of an economic community only when prices are permitted freely to adjust themselves to equilibrium positions. With civilizations characterized by the prevalence of such "true rights" he contrasted others in which individual rights were "vitiated" by the exercise of price control and the ensuing economic disorder. Combining this theoretical analysis with far-reaching political considerations, Rueff identified "price control" as the first step on the way to the establishment of a totalitarian regime. But in spite of his outspoken preference for the competitive exchange economy, he conceded that a system of "true rights," respected by the government, could also exist under a socialist order if the functioning of a free price system were safeguarded by the observance of sound principles of monetary and financial policies.[92]

"Neomarginalism," a version of the Austrian doctrine, found its most convinced and consistent French defender in François Perroux.[93] But Perroux's point of view met with the usual well-known objections, voiced by Jean Marchal, Bertrand Nogaro, and others, that marginal utility analysis does not account for the prices of the productive factors and for the value of money; that it is impossible to establish for each individual a scale of utilities; that subjective values are strongly influenced by institutional factors; and that the concept of "averages" prevails over marginalist concepts in the spheres of administered prices, wage fixing, price differentiation, and so on.[94] He strongly objected to the exaggerated use that he believed was made by the deductive method in formulating the leading economic doctrines, and considered it the main task of the economist to determine the human action behind economic phenomena and to analyze specific historically determined facts. Perroux recognized the limits of the theory of marginalism, but he insisted upon maintaining this theory as the only available general foundation of economics until it might be possible to replace it by another better adjusted to the "dynamics" of the human mind.

The Paretian conception of economics as "applied mathematics" was mainly advocated by some engineers and trained mathematicians. They considered the rigid interdependence of all economic magnitudes as an irrefutable argument in favor of the functional approach to economic theorizing and regarded equilibrium analysis of the Paretian type as an ideal demonstration of the principles underlying the optimum allocation of the available economic resources.[95] In a more cautious formulation of the principles of Walrasian economics, Maurice Fréchet defined the boundaries set to their application by the exercise of free will and the play of chances.[96] But he contested the view that the use of mathematical methods is incompatible with the treatment of the time element.

Adopting a defensive position, Firmin Oulès, a successor of Walras in the chair of economics at Lausanne, endeavored to demonstrate that rigorous application of the equilibrium concept and of the principle of the general interdependence of prices was the outstanding feature of the Walrasian system, and that the discovery, elaboration, and perfection of the Walrasian theories had been achieved independently of the use of mathematics.[97]

The adversaries of the school of Lausanne concentrated their attacks on the purely hypothetical features of the Walrasian and Paretian models; they insisted on the search for causal instead of functional relationships between economic magnitudes. They criticized the tendency of the mathematicians to substitute "scientific pseudodemonstrations" for the treatment of fundamental problems such as the formation of prices, and they assigned the carefully equilibrated Paretian models to the realm of esthetics rather than to the sphere of scientific economics.[98]

The convinced adherents of the inductive method of economic research adopted a radical position. Bertrand Nogaro considered it the main task of the economist to determine the human action behind the economic phenomena and to analyze specific historically determined facts.[99]

Gaëtan Pirou, another leading teacher of economics, attempted to reconcile the use of "positive" methods with the application of equilibrium analysis. He suggested that the antagonism to deductive reasoning was mainly motivated by the belief that economic theorems had to be verified by observation and experience. He proposed to continue equilibrium analysis at least as long as a reconstruction of economics on the lines of positivist methodologies was still in the stages of partial analyses and fragmentary verities.[100]

The economists who derived their methodological views from sociologist Dürkheim's teachings accepted his principles that society is an emergent "psychical" (but not psychological) "reality," that social facts are external to the individual, but that a "social determination" of human behavior is imposed by the value system that prevails in the society.[101] The term *conscience collective* (or *group mind*) was Dürkheim's expression to emphasize the idea that the individual exists only within and by virtue of the group of which he is a member. This line of analysis was continued by M. Mauss and others of Dürkheim's disciples, who went far toward demonstrating the influence exercised upon the organization of economic life by religious creeds and other nonmaterial factors.

This conception of a society unified by mental factors was hardly compatible with the choice of marginal utility analysis as the starting point for economic theories. The main economic phenomena that provided material for Dürkheim's sociological investigations were the division of labor in society and the relations between economic institutions on the one hand and elementary forms of religious life on the other. A characteristic feature of Dürkheim's technique was the method of "concomitant variations," which can be used to compare cases in which two phenomena are simultaneously present or absent.[102] But Dürkheim's categories of social organization, though allegedly derived from observation, appear to have been rather categories of a Cartesian type; they are unsuitable to provide the background for an empirical theory of social change.[103]

François Simiand, one of the most distinguished of Dürkheim's disciples, undertook to elaborate methods of "positive" economic analysis in the light of the master's teachings.[104] He found that the traditional methods of economic research were vitiated by the importance attached to teleological factors of the type associated with end-means relationships. He qualified even the use of the equilibrium concept as an attempt to introduce economico-political considerations into the study of economic phenomena. Another object of his criticism was the method of isolating economic analysis, which implied that economic behavior, ruled by the profit motive in a competitive exchange system, could be assumed to operate independently of the influence of any other social factors. Hence, he proposed to establish a science termed *economic sociology* and designed to determine causal relationships between well-circumscribed ranges of economic phenomena and concomitant social events or developments.

Simiand's economic sociology is not to be confounded with a discipline suggested by various members of the German historical school and bearing a similar name. But in spite of conspicuous methodological differences, the two disciplines had this much in common—their theoretical findings were held to be strictly conditioned by the circumstances prevailing at a given time under the rule of a given civilization. Time series of statistical magnitudes provided the material for this "experimental" approach to economic analysis, which Simiand applied especially to a study of the development of wages as influenced on the one hand by gold discoveries and credit expansions and on the other hand by the psychological determinants of the economic behavior of employers as a secondary factor.[105]

In his interpretation of statistical series, Simiand placed particular emphasis on the differentiation of social groups according to their attitudes toward monetary earnings and economic effort. This differentiation also provided the starting point for his theory of economic progress.[106] The exceptional care that Simiand took in coordinating his statistical material, in confronting the results of his observations with successive hypotheses, and in formulating his theories was quite remarkable. But his assertion that he had permitted "the facts to speak for themselves" was questioned on the ground that he had introduced into his analysis certain general assumptions concerning the mutual relationships of economic variables, a procedure that implied the application of abstract deductive reasoning. For example, Simiand held that the antecedents of a phenomenon extending over time are to be regarded as its causes that can be connected with it by the most general relationship.[107]

The influence of Simiand's "positivism" was felt especially in the field of business cycle analysis as pursued under the direction of André Piatier by the French Institut de Conjoncture.[108] Piatier insisted upon abandoning the search for causes in favor of the search for functional relationships between economic magnitudes and for mutual dependencies between economic events. His approach to business cycle analysis was similar to that adopted in constructing the "Harvard economic barometers"; and he attributed the errors in forecasting committed by the Harvard economists at the beginning of the Great Depression to the faulty application of their methodological principles. In view of the difficulties involved in securing currently complete statistical information, Piatier supplemented the use of "external" or "barometric" procedures with continuous "internal" studies dealing with tendencies and developments not amenable to numerical expressions.[109] However, it is doubtful whether procedures of this kind are fully compatible with Simiand's methodological principles.

Other economists applied the results of "experimental psychology" to the analysis of economic behavior. P. L. Reynaud grouped the various classes of the population according to the degree to which they observe the principles of economic rationality.[110] His studies resulted in modifying certain aspects of marginal utility analysis, especially the treatment of price-cost relationships.[111] According to a widespread view, research carried out in terms of sociological categories had to precede short-run analysis of the deductive or mathematical type and had to supply the latter with the material needed to formulate adequate concepts. Thus, Louis Baudin emphasized the prevalence of "irrational" economic behavior and the existence of far-reaching "psychological" differences affecting economic behavior.[112]

As time went on, many well-known economists, such as Ernest Teilhac, Robert Mossé, Emile James, and Jean Marchal, joined in the protests against the application of mechanical principles to the "science dealing with man." The idea that any rigid isolation of economic analysis is likely to lead to erroneous conclusions was elaborated by various authors, and increasing importance was attached to sociological factors as indispensable elements of economic analysis.[113] The "structural" aspects of the various economies were carefully examined and a distinction was drawn between "economic institutions," characterized as creations of a political type, and "economic structures," the outcome of technical and material conditions which, subjected to slow and gradual changes, can provide the basis for a variety of institutions. Elaborating the idea that the various structures are ruled by definite norms, Pierre Dieterlen undertook to determine statistically for a group of countries certain relations between aggregates of economic magnitudes (such as volumes of production, savings, private revenues and public charges, prices of different categories of goods, etc.) and to compare the results of these measurements for the period 1875–1913 with similar measurements made for 1920–38. This investigation provided an interesting contribution to the well-known problem of the degree to which economic structures are more or less petrified by the desire of individuals to maintain a certain level of income and a certain way of life.[114]

One of the most consistent attempts to apply sociological concepts to the study of economic problems was made by François Perroux in his theory of "domination."[115] The role played by powerful individuals or firms in influencing economic conditions and developments had been emphasized by authors attached to divergent schools, by adherents of socialist creeds, by economists of marginalist persuasion (such as F. von Wieser and Richard Strigl), by mathematical economists (such as Ragnar Frisch), by members of the institutionalist movement (such as John Commons), and by students of the functioning of the American industry. In a elaborate classification of economic structures by Walter Eucken, positions of power occupied an important place. But within the context of nominalistic reasoning, exercise of power and constraint were generally treated as noneconomic forces which can be disregarded in establishing economic theories.

Perroux, however, started from the proposition that the modern economy is characterized by a variety of open or hidden relations between dominant and domineered firms. He placed particular stress on the equilibrium conditions of "the markets" influenced by dominant concerns. Disequilibria were likely to be created by the dissymetrical irreversibility and cumulative effects of "domination." The postulate of laissez-faire which had been identified with freedom of individual economic activity had resulted in securing unhampered freedom of action for the dominant firms. Without developing a fully elaborated "theory of domination," Perroux examined various situations in which the policies pursued by dominant firms were effective: he described their methods of carrying out their objectives, the means of resistance available to the domineered enterprises, and the mutual adjustment of dominant and domineered plans. He showed that dominant positions are frequently not due to the possession of economic power, strictly speaking, but to the fact that some economic units belong to a privileged "economic zone."

Perroux warned against confounding the exercise of economic power with monopolistic control of markets, and applied his leading ideas to the analysis of "macrodecisions" made by governments or large private organizations such as cartels, trusts, or employees' and workers' associations. Quite generally, he argued, the principles of economic rationality are disregarded by those who make these decisions, which are frequently fraught with far-reaching and important consequences.

Perroux qualified the use of the equilibrium principle for purposes of economic analysis as a technique for eliminating intentions and global decisions from economic analysis. Elaborating on this line of thought, he applied his theory to the relations between dominant and domineered nations and to a scheme of stages in the evolutionary history of the economy. Some of this work was undertaken while Perroux served as head of the Institut Scientifique d'Economie Appliquée.[116]

The structural aspects of the economy were also studied by Jean Lhomme, who emphasized certain sociological characteristics of the various classes, their cohesion, the consciousness of the collective power, and similar factors.[117] Closer examination of the vaguely circumscribed concept of social classes led to the establishment of "group characteristics" designed to represent "ideal types" of social configuration.[118] Sociological considerations of this type loomed large in the discussions that turned on the "reconstruction" of the French economy as envisaged by the "Plan Monnet." It was a moot question to what degree the rigidity of an existing "structure" of the population is likely to obstruct attempts to harmonize, within the framework of a unified economic scheme, conflicting economic plans of individuals and groups.

Socioeconomic analysis was also applied to specific economic problems, such as inflation, conceived of as the outcome of the actions of certain groups or as their reactions to the course of economic events.[119] Business fluctuations were interpreted in terms of causal (technical and psychological) relationships between social groups differentiated according to their plans of production, consumption, savings, etc.[120] The authors of such studies were motivated by strong opposition to the belief in the monism of causes and in oversimplified explanations of the course of economic events, as based on correlations, covariations, and statistical regularities.

The discussion of problems connected with the Marxian doctrine was stimulated by the conspicuous role of the communist party in France. Some attempts were made to show fundamental similarities between Keynesian theories and important elements of the Marxian doctrine. Another study was designed to demonstrate that all relevant aspects of modern capitalism had been well analyzed by Marx, including the disproportion between savings and investments, the conditions of permanent unemployment, the stickiness of fixed capital, the increasing imperfection of the markets, the predominant role of monopolies, and so on.[121] Problems of centralized economic planning were examined in lively discussions.[122]

But some socialist authors who dealt with problems of Marxism abandoned the method of dialectic materialism. Thus, the principles of the Marxian doctrine were combined with an appeal to Christian moral precepts, or some leading Marxist ideas were shown to be compatible with the official social doctrine of the Catholic Church.[123]

The conflicting trends which pressed their stamps on French economic literature were reflected in the leading textbooks. Various French economists spoke of a "crisis" which had occurred in the development of economic reasoning. The gap which was found to exist between the abstract and vague generalities of theoretical economics and the problems of daily life was emphasized by Jean Fourastié, Andre L. A. Vincent, Alfred Sauvy.[124] Jean Marchal insisted that the structure of the economy, which had been determined by individualistic principles, was being fundamentally transformed under the influence of associationist movements, and that it was necessary radically to modify the assumptions which had provided the background for the traditional economic theories.[125]

Surveying the development of French economic reasoning from 1945 to 1952, André Marchal observed that the "physiognomy" of economics had been determined in each country by a specific national mentality and by national traditions.[126] In Germany, he stated, this physiognomy was strongly influenced by historical and philosophical tendencies; in England, notwithstanding the Anglo-Saxon pragmatism, by a traditional deductive methodology; in the United States, by predilection for quantitative and statistical analyses; and in France, by the preference for psychological and sociological problems.

The prevailing tendency toward individualism and eclecticism prevented the French students of the social sciences from setting narrow limits to their research. When the "deterministic" belief in inevitable equilibrium and disequilibrium positions was abandoned, the fundamental problems to be solved consisted in determining the instrument for bringing about desired transformations of the economy.

Chapter 29
Further Discussion of Older Problems:
Production and Distribution

——

DISTRIBUTION THEORY

AFTER THE FIRST World War, it was generally recognized that the Ricardian outlook on the long-run development of distributive shares had been disproven by experience. There was no confirmation of the alleged tendency of profits to fall, the share of land rent in the national dividend was obviously declining, and the share of wages showed a remarkable stability in most countries, accompanied by perceptible increases in real wages brought about by the rising productivity of labor.

Hardly any reliable assumptions could be formulated as to the future development of the distributive processes. Even in countries where the economic structure had not been affected by revolutionary changes, important elements of that structure had been considerably modified by inflationary price movements, intensified monopolistic control of important markets, technological innovations, enhanced elasticity of substitution between productive services, measures of fiscal policy, and the like.[1] Almost everywhere it was difficult to determine the influence exercised by demographic and other sociological changes on the prevailing distribution of income.

The traditional association of the theory of distribution with the three main classes of the population had been seriously criticized when marginal productivity analysis was applied to the determination of the shares of the productive factors in the value of the product. Three different magnitudes were used to define marginal productivity: the physical product, the value of the product, and the increase in yield. A consistent method was thus available for deriving the values of the productive services from their marginal contributions to the values of their products, regardless of the roles of these services as sources of income. The *personal* aspects of the distributive processes were superseded by the *functional* characteristics of the productive services, and various authors contrasted these characteristics with the institutional nature of interest on capital, profit, and rent as sources of personal income.

Regardless of its theoretical foundation, the concept of marginal productivity lost much of its apparent attraction when it was put to the test of practical experience.[2] The hypothetical nature of the concept of "marginal contribution" to increases in the yield of productive processes was well characterized by L. M. Fraser's statement that we are no more in a position to identify that part of the total product that is due to any one participating agent than to decide how much of the beauty of a Beethoven symphony is due to the violins and how much to the trumpets or to the flutes.[3]

The intricacies involved in marginal productivity analysis were multiplied when account was taken of the existence of overhead costs, when a distinction was drawn between average and variable costs, and when free competition was no longer regarded as the prevailing form of organizing productive and marketing processes. John M. Clark argued that with the increasing size of enterprises and increasing volumes of investments, overhead costs were rising in importance; he questioned the validity of the traditional view that uniformity of prices for identical products was the rule and that prices were determined by costs of production. Clark tried to show that overhead costs were largely responsible for certain characteristic features of the price and production policies of industrial enterprises, such as price discrimination or selling below cost in periods of slackening sales.[4] Edward H. Chamberlin took account of the fact that in monopolistic situations the total yield is insufficient to reward all productive factors in accordance with the value of their marginal product.[5] He proposed to substitute for the concept of "value of the marginal physical product" the concept of "marginal revenue product," which he defined as the net anticipated addition to the money revenue of the firm attributable to the addition of one more unit of a factor. Attacking the problem from another angle, some German authors raised the question of the degree to which reasoning in terms of marginal productivity was connected with the institutional characteristics of the exchange economy. Thus, Erich Preiser argued that in economics in which not all incomes were earned by labor, the functional distribution of incomes was also influenced by the effects of institutional factors on the supply conditions of the productive agents.[6]

F. H. Knight was the outstanding Anglo-Saxon author who endeavored to develop the significant consequences of marginal productivity analysis. He raised strong objections to the procedure of applying the concept of "productive factors" to generic terms such as *land* and *capital,* since the shares in the yield of productive processes could be related only to specific inputs of land, labor, and capital.[7] He proposed to replace the traditional, somewhat problematic distinction among the three productive factors with another based on their substitutability in the various economic processes. His theory connected profits with the aleatory features of the exchange economy, and he established a clear distinction between interest on capital and profit.[8]

Knight adopted a productivity theory of interest, which he combined with J. B. Clark's conception of capital as a homogeneous fund of exchange values that is perpetually maintained through replacement and enlarged by increments. His capital concept was closely related to his equilibrium analysis. Since he applied the equilibrium principle directly to relationships among economic magnitudes, he had to reduce the latter to a common uniform denominator, a unit of exchange values; capital assets, as defined in that context, signified abstract amounts of accumulated exchange values.[9] Thus, the struggle over the definition of the concept of capital which, about thirty years before, had been waged between Eugen Böhm-Bawerk and Clark flared up again in a somewhat modified form, since according to the Austrian doctrine a fundamental distinction was drawn between capital, a physical magnitude the price of which could be reduced to the cost factor, and the original factors of production land and labor, whose rate of services was held to be independent of their costs.[10]

Knight's theory of capital was attacked by Friedrich A. Hayek, who vigorously defended the basic propositions of the Wicksellian definition of the real rate of interest;[11] that capital was to be conceived of as the sum of produced physical means of production, that the equilibrating forces of the economy were indirectly regulated by the level of interest on capital, and that interest was derived from the preference of present over future goods. The definition of capital in terms of physical elements of the productive processes was indispensable to the Wicksellian model, in which the equilibrium of the economy was not brought about by shifts in exchange values but by the rate of interest, which was regarded as the instrument for adjusting the length of the economic processes to the available supply of capital.[12]

In their elaboration of Böhm-Bawerk's concept of "periods of production" the Austrian economists established three stages of the productive processes: the period during which the capital goods were manufactured, the lifetime of these goods as sources of output, and the durability of the final products. A direct correlation was assumed to exist between the length of the period of production on the one hand and the quantity of goods produced during that period and the average durability of these goods on the other.[13] Additional consideration led to the proposal to use the amounts of time spent on the performance of roundabout productive processes to measure the quantity of capital invested in these processes, and thus to reduce the measurement of capital to homogeneous units.

In his criticism of the Austrian theory, Knight endeavored to show that insuperable difficulties were involved in the attempt to identify capital as the results of accumulated land and labor or to connect a clear concept with the vague expression "length of the productive process."[14] His arguments for rejecting the Austrian theory could be summed up in three propositions: (1) that all productive services were to a certain degree augmentable; (2) that investments could be subjected to diminishing returns, even though all productive agencies were freely augmentable; and (3) that no regular and necessary correlation existed between increases in capital investments and lengthening of the periods of production.

English and American economists took a lively interest in that controversy. Arthur C. Pigou, Thomas N. Carver, and Frank Fetter supported the Austrians. Irving Fisher's "impatience theory" of interest was based on Böhm-Bawerk's idea of the preference for present over future goods. Fisher paid particular attention to the effects of roundabout processes of production on increases in the yield.[15]

A certain clarification of some of the disputed issues was achieved in a discussion between Knight and Nicholas Kaldor, in which Kaldor rejected as untenable Knight's contention that diminishing returns could exist even though all productive services were augmentable.[16] But he qualified the "law of roundaboutness" as a "roundabout way" of expressing the law of nonproportional returns. What was termed "increases in the quantity of invested capital" could mean increases in the investment periods of the relatively augmentable factors or decreases in the marginal productivity of the services of the relatively nonaugmentable factors. An index of capital intensity could be established on these lines, but it could not measure the absolute quantity of capital; it was rather doubtful to what degree such an index reflected conditions of "roundaboutness" as envisaged in the Austrian theory.[17] Having thus defended the Austrian theory against some unjustified objections by Knight, Kaldor questioned the relevance of the theory on two grounds. He doubted whether the concept of "investment period" could be applied to the economy as a whole, and whether the method of comparative statics which had provided the methodological background of the theory was applicable to the processes of change which are characteristic of capital accumulation in highly industrialized societies.[18]

The fundamental relation between capital investments and periods of production was subsequently reformulated in the light of the consideration that the actual period which elapses between the investment of a capital asset and its exhaustion can be determined only ex post, and that such a result is irrelevant from the point of view of the expectations which had been instrumental in fixing the period of production.[19]

It might not be amiss to mention some secondary questions which were brought up in the course of these discussions. Knight characterized the rate of savings which determines the growth of capital as an independent variable, influenced by institutional and sociological factors.[20] He denied the possibility of determining a long-run supply curve of capital. His firm belief in the viability of the exchange economy was reflected in his assertion that under conditions of continuous changes in wants and technology, capital accumulation at a positive rate could be considered assured.[21] But pessimistic observers of the economy, such as Oskar Lange and D. McCord Wright, suggested that under stationary conditions capital accumulation might lead to situations in which, due to the effects of diminishing returns, net capital would supply no yield.[22] The concept of a "long-run" equilibrium rate of interest was dismissed as undefinable, largely because of the influence of incalculable risks.[23]

In these discussions of nonmonetary theories of interest on capital, the concept of capital, whether defined in physical or in value terms, was associated with the growth of the economy, and the level of the rate of interest was connected with the development of productive processes and technical coefficients. A different, entirely static, concept of capital was used by the adherents of a third nonmonetary theory of interest, who defined interest as a payment for "abstinence," "postponement of want satisfaction," "waiting," and the like. But this theory, which had been suggested by Nassau Senior and endorsed by John Stuart Mill and Alfred Marshall, was less designed to provide an explanation for the source of interest on capital than to provide a basis for the analysis of the relationships between changing rates of interest and changes in the rate of savings.[24]

The confusion produced by conflicting definitions of capital as a physical factor of production was intensified by the existence of theories of interest that identified capital with stocks of means of payment, and interest on capital with the price paid for loanable funds. The need to develop monetary theories of interest was due to the fact that in an economy in which goods and services are exchanged in terms of their "real values," without the intervention of money, no uniform rate of interest exists to secure equality between the demand for and the supply of loans. Similarly, the conditions of discount and capitalization are rendered indeterminant by pluralities of discount rates and of relationships between the prices of the productive services and the prices of the final goods. Hence, if lending and borrowing had to be included among the characteristic features of a "static" economy, application of equilibrium analysis was dependent upon the assumption that interest on capital could be defined in monetary terms.[25]

The theories of interest advanced by some Swedish disciples of Knut Wicksell were examples of a monetary theory of interest. Joseph Schumpeter, who adopted a rather narrow definition of a static economy, associated the existence of such an economy with the absence of interest on capital, and connected the origin of interest with some dynamic features of the competitive economy and the need of employers for loan capital.[26] He defined interest as a premium for the use of money presently available and reckoned it among the costs of production. According to his theory, the rate of interest was determined *ex ante* by the estimates of the marginal capitalists, as distinct from the rate of profit, which resulted from the difference between the efficiency of capital and the rate of interest and could be determined only after the termination of the relevant economic processes.

Eventually, John Maynard Keynes placed a sharply formulated monetary theory of interest into the center of economic discussions. That theory was not intended to account for the origin of interest on capital; it dealt with the factors which determine the rate of interest on borrowed capital, and related that rate to the "liquidity preference" of the savers, hence to a psychological attitude. The ensuing controversy with the adherents of the "loanable funds" theory was settled by a sort of compromise, and the essential differences between the leading monetary and nonmonetary theories of interest were clarified when it was shown that the Keynesian rate of interest had its counterpart in the Wicksellian loan or market rates, whereas Wicksell's "real" or "natural" rate of interest corresponded to the Keynesian marginal efficiency of capital.

In the course of these discussions, it was found advisable to differentiate among various kinds of more or less fixed returns on economic resources.[27] Marginal rates of return on securities were distinguished on the one hand from those on cash holdings and on the other hand from returns on investments in productive processes, while subdivisions were established for rates of return on bonds, shares, inventories, and so on. In the light of these distinctions each of the various theories of interest was found to emphasize specific aspects of interest on capital. The time preference theory could be associated with the marginal rate of return on capital used for purposes of consumption, and the marginal productivity theory with the marginal rate of return on investments for purposes of production. The liquidity preference theory was found to account for the marginal rate of return on cash, and the loanable fund theory for the marginal rate of return on securities. Changes in the demand for or supply of loanable funds brought about by changes in the rate of interest could be explained only in accordance with the loanable fund theory.

The traditional conception of interest as the price paid for the use of capital was obviously backed by the view that individualistic motives had free play in deciding upon that price. However, the Keynesian "liquidity theory" of interest could be interpreted as a device which provided the monetary authorities with arguments in favor of active economic policies.[28] That change from the analytical "microeconomic" theory to the Keynesian "normative" and "macroeconomic" approach had a significant counterpart in a change of the correlation between the movement of prices and the behavior of the rate of interest. A close correlation between these two movements, which had been observed for a period of more than one hundred years,[29] had ceased to obtain after 1932, when the discount policies of the Central Banks were subordinated to the instructions of political authorities and savers were excluded from determining their share in the social dividend any more. Viewed from that angle, the Keynesian conception of the rate of interest had less the nature of a theory strictly speaking than the character of a "condensed exposition of empirical observations."[30]

Up to the First World War profit theory had been a stepchild of economic reasoning, as compared with the close consideration given in the various economic doctrines to other features of the distributive process. David Ricardo did not suggest any clear theory of profit; Marshall practically identified profit with a salary earned by the employers. There was no separate place for profit in the equilibrium models of the mathematical school. Some members of the Austrian school who paid special attention to employers' profits treated them as analogous to absolute or differential rents. A vague definition of profit as compensation for the contributions made by capitalist employers to productive processes was quite common. Orthodox Marxists continued to defend the concept of profit as "surplus value" withheld from the earnings of labor; they used the theory of the falling rate of profit as the main argument in support of the breakdown theory. Other socialist authors, such as the Fabians, who did not share that reasoning, motivated their proposals of social reform with the argument that profit was "unearned income."[31]

A promising approach to the analysis of profit had been made by J. B. Clark, who connected that source of income with "dynamic" market conditions. This was elaborated on by Schumpeter, who attributed the existence of profits to discrepancies between prices and costs brought about by innovations and technical improvements. Although Schumpeter had developed that theory in connection with his analysis of cyclical fluctuations of the capitalist machinery, he considered it equally applicable to planned economies in which specific norms would be established for the appropriation and use of profits. According to his theory, the daring entrepreneur created the conditions for the existence of profits. There was no profit without evolution, and no evolution without profit. But in view of the temporary nature of such earnings, Schumpeter hesitated to regard them as revenues of the same type as wages and interest on capital.[32]

Certain dynamic elements were also introduced into the concept of rent, which had preserved its traditional connection with scarcity relationships, when it was generally applied to the difference between the lasting yield of a productive factor and its supply price. Thus, rent was defined as a surplus return earned by an agent of production in a particular industry over and above its opportunity costs.[33] But the empirical generalization, which had been characteristic of the Ricardian concept of rent, was transformed into a universally valid proposition dealing with the relationships between changes in the value of products and changes in the value of scarce productive services required in variable proportions for productive processes.[34]

A dynamic approach to economic analysis was equally reflected in Knight's theory of profit.[35] Starting from a careful examination of the conditions of a perfectly balanced economy, he ascribed the existence of profit to the failure of the competitive forces to achieve full equalization of prices with costs of production. In a characteristic passage Knight asserted that every movement in the world "could clearly be seen to be progress toward an equilibrium."[36] He held risks and uncertainties mainly responsible for the divergencies between the actual forms of competitive behavior and the theoretical pattern of perfect competition. Of paramount importance for Knight's profit theory was his definition of risks as calculable, insurable exposures to mischance, as contrasted with "uncertainties" or similar exposures to which the law of large numbers cannot be applied. Whereas protection against risks, as provided by insurance, could be transformed into a cost element, no such protective devices appeared to be available in the case of uncertainties. In mathematical terms, risks were defined as the known parameters of frequency distribution, whereas knowledge of both the frequency distribution and its parameters was lacking in the case of uncertainties.[37] The existence of uncertainties implied that, as a rule, well-considered choices had to be made between smaller rewards more confidently anticipated and larger ones less confidently anticipated. The accuracy of judgments concerning the outcome of uncertain actions or events obviously depended on individual capacities to evaluate that outcome correctly. Since Knight placed primary emphasis on the difference between foreseen and unforeseen changes, he attached only secondary importance to the distinction between changes brought about by deliberate actions and others occurring independently of such action. He denied enterpreneurial status to the salaried manager who did not directly assume any risk, and attributed that entrepreneurial quality to the shareholder.[38]

The definition of the borderline between risks and uncertainties was the object of considerable discussion. Some French economists discussed the intricate question of how to draw a clear line between calculable and uncalculable happenings (transformable and nontransformable risks). They distinguished a considerable variety of profits, such as individual and social profits; profits resulting from creative activity, imitation, adaptation, friction, competition, or "domination"; "concerted" profits; windfall profits; profits connected with structural, conjunctural, evolutionary events; and so on.[39] Subsequent refinements of Knight's theorem led to the conception of profits as incidents in the allocation process resulting from disequilibria in the general interdependent price system.[40] Only unanticipated, nonfunctional, residual revenues resulting from errors in forecasting were held to constitute profits strictly speaking, since only gains of that type could be related to nontransformable or not transformed uncertainties.[41] That conception of profit as the outcome of expectations, conjectures, and mutually incompatible assumptions was distinguished from the concept of profit as a figure recorded *ex post* by the accountant.[42] Hence, viewed from the *ex ante* angle, profit was regarded as a residual element. In the light of *ex post* considerations, profit appeared on the balance sheet as actually realized returns on investments.[43] But Knight's theory did not account for the existence of all profits; many random events and employers' activities provided additional chances for profit that would be eliminated only under the perfectly stable conditions of free competition.[44]

In his analysis of the effects of imperfect competition, Robert Triffin contrasted the "dynamic" origin of profits with the institutionalist nature of their appropriation.[45] He discussed characteristic forms of distributing profits between entrepreneurs and owners of capital. In his view, obstacles to the freedom of entry into various industries were an important source of profit. In accordance with the principle of opportunity costs, the existence of excessive profit was indicative of a defective allocation of resources. R. G. Hawtrey pointed to the "opportunity cost" of the entrepreneur's own services as a possible source of abnormal profit.[46] These and similar discussions led to the conclusion that the profit rate was determined to a far greater degree by the rate of innovation and the type of entrepreneurial activity than by the existing capital stock and its relations to population and resources.[47]

In passing, mention may be made of another approach to profit theory, which reflected the tendency of various French economists to study economic phenomena against their sociological background. As developed by Jean Marchal in particular, the theory started from the proposition that the functions of those who supply productive factors (workers and capitalists) differ significantly from the functions of the entrepreneurs who endeavor to influence the structure of the market.[48] Hence, Marchal defined profit as income resulting from attempts to "disjoin prices." Without suggesting a clear principle of classification, he distinguished three main types of profit: (1) that of small businesses who combine various functions in their operations; (2) that derived from the monopolistic positions of large corporations; and (3) that of *rentiers*, who can shift their assets from one area to another and whose decisions are motivated more by expectations than by actual market conditions.

Another distinction among different categories of profit was advanced by P. L. Bernstein,[49] who criticized traditional profit theory on the grounds that it ignored important sociological aspects (especially of the profit policy of large concerns), that it failed to take account of the tendency to minimize the burden of taxes, and that it paid no attention to windfall profits and to the question of whether or not the capitalist was trying to maximize the amount or the rate of profit. Bernstein proposed the abandonment of the search for a single profit theory and the development of a system of such theories.

Contributions to the study of the behavior of firms and their managers were supplied by various investigations which started from the Marshallian definition of profit as a reward for specific entrepreneurial or managerial functions. But it was difficult to reconcile that definition with the fact that neither the items on the balance sheets nor the income statements available to the managers of firms provided a basis for the determination of the elements of theoretical profit calculations, such as marginal costs and marginal revenues.[50] The general validity of the assumption that maximization of profits is to be regarded as the guiding principle of entrepreneurial activity was questioned on the ground that the entrepreneur has to take account of the ever-present possibility of losses.[51] As a result, the use that can be made of the profit-maximizing assumption for purposes of economic analysis has remained a controversial topic.[52]

In the light of such considerations, it has been suggested that techniques should be developed to determine and measure uncertainties,[53] as well as a "realistic" theory of entrepreneurship.[54] Some authors proposed to base the analysis of the "rational behavior" of firms on expectations and the influence of income variables.[55] Different kinds of profit structure were distinguished according to the observable preference for liquidity and flexibility in the composition of the assets.[56] Observations of that type were preparatory to a discussion of the theoretical aspects of decision making in the 1950s.

The existence of widespread unemployment that created misery and hardship after the First World War caused various adherents of Ricardian economics to ascribe the development of a "hard core of unemployment" primarily to the increasing rigidity of the wage structure brought about by the conclusion of collective agreements, fixing of wage minima, the operation of unemployment compensation schemes, and similar measures of socioeconomic politics. An outstanding representative of that view was Jacques Rueff. He insisted that labor markets were under the pressure of bilateral monopolies that rendered wages indeterminate, and that disequilibria between the demand for and the supply of labor were bound to result from measures designed to keep the price of labor at higher levels than was economically justified.[57] But the statistical methods Rueff used to support his propositions were criticized by adherents of the prevailing wage policies,[58] and the effects of these policies were discussed in a vast literature.[59] Arthur Cecil Pigou regarded the zone of wage indeterminateness as relatively narrow.[60] John R. Hicks, who studied the theoretical background of collective bargaining, considered wage agreements as instruments that indicate the degree of resistance of the parties involved to the position adopted by their opponents.[61]

Marginal productivity analysis provided the main avenue of approach to a consistent theory of wages.[62] In the United States that analysis occupied a privileged position in J. B. Clark's doctrine; it was used to explain the level of wages in various investigations.[63] A remarkable study of that type was prepared by Paul H. Douglas, who used ample statistical material to establish the relationships between changes of wages and changes in the volume of employment.[64] Marginal productivity analysis also provided a principle for interpreting the concept of the "exploitation of labor." Pigou identified that concept with situations in which wages paid to labor were lower than the value of their marginal physical product would have been under conditions of free competition.[65] The same definition was taken over by Joan Robinson,[66] but it met with the objection that all factors were "exploited" under monopolistic situations. Chamberlin's concept of "marginal revenue product" was considered an appropriate standard for defining the conditions under which "exploitation" of labor takes place.[67]

The application of marginal productivity analysis to the wage problem was, of course, open to the objection mentioned above, that it was practically impossible to disentangle the specific contributions of the various productive factors at the margin of their application.[68] Other criticisms of marginalist methods as used for purposes of wage analysis were based on investigations into the behavior of American businessmen.[69] It was found that the managements of firms tended as a rule to adjust their demand for labor to expected sales rather than to the prevailing wage rate, as would have corresponded to the application of the marginal productivity principle. The ensuing discussion centered on the question of the degree to which that principle was at least indirectly instrumental in determining the factors which the employers considered relevant to their employment decisions. Fritz Machlup, who defended the applicability of marginal productivity analysis, admitted that small changes in the relative prices of the productive agents were not sufficient to provoke technological changes, and that the influence of marginal productivity considerations, though generally prevailing, was modified by the effects of various other factors.[70]

The influence of marginal productivity conditions on wage determination appeared to be reflected in the long-term relative constancy of the shares of capital and labor in the national dividend, both in the United Kingdom and in the United States.[71] But the question of the degree to which such trends might be modified by the effects of collective bargaining as supported by full employment policies remained open.[72] Especially in the United States, the influence of collective bargaining on the distribution of the national dividend was the object of prolonged controversies.[73]

A "balanced wage structure" was defined as a wage system in which wages are rising on the average as fast as average productivity rises in the economy and similar rates of pay obtain for services that are similar in terms of skill, experience, and training. Some attempts were made to define the conditions responsible for departure from such a wage structure and for a wide disparity of wage rates.

The assumption that employers tend to equate marginal costs and marginal revenue was also questioned by some followers of Keynes in prolonged discussion of the Keynesian proposition that in depression periods no increase in output and employment could be expected to result from declines of money wages. The general validity of that proposition became doubtful, however, when account was taken of situations in which price declines lagged behind falling wages, in which wage reductions caused employers to substitute labor for other productive factors, or in which investment opportunities were improved by shrinking wage bills.[74] But even after these disputed issues had been clarified, wage analysis remained one of the most controversial topics of economics.

That situation was reflected in international discussions of the inflationary effects of full-employment policies, the delimitation of the bargaining power of trade unions and managements, and the definition of the role to be assigned to money wages as distinct from real wages. Considerable divergencies of opinion could be registered as to the necessity of putting the results of wage theories to the test of practical experience and as to economic and social implications of trade union policies.[75]

MONOPOLY AND COMPETITION

The paramount position attributed by the post-Ricardian economists to the principle of "free competition" was not questioned by Wicksell and the majority of his disciples. They were convinced that reliance upon that principle provided the instrument for transforming innumerable erratic variables of production and marketing into definable elements of a mechanical model of the economy. Moreover, the assumption that equilibrium conditions were established under the rule of free competition provided the basis for combining into systems of manageable simultaneous equations the magnitudes which the members of the competitive communities were supposed to maximize (utilities, profits, volumes of production and sales, and the like).[76]

That approach to equilibrium analysis was reflected in the attitude adopted by the Ricardian and post-Ricardian economists toward monopolies of all kinds.[77] Francis Ysidro Edgeworth characterized that attitude when he observed that the "abstract economists" would be deprived of their occupation if the economy were permeated by monopolies. He added that only "the empirical school, flourishing in a chaos congenial to their mentality," would survive.[78]

Methodological considerations played a conspicuous role in the post-Ricardians' aversion for monopolistic situations and their unwillingness to deal with the problems which resulted from such situations. "Competitive values" were assumed to regulate the functioning of the economy, but the concept of "free competition" was not always clearly defined. As generally understood, it included among its main attributes the existence of a considerable number of independent producers, buyers, and sellers who were well informed about the market conditions; freedom of access to the productive factors and the market; homogeneity of products; absence of friction impairing the mobility of capital and labor; and stability of the monetary unit.

On the other hand, it was quite obvious that in few if any markets were general conditions at all similar to those posited by equilibrium analysis. Alfred Marshall, who endeavored to adjust his teachings to reality, as much as possible, did not even suggest an unambiguous definition of "free competition."[79] Keynes qualified that principle as an "apparatus of the mind," a "technique of thinking."[80]

The first hypothetical economist to pay full attention to the theoretical problems of monopolistic situations was Antoine Augustin Cournot. His treatment of these problems provided the pattern for several decades.[81] The firm which operates a monopoly was assumed to be faced with given demand functions for its products and given supply functions for its productive resources, and to pursue a policy of profit maximization. The problems of price differentiation which were adumbrated by Jules Dupuit were highlighted by Edgeworth and Pigou, and von Wieser contributed an analysis of markets graded according to the purchasing power of the buyers.

Less agreement was reached on the treatment of "duopolies," or cases in which two competing firms produce an identical product. Cournot had formulated the problem in terms of partial equilibrium analysis, and had assumed that each of the duopolists could ignore changes in the quantities offered by his competitor.[82] A prolonged controversy developed many years later when Joseph Bernard objected to some assumptions made by Cournot, and arrived at the conclusion that in oligopolistic situations prices were fixed by processes of mutual underbidding.[83] According to Edgeworth, no unequivocal answer could be given to that problem, since no equilibrium prices resulted from the application of the principle of profit maximization to the price and production policies of the two parties.[84] Pigou emphasized the indeterminateness of the allocation of resources which was characteristic of duopolistic markets.[85] Arthur Bowley observed that a duopolist could not behave "rationally" when the behavior of his rival, though equally "rational," was unknown to him.[86]

In the course of subsequent discussions, Cournot's attempts to arrive at a determinate solution of the problem of duopolist pricing were defended by Luigi Amoroso and Knut Wicksell but objected to by Ferdinand Zeuthen and Edward H. Chamberlin.[87] Harold Hotelling favored a determinate solution on the ground that discontinuities in the price structure are abhorred in the markets as a vacuum is abhorred in nature.[88] In his *Mathe-*

matical Groundwork of Economics, Bowley attempted to build a bridge between the two extreme positions,[89] and thus paved the way for the analysis of situations ranging between cases in which "conjectural variations" of both duopolists are zero (Cournot's case) and cases of price cutting in which a duopolist has derived a conjectural variation from the reaction curve of his rival, on the assumption that the rival will considerably expand his output. A new category of duopolistic situations was formed of cases in which price cutting was terminated by "tacit combinations" and prices were fixed at levels higher than those which corresponded to Cournot's assumptions.[90]

The term *bilateral monopoly* was applied to cases of exchanges between a group of buyers and a group of sellers, each acting in combination. Practically general agreement was reached on Edgeworth's view that no equilibrium can be defined on the simple assumption that each party is seeking its maximum advantage. The role played by the cost element was emphasized in other studies of monopolistic situations.[91] The relationship between prices and costs of monopolized commodities was analyzed in terms of marginal receipts and marginal costs, and account was taken of changes in the elasticity of demand, of varying costs, and of substitutability of different products.

In his treatment of situations in which the monopolistic buyer of a productive factor is faced with a monopolistic seller, Pigou suggested the analysis of the "degree of resistance" offered by each party when threatened by prolonged or unsuccessful negotiations. Zeuthen proposed to adjust such situations to probability calculations.[92] Hicks discussed the problem of resistance in its application to collective bargaining in the labor market.[93]

The treatment of monopolistic conditions could provide some clues to the analysis of situations in which, as formulated by Pareto, the sale of otherwise identical commodities was differentiated by circumstances of credit, services, and the like.[94] But greater difficulties were involved in the analysis of limited monopolies exercised by organized groups of producers and traders, such as trusts, mergers, interlocking directorates, or cartels. These monopolies were the object of a vast, mainly German, descriptive literature and a number of reports submitted to the World Economic Conference held in Geneva in 1927.[95] Various attempts were made to establish a satisfactory typology of the forms of market control. The criteria adopted with this end in view were mostly derived from some characteristic features of the markets, such as substitutability of products, elasticity of demand, and the like. Less importance was attached to characteristics of the controlling bodies, such as the number of firms participating in the combinations or restrictions imposed on freedom of entry into the market. It was doubtful whether "abnormal profits" or "price rigidity" could be used to define and differentiate such monopolistic situations, since exaggerated profits and lack of price flexibility were also characteristic features of some competitive markets.[96]

In accordance with a suggestion made by Otto von Zwiedineck-Südenhorst, particular importance was attached to a "historical" element, the "principle of inertia," as a determinant of monopolistic price fixing.[97] Practically all analysts of monopolistic situations agreed that market control involving price maintenance and restrictions of production was greatly intensified during depression periods. Advocates of "collective monopolies" hailed such measures as promising attempts to stabilize the economy, but that view was incompatible with almost all business cycle theories.

In a remarkable study of duopolistic and other oligopolistic situations, Heinrich von Stackelberg elaborated the idea that in the majority of markets prices show no tendency to reach equilibrium positions, but remain indeterminate.[98] He started from the simple case of two sellers competing in a market and discussed the alternatives confronting them, showing how the number of alternatives increased with the number of sellers striving for leadership in the market. He reduced the great variety of conditions of restricted competition to a limited number of types and paid special attention to oligopolist situations in which the market was divided among several sellers through product differentiation but was not closed to the entry of new firms. In his treatment of such cases, he assigned a particular market to each differentiated product, and argued that varying elasticities of demand for such products enabled each producer to adopt an active or a passive attitude not only with regard to the volume of output but also with regard to price. The main cases Stackelberg distinguished were oligopoly, monopoly, and limited monopoly of supply and demand, and bilateral monopoly.[99]

In the light of his finding, Stackelberg attributed the instability of the capitalist economy to a "crisis of structure" created by the lack of determinateness, which he held responsible for the tendency of producers and traders to enter into open or tacit combinations. Hence, he arrived at the conclusion that adequate stability of the economy should be undertaken by consistent price and production policies operated by the government. It was a moot question to what degree that conclusion was likely to lend theoretical support to the policies advocated by fascist and national socialist economists.

The Marshallian economists had adjusted their theoretical considerations to the principles of partial equilibrium analysis. But they were confronted with the problems involved in noncompetitive markets when the much-discussed question of the "empty boxes" was raised in an article by Sir John Clapham, a distinguished student of economic history.[100] Clapham attacked the usefulness of the distinctions which Marshall had drawn between external and internal economies and among industries with increasing, constant, and falling returns. He showed that in each industry elements of all three types of return were inextricably mixed and that it was hardly possible to assign an industry to a clearly defined category. Special difficulties were involved in defining industries characterized by increasing returns. However, the classification of the industries according to the nature of their returns was not a purely academic matter; the functional relationship between costs and yield played a significant role in Marshallian welfare economics. Pigou's reply was not very convincing, and Clapham observed that he had been paid with a check drawn on the bank of an unborn William Stanley Jevons.[101]

The significant connection between Marshall's classification of industries and the competitive aspects of their markets was brought out in full relief by Piero Sraffa. Sraffa recalled that the law of decreasing returns had played a prominent part in the Ricardian theory of distribution, whereas the law of increasing returns had been associated with the generalized effects of the division of labor, and that, subsequently, both laws were merged in the single law of "nonproportional returns."[102] It was obvious that, after having secured a substantial reduction of its cost of production, a firm operating under conditions of increasing returns could gradually displace all its competitors. In order to account for the maintenance of free competition among firms with increasing returns, Marshall had referred to the effects of external economics; but Sraffa showed that the economics which are derived from the growth of an industry and are "external" from the point of view of the individual firm are practically insignificant. Moreover, he argued that a relatively large number of manufacturing enterprises operate under conditions of individual diminishing costs or of constant or proportionate costs when their production is increasing. However, that observation was incompatible with the teachings of equilibrium analysis, according to which for the industry, marginal costs in the short run and average costs in the long run had to be at a minimum and expansion of output had to be accompanied by increasing costs.[103] About the same time, Knight criticized Pigou's use of "external economies" on the ground that an external economy is "internal" to another industry and is likely to disappear when it has been fully exploited—unless it is preserved in the second industry through monopolistic devices.[104]

Sraffa concluded that traditional equilibrium analysis was inapplicable to industries operating under increasing returns. Cournet who was aware of the problem was loath to accept that conclusion. But Sraffa proposed to solve the problem with the assumption that in many apparently competitive markets demand was, in fact, determined by the preference of groups of buyers for the products of individual firms. The unified market of an "industry," which was basic to the Marshallian partial equilibrium analysis, was thus transformed into a loosely coordinated range of more or less monopolistic situations characterized by varying degrees of elasticity of demand.

In the course of the ensuing discussion, Robbins and Sraffa questioned the usefulness of the concept of the "representative firm," which was defended by Dennis Holme Robertson and G. F. Shove as an instrument for analyzing industries with increasing costs.[105] R. F. Harrod contributed an article in which he proposed the analysis of the behavior of monopolists in terms of marginal costs and marginal revenue.[106] Jacob Viner, however, remained true to the principles of the Marshallian analysis, and undertook a thoroughgoing discussion of the influence of different cost conditions upon the supply curves in cases of short- and long-run equilibria, increasing and constant costs, net internal and external economics, and diseconomics.[107]

Other economists who were less impressed by the Marshallian methods disregarded the concept of "industry" and analyzed the behavior of individual firms on the assumption that the latter were permitted a certain degree of freedom of action in manipulating prices and selling expenditures.[108] Additional assumptions were introduced in order to arrive at determinate solutions. Several types of markets were distinguished according to the reactions of sellers to the moves of their competitors. Thus "price adjustment markets" were distinguished from "quantity adjustment" markets. The behavior of sellers who anticipate the reactions of rival sellers was distinguished from the behavior of those concerned only with the expected attitude of buyers.[109]

In these discussions, special attention was given to restrictions imposed upon the entry of new firms into a market.[110] Uncertainly concerning the outcome of competitive struggles and indivisibility and immobility of productive resources were listed as important factors contributing to the spread of monopolistic practices. The theory of monopolistic behavior was challenged to deal with markets of nonhomogeneous products and with the substitutability of goods.

These methodological developments prepared the way for the elaboration of two noteworthy studies which were intended to give problems of "restrictive competition" their due place within the framework of Marshallian economics. The author of one study was a Cambridge economist, Joan Robinson, the author of the other, Edward H. Chamberlin, was a Harvard economist.[111] Both authors adjusted their analyses to the Marshallian concept of the isolated market of an "industry" and disregarded the problems involved in the competition between firms belonging to different industries. They adopted the static approach and ignored the influence of the time element on competitive processes, they both applied the principle of profit maximization to the policy pursued by the individual firm, and they used the "downward sloping demand curve" as a criterion for

distinguishing monopolistic competition from free competition in markets with homogeneous products.[112] Moreover, Robinson and Chamberlin centered their analyse on the
same problem: the competition between sellers—whether few or numerous—of a nonhomogeneous product.[113] But they differed markedly as to their formulations of the
problem, the specific assumptions which they made, and the technique which they
used.[114]

Robinson's approach was perhaps influenced by the market conditions which prevailed during the Great Depression. Adopting a procedure recommended by Sraffa, she
started her analysis with a study of pure monopolies and wound it up with a discussion of
equilibrium conditions obtaining under perfect competition. She emphasized two equilibrium conditions: equality of marginal revenue to marginal cost, and equality of average
revenue (or price) to average cost.[115] But she analyzed situations of ''imperfect competition'' only on the assumption that every firm but one in the given industry is in equilibrium, and ignored the reactions of other firms to the monopolistic competitor. Applying
the marginal revenue technique, Robinson arrived at the conclusion that under imperfect
competition profits were maximized when the expansion of the firm's output was determined by the intersection of the marginal cost curve with the marginal revenue curve, not
by the intersection with the average revenue curve, as was the case under free competition. Thus, the firm could maximize its profits at prices higher than those obtainable under
competitive conditions. The marginal revenue technique was not applicable to cases in
which the behavior of a firm could not be isolated from that of its competitors.

Chamberlin opposed the concept of ''monopolistic competition'' to the traditional
concept of ''monopoly'' and applied it to market situations characterized by product
differentiation and cross elasticities. (The cross elasticity of demand for a good is the
relative change in the demand for the good divided by the relative change in the price
charged for a second good.) He considered interdependence of price and production
policies specific features of oligopolistic situations, and emphasized the importance of
selling costs, which were ignored in the theory of pure competition. He extended his
analysis to cases marked by varying degrees of free entry into the market; he took account
of varying numbers of sellers and of changes in selling costs. Chamberlin discussed
several practices used by competing firms in the struggle over privileged market positions.
But, prompted by the intention to arrive at more or less definite solutions, he, like
Robinson, formulated his assumptions with a view to their analytical convenience rather
than to their relevance for reality,[116] and he placed the monopolistic firms under pressure
of market forces compelling them to adjust their behavior to certain conditions beyond
their control.[117]

The intensified study of monopolistic situations led to a clarification of the concept of
competition. Chamberlin identified ''pure'' competition with the existence of perfectly
elastic individual demand curves, consumers' indifference as to their choice among homogeneous products, and absence of conscious influence on prices exercised by the sellers.
In his view, the concept of ''perfect'' competition[118]—which he regarded as imaginary—
included among its characteristics perfect knowledge of market conditions by the sellers,
free mobility of resources, perfect adaptability of the productive factors, and absence of
friction.[119] According to these definitions, the prices paid for homogeneous products and
their marginal costs were equalized under the rule of perfect competition. That criterion
had already been established by Cournot. Perfect ''rationalization'' of production was
expected to be achieved when each firm endeavored to maximize its returns under conditions of perfect competition.[120] But in a dynamic competitive economy, considerable

profit could be earned when freedom of entry into the market was not perfect;[121] more-over, uneven profits resulting from the introduction of ''innovations'' could lead to evolutionary processes. Free competition became a market phenomenon ''stripped of its main social and normative claims'' when the condition of free entry was no longer considered one of its characteristic features.[122]

Terminological considerations of that type caused Chamberlin to avoid the use of the expression ''imperfect competition.'' As distinct from Robinson, he did not regard pure competition as in any sense ideal and conducive to the achievement of optimum social welfare. He objected to the principle of marginal cost pricing as a criterion of welfare economics and to the exclusion of selling costs from economically justified pricing.[123] He held free competition responsible for the development of excess capacity, and qualified ''aggressive pricing'' under conditions of product differentiation as indispensable for economic progress.[124]

In his critical analysis of the theory of restricted competition, Triffin ascribed the disappointing results of the two studies to the fact that they had adjusted the formulation of their problems to the principles of the Marshallian partial equilibrium analysis. He con-strasted that approach with the Walrasian concept of the economy, which placed the individual firm in the center of an interdependent system of economic relationships. In accordance with that conception, Triffin defined the firm quite generally as an economic unit that maximizes its profits; he used the principle of substitutability at the margin to classify units of a good as ''the same commodity.''[125] Along that line of reasoning, he objected to the view that the standard for distinguishing monopolistic from competitive conditions was to be found in the degree of control of the seller over price (the slope of demand curve). He saw competition as marked by definite relationships between sellers and buyers, and market situations could best be classified according to the degree to which the sales or costs of a firm were affected by changing prices of other firms.[126] Hence, in formulating the ''problem of entry,'' account should be taken of interdependence in selling and interdependence in buying, as affected by the closing down of existing firms and the establishment of new firms.

Other discussions dealt with the behavior of prices under monopoly and competi-tion,[127] with the influence of the structure of the markets on income distribution,[128] with the effects of restricted competition on the allocation of resources and the utilization of the available productive capacities. Different degrees of competition were compared as to their efficiency; particular attention was given to certain characteristic aspects of imper-fectly competitive situations, such as varying numbers of competitors, different degrees of free entry into the market, and the diversities in cost and demand functions and their competitive bearings.[129]

In statistical studies of price rigidities done in England and the United States during the thirties, ''kinks'' were shown to be characteristic of the demand curves for products of oligopolists. According to Bowley's principle of ''conjectural variation'' it could be expected that rivals would quickly match price reductions but avoid frequent price changes because of the costs involved in such adjustments.[130] No agreement was reached on Harrod's criticism of the traditional assumption that the entrepreneur's behavior was determined by the principle of short-term maximization of profits. He had argued that under conditions of imperfect competition, guidance to price determination was provided by considerations of long-term marginal revenue and ''full-cost'' policies.[131] Moreover, he questioned the widespread view that excess capacity is frequently to be found in the case of imperfect competition with free entry.

450   HYPOTHETICAL ECONOMICS

In other discussions, the problem of oligopolistic competition was approached from the angle of Hotelling's assumption concerning the limited elasticity of demand as a characteristic of oligopolistic situations.[132] Competitors were assumed to take account of their rivals' possible reactions to their decisions.[133] Methods of market control, profit sharing, collusion, and obstacles to collusion were the objects of various studies. William J. Fellner developed a theory of oligopoly and bilateral monopoly on the assumption that there exists a tendency to maximize the joint profits for groups participating in monopolistic markets of that type.[134]

Chamberlin spoke of "product equilibrium" in characterizing situations in which not prices but the quality of the product and services rendered to the buyers were the object of competitive activities.[135] In later versions of his theory, he abandoned various assumptions which had been suggested by the Marshallian setting of the problem, and placed the individual firm into a vast network of interrelated markets in which each producer and seller was assumed to adjust his prices, production, or selling outlay to changing market conditions.[136] Consequent upon that reformulation of the concept of monopolistic competition, the problems connected with the concepts of "large numbers" and "entry" were dealt with in the discussion of the distribution of resources, and the Marshallian concept of "representative firm" was deprived of any definable meaning.[137]

Almost general agreement was reached on the view that it was necessary to include a number of factors regarded as "noneconomic" in the analysis of oligopolistic situations but that considerable elements of competition, varying in degree, were present in all oligopolistic markets.[138] The need for extensive empirical studies dealing with such markets was emphasized by a number of authors, such as George Stigler, Fritz Machlup, K. W. Rothchild, and E. Schneider. In his analysis of American pricing processes, E. G. Nourse characterized imperfect competition as the prevailing form of business enterprise and considered "reasoned and intricately purposive action" as the main features of the competitive behavior.[139] Various authors emphasized the dynamic nature of competitive as well as noncompetitive processes. Hayek argued that the distinctive traits of such processes are assumed away when the principle of "competitive equilibrium" is applied to economic analysis.[140] Clark characterized the theory of competition as a framework in which various models of dynamic processes must find their places.[141] Factors that equilibrium analysis had excluded from its theoretical considerations as exogenous were regarded as endogenous variables. Clark included such factors as changes in technology, changes in the tastes of buyers and in market conditions, the attitudes of sellers toward the moves of their rivals, the long-run or short-run "economic horizons," and so on. The roles played by product variation and differentiation in processes of monopolistic competition were the object of various studies.[142] Consideration was also given to the distribution of profit between the entrepreneurs and the owners of scarce productive factors.[143]

Considerable difficulties were involved in tackling the question of how to measure the "degree" of monopoly. Oskar Morgenstern suggested measuring the strength of economic power by the amount of indeterminateness that it introduces into the economic process.[144] The level of profit could hardly be used to establish a measure of monopoly, since it was hardly possible to devise a theoretically satisfactory method of separating the effects of monopolistic market control from the effects of other factors on the rate of profits.[145] It was obvious that the "accounting rate" of profit did not supply a reliable criterion;[146] the same was true of other standards, such as the number of competitors and the scope of industrial concentration, uniformity of price quotations and price flexibility, utilization of productive capacity, rate of business mortality, and the like.[147]

A certain agreement was eventually reached on a formula proposed by Abba P. Lerner.[148] He started with the assumption that under free competition profits are maximized when marginal costs are equal to marginal revenue. Hence, he argued that the degree of monopoly could be measured by relating it to the difference between selling price and marginal revenue. The desired formula was provided by the ratio of that difference to the price, an expression which was the reciprocal of the elasticity of demand. In the ensuing discussion, the formula was found to be significant when used to test the economic justification of the allocation of productive factors, but it was hardly fit to determine the degree to which the value of the output differed from that which would have been reached under competitive conditions. It was unclear whether short-run marginal costs, as used in Lerner's formula, might not be replaced by long-run costs.

Lerner's formula was also referred to for measuring changes in the degree of monopoly which take place in particular industries in the course of business fluctuations.[149] Michael Kalecki developed the formula into a method of evaluating the degree of monopoly power for an entire economy, and applied that method to the explanation of the income distribution between labor and other classes of the population.[150]

The theory of oligopoly was welcomed by all authors and teachers of economics who had decried the "lack of realism" of Ricardian and post-Ricardian doctrines. The adversaries of laissez-faire policies who had taken refuge in some vague institutional analyses were provided with a chance to back up their political attitude with the prestige of theoretical soundness.[151] But the outright theoretical results of the study of restrictive competition were so meager and the effects of that study on equilibrium economics so destructive that it was described as a "ticket of admission to institutional economics."[152]

In fact, the attempts to provide a theoretical background for the analysis of product differentiation and lack of free entry were overshadowed by a vast descriptive literature dealing with various aspects of national and international market control, as operated by cartels and trusts, and implemented through patent agreement and other restrictive devices. That literature found fertile soil especially in the "totalitarian" countries, in which market control was organized and regulated by the public authorities.[153] In the United States the policy of price administration which was practiced by the National Recovery Administration as a remedy for the Depression was soon abandoned. It gave place to a public attitude which regarded concentration and abuse of economic power as a major economic problem,[154] and the alleged decline in competition was thought to be responsible for some of the worst features of the Depression. The investigations carried out by the National Economic Committee were intended to provide a full picture of the degree of economic concentration and its influence, especially on the behavior of prices.[155] The committee failed to provide satisfactory material for the formulation of long-range economic policy. This was ascribed to the fact that the politicians who had decided on the research work of the committee were committed to the ideal of an economic world composed of competitive, independent, relatively small business units. But the markets analyzed by the committee were ruled by gigantic monopolistic enterprises, and the politicians had no approach to the problems of such markets.[156]

Official inquiries were supplemented by private studies dealing with the financial concentration of the American industry,[157] with the effects of monopolistic practices on prices and cumulative deflationary price movements,[158] and with the statistical aspects of price flexibility, such as the difference in frequency and amplitude of price changes as observable between various series of prices.[159] Economic policies designed to regulate the distribution of resources and to prevent monopolistic practices from interfering with economic progress were extensively discussed.[160]

The predominant role played in these discussions by problems of pricing and production control was eventually challenged by adherents of the Keynesian doctrine, who approached economic analysis from the angle of expenditures viewed as a macroeconomic problem and could hardly reconcile the monopolistic outlook on "economic stagnation" with confidence in a spontaneous revival of "aggressive competition." They insisted upon stimulating investment activity through raising prices and large-scale programs of public orders.

Looking for evolutionary trends characteristic of Western democracies, some interpreters of economic history pointed to the spread of monopolistic enterprises in support of the proposition that the capitalist order is bound to give way to a socialist organization of production and distribution. Considerations of that type provided the background for a widely read socioeconomic analysis by James Burnham,[161] who elaborated the idea that the economic organization of the leading industrialized nations was increasingly dominated by a new class of people, the managers of the large enterprises, who were scornful of the owners of capital and capitalist conceptions, and increasingly imbued with the desire to adjust production and trade to large-scale plans established and carried out on monopolistic lines.

Another prophet of the inevitable spread of socializing tendencies was Schumpeter,[162] whose theory of economic development was based on the assumption that the existence of monopolistic situations created by "daring employers" was prerequisite to the spread of technological improvements and progress. He questioned the Ricardian view that competition was indispensable for securing optimum productivity and pointed to the achievements of large-scale enterprises which produce for more or less monopolistic markets. He credited them with superior efficiency in organizing the allocation of resources, in enhancing the productivity of economic processes, and in adjusting wages and working conditions to the progress in productivity. He pointed to their capacity to attract enormous amounts of capital, to embark on long-range planning, and to expand their enterprises. He saw in their price and production policies factors that contribute to the stabilization of the economy.[163]

From the logical connection which he established between his "dynamic" theory of profit and the role played by innovations, Schumpeter drew the conclusion that overwhelming socializing tendencies were created by the increasing influence of trained specialists on decision making in many lines of production, by the ensuing "depersonalization" of economic progress, and by the "evaporation of the substance of private capital" through concentration and trustification of capital. In his view, the trend toward centralized planning was intensified through changes in employers' attitudes toward risk taking, which were due to the fact that the entrepreneurial profits were squeezed out by rising wages. That process was likely to lead to the disappearance of the bourgeoisie as a class. But Schumpeter's analysis of economic developments met with much skepticism. Hardy showed that Schumpeter failed to take account of "economic nationalism" as a characteristic feature of a socialist state, and that he attached practically no importance to the loss of freedom which could be considered the inevitable result of the introduction of centralized economic planning.[164]

Another attempt to assess the impact of monopolistic organizations on economic progress was made by John Kenneth Galbraith, who advanced the proposition that technological progress, as promoted by entrepreneurial activity, had been almost exclusively achieved in those sectors of the economy which were not primarily influenced by the working of impersonal forces, but in which the markets were controlled by powerful units or blocs.[165] To these units, Galbraith juxtaposed "countervailing powers"—organizations existing at the opposite side of the market and neutralizing the excess of power exercised by the economic blocs. He considered inflationary price movements as the greatest danger to the maintenance of that, on the whole, desirable structure of the economy.

The view that the existence of countervailing power could be regarded as a suitable substitute for a competitive organization of the economy was the object of various critical comments.[166] Adherents of the principle of competition favored such diffusion of economic power as was required to permit continued adjustment of the economy to changing market conditions and progressive equalization of incomes.[167] Several attempts were made to define a concept of "workable competition" suitable for prescribing norms of "rational" economic behavior in markets characterized by product differentiation and similar noncompetitive conditions.[168] These proposals dealt with the structure of the market (number of traders, moderate quality differentials, and the like), norms of conduct (absence of collusion, observance of fair tactics, and so on), and norms of performance (efficiency profits, prices, allocation of resources, barriers to free entry, and the like). Particularly noticeable was Clark's proposed definition of "workable competition," which considered exercise of an adequate degree of market control as prerequisite to the assumption by entrepreneurs of the risks and uncertainties associated with the introduction of innovations in productive processes.[169] Other discussions of entrepreneurial behavior were ruled by the intention to classify it according to quasi-rational types in order to arrive at a criterion for distinguishing socially undesirable monopolistic enterprises from others considered neutral or even favorable to general economic welfare. But, regardless of intentions pursued by the various authors, their studies resulted in dissolving the theory of restrictive competition into a "myriad of disconnected compartments, without subjecting the fragments to a useful unifying principle."[170]

In view of the difficulties involved in establishing a satisfactory groundwork for the analysis of oligopolies, some authors were tempted to abandon the usual approach to the problem and to suggest the application of analogies drawn from other lines of activities, such as military strategy and tactics.[171] The oligopolist's behavior was shown to be strongly determined by considerations of security, which frequently cause him to keep his prices stable but are sometimes responsible for prolonged price wars.[172] The existence of oversized firms and interlocking directorates was attributed to the desire to provide oligopolistic firms with a strong financial background.

The functioning of the capitalist economy was equally the object of divergent interpretations in Western and Central Europe after the competitive economy had reasserted itself in Germany and Italy.[173] Especially controversial was the question of whether a tendency toward increasing industrial concentration is inherent in the capitalist society.[174] The results of the theoretical discussions were rather disappointing. Some European economists who rejected competition as an efficient form of market organization were opposed by convinced adherents of the principle of competition, who attacked monopolistic devices as instruments of economic rigidity, destabilizing factors, and impediments to economic progress. Considerable skepticism prevailed as to the possibility of exercising effective control over monopolized markets.

The American participants were practically unanimous in emphasizing the high degree of workable competition which exists in the United States. But no convincing explanation was offered for the divergencies between American and European patterns of monopolistic competition.[175] The problems connected with the competitive and the monopolistic organizations of the economy were discussed at a meeting organized in 1951 by the International Economic Association.[176].

Chapter 30
Further Discussion of Older Problems: Planning and Welfare

DISCUSSION ABOUT PLANNING

THE DISCUSSION of "hypothetical" planning was closely connected with the increasing attention given to the problems of restricted competition since it appeared necessary to elaborate the fundamental distinctions between planning under competitive conditions and "monopolistic" planning, as designed to reduce the risks involved in operating competitive enterprises or as exercised under the influence of organismic or dialectic reasoning.[1] Research into the actual behavior of firms in organizing production and sales was also frequently stimulated by the desire to achieve closer touch with reality in analyzing various aspects of business administration.

The problems involved in decision making, in expectations and anticipations, had been virtually ignored by the Ricardian and post-Ricardian economists who had endeavored to adjust their hypothetical model of the economy to mechanistic principles. Their consistent use of the equilibrium concept to coordinate the relationships of economic magnitudes was backed by the explicit or implicit belief in the ultimate harmony of individual objectives, which was assumed to be secured by the operation of economic forces working independently of any conscious human activity. In the light of that approach to economic analysis, an otherwise unmanageable network of individual economic operations was transformed into a system of calculable and strictly determined planning procedures of "economic men." Rational economic behavior meant striving for the largest possible share of the available exchange values.

After the cost of production theory of value had been superseded by the subjective theory, a purely hypothetical unit of value (the *numéraire*) was introduced into Walrasian economics in order to preserve the mechanistic features of the economic system. The innumerable processes of hypothetical competitive economic planning which take place in the economy were coordinated in accordance with two main assumptions: (1) that the marginal utilities of goods for each individual were continuously equalized, and (2) that rational economic behavior of the entrepreneurs resulted in equalizing the marginal productivities of the productive factors. A system of interdependent prices was assumed to keep the behavior of the markets within the range of predictability. But the Walrasian suggestion that the general establishment of equilibrium prices could be assured through processes of "groping" met with serious objections. The postulated "higgling" of the markets was shown to be terminated not through intellectual processes but through acts of willful decisions. The assumption of perfect foresight on the part of economic individuals was shown to be incompatible with equilibrium analysis.[2] The endeavor by the Walrasian economists to render all elements of their system determinate only accentuated the purely imaginative aspects of their doctrine.

Within the the framework of the Austrian version of marginalism, subjective estimates of the marginal utilities of consumers were regarded as important elements of producers' and traders' decision making. Böhm-Bawerk attempted a coordination of innumerable hypothetical plans. He assigned to the rate of interest the function of determining the economically justified duration of the various periods of production; the volumes of desirable investments and their distribution among the promising channels of economic activity were thus indirectly defined. Moreover, the concept of "economic rationality" was given an expression in quantitative terms when the entrepreneur was assumed to adjust his production to the principle of marginal productivity and to be guided by the tendency to maximize his profits. But on closer analysis the concept of "economic rationality" turned out to be open to varying interpretations.

It soon became apparent that the principle of marginal productivity, though well established on theoretical grounds, did not provide reasonable guidance for practical economic behavior. Similarly, doubts were cast on the principle of profit maximization, described by F. H. Knight as a law of the empirical type which, as a first approximation to reality, could be used to explain the existence and the behavior of the firm.[3] Other economists sought the reasons for the existence of the firm and for the size of the firm in the cost-saving functions of the entrepreneur.[4] The view that striving for profit maximization was frequently not the most desirable policy to be pursued by a firm was advanced by several economists.[5] In addition, analysts of business behavior argued that frequently no method was available to define maximum profits, even if a firm wanted to pursue that policy.[6] Regardless of the emphasis placed by economic theory on marginal revenues and marginal costs, businessmen were found to adjust their prices to the rules of the "full cost principle," according to which prime costs were increased by a conventional fraction of costs. In a study prepared by a research group of Oxford economists, that economic attitude was found to be typical of the average British firm.[7]

These economists questioned the usefulness of such concepts as marginal and average revenue and marginal and average costs, and insisted that dependence of demand on present as well as future prices made it impossible to derive marginal revenue from any single demand curve.[8] Consequently, they objected to the use of the marginal cost principle in drawing distinctions among competition, monopoly, and monopolistic competition of different types, and insisted that the price policy of the various firms was commonly determined by factors which could be accounted for only in the light of the history of the industry.[9] In the markets of the majority of the American firms, non-economic forces were shown to exercise a significant influence on price determination, with the result that even in competitive markets costs of production were not generally reduced to a minimum, and allocation of resources was far from being perfectly rational.

The perceptible changes in the behavior of American business executives since about the beginning of this century were attributed to numerous factors: modifications of accounting procedures, adoption of flexible administrative procedures, introduction of policies of long-range planning and of refined methods of market analysis, and so on. Other important changes have occurred in ''industrial relations,'' the relations between employers and employees. The tendency to maximize profit appears to have given way to the tendency to maximize ''the present value of an indefinitely long series of secure and socially permitted profits.''[10]

Some economists considered as entirely imaginary the concept of a firm which was alleged to maximize an income variable called ''net revenue'' which was unknown to the accountant.[11] A new approach to expectations and anticipations was adopted in some ''dynamic'' models of the economy, and more or less consistent attempts to take account of the risk factor as an element in influencing individual economic planning were eventually made in econometric studies. The history of the analysis of employers' planning in a competitive economy is another telling contribution to the proposition that the development of a science is primarily dependent upon the development of its methodological devices.

The methodological principles of the Ricardian and post-Ricardian economists had a counterpart in their belief that any interference with individual planning was bound to upset the adjustment of productive activities to the prevailing market conditions and to disturb the optimal allocation of resources. Viewed from that angle, the phrase ''economic planning on national lines'' was contradictory. Strong objections were also raised to the planning devices of monopolistic or semimonopolistic concerns or organizations.

To the extent that the belief in the blessings of free competition had survived the incessant attacks of the adversaries of the capitalist economy, that belief was deeply shattered during the Great Depression when practically all governments felt obliged to interfere with the functioning of the economy in order to stem the tide of rapidly declining business activity. Especially noteworthy was the break with the traditional policy of laissez-faire in the United States, where economists and politicians vied with each other in recommending remedial economic measures.[12] Conservative authors centered their proposals on the protection of domestic markets against foreign competition. More radical reformers proposed the introduction of far-reaching measures of credit control, public works programs, and the like,[13] or an organization of industries on a cooperative basis,[14] or the subordination of the industries to the control of holding companies,[15] or the application of principles of ''scientific management'' to the industrial organization.[16] Theoretically better founded were other, but equally utopian, plans which visualized the establishment of large schemes of production[17] or consumption[18] guaranteed by the government. Almost all these reformers manifested a remarkable predilection for monopolistic methods of market control[19] and for inflationary methods of financing their plans.[20]

In fact, the idea of organizing the expansion of production along the lines of a sort of collective monopoly played a conspicuous role in the emergency measures of the ''New Deal'' introduced by the Roosevelt administration. But that phase in the history of American economic policy soon came to an end, and the upswing of business activity coincided with a renewed wave of theoretical interest stimulated by the teachings of Keynes's *General Theory*. The younger generation of American economists agreed almost unanimously on the belief that the exaggerated propensity to save had been the ultimate cause of the Depression, and that various methods of monetary and credit policy were available to supplement deficient expenditures on consumption goods.

The question of the degree to which the American economy was being gradually permeated by elements of collective planning was the object of widely divergent views. In a discussion of the long-term trends of American capitalism which took place in 1949, H.B.S. Keirstead emphasized the existence of a strong trend toward industrial concentration and advocated the establishment of appropriate government control of business activity.[21] Sumner H. Slichter questioned the wisdom of various planners who requested the enforcement of a ''national'' economic budget. Schumpeter considered a gradual transformation of a ''disintegrating capitalism'' into a ''socialist economy'' inevitable. In support of that thesis, he argued that the system of private enterprises was overburdened with public charges and was regulated beyond its power of endurance, and that the social framework of society was weakened by the effects of ''perennial'' inflationary pressures. Discussions of that type recurred time and again without leading to definite conclusions.

Symptomatic of the confusion which beclouded the thinking of many socialist authors was the fact that the problems involved in organizing an economy along ''collectivist'' lines were hardly ever clearly formulated. Application of advanced methods of technology and ''scientific management'' was expected to result in the elimination of the wasteful methods of the ''anarchical'' system of free competition, and to secure enormous increases in productivity. Students of the natural sciences were particularly fascinated by the idea that the rapid progress achieved in securing conscious control of natural forces could be accompanied by a similar control of economic activities organized by central bodies of experts. According to a widespread view, held especially by adherents of the technocratic movement, economic calculations in terms of ''values'' could be replaced by calculations in terms of ''energy'' or similar standards derived from the physical sciences, and could thus be adjusted to ''rational'' principles.

The masters of the school of Lausanne, Walras and Pareto, were the first authors to apply the tools of consistent theoretical analysis to the examination of the possible functioning of a socialist economy. They formulated the fundamental problems of centralized planning in accordance with the proposition that it was necessary to organize a system of interdependent prices which would secure the adjustment of supply to the effective demand displayed by the members of the community. But Pareto emphasized the formidable difficulties involved in any attempt to substitute such prices for those arrived at through individual transactions under the rule of free competition. In an article published in 1908, Enrico Barone examined more closely the tasks of the ministry of production of a socialist state.[22] On the assumption that definite amounts of purchasing power were allotted to the members of the communist society, Barone showed the range of practically insoluble calculations which would have to be performed in order to determine the demand functions for consumers' goods, the supply functions of labor, and saving, if freedom of choice as to consumption, saving, and employment of labor were to be preserved, costs of production minimized, and productive factors allocated in accordance with the principles of economic rationality.[23]

Another attempt to apply marginal utility analysis to the problems connected with the organization of a communist society was made by Friedrich von Wieser in his *Treatise on Social Economics*.[24] On the assumption that optimum want satisfaction of the members of the community and optimum allocation of resources were the ultimate objectives of the economy, Wieser arrived at the general conclusion that production had to be organized in every line in such a way that marginal productivity of all resources was equalized in all uses. It is an open question as to what degree elements of "social valuation" were implied in Weiser's definition of the demand functions. In these discussions it was assured that, regardless of the rules applied to capital accumulation, to the distributive processes, and to the definition of public expenditures, the values of the productive factors were the determinant elements in the process of organizing rational plans of production, and that these values were in turn derived from the relative shares of the productive factors in the values of their products.

Ludwig von Mises is to be credited with having confronted the advocates of socialism with the full array of problems which need to be taken into account when an economic system is to be operated in accordance with the principles of "economic rationality."[25] He argued that observance of these principles could not be assured unless determinate prices for the productive factors were established in competitive markets and unless competitive processes could be relied upon to secure the interdependence between these prices and those of consumption goods. If these methods of price determination were replaced by arbitrary decisions by central authorities or by managers of monopolistic concerns, considerations of marginal productivity were ignored and rational allocation of resources was rendered impossible.

Similar ideas were later summarized in the statements that the "economic calculus" or the pure logic of choice helps us, at least by analogy, to see how problems of choice are solved by the price system; that a single mind could solve these problems only by constructing and constantly using rates of equivalence or values or "marginal rates of substitution," that is, by attaching to each kind of scarce resource a numerical index which reflects its significance in the whole means-end structure.[26]

Considerations of that type caused some socialist authors, such as Maurice H. Dobb, to reject the "sacredness of consumers' preferences," to emphasize the need to establish "collective choices," and to minimize the economic importance of the preference for present over future goods.[27] As opposed to the ex post coordination of productive processes which takes place under the rule of a decentralized pricing system, Dobb put forward the advantages he ascribed to the possibility of securing ex ante adjustments of "productive processes in a planned economy.[28] But E.F.M. Durbin admitted that in a planned economy it might be advisable to apply the principles of marginal productivity to the mutual adjustment of the productive factors and to use the principles of equilibrium analysis to determine the depreciation allowance and the profits to be attributed to the capital goods.[29]

In his contribution to these discussions, Arthur C. Pigou availed himself of certain criteria of welfare economics to compare a system of planned socialism with one of the competitive type.[30] In favor of socialism, he listed the prospects of reducing inequalities of income, of remedying employment conditions, and of including social costs in processes of price determination. He agreed with Dobb's proposition that one should disregard—on grounds of nonrationality—the preference actually shown by individuals for present over future want satisfaction. But he questioned the capacity of a socialist regime to take full advantage of technological efficiency and to master the administrative difficulties involved in operating innumerable economic departments.

These discussions were enlivened by an interesting interlude provided by the writings of several authors who had been trained in the refined methods of marginalism and who fully appreciated the functions fulfilled by an interdependent price system in determining the economically justified allocation of the productive factors. As a result, they considered it advisable to organize a "workable collectivistic economy" in accordance with

Barone's proposition that the determination of prices and volumes of production in a socialist economy should be adjusted to the rules established for a perfectly competitive economy.[31] The main problem to be solved consisted apparently in substituting for Barone's innumerable equations a system of manageable administrative devices.

With this purpose in mind, Lange proposed to start the operation of the collectivist economy from a system of prices fixed for capital goods and intermediary products by a control board. The plant managers would be requested to combine productive factors in such a way that for a given output average costs would be at a minimum and prices would be adapted to marginal costs.

Lange's scheme provided an instructive analysis of an imaginary centralized economy functioning according to the rules of perfect competition, but it is doubtful whether even its author believed that it could ever be put to the test of practical application.[32] Henry Dickinson proposed to use strict observance of the marginal cost principle as the criterion of price determination and to establish a "marginal cost equalization fund" into which industries with increasing costs would pay a tax and out of which industries with decreasing costs would be subsidized.[33] In a prolonged discussion of the principles of price determination to be observed in a planned economy, Durbin advocated the application of average costs, whereas Abba P. Lerner insisted that prices had to be adjusted to marginal costs.[34]

In additional discussions, account was taken of a variety of problems likely to confront the masters of a collectivist economy: how adjustment of prices to changing market conditions and marginal costs could be assured, how inflationary pressures could be avoided and optimum allocation of resources be achieved,[35] how managerial initiative could be stimulated, how individual firms could be assisted in assuming financial risks, how directives could be established to determine investment policies and to fix the rate of capital accumulation and the distribution of capital among the various lines of economic activity, and so on.[36] Adversaries of collectivism emphasized the problematic aspects of these schemes: their inherent association with autarkic and protectionist policies designed to reduce the dependence of the planned economy on supplies from abroad; their tendency to discourage risk taking;[37] their reliance on inflationary methods of financing investment;[38] and the overall weakness of theoretical, mathematical, or logical models of planned economics.[39]

In a comprehensive analysis of the problems of the planned "welfare economy," Lerner admitted that enormous difficulties were involved in controlling the allocation of resources through a central agency, and that the investment decisions of the planning agencies could be determined only by political considerations.[40] He considered it advisable to divide a planned economy into a competitive sector and a noncompetitive sector and to assign to the latter all industries based on the use of indivisible factors. The managers of these monopolistic concerns should be required to adjust their economic decisions to the principles underlying the behavior of perfectly competitive markets. Adequate aggregate demand and a continuous high level of output and employment should be secured through methods of "functional finance."

It has been one of the strange episodes in the history of economic reasoning that radical minds, bent on overthrowing the existing economic order, nevertheless believed— or pretended to believe—that, contrary to any historical experience, the pattern for the organization of a "planned" economy could be supplied by a model of the Walrasian type in which full reliance was placed on the automatic working of equilibrating forces. The belief that Walrasian economics could provide the guiding principles for the organization of a planned economy was carried to its extremes by the French economist Maurice Allais. Starting with the argument that under perfect competition in an equilibrated economy interest on capital is bound to disappear, Allais proposed to nationalize the soil and to express price in terms of a money of account based on a unit of unskilled labor time. The circulating means of payment should be gradually devalued in order to discourage capital accumulation.[41]

The authors of such programs of hypothetical, even fictional, planning overlooked the obvious fact that the functions ascribed to human reason by the adherents of Walrasian economics differ radically from those which the leaders of a planned economy must attribute to their own reason if they want to fulfill the tasks involved in directing such an economy. It is equally absurd to expect that the managers of monopolistic concerns would capable of adjusting their economic behavior to an ill-defined fiction, such as the functioning of a perfectly competitive economy in which money provides only a convenient unit of account. The operation of a planned economy is hardly compatible with the objectives of a democratic society in which production is primarily determined by the wants of individuals and their purchasing power. The government of a socialist state engaged in long-range planning has to be protected by institutional devices against the danger of being overthrown by a hostile opposition. The moral and political background of such devices can be supplied only by social philosophies which are opposed to the methods of hypothetical reasoning and which provide their adherents with the instruments to enforce uniformity of belief and subordination of individual freedom to the dictates of the government.

The proposals of some less radical hypothetical reformers reflected the widespread view that the deficiencies of the capitalist economy could best be remedied by reducing the risks involved in the competitive organization of production and trade. Hence, their plans were designed to assure full utilization of productive resources and to guarantee a certain degree of income security, not only to the wage earners but also to the recipients of income from professional occupations and from the ownership of capital assets.[42] Other schemes were suggested by the theorem of economic stagnation.

The system of planning and economic control that was practiced in England during the Second World War greatly appealed to the leaders of the Labor party. When called upon to form a government, they proposed the nationalization of a number of key industries, and a lively discussion turned on the problems of "democratic planning" as outlined in the official economic survey of 1947. On the one side were the advocates of the planned economy, who insisted upon the task of the government to control the use of the available resources in the national interest.[43] On the other side were the adherents of the competitive economy, who protested against any far-reaching interference with the functioning of the economy. Harrod argued that the recovery of the English economy was retarded by "overinvestment" and ensuing "inflationary pressures." John Jewkes analyzed the reasons advanced in favor of the policy of central planning and pointed to the obsession with material ends as a fundamental weakness of the planned society. James M. Meade admitted the need for a reasonable degree of state intervention, and recommended control of monopolistic industries in which average costs were far below marginal costs, but he defended the competitive economy and free determination of prices and output.[44] Considerations connected with problems of economic productivity and efficiency had to be weighed against postulates derived from principles of social justice, equity, and humanitarian doctrines.[45] It was especially doubtful whether the application of large-scale measures of planning was compatible with the exercise of the traditional freedom of occupational choice.[46]

The experience derived from the operation of the nationalized industries led to the conclusion that there was no reason to suppose that under public ownership investment plans would be wiser, that production would be more efficient, that the search for export markets would be keener, or that management would be more flexible and more enlightened.[47] No agreement was reached on the intricate problem of how far the operation of the nationalized industries should be governed by commercial considerations and how far by political objectives.[48] It remained equally an open question as to how to find a reasonable basis for the assessment of the capital needs of these industries. Even cautious left-wing economists, such as C.A.R. Crossland, admitted that the nationalized industries had failed to contribute significantly to the process of capital accumulation and to the improvement of social relationships.[49] The ultimate fate of the British economy will hardly be determined exclusively by considerations of "economic rationality."

Problems of centralized planning were placed on the agenda of one of the first conferences organized after the Second World War by the German Association for Social Politics.[50] Widely divergent views were advanced on the question of whether and to what degree a planned economy was to be regarded as superior to the exchange economy. Similarly divergent views were expressed as to what principles of "social justice" should be followed in the distribution of incomes and wealth, what methods should be used to assure the efficiency of planning devices, and the like. These discussions did not contribute significant new ideas to the problems involved in economic organization.

WELFARE

The problems treated under the somewhat ambiguous heading of "welfare economics" were originally formulated in accordance with the utilitarian principle that the welfare of a society or community is equal to the sum of the welfare of its individual members. The Ricardian economists had oversimplified these problems on the assumption that, under the rules of free competition and free trading, production was maximized an optimum allocation of resources was assured unless the functioning of the economy was disturbed by outside factors. In their model of the economy, "riches," the objects of immediate want satisfaction, were excluded from any consideration in favor of "wealth," the economic magnitudes which could be reduced to a common standard of value.

Although problems connected with the increases and distribution of "riches" had aroused the interests of various Ricardian economists, Alfred Marshall is to be credited with having given these problems a definite position in post-Ricardian economics. The subjective approach to value analysis played a significant role in their formulation under the heading of "welfare economics," since the welfare of the community was identified with the maximum want satisfaction of its members, utility being defined as a measurable function of a given commodity; interpersonal comparability and measurability of want satisfaction were considered reasonable assumptions in welfare economics.[51] Marshall was convinced of the validity of his proposition that a shilling's worth of gratification to one Englishman might be taken as equivalent to a shilling's worth to another, until cause to the contrary was shown. [52] Similarly, the Marshallian concept of consumers' surplus was suggested by the assumption that differences in marginal utilities as expressed monetary terms could be compared with each other. In accordance with this reasoning, general increases in want satisfaction could be brought about by shifts in demand from goods produced under conditions of decreasing returns to goods produced under increasing returns.

Ideas of that kind provided the background for Pigou's elaborate discussion of welfare economics.[53] Pigou defined the quantity which was to be maximized as that part of social welfare that can be brought directly or indirectly under the measuring rod of money.[54] Conceived of as a "realistic" positive theory, economic welfare was to be studied in terms of quantities of values and their distribution. In a more or less axiomatic manner, Pigou assumed that—with the exception of some special circumstances—welfare was increased when the volume of aggregate real income was enlarged, the steadiness of its flow better assured, the dissatisfaction caused by its production reduced, and the distribution of the national dividend changed in favor of the poor. He brushed aside objections to interpersonal comparisons of want satisfactions and dissatisfactions, and based his comparisons of different degrees of welfare reached at different periods on how far their interpersonal comparability was justified and whether maximum or optimum welfare could be identified with the production of a maximum amount of exchange values.

The problem of how to measure utilities had been the object of various unsuccessful attempts at solution on the part of Irving Fisher. In a renewed endeavor by Ragnar Frisch,[55] the marginal utility of money was derived from the marginal utility of income, and refined mathematical methods were used to measure changes in that marginal utility. These methods were adjusted to the available material according to whether that material showed quantities of goods consumed at different prices, or changing quantities consumed at constant prices, or only the size of nominal incomes and total sum spent on consumption. But Frisch's procedures were also vulnerable to the general objections to measurability of utilities.[56] He applied the results of his measurements to the solution of practical problems, such as adjustment of income tax legislation to different principles of justice.

These objections had a counterpart in other objections to the interpersonal comparability of utilities and even to intertemporal comparisons of utilities experienced by the same individual. The often-quoted attempt by John R. Hicks and R.G.D. Allen to reformulate value theory[57] contributed greatly toward discrediting the application of cardinal numbers to the measures of utilities. As elaborated in the methodological discussions of Lionel Robbins, these considerations resulted in questioning the scientific validity not only of "welfare economics" as commonly understood but also of almost all recommendations of economic policy, including the free trade principle.[58]

Under these conditions, skeptical minds could regard it as an "obsolete sport" to rationalize the competitive system into an engine of welfare.[59] Authors who continued to praise competition, condemn tariffs, and advocate a "neutral" monetary policy were said to preserve that attitude "out of sheer habit."[60] The phrase "euthanasia of welfare economics" was used to characterize the results of a study which implied that the economist abandoned his scientific neutrality when he expressed preference for any measure of economic policy, unless it could be shown that nobody's interests were damaged by the effects of the measure, and even in that case a hidden normative principle was held to be implied in his acceptance of the existing distribution of incomes and wealth.

The welfare economists of the Cambridge school protested against the limitations imposed on their doctrine by these considerations.[61] Harrod regarded interpersonal comparability of utilities as an indispensable element of economic analysis.[62] Colin Clark believed that nothing would be left—except possibly the theory of the trade cycle—when economics was deprived of the concept of welfare.[63] Frank H. Knight argued that the need to justify progressive taxation and reductions of the inequality of incomes was too urgent to be dismissed because no way had yet been found to prove the underlying assumptions and no perfect standard had been discovered to measure utilities.[64] Marcus Fleming suggested a "cardinal concept" of welfare by assigning numbers to the different degrees of welfare associated with indifferent hypothetical situations under a given ethical system, and to the different degrees of well-being which the several individuals experience in these situations.[65] Thus, he expected to substitute ethical for economic evaluations and to replace the measurement of utilities with the measurement of welfare situations.

In accordance with a proposition elaborated by various sociologists, in particular by Pareto, no society can exist unless its members have agreed—explicitly or tacitly—on a common value system. In the light of such considerations, the value system which is basic to the capitalist society was examined by several authors who were equally critical of the utilitarian social philosophy, the attitude adopted by outspoken adversaries of the capitalist order, and the normative precepts derived from the teachings of religious denominations.[66] Thus, John M. Clark looked for the assistance of neighboring disciplines, such as psychology and sociology, to arrive at a "dynamic interpretation" of the functioning of the economy and the establishment of "social values" as distinct from the values that dominate the marketplace.[67] In addition, he insisted on a determination of the costs of production that accrue to society, as distinct from the costs covered by private cost accounting. Among the social values that could be expected to meet with general approval, he listed striving for economic stability, for maximum progress and growth of the economy, and for full employment of the available resources, especially of labor. In his search for a solution to a similar problem, Marshall had advised the economist to use "ethical instincts" and "common sense" as ultimate arbiters in cases in which a cause that appears to promote economic welfare may be detrimental to welfare as viewed from a noneconomic angle.

On closer examination, these social objectives were found to be not fully compatible with each other. Even authors who accepted "maximization of individual welfare" as the supreme end of society questioned the prevailing "materialistic" interpretation of the concept of welfare and objected to the view that the definition of maximum welfare was to be based on the existing distribution of incomes.[68] It was doubtful that the achievement of noneconomic objectives, such as political security of the community, could claim precedence over maximization of real incomes. In support of such views, Stigler referred to a proposal advanced half a century before by John N. Keynes: to develop a science of "applied ethics" designed to define the objectives which are basic to the existence of the community.[69]

At this juncture, the advocates of a "science of welfare economics" were confronted with the verdict that it was impossible to set up standards of judgment based on purely economic considerations and free from any political or moral ideas or motivations. They were also faced with the objection that it was impossible to define a maximum degree of welfare and to determine processes which are likely to lead to that goal.

As in other similar cases, a way out of the impasse was provided by methodological considerations which resulted in the development of analytic instruments such that the apparently insoluble problems were reformulated in a more amenable manner. These instruments were systems of indifference and preference curves which had been used by Pareto and Barone in their studies of the distributive aspects of welfare economics.[70] It thus happened that welfare economics was transformed into "a department of thought" which owed its unity not so much to the "natural boundaries" of the subject matter which it discussed as to the limitations of its tool chest.[71]

With the aid of systems of indifference and preference curves, Pareto and Barone had circumvented direct measurement of utilities and established standards of efficiency by setting up comparable optima of want satisfaction. Barone had proposed to measure increases and decreases of individual welfare in terms of changes in the money income needed to maintain the original level of welfare. Pareto's *"maximum d'ophélimité"* was based on the consideration that a situation could be regarded as superior to another when the change had made some individuals better off and none worse off. But absolute positions of maximum welfare could not be determined with this method.

This approach to welfare analysis was combined with the reformulation of value theory suggested by Hicks and Allen, in which the concept of marginal utility was replaced by the concept of the marginal rate of substitution.[72] Hence, the individual was assumed to determine his outlays on any one commodity in such a way that he would be on the margin of indifference between the last small increment of that commodity and an additional alternative increment of any other commodity that might be substituted. Similar reasoning was applied to the determination of the isoquants, or equal products curves, representing the indifference curves in production theory.[73]

Aversion to the psychological interpretation of value theory caused various mathematical economists to object to the interpretation of "preference" and "indifference" as mental states determined by some sort of "introspection." They insisted upon defining these categories as forms of economic behavior. By pursuing that reasoning, the concept of "behavior lines" was substituted for the concepts of preference and indifference curves, and the transfer of an individual into a "higher behavior line" was no longer interpreted as a change in the degree of want satisfaction, but rather it was regarded as a change in his "chosen position." The consumer's preference, as revealed by his act of choosing, was related to observed or potentially observable market phenomena.[74] Utility analysis, which had provided the starting point for the mathematical approach to economics, was to be superseded by a theory of "rational choice."

Since progress in maximizing welfare was identified with improvements in the allocation of resources and increases in the efficiency of the economy, the economist who availed himself of such an approach appeared to have been provided with a sound theoretical basis for making policy recommendations without being influenced by normative considerations.[75] In fact, Harold Hotelling used the same conception of economic efficiency to determine the effects of specific measures of economic policy, such as the use of the receipts of general taxation to finance the construction of bridges and tunnels.[76]

In a generalized "efficiency analysis," Hicks undertook to define the theoretical conditions prerequisite to the adjustment of the economy such that the changes made could be regarded as improvements in the efficiency sense.[77] He took account of the influence of imperfect competition but, when faced with the treatment of the indirect effects of economic measures on consumption, he felt obliged to make the problematic assumption that these effects would tend to offset each other.

Moreover, since the indifference curves were derived from static conditions, any factors which might be responsible for inconsistent behavior had to be ignored,[78] and no account could be taken of consumers' behavior which was motivated by uncertainty and risk.[79] No conclusive answer was given to the fundamental question of whether, in fact, any reference to psychological factors had been eliminated when the theorems of rational behavior were derived from the questionable assumptions underlying the principle of "rational choice." On close examination it was found that the measurement of utilities was implied in the comparison of the size of changes in behavior positions.[80]

Additional objections to the use of indifference curves or behavior lines for purposes of welfare analysis were raised by critics who argued that the construction of such curves was obviously dependent on the prospect of obtaining from the individuals concerned reliable answers about their indifference or preference as to almost infinite numbers of combinations of goods, although such judgments might be subjected to frequent changes under the influence of varying events.[81] Could it legitimately be assumed that all utilities were perfectly divisible, that all utility indexes could be arranged in continuous lines, and that human behavior was exclusively motivated by the principles of "rational behavior"?

When a more realistic approach was adopted, the discussion shifted to a definition of the criteria which would enable the observer to determine the effects of measures of economic policy in the light of welfare economics. Pareto had assumed that welfare or "collective" satisfaction was increased in a perfectly objective sense by all changes in the course of which those who gained could indemnify those experiencing losses and would still have some gain left. That suggestion, which had been amplified by Barone, was taken up by Nicholas Kaldor, who requested the economist to recommend such economic changes as would result in improving the efficiency of the economic system on the assumption that any losers could be compensated for their losses by public authorities. The question of whether the compensation should actually be made was to be dealt with on grounds of political expediency. Kaldor believed that whenever increases in physical productivity and aggregate real income had been brought about by methods of economic policy, appropriate measures of taxation and compensation would be available to keep intact the previous income distribution.[82]

This reformulation of the problems of welfare economics implied a return to the separation of the productive and the distributive aspects of the economy. It provided Hicks with the opportunity of redefining the much-criticized Marshallian concept of "consumers' surplus" by identifying that concept with the sum of money a consumer would be required to pay after some change was made if he were reduced to the same behavior line (the same level of satisfaction) as before the change.[83] I.M.D. Little criticized the usefulness of the concept of consumer's rent for welfare comparisons.[84]

Tibor Scitovsky insisted even more strongly than Kaldor upon separating the problems of efficiency from those of the distributive process;[85] but it remained a moot question as to whether the problem of allocating resources could be treated separately from that of income distribution.[86] The payment of compensation for losses caused by measures of economic policy was the object of various discussions.[87]

The definition of efficiency standards in terms of the existing distribution of incomes and the determination of aggregate values in terms of the prevailing distribution of values were obviously promoted by conservative social philosophies. A more egalitarian approach was adopted by Abba P. Lerner, who applied the method of interpersonal comparability of utilities and assumed that the law of diminishing marginal utility was applicable to incomes expressed in monetary terms.[88] Oskar Lange elaborated the proposition that achievement of optimum general welfare was dependent upon adjustment of prices to marginal costs and that such adjustment was unattainable in an exchange economy.[89] Hence, he requested the establishment of a "dominant system of social values," which could be used in deciding among general systems of economic order.[90] In the light of those discussions it was pretty apparent that the fight for the establishment of generally valid principles of welfare economics was at least partly motivated by animosity toward the competitive economy and the endeavor to justify the adoption of systems of centralized planning.[91]

A final attempt to provide a more solid logical foundation for the definition of welfare economics was made by Abram Bergson, who proposed to aggregate individual value schemes in order to arrive at a sort of collective utility function (termed "social welfare function") by combining preferences exhibited by each individual, not only with regard to his personal satisfaction but also with regard to the state of the entire community and to the distribution of welfare among its members.[92] Within such a schema, account could be taken of risks and uncertainties, of the effects of external economics and diseconomics, of individual judgments concerning income distribution, etc. Optimal situations could be compared by arranging all possible utility distributions according to their relation to an ideal welfare function. In passing, reference may be made to a discussion of the question of whether and within what limits interpersonal comparisons of utilities are to be regarded as statements of facts which are not affected by value judgments. I.M.D. Little reasonably argued that individuals' judgments concerning their satisfaction, happiness, real income, or welfare, and comparisons based on such judgments, were statements of fact. But the proposition to define the general standard of welfare in accordance with individual desires was apparently derived from a value judgment.[93]

Critics of this complex approach could refer to previous inconclusive discussions of the decision process and its influence on individual valuations.[94] Wants had been shown to be inherently unstable, and unfit to supply reliable data for judgments concerning want satisfactions.[95] More or less general agreement of a community on a certain uniformity of preference was obviously prerequisite to the construction of a satisfactory welfare function, and value judgments were likely to be implied in the allocation of relative weights to the individual preferences aggregated in the "social value functions."[96] Kenneth J. Arrow pointed out a fundamental "summation problem" in his discussion of contradictory conclusions which may result from procedures involving choices among alternatives.[97] Such contradictions could be avoided only when the alternatives could be arranged on a linear scale, and when all members of the voting group had agreed on the order underlying the arrangement of the alternatives.[98]

The outcome of these extended and increasingly intricate discussions was not very encouraging. The various attempts to establish "objective criteria" for measuring social welfare had obviously quite frequently served the purpose of covering up the recommendation of specific systems of social organization; it was hardly possible to escape the conclusion that economic welfare was a topic "in which rigor and refinement were probably worse than useless."[99] The adoption of a system of value judgments was generally considered prerequisite to the analysis of problems of economic welfare.

Jan Tinbergen pointed to the "multidimensional" aspects of the welfare problem and proposed to substitute for the analysis of these problems the search for consistent methods dealing with the determination of the effects of policies designed to increase productivity.[100] With the aid of various models, he showed that, dependent upon changing economic conditions, expenditures on consumption and investment, the volumes of real income earned from labor, and the degree of employment were all affected to varying degrees by measures of economic and social policy, and that, consequently, the choice of such measures was to be adapted according to the importance attributed to capital supply, the level and distribution of incomes, and general working conditions.

In another connection, Tinbergen proposed a program of research designed to adjust welfare economics to the problems of income distribution as established in accordance with certain principles of social justice. This purpose should be served by comprehensive statistical investigations into frequency distributions of characteristics of persons and jobs, the elasticity of substitution between capital and labor, and other factors which throw some light on the questions of how incomes are generated within a nation and how international differences in incomes can be explained. Special importance was to be attached to the various attempts to use the vague concept of ''equality'' as a basis for the definition of social justice and social welfare by defining the concept in terms of quantitative, economically relevant characteristics.[101]

Chapter 31
Discussions about Money
and Monetary Reform

THE QUANTITY EQUATIONS AND THE CASH BALANCE APPROACH

FOR ALMOST TWO decades after the end of the First World War, each of the four leading schools of nominalistic economic reasoning (the British, the Austrian, the Lausanne and the Stockholm schools) pursued its research more or less independently of the others. Each preserved the principles, methods, and directives set up by its founders, but was faced with national economies which had been deeply unbalanced by the effects of the war, devastating inflationary movements, and the disruption of international trade relations.

One of the first problems to be solved consisted of explaining the origin and nature of inflationary price movements and their economic consequences in the light of the available monetary theories, and of suggesting ways and means to reestablish a sound monetary order. The starting point was provided by the traditional assumption that the means of payment are superimposed on an exchange system of ''real values'' or relative prices which are attached to the goods in the markets through the competitive bidding of producers and consumers. This fundamental approach to the pricing processes was well characterized by Knut Wicksell. The deliberate elimination of the function of money, he stated, the conception of trade as being in the final analysis an exchange of goods, the conception of capital as real capital instead of a sum of money, and the conception of wages as real wages—these were the decisive steps which gave a scientific character to political economy.[1]

Monetary theory had to define the exchange value or purchasing power of money; it had to supply the equation for determining the multiplicative factor which transforms relative into absolute prices.[2] R. G. Hawtrey said quite bluntly that monetary theory might be described as nothing more than the theory of how the value of money is determined.[3] Hence, monetary analysis was charged with the task of disentangling the value of money from the effects of ''nonmonetary causes'' and of ''defining the general level of prices.'' A considerable number of books and articles which dealt with the relations between money and prices adjusted their analyses to this setting of the monetary problems.

Irving Fisher's equation of exchange could hardly survive the barrage of criticism to which it had been exposed. It was defended by some adherents of the mechanical approach to economics.[4] But since the static equations of the transaction type were based on the assumption that the velocity of circulation of the means of payment and the volume of transactions were more or less constant, the usefulness of these equations was noticeably impaired during the Great Depression when income velocity as well as the volume of outputs fluctuated considerably.[5] Under these conditions, variables of unknown magnitudes had to be taken into account in order to determine the effects on prices of changes in the money supply, and the quantity equations enjoyed any consideration mainly in textbooks as pedagogical instruments of price analysis. Moreover, the validity of Fisher's equation was occasionally upheld in defense of the view that basic economic maladjustments cannot be corrected by monetary measures.[6]

James W. Angell carefully analyzed Fisher's equation. He endeavored to clarify the exact meaning of its constituent elements and distinguished several categories of money according to this behavior.[7] He found that for a given level of activity the demand for money may vary greatly according to the character of the economic organization and the prevailing forms of payment, and that only a part of the money supply may be in circulation. Hence, he arrived at the conclusion that the formulas of the quantity theory cannot give adequate expression to the immense variety of changes in prices resulting from changes in the quantity of the circulating means of payment.

Prolonged attempts to establish a consistent theory of money were dominated on the one hand by the income approach endorsed by the Austrian school and on the other by the cash balance approach adopted by the Cambridge economists. As developed with the aid of these tools, monetary analysis was linked with general economic theory.

The Cambridge economists remained true to the principles of static Marshallian economics; they centered their analysis on individual decisions reflecting preference for holding cash instead of other forms of wealth. Moreover, they dropped the traditional connection of changes in prices with changes in the quantity of money and looked for some links between monetary theory and the analysis of the national income.

Dennis Holme Robertson introduced the concept of "income velocity" into monetary theory and identified it with the average number of days in which each unit of money is brought to the market.[8] He discussed problems of income velocity on the assumption that consumers' outlays are derived from the income which becomes disposable during an immediately preceding period, as short as one day or a small number of days. He thus anticipated the ex ante method adopted by members of the Stockholm school, but he did not take account of expectations and ignored the existence of incomes of different types, as well as the spread of expenditures over more or less extended periods. Robertson used the terms *induced lacking* and *induced dislacking* to denote cases in which hoarding and dishoarding are not motivated by spontaneous alterations of cash balances but are designed to protect the real value of such balances from being affected by inflationary or deflationary processes.

The concept of "income velocity" was considered a useful instrument of economic analysis because it points to the ways in which increases in the quantity of money affect the income stream.[9] But the concept was qualified as "hybrid," since it was applied to an average relation between all cash balances and the national income, whereas most balances are held against the purchase of "unfinished" output, the value of which constitutes only a part of the national income.[10]

The discussion of monetary theories reached a new stage after the publication of John Maynard Keynes's great *Treatise on Money*,[11] a comprehensive and impressive attempt to connect the study of monetary problems with general economic theory. Qualifying the equations of the quantity theory of money as mere identities, relating the "turnover of the monetary instruments to the turnover of things traded for money," Keynes defined the general price level as a function of the ratio of the earnings of the community to total output. He adjusted his equations to this definition. In view of the fact that the purchasing power of money varies between different types of expenditures, he distinguished a number of different levels, and contrasted the "consumption" standard (the "purchasing power of money") with (1) the earnings standard (the labor power of money), (2) the standard of living index, and (3) currency standards (such as the cash transaction standard and the cash balances standard).

As had been done by Knut Wicksell, Keynes attached considerable importance to changes in the purchasing power of money and connected them with changes in the rate of interest. Analysis of savings and investments, as influenced by the rate of interest, was thus linked with monetary theory. Keynes defined the rate of interest which keeps the price level of output constant as the "natural rate of interest, and considered constancy of profits and equality of savings and investments prerequisite to the stability of the price level. Consequent upon this formulation of the theory of money, the stability of the price level was affected when the distribution of investments among goods of consumption and investment goods did not coincide with the distribution of incomes among consumption expenditures and savings.[12] Thus conceived, the use of money as a store of value appeared to be a main source of disturbances affecting the productive and distributive processes. But, true to the Marshallian tradition, Keynes ignored the time lag between the receipt of incomes and their expenditures. He condensed in a single equation the elements of a process which passes through several stages. His concepts of income, savings, and investments were adjusted to these premises.[13]

Keynes criticized Wicksell for having failed to draw a clear distinction among the functions of the market rate of interest as the capitalization factor, its role as an element of costs of production, and its influence on the volume of credit. But his own equations were open to the objection that they failed to show the transition from one equilibrium position to another; that some elements of the equations were not independent of each other; that some concepts, such as those of savings and investments, were not clearly defined;[14] and that the treatment of lags which was designed to explain the existence of profits was far from being unambiguous.

The cash balance approach to monetary analysis continued to occupy the Cambridge economists. They distinguished three types of money kept out of circulation: (*a*) working balances, involved in advancing credits to consumers; (*b*) financial balances, used for speculative and/or holding[15] purposes; and (*c*) idle balances, hoards, and contingency and liquidity reserves. Hence, the concept of velocity of circulation was related to individual decisions. The ratio of spending to holding money and the ratio of savings to investment were considered instrumental in determining the price level. Special attention was paid to the size of the working balances and the definition of the concept of hoarding.[16]

Arthur Marget's discussion of the Keynesian version of the cash balance approach was a specimen of his scholarship. He showed that the objections raised by Keynes to the quantity theory of money did not deal with this theory but with Fisher's transaction type of quantity equation. The Keynesian price theory, Marget argued, was misleading, since it assumed that price movements are directly influenced by changes in the rate of interest. Questioning the functions Keynes assigned to the national dividend, Marget emphasized the connection between the quantity of money and the level of incomes on the one hand and the relation between the incomes received and the corresponding expenditures on the other.[17]

In interpreting Fisher's equation, Marget carefully defined the meaning of the elements of the formula. He introduced the concept of velocity of circulation of goods and availed himself of the Walrasian concept of *"demande d'encaisse"* to characterize specific forms of demand for money. He endeavored to demonstrate that Fisher's variables and equations could be adjusted to different theories: those based on a simplified balance concept and those which took account of the time element.[18]

About the same time a new approach to the analysis of monetary problems was suggested by John R. Hicks, who found that three theories of money were combined with each other in Keynes's *Treatise on Money:*[19] (*a*) a quantity theory based on the relations between savings and investment; (*b*) a theory based on the functions which Wicksell had attributed to the natural rate of interest; and (*c*) a theory in which the price level of investment goods was linked with the relative preference of investors for liquidity or for profit. Hicks proposed to conceive of monetary theory as a sort of generalized banking theory using capital accounts or balance sheets instead of income accounts.

Viewed from this angle, the main task of monetary theory consisted of determining the varying reactions of individuals and groups of individuals to changes in their wealth. Hicks distinguished groups whose members are insensitive to such changes from others whose members are likely to react positively and from a third type characterized by reducing the demand for money consequent upon increases in wealth. Fluctuating price movements of varying degrees could be explained as the effect of such reactions. This analysis of much-discussed problems aroused considerable attention.[20]

THE INCOME APPROACH

The Austrian economists developed the income approach to monetary theory and derived the value of money from its significance as a unit of wealth and income. They placed special emphasis on the function of money as an instrument for transferring values from one period to another, and considered the "efficiency of money," as defined by Joseph Schumpeter, an important determinant of the value of money.[21] Schumpeter's analysis of the value of money proved helpful in explaining the behavior of prices in the German war economy when considerable intervals developed between the receipt and the expenditure of income, and sterilization of large amounts of money was an important factor in facilitating price adjustments.[22] But Schumpeter's assumption that the efficiency of money represented an almost constant factor was open to serious objections.[23]

The prevailing view that the value determination of money is to be analyzed in terms of impersonal and mechanical processes was incompatible with the principles of the income approach according to which the exchange value of money is derived from the combined effects of innumerable estimates of the subjective value of units of income.[24] Various price levels were distinguished in accordance with this theory. The purchasing power of money over consumer goods was found to be the best available "all-purpose index."

In his study of the meaning of index numbers, Gottfried Haberler connected the interpretation of such indices with the theory of choice; he characterized them as instruments for measuring changes in individual purchasing power.[25]

Various compartments of the economy were differentiated according to the distributive aspects of the stream of money: the spheres of incomes, of enterprises (business sphere), and of financial transactions.[26] The general velocity of circulation was conceived of as a weighted average of particular velocities; special attention was drawn to the influence exercised on circuit velocity by the "coefficient of differentiation," or the number of transactions required to put a product through all stages of the productive process.[27]

The concept of a general price level designed to measure the "outer objective" exchange value of money was rejected by some convinced adherents of the income approach. They contrasted this concept with that of the "inner" objective value of money derived from individual valuations. They abandoned the traditional conception of money as a "veil" superimposed on the real exchange economy and endorsed the concept of "neutral money which had been suggested by Wicksell in his search for a connecting link between general economic theory and monetary theory. They argued that the idea of "neutral money" had been anticipated in the Ricardian model of the economy in which the volume of the circulating means of payment was kept constant, any amount of money earned or received was immediately spent, and equilibrium conditions were defined in accordance with Jean Baptiste Say's law of market. The neutrality of money was considered assured when changes in its volume had no influence on relative prices or when such changes had the same effect on relative prices as would obtain under analogous circumstances in a barter economy.

A reformulation of the concept of "neutral money" became necessary, however, when it was realized that account had to be taken of the time element in order to secure a closer approximation to reality. Friedrich A. Hayek started from the consideration that a break in the reaction mechanism of the equilibrating forces was bound to occur when changes in the volume of money did not affect all prices at the same time and in the same proportion.[28] To the view that equilibrium analysis could be applied only to a static system,[29] he opposed the theorem of an "intertemporal equilibrium of prices"; to the traditional assumption that all movements of the general price level are caused by changes in the quantity of money, he opposed the argument that the general level could very well be altered by cost reductions which are due to technological improvements and are reflected in declining prices unless interfered with by credit expansion. Hence, the equilibrium of demand and supply was to be assured by measures designed to keep constant the volume of the circulating means of payment multiplied by the velocity of circulation of the monetary unit. Any change in the velocity of circulation was to be compensated by a reciprocal change in the amount of the circulating means of payment.[30]

It may be mentioned in passing that a few years later Robertson suggested that the American economic crisis of the thirties was a "nemisis for ill-considered efforts to hold up prices in the face of falling costs." He qualified the stabilization of the level of wholesale prices which took place between 1922 and 1929 as a vast attempt to destabilize the value of money in terms of human effort.

In elaborating the concept of "neutral money," Hayek attached special importance to the incidence of "forced savings" as a cause of economic disturbances.[31] He carefully surveyed the views of Ricardian and post-Ricardian authors who had taken account of the sacrifices in consumption imposed on those whose income did not rise proportionately with inflated prices.[32] Included in this survey were Jeremy Bentham, Henry Thornton, Douglas Stewart, Thomas Robert Malthus, John Stuart Mill, and Léon Walras.

Keynes questioned the usefulness of the concept of forced savings on the ground that under conditions of less than full employment of the available resources, no inflationary price increases are likely to result from increases of the circulating means of payment. This argument was refuted by Robertson.[33] Closer analysis of the influence exercised by expanding volumes of money on the behavior of prices led to the distinction of different situations brought about by the elasticity of the supply of goods in response to "inflated" demand.[34]

A thorough discussion of the conditions which money must fulfill in order to remain "neutral" was contributed by J. G. Koopmans,[35] who joined Hayek in endorsing Wicksell's analysis of the conditions of monetary equilibrium. But these conditions were shown to be outright utopian, since they included the requirements that the volume of the means of exchange remain unchanged, that there be no hoarding or dishoarding, and that incomes and outlays be equal at any moment. Even in an economy ruled by perfectly free competition, equilibrium and optimum allocation of resources could not be secured by stabilizing the volume of money. Price movements could be initiated by the effects of cost reductions, and cumulative changes of prices could be brought about by variations in demand and in the time lags between the receipt and the expenditure of income occurring before a previous equilibrium of supply and demand had been reestablished by compensatory movements.

The concept of compensatory movements played an important role in the discussion of the practical problem of whether large expenditures for various purposes such as reparations, speculative purchases of securities, or wage increases are bound to reduce the volume of purchasing power available for all other expenditures. So-called qualitative repercussions were shown to occur when transfer of purchasing power was accompanied by substantial alterations of the demand for goods and services.[36]

The search for a clear definition of the concept of neutral money was finally discontinued when equilibrium analysis of the traditional type was found to be unsuitable for dealing with the behavior of an economy in which the need to hold money results from conditions of "insecurity," economic friction, and other factors, later analyzed under the heading "liquidity preference." In a notable examination of the issues involved in the quest for neutral money, Paul N. Rosenstein-Rodan argued that intertemporal contracts are referred to when account is taken of the functions of money to serve as a store of values and a standard of deferred payments. He suggested that, independently of any other considerations, this aspect of economic analysis is likely to explode the framework of a timeless static economy.[37] He insisted that the value of money is derived from continuously changing values of indeterminate masses of commodities and that it is misleading to draw a distinction between the "external" and the "internal" values of money.

The contributions to monetary theory by Wicksell and some of his disciples provided Rosenstein-Rodan with a valuable background for introducing the concept of anticipations into price analysis, for pointing to dynamic processes connected with the accumulation of savings, and for defining the role of the money rate of interest as an instrument for establishing the equilibrium among investments, length of productive processes, and the capital market. The fragmentary Wicksellian analysis of expectations was to be developed; his "dynamic theory" of money was to be linked with a dynamic theory of prices. Rosenstein-Rodan credited the Cambridge economists with having analyzed the demand for money in accordance with the general principles of economic theory. He also drew attention to Hicks's endeavor to include uncertainty among the elements of decision making. Thus, an attempt was made to amalgamate monetary theories which had started from different conceptions of the price system.

PROBLEMS OF MONETARY REFORM

The theoretical discussions of monetary problems provided the background for the controversies that dealt with two burning practical problems of the twenties and thirties: the maintenance of the gold standard and the stabilization of the price level. The problem of how to stabilize the price level is not to be confounded with the problem of how to establish a "neutral money." The introduction of methods designed to stabilize the price level implies recognition of the fact that a mutual relationship exists between prices and the value of money, hence, that money is not "neutral." Return to the gold standard was regarded by many economists as a prerequisite for the reestablishment of sound international commercial relationships.[38] Others recommended certain adjustments of that standard to the conditions of the postwar world, in particular, to widespread adoption of the gold exchange standard.[39] Schumpeter, who regarded recurrent credit expansions as indispensable elements of economic growth, argued that under the liquidity provisions of the gold standard, such expansions were kept within limits and had their corollaries in the price deflations that occurred after the termination of the booms. He questioned the importance of the arguments against the maintenance of the gold standard, but agreed with Keynes on the proposal to adjust monetary policy to the dangers involved in the combined effects of the law of decreasing returns and the reductions of the rate of technical advancement.[40]

In fact, belief in the virtues of "sound monetary policies" caused various countries with inflated currencies to return to the principles of the gold standard and to subordinate their price and employment policies to the restrictions imposed by the maintenance of a fixed parity of exchange.

The adversaries of the gold standard elaborated the argument that the conditions which might have justified the maintenance of that standard had ceased to prevail in the postwar world.[41] They pointed especially to the fact that the flow of gold was no longer directed to the countries with the lowest price level; they emphasized the deflationary bias inherent in the operation of that money device. In England, Keynes played a leading role in the unsuccessful fight against the return to the prewar parity, and defended with telling arguments the need to maintain a rising domestic price level against the traditional monetary policy, which he held responsible for deflationary price movements, depression, and unemployment.[42] The monetary policy which he recommended implied a considerable latitude in manipulating the rate of exchange.

Gustav Cassel, a violent adversary of the gold standard, endeavored to demonstrate that prerequisite to the maintenace of a world-wide stable price level was an annual increase in the available gold stock at a rate of 2.8 percent.[43] Since such increases were outside the range of reasonable expectations, he predicted prolonged deflationary price movements unless the standard were abandoned. However, strong objections were raised to his statistical methods of calculating monetary requirements, and to his attempt to show

the existence of a strict causal relationship between changes in the gold stock and variations of the price level.[44]

In the course of these discussions an increasing number of economists agreed that
general deflationary price movements are an unqualified evil and that stabilization of the
"general price level" is to be regarded as a goal of economic policies. The treatment of
this problem was clearly to be distinguished from the hopeless task of securing the
"neutrality" of money. However, as mentioned above, there remained the question of
whether the price level to be stabilized was the level of wholesale or of retail prices, or the
purchasing power of wages, or the purchasing power of fixed incomes.[45]

In the United States a policy of price stabilization was advocated by Carl Snyder,[46]
who proposed a yearly expansion of the circulating media at a rate of three or four percent
or such rate as would be appropriate to the secular increase in productivity. Keynes, who
examined the merits of various types of price levels in his *Treatise on Money*, indicated
his predilection for the stabilization of a standard of consumption. Haberler supported the
idea of keeping constant the average rate of earnings of the factors of production. Some
French economists requested that all claims to present and future payments be stabilized.[47] Whichever level was chosen, it was evident that the interests of certain groups
of the population were promoted and the interests of others were neglected. But no clear
answer was given to the question of whether measures of monetary policy provided
effective instruments for remedying strains which appeared to be deeply rooted in the
industrial organization.[48]

After the arguments in favor of the stable money policy had been exhausted, proposals of more or less radical monetary reforms were launched in the United States under
the slogans "hundred percent reserve" plans and "commodity reserve standards." The
reserve plans were designed to restrict the lending facilities of the banks to the accumulated deposits and to establish a sharp separation between the clearance functions of the
banks and their lending and investing functions.[49]

The commodity reserve schemes were motivated by the idea of substituting for the
metallic standard the combined values of a basket of commodities. These commodities
should continuously be bought and sold by the monetary authorities in such quantities that
the price of the basket would be held within narrow limits, whereas no limits would be set
on variations of the prices of the commodities.[50] Critics of these proposals argued that it
was hardly possible to include perishable agricultural commodities among the elements of
the basket, although it was highly desirable to stabilize the prices of these products. They
also pointed out the difficulties involved in operating commodity reserve plans.

The German National-Socialist government paid special attention to price problems,
since its comprehensive investment program was largely financed by borrowing and was
fraught with the danger of creating inflationary price movements. Mention may be made
of a study by Carl Föhl in which these problems were treated.[51] He developed the model
of an economy in which a "circular flow of values" was taking place and proposed to
analyze this flow by differentiating the channels through which it was distributed. This
discussion of credit expansion was influenced by the Keynesian proposition that no
inflationary price movements result from such expansion when investments, financed by
credits, are made in an economy which is operated at less than full employment of the
available resources, especially of labor.

The belief in the stimulating effects of credit expansion on economic activity was
kept alive in France by some economists who proposed to counteract excessive inflationary price movements with appropriate measures such as enforced savings and the skim-

ming off of redundant money by public loans.[52] But they had no satisfactory answer to the argument that inflationary price movements are bound to result in tensions, in maladjustments, and in discrepancies between two movements: a flow of commodities and a flow of incomes.

The French economist Pierre Dieterlein emphasized the well-known cumulative effects of rising prices.[53] He distinguished the characteristics of "induced" inflation from those of "autonomous" inflation. The Swedish economist Bert Hansen studied the rhythm of inflationary movements and examined the effects of inflationary conditions on the market of products, as distinct from the corresponding effects on the markets of the productive factors.[54] Some economists, such as James S. Duesenberry, ignored the more or less quantitative aspects of inflationary movements and centered their attention on the different attitudes toward money adopted by various social groups.[55] He showed the fate of the monetary unit to be dependent upon the combined effects of these attitudes. Applying François Perroux's "theory of domination" to monetary policies, Henri Aujac conceived of inflation as a consequence of the decision of a "dominant" group to break down the constraint exercised by existing monetary relationships.[56]

Emile James, who surveyed these developments, observed that analysis of group behavior could be a useful tool for explaining the spread of inflationary price movements. He pointed to the influence exercised on such movements by producers' interests, balance of payments disequilibria, and income disparities.[57]

Chapter 32
Discussions about
the Business Cycle

—

GENERAL OBSERVATIONS

VARIOUS METHODOLOGICAL discussions which started from equilibrium analysis centered on the question of why disturbances of equilibrium positions were permitted to develop into general prolonged disproportionalities betweeen supply and demand. In order to account for those disproportionalities, the authors of many nonmonetary business cycle theories looked for random variables affecting the economic system from outside and causing changes in supply and demand conditions. They connected the periodicity of the crisis with either the originating factors or the response mechanism of the economy to these factors. Hence, J. M. Clark proposed to draw a distinction between originating (genetic) theories and theories of response (functional theories). Increases in the population, changes in techniques of production or distribution, and managerial factors were listed among the causes of the impingements, but theories of this type were faced with particular difficulties when challenged to account for the rhythm of the impingements and for the forces which were instrumental in producing the cyclical movement of business activity.

No effective measures of counteracting crises and depressions appeared to be available when the existence of the cyclical movements was attributed to the response mechanism and when instability was regarded as a characteristic attribute of the capitalist economy. Views of this kind were shared by most authors who emphasized growing disproportionalities in the expansion of the different sectors of the economy as a significant feature of the prosperity period.

The assumption that the cyclical behavior of business activity is somehow inherent in the functioning of any market economy was basic to the construction of the so-called business barometers which flourished in the United States during the twenties. These barometers were the work of pioneers who grasped the importance of time series of economic variables for an understanding of the functioning of the economy. But they made no attempts to supply theoretical considerations in support of their interpretations of the statistical data which they used to predict the trend of business.

The *Harvard Business Barometer,* which was published regularly by a Committee of Economic Research connected with Harvard University, enjoyed a considerable reputation. It was composed of three series of data considered representative of the behavior of the economy: one showed the effects of stock exchange transactions, the second dealt with the concept of business transactions, and the third reflected the behavior of interest rates. The combination of these time series and the interpretation of their movements were backed by the problematic proposition that a "trend" as a basic movement could be determined and separated from the curves which were assumed to oscillate around the trend line.

Similar reasoning provided the directives for an American semiofficial *Report on Recent Economic Changes,* published in 1929, which predicted the abatement of cyclical fluctuations and an impending accelerated phase of productivity. The results of these prognostications were soon belied by the devastating effects of the Great Depression. The authors of the *Harvard Barometer* were pehaps typical representatives of a large number of economists who were hardly aware of the fact that the concept of a "business cycle" was a fiction; that the "wavelike movements," the "oscillations," and the "secular trends" were abstract pictures of a highly complex reality; and that the curves which filled their charts were related to reality only to the degree that they were correctly interpreted as the combined result of many, partly unknown, factors which had cooperated in producing the variables included in the time series. No plausible arguments were advanced for the assumption that, when extrapolated, the charts would indicate the course of economic developments to come.[1]

Compared with any other business cycle theories, monetary theories enjoyed the advantage that the factors which they considered responsible for producing the fluctuations were expanding and contracting volumes of purchasing power expressed in monetary magnitudes. The main problems which these theories had to solve consisted of explaining the periodic variations in the volumes of purchasing power and determining the effects of these variations on the behavior of business activity. Problems of this type were well outlined of business activity. Problems of this type were well outlined by John R. Hicks, who started from a Paretian model of static market conditions and showed how the price system could be interfered with by the accumulation of net savings and how the assumed equilibrium of supply and demand had to give way to entirely different assumptions when disappointed expectations were caused by changing prices, when shifts in investments were induced by changes in business prospects, and so on.[2]

A direct causal relationship between the credit policy of the commercial banks and the fluctuating behavior of business activity was established by all cycle theories which were influenced by Böhm-Bawerk's and Knut Wicksell's definition of the strategic position of the rate of interest in determining the expansion or contraction of productive processes.[3]

The authors who belong to this group also attributed to the rate of interest a significant role in determining the relationships between the "real exchange" system, assumed to be ruled by equilibrating forces, and the "monetary system," which was held to be superimposed on the real exchange system and to be the source of its alternating expansions and contractions. The delay in the adjustment of the real exchange system to new equilibrium positions was frequently ascribed to different elasticities of the sectors of the price system and to discrepancies between savings and investments. The business cycle theories which adopted this approach will be discussed under the heading "double system theories."

The existence of more or less constant relations between certain economic aggregates appeared to be prerequisite to the establishment of a generally applicable business cycle theory. Particular importance was attached to the "acceleration principle" which had first been used by Albert Aftalion and was more carefully analyzed by C. F. Bickerdike and John M. Clark. This principle was derived from the observation that fluctuations in the production of fixed capital equipment were followed by more than proportionate fluctuations in the production of consumer goods; in addition, it was found that the size of the fluctuations in the output of capital goods was determined by the durability of the stock of invested capital. Hence, the "accelerator" or "coefficient of acceleration" was defined as the ratio between the current increase in the stock of capital equipment and the current increase in the flow of final output produced with that equipment.[4]

Critics of the accelerator as a reliable instrument of economic analysis pointed to the limits to its constancy.[5] Simon Kuznets, who constructed a series of model sequences dealing with the relations between the production of capital goods and finished products, arrived at the conclusion that the acceleration principle could be related to secular change, but that its importance for business cycle research was hardly significant.[6] However, the temptation to ignore these limits was very strong.

A constant relationship of another type was frequently assumed to exist between changes in current output and induced (net) investments made by producers in response to such changes. However, considerable practical difficulties were involved in differentiating net investment from the *reinvestment* required to keep the capital stock intact, since replacements were generally combined with improvements in technical procedures.[7]

Wesley C. Mitchell's comprehensive studies of the cyclical behavior of business activity[8] represented in some respects the most effective attempts to discover regularities or constants in the mutual relationships of fluctuating economic magnitudes, to determine shifts in the relative importance of the different sectors of the economy and changes in their characteristics. In his analysis of the duration and the international coincidence of the various cycles and their amplitudes, he drew the attention of economists to the problems connected with economic trends and economic growth.[9] According to his findings, the behavior of seven American series of cyclical movements and the duration of business cycles in various other countries had not been influenced perceptibly by secular and structural changes. But the variety of movements shown in the course of his descriptive analysis suggested considerable caution as to generalized interpretations of the movements and of relationships likely to reflect only the effects of passing conditions and random factors. From business cycles strictly speaking, varying in duration between seven and eleven years, Wesley C. Mitchell and Arthur Burns distinguished minor fluctu-

ations averaging about forty months. These cycles, which did not show a considerable
degree of regularity, had also been analyzed by Willard L. Thorp, who derived his
material from comphrehensive collections of reports about business conditions in different
countries.[10]

A characteristic feature of Mitchell's analysis was his emphasis of the apparent
international synchronization of the various phases of the cyclical movements. But he did
not attempt to substantiate his "bold hypothesis" that a common cause might be basic to
this phenomenon.

Logically connected with the interpretation of the international aspects of the cyclical
movements was a question raised by Oskar Morgenstern, at that time head of the Austrian
Institute for Business Cycle Research: whether the spatial units which provided the arenas
for determining the course of these movements should not be defined in accordance with
economic considerations rather than in accordance with national boundaries, as was
commonly done for reasons of administrative convenience.[11] Morgenstern proposed to
apply business cycle analysis to large regions characterized by typical forms of economic
behavior, and to give special attention to the problem of how the fluctuations were
transmitted from one region to another. But sporadic discussions of this problem were
inconclusive. Some vague references were made to the importance of structural conditions
for the transmission of economic fluctuations.[12] Other authors, however, found no satisfactory proof for the view that factors operating on an international scale could be held
responsible for the cyclical behavior of the various national economies.[13]

SIMPLE MONETARY THEORIES

Analysis of inflationary price movements which occurred after the First World War
provided strong support for monetary theories which connected the expanding business
activity of the upswing with increases in the credit supply and held credit restrictions
responsible for bringing about crises and depressions. Howard S. Ellis drew a distinction
between "exogenous" monetary theories, which regarded the credit factor as a necessary
condition of cyclical oscillations, and "endogenous" theories, which qualified this factor
as the sufficient condition of such oscillations.[14] Probably more significant was another
distinction: the authors of some theories considered credit expansion as as prerequisite to
beneficial evolutionary processes and economic growth. In other theories, however, credit
expansion played a less unequivocal role, and was held responsible for interfering with the
smooth functioning of the economy; hence, pursuance of appropriate banking policies
could be expected to mitigate, perhaps even to eliminate, crises and depressions.

One of the most radical versions of the monetary approach was L. Albert Hahn's
"economic theory of the bank credit,"[15] advanced under the impact of the devastating
inflationary price movements which pervaded the German economy after the end of the
First World War. Hahn was a German banker who practiced in Frankfort. A characteristic
aspect of his purely monetary conception of the functioning of the economy was his
definition of interest as the price paid for the confidence granted by the creditor to the
debtor. Without adjusting his theory to the principles of equilibrium analysis, he examined the economic effects of the decision of the German Central Bank to renounce the
application of effective methods of discount policy and to discount unlimited amounts of
bills of exchange. He concluded that "permanent prosperity" could be financed through
the continuous creation of unlimited credit. The experiences under the pressure of the

fantastic depreciation of the German currency were reflected in Hahn's analysis of the far-reaching effects of forced savings on the distribution of the national dividend.[16]

The conception of the trade cycle as an exclusively "monetary phenomenon" was shared by R. G. Hawtrey.[17] This concept of monetary equilibrium was determined by Alfred Marshall's "cash balance principle," according to which, under equilibrium conditions, no person could be tempted to alter the size of his cash balance.[18] Hence, monetary equilibrium was characterized by equality between the creation and the cancellation of money in any period, and by constancy in the rate of turnover of money, as defined by the relation between consumers' outlays and the "unspent margin." Although Hawtrey conceded that the equilibrium of the economic could be disputed by a variety of factors, he connected the specific form of the trade cycles, and especially their periodicity, with the behavior of traders who were tempted by cheap short-term credits to enlarge their purchases and supplied the banks with a stream of capital resulting from their profits. Hawtrey explained crisis and depression as a consequence of the credit squeeze brought about by the increased demand for cash which was mainly due to rising wages. But far more significant than his attempt to make the behavior of the traders responsible for business fluctuations were Hawtrey's discussions of the international credit mechanism. In analyzing the cumulative processes of credit expansion and credit contraction, he showed how the fluctuations were transmitted from one member of the international trading community to another.[19]

Proposals of reform, which Hawtrey derived from his theoretical considerations, centered on the adoption of banking policies designed to control the income stream and to stabilize the price level of the factors of production.[20] The monetary system which he recommended was ruled by the principle of the gold standard, but the international demand for gold was to be reduced, as far as possible, by spreading the use of the "gold exchange standard" and by curtailing the gold reserves of the central banks.[21] Coordination of the credit operations of these banks was another important element of his proposed reforms.

Similar ideas were elaborated in the "Macmillan Report" submitted to the English Parliament in 1931, but they were rejected because of their possible effects on public debts. The government preferred to devaluate the pound.

Some elements of a monetary business cycle theory were implied in the analysis of price movements by John Maynard Keynes in his *Treatise on Money*. Keynes started with the assumption that changes in the rate of interest are of primary importance in influencing decisions to save and to invest, and he regarded profit as the source of inflationary movements affecting first the prices of productive factors and proceeding spirally until the prices of products were affected. He pointed out a process in the course of which "profit inflation" leads to "commodity inflation," characterized by a price structure in which prices of consumption goods are in advance of the prices of productive services, particularly of wages.[22] The last stage of this process, qualified as "income inflation," is reached. When the rate of earnings rises, due to enhanced competition for the productive factors. A corresponding process could be observed when profit deflation is followed by commodity deflation and finally by income deflation.

The elements of various monetary theories were combined in this analysis. Keynes assumed that an economic policy which would keep the price level of investment goods equal to their cost would assure a continuous adjustment of the market rate of interest to the "natural rate," that is, the rate which would equalize savings and investments. He considered it necessary to adjust foreign trade and foreign lendings to the requirements of

domestic price stabilization. He shared with some adherents of purely monetary business
cycle theories the tendency to minimize the influence of credit expansions and inflationary
price movements on the structure of productive processes.

In his Harris Foundation lecture, published in 1931, Keynes voiced strong opposition
to deflationary policies.[23] He argued that the gap between the long-term and the short-
term rates of interest had been largely responsible for aggravating the depression of the
thirties, since variations in the long-term rate, being beyond the control of the central
banking system, had caused considerable fluctuations in the value of fixed capital. As
recovery measures he recommended, apart from reductions of the long-term rate of
interest, mainly the execution of large-scale programs of public construction.

Irving Fisher contributed to the business cycle discussion the proposition that the
development of the boom was associated with "overindebtedness" occurring in the
course of inflationary processes when the rate of interest lagged behind the rate of
profit.[24] Using the method of approximation, he attempted to show how interest rates fail
to be adjusted to changes in the price level that take place during inflationary and
deflationary movements. He analyzed the contractions of the income stream forced upon
the economy through the process of debt liquidation, and connected this process with the
heavy decline of prices occurring during the depression.

Other analysts of business fluctuations agreed with Fisher on the deflationary effects
of debt liquidations, but they considered "overindebtedness," as linked to overinvestment, a secondary factor in determining the fluctuating behavior of the economy. Moreover, the volumes of indebtedness incurred during boom periods by the various firms
appear to have been greatly overestimated by Fisher as well as by Keynes.[25]

MONETARY DOUBLE-SYSTEM THEORIES

Knut Wicksell's "dynamic" approach to economic analysis, as elaborated by Ludwig von Mises, was basic to the business cycle theories advanced by Friedrich A. Hayek
and other adherents of the Austrian school. In these theories, primary attention was given
to the changes produced in the structure of the real exchange system by changes in the
purchasing power of money. Hayek's analysis can conveniently be used as a specimen of
the reasoning adopted by the members of this group.[26]

In accordance with the principles of Austrian marginalism, Hayek started on the
assumption that the prices of future goods reflect the time preference for present goods
and that the rate of interest fulfills the function of adjusting the length of the periods of
production to the capital available for investment purposes. For Böhm-Bawerk's concept
of capital as a uniform productive factor, Hayek substituted a definition of capital as a
congeries of resources weighted according to their relative values.

In the light of these premises, Hayek argued that the equilibrium of the economy is
maintained when money is kept neutral, since in that case increases in voluntary savings
are followed by corresponding reductions in the demand for goods of consumption,
reductions in the rate of interest, increasing profit margins, and economically justified
extensions of the periods of production. Hayek assigned to the Wicksellian "equilibrium
rate" of interest the role of assuring equilibrium between the amounts saved and the
amounts spent on goods of consumption, and also the function of securing such a distribution of new savings between the production of future and present goods that the marginal
net products yielded by the investments of the two types are equal in value. Sharing the

optimistic views of other authors of monetary business cycle theories, Hayek was convinced that unlimited investment opportunities are always available and that the market
rate of interest can always be fixed at a level which is lower than the ratio of anticipated
returns to the cost of investments (the rate of profits).

This model of the economy, operating under the rule of neutral money, was, of
course, an abstract construction when compared with the behavior of an economy in
which the banks failed to adjust the rates of interest to the "natural" rates as determined
by technical progress. In his discussion of banking policies as the source of inflationary
movements, Hayek referred to a long list of similar analyses, beginning with Henry
Thornton's evidence before the Committee on Bank Restriction in 1797. Hayek showed
how credit expansion initiated by one commercial bank would enable others to participate
in multiplying their credit facilities without impairing their liquidity, since, according to
his estimates, under the rule of a 10 percent reserve system the credit creation of the banks
could amount to nine times their original volume of deposits.

Such credit expansion was likely to lead to unjustified expansions of the periods of
production, to disproportionate increases in the production of capital goods, and to the
application of misleading methods of bookkeeping. To the use of such methods, Hayek
attributed serious distortions of rational economic behavior in prosperity and depression
periods, especially the practice of making erroneous capital and profit calculations.[27]

Elaborating on these considerations, Hayek arrived at the conclusion that the collapse
of the boom is to be attributed to a shortage of loan capital for financing overexpanded
periods of production and to the rapidly increasing demand for goods of consumption
when paper profits result in swelling employers' incomes and when workers' earnings are
expanded by rising wages and payment for overtime. In analyzing these processes, Hayek
attached particular importance to the "Ricardo effect," the proposition that wage increases are bound to reduce the profitability of productive processes in inverse proportion
to the share of capital as a productive factor.[28]

In the revised version of his business cycle theory, Hayek discussed the influence of
the "deceleration" principle, the progressive substitution of less capitalistic methods of
production for more capitalistic methods during the later stages of the prosperity period.[29]
Thus, he described the cycle as the result of changes in the ratio of capital to output
brought about by changes in the rate of profit and changes in the wage levels. The function
of the depression period consisted in providing the conditions for the establishment of a
new equilibrium of the real exchange system,[30] at less than full employment of the
available productive resources.

Other authors who adopted similar interpretations of the business fluctuations emphasized the effects of "secondary" deflationary price movements occurring in prolonged
depression periods.[31] They argued that, due to the cumulative nature of these movements,
contraction of productive activities might exceed, in the final analysis, the volume of
overinvestments made during the prosperity period.[32] and that the process of readjustment
taking place in the depression period might also affect industries which had not experienced undue expansion.[33]

Hayek's highly consistent and clearly reasoned theory represented an effective elaboration of the leading ideas of the Austrian school of marginalism and found many
adherents outside of Austria, especially among English economists. But sooner or later
critical objections were raised to some significant features of this theory, especially to the
choice of equilibrium conditions at full employment as the starting point of the cyclical
movement, since under these conditions no labor would be available for the assumed

expansion of productive processes. Swedish economists emphasized the fact that Hayek's analysis was hardly suitable to take account of the problems connected with risks and uncertainties.[34] Marshallian economists objected to the role assigned to the shortage of savings in explaining crises and depressions, and to the strategic position attributed to the rate of interest in determining the length of the periods of production, independently of the influence of technological changes.[35] They minimized the alleged connections between the rate of profit and the substitution of labor by capital and vice versa.[36] Other objections were raised to Hayek's proposition that toward the end of the boom a crisis is precipitated by increasing competition for productive services. This view was countered with the argument that enhanced demand for these services could be met by the completion of roundabout processes of production which had occurred during the upswing.[37] The validity of this argument was strengthened by the results of statistical investigations which failed to confirm Hayek's assumption that productive services are shifted to consumers' industries during the later stages of the prosperity period.[38] His contention that shrinkages in the technical structure of production were taking place during the Depression was also open to serious doubts.[39] The Austrian approach to business cycle analysis was finally eclipsed by the elaboration of the dynamic aspects of the Keynesian theory of employment.

NONMONETARY THEORIES

The term *nonmonetary theories* may be used to cover a number of heterogeneous theories which connected the origin of business fluctuations not with changes in the volume of the means of payment but with other factors. In passing, a group of theoretically weak underconsumption theories may be briefly characterized. They found fertile soil in the economic atmosphere of the twenties and the first half of the thirties, and developed in various versions the old idea that the unemployment conditions of depression periods were caused by disproportionalities between the amounts invested and the amounts spent for consumption purposes. As a specimen of a theory of this type, P. W. Martin's business cycle theory may be mentioned. Martin argued that, owing to a sort of "short circuit" of the circulation of money, the reward for the use of the productive factors was largely spent on capital goods instead of being used for the purchase of consumption goods.[40]

An oversavings theory devised by the Americans William T. Foster and Waddill Catchings was widely advertised. Foster and Catchings attributed the fluctuating behavior of the economy to unequal distribution of incomes, the ensuing lack of demand for consumption goods, and excessive individual and corporate savings.[41] While they shared the belief of many authors of oversaving theories that sufficient outlets were available for any level of savings, they had no answer to the obvious question of why productive capacity, financed out of savings, did not generate sufficient income to absorb the additional output.

These theoretical discussions had a practical counterpart in the "social credit scheme" of Major Paul H. Douglas, which was designed to maintain a continuous flow of spending financed by subsidies to be granted to consumers out of public funds. Schemes of this type were put to the test of experience in the Canadian province of Alberta and in New Zealand.

The expression "industrial fluctuations," used by Dennis Holme Robertson and Arthur Cecil Pigou to denote cyclical movements, was indicative of their tendency to connect these movements with factors related to the technical aspects of industrial production.[42] True to the Ricardian conception of the economy as a system fundamentally determined by the operation of equilibrating forces, they based their explanation of the cyclical form, the regularity, and the periodicity of the fluctuations on the response mechanism of the system and attached only secondary importance to the search for the origin of the disturbances.

Thus, Robertson pointed to "explosive forces" of industrial progress and distinguished necessary and desirable industrial fluctuations, inherent in the nature of economic progress, from undesirable fluctuations. He attributed the latter to the induced effects of errors caused by the stress of competition, by the time involved in adjusting production to changes in demand, and by mistaken banking policies and ensuing price movements. But he listed the effects of credit expansion only among the contributory factors, and centered his analysis on the study of structural problems, which he connected with the adjustments required by alterations in cost elements and in demand.[43]

In his study of elasticities of demand, Robertson analyzed certain factors which could be held responsible for "inappropriate" responses to demand, such as discontinuous additions of large volumes of fixed capital, the burden of overhead charges, excessive costs of nonoperation, and exaggerated expansions of otherwise justified investments. He associated the periodic recurrence of upswings with the coverage period of amortization and the periodic renewal of machinery calling for large-scale investment, and regarded the length of productive processes (the "gestation of capital goods") as a factor which contributed toward extending the length of prosperity periods. In analyzing industrial fluctuations of the past, Robertson illustrated the part played by certain technological innovations in initiating prosperity periods of remarkable intensity. Since he was convinced that fluctuations of business activity were deeply rooted in the nature of industrial production, he limited his recommendations to measures of conservative bank policies and wage policies, and ridiculed what he called "boom shyness," the popular conviction that to avert a slump it was necessary to avert a boom.[44]

Pigou's analysis of industrial fluctuations was also marked by the search for the response mechanism of the economy. He drew a clear line between the "impulses" which he considered instrumental in initiating the cyclical movements and the factors to which he attributed primary effects on the intensity and the course of the movement.[45] The list of impulses included harvests, inventions, changes in demand, and monetary expansion. He agreed with Robertson on connecting the response mechanism with the life span of the durable goods and with the "replacement cycle." The acceleration principle (which he termed the "principle of derived demand") provided him with an instrument to explain the intensity and amplitude of the fluctuations in the production of capital goods as compared with the fluctuations in the production of consumption goods. A remarkable feature of Pigou's theory was the role which he assigned to psychological factors (errors in the anticipation of future market conditions, errors committed in duplicating plans and equipment, and the like). In the light of this psychological approach, he qualified the fluctuations as alternating waves of optimism and pessimism.

"Contagion of confidence," as a psychological element in stimulating business expansion, was also emphasized in the theory of Frederick Lavington.[46] Frank W. Taussig[47] and William Beveridge[48] referred to errors committed especially by producers in competitive industries in their discussions of business fluctuations. In Marco Fanno's theory a monetary approach was combined with the introduction of a response mechanism which included lack of human foresight as a primary element.[49]

John M. Clark started his contributions to business cycle analysis with a study of the relation between the demand for finished products and the demand for capital goods,[50] and subsequently centered his attention on the role played by institutional "strategic factors" in transmitting the effects of random disturbances in the course of business fluctuations.[51] He discussed the determinants of the timing and the intensity of fluctuations, such as changes in prices, in employment, and in the supply of credit, and expansions and contractions of basic industries and of wholesale and retail trades. He emphasized the importance of the acceleration principle, especially as manifested in influencing derived demand in construction industries, and pointed to large volumes of fixed investments as the main cause of the instability of the economy, which was also "destabilized" by the elasticity of the credit system and the discrepancy between increases in expenditures on consumption and increases in national income and savings. In other studies Clark applied the "multiplier effect" to government expenditures and raised the question of why and how these secondary effects were likely to come to a stop.[52]

The relation between the demand for finished products and the demand for capital goods was carefully reexamined by Simon Kuznets, who also investigated the importance of this relation for business cycle analysis.[53] Considerably impressed by Adolph Löwe's critical comments on the nonmonetary business cycle theories and their compatibility with equilibrium economics, Kuznets elaborated the idea that equilibrium economics was inconsistent with any theories that did not connect periodic fluctuations with factors affecting the economic system for outside.[54] He followed Paul N. Rosenstein-Rodan in accepting the propositions that for purposes of business cycle analysis the assumed interdependence of all economic magnitudes should be replaced by the recognition of variable irreversible relationships of dependence, and that account should be taken of differences in time coefficients resulting from varying and disproportionate reactions of producers, buyers, and sellers to changes in market conditions.[55] In accordance with this approach, accumulation of random changes could be assumed to be brought about by a sequence of disturbances under conditions of unequal time coefficients of response. Prolonged oscillations of the system could thus be produced. R. W. Souter objected to this reasoning, however, and insisted upon interpreting the fluctuations as deviations from the path of moving equilibria, caused by the operation of some fundamental economic forces.[56] The problems in this discussion were taken up in the attempts to develop outright dynamic methods of business cycle analysis.

The most comprehensive study in which the "impulse principle" was applied to the explanation of cyclical economic processes was Joseph Schumpeter's business cycle analysis.[57] It was designed to elaborate on the "dynamic" approach which he had adopted in his analysis of "economic development" more than a quarter of a century before. Schumpeter conceived of the recurrent expansions and contractions of productive activities as processes inherent in the behavior of the capitalist economic order and adjusted his model of the economy to the task of combining business cycle analysis with an analysis of economic growth. Thus, he raised some fundamental problems which later became the object of extensive discussion.

The evolutionary processes taking place in Schumpeter's model of the economy are determined by the relations among five variables: physical output, price level, the volume of the means of payment, total income, and net borrowing. The fluctuations of the economy are assumed to be initiated by "innovations" introduced by "daring employers" into an orginally static Walrasian system during periods when the risk of failure is not considerable. Innovations are defined in terms of cost reductions not resulting from reduction of prices of productive factors. Hence, they are assumed to promote economic growth through the production functions, and the forces which are instrumental in stimulating the application of innovations are to be distinguished economically and sociologically from the processes which initiate inventions. Thus conceived, the development of the economy is determined by the combined effects of three factors: innovations, the principle of profit maximization, and the credit mechanism.

The response mechanism is supplied by the competitive behavior of large groups of conservative producers. Using the method of progressive approximation, Schumpeter started from the model of a two-phase cycle and introduced secondary factors to show how business activity is intensified during the upswing and how deflationary trends are aggravated during depression periods in which the equilibrium of the system is eventually reestablished. He supplemented his theoretical discussion with ample descriptive studies of the cyclical development of the English, American, and German economies. In these studies he distinguished three types of cyclical movement, which he termed "Juglar cycles," "Kitchin cycles," and "Kondratieff cycles." He credited Clement Juglar with having been the first to provide a clear picture of recurrent fluctuations extending over seven to eleven years. The existence of the relatively short "Kitchin cycles," covering about forty months, had been established for Great Britain and the United States at the beginning of the twenties.[58] Time series of bank clearings, interest rates, and wholesale prices had been used to determine their course and their periodicity. The large cycles, associated with the Russian N. D. Kondratieff, were spread out over several decades and were defined in terms of moving averages derived from statistics of prices, interest rates, and volumes of production. Schumpeter suggested to count, historically as well as statistically, in every individual case three Kitchin cycle to a Juglar cycle, and six Juglar cycles to a Kondratieff cycle. He connected each of the large waves outlined by Kondratieff with revolutionary events in economic history: the first cycle, beginning around 1790, with radical technical improvements in the textile industry and in iron and coal production; the second wave, beginning around 1845, with the rapid expansion of railroad construction; and the third, beginning about 1898, with the large-scale introduction of electricity as the source of power and the transformation of the chemical industry through the application of new processes.

But the voluminous statistical material which Schumpeter accumulated failed to supply sufficient evidence to demonstrate the alleged regularities of the cyclical movements. Various objections were raised to his assumption that high entrepreneurial ability and energy clustered in recurrent periods instead of manifesting themselves in a continuous stream.[59] Schumpeter's emphasis on the impulses supposed to generate the cycles was contrasted with the secondary importance which he attached to the response mechanism.[60] This mechanism centered on the idea that large profits resulting from the introduction of technical innovations were whittled down by competitive processes. But critics of Schumpeter's theory found that a far better approach to reality was achieved in a model of the Russian Eugen Slutsky, in which a probability distribution of random causes was combined with a slow absorption of the effects of important innovations.[61] Serious doubts were also cast on Schumpeter's assumption that the same principle, the clustering and diffusion of innovations, could be used to explain all business cycles, regardless of their character, incidence, intensity, and duration.[62]

The business cycle theories which had been advanced prior to the First World War
and during the interwar period were surveyed by Gottfried Haberler in an excellent study
prepared under the auspices of the Secretariat of the League of Nations.[63] Haberler
distinguished five main groups of theories: purely monetary, overinvestment, underconsumption, psychological, and harvest theories. The "psychological" theories did not
form a clearly defined group, but were characterized by the fact that their authors placed
particular emphasis on psychological factors in their analysis of the reaction mechanism of
the economy. The theories of Keynes, Lavington, Pigou, and Taussig were included in
this group. The overinvestment theories were subdivided into three groups: monetary,
nonmonetary, and those based on the acceleration principle.

Habeler's survey provided a comprehensive picture of the varying importance which
had been ascribed to some significant economic phenomena in determining the fluctuating
course of economic events. Especially striking were the divergent roles attributed to
disproportionalities in the expansion and contraction of various sectors of the economy; to
income distribution and its effects on consumption, savings, and investments; to the rate
of interest and the efficiency of capital; to changes in the volumes of money and credit; to
innovations; to the length of productive processes; and to changing attitudes of producers
and consumers.

The difficulties involved in explaining the collapse of the boom were reflected in the
variety of attempts to account for this phenomenon. The downturn was attributed to
disturbances affecting economic systems from the outside, scarcity of capital goods
(mentioned by overproduction theories), shortages of the credit supply (characteristic of
"overinvestment" theories), insufficient demand for consumer goods (referred to by
"underconsumption theories), general increases in costs of production and declines in
efficiency, and vertical and horizontal maladjustments in the structure of production due
to shortage of capital. Vertical maladjustments were connected with decisions concerning
the distribution of income between savings and investments; horizontal maladjustments
were related to decisions concerning the distribution of expenditures between different
lines of consumption goods or between different cost factors.

In a positive "eclectic" business cycle analysis, Haberler combined the most reliable
elements of other theories into a coherent picture of the fluctuating course of economic
events. He used the acceleration principle to explain the maladjustments which take place
during periods of expansion, but did not find any reason to hold monetary factors responsible for terminating the boom. His discussion of measures of business cycle policy
centered on the idea of stabilizing per capita incomes. In the last chapter of his treatise,
Haberler dealt extensively with the "international aspects of the cycle" and the spreading
of cyclical movements.

The list of authors who advanced business cycle theories could be supplemented by
another list of those who questioned the prospect of establishing a universally valid
business cycle theory.[64] A number of economists agreed with Clark's proposal to forget
the "glittering prize of achieving the theory of the trade cycle" and to concentrate on the
study of the "strategic factors" and their possible manipulation through adequate measures of economic policy.[65]

Almost insuperable difficulties were involved in the task of defining the relations
between the "Juglar cycles," the objects of traditional analysis, and other observable
recurrent fluctuations of economic activity. The methods used in establishing the long
waves of business activity were exposed to many objections. In the Soviet Union,
Kondratieff's theory of the long waves was violently attacked because it failed to reflect

the operation of antagonistic forces which Marx ascribed to the capitalist economy and also because it was incompatible with the Leninist thesis that the First World War had started a prolonged phase of revolutionary social movements and hostilities between capitalist economies.[66]

As Kondratieff had connected the long waves with the discontinous replacement of capital goods, his Western critics argued that he had failed to account for the operation of endogenous forces which could be considered responsible for generating these movements, that he had also ignored the possible existence of exogenous causes, and that he had eliminated all minor fluctuations from the time series of statistical variables which were basic to his graphs, although it could be assumed that long waves (provided their existence could be demonstrated) were working through shorter cycles.[67]

Some authors who discussed the problem of long waves, such as Gustav Cassel and Robert A. Lehfeldt, denied the cyclical nature of these phenomena and attributed their existence to changes in the available stocks of monetary gold; others held the credit mechanism or combinations of monetary and sociological factors responsible for the long waves.[68]

Kondratieff's long waves had counterparts in the long waves of rising and falling prices established by François Simiand[69] and the "long waves of unemployment" defined by the Swiss economist Manuel Saitzew.[70] The existence of the "Kitchin cycles" was connected with the accumulation and clearance of inventories which is marked by more or less regular successions. Dampening effects on the cycles were attributed to changes of the "inventory accelerator" (the ratio of stocks to output and sales); increasing vertical integration of various industries, and to technical innovations which were also expected to bring about a gradual dampening of the amplitude of these cyles.[71]

Long cycles of residential construction, which in some respects provided a counterpart to the Juglar cycles, were characteristic of the behavior of the American economy. Their causes, their incidence, their scope, and their relationship to the trade cycles were repeatedly studied and interpreted.[72] These studies were supplemented by others dealing with cycles of transport building and shipbuilding.

BUSINESS CYCLE POLICIES

It is not within the scope of this study to deal with the various aspects of economic policies, but it might not be amiss to give a short account of the attempts made during the Depression of the thirties to derive measures of economic policy from the results of business cycle analysis. The proposals to deal with the depression can be divided into two broad groups.[73] The adherents of the "monetary school" believed that the relations between the elements of the economic "system of physical magnitudes" had not been affected by "genuine" disturbances, and were not in need of radical readjustment. Authors who shared this view laid the blame for the depth of the depression on mismanagement of the monetary system. They pointed to the deflationary effects of the foreign trade policy of France and the United States, which had led to the absorption of large parts of the available gold supply. Others elaborated the idea of "vicious" deflationary spirals which they ascribed to the secondary effects of shrinking prices and wages. Hence, they recommended a policy of "reflation" designed to restore general purchasing power, primarily through measures of discount and open market procedures, and they requested regulation of wage rates and of the prices of raw materials.[74]Since there was no prospect of achieving international monetary agreements, they regarded abandonment of the gold standard as a prerequisite to the pursuance of unfettered domestic reflationary policies.

A different approach was adopted by the adherents of the "structural school," who argued that during the preceding prosperity period serious dislocations had taken place in the sphere of physical production, that no sound recovery could begin before a mutual readjustment of the productive processes had been effected through reductions of costs, writing off of economically unjustified investments, and other deflationary procedures. They defended the gold standard, they recommended maintenance of the price structure as established at or near the bottom of the Depression, and they insisted that no measures were available to control the velocity of circulation of the means of payment or the distribution of the supply of money among the various sectors of the economy. A policy of this type was advocated by several members of the Austrian school.

Adherents of monetary business cycle theories objected to the execution of public works programs as a means of initiating an upswing. Hawtrey believed that credit expansion, achieved through measures of discount policies, would have the same effect on the volume of employment as expenditures on public works, financed by loans.[75] Cassel raised a number of objections to public works programs and recommended downward adjustment of wages to the demand for labor as an effective method of combating unemployment.[76]

The International Labour Office recommended the adoption of a comprehensive world-wide program of public works, but made no attempt to support its proposal with theoretical arguments.[77] Several authors approached the problem of public works from the theoretical angle.[78] It later became prominent in the discussions of the Keynesian theory of employment. But during the thirties, antidepression policies pursued by the various countries represented, as a rule, rather inconsistent mixtures of the methods considered available for breaking the vicious spiral of declining investments and outputs, falling prices, and losses of income. These policies were not influenced by theoretical considerations and were supplemented by protectionist measures. Each national economy came to be regarded as an isolated unit needing defensive weapons against the disrupting effects of international deflationary price movements. The world-wide protectionist trend was intensified by the aggressive economic policies pursued by some totalitarian regimes. After England abandoned the gold standard in 1931, this standard was preserved for some time by only a few creditor countries (France, the Netherlands, and Switzerland), whose capitalists and bankers were not entangled in the network of international short-term debts. In the countries which devalued their currency, reflationary price movements were frequently supported by measures of exchange control designed to isolate the domestic price system from the movement of prices in markets abroad. Japan was the only country that adopted an inflationary policy.

Part X

The "New Economics"

Chapter 33
Discussions of
the Stockholm School

IN PREVIOUS CHAPTERS I have made repeated references to the fact that the reformulation of older problems and the formulation of new ones were largely connected with the abandonment of assumptions which had been basic to Ricardian and post-Ricardian economics. Four of these assumptions were of particular importance: (1) that free competition establishes itself as the normal form of economic organization, unless disturbed by government intervention; (2) that free competition guarantees full employment of the available resources, and their optimum allocation; (3) that equilibrium analysis, ignoring the time element, provides the safest approach to the understanding of the relationships of the economic magnitudes; and (4) that money is to be treated as a veil which is superimposed on the "real exchange system," and its functions can be disregarded in establishing economic laws and regularities.

Knut Wicksell earned his outstanding position in the history of economic reasoning particularly through his consistent endeavor to free his model of the economy from some of the fetters imposed by these assumptions. He gave the time element a significant position in economic analysis, on the one hand through the strategic role which he attributed to the market rate of interest in influencing investments and the expansion of economic processes, and on the other hand through the importance which he attached to anticipations and expectations as determinants of economic behavior. Wicksell discarded the belief that the functioning of the economy could be studied independently of the influence exercised by monetary factors on the behavior of prices, investments, and the formation of incomes. He placed the analysis of the relationships between the "real exchange system" and the "monetary system" into the center of his scientific preoccupations. He realized that savers' decisions were made independently of those of investors,

489

and that the equilibrium of the economy might be endangered by the resulting discrepancies between the amounts withheld from consumption and those invested for productive purposes. He pointed to cumulative processes of price movements, and argued that such movements could not be dealt with on the assumption that the plans of the members of the economic community are mutually compatible. In establishing his model of the economy, Wicksell made ample use of aggregates such as total income of the community, total demand for consumption goods, total investment, total volume of production, and total supply of money. From his analysis of the relationships of these magnitudes he drew the conclusion that no position that the economy reached in the course of economic processes could be regarded as an equilibrium position, and that, consequently, it was possible to start the study of the expansions and contractions of business activity at any point of the fluctuations, depending on the assumptions made about the conditions of production and distribution and the behavior of producers and consumers.

Wicksell's methodological considerations were clarified in his prolonged discussions with David Davidson.[1] They provided a sort of unified framework for price and income analysis, monetary theory, and the study of business fluctuations. Some of his leading ideas were elaborated by members of the Austrian school. Others provided the starting point for studies by some outstanding Swedish economists, who formed the so-called Stockholm school of economics about the middle of the thirties. The Stockholm school centered around Gunnar Myrdal, Eric Lindahl, and Bertil Ohlin; other members of the group were Fabian von Kock, Karin Kock, Dag Hammarskjöld, Tord Palander, Erik Lundberg, Ingvar Svennilson, and Richard Sterner.[2] They combined their Wicksellian approach to economic analysis with an outspoken reaction to the utilitarian philosophy of some teachers of the Wicksellian generation; they showed a remarkable ingenuity in developing the monetary and dynamic aspects of Wicksell's teachings. Moreover, they endeavored to adjust these teachings to the changes in the structure of the economy brought about by the effects of the Great Depression and by the social reforms carried out under the pressure of strong political parties.

According to Wicksellian theory, the functioning of the economy was largely determined by the divergence between the monetary rate of interest and the real (natural) rate of interest. To that divergence, Wicksell ascribed the origin of cumulative inflationary and deflationary price movements. Such a formulation of the problems of price analysis—which differed radically from the approach adopted by the advocates of the quantity theory—led Wicksell to analyze the conditions which were basic to the establishment of the monetary equilibrium of the economy.[3]

The first noteworthy theoretical studies published by members of the Stockholm group were designed to clarify the monetary aspects of the Wicksellian theory. In other studies account was taken of the time element, of anticipations and expectations, and of differences between ex ante and ex post relationships of economic aggregates. The Swedish economists adjusted their business cycle analysis to considerations derived from these studies, and suggested consistent schemes of antidepression policies. Last but not least, in their treatment of problems of dynamic economics, they introduced "period" and "sequence" analysis, and thus contributed to the modification of the traditional methods of equilibrium analysis.

Gunnar Myrdal, who undertood the task of interpreting and testing the three somewhat ambiguous Wicksellian equilibrium conditions of the monetary sector of the economy, was faced with considerable difficulties when he attempted to attach a precise meaning to the Wicksellian concept of the "real" or "natural" rate of interest.[4] That concept had been derived from the model of an imaginary economy with a single productive factor, all services of which were strictly determined in accordance with marginal productivity analysis. Hence, in order to take account of the conditions of the monetary economy, Wicksell's rate of physical productivity had to be replaced by the concept of a monetary rate of return on new investment. In accordance with Wicksell's first equilibrium condition, the loan or market rate of interest was to be equal to the "ex ante" efficiency rate of capital.[5] But Myrdal considered that condition unsatisfactory, since it failed to determine for the system as a whole the level of investment, the level of profits, and the time rate of investment that would prevent cumulative processes from taking place.

Wicksell's second equilibrium condition pointed out the coincidence of the demand for and the supply of loan capital, hence the identity of savings and investments. But the ex ante establishment of equilibrium conditions in the capital market was obviously dependent upon the existence of coincident expectations on the part of savers and investors, and such coincidence could not be assumed to occur in the normal course of events. Wicksell had made repeated allusions to expectations as important elements of decision making. In his doctoral dissertation on price formation, Myrdal introduced that idea under various simplifying assumptions into his analysis of equilibrium prices. He showed how the behavior of the economy was affected by discrepancies between planned savings and investments, and how deviations from equilibrium positions were produced by imperfect foresight, imperfect competition, underutilization of resources, and the like. The complex formula for the "normal" market rate of interest, which Myrdal established with the aid of some simplifying assumptions, could hardly be adjusted to reality. According to that formula, the market rate of interest was to be regarded as "normal" when it corresponded to a margin of profit that was reached by establishing conformity of total gross investments with total amounts of savings plus total anticipated changes in the value of existing real capital.

Wicksell's third condition of monetary equilibrium was perhaps prompted by the intention to supplement the other purely abstract conditions with an operational formula. It provided in some respects a bridge to the quantity equations, since it required the adjustment of the market rate to the task of securing a stable general level of the prices of the finished products. But that equilibrium condition was opposed on the ground that it was incompatible with the postulated equilibrium between the loan rate of interest and the productivity rate of new capital investment. Increased productivity, when accompanied by a constant price level, was likely to lead to exceptional profits and speculative ventures, whereas declining productivity, as attended by a constant price level, was likely to initiate a depression.[6]

Thus, when the "natural" rate of interest was interpreted as a monetary rate, important aspects of the Wicksellian definition of the monetary equilibrium were found to be untenable. Any rates of interest, when properly adjusted, were shown to be compatible with any change in the price level; the management of the rate of interest did not appear to provide an efficient instrument for preventing the occurrence of profits and losses due to price adjustments. It seemed hardly possible to define a monetary equilibrium in terms of prices or of relationships between price levels, and Myrdal considered the concept of monetary equilibrium as nothing more than an instrument for classifying the expectations entertained by individuals at any period of time.

One of the most interesting aspects of Myrdal's testing of equilibrium conditions was the emphasis which he placed on anticipations and expectations. Some other "dynamic"

features of the Wicksellian doctrine were elaborated by Eric Lindahl,[7] who developed the
idea of applying equilibrium analysis to economic relationships extending over time. In
his attempt to establish a general "dynamic" theory, Lindahl considered it necessary to
make definite assumptions concerning individual behavior as manifested under varying
conditions: assumptions about the adoption of economic plans, about the principles underlying the adjustments of plans to changes in expectations, and the influence of outside
factors on the adjustment processes. When analyzing the adjustment process, Lindahl
introduced the notion of the "period of registration," which was defined as the period that
elapsed between two successive reconsiderations of economic plans; it was assumed to
come to an end when plans were changed. Faced with the fact that the decisions of
entrepreneurs were not coordinated, Lindahl established this corrdination for the end of
the period of registration on the assumption that all plans were mutually adjusted at
regular intervals and that, by averaging the price estimates of the entrepreneurs, definite
shapes could be given to the price movements. Thus, he substituted a series of discontinuous phases for a continuous process, and could define for each of these phases
equilibrium conditions in accordance with the usual equations.[8] The obvious objection
that changes in equilibrium positions are not likely to occur only at the end of registration
periods could be met by greatly reducing the length of these periods. But under these
conditions, the analysis was exposed to the danger of being transformed into a descriptive
treatment of rapidly changing events. Johan Akerman pointed to the discrepancy which
existed between the conception of the economy as a simple summation of individual
competitive plans and the actual conditions of the economy, where imperfect competition
prevailed and the productive factors were neither absolutely mobile nor absolutely
divisible.[9]

In his analysis of monetary problems, Lindahl adopted Wicksell's general criticism
of the quantity theory of money, regarded cash holdings as variable, and ascribed to the
movements of the quantity of money a more or less passive role. He studied the cumulative price movements which Wicksell had associated with changes in the rate of interest,
and analyzed the effects of such processes on the value of capital, the costs of its
reproduction, and the relation between the available loan capital and new investments.
Thus, he opened a wide field for discussion of problems of monetary and fiscal policies.[10]

The Wicksellian doctrine also provided the background for a series of treatises
prepared at the beginning of the thirties under the auspices of the Commission on Unemployment.[11] These studies dealt with the causes of unemployment (Gösta Bagge), the
industrial rationalization and its effects (Gustaf Åkerman), the diffusion of economic
fluctuations (Dag Hammarskjöld), the economic effects of financial policies (Gunnar
Myrdal), wages and unemployment (Alf Johannsson), and monetary policy and other
measures of combating unemployment (Bertil Ohlin). The factors which were considered
responsible for the contraction of business activity and unemployment were discussed in a
concluding report by Hammarskjöld. The report examined the ex ante and ex post effects
of saving on the relationships between monetary demand and the volume of output, and
applied period analysis to the establishment of various models of the economy which were
designed to throw some light on particular phases of the processes of expansion and
contraction.[12]

A significant theoretical result of these studies was the proposal to substitute for
Wicksell's fluctuating level of prices a fluctuating level of incomes as the variable to be
considered instrumental in adjusting savings to the rate of investments. Gains and losses
reflected in changing incomes were regarded as the main elements of that process of

adjustment, and changes in the price level, produced by changes in income, were held responsible for changes in the distribution of income. The Swedish economists questioned the effectivness of monetary measures as a means of initiating the upswing, but recommended the exercise of an appropriate discount policy as a method of arresting exaggerated credit expansions during boom periods.

The policy of combating unemployment through public works programs financed by loans was the object of prolonged discussions and was vigorously defended by the Minister of Finance, Ernst Wigfores. Adversaries of that policy (Lundberg, Cassel, Eli Filip Heckscher, and others) argued that private enterprise might be crippled by state-subsidized production, which might become a permanent economic institution. Theoretical arguments against the proposed credit policy were derived from the view that the contraction of business activity that took place during the Depression was a necessary correction of misdirected investments caused by the overexpansion of credit. This approach to business cycle policy was similar to that adopted by members of the Austrian school, who were strongly influenced by Wicksell's teachings. Consistent adherents of reasoning of that type, such as Johan Åkerman, were convinced that reductions of the rate of interest could have the desired lasting effect only when justified by increased savings and combined with wage reductions.

Defenders of public works policy pointed to the creation of new income which was likely to result from increased public expenditures. In his study of the monetary aspects of employment policies, Ohlin gave some examples of the multiplier effects of such expenditures on government revenues. Johannsson's study of the wage problem concluded that, as compared with other more relevant factors, changes in wages were relatively unimportant in determining the course of business cycles. But he admitted the need for wage reductions as a means of obviating exchange difficulties in the event of an isolated upturn of the Swedish economy. Frequent expression was given to the view that stabilization of the value of money, maintenance of stable and full employment, and maintenance of equilibrium in the balance of payments were perfectly compatible objectives of economic policy.[13] But increasing recognition was given to Davidson's view that the official price policy, instead of tending to stabilize the price level of consumption goods, should permit that price level to vary inversely with increases or declines in productivity; hence, that stabilization of the price level of the productive services should be the ultimate object of the price policy. The Swedish economic policy of the thirties was credited with having avoided many mistakes committed in other countries. But the measures of economic policy recommended in the theoretical discussions were drawn upon only to a limited extent.

Considerations which played significant roles in the Keynesian theory of employment were anticipated in these discussions. But, as distinct from Keynes and his followers, the Swedish economists regarded unemployment as a purely cyclical phenomenon and ignored "propensity to consume" as a relevant economic factor.[14] They were convinced that any equilibrium positions reached by the economy were highly unstable, since price rises occurring at greatly varying rates in different sectors of the economy or wage increases lagging behind price increases were likely to lead to substantial changes in the distribution of incomes. In their view, the existence of inflexible prices was a factor which aggravated the effects of market imperfections. Their employment policy, as formulated by Ohlin, centered on three populations: (a) the aggregate volume of real investments was to be adjusted to the willingness to save; (b) the average wage level was to be prevented from rising more quickly than the corresponding increase in productivity calculated for the industry as a whole; and (c) maintenance of industrial peace was of paramount importance. Ohlin compared the undesirable effects of "overemployment" brought about by economically unjustified expansion of productive activity with the dangers involved in underemployment of the available resources.

Process analysis as initiated by other Swedish economists was further developed by Lundberg in some remarkable studies dealing with the behavior of a "dynamic economy."[15] In a critical survey of the methods of equilibrium analysis, he questioned the usefulness of the partial equilibrium approach, since partial systems could hardly be adjusted simultaneously to changing conditions. He insisted that the most important problems were obscured when economic analysis was simplified by bold assumptions such as neutrality of money, perfect foresight of producers and consumers, and the like. He recommended the establishment of significant "total categories" for the economy as a whole, and suggested studies of the variations in the elements of the general equilibrium system brought about by changes in monetary aggregates such as total income, purchasing power, and the like.

In the light of these considerations, Lundberg classified some recent economic theories according to the degree to which they assigned appropriate positions to factors which are adaptable to changing economic conditions, as distinct from factors which are excluded from the nexus of the interdependent elements of the economic system. Thus, he questioned the explanatory value of the theories of Eugen Böhm-Bawerk and Wicksell in which the supply of real capital was assumed to adapt itself to given data simultaneously with the rest of the variables (such as total employment of the economy, total income, consumption, expenditures, and savings). He questioned the assumptions which were basic to the Keynesian theory of employment on the grounds that the independent magnitude of the model, the quantity of money, was connected with the functioning of the economy through a stable factor, the multiplier; that savings were qualified as mere residuals of expenditures; that income, savings, and investments were defined as ex post magnitudes; and that no account was taken of possible variations in the relations between the values of new investments and expenditures for consumption purposes, which might occur in the course of expansions or contractions of the economy.

The models which Lundberg had in mind were designed to show the determination of all variable factors in a process of sequence analysis based on the concept of a balanced growth of the economy. He defined the period to be chosen for purposes of process analysis as a sort of "operational time" corresponding to the "dynamic relations" between income and expenditure, buying and selling, change in earnings and productive activity. In an instructive survey of various economic models, he qualified Wicksell's unit period as the length of time required to produce consumption goods (a year), Keynes's period (suggested in the *Treatise on Money*) as a credit cycle disrupted by an increased flow of consumption goods, Johannsson's[16] period as one stage out of four stages of production, and Robertson's period as a time span determined by the relation between the period of production and the velocity of circulation of money. Hammarskjöld's unit period was defined by the intervals between successive profit registrations and was independent of periods of production.[17]

Lundberg regarded all these definitions of the basic period as defective, since they failed to take account of variations in savings and fixed capital investments. In his view, the unit period was a device for averaging the speed of psychological reactions of groups of producers and consumers on the assumptions that these reactions did not change perceptibly during the period and that divisions into subgroups were possible when rendered advisable by the existence of time lags in reactions. Lundberg admitted, however, that it was unrealistic to assume simultaneous changes in operations at discontinuous points in time, since individual reactions to changing economic conditions might be spread over indefinite periods.[18] He discussed differences in time lags that he found to exist between changes in demand and changes in output, between the construction of capital goods and their use, between changes in the rate of interest and their effects on investments, and between the receipt of certain kinds of income and the decisions to make corresponding expenditures.

In his analysis of the reaction patterns of various economic groups, Lundberg took account of the institutional background of economic behavior as well as of banking and fiscal policies as important factors influencing changes in saving, investment, and consumption plans. But the introduction of subdivisions could not be carried on very far, since it implied the danger of leading to partial equilibrium analysis instead of supplying for the entire economy a picture of combined patterns of reactions to changes in investment, saving, consumption, and so on. Hence, Lundberg was obliged to take recourse to the usual assumption that variable magnitudes change discontinuously and that the concept of a rate of flow at a point of time can be replaced by the concept of an amount related to a period of time. In accordance with that step-by-step analysis, he had to assume that changes of the plans occurred only at the end of each period, and that the plans were made on the basis of previous experience.

In the light of simplified models, Lundberg attempted to give precise meaning to the assumptions underlying various business cycle theories, and to define the coefficients of instability for the reactions of the models to certain changes in their elements: to changes in consumers' outlay, in saving or investments, and the like. He ascribed to his models the merit of demonstrating conclusively the defects of practically all theories designed to provide a uniform explanation for all business fluctuations and crises.

But, though highly instructive, these studies in the field of process analysis amounted only to the outline of a new methodology, without being expanded into a consistent doctrine. The disintegration of the Stockholm school which took place during the Second World War destroyed the prospect of developing such a theory. The Wicksellian tradition lost its cohesive force when "minor differences in interpreting the relative importance of the various methods" became differences of "crucial importance" for the members of the Stockholm group, and when some leading members of the group became deeply engaged in politics or were appointed to responsible official positions.[19] To the younger generation of Swedish economists the relatively simple Keynesian theory of employment offered greater attraction than intricate reasoning in terms of period and sequence analysis. Adoption of the Keynesian theory was hardly regarded as a "revolutionary" event, since various characteristic features of that theory had been included among the teachings of Wicksell and his disciples.[20]

The approach to economic analysis eventually adopted by Lundberg and his followers was determined by a synthesis among a version of the quantity theory of money, the Keynesian theory of the influence of the supply of money on the rate of interest, and the Wicksellian theory of the effects of interest rates on investments. In their view, the critical problem consisted in determining how the propensities to spend, to lend, and to borrow, as manifested by different groups of firms or individuals, are affected by changes in the level and structure of interest rates and by consequent variations in the supply and distribution of liquidity.[21] But in view of the uncertainties which surround decision making by firms or individuals, it was found impossible to disentangle either on theoretical grounds or by means of statistical investigations, the effects of changes in the rate of interest and in the supply of money. Highly simplifying assumptions had to be made by the Swedish Konjunkturinstitut in the economic surveys prepared under Lundberg's direction.[22] These studies dealt especially with the problem of determining what degrees of government intervention are involved for various measures of economic policy and the disturbances to the economy which are likely to result from the execution of far-reaching measures of control.[23]

Chapter 34
Keynes's Theory of Employment, Interest, and Money

THE PROPOSITION THAT any progress in economic reasoning is conditioned by the abandonment of some fundamental assumptions of Ricardian economics has been most dramatically illustrated by the eventful history of John Maynard Keynes's *The General Theory of Employment, Interest and Money*—a work which was hailed as the beginning of a new era in the development of economic thought.[1] During the first ten or twelve years after its appearance, *The General Theory* received more attention that Alfred Marshall's *Principles of Economics* had received in over fifty years.[2] It stimulated economic thinking in the Anglo-Saxon countries to a degree which can be compared only with the—infinitely slower—effects of *The Wealth of Nations,* by Adam Smith.

A generation of enthusiastic disciples endorsed the leading ideas of the Keynesian teachings and developed them in many directions. In due course, they succeeded in converting leading British and American politicians and business executives to the economic policies advocated by Keynes and adjusted their own research to the task of implementing these policies.

The General Theory has been considered as the product of a depression period in which the foundations of the capitalist economy were shaken by a stagnation of business activity of apparently indefinite duration.[3] If this view is accepted, this work occupies an exceptional place in the history of economic reasoning, since virtually all other more or less radical transformations of prevailing economic doctrines were not suggested by the impact of striking economic events, but were prompted by methodological considerations or deep-seated aversion to the existing economic order.

In fact, in the midst of an economic crisis, when the air was filled with schemes of collectivist economic planning, Keynes advanced a new theoretical interpretation of the capitalist economy which opened the way for the adoption of measures designed to direct the functioning of the economy into desired channels without interfering with the general principles underlying its behavior. Keynes's theory was adjusted to the reasoning of those trained in Marshallian equilibrium analysis, but, although imbedded in a vast array of intricate, partly critical and partly constructive discussions, its leading ideas could be expressed in popular language.

Keynes claimed to have developed a "general theory of employment" because he demonstrated that the equilibrium of the economy can be established at various levels of employment of the available resources and that full-employment equilibrium is but a single case out of a wide variety of economic conditions. He thus discarded the fundamental Ricardian assumption that full-employment equilibrium is an indispensable ingredient of any theoretical model of the economy.

Centering his analysis on characteristic features of cyclical unemployment, Keynes effectively attacked a prevailing view which he had shared when writing his *Treatise on Money:* the view that there exists a tendency to bring about equilibrium positions at full employment through gradual adjustment of wages and prices to changing market conditions. In his frequent allusions to the discussions between Ricardo and Malthus, he extolled the merits of the Malthusian emphasis on short-term problems and expressed his deep regret about the victory of the Ricardian long-term approach to economic analysis over the Malthusian formulation of short-term issues. As Thomas R. Malthus had done more than a century before, Keynes insisted on the importance of "effective demand" for the maintenance and expansion of economic activity. He took the Ricardians to task for having misled the thinking of many generations of economists through their equilibrium analysis, which was governed by Jean Baptiste Say's law of markets[4] and excluded the existence of equilibrium positions at less than full employment; even large-scale prolonged unemployment of available resources had been ascribed to "frictions," to be remedied by adjusting wages to the prevailing conditions of the labor market.

Arthur Cecil Pigou's theory of unemployment was a special object of Keynes's strictures.[5] Pigou availed himself of the concept of a wage fund to justify the propositions that at a given rate of real wages the quantity of labor demanded by the aggregate of all industries could vary only in precise proportion to the quantity of wage goods available for the payment of wages, and that downward revisions of wages could be expected to stimulate the expansion of business activity.

Strongly opposed to this approach to the unemployment problem, Keynes argued that workers had a definite predilection for bargaining in terms of money wages, and that, when marginal prime costs were rising with expanding output, real wages were not affected by nominal wage reductions. Quite generally, he believed that in analyzing the behavior of the economy as a whole, the function of wages as a cost element of the firm was insignificant. He attacked the wage problem from the side of demand, and placed primary emphasis on the general deflationary effects of declining wages and on the rigidity of the wage system when it was faced with a downward movement. To the view that downward revisions of wages could be expected to stimulate the expansion of business activity, Keynes opposed the "great puzzle of effective demand" with which Malthus had wrestled and which could live only furtively below the surface in the underworlds of Karl Marx, Silvio Gesell, and Paul H. Douglas.[6]

As a long-term wage policy, Keynes recommended a combination of rising wages and stable prices which, assisted by the effects of technological improvements, would secure participation of the workers in the fruits of enhanced productivity and lead to the transfer of workers from less productive to more productive processes.

In the light of these considerations, the "classical economists" (by which Keynes meant all leading English economists of the Marshallian school, such as Marshall, Edgeworth, and Pigou) had adopted a misleading model of the economy in which "the calculus of probability—mention of which was kept in the background—was capable of reducing uncertainties to the same calculable status as that of certainty itself."[7]

The Marshallian treatment of the rate of interest was another object of Keynes's criticism. Placing demand into the center of his analysis, he defined the ''consumption function'' as a schedule which relates expenditures on goods of consumption to income levels. Marshall and his disciples, Keynes argued, had thoroughly misunderstood the relation of the rate of interest to the consumption function, since they assumed that the demand for consumption goods increased along with the decline of the rate of interest, and that this rate was bound to decline when the demand for loan capital was reduced by declining investments. (The functions which Keynes assigned to the rate of interest in relation to demand will be discussed in another connection.)

If the forces operating in the exchange economy could not be relied upon to establish full-employment equilibrium, pursuance of an appropriate economic policy appeared to be indispensable in order to prevent the disintegration of a decaying economy. Such a policy, Keynes believed, was incompatible with the traditional conception of the economy as an interplay of prices and wages. This ''microeconomic'' view was to be replaced by a ''macroeconomic'' view based on the relations between economic aggregates. In his model of the economy, Keynes paid particular attention to aggregates which could be influenced by measures of economic policy, such as national income, total consumption, volumes of savings and investments, and the like.[8]

In spite of these criticisms of Marshallian economics, however, Keynes was so deeply imbued with the Marshallian tradition that his model of the economy showed many characteristic features of a static Ricardian real exchange system.[9] Econimic activity was assumed to be ruled by the principles of free competition and profit maximization, prices were expressed in stable wage units paid per unit of labor time, prices were elements of a fixed and uniform price level, and neither the quantity and quality of plants and equipment nor the existing methods of production were allowed to change. Moreover, the model was impervious to the influence of outside factors. The volume of employment was regarded as an adequate index of output, and was measured in terms of ''labor units.'' Hours of ''special'' labor were reduced to hours of ''ordinary'' labor in proportion to their re-muneration. The hypothetical wage unit was defined as the money wage of the labor unit; it was assumed to be independent of the fluctuations of monetary values and provided the basis for the construction of a ''real exchange'' system.

Faced with the task of defining the relations between relevant economic aggregates, Keynes appears to have followed pretty closely the pattern established by Marshall for analyzing the short-term equilibrium conditions of an industry.[10] His ''aggregate supply'' function corresponded to the Marshallian supply functions of the firm; his concept of ''social dividend'' reflected the value of the Marshallian ''current output'' of the firm. Marginal analysis, which he applied to economic aggregates, had its prototype in Marshall's treatment of the behavior of the firm.

When the Keynesian model of the economy is reduced to its elements, its ''ultimate independent variables'' are found to consist of: (a) three fundamental psychological factors, namely, the propensity to consume, the liquidity preference, and the expectation of future yields from capital assets (the propensity to invest); (b) the wage unit; and (c) the quantity of money fixed by the central bank. These variables, Keynes said, determine the national income and the quantity of employment.[11]

It was one of the original features of the Keynesian model of the economy that it was designed to reflect the relationships between the available resources and the distribution of purchasing power among the main channels of the economy. In the formula $I + C = Y$, investment and consumption were defined as the constituent elements of inccme. Disregading all problems connected with the flow of income, Keynes held the relationship between investment and consumption to be directly responsible for the existence of equilibrium conditions at less than full employment. In analyzing these relationships he emphasized an idea which also had played a significant role in Wicksell's interpretation of the capitalist economy: that no institutional devices exist in this economy to adjust the amounts actually invested to the amounts not spent and available for investment.

Elaborating on this idea, Keynes suggested that throughout economic history a remarkable tendency had existed for the propensity to save to be stronger than the inducement to invest.[12] In the light of these conditions, he formulated a sort of "psychological law" according to which there has existed, for each stage of cultural and industrial development, a more or less fixed relation between increases in income and increases in consumption.[13] Using the term "propensity to consume" to denote the relation of consumption outlays to total income, Keynes advanced the proposition that in highly industrialized societies increases in consumption have a strong tendency to lag proportionately behind increases in income. In various passages of *The General Theory*, he expressed his aversion to the "bourgeois" virtue of thrift and to all features of the capitalist society which imply preference of future over present consumption, such as excess savings, high rates of interest, the incentive given to saving by the hereditary principle, and the like.

In an often-quoted dictum, Keynes looked forward to the "euthanasia" of the *rentier* class, its gradual elimination through the progressive reduction of the rate of interest to zero. Viewed from this angle, the growth of the economy was retarded rather than promoted by the "abstinence" practiced by the capitalists. One of the main arguments which had been advanced in favor of considerable inequalities of the distribution of wealth could thus be considered irrelevant.

Keynes was convinced that he could derive his "psychological law" both a priori from our knowledge of human nature and from the detailed facts of experience. But he did not state explicitly whether he connected the discrepancy between the propensity to save and the inducement to invest with institutional factors or simply with the development of wealth in society.

According to the assumptions underlying the Keynesian model of the economy, the "normal" or "equilibrium" level of economic activity was brought about when "intended" savings were equal to "noninduced" investment, or investment not dependent upon the secondary effects of monetary expansion.[14] The demand for money—as determined by the volume of investments—was related to the difference between two variables: the profit expectations of the entrepreneurs and the rate of interest.

Profit expectations were associated with the "marginal efficiency of capital," which was defined as the rate of discount that makes the present value of the future returns of a capital asset equal to the supply price of that asset. In other words, the demand for capital goods was held to depend upon the excess of the discounted value of their expected earnings over their price. Keynes practically identified his concept of "marginal efficiency of capital" with Irving Fisher's "rate of return over cost" and Marshall's "marginal utility of capital," that is, with the profits which could be expected from new investments. However, as distinct from the two other authors, he applied marginal utility analysis not to specific assets but to economic aggregates.[15]

In his discussion of profit expectations, Keynes occasionally dealt with different aspects of uncertainty and speculation and alluded to the time factor as an important element in modifying decisions concerning expansion or contraction of business activity.

He discussed a theory of "shifting equilibria," which was designed to analyze successive equilibrium positions on the assumption that changing views about the future are capable of influencing present decision making.[16] In another connection, he characterized disappointed illusions about future yields of investments as the cause of psychological shifts in the "marginal efficiency of capital," thus modifying the original meaning of the latter term.[17] But such observations did not imply serious departures from the Marshallian view that expectations, being variables of a psychological type, are to be regarded as indeterminate factors which remain outside the circumscribed sphere of economic analysis strictly speaking.

The Keynesian conception of the rate of interest—the second main determinant of the demand for money—differed perceptibly from the role assigned to this factor by the Marshallian economists who derived the level of the rate of interest from the interaction of the supply and demand schedules for savings. According to this view, the saving-investment equilibrium was established by the movement of the rate of interest.

Keynes rejected Marshall's proposition that a rise of the price for savings tends to increase the volume of savings; he sharply criticized Gustav Cassel's view that a fall of the rate of interest below a certain level might lead to an excess of consumption over savings.[18] Some authors of monetary business cycle theories had attached particular importance to the mismanagement of the rate of interest practiced by commercial banks. Within the framework of the Keynesian theory, however, a "wrong rate of interest" was natural, durable, in a certain sense inevitable in the free system.[19] In support of this proposition, Keynes attributed to the owners of capital a specific psychological attitude, a "liquidity preference" or desire to hoard which was stimulated by the "speculative motive." Hence, he defined the rate of interest as the price to be paid in order to overcome the borrowers' predilection for assets in liquid form; he identified this rate with the factor which adjusts at the margin the demand for and supply of hoards.[20]

The rate of interest was assumed to affect the demand for investments indirectly through its influence on the discount rate used in determining the value of expected future earnings. The discount rate was in turn assumed to be influenced by considerations of risk and uncertainty. Keynes suggested that, as distinct from hoarding for speculative purposes, accumulation of cash for transaction or precautionary reasons is not affected by changes in the rate of interest. According to this theory, the desire to hold cash balances can lead to increases in the rate of interest even when investments are declining, and the rate of interest can fluctuate for decades about a level too high to be compatible with full employment.

The concept of a stagnant economy in which equilibrium between savings and investments exists at conditions of less than full employment was derived from this interpretation of the functioning of the economy. Stagnant economic conditions of indefinite duration could be brought about when reduced total income, caused by reduced investment, would lead to reduced savings. The decline of savings would continue to a point at which all savings were invested, and stable total expenditures would be adjusted to stationary total incomes.

In a short survey of the economic conditions of the nineteenth century, Keynes observed that during this period the growth of the population—as combined with the influence of inventions, the opening up of new territories, and the existing propensity to consume—seemed to be adequate to secure a marginal efficiency of capital which, at the generally accepted rate of interest, was compatible with a satisfactory level of employment.[21] These conditions, however, do not prevail in a wealthy country in which large amounts of capital are accumulated, the supply price of capital goods is raised, and the opportunities for further investment are correspondingly reduced.[22] In such a country none of the three factors which Keynes considered indispensable for assuring the equilibrium of the system at full employment can be expected to contribute effectively to the achievement of this goal. The marginal efficiency of capital appears to be lacking stability and to show a downward trend. The propensity to consume declines under the rule of a "psychological" law. The rate of interest can be expected to rise even when the demand for loans is declining.

Keynes supplemented these considerations with an analysis which showed how investments depended upon a variety of partly exogenous factors, and how, even under conditions of full employment, adjustment of investments to the level of the available savings is in no way assured. He contrasted the results of this analysis with the conviction expressed in John Stuart Mill's dictum that "the laws and conditions of the production of wealth partake of the character of physical truths."

In order to offset the decline in the propensity to consume, Keynes proposed the imposition of steeply progressive income taxes. He recommended the use of exchange control, prohibition of capital exports, and other measures designed to counteract the pressure of deflationary trends; he regarded issuance of public loans and execution of public works programs as important elements of a "socialization" of investment activities. Occasionally he even expressed a certain predilection for various types of usury laws and for "stamped money" as advocated by Silvio Gesell.[23]

As a long-range wage policy, Keynes proposed a combination of rising wages and stable prices which, assisted by the effects of technological improvements, would secure participation of the workers in the fruits of enhanced productivity and lead to the transfer of workers from less productive to more productive processes.

Keynes's treatment of the rate of interest was in many respects reminiscent of the economic policy defended by some mercantilist authors. Keynes was well aware of this similarity, and he devoted a special section of his book to a discussion of some of their leading ideas.[24] He praised their "wisdom" as manifested in their intense preoccupation with the task of keeping down the rate of interest, and their readiness to restore the monetary stock by devaluation if it had become plainly deficient through an unavoidable foreign drain, a rise in the wage unit, or any other cause. He was quite emphatic on contrasting these views with those of the Ricardian economists, who established a causal relationship between changes in the rate of interest and the supply of loanable funds and ignored the importance of money as a store of value.

In discussing the effects of monetary expansion, Keynes introduced into his analysis a new instrument, the "investment multiplier," based on the relation between an increment in investment and an increment in income. This "tool" was a version of the "employment multiplier," which had been suggested by R. F. Kahn in a study designed to defend the execution of public works programs as means of creating employment.[25] The "multiplier idea" had been alluded to in various previous studies of the fluctuating behavior of the economy.[26] Kahn's achievement consisted, above all, in analyzing the relations between two static situations—that before and that after the execution of public orders—on the assumption that all productive factors, including labor, were in perfectly elastic supply. This assumption was at variance with the post-Ricardian proposition that the main object of economics was the study of the adjustment of "Scarce means to rival ends." The employment multiplier provided a factor for determining the total volume of employment which could be expected to result from a stream of employment created by public orders. The definition of this factor was based on the consideration that the employment created by the public orders would increase the demand for consumption goods and would thus bring about additional employment of a gradually declining size. The formula for this multiplier reads: "primary employment plus secondary employment divided by primary employment."

Keynes's "investment multiplier" did not reflect changes in volumes of employment, but increases in purchasing power resulting from new public investments. Keynes facilitated his analysis by making some bold assumptions, such as that all earners of income renounced all profit-seeking activities and adjusted their consumption expenditures to the rate determined by the marginal propensity to consume.[27] Other assumptions served the purpose of separating the streams of income derived from previous investments from the increments in income which could be attributed to the public orders. These increments in income were said to enhance the demand for consumption goods to the extent that they were not absorbed by "leakages" brought about by accumulation of cash reserves, hoarding, repayments of debts, payments for imports, etc. In Keynes's multiplier formula $1/1\text{-}K$, the letter K indicated the increase in consumption taking place during an initial period, and the formula was designed to define the factor by which this initial increase in purchasing power is to be multiplied in order to determine the total increment in purchasing power resulting from the public order.[28] Since Keynes applied his formula exclusively to the conditions of prolonged depression periods, he, like Kahn, availed himself of the assumption that the productive factors were in ample supply and that no inflationary price movements resulted from the methods of financing the expansion of production.

In his *General Theory*, Keynes did not advance a business cycle theory strictly speaking, but he pointed to some significant relationships between his interpretation of unemployment conditions and the fluctuations of business activity. He connected the termination of the boom with the alleged tendency of consumption to lag behind the increase in incomes. He pointed to his proposition that the marginal efficiency of capital declines along with the increase in capital stocks, and suggested that during the boom the yield of new investments is gradually reduced even below the level of the lowest rate of interest still compatible with the existing propensity to hoard. Hence, he ascribed the collapse of the boom to sudden changes in the efficiency of capital and observed that the provision of sinking funds and depreciation allowances far in excess of current requirements for repair and renewal might be an aggravating factor. During a depression, he argued, the capital stock accumulated during a boom is whittled down through depreciation and obsolescence. An increase in the marginal efficiency of capital is thus rendered possible when demand recovers after prolonged delcines and when markets are expanding.

Keynes's outlook on the future of the capitalist economy was based on his model of the real exchange economy. It was ruled by the combined prospect of the increasing propensity to save and the drying up of investment opportunities.[29] Owing to the rapidly advancing accumulation of stock, the marginal efficiency of capital was bound to decline and the income-generating power of new investments was gradually reduced.

These long-term considerations encouraged some leftist adherents of the Keynesian doctrine to establish close comparisons between that doctrine and the Marxian teachings.[30] They attempted to demonstrate that Karl Marx had anticipated the theory of effective demand, and that the Marxian theorem of the falling rate of profit could be used to establish an economic model with "behavior equations" similar to those which were characteristic of Keynes's conception of the economy.[31] From Keynes's demonstration that under conditions of full employment there was nothing to assure equality between investments and the level of available savings, some leftist adherents of the Keynesian doctrine derived the conclusion that profit expectations had ceased to be indispensable as incentives to the expansion of productive activity, and that it was no longer necessary to include profit among the costs of production.[32] But these comparisons were rendered almost meaningless by the fact that they ignored the fundamental difference in methods of reasoning which exists between the Keynesian approach and its Marxian counterpart.

Keynes was convinced that during his time there was no more reason to socialize economic life than there was before.[33] Although *The General Theory* was intended to dispel the optimistic Marshallian views concerning the functioning of the exchange economy, Keynes expressed in various passages of his work his belief in the beneficial effects of the free competitive forces, of private initiative, and of individual responsibility.[34]

Chapter 35
Discussions of
the "New Economics"

―――

INTERPRETATIONS OF THE KEYNESIAN THEORY

FOR ABOUT TEN YEARS after the appearance of *The General Theory of Employment, Interest and Money,* the main Anglo-American economic discussions centered on the interpretation and the development of the ideas advanced in this work. Its admirers—and there were many—disagreed less on the importance of John Maynard Keynes's theory for the advancement of economic reasoning than on the question of how to define its original and fundamental contributions to their science. Some authors, such as Roy F. Harrod, were convinced that Keynes's greatest merit consisted in having paved the way for the development of a dynamic theory.[1] Others, such as Paul A. Samuelson, attributed the "broad significance" of the theory of employment to the fact that it provided a relatively realistic, complete system for analyzing the level of effective demand and its fluctuations.[2] Still others derived the "tremendous appleal" of Keynes's work from the fact that here, for the first time in the history of economic thought, a general equilibrium analysis was presented in easily manageable macroeconomic terms.[3] Keynes was credited with having made a number of valuable contributions to economic theorizing, having made a brilliant analysis of the demand for money, having introduced some relevant psychological factors (such as liquidity preference expectations), having advanced a highly significant concept of the national income, and having defined the variables which determine its changes.

Although *The General Theory* was designed to lead the exchange economy out of the trough of a deep depression, both open and secret adversaries of the competitive order used its attack on the bourgeois virtues of thrift and hoarding and its insistence on the application of "rational principles" to the regulation of production to justify their view that the inequitable distribution of wealth was one of the primary evils of the Western society. They had been taught that the growth of national wealth, far from being dependent upon the "abstinence" of the capitalists, was instead impeded by excessive accumulation of capital. They argued that since profit expectations had ceased to be indispensable as incentives to the expansion of productive activity, it was no longer necessary to include profit among the costs of production.[4]

The enthusiasm displayed by the protagonists of the "Keynesian revolution" found a counterweight, however, in the critical examination of the new doctrine by more conservative economists, who pointed to the narrow, static, short-term aspects of the Keynesian analysis and questioned the general validity of almost all its leading propositions. Strong objections were also raised to Keynes's interpretation of the views of the "classical" economists and to his claim that his theory implied a radical departure from their economic analysis.[5]

Even lenient critics of *The General Theory* questioned the adequacy of the Keynesian model of the economy, in which the rate of interest was determined by the quantity of money and the liquidity preference, the liquidity preference was determined by the level of incomes, the level of investment was determined by the rate of interest and the marginal propensity to consume, and income output and employment were determined by the level of investment and the marginal propensity to consume. In addition, people objected to the establishment of simple linear relationships between a few constituent elements of the national income, the choice of a "wage unit" as the standard for reducing all economic aggregates to a uniform denominator, the excessive use of the *ceteris paribus* clause, the extremely mechanistic nature of the model (which excluded any reference to entrepreneurship), and the static structure of the model which rendered the analysis unsuitable to take account of changes in the ratio of the disposable income as related to the amounts of money held in successive periods).[6]

Some critics took exception to the application of marginal analysis to economic aggregates such as national income, total expenditure, global savings, and the like.[7] On closer examination, such a procedure could be considered justified only when it was assumed that the individual units of which the economy is composed are operating under a regime of perfect competition. Other critics raised the question of whether Keynes connected the discrepancy between the propensity to save and the inducement to invest with institutional factors, or associated it simply with the development of wealth in society. But convinced followers of the Keynesian doctrine countered these and other objections with the argument that the true greatness of *The General Theory* could never have been achieved had its author been fully dependent on the analytical tools he forged.[8]

The Keynesian terminology provoked prolonged and tedious controveries. A considerable confusion resulted from the "accounting equality" which Keynes established by identifying "savings" and "investments" in his fundamental equation.[9] What he had in mind were ex post, or actually invested, savings, as distinct from ex ante, or planned, savings.[10] However, it soon became apparent that the issue created by this definition was not simply terminological, since in accordance with this formulation of the savings-investment relation all cumulative processes connected with "savings" were excluded from the analysis, and no distinction could be drawn between investment financed by inflationary credit or dishoarding and investment financed by the current supply of voluntary savings.[11]

The static conception of savings adopted by Keynes met with much opposition and was contrasted with three other concepts which implied that the behavior of savings might give rise to disequilibrium positions:[12] the concept used by Keynes in *Treatise on Money;* the concept suggested by Dennis Holme Robertson in support of period analysis;[13] and the concept of "unintentional" savings advanced by the Stockholm school and used to develop the distinction between ex ante and ex post savings.[14] The defense of the Keynesian position was supported by the arguments that it reflected the behavior of savers, investors, and entrepreneurs under equilibrium positions at full employment and that it avoided the difficulties involved in defining the unit period for purposes of process analysis.

Another subject of prolonged discussion was Keynes's definition of the rate of interest as the rate that equates the supply of and the demand for money. This conception was incompatible with the "loan fund theory," which made the supply of credit for lending purposes a determinant of the rate of interest.[15] Various attempts to qualify the choice between the two definitions as a matter of convenience rather than as a theoretical issue were not very convincing.[16] Some of these attempts were partly suggested by the idea of transforming into ex post concepts the ex ante concepts used by the loan fund theory;[17] others reflected the view that both variables should be formulated in the ex ante sense.[18] But these proposals were shown to be untenable, since the liquidity preference theorem which provides the background for the Keynesian concept of interest is an element of his equilibrium analysis, whereas the loanable funds theory is applicable to the flow of hoarding and dishoarding which occurs independently of equilibrating tendencies. Two telling arguments were advanced in favor of the loanable funds theory: that it is compatible with a differentiation of rates, and that it can be adjusted to dynamic aspects of the economy, such as "security preferences" and the like.[19]

Keynes's formulation of the concept of liquidity preference was generally considered an original and useful instrument of economic analysis, but various authors criticized the exaggerated importance which Keynes attributed to hoarding for speculative purposes. They stressed the quest for security and the risk element as more significant factors among the incentives to save and the motives to keep assets in liquid forms.[20] Joan Robinson was rather isolated in defending Keynes's emphasis on hoarding for speculative purposes as a motive of liquidity preference.[21] The relation established by Keynes between the liquidity preference theory and the rate of interest was questioned by Robertson, who observed that this theorem was hardly suitable to deal with situations in which changes of the rate of interest are brought about by changes in the velocity of circulation.[22] Jacob Viner considered Robertson's flow analysis as applied to the study of the effects of hoarding far superior to the liquidity preference method.[23]

Similarly, serious doubts were cast on the correlation which Keynes established between liquidity preference and the increasing importance attached to the risk element. Both consumption and investment were shown to react irregularly to changing ideas, techniques, and resources; it was doubtful whether the course of these reactions could be adjusted to the requirements of equilibrium analysis.[24] In fact, after the Second World War, American investment activity was strongly stimulated by the demand which had accumulated and was supported by large volumes of liquid means.

Another disputed element of Keynes's theory was the role which he attributed to the liquidity preference in determining the unemployment equilibrium.[25] His broad distinction between liquid and illiquid funds could not be maintained in the light of experience.[26] There was considerable agreement on the proposal to distinguish different degrees of liquidity and to arrange assets of various types on a scale beginning with cash and ending with specific finished goods.[27] The "asset theory" of money was an interesting contribution to the liquidity preference problems raised by Keynes. The authors of this theory drew a distinction between payments for the safety of assets and payments for plasticity and lucrativeness of assets.[28] They arrived at the conclusion that increased liquidity preference could lead to a fall in the rate of return of short-term government paper, hence to a decline of the rate of interest, a result which was incompatible with the Keynesian assumptions.

The apparently well-defined concept of "marginal efficiency of capital" lost much of its significance as a methodological tool when it was shown to be a purely theoretical notion, since the distinction between newly invested and old capital did not meet the test of practical application. Even the theoretical validity of this concept was questioned on the ground that it failed to take account of revisions of economic plans and their cumulative effects on supply and demand functions.[29]

Many American economists welcomed the consumption function as a promising approach to income analysis and endorsed the Keynesian theorems that total expenditures on consumption goods increase at a smaller rate than the national income and that the fluctuations in the production of capital goods are mainly due to the decline of the average propensity to consume.[30] On closer analysis, however, these theorems appeared in a different light when account was taken of the effects of capital gains, expectations of future gains, accumulated savings, and other economic factors providing links between the microeconomic approach and the formation of aggregates.[31]

Critics of the Keynesian analysis refused to qualify the behavior of the consumption function as a "psychological law" and regarded it simply as a tendency that should be tested and verified by statistical methods.[32] Extensive investigations into the relationships between consumption, savings, income, and other economic variables were organized in the United States by the Research Center of the University of Michigan. The theoretical and practical problems involved in such studies were discussed at various meetings of the International Association for Research in Income and Wealth. The Keynesian propositions were confirmed by some studies of family budgets. Other studies showed that shifts in the marginal propensity to consume occurred in the course of business fluctuations as direct or indirect reactions to increases in investments, varying in intensity and in temporal and spatial distribution.[33] Long-range statistical investigations into capital formation indicated that in the United States, in a period covering half a century, the propensity to consume exhibited a long-range upward trend and that it was hardly possible to predict the effects on consumption expenditures of changes in income which occur in societies with unequal income distribution.[34] Drastic redistribution of income was regarded as a measure likely to discourage investment activity.[35]

Samuelson's "revealed preference" theorem was designed to provide a method of testing consumers' behavior.[36] The attitude of a "representative" consumer toward a given collection of goods was to be tested by comparing his expenditures on different combinations of these goods in different price situations.

Milton Friedman undertook to replace Keynes's analysis of the consumption function with a theory of his own.[37] Rejecting the Keynesian psychological approach in favor of analyzing the "rational behavior" of the "economic man," he considered "permanent" consumption a stable proportional function of "permanent" income, and contrasted his concept of a homogeneous consumption function with the "stockless" Keynesian theory. He took account of the influence of expectations on the consumption function in order to emphasize the dynamic aspects of consumers' behavior.

Serious difficulties were involved in interpreting the Keynesian propositions that the propensity to consume and the rate of new investments determine between them the volume of employment.[38] The Keynesian multiplier analysis, which was closely related to the discussion of the consumption function, was considered incomplete for a variety of reasons:[39] it disregarded the influence of the time element on the process of transforming investments into additional incomes; it ignored situations in which productive resources are in short supply; and it did not take account of possible secondary effects of government spending, such as the creation of additional savings, changes in the distribution of income and investments, changes in the marginal propensity to consume, discouragement of private investment by the execution of large-scale public orders, and so on.[40]

The multiplier formula could not be regarded as a reliable instrument for measuring changes in economic aggregates caused in an equilibrium system by outside influences.[41] The results of such measurements varied along with varying assumptions.[42] No definite answers were given to the related questions of how to determine the marginal propensity to consume for a population or a region and how to define the average interval of time which elapses between the receipt of income by one group of the population and the transfer of that income (or a part of it) to another group through purchases of consumption goods and services.[43] Estimates concerning this average time interval have varied between two months and six months. The problems of how to apply multiplier analysis to decreases in investments and how to use it for forecasting purposes were relegated to the category of unsettled questions.[44]

Finally, some authors objected to the very conception of the multiplier as an instrument of income analysis and refused to regard it as a stable factor.[45] They argued that the effects of new investments on the creation of new incomes might be offset by changes in prices, wages, interest rates, and varying rates of consumption and savings.[46] Robertson suggested that in a world of fluctuating magnitudes the multiplier does not constitute much advance over crude monetary weapons of thought.[47]

Intricate problems were involved in the prolonged discussions of Keynes's attacks on the Marshallian economists. Keynes was thought to have misinterpreted the quantity theory of money and the role played by Jean Baptiste Say's law of markets in the Marshallian literature, and to have exaggerated the importance attached by Pigou and other Marshallians to the flexibility of wages as an efficient instrument for combating depressions and unemployment.[48]

Keynes's criticism of the quantity theory of money was supported by the argument that the applicability of this instrument of economic analysis was considerably limited because of the rigid underlying assumptions, such as absence of hoards, full employment, and the proportionality of increases in effective demand and increases in the quantity of money. In extensive studies, however, Arthur W. Marget demonstrated that Keynes had mistaken the quantity equations for the quantity theory and that the latter, when reasonably interpreted, can be developed into an effective tool for analyzing relations between economic aggregates.[49]

Various objections were raised to Keynes's view that Say's law of markets was a constituent element of the model of the economy adopted by the post-Ricardian economists. This law had been disregarded, at least tacitly, by all economists who had freed their models from some "heroic" Ricardian assumptions, such as that all savings are instantaneously investments and that the behavior of the economy is not affected by monetary factors.

The biting attacks launched by Keynes on Pigou's theory of unemployment were closely connected with the Keynesian formulation of the wage problem. Flexibility of the wage structure as recommended by Pigou and other post-Ricardian authors was contrasted with the rigidity of the wage structure postulated by Keynes.[50] This wage structure, which was prerequisite to the Keynesian analysis of equilibrium conditions at less than full employment, was backed by two disputed assumptions: (a) that wages are impervious to downward movements, and (b) that workers have a "nonrational" preference for increases in money wages and are powerless to remedy conditions of "involuntary" employment through concessions in terms of wage reductions. The problematic concept of "involuntary" unemployment, as defined by Keynes, implied that a worker's unemployment resulted from his refusal to accept employment at a reduced monetary rate although he is willing to work at a reduced real rate. The conception of wages as a function of money wages was qualified as an "arbitrarily assumed exogenous element," and no reasonable arguments were found to call any given rate of employment or unemployment "involuntary" if it was determined by the decision to give conscious preference to higher money wages as opposed to higher real income.[51]

Keynes tried to minimize the effects of declining wages on business activity, and argued that output is affected by a general wage reduction, mainly through the ensuing decline of the rate of interest. But he regarded any reduction of this rate as too small to eliminate the deflationary gap since, due to the operation of the liquidity preference, ex ante savings are bound to exceed investments at all positive interest rates.[52] This reasoning, termed the "Keynes effect," provided the background for the "stagnation theorem," and was open to the objection that the fall of wages, when accompanied by declining prices, is likely to enhance the real value of liquid assets (cash balances and the like) and thus to stimulate demand independently of changes in the interest rate. Favorable effects on business confidence could thus be expected from downward movements of wages.[53] The stimulating effects on demand which might result from the increased value of cash balances brought about by a reduction of wage rates were termed the "*Pigou effect.*"[54]

In the ensuing discussion, Pigou agreed with Keynes on the view that reductions in money wages would affect the volume of employment only when attended by reductions in the rate of interest.[55] Other critics of the Keynesian wage theory did not make such concessions. L. Albert Hahn[56] insisted on maintaining the Ricardian proposition that unemployment would be reduced and aggregate wages would be increased by downward adjustments of wages. Jacques Rueff emphasized the self-adjusting effects of the price mechanism under the gold standard as well as under a paper standard.[57] Eventually, Keynes felt obliged to take account of situations in which employment conditions could be improved by wage reductions, but he consistently objected to the idea that such reductions could be relied upon to reestablish full employment.[58]

Certain problems involved in this controversy were clarified when attention was drawn to various situations in which general declines of wage rates could lead to improved profit expectations, to increased investments with multiplier effects, reductions in the rate of interest, substitution of labor for other factors, and enhanced demand for consumption goods.[59] Some economists recommended "selective" wage cuts to be applied during a depression as a measure of alleviating unemployment. The chances of stimulating investments through wage reductions were considered particularly favorable when such reductions were made in noncompetitive or outright monopolistic industries.[60] In the effective antidepression policies adopted during the thirties by Sweden and Australia, wage reductions were combined with credit expansion. Some studies made in the United States arrived at the conclusion that the effects of collective bargaining on the course of longer cycles were almost totally negligible.[61] The influence of changes in wages and prices on the volumes of employment was found to be "surprisingly obscure."[62]

On final analysis, it appeared that the only generally valid argument against wage reductions as an antidepression policy could be derived from the resistance of the wage structure to downward revisions. But this resistance is an institutional factor, and within the strictly theoretical framework of *The General Theory* such an argument was no doubt an alien element.

THE STAGNATION THEOREM

In various passages of his work Keynes stated explicitly that his proposals were designed to prevent deflationist policies and erroneous institutional devices from undermining the efficiency of the competitive economy. But some analysts of the Great Depression suggested that the essence of the Keynesian message was summarized in those passages of *The General Theory* in which Keynes argued that the rate of interest could never be reduced to levels low enough to meet the progressive decline in the marginal efficiency of capital,[63] and that, consequently, no mechanism was available to restore full employment in the highly industrialized countries and that economic progress or growth could be achieved only through changes in technique, population and institutions.[64] Starting from these aspects of *The General Theory*, some adherents of the Keynesian doctrine elaborated on the view that in the capitalist system which we know, abstinence "does not create real wealth but leads to waste and that sound finance is the cause of bankruptcy."[65] Other adherents of the doctrine developed Keynes's arguments into the "stagnation thesis," or "theory of economic maturity," according to which at the advanced stages of industrialization economic growth is more or less arrested, owing to the combined effects of factors such as declining birth rates, progressive exhaustion of natural resources, slowing down of technological progress, "closing of the frontiers," increasing government interference with economic activities, intensified taxation, wage regulations, and restrictions imposed on foreign trade.

In the light of this approach, Hansen analyzed the demographic, geographic and technological arguments in favor of the stagnation thesis.[66] He pointed to the undesirable saving processes which take place in the industrialized countries, the disproportionate accumulation of capital stocks barred from being invested in risky enterprises, the tendency of large concerns to finance the expansion of their plants out of their own reserves, and the increasing volume of hoarded assets. As viewed from this angle, the capitalist economies had arrived at a critical stage in the struggle for their existence: they had to choose between "democratic planning" and "totalitarian regimentation."[67] It may be mentioned that Hansen shared with Keynes the belief that competitive struggles for markets are paramount among the causes of modern warfare, and that a general pursuance of full-employment policies could be expected to eliminate this cause.

A study published by seven Harvard and Tufts economists started from the proposition that the factors of growth upon which their country's economic life had depended were no longer operating.[68] They contrasted a highly flexible investment demand with the existence of large volumes of inflexible savings, which they considered a characterstic feature of the American economy. Hence, they argued that private enterprise, "even at its best," was unable to absorb the whole of the savings piled up in the economy. Convinced of the validity of these judgments, the seven economists strongly recommended a policy of monetary expansion through continued deficit spending, combined with radical measures of fiscal and tax policies.[69]

Within the context of business cycle analysis, the theory of "economic maturity" led to the view that increases in per capita real income are likely to enhance the amplitude of the cyclical fluctuations, and that declining marginal efficiency of capital contributes to the intensification of the violence of depressions and to the weakening of the forces which promote a recovery. A special version of the stagnation theorem was its association with the proposition that the risk of losing one's assets is greater the larger the volume of investment in relation to the entrepreneur's capital.[70] This "principle of increasing risk" was referred to by J. Steindl to explain the reluctance of many employers of the competitive sector of the economy to embark on large-scale investments requiring a high proportion of borrowed capital.[71]

We have mentioned how considerations of this type provided the background for the view that profit expectations had ceased to be indispensable as incentives to productive activity and that it was no longer necessary to include profit among the costs of production.[72] Some liberal English economists were deeply impressed by Keynes's view that "a somewhat comprehensive" socialization of investment would provide the only means of securing an approximation to full employment.[73] Sir William Beveridge, England's outstanding student of unemployment problems, undertook an extensive analysis of the English economy in which he carefully examined the prerequisites of a policy of full employment.[74] He defined "full employment" as a situation of the labor market in which the number of vacant jobs available at "fair wages" and acceptable by the workers would always exceed the demand for jobs. In his view, large-scale increases in public outlays, control of the location of industry, and "organized mobility of labor" were indispensable for securing full employment, but he was perfectly aware of the dangers likely to result for individual liberty from the execution of such an effective full-employment policy. He minimized these dangers, however, since he was convinced that, if full employment was not kept and won, no liberties were secure, for to many they would not seem worthwhile.[75]

A somewhat similar approach to the employment problem was adopted by a group of young economists from Oxford University. They combined a critical examination of various post-Ricardian economic theories with a program of economic policies which was designed to protect the country from the effects of economic disturbances which might occur in other countries through measures of tariff regulation, exchange control, currency depreciation, and the like.[76] The difficulties involved in pursuing a full-employment policy were clearly recognized in only one essay, contributed by G.D.N. Worswick. But radical measures of employment policy met with a considerable array of objections. Since they were intended to guarantee the continued existence of a sellers' market, they could be applied only at the risk of substantial cost-price maladjustments.[77] Hence, many critics of the Keynesian wage theory agreed on a policy designed to prevent the average level of wages from rising faster than the average increase of productivity.[78]

The confusion which followed upon the popularization of the Keynesian theory was well characterized in a series of articles published by the English weekly *The Economist*.[79] Various doubtful propositions were shown to have been associated with this theory, such as the view that deficiencies in the monetary machinery were mainly responsible for the instability of the economy, that "cheap money" was desirable under any circumstances, that internal prosperity could be achieved without taking account of international markets, and that investment automatically generates savings equal to itself.

Nine-tenths of all measures of practical full-employment policy could be shown to lead to inflationary price movements. In fact, a general though intermittent upward trend of prices was a characteristic feature of postwar economic history.[80]

The arguments in favor of the stagnation theorem were critically analyzed in a rapidly increasing literature. A number of objections were raised to Keynes's treatment of capital accumulation and his statements that in the twentieth century increases in output had become proportionately smaller than the expansion of the capital stock, and that increases of the capital stock had depressing effects on the marginal efficiency of capital.[81] The proposition that progressive unfavorable changes in "deepening of capital" (that is, a more than proportionate rise in the capital stock compared with output) had taken place was considered untenable because it was impossible clearly to define the economic effects of technological improvements.[82]

In the discussions of the American version of the stagnation theorem, theoretical arguments were combined with considerations derived from institutional factors. Quite a number of authors endeavored to demonstrate that the application of the stagnation theorem to the American economy had presented a distorted picture of American capitalism.[83]

Statistical investigations into the trend of the consumption functions showed for the United States no decline of the average propensity to consume.[84] For Great Britain the average propensity to consume showed even a rising tendency. But it is hardly necessary to dwell upon the details of this controversy, since the interest in the discussion of the stagnation theorem was exhausted when a prolonged prosperity period set in after the Second World War in England, the United States, and almost all countries of the European continent. About twelve years after the publication of The General Theory, it was obvious that in the "mixed economies" the alleged "discrepancy between the propensity to save and the inducement to invest no longer presented itself in its historical form."[85] Impressive arguments could be advanced for the view that adverse sociological and economic effects were likely to result from far-reaching interference with the flexible methods of capitalist economic expansion.[86]

The Anglo-Saxon discussions of the Keynesian theory had a counterpart on the European continent. The view that The General Theory could claim general validity met with widespread skepticism. The members of the Stockholm school centered their criticism on the static aspects of the Keynesian model. Eric Lundberg considered the looser theoretical constructions of Keynes's Treatise on Money a far more fruitful approach to reality than the equilibrium approach of The General Theory.[87]

In France, François Perroux took the lead in spreading the knowledge of the Keynesian theory.[88] But in his attempts to adjust this theory to the prevailing French economic philosophy he arrived at the conclusion that the Keynesian assumptions were open to many questions when examined in the light of experience. He found that the Keynesian "mechanism of global quantities" was no better method of economic analysis than the "microeconomic mechanism of the general price level" and that, owing to his macroeconomic approach, Keynes had failed to take account of the specific aspects of the various sectors of the economy and of the factors operating in these sectors. Perroux felt that it was doubtful whether "full employment" was a well-defined economic goal worthy of attainment and whether Keynes, having opened the way to large-scale government intervention, had succeeded in establishing sound principles of a rational economic policy.

Other French economists questioned the importance attributed by Keynes to the rate of interest and marginal efficiency of capital as determinants of investment activity.[89] In an extensive discussion of the stagnation theorem and full-employment policies, a large number of representative French economists agreed to reject the Keynesian approach to economic analysis.[90] They argued that in the Keynesian analysis a short-term, "normative" critierion—full employment—was used to establish a general theory of long-term validity, and that this theory had failed to take account of the distinction between exogenous and endogenous factors.

Some economists requested a return to post-Ricardian methodology. Others, led by Albert Aftalion, wondered whether it was sensible to establish general theories of economic development. They insisted upon closer adjustment of theoretical reasoning to observable facts. Some convinced Marxists pointed to the analogy between the idea of "economic frontiers" elaborated by the defenders of the stagnation theorem and the Marxian attempt to demonstrate the limits set to the development of capitalism.

But even the critics of *The General Theory* recognized its stimulating effects on economic research. Henri Guitton elaborated the idea that all theories of growth and stagnation are implicitly prompted by the tendency to extrapolate short-range observations, whereas the human mind is poorly equipped for the treatment of secular developments. He proposed a modified stagnation theorem based on the formula "of secular disparity between the increases in a potential and in an actual global income."[91] But he qualified the theorem of "economic maturity" as ill conceived and suspect because of its "biological" connotations.[92]

Various German economists considered the Keynesian theory inadequate to analyze the conditions of countries in which foreign exchange reserves are limited and investment policies differ widely from those prevailing in Anglo-Saxon countries.[93] In Switzerland, a group of distinguished authors protested in a symposium against proposals to pursue radical policies of full employment implemented by inflationary movements and planning procedures.[94]

In Italy, the Keynesian doctrine was opposed by some leading economists of the mathematical school. Outstanding members of that group were Giovanni Demaria, Constantino Bresciani-Turoni, and Antonio De Viti de Marco.

The question of how much *The General Theory* had definitely contributed to the development of economic thought was discussed in 1956 at a meeting of the American Economic Association.[95] Almost all speakers agreed that Keynes's influence had been paramount in the field of economic policy. In the field of economic analysis, he was credited with having assigned a well-defined place to the marginal efficiency of capital. Fighting against the old "ideology of scarcity, frugality and abstinence," he definitely discarded the conception of unemployment as the effect of "friction," and replaced this conception with a theory which held economic and social factors responsible for the failure of the available resources to achieve full employment. Many problems which had occupied the minds of business cycle analysts could be ignored in the light of his theorems. His method of formulating new problems suggested extensive studies in many fields of economic research, such as those connected with the relations between income and consumption function, with the flow of money, effective demand, the marginal efficiency of capital, the role of savings, and multiplier analysis.[96]

Last but not least, Keynes supplied economists with a language and a conceptual framework of the economy that the public understood and appreciated.[97] He contributed to the development of economic methodology mainly through his stimulus of the discussion of methodological problems.

SUMMARY AND EVALUATION

It might not be amiss to summarize in a few passages the position occupied by *The General Theory* in the history of economic reasoning. Until the middle of the thirties, the interests of the Anglo-Saxon economists centered mainly on problems which had been inherited from the past but reexamined in the light of the experiences during periods of inflationary and prolonged deflationary price movements. These experiences were reflected in various attempts to reformulate monetary theories and to elaborate business cycle theories of the monetary type.

The differences between the leading schools of marginalism were discussed in a lively manner, but the struggle between the psychological and the mathematical schools of economics was intensified rather than settled. Significant problems raised by Knut Wicksell were elaborated by his disciples. They endeavored to define the equilibrium conditions of the monetary system, and to determine the relations between expectations and their fulfillment in the field of investments and other economic activities. They took account of the time element and of shifts in equilibrium positions. Moreover, they proposed to replace the prevailing conception of the economy as a system of interdependent prices by the conception of interdependent incomes. This was a new approach to the problems connected with the stability of the economy; it introduced a method of shifting equilibria for the analysis of the dynamic aspects of the economy.

Apart from a few exceptions, the economic policies pursued by the various countries in the course of the Great Depression were not influenced by consistent lines of theoretical considerations. Chaotic intermittent economic relations resulted from the abandonment of the gold standard which had formerly secured far-reaching coordination of monetary policies.

One of the striking aftereffects of the Great Depression was the conviction, shared by increasing numbers of Anglo-Saxon economists, that the traditional assumptions of Ricardian and post-Ricardian economics were inapplicable to the analysis of the highly industrialized economies in which the market place, as the arena of competitive forces, had been replaced by monopolistic control of production and prices, and striving for maximizing profits had ceased to be a decisive motivating factor. Moreover, many analysts believed that the economy had lost the elasticity required to secure uninterrupted adequate growth. Large-scale unemployment was regarded as a more or less permanent characteristic of a stagnant economy.

In the Keynesian theory of employment, two main factors were held responsible for the stagnant behavior of the economy: a decreasing propensity to consume, relative to the increase of incomes, and a declining efficiency of capital (the rate of profits), relative to the accumulation of stock. Hence, Keynes insisted on the need for remedial public policies and provided welcome arguments for a radical change of the social functions of economists, whom he qualified as indispensable advisers on economic policies.

But the Keynesian doctrine exercised a relatively limited influence on theoretical economics, when compared with the impact of the streams of thought which became prominent after the middle of the forties. As had happened before in the history of economic reasoning, the general trend of this reasoning was directed into new channels by radical changes in the Western intellectual climate. These changes, which originated in the natural sciences, were marked by three main tendencies: (*a*) a trend to give advanced mathematical methods exclusive predominance in all fields of economic research; (*b*) a trend to substitute, as far as possible, "operational" concepts for abstract concepts as the starting point of deductive reasoning; and (*c*) a trend to take account of the time element in defining the relations between the phenomena under observation.

The traditional structure of economic research was deeply affected by the increasing influence of these trends of thought. Dynamic elements were introduced into economic analysis in three ways: through changes in the methods of business cycle analysis, through extensive studies dealing with problems of progress and development in industrially advanced as well as in backward countries, and in connection with an intensified analysis of decision making, since anticipations and expectations played an important role in formulating the various theories of choice.

Deeply impressed by the progress achieved in the natural sciences, increasing groups of Anglo-Saxon, Dutch, and Scandinavian economists arrived at the conclusion that the use of advanced mathematical methods is characteristic of any science. Hence, they chose to adjust the formulation of all relevant economic problems to mathematical treatment, and to adjust advanced mathematical methods to the treatment of these problems. They rejected the traditional formulation of mechanistic equilibrium analysis as a problem of maximizing certain variables (utilities or profits). They rejected the traditional assumptions that the producers and traders of the exchange economy are placed, under the rule of free competition, into markets in which they have complete knowledge of the prevailing fixed conditions and are pursuing their efforts to maximize their profits in complete isolation from each other. The adoption of such misleading assumptions was held to have led to the failure of the school of Lausanne to use appropriate mathematical methods in constructing their model of the economy.

The study of the problems of decision making was developed in many directions and adapted to the task of defining the "rational" behavior of the firm. Economic research was thus extended into fields which previously had been completely ignored, and new methods were devised to deal with the problems involved in the new types of research.

The tendency to achieve the closest possible touch with reality led to the construction of models representing more or less adequate pictures of the functioning of national economies. These models were frequently used to determine the possible effects of measures of economic policy. On a lower level of abstraction, research of this kind was supplemented with statistical investigations into the development of national income and wealth, and into the course of productive and distributive processes. The transformation of economics into "econometrics," a science of applied mathematics, was supported by the elaboration of refined methods of statistical analysis and substantially assisted by technological improvements such as the use of electronic computers. The application of these methods to economic research was hailed as a most promising achievement, especially by many American economists.

One of the last pillars of Ricardian economics was eliminated when the concept of the "real exchange economy" was dropped and monetary factors were assigned a decisive influence on the behavior of important economic aggregates.

In the course of these methodological developments the marginalist doctrines were displaced from the dominant position which they had occupied for about half a century. The eclipse of these doctrines was accelerated by the victory of the methods of macro-economic analysis. But no serious attempts were made to direct the prevailing, partly conflicting, trends into a unifying stream. At least in the Anglo-Saxon countries, especially in the United States, the search for a comprehensive doctrine was superseded by the search for methods of solving specific problems which could be formulated in operational terms. This attitude was well characterized by Howard S. Ellis in the preface to *A Survey of Contemporary Economics,* published in 1948.[98] The day of the exhaustive economic treatise, he wrote, might have passed; its place might be taken by compendia consisting of essays on specific topics, each contributed by a specialist in his field—"less personal, less literary and less unified, perhaps, but it is to be hoped less intuitive, less prescinded, and no less inspiring."

Chapter 36
Methodological Discussions
of Dynamic Analysis

DYNAMICS VERSUS STATICS

THE RICARDIAN ECONOMISTS and the majority of their successors who adopted the static approach to economic analysis had devised a "theoretical wonderland which was beset with inconsistencies."[1] John Stuart Mill realized the fundamental problem of how to reconcile the alleged operation of equilibrating forces with changes occurring over time in the relations among economic magnitudes, and drew a distinction between the "static" and the "dynamic" problems of the economy. In accordance with a suggestion by Auguste Comte, Mill defined as "static" such regularities as are not subject to change. Among the "dynamic" aspects of the economy, he included irregular changes produced by population movements, technical progress, and increases in capital. But these dynamic aspects remained outside the pale of theoretical considerations, and the *ceteris paribus* clause fulfilled the function of impounding the effects of all factors not amenable to equilibrium analysis. William Stanley Jevons identified "statics" with the conditions of economic forces at the equilibrium level and used the term "dynamics" to denote changes in the relations of these forces that lead equilibrium. John Neville Keynes found that the dynamics of political economy "was exceptional in its dependence upon the historical method of treatment,"[2] since no deductive methods were available to deal with deviations from equilibrium positions. No particular attention was given to Maffeo Pantaleoni's observations that economic statics was to be regarded as a special case of economic dynamics, and that endless fluctuations might be caused by the operation of certain dynamic factors.[3]

John B. Clark made a notable attempt to extend economic analysis beyond the static sphere into that of dynamic problems. He connected dynamic situations with changes of five factors: population, capital, methods of production, industrial organization, and consumers' wants. But his discussion of dynamic conditions was limited to disturbances of equilibrium positions starting from the supply side. No clear distinction was made between the static and the stationary states of the economy. The competitive order was prerequisite to Clark's conception of the static state.[4] The discussion of the roles attributed to capital and interest on capital within the context of the Austrian marginalistic theory provided various incentives to take account of the time factor in formulating economic problems.[5] Eugen Böhm-Bawerk's analysis of the relations between present and future want satisfactions, the *agio* theory of interest, and the theorem of the roundabout ways of production all make reference to the time element. Knut Wicksell associated the time factor with the use of capital, as distinct from the use of land and labor.

But although the connection between the time element and the term "dynamics" was quite obvious, considerable confusion beclouded the meaning of the term. A member of the historical school who surveyed the literature dealing with this topic distinguished no less than eight different conceptions of the relation between statics and dynamics.[6] Organismic economists related their "dynamic" analysis to the specific characteristics of the national economies and emphasized structural changes of economies as distinct from the fluctuating behavior of economic magnitudes.[7] Werner Sombart associated the ideas of "actuality" and "potentiality" with the concept of "dynamics," and argued that the latter concept could reasonably be applied only to specific national economies.[8]

Some Austrian economists made noteworthy efforts to clarify these methodological and terminological issues.[9] They insisted upon dissociating the meaning of the terms "static" and dynamic" as applied by economics from the meaning attached to these terms by the science of mechanics. According to their view, methods of static analysis had been introduced into economics only to gain a starting point for research into conditions of change. They ascribed static conditions to an economic system which, having constant specific properties concerning technology and the organization of production and distribution, proceeds directly from one equilibrium position to another. Thus conceived, the term "static conditions" was applicable to "progressive" economies in which wage rates and the yields of investments were assumed to be determined under the rules of perfect competition, and in which the distributive processes were ruled by the principle of marginal productivity. Constancy over time of the prices of goods and services and of the volumes of capital was not regarded as a characteristic feature of static—as distinct from stationary—conditions.

Antoine A. Cournot had suggested the method of "small variations" as a procedure of transforming into discontinuous changes the changes in the relations among the elements of a system of interdependent variables. According to this method, every equilibrium position was assumed to be adjusted to the preceding position during an infinitely small period. This procedure was recommended by Enrico Barone.[10] Joseph Schumpeter applied the term "static" to a system in which the changes of data were small and continuous.[11] But the method of small variations was considered inapplicable when the equilibrium of the system was modified by the changes.

The method of "comparative statics" was considered an instrument for establishing direct comparisons between successive equilibrium positions when the process leading from one position to another was ignored.[12] Böhm-Bawerk's analysis of the capitalist production provided an outstanding example of the application of this method.

Frank H. Knight, a consistent advocate of equilibrium analysis, defined three methods of dealing with economic relationships.[13] He considered the "static" method appropriate for determining equilibrium conditions existing at a given moment; to the "kinetic" method he attributed the task of analyzing the establishment of equilibrium situations over short periods, when general conditions could be assumed to be constant. He distinguished "processes" involving passive and mechanical individual behavior from procedures or manifestations of creative unpredictable activity.[14] "Dynamic" methods, he argued, had to be applied to the analysis of long-term processes, when account was to be taken of historical and institutional factors and changes of data. But Knight was convinced that scientific treatment of economic processes could not be extended beyond adjustments, over time, of one equilibrium position to another.

The idea of conceiving of the behavior of the economy as a process of moving equilibria appealed to various economists. Luigi Amoroso advanced a program of studies dealing with the successive adjustments of the economy to new equilibrium positions.[15] Abba P. Lerner insisted upon maintaining the assumption that the economy does not seriously depart from short-term equilibrium positions.[16]

However, this view was incompatible with John M. Clark's proposition that the key to dynamics is the treatment of processes which do not tend to establish a complete or definable static equilibrium.[17] He suggested that special studies be prepared dealing with the forces of mutual adjustment which determine economic life in the sectors in which free competition is operating and in those in which competition has been superseded by monopolistic organization of the markets. Moreover, he requested that due regard be given to the institutional framework of society and its influence on the course of economic processes.

Simon Kuznets elaborated the idea that, as distinct from static analyses, economic dynamics do not deal with the relations between individual activity and the resulting social phenomena, but rather with changes of "social phenomena" over time. Hence, he considered the use of economic aggregates as a characteristic feature of dynamic economics and proposed the collection of statistical material in order to provide a basis for inductive generalizations. In accordance with this approach, the concept of a succession of equilibria was to be replaced by the concept of "motion" generated by the influence of steadily operating forces.[18]

Fundamental problems of economic methodology were thus involved in the question of how to define "dynamics," above all, (1) the problem of whether and to what degree the economy can be assumed to be governed by equilibrating tendencies, (2) the problem of whether the development of a "dynamic" theory is conditioned by the use of economic aggregates, and (3) the problem of how to define the criteria for determining the aggregates.

The time element as a characteristic feature of the dynamic approach was emphasized in a prominent article by Paul N. Rosenstein-Rodan.[19] He showed that the application of equilibrium analysis is conditioned by three assumptions: that the reactions to any changes in economic data occur simultaneously, and that they are of the same duration and of the same velocity. Hence, prolonged disturbances of equilibrium positions are bound to be caused by divergent reactions, and traditional economic analysis is to be supplemented by the study of the processes which take place when the equilibrium tends to be reestablished.

More or less consistent research into changes in economic relations over time began in studies in which variations in the equilibrium values of prices and sales were analyzed in accordance with methods of comparative statics.[20] This development reached second stage when regard was paid to "lags," or differences in the time required for the mutual adjustment of economic magnitudes during processes of production, marketing, spending, and the like. Dennis Holme Robertson introduced lags between the receipt of income and expenditures into period analysis; lags of output after changes in the volume of sales were taken into account in the sequence analyses of the Stockholm school.[21] During a third stage, attention turned to general price movements and their effects, as distinct from the effects of changes in individual prices. In surveying this stage, Jan Tinbergen referred to the studies of prices, supply and demand, etc., by Mordecai Ezekiel, L. A. Leontief, Henry L. Moore, George F. Warren and Karl Pearson, Arthur C. Pigou, Henry Schultze, Hans Staehle, and others. He considered it advisable to transform the Walrasian model into a simplified "dynamic" scheme in which a moving equilibrium as a guiding principle was combined with the idea of an "economic horizon" assumed to be established by each economic unit at the beginning of every period. Taking account of expectancies and lags, Tinbergen proposed to use mathematical procedures particularly to analyze the relations between production and consumption of nonperishable agricultural products.[22]

In a similar vein, Roy F. Harrod suggested that the main task of dynamic analyses was to deal with the influence of expectations and time lags on the processes leading to the establishment of new equilibrium conditions.[23] He pointed out the possible existence of forces which might modify a prevailing trend in the course of these processes.

Eventually a remarkable international group of economists, including Ragnar Frisch (Norway), Eric Lundbert (Sweden), and E. Schneider (Germany), agreed with Tinbergen and Harrod on two propositions: (1) to use the terms "statics" and "dynamics" exclusively for defining methods of formulating and analyzing theoretical problems, and (2) to adopt the time element as a criterion for separating the dynamic from the static approach.[24] Hence, expressions such as static or dynamic conditions or systems and the like had to be avoided. The *static* methods were held to be applicable to situations in which all variables refer to the same point of time and are explained through data relating to the same time. Methods of *comparative statics* were considered appropriate for dealing with changes over time by comparing data which belong to successive equilibrium situations.[25] But procedures of advanced mathematics had to be used to analyze processes of transition leading from one equilibrium position to another. Special problems had to be solved in analyzing cumulative movements involving repeated adjustments to changing data with no recognizable tendencies to establish equilibrium positions. "Unstable equilibrium conditions" were defined as conditions under which a system tends to move away from equilibrium values whenever a change in its variables occurs.[26]

Frisch defined "dynamic laws" as laws in which time variables and derivatives of them appear.[27] He characterized the difference between statics and dynamics as a "distinction between two ways of thinking." Paul A. Samuelson added to the three kinds of economic analysis distinguished by other authors a fourth type, the study of historical-causal characteristics.[28] Historical analysis was designed to deal with situations in which certain relevant data (movements) are taken as unexplained, possibly because their explanation is held to be outside the sphere of economics. To illustrate the need to combine the dynamic with the historical approach, Samuelson referred to technological changes and included among "historical data" such changes, to which the economy reacts noninstantaneously or in a dynamic fashion.

I have given this lengthy and somewhat tedious history of the concept of economic dynamics in order to facilitate the understanding of the intricate problems involved in adjusting the concept of time to the requirements of the equilibrium analysis. The treatment of the problem of continuity was beset with similar difficulties.[29] Robertson and Lundberg, who wrestled with it, resorted to methods of comparative statics and of sequence and period analysis. Individual plans of production and consumption were artificially synchronized in "registration periods," but the usefulness of these methods for a study of dynamic problems diminished along with the adjustment of these periods to reality.

The assumption of "uniformity of lags" introduced for purposes of synchronization was also resorted to in models in which change was assumed to be continuous and time was measured in terms of changes in one or more variables of the system. The gestation period of capital goods used in Michael Kalecki's dynamic scheme model was a case in point.[30] More or less arbitrary assumptions were involved in all analyses in which continuous events were transformed into discontinuous processes. The use of concepts implying continuous movements was another method of coping with the problem of continuity. Such concepts played a significant role in post-Keynesian dynamics.

THE DYNAMIC ELEMENTS OF POST-KEYNESIAN ECONOMICS

Keynes virtually ignored various previous attempts to develop a "dynamic" methodology in *The General Theory,* which remained true to the traditional static approach. But few economists accepted the proposition advanced by some adherents of the Keynesian doctrine that business cycle analysis could be considered obsolete in the light of the stagnation theory and the theorem of economic maturity.[31] Some skeptical minds raised the question of whether Keynes had rendered economics a service or a disservice by attempting to push the analysis of economic fluctuations back into an abstract framework of equilibrium theory.[32] They pointed to the paradoxical fact that he had applied equilibrium analysis to situations which were altogether lacking in objective stability.[33] His analysis was qualified as "metastatic," since the hypothesis of perfect foresight was not referred to either explicitly or implicitly, whereas the variables of his economic model were not dated.[34] Observations of this type were elaborated in various studies which emphasized some aspects of the Keynesian theory connected with the idea of changes over time[35] and some elements of this theory providing a bridge to business cycle analysis.[36]

Keynes called his theory a theory of "shifting equilibrium," designed to explain a system in which changing views about the future are capable of influencing the present situation. "The importance of money," he said, "essentially flows from its being a link between the present and the future."

Other references to "dynamic" factors were implied in various "antinomies" which were basic to *The General Theory*—the antinomy between the rate of saving and the rate of investment, and the antinomy between the tendency of the liquidity preference to enforce upward movements of the rate of interest and the tendency of the marginal efficiency of capital to decline. The concept of "positive savings" could be interpreted as implying processes of continuous change.[37] A time schedule of another type could be connected with the marginal efficiency of capital, which was assumed to show considerable variations, reflected in changing rates of profit. Moreover, a link was established between present and future positions when the concept of liquidity preference was applied to the fluctuating behavior of transaction balances. Finally, the time element was of primary importance in determining the operation of the multiplier. The far-reaching use of the multiplier concept in post-Keynesian economics was mainly due to the fact that it supplied patterns of continuous, more or less fixed relations between investment and income. Hence, some comments on the role assigned to this instrument within the context of dynamic analysis appear to be in order.[38]

Keynes's distinction between the instantaneous and the process multiplier was elaborated by L. Alvin Hansen, who suggested the use of two additional types of multipliers: the "period analysis multiplier" and the "timeless or comparative statics multiplier."[39] Of paramount importance was the period analysis multiplier, which was used by Robertson, Fritz Machlup, and others. It took account of the time lags involved in reactions to the expansion of investment activities.

Machlup distinguished four periods which were suitable for multiplier analysis:[40] the transaction period, the plan adjustment period, the income adjustment period, and the equilibrium adjustment period. He gave definite preference to the transaction period as defined by the assumptions that dates of receipts and of outlays are usually fixed and that no disbursement can take place without preceding receipts. When the "income generation period" was applied to the determination of the multiplier, the overall time lag of the latter was identified with the length of time it takes for the money in active circulation to complete a circuit from income recipient to income recipient. The reasoning which was basic to this definition was similar to that used in defining the concept of income velocity.[41]

The implications of the multiplier theorem were more fully realized when it was applied to various situations in which new purchasing power is injected into the stream of income. Income earned at any time could be conceived of as a result of current injections of investments augmented by fractions of income produced by preceding investments. In various studies the investment multiplier was assumed to be a measureable, endogenous factor of the economic mechanism capable of assimilating and propagating exogenous shocks.[42] But the expansion of multiplier analysis complicated this analysis and increased the difficulties involved in determining the various time lags.[43] The complexity of multiplier analysis caused R. M. Goodwin to suggest the establishment of a "matrix multiplier," a compound multiplier representing the weighted average of the multipliers determined for the various industries or sectors of the economy.[44] But this concept was found to be useless for practical purposes.

The "acceleration principle" was another instrument of economic analysis which was based on more or less fixed relations among relevant economic variables. Hence, it was frequently applied to the construction of dynamic models of the economy. Keynes, whose analysis centered on situations in which idle plant capacity can be utilized when demand is stimulated by increased purchasing power, ignored this principle, since it is ineffective in depression periods.[45]

The acceleration principle had been derived from the relation between current increases in the stock of capital equipment and the current increase in the level of output; it was interpreted as "the ratio of induced investment to a preceding change in income or output." "Induced investment" was defined as investment made in response to changes in current output. It was contrasted with "autonomous" (spontaneous) investment, which was identified with investments in capital goods of long duration, investments connected with inventions and discoveries, or investments made by public authorities. The distinction between induced and autonomous investments was elaborated by Hansen, Harrod, and Lloyd A. Metzler.

Considerable difficulties were involved in devising practical methods of separating induced, or "net," investment, as determined by consumers' demand, from replacement expenditures and "autonomous" investment. No statistical procedures were available to separate replacement of outworn or obsolete machinery from improvements of a capital stock and additions to it. It would have been misleading to apply the acceleration principle to gross instead of net investments.

Highly intricate conditions were listed as prerequisite to the definition of a constant coefficient of acceleration: homogeneity and perfect divisibility of capital equipment, constant returns to scale, constant coefficients of production, pursuance of the economic principle, and perfect foresight.[46] The use of a fluctuating accelerator for purposes of business cycle analysis was also hedged by important reservations: it was very doubtful whether the concept of "induced investments" had a definable counterpart in reality,[47] and whether and within what limits the accelerator could be considered a reliable instrument for a theory of investment.[48] When reasonably interpreted, the acceleration principle meant that investments are stimulated by rising incomes and consumption and retarded by declining income. But no precise relationships could be established between changes in the rates of growth or decline of incomes and corresponding changes in the rates of investment activity.[49]

Advocates of the acceleration principle were also faced with the paradoxical situation that the principle was inoperative in periods of full employment, when demand was increasing, and again in periods of underemployment, when increasing demand could be met by drawing upon available idle capacities.[50] Objections of this type did not prevent some convinced adherents of the Keynesian doctrine from insisting that the relations between relevant economic aggregates are determined by fixed or varying numerical values of the coefficient of acceleration and the multiplier. The predilection shown by some economists for the multiplier principle was probably suggested by the importance that they attached to autonomous investments, whereas the predilection of others for the acceleration principle was symptomatic of their view that special attention should be paid to induced investment.

The "dynamic" interpretation of the Keynesian doctrine was likely to lead to the conclusion that the growth of the economy is produced by the interaction of two sets of divergent motives: those that determine the rate of savings and those that are instrumental in promoting long-term capital investments. A relatively simple procedure of adjusting these considerations to business cycle analysis consisted in separating the forces that determine the growth of the economy from the factors that create the cyclical movements. In accordance with this reasoning, Harrod interpreted fluctuations of business activity as oscillations taking place along a trend line that defines the growth rate of the economy.[51]

Chapter 37
Dynamic Models

———

MODELS OF THE KEYNESIAN TYPE

As was suggested by Paul A. Samuelson, the "revolutionary nature" of Keynes's *General Theory* became apparent only after the publication of some models of the economy in which mathematical methods combined with elements of dynamic analysis were applied to the fundamentally static Keynesian model.[1] The economists who embarked on such studies ignored the influence of monetary factors on relevant economic aggregates and remained true to the Keynesian concept of the economy as a "real exchange system." The multiplier, based on more or less fixed relations between economic variables, provided a welcome instrument for dynamic analysis. The accelerator, an instrument of a similar type, did not enjoy the same general application.

Samuelson was one of the first adherents of the Keynesian theory to use the combined effects of the multiplier and the acceleration principle to produce models of steady growth, of cyclical movements, and of equilibrating processes.[2] He pointed to the size of the coefficient of acceleration, the role of the consumption function, and the introduction of suitable lags between the receipt of incomes and disbursement as characteristic features of such a model. A more elaborate attempt to apply the principles of the Keynesian theory to the study of "dynamic" problems was made by Roy F. Harrod, who connected the existence of such problems with changing rates of output.[3] His study was designed to define the self-perpetuating "warranted" rate of economic growth which would keep savings and investments in balance, hence, a rate determined jointly by the propensity to save and the quantity of capital required to produce a unit increment of total output as determined by the prevailing technological conditions.

The consistency of the "warranted rate" was dependent upon the logical validity of the implied assumption that, on balance, entrepreneurs increase production at the same rate which had prevailed in the past period. In describing the "equilibrium path" along which the economy is supposed to move, Harrod related investments to the difference between current income and last period's income; he assumed that equilibrium positions of the economy are maintained at full employment by a proper time sequence of investment flows and that the expansion of the economy is mainly determined by the effects of the accelerator. He held divergencies between ex ante savings and ex post investments responsible for cumulative expansions and contractions of the economy, and interpreted prosperities and depressions as zones of disturbances oscillating around a line of steady growth. The economic policies recommended by Harrod centered on the execution of public works, adoption of anticyclical methods of public budgeting, and establishment of buffer stocks financed by the government.

Harrod elaborated his leading ideas in subsequent publications.[4] But his "unrealistic" assumptions were exposed to many doubts. Various critics objected to the proposition that the economy is developing along a strictly linear path at constant, proportionate rates of growth. They argued that Harrod ignored differences in the composition of output, capital, and real income, that he regarded the propensity to save and the increase in productive capacity as stable functions,[5] and that in a competitive exchange economy slim prospects exist for the combined results of independent investment decisions to coincide with the "warranted" conditions of growth.[6] The assumed stability of prices and wages was characterized as the "Achilles heel" of various business cycle theories of the Keynesian type.[7] The French economist Alfred Marchal qualified the trend as an average calculated ex post from observed oscillations and considered it an arbitrary assumption to define the trend as the pivot on which the economic mechanism turns.[8] It was a moot question whether the model of the economy could be adjusted to the principle of decision making under uncertainty.[9]

The conception of a fundamentally unstable economy was basic to a model suggested by Joan Robinson. Her model was designed to serve intentions supported by some of its characteristic features, such as: that all values were measured in terms of the average price of a man hour of labor, that the community was assumed to consist of three classes, and that divergencies between the rates of interest were ignored.[10]

A third attempt to apply Keynesian ideas to the construction of a dynamic model was made by L. Alvin Hansen in a study designed to prepare the theoretical background for an anticyclical fiscal policy.[11] Hansen organized his analysis in accordance with the "stagnation theorem,"[12] and pointed to three factors which he considered detrimental to economic growth: the slope of the consumption function, the progressive exhaustion of investment possibilities of the autonomous type, and the tapering off of the rate of increase in physical output after full employment of the productive factors had been reached. His countercyclical program of public policies included built-in institutional devices, measures of government intervention, and promotion of structural changes in the economy. The view that the capitalist economy was inherently unstable and exposed to the danger of stagnation was also basic to an economic model outlined by Benjamin Higgins, who used a combination of the "relation effect" and the "cobweb" theorem to account for the propagation of "random shocks" affecting the economy.[13]

Evsey D. Domar wrestled with the Keynesian proposition that the elimination of hoarding would assure full employment of the available resources.[14] He endeavored to show that Keynes had disregarded the effects of changes in the quantity of capital on changes in the productivity of capital. Applying Harrod's idea of a warranted rate of growth to the determination of various economic aggregates, Domar argued that unused capacity develops when investment and, consequently, income do not grow at a rate equal to the propensity to save and the "average productivity" of investment. In addition, he studied the effects of increases in production capacity and of the expansion of national income, and arrived at the conclusion that crises and unemployment occur when productive capacity has been increased permanently, whereas the expansion of income had been only temporary and is gradually diminishing in accordance with the multiplier theorem.[15] Domar countered the objection that his analysis failed to take account of many factors affecting the behavior of the economy[16] with the argument that model building is not intended to provide "factual statements" about real processes, and that different and even contradictory models could legitimately be set up regarding the same process.[17] Hence, methodological questions loomed large in the discussions of dynamic model building.

After the validity of the stagnation theorem had been disproved by actual economic developments, Hansen outlined a new dynamic model in which he used the mechanical interaction of the multiplier and the accelerator as the main instrument for explaining the cyclical movements as "cycles of investment."[18] But he was found to have rationalized "changes of economic processes into some general theory, at the risk of exaggerating the area of its application."[19]

OTHER DYNAMIC MODELS OF THE ECONOMY

The most distinguished place among the various versions of "dynamic" models of the economy was occupied by studies by John R. Hicks, who was particularly careful in preparing the methodological background of his economic analysis.[20] In accordance with the prevailing trend, he adjusted his model to the principles of a "real exchange system" of the economy and considered it his first task to define the conditions of a stable production equilibrium in an economy of the nonstatic type. The microeconomic approach appeared to provide the most suitable instrument for dealing with this problem. Taking his start from a Walrasian equilibrium system, he applied the indifference curve technique to the formulation of a theory of consumers' demand. This discussion of the equilibrium of the firm was ruled by the equality of marginal cost and marginal revenue.

Hicks defined dynamics as that part of economic theory in which every quantity must be dated. In the second part of his study he transformed the process of continuous change into a succession of equilibrium positions maintained for relatively short periods (weeks) in four markets (for products, for factors, for direct services, and for intermediate products). On the assumption that goods of the same type but available at different dates are different goods, he adjusted his "dynamic" analysis to his fundamentally static approach. The equilibrium positions were assumed to be connected with each other through plans of economic units made in accordance with "reliable expectations," such as stability of prices and mutual "consistency" of the plans.

But considerable difficulties were involved in defining "consistency" of this type when account was taken of the interdependence of the plans and the mutual effects of changes made during the execution of the plans. Some critics raised the question of whether stability of prices could reasonably be included among the assumptions of economic analysis.[21] Others objected to the treatment of the stability of multiple markets. Contrary to Hicks's assumptions, perfectly stable production equilibrium could not be regarded as a reasonable hypothesis.[22]

Hicks provoked considerable discussion later with another study, in which he attempted to develop a strict business cycle theory.[23] He transformed Harrod's theory of oscillations around a trend of warranted growth into a theory of cyclical fluctuations around a means, and eliminated the close connection which Harrod had established between the cycles and the growth of the economy. In order to simplify his analysis, he assumed that investment functions are constant and marginal propensities to consume are fixed. In his picture of an imaginary cycle, the "trend" was connected with the rate of growth of "autonomous" investment, as determined by technological progress and increases of the population. The relation of autonomous investment to induced investment was made dependent on the propensity to save. The boom was shown to be stimulated by waves of technological improvements accompanied by the tendency of increases in income and spending to exceed the rate of increases in output. The multiplier, expressed in units of output, had a stabilizing rather than disturbing influence on the behavior of the economy, whereas the "acceleration principle" was responsible for fluctuations in output, since its operation interfered with the proportionality between the rate of investment and the rate of increase in income.[24]

Hicks listed some limiting factors to explain the downturn, among others a decline of profitable investment opportunities when all resources were fully utilized. A temporary depression equilibrium was established in the model when the maximum possible rate of disinvestment had been attained; a new expansion could be expected to be initiated by increasing autonomous investments. Since investment of this type was assumed to be operative during a depression, the growth of the economy at a certain potential rate could be assured at any time through nonproductive public investments.[25]

In his discussion of the interaction of the multiplier and the accelerator, Hicks availed himself of the lag analysis suggested by Samuelson[26] and referred to varying numerical relations of these two factors in order to account for differences in the amplitudes of the fluctuations. Thus, he developed a "nonlinear" system in which the trend toward stabilization could vary independently of the initial displacement. From free cycles marked by low autonomous investment, a weak multiplier, or a weak accelerator, Hicks distinguished constrained cycles, driven by expansionist forces until output at full capacity was reached. But differences in the composition of investments were considered a more convenient criterion for a grouping of cycles in accordance with their amplitude.[27]

A number of methodological issues came up in the ensuing discussion of this business cycle theory. Doubts were cast on the purely mechanical conception of the economy and on Hicks's use of the multiplier and the accelerator in interpreting the recurrent successions of prosperity and depression.[28] Critics objected to the behaviorist background of his theory and his treatment of consumers' spending, his failure to apply ex ante analysis, and his method of connecting the growth of the economy with the effects of autonomous investments expanding at a constant rate.[29] In the light of statistical evidence, the behavior of the accelerator differed perceptibly from the course Hicks attributed to it. Its influence was spread in shifting degrees over the entire cycle.[30] The claim that the influence of monetary factors had been completely ignored in establishing the theory was questioned because the existence of a perfectly elastic credit supply was prerequisite to the alleged correspondence between the rate of autonomous investment and the rate of growth.[31] In a discussion of the turning points, the argument prevailed that the combination of the Keynesian consumption function with the principle of acceleration permitted an explanation without having recourse to limiting factors.[32]

Some other dynamic models of the "real exchange" type were constructed by mathematically minded economists who conceived of the economy as a mechanical system of fluctuating, functionally related variables. They differed widely as to the importance which they attached to the mechanism considered instrumental in transforming the effects of impulses into oscillating movements of economic aggregates. They neglected the acceleration principle as an instrument of economic analysis and showed significant preference for the use of lags between decision making and the execution of the decisions, between the receipt of incomes and expenditures, between output and sales.

Since their approach to dynamic analysis was influenced by sociopolitical motivations, these economists were looking the disequilibrating forces, agents of prolonged and deep depressions. The models of Michael Kalecki, Nicholas Kaldor, and R. M. Goodwin are characteristic of this group. Kalecki developed a model of a fundamentally unstable economy driven by endogenous forces, but did not attempt to define a trend.[33] He undertook to determine the necessary and sufficient conditions to be fulfilled in order to produce the cumulative processes of expansion and contraction of business activity as connected with the combined results of the irregular flow of autonomous investments and the lags between investment decisions and their execution. According to his estimates, this lag amounted to half the construction period of investment of goods, or three to six months on the average. In his analysis of the upswing, he attributed to the multiplier stimulating effects on investment decisions; he related the eventual decline in profitability to increases in capital equipment and to a tendency of the rate of investments to exceed, toward the end of the expansion period, the level necessary for the maintenance of the capital equipment. Inverse movements were assumed to take place during the depression until the rate of investment had fallen below the level necessary to maintain this equipment.[34]

Kaldor and Goodwin followed Kalecki in adjusting their theories to the concept of the economy as an inherently unstable mechanism. Both authors introduced nonlinear investment functions in order to adjust their models to the fluctuating character of recurrent expansions and contractions. They referred only indirectly to the acceleration principle as a factor relating investment decisions to the stock of capital and national income.

Kaldor followed Kalecki in his attempt to define the necessary and sufficient assumptions for a cyclical movement to result from the combined operations of the multiplier and the demand function. He derived disturbances of equilibrium positions from divergencies between ex ante savings and ex ante investments. To time lags he ascribed only the function of influencing the length of the cycles, but not their existence. In the light of this model, in which investment opportunities were declining along with capital accumulation, only very remote chances existed to "even out" the fluctuations through measures of anticyclical investment policies.[35]

Goodwin regarded the cycles as indispensable elements of economic growth, referred to changes in capital stock as a central explanatory variable, and used a not clearly defined concept of "innovational investment" as combined with inventory movements and the multiplier mechanism to explain expansion of output.[36]

The theorem of the declining efficiency of capital was endorsed by Kenneth K. Kurihara,[37] but he assumed that the effects of this factor were counteracted by expanding incomes, "deepening of capital" through technical improvements, and progressive reductions of the rate of interest in relation to the marginal efficiency of capital. The mechanistic approach which was characteristic of these models was also applied to the analysis of cycles of residential construction, inventory cycles, and other specific fluctuating movements of economic activity. Thus, Lloyd A. Metzler suggested a relatively simple model in which the interaction of the multiplier principle with the accelerator was used to explain fluctuations in business inventories on the assumption that past experience determines demand and that demand increases more slowly than supply.[38] But attempts to verify the application of the acceleration principle to inventory cycles yielded rather negative results. In his study of inventory investment, Ragnar Nurkse attached particular importance to autonomous investment, which has no systematic relation to the income level.[39]

The strictly mechanical approach to dynamic economic analysis was attacked in prolonged discussions. Adherents to this approach were said to "overexaggerate" observed trends, neglect cost-price relations, ignore the problems involved in expectations and anticipations, minimize the influence of monetary factors, and attach unjustified importance to the stability of the consumption function and to the distinction between induced and autonomous investments.[40] The prevailing Ricardian conception of the economy as the arena of competitive struggles for markets was also the object of critical comments.[41]

At a meeting of the American Economic Association held in December 1948, James W. Angell raised the question of how much of the "total reality" of the fluctuations must be accounted for in order to make an explanation satisfactory.[42] Arthur F. Burns stated bluntly that the explicit and systematic introduction of expectations and anticipations had marked the passing of the mechanical age in business cycle theory.[43] The treatment of problems of dynamic analysis as adopted by various authors was, to a considerable degree, influenced by sociopolitical considerations. Adversaries of the capitalist economy looked for combinations of disequilibrating forces which could be used to demonstrate the incidence of prolonged and deep depressions. Intricate problems which had played a role in the discussions of the stagnation theorem appeared in new versions. Thus, Robinson, H.B.S. Kierstead, Domar, and Kalecki pointed to the growing concentration of industry as a factor in arresting economic growth. Kalecki attributed a similar role to the policy of accumulating large reserves as practiced by oligopolistic concerns. Another instrument for evidencing an inevitable decline of the capitalist economy was the theorem of the decreasing profitability of investments as correlated with the accumulation of capital.

But in the light of statistical analysis, the long-term trend underlying the cyclical movements showed that the quantity of capital had increased relative to labor. The much-discussed "diminishing productivity of capital" had been more than compensated by the effects of technological progress; moreover, the concept of "capital as a homogeneous aggregate" became vague and nebulous when technical improvements were taken into account. The "shock resistance" of the economy had probably been effectively enhanced in many countries by "built-in stabilizers" such as high taxes imposed on large incomes and corporate savings, social security systems, and similar devices designed to maintain the purchasing power of the large masses.[44] But the effects of such stabilizing measures could hardly be assessed with any degree of accuracy.[45]

Arthur Smithies surveyed the results of some dynamic analyses of business fluctuations as connected with the growth of the economy.[46] He established a series of models of the economy by combining various elements of dynamic theories in order to demonstrate how fluctuations can be generated by the process of growth, how growth can occur without fluctuations, and how fluctuations can occur independently of growth. He considered it a very useful exercise to exhibit a variety of such possibilities. But serious objections were raised to the practice of restricting model building to the "real exchange" economy and neglecting the influence of the rate of interest and monetary factors on the behavior of the economy.[47] The use of highly abstract aggregates as elements of model building was another object of criticism.[48] Finally, increasing groups of skeptics questioned the usefulness of models which had no reference to reality.

On the European continent the Anglo-Saxon methods of model building met with strong opposition. French economists had no use for oversimplified models of the economy adjusted to specific economic policies, such as those derived from the Keynesian doctrine.[49] André Marchal stressed the importance of the nexus of causality and insisted upon relating the variables of each period to the variables of the preceding period.[50] Léon Dupriez considered the Keynesian concept of "aggregative equilibria" incompatible with the principle of the general interdependence of the price system.[51] He attacked the method of analyzing business cycles in terms of successive equilibrium positions, since it implied the necessity of holding outside factors responsible for the origin of the cyclical oscillations. He conceived of the economy as a network of price movements and took account of the acceleration principle and the multiplier in developing his model.

Other French economists emphasized the need to form homogeneous economic aggregates. They distinguished technicoeconomic aggregates, mainly of the statistical type, from sociological aggregates. They requested intensified research into the vertical and horizontal structure of the various economies in order to determine the influence of changes in monetary and other factors on the sectors of the economy.

Many Italian authors joined their French colleagues in resisting the mechanistic approach to business cycle analysis.[52] Giuseppi Ugo Papi found that the rising "trends" exhibited in the course of fluctuations were the result of a posteriori considerations.[53] Marco Fanno objected to the conception of business cycles as oscillations around general equilibrium positions.[54] He followed Goodwin in attempting to establish a close interaction between the factors of propulsion considered instrumental in generating the movements and the factors which determine the progressive expansion and contraction of the economy. This analysis may be contrasted with the view of Gustavo del Vecchio, who regarded each cycle as an independent phenomenon and rejected any attempts to apply the same model to several cycles.[55]

At a conference organized in 1952 by the International Economic Association, postwar business cycle analysis was put to the test of practical application.[56] The discussions of the participants were prepared by a series of papers which surveyed postwar economic developments in a number of countries. Summarizing the results of these reports, Eric Lundberg distinguished four lines of approach to the business cycle problem: (1) the theories of the Oxford economists based on "strategic relations"; (2) the methods of mathematical statistics used by the econometricians; (3) the mathematical models which could not be tested by statistical methods since they were based on abstract assumptions and included a limited number of variables; and (4) the theories of "literary schools" marked by distinct preference for "open systems" permitting economists to take account of exogenous factors. But Lundberg suggested that because of threat of war and the international imbalance, the course of events had been abnormal to a degree which was likely to render idle any attempt to write the economic record of the postwar years in terms of a theory of normal cyclical movements. This view was supported by E.A.G. Robinson, who believed that the European cycles had departed from the traditional form; their origin was likely to be sought in exogenous factors. J. J. Polak questioned the validity of all busines cycle theories and qualified cycle theory as a particular eclectic section of dynamic economics.

The explanatory value of oversimplified mechanical models met with widespread mistrust.[57] Advocates of the "realistic" approach to dynamic analysis proposed to limit the use of "abstract models" to the tasks of illustrating economic phenomena of the past and implementing research into the effects of specific measures of economic policy. The respresentatives of national institutes of economic research were virtually unanimous in ignoring generalized business cycle theory. Lawrence Klein insisted on the use of econometric methods because they enable the economist to adjust his analysis to the requirements of a mathematical equation system independently of any strict business cycle theory.

The cyclical movements of certain European countries (Denmark and France) were shown to have been generated by domestic factors, but considerable emphasis was placed on the international propagation of such movements. Jacques J. Polak suggested the preparation of a special model suitable for analyzing the postwar spread of cycles. He argued that, as distinct from prewar conditions, a shortage of exchange reserves and the operation of import controls had resulted in impairing the responses of imports to changes in income and exports. He outlined a mechanism according to which the intensity of the changes in import policy and the length of the adjustment period were particularly relevant.[58]

Robinson's view that the United States played a predominant role in initiating worldwide business fluctuations was shared by other economists. Of course, there was no doubt that, as compared with previous times, the structure and behavior of the American economy had undergone considerable changes. But no definite answer was given to the question of whether and to what degree stabilizing effects had resulted from the accumulation of high volumes of corporate savings, as combined with a high level of investment at full employment. No agreement existed as to the role to be attributed to credit control, programs of public works, and other countercyclical measures of public policy. Several economists pointed to the dangers involved in the growing rigidity of the cost-price structure and in processes of "chronic inflation." The effects of "wage inflation" as an important element in the general reaction mechanism of the economy were repeatedly stressed, and the lack of a reliable theory of wages was considered by some experts as one of the weakest links in business cycle analysis.[59] No reasonable prospects of establishing reliable patterns of international cycles appeared to exist, and it remained a moot question how to provide protection against the international spread of depressions.

In the course of these discussions, divergencies of view were accentuated rather than attenuated by compromises. The adherents of the ''realistic'' approach to business cycle analysis were radically opposed to the methodological principles of some Keynesian economists, who insisted upon constructing abstract models of imaginary economies. Similarly, no bridge appeared to be available between Trygve Haavelmo's proposal to include ''hazy variables,'' such as expectations, among the instruments of business cycle analysis and the conviction of some Keynesian economists that the establishment of fixed relations between some economic aggregates was prerequisite to business cycle analysis.

Part XI

International Relations

Chapter 38
International Trade Theory

———

THE RICARDIAN and post-Ricardian theories of international trade were developed against a background of five not fully integrated assumptions: (1) that the international exchange of goods was to be analyzed in terms of real, as distinct from monetary, costs; (2) that this exchange was to be conceived of as an equilibrating process carried on under conditions of limited mobility of factors; (3) that the price mechanism provided the instrument for the mutual adjustment of the balances of trade; (4) that the functioning of the price mechanism was to be analyzed in accordance with the quantity theory of money; and (5) that the general application of the free trade principle was a reliable method of promoting the welfare of all members of the international trading community. The free market economy was believed to lead to an equalization of the domestic remunerations of like factors of production and to the maximization of total production. Observance of the rules of the gold standard was considered prerequisite to the operation of the price mechanism as an instrument for directing the flow of gold to the countries where its purchasing power was higher than in other parts of the trading community.

Some modifications which were suggested over the course of time did not affect the main body of the traditional doctrine. Charles F. Bastable pointed to the effects of variations in the elasticity of demand; moreover, as George Wheatley and Mountifort Longfield had done before him, he showed that balancing of international accounts might be facilitated by changes in relative incomes independently of gold movements and price changes.[1] Bastable's method of measuring "real costs" in terms of quantities of "productive power" was taken over by Francis Ysidro Edgeworth, who paid special attention to the problems involved in determining a country's gain from foreign trade.[2] Maffeo Pantaleoni and Enrico Barone analyzed certain monetary aspects of international commercial relationships.

The Austrian economist Richard Schüller emphasized differences in the costs of production as a decisive factor in determining competitive conditions in national as well as international trade. To the importance the Ricardians attached to demand he opposed the influence of supply conditions on the structure of foreign trade. A third, equally remarkable feature of his discussions was an analysis of the desirable effects which the imposition of import duties might have on the utilization of idle domestic resources, especially unoccupied labor.[3]

For more than half a century after the labor cost theory had been displaced by marginal utility analysis, the theorem of comparative costs, as based on the labor cost theory, continued to provide the backbone for the prevailing theory of international trade. Alfred Marshall extended the life span of the theory of comparative costs,[4] when he used it to construct hypothetical "bales" composed of constant quantities of a country's capital and labor, and designed to facilitate the measurement of demand. But that instrument of trade analysis was not applicable to situations in which the output of the various commodities was subjected to increasing or decreasing returns, or in which the factors of production were not employed in constant proportions. Marshall's proposal to measure gains from foreign trade in terms of producers' and consumers' surpluses was open to the objections which had been raised to the measurability and comparability of utilities.

The idea of using a country's units of productive power to measure its participation in international trade also provided the basis for Marshall's definition of the "terms of trade," that is to say, the rate at which one country's products were exchanged for those of another country. The terms of trade could be established most conveniently by calculating the ratio of average export prices to average import prices. They were shown to be generally favorable for countries with a highly elastic demand for imports, as contrasted with countries which combined high and rigid demand for imports with elastic markets of their export goods.

A notable episode in the history of the theory of comparative costs was the Rumanian economist Mihail Manoilesco's use of that theory in an attempt to refute the general validity of the free trade principle.[5] He raised the question of whether the determination of labor costs should be based on marginal returns in industry or in agriculture, and argued that the value of the products exported by an agricultural country was relatively much lower than the value of industrial commodities imported by that country. Hence, he considered a protectionist tariff advantageous for such a country if it promoted shifts of agricultural workers to industrial enterprises.

A last well-reasoned attempt to defend the theorem of comparative costs was made by Jacob Viner in his outstanding analysis of the development of the theory of international trade.[6] Viner argued that the post-Ricardian advocates of that theorem formulated it in terms of real costs, not in terms of labor costs, and could avail themselves of the assumption that at least a rough proportionality exists between market prices and real costs. But he admitted that such a correspondence is lacking where proportions between labor costs and capital costs are variable.

The problems involved in the international balancing mechanism attracted the special attention of Frank William Taussig, who devoted a large part of his scientific endeavors to the preparation of a comprehensive study of international trade relationships.[7] He transformed the "costs of production" of the traditional costs formula into monetary values by applying wage rates to absolute costs. Thus, differences in costs between two countries were related to various factors which affected the productivity of labor, such as differences in wage levels, in industrial developments, and in equipment and organization of productive processes.

In addition, Taussig initiated a series of remarkable studies which dealt with international balancing processes that had taken place under well-defined, extraordinary conditions.[8] These studies provided ample confirmation of his observations that frequently the range of price movements involved in the balancing processes was far too insignificant fully to account for these processes, and that the size of the gold transfers was very small when compared with the deficits which had to be liquidated. The assumptions made by the traditional theory were obviously not sufficient to explain the adjustments which took place in the course of the balancing processes.

James W. Angell studied changes in the general price level and in exchange rates with regard to their effects on the cost structure and on the supply and demand conditions of two trading partners.[9] Problems of factor mobility were discussed by John H. Williams, who objected to the sharp distinction commonly drawn between the alleged mobility of productive factors within a country and their lack of mobility between different countries.[10] Frank D. Graham questioned the validity of the assumption that international values were primarily influenced by the intensity of demand, whereas costs of production were assumed to be determined by domestic values.[11] Applying the concept of marginalism to exported and imported commodities, Graham argued that such commodities were in a zone of indifference with regard to their production for domestic markets or for export purposes. He attempted to demonstrate that import restrictions were likely to serve merely the interests of specific industries at the expense of others, and that it was disadvantageous for a country to exchange goods produced under the law of decreasing returns for goods produced under increasing returns.[12] T. O. Yntema and Jacob L. Mosak made remarkable attempts to give exact mathematical precision to the international balancing processes.[13]

During the twenties and early thirties, mathematical studies did not attract as much attention as discussions concerned with disturbances of international commercial relationships, the reestablishment of the equilibrating functions of the London money market, and the return to the gold standard. The catastrophic disruption of the international commercial and financial systems was generally ascribed to the war and its aftereffects, but some acute observers endeavored to show that the ultimate reasons for these tragic events had to be sought in deep-seated changes which had occurred in various spheres of the international exchange of goods. In accordance with these observations, a vast international network of trading had been established in the nineteenth century among the tropics, characterized by oversupply of labor; the Great Plains, with vast fertile regions and scarce labor; and industrialized Europe, which combined a large supply of capital with limited agricultural potential. The smooth functioning of the international exchange of goods which had been adjusted to these conditions had been endangered when intensified farming was promoted in some European countries, when the United States (whose territories were included in the Great Plains area) was increasingly industrialized, and when the terms of international competition were undermined by changes in technology.[14]

Prolonged international discussions dealt with the problem of how to determine proper rates of exchange for countries with depreciated currencies. The purchasing power parity theory, strongly advocated by Karl Gustav Cassel, promised to provide a reliable method. That method was ruled by the ideas that for each pair of countries, the "equilibrium rate" of exchange corresponded to the quotient of their general price levels and that the price levels were determined by the volumes of the circulating means of payments.[15] As modified in Cassel's contribution to the Financial Conference held at Brussels in 1920, the formula read that the parity of exchange of a country was equal to the old rate multiplied by the quotient of the degrees of inflation of both countries.[16] But on closer examination, even this "comparative" version of the purchasing power parity theory was found to be applicable only to cases in which all prices and incomes of the two countries had been affected by inflationary movements while the conditions of production and marketing had remained unaltered.[17] Moreover, the balance of payments could be influenced by various factors that did not influence the price levels, such as transfer of capital, changes in supply and demand conditions, or speculative selling of depreciated currencies. Cassel's formula for calculating purchasing power parity was criticized for its choice of a basic year, for its choice of which commodities to include, and so on.[18] The limited support that the purchasing power parity theory enjoyed in financial circles was lost during the thirties, when balancing procedures were increasingly influenced by speculative transfers of capital and competitive devaluation.[19] During the prosperity period of the twenties, the international credit system had been burdened with huge volumes of short-term loans, which had been used to finance long-term investments and were frozen when they were recalled at the outbreak of the crisis. The ensuing balance of payments difficulties were considerably enhanced by erratic migratory movements of capital. Because of these erratic capital movements, considerable doubt was cast on the view that a country's balance of payments could derive lasting improvement from fluctuating exchange rates.[20]

A new phase in the development of the theory of international trade was initiated at the beginning of the thirties, when two attempts were made to replace the obsolete theorem of comparative costs with far-reaching reformulations of the problems involved in the international exchange of goods. Gottfried Haberler, who based his remarkable analysis of these problems on the principles of marginalism, availaed himself of the theorem of opportunity costs, and substituted for the Ricardian conception of "real costs" the concept of utilities, which must be forsaken in order to make productive factors available for more profitable uses.[21] The slope of "product substitution curves" showed the ratios of the marginal costs of two products produced by a country with given amounts of productive factors; the slopes of the points at which these curves were tangential to the community's highest indifference curves of consumption measured the domestic opportunity costs of one product for another, indicating the gain to be made by exchanging the products at different, exogenously determined, international prices. A theoretical procedure was thus suggested to measure gains from international trade and to demonstrate how a country could achieve a higher community indifference curve—to the advantage of its inhabitants—through appropriate adjustments of imports and exports. According to Haberler's findings, national and international markets did not differ significantly as to the formation of comparative costs when differences in productive efficiency were due to natural causes or other conditions which would not easily be modified. But where important cost elements could be changed by suitable measures, such adjustment of costs could be expected to yield substantial comparative advantages. Under conditions of free trade and perfect elasticity of supply and demand, the trading communities could be expected to achieve optimum allocation of the available resources and maximization of the sum total of their incomes. But the problem of comparative costs was completely obscure when restrictive measures interfered with competition, since the validity of the free trade theorem was dependent upon the proportionality of relative prices and marginal costs.[22]

In the ensuing discussions of Haberler's analysis, various objections were raised, especially to some of his simplifying assumptions. The economic model to which he applied his considerations was ruled by conditions of static equilibrium and perfect competition. He availed himself of the *ceteris paribus* clause to impound the influence of a variety of factors, such as costs of transportation, changes in productive services and in money and credit supply, and technological conditions. Viner argued that the product substitution curve could not be regarded as fixed when account was taken of technological changes, and that the quantitative relationships between the productive factors were determined by prices which were not independent of international transactions.[23] Even more fundamental from a methodological point of view was the question of whether an unambiguous and useful meaning could be attached to indifference curves of consumption established for a country as a whole.[24] Bertil Ohlin objected to the development of a "pure theory" of international trade in which equilibrium analysis was applied to "real" as distinct from monetary magnitudes,[25] and considered any theory of international trade incomplete unless it dealt with the foreign exchange mechanism and the transfer of capital.

The problems involved in the international balancing mechanism provided the starting point for a theory of international trade suggested by the Swedish economist Eli Filip Heckscher, the author of outstanding contributions to the history of mercantilism and the economic history of Sweden. Heckscher pointed to the relative scarcity or abundance of the various productive factors as important elements in influencing the flow of international trade and the ensuing distribution of incomes.[26] Application of marginal productivity analysis provided him with a unified theory of distribution and with the instruments to demonstrate that in each country international trade tended to enhance the demand for relatively abundant factors and to reduce the demand for relatively scarce factors. An equalizing effect was thus exercised on the relative returns to land, labor, and capital throughout the entire area covered by that trade.

In the light of such considerations, Ohlin, Heckscher's disciple, showed that the fundamental assumptions underlying the Ricardian theorem of comparative costs were incompatible with the results of experience to such a degree that all propositions derived from the theorem were virtually useless. In his constructive analysis, Ohlin started from the spatial distribution of productive factors and drew a broad distinction between "regional trade" (marked by unlimited mobility of all factors and products) and interregional trade (characterized by restricted mobilities).[27] International trade was to be regarded as a segment of interregional trade. Starting from Heckscher's propositions, Ohlin introduced the spatial distribution of labor, capital, and means of transportation as the basic elements of the pricing process, and concluded that each of the various regions tended to expand those lines of production for which it was best equipped, and that interregional expansion of trade was rendered profitable by economies which resulted from large-scale production, irrespective of differences in the prices of the productive factors. Mobility of goods could be expected to operate toward equalizing the relative returns of the productive factors and, hence, toward equalizing their prices. That proposition was occasionally termed the "Heckscher-Ohlin law of factor price equalization." In the descriptive parts of his work, Ohlin modified his rigid assumption in order to achieve a better approach to reality. Using the method of successive approximations, Ohlin showed how the balance of imports and exports was influenced by the rate of exchange and how it could be established through relative shifts in purchasing power or changes in money incomes, unaccompanied by changes in relative prices.[28]

Ohlin's ideas were elaborated on in some subsequent studies dealing with the effects of international trade on the equalization of the prices of the factors of production.[29] But the practical results of these studies were impaired by the rigid assumptions which were made in formulating the theoretical problems.[30] Similar methods were applied to the analysis of the influence of international trading on the functional distribution of incomes. They led to the proposition that, unless rendered ineffective by retaliation, a protective tariff tends to secure to the relatively scarce productive factors increased shares in the value of the product. Labor in a thinly populated country was mentioned as an instance in point.[31]

Repeated attempts to establish standards for the measurement of gains from international trade were inconclusive. What could be measured were increases in the volume of available commodities and such reductions in expenditures on productive services as could be ascribed to increased imports. Viner suggested measuring total gains from exports with the aid of index numbers calculated by dividing the index of total export values by the index of import values.[32]

Ohlin applied his theory with considerable success to the problems of capital transfer, which were discussed in connection with the German reparation payments. According to the so-called orthodox theory, which was traced back to Henry Thornton and John Stuart Mill, payment of capital imposed upon a country had to be liquidated by increased exports effected at reduced prices under the pressure of deflationary movements. In his discussion of the international transfer of capital, Taussig based his analysis on these assumptions. He regarded reductions in purchasing power that occurred in the capital-exporting country as the results of credit restrictions rather than as automatic effects of capital transfers. Reasoning on these lines caused Keynes to raise the question of whether the transfer of the reparation payments could be effected at all in view of the low degree of the relevant price elasticities.[33]

But according to Ohlin's theory, the transfers could be effected largely through changes in purchasing power and their influence on balances of payments.[34] In fact, the execution of the reparation program did not lead to perceptible changes in price relationships. Owing to the reduction in purchasing power which took place in Germany, productive factors were made available for the production of export goods and of commodities which took the place of others which might have been imported. In the countries which received the reparation payments, increases in purchasing power enhanced the demand for domestic products and thus diverted productive factors from being allocated to the production of export goods.[35] Ohlin also emphasized the long-run effects of such shifts in productive factors upon the German demand conditions, and attached only secondary importance to measures of credit policy as instruments influencing demand. Applying similar considerations to the relationships between lending and borrowing countries or regions, he argued that the lending region had an effective demand for a lesser portion of the total production of the two regions and the borrowing country a demand for the greater portion, and that the balance was to be adjusted accordingly. August Lösch adopted another approach to the transfer problem. He emphasized the spatial nature of the changes in prices produced by the transfer and the dampening effects of the gradual propagation of these changes. In the light of his reasoning, these processes occurred independently of differences in currency standards and were rendered possible only by credit creation, which in turn had important effects on the price movements.[36]

In the course of these and related discussions, it became apparent that international commercial relationships were frequently affected by differences in the degree to which productivity was modified in the trading countries. Enhanced exports which provided unemployment for otherwise unutilized resources could lead to induced expansions of income, thus stimulating investments and imports independently of changes in prices.[37] Supported by the inflow of gold, export surpluses could be maintained for considerable periods, and economic policies designed to assure the continuation of surpluses could be considered justified under these circumstances.[38]

When the Keynesian theory of employment was applied to the conditions of international trade, the monetary aspects of that trade were emphasized and attention centered on balance of payments processes and their relations to income and employment. Keynes characterized the international gold standard as the most efficacious method of setting each country's advantage at variance with its neighbors, since it made domestic prosperity directly dependent on competitive pursuit of markets and a competitive appetite for precious metals.[39] Convinced adherents of the Keynesian theory rejected without reservation the use of deflationary measures as instruments for overcoming balance of payments difficulties, and placed imports as a source of "income deflation" on a footing equal to the "leakages" of the multiplier theorem. Interestingly, R. F. Kahn, who suggested the use of the multiplier principle, later modified his original view that all imports are to be counted among the factors that are likely to produce "leakages" in the process of spreading the effects of public works programs.[40]

Some disciples of Keynes, particularly Joan Robinson and Roy F. Harrod, ascribed the performance of balancing processes primarily to induced movements of income and employment and minimized the role played by price movements in these processes. They assumed that the price elasticities of demand were very low, and argued that increases in exports would lead to increased imports, even without price changes, by way of changes in output, employment, and income. According to Robinson, the secondary effects of the expansion of exports were particularly significant when considerable shares of the resulting advantages went to workers with a high propensity to consume. The multiplier principle was used to demonstrate how incomes created by export surpluses were reduced through "induced" imports. The existence of continued export surpluses was connected with induced savings spent to finance foreign loans.[41] Since the demand for loans was assumed to be insensitive to the rate of interest, the influence of bank policies on the balancing processes was considered negligible.[42]

The models used in these discussions were based on the principle of comparative statics, hence no account was taken of the mechanism leading from one equilibrium position to the other. Fritz Machlup adjusted multiplier analysis to the "dynamic" aspect of internatinal trade on the assumptions that all prices and implicitly all marginal costs remained unchanged and that the marginal propensity to import and the marginal propensity to consume remained constant.[43] Since "autonomous" changes (not induced by changes in incomes) in exports and imports differ conspicuously from induced changes, he developed a specific formula for each group of cases, and illustrated the functioning of the multiplier under varying assumptions. But these and similar attempts to develop dynamic versions of multiplier effects had only very limited prospects of practical application, in view of the rigid assumptions which had to be made in order to reduce highly complex problems to manageable proportions.

Ragnar Nurkse suggested the term "marginal propensity to import" to denote the relation of a unit increment of income to the change in imports.[44] He analyzed the relationships between varying magnitudes of that propensity on the one hand and changes in national income and in the import-export balance on the other. He defined the "export multiplier" as the increment in national income generated by a rise in exports as compared with the increment in exports, and extended his studies to the transmission of fluctuations in economic activity and employment.[45] The adjustment problem and the "propagation problem" were thus approached from the angle of dynamic changes in incomes and employment. These fluctuations were shown to be spread abroad through their effects on the demand for imports; lags in the propagation process of the multiplier mechanism were shown to lead to gaps in the balance of payments. Closing of the gap was related to changes in the flow of domestic incomes. Thus, international balancing processes could be analyzed in accordance with a general schema on the assumptions that prices remained unchanged and that exchange rates were not altered. But no conclusive answers were given to the questions of the degree to which the adjustment of trade balances could definitely be attributed to the operation of the multiplier and whether the relations between consumption and income and between imports and income could be assumed to be as stable as was postulated by the multiplier theorem.[46] Since pursuance of full-employment policies could be expected to prevent induced movements of output and employment from playing a significant role in balancing international accounts, convinced adherents of the Keynesian doctrine arrived at the conclusion that, barring the use of direct controls, the balancing process would be performed again through price changes. But it was considered imperative to prevent such price movements from having deflationary effects.

The theoretical analysis of the exchange of goods taking place under fixed exchange rates and under the influence of depreciation was not extended beyond the case of two countries trading two commodities.[47] Possible improvements of the balance of trade brought about by depreciation were shown to depend on the degree of elasticity in the supply of and demand for exported and imported commodities;[48] the view prevailed that such effects were predominantly of the short-run type. This view was reflected in the provisions of the International Monetary Fund and the proposed charter of the International Trade Organization.[49] A careful and painstaking analysis of the problems involved in the equalization of the balance of payments was prepared by J. E. Meade, who distinguished the actual balance of payments deficit from the "potential" deficit and defined the latter as "the amount of accommodating finance" that it would have been necessary to provide in any period in order to avoid any depreciation of the exchange rate or adoption of measures specially designed to restrict the demand for foreign currencies. "Potential" deficits (and the corresponding "potential surpluses") could be considered as the proper measures of balance of payments equilibria. The analysis of balancing procedures was the special object of Meade's studies.[50]

When the concept of "immobility of factors" was combined with the notion of "restriction of entry" into a given industry or a given economic collectivity, important features of the theory of imperfect competition became applicable to the theory of international trade.[51] The question was raised whether it might be possible to reduce all valid distinctions between international and domestic trade to one resting upon differences in degrees of restrictions imposed upon free entry. Such restrictions could be related either to spatial occupational immobility or to forces which retard the freedom of factor movement.[52]

Considerable agreement was reached on the proposition that a country's interests could effectively be promoted by trade restrictions, especially by protective tariffs, unless foreign demand was very elastic or the advantages derived from the restrictions were impaired by retaliatory measures.[53] But considerable difficulties were involved in attempts to measure the gains resulting from protective tariffs. As a rule, studies of this type were adjusted to the principles of "welfare economics," according to which an economic change is desirable if it leads to an increase in real national income without involving an undesirable change in the distribution of income.[54] Meade undertook a comprehensive analysis of the welfare aspects of foreign trade policies, and made allowance for a morally justifiable redistribution of incomes.[55]

Writing in 1946, Jacob Viner attempted to refute the widespread view that owing to the operation of the law of diminishing returns and the growing density of population most countries had to restrict their participation in international trade in favor of the domestic production of agricultural commodities. He attributed the decline in the absolute importance of world trade to the autarchic policies pursued by many countries; he criticized the general tendency to underestimate the contribution which foreign trade makes to general well-being and said that its contribution to economic instability was frequently exaggerated. Strongly opposed to the policy of bilateral trading as supported by Keynes, he emphasized the need for imports rather than exports. Viner also raised the question of whether there is and can be a relevant general theory of international trade for a world of planned economies, state trading, and managed instability of exchange rates.[56]

Haberler strongly objected to that "mournful" view, and defended his belief that the basic principles of a well-organized modern theory could be traced back to the early nineteenth century in its three interrelated branches: the theory of the balance of payments mechanism; the equilibrium theory of the international division of labor; and the theory of the welfare aspects of trade, as applied in the free trade doctrines and the doctrines of trade restrictions.[57] Modern analysis, he argued, operates with shapes and shifts of supply and demand curves of one currency in terms of another. These curves are derived from supply and demand curves of exports and imports, which are deduced from supply and demand curves of consumers and producers, which in turn can be connected with utility and production functions. Thus, in his view, international trade theory had been successfully integrated with the general theory of money, business cycle theory, and employment doctrine on the one hand, and with pure equilibrium theory on the other. But he admitted that almost all theorizing on the balancing mechanism was "competitive" theory—and this in a world abounding with monopolies, oligopolies, monopolistic competition, and other imperfections and impurities of competition. Other economists were less satisfied with the achievements of the theory of international trade, and pointed especially to the lack of a consistent approach to the dynamic processes of the international exchange of goods.[58] They argued that the study of these processes was limited to a few select cases and that only a couple of tentative steps had been taken toward the establishment of a bridge between the analysis of international trade relationships and research into the international propagation of business fluctuations.[59] Moreover, the treatment of various problems such as international price movements, terms of trade, gains from trade, or the effects of tariffs still showed the poorly coordinated traces of three different approaches, of which one started from the application of the principle of opportunity costs to the analysis of international trade relationships, the second from the spatial distribution of the productive factors, and the third from the effects of induced demand and the operation of the multiplier.

The discussion of economic policies is outside the scope of this analysis, but since problems of foreign trade policies have significantly affected the treatment of theoretical issues, it might not be amiss briefly to point out some fundamental relationships between certain theoretical considerations and the main patterns of foreign trade policies. Three patterns of such policies could be clearly distinguished during the interwar period, each modified by one of the prevailing modes of reasoning. Hypothetical reasoning, as practiced by leading nineteenth-century social philsosophers, was reflected in the principles of multilateral trading. Basic to these principles was the assumption that foreign trade was the combined result of innumerable competitive private transactions performed under conditions of full employment of the available resources, expanding demand, and neutrality of the monetary factors. Foreign trade was held to differ from domestic trade by the fact that imperfect occupational mobility of a country's productive services prevented the "real" costs of production of its export goods from being equalized with the real costs of production of other countries. The proposition that the free movement of prices was to be relied upon to perform the balancing mechanism was an outcome of the same pattern of reasoning which led to the establishment and the strict observance of the gold standard. The operation of mechanical forces was held to assure optimum effects of the international division of labor. But the arguments advanced in favor of multilateral free trading lost much of their persuasive power, and it became increasingly obvious that there exists "neither among economists, nor among laymen, any large or influential body of opinion which believes in an inherent or fortuitous complete or even predominant harmony between national interests properly conceived and the interests of the world at large.[60]

It would be a mistake, however, to assume that all measures of protectionism are incompatible with the methods of hypothetical reasoning as applied in the decision making of producers and traders. Perfect compatibility obtains for all measures of economic policy which do not interfere with the interdependence of the international price system but result only in the modification of existing cost-price relationships in favor of certain groups of producers and traders. Protective tariffs and payment of import subsidies, as distinct from quantitative trade restrictions, are measures of that type. Leading advocates of the free trade policy, such as Mill, Marshall, Edgeworth, and Taussig, attributed unconditional blessings to that policy only when it was observed on a world-wide scale, but they admitted that a country or important sectors of its population could derive considerable advantages from protectionist measures, especially when such measures were designed to promote the development of infant industries.[61]

The conceptual approach to protectionism adopted by many adherents of the German historical school was quite different. Their considerations started from the power policies of "national states," regarded as integrated wholes and fighting with other states over the share of limited supplies of raw materials, limited national and international outlets for their export goods, and limited prospects of profitable capital investments. There was no room within the framework of that reasoning for concepts such as the international interdependence of the price system or the operation of equilibrating forces in the mutual adjustment of balance of payments.

Viewed from that angle, foreign trade policy was not simply designed to promote the interests of individual firms or industries; it was conceived of as one of the most effective instruments of national power policies and was to be adjusted, as closely as possible, to expansionist nationalistic objectives. The conclusion of bilateral trade agreements and the operation of a network of international cartels as practiced by the German national socialist government had their origin in reasoning of that type.[62] These measures were supplemented by others designed to isolate the domestic price system through import regulations and exchange controls and to subject imports to discriminating treatment.[63]

Under the impact of the Great Depression of the thirties, the principles of bilateral trading were also adopted by many countries which did not pursue aggressive power policies but wanted to adjust their commercial relations with other countries as closely as possible to their national interests. According to a widespread belief, these interests could best be served when other countries with export balances in bilateral trading were required to spend such surpluses on exportable commodities of the less privileged trading partner, regardless of whether these commodities could be purchased more advantageously in other markets. Clearing accounts were operated in order to assure the equilibrium of exports and imports between the partners to bilateral trade agreements. The methods applied in operating bilateral agreements were far from uniform, but strong elements of organismic reasoning provided the background for all these agreements.

A third method of reasoning was instrumental in determining the foreign trade policies pursued by the Soviet Union. Since the influence of incalculable outside factors represented a serious danger to the fulfilment of the long-term plans, the organization of exports and imports had to be strictly adjusted to the requirements of the plans, and dependence upon foreign unreliable markets had to be reduced to a minimum.[64] Hence, foreign trade was carried on along monopolistic lines through bilateral agreements which were, above all, designed to cover the country's import needs.[65] But political considerations were permitted to play a considerable role in determining the choice of foreign markets. The economic relationships of the Soviet Union to the satellite countries of Eastern Europe were ruled by the intention to adjust the economic development of these territories as closely as possible to the objectives of Russian planning.[66]

The lessons taught by the chaotic international commercial relationships of the interwar years were not lost on the Western democracies, and caused them after the termination of the Second World War to adopt a new approach to the settlement of international economic difficulties and frictions. The establishment of a new order of international commercial and financial relationships was prepared by well-coordinated actions designed to assure to all countries the freedom of pursuing domestic policies of full employment and to prevent the adoption of measures likely to shift the burden of unemployment from one country to its trading partners.[67] In order to prepare the way for the abolition of discriminatory trade restrictions and for the operation of a system of fixed exchange rates, it was considered necessary to provide for a common pool of liquid reserves which would assist the various countries in overcoming temporary balance of payments difficulties and to promote the correction of "fundamental" balance of payments equilibria through adjustments of exchange rates, but allowance was made for the adoption of discriminatory procedures when excessive demand for imports threatened to exhaust the available foreign exchange reserves.

The principle of multilateral trading was virtually institutionalized in the course of these developments. The International Monetary Fund was created for the purpose of securing the operation of a world-wide system of sound "realistic" exchange rates. The Marshall Aid Program, as carried out through the Organization of European Economic Cooperation and its affiliated agencies, supplied effective measures for the economic recovery of the European countries and toward closing the "dollar gap" which had resulted from the extraordinary demand for American capital goods. As distinct from the static concept of a "deficit in the balance of trade," strong dynamic elements were implied in the idea of the "dollar gap," which was defined as a lack of equilibrium in balances of payments covered up by assistance from abroad or prevented from being effective by means of economic policy such as import restrictions, artificial promotion of exports, and the like.[68] The General Agreement on Tariffs and Trade was established as an instrument for assuring observance of the principles of multilateral trading through concerted action of the contracting parties. A more ambitious instrument of that kind, the International Trade Organization, was the object of extensive international discussions in 1948 but failed to be realized. Other agreements were intended to defend the Western democracies against the aggressive economic policies of the Soviet Union. The history of postwar international trade relationships provides an excellent illustration of the role played by conflicting patterns of thought in economic organization.

APPENDIX A
THE THEORY OF LOCATION

THE STUDY OF location problems, as undertaken in the pioneer works of Johann von Thünen, Wilhelm Launhardt, and Alfred Weber, had been approached from the angle of the "low cost" principle.[69] This formulation of location problems also prevailed in some subsequent discussions of various aspects of the theory of location, though wide differences developed as to the objectives to be pursued and the procedures to be adopted. The disciples of Alfred Marshall did not attempt to develop the theoretical aspects of the problems of location. Their master had complained of the difficulties involved in the study of the influence of space and time on economic conditions. But he had limited his discussion of spatial problems to certain observations concerning the conditions that are favorable to the development of industries. It is hardly possible to present a coherent and consistent picture of these discussions. In view of their fragmentary nature and their very limited results, it will be sufficient to outline some of the divergent attempts to adjust the study of spatial conditions to the principles of the general economic theory.

The analysis of the problems connected with the location of specific enterprises or industries can conveniently be distinguished from the research into the conditions of regional economic development. Oscar Engländer[70] drew a distinction between a theory of markets and a theory of location; to the theory of location he assigned the special problem of determining the influence of the costs of transportation on the establishment of enterprises. He analyzed the relations between patterns of local price differences and the location of economic activities, and supplemented his theoretical considerations with extensive research into the adjustment of railway tariffs to the costs of transportation.

Andreas Predöhl abandoned the low cost principle, which had previously provided the directives of spatial research, and instead used the principle of substitution in an attempt to elaborate a general theory of location based on the assumption that optimum allocation of productive resources was secured when the last units of two productive factors or groups of such factors used in a productive process had the same price. The logical difficulties involved in that reasoning became apparent, however, when Predöhl attempted to illustrate specific substitution operations. The validity of his equations was restricted to cases in which only two factors of production were required and the scale of productive processes was fixed.[71] Moreover, objections were raised to Predöhl's procedure of transforming all differences in space and quality into quantities of "use units."[72] Hans Ritschl availed himself of Weber's distinction of economic strata to determine shifts in the location of industries.[73] He attached special importance to changes in freight rates as a factor promoting such shifts.

Considerations prompted by the dynamic aspects of regional developments caused Tord Palander to reject the application of equilibrium analysis to spatial problems.[74] In his treatment of these problems, he emphasized the influence of costs of transportation, changing technologies, and factors affecting free mobility of capital and labor. In his view, the price discrepancies existing in regional markets were symptoms of monopolistic situations enjoyed by groups of producers and traders.[75] Because of methodological difficulties, Palander limited his discussions to the analysis of some special problems, such as employers' reactions to differences in local conditions of production, competitive struggles of transportation firms, and the like.

But the equilibrium approach prevailed in most other studies of spatial problems. Leonhard Miksch emphasized the importance of the method of substitution.[76] Walter Isard suggested that oligopoly theory was even more vital in spatial than nonspatial economies. On the one hand, he was looking for "empirical regularities" in the space economy; on the other, he attempted to give a mathematical formulation to location theory, conceived of as a maximization problem.[77] With this end in view, he connected all problems of location with a condition of equality between ratios of transportation rates and marginal rates of substitution of transportation inputs. Isard introduced the abstract concept of "distance input," defined as the movement of a unit weight over a unit of distance, and identified the price of a distance input with the transport rate. He also used the transportation aspects of interregional trade to establish a connection between location theory and the theory of international trade.[78] Bertil Ohlin adjusted his analysis of spatial problems to his formulation of the theory of interregional trade.[79] He started his analysis by considering a given district in which the choice of the special locations for various industries was solved for fixed productive factors, including costs of transportation and transportation facilities, the tendencies toward agglomeration, and the conditions of the labor force as influenced by previous occupations. Thus, the choice of a location was shown to be due to certain determinant elements of the pricing processes, and the inter-regional problems problems were connected with the lack of mobility of the productive factors.[80]

The German economist August Lösch developed a simplified static model of a regional economy which was assumed to operate under conditions of monopolistic competition.[81] In his highly abstract considerations, he distinguished three main causes of spatial differentiation: economies of scale, transport costs, and agriculture's need for space. He qualified agricultural production as "areal" (as distinct from "punctiform"), and elaborated the idea that selling by a punctiform industry to areally spaced customers was characterized by "price funnels"; Thünen had shown that selling by areal agriculture to a punctiform city proceeded by "crop gradients."

In his analysis of the conditions of the optimum location of the individual firm, Lösch formulated the problem in terms of a maximum proposition, but to the usual assumption that firms tend to maximize their profits he opposed, as a "collective tendency," a trend toward maximizing the number of independent enterprises. His systems of networks, which were designed to illustrate the conditions for the most advantageous location of the various industries, were based on the assumptions of free competition, uniform distribution of the population, and maximum demand for the product of each producer. But he admitted that only practical trial and error tests could supply realistic solutions to the problems of optimum location.

Organismic views, as developed by the German historical school, caused Lösch to abandon the traditional definition of economic regions in terms of factor mobility, homogeneity, and self-sufficiency, and to substitute for that definition a "Gestalt" concept based on the interplay of markets and of the relationships between production and consumption units. He agreed with Ohlin that factor endowment was a characteristic feature of an economic region and that changes in production were significantly affected by variations in the combinations of the factors. But he objected to Ohlin's method of

reducing spatial differences in prices to variations in freight costs, and he attached far
more importance than Ohlin to demand.

Lösch's theory of international trade, which he had developed in accordance with his
basic assumptions, was designed to show the influence of long-run changes in international supply and demand conditions on price movements leading to low levels of prices in
regions with declining purchasing power and high prices in regions where purchasing
power was increasing. From the ensuing redistribution of the productive factors, Lösch
derived changes to the spatial configuration of industries. Although the merits of Lösch's
analysis were pretty generally recognized, various objections were raised to the highly
artificial structure of his model of economic regions.

APPENDIX B
INTERNATIONAL MONETARY RELATIONS
AFTER THE SECOND WORLD WAR

The followers of John Maynard Keynes more or less disregarded the "neomercan-
tilistic" views that Keynes proclaimed in his remarks about the predecessors of Adam
Smith. But they endorsed his dictum that the international gold standard was the "most
efficacious method of setting each country's advantage at variance with its neighbours,"
since it made domestic prosperity directly dependent on "competitive pursuit of markets
and a competitive appetite for precious metals." In their theoretical treatment of the
problems of international economic relations, Keynes's disciples were faced with some
issues that had been well formulated in preceding discussions. They were challenged to
analyze the exchange mechanism operating under fluctuating rates of exchange and had to
weigh the advantages of fluctuating rates against the disadvantages. Moreover, they had
to explain the adjustment mechanism that takes place when movements of income are
assumed to be the primary motion of balancing processes, as distinct from prices that
fulfill this function under the gold standard.

As I have mentioned earlier, the discussion of the problem of exchange stability was
initiated in 1920 by Charles F. Bickerdike, who pointed out the unfavorable influence of
fluctuating rates on the adjustment of balances of payments. The treatment of this topic
was taken up by Joan Robinson, who analyzed four measures of economic policy as to
their effects on balances of trade: (1) exchange depreciation, (2) wage reductions, (3)
export subsidies, and (4) import restrictions brought about by tariffs and quantitative
controls of imports.[82] The results of her analysis of flexible exchange rates were similar to
those Bickerdike had arrived at in 1920: she said that violent fluctuations of these rates are
likely to occur when the demand for foreign products has small price elasticity. But Arthur
J. Brown, who treated the same problem, attributed a much higher price elasticity than
Robinson to the demand for exports, and derived from this assumption a stabilizing effect
on balances of payments.[83]

Frank D. Graham, who recommended the adopted of variable exchange rates as a
temporary measure, suggested, as he had done before, the introduction of a system of
commodity reserves as a means of supporting price stabilization.[84] In accordance with the
assumption that price elasticities of demand are very low, the adherents of the Keynesian
doctrine argued that increases in exports bring about enhanced imports without leading to
noticeable price changes through their effects on output, employment, and income.[85]

Ragnar Nurkse defined the equilibrium rate of exchange as a rate at which for a considerable period (at least a year) foreign payments and receipts are equalized without additional restrictions on trade.[86] But no sound principle could be suggested to establish an equilibrium rate when the balancing of a country's payments and receipts occurred under conditions of severe unemployment or inflationary price movements.

The discussion of theoretical problems surrounding the international adjustment process proceeded against the background of changing international foreign policies toward the end of the Second World War. Strong movements in favor of planned economies asserted themselves in Great Britain and other countries of Western Europe. A number of economists expressed the fear that pursuance of a successful "full-employment policy" might be impossible unless quantitative trade restrictions and bilateral trade agreements provided protection against the disrupting influence of the "instability" of the American economy.[87]

An important role in these discussions was also played by the argument that, owing to the superiority of its industry, the United States was likely to enjoy continuous surpluses in its balances of payments and to "suck in" gold. Low price and income elasticity of American demand for imports and high income elasticity of foreign demand for American exports were listed as contributory factors.[88] Although conflicting views existed as to the degrees of elasticity of demand in foreign trade, virtually all students of international relations agreed that special dangers were involved in speculative capital movements induced by prospective changes in exchange rates. Hence, many economists proposed to use quantitative trade restrictions and exchange control rather than flexible exchange rates as instruments of balance of payments policy.

A new period in the history of international economic relations started after the termination of the Second World War. The end of the hostilities was not yet in sight when the British government took the initiative in advancing an ambitious plan designed to deal with the burning question of how to provide adequate means for settling prospective balance of payments deficits of the European countries. The author of this plan was John M. Keynes, who proposed to substitute a comprehensive international credit system for gold as the primary instrument of monetary reserves. A generally accepted monetary unit was to be issued and the credit system was to be organized on the pattern of commercial banking.[89]

This ambitious scheme was rejected by the American government, but prolonged negotiations held at Bretton Woods, New Hampshire, led to the creation, in 1946, of the International Monetary Fund. The International Monetary Fund was designed to coordinate the monetary policies of the various countries, to serve as an intermediary between lending and borrowing countries, and to facilitate the settlement of temporary balance of payments deficits. The proposed functioning of this international machinery was less influenced by theoretical considerations than by the results of practical experience during the interwar period, when international economic relationships had been disrupted by "competitive devaluation."

Adherence to the principle of fixed exchange rates prevailed over the idea of permitting fluctuating rates to find changing equilibrium levels, and widespread agreement existed on the view that rates had to be linked with gold as the ultimate instrument of monetary reserves. Gold parities were to be adjusted to the international economic conditions of the various countries, but the idea of regarding gold as the exclusive reserve asset was discarded, since the supply of monetary gold could not be expected to cover the needs of an expanding international trade. Hence, the American dollar and the British pound sterling were defined as the "key currencies" of a gold exchange standard in order to fill the gap between the available gold reserves and the amount of needed reserves.

The fulfillment of at least three conditions was prerequisite to the smooth functioning of the projected monetary system: the key currency countries had to have ample gold reserves to maintain the stability of their currencies; they had to supplement the demand for gold by creating sufficient liquid claims against their own currencies; and the United States had to take appropriate measures to maintain the exchange rate of the dollar at a fixed parity (thirty-five dollars per ounce of gold).

The International Monetary Fund's reserves available for lending purposes were built up out of contributions by the member countries and later were repeatedly enlarged. The exercise of "drawing rights" was made dependent upon the adoption of such economic policies as were consistent with the objective of establishing and maintaining stable exchange rates and of exercising liberal foreign trade policies.[90] Hence, from the outset a close connection was established between the objectives of international monetary and international trade policies.

Modifications of exchange rates were permitted only when approved by the board of the fund and when necessary to correct "fundamental" balance of payments disequilibria. Disequilibria of this type were assumed to exist when a country's balance of payments deficit coincided with a relatively high degree of unemployment or when a persistent surplus of the balances of payments was accompanied by domestic overemployment and inflationary price pressures. An international authority was thus charged with the task of supervising the observance of the rules of a monetary order agreed upon by the member governments, whose range eventually covered all those of the noncommunist type. An important role in promoting the coordination of national economic policies was played by regional organizations such as the Sterling Bloc, dominated by Great Britain, and the Organization for European Economic Cooperation.[91]

The stabilization of international monetary relations and the expansion of the monetary mechanism proceeded by stages. During a transition period which lasted until about 1957, intricate problems of monetary relationships resulted from the unequal distribution of the gold reserves among the trading nations and the relatively slow increases in the monetary gold supply. The much-discussed dollar shortage, or "dollar gap," was defined as a "lack of equilibrium in balances of payments covered up by assistance from abroad or prevented from being effective by measures of foreign trade policy such as import restrictions, artificial promotion of exports and the like."[92] Owing to its vast industrial superiority, the United States was able to "suck in" the available gold supply and to render virtually all European countries dependent upon its monetary and commercial policies.

The organization of the international monetary mechanism was a manifestation of a spirit of international economic cooperation unknown in the history of economic reasoning. The execution of the Marshall Plan was another achievement suggested in the same spirit.[93] It prepared the way for the rapid recovery of the European countries and for a gradual redistribution of the monetary gold stock. Reestablishment of multilateral trading was effectively promoted by the European Payments Union, created in 1950. It provided the framework for a multilateral compensation mechanism of the majority of European countries.[94]

A third instrument of international economic cooperation grew out of the abortive attempts to create a comprehensive international organization for the promotion of foreign trade. Beginning with 1947, expansion of world trade was effectively supported by tariff reductions made in accordance with the General Agreement on Tariffs and Trade (GATT). The creation of a broad European common market was prepared by the establishment of the European Economic Community, which was followed by the conclusion of the European Free Trade Association. A strong economic counterweight was thus established to oppose the overwhelming economic power of the United States and the foreign trade policies of the Soviet bloc. The organization of trade with the communist countries was beset with many difficulties and only slowly assumed substantial proportions.

The spirit of international cooperation also provided the incentives for the establishment of financial institutions designed to organize effective assistance to underdeveloped countries. This task was assigned to the International Bank for Reconstruction and Development, known as the World Bank, which undertook to grant loans to governments on a strictly commercial basis. The functions of the World Bank were subsequently supplemented by its affiliates, the International Finance Corporation and the International Development Association. Special development banks were established for certain regions, such as Latin America or Southwest Asia.

About 1958, at the beginning of the second stage in the development of international economic cooperation, a sound organization of the international monetary mechanism had been well established. Almost all industrialized and some less developed countries had stabilized their foreign exchange rates and achieved free convertibility of their currencies. The European Payments Union, which had fulfilled its mission, was dissolved; the European Monetary Agreement assumed the task of facilitating the settlement of mutual transactions of the European countries.

But the assistance granted to underdeveloped countries by the international institutions did not come close to satisfying the demands of the representatives of the ''developing'' areas. These institutions insisted that the economic and social progress of the backward countries must be the central concern of international economic relations, and they requested that these countries be allotted a privileged position in the organization of world trading. The discussion of these problems reached a climax in the spring of 1964 at the Conference of Trade and Development, held in Geneva under the auspices of the United Nations (UNCTAD). Raul Prebisch, the general secretary of the conference, showed that in the course of the twentieth century the industrialized countries had developed their own agricultural products, and that the producers of primary commodities were faced with competition from cheaper substitutes. Hence, radical changes in the existing pattern of comparative advantages were needed to secure the progress of the ''developing'' regions.[95]

The resolutions passed by the conference reflected these demands: (1) conclusion of commodity agreements to assure safe markets and fair prices for the traditional products of the developing countries (at the time of the conference international commodity agreements existed for only four products: wheat, coffee, sugar, and tin), (2) preferential treatment enabling these countries to develop the production of exportable manufactures, and (3) expansion of trade among the developing countries and trade with the planned economies of the Soviet bloc. Losses incurred by the developing countries from adverse movements of the terms of trade should be compensated out of special funds. But the fulfillment of these demands was largely dependent upon the development of the world economy and the balance of payments conditions of the industrialized nations.

Although the achievements of the International Monetary Fund and the organization of the international monetary machinery were generally recognized, the smooth functioning of this machinery was jeopardized by important changes in international monetary relations which started at the beginning of the sixties. They were connected with the behavior of the reserve currencies which filled the gap between the supply of monetary gold and the requirements of the rapidly expanding world trade.

The stability of the pound was exposed to repeated severe attacks which had to be warded off by emergency measures taken by the International Monetary Fund and a number of financially strong countries in accordance with the "Agreement to Borrow" concluded in 1962. But because of inadequate increases in the supply of monetary gold, the international monetary system was more and more transformed into a credit system characterized by an "overhang of dollars," that is, short-term loans granted to the United States by other countries. Simultaneously, U.S. gold reserves were whittled down by substantial payments deficits, a situation which was bound to undermine the confidence in the stability of the dollar. The monetary authorities of the leading countries were thus faced with the paradoxical problem: any reduction of American balances of payments could be expected to endanger the liquidity of the international monetary system; on the other hand, unless these deficits were considerably reduced, the usefulness of the dollar as a reserve currency was open to serious questions.[96]

The functions of the dollar as a reserve currency were discussed in a vast literature, and the problem of how to organize the international monetary system was the object of widely varying views which were partly influenced by political considerations.[97] The old struggle between the advocates of the gold standard and the protagonists of the principle of flexible exchange rates flared up with renewed intensity. Acceptance of one of these two alternatives implied adjustment of the rates of exchange to the available gold stocks; the question of how to supplement insufficient gold stocks with reserve assets could be ignored.

Economists who favored a return to the gold standard, such as Jacques Rueff and Michelangelo Heilperin, recommended a substantial reevaluation of the price of gold in order to provide adequate gold reserves for some time to come. But they minimized the disturbances likely to result for the international monetary mechanism from the proposed change in the value of gold; they ignored the fact that in most industrialized countries the wage and price structure was resistant to downward movements and that the full-employment policy pursued by many countries provided another obstacle to the successful operation of the gold standard. Hence, virtually all bankers were opposed to a return to this monetary order.

The principle of flexible exchange rates was hardly better when put to a renewed test of practical experience, although it was endorsed—frequently with some reservations—by a considerable number of economists. These economists derived their attachment to this principle from their belief in the equilibrating effects of freely moving goods, capital, and labor. This attitude was represented in the Anglo-Saxon countries by Frank D. Graham, Charles R. Whittlesey, Milton Friedman, Gottfried Haberler, and Fritz Machlup; and on the European continent by Friedrich A. Lutz, Alfred Amonn, L. Albert Hahn, Fritz W. Megan, and Erik Lundberg. They emphasized that under a system of flexible exchange rates monetary and fiscal authorities would be free to pursue policies of full employment or price stabilization without regard to balance of payments considerations. But they were strongly opposed by leading bankers, who feared that abandonment of well-coordinated monetary policies might give free rein to misguided speculation and inflationary trends.

Hence, the large majority of reform proposals centered on the question of how to preserve the system of stable exchange rates and to provide monetary reserves which could be expanded proportionately to the requirements of the growing world economy.

Reliance on gold to guarantee the value of the various currencies had to be supplemented by relying on the financial capacity and the wisdom of an international authority charged with the issuance of widely acceptable monetary units and with the control of their use and distribution. A great variety of proposals were made with a view to implementing these objectives, and the staff of the International Monetary Fund contributed effectively toward clarifying disputed issues. Many proposals were strongly influenced by the ideas to use current or accumulated balance of payments surpluses to expand the borrowing potentials of countries with temporary balance of payments deficits,[98] to transform the short-term liabilities of the key currency countries into long-term debts, and to supplement the reserve currencies with some international fiduciary money.

The most radical of these proposals, the "Triffin Plan," aimed at entrusting the International Monetary Fund with the function of issuing fiduciary money on the pattern of a national central bank.[99] The central banks of the member countries were expected to hold certain portions of their reserves with the fund and could be granted overdraft facilities to cover deficits in their balances of payments. Many monetary authorities, however, were very reluctant to render the elasticity of the international liquidity dependent upon the decisions of a board with ill-defined responsibilities. But on the other hand, they realized that no expansion of the volume of international reserves could take place unless at least the amounts withdrawn to cover balance of payments deficits ceased to be repayable on short notice.

Hence, a much-discussed group of proposals was ruled by the intention to strengthen, as far as possible, confidence in the reliability of the supplementary reserve currency and in the methods of administering the international monetary system. These proposals were more or less elaborated versions of the "Bernstein Plan." They envisaged the creation of a "composite reserve unit" (CRU) linked with gold and guaranteed by the economic power of a number of leading industrialized countries. The reserve units to be issued according to this plan were designed to be used exclusively for liquidating mutual obligations of ten highly industrialized countries participating in this scheme.

In subsequent proposals, various characteristic features of this plan were modified, such as the definition of the range of the participating countries, the methods of fixing the volumes of the circulating reserve units, the determination of the shares of the participating countries in the volume of the reserve units, and the way of linking the units to gold.

As a remarkable version of this pattern, the "Roosa currency plan" may be mentioned.[100] The participating countries were requested to match with equal contributions special accounts expressed in "fund units." A stable dollar price for gold and a system of fixed exchange rates had to be maintained. The fund units were designed to supplement the gold reserves and the key currency reserves. The governors of the fund account were requested to fix the amount of units annually to be created and to allot the participating countries' shares according to the position occupied by their currencies in international trade and finance.

In the negotiations of the national monetary authorities, any radical solutions to the liquidity problem were discarded and preference was given to the establishment of "special drawing rights," which might not be repayable but would be used as part of a country's reserves. Thus, two main problems came to occupy a prominent place in the organization of international economic relations: the settlement of the liquidity of the

monetary system and the promotion of growth and progress of the underdeveloped countries. Compared with these problems, the tariff issues faded into the background.

Chapter 39
Economic Growth and
Economic Progress

ECONOMIC GROWTH OF INDUSTRIALIZED COUNTRIES

UNTIL THE FOURTH decade of the present century, problems of economic growth were
ignored by almost all post-Ricardian economists. Their theories had been built around the
problems of pricing and allocating scarce resources in an optimal way, and they remained
true to the essentially static Ricardian approach to economic analysis. The Ricardian
treatment of the evolutionary aspects of the economy was based on "empirical laws"
which were falsifiable: a gradually intensified process of declining profits was derived
from the combined effects of the Malthusian population theory and the theorem of ever-
diminishing agricultural returns. Thus, virtually all European economies appeared to be
headed toward more or less stationary conditions. The final stage of such a development
could be delayed by technological improvements and by the effects of free trade, which
was expected to secure the advantages of comparative costs, relatively low prices of
agricultural products, and rising wages and profits.[1] These not very promising aspects of
economic growth were later associated with certain structural changes in the economy.
John Stuart Mill and Alfred Marshall were aware of these changes. Marshall discussed
problems of this kind in book 4 of his *Principles of Economics,* and recommended the use
of biological analogies in dealing with the evolutionary features of economic life.[2] These
problematic suggestions were ignored by his disciples. But Allyn Abbott Young applied
the Marshallian concept of external economies to the analysis of industrial expansion in a
widely read article published in 1928. He argued that such economies could be created in
enlarged markets for the industries which had initiated the expansionist movement, and
that these movements and the resulting changes would become progressive, propagating
themselves in a cumulative way.[3] The expansion of one industry could thus create markets for another. But these suggestions were extended to some significant practical consequences only much later.

The indifference to the problems of economic growth shown by the post-Ricardian
and marginalist economists provides a good example for the overwhelming influence of
methodological considerations on the choice of scientific problems. No tools appeared to
be available to analyze long-range developments. The economic movements which were
taken into consideration were almost exclusively of the short-range type: sustained periods
of economic expansion related to the effects of wars, the settlement of new territories, and
other extraordinary political and sociological events.[4] Joseph Schumpeter's theory of
economic developments was a unique attempt to conceive of the trade cycles as the very

ECONOMIC GROWTH AND ECONOMIC PROGRESS 551

elements of economic expansion. The general post-Ricardian approach to the problems of economic growth may be contrasted with the Marxian attempt to use evolutionary concepts to identify the expansion of the capitalist economy with a self-destructive process.

The treatment of the problem of economic growth was not considerably modified when the validity of the Malthusian demographic analysis was proved false by declining birth rates.[5] However, special mention may be made of the "prosperity theory" advanced by the German economist Paul Mombert in the second decade of this century.[6] Basic to this theory was the assumption that gradually improving standards of living resulting from a declining rate of population growth might exercise a favorable influence on the development of "rational" economic behavior.

Increased interest in the problems of long-term economic growth asserted itself only after the Second World War, when repeated attempts were made to develop some dynamic aspects of the fundamentally static Keynesian theory. The analysts who regarded the cyclical movements as deviations from a trend had to adopt a long-run approach to business cycle research and were faced with the difficult, previously neglected, problem of how to account for the forces producing the trend—the growth of the economy, as distinct from the factors considered responsible for other movements which produce the cycles.[7] After the stagnation theorem had been replaced by an optimistic outlook on the development of capitalist societies, the study of economic growth received additional stimulus from ever-intensified attempts to demonstrate that the competitive organization of the economy was superior to its communist counterpart.

When viewed from the analytical angle, economic growth was commonly measured in terms of increases in capital accumulation or in gross national product. The related idea of "economic progress" was identified with the relation of national production to the size of the population. The annual income per capita was also regarded as an appropriate index of progress. Hence, in highly industrialized countries, such as Great Britain and the United States, measurements of economic growth in terms of national income became the object of extensive studies centering on the ratios of the national dividend to accumulated capital and to newly formed capital (savings). The problems involved in defining "national capital" and "national income" for purposes of international comparisons were treated in extensive discussions.[8]

Various attempts to give a wide scope to the concept of economic progress centered on determining the constituent elements of this concept. Proposals dealing with this topic ranged from the establishment of a limited number of economic characteristics to the enumeration of many factors, including factors of an institutional nature. When the latter procedure was adopted, the social philosophy and even the temperament of the observer were permitted to play a certain role in assessing the weight of the criteria and in interpreting the results of the analysis.[9]

Moses Abramowitz, who contributed an instructive article on this topic, placed special emphasis on the problem of how to explain long-run changes in the factors that can be regarded as immediate determinants of the level of output and on the corresponding problem of defining the effects of such changes upon output.[10] His list of "determinant" factors included, apart from land, labor, and capital, various psychological and other characteristics of the population, commercial and financial organization, the legal and political framework of economic life, discoveries, and exploitations of knowledge. Specific conceptions of economic progress were shown to be coordinated with corresponding patterns of economic organization.

In the discussions of the problems of economic growth some authors regarded changes in the composition of output or in certain trends of saving-income ratios as important factors in determining economic expansion. Giuseppe Ugo Papi attached particular importance to changes in the relationships of the productive agents.[11] Colin Clark proposed a classification of "objective criteria" of economic progress and grouped the various countries according to the participation of primary, secondary, and tertiary activities in the national dividend.[12]

The French economist François Perroux criticized the traditional indices of economic growth on the ground that they told nothing about changes in welfare as connected with costs in human life, individual freedom of choice, and other "social costs."[13] In order to supply a satisfactory theory to the statistical analysis of economic progress, Perroux proposed to divide the huge number of variables and interdependencies which affect progress into three groups characterized by the terms *creation, propagation,* and *signification.*

Attempt to use the rate of economic growth for purposes of economic forecasting were generally considered impracticable in view of the enormous variety of unpredictable factors which might be instrumental in determining the volume of investments in years to come and the distribution of the investments among the various lines of productive activity. Planned economies, however, are supposed to expand at predetermined rates of growth. But adherents of the various versions of the "stagnation theorem" pointed to the "inevitable" decline of the ratio of net investment to total output as an important factor in slowing down economic growth.[14] The French economist Pierre Dieterlen developed a special version of the theory of "economic maturity"; he argued that the "widening" and "deepening" of markets were adversely affected by conjunctural and structural changes and that large-scale destruction of prior investment was frequently caused by rapid technological innovations.[15]

Evsey D. Domar wrestled with the proposition that under the rule of free competition optimum allocation of resources at a point in time is ruled by conditions which differ from those which are conducive to the achievement of an optimum rate of growth.[16] Starting from R. F. Harrod's concept of "warranted" growth, Domar related intended savings to levels of income and argued that the maintenance of equilibrium positions is dependent upon the adjustment of a steady growth of savings and investments to the increasing productivity of the economy. His model of the economy reflected a "natural rate" of growth, output, and productive capacity assumed to be in balance when inflation and unemployment are avoided.[17] Demand was represented by investment as an independent variable; government expenditures on goods and services were introduced as additional elements of demand. Consumption was tied to investment by a Keynesian functional relationship.

But the results of investigations into the relations between actual changes in consumption and changes in investments were inconclusive, and no definite function could be assigned to autonomous investment as an element of demand.[18] Considerable difficulties were involved in the task of suggesting simple variables for supply, where highly complex factors are operating, such as changes in the composition of the labor force, institutional and geographical conditions, technological progress, and the like. For the sake of simplifying the measurement of output over time, output was assumed to be a function of hours worked, inflated by some increase in manhour productivity. However, no satisfactory methods were devised to measure the productivity of labor and capital.

The problems involved in devising models of economic growth have challenged the sagacity of a number of authors. Their methods of establishing the Keynesian doctrine frequently provided the pattern for determining the relations between significant variables of the models.[19] Given capital coefficients played a predominant role in Hans Brems's and Robert Eisner's attempts to illustrate the rate of growth.[20] Models with fixed production coefficients for labor input and for capital stock were suggested by Daniel Hamberg, Petrus J. Verdoorn, and other authors dealing with input-output analysis.[21] The proposition that substitution between total labor input and capital stock in a transitional production function is a distinct possibility was a characteristic feature of the models of Jan Tinbergen, Trygve Haavelmo, and Robert Solow.[22]

The tendency to simplify the models led people to ignore important aspects of actual economic dynamics, such as varying price levels, varying rates of interest, the influence of technological change, and the like. Various unverified assumptions were important elements of some models of this type, such as the assumptions that the economy grows under the rule of a constant average propensity to save or of a constant per capita consumption standard. Their "operational value" was questioned on good grounds.[23] The assumption that current output and capital grow steadily at the same proportional rate over time was a characteristic feature of the models of the "golden age." During subsequent periods some highly industrialized countries appear to have actually experienced something like this steady rate.[24]

Technological progress, regarded as a destabilizing factor within the context of equilibrium analysis, could be expected to be a stabilizing element when viewed from the angle of economic growth. Accordingly it was assumed that the incidences of technological and organizational innovations show a certain regularity.[25] The effects of these improvements on savings of labor and natural resources were said to have prevented a consistent fall in the profitability of newly accumulated capital and to have provided favorable conditions for increases in real wages. In view of the close analogy between capital accumulation and augmentation of technical knowledge, technical progress could possibly be made a consistent part of capital theory. When the flow of innovations was assumed to be a continuous process, problems of technological and organizational innovation were included among the objects of economic research.[26] But the contributions to the analysis of innovations have remained in the sphere of empirical research, and the general discussions of innovations and their role in influencing economic developments have not been backed by a consistent theoretical approach.

Innovations which modify methods of production were contrasted with "inventions" which affect the product.[27] Neutral innovations were distinguished from capital-saving and labor-saving innovations, and the effects of labor-saving innovations were differentiated according to whether their application coincides with conditions of undersupply of labor, oversupply of labor, or full employment. Special attention was given to the influence of innovations on cyclical and structural employment. Capital-saving inventions do not appear to have provoked large-scale and sudden disinvestments.

The proposition that there exists a tendency for innovations to have a labor-saving bias has been supported by the argument that the relative share of labor in productive processes is larger than the share of capital.[28] It remained a moot question whether innovations counteract the favorable influence of capital accumulation on wages.

The prolonged endeavors to define the concept of economic progress, to apply standards of measurement to changes of economic growth, to devise models of economic growth, and to analyze the politicoeconomic aspects of economic growth were accompanied by numerous attempts to establish outright "theories of economic progress" or at least to indicate certain factors which could be assumed to determine the conditions of economic progress. In these theories a significant role was attributed to a distinction drawn among primary, secondary, and tertiary sectors of the economy as determined by their functions within the general framework of economic activities.

The first economist to suggest a clear and consistent distinction of that kind was Allen G. B. Fisher, who based that differentiation on the structure of consumers' demand. He contrasted the production of food and raw materials with the manufacturing industries and with the service industries.[29] In a subsequent study he emphasized the importance of the tertiary sector as a field of effective employment policies. In his analysis of economic progress he studied the varying degrees in which the three sectors participate in the process of reducing costs of production.[30]

The choice of demand as a criterion for distinguishing the sectors was criticized by Martin Wolfe. Wolfe proposed to base the distinction on modes of production and to assign to the primary sector those industries in which an increase in productivity is limited by natural growth forces, to the secondary sector those industries in which such limitation is brought about by mechanical factors, and to the tertiary sector the industries operated by relatively unaided human skill.[31]

Colin Clark's much-discussed theory of economic progress centered on another idea. Clark argued that, due to the spread of technological improvements, industry and agriculture had been enabled to supply their products at gradually reduced costs and amounts of labor.[32] His somewhat vague distinction of three sectors of the economy was based on their participation in technological improvements, their relative productivity, and the nature of the demand for their products.[33] In his comparative studies of the prospective developments of the various nations, he availed himself of the relationship between selected economic aggregates. But critical objections were directed especially against Clark's use of income statistics to compare economies of widely different types.[34]

A fourth author who distinguished three economic sectors for purposes of analyzing economic progress was the French economist Jean Fourastié,[35] who applied the term *tertiary sector* to activities characterized by relatively small technical progress. He suggested that certain effects of technological improvements are antagonistic to changes in demand, and he attributed the instability of the economy to the constant transfer of human labor from the saturated (agricultural) sector to the other sectors, and to uninterrupted but irregular increases in the yield of human labor.

Walt W. Rostow started his analysis of primary, supplementary, and derived growth sectors on the assumption that increases in output are mainly dependent on two variables: the labor force and the capital stock of the community.[36] He related the rate of change of these variables to six—more or less arbitrarily chosen—propensities, namely, the propensities to develop fundamental science, to apply science to economic ends, to consume, to seek material advancement, to accept innovations, and to have children. Thus, he undertook to explain economic growth in terms of varying community responses to the challenges and opportunities offered by economic environments. But it remained an open question to what degree these propensities could be relied upon to establish stable and independent relations between economic aggregates.[37] Other critics emphasized the difficulties involved in identifying the various sectors.[38]

Elaborating on his ideas, Rostow advanced a highly successful "dynamic" theory of economic development in which he differentiated among the various sectors of the economy according to the role played by the composition of the investments. He showed how, during the period of the "take off," the undeveloped, traditional, stagnant economy is transformed, through adjustments of society's attitudes toward certain aspects of general and applied science, toward changes in technology and methods of work, and toward new forms of risk taking.

In the light of this theory, the "transition to maturity" is brought about by raising the rate of investment to a level which perceptibly outstrips population growth as accompanied by the development of several sectors of manufacturing. Rostow considered nationalistic motivation an important factor in determining the part played by governments in promoting the transition to modern societies. Analyzing the structure of the highly industrialized countries, he arrived at the conclusion that too small a share of the national income is available to the public sector, as compared with the share allotted to private economic activity. He illustrated his theory with many examples taken from the history of various countries; particularly striking is a comparison of the industrial development of the United States with the process of growth experienced by Russia in his second book on this topic, *The Stages of Economic Growth: A Non-Communist Manifesto*.[39]

Rostow did not claim absolute validity for his method of typifying the course of economic development. He suggested that his analysis was mainly designed to dramatize not only uniformities in the sequence of processes of growth but also the uniqueness of each nation's experience. Critics of his theory utilized the difficulties involved in establishing exact statistical identification of the various sectors and objected to the impression of discontinuity he created by singling out a small sector of growth industries.

Applying his theory to modern political issues, Rostow argued that seizure of political power by communist minorities is easiest in "precondition periods" in which a society has acquired a considerable stock of social overhead, capital, and modern know-how, but lacks the coherence and organization to move decisively forward in any sustained direction. He warned the nations which now live in the stage of high mass consumption that their fate is going to be substantially determined by the nature of the precondition process and the take-off in distant nations.

The methodological problems implied in the theories of economic progress were discussed by a group of economists at an international conference held at Santa Margherita Ligure in 1953.[40] Many Anglo-Saxon participants insisted on limiting the discussions strictly to the economic aspects of the problem. French and Belgian scholars, however, elaborated various issues involved in developmental processes. Henri Guitton brought up questions connected with changes in human behavior and with checks on progress. André Marchal attempted to disentangle the forces governing the short-term mechanism from more permanent long-term variables. He proposed to substitute structural analysis for aggregate analysis, sectional concepts for global ones, variable coefficients for constant and stable ones, and differentiated models for undifferentiated schemes. Summarizing his ideas, Marchal defined economic progress as the passage from one coherent complex of structures to another and considered long-range historicostatistical research into the conditions surrounding the economic mechanism indispensable for arriving at the establishment of "interstructural laws." The concept of such laws had been suggested by J. Åkerman and was discussed in a paper by the Swedish economist Eric Dahmen. Rostow defended his approach to the theory of economic progress,[41] but A. K. Cairncross raised objections to the division of the economy into sectors and Gottfried Haberler protested the use in historical analyses of doubtful concepts such as "stable propensities."

Special care was taken to define the relations between the conditions of labor supply and "widening" or "deepening" productive processes. Haberler argued that capital shortage did not seriously retard economic progress and that lack of capital could produce important bottlenecks only in the short run. This view enjoyed considerable support—for example, in a paper by Cairncross on the place of capital in economic progress. According to Cairncross's calculations for Great Britain, there had been no significant trend in the capital output ratio over a period of seventy or eighty years. In his view, capital accumulation, taken by itself, could account for at most one-quarter of the recorded rate of economic probress.[42] These observations were supplemented by Domar's findings concerning the relative stability of capital output ratios in the American economy. The need to develop a satisfactory theory of capital formation was repeatedly stressed, but no conclusive answer was given to the questions of whether deepening of capital was to be considered an index of economic progress and whether "human capital" should be included in the numerator of the capital output ratio.[43]

The attempts to account for the economic growth of individual countries may be contrasted with an evolutionary scheme advanced by Andreas Predöhl and designed to characterize the progressive industrialization of the world.[44] Predöhl distinguished three states in the industrialization of the world: (1) a phase of "integration," during which the Western European industrial core was created, with belts of decreasing intensity of agricultural utilization arranged around this gravitation field; (2) a phase of "expansion," reaching from the middle of the nineteenth century to 1931 and ending with the existence of two large industrial gravitation fields and a "biconcentric" world economy; and (3) a phase of "intensification," which started at the end of a period of large-scale migration and territorial expansion and was marked by the growth of a third industrial gravitation field in Soviet Russia. The industrialization of underdeveloped countries was shown to be a characteristic feature of that third phase.

A few lines may be added about the studies which have dealt with the economic growth of the United States. They have treated a wide variety of topics, such as the part played by entrepreneurs in influencing economic growth and technological advancement, or the problems of capital formation and income distribution as connected with economic progress.[45] The National Bureau of Economic Research has made valuable contributions to these studies. The American Economic Association devoted ten sessions of a meeting held in New York in 1955 to exhaustive discussions of problems of this kind.[46] In the discussions of the measures to promote economic growth, emphasis was placed on the proposition that the functions of central banks are to be restricted to the tasks of maintaining exchange rates and assuring stable price levels and such monetary and credit conditions as are prerequisite to full employment of the available resources.[47]

Various attempts were made to measure the steadily growing importance of innovations in the growth of output of the United States and to determine the relations between the size of a firm and its participation in research and in technological and organizatory changes. Studies of this type were connected with those dealing with monopoly power and market control.[48]

John Kenneth Galbraith challenged the widespread conviction that maximizing production is one of the main goals of economic policy in a stimulating book *The Affluent Society*. He argued that this goal is relevant in a world in which the large majority of the population is stricken by poverty.[49] Galbraith contrasted the economic conditions obtaining in such a society with the characteristics of the American affluent society, in which dangerous processes creating consumers' demand are supported by complex processes of debt accumulation, while the stability of the economy is undermined by inflationary trends of profits, prices, and wages. He agreed with Rostow on the proposition that the public sector of the economy is far too limited in comparison with the private sector, and recommended a fiscal policy which would automatically make available to the public authorities an adequate pro-rata phase of increasing incomes. Thus, a "social balance" was to be established between privately produced and marketed goods on the one hand and publicly produced services on the other. But these ideas met with many critical objections and did not perceptibly affect the development of economic reasoning.

ECONOMIC GROWTH OF UNDERDEVELOPED COUNTRIES

An adequate definition of the ambiguous term *underdeveloped countries* can perhaps be derived from the consideration that these countries exhibit varying combinations of three characteristics: the existence of unutilized resources, a low standard of living of the large masses of the population, and a prevalence of "Malthusian pressures."[50] In other definitions, the main emphasis was placed on limited capacity to accumulate capital, limited capacity to import, and unsatisfactory utilization of available resources.

The problems connected with the advancement of "underdeveloped" countries became prominent only after the Second World War, along with the gradual dissolution of the overseas empires of the European colonial powers. The new approach to these problems differed conspicuously from their treatment in the past, when the economic organization of colonies, dependencies, and other nonindustrialized territories was frequently adjusted to the interests of the entrepreneurs and capitalists of the ruling powers.

Varying appeals were advanced in support of the claims of underdeveloped countries to be assisted in their striving for economic betterment; to a doctrine of natural right, to evolutionary and nationalistic philosophies, to religious and humanitarian considerations, and finally to reasons of political expediency. At the Montreal Conference of the Commonwealth Ministers, held in 1958, India's Finance Minister, Morarji Desai, asserted that the contrast between living standards in underdeveloped Asian countries and those in the western world "was the greatest international problem of our time."[51] The political implications of these claims were intensified when the Soviet government developed an effective policy of assistance intended to promote the attachment of economically backward countries to the orbit of Moscow. These aspects of the problem were accentuated by the ensuing rivalry between Moscow and Peking. Thus, in the course of time, a variety of frequently conflicting ideas and interests contributed to the shaping of the steadily accumulating reports on conditions of underdeveloped countries and the policies to be adopted for purposes of economic advancement.[52] Theoretical considerations were influenced partly by various concepts derived from the Keynesian approach to economic analysis, partly by categories established by welfare economics, and partly by the idea of government planning adjusted to principles of economic rationality.[53]

According to the Ricardian doctrine, increases in the international exchange of goods and services could be expected to promote general equalization of factor prices and incomes among different countries. But this proposition was frequently at variance with experience.[54] The free play of economic forces appears in many cases to have aggravated the existing divergencies in economic developments.[55] Moreover, crises and depressions of world-wide scope appear to have perceptibly retarded the advancement of monocultural economies which are very sensitive to declines in their export trade.[56] When measured on a per capita basis, the import capacity of such regions often exhibited a declining trend. In addition, their economic growth was frequently interfered with by the tendency to promote the importation of consumption goods at the expense of capital goods.[57]

The results of trade statistics compiled by the United Nations Economic Commission for Latin America provided the background for the so-called theory of peripheral economies, according to which between 1880 and 1940 a continuous deterioration had taken place in the relations between the prices of raw materials exported by the Latin American countries and the prices of industrial products imported by them.[58] The defenders of that theory, led by the Argentine economist Raul Prebisch, the general secretary of the commission, alleged that technological progress, whether applied to industry or to the production of raw materials, had been exploited to the advantage of the industrialized countries.[59] But the sweeping conclusions drawn from this material by Latin American economists were hardly consistent with the results of careful statistical examination.[60]

The discussions of the economic conditions of underdeveloped countries have abounded with problems which have been approached from widely varying points of view and which do not lend themselves to simple, unequivocal solutions. In the demographic sphere, the Malthusian population theory has enjoyed a resurrection when, owing to improved hygienic conditions, death rates declined rapidly in some Asian and African countries, whereas agricultural production did not keep pace with the rapidly mounting food requirements. Egypt and India are typical examples of countries in which such "population explosions" were taking place.

Closely related to these topics has been the question of how to organize agricultural production and how to adjust its methods to the conditions of the population movements and to the requirements of domestic and foreign trade. The economic backwardness of many underdeveloped countries in important lines of agricultural and industrial activity was due to a lack of education and training facilities. The problems connected with the definition of economically desirable factor proportions and the choice of techniques adjusted to the specific conditions of such countries were widely discussed. Superior techniques were frequently found to be too specialized to be useful in backward regions. At the international economic conference held at Santa Margherita Ligure in 1953, some experts insisted that in underdeveloped regions a slow transformation of indigenous techniques was preferable to the introduction of modern tools and machinery. But others argued that growth and progress might be stifled by such a policy.

It has remained a moot question whether the principle of profitability should be strictly observed in deciding on the allocation of resources, and no agreement has been reached on the question of the extent to which investment policies should be determined by the objective of promoting export industries.[61] Advocates of active foreign trade policies have argued that the advantages which could be gained from specialization and extensive participation in international trade are likely to outweigh those attainable through tariff protection applied to a more or less balanced economy. Extensive discussions have turned on the methods of financing investments in underdeveloped countries.[62] Conspicuous differences were found to exist between the saving and investment habits of Eastern countries and the corresponding habits which had prevailed at the beginning of the period of industrialization in European countries and in the American colonies.[63] Careful analysis of the conditions under which the rate of savings could be increased in various underdeveloped countries led to the conclusion that redistribution of incomes in favor of the poorer classes might be detrimental to capital accumulation and probably would be so to economic growth.[64] The related problem of defining the role of inflationary measures as a means of promoting industrial progress was the object of widely divergent views. Earl Hamilton analyzed in remarkable studies the influence which revolutionary movements of prices had exercised on the economic development of various European countries.[65]

Adherents of Keynesian monetary policies strongly recommended promotion of industrial activity through rising prices.

Arthur Lewis was one of the most convinced representatives of this group.[66] He developed his ideas within the framework of a theory of economic growth adjusted to the conditions of underdeveloped countries. Contrasting a "capitalist, industrialized" sector of such countries with a "stagnant, agricultural" sector, he showed how economic growth, defined in terms of per capita output, is dependent upon the expansion of savings and investment in the capitalist sector, accompanied by the gradual absorption of the population of the stagnant sector. This model provided Lewis with a framework for a discussion of a variety of topics arranged around the general proposition that one of the best indices of economic growth is provided by changes in the ratio of the manufacturing population to the agricultural population. Viewed from this angle, inflationary policies are means of creating "useful capital." Careful planning and public guidance are indispensable in organizing economic activities.

In fact, in many underdeveloped countries inflationary credit expansion has been considered prerequisite to the promotion of industrialization in view of the limited prospects of securing substantial amounts of capital through other methods.[67] Arguments in favor of the inflationary bias were derived from autarkic tendencies, the lack of markets for public loans, and the lack of confidence in the stability of the domestic currency.[68]

But prolonged and cumulative inflationary movements were bound to impose "forced savings" on large masses of the population and to lead to increased social tensions.[69] The effects of such movements on underdeveloped countries were discussed in a vast literature. Adherents of inflationary policies requested that these effects be analyzed separately for the market sphere and for the subsistence sphere.[70]

Hence, highly intricate problems were involved in the attempts of international agencies[71] and Western governments[72] to promote the economic development of backward areas. The United Nations Assembly's original attitude toward these problems was outlined in a report submitted in 1951 by a group of experts.[73] It centered on the question of how to determine the amount of capital to be contributed by outside sources in order to permit an annual growth of output of 2.5 percent for the underdeveloped areas on the assumption that the social and economic factors which prevailed in these territories would remain unaltered. The proposals of the experts were marked by a distinct predilection for government planning and activity in almost all economic spheres; they included government participation in investments, application of credit control and fiscal policies, exchange control, and pursuance of other methods of foreign trade policies. In subsequent discussions, objections were raised to the terms of reference laid down by the United Nations and to the uncritical acceptance of the terms by the experts.[74] Prolonged discussions have dealt with various factors which limit the economic development of backward areas, such as exiguity of markets for their products,[75] misdirected investments resulting from erroneous planning or from conflicts between private and public interests,[76] or "hidden unemployment," that is, inadequate and inefficient use of labor, especially in small agricultural enterprises of densely populated countries.

The chances of making progress are slim in countries where the governments do not enjoy a reasonable degree of stability and are lacking the assistance of a staff of efficient and reliable civil servants.[77] Attempts to promote economic progress in underdeveloped countries have frequently been frustrated by social and cultural patterns adverse to factor substitution, mobility of labor and capital, or even expansion of the domestic market.[78] Hence, increasing emphasis has been placed on education and institutional reforms as prerequisites of the economic advancement of many underdeveloped countries.[79] It has been argued on good ground that a "take-off" requires the appearance of an indigenous entrepreneurial class and political regime that is at least not hostile to it.[80] But reliance on the price system as the method of organizing economic activity is dependent upon the prevalence of a nominalistic pattern of thought, and such a pattern is frequently incompatible with the modes of reasoning which are predominant in many regions of Africa and Eastern Asia.

An important obstacle to economic advancement has been the penury of "fixed social capital," that is to say, of means of communication and transport, public services, and the like.[81] Prospects of private investment opportunities are generally dependent on improvements of this kind.

In quite a number of underdeveloped countries continuous economic advancement has been jeopardized by the accumulation of large amounts of foreign short-term debts. Thus, relatively high percentages of their balances of payments have been absorbed by the obligations resulting from these debts.[82]

Many observers have agreed that assistance, to be effective, has to be carefully adjusted to local conditions, and that a cautious attitude should be adopted toward ambitious plans of rapid industrialization which are inconsistent with a country's limited capacity to absorb substantial investments in relatively short periods. The question of how to assure the most productive use of that assistance has been carefully examined by international bodies, especially by the World Bank, and attempts have been made to establish certain "performance criteria."

THEORIES OF ECONOMIC PROGRESS

Theoretical considerations were introduced into the analysis of economic growth by applying the criterion of "marginal social productivity," according to which capital and labor are combined in such relations that marginal productivities of the services are equalized in all uses.[83] Ragnar Nurkse and others elaborated the idea suggested by Allyn Abbott Young in 1928 that mutual external economies might be created by a wave of new investment in different branches of production, enlarging the market and thus breaking the bonds of the stationary equilibrium of underdevelopment.[84] They argued that economies of this type could result from horizontal complexities of industries as well as from vertical complexities, when industries at different stages of production are simultaneously expanded.[85] Hence, advocates of this policy recommended it even for countries with an abundant supply of labor and supported it with considerations derived from the complementarity of many industrial processes. They considered it particularly suitable for promoting the economic progress of countries which cannot count on vigorous expansion of the export sector.[86]

But some attempts to test the validity of the theory of "balanced growth" in the light of historical experience and to determine the degree to which past economic growth has been the result of simultaneous processes of opening up and widening domestic and foreign markets were inconclusive. Three main factors had been instrumental in bringing about unbalanced developments: competition for markets, competition for factors, and introduction of cost-reducing innovations.[87]

Alexander Gerschenkron described "eruptive" processes characteristic of the industrialization of some backward European countries.[88] He emphasized the influence of technological progress emanating in the nineteenth century, especially from England, and showed that frequently a "big push" was needed to break down the economic stagnation of those countries. Studies of this kind provided support for the view that economic progress of underdeveloped countries is to be initiated by speeding up investment processes, especially in manufacturing industries, and by government control of industrial developments. A particularly well-reasoned version of a theory of "accelerated investment" was suggested by Walter Galenson and Harvey Leibenstein, who considered the marginal productivity criterion inapplicable to investments in countries with low per capita incomes, great scarcity of capital, and an abundance of labor. In these cases they proposed to apply the principles of "maximizing the reinvestment quotient," that is, maximizing the capital equipment per worker, even if labor was in surplus supply.[89] In the light of this theory, the much-criticized policy of establishing iron and steel plants in underdeveloped countries was given a new aspect; it was defended on the ground that such plants have higher aggregate effects on additional investments than any other enterprises. Since the advocates of this view insisted upon maximizing productive capacity and output over time, they were ready to sacrifice to this aim increases in the employment of the labor force, present gains in productive capacity, and general improvement of the standard of living.

Other versions of this theory were elaborated by Benjamin Higgins, Albert Hirschmann, and François Perroux.[90] Higgins argued that the development of poor and stagnant economies is marked by discontinuous structural changes and by resource allocation not determined by the forces of the market. A graduated approach, he asserted, is almost certain to be self-defeating. As seen by Hirschmann and Perroux, in underdeveloped countries it was necessary to create tensions and disequilibria which would act as stimuli in provoking further change and facilitating subsequent decision making. Hence, they argued that capital-intensive processes should be applied to the key sectors of underdeveloped countries even though hand-operated processes prevailed in other sectors and in auxiliary processes within the modernized sector. Hirschmann spoke of the "uncharted territory" of efficient sequences and development strategies.[91] In support of the policy of accelerated investment he proposed the use of discriminating tariffs, the application of multiple exchange rates, administered allocation of resources, granting of monopolistic power to certain groups of producers, and the like.[92]

Intricate political questions were involved in the problem of how to distribute among the "donor countries" the burden of providing aid to underdeveloped territories. In a frequently advanced proposal, the amount to be contributed by each donor country was expressed in terms of a percentage of the national income. The allocation of bilateral aid was clearly influenced by political considerations. British assistance went to Commonwealth countries, French assistance to former French colonies, American assistance preferably to Latin America. International bodies strongly objected to the practice of tying bilateral aid to procurement in the country providing the aid.

The tasks involved in promoting the economic growth of the developing countries have been complicated by the fact that Western economists have tended to identify noneconomic motivation, which prevails in such regions, with "irrational" motives.[93] It has been observed on good grounds that in these countries the response to the stimulus of price and income variations differs widely from the response mechanism obtaining in "capitalist" countries, that similar differences exist as to saving and investment habits, and so on. Attention has been drawn to the principle of "nonstriving for income maximization" which is characteristic of many underdeveloped countries[94] in which free competition is not a workable form of economic organization. Avoidance of any risks extending over lengthy periods is closely associated with economic behavior of this type.

If the results of our economic reasoning are not very meaningful when imparted to the inhabitants of such regions,[95] it might be advisable to study carefully those varying manifestations of economic behavior in the light of conflicting patterns of reasoning and to devise methods of economic organization and economic policies which can be adjusted to the thinking processes prevailing in territories of that kind.

Striking phenomena were discussed by Trygve Haavelmo in a remarkable essay on "economic evolution" in which econometric methods were applied to the construction of various models of economic growth.[96] Haavelmo was impressed by two observations: that the inhabitants of some large backward regions had once enjoyed periods of high cultural development and well-being, and that countries which had existed side by side under similar economic conditions had experienced widely divergent developments. Hence, he considered it advisable to substitute for investigations into evolutionary dissimilarities a careful research into alternative evolutionary possibilities for given regions. In his macroeconomic models, he included a number of variables indicative of evolutionary processes, for example, population, capital, level of education and technical knowledge, and rate of production. These models were designed to be tested in the light of statistical and other data and to be used to interpret differences in economic behavior. However, the question of whether phenomena qualified as "shocks" could be included among the "endogenous" factors of an evolutionary theory remained open. Haavelmo gave some mathematical illustrations of various processes through which random disturbances could be absorbed or propagated in dynamic models. But even small initial dissimilarities between two economies could be shown in the long-run to cause very large, almost irreparable differences. In pursuance of these analyses, Haavelmo raised a question which reaches to the root of the econometric approach: whether an economic theory which deals too mechanically with the human element can escape the risk of becoming analytically empty.

Chapter 40
Econometric Problems

———

WILLIAM STANLEY JEVONS was perhaps the first economist to suggest the filling of empty boxes of abstract arguments with quantities supplied by statistical investigations. He proposed to study demand curves corresponding to the actual changes of quantities over time. Statistical investigations into the development of prices and wages were, in fact, undertaken in England in the second half of the nineteenth century, but their analytical importance was not very significant.

The first consistent attempts to use comprehensive volumes of time series of economic variables to analyze the behavior of specific national economies were made only in the second decade of this century. The works of Wesley C. Mitchell and Warren M.

Persons were governed by the conviction that the oscillations of an exchange economy could best be understood by observing the movements of prices, wages, economic aggregates, and other economic indicators reflecting the varying behavior of consumers, producers, traders, and other members of the economic community.[1] Economic research without a theory was a characteristic feature of this method. Persons's work was preparatory to the construction of the three-curve business barometer published by the Harvard University Committee on Economic Research.

Statistical studies were designed to test certain economic theorems or to illustrate inferences drawn from them. Thus, Henry L. Moore tried to determine for a series of agricultural commodities (corn, potatoes, cotton, etc.) the "coefficient of elasticity," or the percentage rise in demand which corresponds to a drop of 1 percent in the price.[2] He distinguished "elastic" demand curves from "variable" demand curves marked by irregular shifts. In his search for a "general law" of supply and demand, Moore established moving equilibria of quantities of production and prices as distinct from oscillations or deviations from such equilibria. He attributed the oscillations to the influence of exogenous factors and pointed to the "business cycle paradox," the fact that rising prices frequently did not result in reduced demand.

A similar approach to economic analysis was adopted by two other outstanding statisticians, Wassily W. Leontief and Henry Schultz, who undertook to study the oscillations of production and price around an assumed "normal" or secular trend.[3] Schultz did not explicitly introduce the time element as a variable into the demand equations, but rather he made adjustments in some variables which reflected changes probably due to the time factor. Paul H. Douglas attempted to verify the theory of marginal productivity in the light of wage statistics.[4] Charles F. Roos analyzed the fluctuating behavior of markets of durable goods such as automobiles and housing.[5] Oskar Lange suggested the use of price dispersions for measuring disturbances of equilibrium positions.[6]

A striking picture of fluctuating market conditions was presented by the "*cobweb theorem,*" which was derived from the statistical analysis of curves of supply and demand. A lag between supply and demand, frequently caused by natural conditions of production, was shown to be responsible for the fact that, in some markets at least, a full period of production had to elapse before planning of supply could be adjusted to changes in prices, whereas demand reacted instantaneously to such changes. Hence, at any time the supply was a function of a market price which had prevailed at an earlier period, while prices and production apparently fluctuated indefinitely after having been displaced from their equilibrium positions.[7]

The theoretical foundation of the theorem was supplied in three papers published in German periodicals by Henry Schultz, Jan Tinbergen, and Umberto Ricci.[8] The authors based their analyses on statistical material derived from markets of agricultural products (corn-hog cycle), minerals and metals, and manufactures, and from data on residential construction and utilities.[9] The results of these studies were incompatible with the assumptions underlying the traditional equilibrium analysis of the competitive market economy. Industries to which the cobweb theorem was applicable could be expected to be occupied at any time below the capacity reached during the last period of expansion.[10]

These findings were supplemented by various observations which confirmed the view that disequilibrating forces are permanently operating in the exchange economy. Thus, Tinbergen remarked that oscillations in the production of durable goods are likely to be wider than oscillations in the production of short-lived commodities, since only the addition to the existing stock, and not the volume of the entire subsequent supply, is determined by the prices prevailing at the time when investments in the production of durable goods were decided upon.

In pursuance of this approach to economic analysis, promising methodological and statistical work was devoted to problems of "social accounting" involving the measurement of the national income and its components and of the formation of the capital stock.[11]

The use of numerical data for purposes of economic analysis, as supported by the refinements of statistical methods, was stimulated by the increasing antagonism to the deductive method and to the construction of imaginary pictures of the economy which had no noticeable relation to reality. This antagonism was also a motivating factor in promoting the inductive research of the institutionalists; but whereas the adherents of this movement avoided any theoretical interpretation of statistically established relations between economic variables, the statistical studies of Moore, Leontief, Schultz, and other economists were guided by the search for well-defined regular relations between economic aggregates and for economic "laws."

This motivation for inductive research found a clear expression in Tinbergen's attempt to test the explanatory value of various business cycle theories in the light of statistical experience. His study, a landmark in the history of economic statistical analysis,[12] was initiated by Alexander Loveday, Director of the Financial Section of the Secretariat of the League of Nations. It was designed to provide a supplement to the comparative analysis of business cycle theories which had been prepared by Gottfried Haberler under the title *Prosperity and Depression*.

Tinbergen based his analysis on a carefully organized quantifying pattern of a business cycle theory. The variables included in the model were aggregates or suitably weighted averages of measurable economic magnitudes. They were expressed as deviations from a trend regarded as "normal" and were interconnected by multiple correlation analysis. Supplementary data referred to in various business cycle theories as particularly relevant for the analysis of the fluctuations were drawn upon in order to narrow the scope of "significant" interrelations and to test the relation of these data to the original variables. The term *interrelation* signified that fluctuations of one variable were connected with those of the others through appropriate coefficients.

Surveying the results of his findings, Tinbergen characterized as "open systems" various business cycle theories (for example, those of John M. Keynes and Friedrich A. Hayek) in which the number of variables was larger than the relations that were precisely and explicitly stated. The irregularities shown in the behavior of the cycles provided strong arguments against the view that simple correlations between time series of economic aggregates could be used for purposes of business forecasting. Many assumptions, generally made by business cycle analysts, were confirmed in the light of statistical research, but the principle of acceleration was found to be not particularly effective in influencing investment activities, which appeared to depend on profit expectations rather than on changes in consumers' demand.[13] The period required for the construction of physical capital appeared to be instrumental in shaping the form of the cycle. No adequate proof was available for the view that reductions in investment activity which occurred toward the end of the prosperity periods were due, at least in part, to increased demand for labor by consumers' goods industries.[14]

The objections raised to Tinbergen's procedures, especially by Keynes, centered on the argument that it is impossible to avoid "spurious correlations" unless all significant elements of the abstract theories are measurable and are substantially independent of one another.[15] Keynes questioned the use of the method of multiple correlation on the ground that it provided only quantitative precision to what was already known in qualitative terms as the results of a complete theoretical analysis. But Tinbergen was very successful in defending his methods.[16]

Some aspects of the problems involved in testing economic theorems were carefully examined by Trygve Haavelmo.[17] He emphasized that a theoretical formula or model obtains economic meaning only after a corresponding system of quantities or objects in real economic life has been described and identified with those in the model. His definition of "true" variables was based on his approach to the problem of testing, which implied that the theory under review be so formulated that the underlying assumptions represent statistical hypotheses, that is to say, statements regarding certain probability distributions. Probability can be interpreted simply as a measure of our a priori confidence in the occurrence of a certain event.

In support of these propositions, Haavelmo suggested that some design of actual experiment exists in economists' minds when they are building their theoretical models; hence, he requested that every theory be accompanied by a well-described design of experiments. The problem of testing economic theorems can then be treated in accordance with the methods of testing statistical hypotheses, that is, by specifying in what respect the hypotheses might be wrong.

The "testing controversy" was a characteristic episode in the development of the intellectual movement directed toward applying advanced methods of mathematics to the analysis of actual economic processes, as distinct from the use of such methods to construct pictures of a static imaginary economy. The scientific convictions of many English, American, Scandinavian, and Dutch economists had been well summarized in a dictum by Lord Kelvin, who asserted that your knowledge is of a meager and unsatisfactory kind unless you can measure what you are speaking about and express it in numbers.[18]

The Econometric Society, founded in 1930, became a rallying point for those who endeavored to organize appropriate procedures for collecting relevant statistical data and to prepare effective tools for adjusting these data to the purposes of economic analysis. The first issue of *Econometrica*, the literary organ of the society, was published at the beginning of 1933. In the leading programmatic article, Ragnar Frisch elaborated the idea that prerequisite to a real understanding of the quantitative relations in economic and social life was the unification of statistics, economic theory, and mathematics. Others, such as John R. Hicks,[19] proposed to separate "econometrics," a new science, from mathematical economics, on the one hand, and from economic statistics (social accounting) and genuinely statistical, but not genuinely economic, analysis of economic data on the other. They considered it a bad methodological preconception to attribute vigor and validity to economic laws of the deductive type, based on a priori assumptions and arrived at independently of any reference to empirical human behavior.[20] Hence, they insisted upon using exclusively "operational" concepts, adapted to the setting of practical economic problems, and upon establishing "operationally meaningful" theories which could be tested in the light of statistical experience.[21] But this postulate was frequently ignored.

Identifying mathematics with the rules of deductive logic and statistics with the rules of inductive logic, Jacob Marschak characterized econometrics as the application of inductive logic to economics.[22] George L. Shackle qualified econometrics as attempts to write equations with actual numerical values assigned to the parameters.[23] At least twenty definitions of econometrics were advanced over the course of time. They differed according to the emphasis placed on problems of measurement, on statistical methods, and on the combination of economic theory, mathematics, and statistics.[24] Eventually, some agreement was reached on defining econometrics as a special type of economic analysis in which the general theoretical approach, often explicitly formulated in mathematical terms, is combined—frequently through the medium of intricate statistical procedures—with empirical measurements of economic phenomena.[25]

Ragnar Frisch initiated the search for procedures adapted to the task of constructing econometric models of the economy.[26] In his "pendulum" model the fluctuating movement was brought about by erratic shocks of even frequency distribution which were propagated by processes of interconnected changes in certain sets of economic relations. He pointed out sequence analysis as a method of showing how, in markets which are not organized, the values of the variables are gradually adjusted to changes in the data. Such analysis was to be based on definite assumptions concerning the economic attitude of those who are engaged in the task of discovering differences between the quantities of goods available and the quantities demanded.[27] "Structural data," or measured quantities, were needed to characterize the theoretical model of the economy. As used in this connection, the term *structural* was designed to cover a set of numerically known constants which determine changes in independent variables and are included in the equations defining the model.[28] The effects of increased cash balances during expanding business activities and of the acceleration principle served as shocks to start indigenous cyclical movements.[29] The length of the cycles and their tendency toward "damping" were connected with the "structure" of the system, the intensity of the fluctuations and their amplitude were related to factors affecting the system from outside. Appropriate mathematical operations permitted Frisch to take account of both the tendency to regularity and the tendency to irregularity which are characteristic of the fluctuating behavior of the economy. These ideas were elaborated by Paul Samuelson, who combined the effects of the multiplier and the acceleration principle to produce models of steady growth, of cyclical movements, and of equilibrating processes, depending on the size of the coefficient of acceleration, the choice of the consumption function, and the introduction of appropriate lags between the receipt of incomes and their disbursement.[30]

The great step which led to the construction of econometric models of specific national economies was taken by Jan Tinbergen. He conceived of the irregular movements "which we are accustomed to call business cycles" as the result of the cooperation of essentially two factors: a "mechanism capable of performing characteristic cyclical movements," and "exogenous shocks" as initial movers.[31] In his study of American business cycles, he attempted to adjust the construction of his model as closely as possible to the actual behavior of the American economy. His use of lags enabled him to characterize business fluctuations as a normal attribute of the model; he analyzed the cycles in terms of deviations from a trend, and connected two main aggregates, national income and demand, through appropriate assumptions concerning the reactions of demand to changes in income. In order to account for the lags in the adjustment processes of the system, he endeavored to give mathematical precision to the reactions of groups of individuals or firms to changes in prices, income, and the like. Profit provided incentives for investment, and behavior parameters provided the instruments for propagating cyclical movements produced by external disturbances. This model, in which about fifty relations were established among seventy different economic factors, became a paragon for the treatment of some important aspects of econometric business cycle analysis: the definition of the "systematic terms" of the equations (indigenous changes and explanatory values), the determination of the mechanism involved in the mutual adjustment of the variables, and the interpretation of the cumulative processes initiated by the disturbances of equilibrium positions.[32]

About ten years later, Lawrence R. Klein constructed a more elaborate model of a similar type. He introduced sixteen endogenous variables[33] to determine the functional relationships between the elements of the American economy and added thirteen exogenous variables which were assumed to influence the behavior of the economy without being determined by the processes described in the model. Less designed to explain the origin and behavior of business cycles than to supply an instrument for forecasting purposes, this model was to be revised every year. A new model of the American economy was published by Klein and Arthur S. Goldberger in 1955, and similar models were constructed for some other countries.[34]

Current and more simplified statistical observations of the behavior of national economies were suggested by the expectation that forecasting the numerical development of certain relevant economic variables might be facilitated by studying the behavior of some economic reaction coefficients. The difficult problem of timing appropriate measures of economic policy would thus be approached from the econometric angle, and research of this kind was effectively organized in several countries by statistical institutions headed by outstanding scholars. Such institutes were established at Oslo (for Norway), at The Hague (for the Netherlands), at Cåmbridge (for the United Kingdom), at Paris (for France), and at Vienna (for Austria).

These efforts received theoretical support from Tinbergen's studies of the effects of measures of economic policy or "political parameters." In a growth model of the economy, he distinguished instrumental variables which can be influenced directly, endogenous variables which can be influenced indirectly, and data which are beyond the reach of the decision maker.[35] The model was required to include as many independent equations as endogenous variables. One of the main problems consisted in defining the conditions for a mutual compatibility of the economicopolitical targets.

Economists and statisticians competed with each other in clarifying the methods to be used in preparing econometric models. Various techniques, suggested, above all, by Haavelmo and Tjalling C. Koopmans, were designed to provide a priori procedures for drawing inferences from statistical observation and for assessing the precision achieved by these procedures.[36] Three instruments of statistical thinking were considered prerequisite to the selection of a group of admissible hypotheses—to be followed by the selection of one specific hypothesis or the choice of a "structure," that is to say, a minimum of information about numerically known constants defining the relations between relevant economic magnitudes. The "identification problem" to be solved by the statistician consisted in determining whether the evidence used to select the final hypothesis could be considered consistent with at most one hypothesis.[37]

Three instruments of statistical analysis were particularly important. The theory of testing hypotheses was suggested by Jerzi Neyman and E. S. Pearson, the theory of estimation was developed by Ronald A. Fisher, and the theory of decision making was proposed by Abraham Wald. Other refinements of statistical techniques were achieved in the fields of sampling and "design of experiments," in which the observer can influence the number and character of the observations.

Fundamental to the application of these techniques were the assumptions that there exists a stable universe and that the available observations can be interpreted in accordance with a probability law or stochastic processes about which some incomplete knowledge is available a priori.[38] The Cowles Commission for Research in Economics spent considerable effort on the development of new procedures for defining appropriate "structures" of economic models.

Some differences are of view arose as to the distribution of the functions among those participating in the elaboration of econometric models. Koopmans recommended a more or less clear separation between the jobs of the economists responsible for devising the theoretical framework of the models and the statisticians to be charged with the task of implementing this framework in the light of available statistical material and with the task of testing the underlying assumptions as to their compatibility with actual facts.[39] But Leontief protested against Koopmans's emphasis on the logical consistency of the theoretical approach to business cycle analysis.[40] In his view, primary importance was to be attached to the "effective operational relationship of the theory to observed facts" and to the "conceptual stratification of amorphous statistical material." He insisted on the need for intensified statistical research into economic relationships, and assigned to the economist primary responsibility for translating his problems into mathematically manageable symbolic terms and for making appropriate use of special tools developed in the spheres of applied mathematics and statistical techniques. In accordance with this view, the quantitative approach to economic analysis was to be reserved for economists perfectly familiar with the use of statistical material and the application of advanced statistical procedures.[41]

In such discussions, a sharp light was cast on the significance of a trend which was tending to determine the future of economics as an exact science. This trend, its general character, and its possible effects on the development of economics were the object of varying interpretations.[42] Convinced advocates of econometrics insisted that the abstract language of mathematics imposes the necessity of formulating unambiguous concepts and of presenting exact reasons for divergent results derived from different assumptions.[43] Their claim met with the consideration that the use of broad definitions, though giving "spurious" exactness to the mathematical presentation, could permit the symbols to fit a wide variety of concepts. Moreover, inexactness of the definitions could lead to the use of the same symbol for what are significantly different concepts.[44]

John M. Clark and George Stigler did not question the advantages resulting from the application of mathematics to economics. However, they requested that the mathematical methods used in economic investigations be translated into words so that those not trained in advanced mathematics would be able to understand the significance of the econometric studies.[45]

Some fundamental methodological objections were raised to various econometric procedures which were designed to bridge the gap between abstract, but logically consistent, pictures of the economy and the representation of "economic reality." Schumpeter qualified mathematical models of economic relations as sterile, and argued that one and the same behavior of time series of economic variables could be accounted for analytically in a number of ways and that statistical material did not provide reliable instruments for verifying the results of deductive processes, since its constituent elements were exposed to many disturbing influences.[46] Hence, he insisted upon restricting the function of historical and statistical facts to the role of determining the pattern of the theoretical analysis. Such skepticism was shared by other economists, who criticized the more or less arbitrary assumptions used in constructing econometric models. They objected to the logical isolation of the fluctuations, to the methods adopted for separating cyclical from secular forces, and to the principle of ignoring all factors which cannot readily be cast into a quantitative form.[47]

Some advocates of econometric models did not claim for these models the merit of increasing our ability to explain or to predict business fluctuations. They admitted that their equations represented only a set of hypotheses as to the possible functioning of certain "economies." They realized that a high correlation coefficient between dependent and independent variables might be due to the influence of variables not included in the model.[48] Herman O. R. Wold emphasized this varying nature of many of the factors which render econometric analysis complex and difficult.[49] He warned against placing overoptimistic hopes on the development of the econometric methodology. Commenting on cautious statements of this kind, Dennis Holme Robertson ridiculed the "art of predictional arithmetic" and observed, "The proposition that the connection between the variables must sometimes be taken to be stochastic rather than functional, is now the 'dignified way of saying that it is all largely a matter of guess-work after all.' "[50]

At the opening of a session of the Econometric Society held in Kiel in 1955, Frisch protested against the belief that the network of theorems established within the very refined and very abstract field of mathematics would solve the economic problems more or less by itself.[51] He pointed out the "enormous distance" which well-trained, sophisticated mathematicians will have to cover before they reach a point where they would begin to understand the "basic reality of the classics."

In a broad survey of the effects of econometrics on economic theory made in 1958, Haavelmo arrived at the conclusion that the concrete results of the efforts at quantitative measurement often seemed to get worse the more refinement of tools and logical stringency were called into play,[52] and that econometricians have been living in a dream world of large but somewhat superficial and spurious correlations. He characterized "some notions of permanent preference schedules" as the usual starting point of econometric analysis, but added that the only trace left of the whole background structure of intricate complexities could eventually be found in the presumably constant parameters of the net relations between statistically observable data of prices, quantities, etc.[53] Another critical observer found that, as a rule, the econometric models were selected on the basis of their explanatory value rather than on the basis of their predictive power, and that the search for meaningful specified (or interpreted) theories which could stand a chance of being refuted constituted a program of research rather than an achievement.[54]

Koopmans developed similar considerations in a carefully reasoned survey of the logical foundations of economics, the application of mathematical methods to economic research, and problems of the econometric methodology.[55] He qualified economic theory as a sequence of conceptual models that seek to express in simplified form different aspects of an always more complex reality. The difficulties involved in dealing with economic dynamics had been so great that the tools had suggested the assumptions, rather "than the other way around." For the time being, the establishment of a sort of "economic weather station" was to be regarded as the ultimate goal of econometric analysis. Hence, he recommended the use of quarterly or monthly instead of annual statistical data; breakdowns by industry or process in the study of technology, production, and investment; and breakdowns by types of consumers and by commodity class in the study of consumption. Since econometric methodology was still in an early, experimental stage, he proposed to channel the available resources of research into concentrated studies of the specific types of human behavior.

Discussions of this kind have probably helped bring about some changes in econometric analysis. The method of using comprehensive economic aggregates as elements of model building was replaced by the tendency to place more reliance on data concerning production, inventories, and the behavior of prices and wages.[56] Thus, the National

Bureau of Economic Research developed a technique of determining certain economic variables which, in the past, had influenced the course of business fluctuations. The behavior of these series was considered indicative of impending changes in business activity.

In a presidential address delivered in 1956, Haavelmo[57] elaborated the idea that econometric studies had been highly effective in screening economic theories and in making them more specific by confronting them with economic facts. This general "repair work," applied to the logical consistency of theories, had liquidated the battle between "measurement without theory" and "theory without measurement." An important group of problems which could best be treated with mathematical methods had been suggested by period analysis as an element of economic dynamics. New vistas were opened up when important elements of the theory of probability and methods of statistical inference were applied to model building. Hence, the art of formulating models and of rendering them logically valid had made great progress. But, having surveyed these remarkable achievements, Haavelmo conceded that their positive results had been disappointing: the explanatory value of the models had been poor, and their usefulness for purposes of prediction was insignificant. He attributed these shortcomings of the models above all to the lack of a satisfactory economic theory, and pointed out the need to devise new methods of choosing fruitful economic hypotheses.

The theoretical and technical aspects of econometric business cycle analysis did not perceptibly affect the development of extensive statistical research into the flow of incomes and expenditures as a prerequisite of decision making in various fields of economic and financial policies.[58] In the United States, publication of national surveys of financial transactions was integrated with statistical surveys of sources of income and the allocation of income to expenditure and savings.[59] The publication of similar accounts was organized in the Netherlands, Germany, and France.

Theoretical problems were involved in establishing criteria for distinguishing relevant sectors of the economy in accordance with homogeneity of behavior and in determining the influence of the various sectors on inflationary, deflationary, reflationary, or disinflationary movements.[60] Additional problems suggested by the interpretation of these accounts were connected with the adjustment of ex post variables to ex ante situations: with the origin of inflationary and deflationary pressures, with the roles played by the various parts of the monetary and financial mechanism in favoring or restraining initial disturbances, with the definition of the meaning of financial disequilibria, and with the integration of national income accounts and financial statistics for purposes of model building.[61]

Econometric analyses of economic variables have been widely used by many governments to provide dynamic frames of reference for projecting guidelines for the development of the economy.[62] The potential growth of the national economy or of its sectors has been measured, for considerable periods to come, in terms of highly hypothetical assumptions concerning the stability of relevant economic factors such as production and consumption, investment, and price and wage levels. Balance of payments problems have strongly stimulated work of this type in the United States, France, Canada, the Netherlands, Japan, India, Pakistan, Sweden, Israel, and Puerto Rico. In Sweden, the potential development of the economy has been calculated under alternative assumptions concerning government policies and programs.[63] A comprehensive literature has dealt with the problem of directing the development of large, complex economies.[64]

A remarkable counterpart to the dynamically oriented study of the flow of monetary funds was provided by comprehensive research designed to apply the rigid principles of general equilibrium theory to the detailed statistical analysis of the relations between interdependent industries. Termed *input-output analysis*, statistical operations of this kind established "decision models" which could be used to determine the effects of various measures of economic policy on investment activities and to probe the reactions of industrial production to changes in prices or in productive processes.[65]

Leontief, the originator of input-output analysis, developed special statistical techniques for the collection and coordination of data indicating for the various American industries how the output of their activities was allocated among other industries and how their inputs (the productive factors) were obtained from other industries. Thus, the external balance between the various sectors of the national economy was described in terms of supply of and demand for the various kinds of goods and services.[66]

The balanced picture of input-output analysis, as reflected in a system of simultaneous equations, was achieved through many simplifying assumptions, such as constancy of coefficients of production, of relative wages and prices, of technological factors, and the like. The equilibrium principle underlying this analysis had a normative connotation, and the concept of "balanced identities," as applied to the interdependent relations of industries, corresponded to the structure of a centralized planned economy rather than to the behavior of the market economy where the mutual adjustment of supply and demand is brought about by the price mechanism.[67]

Input analysis has many practical applications. It could be used to calculate the compensatory increase in civilian expenditures following a reduction of outlays for armaments, it could be helpful in determining the direct and indirect effects of taxes levied on various industries, it could provide a basis for analyzing the conditions of geographical and industrial sectors of the economy, or it could establish a starting point for models of economic growth.

Although the importance of input-output analysis was widely recognized, objections were raised to various technical aspects of the analysis, such as the method of forming aggregates, the classification of industries, and so on.[68] Moreover, some skeptics observed that account should be taken of institutional and psychological factors when the picture of input-output analysis is extrapolated into the future.

Studies of the relations between quantities of output and various elements of productive input were developed in various directions,[69] and the question was raised whether some dynamic elements could be introduced into Leontief's model.[70] Input-output research on an experimental scale was also undertaken in various European countries, among them the United Kingdom.

When applied to microeconomic relationships, input-output analysis provided a promising starting point for the construction of "conceptual models" designed to examine suitable forms of organizing the allocation of resources in cases in which the choice among appropriate processes is relatively limited and discontinuous treatment offers real advantages. The terms *activity analysis, theory of allocation of resources,* and *linear or mathematical programming* have been used interchangeably to denote the development of rigorously specified optimal economic behavior patterns under certain simplifying assumptions about the dimensions of economic activity. The application of input-output analysis to problems of this type was suggested by R.G.D. Allen and elaborated on by George B. Dantzig and Marshall K. Wood.[71]

Linear models of production are based on the assumption that constant ratios obtain between the inputs and the outputs of each process of production. They have most advantageously been applied in cases in which the quantities of resources are specified or the supply of one or more factors of production is so limited that it is obtainable at constant unit costs only up to a maximum quantity and not at all beyond that quantity. Additional assumptions as to changes in volume and price of inputs were made in order to define the conditions under which increases in output are economically justified.

Since the empirical constants which characterize economic processes can frequently be determined, and since controllable variables can be introduced into the calculations, mathematical programming soon became an important chapter in the theory of business administration. The sphere of economic activity which offered special chances for its successful application included problems of determining optimum product under given purchase and selling prices; machine productivities and capacities; problems of optimum storage, shipment, and distribution of goods; and problems of optional labor allocation.[72] Special attention was paid to the problem of assessing the possibilities and limitations of the price system as a method of allocating resources and to the related problem of developing methods to be used when definition and evaluation of efficiency prices prove to be impossible.

Starting from the application of programming to conditions of static equilibrium, intensive studies by Frisch and others extended the scope of this analysis to "dynamic" problems connected with the interrelation of successive periods of production and to programs of efficient capital accumulation.[73] Thus, close relations were established with the theory of dynamics and with the approach to decision making.

Chapter 41
Theory of Decision Making

THE THEORY OF CHOICE

As mentioned in the preceding chapter, the development of econometrics was perceptibly influenced by the theory of decision making, a borderland among economics, statistics, and psychology. Some students of this theory prefer to use a broader term and to speak of the theory of *choice*, to indicate that unconscious, or at any rate unreflective, choices are also included in the analysis.[1]

The twentieth century was well advanced before due attention was paid to the procedures used by producers and traders, managers of large firms, and other agents of economic processes in deciding on the steps considered necessary or adequate to achieve desired aims. The problems involved in these procedures turned out to be fundamental to the understanding of the functioning of the economy, and a wide variety of logical devices were restored to in order to adjust these problems to scientific analysis. The traditional Ricardian concept of economic decision making as a deterministic process imposed upon producers and traders by the "laws" of a strictly competitive market was found to be utterly inadequate. The dynamic factor of expectations was made an important element of the analysis; principles of probability were applied to analyze a wide range of decision making. These methods were supplemented by statistical research, experimental procedures, and attempts to define the psychological effects of disappointed expectations and to apply a version of "social determinism." Some fundamental problems of decision making were formulated in terms of highly advanced mathematical methods. The results of virtually all prevailing doctrines were challenged when the theory of decision making was pursued to its consequences. Inasmuch as research into the various aspects of decision making is still in progress, my purpose will be served by giving a brief outline of some problems involved in the vast field of psychological and sociological processes.

The principle of "rational behavior" provided the general background for this theory. It was defined as behavior in accordance with some ordering of alternatives in terms of relative desirability.[2] Such behavior was frequently qualified as a normative rather than analytical concept. Over the course of time, it became the object of varying interpretations.

In the relatively rare cases in which conditions of "perfect foresight" obtain, the choice of the decision maker is determined by a rule which implies that the order of his preferences is to be adjusted to the consequences of his actions. Under conditions of uncertainty, however, the consequences of his actions are not completely known at the time the choice must be made, and his order of preferences might be affected by information which is to be secured at the cost of scarce resources.

Ex post analysis and reasoning in terms of the "as if" formula, as combined with the use of *ceteris paribus* clause, were the main instruments applied by Ricardian and post-Ricardian economists to impound any hypothetical elements of decision making and any changes in planning occurring in the market economy. William Stanley Jevons realized the importance of expectations for economic analysis, although he simplified his analysis by assuming that a general tendency to maximize the mathematical expectations of gains prevailed, in other words, the weighted arithmetic means of the utilities, the weight being supplied by the probabilities.[3] A similar interpretation of expectations in terms of measurable utilities was also basic to the theories of welfare economics advanced by Alfred Marshall and Arthur Cecil Pigou, who argued that it is the utility of satisfaction anticipated which guides consumers' choices.

The Paretian indifference and preference analysis was designed to provide a pure theory of choice adapted to the marginalist principles of the school of Lausanne. In their "rational model" of choice, Vilfredo Pareto and his disciples started from conditions of certainty and derived the demand functions from the principle of maximizing utilities through choices among commodity bundles. They took account of relations of complementarity and rivalry between different commodities and used the income nexus to connect all these relations.[4]

Critics of the Paretian methods listed a number of factors apart from prices and incomes which should be included among the determinants of consumers' behavior.[5] They questioned the assumption that the individual is never at a loss to evaluate the importance which he attaches to a particular combination of goods, and pointed out the dependence of one consumer on choices made by others. The development of ex ante analysis was bound to draw the attention of some economists to the role played by expectations in processes of decision making; but Dennis Holme Robertson and the economists of the Stockholm school who adopted this approach treated expectations only implicitly as links between past and present effectively realized data. Various bold assumptions enabled them to synchronize disparate results of decision making. A characteristic instrument of their analyses was the ''registration period,'' in which the intervals between planning and the execution of the plans were adjusted to equal lengths for all economic units. Some intricate problems of decision making were thus made amenable to methods of comparative statics.

Johan Åckerman emphasized the need to establish a close connection between microeconomic decision making and macroeconomic formation of economic aggregates.[6] He objected to the usual method of devising aggregates of economic relationships without regard to the fact that far-reaching conflicts of interest exist between economic units, and that the various units differ greatly as to their influence on price determination and other economic conditions. Hence, he believed that serious methodological errors were involved in the method of synchronizing decisions and actions as if they presented the effects of a sort of overall planning ruled by a unified will.

The risk problem provided another starting point for research into important aspects of decision making. Risks surrounding entrepreneurial activity were frequently discussed in descriptive studies. In the literature dealing with insurance problems risks of various types were extensively treated from the actuarial angle. The theory of probability supplied the principles for distributing among those exposed to them the burden resulting from calculable risks. Frank H. Knight is to be credited with having formulated the risk problem as a determinant element of decision making.[7] In his attempt to develop a sort of dynamic theory of profit, he contributed greatly toward clarifying some fundamental aspects of economic behavior.[8] He applied the term *risk* to cases which are amenable to a priori statistical probabilities in evaluating events to come or the future effects of actions or nonactions. He supplemented this definition by contrasting the probabilistic features of risks with situations of ''uncertainty'' which are in some sense unique and objects of two judgments: an estimate in which events to come are evaluated, and another judgment concerning the reliability of this estimate. As seen by Knight, the existence of uncertainties had been a major factor in promoting the development of the free enterprise system.[9]

In the discussions of decision making under conditions of uncertainty, primary attention was paid to the definition of suitable methods of securing optimum use of available complex information[10] and of ''rationalizing'' decision making in private and public life. However, widely divergent views developed as to the methodological aspects of this issue.

Some authors of post-Keynesian ''dynamic cycle'' theories pointed out conflicting interests of investors and different degrees of certainty shown by investors in their estimates of their future liquidity requirements.[11] The definition of some economic aggregates was adjusted to the idea that certain price movements (of securities, agricultural products, and the like) reflect a sort of consensus of expectations.[12] Theoretical discussions of this kind started from the observation that the existence of a ''general bias'' in market expectations could be accounted for by the influence of risk premiums.[13] Conservative bias was differentiated from exaggerative bias, and some attempts were made to devise methods to define the ''necessary'' inaccuracy in market expectations.

Analysts of decision making went to considerable effort to devise methods of measuring the probable incidence of future events when normal statistical procedures failed to provide a solution. Their distinction between ''subjective'' and ''objective'' probability was derived from the consideration that there exists a risk preference function which indicates how the individual evaluates his probability distribution of utility under conditions of subjective risk.[14] Situations of this type were contrasted with others in which a certain objectivity can be attributed to estimates of the probability for happenings to which frequency ratios of some kinds of repetitive event appear to be applicable. Harold Hotelling proposed to apply the term *probability* exclusively to cases of the objective type and to speak of cases of *credibility* when hypotheses concerning future events are related to uncertain conclusions.[15]

The problems involved in treating objective and subjective probabilities were approached from two angles. Adherents of the "frequency theory of probabilities," such as Jerzi Neyman, E. S. Pearson, and Abraham Wald,[16] used frequency rates of repetitive events to determine their occurrence objectively. Another procedure was adopted by the school of "subjective probability," which tried to establish a link between utility and probability. The members of this school started with the assumption that the decision maker is motivated by the objective of maximizing the expected utility value of the gains which could possibly be derived from uncertain events. They distinguished two types of uncertainty: one related to the probability implied in the assignment of a hypothesis to a certain class or model, the other to the probability distribution of future events or observations associated with the hypothesis. Hence, in the planning mind, each venture or asset was held to be represented by a probability distribution involving the assignment of a numerical probability to each hypothesis about the gain or loss which will finally be experienced when the venture is wound up.[17] In order to determine the valuation of capital assets on the basis of the risks and uncertainties involved, it was consequently assumed that the entrepreneurs constructed, at least tacitly, a sort of probability distribution of the prospective earnings and calculated their risk premium accordingly.[18] Albert G. Hart, who analyzed the planning of the firm, assumed that a businessman's knowledge about his contingencies can be adjusted to insurance principles, and that the businessman will maximize his net receipts over a period embracing as many decisions as possible.[19] But the authors of such decision models conceded that drastic approximations were needed to bring real-life choices within the reach of maximizing techniques.

Milton Friedman and Leonard J. Savage suggested an "expected utility" hypothesis to establish a connection between economic behavior adjusted to choices among alternatives regarded as certain and economic behavior in cases involving risk.[20] This hypothesis was based on the assumption that there exists some utility which corresponds to each uncertain alternative and that individuals seek to maximize expected utilities. An income which is equal to the utility expected to result from its expenditure was qualified as the "certainty equivalent."

Kenneth J. Arrow followed Hart in emphasizing the dynamic aspects of decision making, and developed a "general possibility theorem" as applied to problems of choice.[21] This theorem was designed to establish alternative criteria of choice, to analyze the empirical flexibility of the criteria, and to define·their inner consistency.[22] In a subsequent paper Arrow applied his analysis of decision making to the purposes of public policy.[23] He qualified public policies as "sequential" and "uncertain," since the decisions made in one period affect those to be made in the next, and since the model of the economy does not permit perfect predictability. The collection of information was to be adjusted to different concepts of time (sequential, computational, or cumulative). Increased and well-organized information could be expected to reduce the scope of arbitrary decision making.

But the ambitious concept of a "general theory" of maximizing utilities was open to the objection that only a limited set of variables can be optimized.[24] Doubts were cast on the proposition that expected utilities can be the object of reliable measurements,[25] since uncertainty introduces into the realm of decision making a "qualitatively new dimension" and since changing wants and unpredictable events cannot be adjusted to the calculus. This calculus was said to be applicable only in cases in which ignorance about single events and knowledge about groups of events can be joined together in a single statement, whereas it is "commoner in economics to have ignorance about both."[26]

G. L. Shackle was one of the most outspoken critics of the attempts to apply probability analysis to a wide range of cases marked by uncertainty.[27] He argued that it is impossible to determine the probable effects of a decision when no frequency ratios can be established through divisible seriable experiments and when the decision to be made is unique for each individual. Adopting an outright psychological approach to the theory of choices under uncertainty, he defined expectations as anticipations of future situations which can be arranged on a scale measuring the degree of the planner's belief that a specific action on his part will make the desired situation come true. In order to determine a person's degree of belief in two different outcomes of some course of action, Shackle proposed to imagine the intensity of shock or surprise felt by the planner upon hearing that his anticipation had been false. The degree of "potential surprise" would be greater, the more extreme had been the outcome contemplated. As elements of decision making, Shackle listed certain "intervening variables," such as the subjective valuation of the outcome, a preference pattern of the decision maker (the gambler's preference for speculative purchases of assets), the effects of taxation on investments, the behavior in cases of bilateral monopolies, and the like. The importance which he attached to uncertainty as an economic factor was reflected in his view that interest on capital is to be regarded as a manifestation of uncertainty. But his proposal to exclude all elements of probability from the theory of decision making was not left unchallenged.[28]

Shackle's attack on the theories of decision making was supported with similar arguments by some French authors. Maurice Allais believed that the American school of probability theorists, as represented by the words of Friedman, Savage and Jacob Marschak, had committed the error of neglecting the "dispersal of psychological values."[29] He pointed out that distributions with "smaller variance" would be preferred by the prudent decision maker, while the gambler favors risk taking. He defined "rationality" vaguely as preference ordering of the field of choice, and insisted on the use of objective probability where available. The problem of rationality, as connected with the theory of choice, was attacked from another angle by Maurice Fréchet, who drew a distinction between rational and irrational probabilities.[30] D. van Dantzig rejected the search for optimal but fictitious solutions to the problem of decision making; he challenged the role assigned to utility analysis in the theory of choice and qualified as "unrealistic" the axioms of the theory of subjective probability.[31]

In the course of these discussions, it became increasingly apparent that the problems of decision making had been oversimplified when strenuous attempts were made to extend the applicability of the probability calculus to a wide range of cases beset with uncertainties. Particularly misleading were the assumptions that actual behavior could be identified with "rational behavior" and that others' irrational behavior played no role in influencing the planning of the decision maker.[32] The theory of decision making was thus deprived of a promising avenue of research.

THE THEORY OF GAMES

A new chapter in the history of decision making was opened in 1944 with the publication of *Theory of Games*, by John von Neumann and Oskar Morgenstern.[33] The remarkable achievement of this work was that it elaborated a theory of "multipersonal choices" dealing with economic situations in which choices made by different individuals are characterized by mutual dependency. The economic situations covered by this theory were assigned to the sphere of "nonprobabilistic uncertainty" and were shown to be similar to those which confront the participants of certain games of strategy in which the players can fix only certain variables. The methods used were derived from branches of advanced mathematics, and the scientific bearing of this work was commonly believed to be far greater than the significance of the immediate purposes it was intended to serve.

According to the principles adopted by the school of Lausanne, the use of mathematical methods was limited to the task of providing condensed expression in symbol form for theorems established by deductive reasoning. Consequent upon the introduction of econometric methods, the application of advanced mathematical procedures was extended to the construction of models designed to achieve the closest possible approach to reality. The theory of games had "revolutionary" effects, however, as its authors undertook to adjust methods of advanced mathematics to the objective of formulating new concepts and new problems and to derive new theorems from these concepts. This aspect of the theory opened the prospect of making economics and mathematical economics homogeneous at a certain stage of development.[34]

A striking analogy was found to exist between the strategies of players participating in games of chance and the procedures of marketing pursued in certain economic situations, above all in cases in which monopolists of various types either are acting alone or are taking advantage of "cooperation" with some competitors. In order to facilitate the formidable task of adjusting decision making under conditions of nonprobabilistic uncertainty to mathematical treatment, the authors of the theory of games made some simplifying assumptions.[35] As a first approximation they adopted the static approach on the ground that a theoretical "game of strategy" is bounded by time. But they introduced into their analysis certain dynamic elements, such as varying anticipations and negotiations about mutual understandings of the partners in a game.

The "constant-sum" character of the games (including the "zero-sum" case) was another simplifying assumption. In games of this kind a given sum is to be divided among the participants, and only their relative shares are significant; the additional assumption that the sum of the shares might amount to zero means that a diversity of interest exists among the parties participating in the distributive processes.

A radical change of the methods used in analyzing decision making was introduced by the assumption that, instead of trying to maximize utilities, each partner in a game (or each competitor in a market) adopts a strategy that yields a minimal gain at least as high and possibly higher than the minimal gain which could be expected to result from any other strategy. This assumption, termed the *minimax principle*, pointed out the intention to minimize maximal loss or risk, as distinct from the tendency to maximize minimal gain. Abraham Wald had suggested a similar formula: he assumed that an individual will order the consequences of his actions according to a rule which implies that he chooses that action which under the alternative hypotheses maximizes the minimum return.

Another significant methodological device was introduced by drawing a distinction between essential and nonessential games. Participants in nonessential games were assumed to be unable to modify their shares in the outcome of the game. In a modern economy the prevailing conditions are obviously favorable to situations that are analogous to essential games, as is shown by the spread of trade associations, cartel agreements, mergers, and interlocking directorates.

In certain well-defined two-person games, determinate solutions were found to result from the use of "rational strategies." When one of two players reveals his minimax strategy, the other cannot do any better than to use his corresponding strategy. The two strategists meet at the so-called saddle point and have a tendency to stay at this point in an equilibrium position. In other cases, the minimum profits of the partners in a two-person game do not add up to the maximum attainable. The area of indeterminacy can be measured by the residual, and the skill of the superior partner decides the allocation of the difference. In situations of this kind, "offensive" strategies appear to be inapplicable.

Starting from relatively simple models of two-person games, Neumann and Morgenstern developed a considerable variety of more complex problems marked by conflicting interests and the application of "mixed strategies" involving the introduction of elements of chance into decision making. The distribution of the shares among the participants and the definition of the sums of the shares were qualified as elements of processes of "imputation," whereas the "rules of the game," the background against which the transactions are performed, were considered formalized in the "characteristic functions." The problems to be solved consisted of selecting out of the range of processes of imputation those processes which are consistent with the rules of "rational" behavior. It was shown that decision making of this kind involved intricate questions, such as entrance into combinations and alliances implying the threat of defection, payment of compensation, and the like. A clear definition of "rational behavior" appears to have been possible only in the case of the zero-sum two-person game; when the principle of rationality and the equilibrium principle conflict, one of the principles has to be sacrificed.

In the course of analyzing rational behavior in accordance with the theory of games, the authors of this theory abandoned the definition of "utility" as a psychological concept adopted by marginalist schools in favor of a behaviorist approach. They availed themselves of the proposition that "measurement is always invented, never discovered,"[36] and they qualified the concept of "utility" as a measurable variable and applied to it arbitrary measures subject to certain conditions. Backed by their methodological approach to decision making, they gained a firm foothold for a critical analysis of the Walrasian model of the economy as ruled by the principle of counting equations and unknowns and as based on simple maximum calculations applied to the behavior of firms and consumers. The methods used by the school of Lausanne were shown to be utterly inadequate to solve the problems involved in the functioning of the exchange economy.

The theory of games initiated an extensive literature. The various mathematical and logical aspects of the theory were explored; its importance for the development of economics was critically examined. Distinguished economists such as Roy F. Harrod and Ferdinand Zeuthen endorsed the proposal to disregard the psychological aspects of utility and to apply cardinal numbers to the measurement of utilities.[37] Utility analysis could thus be adjusted to the problems of dynamic economics.

But other economists raised the question of whether the concept of "utility" was likely to provide an appropriate object of choice within a theoretical analysis of rational behavior. They proposed to apply the principle of maximizing to other variables (such as minimal expected gain, or some weighted average of the maximal and minimal expected gains, and the like), combined with the proviso that there must not exist another strategy promising a better or a worse outcome (the principle of admissibility).[38] According to this view, the theory of games was to be interpreted not in terms of measured utilities but exclusively in terms of monetary magnitudes.[39]

Much attention was paid to "minimax" solutions applied to certain two-person games because it permitted a clear definition of the rationality of the players and could lead to an equilibrium position. Some discussions dealt with the strategy to be pursued when more than two people participate in the game. The development of operation research was strongly influenced by the theory of games. Intricate problems of decision making are involved when those opposed to each other in an economic situation have simultaneously both common and opposite interests.[40] Some attempts were even made to devise complex mathematical methods for the treatment of "preference structures" which, because of their nonquantitative nature, do not permit numerical representation.[41]

Several logicians proposed to interpret the solutions offered by the theory of games in terms of normative rather than behaviorist propositions. They doubted whether the perfectly rational individual envisaged by this theory could ever be found in reality. However this question is answered, the authors of this theory can claim the merit of having opened up a vast field of research extending far beyond the scope of their analysis. In the field of economics a new methodological approach was secured to the study of oligopolistic decision making and the formulation of market policies under conditions of imperfect competition.

These efforts to establish reliable theoretical foundations for analyzing economic behavior were supplemented by various studies designed to ascertain, through experience and observation, the actual behavior of producers and consumers in deciding upon their plans and the execution of their plans.[42] These studies were carried out in support of different fields of research, such as "management science, engineering economics, operation research," and the like. Moreover, techniques of experimental testing were developed to verify various hypotheses concerning economic behavior under certain well-defined conditions.[43] The results of these investigations were expected to facilitate the analysis of such behavior and to provide guidelines for the application of monetary and fiscal policies.

Concluding Observations

——

THE PRECEDING DISCUSSIONS attempted to provide an answer to a question raised by various economists: why are continuous and intensive efforts being spent on elaborating and teaching the history of economic thought, whereas the history of the natural sciences has been conceived of as an integral part of the general development of scientific reasoning and has never been made a constituent element of academic curricula? The special position assigned to the history of economic thought has been due to the fact that economics, along with other social sciences, has been the arena of ever-renewed struggles of antagonistic patterns of thought. Widely divergent interpretations have thus been applied to the term *economics;* no agreement has been reached as to the formulation of fundamental economic problems and the choice of appropriate methods for treating these problems. Under these circumstances, no full understanding of economic problems and their analysis can be achieved unless account is taken of their historical setting.

According to the prevailing view, the thinking of the economists has been influenced primarily by their endeavor to answer the burning problems of their day. The general validity of this view is open to serious doubt; on closer examination, it appears that at least the methods used by the various schools of economics were determined by general intellectual movements which developed independently of any economic conditions and relationships.

Scholastic economics were dominated by medieval moral theology; the adoption of a version of nominalistic reasoning by a group of Franciscan monks provided the initial stages for the mercantilistic approach to economic problems. Ricardo borrowed a mechanistic system concept from the natural sciences and applied the equilibrium principle to the relations between economic variables at a time when the "industrial revolution" could be expected to throw dynamic evolutionary problems into the center of economic thought.

The static conception of the economy prevailed for over a century in the Anglo-Saxon countries in spite of its incompatibility with the results of daily experience. The emergence of marginalist theories was exclusively due to an intellectual movement and cannot be accounted for by the incidence of economic events. The approach to economic analysis adopted by the German historical school was not connected with the special conditions of the German economy, but bears the marks of the teachings of the "idealistic" philosophers. Of course, socialist authors derived their inspiration from problems of their times, but they had to rely on outside sources in choosing their methods.

As has happened several times before, economic thought appears to have arrived at a crossroad after the middle of the present century. This is true of the communist version of economic planning, as well as of the pattern of economic reasoning prevailing in Western industrialized countries. Bolshevist politicians have resorted to tortuous redefinitions and interpretations of the Marxist doctrine in order to adapt the concepts and theorems of "dialectic materialism" to the aim of justifying the objectives of national power politics and to the task of transforming a predominantly agricultural economy into a highly industrialized one. Time and again, Soviet economists have been officially reprimanded for lack of courage and ingenuity in establishing a satisfactory Bolshevist economic doctrine. Stalin's successors finally appear to have forsaken the belief that the "laws" underlying the organization of the socialist economy can be discovered with absolute finality when the methods of dialectic materialism are properly applied.

The process of reformulating an allegedly irrefutable doctrine has reached a stage in which the endeavor to develop a rational economic policy has resulted in the elimination of some untenable elements of the communist creed, such as the proposition that interest on capital is incompatible with the principles of socialist planning. Account has been taken of the concept of the "market" when at least a limited role has been assigned to supply and demand as determinants of prices. Increasing recognition has been given to the profit motive as an incentive to remedy inefficient plant management. But considerations of power policy have remained a predominant factor in determining the investment policy of the Politburo.

It is a moot question whether the belief in the final breakdown of the "capitalist economy" will be preserved as a constituent part of the Marxist-Leninist mythology, in spite of a prolonged period of "coexistence." But in the course of all post-Stalinist reinterpretations of the Marxist doctrine, the unified structure of Bolshevist planning has been undermined by the tendency of some communist countries of Eastern Europe to adopt methods of their own in planning their economies and to intensify their contacts with the Western world. Repeated attempts by the Soviet government to create a closely knit economic bloc of communist countries met with failure.

Even more striking has been the break in Western economic reasoning in the aftermath of the Second World War. Organismic reasoning ceased to play a significant role in the regions of Central and Southern Europe where it had provided the logical background for nationalistic power policies and for the adjustment of the economies to the objectives of these policies.

Toward the end of the thirties, some enthusiastic adherents of the Keynesian theory of employment hailed that theory as a revolutionary event in the history of economic reasoning. Their claim proved to be unjustified, although the stimulating effects of the Keynesian analysis should not be minimized. In England and, above all, in the United States that analysis initiated lively and promising intellectual movements, introduced the "macroeconomic" approach to economic analysis, and provided a theoretical background for an active economic policy. But far more important in its lasting effects on economic reasoning was the increasing influence of a philosophical trend which centered on the proposition that thinking in terms of magnitudes is prerequisite to any formulation of theoretical problems and that the use of refined mathematical procedures is indispensable to the advancement of any science. Thus, mathematical techniques were adjusted to the tasks involved in establishing schemes of input-output analysis and of linear programming; such techniques were widely used in devising dynamic macroeconomic models of the economy. Probabilistic and nonprobabilistic methods were applied to the development of theories of pure choice and decision making. The adherents of the econometric movement endeavored to elaborate new mathematical and statistical techniques designed to provide realistic pictures of the functioning of specific national economies. Leading representatives of that movement did not deny the need for abstract theoretical considerations as the starting point of any economic research. But they insisted upon adjusting their scientific tools to such magnitudes as can be expressed in time series of statistical figures; they questioned the usefulness of any theory that cannot be tested in the light of statistical experience and does not open the way for the establishment of reliable forecasting procedures.

In the course of these developments, the economy became the object of a bewildering diversity of interpretations. That situation can best be illustrated by surveying some attempts to account for the fluctuating behavior of the economy. Business cycles were analyzed in terms of purely mechanical theories based on some oversimplified assumptions concerning the effects of individual economic behavior. They were explained as the result of disturbances inflicted from outside on the functioning of the economy dominated by equilibrating tendencies, and they were ascribed to mistaken credit policies which lead to the overexpansion of certain sectors of economic activity. They were qualified as the movement of oscillations around a definable trend and regarded as an inherent element of economic growth. In accordance with a strictly mechanical interpretation of the relationships between economic magnitudes, the fluctuations were attributed to external or internal shocks propagated through the reactions of various elements of the system. Finally, it was suggested to replace the search for a general business cycle theory with a combination of several theories adjusted to the varying course of economic events. Business fluctuations were also interpreted as the result of random variations of economic factors which defy the research for laws or regularities.

For lack of a unified economic theory, it became common practice to pursue research into special topics more or less independently of their connection with related problems. Specialization and departmentalization of economic analysis and teaching assumed increasing proportions, especially in the United States, and considerable progress was made in adjusting various techniques—particularly statistical procedures—to the treatment of specific problems.

Paramount among the specific fields to be treated by statistical procedures has been the construction of econometric models of specific national economies. These models have been designed to serve purposes of prediction and to facilitate the application of measures of economic policies. Hence, special emphasis has been placed upon including in the models those variables that can be used to implement such measures. Econometric treatment of the general features of national economies has been supplemented by studies dealing with specific fields of investigation which lend themselves to statistical operations such as the monetary flow, savings and investments, and the like. A broad sphere of dynamic aspects of the various economies has thus been opened up to economic research.

The prospect of stabilizing the behavior of the exchange economy has been considerably enhanced in the second half of this century. Owing to the effective application of various measures of economic policies, business cycles of perceptible intensity appear to have been mitigated in some highly industrialized Western countries. In these countries, the behavior of the economy was characterized by a prolonged expansion of business activity interrupted by more or less short-lived "recessions." These periods of slackening activity were qualified as "inventory cycles" or as symptoms of a fundamental instability of the economy. The choice of remedial measures was mainly influenced by the role ascribed to monetary factors in promoting or retarding the course of business activity. Policies derived from the Keynesian approach to monetary analysis were likely to lead to inflationary movements of prices and wages. Hence, conservative economists insisted on preventing any "overheating" of the economy through excessive expansion of credit supply.

Another characteristic feature of the midcentury economicopolitical climate has been a trend toward intensifying international economic cooperation. This trend has manifested itself in attempts to liberalize international trade relations, to establish regional economic communities, and to implement schemes of promoting the economic advancement of underdeveloped countries. Far-reaching international cooperation has been considered indispensable for dealing with the question of how to assure adequate volumes of internationally acceptable reserve currencies. Political considerations have played a major role in the negotiations which have turned on the problem of "international liquidity."

The vigor and zeal displayed in attacking a wide variety of topics are no doubt an encouraging sign of intellectual vitality. But in the long run, no social science can enjoy satisfactory progress unless it is backed by a consistent doctrine which assures the coherence of its divergent parts, especially as viewed from the methodological angle. The establishment of such a doctrine appears to be dependent upon the settlement of a number of controversial issues which, time and again, have been relegated to the background. Issues of that kind are: Can high abstractions be relied upon to provide a sufficient basis for economic theorizing, and can the functioning of the economy be explained in terms of a single general theory? How far can the functioning of the economy be analyzed on the assumption that it is ruled by forces which tend to establish equilibrium positions? Is it justified to conceive of the economy as an outright mechanism and to regard refined mathematical procedures as the primary tools of economic analysis? Is it possible to establish a bridge between microeconomic analysis and analysis in terms of economic aggregates? What methods are available for adjusting the definition of such aggregates to the requirements of theoretical analysis? Is it desirable to take account of psychological and/or sociological factors in constructing models of the economy? Finally, what methods are to be chosen to establish a consistent system of economicopolitical objectives and to adjust economic research to these objectives?

Such a survey of methodological issues leads back to one of the fundamental propositions of my study: that the most significant and lasting changes in the development of economic reasoning were produced by, or were at least intimately connected with, attempts to redefine methods of economic analysis. In the light of that proposition, it appears that struggles of conflicting methodological principles and their application to a science should not be interpreted as a symptom of weakness and indecision; they are indispensable to the advancement of scientific research, and their outcome will play a decisive role in determining the future of economics.

Appendixes

Appendix A
Prolegomena to a History
of Economic Reasoning

—

INTRODUCTION

IT IS ALMOST a truism that the history of economic reasoning is imbedded in the history of Western thought. That relationship has been recognized by various authors, above all by James Bonar in his *Philosophy and Political Economy*. But in more recent times comparatively little attention has been given to the task of elaborating the connections which obviously exist between the emergence and development of the various economic doctrines on the one hand and leading philosophical movements on the other. Either the history of economic ideas has been treated as an isolated proposition, more or less divorced from attendant intellectual movements, or, under the influence of the "economic interpretation of history," main emphasis has been placed on the relationships which were found to exist between the economic conditions prevailing during historical periods and the doctrines advanced for explaining the shape and the course of economic events. Some students of the development of economic thought have even suggested that the various economic doctrines which have gained prominence were intended—deliberately or unconsciously—to rationalize and defend economic interests of specific classes of the population.

Of course, there is no doubt that changes in the emphasis placed on varying economic problems were frequently brought about by structural changes of the economic organization which required explanation in terms of consistent theories. But recognition of this fact is fully compatible with the proposition that, ultimately, the organization of

This essay originally appeared in *The Quarterly Journal of Economics* 65, no. 1 (February 1951).

economic life as well as the theories advanced for explaining the operation of the economic machinery have reflected the principles of reasoning which have determined social and economic behavior.[1] These principles were suggested by leading social philosophers, the educators of the ruling classes of the population. Hence, both the forms of social and economic organization and the fundamental conceptions of economic phenomena can, broadly speaking, be regarded as functions of the same variable, namely, methods of reasoning. Relatively rare have been the cases in which schools of economics have endorsed patterns of thought not generally prevailing in their countries. In the last analysis it has always been a method which has decided the object and the scope of economics as of any other science.

It is obviously no easy task to determine the relationships which are bound to exist between the history of economic reasoning and the history of the development of modes of cognition. There does not exist a ready-made history of the latter development which would provide a scheme for grouping economic doctrines. Such a scheme can, however, at least tentatively be derived from the consideration that the development of Western reasoning has been influenced predominantly by a secular struggle between two divergent conceptions of the intellectual faculties of the human mind. According to one conception, mind has been endowed with the capacity of adjusting its concepts exactly to the real order of outside phenomena. Basic to that conception has been the principle of "identity of thinking and being," according to which the human intellect is able to achieve "full insight" into the nature and essence of things and events with the aid of concepts regarded as eternally valid or at least absolutely valid under certain historical conditions. The term *essentialistic* may be applied to all doctrines whose methods are predominantly determined by that principle.

In polar opposition to the essentialistic patterns of thought stands the "hypothetical" pattern, the adherents of which are inclined to question the real existence of any concepts outside the mind or at least the faculty of the intellect to grasp such concepts. Hence, the methods of hypothetical reasoning have been derived from the belief that all abstract notions are freely formed by the mind in accordance with rules which are likely to differ from those underlying the course of actual events. These methods imply that any attempts to arrive at an understanding of such events must start from assumptions which can be considered the more useful and reliable the better they assist the student in establishing causal or functional relationships between the phenomena under observation and enable him to devise a consistent body of doctrine.

In view of the polar opposition which exists between these two patterns of reasoning, a variety of mixed modes of cognition has developed, uniting elements of both patterns in different combinations. At least a tentative attempt can be made to distinguish and analyze schools of economics with a view to defining the specific methods of thought adopted and observed by their members in their approach to the study of economic phenomena. In the light of that distinction, it can easily be shown why wide divergencies have obtained between the leading schools as to the setting of their problems, and why certain problems which have played a predominant role in the doctrines of some schools have been considered irrelevant and have been disregarded by others.

Subgroups of the main schools can be established when account is taken of differentiation of methods which has frequently occurred within the context of a given pattern. Along with the refinement of epistemological considerations, increasing emphasis has been placed on the system concepts used in coordinating the relationships between economic phenomena; in many cases the system concept explicitly or tacitly chosen by an author can be regarded as indicative of his adherence to a specific school.

Modern history of economic reasoning can conveniently start from Scholastic economics as laid down in the doctrines of St. Thomas Aquinas. These doctrines were based on a rigid essentialistic pattern, commonly termed *universalism*. [2] In the Middle Ages the firm belief in a hierarchical structure of eternally valid general notions found its counterpart in an equally rigid social and economic organization. The medieval era came to a close when that belief was attacked by thinkers who questioned the real existence, outside of the mind, of abstract concepts and claimed for the intellect full freedom to form concepts in accordance with rules of its own. In the course of that secular struggle, mixed patterns of various types emerged in various countries and dominated over longer or shorter periods the thinking of the educated classes. The following survey is designed to indicate how that process was reflected in the development of economic reasoning.

BACONIAN AND CARTESIAN ECONOMICS

Franciscan monks in England and France received from Arabian sources the knowledge of the principles of hypothetical—also termed *nominalistic*—reasoning. Their fight against the Scholastic methods resulted in displacing these methods from the dominant position which they had occupied for almost a thousand years. Increasing groups of educated laymen participated in the endeavor to free the mind from the fetters of the medieval conceptual structure; merchants and bankers were particularly receptive to the hypothetical approach which permitted indefinite expansion of venturesome business activity. In Italy a similar transformation of the medieval economic organization was initiated in the wake of the crusades, after commercial relationships had been established with Greek traders. During the period of the Renaissance, Italy was the main arena of violent struggles between conflicting methods of reasoning. New patterns developed, still mixed with strong elements of Scholasticism. But England appears to have been the only country where, during the sixteenth and seventeenth centuries, hypothetical reasoning secured a strong hold over the minds of the social philosophers and of businessmen.

That reasoning supplied new logical instruments for the study of the relationships between social and economic phenomena. For the most part these instruments were borrowed from the atomistic and mechanistic approach adopted by the natural sciences. The bold idea of using mechanistic conceptions for coordinating social and economic events was among the most outstanding and amazing achievements of hypothetical reasoning. As used by English authors in the seventeenth and eighteenth centuries, the equilibrium concept in its purely mechanical quantitative form tended to supersede the qualitative and normative Scholastic concept of equivalence. [3]

If the views of the considerable group of authors generally referred to by the misleading term *Mercantilists* have anything characteristic in common, it is the continuously intensified application of methods of hypothetical reasoning and, within that context, of the equilibrium concept, in their discussions of economic problems. The progressive isolation of these problems from any considerations connected with other aspects of social life was itself symptomatic of the use of nominalistic methods, since no real existence outside the observer's mind was assigned to the economic sector which was more or less arbitrarily divorced from its intimate relations with all other spheres of human activities.

When reason was denied the power to supply absolutely valid notions, there remained as sources of knowledge primarily observation and experience. That was the gist of the Baconian epistemology. In the second half of the seventeenth century, Sir William Petty endeavored to develop methods designed to render that epistemology applicable to economic investigations. In his *Political Arithmetic* he transformed the teleological qualitative concepts of the Scholastic sociology into measurable magnitudes and prepared the way for thinking in quantitative terms.[4]

Simultaneously, nominalistic reasoning led to the rejection of the Scholastic belief in the real existence of religious or political collectivities independent of the will of their members. In the field of political theory the individualistic doctrine of the social contract was derived from that approach which allotted to the will ascendency over reason. Reason was assigned the subordinate function of teaching the means for achieving objectives prescribed by individual wills or interests. In his analysis of the faculties of the human mind, John Locke, the great protagonist of nominalistic reasoning, successfully undermined the Scholastic clear-cut distinction between good and evil. With his theory of indifference he introduced a new category of morally indifferent actions and motives. Pursuance of self-interest, especially in the economic sphere, could be qualified as morally indifferent, and pursuance of gain for its own sake could be included among morally legitimate forms of conduct.

The theory of the social contract was supplemented and subsequently displaced by the utilitarian philosophy which was derived from the consideration that in the last analysis all social relationships represented an interplay of individual interests. When developed to its consequences, that philosophy resulted in establishing a maximization principle as a fundamental element of individual behavior. When applied to economic activity, that principle was expressed by the formula of striving for maximum gain. In this specific field a quantitative expression could thus be given to an otherwise vaguely defined concept. But the English philosophers of the eighteenth century were deeply concerned about the question of how to establish principles of socially desirable conduct when reason was unable to provide absolutely valid norms for distinguishing between good and bad, true and false notions.

In the course of the cognitive process which led to thinking in quantitative terms, the problem emerged how to reduce to a common denominator all the innumerable phenomena of the exchange economy which found their monetary expression in fluctuating prices.

The value theory of the Mercantilists was an outcome of the logical requirements imposed by thinking in terms of the equilibrium concept. Their theory was still strongly influenced by the substance concept of the goods which had been a backbone of Scholastic economics. The substance concept implied a distinction between the "essential attributes" of a good and its purely "accidental" characteristics. The Scholastics had derived one of the essential attributes of the goods—their "intrinsic goodness"—from the utility of the class or genus to which the things belonged in accordance with a pre-established classification of all things and beings. From the outset they were faced with the so-called paradox of value—the much-discussed fact that the price or exchange value of a thing did not reflect the utility attributed to the class. That problem was met as early as the sixteenth and seventeenth centuries by some Italian economists, who pointed to scarcity relationships as a determinant of exchange values.

The English Mercantilists, however, apart from a few exceptions, clung tenaciously to the idea of expressing the "inner goodness" of the things in quantitative terms, in terms of a denominator to which all values could be reduced. Sir William Petty appears to have been the first to wrestle with the problem of how to define a standard of value common to all goods. As a rule, John Locke is credited with the idea of deriving that standard from the amount of labor spent in producing the goods. It is likely that the choice of that standard was suggested by a principle of explanation which in the mercantilist period was used by students of the natural sciences in order to account for measurable qualities of things. They derived the unit of measurement from a force believed to be responsible for producing the quality. The "phlogiston" theory was an outstanding example of that reasoning. Since labor was considered the force which was predominant in producing the things, it appeared quite reasonable to attribute to that force the functions of producing the value of the things and to provide the standard for measuring values. Locke's theory of "objective" value soon superseded the Scholastic qualitative definition of the value concept. His theory was accepted by the majority of mercantilist authors and suggested the idea that the general behavior of the exchange values was largely independent of the influence of monetary factors. Combined with the equilibrium concept, the labor cost theory permitted a more refined formulation of the balance of trade doctrine; it provided the basis for the quantity theory of money, for various explanations of interest on money, and eventually for a theory concerning the international distribution of the monetary metals. It is a remarkable fact that the view which rendered labor responsible for the creation of exchange values maintained a dominant position in economic reasoning for several generations after the natural sciences had completely abandoned the belief in the power of forces to create measurable qualities of the things.

In pursuance of the mechanistic approach to the understanding of economic phenomena, the Mercantilists adopted also the Baconian advice to replace the scholastic teleological approach by the search for causal connections. The search for such connections was predicated upon the belief in the existence of automatic forces operating in the economic sector independently of the will of the individuals. That belief was explicitly expressed by Sir William Petty and subsequently emphasized by various mercantilist authors. It found its first consistent application in Hume's refutation of the traditional balance of trade policy. He described the price mechanism as a self-regulating force determining the allotment of the monetary metals among the trading nations. Hume's contemporary, Richard Cantillon, extended the use of nominalistic concepts and methods considerably beyond the range of their customary application. He outlined a scheme for the mutual relationships of productive and distributive activities, applied the equilibrium concept to cost-price relationships, and ventured to support his theoretical considerations with fully constructed hypothetical cases.

In turn, reliance upon the principles of causality provided a strong logical support for the demand of merchants and bankers that their business be left free from government interference. The attitude of these businessmen was increasingly ruled by the principle that, in the last analysis, rational economic behavior should consist in choosing from among available alternatives and should be ruled by assumptions as to probable conditions of markets. Thus, during the mercantilist period, the way was prepared for the so-called industrial revolution by the abandonment of the rigid Scholastic conceptual system which had imposed strict rules of economic conduct.

German economists of the historical school have taken great pains to define the "spirit of capitalism" predominantly in terms of moral characteristics. On closer examination, it appears that the spread of capitalistic modes of production and distribution was primarily due to the increasing application of hypothetical methods of thinking to economic behavior.

The gradual process of that logical transformation of medieval economic ideas could be demonstrated by analyzing the changes which took place in practically all fields of business activity. The revolution of the price system which occurred in the wake of the influx of gold and silver provided a strong support for the tendencies which had been inaugurated in England and France by changes in the prevailing patterns of thought. These changes manifested themselves particularly in the spheres of banking and finance. They found their most striking expression in the roles assigned to velocity of circulation and credit by imaginative thinkers such as John Law.[5] In order to appreciate the logical aspects of John Law's scheme, it may be recalled that about fifty years prior to its realization the protagonists of hypothetical reasoning had still been engaged in a prolonged struggle over the prohibition of usury, one of the most tenaciously defended bastions of Scholastic reasoning.

In Spain, however, where the firm hold of the Church over social life had prevented hypothetical reasoning from achieving any perceptible influence upon business activity, the medieval structure of the economy was scarcely affected by the acquisition of the treasures of the Incas and the exploitation of the silver mines of Mexico. Wide prospects for commercial and industrial ventures were left unutilized, and the material welfare of the Spanish population was reduced rather than increased by the influx of the precious metals, which were quickly spent on imported luxury goods.

On the other hand, the emergence of the Physiocratic doctrine is likely to indicate that even in the middle of the eighteenth century hypothetical reasoning had failed to reach in France the same dominant position which it occupied in England. From the Scholastics, Descartes had taken over the belief in the power of reason to establish eternally valid concepts revealing absolute truth. The Cartesian philosophy, in Malebranche's version, supplied the logical background for the thinking of the Physiocrats. They transformed economics into a science capable of expressing, in a self-evident mathematical form, the normative principles taught by the sovereign laws of nature. Violation of these principles out of ignorance was to be prevented by adjusting the positive laws to the invariable rules of the natural laws. Malebranche's teachings were probably responsible for the idea of ascribing to nature the exclusive power to create exchange values and of considering human activities as passive rather than active elements in the functioning of the economic machinery. The distinction between ''productive'' and ''sterile'' classes of the population was characteristic of that sociophilosophical attitude. The analysis of the distributive process presented in the *tableau économique* claimed absolute validity. The demand of the Physiocrats for freedom of trade was not derived from utilitarian considerations but from a natural individual right alleged to be self-evident.

Viewed from the angle of the development of methods of economic reasoning, Adam Smith's contribution consisted mainly in the definite establishment of economics as an independent science. This was, of course, a remarkable intellectual achievement. He fulfilled that task by combining all the more or less disconnected economic theories of his mercantilist predecessors into a well-coordinated doctrine which was permeated by the idea that free competition was prerequisite to the full operation of self-regulating economic forces. But, as distinct from some outstanding Mercantilists, such as John Locke and David Hume, he avoided facing outright methodological issues. On the one hand, he did not share the belief of the Physiocrats in the faculty of reason to supply absolutely valid rules of economic conduct. On the other hand, he was reluctant to apply hypothetical methods consistently to the setting of economic problems. It is a debatable question whether the great influence exercised by his work was not increased rather than diminished by his tendency to suggest various, partly conflicting views in defining his fundamental economic concepts.

BENTHAMITE ECONOMICS

Ricardo's work signified a great step toward the development of a consistent doctrine adjusted to the principles of hypothetical thinking, although Ricardo did not care about explaining the methods which he used in constructing his economic system. These methods were derived from the teachings of the associational psychology which had been elaborated in the course of the second half of the eighteenth century and were later synthesized by James Mill. They started on the assumption that a multitude of scattered sensations provide the material of thinking and that these sensations are combined with each other by the operation of a few simple laws of mutual attraction. Associations which are common to large groups of individuals were qualified as "truth," as logical judgments reflecting reality. In accordance with this mechanistic construction of the behavior of the mind, the inner consistency of concepts and of associations of concepts was considered the criterion of any exact science, regardless of whether it dealt with physical bodies or social relationships. The application of the principles of mechanics, especially of the equilibrium concept, to economic analysis was thus given a theoretical justification.

James Mill prevailed upon Ricardo to elaborate an economic doctrine in accordance with these epistemological maxims and with the felicific calculus suggested by Bentham's version of the utilitarian philosophy. Ricardo approached the solution of that problem on the assumption that each individual is the best judge of his pleasures and pains; that in the field of economic activities, pleasures and pains are expressed in gains and losses and can be reduced to a common denominator, a standard unit of value; that, as suggested by Adam Smith, under a system of free competition, each individual producer was limited in his efforts to maximize his gains by similar efforts of other members of the economic community, since the economic system consisted of a more or less unchangeable volume of values and was kept in balance by the self-regulating behavior of the price mechanism.

Although the premises underlying the Ricardian economic system differed widely from those adopted by the Physiocrats, the ultimate objective of both doctrines was the same: to determine the laws which regulate the distributive process. In comparing the premises of the two systems, it can easily be shown to what an extent the principles of hypothetical reasoning were predominant in the Ricardian approach. Yet, even his approach still preserved certain important elements of Scholastic thinking. One element of that type was the traditional grouping of the population into three economic classes: landowners, capitalist employers, and workers. That grouping provided the directives for the distinction of three sources of income and for the explanation of each of these types of income in terms of a specific law.

Even more important for the structure of the Ricardian doctrine was the preservation of a mainstay of Scholastic economics: the belief in the substance concept of the goods. That hardly any English economist of the Ricardian period questioned the validity of that concept was the more remarkable, as it had been practically abandoned in the eighteenth century by some Italian and French authors of nominalistic persuasion. F. Galiani, the

Abbé de Condillac, and Turgot had suggested an outright subjective theory of value based upon individual estimates of the importance of individual goods, as determined by scarcity and usefulness. A value concept of that type, however, appeared to be incompatible with the consistent application of the equilibrium principle to economic analysis. The logical need to reduce all magnitudes included in the economic system to a common standard of value was probably responsible for the survival of the mercantilist idea to derive that standard from a unit of common labor spent on the production of the goods.

For Adam Smith it had been an open question whether embodied or commanded labor was better apt to serve that purpose. Ricardo decided to make the value-creating power of labor a cornerstone of his doctrine, although in his more cautious statements he appears to have been aware of the purely hypothetical nature of his value concept and to have attributed to labor only the function of measuring exchange values. The standard unit of labor time—which neither Ricardo nor his followers cared to define—supplied the "atom," the hypothetical unit for the construction of an economic system which was assumed to be kept in equilibrium like its prototype, the Newtonian system. Maintenance of that equilibrium was held to be assured by the operation of forces which did not permit any exchange values to be eliminated without being replaced by others equal in quantity.

The smooth functioning of the equilibrating forces appeared, however, continuously endangered by the impingement upon the system of two outside factors, operating independently of those forces: population movements and technological improvements. The Malthusian population theory was designed to account for the adjustment of the population to the requirements of the equilibrium system. In accordance with the less conspicuous "compensation" theory, the effects of technological changes were held to be similarly adjusted.

With admirable ingenuity Ricardo attempted to obviate all the logical difficulties created by the starting point of his doctrine: the substance concept of the goods and the closely allied labor cost theory. His greatest achievements consisted in devising new methods of hypothetical reasoning and in formulating fundamental problems so pointedly that subsequent generations of economists were reluctant to improve upon his setting of the problems. The apparent inner consistency of the Ricardian doctrine saved it from being completely discarded even after some of its fundamental premises had been found to be untenable.

Without being significantly modified, Ricardo's doctrine was refined by his orthodox followers. The methods which he had introduced were clarified by Senior, who pointed to the distinction between hypothetical laws—derived from assumptions—and empirical laws, based on the analysis of observed facts. For Ricardo's labor cost theory Senior substituted another which was better adjusted to the felicific calculus: he qualified wages as a reward for disutilities and interest on capital as a reward for abstinence from immediate consumption. But reduction of all pains and pleasures to a common denominator was even less compatible with observation and experience than reduction of all exchange values to a standard unit of labor.

The methods of hypothetical reasoning as derived from the utilitarian epistemology were eventually laid down with great perspicacity by John Stuart Mill, who presented the Ricardian doctrine in its final elaborate form. It has often been observed that this presentation was in no way intended to glorify the structure or the achievements of the capitalist economy. Within the context of that doctrine the institution of private property—which semischolastic reasoning had derived from a "natural" law—was assigned the indispensable role of providing the basis for the functioning of the exchange economy; the introduction of the concept of the "economic man" served the purpose of demonstrating that the tendency to maximize profits was the rational principle of a balanced economic system. That this concept was made a constituent element of an economic doctrine generally accepted in England about the middle of the nineteenth century seems to provide a strong argument for the thesis that the development of economic reasoning occurred to a high degree independently of the actual course of economic events. It was—to put it mildly—a strange fiction to equip the agent of the hypothetical economic system with perfect foresight, whereas, practically, economic conduct of any kind was ruled by estimates of indeterminate chances, prospects, and risks. Similarly, the conception of an economic system, governed by equilibrating forces, was in striking contrast to the economic developments in an age of industrial revolution marked by recurrent alternations of prosperity and depression periods. Such developmental processes were assigned to a sphere which was held to be beyond the reach of theoretical analysis because it did not lend itself to the application of rigid mechanistic principles.

The dominant position occupied by the equilibrium concept in the minds of the Ricardian economists not only determined the structure of their doctrine but also provided the directives for the official economic policy. The rules of the gold standard, to mention only that example, were derived from the equilibrium concept. It is a moot question to what degree that concept, when applied to the solution of politicoeconomic issues, lost its original hypothetical character, and to what degree the alleged equilibrium of the system was treated as the reliable ultimate effect of forces operating in reality within the economic machinery.

The refinement of the Ricardian doctrine, strictly speaking, was accompanied by the development of three distinct versions of classical economics which reflected in various forms the influence of residues of Scholastic reasoning. One version was apparent in the attacks of the so-called Ricardian Socialists on the capitalist order. The authors, covered by this name, eliminated all hypothetical elements from the labor cost theory and advocated a "natural" right of the workers to the full value of their product by virtue of the untenable argument that exchange values were exclusively created by labor. Implicit in that argument was a revival of the mercantilist substance concept of goods, combined with a belief in self-evident "natural" individual rights. Some utopian plans of Ricardian Socialists were even based on the conviction that it was possible to operate an economic machinery in which, for practical purposes, exchange values were expressed in amounts of labor spent on the production of the goods.

The French version of the classical doctrine was prepared by J. B. Say, more than a decade before the publication of Ricardo's *Principles*. Influenced by the teachings of Condillac and Turgot, he adopted an explanation of exchange values in terms of scarcity and utility without, however, clearly defining his value concept. He and his disciples, who determined the structure of the nineteenth-century French economic doctrine, refused to accept the Ricardian methods of economic analysis without suggesting more appropriate methods. They did not care about establishing a consistent conception of the "economic system" or about supplying a theoretical basis for the principles of economic liberalism of which they were convinced advocates. Practically all their discussions remained in the sphere of lower abstractions, and dealt with problems of economic policies rather than with outright theoretical issues. Auguste Walras and, to a much higher degree, Augustin Cournot occupied exceptional positions. They realized the implications of the equilibrium concept as a tool of hypothetical reasoning.

The German version of the classical doctrine was to a remarkable degree interspersed with elements of Scholasticism. Throughout the seventeenth and eighteenth centuries the rigid principles of the Aristotelian logic, which had provided the backbone of the Thomistic philosophy, strongly appealed to the minds of the German teachers of the social disciplines. The writings of the "Cameralists," who expounded a theory and practice of economic and political administration, bore the imprint of that methodological approach. In their teachings they followed the logical principles established by Leibniz and popularized by C. Wolff. Even those German economists who, in the first decades of the nineteenth century, endorsed the liberal economic policy advocated by Adam Smith, exhibited a significant hostility toward the methods of hypothetical reasoning, and rejected the application of mechanistic ideas to economic analysis. Their attitude received strong support from the Kantian epistemology, according to which recognition of the rules of "practical reason" was incompatible with the search for causal laws in the realm of social relationships. Organismic ideas prevailed in the German approach toward social and economic collectivities. Some authors, such as Adam Müller, even adopted an outright Scholastic approach to economic and social problems.

During the entire nineteenth century, only two outstanding German economists used Ricardian methods in their analyses: J. H. von Thünen, who made remarkable contributions to the problem of the ground rent and suggested the idea of marginal productivity, and K. Rodbertus-Jagetzow, who availed himself of the labor cost theory in order to elaborate a socialist doctrine. Neither of them was attached to the academic profession.

INTUITIONAL ECONOMICS

German philosophers, such as Fichte and Schelling, who belonged to the so-called idealistic school, prepared the soil for the emergence of a specific pattern of thought which, for want of a better term, may be called "intuitional" or "organismic." Its logical principles were never clearly defined, but all the various authors and students of the social sciences who adopted it had in common the fact that they had lost the belief in the existence of eternally and absolutely valid concepts and nevertheless longed for knowledge of reality. They were searching for the substances of things and beings. As a rule they resorted to a sort of "intuition" in order to grasp the essential characteristics of complex phenomena in their totality. They segregated these characteristics from accidental or fortuitous features in order to arrive at an "insight" into the true nature of events. They were inclined to attach reality to complex social collectivities such as nations and national economies, religious bodies, and classes of the population. They devised concepts of such collectivities in accordance with the "organic" principle and regarded the parts as living members of a "living whole," subject to growth, maturity, and eventually decline in vitality and energy.

Application of the organic principle to sociological and economic analysis was obviously incompatible with the atomistic and mechanistic approach adopted by the Ricardian economists. Deep-seated aversion toward that approach was frequently defended on the ground that, as taught by the philosopher Fichte, the "German mind" was especially gifted for the use of intuitive methods and organismic concepts.

That pattern of thought provided the background for the German historical school of economics which was initiated by a few preliminary attempts to outline a program of research designed to stimulate purely descriptive analysis of economic events, institutions, and sociophilosophical ideas. As Roscher, Knies, and Hildebrand, the authors of such programmatic essays, believed, it would be possible, in a not too distant future, to derive sociological and economic "evolutionary" laws from the comparative analysis of the accumulated material. The methods suitable for achieving that purpose were, however, never clearly indicated. Ambiguity and vagueness were also characteristic of various concepts frequently used by members of the historical school. The concepts of "economic forces" and "evolution" are instances in point.

The German historical school took its start in the 1850s. In accordance with its epistemological principles, it oriented its thinking within a sphere of concepts loaded with relatively high numbers of characteristics. Since no consistent principles were developed for the selection, definition, and coordination of these concepts, ample room was left to the "intuition" of the various authors. In due course, especially after the victories of Prussia in the wars with Austria and France and after the creation of the German empire, nationalistic ideas and aspirations provided an important selective principle.

The so-called historicoethical school, which spread rapidly under the leadership of Gustav Schmoller, displayed an outright hostile attitude toward economic theorizing which availed itself of the methods of hypothetical reasoning. The ideas of this school centered on the German national economy, which was conceived of as strictly opposed to all other national economies, and on the growth and power of the Reich and the measures to be adopted for promoting its unity, inner coherence, and power. The term *social economics*, used for denoting the content of several textbooks, was indicative of the mixture of economic and sociological problems which constituted the topics of their teachings and were largely treated from a nationalistic, political point of view. The large majority of the members of the school devoted their unrelenting efforts to the descriptive analysis of economic and social events and social conditions and to the examination and recommendation of practical economic policies. Chronological sequences of events were frequently presented as stages of an ill-defined "evolutionary" process. Only a few noted German economists, who remained outside the historical school, expounded economic doctrines mainly in the form which they had received in the work of Adam Smith.

In the first decade of the twentieth century Werner Sombart, the author of comprehensive volumes on the development of capitalism, and Max Weber, the noted sociologist, sounded a note of warning against the vitiation of scientific objectivity through the use of normative concepts tinged with political or ethical connotations. They urged the establishment of a "value-free" social science. Under the influence of the teachings of some neo-Kantian philosophers, Max Weber emphasized for the social sciences—the sciences of the mind—the need for methods based on insight into motives and aims (*verstehen*), as distinct from the methods of the natural sciences, designed to provide knowledge of causal relationships (*begreifen*). As a most effective instrument of scientific analysis, Weber recommended for the social sciences the construction of so-called ideal types. That device implied an invitation to use one's intuition in selecting, more or less arbitrarily, certain characteristics of complex social phenomena in order to set up standards for comparative analyses.

For German teachers who refused to adhere to the historical school, the intuitional aspects of the organic philosophy provided a strong incentive to use their imagination in constructing new doctrines composed of (sometimes heterogeneous) elements of various theories. Thus, to mention only one instance in point, Franz Oppenheimer developed a doctrine which combined a rigid labor cost theory with the idea of a "monopoly" exercised by landed property and the conception of a circular, ever-expanding flow of goods within the economy, conceived of as a sort of organism. The incontestable ingenuity of some doctrines of this type provided no compensation for their questionable logical foundation. Each attracted some followers, but they remained isolated products of eclectic thinking.

DIALECTIC ECONOMICS

The search of German philosophers for the "substance behind the shadow" was responsible for the emergence of the dialectical pattern of reasoning which gained prominence in the first half of the nineteenth century. Its logical structure was far superior to that of its intuitional counterpart. As outlined by Hegel, its originator, dialectic reasoning is based on the idea of conceiving the flux of constantly changing events as an evolutionary process. In order to understand that process as a struggle of antagonistic forces operating in reality, the mind has to avail itself of the contradictions which are basic to our reasoning and to conceive of that process as a sequence of stages developing toward a predetermined end. During each stage the antagonisms gain in intensity and are eventually transformed through a revolutionary act into a new synthesis which contains the elements for the development, upon a higher level, of new sets of antagonistic forces.

As distinct from Hegel, who applied his method mainly to the analysis of history and the philosophy of law, Karl Marx and Friedrich Engels used it in order to prove with "irrefutable" scientific arguments the thesis of the inevitable breakdown of the capitalist economy and its final replacement by a communist order. They pursued that objective by analyzing the functioning of the capitalist machinery, conceived of as a historically determined stage in an age-long evolutionary process. As taught by Hegel, however, dialectic reasoning did not, like hypothetical reasoning, permit the conceptual isolation of economic phenomena from their interconnection with all other spheres of social life. In order to obviate that logical difficulty, Marx and Engels adopted the ingenious device of combining Feuerbach's materialistic philosophy with Hegel's dialectics, and made the "modes of production and distribution" the main arena of the antagonistic forces operating in reality. All other social institutions, all political and social events, even intellectual and moral attitudes were conceived of as a "superstructure," the evolutionary developments of which were made dependent upon the underlying developments of their economic basis. The "materialistic interpretation of history" permitted its authors to preserve the conception of a unified evolutionary social process and relieved them of the task of analyzing the evolutionary development of noneconomic institutions and events. It is worth mentioning that neither Marx and Engels nor their followers ever suggested clear definitions of the "modes of production and distribution" or of the concept of the "superstructure." Nor did they indicate exactly the mutual relationships between these two spheres of social life. When viewed from the angle of hypothetical reasoning, both these concepts are the result of highly complex abstractions and consequently cannot be interconnected in accordance with the principle of causality which is applicable only to the relationship between individual phenomena.[6]

Like the German philosophers of nationalistic persuasion, the advocates of the materialistic interpretation of history were convinced that their superior methods of reasoning were accessible only to selected groups. They argued that those connected with the existing order of society were, by their proprietary interests, inherently unable to understand these methods. By virtue of this argument any objections and criticisms formulated in accordance with other patterns of reasoning could be thrown out as fundamentally erroneous or irrelevant.

In his *Kapital* Karl Marx attempted to describe the development of the capitalist machinery as driven relentlessly by the impact of antagonistic forces toward its final catastrophe. From the Ricardian doctrine he took over at least three important elements: the labor cost theory, the tendency of entrepreneurs to maximize their profits, and the mechanical interpretation of the functioning of the economic machinery. Of course, Marx carefully eliminated all traces of hypothetical reasoning from the Ricardian concepts and attributed to labor, as "crystallized" in a commodity, a real power to create exchange values equal in volume to the labor spent. But he did not succeed any better than Ricardo in solving the question of how to reduce labor of different kinds to a standard unit of labor time. Equipped with that objective value theory, he undertook to lay bare the "fetish" nature of money. His logical device of transforming conceptions into "essences" enabled him to attach reality to abstract notions, such as "socially necessary" labor time, and to the results of arithmetic operations, such as averages, sums total of exchange values, or profits, and the like. He applied the same logical procedure to the concepts of social collectivities, such as classes of the population, as characterized by their relation to the ownership of means of production. The doctrine of the class struggle was a bold attempt to attribute real existence to an alleged antagonism between two classes of the population and to place that antagonism in the center of a predetermined evolutionary process.

Marx used the dialectic method for splitting up all fundamental economic concepts into two mutually antagonistic concepts. Thus he divided exchange values as created by labor into two parts: one allotted to the workers as payment for their labor power, the other withheld by the entrepreneurs as "surplus value." Similarly he split the total volume of exchange values created by productive processes into two parts, of which one was exclusively spent on commodities used for consumption, the other largely on capital goods. The economic machinery of a capitalist economy and its markets was likewise broken up into two sectors. A considerable fraction of the total labor force—the industrial reserve army of the unemployed—was pointed to as the antagonistic element operating against increases of the earnings of those employed.

According to the Ricardian doctrine, profits were a residual element in the national dividend; and a tendency of profits to fall was likely to result from the rising share of land rent combined with a constant level of real wages. That trend was expected eventually to lead to a more or less stagnant state of economic activity. According to the dialectic Marxian doctrine, however, a rapidly intensified fall in the rate of profits was held to be the lever which was bound to render the economic machinery inoperative. In that context the rate of profit was the ratio between the surplus value (withheld by the employers from the exchange values of the products) and the sum total of capital and wages spent in producing the commodities. Since surplus values could be created only by labor, that ratio was bound to fall to the extent that cooperation of labor was replaced by the adoption of labor-saving devices. Thus the Marxian labor cost theory served the purpose of revealing a fundamental contradiction in the behavior of the capitalist employer, whom relentless competition placed under a persistent pressure to substitute machinery for labor and thus to deprive himself more and more of the use of the force which alone could provide profits. In turn, the falling rate of profits exerted a constant pressure to expand the productive machinery and to increase the volume of goods offered for sale in markets in which the demand was constantly declining, owing to the displacement of wage earners through labor-saving devices.

Thus for the rational capitalist employer of the classical doctrine, Marx substituted the inherently irrational entrepreneur who, blinded by the profit motive, was compelled to undermine the basis of his own existence. In his search for "objective reality" Marx believed himself to have demonstrated that the capitalist economy was torn asunder by the operation of relentless antagonistic forces. What he did not even attempt to explain was the persistently self-destructive behavior of the entrepreneur.

An intricate logical problem was involved in the Marxian proposition which implied the subjection of a mechanical hypothetical system, as devised by Ricardo, to the working of an evolutionary process. Since a mechanism presupposes rigid relationships between its constituent elements; it cannot be subjected to such a process without being immediately disrupted. The combination of two logically inconsistent principles was in itself sufficient to provide the premises for demonstrating the inevitable breakdown of the capitalist machinery. The task which the Marxian analysis had to fulfill consisted less in evidencing that outcome of the dialectic evolutionary process than in explaining why the breakdown did not occur at the earliest possible moment. In his discussion of the ever-recurrent crises, Marx dealt with that question without, however, suggesting a consistent business cycle theory.

The Marxian analysis of the capitalist machinery shared the fate of all "essentialistic" doctrines which claim to provide full knowledge of the laws which determine the course of cosmic events.[7] Only a single interpretation of such a doctrine can be accepted as binding; any deviations from that interpretation are to be condemned as "heretical," since they are likely to cast doubt on the validity of the logical principles underlying the doctrine. The function of protecting the Marxian doctrine against that danger was assumed by the so-called orthodox Marxists who devoted their most important contributions to the question of why the capitalist economy had been able to recover, time and again, even from its most severe crises. The problematic theory that the glut in the capitalist market, created by inevitable overproduction, could be relieved by means of exports to "noncapitalist" areas also served the purpose of explaining modern wars as the inevitable concomitants of the struggle of the "imperialist" nations for colonial markets.

Beginning with the twentieth century, the role of the heretics was played by the so-called Revisionists who abandoned the dialectical methods and were even inclined to drop the rigid labor cost theory. They adopted the principles of organismic reasoning and expected that the socialist economy of the future would be brought about not through a catastrophic revolutionary collapse but through a gradual process. They attached particular importance to the restriction of the area of free competition through the formation of monopolistic concerns and employers' organizations, on the one hand, and to the increasing strength of the trade unions, on the other. They propagated the slogan of "industrial democracy," involving participation of workers' representatives in the management of large concerns. The methods which they used in their economic treatises were descriptive, similar to those adopted by the German historical school.

REFINEMENT OF HYPOTHETICAL REASONING

It was perhaps no mere coincidence that in the 1870s three thinkers, independently of each other, introduced the principles of marginal utility analysis into economics and thus prepared the way for a far-reaching revision of Ricardian economic concepts and methods. One of these thinkers, Jevons, lived in England, another, Walras, in Switzerland,

and a third, Menger, in Austria.[8] The simultaneous emergence of the idea that, in the last analysis, the origin of all economic values, including exchange values, is to be looked for in individual estimates of the importance of individual goods was probably due to the abandonment of the substance concept of goods and to the final elimination of the Scholastic principle that "equivalence" was a prerequisite to all exchange transactions.

The new setting of the value problem definitely deprived the productive process of its alleged power to create exchange values and attributed that function exclusively to processes connected with the exchange of goods. The idea of "exchange" could be extended to all situations in which acts of preferential treatment were applied to scarce means of want satisfaction. Economics could be defined as the science dealing with scarcity relationships, with their transformation into measurable magnitudes, and with rational methods of distributing scarce goods.

Marginal utility analysis provided a single principle for explaining indiscriminately the value of all goods and services in terms of the diminution in want satisfaction caused by the loss of a unit out of an available stock or in terms of the increment in want satisfaction achieved by adding another unit to an available stock of goods. If all values were, in the last analysis, determined by the marginal utility of the goods for consumption, the setting of the cost of production problem, as formulated by the classical economists, could be reversed, and the value of the productive factors could be derived from the value of their products. In accordance with the "opportunity cost" principle, cost could be defined as utilities sacrificed or forgone in order to secure more useful goods and services. Application of that principle opened the way for a uniform explanation of the distribution of the value of the product among the contributing productive services, and deprived the traditional distinction of three main productive factors of much of its importance. Since the source of all exchange values was sought in market transactions, the idea of "rent"—an element of prices not attributable to productive services—gained a meaning which extended its scope of application far beyond that of the classical concept of ground rent.

The concept of marginal utility found a counterpart in the concept of marginal productivity which could be used independently of marginal utility analysis strictly speaking. Marginal productivity analysis started from the assumption that increases in the use of each productive service could reasonably be continued up to the point at which the value of the product of the last unit of the service, when added to the result of the productive process, was equal to the cost of the unit. Especially the price paid for labor could be derived from the value of its marginal product, and differences in the level of wages could thus be accounted for.

It was obvious that abandonment of the attempts to reduce all exchange values included in the economic system to a common uniform standard unit necessitated a reformulation of all problems connected with the application of the equilibrium concept to the economic system. The Ricardian proposition that the system consisted of a more or less fixed volume of uniform exchange values had to be dropped. Maintenance of the system's equilibrium appeared to depend upon individual behavior, on the assumption that each individual equalized the marginal utilities of all goods entering into his sphere of consumption, that is to say, abstained from consuming or acquiring any good, the marginal utility of which was lower than that of an equally available and desired good. The economic man of the Ricardian doctrine, whose behavior was motivated by the desire to maximize his share in the available exchange values, was replaced by the rational entrepreneur, whose behavior is determined by the principle of marginal productivity. Thus the maximization principle as the lever of economic activity was not discarded but received a new formulation which permitted recognition of a wide range of degrees in the entrepreneur's or capitalist's "striving for gains."

Further development of economic reasoning was determined by the ingenuity exhibited by leading thinkers in mastering the intricacies of marginal utility analysis through simplified assumptions designed to preserve the applicability of the equilibrium concept to the relationships of economic magnitudes. This process has extended over many decades and has not yet led to a satisfactory setting of the fundamental problems involved in that analysis. In the course of these discussions various questions which for a time had received primary attention were superseded by others which subsequently shared the same fate. The progress made in refining the methods of hypothetical reasoning was quite remarkable.

From the outset the formulation of economic problems varied in accordance with the divergent approaches adopted by the initiators of marginal utility analysis. This trifurcation has continued to exercise a significant influence up to the present day. The thinking of Jevons was still deeply rooted in the utilitarian philosophy and the Ricardian doctrine. He tried, as far as possible, to adjust his concepts to those established by that doctrine and based his concept of the economic system upon a calculus of pleasures derived from the enjoyment of desired goods, and of pains caused by the disutility of labor spent on their production. Hence, he argued that under static conditions the equilibrium of the system was assured when the fund available for the demand of each individual (the latter's income) was so distributed among the individual's requirements that the "final increments" of all commodities acquired by him were equal in utility. Jevons did not, however, become the founder of a school strictly speaking. A few English economists, such as Smart, Edgeworth, and Wicksteed, who fully endorsed the principles of marginal utility analysis, adopted rather important features of the two other versions of that analysis.

Jevons emphasized the strictly hypothetical foundations of his economic theory when he explicitly stated that it was his ultimate objective to transform economics into a science of applied mathematics. That objective was even far more consistently pursued by Walras. As a Frenchman he had not been educated in the Ricardian doctrine and practically ignored its conceptual structure. His much-admired intellectual achievement consisted in defining, as exactly as possible, the conditions which had to be fulfilled, according to the marginal utility principle, in devising a perfect model of a purely hypothetical, stable economic system, exclusively governed by equilibrating tendencies which were assumed to operate under the rule of unimpaired free competition. All problems not immediately connected with the behavior of equilibrium prices in a competitive economy were outside the scope of that analysis; the latter was based on a set of rigorously defined assumptions regardless of the degree to which these assumptions corresponded to the results of observation and experience. Among these assumptions was the introduction of a purely abstract hypothetical unit of value, the *numéraire,* which served the purpose of eliminating all fluctuations in the value of the means of exchange. Another assumption made by Walras was the proposition that the equalization of the level of marginal utilities could be conceived of as a process in the course of which want satisfactions, split up into infinitesimal fractions, continuously decreased in intensity. That assumption provided the logical prerequisites for the application of refined mathematical methods to the analysis of the equilibrating tendencies. His mathematical approach caused Walras to abandon the search for causal relationships and to establish purely functional relationships between the prices which formed the elements of his economic system.

The aloofness of the Walrasian doctrine, its mathematical bent, and its reliance on intricate methods of hypothetical reasoning were responsible for the isolated position which it occupied for several decades. The Italian Pareto, Walras's most distinguished follower, intensified even his master's abstractions and strongly objected to the connection of any psychological considerations or causal relationships with economic analysis. His construction of "ophelimity indices," indicating the order in which an individual may group different combinations of quantities of goods in accordance with his scale of preferences, was based on the idea that the unit of want satisfaction, derived by an individual from the increment in the quantity of a good, was dependent upon the availability of variable quantities of complementary goods. With the aid of indifference curves, which Pareto derived from these indices, he expected to establish a "photographic picture" of each individual's economic aspirations. To this picture he juxtaposed similar lines representing the obstacles to be overcome in the individual's striving for want satisfaction; costs of production were among the main elements of obstacles. Equilibrium positions were established at the points where the equilibrium of the desires and the equilibrium of the obstacles met. Thus Pareto endeavored to develop a purely mathematical theory of exchange and used the principle of marginal productivity for applying the ideas of preference and indifference to a mathematical presentation of productive processes in order to arrive at his ultimate goal, the presentation of an equilibrated economic system as a system of innumerable equations.

It has remained a moot question whether, with the construction of indifference and preference curves, Pareto had in fact eliminated any reference to psychological considerations underlying the concept of marginal utility. Even more justified doubts were cast in prolonged discussions on Pareto's fundamental assumptions which implied practically perfect divisibility of the goods and treatment of utilities as measurable magnitudes. The epistemological problems involved in these discussions have turned on the intricate question to what degree scientific analysis can be permitted to operate with assumptions which are inconsistent with the results of observation and experience. The use of "fictions" and the scope of application of these instruments of hypothetical reasoning are closely related to that question.[9]

As distinct from the utilitarian approach adopted by Jevons and the mathematical approach initiated by Walras, marginal utility analysis, as taught by Carl Menger, was rather a study in applied psychology, adjusted as closely as possible to the results of everyday observation. Menger and his followers ignored all problems connected with pain and disutilities in formulating their concept of marginal utility. In addition, they carefully avoided the temptation to transform utilities into measurable magnitudes. Among the outstanding characteristics of the psychological approach was the contention that marginal utilities can be scaled and compared with each other merely as to their degrees.

Menger's position was peculiar insofar as he was faced from the outset with the hostile attitude of the German economists of organismic persuasion, who were horrified by the idea of basing economic analysis upon individual behavior instead of starting from the national economy, conceived as an integrated whole, with the individuals as fully dependent constituent elements. In Menger's famous "Methodenstreit" with Schmoller, the struggle turned on the validity of methods of hypothetical reasoning as an appropriate instrument for the establishment of general causal laws underlying the relationships between economic phenomena.

The methods which Menger defended with great acumen were derived from the same logical principles which had been adopted by Ricardo and explained by J. S. Mill. But

Menger not only eliminated the Ricardian substance concept of goods, he also practically ignored the idea of applying the equilibrium concept to the economic system; in fact, he did not even suggest any clear concept of such a system. The range of problems which he tried to solve was far more limited than that contemplated by Jevons or Walras. He devoted his deductive reasoning mainly to a revision of certain Ricardian theories which had been formulated in terms of the assumption that all exchange values could be reduced to a common denominator and that the productive process was the main source of exchange values. Consequent upon that approach the Ricardian economists had centered their attention on the supply of goods, whereas the demand for goods was the starting point of Menger's analysis. Since he considered the demand for goods of immediate consumption to be the ultimate source of all values, he raised the question of how to derive the value of the productive services from the value of their products.

Menger's disciples did not modify substantially the setting of the problems as formulated by their master. True to his conception of economics as an exact science, they availed themselves predominantly of the methods of deductive reasoning, based on carefully defined premises. Almost all those who belonged to the first generation of that school practically disregarded all questions connected with the dynamic aspects of the economy. They endeavored rather to elaborate various aspects of the opportunity cost principle which identified costs with marginal utilities forgone in favor of greater ones. Thus they reformulated the Ricardian setting of the problems of cost, interest on capital and profits, wages and rents, with the purpose in mind of accounting for all these phenomena in accordance with a single principle, that of marginal utility. As Jevons had done before, they made various, hardly successful attempts to explain in terms of the same principle the formation of prices in the exchange economy under competitive conditions.

In his theory of interest and even more in his economic analysis of the social system, F. von Wieser showed some inclination to permit the substance concept to have a certain influence upon his reasoning. But Böhm-Bawerk's lifetime work can perhaps be characterized as an incessant fight against that concept in all its forms. This attitude pressed its stamp on his comprehensive discussion of the numerous theories of capital and interest which he subjected to (partly devastating) criticism. His own theory of interest—the so-called agio theory—was based on a logical development of the idea that subjective valuations were the ultimate source of all values and the determinants of all value relationships. From that view Böhm-Bawerk derived the idea of interpreting interest on capital as a difference between a higher value of the use of goods readily available and a lower value of the use of the same goods available in a more or less distant future. Viewed from that angle, all productive services had the nature of future goods, increasing in value simultaneously with their gradual transformation into goods of immediate consumption; especially land rent appeared as the share of a productive service, supplying an infinite series of future yields, the discounted value of which was gradually declining to zero.

Böhm-Bawerk's reliance upon the time element to explain the source of interest on capital met with various objections. Far more important for the development of economic reasoning was the strategic position which he assigned to the level of interest as an instrument for regulating the behavior of the economic system. He argued that the productivity of industrial enterprises was increased with the lengthening of the period of production and that the average period of production was in turn determined by the rate of interest. Thus, without suggesting a clear concept of the economic system in terms of the Ricardian equilibrium concept, he radically transformed the significance of the rate of interest which had played a predominantly passive role in the classical doctrine.

The Swedish economist Knut Wicksell, who contributed greatly toward developing marginal utility analysis on the lines initiated by C. Menger, combined Böhm-Bawerk's approach with monetary considerations which had been practically neglected by the Austrian school. He demonstrated that the rate of interest which Böhm-Bawerk had in mind was a "real" rate, characteristic of an economy which was not affected by changes in the volume of the circulating means of payment. The distinction which he drew between that rate and the "market" rate of interest, as fixed by the credit institutions, pointed to disturbances of the balance of the economic system which were likely to result from prolonged discrepancies between the two rates of interest. Implied in that reasoning was a logical differentiation between two aspects of the economic system: a monetary system, ruled by equilibrium conditions of its own, and a system of productive processes. In pursuance of that approach Wicksell undertook to determine the equilibrium conditions of the monetary system as influenced by the market rate of interest, and thus raised a set of new problems involving far-reaching implications.

MODIFIED RICARDIAN ECONOMICS

It is an open question, which could be answered only within the context of a history of Western reasoning, why the overwhelming majority of the British economists, led by Marshall, abstained from developing the methods of hypothetical reasoning into instruments of more rarified abstractions, although these methods had received the first consistent formulation in their country. With all the new admirable methodological devices which Marshall introduced into his scientific analysis, he remained within the sphere of abstractions established by the Ricardian school and preserved especially the attachment of that school to the substance concept of goods. He made ample and highly effective use of marginal productivity analysis which was compatible with that concept, but he applied the idea of marginal utility only to situations connected with the demand for goods and assigned to problems of demand a subordinate place, similar to that which it had occupied in the Ricardian doctrine. His simile of the two blades of a pair of scissors reflected his decision to derive exchange values primarily from the "real" costs of production and to ignore the idea of opportunity costs. He preserved the classical setting of the problems of distribution, which consisted in developing specific theories for explaining the shares allotted to the productive services in the value of the products.

But since he had lost, along with the abandonment of the labor cost theory, the logical instrument which had enabled Ricardo to apply the equilibrium concept to the construction of a consistent economic system, he limited his equilibrium analysis mainly to partial equilibrium situations in which the value of the monetary unit could be assumed to remain unaltered. To this field he applied methods of refined mathematical analysis and opened new avenues of deductive reasoning by varying the conditions under which free competition could be considered to be operating.[10] Due to his outstanding influence as the head of a firmly established school, the classical tradition was preserved in England for almost two generations.

Simultaneously with Marshall, the works of J. B. Clark initiated the development of a school of American economists. Independently of the European originators of the marginal utility principle, he made a start of his own on similar lines, and centered his scientific efforts upon analyzing the distributive processes of the economy in the light of that principle and the closely allied principle of marginal productivity. He abandoned the

Ricardian tradition in that he started with the model of a hypothetical, stationary, economic system in which the quantities of the productive services were not allowed to vary; the return of each productive service was determined by the marginal productivity of its unit; and the returns of all these units were equalized. Like the other adherents of marginal utility analysis, he was faced with the difficulty of deriving a standard unit of exchange values from individual estimates of utilities. He obviated that difficulty with the aid of a hedonistic version of marginal utility analysis and of various additional assumptions—such as that all labor could be expressed in units of disutilities supposed to be homogeneous for all workers, and that under equilibrium conditions marginal utility could be assumed to be equal to marginal disutility. Thus he tacitly transformed Ricardo's hypothetical unit of labor costs into a homogeneous unit of disutilities. On the assumption that in the stationary economy the supply of all productive factors was fixed, Clark refused to draw a distinction between capital and land as productive factors and derived the rate of interest from the marginal productivity of an abstract quantum of productive wealth.

Thus Clark preserved the general structure of the Ricardian mechanical concept of the economic system, but suggested new interpretations of the main Ricardian theories. His attempt to demonstrate that all productive activities were rewarded in accordance with their contributions at the margin of utilization and that the exchange values of the goods as fixed in the markets reflected "social utilities" was, however, refuted by the large majority of his disciples. Subsequently Clark supplemented his analysis of the stationary model by the introduction of dynamic factors which he described without attempting to suggest generally valid laws with regard to their effects upon the structure of the economic system. He characterized the progressive changes of that structure as a movement of successive equilibrium positions and pointed to the intricate problems involved in the behavior of an economy affected by the impact of noneconomic factors.

Although many American economists showed a considerable tendency to preserve, as far as possible, the Ricardian approach to economic analysis, their discussions were strongly influenced by the concepts and theories advanced by the psychological school of marginal utility analysis. These discussions turned on questions such as whether utilities could be reduced to a standard unit of measurement, whether prices could supply such a standard; how to define the concept of "opportunity costs" and how to derive the value of the productive services from the value of the goods of consumption; whether interest on capital was to be explained in accordance with the marginal utility principle or in accordance with a general productivity ascribed to capital. Frank Fetter, F. W. Taussig, H. J. Davenport, and I. Fisher, to mention only a few names, contributed greatly toward clarifying disputed concepts and problems.

Since it was impossible to reduce marginal utilities to a common denominator, insurmountable difficulties were involved in deriving a system of prices directly from marginal utility analysis. Hence, some economists took the radical step of eliminating the value problem entirely from the scope of economic research and of limiting economic theory to the analysis of economic phenomena which could be expressed in directly measurable magnitudes or prices. They considered a system of simultaneous equations describing price relationships, sufficient for supplying a picture of the behavior of the economic machinery. The Swedish economist Gustav Cassel was among the most important representatives of that view, which met with the objection that it excluded from economics the search not only for the origin of prices but also for changes in price relationships.

VARYING ASPECTS OF THE EQUILIBRIUM CONCEPT

Ricardo had used the equilibrium concept to devise a timeless model of the economic system. The balance of the system was achieved with the aid of a maximization principle: competitive striving for the greatest possible individual share in a more or less fixed volume of exchange values. Problems connected with "riches" or "wealth," that is to say, with individual want satisfaction, were eliminated from the structure of the system; consistent reasoning in terms of a hypothetical distributive process led to the theory of a gradually falling rate of interest which would eventually result in arresting economic expansion and in petrifying the economic system. Marx started from a similarly constructed mechanical system, but submitted it to the disrupting effects of an evolutionary process—a logically highly problematic procedure; he used his version of the rapidly falling rate of profits to demonstrate the inevitable breakdown of the capitalist machinery.

There was no place within the context of hypothetical reasoning for a concept of "evolution" which implied a succession of stages tending toward a predetermined goal and, consequently, marked by teleological features.[11] Instead, a vague concept of "development" was used to characterize structural alterations of an economy or lasting changes in the relationships of relevant economic magnitudes. Changes of the latter type were subsequently adjusted to the requirements of equilibrium analysis with the aid of the concept of moving equilibria.

With the introduction of marginal utility analysis the maximization principle, as used by Ricardo, experienced a fundamental modification. That modification was most consistently carried out in the highly abstract and rigidly stationary Walrasian system. All exchange values of which the system was composed were derived from individual estimates of utilities balanced at their margins, while balancing of marginal productivities on the part of the employers ensured equilibrium from the supply side. Subsequent introduction of indifference curves through Pareto reflected a refined formulation of the marginal utility idea and, at the same time, served the purpose of eliminating any reference to a hedonistic or psychological foundation of that idea.

Marshall, who preserved the Ricardian maximization principle but abandoned the belief in a rigid unchangeable unit of exchange values, applied the equilibrium concept mainly to specified situations in which a stable monetary standard could reasonably be assumed to prevail. J. B. Clark started his analysis from the model of a stationary economic system similar to that which Ricardo had imagined as the outcome of his long-run considerations. He visualized economic progress as a process in which the economic system proceeded from one equilibrium position to another and supplemented that construction by introducing "dynamic" factors on the demand and supply side in order to account for changes in the structure of the economic machinery. Thus he outlined a pattern of indefinite expansion, without, however, suggesting the possibility of establishing hypothetical laws for defining that pattern.

At first, most members of the psychological school of marginal utility analysis ignored the equilibrium conditions of the system as a whole. Böhm-Bawerk, however, pointed to the rate of interest as the strategic factor which was likely to assure the smooth functioning of the economic machinery. But he disregarded the question of how the adjustment of productive processes to the available supply of capital could be secured under a monetary standard the value of which was fluctuating. In due course Knut Wicksell juxtaposed the volume of monetary capital to that of "real" capital as defined by

Böhm-Bawerk; he suggested a definition of the equilibrium conditions of the monetary system. Maintenance of the equilibrium of that system appeared to be prerequisite to the maintenance of the equilibrium of the productive and distributive processes. The Ricardian equilibrium concept had been entirely independent of the functioning of the monetary machinery.

Joseph Schumpeter made the first ambitious attempt to establish the pattern of an economic system subjected to a process of moving equilibria. He started his analysis from the conditions of a stationary economy, as J. B. Clark had done before him, but described these conditions in accordance with the premises which had been formulated by Walras. In such an economy all individuals were assumed to have achieved the highest possible degree of want satisfaction available to them with the means at their disposal; the equivalents for the services rendered by soil and labor were the only forms of income; no income was earned on capital or entrepreneurial activity. In order to account for the behavior of an economy under "dynamic" conditions, Schumpeter introduced a sort of dialectical device by distinguishing between the traditionally minded employers of the stationary economy and daring entrepreneurs motivated by the expectation of increasing the yield from their industrial activity. Simultaneously he accepted, at least tacitly, Wicksell's distinction between the two aspects of the economic system and placed great emphasis on the faculty of the banks to create the money capital needed for industrial expansion. The dynamic features of that economic system were accentuated by the assumption that the profits of the daring entrepreneurs, which genetically constituted the sources of interest on capital, were, time and again, swept away by increasing competition. Thus Schumpeter introduced factors operating outside the economic system, strictly speaking, in order to account for the sequence of moving equilibria.

No such problem existed for those who applied intuitional reasoning to the construction of the economic system. The majority of those who cherished the idea of a "national economy" operated with vague organic analogies; they made a more or less metaphysical collective spirit or will responsible for the coherence of their economic systems and freely used "forces" of various kinds to explain structural, developmental, or "evolutionary" changes of the economy. Not only the behavior of each national economy but also any changes of that behavior were regarded as the combined results of specific, historically conditioned circumstances. Any mechanical interpretation of the economic system was, of course, rejected by the adherents of neo-Scholastic patterns. The Viennese economist Spann, the most remarkable representative of that method of reasoning, even suggested a strictly hierarchical system of economic concepts as a starting point of economic analysis. The list of attempts to devise nonmechanical economic systems could be greatly expanded.

In this connection a separate position was occupied by the American institutionalists whose thinking was strongly influenced by Veblen's view that economic analysis should be directed by, and subordinated to, sociological considerations. Although their epistemological approach showed considerable resemblance to that of the German historical school, their main economic concepts were still determined by the classical tradition and they avoided the use of organismic concepts. They rejected marginal utility analysis as well as the traditional application of the principles of mechanics to the study of economic phenomena, and emphasized the influence of historical conditions, especially legal and judicial institutions, upon the functioning of the economy. W. C. Mitchell, an outstanding member of that group, developed with great energy and skill a method for comparing the results of the descriptive analysis of carefully defined specific economic situations.

The varying applications of the equilibrium concept to economic problems were reflected in the widely divergent attempts to explain crises and depressions which had become a regularly recurrent phenomenon in the course of the nineteenth century and attracted increasing attention. In accordance with the classical conception of the economic system, such disastrous events were looked upon as disturbances of an otherwise equilibrated machinery, brought about by factors operating from outside, such as wars, poor harvests, mismanagement of the currency, and the like. Malthus, who did not share Ricardo's belief in the existence of equilibrating forces, was among the first to attribute general dislocations of the economic machinery to a factor inherent in the economic system: the lack of effective demand for the goods produced with accumulated capital.

That view was not acceptable to the Ricardian economists. The falling rate of profit, which Ricardo had made responsible for gradual structural changes of the economy, suggested the idea, shared by J. S. Mill, among others, that crises were time and again produced by the tendency of investors to ignore the decline in the rate of profits and to embark on economically unjustified speculative ventures. Other Ricardians stuck to the conviction that the periodic recurrence of crises could be explained only by the impingement upon the economic system of outside forces, characterized by periodic recurrence. Jevons's sun spot theory was the most consistent and elaborate explanation of that type.

Socialist authors, such as Sismondi, Proudhon, and, above all, Rodbertus, used a crude labor cost theory to demonstrate that crises were due to the exploitation of workers and the ensuing unequal distribution of incomes which was alleged to cause "underconsumption" and lack of purchasing power for absorbing the commodities produced in excess of effective demand. That reasoning implied that disequilibrating forces were continuously operating within the economic machinery. Marx did not suggest a coherent explanation of crises, but some nondialectic aspects of his discussions were used toward the end of the nineteenth century by the Russian author M. Tugan-Baranowsky to outline the scheme of an economic system in which the sector devoted to the production of capital goods was expanding disproportionately in relation to increases in the production of consumers' goods. That crisis theory was substantially endorsed by the German "Revisionists."

The explanation of crises advanced by French economists was in line with their interpretation of the functioning of the economic system. They had never subscribed to the Ricardian rigid equilibrium analysis and felt free to make institutional factors responsible for alternating expansions and contractions of business activity. In addition, a firm belief in the power of credit to determine the volume of that activity had been a heritage of French economic reasoning since the time when Law had ascribed to credit an almost magic influence upon production and trade. Juglar is regarded as the first author who, in 1862, approached the problem of crises from the monetary angle; he was also among the first to emphasize the recurrent nature of crises and qualify them as a distinct phase in a wavelike behavior of economic events. He suggested a chain of causal relations, starting with credit expansion and ensuing price increases during the upswing, followed by the adverse effects of changes in the price structure upon the balance of trade, and leading eventually to credit restrictions enforced by the necessity of tightening the rate of discount in order to protect the available foreign exchange reserves. Juglar's business cycle theory was adopted with various modifications by other French economists.

The introduction of marginal utility analysis and the emergence of many new intricate problems connected with that doctrine appear to have deflected the attention of the leading economists for about forty years from the fluctuating behavior of the economic machinery. In 1912 Schumpeter suggested, along with his far-reaching transformation of the Walrasian static conception of the economic system, a new interpretation of business fluctuations which he characterized as phenomena inherent in the behavior of an expanding capitalist economy. Within the context of his theory of capitalist development, prosperity periods, initiated by daring entrepreneurs and supported by credit expansion, were bound to alternate with depression periods after enhanced competition had deprived the daring entrepreneurs of their gains. Depression periods represented a temporary return of general economic conditions to a predominantly stationary state.

About the same time, Mises developed Wicksell's theory of interest into a monetary business cycle theory. He ascribed the upswings to the tendency of the banks to keep the market rate of interest below the equilibrium rate which caused employers to embark on productive processes of longer duration than would be justified by the available volume of means of subsistence and savings. Crises ensued when, out of liquidity considerations, the banks were compelled to set the market rate of interest at a level exceeding the prevailing rate of profits.

This short survey of business cycle theories, which were advanced prior to the First World War, indicates that a broad distinction could be drawn between monetary theories and nonmonetary theories. Schumpeter's view represented a combination of both approaches to the problem. The nonmonetary theories reflected, as a rule, a deterministic attitude with regard to the behavior of the economic system; they enjoyed preference on the part of various socialist authors. For those who emphasized the influence of monetary factors upon alternating expansions and contractions of business activity, it remained an open question whether business fluctuations could not be eliminated or, at least, greatly reduced in intensity through appropriate modifications of the credit machinery.

The adherents of organismic reasoning, true to their general epistemological attitude, considered each crisis or depression an individual phenomenon of a national economy to be explained in terms of specific causes. Sombart's crisis theory was, in some respects, an exception; he connected the periodic recurrence of crises with variations in the gold output and with changes in the structure of the economy through a process in which raw materials produced by agriculture were superseded by materials derived from minerals and metals. Spiethoff, who equally belonged to the historical school, concentrated his research on devising a pattern of business fluctuations based mainly on expansions and contractions of the output of heavy industry.

CONCLUDING OBSERVATIONS

In reviewing the development of economic reasoning up to the beginning of the First World War, the part played by the equilibrium concept, especially in Anglo-Saxon economics, can hardly be overemphasized. The purely hypothetical nature of that concept as applied to the relationships of economic phenomena is quite evident; neither at a first glance nor on closer analysis do these relationships reveal specific characteristics which would suggest their coordination in terms of an outright mechanical order. The equilibrium idea was the magic wand which rendered these relationships accessible to consistent analysis and eventually provided the logical instruments for combining them into more or less carefully devised hypothetical systems. The effective use made of the equilibrium idea in its various forms and modes of application strongly influenced not only theoretical reasoning but also considerations of economic policy. Thus the institutional setup of the capitalist order appears to have been gradually adjusted to ideas which were closely connected with the equilibrium concept. Consequently, theories in which that concept was predominant had a better chance of explaining the functioning of the economic machinery than others which ignored it.

It is as yet an unsolved question to what degree the alleged mechanical economic laws were purely fictitious, but there is hardly any doubt that the widespread belief in the real existence of these laws made them a powerful agent in shaping the economic developments of the capitalist era. On the other hand, regional differences in the economic structure can, at least in part, be related to differences in prevailing methods of reasoning.

Even when schools of minor importance, such as the neo-Scholastic school, are disregarded, there existed in the first decade of the twentieth century at least six schools of economics, each marked by a specific concept of economic system. The Anglo-Saxon neoclassical school had preserved the Ricardian concept; the French school—like a group of German "liberal" economists—had preferred the vague concept underlying the teachings of Adam Smith, and was looking for historical "empirical" regularities rather than for the establishment of hypothetical laws of the Ricardian type.

A highly abstract concept of the economic system, based partly on fictitious assumptions, had been developed by the leaders of the mathematical school of Lausanne. The "psychological" Austrian school had introduced the idea of a twofold system, one applicable to the sphere of production, the other to the monetary sphere.

The German economists of the historical school had adopted an "intuitively" defined organismic concept of the economic system; the followers of the Marxian doctrine a dialectic evolutionary concept, based on the belief in the real existence of disequilibrating forces operating within the capitalist economy.

The concepts adopted by socialist authors other than Marxists could be grouped according to their adherence to the Ricardian, the French, or the German interpretation of the functioning of the economic machinery. Their views were qualified as "utopian" by the orthodox Marxists, who claimed for their own views the privilege of representing "scientific" socialism.

These differences in fundamental concepts reflected deep-seated divergencies in principles of reasoning which rendered mutual understanding very difficult, in many cases even impossible. These difficulties were accentuated by the fact that the adherents of certain schools—especially some protagonists of the German historical school and all orthodox Marxists—not only considered their methods of reasoning far superior to any others, but declared their opponents inherently incapable of understanding and applying those methods.

The epistemological problems involved in the struggle between conflicting doctrines were by no means overlooked. They received increasing attention during the greatly intensified conflict which ensued in the course of the subsequent development of economic reasoning.[12]

Appendix B
Patterns of Economic Reasoning

WHOEVER EMBARKS on the study of the history of economic thought is faced with the question of explaining why the meanings of commonly used terms vary so greatly between the different schools—why some concepts and problems which are of fundamental importance for certain schools are irrelevant or at least hardly significant for others.

There is hardly any doubt in my mind that in many cases varying definitions of economic concepts are due to the pervading influence of conflicting methods of reasoning or patterns of thought.[1] Each pattern causes its adherents to adopt a specific approach in formulating and solving their problems. Viewed from that angle, the history of economic thought, reflecting the general development of Western reasoning, is largely a history of applied logical procedures. That proposition may be contrasted with the widespread view that the development of economic thought has been strongly influenced by the changing structures of economic life and the related view that many, perhaps all, economic doctrines reflect in their essential aspects the material interests of specific classes of the population. Such relationships may be found to obtain in certain cases, but their importance is hardly significant when compared with the control exercised by the modes of thought which have alternatively determined the character of the prevailing thinking processes.

In order to facilitate the difficult task of conveying a clear distinction between different methods of reasoning and of arranging schools of economic thought accordingly, I should like to start with a discussion of the divergent meanings attached by the various schools to a general concept which has been fundamental to economic thinking of all types: the concept of economic system or economic model; that is to say, the set of principles used by an author or a school for combining economic relationships into a more or less unified and coherent picture. The system concept adopted by a school reveals the basic logical rules observed by its adherents in defining, coordinating, and integrating the elements of economic life considered relevant for the understanding of any economic relationships and processes.

In accordance with the rules of reasoning which the nations of Western Europe had inherited from the Greek classical philosophers, two conflicting system concepts were competing with each other when the first attempts were made to transform the perplexing variety of economic happenings and events into simplified pictures. The schools whose adherents believed in the power of reason to grasp reality and fully to understand the teleological aspects of economic life were inclined to adopt an organic concept which could be easily combined with the belief in imminent ends of various human collectivities.

Other schools, however, that did not believe in the power of reason to teach us the essence of things and their real meaning, that ascribed to reason only the faculty to formulate the hypothetical conditions under which causal relationships between outside events could be assumed to exist, decided upon the use of mechanical system concepts.

The choice of a rudimentary concept of mechanic economic system by the English Mercantilists of the seventeenth century has been among the most amazing and momen-

This essay originally appeared in *American Economic Review* 43, no. 2 (May 1953).

tous events in the history of Western thought. It has determined the development of the reasoning of the Ricardian, post-Ricardian, dialectic, and marginalist schools to such extent that the history of these schools can almost be identified with the history of the changes which in the course of two centuries were made in incessant attempts to apply mechanical principles to the construction of economic system concepts. Particularly remarkable have been the various efforts to transform a rigid equilibrium concept into a more flexible tool of economic analysis fit for coping with the dynamic nature of economic events and processes.

The adherents of the German historical school and the followers of similar intellectual movements, however, repudiated the use of mechanical principles for purposes of economic analysis and made continued efforts to construct organic concepts of social collectivities to which biological characteristics were applicable. Thus, national economies were quite commonly conceived as integrated wholes. A sort of intuition was used—consciously or implicitly—for interpreting the relationships between the parts and the whole of such organic collectivities, and the diversity of imaginative intuition was reflected in the variety of definitions and explanations advanced by members of the school for characterizing national economies.

Far more carefully devised than the various concepts of organic system was the dialectic concept used by K. Marx for evidencing the inevitable breakdown of the capitalist order. Although one might expect that only an organic concept was compatible with the evolutionary aspects of dialectic reasoning, Marx availed himself of the hypothetical, atomistic mechanic system concept of Ricardian economies as a starting point, but transformed the equilibrating tendencies operating within the Ricardian system into mutually antagonistic forces working in reality toward the disruption of his system. A machinery the operation of which was determined by so grossly disparate elements could not function at all, and the main task of the Marxian analysis did not consist in demonstrating the necessity of the collapse of that machinery; that necessity was logically implied in the construction of the system. What Marx had to explain, and what he could not explain, was the functioning of a fundamentally mechanical system in which disequilibrating tendencies were continuously operating.

Thus, when economic reasoning unfolded in the course of the nineteenth century, at least three radically different concepts of economic system were being applied: an organic, a mechanic, and a dialectic. They provide an adequate basis for a first general classification of economic doctrines. Subdivisions can be established by differentiating various versions of these system concepts.

In order to clarify the connections which have existed between the development of economic thought and the general history of Western reasoning, it appears appropriate to extend our discussions beyond the pales of economic analysis strictly speaking and to refer to some metaeconomic concepts which have played important roles in determining the formation of economic systems. The metaeconomic concepts which I have in mind have been borrowed from other sciences or from popular reasoning and have subsequently been adjusted in varying degrees to the purposes of economic analysis. I have selected five such concepts which have played outstanding roles in the history of our science: the equilibrium concept, the maximization principle, the notion of time, the idea of freedom, and the conception of law. The meaning of each of these notions has varied widely according to the methods of thought which have supplied the logical setting for their definitions.

THE CONCEPT OF ECONOMIC EQUILIBRIUM

The importance of the equilibrium concept for the development of Western thought has been so great that one might be tempted to include the concept—at least in a rudimentary form—among the self-evident synthetic categories of our process of thinking were it not for the fact that mechanical ideas have been practically ignored by the peoples of the Far East before they came into closer contact with the Western World.

Led by Saint Thomas Aquinas, the Schoolmen of the later Middle Ages elaborated an economic doctrine which was largely derived from Aristotelian views. The equilibrium concept appeared in the form of equivalence, and the normative connotations implied in the idea of equivalence permeated all Scholastic economic precepts: what was given should be equal in intrinsic value to what was taken. That maxim was reflected in the concept of just price and just wage, of money, in the ideas of commutative and distributive justice, and in the prohibition of usury.

It is not necessary to discuss in this connection the remarkable phases of the prolonged logical struggle waged mainly in Italy and England during the mercantilist period against the principles of Scholastic reasoning. In the course of this struggle, reason was deprived of its predominant position as a reliable instrument of discovering the truth with the aid of absolutely, eternally valid concepts. Instead, emphasis was placed on the function of individual wills in organizing human collectivities in accordance with the interests of the individuals. The utilitarian principle which made its appearance had been anathema to the Scholastics.

In a world in which reason was no longer relied upon to teach the rules of lawful and just behavior, a purely mechanical equilibrium concept borrowed from the natural sciences was resorted to in order to establish a firm starting point for an understanding of the relationships of economic phenomena. The equilibrium concept appeared in various rudimentary forms: in the form of the proposition that what was somewhere gotten was somewhere lost; in the application of the balance idea to the measurement of gains and losses in foreign trade and to the explanation of prices in accordance with the quantity theory of money. More refined uses made of the equilibrium concept led to the proposition that prices tended to be equal to cost and to the analysis of the international distribution of monetary metals in terms of the simile of the behavior of liquid in communicating vessels. Eventually that process culminated in the conception of a hypothetical economic system as an equilibrated mechanism and in the elaboration of all conditions which were needed for assuring the operation of that mechanism.

It is very likely that the application of the equilibrium concept to the construction of an economic system has provided a way of escape from the hopeless undertaking to devise an economic system which would have included among its logical premises all the uncertainties and risks confronting an individual's economic behavior under the competitive order.

Three important consequences followed from the construction of a mechanical economic system: First, that the system was to be conceived as a self-regulating mechanical relationship of magnitudes to be reduced to a common denominator, a standard unit of value. Second, the belief that, if the system tended to maintain all its constituent elements in general equilibrium, noninterference with its functioning was the best method of assuring the most beneficial effects of individual economic activities. Thus, regardless of the philosophical utilitarian origin of the idea of free competition and its blessings, that idea received strong support from the mechanistic construction of the economic system.

Finally, since such a mechanistic construction was inapplicable to any other spheres of human activity, analysis of the economic system could be completely divorced from the discussion of other sectors of social life and the search for laws of causality could be made a main object of economic analysis.

That rigid equilibrium concept which required reduction of all elements of the economic system to a common denominator, an objective standard unit of value—as distinct from fluctuating prices—dominated Anglo-Saxon economic reasoning almost until the end of the nineteenth century. Phenomena which were incompatible with the assumed self-regulating tendencies of the system were held to have been caused by forces operating from outside the system and, consequently, were placed beyond the reach of the economist's reasoning.

A new chapter started in the history of the equilibrium concept as applied to economics when the labor cost theory was superseded by the theory of subjective value. The emergence of marginal utility analysis signified a victory of hypothetical reasoning in the fight against the substance concept of the goods and the traditional Scholastic belief that the value of a good must be conditioned by some quality inherent in the good. On the other hand, the application of the equilibrium concept to the system as a whole met with extraordinary logical difficulties when two fundamental assumptions of Ricardian economics had to be abandoned: that all exchange values could be reduced to a common, invariable denominator, a standard unit of cost, and that equal values were exchanged for each other in each exchange transaction. Instead of starting from the search for forces tending to maintain the balance of the system as a whole, marginal utility reasoning requested its adherents to start on the assumption that every individual permanently tended to equalize his marginal utilities and thus to keep in balance his entire system of want satisfaction; that, moreover, on the supply side each producer continuously performed a corresponding balancing process by continuing his production up to the point at which his returns and the marginal productivity of his resources were equalized.

The differences which developed between the mathematical and the psychological versions of marginalism were reflected in divergencies made in the use of the equilibrium concept. Motivated by the desire to apply series of simultaneous equations to the analysis of their hypothetical economic systems, the adherents of mathematical economics did not hesitate to assume indefinite divisibility of goods and utilities, interpersonal comparability of utilities, and similar fictitious devices. A substantial array of these and additional fictions were introduced by Walras into his bold construction of a perfectly equilibrated system; other somewhat less extravagant fictions were used in other versions of marginal utility analysis.

The followers of the psychological school, however, never came under the spell of the rigid Ricardian equilibrium concept. They regarded utilities as nonmeasurable and indivisible stimuli of demand and did not even look for a method fit for reducing marginal utilities to mutually comparable magnitudes. Böhm-Bawerk made the equilibrium of the economic machinery dependent upon the maintenance of the equilibrium rate of interest as the strategic factor operating toward the mutual adjustment of the various productive processes. Thus, he was among the first economists to emphasize such adjustment over time as an indispensable element of securing the equilibrium of the system.

It is well known how Knut Wicksell developed these ideas and ultimately substituted for the Ricardian rigid equilibrium concept another concept which proved to be a far more flexible instrument of economic analysis. He made the stability of the system dependent upon the coincidence of the real rate and the market rate of interest; he established a new monetary equation which identified that part of the national income that is not saved with the total volume of goods of consumption multiplied by their prices. Thus he questioned the classical myth that money was simply a veil to be lifted in order to understand the functioning of the economic machinery. He pointed to expectations as an important element in determining employers' decisions. Finally, he suggested even the existence of two economic systems with different equilibrium conditions—a system of productive operations and a monetary system—and attempted to define exactly the equilibrium conditions of the monetary system. Thus he outlined the equilibrium problems which were elaborated by his Swedish disciples and provided the framework for the development of the Austrian business cycle theory.

Another attempt to take account of the time factor in devising a more flexible equilibrium concept than that used by the Ricardians was made by Schumpeter, who transformed the Walrasian system into a system of moving equilibrium positions. The forces operating within that system were arranged in accordance with a sort of dialectical scheme.

Business cycle analysis of the interwar period was largely influenced by the idea that the disruptions of the equilibrium of the economic system were caused by the alternative expansions and contractions of the means of payment. A new formulation of the equilibrium aspects of the economic system was advanced by Keynes. He placed great emphasis on the lack of any connection between the propensity to save and the propensity to invest and dropped the Ricardian assumption that there exists for the economic system a tendency to establish its equilibrium at a level of full employment of the available resources. He requested the development of a theory of shifting equilibrium designed to analyze a system in which changing views about the future are capable of influencing the present situation. Thus the Keynesian theory marked another step in the development of a doctrine which started from the Ricardian equilibrium system and advanced by removing one after another the assumptions which Ricardo had made in order to justify the application of equilibrium analysis to an imaginary real exchange economy operating independently of the influence of money and credit.

The American Institutionalists—who can hardly be said to have formed a coherent school—occupy a separate chapter in that history. They refused to apply the equilibrium concept and other concepts of high abstraction to economic relationships; on the other hand, since they did not adopt the methods of organismic reasoning proclaimed by the German historical school, they did not develop any clear concept of economic system.

The Ricardian mechanical conception of the economic machinery was also responsible for a considerable number of socialist doctrines designed to evidence the existence of mutually antagonistic, disequilibrating forces operating within the capitalist economy. That was, above all, true of the Marxian doctrine, which emphasized disproportionate expansions of the various sectors of the economy as the source of continuously intensified disequilibria. In contrast to the alleged behavior of the capitalist economy, a definite equilibrium concept appears to have been introduced into bolshevist reasoning. Stalin's scheme of abolishing private property of land and of mechanizing agriculture was explicitly motivated by the intention to establish, as quickly as possible, the equilibrium between agricultural and industrial production.

THE MAXIMIZATION PRINCIPLE

Next to the equilibrium principle in its various forms, the idea of "maximization" has been an important metaeconomic logical category—frequently intimately connected with the equilibrium concept through the proposition that what was to be maximized was a share in a limited supply. In that case the share of any partner could be increased only at the cost of others. Thus the economic policy of striving for export surpluses as pursued in the mercantilist period was suggested by the belief that the total volume of wealth available for all countries and embodied in the precious metals was a given, more or less fixed, magnitude, so any gain in the struggle for wealth and power could be secured only at the expense of other competitors.

Subsequently, after general relative scarcity of goods had been recognized as a factor which was fundamental to any economic considerations, the idea of maximization provided a "rational principle" to quite a number of economic doctrines, that is to say, a principle which, when generally observed, could be assumed to assure the smooth functioning of the system envisaged by the doctrine. Especially did the doctrines that questioned the power of reason to establish absolutely valid rules of social behavior resort to the formal maximization principle which appeared to provide an objective, measurable goal for individual and collective actions. The classical instance in point was the Utilitarian philosophy which made striving for the satisfaction of self-interest the guiding principle of human behavior and elevated the principle of maximizing happiness to the rank of an incontestable ultimate end. Simultaneously the apparently insoluble problem of how to transform happiness into a measurable magnitude was approached from the economic angle. Striving for maximization of earnings in form of exchange values could be established as a rational principle of economic behavior if it could be shown that pursuance of that objective was consistent with the interests of others and those of the community. That problem was answered by Adam Smith to the satisfaction of his contemporaries. In Ricardian economics, maximization of gains was transformed into maximization of the individual shares in a national dividend which was assumed to consist of a more or less fixed volume of exchange values expressed in units of labor costs. There is no doubt that the use of the maximization principle contributed greatly toward transforming economics into an exact and dismal science. Among the psychological and economic magnitudes which on different occasions were suggested as objects of maximization were the utilitarian categories of pleasure, happiness, want satisfaction; the marginist categories of utility, ophelimity, social utility; and the economic categories of welfare, real income, national income, profits. Even after the intimate connection between the utilitarian philosophy and equilibrium economics had been significantly reduced, the leading Anglo-Saxon schools of economics, headed by A. Marshall and J. B. Clark, maintained, on the whole, the Ricardian setting of the maximization problem.

The members of the German historical school, who abhorred the idea of quantifying economics, returned more or less explicitly to the mercantilist idea of the struggle of the world powers over their shares in the world markets. In the Marxian analysis of the capitalist economy, striving for the maximum possible gain was presented as a sort of original sin of the capitalist employer and combined with an alleged uncontrollable passion of the capitalist for maximizing the accumulation of capital and for investing it in productive processes regardless of the prevailing market situation. On closer analysis, the maximization principle—as the rationale of the employer's behavior—appears to be the real source of the disruptive tendencies attributed by Marx to the operation of the economic forces.

With the introduction of marginal utility analysis, the maximization principle assumed new aspects. The relatively simple idea of how to maximize shares in a national dividend was superseded by the idea of maximizing marginal utilities and marginal productivities. The problem of how to maximize utilities expressed in cardinal numbers was replaced by the problem of how to maximize ordinal magnitudes. The problem of how to maximize production was transformed into the problem of how to allocate available resources in such a way that the marginal increment of return from the unit of the resources was equal in all alternative uses.

A central position was assigned to the maximization idea in welfare economics, the problems of which turn on the question of how to maximize economic advantages and minimize costs. In due course these studies were faced with the intricate problem of how to measure and compare individual utilities and disabilities. In more recent discussions considerable doubt has been cast on the applicability of the maximization principle to the analysis of the normal behavior of the businessman.

THE NOTION OF TIME

Most puzzling has been the role played by the concept of time in the history of economic reasoning. In accordance with the principles of Aristotelian logics, the Scholastics were requested, in the words of Whitehead, to derive the historical world of change from a changeless world of ultimate reality. Practically all aspects of medieval thinking point to the timelessness of the mental attitude of Scholastic theologians and their contemporaries.

Although Francis Bacon, the great teacher of many mercantilist economists, had recommended observation and experience as the primary instrument of analysis, the Mercantilists were prevented by their predilection for the mechanical approach from including the time element among the factors to be taken into account in establishing relationships between economic phenomena. Leading eighteenth-century economists, such as D. Hume and Adam Smith, did not overlook the importance of historical change, but the theoretical concept of economic system which grew out of mercantilist thinking, the economic regularities and laws which were sought after, were dominated by the equilibrium concept and considered applicable regardless of time and place. In the Ricardian economics, all vestiges of the historical approach were eliminated; the "economic man" was the timeless agent of a well-balanced, fictitious economic machinery in which the use of the productive factors was assumed to be perfectly flexible and the relation of prices to changing market conditions was assumed to be almost instantaneous; savings were supposed to be fully invested without delay; the time-involving function of money to serve for storing up values was ignored; and so on. Some leading post-Ricardian economists, such as Jevons and Walras, dreamt of economics as a science of timeless applied mathematics.

Within the context of post-Ricardian economics, A. Marshall gave a limited consideration to the time element. In an often-quoted dictum, he pointed to the element of time as the center of the chief difficulty of almost every economic problem. In his study of the short-run and the long-run equilibria of hypothetical-representative firms, he measured time in terms of intervals dependent upon the modifiability or fixity of the forces operating on the supply side. The term *operational* measures of time was later applied to such varying standards of measuring time.

In this connection F. H. Knight spoke of kinetic methods designed to show how the equilibrium is established over short periods when general conditions are assumed to remain unchanged. Knight reached also into the time problem in his proposal to explain profits as surpluses derived from uncertainties.

The members of the Austrian school, who were not tempted to apply a rigid equilibrium concept in devising their economic system, did not assume timeless reactions of prices or other economic magnitudes to changes in market conditions. As suggested by Böhm-Bawerk, two special aspects of the time problem attracted their attention: the subjective time preference for present as compared with future goods and a sort of operational objective concept of time connected with Böhm-Bawerk's average period of production. Extensive discussions have turned on the relevance of the time factor for the explanation of interest on capital.

Among Knut Wicksell's most promising contributions to Böhm-Bawerk's theories of interest and capitalist production was his reference to expectations as a significant element of economic processes. Such expectations, whether entertained by employers, consumers, or savers of capital assets, are psychological phenomena involving a concept of subjective time. It was realized that for purposes of equilibrium analysis, subjective time was to be translated into operational time and the latter into calendar time—the time underlying the general course of actual economic events. Only calendar time is not measured by changes closely connected with the purposes of measurement.

Wicksell's suggestions were elaborated by his Swedish followers in studies in which methods of sequence analysis were used for examining hypothetical cases of discontinuous change. Special attention was given to the so-called unit period—the period of adjustment during which one or more significant variables were assumed not to change.

The process of change was transformed into a series of temporary equilibria by economists such as Hicks who attempted to adjust the Marshallian models to conditions obtaining under the influence of expectations of future prices. The stability of the equilibrium system appeared to be seriously weakened when account was taken of expectations. Considerable discussions have turned on the question of whether stability is likely to be promoted by the greatest possible flexibility of the price system or whether, as suggested by Keynes, rigidity of the wage level is to be counted among the measures fit for promoting stability.

In the course of the development of monetary and business cycle theories, two important ideas connected with the time factor were added to the arsenal of our instruments of analysis: the multiplier—intended to determine the relation between changes in investment and changes in income—and the acceleration principle, according to which every fluctuation in the demand for finished goods leads to far stronger fluctuations in the demand for producers' goods needed for producing the finished goods. When account was taken of these factors, as a rule a discontinuous concept of time has been used.

Still in a more or less preliminary stage is the difficult problem of how to allow for changes in economic relationships assumed to be continuous.

The difficulties which the adherents of hypothetical reasoning experienced in dealing with the time factor were largely ignored by the followers of those nineteenth-century philosophies which preserved the belief in the power of reason to grasp the "intrinsic" reality of outside events with the aid of appropriate concepts. Since they considered continuous change an "inherent" element of the "real" course of events, the logical operations which they performed were alleged directly to reflect such continuous processes.

Such logical operations were characteristic of the methods used by the German historical school. The very nature of the school indicates the importance which its adherents attached to the element of time as a factor indispensable for the understanding of any economic phenomena. In sharp opposition to the timeless hypothetical laws of Ricardian economies, they hoped to discover historical laws determining for specific periods and nations the rules or regularities underlying changes in economic relationships. Quite commonly they circumvented the difficulties involved in dealing with the concept of continuous change by the use of biological analogies which included attributes such as continuous growth and decline, expansion of economic forces, structural developments, and the like. The term *organic time* might be used to denote the time span which covers the growth and decline of an organism. A similar concept was used by those German economists who distinguished ''stages'' in the history of developmental economic processes. Each stage was believed to be marked by growth and decline of its characteristic features. The scientific results of vague analogies drawn between collectivities and organisms were not very significant.

Again another concept of time—that of ''evolutionary'' time—was used by the adherents of dialectic reasoning, especially by Marx. For dialectic reasoning of the materialistic type, continuity of time was of outstanding importance, since that reasoning was intended to convey the idea of incessant changes occurring in reality in the structure of production, and in economic and social relationships, up to the point at which a revolutionary climax is reached in the clash between antagonistic forces. The continuous growth of an antagonism inherent in the capitalist order was alleged to be reflected in its full reality in the contradictions of a logical process. In his schemes of simple and expanding production, however, Marx appears to have resorted to the use of a concept of discontinuous time. These problematic schemes were further elaborated by some adherents of his doctrine.

Where the concept of time entered into economic reasoning, the meanings attached to the concept showed considerable differences. The more or less indifferent concepts of calendar time and continuous and discontinuous time have been associated with all methods of reasoning. Within the framework of hypothetical reasoning, the concept of discontinuous time has been used in connection with the methods of comparative statics and sequence analysis. Also of the hypothetical type have been the concepts of subjective time and of operational time. The concept of organic time has been widely used by members of the German historical school; the concept of evolutionary time has been indispensable for dialectic reasoning.

THE CONCEPT OF FREEDOM

A discussion of the concept of freedom as a metaeconomic category can conveniently take its start from a definition of freedom as the faculty or the right to choose among various alternatives. A concept of this type was implied in the Scholastic notion of ''freedom of the will,'' which was the counterpart of the power of reason to teach with finality what is right or wrong, what is true or false. The ''terrible'' Scholastic power of reason limited the choice of the will to very narrow ranges of behavior, since there was nothing adiaphorous in the medieval world and everybody was assigned a fixed place in a strictly hierarchical organization. The fight for individual liberties began with the fight for the freedom to formulate new concepts and new teachings which were independent of the decisions of clerical authorities. In the course of that struggle a logical foundation for individual liberties and social institutions such as private property was sought after in innate ideas or natural rights. Later, when the belief in innate ideas and natural rights was eliminated, reason was assigned the subordinate functions to show the most adequate means of achieving objectives chosen by the will and to explore and evaluate the chances of reaching constantly shifting ends. Randomness of wants, as that principle has been termed, became a cornerstone of the utilitarian philosophy. Along with the increasing use made of the methods of hypothetical reasoning, liberty of thought, tolerance, and democratic procedures became closely associated ingredients of social organization.

That spiritual development provided the background for unfolding mercantilist thinking. The request for economic freedom which the Physiocrats derived from a natural individual right was based by the advanced Mercantilists on the belief that the functioning of a mechanical system governed by causal interrelationships would be disturbed rather than helped by measures of government interference. That idea of transforming the principles of free competition into an ingredient of a causally determined order was forcefully presented by Adam Smith and used by Ricardo as the starting point of a logically consistent doctrine.

The hypothetical aspects of that approach were even more consistently developed in the doctrines of the marginal utility type in which any normative connotations were eliminated from the concept of free competition. It was assumed that the freedom of each individual to balance his marginal utilities and disutilities was limited only by a similar freedom of all competitors, that assumption was conceived as the logical basis for assuring the most rational or economic use of a limited supply of productive resources confronted with a much larger demand. The hypothetical features of the concept of free competition were given new emphasis in the recent studies dealing with the limited role played by perfect competition in actual economic organization.

The importance of individual freedom and free competition for the organization of society was belittled or even ridiculed by almost all schools of thought which rejected the methods of hypothetical reasoning. Most adherents of the German historical school who identified public interest with national power politics favored the establishment of public as well as private monopolies as instruments of such politics. They applied the Darwinian principle of the survival of the fittest to an alleged struggle waged between conflicting nations. The idea of individual freedom was lost where such reasoning was firmly established.

Under the rule of dialectic reasoning, adopted by Marx, all hypothetical features of Ricardian economics were transformed into antagonistic forces operating in reality; these forces were said to find their expression in the self-development of the modes of production and distribution and in the evolutionary class struggle. The workers were shown to be engaged in a heroic struggle, not for individual liberty but for the liberation of their class and the annihilation of the employers. The liberty promised after the establishment of the communist so-called stateless society was an ill-defined metaphysical concept.

Hence, within the context of deterministic doctrines the concept of free competition has been either eliminated as far as possible or transformed into a fateful struggle for existence. Individualistic doctrines have originally included freedom of competition among the precepts taught by natural law. Later, freedom was conceived as a rational principle of an economy functioning in accordance with the laws of economic causality. Finally, it was used in a purely hypothetical form for the construction of imaginary mechanical economic systems.

THE CONCEPT OF LAW

The fight which was waged over the liberation of the methods of thought from the fetters of medieval reasoning was clearly reflected in the gradual development of the concept of causal law as applied to social relationships. All notions of the Scholastic sociology or economics included normative elements; all "laws" which corresponded to these notions were precepts, formulated as eternally valid, absolutely binding commands. Subsequently the development of the doctrine of natural laws was indicative of the strong desire to find in an innate faculty of reason a justification for the vindication of certain individual rights. The ensuing application of mechanistic conceptions to the relationships between economic magnitudes suggested the search for laws of nature or causal laws of an economic or sociological type, but until late into the eighteenth century the borderline between normative and causal laws remained blurred and ill defined.

The first thinker who quite clearly used the term *law* in the causal sense for defining rules underlying relationships between economic phenomena appears to have been Ricardo. The catalogue of the fundamental laws of Ricardian economics, based on the distinction between hypothetical and empirical laws, was established by Senior and elaborated by J. S. Mill. Whereas empirical laws, derived from observation and experience, were considered falsifiable, hypothetical laws, derived from assumptions, served the purpose of constructing imaginary models of economic relationships which were frequently far removed from the results of actual observation. Such constructions were considerably encouraged by the application of marginal utility and marginal productivity analysis. The same was true of the search for causal or functional relationships between economic magnitudes.

Simultaneously the maxim that reason was unable to establish generally valid normative rules of behavior led to the consequence that formulation of principles of economic policy was beyond the scope of scientific economics. When the principles of hypothetical reasoning were strictly applied, it was even questionable whether it was possible to establish economic laws of the causal type. The relationships between economic phenomena were regarded as purely functional for purposes of theoretical economic analysis.

The concept of hypothetical laws was incompatible with the logical principles of economic or sociological schools which believed in the power of reason to discover the substance of things and to teach the real laws underlying the course of actual events. But never fulfilled were the ambitious hopes of the members of the historical school to arrive at a full understanding of the development of the various national collectivities and economies through the discovery of "historical" laws, reflecting the individuality of these collectivities.

Again radically different from hypothetical laws and the historical laws are the "evolutionary" laws advanced within the context of the dialectic method of reasoning. Absolute validity has been claimed for these laws because of the reputedly infallible methods used in establishing them. Examples of laws of that type are the law of the class struggle, the laws of capital accumulation, the law of the falling rate of profit, and the like.

Among all the metaeconomic concepts, the concept of law has probably been the object of the most divergent meanings. It has been used for denoting moral or legal precepts derived from revelation, from an innate faculty of reason, or from the will of authorities, however constituted; for denoting the existence of regular causal relationships suggesting identity in time or of purely hypothetical relationships assumed to follow from exactly defined assumptions in accordance with rules of hypothetical reasoning; for denoting the results of empirically determined regularities frequently found with the aid of statistical methods; for denoting certain regular relationships discovered through intuitive penetration into the meaning of the course of predominantly historical events; and, finally, for denoting the rules underlying the course of teleologically determined social processes and discovered with the aid of dialectic methods alleged to reflect exactly the rules of evolutionary processes occurring in reality.

CONCLUSIONS

If the preceding distinction of patterns of thought is fairly correct, it would be futile to suggest compromises between schools which fundamentally differ as to the methods of setting and solving economic problems. If effected, such compromises might result in beclouding deep-seated differences in the approach to fundamental aspects of economic life and in preventing the clarification of important issues.

It is obvious that in some important respects the foregoing discussion reaches beyond the narrower limits of economics. The principles suggested for the grouping of the economic doctrines could easily be adjusted to the task of classifying the doctrines in practically all other social sciences.

Appendix C
Further Metaeconomic Concepts
——

RATIONALITY

Since the formulation of the relations between will and reason was of paramount importance for differentiating the various patterns of thought, it might be convenient to start this survey with some observations concerning protean aspects of the notion of "rationality."

In the light of Scholastic methods the power of reason was supreme, and human will, believed to be influenced by the "weakness of the flesh," was strictly subordinated to absolutely valid precepts derived from the hierarchical scale of general notions. Tertullian's dictum *"credibile quia ineptum est"* (frequently cited as *"credo quia absurdum"*)—"I believe it because it is absurd"—points to the sharp distinction drawn by the Scholastics between the commands of faith and those of reason. But throughout the Middle Ages the Scholastics successfully endeavored to demonstrate the logical consistency of their tenets.

A similar subordination of the will to reason was characteristic of the physiocratic philosophy. Quesnay's remarkable achievement consisted in establishing a "self-evident" natural order providing the guiding principles for a sort of linear progress in pursuance of general welfare. Exercise of rationality required adjustment of economic institutions and economic behavior to this order.

Where organismic concepts prevailed, reference was frequently made to a poorly defined "common will" and the members of the community were required to adapt their economic behavior unconditionally to the rules and regulations issued by an authority vested with the power of establishing, interpreting, and carrying out the intentions of the common will. Some supreme objectives—a mission—were ascribed to the community, conceived of as an "organism"; they provided the directives for decisions qualified as "rational," but this term does not appear to have played an important role in the context of a philosophy that emphasized the power of the will rather than the power of reason.

When defined in accordance with Marxian dialectics, the concept of rationality was applicable only to members of the working classes, who were said to be engaged, consciously or unconsciously, in waging the class war, and thus to adapt their behavior to the inexorable laws of evolutionary processes. According to these laws, the behavior of the Capitalists was to be qualified as inherently irrational. It was bound to lead to the progressive accumulation of capital in the hands of a few employers, to a constantly declining rate of profits, to increasingly intensified crises and depressions, to the break-down of the capitalist order, and to the final victory of the proletarian revolution.

The Bolshevists of the Stalinist type interpreted the Marxian doctrine to the effect that consummate exercise of the dialectic methods enabled the leaders of the Communist party to gain full insight into the "laws" to be applied to the organization of the planned economy. Fundamental to these laws was the idea of expanding the heavy capital goods producing industries at the cost of other sectors of the economy and of mechanizing, as far as possible, all economic processes. Application of these "laws" was hailed as the realization of socialist economic rationality, and any attempts to question the validity of these laws were prosecuted. There is no room for a discussion of individual economic rationality within the framework of a dictatorship that extends its control to all spheres of life. Still unanswered are the questions of how and to what degree the concept of eco-nomic rationality will be modified in the course of the discussions that have dealt with problems of planning in the post-Stalinist period; the leading authorities of various com-munist countries have started gradually to introduce some salient features of the market economy into their planning devices in order to secure a "rational" allocation of the available resources.

The relation of will to reason, as defined within the context of nominalist reasoning, was succinctly expressed in Pareto's dictum that the choice among ultimates belongs to the sphere of nonlogical actions. Hence, such choice could never be subject to logical judgments. This dictum was supplemented by the formula "randomness of wants," which was derived from the Benthamite utilitarian philosophy and implied that, as viewed from the economic economic angle, no distinction was to be made between wants of different kinds.

The function of reason was, consequently, limited to the task of teaching the appro-priate means for achieving desired ends. The Ricardian economists were convinced that strictly competitive behavior combined with striving for maximization of profits resulted in assuring, as completely as possible, the objectives of the economy, namely, maximum production of desired goods, economically advisable allocation of resources, and best available distribution of incomes. Economic behavior, determined by these principles, was characterized as observance of the rules of a game agreed upon by the parties to it. The movement of prices was relied upon to secure the equilibrium of the economic forces. Post-Ricardian economists protested against the attempts of the "technocrats" to adjust the organization of the economy to the principles of technological rationality, and identi-fied rational "economic" behavior with the observance of the principles of marginal utility and marginal productivity.

The apparently well devised definition became, however, the object of conflicting interpretations when due recognition was given to the widespread existence of noncompetitive market conditions, when account was taken of the effects of risks and uncertainties on decision making and attempts were made to establish models of choice, lending themselves to mathematical treatment. Rational behavior now was defined as behavior in accordance with some ordering of alternatives in terms of relative desirability. The concepts of subjective and objective probability played a significant role in elaborating this definition. Another approach to the problem of rationality was suggested by the idea of abandoning theories based on generalized, nonverifiable assumptions and replacing them with a theory of choice derived from observation and experience.

The usefulness of the concept of rationality for economic analysis was eventually questioned on the grounds that in actual situations the decision maker is faced with a range of complex choices, that the utility function is highly unstable over time, and that individual actions are partly controlled by the realization of their repercussion on the action of others.[1]

In the light of these considerations, rational economic behavior, far from being amenable to a clear-cut definition, turned out to signify an attitude frequently affected by irrational assessment of previous information and characterized by adjustment of decision making to changing unforeseeable conditions. Hence, increasingly complex methods of operational research were devised by students of business administration for restricting the range of choices among alternative solutions.

SYSTEM

Turning to the concept of "system," we are faced with a variety of methods that were used in forming logically coordinated mental pictures of the elements to be combined for purposes of analyzing the behavior of the "economy." The definition of the constituent parts of the "economic system" and the determination of their relationships to the whole were of primary importance in forming the various organic, dialectic, or mechanical system concepts. The first attempt to suggest a consistent model of the economy was made by the Physiocrats, who based their analysis of the "natural order of an agricultural kingdom" on a volume of exchange values created by nature in the course of each economic period and distributed during that period among the main—productive and sterile—classes of the population. This strictly mechanical scheme reflected a Cartesian conception of the forces that are operating in the universe. It was described in mathematical terms and its functioning was illustrated by a graphical presentation.

The Baconian methodology, as influenced by Newtonian cosmology, provided the logical background for the vaguely defined concepts of "economic system" suggested by Adam Smith and some eighteenth-century Italian economists. The Ricardian model of the economy owed some of its main characteristics to the principles of the associationist psychology; in other respects it reflected certain characteristics of Scholastic reasoning, since it was intended to reveal the "substance" of the economy behind the screen of fluctuating prices. Influenced by a deterministic philosophy, Ricardo elaborated the picture of an economy driven by forces beyond the control of individuals. The mechanistic aspects of this model were accentuated by the elimination of the time element from economic analysis. It had a counterpart in an atomistic conception of the social community, a group of individuals acting independently of each other.

The methods of hypothetical reasoning used in elaborating the Ricardian doctrine were made explicit by Cairnes and John Stuart Mill. In the light of these methods, all economic magnitudes that could be reduced to a common denominator (a unit of exchange values) were coordinated in accordance with mechanical principles; a number of assumptions were introduced to determine the movement of the exchange values and to establish their distribution among the main classes of the population. Thus, an abstract economic system was logically isolated from the other sectors of the society that did not lend themselves to the application of mechanical principles.

The use of highly abstract concepts as means of economic analysis, the application of the principle of causality to the explanation of economic relationships, and the mechanical aspects of the Ricardian system were rejected by the adherents of intuitional reasoning, who believed that reality could be directly grasped with the aid of "organismic" notions tinged with biological characteristics. The definition of the "structure" of the economy played a considerable role in their discussions.[2] But formidable problems were involved in accounting for the "organic unity" of the economy, its supraindividual objectives, the relations of the parts to the whole. Even after long discussions, no effective methods were available for establishing a consistent "organic" model of the economy.

The Marxian picture of the capitalist economy was also designed to reflect "reality" fully; it owed its characteristic features to the methods of dialectic materialism, and was intended to demonstrate the operation of antagonistic forces leading to a preestablished goal, the breakdown of the capitalist economy. With this end in view, an abstract mechanical model, composed of exchange values, like its Ricardian prototype, was exposed to the disrupting effects of disproportionate expansions and contractions of its two sections, the section producing capital goods and the section producing consumers' goods. Since such a mechanism was bound to be disrupted in the course of the first crisis, Marx felt obliged to devote large parts of the second and third volumes of *Kapital* to a discussion of the factors that had permitted the capitalist system to survive even long periods of deep depressions. Rosa Luxemburg's problematic theory of "economic imperialism," as adopted by Lenin, provided the Bolshevist party with an official interpretation of Marxism according to which the capitalist order, passing through the last phase of its history, owed its prolonged existence to the ruthless exploitation of the "noncapitalist" territories. This final stage of a long evolutionary process was designated as "monopoly capitalism" and the wars of the colonial powers were explained as desperate fights over markets.

The system concept adopted by the Soviet planners has not been clearly defined. It appears to be of a mechanical type and to be characterized by the steady expansion of the capital-producing industries at the expense of the other sectors of the economy. The rate of investments has probably been defined by more or less arbitrary decisions prompted by power policies. During the initial violent fights over the organization of the Soviet economy, Stalin proclaimed the principle that the highly mechanized industrial sector had to be developed far more rapidly than the agricultural sector. Hence, for more than two decades the Soviet economy was subjected to highly disproportionate expansions of its constituent elements. Some attempts to correct these discrepancies were made, but only after the end of the Stalinist regime. More refined models of the economy were suggested by some Russian economists who applied input-output analysis and other econometric methods to centralized planning of their economy.

The original, vaguely conceived, system concepts of the Ricardian economists were consistently elaborated by authors of mathematical persuasion who eliminated from their considerations any reference to causal relationships between economic magnitudes and all logical obstacles to the timeless mutual adjustment of all elements of the system to equilibrium positions. Thus, the Walrasian and Paretian models were based on bold assumptions, such as complete interdependence of the price system, strict observance of marginalist principles, and the rules of perfect competition. Any economic phenomena the existence of which could not be reconciled with this imaginary static model were excluded from the sphere of theoretical economics. The exclusive use of mathematical methods was considered indispensable for the establishment of a consistent system, and the transformation of economics into a science of applied mathematics was frequently defended with the argument that the rules of mathematics—like those of logic—represented instruments of a higher, absolutely valid order. It is a moot question whether, as was asserted by Schumpeter, any analysis of the functioning of the capitalist economy has to start from this model as the first stage in a process of approximation.

The conception of the economy as a system of functional relations between exchange values was questioned by the economists who adopted the psychological version of marginal utility analysis and insisted upon defining these relations in terms of causes and effects. They applied equilibrium analysis not only to a system of "real" exchange values but also to the monetary system; they attempted to define the relationships of these two systems, and relied on the rate of interest as the instrument for securing the mutual adjustment of the productive processes.

The Marshallian principles were not backed by a consistent general system concept; pictures of circumscribed sectors of the economy provided the main objects of abstract partial equilibrium analysis. A considerable variety of more or less vaguely defined models of the economy were, however, suggested by the authors of business cycle theories who endeavored to explain the fluctuating behavior of the economic magnitudes. Models in which this behavior was attributed to "exogenous" causes vied with others in which forces inherent in the economy were made responsible for the cyclical movements and their periodicity. Models in which the influence of monetary factors was practically ignored competed with others in which primary importance was attached to alternating expansions and contractions of the means of payment. Models of the latter type gained the upper hand during the interwar period, but no agreement was reached on the fundamental problem of how to account for the lack of stability of the economy.

A new approach to model building was inaugurated by the introduction of "macroeconomic" analysis, which started, not from phenomena directly reflecting individual behavior but from aggregates of economic magnitudes and their mutual relationships. Economic growth was another aspect introduced into model building. Mechanistic concepts of the economy prevailed in various "dynamic" models in which certain fixed coefficients were assumed to determine the relations between relevant economic aggregates, and the cyclical movements were included among the factors of economic growth. In models of this type the economy was conceived of as the object of circular motions brought about by propelling impulses propagated by a reaction mechanism.

The traditional hypothetical approach to economic analysis experienced some radical changes when it was realized that large and important sectors of the economy were permeated by monopolistic elements and that striving for maximization of profits could not be assumed to provide a rational principle for constructing models of the economy. The emergences of theories of monopolistic and imperfect competition, of the French theory of dominant economic factors, and of the theory of games were landmarks in this development. They called for a revision of the concept of the isolated economic unit.

In due course a considerable group of econometricians objected to the exclusive use of deductive reasoning for model-building purposes. They insisted upon establishing models of the behavior of specific historically determined economies, and upon verifying the validity of these models in the light of subsequent experience.

DEVELOPMENT AND EVOLUTION

The varying meanings attached to the concept of time had a counterpart in the interpretations of the terms *development* and *evolution*. Both concepts imply that subsequent events are somehow prepared through changes that have occurred in preceding periods. The Scholastics distinguished various phases in the history of mankind but the rigid hierarchical structure of their concepts prevented them from applying the idea of development to the succession of these phases. Hence, these phases were separated from each other by metaphysical forces. The Baconian Mercantilists were also lacking a clear concept of economic or historic developments, and the doctrine of the Physiocrats was characterized by an outright though static picture of a distributive process.

During the period of enlightenment, various authors elaborated the idea that continuous linear progress was taking place in the sphere of knowledge, in the utilization of the forces of nature, in general well-being, even in the realm of morality. The application of a measuring rod or the use of normative concepts was implied in the idea of "progress." But others questioned the optimistic outlook to the future which was associated with these visions, pointing to the dismal effects of the propensity of the human race to propagate. Ricardo and his followers adopted the Malthusian population theorem and the "law" of the declining agricultural productivity; starting from these premises, they arrived at the conclusion that the economy was headed toward a final stage of static or stagnant conditions. Reference to these vaguely defined processes contrasted sharply with the structure of the Ricardian methodology, which did not include among its instruments the concept of development.

The question of how to transform continuous into discontinuous processes was only one of the difficulties involved in the task of defining a consistent concept of "evolution" in accordance with the principles of nominalistic reasoning. Another difficulty resulted from the logical requirement that any allusion to teleological propositions had to be carefully avoided. Hence, research dealing with gradual changes had to be restricted to ex post analysis, and the course of the changes had to be related to the incidence of random events. The Darwinian theory of the survival of the fittest was established in accordance with these principles. It was exclusively applicable to past developments and deliberately failed to indicate any trends leading to a predetermined goal. Some adherents of "social Darwinism" attempted to extrapolate alleged trends of evolutionary social processes, but studies of this type were not very successful.

J. Schumpeter used a developmental scheme in his broad economic analysis, especially to explain the fluctuating behavior of the economy. He drew a sharp distinction between economic magnitudes, but he did not attach particular importance to continuous changes which, in his view, could be conceived of as infinitesimally small mutual adjustments of demand and supply. The main factors that he held responsible for the alternating expansions and contractions of business activity were technological and managerial innovations and their effects on production and trade. Thus, whereas he emphasized the incidence of certain shocks and impulses, he failed to show the operation of the propagation mechanism.

Authors who adopted methods of organismic and dialectical reasoning experienced no difficulties in endowing their concepts of evolutionary processes with the characteristics of continuity and teleology. The economists and sociologists of the German historical school who conceived of the national economies as "integrated wholes" applied to them organismic concepts such as juvenile growth, virility, and senescense. In addition, they attributed outstanding cultural missions to certain peoples of their own choosing. They suggested various principles for establishing "stages" in the development of national economies, but failed to indicate the factors that could be considered instrumental in initiating the transition from one stage to the other. Hence, no allusion to evolutionary processes was implied in the concept of stages. Some socialist authors availed themselves of the methods of the historical school to elaborate a "theory" of "evolutionary socialism," which pointed to a gradual transformation of the capitalist economy into a planned organization of productive and distributive processes. As mentioned above, a logically more consistent concept of social evolution was basic to the "materialistic interpretation of history," according to which the class struggle, conceived of as a sort of metaphysical factor, was instrumental in producing evolutionary processes of a strictly deterministic type. The continuity of these processes was held to be interrupted from time to time through revolutionary events that created antagonisms of a higher order and resumption of the processes on a higher level. Establishment of a classless communist society was regarded as the ultimate goal of this teleological scheme.

When faced with problems involving continuous processes, students of nominalistic persuasion had to transform these processes into successive equilibrium positions of the least possible duration. This difficulty was circumvented by the adherents of social philosophies that attributed to reason the power of grasping the "intrinsic" reality of social or economic processes. "Continuous change" could thus be included among the "inherent elements of reality."

A method of this type which was frequently used by authors of intuitional persuasion consisted in applying biological analogies to the analysis of economic collectivities conceived of as integrated wholes. But such analogies were never clearly defined.

Far more consistent and far better developed was the concept of "evolutionary" time which was implied in the Marxian doctrine of dialectic materialism. According to this doctrine, the continuity of economic and social processes is directly reflected in the play of antagonistic concepts used to explain the incessant changes taking place in the development of the capitalist economy. This development is characterized as a succession of increasing disproportions between the main sectors of the economy and of ensuing intensified economic and social tensions and crises. The idea that the incessant action of the antagonistic forces operating within the capitalist economy is leading to a predetermined goal is an essential element of the logic of "scientific" as distinct from "utopian" socialism. The laws of human reasoning, when adjusted to the principles of dialectic materialism, are believed to reflect exactly the evolutionary laws that are leading with absolute finality to the breakdown of the capitalist society.

The apparent consistency of the Marxian evolutionary interpretation of history was lost in its bolshevist version. The concept of "dialectic dynamic growth" used by Stalin in defense of his first five-year plans was perhaps only an appropriate phrase designed to interpret, in dialectical terms, the decision to apply disproportionate rates to the expansion of the various sectors of the economy. Any official attempts to use the dialectic phraseology to justify the methods of bolshevist planning were virtually abandoned after the end of the Stalinist regime.

CLASS

The widely used and frequently misused concept of class can also be shown to be the object of conflicting interpretations. It has been indispensable for all economic doctrines that did not isolate their analysis completely from the body of noneconomic social relationships. The Scholastics regarded rules of parentage as the primary factor that divided the population into classes. These rules were believed to be of man-made origin, and consequently modifiable. The Physiocrats, as well as the Mercantilists, preserved certain features of the Scholastic class concept, especially the view that the various classes and their subgroups were differentiated by occupational characteristics. Hence, the main distinction between the classes was derived from economic considerations connected with the division of labor. The Mercantilists distinguished three main classes: landowners, manufacturers, and workers. The juxtaposition of the "productive" and the "sterile" classes of the population, as made by the Physiocrats, reflected the methodological aspects of their doctrine.

Adam Smith adopted the mercantilist tripartite distinction of classes and used it to implement his analysis of the distributive process. Each of the three main shares in the national dividend—rent, interest on capital and profit, and wages—was connected with a specific source of income—land, capital, and labor—and allotted to one of the main classes of the population: landowners, owners of capital, and workers. He thus prepared the way for the formulation of the Ricardian laws of distribution, and this setting of the problem was taken over by the Marginalists of the psychological school, who endeavored to explain the various sources of income in terms of a single principle.

Many members of the historical school availed themselves of the class concept to elaborate the sociological structure of the economy. Others centered their studies on the task of attenuating the class conflicts in the interest of national unity.

But with the intensified refinement of nominalistic methods, the concept of class as an appropriate instrument of theoretical analysis met with increasing skepticism. The traditional procedure of associating each main class with the receipt of a specific type of income was hardly compatible with considerations derived from the broadening of the rent concept and from the application of marginal productivity analysis to the distribution of the value of the product among the productive factors. Justified objections were raised to the widespread view that the concept of class was a sort of self-evident, indispensable economic category; various principles were suggested for dividing the society into economically relevant groups adjusted to the specific purposes pursued by theoretical or practical research.

This treatment of the concept of class was, of course, incompatible with the convictions of the socialist authors who insisted on defining wages as a fundamental social category and relied on the idea of conflicting class interests as a telling argument in support of their attacks on the capitalist economy. Within the context of the Marxian doctrine, the two antagonistic classes of society were treated as real entities pitted against each other in an unrelenting struggle marked by the succession of several stages. "Blinded" by their propertied interests, the members of the "exploiting" classes were disqualified from availing themselves of the methods of dialectic materialism.

The dialectic formulation of the class struggle provided the leaders of the bolshevist revolution with some of their most effective slogans, which they combined with the assertion that in the "classless" communist society the state will "wither away." But in some later versions of Lenin's theory of economic imperialism the workers of the capitalist countries were shown to have been affected by capitalist interests and thus to have lost class consciousness and the fighting spirit attributed to them by the materialistic interpretation of history. In his blueprint of the planned economy, Lenin did not entrust organized labor with the leadership but rather assigned this task to the Communist party, a group of political revolutionaries. In all communist countries the alleged "dictatorship of the proletariat" has turned out to be the dictatorship of a few party chieftains.

VALUE

Critics of the Ricardian and marginalist models of the economy have repeatedly raised the question of whether the concept of "value" is an indispensable instrument of economic analysis. As a matter of fact, this concept was ignored by all doctrines that restricted their analysis to directly observable phenomena; it was disregarded by others, which, though conceived on a level of high abstraction, introduced various hypothetical standard units to reduce the economic variables to a common denominator.

The history of the value concept starts with the Scholastics, who considered "value" as an inherent, constituent element of the "substance" of a good. They attempted to discover the divine plan of creation according to which all things and beings were believed to be arranged in a hierarchical order reflecting their importance for the well-being of mankind. Hence, at an advanced stage of the Scholastic doctrine, when the principles of economic behavior were consistently analyzed as a part of moral theology, Saint Thomas Aquinas and his followers derived the exchange value of the goods as expressed in prices from the utility of the classes to which the goods were assigned by the divine order.

The Scholastic concept of value provided the basis for the principle of equivalence in buying and selling, and the "just price" of a good was considered invariable unless the good was so transformed that it was transferred into a higher or lower class of utility. But this rigid definition of exchange values was abandoned by some Scholastics of nominalist persuasion, who referred to the estimates of buyers and sellers to account for the formation of such values.

The Baconian Mercantilists preserved the substance concept of the goods. But they replaced the Scholastic concept of "inner goodness" with a quantitative concept of measurable magnitudes incorporated in the goods; moreover, they introduced into economic reasoning the idea of "objective" exchange values as a lasting essential characteristic of the goods and opposed this concept to the fluctuating market prices. The term *productive labor* was applied to activities that resulted in creating exchange values. Adam Smith, who inherited this setting of the value problem, did not arrive at a clear solution. The attempts of Galiani and Turgot to eliminate the substance concept of the goods and to develop a value theory based on estimates of the usefulness of individual goods did not appeal to their contemporaries. The idea that value is a quality permanently inherent in a good prevailed and Ricardo's cost of production theory provided the background for the conception of the "real exchange system" as the true object of economic analysis and for the formulation of the problems involved in productive and distributive processes.

The Ricardian concept of a standard unit of exchange values—virtually a hypothetical concept—was prerequisite to the construction of an economic system in which all magnitudes were reduced to a common denominator. The principle of equivalence as applied to the performance of exchanges was preserved by the Ricardians. But some French and German economists, who did not care about establishing a consistent model of the economy, simply referred to relationships of utility and scarcity to account for the exchange values of the goods.

Of an entirely different type was the value concept adopted by the members of the German historical school. They were looking for a common will or an objective spirit as the source of "social values" and regarded the market prices as the expression of such values. But later the concept of "social values" was frequently freed from its association with metaphysical conceptions and simply used to emphasize the influence of ethical or political ideas on the formation of certain market prices.

The "paradox of value" was solved when the substance concept of goods was abandoned and the utility of a good, instead of being connected with the class to which the good was assigned, was derived from individual estimates of the unit of the good. The formulation of the value problem in terms of marginal utility analysis provided the starting point for the theorizing of the Marginalists of psychological persuasion; a chain of causation could thus be established, reaching from subjective estimates of utilities to the explanation of the value of the productive factors. Marginalists of the mathematical school who endeavored to keep their analysis within the framework of functional relationships of the economic magnitudes had little use for the concept of value. They rejected the search for causal relationships between economic phenomena, and developed a conception of the economy as a system of interdependent prices, assumed to be entirely free from any connection with social relationships. For several decades, repeated attempts were made to find satisfactory solutions to the questions of how to measure utilities and how to qualify interpersonal comparisons of utilities. Students of welfare economics resorted to systems of indifference and preference curves to circumvent these tricky questions. The discussion of the problems connected with the concepts of value and utility faded into the background when the schools of marginalism were displaced from their leading position, at first by the "Keynesian revolution" and later by the development of econometric analysis. As viewed from the econometric angle, the concepts of value and utility did not lend themselves to "operational" research.

It is hardly possible to overemphasize the role played in the structure of the Marxian doctrine by the labor cost theory of value which was suggested by a misinterpretation of the Ricardian value concept. As used by Marx, this theory led to various insoluble problems. It was virtually disregarded by Marx in the discussion of the rate of profit and considered untenable by German "Revisionists." But the economists of the Stalinist period were nevertheless obliged to pay lip service to it, as well as to the principle that payment of interest on capital is incompatible with bolshevist planning. The influence of the labor cost theory on the Stalinist wage and price policy was hardly noticeable, however, and after the end of the Stalinist period an increasing tendency made itself felt to adjust prices to supply and demand conditions.

A few observations may be made on the concept of surplus value as applied to unrequited yields accruing in the course of economic processes. This concept was introduced into economic reasoning by the Physiocrats, who defined agricultural products as a free gift of nature and the exclusive source of exchange values. A reference to surplus values was implied in the Ricardian definition of rent, which later was applied to a large variety of similar situations. The normative idea of the accrual of unearned value increments was involved in the rent concept. As an outright nominalistic notion, the concept of consumers' rent, an outcome of marginal utility analysis, was added to the list.

But the idea of surplus value could also very effectively be used to analyze the "destabilizing" effects of incomes diverted from their economically justified uses. Thus, a dramatic role was assigned to misapplied values in the Marxian treatment of the antagonistic aspects of the capitalist economy. The surplus values withheld from the workers' earnings were identified with the profits amassed by the capitalist employers in the process of self-destructive capital accumulation. The bolshevist interpreters of this doctrine conceded that the Marxian "law of value" continued to function in the socialist economy, but they insisted that it was deprived of its antagonistic effects, since the "socially necessary" costs of production were only one of the factors taken into account in the process of authoritarian price fixing.

This further discussion of metaeconomic concepts, which could be extended in many directions, may be considered sufficient for illustrating the proposition that the history of Western social, sociological, political, moral, and economic doctrines could well be coordinated in accordance with a uniform principle derived from the differences in the logical background of the doctrines. Thus, the way could be prepared for a consistent "logical" interpretation of the development of Western reasoning, and for a study of the influence of the various patterns of reasoning on the course of social events.

Notes

BOOK I

CHAPTER 1

1. Prior to the twelfth century, the commentaries on some Aristotelian writings prepared by Boethius (480?–524?) provided the only Latin source for the knowledge of Aristotelian teachings. This information was not only very fragmentary but also vitiated by the fact that Boethius attempted to reconcile the Aristotelian logic with Neoplatonic methods.

2. The spread of the Aristotelian literature was actively promoted in the thirteenth century by the German emperor Frederic II (d. 1250), who surrounded his court with Arabian philosophers.

3. It is, of course, outside the scope of this study to discuss the intricate question of how far the Scholastics—as influenced by Arabian philosophers—misunderstood and misinterpreted the Aristotelian teachings.

4. Thomas Aquinas was canonized in 1323. The methods of reasoning taught by him were declared binding by the Catholic Church only much later, in the encyclical *Aeterni Patris,* dated 4 August 1879.

5. See Carl Prantl, *Geschichte der Logik im Abendlande,* 2 vols. (Leipzig, 1855–67), pt. 2.

6. See Ernst Cassirer, *Substance and Function,* trans. William C. Swabey and Marie C. Swabey (Chicago, 1923), chap. 1.

7. See Ernest Addison Moody, *The Logic of William of Ockham* (New York, 1935), p. 15.

8. Thus, the program of the University of Paris as set up in the middle of the thirteenth century included grammar, rhetoric, and dialectic in the "Trivium" as separate branches. The teaching of dialectics (logic) was based on the *Organon*, a collection of Aristotle's logical treatises.

9. Since Joseph Alois Schumpeter (*History of Economic Analysts* [New York, 1954], p. 85) has credited me with the authorship of the "doctrine of universalism," I should like to emphasize that I have never used the term *universalism* in the sense applied to it by Othmar Spann.

10. In this connection, see also Erich Rothacker, *Logik und Systematik der Geisteswissenschaften* (Munich, 1927), p. 67.

11. The concept of the *universitas* as a body uniting its members in a superior unity was derived from Roman law, as distinct from the term *societas,* which was applied to organizations formed by agreements of their members.

12. Thomas Aquinas, *Summa contra Gentiles,* chap. 3. About the Aristotelian view that the state was by nature clearly prior to the family and the individual, see Sir Paul Vinogradoff, *Outlines of Historical Jurisprudence,* 2 vols (Oxford, 1922), chap. 6.

13. *"Naturale autem est homini ut sit animal sociale et politicum, in multitudine vivens, magis etiam quam omnia alia animalia"* (Thomas Aquinas, *De Regimine Principum*).

14. *Tota communitas quasi unus homo reputatur* (the whole community can be conceived as a single individual) (Thomas Aquinas, *Summa Theologica,* II. I, q. 81).

15. Idem, *Summa contra Gentiles,* chap. 3.

16. The political philosophy of the Scholastics recieved a definite shape only after a translation of Aristotle's *Politics* into Latin had been made available by William of Moerbeke in 1260. The political community which Aristotle had in mind was the Greek city-state, and he made a careful collection of the constitutions of such states.

17. Aquinas, *Summa Theologica,* II. II, q. 58.

18. Idem, *De Regimine Principum,* bk. 1, chap. 6.

19. Saint Thomas dealt with the theory of justice and law in *Summa Theologica,* I. II, q. 90–100.

20. The Scholastics spoke of *"synteresis"* to account for an inborn faculty of the human mind to grasp the principles of a natural law prescribing the rules of morally lawful behavior (*habitus primorum principiorum innatus*).

21. For the Aristotelian distinction between what is right according to natural law and what is right according to human convention, see Vinogradoff, *Historical Jurisprudence,* 2: 40.

22. The natural law doctrine of the Stoics and its interpretation on the part of the Scholastics have been the object of extensive learned discussions. About the influence of Stoic ideas on the juridical doctrine of the Scholastics, see R. W. Carlyle and A. I. Carlyle, *A History of Medieval Political Theory in the West* (Edinburg and London, 1903), I: 145.

23. The material for the *Digests* or *Pandects,* which constituted the essential part of the Justinian codification of the Roman law (prepared between 528 and 533 A.D.) was supplied by eminent jurists who had been given the *"jus respondendi,"* the privilege of rendering opinions in disputed cases.

24. The first outstanding medieval "glossator" of the Roman law was Irnerius; his most remarkable successor was Accorso (Accursius) (d. 1252?).

25. Aquinas, *Summa Theologica,* I. II, q. 97, art. 2.

26. Idem, *De Regimine Principum,* bk. 1, chap. 3. It is very likely that only book 1 and chapters 1 to 4 of book 2 of the *De Regimine* were written by Saint Thomas; the other parts were prepared by his disciple, Ptolemy de Lucca, but can be assumed to reflect Thomistic views.

27. Idem, *Summa contra Gentiles,* book 3, chap. 134.

28. Idem, *Summa Theologica,* II. II, q. 77, art. 1.

29. This mental attitude can also be illustrated by the widespread method of piling up quotations from authoritative writings in order to provide corroborative evidence for the validity of a disputed view. Saint Thomas demonstrated his doubts concerning the reliability of this procedure when he regarded the argument from authority as the weakest of all, where human reason was involved (*Summa Theologica,* I. q. 1, art. 8 ad secundum).

30. Very characteristic was the definition of "election" by Saint Thomas in his discussion of the right to elect the civil authorities (*Commentarii in Polit. Aristotelis lib.* III lectio 14): *Electio per se est appetitus ratione determinatus.* Primary emphasis was placed on the role of reason in determining the process of choosing.

31. The name *Patristic Fathers* has been given to the theologians who, during the first four centuries of the Christian era, developed the doctrines of the church in accordance with Neoplatonic principles of reasoning.

32. For a discussion of the Scholastic conception of private property, see George O'Brien, *An Essay on Mediaeval Economic Teaching* (London, 1920), pp. 38 ff.

33. A final sentence in favor of the possession of property was pronounced by the Pope John XXII in 1307.

34. Aquinas, *Summa Theologica,* II. II, q. 66: *"Proprietas possessionum non est contra jus naturale, sed juri naturali superadditur per adinventionem rationis humanae."*

35. Ibid., II. II, q. 32, art. 5.

36. John Duns Scotus, *Sententiae,* IV. 15, q. 2. See the quotations from the writings of sixteenth-century Schoolmen in Bernard William Dempsey,

Interest and Usury (Washington, D.C., 1943), p. 131.

37. Aquinas, *Summa Theologica,* II. II, q. 61, art. 2.

38. The Aristotelian view was reproduced in idem, *De Regimine Principum,* bk. 2, chap. 10.

39. See below about the Aristotelian conception of money. Plato's monetary views were very vague. He connected the introduction of money with acts of legislation and raised objections to the use of gold and silver for monetary purposes.

40. The latter interpretation has been advocated by Schumpeter, *Economic Analysis,* p. 61.

41. Aquinas, *Summa Theologica,* II. II, q. 77, art. 1.

42. About the identity of the terms used by Aristotle to denote "justice" in exchange transactions as well as "justice" in criminal prosecution, see Vinogradoff, *Historical Jurisprudence,* vol 2, p. 46. The idea of equivalence also played a role in the *lex talionis* of the Mosaic law.

43. About allusions to a rudimentary theory of subjective value which can be found in Aristotelian writings, especially in the *Topics,* see an article by Oskar Kraus in *Zeitschrift für die Gesamte Staatswissenschaft* (1905).

44. See Edmund Schreiber, *Die volkswirtschaftlichen Anschauungen der Scholastik* (Jena, 1913), p. 162; Dempsey, *Interest and Usury,* p. 214.

45. Aquinas, *Summa Theologica,* II. II, q. 77, art. 11.

46. In his *Nicomachean Ethics* (chaps. 5 and 8), Aristotle suggested that the Greek expression for money, *nomisma,* was etymologically connected with the Greek term *nomos,* which read "law" in the Scholastic translation. See Aquinas *Commentarii in Ethic. Aristotelis,* bk. 5, lectio 9. More recently, however, the term *nomos,* as used in that connection, has been given another interpretation according to which it did not signify "law," but "custom" or "use." If that translation is correct, the Schoolmen might have misinterpreted the Aristotelian views concerning the origin of money. See Filippo Carli, *Studi di storia delle dottrine economiche* (Padua, 1932), p. 49.

47. The Roman jurists who ignored the Aristotelian writings attributed to money a value of its own. They emphasized that the expression *pecunia,* used to denote the general means of exchange, was derived from *pecus,* or cattle, which had originally served the purpose of facilitating exchanges. On the other hand, in an often-quoted passage of the *Pandects* dealing with the contract of sale (1, Dig. XVIII, 1), the Roman jurist Julius Paulus appears to have subscribed to the theory of the conventional origin of money and to the view that the value of money was primarily based on its quantity. Considerable discussion has turned on the question of whether a reference to the quantity theory of money was implied in that dictum.

See Hugo Hegeland, *The Quantity Theory of Money* (Goteborg, 1951), p. 11.

48. In more recent studies, the origin of the monetary functions of various goods (including precious metals) has been connected with the use of these goods for discharging obligations of primitive men to their gods. See Bernhard Laum, *Heiliges Geld* (Tübingen, 1924). Wilhelm Gerloff, *Die Entstehung des Geldes,* 3rd ed. (Frankfort, 1948) has suggested that the monetary functions of certain goods originated from the desire to hoard them, since their possession secured social prominence.

49. Duns Scotus has been credited by Schumpeter (*Economic Analysis,* p. 93) with having discussed the condition of competitive equilibrium which came to be known in the nineteenth century as the "law of cost." However, the concept of "cost" adopted by the Scholastics did not refer to competitive costs but to equal costs prescribed to the producers by the existing rules and regulations. Moreover, the principle of price fixing to which Duns Scotus applied his rule of costs was hardly compatible with the principles underlying the competitive economy.

50. Albertus Magnus, *Sententiae,* III. 37.

51. Aquinas, *Summa Theologica,* I. II, q. 95, art. 4.

52. The establishment of the principle that in trading one party could gain only what the other lost was ascribed to the Latin patristic author Saint Jerome, *Epistula ad Hadib.* In their discussions of the concept of commutative justice, the Thomists of the sixteenth century argued that if a thing was sold at an excessive price because of its special utility to the buyer, the seller took advantage of a utility to the existence of which he had contributed nothing. See Dempsey, *Interest and Usury,* p. 139.

53. Aquinas, *Summa Theologica,* II. II, q. 77, art. 2.

54. For a discussion of the Scholastic attitude toward monopolies and market control, see Raymond De Roover, "Monopoly Theory Prior to Adam Smith," *Quarterly Journal of Economics* (November 1951).

55. See, for instance, Richard H. Tawney, *Religion and the Rise of Capitalism* (New York, 1926), p. 36; Rudolf Kaulla, *Theory of the Just Price* (London, 1940) (translation of a German essay).

56. Aquinas, *Summa Theologica,* II. II, q. 78. The treatise *De usuris,* by Aegidius Lessines, mentioned above lists various exceptions to the rigid principle of equivalence.

57. Duns Scotus, *Sententiae,* IV, 15, q. 2.

58. Richard of Middletown, *Quodlibeta,* II, q. 23: "*quomodo justae mercationes in quibus tantum dat emens, quantum accipiat sunt lucrativae?*"

59. According to the rules laid down in the Roman *Pandects,* a thing was worth as much as the price it could fetch. The rule stated: *Res tantus valet quantum vendi potest.* If a judge was called upon to determine the price of a commodity, the market price which was held to correspond to the usefulness of the good was considered the appropriate price, and mere personal likings were explicitly disregarded.

60. Among these authors were Saints Jerome, Chrysostom, and Augustine.

61. See William Cunningham, *An Essay on Western Civilization* (New York, 1913), 4: 35.

62. "*Sicut aliquis mercenarius locat operas suas, ita etiam aliqui locant domum vel quaecumque alia huiusmodi*" (Aquinas, *Summa Theologica,* I. II, q. 105).

63. "*Jus naturale habet quod homo vivat de labore suo. Dignus est enim operarius mercede sua*" (idem, *Quaestiones quodlibitales,* XII a. 30).

64. Idem, *Summa Theologica,* II. II, q. 55, art. 1.

65. "*Vili velle emere et care velle vendere, vitium est*" (*De Trinitate,* 13).

66. That principle was pronounced in the *Decretum Gratiani,* Dist. 88, causa 11.

67. It is moot but irrelevant to ask whether Saint Thomas misinterpreted the Aristotelian distinction. See Schreiber, *Anschauungen der Scholastik,* p. 28.

68. Aquinas, *Summa Theologica,* II. II, q. 87, art. 4; q. 77, art. 4.

69. Alexander of Hales, *Universae Theologiae Summa,* III, q. 50.

70. Duns Scotus, *Sententiae,* distinguished between *commutatio oeconomica,* the exchange for purposes of consumption, and *commutatio negotiativa,* the exchange for resale at a higher price. To the latter Duns Scotus applied the term *pecuniaria vel lucrativa.*

71. See Schreiber, *Anschauungen der Scholastik,* p. 9.

72. Some objections to the business of moneylenders were made by Roman authors of Stoic persuasion, such as the elder and the younger Cato and Seneca. But according to the almost general conviction of the Greek and Roman politicians and jurists, lending of money, unless done at excessive rates, was considered to be perfectly in harmony with generally accepted moral standards.

73. A *capitulare* issued under Charlemagne in 789 limited the scope of the prohibition to the clergy.

74. See the extended analysis of the medieval attitude toward usury in Tawney, *Religion and Capitalism,* p. 36 ff.

75. See Schreiber, *Anschauungen der Scholastik,* pp. 93, 230.

76. About the question of the extent to which Jews were exempted from the application of the prohibition of usury, see Wilhelm Endemann, *Studien in der romanisch-kanonistischen Wirtschafts und Rechts-*

lehre, 2 vols. Berlin, 1874 and 1883), 2: 383. The exemption granted to the Jews was mainly based on a provision of Deuteronomy 23: 20, in which the Jews were permitted to "lend upon usury unto a stranger" (*nokri*). About the medieval interpretations of that passage, see Benjamin N. Nelson, *The Idea of Usury* (Princeton, 1949), chap. 1. The debtors of the Jews played a prominent part in the terrible prosecution of Jews which occurred in 1348 in Switzerland and in some German cities.

77. See Schreiber, *Anschauungen der Scholastik*, p. 98. Among the Scholastics who contributed to the development of reasons in favor of the prohibition, Alexander of Hales and Vicentius of Beauvais (d. 1264) may be mentioned. Practically all Scholastic arguments of that type were finally listed and refuted by the French jurist Charles Dumoulin in his *Tractatus Commerciorum et Usurarum* (Paris, 1546). See the English translations in Arthur Eli Monroe, ed. and trans., *Early Economic Thought* (Cambridge, Mass., 1924), p. 109.

78. "*Omnes aliae res ex se ipsis habent aliquam utilitatem, pecunia autem non, sed ex mensura utilitatis aliarum rerum. Unde accipere majorem pecuniam pro minori nihil alius videtur quam diversificare mensuram in accipiendo et dando, quod manifeste iniquitatem continet*" (Thomas Aquinas, *Sententiae*, 3, Dist XXVII, q. 1).

79. Aquinas, *Summa Theologica*, II. II, q. 78, art. 2.

80. The same idea was expressed by Aquinas, *Sententiae*, III, 37, q. 1.

81. See Alberto E. Truggenberger, *San Bernardino da Siena* (Bern, 1951), p. 85. As expressed effectively by Saint Bernardino, that argument implied that it was against the principles of natural law to claim from an affair exposed to various risks and contingencies a safe advantage involving no danger of loss or damage.

82. See William J. Ashley, *An Introduction to English Economic History and Theory*, 2 vols. (London, 1888 and 1893), vol. 1, pt. 2, p. 402.

83. Since the canonists permitted the receipt of profits resulting from the use of investments but objected to the identification of loans and investments, they have been credited with the earliest attempt to distinguish capital from money. See H. Sommerville, "Interest and Usury in a New Light," *Economic Journal* (December 1931), p. 648.

84. Aquinas, *Summa Theologica*, II. II, q. 78, art. 2.

85. The *Aurea quodlibeta* of the Thomist Henry of Ghent (d. 1293) was the first treatise in which purchases of annuities were discussed from the point of view of their legality in accordance with the canon law. The list of licit contracts was considerably enlarged by the Franciscan Richard of Middletown,

mentioned above. See Schreiber *Die Volkswirtschaftlichen Anschauungen*, p. 131.

86. See Dempsey, *Interest and Usury*, p. 165.

87. See Tawney, *Religion and Capitalism*, p. 37. See below, pt. 2, chap. 3.

CHAPTER 2

1. Thomas Aquinas, *Summa Theologica*, I, q. I. art. VII.

2. The writings of Roscellinus were condemned at the Council of Soissons (1092) and annihilated.

3. These discussions were surveyed in the *Metalogicus* of John of Salisbury (d. 1180), a disciple of Abelard.

4. In 1267 Roger Bacon addressed his opus majus to Pope Clement IV. But his attacks on leading contemporary Scholastics and his heretic views were reprimanded by the authorities, and from 1278 to 1292 he was kept in confinement.

5. See Ernest Addison Moody, *The Logic of William of Ockham* (New York, 1935).

6. Ockham used the expressions *institutio, intentio*, and *conceptus formatus* to define the subjective general concepts formed by the mind. See Carl Prantl, *Geschichte der Logik im Abenlande*, 2 vols. (Leipzig, 1855–67), pt. 3, p. 344.

7. The Turkish philosopher al-Farabi (d. 950) has been credited with having identified the *universalia post res* with the generic, purely abstract concepts of the Epicurean epistemology, as distinct from the Aristotelian general notions, or *universalia in rebus*, and the Platonic ideas, or *universalia ante res*.

8. In 1328, when Ockham and other Franciscans were threatened with excommunication, he fled to the German emperor Lewis IV (King of Bavaria) and sided with him in the struggle against the pope. He supported the emperor's cause in the *Tractatus de potestate imperiali* (1338). Another partisan of the emperor, Marsilius of Padua, in his *Defensor fracis* (1326), referred to the principles of the natural law in support of the sovereignty of the community of the people within the church.

9. See Prantl, *Geschichte*, vol. 3, p. 3 ff. and vol. 4, p. 15 ff.

10. See John S. Zybura, *Present Day Thinkers and New Scholasticism* (1926), p. 325.

11. Outstanding Ockhamists of the fourteenth and fifteenth centuries were Jean Buridan, Nicole Oresme, Albert of Riggendorf (d. 1390), Pierre d'Ailly (1350–1425), Saint Antoninus of Florence, and Gabriel Biel.

12. "*Indigentia humana est mensura naturalis commutabilium*" (Jean Buridan, *Questions in Aristotelis Ethica Nichomachea*, V. q. 16).

13. Ibid., IX q. 1.

14. See Emile Bridrey, *La Théorie de la monnaie au XIVe siècle: Nicole Oresmie* (Paris, 1906). In French ordinances of 1346 and 1361, the royal privilege of changing the content of the coins was strongly emphasized.

15. He dealt with that question in his *Commentaries on Aristotle's Ethics*, V. 17, and *Politics*, I. 11. See also Arthur Eli Monroe, *Monetary Theory before Adam Smith* (Cambridge, Mass., 1923), p. 26.

16. Nicole Oresme, *De origine, natura, jure nec non de mutationibus monetarum* (1373). Oresme's treatise was "rediscovered" in 1857 and hailed as a great achievement by the German economic historian W. Roscher in 1863. It was the object of considerable discussions. For an extract, see Arthur Eli Monroe, ed. and trans., *Early Economic Thought* (Cambridge, Mass., 1924).

17. The Latin expressions used for debasement of the currency were *mutatio* and *augmentum*.

18. It may be mentioned in passing that Buridan and Oresme emancipated themselves in their cosmology from the traditional medieval teachings. They adopted a theory of the diurnal rotation of the earth according to which the earth, within a sphere of fixed stars, made a daily turn around its own axis. See the literature cited by Dana Bennett Durand, "Tradition and Innovation in Fifteenth Century Italy," *Journal of the History of Ideas* (January 1943), p. 11.

19. See Monroe, *Monetary Theory*, p. 26.

20. Heinrich von Langenstein, *Tractatus bipartitus de contractibus emptionis et venditionis*.

21. Jean de Gerson, *De contractibus*.

22. Johannes Nider, *Compendiosus Tractatus de contractibus mercatorum* (1435). See Robert Zuckerhandl, *Zur Theorie des Preises* (Leipzig, 1889), p. 36.

23. Antoninus of Florence, *Summa theologiae moralis*, 3 vols. (Venice, 1485), especially pt. 2, Tit. 1, chaps. 8 and 16.

24. "*Emptor vult sibi rem emptam potius quam pretium et venditor e converso.*"

25. According to Alberto E. Truggenberger, *San Bernardino da Siena* (Bern, 1951), the formulation of some of the economic precepts taught by Saint Antoninus had been borrowed from Saint Bernardino's *Quadragesimo de Evangelio Aeterno*.

26. Gabriel Biel, *Sententiae*, IV Dist. 15 qu XII para. 5 (quoted in Hector Meredith Robertson, *Aspects of the Rise of Economic Individualism* [Cambridge, Mass., 1933], p. 57).

27. The Council of Constance (1414-16) dealt with the question, which was finally settled by a decision of Pope Martin V (1425) in favor of permitting the repurchase.

28. An outstanding defender of loans of that type was Laurentius de Rodulphis, *Tractatus de usuris* (1403) (see Edmund Schreiber, *Die volkswirtschaft-*

lichen Anschauungen der Scholastik [Jena, 1913], p. 211).

29. In Central and Northern Europe, bookkeeping spread only after the middle of the sixteenth century (see Werner Sombart, *Der moderne Kapitalismus*, 2 vols. [Leipzig, 1902], 1: 319.

30. See Amintore Fanfani, *Catholicism, Protestantism and Capitalism* (London, 1935), p. 162.

31. A Venetian law "*De litteris cambii*" was promulgated in 1272.

32. About a century later, the "or bearer" clause also found its way into Northern Europe.

33. De Rodulphis, *De usuris*. The classification suggested by Laurentius was taken over by Antoninus of Florence. In 1442 the practice of dealing in bills of exchange was described by a Florentine author, Uzzano, in a book entitled *Practica della Mercatura*. Various other publications of a similar type are listed by Robertson, *Economic Individualism*, p. 48.

34. Procedures of that type were defined and condemned as unlawful in a papal bull of 1566.

35. The fairs of Champagne which were mentioned in the tenth century reached world-wide importance in the twelfth century; the Flemish fairs flourished in the twelfth and thirteenth centuries. The most important instruments of trade were developed at the Italian fairs.

36. The School of Salamanca was founded by Francisco di Vitoria. In 1534/35, he delivered a course of lectures on the *Secunda Secundae,* or moral theology of Saint Thomas, which was subsequently published. Among the topics he discussed were various problems of commercial ethics. See M. Grice-Hutchinson, *The School of Salamanca* (Oxford, 1952), p. 42 *passim*.

37. In the sixteenth century, the main Spanish fairs were held at Medina del Campo, Rioseco, and Villelon.

38. A history of the maravedi was written by Diego de Covarrubias, *Veterum numismatum collatio* (1550).

39. A handbook of that type was Tomas de Mercado, *Tratos y contratos de mercederes* (Salamanca, 1569).

40. See quotations from the works of Saraviu de la Cella, Diego de Covarrubias, and Francisco Garcia in Grice-Hutchison, *Salamanca,* pp. 48 and *passim*.

41. See Bernard William Dempsey, *Interest and Usury* (Washington, D.C., 1943), pp. 95, 144 ff.

42. That explanation was referred to in the treatise of Diego de Covarrubias.

43. Martin de Azpilcueta Novarro, *Comentario resolutorio de usuras* (Salamanca, 1556). See Grice-Hutchinson, Salamanca, p. 95.

44. Domingo de Soto, *De justitia et jure* (Salamanca, 1553). Do Soto was confessor of Charles V and the emperor's representative at the Council of Trent.

45. Luis Molina, *De justitia et jure* (1597), II Disp. 406 and 410, cited in Dempsey, *Interest and Usury*, p. 157. About the moot question in these passages, Molina pointed to the quantity theory of money. See Hugo Hegeland, *The Quantity Theory of Money* (Goteborg, 1951), p. 21.

46. See the quotations from the dissertations entitled *De justitia et jure* by the Jesuits Leonard Lessius and Cardinal Juan de Lugo in Dempsey, *Interest and Usury*, p. 159. The last edition of de Lugo's authoritative treatise written in 1642 appeared in 1892.

47. Banks for clearing purposes were created at Geneva (1586), at Venice (1587), at Amsterdam (1609), and at Hamburg (1619).

48. See translations of the report and the reply to it in appendix 1 of Grice-Hutchinson, *Salamanca*.

49. Juan de Lugo, *De justitia et jure* (Lugduni, 1642), Disp. 26, para. 96, cited by Dempsey, *Interest and Usury*, p. 170.

50. See the quotations from de Lugo, *De justitia et jure*, and Leonard Lessius, *De justitia et jure*, in Dempsey, *Interest and Usury*, p. 159.

51. The Neoscholastic economist Heinrich Pesch (*Lehrbuch der Nationalökonomie*, 5 vols. [Freiburg, 1905–23], 5: 729) has criticized such a formulation of the exceptions to the prohibition on the ground that the validity of the exceptions was made dependent upon considerations connected with individual situations. He argued that the existence of a uniform rate of interest was not consistent with the principles of reimbursement for a damage or for loss of a gain. See Richard E. Mulcahy, *The Economics of Heinrich Pesch* (New York, 1952), p. 156.

52. About this question, see a discussion in *Economic Journal* (December 1931) and (March 1932).

CHAPTER 3

1. The term *national states* owes its origin to the influence of organismic reasoning, which developed in the nineteenth century. Hence, that term is not quite adequate to denote the European realms and principalities that were consolidated by ambitious rulers and that endeavored to assert their independence of the imperial supremacy after the end of the Middle Ages. But, if correctly interpreted, the term can be used for the sake of convenience. Equally for reasons of convenience, the names of modern political communities (England, France, etc.) will frequently be used to define territories and regions of a period in which the political configuration conspicuously differed from that of more recent times.

2. Jakob Christoph Burckhardt, *Die Kultur der Renaissance in Italien* (Basel, 1860), trans. S. G. C.

Middlemore, as *The Civilisation of the Period of the Renaissance in Italy* (London, 1878).

3. On this question, see Paul Oskar Kristeller and John Herman Randall, Jr., "The Study of the Philosophies of the Renaissance," *Journal of the History of Ideas* (October 1941).

4. For the following discussion, see, among others, Paul Oskar Kristeller, "Renaissance Philosophies," and the bibliography cited at the end of it, in Vergilius Ferm, ed., *A History of Philosophical Systems* (New York, 1950), chap. 18.

5. See H. Randall, Jr., "The Development of Scientific Method in the School of Padua," *Journal of the History of Ideas* (April 1940), p. 127.

6. The Alexandrinists adopted a version of Aristotelianism advanced by the Greek commentator Alexander of Aphrodisias.

7. Giovanni Botero, *Della ragion de statò* (Venice, 1589).

8. The individualistic idea of a social contract as the origin of political organization was advanced by the Greek Sophists. It was taken over by the Epicureans, who recognized only the will of individuals as the ultimate source of social relation.

9. Jean Bodin, *Les Six Livres de la République* (Paris, 1576). An English translation prepared by Richard Knoller was published in London 1606.

10. In reply to these conceptions of the royal powers, the defenders of the supreme authority of the Church in matters spiritual and temporal insisted upon the right of the people to assist the Church in the struggle with impious, disobedient, or unjust rulers. The antiroyalist struggle was elaborated upon by various Jesuits, such as Juan de Mariana, *De rege et regis institutione* (Toleti, 1599), and Francisco Suarez, *Tractatus de legibus, ac Deo legislatore* (Coimbra, 1612).

11. See, for example, Noccolò Machiavelli, *Discorsi sopra la prima deca di Tito Livio* (Florence, 1531), introduction to bk. 2. See also Giovanni Botero, *Delle cause della grandezza de le citta* (Venice, 1589).

12. See Eli Filip Heckscher, *Mercantilism* (Stockholm, 1931), translation of 2nd ed. rev. Mendel Shapiro (London, 1935), vol. 1.

13. Francis Bacon, *Essay of Seditions and Troubles* (London, 1625).

14. See, among others, Giorgio Tagliacozzo, *Economisti Napolitani dei Sec. XVII e XVIII* (Bologna, 1937).

15. About the anticapitalistic policy pursued by the Church in the sixteenth century, see Amintore Fanfani, *Le origine dello spirito capitalistico in Italia* (Milan, 1933), chap. 4.

16. See Anthony Charles Deane, *The Life of Thomas Cranmer, Archbishop of Canterbury* (London, 1927).

17. Richard Hooker was the author of a treatise entitled *Laws of Ecclesiastical Policy* (1594–97).

18. See Richard H. Tawney, *Religion and the Rise of Capitalism* (New York, 1926), p. 9.

19. See John R. McCulloch, *The Literature of Political Economy* (London, 1845).

20. See Gustav Schmoller, *The Mercantile System and Its Historical Significance* (New York, 1902), a translation of an article published in 1883.

21. Heckscher, *Mercantilism,* II, p. 363.

22. See Eric Roll, *History of Economic Thought* (New York, 1942), p. 58.

23. See Edwin Cannan, *A History of the Theories of Production and Distribution in English Political Economy, 1776–1848* (London, 1894).

24. See Clarence E. Ayres, *The Theory of Economic Progress* (Chapel Hill, 1944).

25. Various versions of this view have been advanced by Henri Pierenne, Richard H. Tawney, Georg A. H. von Below, and Jacob Strieder.

26. Werner Sombart, *The Quintessence of Capitalism,* trans. M. Epstein (London, 1915). See below, chapter 14, "The German Historical Schools."

27. See Werner Sombart, *Die Juden und das Wirtschaftsleben* (Munich, 1911), trans. M. Epstein, *The Jews and Modern Capitalism* (London, 1913).

28. Max Weber, *Die protestantische Ethik und der Geist des Kapitalismus* (Tübingen, 1904–5, trans. Talcott Parsons, as *The Protestant Ethic and the Spirit of Capitalism* (London, 1930).

29. Among the main sources of Weber's analysis of the moral attitude of the seventeenth-century Puritans were books and pamphlets such as Richard Baxter's *A Christian Dictionary* (London, 1673).

30. Weber's views were accepted by Ernst Troeltsch, *Die Soziallehren der christlichen Kirchen und Gruppen* (Tübingen, 1912, trans. Olive Wyon as *The Social Teaching of the Christian Churches* (New York, 1931); Gerhard von Schulze-Gaevernitz, *Britischer Imperialismus und englischer Freihandel* (Leipzig, 1906); and William Cunningham, *Christianity and Economic Science* (London, 1914), chap. 5.

31. See J. B. Kraus, *Scholastik, Puritanismus und Kapitalismus* (Munich, 1930), p. 245 ff.

32. See Tawney, *Religion and Capitalism,* p. 241. See also Georg Wunsch, *Evangelische Wirtschaftsethik* (Tübingen, 1927), pp. 29, 33 ff.

33. See Tawney, *Religion and Capitalism,* p. 85; Kraus, *Scholastik* passim; Hector Meredith Robertson, *Aspects of the Rise of Economic Individualism* (Cambridge, Mass., 1933), p. 164; and Amintore Fanfani, *Catholicism, Protestantism and Capitalism* (London, 1935), p. 149.

34. The main reason why some peoples of the Far East, such as the inhabitants of India and China, never developed capitalist forms of production and trade can perhaps be connected with the fact that they failed to establish concepts of a hypothetical type, which are basic to the competitive organization of the capitalist economy. It is even doubtful whether and to what degree they developed clear concepts of higher abstraction.

35. As early as 1663, a book of inventions was published by Somerset, the second marquis of Worcester. About 1682 Daniel Defoe published *Essay on Projects.*

36. The transformation of common land into private property and the dispossession of the small farmers was practiced mainly by the Tudor aristocracy which had grown up under Henry VII and Henry VIII. The large estates created during that period were frequently operated in accordance with outright commercial principles. A certain degree of security against being dispossessed at the expiration of a lease existed only for the copyholders whose right to transmit their holdings to their sons was attested to by copies of the ancient manorial court records. See R. H. Tawney, *The Agrarian Problem in the Sixteenth Century* (London, 1912).

37. The "statute of monopolies," which was passed in 1624 after long and quarrelsome discussions, placed various restrictions on the issuance of "letters patent of monopoly" and limited the protection of new inventions to fourteen years. It did not affect the privileges of the guilds and the chartered companies. A new outbreak of attacks against monopolistic practices occurred at the beginning of the 1640s; in 1641, the Long Parliament declared null and void a number of monopolies and prohibited granting of monopolies concerning the production of commodities for domestic consumption.

38. The activities of the company were effectively defended in John Wheeler's *Treatise of Commerce* (London, 1601).

39. The English East India Company was founded in 1600; in 1661 it was granted the right to carry on war and to make peace in non-Christian countries.

40. See Heckscher, *Mercantilism,* II: 114, for quotations from the words of Antoine de Montchrétien, Nicholas Barbon, William Petyt, Charles Davenant, and Johann Joachim Becher.

41. In England, a period of consistent protectionism started in the second half of the fifteenth century under Edward IV. In the second half of the sixteenth century (1563), import prohibition was extended to a large number of manufactured articles. In the first half of the seventeenth century (under King James I), an additional comprehensive system of import duties was established. In France, Colbert's unified import tariff was introduced in 1664.

42. See Joseph Catry, "La Liberté du commerce international d'après les scolastiques," in *Revue générale de droit international public* (Paris, 1932), p. 193.

43. See Bruno Suviranta, *The Theory of the Balance of Trade* (Helsingfors, 1923), p. 150.

44. See Edgar Furniss, *The Position of the Laborer in a System of Nationalism* (Boston, 1920), p. 20.

45. Cannan, *Production and Distribution*, p. 3.

46. About the identification of the wealth of a nation with its possession of precious metals, see Charles W. Cole, *French Mercantilist Doctrines before Colbert* (New York, 1931), p. 6. See also Jacob Viner, *Studies in the Theory of International Trade* (New York, 1937), p. 17, for an extensive list of citations from English Mercantilists.

47. Arthur Eli Monroe, *Monetary Theory before Adam Smith* (Cambridge, Mass., 1923), p. 31.

48. Sigismondo Scaccia, *Tractatus de commerciis et cambio* (Rome, 1619), quoted in Robert Zuckerkandl, *Zur Theorie des Preises* (Leipzig, 1889), p. 132.

49. Gasparo Scaruffi, *Alitinonfo* (Reggio, 1582).

50. In accordance with careful research carried out by Elizabeth Lamond, the treatise, ascribed to an anonymous author W. S., was written about 1549 by John Hales, member of Parliament in 1548 and later chairman of the Midland Committee of the Depopulation Commission appointed by Protector Somerset. Others have attributed the authorship of the "discourse" to Sir Thomas Smith. See A. F. Chalk, "The Rise of Economic Individualism," *Journal of Political Economy* (August, 1951), p. 334.

51. The enclosing of common land in order to transfer it to private property was attacked by various social philosophers such as Thomas More and religious reformers such as Sir Hugh Latimer in the 1530s and by William Land in the 1630s. The related problem of depopulation was repeatedly dealt with by royal commissions and statutes. See Tawney, *Religion and Capitalism*, p. 255. Another object of endless criticism was the exploitation of tenant farmers by the rich landlords who had acquired large estates after the secularization of ecclesiastical possessions. These developments, especially the dispossession of the hereditary tenants, signified revolutionary changes in the traditional conception of property rights. The defenders of such changes argued that it was in the public interest to have the land applied to the best purposes. See, for instance, Samuel Fortrey, *England's Interest and Improvement Consisting in the Increase of the Store and Trade of this Kingdom* (Cambridge, 1663). Arguments of that type were characteristic of the degree to which adherence to tradition had been superseded by considerations of expediency.

52. For similar passages from contemporary writings in which striving for gain was defended against moral and religious precepts, see Chalk, "Economic Individualism."

53. Bodin, *Les Six Livres de la République*.

54. Idem, *Réponse aux paradoxes de monsieur de Malestroit touchant l'enchérissement de toutes les choses* (Paris, 1568). See Arthur Eli Monroe, ed. and trans., *Early Economic Thought* (Cambridge, Mass., 1924), p. 127.

55. That view had been defended by Johann de Malestroit, member of the royal council and controller to the mint, in an essay, "Les Paradoxes sur le faict des monnoyes" (Paris, 1566).

56. The inflationary price movement of the sixteenth century affected France three or four decades earlier than England. Bodin discussed that movement in his *Discours sur le rehaussement et diminution des monnoyes* (Paris, 1578).

57. About a similar explanation of the general rise in prices advanced by some Dominican theologians of the University of Salamanca, see chapter 2, "The Disintegration of Thomistic Reasoning."

58. It is noteworthy that the famous astronomer Nicholas Copernicus in his essay "Monetae cudendae ratio" (1526) had advanced a statement which implied that the prices of the commodities increased or decreased in accordance with monetary conditions (*ad monete conditionem*). See Paul Harsin, *Les Doctrines monétaires et financières en France du XVIIe au XVIIIe siècle* (Paris, 1928); Filippo Carli, *Studi di storia delle doctrine economiche* (Padua, 1932), p. 75. The Copernican treatise was published in a French translation in 1864 by M. L. Wolowski.

59. See Hugo Hegeland, *The Quantity Theory of Money* (Göteborg, 1951).

60. It has been suggested that the balance of trade idea was anticipated as early as the fourteenth century by a high official of the English mint. See William Cunningham, *The Growth of English Industry and Commerce, Early and Middle Ages* (Cambridge, 1922), p. 395. This view, however, is inconsistent with the fact that in the fourteenth century the validity of the principle of the commutative justice was still generally recognized. See Max Beer, *Early British Economics* (London, 1938), p. 76.

61. See Eli Filip Heckscher, "Natural and Money Economy," *Journal of Economic and Business History* (1930–31).

62. See Edmond Silberer, *La Guerre dans la pensée économique du XVIe au XVIIIe siècle* (Paris, 1939). See pp. 97 ff. for quotations from mercantilist sources emphasizing the importance of money for purposes of national power policies.

63. Marshal Gian Jacomo Trivulzio (1440?–1518) has been credited with the authorship of the often-quoted dictum about the three things which he

considered necessary for warlike preparations: "*Tre cose ci bisognano preparare, danari, danari e poi danare.*"

64. *An Apologie of the Cittie of London,* written about 1578 and reprinted in John Stow, *A Survey of London* (London, 1598); quoted in Beer, *Early British Economics,* p. 133.

65. In 1588, John Mellis published a treatise entitled "Briefe Instruction and Manner How to Keep Books of Accounts after the Order of Debitor and Creditor." This instruction was a translation of a section of a treatise published in 1494 by the Venetian Luca Paccioli under the title *Summa de arithmetica, geometrica, proportioni e proprotionalita.* (See R. D. Richards, "Pioneers of Banking in England," *Economic Journal,* supplement (January 1929), p. 501. About the use of the term *balance* for bookkeeping purposes, see Viner, *International Trade,* p. 32.

66. The Royal Exchange had originally been a *bourse* established by Florentine merchants. The name *Lombard Street* points to the historical background of that settlement. Later, the supervision of all transactions in foreign exchange was exercised by an officer of the crown. The most successful royal exchanger was Sir Thomas Gresham, financial adviser to Queen Elizabeth. For valuable source material concerning the exchange policy, monopolies, customs, and other economicopolitical problems of the Tudor period, see Richard H. Tawney and Eileen Power, *Tudor Economic Documents,* 3 vols. (London, 1924).

67. Similar treatment of foreign merchants was a common practice exercised by medieval towns. The statutes of employment had been introduced at the end of the fourteenth century.

68. Gerard Malynes wrote a number of essays on economic questions. In 1601, he published *Canker of England's Commonwealth,* a treatise in which he reproduced the views of the commission of which he was a member. The merchants were especially antagonized by his pamphlets (*Consuetudo vel Lex Mercatoria* (London, 1622) and *The Center of the Circle of Commerce* (London, 1623).

69. It is to be recalled that, at the beginning of the seventeenth century, prices were much lower in England than in neighboring countries such as France and the Netherlands, which had been much earlier and more strongly affected by the influx of precious metals from the West Indies. Hence, English exports were sold at low prices and English importers bought dear. In other words, the terms of trade were unfavorable to England.

70. The prohibition of charging or paying interest on money was circumvented by a common practice according to which an English merchant borrowed money abroad with the understanding that he would repay the loan at a rate which was more advantageous to the lender. The qualification of exchange transac-

tions as "usury" was also suggested in other contemporary writings, such as Sir Thomas Culpeper, *A Tract against the High Rate of Usurie* (London, 1621; reprint ed. 1668 in enlarged form).

71. The Ordinance of the Staple was a heritage from the arsenal of medieval trade restrictions.

72. See John Maynard Keynes, *General Theory of Employment, Interest, and Money* (London, 1936) p. 345, and Joseph Alois Schumpeter, *History of Economic Analysis* (New York, 1954), pp. 314, 345, 364.

73. The charter of the Merchant Adventurers Company dated from the beginning of the fifteenth century. From the sixteenth century onward, the company had virtually monopolized the English export trade in cloth and had been successful in promoting a commercial policy which encouraged the exportation of "wrought" or fabricated goods, as opposed to the traditional exportation of English staples such as wool, tin, corn, and leather. The privileges of the Hanseatic League, which was largely engaged in the export trade in these latter goods, had been withdrawn in 1578.

74. Edward Misselden, *Free Trade or the Means to Make Trade Flourish* (London, 1622); *The Circle of Commerce or the Ballance of Trade* (London, 1623). See, among others, E. A. J. Johnson, *Predecessors of Adam Smith* (New York, 1937), p. 61.

75. For the views on exchange control expressed by contemporary Dutch authors, see Etienne Laspeyres, *Geschichte der volkswirtschaftlichen Anschauungen der Niederländer* (Leipzig, 1863), p. 283.

76. For the question of whether the term *balance of trade* had been used by previous authors and the spread of that expression, see Viner, *International Trade,* p. 9.

77. Thomas Mun's treatise, entitled *England's Treasure by Forraign Trade,* was written about 1630, but published only in 1664, by his son, after its author's death. The delay in the publication has been ascribed to the fact that the treatise was mainly directed against the policy of the government which had issued an ordinance on bullion in 1622. The embargo on the exportation of bullion was abolished (except for English coin) late in the eighteenth century. See Johnson, *Predecessors,* p. 77.

78. The distinction between the export of manufactures and the export of raw materials had also been made by John Hales.

79. The idea that all available labor supply should be employed for production purposes had found its practical expression in the Elizabethan Statute of Artificers (1563), which remained in force until the beginning of the nineteenth century and prescribed work as a general obligation for all persons not

privileged by their social status. Preference was given to work in agriculture.

80. Neither Mun nor any other seventeenth-century author used the term *favorable balance of trade*. That expression appears to have come into use only in the second half of the eighteenth century.

81. Thomas Mun, *England's Treasure*. About the various editions of this book, see Johnson, *Predecessors*, p. 334.

82. Antonio Serra, *Breve trattato delle cause che far abbondare l'oro in un regno dove non sono miniere* (1613). See Tagliacozzi, *Economisti Napolitani*, p. xxix.

83. The industrial policy was initiated by an edict of 1581 and continued by an edict of 1597.

84. See René Gonnard, *Histoire des doctrines économiques*, 3 vols. (Paris, 1927), 1: 115.

85. See ibid., 1: 180, and Cole, *Mercantilist Doctrines*.

86. See Colbert's *Lettres, instructions et memoires*, published by Pierre Clément (Paris, 1861-83).

87. See Cole, *Mercantilist Doctrines*, p. 227.

88. Juan de Mariana, *De monete mutatione disputatio* (1609).

89. Geronimo Ustariz, *Theorica y practica de comercio y de marina* (Madrid, 1724). See Andres V. Castillo, *Spanish Mercantilism* (New York, 1930).

90. Charles Ganilh, *La Théorie de l'économie politique* (Paris, 1815).

91. Bernardo Davanzati, *Lezione delle monete* (1588), trans. John Toland as *A Discourse upon coins* (London, 1646). About Davanzati's price theory, see Zuckerkandl, *Theorie des Preises*, and Gino Arias, "Les Précurseurs de l'économie monétaire en Italie: Davanzati el Montanari," *Revue d'économie politique* (1922), p. 737.

92. Viner, *International Trade*, p. 41, has listed a series of quotations from English authors who, prior to John Locke, expressed similar views.

93. This depression, which especially affected the clothing trade, led to debates and inquiries in the House of Commons; traders and businessmen were blamed for having contributed to the disappearance of the precious metals and to the embarrassing scarcity of money. See Heckscher, *Mercantilism*, 2: 223.

94. Rice Vaughan, *A Discourse of Coin and Coinage* (London, 1675), written in 1649, quoted in Beer, *Early British Economics*.

95. See Tawney, *Religion and Capitalism*, chap. 1 and 2, and the literature mentioned in the notes to these chapters.

Luther, in his *Long Sermon on Usury* (1520) and in his *Tract on Trade and Usury* (1524) drew his doctrines from the strictest interpretations of ecclesiastical jurisprudence. See also Benjamin N. Nelson, *The Idea of Usury* (Princeton, 1949), chap. 2.

96. It is doubtful whether the bull *Detestabilis* of Pope Sixtus V, which was directed against the perpetration of usury, was applicable to the contract.

97. See August Maria Knoll, *Der Zins in der Scholastik* (Innsbruck, 1933); Robertson, *Economic Individualism*, chap. 6; James Brodrick, *The Economic Morals of the Jesuits* (London, 1934), p. 143.

98. Cunningham, *Christianity and Economic Science*, p. 43.

99. John Calvin, *De Usuris Responsum in Epistolae et Responsa* (Geneva, 1617), quoted by Robertson, *Economic Individualism*, p. 117.

100. See Amintore Fanfani, *Catholicism, Protestantism and Capitalism*, p. 191, See also Tawney *Religion and Capitalism*, p. 109. For the Calvinist, good works were not a way of attaining salvation; rather, they were regarded as proof that salvation had been attained.

101. Charles Dumoulin, *Tractatus commerciorum et usurarum* (Paris, 1546). See Monroe, *Early Economic Thought*, p. 105.

102. Thomas Wilson, *A Discourse upon Usury* (London, 1584) cited by Tawney, *Religion and Capitalism*, p. 179.

103. Similar references to the views of medieval authorities were advanced in another contemporary treatise, Miles Mosse, *The Arraignment and Conviction of Usury* (London, 1595).

104. Paramount among such writings were W. Ames, *De conscientia et eius jure* (London, 1631), Baxter, *Christian Dictionary*, and the widely used textbook of Puritan morals, John Bunyan, *The Pilgrim's Progess from this World . . .* (London, 1678). In popular words designed to teach the rules of Christian conduct in varied conditions of life, considerations of expediency gained the upper hand. Such was the case in Richard Steele, *The Tradesman's Calling* (London, 1684).

105. For the German countries, the prohibition of usury was abolished by a recess of the Imperial Diet of 1654.

106. About the treatment of the prohibition of usury by Dutch authors, see Laspeyres, *Geschichte der Volkswirtschaftlichen Anschauungen*, p. 258: Hugo Grotius, *De jure ac pacis belli* (Amsterdam, 1625), L b. II, chap. 12, did not object to the prohibition, but refused to accept the arguments derived from the alleged sterility of money and from the use that could be made from money.

107. Culpeper, *Tract against Usurie*.

108. Josiah Child, *Brief Observations* (London, 1668), reprinted in *A New Discourse of Trade* (London, 1692).

109. Claude du Saumaise, *De Usuris* (Lugduni, 1638). Saumaise dealt with the same problem in other writings, particularly in *De modo usurarum* (Lugduni, 1639) and *De foenore trapezitico* (Lugduni, 1640).

110. See the highly instructive discussion of the usury controversy in Eugen Böhm-Bawerk, *Capital and Interest,* trans. William Smart (Edinburgh, 1890), III. Like most other students of the prohibition, Böhm-Bawerk, though strongly emphasizing the logical aspects of the arguments advanced in favor of the prohibition, made moral considerations responsible for the insistence of the clerical authorities upon the introduction and maintenance of that much-disputed measure.

CHAPTER 4

1. Bacon ascribed to physics the task of reducing the complex concepts gained by experience to a bundle of abstract and simple "qualities." The conception of heat as a quality which could be transferred from one body to another was an outcome of that reasoning; another quality of that type was the property of combustibility, which was held to be mixed with the bodies. Combustibility was believed to reach the highest degree in sulphur; likewise, solubility in salt. Mercury was regarded as the expression of all metallic properties.

2. Isaac Newton, *Principia philosophiae naturalis* (London, 1686).

3. It may be mentioned in passing that the use of the term *philosophy* in the title of that treatise reflected a tradition which had developed under the rule of Thomistic Scholastics, when reason was credited with the faculty of deriving absolutely valid knowledge from abstract concepts, and "philosophy" signified the sum total of such knowledge. When the methods of nominalistic reasoning were consistently developed and exclusively applied in the "sciences" strictly speaking, the term *philosophy* was used to denote discussions of general principles freed from the influence of theological speculations.

4. The term *attraction* as used in this connection was intended to signify only a certain numerical value indicating the measure of acceleration which a body undergoes at each point of its path.

5. Analytical imagination can be distinguished from intuitive imagination, used to form concepts of unified aggregates.

6. Michel de Montaigne (1533-1592), Pierre Charron (1541-1603), and François Sanchez (d. 1634) were outstanding representatives of that line of thinking.

7. Gassend's main work was *Syntagma philosophiae Epicuri* (1659).

8. The *Discours sur la méthode* was included in the *Essais philosophiques.* Descartes elaborated on his leading ideas in his *Principia Philosophiae* (Amsterdam, 1644).

9. In his view, the principle of the unity of na-

ture was violated by the "vacuum" left between the atoms of the Newtonian cosmological system.

10. These criticisms were renewed in 1669 by Pieter de la Court. See Etienne Laspeyres, *Geschichte der volkswirtschaftlichen Anschauungen der Niederlande* (Leipzig, 1863), p. 89 ff.

11. Roger Coke, *Reasons of the Increase of Dutch Trade* (London, 1671); *England's Improvement* (London, 1675).

12. Philanglus, *Britannia Languens* (London, 1680); its authorship has been attributed to William Petyt.

13. See Eli Filip Heckscher, *Mercantilism* (Stockholm, 1931); translation of 2nd ed. rev. Mendel Shapiro (London, 1935), 2: 17, for utterances of Colbert about the role played by Holland in the drama of European power politics.

14. The Holy Inquisition, instituted in 1478 and abolished only in the first quarter of the nineteenth century, was a powerful instrument for safeguarding compliance of all aspects of life with the precepts of orthodox thinking.

15. In order to explain the destruction of the Spanish trade which began with the latter part of the fifteenth century, Lord Keynes (*General Theory of Employment, Interest, and Money* [London, 1936], p. 337) has referred to the "effect on the wage unit of an excessive abundance of the precious metals." Why did similar inflationary processes have entirely different effects in other countries?

16. *De jure belli ac pacis* (Amsterdam, 1625) chap. 1, sec. 10.

17. Samuel Pufendorf, *De jure naturae et gentium, libri octo* (London, 1672).

18. As used by the advocates of seventeenth-century natural law, the term *jus gentium* signified "international law," or the law that is basic to the relations among the various nations. See also Overton H. Taylor, "Economics and the Idea of Natural Laws," *Quarterly Journal of Economics* (February, 1930), p. 209.

19. An English translation by Ralph Robinson of the *Utopia* appeared in London in 1551.

20. See Ernst Troeltsch, *Die Soziallehren der christlichen Kirchen und Gruppen* (Tübingen, 1912), trans. Olive Wyon as *The Social Teaching of the Christian Churches* (New York, 1931).

21. Tommaso Campanella, *Civitas solis* (1623); Francis Bacon, *New Atlantis* (London, 1627). More important has been the *Oceana* of James Harrington (London, 1656), which was based on the idea that the distribution of property, especially of landed estates, was reflected in the distribution of political power.

22. Johannes Althusius, *Politica* (Nassau, 1603).

23. Grotius considered the state the outcome of a contract freely entered into by its members. In a very

characteristic passage of his work, *De jure belli ac pacis* (vol. 2, chap. 6, sec. 4), he argued that the social contract was intended to create a "permanent and immortal" community, but that the members of the community could not be held to be incorporated in the latter like the parts of an organic body, which cannot exist without and apart from the body.

24. A certain confusion has been created by the fact that the term *individualistic* has been applied not only to social philosophies of the Baconian type but also to various philosophies of the Renaissance period which emphasized the difference between the qualities of outstanding individuals and those of the large masses of the population.

25. Joseph Alois Schumpeter (*History of Economic Analysis* [New York, 1954], p. 121) has proposed to denote that "working hypothesis" by the phrase *analytic equalitarianism* in order to distinguish it from the *normative equalitarianism* taught by the Christian doctrine.

26. See above, chapter 1, "Thomistic Economics."

27. Joseph Lee, *A Vindication of Regulated Enclosure* (1656), cited in Richard H. Tawney, *Religion and the Rise of Capitalism,* (New York, 1926) p. 259.

28. Thomas Hobbes, *Leviathan* (London, 1651).

29. The term *philosophical sensualism* or *sensationalism* was later used to denote that conception of the human mind.

30. "*Fertur unusquisque ad appetitionem cius quod sibi bonum est, idque naturali necessitate non minor quam qua lapis deorsum fertur*" (Thomas Hobbes, *De cive* [Amsterdam, 1642] I, sec. 7).

31. Idem, *De corpore politico* (London, 1650), I, chaps. 1 and 2; chap. 9; and *Leviathan.*

32. See idem, *Leviathan,* I, chaps. 14 and 15.

33. See the analysis of the Hobbesian philosophy in Talcott Parsons, *The Structure of Social Action* (New York, 1937), p. 88 ff. *Randomness* describes a situation which is not capable of intelligible analysis but which possibly conforms to established laws of probability (p. 91).

34. It may be mentioned that in his *Leviathan,* Hobbes especially rejected the Scholastic value theory. The just value, he said, is that which the contractors may be content to give.

35. The term *psychogenetic* has occasionally been used to characterize Locke's method.

36. That comparison had been suggested in the third century B.C. by the Stoic philosophers Zeno and Cleanthes.

37. John Locke, *Essay concerning Human Understanding* (London, 1690), I, chap. 2, par. 5.

38. Ibid., II, chap. 22, par. 2.

39. To the development of the associationist psychology, Locke contributed his observation that

random associations played an important part in all thinking processes. See James Bonar, *Moral Sense* (London, 1930), p. 19.

40. See Wilhelm Windelband, *Die Geschichte der neueren Philosophie,* 2 vols. (Leipzig, 1904-11), 1: 267.

41. Locke, *Human Understanding,* IV, chap. 6.

42. Ibid., I, chap. 3, par. 3.

43. Ibid., IV., chap. 21, par. 3.

44. Ibid., II, chap. 28, par. 5.

45. In his *Two Treatises of Government* (London, 1690), II, chap. 9, Locke said that preservation of their property was the great and chief end of men uniting into commonwealths and putting themselves under governments.

46. About the logical connection between democratic procedures and the methods of nominalistic reasoning, see my *Conflicting Patterns of Thought* (Washington, 1949), chap. VIII.

47. Locke, *Human Understanding,* L. I, chap. 9, par. 6.

48. It may be mentioned in passing that Locke also pointed out the dangers implied in the use of language because it permits different meanings to be attached to the same symbol.

49. Among the principles established by Bacon was the maxim that "utility" should be the end of all knowledge.

50. Petty was a charter member of the Royal Society for Improving Natural Knowledge, founded in 1662.

51. *The Economic Writings of Sir William Petty* was edited by Charles Henry Hull in 1899 (Cambridge).

52. *Naturam expellas furca, tamen usque recurret.*

53. The remarkable treatise which contained that estimate was entitled *Natural and Political Observations and Conclusions upon the State and Condition of England.* It was written in 1696, but published only much later, in 1804, by George Chalmers.

54. The theory of probability attracted the attention of Newton; Blaise Pascal published a book on probabilities in games of chance in 1660, and Jacques Bernouilli his *Ars conjectandi* in 1713. About the connection between the theory of probability and the development of statistical methods, see Harold Ludwig Westergaard, *Contributions to the History of Statistics* (London, 1932).

55. Sir Dudley North, *Discourses upon Trade* (London, 1691), preface.

56. Tawney, *Religion and Capitalism,* p. 237.

57. See August Oncken, *Die Maxime Laissez-faire et laissez passer* (Bern, 1886).

58. Philanglus, *Britannia Languens.*

59. John Pollexfen, *England and East India Inconsistent in their Manufactures* (London, 1697),

written in reply to Charles Davenant, *An Essay on the East India Trade* (London, 1692).

60. See Heckscher, *Mercantilism,* 2: 99.

61. Two reprints under different titles appeared in 1690 and 1693. Subsequent editions were published under the title *A New Discourse of Trade.* Since Child's views were obviously influenced by his financial and commercial positions, his predilection for "freedom of trade" has frequently been connected with his business interests. See especially Sven Helander, *Weltwirtschaftliches Archiv* (1923), p. 234.

62. In his study on Ireland (1662), Sir William Petty had also mentioned that "paradox" credited the rents paid to absentee landlords with the merit of securing Ireland's favorable balance of payments.

63. Davenant, *East India Trade.*

64. North, *Discourses upon Trade.*

65. See, for instance, Samuel Fortrey, *England's Interest and Improvement Consisting in the Increase of the Store and Trade of This Kingdom* (Cambridge, 1663); Roger Coke, *A Discourse of Trade* (London, 1670) and *England's Improvement*; and Philanglus, *Britannia Languens.*

66. Prohibitions in the trade with France were introduced in 1678 and, subsequently, extended in 1689, 1691, and 1705. The struggle between the Whigs and the Tories over the principles of commercial policy was taken up again in 1712.

67. Locke, *Two Treatises,* II, chap. 6, par. 37.

68. Ibid., II, chap. 5, par. 37 and 43.

69. William Petty, *A Treatise of Taxes and Contributions* (1662). See Arthur Eli Monroe, *Early Economic Thought* (Cambridge, Mass., 1924), pp. 211 ff.

70. William Petty, *The Political Survey of Ireland* (London, 1719). See Monroe, *Early Economic Thought,* p. 218.

71. See Emile Meyerson, *Identity and Reality,* trans. Kate Lowenborg (London, 1930), p. 333.

72. The Russian economist Petr Struve has pointed to the logical analogy between the "phlogiston" theory and the labor cost theory of value. (About the phlogiston theory, see below, chapter 6, "Cameralist Economics.") In both cases, a measurable quality of the things was causally connected with the force which was alleged to produce that quality and its varying degrees. See Alexander Bilimovic, in Hans Mayer, ed., *Die Wirtschaftstheorie der Gegenwart* (Vienna, 1932), 2: 103.

73. In passing, it may be mentioned that considerable discussions turned on the techniques of coinage and the so-called seignorage, the right of the princes to impose taxes on the coining of money for private persons. A remarkable treatise dealing with these and related questions was Rice Vaughan, *A Discourse of Coin and Coinage* (London, 1675), written about 1635.

74. See Schumpeter, *Economic Analysis,* p. 299.

75. See Filippo Carli, *Studi di Storia delle dottrine economiche* (Padua, 1932), p. 61.

76. Petty characterized silver, gold, and jewels as wealth at all times and places.

77. See Jacob Viner, *Studies in the Theory of International Trade* (New York, 1937), p. 77.

78. North, *Discourses upon Trade.*

79. Isaac Gervaise, *The System or Theory of the Trade of the World* (London, 1720).

80. Jacob Vanderlint, *Money Answers All Things* (London, 1734).

81. William Potter, *The Key of Wealth, or A New Way for Improving of Trade* (London, 1650).

82. About Potter's proposal to issue bills drawn on the security of real estate, see below, sec. 5.

83. See Marius Wilhelm Holtrop, "Theories of the Velocity of Circulation of Money." *Economic Journal,* supplement (1929), p. 505.

84. See, for instance, Charles Davenant, *Discourses on the Publick Revenues and on the Trade of England* (London, 1698).

85. Geminiano Montanari, *Breve trattato del valore delle monete* (1680), and *Della Moneta* (1683). Montanari was a professor of mathematics and astronomy in Bologna and Padua.

86. Nicholas Barbon, *A Discourse of Trade* (London, 1690).

87. Similar ideas were expressed in the anonymous *Essay on Money, Bullion and Foreign Exchanges* (1718) (quoted in Robert Zuckerkandl, *Zur Theorie des Preises* [Leipzig, 1889], p. 8).

88. Sir Thomas Culpeper, *A Tract against the High Rate of Usurie* (London, 1621).

89. Petty, *Taxes and Contributions.*

90. About a hundred years later a similar idea was suggested by Anne Robert Jacques Turgot. See below, chapter 5, "Refined Mercantilism." Petty expressed his opposition to the legal limitation of the rate of interest in *Quantulumcunque concerning Money* (London, 1682).

91. Davenant, *Publick Revenues.*

92. John Locke, *Some Considerations of the Consequences of Lowering of Interest, and Raising the Value of Money,* in *Works,* 3 vols. (London, 1714).

93. North, *Discourses upon Trade.*

94. Sir Josiah Child, *A New Discourse of Trade* (London, 1692).

95. Barbon, *A Discourse of Trade.*

96. The term *stock* was quite generally used to denote means of production other than labor.

97. About this interpretation of Barbon's theory of interest, see Schumpeter, *Economic Analysis,* p. 330.

98. Child, *A New Discourse of Trade.* For views of the Dutch economists, sae Laspeyres, *Geschichte der volkswirtschaftlichen Anschauungen,* p. 87.

99. Sir William Petty, *Political Arithmetick* (London, 1690).

100. Davenant, *Publick Revenues*. About the position adopted by adversaries of the East India Company, such as Pollexfen, and the doubts expressed by Davenant concerning the final effects of the issuance of paper money, see Heckscher, *Mercantilism*, 2: 233.

101. North, *Discourses upon Trade*. See also John Cary, *An Essay on the Coin and Credit of England* (Bristol, 1696) and *An Essay towards the Settlement of a National Credit* (London, 1696).

102. William Potter, *The Key of Wealth*; and Nicholas Barbon, *A Discourse of Trade*.

103. John Asgill, *Several Assertions Proved in Order to Create Another Species of Money than Gold and Silver* (London, 1696).

104. The full title of Law's essay was *Money and Trade Considered with a Proposal for Supplying the Nation with Money* (Glasgow, 1705). For a French version, see *Economistes-financiers du XVIIIe siècle*, ed. Guillaumin (1843).

105. The monetary views of Law, like those of many other economists, are likely to show that the importance which has commonly been attached to the distinction between "metallic" and "nonmetallic" monetary theories has been greatly exaggerated. It might be more advisable to emphasize the distinction between theories influenced by nominalistic reasoning and theories influenced by other patterns of thought.

106. This idea appealed to several subsequent authors of the nineteenth century, such as Jean Baptiste Say, Pierre J. Proudhon, and Bruno Hildebrand.

107. Heckscher, *Mercantilism*, 2: 25. Heckscher even made this "fundamental disharmony" responsible for the commercial wars of the mercantilist period.

108. The so-called South Sea Bubble, which ended in 1720 with the breakdown of a speculative scheme, was the result of fraudulent operations and not connected with inflationary manipulations of the currency.

109. See below, chapter 5, "Refined Mercantilism."

110. See René Gonnard, *Histoire des doctrines de la population* (Paris, 1923); James Bonar, *Theories of Population from Raleigh to Arthur Young* (London, 1931).

111. See the discussion of this aspect of mercantilism in Edgar St. Furniss, *The Position of the Laborer in a System of Nationalism* (New York, 1920).

112. Giovanni Botero, *Della ragion de statò* (Venice, 1589).

113. Petty, *Political Arithmetick*. Reliable data on the size of the population were lacking for England as well as for all other countries. Hence, the methods used to determine population figures were the object of various controversies.

114. William Petty, *Another Essay in Political Arithmetick concerning the City of London* (1683), and idem, *An Essay concerning the Multiplication of Mankind*, 2nd ed. rev. (London, 1686).

115. Philanglus, *Britannia Languens,* or Barbon, *A Discourse of Trade*.

116. John Cary, *Essay on the State of England in Relation to Its Trade, Its Poor, and Its Taxes* (Bristol, 1695).

117. For characteristic questions reflecting mercantilist views on pauperism, see Furniss, *The Position of the Laborer*, pp. 30, 40 ff. See also E. A. J. Johnson, *Predecessors of Adam Smith* (New York, 1937), chaps. 12, 14.

118. Cary, like Pollexfen, was an adversary of the trade policy advocated by the East India Company.

119. In his *Treatise of Taxes and Contributions,* Petty enumerated among superabundant occupations those of government officials, lawyers, doctors, clergy, merchants, and retailers.

120. John Pollexfen, *A Discourse of Trade, Coyn, and Paper Credit* (London, 1697).

121. About various meanings attributed to the term *art* by the mercantilist authors, see Johnson, *Predecessors*, chap. 13.

122. Sir William Temple, *Observations upon the United Provinces of the Netherlands* (London, 1673).

123. Petty, *Taxes and Contributions*, ch. 6.

124. See the chapter on *The Triumph of the Economic Virtues* in Tawney, *Religion and Capitalism*, pp. 227 ff.

125. See Johnson, *Predecessors*, p. 304, and the discussion of the mercantilist "fear of plenty" in Heckscher, *Mercantilism*, 1: 114.

126. The term *balance of industry* appears to have been suggested by Josiah Tucker in his treatise *The Elements of Commerce and Theory of Taxes* (Bristol[?], 1755).

127. Barbon, *A Discourse of Trade* and *A Discourse concerning Coining the New Money Lighter* (London, 1696).

128. *Considerations on the East India Trade* (London, 1701). The authorship of this treatise has been ascribed to Henry Martin, who later was hired by the Whig interests to defend the case of protectionism. The general tenor of the work was rather liberal and showed the influence of Petty's ideas. (See Johnson, *Predecessors*, p. 348, n. 31.)

129. Theodore Janssen, *General Maxims in Trade* (London, 1713).

130. The infant industry argument had been emphasized by earlier authors, such as Andrew Yarranton, *England's Improvement by Sea and Land* (London, 1677), cited in Schumpeter, *Economic Analysis*, p. 349.

131. The pamphlets issued in 1713–14 twice a

week by the protectionist group were edited by Charles King. In 1721 they were published in three volumes under the title *The British Merchant or Commerce Preserv'd*. See the discussion of "all round protectionism" in Heckscher, *Mercantilism*, 2: 152 ff.

132. The periodical of the Tories issued in 1713-14 was entitled *Mercator or Commerce Retrieved*.

133. Petty, *Political Arithmetic*.

134. Child, *A New Discourse of Trade*.

135. Daniel Defoe, *A Plan of the English Commerce* (London, 1728). See Heckscher, *Mercantilism*, 2:171.

136. Child, *A New Discourse of Trade*, chap. 1.

CHAPTER 5

1. An English translation of Cantillon's essay was published in 1932 by the Royal Economic Society. See also Arthur Eli Monroe, ed. and trans., *Early Economic Thought* (Cambridge, Mass., 1924), p. 247.

2. Especially Malachy Postlethwayt's *Universal Dictionary of Trade and Commerce*, 2 vols. (London, 1751-55), contained many passages from Cantillon's work, strewn over various articles. Postlethwayt also used various pages from the *Essai* in his treatise *Great Britain's True System* (London, 1757).

3. Adam Smith, *The Wealth of Nations*, 2 vols. (London, 1776), I, chap. 6.

4. The merits of Cantillon's treatise have been emphasized more recently in Friedrich A. Hayek's introduction to the German edition of Cantillon's *Essai* (Jena, 1931), in Amintore Fanfani, *Dal Mercantilismo al liberalismo* (Milan, 1936), and Joseph Alois Schumpeter, *History of Economic Analysis* (New York, 1954), p. 217.

5. Cantillon, *Essai*, part I, chap. 10 and 11.

6. Ibid., part II, chaps. I, II.

7. Cantillon also discussed the reasons which had caused Isaac Newton to reduce the nominal value of the gold piece and to settle the English guinea at twenty-one shillings. His final arguments were directed against the maintenance of the double standard.

8. See Arthur W. Marget, *The Theory of Prices* (New York, 1938), 1: 306.

9. Hume's treatises were reedited under the title *Essays Moral, Political and Literary*, ed. T. H. Green and T. H. Grose (London, 1875).

10. Among these writers were George Whately, *Principles of Trade* (London, 1774), and François Veron de Forbonnais, *Principes et observations économiques*, 2 vols. (Amsterdam, 1767).

11. David Hume, "Essay of Money," in *Essays Moral, Political and Literary*.

12. Idem, "Of Public Credit," in *Essays Moral, Political and Literary*.

13. Criticisms of public loans were also elaborated by Malachy Postlethwayt, *Britain's Commercial Interest Explained and Improved*, 2 vols. (London, 1757). These views may be contrasted with those of some French economists, such as Isaac de Pinto, *Traité de la circulation et du crédit* (Amsterdam, 1771), who attributed to public debts highly favorable effects on national prosperity.

14. David Hume, *Of the Balance of Trade* (Edinburgh, 1752). See Monroe, *Early Economic Thought*, p. 326.

15. About some objections raised by Hume's friend James Oswald of Dunnskier against these rigidly mechanistic views, see J. M. Low, "An Eighteenth Century Controversy in the Theory of Economic Progress," *Manchester School Studies* (September 1952), p. 314.

16. Thus, in order to promote the importation of rum from the southern colonies, Hume recommended an import duty on spirits. In order to expand the sales of domestic textiles, he favored an import duty levied on German linen.

17. David Hume, "Of Interest," in *Essays Moral, Political and Literary*.

18. Josiah Tucker, *The Elements of Commerce and Theory of Taxes* (Bristol[?], 1755), and *A Brief Essay on the Advantages and Disadvantages Which Respectively Attend France and Great Britain with Regard to Trade* (London, 1749). See Jacob Viner, *Studies in the Theory of International Trade* (New York, 1937), p. 53.

19. See Low, "Eighteenth Century Controversy," p. 320.

20. Robert Wallace *Characteristics of the Present Political State of Great Britain* (London, 1758).

21. Joseph Harris, *An Essay upon Money and Coins*, 2 vols. (London, 1757-58). See the discussion of that formulation of the quantity theory in Hugo Hegeland, *The Quantity Theory of Money* (Göteborg, 1951), p. 38.

22. A similar mercantilist position was advocated by Matthew Decker in *An Essay on the Causes of the Decline of the Foreign Trade* (London, 1744).

23. Sir James Steuart, *An Inquiry into the Principles of Political Economy* (London, 1767).

24. Steuart had been exiled after the battle of Culloden (1746) and lived in France, Germany, Italy, and the Netherlands between 1745 and 1764.

25. See Schumpeter, *Economic Analysis*, pp. 296-97.

26. Among the Mercantilists who had emphasized the tendency of the human race to propagate, Petty and Cantillon have already been mentioned.

27. *Political Economy*, II, chap. 22.

28. About Genovesi as a scholar and teacher, see

Giorgio Tagliacozzo, *Economisti Napolitani dei Sec. XVII e XVIII* (Bologna, 1937).

29. Genovesi's works, together with most other Italian economic writings of the pre-Ricardian period, were republished in Pietro Custodi's *Scrittori classici italiani di economia politica,* 50 vols. (Milan, 1803–16).

30. See Amintore Fanfani, *Catholicism, Protestantism and Capitalism,* (London, 1935), p. 134 ff.

31. As suggested by Beccaria, the formula read: *la massima felicità divisa nel maggior numero.* See chapter 7, "Cortesian Economics."

32. *La natura che va sempre all equilibrio dove sia bene avviate ne bruscamente arrestata vi dara in poco da tempo una presso equale diffusione di stabili d'industris, di danaro* (Lezioni, pt. 2, chap. 9, sec. 10).

33. Lezioni, *Conclusione,* sec. 12.

34. See chapter 8, "The Concept of Subjective Value."

35. See Pietro Verri, *Bilanci del commercio dello stato di Milano,* ed. Luigi Einaudi (Turin, 1932).

36. About the work of Ortes, see Roberto Michels, *Introduzione alla storia delle dottrine economiche e politiche* (Bologna, 1932), p. 169, and Albino Uggi, "La teoria della populazione de Giammaria Ortes," *Giornale degli Economisti e annali di economia* (January, 1928).

37. Giovanni Rinaldo Carli, *Breve ragionamente sopra i bilanci economici delle nazione* (1770).

38. Girolamo Belloni, *Del commercio dissertazione* (Rome, 1750).

39. Giovanni Rinaldo Carli, *Delle monete,* 3 vols. (Venice, 1754–60).

40. Lezioni, pt. 1, chap. 2, sec. 22: *"Ne stimerei fuor d'ogni probabilità che un giorno non potessere quelle colonie esser le nostre metropoli."*

CHAPTER 6

1. See above, chap. 2, sec. 1.

2. Ernst Troeltsch, *Protestantism and Progress* (New York, 1912), p. 44.

3. *Die drei Flugschriften über den Münzstreit der sächsichen Albertiner und Ernestiner um 1530,* ed. Walter Lotz (Leipzig, 1893).

4. See Louise Sommer, *Die oesterreichischen Kameralisten,* 2 vols. (Vienna, 1920), vol. 1.

5. Wilhelm von Schröder, *Disquisitio politica vom absoluten Fürstenrecht* (1686).

6. Johann Joachim Becher, Politische Discurs von den eigentlichen Ursachen des Auf- und Abnehmens der Städt Länder und Republicken (Frankfort, 1668). This book enjoyed no less than five editions; the last appeared in 1759.

7. Samuel von Pufendorf, *De jure naturae et gentium, libri octo* (1672). See above, chap. 2, sec. 2, about the role of Pufendorf as an advocate of the doctrine of natural law.

8. See Albion W. Small, *The Cameralists* (Chicago, 1909), p. 6 sq. Members of the German historical school have taken great pains to analyze the works of the Cameralists. The first comprehensive study in which these works were carefully registered was Robert von Mohl, *Die Geschichte und Literatur der Staatswissenschaften,* 3 vols. (Erlangen, 1855–58). See also Kurt Zielenziger, *Die alten deutschen Kameralisten* (Jena, 1914).

9. See Small, *The Cameralists,* p. 588.

10. Small, *Cameralists.*

11. Veit Ludwig von Seckendorf, *Teutscher Fürstanstaat* (Frankfort, 1656), a widely read treatise.

12. Becher, *Politische Discurs.*

13. Joseph Alois Schumpeter, *History of Economic Analysis* (New York, 1954), p. 283.

14. Wilhelm von Schröder, *Fürstliche Schatz- und Rent Kammer* (Leipzig, 1686).

15. See my article on the development of Austrian statistics in *Statistische Monatschrift* (Brünn, 1913).

16. Herman Conring, *Staatsbeschreibung* (1660).

17. See Wilhelm Stieda, *Die Nationalökonomie als Universitätswissenschaft* (1906).

18. From his comparative study of languages, Leibniz drew the conclusion that German was the mother of all other languages and that the "essence" of the European spirit was to be sought among the Germans.

19. Two earlier textbooks which belonged to this group may be mentioned: Georg Heinrich Zincke, *Grundriss einer Einleitung der Cameralwissenschaft* (1742), and Joachim Georg Daries, *Erste Gründe der Cameralwissenschaften* (Jena, 1756).

20. For a detailed analysis of the writings of Justi and Sonnenfels, see Sommer, *Die oesterreichischen Kameralisten.*

21. Johann Heinrich Gottlob von Justi, *Staatswirthschaft oder Systematische Abhandlung aller ökonomischen und Cameralwissenschaften* (Leipzig, 1755).

22. See Karl Pribram, *Geschichte der osterreichischen Gewerbepolitik* (Leipzig, 1907), 1: 120 ff., 268.

CHAPTER 7

1. See Fritz Karl Mann, *Der Marschall Vauban* (Leipzig, 1914); Daniel Halevy, *Vauban* (Paris, 1923).

2. Pierre Le Pesant de Boisguillebert frequently

spelled Boisguilbert, *Le Détail de la France* (Rouen, 1695), *Traité des grains* (1702), *Factum de la France* (Rouen, 1707), and *Dissertation sur la nature des richesses, de l'argent et des tributs* (1707). See Félix Cadet, *Pierre des Boisguilbert* (Paris, 1870). S. L. McDonald, "Boisguilbert," *Quarterly Journal of Economics* (August 1954). His works were reedited by Eugene Daire in the *Collection des principaux économistes* (Osnabrück, 1846).

3. See René Gonnard, *Histoire des doctrines économiques*, 3 vols. (Paris, 1921), 1: 245.

4. See Alfred Espinas, "La Troisième Phase et la dissolution du mercantilisme," *Revue internationale de sociologie* (1902).

5. Charles Dutot, *Réflexions politiques sur les finances et le commerce* (London, 1739).

6. The treatise was entitled *Traité de la richesse des princes et des moyens simples et naturels pour y parvenir*, by M.C.C.C. d. P. d. B. allemand. (See A. Tautscher, "Der Begründer der Volkswirtschaftslehre in Deutscher, *Schmoller's Jahrbuch für Gesetzgebung, Verwaltung und Volkswirtschaft*" [1940].)

7. François Veron Duverger de Forbonnais, *Elémens de commerce*, 2 vols. (Leyden, 1754, 1766), *Principes et observations économiques,* 2 vols. (Amsterdam, 1767). See below, sec. 4.

8. Related by Anne Robert Jacques Turgot, *Eloge de Gournay* (Paris, 1759).

9. See Gustave Schelle, *Vincent de Gournay* (Paris, 1897), p. 322.

10. D'Argenson's full name was René Louis de Voyer de Paulmy, Marquis d'Argenson. He attacked the economic policies of the government in a number of anonymous articles. His *Mémoires* were published in 1857–58, a hundred years after his death. See August Oncken, *Die Maxime Laissez-faire et laissez passer* (Bern, 1886), and Luigi Einaudi, *Saggi bibliografici e storici intorno alle dottrine economiche* (Rome, 1953), chap. 4.

11. See above, chapter 3, "The Transition Period."

12. See Ernst Mach, *The Science of Mechanics,* trans. Thomas J. McCormack (Chicago, 1893), p. 463.

13. Charles de Montesquieu, *De l'esprit des lois* (Geneva, 1748), trans. Thomas Nugent, as *The Spirit of Laws* (London, 1776).

14. The first to draw such a distinction was probably the bishop George Berkeley.

15. François Marie Arouet [Voltaire], *Lettres sur les Anglais* (Rouen, 1734), and *Métaphysique de Newton* (Amsterdam, 1741).

16. Etienne Bonnot de Condillac, *Essai sur l'origine des connaissances humaines* (Amsterdam, 1746), and *Traité des sensations* (London and Paris, 1754).

17. See chapter 6, "Cameralist Economics."

18. Claude Adrien Helvétius, *De l'esprit* (Paris, 1758).

19. Morelly, *Code de la nature* (Paris, 1755).

20. Gabriel Bonnet, Abbé de Mably, *De la législation ou principes des lois* (Amsterdam, 1776). See below, section 6.

21. Jacques Pierre Brissot de Warville, *Recherches philosophiques sur le droit de propriété et sur le vol* (Paris, 1780).

22. Jean Jacques Rousseau, *Discours sur l'origine et les fondements de l'inégalité parmi les hommes* (Amsterdam, 1755), and *Le Contrat social* (Amsterdam, 1762).

23. See, more recently, Alfred Cobban, "Political Thought of Rousseau," *Political Science Quarterly* (June 1951).

24. The works of Quesnay were reedited in 1888 by August Oncken under the title *Oeuvres économiques et philosophiques de F. Quesnay* (Frankfort).

25. See *Oeuvres de Quesnay*, p. 745, and Elie Halévy, *The Growth of Philosophic Radicalism,* trans. Mary Morris (London, 1928), p. 267. See also Benedikt Güntzberg, *Die Gesellschafts- und Staatslehre der Physiokraten* (Leipzig, 1907), and Thomas P. Neill, "The Physiocrats' Concept of Economics," *Quarterly Journal of Economics* (November 1949).

26. "*Les sensations sont les motifs ou causes déterminantes de la raison et de la volonté décisive*" ("Evidence," in *Encyclopédie*, para. 56).

27. "*Evidence, une certitude à laquelle il nous est aussi impossible de nous refuser qu'il nous est impossible d'ignorer nos sensations actuelles.*"

28. Malebranche contrasted knowledge of the relation of perfection (*rapports de perfection*), or the unchangeable precepts of the moral order, with the knowledge of the quantitative relation (*rapports de grandeur*), the laws of physical nature.

29. See Quesnay's article "*Le Droit naturel,*" contributed to the *Encyclopédie*.

30. About the conditions of French agriculture in the second half of the eighteenth century, see A. G. Pundt, "French Agriculture and the 1788 Crisis," *Journal of Political Economy* (December 1941). About the effect of the liberalization of industry and trade on French economic life, see Henri Sée, *Economic and Social Conditions in France during the Eighteenth Century,* trans. Edwin H. Zeydel (New York, 1927).

31. *Physiocratie*, 6 vols. (Paris, 1768), 4: 9. That publication was a collection of Physiocratic writings.

32. François Quesnay, *Maximes générales* (Paris, 1775), para. 4.

33. Victor Riquetti, Marquis de Mirabeau, *La*

Philosophie rurale (Amsterdam, 1763), cited in René Gonnard, *Le Développement de la pensée économique,* p. 14.

34. François Qyesnay, "Dialogue sur les travaux des artisans," *Journal de l'agriculture* (November, 1766).

35. August Oncken, *Geschichte der Nationaloekonomie,* 2 vols. (Leipzig, 1902), vol. 1.

36. See, for instance, Alexander Bilimovic, "Das allgemeine Schema des wirtschaftlichen Kreislautes," *Zeitschrift fur Nationalokonomie* (Vienna, 1944).

37. Bertrand Nogaro, *Le Développement de la pensée économique* (Paris, 1944), p. 23.

38. Eduard Heimann, *History of Economic Doctrines* (Oxford, 1945), p. 17.

39. About the methodological principles adhered to by Quesnay on the one hand, and by some of his disciples on the other, see Neill, "Physiocrats' Concept of Economics."

40. About the life, activities, and writings of Pierre Samuel Du Pont de Nemours, see Gustave Schelle, *Du Pont de Nemours et l'école physiocratique* (Paris, 1888).

41. Pierre Samuel Du Pont de Nemours, *Origine et progrès d'une science nouvelle* (Paris, 1768).

42. There exists voluminous literature, especially in French and German, dealing with many aspects of the Physiocratic doctrine. For a general survey, see Henry Higgs, *The Physiocrats* (London and New York, 1897; and George Weulersse, *Le Mouvement physiocratique en France* (Paris, 1910), and *Les Physiocrates* (Paris, 1931).

43. A similar attitude had been adopted by a group of French theologians including Jacques Bossuet and François Fenelon; they were apologists of the French monarchy.

44. The distinction of stages had been adumbrated in an early essay of Anne Robert Jacques Turgot, *Discours sur l'histoire universelle;* that classification was later elaborated upon by Du Pont de Nemours, Mirabeau, and Mercier de La Rivière.

45. "*Les ordonnances des souverains qu'on appelle lois positives ne doivent être que des actes déclaratoires de ces lois essentielles de l'ordre social*" (Du Pont de Nemours, *Origine et progrès*).

46. Paul Pierre Mercier de la Rivière, *L'Ordre naturel et essentiel des sociétés politiques* (Valencia, 1823).

47. Guillaume François Le Trosne, *De l'ordre social: ouvrage suivi d'un traité élémentaire sur la valeur, l'argent, la circulation, l'industrie et le commerce intérieur et extérieur* (Paris, 1777), chap. 7; Mercier de la Rivière, *L'Ordre naturel.*

48. See Quesnay, *Oeuvres de Quesnay,* p. 391.

49. Quesnay, "Grains" and "Fermiers," in *Encyclopédie.*

50. Nicolas Baudeau, *Principes de la science morale et politique sur le luxe et lois somptuaires* (1767).

51. Quesnay, *Maximes générales.*

52. Mirabeau, *Philosophie rurale.*

53. Anne Robert Jacques Turgot, *Mémoire sur les prêts d'argents* (Paris, 1789), written in 1769.

54. Victor Riquetti, Marquis de Mirabeau, *Théorie de l'impôt* (Paris[?], 1760).

55. See, for instance, Wilhelm Hasbach, *Die allgemeinen philosophischen Grundlagen der von François Quesnay und Adam Smith begründeten politischen Oekonomic* (Leipzig, 1890).

56. Joseph Alois Schumpeter, *History of Economic Analysis* (New York, 1954), p. 233.

57. See Güntzberg, *Die Physiokraten,* p. 31.

58. Le Trosne, *De l'ordre social.*

59. Karl Marx, *Theorien über den Mehrwert,* ed. Karl Kautsky, 3 vols. (Stuttgart, 1905-10), vol. 1.

60. See Overton H. Taylor, *Economics and Liberalism* (Cambridge, Mass., 1955), p. 82.

61. See Norman J. Ware, "The Physiocrats: A Study in Economic Rationalization," *American Economic Review* (1931), p. 607.

62. Fernando Galiani, *Dialogues sur le commerce des blés* (London, 1770). About Galiani's criticisms of the Physiocratic doctrine, see Gino Arias, "Ferdinando Galiani et les Physiocrates," *Revue des sciences politiques* (1922).

63. Jean L. Graslin, *Essai analytique sur la richesse et sur l'impôt* (Paris, 1767). See also Filippo Carli, *Studi di storia delle dottrine economiche* (Padua, 1932), p. 43.

64. Jacques Necker, *Sur la législation et le commerce des graines* (Paris, 1776).

65. Gabriel Bonnet, Abbé de Mably, *Doutes proposés aux économistes* (Paris, 1768). Mably also attacked the Physiocratic conception of private ownership of land as a natural right. His communist views were mentioned above in another connection.

66. Forbonnais, *Principes et observations économiques.* Another notable advocate of the ideas of refined mercantilism was Isaac de Pinto, *Traité de la circulation et du crédit* (Amsterdam, 1771), who extolled the advantages of a rapid circulation of the means of payment and of public debts.

67. Johann August Schlettwein, *Grundfeste der Staaten oder die politische Okonomic* (Giessen, 1779).

68. Jakob Mauvillon, *Physiokratische Briefe an den Herrn Professor Dohm* (Braunschweig, 1780).

69. Jean Herrenschwand, *De l'économie politique moderne* (London, 1786). That essay was first published in the *Ephémerides* for 1772.

70. See Karl Grünberg, *Die Bauernbefreiung in Böhmen, Mähren und Schlesien* 2 vols. (Leipzig, 1894), 1: 314. Karl Pribram, *Geschichte der oesterreichischen Gewerbepolitik* (Leipzig, 1907), p. 345.

71. See about this development Güntzberg, *Die Physiokraten,* chap. 6.

72. Adam Smith, *The Wealth of Nations,* 2 vols. (London, 1776), bk. 4, chap. 9.

CHAPTER 8

1. Fernando Galiani, *Della moneta* (Naples, 1750). An English version of this essay is included in Arthur Eli Monroe, ed. and trans. *Early Economic Thought* (Cambridge, Mass., 1924), p. 281.

2. About divergent interpretations of Galiani's value theory on the part of nineteenth-century Italian economists, see Augusto Graziani, *Storia critica della teorie del valore* (Milan, 1889), chap. 5. About the difficulties involved in defining Galiani's position in the history of economic reasoning, see Luigi Einaudi, *Saggi bibliografici e storici intorno alle dottrine economiche* (Rome, 1953), p. 271.

3. "Siano persuasi i leggitori che con tanta ezatteza corrispondono le leggi del commercio a quella della gravità e de fluidi, che niente piu. Qualche la gravità nella fisicà e il desiderio de guadagnara o sia di vivere felice nell'huomo" (Galiani, *Della moneta,* I, chap. 2).

4. See Eugen Böhm-Bawerk, *Capital and Interest,* trans. William Smart (Edinburgh, 1890), passim.

5. For a discussion of Böhm-Bawerk's theory of interest, see below, bk. 2, pt. 3.

6. Giovanni Battista Vico was the author of *Principi di una scienza nuova d'intorna alla comune natura delle nazioni* (Naples, 1730).

7. About Galiani's relations to Vico, see Giorgio Tagliacozzo, *Economisti napoletani dei Sec. XVII e XVIII* (Bologna, 1937), pp. xvi, xli, and Eduard Ganzoni, *Ferdinando Galiani* (Zurich, 1938).

8. About eighteenth-century authors who adopted a subjective concept of value, see Augusto Graziani, *Storia critica,* chap. 5.

9. Anne Robert Jacques Turgot, *Discours sur les progrès successifs de l'esprit humain* (1750).

10. Similar ideas were later introduced into the body of their doctrine by some Physiocrats, such as Mirabeau. See above, the section on the philosophical background of the Physiocratic doctrine.

11. That essay was written in 1766 at the request of two Chinese students, and was published in 1769. Another—unfinished—essay entitled "Valeurs et monnaie" was published in 1770. About Turgot's life and achievements, see Gustave Schelle, *Turgot* (Paris, 1909). Schelle was also the editor of a collection of Turgot's writings *Oeuvres de Turgot et documents le concernant, avec biographie et notes* (Paris, 1913).

12. "Tant que l'on considère chaque échange en particulier, la valeur de chacune des choses échangées

n'a d'autre mesure que le besoin ou le désir et les moyens des contractants balancés de part et e'autre, et n'est fixé que par l'accord de leur volonté" (Anne Robert Jacques Turgot, *Réflexions sur le formation et la distribution des richesses* [Paris, 1766]).

13. Ibid.

14. Idem, *Mémoire sur les prêts d'argent* (Paris, 1789). See the discussion of the *Tableau économique* in chapter 7.

15. Böhm-Bawerk, *Capital and Interest,* chap. 4.

16. See the section on conflicting social philosophies in France, in chapter 7. Condillac's economic treatise was entitled, *Le Commerce et le gouvernement considérés relativement l'un à l'autre* (Amsterdam, 1776).

17. "Le plus ou moins de valeur des choses," he said, "est fondé—l'utilité restant la même—sur leur abondance, ou plutôt sur l'opinion que nous avons de leur rareté ou de leur abondance."

18. The Physiocrats' position was defended by Le Trosne.

19. "L'inégalité de valeur," said Condillac, "suivant les usages et les opinions des peuples, voilà ce qui a produit le commerce et ce qui l'entretient."

CHAPTER 9

1. Mandeville's pamphlet was first published as a satirical poem in 1706, under the title "The Grumbling Hive, or Knaves Turned Honest." In 1714 it was republished in prose in an enlarged edition, entitled *The Fable of the Bees: Private Vices, Publick Benefits* (London). Another edition appeared in 1723.

2. George Berkeley, *Alciphron or the Minute Philosopher* (London, 1732). In that essay, written in the form of a dialogue, Berkeley also attacked the "Deists" and the concept of "natural" morality as defended by the earl of Shaftesbury.

3. See Henry W. Sams, "Self-Love and the Doctrine of Work," *Journal of the History of Ideas* (1943), p. 322.

4. Richard Cumberland, *Disquisitio philosophica de legibus naturae* (London, 1672).

5. Anthony Ashley Cooper, Earl of Shaftesbury, *Characteristicks of Men, Manners, Opinions, Times* (London, 1711). The main ideas advanced in that essay had been published in previous studies by its author.

6. Francis Hutcheson, *An Inquiry into the Origin of Our Ideas of Beauty and Virtue* (London, 1725).

7. Idem, *System of Moral Philosophy* (London, 1755).

8. It was also common usage during that period to draw analogies between the motives that determine

human behavior and the operation of physical forces. A verse by Alexander Pope (*An Essay on Man* [London, 1733], III, 6) may serve as an example:

On their own axis as the planets run
Yet make at once their circle round the sun:
So two consistent motives act the soul,
And one regards itself and one the whole.

9. Francis Hutcheson, *Inquiry Concerning Moral Good and Evil,* (London, 1726), III, sec. 8. See James Bonar, *Moral Sense* (London, 1930), p. 76.

10. Jacob Viner, "Bentham and J. S. Mill," *American Economic Review* (March, 1949), p. 360.

11. George Berkeley, *A Treatise Concerning the Principles of Human Knowledge* (Dublin, 1710).

12. The title of the essay which contained these contributions was *Querist* (1735).

13. Wilhelm Windelband, *Die Geschichte der neueren Philosophie,* 2 vols. (Leipzig, 1904-11), 1: 322.

14. It has been emphasized that in spite of his logical radicalism Berkeley did not abandon the fundamental approach adopted by the Aristotelian logic. In his construction of the "presentations"—regarded as the psychical correlates of things—Berkeley applied the Aristotelian procedure of combining characteristics which were common to a variety of individual things or beings. See Ernst Cassirer, *Substance and Function,* trans. William C. Swabey and Marie C. Swabey (Chicago, 1923), chap. 1, 2.

15. The *Enquiry* was a revised edition of Hume's *Treatise on Human Nature: Being an Attempt to Introduce the Experimental Method of Reasoning into Moral Subjects,* 3 vols. (1739-40).

16. See Windelband, *Geschichte,* I: 347.

17. The predominantly passive behavior of the intellect has been questioned by various "positivists" who have otherwise accepted Hume's logical classification of propositions.

18. Hume elaborated on his theory of causality in a treatise entitled *Abstract of a Treatise of Human Nature* (1740).

19. See Bonar, *Moral Sense,* p. 141.

20. See Elie Halévy, *The Growth of Philosophic Radicalism,* trans. Mary Morris (London, 1949).

21. Adam Ferguson, *An Essay on the History of Civil Society* (Edinburgh, 1767), pt. 1, chap. 9.

22. It is not improbable that Ferguson had borrowed some of his leading ideas from lectures of Adam Smith who charged plagiarism. See W. R. Scott, "New Light on Adam Smith," *Economic Journal* (September 1936), p. 406.

23. See Overton H. Taylor, "Economics and the Idea of *Jus Naturale,*" *Quarterly Journal of Economics* (February, 1930), p. 208.

24. See Henry John Bitterman, "Adam Smith's

Empiricism," *Journal of Political Economy* (August, 1940), p. 494.

25. *Moral Sentiments,* 2: 129.

26. These lectures, as reported by a student who attended them in 1763, were edited by Edwin Cannon in 1896.

27. Introduction to *Wealth of Nations.*

28. *Wealth of Nations,* bk. 1, chap. 5.

29. Walter Weisskopf, *The Psychology of Economics* (Chicago, 1955), p. 29, has ascribed this ambivalence to a basic conflict of the period, the conflict between the attitude of the traditional subsistence economy and the new acquisitive work ethics.

30. Prolonged subsequent discussions have turned on the question of how to distinguish "productive" from "unproductive" services. About the role played by the concept of "productivity" in the economic philosophy of *The Wealth of Nations,* see Hla Myint, "The Welfare Significance of Productive Labour," *Review of Economic Studies* (Winter 1943), p. 21.

31. Bk. 1, chap. 10.

32. Bk. 1, chap. 11.

33. See D. H. Buchanan, "The Historical Approach to Rent and Price Theory," *Economica* (June 1929), reprinted in American Economic Association, *Readings in the Theory of Income Distribution* (Philadelphia, 1949), p. 603.

34. Bk. 1, chap. 8.

35. For a discussion of Adam Smith's conflicting theories of profit and interest, see especially Edwin Cannan, *A History of the Theories of Production and Distribution in English Political Economy, 1776-1848* (London, 1894), and Eugen Böhm-Bawerk's *Capital and Interest,* trans. William Smart (Edinburgh, 1890).

36. Bk. 1, chap. 5.

37. Halévy, *Philosophic Radicalism,* p. 268.

38. See James Bonar, *Philosophy and Political Economy* (London and New York, 1893), and Albion W. Small, *Adam Smith and Modern Sociology* (Chicago, 1907); Taylor, "Economics and the Idea of *Jus Naturale,*" p. 232. See also Henry John Bittermann, *Smith's Empiricism and the Law of Nature* (Chicago, 1940).

39. These essays were published after the author's death in 1795 under the title *Essays on Philosophical Subjects by the Late Adam Smith. In a preface to this publication, Dugald Stewart gave an "Account of the Life and Writings of the Author."*

40. In another passage of the *Essays*, Smith argued that the emergence of theistic conceptions in the teachings of the Greek philosophers was associated with their idea that the operations of nature were guided by a plan. Such an idea, he believed, was

inconsistent with the notions underlying polytheistic religions.

41. See Hla Myint, *Theories of Welfare Economics* (Cambridge: Mass., 1943), p. 4.

42. Bk. 1, chap. 7, 10.

43. Edmund Burke, *Thoughts and Details on Scarcity* (London, 1795).

44. Luigi Einaudi, *Saggi bibliografici e storici intorno alle dottrine economiche* (Rome, 1953), p. 95.

BOOK II

CHAPTER 10

1. According to John Stuart Mill, who discovered the axiomatic nature of that principle (*Utilitarianism* [London, 1863]), no reason can be given why general happiness is desirable except that each person desires his own happiness as far as he believes it to be attainable. About Mill's attempt to arrange pleasures according to their desirability and value, see Jacob Viner, "Bentham and J. S. Mill," *American Economic Review* (March 1949), p. 377.

2. Jeremy Bentham, *An Introduction to the Principles of Morals and Legislation* (London, 1780).

3. See Overton H. Taylor, "The Future of Economic Liberalism," *American Economic Review* (May 1952), p. 8.

4. Edmund Burke, *Reflections on the Revolution in France* (London, 1790).

5. John Stuart Mill on Bentham in *Westminster Review* (1838), reprinted in *The Development of Economic Thought*, ed. H. W. Spiegel (New York, 1952), p. 189.

6. The theory of associational psychology had been outlined by David Hartley. His work was continued by Erasmus Darwin (1731–1802) and Horne Tooke (1736–1812). James Mill elaborated that psychology in his *Analysis of the Phenomena of the Human Mind* (London, 1829).

7. Bentham stated explicitly (*Principles of Morals*, chap. 1, sect. 3) that action is good or bad according to the sum total of its consequences.

8. Among the main objections raised against the associationist theory of knowledge was that it considered a frequent empirical coexistence of the elements of an association sufficient for justifying the assumption that they were logically connected.

9. Jeremy Bentham, *Manual of Political Economy* (London, 1798).

10. The doctrine of natural harmony of interest was hardly compatible with the Benthamite definition of the limits set to government interference with the economy. See Viner, "Bentham and Mill," p. 369.

11. For the connection between Bentham's doctrine and Ricardian economics, see Elie Halévy, *The Growth of Philosophic Radicalism*, trans. Mary Morris

(London, 1949). David Ricardo's *Principles of Political Economy and Taxation* was published in London in 1817. About the circumstances that have surrounded the elaboration of the principles, see especially Piero Sraffa's introduction to *Works and Correspondence of David Ricardo* (London, 1951).

12. *Principles of Economics*, 8th ed. (New York, 1950), p. 873.

13. About some problems involved in interpretation, see Sraffa's introduction to *Works and Correspondence of David Ricardo*.

14. J. Bonar, *Philosophy and Political Economy*, 3rd ed. (London and New York, 1922), p. 151. See also Overton H. Taylor, *Economics and Liberalism* (Cambridge Mass., 1955), p. 63.

15. See A. N. Whitehead, *Modes of Thought* (New York, 1938), p. 120. Paramount among the other principles of Newtonian mechanics was the proposition that the position of a mobile body is defined by velocity and time.

16. Overton H. Taylor, "Economics and the Idea of Natural Laws," *Quarterly Journal of Economics* (February 1930), p. 18.

17. See Jacob H. Hollander, *David Ricardo* (Baltimore, 1910), p. 72. See also Roy F. Harrod, "Scope and Method of Economics," *Economic Journal* (September 1938), p. 398.

18. About the importance that Ricardo attached to the problem of proportions, see L. Sommer, "Zum Wirklichkeitsgehalt," *Schweizerische Zeitschrift für Volkswirtschaft und Statistik* (1947).

CHAPTER 11

1. Ricardo ascribed to his theory of value the function of making it possible, in the face of changes in distribution, to measure changes in the magnitude of aggregates of commodities of different kinds, or, what is even more important, to ascertain their constancy (Piero Sraffa, introduction to *Works and Correspondence of David Ricardo* [London, 1951], p. xlix).

2. The intricacies of the Ricardian value theory have been exhaustively discussed by a number of out-

standing economists. It is a moot question to what degree Ricardo was aware of the fundamental methodological issues that provided the background to his reasoning, since he did not explain the methodological considerations underlying his analysis.

3. *The Wealth of Nations*, 2 vols. (London, 1776), bk. 1, chap. 5.

4. Ibid.

5. Ibid.

6. See Walter Weisskopf, *The Psychology of Economics* (Chicago, 1955), p. 29.

7. The idea of "commanded labor" could be used to determine whether the value of the product was large enough to render the labor bestowed on the product "productive." Prolonged subsequent discussions have turned on the question of how to distinguish "productive" from "unproductive" services.

8. About the role played by the concept of "productivity" in the economic philosophy of *The Wealth of Nations*, see Hla Myint, "The Welfare Significance of Productive Labour," *Review of Economic Studies* (Winter 1943), p. 21.

9. In the fourth edition of his *Traité d'économie politique* (bk. 2, chap. 1), Say explicitly rejected the view that the value of the products was founded upon that of the productive agency. He asserted that it is the ability to create the utility that gives value to the productive agency, that this value is proportionate to the importance of its cooperation in the business of production, and forms, in respect to each product, what is called the cost of its production (cited in Marian Bowley, *Nassau Senior and Classical Economics* [London, 1937], p. 78). See also Bertrand Nogaro, *Le Développement de la pensée économique* (Paris, 1944), p. 114.

10. James Martland, eighth earl of Lauderdale, *An Inquiry into the Nature and Origin of Public Wealth* (London, 1804; 2nd enlarged ed. 1809). Lauderdale also published various essays on questions of currency, corn laws, and the like.

11. Alfred Marshall has suggested that throughout his disucssion of the differences between "value" and "riches" Ricardo was trying to say that marginal utility is raised and total utility is lessened by any check to supply (*Principles of Economics*, 8th ed. [New York, 1950], appendix).

12. Weisskopf (*Psychology of Economics*, p. 57) has interpreted Ricardo's distinction between wealth and riches as an analysis which hides a conflict between economic value based on labor and the utilitarian, hedonistic value attitude. Since Ricardo was not a Utilitarian in the strict sense of that term, it is very doubtful whether he was troubled by such a conflict.

13. Adam Smith pointed to the higgling and bargaining of the market as the method commonly used for adjusting to each other "the different productions of different sorts of labor, allowance being made for hardship and ingenuity." Ricardo expressed the same idea by stating that the estimation in which different quantities of labor are held soon comes to be adjusted in the market with sufficient precision for all practical purposes. For a discussion of the reasons advanced by Smith for variations in wages of different occupations, see P. Douglas, *Adam Smith, 1776–1926*, (Chicago, 1928).

14. "In speaking of commodities," said Ricardo, "of their exchangeable value and of the laws which regulate their relative prices, we mean always such commodities only as can be increased in quantity by the exertion of human industry and on the production of which competition operates without restraint" (*Principles of Political Economy and Taxation*, chap. 1, sect. 1).

15. Adam Smith circumvented that problem by assuming without much discussion that the number of useful and productive laborers was everywhere in proportion to the quantity of capital stock employed in setting them to work.

16. Letter of Ricardo to Malthus, 13 July, 1823, quoted in Elie Halévy, *The Growth of Philosophic Radicalism*, trans. Mary Morris (London, 1949), p. 357. In another connection Ricardo emphasized that there is not and cannot be an accurate measure of value. It is a moot question whether the value theory which Ricardo adopted toward the end of his life was not a cost of production theory which included interest and profits among the elements of cost. See Bowley, *Nassau Senior*, p. 85. James Mill, *Elements of Political Economy* (London, 1821), stated explicitly that labor measured value only in a purely ideal sense, that it was the regulator of value and could not serve as a practical measure of it.

17. *The Wealth of Nations*, chap. 10.

18. Within the context of the Ricardian economy, free competition, far from being identified with a general struggle for existence, meant a form of economic organization in which all prices were fully adjusted to costs and everybody was given a chance to earn and to increase his share in the national dividend.

19. For a detailed discussion of that problem, see Hla Myint, *Theories of Welfare Economics* (Cambridge, Mass.: 1943), chap. 4.

20. "The real value of a commodity," said Ricardo, "is regulated by the real difficulties of that producer who is least favored" (*Principles of Political Economy and Taxation*, chap. 2).

21. The equilibrium condition that the total supply of exchange values included in the marketable commodities be always equal to the demand for them was made explicit by Léon Walras (1834–1910) about fifty years later.

22. See the quotations in David H. Macgregor,

Economic Thought and Policy (Oxford, 1949), p. 112, and an extensive discussion of divergent interpretations of Say's law in Joseph Alois Schumpeter, *History of Economic Analysis* (New York, 1954), p. 616 ff. Since Say attached much less importance to his law than Ricardo, continued criticism of the law caused him to loosen the original rigidity of its formulation. In the 1826 edition of the *Traité* he even defined a product as a commodity which fetches an equilibrium price, and thus transformed the law into a tautology. See Gary S. Becker and William J. Baumol, "The Classical Monetary Theory: The Outcome of the Discussion" *Economica* (November 1952), p. 372.

23. Some students of Ricardian economics have suggested that Say's law owed its consistent formulation to James Mill rather than to Say. (See Jacob H. Hollander's introduction to Ricardo's *Notes on Malthus' "Principles of Political Economy,"* ed. Jacob H. Hollander and T. E. Gregory [Baltimore, 1928], and Maurice Dobb, *Political Economy and Capitalism* [London, 1937], p. 40.) In his *Commerce Defended* (London, 1808), James Mill did not refer to Say when he advanced the first clear formulation of the law of markets in those words: "Whatever be the additional quantity of goods which is at any time created in any country, an additional power of purchasing, exactly equivalent, is at the same instant created; so that a nation can never be naturally overstocked either with capital or with commodities." In his *Elements of Political Economy,* Mill added the considerations that in the normal course of economic life no exchange values could be lost and that the volume of these values was kept fairly constant.

24. John Barton, *Observations on the Circumstances which Influence the Conditions of the Labouring Classes in Society* (1817).

25. See Schumpeter, *Economic Analysis,* p. 682.

26. About the wage fund, see below, chap. 23.

27. The effects on the condition of the working classes of the introduction of machinery were discussed by Charles Babbage, *On the Economy of Machinery and Manufacture* (London, 1832). Lack of sufficient data prevented Babbage from determining more or less conclusively the degree to which unemployment was caused by the introduction of labor-saving devices.

28. Smith, *The Wealth of Nations,* bk. 1, chap. 8.

29. Among the authors who recommended more or less radical schemes of agrarian reform were Thomas Spence, *The Meridian Sun of Liberty* (London, 1796); William Ogilvie, *An Essay on the Right of Property in Land* (London, 1782); and Thomas Paine, *Agrarian Justice* (London, 1797).

30. Robert Wallace, *Various Prospects of Mankind, Nature and Providence* (London, 1761).

31. William Godwin, *An Enquiry concerning Political Justice and Its Influence on General Virtue and Happiness,* 2 vols. (Dublin, 1793).

32. The full title of the book was *An Essay on the Principle of Population As It Affects the Future Improvement of Society, with Remarks on the Speculations of Mr. Godwin, Mr. Condorcet, and Other Writers* (London, 1798).

33. As mentioned above, the same formula had been advanced by various distinguished authors, such as Giovanni Botero, Sir William Petty, Robert Wallace, and Giammaria Ortes. An exact mathematical expression of the formula was recently elaborated by Trygve Haavelmo, *A Study in the Theory of Economic Evolution* (London, 1954), p. 9. It is interesting to note that according to estimates made by W. Willcox the population of the earth increased by 371 million from 1650 to 1800; according to additional estimates it increased by 1542 million during the following 150 years (1800–1950). The increase amounted to more than fourfold for the second period as compared with the first period. See Otto von Zwiedineck-Südenhorst, "Menschenzahl und Menschenschicksal," *Zeitschrift für Nationalökonomie* (September 1954), p. 231.

34. James Bonar, *Philosophy and Political Economy,* 3rd ed. (London & New York, 1922).

35. It was an open question to what degree "survival of the unfittest" was promoted by the strict observance of the Malthusian principles on the part of the careful and prudent members of society. See Edwin Cannan, *Review of Economic Theory* (London, 1929), p. 90.

36. William Godwin, *Of Population* (London, 1820).

37. Nassau William Senior, *Two Lectures on Population* (London, 1829).

38. George Julius Poulett Scrope, *Principles of Political Economy* (London, 1833). See Redvers Opie, "A Neglected English Economist: George Poulett Scrope," *Quarterly Journal of Economics* (November 1929).

39. Francis Place, *Illustrations and Proofs of the Principle of Population* (London, 1822).

40. Anne Robert Jacques Turgot, *Observations sur le mémoire de M. de Saint-Peravy* (Paris, 1768).

41. James Anderson, *An Inquiry into the Nature of the Corn Laws* (Edinburgh, 1777); *Recreations in Agriculture, Natural History, Arts, and Miscellaneous Literature,* 6 vols. (London, 1799–1802).

42. See Schumpeter, *Economic Analysis,* p. 265.

43. Sir Edward West, *Essay on the Application of Capital to Land* (London, 1815).

44. Thomas Robert Malthus, *Observations on the Effects of the Corn Laws* (London, 1814); *An Inquiry into the Nature and Progress of Rent and the Principles by which It Is Regulated* (London, 1815).

45. Idem, *Nature and Progress of Rent.* About the disputed question of whether the law of diminishing returns was associated with the original formulation of the Malthusian doctrine, see Lionel Robbins, "Schumpeter's History of Economic Analysis," *Quarterly Journal of Economics* (February 1955), p. 12.

46. Implied in that statement was a reference to the idea of marginal productivity, but that idea received due attention only much later.

47. The law of increasing returns as applied to manufactures was later especially emphasized by Senior.

48. Adam Smith stated quite definitely that in every civilized society the landlords, laborers, and capitalists form "the great, original and constituent" orders and that their revenues "the rent of land, the wages of labour and the profits of stock" together make up the national income (*The Wealth of Nations,* bk. 1, chap. 6).

49. "What is annually saved," said Smith, "is as regularly consumed as what is annually spent, and nearly at the same time too; but it is consumed by a different set of people." In accordance with that definition, "productive consumption," as associated with the concept of "productive labor," was distinguished from the nonproductive consumption of other classes of the population (*The Wealth of Nations,* bk. 2, chap. 3).

50. About a problematic attempt to apply the Ricardian analysis of the distributive process to the actual conditions of England at the beginning of the nineteenth century, see Jean Marchal, "Die Theorie der Verteilung bei den englischen klassikern," *Zeitschrift für Nationalökonomie* (September 1954), p. 462.

51. The thesis that wages are advanced by the employers had been suggested by Cantillon. The conception of capital as "advances" had played a considerable role in the reasoning of the Physiocrats and in the theoretical considerations of Turgot. It is a moot question to what degree—in this as in other respects—Smith was influenced by these ideas. In general, allusion to the idea of a wage fund can be found in the introductory passage to *The Wealth of Nations,* in which the annual labor of every nation is referred to as the fund which originally supplies it with all its necessities. Elaborating that theorem, Smith grouped countries according to whether their funds were increasing, stationary, or diminishing.

52. Malthus expressed that idea most clearly in his *Nature and Progress of Rent.* For the history of the Malthusian wage theorem, see W. D. Grampp, "Malthus on Money, Wages and Welfare," *American Economic Review* (December 1956).

53. Robert Torrens, *An Essay on the External Corn Trade* (London, 1815).

54. Sir Edward West, *Price of Corn and Wages of Labor* (London, 1826).

55. That belief was hardly affected by the results of statistical investigations published in Thomas Tooke's *History of Prices* (London, 1838–57). Tooke did not find any correlation between high prices of agricultural products and high wages.

56. See D. H. Buchanan, "The Historical Approach to Rent and Price Theory," *Economica* (June 1929), reprinted in American Economic Association, *Readings in the Theory of Income Distribution* (Philadelphia, 1949), p. 603.

57. Among these publications were John Gray, *The Essential Principles of the Wealth of Nations* (London, 1797); Thomas Spence, *Britain Independent of Commerce* (London, 1807); and Thomas Chalmers, *Enquiry into the Extent and Stability of National Resources* (Edinburgh, 1808). The pamphlet by Spence was answered by James Mill in *Commerce Defended.* See R. L. Meek, "Physiocracy and Classicism in Britain," *Economic Journal* (March 1951).

58. See Frank H. Knight, "The Ricardian Theory of Production and Distribution," *Canadian Journal of Economics and Political Science* (1935), p. 179 ff.

59. See Joseph Alois Schumpeter, "Das Rentenprinzip in der Verteilungslehre," *Schmoller's Jahrbuch für Gesetzgebung, Verwaltung und Volkswirtschaft* (1907), p. 36. Other criticisms of the Ricardian rent concept will be mentioned in connection with the discussion of the principles of marginalism.

60. In accordance with the legal provisions which were in force at his time, Adam Smith was in favor of fixing at 5 percent the maximum limit set to the rate of interest (*The Wealth of Nations,* bk. 2, chap. 4). In his *Defense of Usury* (1816), Bentham attacked the "impolicy of the legal restraints on the terms of pecuniary bargains." To Smith's view that it was advisable to discourage risky projects by fixing a maximum rate of interest, he replied that such limitation would leave too little margin for the reward of legitimate risks, and that risky projects had been instrumental in creating the manufactures which were the "causes and ingredients of national prosperity."

61. *The Wealth of Nations,* bk. 1, chap. 8. Smith's conflicting utterances on the nature and origin of profit have been repeatedly discussed, especially in Edwin Cannan and Böhm-Bawerk's critical surveys of the theories of production, distribution, and interest on capital. See Edwin Cannan, *A History of the Theories of Production and Distribution* (London 1917); and Eugon Böhm-Bawerk, *Capital and Interest,* trans. William Smart (Edinburgh, 1890).

62. It is probably misleading to assume that in the eighteenth century profit emerged as a "new category of class income" and that its origin had to be looked for in production rather than in exchange (see

R. Meed, *Studies in the Labor Theory of Value* [London, 1956], p. 27). What was new was only the connection which Smith attempted to establish between the labor cost theory and an ill-defined concept of profit.

63. Letter of 13 June 1820, quoted in Sraffa's introduction to Ricardo, *Works and Correspondence,* p. XXXIII.

64. For an attempt to interpret Ricardo's views on profit in accordance with the principles of a productivity theory, see V. Edelberg, "The Ricardian Theory of Profits," *Economica* (1933).

65. Cf. the statement in *The Wealth of Nations* (bk. 2, chap. 3) that "parsimony" and not industry was the immediate cause of the increase of capital. Smith observed that high profits, such as those gained from monopolistic trades, might have adverse effects on parsimony, and hence on the accumulation of capital (bk. 4, chap. 7).

66. That assumption was questioned by Thomas Joplin, *Analysis and History of the Currency Question* (London, 1832). He pointed to the inducements to save which were likely to be connected with changes in the rate of interest. See R. L. Meek, "Thomas Joplin and the Theory of Interest," *Review of Economic Studies* (1950/51), no. 47. In other studies (*An Essay on the General Principles and Present Practice of Banking* [London, 1822] and *Outlines of a System of Political Economy* [London, 1823]), Joplin analyzed the motives which were instrumental in causing the "economists" of society to save parts of their income. Among these motives he mentioned the quest for security. Moreover, he developed the concept of "forced savings" as associated with the effects of inflationary price movements. See Friedrich A. Hayek, *Prices and Production* (London, 1931).

67. Smith and Ricardo considered the entrepreneurs as "capitalists"; J. B. Say and J. S. Mill treated them as wage earners of a particular type. See L. M. Fraser, *Economic Thought and Language* (London, 1937), p. 321.

68. For a comprehensive criticism of Say's theory of interest and similar productivity theories of interest, see Böhm-Bawerk, *Capital and Interest,* chap. 7, sect. 2. Theories of that type provided good illustrations of the unconscious tendency to apply the attributes of "natural categories" to economic concepts which reflect the effects of institutional factors.

69. Lauderdale, *An Inquiry.*

70. Thomas Robert Malthus, *Principles of Political Economy* (London, 1820).

71. The view that profits constituted a part of the costs of production was attacked by Malthus's contemporary, Robert Torrens, in *An Essay on the Production of Wealth* (London, 1821). Without developing a clear theory, Torrens ascribed the origin of profits to market conditions; according to his termi-

nology, *prices* included costs of production plus profits.

72. Mill, *Elements of Political Economy,* and John R. McCulloch, *The Principles of Political Economy* (Edinburgh, 1825).

73. About the interpretation of Ricardo's law concerning the falling rate of profit, see Amadeo Gambino, "Il Ricardo del Ferrare," *Giornale degli economisti e annali di economia* (July 1953).

74. A similar picture of the continuous decline of the rate of profit had previously been suggested by West, *Essay on the Application of Capital to Land.* It may be mentioned that during the period in which such considerations were advanced (1790–1820), land rents actually doubled, the rate of interest was almost doubled, but the wages of workers fell. See Harvey W. Peck, *Economic Thought and Its Institutional Background* (London, 1935), p. 111.

75. Adam Smith asserted that what is bought with money or with goods is purchased by labor as much as what we acquire by the toil of our own body (*The Wealth of Nations,* bk. 1, chap. 5).

76. About the interpretation of the monetary views of J. B. Say and some Ricardian economists, see Becker and Baumol, "Classical Monetary Theory."

77. Henry Thornton, *An Inquiry into the Nature and Effects of the Paper Credit of Great Britain* (Philadelphia, 1807).

78. In his *Manual of Political Economy* (1798), Jeremy Bentham included a chapter entitled "Forced Frugality," in which he compared the issuance of inflationary money with a tax on personal income. Such a tax, he argued, involved injustice, even though increases in the national income might result from the use for productive purposes of the additional supply of capital. See Friedrich A. Hayek, "A Note on the Development of the Doctrine of 'Forced Saving,'" *Quarterly Review of Economics* (November 1932).

79. See Friedrich A. Hayek, *Prices and Production,* chap. 1, about a subsequent analysis by Thomas Joplin of the relations between the rates of interest and fluctuations in the volume of the currency. Other contemporary essays dealt mainly with the effects upon foreign trade of the issuance of inconvertible banknotes. Mention may be made of John Wheatley, *Remarks on Currency and Commerce* (London, 1803). Wheatley suggested that a comparison of levels of domestic purchasing power provided an index for determining the foreign exchange rate of two currencies. That proposition anticipated an idea later termed *purchasing power parity* of money. It was elaborated by William Blake, *Observations on the Principles which Regulate the Course of Exchange* (London, 1810).

80. David Ricardo, *The High Price of Bullion* (London, 1810). About varying interpretations of the Ricardian version of the quantity theory of money, see

Hugo Hegeland, *The Quantity Theory of Money* (Göteborg, 1951), p. 57. As a general rule—to which he admitted some qualifications—Ricardo defended the principle of *ceteris paribus;* increases in the quantity of money will be accompanied by proportionate decreases in the purchasing power of the monetary unit. He was convinced that whenever foreign exchange was under persistent pressure, the cause was to be sought exclusively in excessive increases in the volume of money.

81. See the excellent discussion of the currency controversy in Jacob Viner, *Studies in the Theory of International Trade* (New York, 1937), p. 150. In 1816, gold was made the official standard of the English currency.

82. Ricardo, *Principles of Political Economy and Taxation* (1817), chap. 28.

83. Mill, *Elements of Political Economy,* p. 95.

84. George Julius Poulett Scrope, *On Credit Currency and Its Superiority to Coin* (London, 1830). See Opie, "George Poulett Scrope," p. 119.

85. Malthus published an article on paper currency and another on the high price of bullion in *Edinburgh Review* (1811). See also Lionel Robbins, *The Economist in the Twentieth Century* (London, 1954), p. 50.

86. For an exhaustive analysis of the development of that theory, see Viner, *International Trade.*

87. Robert Torrens, *The Economists Refuted* (London, 1808), and *An Essay on the External Corn Trade.* See E.R.A. Seligman, "On Some Neglected British Economists," *Economic Journal* (December 1903).

88. The possibility of effecting balances in international trade without changes in prices through changes in purchasing power was suggested by John Wheatley, *An Essay on the Theory of Money and Principles of Commerce* (1807), and by various other authors. See Viner, *International Trade,* p. 295.

89. Ricardo, *The High Price of Bullion.*

CHAPTER 12

1. *Letters of David Ricardo to Thomas Robert Malthus,* ed. James Bonar (Oxford, 1887), p. 116.

2. In his *Principles of Political Economy* (London, 1820), Malthus objected to the "disinclination to allow of modifications limitations and exceptions to any rule or proposition," and emphasized that one of the specific objects of his work was to prepare the general rules of political economy for practical application by a frequent reference to experience.

3. Robert R. Torrens, preface to *An Essay on the Production of Wealth* (London, 1821), cited in Marian Bowley, *Nassau Senior and Classical Economics* (London, 1937), p. 38.

4. Thomas Robert Malthus, *The Measure of Value* (London, 1823).

5. In a letter written in 1818 (*Letters to Malthus,* p. 148), Ricardo expressed his astonishment at Malthus's view that natural price as well as market price was determined by supply and demand.

6. Prior to Malthus, Lord Lauderdale (the author of *An Inquiry into the Nature and Origin of Public Wealth* [London, 1804]) had objected to "forced parsimony" in a discussion of a sinking fund proposed for debt retirement purposes. He argued that, proportionately to the reduction which the fund had available for the acquisition of consumer goods through forced savings, the demand for labor was bound to be reduced. Moreover, since in his view limits were placed on the use of accumulated capital by the existing technical knowledge, Lauderdale objected to all measures intended to increase such accumulation at the expense of increases in the production of consumption goods. He favored widespread distribution of wealth and property. See Frank A. Fetter, "Lauderdale's Oversaving Theory," *American Economic Review* (June 1945), p. 265, and Alvin H. Hansen, *Business Cycles and National Income* (New York, 1951), chap. 14.

7. See the discussion of that controversy by George J. Stigler, "Sraffa's *Ricardo,*" *American Economic Review* (September 1953), p. 504. Malthus did not introduce any monetary considerations in support of his problematic arguments.

8. See Ricardo's evidence of 24 March 1819 to the Lord's Committee on the Resumption of Cash Payments, cited in J. W. Hutchison, "Some Questions about Ricardo," *Economica* (November 1952).

9. John Maynard Keynes, *Essays in Biography* (London, 1933), pp. 141, 144. See also James O'Leary, "Malthus and Keynes," *Journal of Political Economy* (1942).

10. See S. G. Checkland, "The Propagation of Ricardian Economics in England," *Economica* (February 1949).

11. The club had been founded in 1821; its statutes, drafted by James Milland, imposed on the members the obligation to diffuse among others the first principles of political economy.

12. See R. L. Meek, "The Decline of Ricardian Economics," *Economica* (February 1950).

13. Thomas De Quincey (1785–1859) emphasized the equilibrium aspects of the Ricardian analysis in his *Logic of Political Economy* (Edinburgh, 1844). See Bowley, *Nassau Senior,* p. 86.

14. It is possible that had the issues been made publicly explicit, Malthus's case might have received the support of the landlords, the protected industrialists, and those who after so many years of war were terrified by the prospect of making the country dependent upon the importation of foreign food (Checkland, "Ricardian Economics," p. 43).

15. Outstanding among the popularized versions of Ricardian economics was Harriet Martineau's *Illustrations of Political Economy* (London, 1832–34).

16. John Maynard Keynes, *The End of Laissez-Faire* (London, 1926), p. 11.

17. Nassau William Senior, *An Outline of the Science of Political Economy*, first published in 1836 as an article in the *Encyclopaedia Metropolitana*. Some changes in Senior's view concerning the attitude of the economist toward practical problems were discussed by Bowley in *Nassau Senior*.

18. Senior, *An Outline*, p. 3.

19. John Elliott Cairnes, *The Character and Logical Method of Political Economy* (London, 1857).

20. Senior was the author of *Elementary Lessons in Logic* (1888). The first requisite of a philosophical language, said Senior (*Lessons*, lesson 33), evidently is that "every general name must have a certain and knowable meaning."

21. The term *law* as applied to causal relationships between economic magnitudes appears to have been used for the first time by Ricardo in the tract on *The High Price of Bullion* (London, 1810). See James Bonar, *Philosophy and Political Economy*, 3rd ed. (London & New York, 1922), p. 195.

22. See Bowley, *Nassau Senior*, chap. 6; about the interpretations of the Aristotelian concept of values, see above, chapter 1, "Thomistic Economics."

23. As mentioned above, Senior's definition of wealth included services.

24. As expressed by Senior, the "law of population" simply stated that the number of persons inhabiting the world is limited only by moral or physical evil, or by fear of a deficiency of those articles of wealth which the habits of the individuals of each class of its inhabitants lead them to require (*An Outline*, p. 26).

25. "Additional labor," said Senior, "when employed in manufactures, is more, when employed in agriculture is less, efficient in proportion" (*An Outline*, p. 81).

26. John Stuart Mill, *A System of Logic, Ratiocinative and Inductive* (London, 1843). The methodology of the social sciences was developed in the sixth book of that work, and also in Mill's *Essays on Some Unsettled Questions of Political Economy* (London, 1844).

27. Mill applied that principle even to the rules of logic and mathematics, although he had to admit that the concepts in the mathematical sciences cannot be established by selection from facts of nature. Since Mill's "theory of abstraction" reflected the principles of associationist psychology, it was open to the objection that it selected, out of a wealth of possible principles of logical order, merely the problematic principle of similarity. See, among others, Ernst Cassirer, *Substance and Function*, trans. William C. Swabey and Marie C. Swabey (Chicago, 1923), chap. 1.

28. Mill distinguished four types of mental operations: thoughts, sensations, emotions, and volitions.

29. Richard Whately also published *Introductory Lectures on Political Economy* (London, 1831).

30. John Elliott Cairnes agreed with Mill on a definition of the economic principle according to which all individuals: (*a*) were motivated by the desire for well-being and for wealth as the means of obtaining it, (*b*) had the intellectual power of judging of the efficiency of means to ends, and (*c*) tended to reach the ends by the easiest and shortest means. But the meaning of perfect foresight as ascribed to the economic man was not clarified and could hardly be clarified since possession of perfect expectation by the members of a competitive economy would be incompatible with the functioning of the competitive order. See Oskar Morgenstern, "Vollkommene Voraussicht und Wirtschaftliches Gleichgeaicht," *Zietschrift für Nationalökonomie* (1935), p. 337.

31. Another contemporary utilitarian economist, George Julius Poulett Scrope (*Principles of Political Economy* [London, 1833]), attempted to determine the attitude of his "economic man" through generalizations from experience. (See Redvers Opie, *Quarterly Journal of Economics* [November 1927], p. 107.)

32. Economic competition implies no feeling of rivalry or emulation. The economic man does not "compete" in the ordinary sense of the word at all. In a perfect market there is no higgling or bargaining (Frank H. Knight, *The Ethics of Competition* [London, 1935], p. 282).

33. That interpretation was accepted by authors who treated general historical problems, such as Henry Thomas Buckle, *History of Civilization in England*, 2 vols. (London, 1857–61), vol. 2. In *Adam Smith and Immanuel Kant* (Leipzig, 1877), the German economist August Oncken characterized the concept of "economic man" equally as an abstraction designed to make the analysis of economic behavior independent of the theory of moral sentiment. But the German philosopher Friedrich Albert Lange, author of a remarkable history of the materialistic philosophy, insisted that the introduction of self-interest as the exclusive economic motive amounted to a fiction, since it was incompatible with the results of observation and experience (*Geschichte des Materialismus und Kritik seinar Bedentung in der Gegenwart*, 2 vols. [Iserlohn, 1876–77], 454). This observation was elaborated with convincing arguments by the Neokantian philosopher Hans Vaihinger (*The Philosophy of "As If,"* trans. C. K. Ogden (New York, 1925), pt. 2, sect. 3), who referred to the concept of economic man in order to illustrate certain aspects of the role played by "fictions" as a methodological device.

34. John Stuart Mill, *On Liberty* (Chicago, 1955).

35. About half a century later, Francis Ysidro Edgeworth observed in a very characteristic passage that, if monopoly should extend over a large part of the economic order, the "abstract economists" would be deprived of their occupations, the investigation of the conditions which determine value. "There would survive only the empirical school, flourishing in chaos congenial to their mentality" ("The Pure Theory of Monopoly" [1897]; reprinted in Edgeworth, *Papers Relating to Political Economy* [London, 1925], vol. 1.)

36. About the logical relationship which was established between the institutions of private property and the Malthusian law of population, see above, chap. 11.

37. The Ricardian doctrine has repeatedly been characterized as the "rationalization" of a value system derived from the philosophy of natural law. See, especially, Gunnar Myrdal, *The Political Element in the Development of Economic Theory,* trans. Paul Streeten (London, 1953), p. 4 and passim. As in every social theory, some value judgments were no doubt implied in various propositions of the Ricardian economists. The choice of a specific pattern of thought involves such a judgment. But the interpretation of the Ricardian doctrine as a rationalization of a natural law doctrine is hardly compatible with the fundamental role played by the method of hypothetical reasoning in the Ricardian teachings.

38. That formulation of the law in terms of incremental returns was later replaced by another which conveyed the idea that when all resources but one (labor) are held constant, output increases in progressively smaller proportions as the ratio of the variable factor to the other factors increases.

39. About the specific aspects of the controversy, see Bowley, *Nassau Senior,* chap. 1.

40. Richard Jones, *An Essay on the Distribution of Wealth and the Sources of Taxation* (London, 1831) (only the first part, "On Rent," was published); and *An Introductory Lecture on Political Economy* (London, 1833). It may be mentioned that Jones's "literary remains" were edited in 1859 by William Newmarch, author of a *Treatise on Inductive Sciences* and *Lectures Dealing with Economic Problems.*

41. Thomas Tooke, *Considerations on the State of Currency* (London, 1826); *An Inquiry into the Currency Principle* (London, 1844).

42. Thomas Tooke and William Newmarch, *A History of Prices and the State of Circulation from 1792 to 1856,* 6 vols. (London, 1838–57). That voluminous work was reedited in 1928 by Sir J. E. Gregory, and was accompanied by a valuable introduction.

43. William Newmarch, "Methods of Investigation As Regards Statistics of Prices," *Journal of the Royal Statistical Society* (December 1860). See Ross M. Robertson, "Jevons and His Precursors," *Econometrica* (July 1951), p. 246.

44. John Rae, *Statement of Some New Principles on the Subject of Political Economy, Exposing the Fallacies of the System of Free Trade, and of Some Other Doctrines Maintained in the "Wealth of Nations"* (Boston, 1834). After having been forgotten for many decades, the book was rediscovered and reedited by C. W. Mixter under the title *The Sociological Theory of Capital* (New York, 1905). See especially the analysis of Rae's theory of interest on capital in Eugen Böhm-Bawerk, *Geschichte und Kritik der Kapitalzinstheorien,* 3rd ed. (Innsbruck, 1914), ch. 11.

45. Samuel Bailey, *A Critical Dissertation on the Nature, Measures and Causes of Value* (London, 1825).

46. About some other critical contemporary discussions of the Ricardian value theory, see E.R.A. Seligman's article "On Some Neglected British Economists," *Economic Journal* (December 1903).

47. John Craig, *Remarks on Some Fundamental Doctrines in Political Economy* (Edinburgh, 1821). See Thomas W. Bruce, "The Economic Theories of John Craig, A Forgotten English Economist," *Quarterly Journal of Economics* (August 1938), p. 698.

48. William Forster Lloyd's *Lecture of the Notion of Value* was published in 1834. See Seligman's article "Neglected British Economists."

49. Mountifort Longfield, *Lectures on Political Economy* (Dublin, 1834). Like Lloyd, Longfield was "rediscovered" by E.R.A. Seligman; see the latter's article "Neglected British Economists."

50. Samuel Read, *An Inquiry into the Natural Grounds of Right to Vendible Property* (Edinburgh, 1829).

51. Scrope, *Principles of Political Economy.*

52. See Knight, *The Ethics of Competition,* p. 255.

53. Among the main defenders of the existing order were Longfield (*Lectures on Political Economy*), Charles Knight (*The Rights of Industry* [London, 1831]), Read (*Right to Vendible Property*), and Scrope (*Principles of Political Economy*).

54. See Anton Menger, *The Right to the Whole Produce of Labor,* trans. M. E. Tanner (London, 1899), with a remarkable introduction by H. S. Foxwell. Foxwell pointed out Ricardo's "crude generalizations," which became positively mischievous and misleading when they were unhesitatingly applied to determine grave practical issues without the smallest sense of the thoroughly abstract and unreal character of the assumptions on which they were founded. For a similar view, see Eugen Böhm-Bawerk, *Capital and Interest,* trans. William Smart (Edinburgh, 1890), p. 317.

55. See Esther Lowenthal, *The Ricardian Socialists* (New York, 1911). For a discussion of the "libertarian alternative," represented by Hodgskin, and the "egalitarian alternative," represented by Thompson, see W. Stark, *The Ideal Foundations of Economic Thought* (London, 1943), pp. 51 ff.

56. Thomas Hodgskin, *Labor Defended against the Claims of Capital* (London, 1825); *The Natural and Artificial Rights of Property Contrasted* (London, 1832).

57. William Thompson, *An Inquiry into the Principles of the Distribution of Wealth Most Conducive to Human Happiness* (London, 1824).

58. John Francis Bray, *Labour's Wrongs and Labour's Remedy* (1839).

59. In his *Misère de la philosophie* (Paris, 1847), which was directed against Pierre Proudhon's propositions, K. Marx quoted Bray extensively, opposing his ideas to those of Proudhon.

60. John Gray, *The Social System: A Treatise on the Principles of Exchange* (London, 1831).

61. Robert Owen's most important writings were *A New View of Society* (London, 1813) and *Report to the County of Lanark* (London, 1821).

62. See G.D.H. Cole, *Persons and Periods* (London, 1938).

63. See Bowley, *Nassau Senior,* pp. 134, 156.

64. About the question of how far the abstinence theory had been anticipated prior to Senior by other authors, see Bowley, *Nassau Senior,* p. 144.

65. See ibid., p. 151.

66. Cited by Bowley, *Nassau Senior,* p. 214. About a hundred years later a similar idea was developed by John R. Hicks, "A Suggestion for Simplifying the Theory of Money," *Economica* (February 1935).

67. See Bowley, *Nassau Senior,* p. 225, about the controversy that was provoked by Torrens's contention that one-sided free trade would bring about a fall of prices and depression in the free trade country.

68. John Stuart Mill, *Principles of Political Economy with Some of Their Applications to Social Philosophy* (Boston, 1848). A seventh edition was published in 1871.

69. A widespread, less elaborate textbook which was based on Mill's *Principles* was Henry Fawcett, *Manual of Political Economy* (London, 1863).

70. This approach led to studies dealing with the statistical analysis of the capital stock. See Sir Robert Giffen, *The Growth of Capital* (London, 1889).

71. A. C. Pigou has suggested that Mill's wage fund conception was influenced by the situation that about the middle of the nineteenth century the predominant part of wage goods consisted of food which became available annually at English harvest time ("Mill and the Wages Fund," *Economic Journal* [June 1949], p. 179).

72. Mill's frequently quoted dictum that "demand for commodities is not demand for labor" has been the object of varying interpretations. See Harry G. Johnson, "Demand for Commodities Is Not Demand for Labour," *Economic Journal* (December 1949), p. 533.

73. The article dealt with William Thomas Thornton, *On Labor: Its Wrongful Claims and Rightful Dues* (London, 1869).

74. Mill, *Principles,* bk. 2, chap. 11.

75. Francis D. Lange, *A Refutation of Wage Fund Theory* (1866).

76. Francis A. Walker's *The Wages Question* (New York, 1876), was one of the first noticeable American contributions to the discussion of Ricardian economic theories. Walker ascribed to wages a residual position among the distributive shares, and argued that wages, being determined by competition among the employers, were bound to rise with the increasing efficiency of labor.

77. In support of this view Mill advanced the general proposition that countries which have enjoyed large production and large net incomes to make savings from were characterized by rates of profit which were "habitually within a hand's breadth of the minimum" (*Principles,* bk. 4, chap. 4). But he admitted the existence of factors contributing to the expansion of the "ultimate boundary of capital."

78. Henry Sidgwick, *The Methods of Ethics* (London, 1874), requested maximization of the product of average happiness and the number of individuals concerned. A similar solution was suggested by Francis Ysidro Edgeworth, *Mathematical Psychics: An Essay on the Application of Mathematics to the Moral Sciences* (London, 1881).

79. About varying views concerning the division of advantages derived from foreign trade, see Luigi Einaudi, "James Pennington or James Mill: An Early Correction of Ricardo," *Quarterly Journal of Economics* (November 1929), p. 165.

80. The changes in Mill's attitude toward Benthamite philosophy have been the object of many comments. See, for instance, Jacob Viner, "Bentham and J. S. Mill," *American Economic Review* (March 1949).

81. The English Land and Labor League, founded in 1869, was influenced by Marxist ideas and requested outright nationalization of land. It was opposed by the Land Tenure Reform Association, founded in 1870, which favored less radical reform measures, above all a tax on unearned increment derived from the sale of land. Among the leading economists who supported these proposals were J. S. Mill, Henry Fawcett (1833–1884), John Elliott Cairnes, and J. T. Rogers. A subsequent step in the development of reform ideas of that type was the publication, by Alfred Russel Wallace, of a book on *Land Na-*

tionalization (London, 1892) and the foundation of a Land Nationalization Society.

82. H. S. Foxwell, introduction to Menger, *Whole Produce of Labor.*

83. John Elliott Cairnes, *Some Leading Principles of Political Economy Newly Expounded* (London, 1874). A similar observation had been made by Longfield, *Lectures on Political Economy.* In his analysis of more or less permanent differences in values and variations in incomes, Senior had equally pointed to the obstacles which exist even "within the same neighborhood and the same country" to the transfer of labor and capital from one employer to another.

84. In his "Introductory Lecture on Political Economy and Laissez-Faire," delivered in 1870 at University College of London, Cairnes also questioned the scientific basis of the maxim of laissez-faire and declared it to be at best a mere handy rule of practice (quoted in Keynes, *The End of Laissez-Faire,* p. 26).

85. William Whewell, "Mathematical Exposition of Some Doctrines of Political Economy," *Cambridge Philosophical Transactions* (Cambridge, 1829, 1831, 1850). See Ross M. Robertson, "Mathematical Economics before Cournot," *Journal of Political Economy* (December 1949).

86. Dionysius Lardner, *Railway Economy* (London, 1850).

87. Henry C. Fleeming Jenkin, "Trade Unions, How far Legitimate?," *North British Review* (March 1868); and *Graphic Representation of the Laws of Supply and Demand, and Their Application to Labor* (Edinburgh, 1870). Jenkin based his wage analysis on a crude supply and demand theory.

88. A "tabular standard" was a monetary standard designed to create a stable monetary unit of deferred payment. A standard of that type had been proposed by John Wheatley, *An Essay on the Theory of Money and Principles of Commerce* (London, 1807). Later similar proposals were made by Joseph Lowe, *The Present State of England in Regard to Agriculture, Trade and Finance* (London, 1822), and George Julius Poulett Scrope, *An Examination of the Bank Charter Question* (London, 1833). Scrope's tabular standard, which made effective use of the index number technique, was to be based on the prices of about one hundred articles "in most general request," weighted according to their consumption.

89. Such a policy was advocated by Thomas Perronet Thompson, *On the Mistreatment of Exchange* (London, 1830). A lively propaganda in favor of a system of managed paper currency was made by Thomas Attwood, who published a series of pamphlets, such as *The Scotch Banker* (London, 1828). See Joseph Alois Schumpeter, *History of Economic Analysis* (New York, 1954), p. 714.

90. It may be mentioned that Ricardo had recommended a modified gold standard as his "ingot plan," which, if put into effect, would have reduced the volume of gold reserves to be held by the bank. The plan provided for full convertibility of notes at fixed prices but only against bullion, and excluded gold from use in daily circulation.

91. Lord Overstone (Samuel Jones Loyd), *Tracts and Other Publications on Metallic and Paper Currency* (London, 1857). The currency theory was equally defended by G. W. Norman, *Remarks upon Some Prevalent Errors with Respect to Currency and Banking* (London, 1838). A third outstanding advocate of that theory was John R. McCulloch, *Treatise on Metallic and Paper Money and Banks* (Edinburgh, 1858).

92. Outstanding advocates of the banking principle were James Wilson, *Capital, Currency and Banking* (London, 1847); John Fullarton, *On the Regulation of Currencies* (London, 1844); and Tooke, *Inquiry into the Currency Principle.*

93. See Charles Rist, *History of Monetary and Credit Theory,* trans. Jane Degras (London, 1940), pp. 214, 223.

94. In the United States, the power of the banks to create credit through the opening of accounts had been appreciated as early as 1790 by Alexander Hamilton in his *Report on a National Bank* (Philadelphia, 1790).

95. See Thomas Joplin, *Analysis and History of the Currency Question* (London, 1832).

96. Nassau William Senior (*Three Lectures on the Value of Money* [London, 1829]) argued that long-run changes in the price level could be brought about only by reductions in the costs of production of the monetary metals and ensuing increases in the volume of mining.

97. See the discussion of Mill's monetary theory in Hugo Hegeland, *The Quantity Theory of Money* (Göteburg, 1951), p. 66.

98. Lord Overstone, *Metallic and Paper Currency,* p. 204.

99. Ibid., p. 167. The use of the term *oscillation* in that passage points to the general habit of comparing economic phenomena with those of the mechanical sphere.

100. Wilson, *Capital, Currency and Banking.* Wilson was the first editor of the "Economist."

101. Thomas Chalmers, *On Political Economy in Connexion with the Moral State and Moral Prospects of Society* (Glasgow, 1832). Chalmers warned that loss of effective demand might result from "not spending" on the part of consumers.

102. John Mills, "On Credit Cycles and the Origin of Commercial Panics," *Transactions of the Manchester Statistical Society* (1867–68).

CHAPTER 13

1. Say's methodological principles have recently been defended against the Ricardian methodology by Bertrand Nogaro, *Le Développement de la pensée économique* (Paris, 1944). In addition to his *Treatise*, which enjoyed several editions, Say published in six volumes a *Cours d'économie politique* (Paris, 1828–29).

2. Almost all of them elaborated their ideas in more or less voluminous textbooks. Their rallying point was the Société d'Economie Politique (founded in 1842), their leading periodical the *Journal des économistes*.

3. The behavior of the French nineteenth-century entrepreneur has been the object of various studies. It has been connected with prevailing popular social philosophies and has been made responsible for the uneven economic development of the country. See, among these studies, David S. Landes, "French Entrepreneurship," *Journal of Economic History* (May 1949); John E. Sawyer, "Strains in the Social Structure of Modern France," in Edward Mead Earle, ed., *Modern France* (Princeton 1951); and David S. Landes, "French Business and the Businessman: A Social and Cultural Analysis," in Earle, ed., *Modern France*.

4. See Emile James, *Histoire des théories économiques* (Paris, 1950), p. 91.

5. Examples of that type were treatises by Jean Gustave Courcelle-Seneuil dealing with industrial, commercial, and agricultural enterprises (*Traité théorique et pratique des entreprises industrielles* [Paris, 1855]) and with banking operations (*Traité théorique et pratique des opérations de barque* [Paris, 1853]). Problems of the gold standard were ably discussed by Pierre Emile Levasseur, *La Question de l'or* (Paris, 1858), and Michel Chevalier, *La Monnaie* (Brussels, 1851).

6. Michel Chevalier was the counterpart of R. Cobden in the negotiations which led to the Anglo-French commercial treaty in 1860 which initiated a temporary abandonment of the French protectionist policy.

7. Clement Juglar, *Les Crises commerciales et de leur retour périodique en France, en Angleterre et aux Etats Unis* (Paris, 1862). In his analysis of business cycles (*Business Cycles: A Theoretical, Historical, and Statistical Analysis of the Capitalist Process*, 2 vols. [New York, 1939]), Joseph Alois Schumpeter used the term *Juglar* to denote (medium) cycles of the type described by him.

8. Clement Juglar, *Du change et de la liberté d'émission* (Paris, 1868).

9. See, for instance, Emile L. V. de Laveleye, *Le Marché monétaire et ses crises depuis cinquante ans* (Paris, 1865). Laveleye enumerated various factors to which he attributed adverse influences on the balance of payments.

10. See, especially, Clément Joseph Garnier, "Crises commerciales," in Gilbert Guillaumin, ed., *Dictionnaire universel théorique et pratique du commerce et de la navigation* (Paris, 1863), and the discussion of the French business cycle theories in Eugen von Bergmann, *Geschichte der nationalökonomischen Krisentheorien* (Stuttgart, 1895), p. 198.

11. Léon Walras, *Traité mathématique des billets de banque* (1879). See Valentin F. Wagner, *Geschichte der Kredittheorien* (Vienna, 1937), p. 360.

12. Barthélemy Charles Dunoyer, *Nouveau Traité d'économie sociale* (Paris, 1825–30), *De la liberté du travail* (Paris, 1845).

13. Claude Frédéric Bastiat, *Sophismes économiques* (Paris, 1846), *Harmonies économiques* (Paris, 1850).

14. For an analysis of Bastiat's reasoning, see an article by John Elliott Cairnes in *Fortnightly Review* (October 1870), reprinted as "Cairnes on Bastiat," in H. W. Spiegel, ed. *The Development of Economic Thought* (New York, 1952).

15. For a criticism of these views, see Eugen Böhm-Bawerk, *Capital and Interest*, trans. William Smart (Edinburgh, 1890), chap. 9.

16. Henry Charles Carey, *Principles of Political Economy*, 3 vols. (Philadelphia, 1837–40).

17. That was the judgment of the eminent historian of economics, Charles Gide, in the survey of the French economic literature which he prepared for the *Wirtschaftswissenschaft nach dem Kriege* (Leipzig, 1925), 1: 34 ff.

18. Two interesting studies may be referred to here: Pierre Paul Leroy-Beaulieu, *Essai sur la répartition des richesses* (Paris, 1881), and Maurice Block, *Le progrès de la science économique depuis Adam Smith* (Paris, 1890).

19. See Luigi Cossa, *Guida allo studio dell'economia politica* (Milan, 1870), trans. 1880); Hermann von Schullern-Schrattenhofen, *Die theoretische Nationalökonomie Italiens* (Leipzig, 1891); and Luigi Einaudi, *Saggi bibliografici e storici intorno alle dottrine economiche* (Rome, 1953).

20. Fuoco's main writings were *Introduzione allo studio della economia industriale* (Naples, 1829), and *Saggi economici* (Pisa, 1825–27). Another treatise, *Magia del credito svelata* (1824), was sold by Fuoco and published under the name of De Wels.

21. Thus, it is probable that his analysis of quasi-rent was influenced by the ideas of the German Heinrich F. von Storch, his application of mathematics to economics influenced by G. Verri, and his cred-

it theory influenced by John Law and Isaac de Pinto. See Luigi Einaudi, *Saggi bibliografici,* chap. 8.

22. Francesco Ferrara, *Lezioni di economia politica* (Turin, 1849–52).

23. Ferrara's theory was criticized from the point of view of Ricardian economics by Luigi Cossa, *La teoria del Valore negli economisti Italiani* (1882). See also Augusto Graziani, *Storia critica della teoria del valore in Italia* (Milan, 1889), p. 93 ff., and Otto Weinberger, "The Importance of Francesco Ferrara in the History of Economic Thought," *Journal of Political Economy* (February 1940), p. 91 ff. The influence of the Ricardian doctrine continued to be remarkably strong in Italy until the late twentieth century. See Luigi Cossa, *Introduzione allo studio dell'economia politica,* 3rd ed. (Milan, 1892); Augusto Graziani, *Ricardo e J. S. Mill* (Bari, 1921); Achille Loria, *Davide Ricardo* (Rome, 1926).

24. Francesco Ferrara, *Esame storico-critico di economisti* (Turin, 1889–91).

25. Antoine Cournot, *Recherches sur les principes mathématiques de la théorie des richesses* (Paris, 1838), trans. Nathaniel Bacon as *Researches into the Mathematical Principles of the Theory of Wealth* (London, 1897). Cournot published many mathematical treatises and some contributions to the history of ideas. His noneconomic work enjoyed due recognition on the part of contemporary students of mathematics and the natural sciences.

26. René Roy, "Cournot et l'école mathématique," *Econometrica* (1933), p. 15.

27. See the elaborate discussion of Cournot's price theory by Hans Mayer in Hans Mayr et al., eds., *Wirtschaftstheorie der Gegenwart,* 4 vols. (Vienna, 1927–32), 2: 153.

28. Auguste Walras, *De la nature de la richesse et de l'origine de la valeur* (Paris, 1832), and *Théorie de la richesse sociale* (Paris, 1849). Walras's attacks on the prevailing value theory were resented by Jean Baptiste Say. See Gaëtan Pirou, *Les Théories de l'équilibre économique* (Paris, 1939), p. 82 ff.

29. Auguste Comte, *Cours de philosophie positive,* 6 vols. (Paris, 1830–42). Some leading ideas of Comte's philosophy had been suggested by Saint-Simon.

30. The "Utopian Socialists" have been the objects of an extensive literature; especially French and German historians of social philosophies have carefully analyzed the various schemes of radical reform. See, among other contributions, Vilfreda Pareto, *Les Systèmes socialistes,* 2 vols. (Paris, 1902–3), and Alexander Gray, *Socialist Tradition: Moses to Lenin* (London, 1946).

31. For an impartial analysis of Sismondi's economic views, see Alfred Amonn, *Simonde de Simondi als Nationalökonom,* 2 vols. (Bern, 1945–49).

32. J.C.L. Simonde de Sismondi, *De la richesse commerciale* (Geneva, 1803).

33. Idem, *Nouveaux principes d'économie politique* (Paris, 1819). The view that this study was not simply the result of a change in Sismondi's political convictions but was designed to supplement his first economic publication by a critical theoretical discussion of the problems of production and distribution has been defended by Amonn (*Simonde de Sismondi*) with good arguments.

34. This may have had something to do with his knowledge of history. Although not a trained historian, Sismondi was deeply devoted to the study of historical developments. He published many volumes dealing with the history of the Italian Republics, of France, and of the downfall of the Roman Empire.

35. Sismondi mentioned occasionally that he had undermined ("j'ai démoli") the existing society, but that he did not have the power to reconstruct it. See Luigi Einaudi, *Saggi bibliografici e storici intorno alle dottrine economiche* (Rome, 1953), p. 172. The term *socialist* as applied to radical social reformers was introduced into the vocabulary of political and economic literature through an article which appeared in February 1832 in the Saint-Simonian journal *Globe.* See Karl Grünberg, ed., *Archivur Geschichte des Sozialismus und der Arbeiterbewegung* (1912), p. 378; and Friedrich A. Hayek, "The Counter-Revolution of Science," *Economica* (August 1941), p. 146. Prior to the establishment of the Soviet regime the term *socialism* was applied to schemes of economic organizations in which common ownership of the means of production was combined with the maintenance of some ill-defined freedom in the sphere of consumption. According to the bolshevist terminology, *socialism* denotes the economic organization of a transition period during which "commodity production" has not yet been completely eliminated. These differences in terminology should be kept in mind if confusions are to be avoided.

36. The main works of Claude Henri de Rouvroy, Comte de Saint-Simon, were: *L'Industrie,* 4 vols. (Paris, 1817); *Du système industriel* (Paris, 1821); *Catéchisme des industriels* (Paris, 1823–24); and *Nouveau Christianisme* (Paris, 1825).

37. This aspect of Saint-Simon's social philosophy has been emphasized by E. S. Mason, "The Rationalization of Industry," *Quarterly Journal of Economics* (August 1931).

38. With that approach some followers of Saint-Simon anticipated certain teachings of Marxism. See A. J. Tiumenev, in Nikolai I Bukharin et al., *Marxism and Modern Thought,* trans. Ralph Fox (London, 1935), p. 256.

39. *Exposition de la doctrine de Saint-Simon* (1828–29). The formulation of the doctrine was

largely the work of Bazard. Enfantin contributed a series of articles to *Le Producteur*, the organ of the Saint-Simonians.

40. About a century later some fascist authors hailed this scheme as a forerunner of the Italian corporative organization of industries. See Herbert von Beckerath, *Wesen und Werden des facistischew Staats* (Jena, 1927).

41. François Marie Charles Fourier, *Théorie des quatre mouvements et des destinées générales* (Lyons, 1808), *Le Nouveau Monde industriel et sociétaire* (Paris, 1829). Fourier's teachings were propagated mainly by Victor Considérant, *Destinée sociale* (Paris, 1834–44). They also gained adherents in the United States.

42. See Wagner, *Geschichte der Kredittheorien*, p. 93.

43. Louis Blanc, *Organisation du travail* (Paris, 1839), Le Socialisme: *Droit au travail* (Brussels, 1848).

44. French students of the history of radical movements have connected the ideas of Louis Blanc with those of Constantin Pecqueur (1801–1887), *Théorie nouvelle d'économie sociale et politique* (Paris, 1842). But Pecqueur was strongly influenced by the Christian socialist movement as represented by François Huet, *Le règne social du christianisme* (Paris, 1853).

45. Pierre J. Proudhon, *Mémoires sur la propriété* (Paris, 1840–42), *Système des contradictions économiques, ou Philosophie de la misère* (Paris, 1846). See Karl Diehl, *P. J. Proudhon: Seine lehre und sein leben*, 3 vols. (Jena, 1888–96).

46. Proudhon's *Contradictions économiques* were the object of vehement criticisms in Karl Marx's *Misère de la philosophie* (Paris, 1847). The Marxian objections centered on the idea that the economic categories (rent, profit, wages, exchange, value, money, and the like) were not absolute and eternally valid concepts but merely the abstract expressions of historical and transitory "production relations."

47. To theses expressed by the slogan "*La propriété c'est le vol*" he opposed the antithesis: "*La propriété c'est la liberté.*" Other slogans which were characteristic of his economic conceptions were "*Constitution des valeurs*" (establishment of real value) and "*mutualité*" (cooperation of the producers).

48. A similar conception of credit was propagated by François Vidal, *Organisation du crédit personnel et réel* (Paris, 1851).

49. Mikhail Bakunin, *God and the State*, trans. Benjamin Tucker (Boston, 1883), and Pëtr A. Kropotkin, *Mutual Aid, a Factor of Evolution* (New York, 1902).

50. A German translation of *The Wealth of Nations* was published as early as 1778.

51. Among the first German textbooks to reflect the principles of economic freedom were those of Graf F.J.H. Soden, Ludwig H. von Jakob (1759–1827), Gottlieb Hufeland, J.F.E. Lotz, and Heinrich von Storch (who taught at Russian universities but was of German origin). Storch published in French a *Cours d'économie politique* (St. Petersburg, 1815).

52. Karl Heinrich Rau, *Lehrbuch der politischen ökonomie*, 3 vols. (Heidelberg, 1826–37). This textbook was widely used at German universities. A ninth edition was published in 1870.

53. Immanuel Kant, *Critique of Practical Reason* (1788).

54. Friedrich Benedict Wilhelm von Hermann, *Staatswirhschaftliche untersuchungen* (Munich, 1832). About some differences between the value theory of Hermann and that of Senior, see Marion Bowley, *Nassau Senior and Classical Economics* (London, 1937), p. 113.

55. Among the authors who adopted that approach were Johann Schön, *Neue Untersuchung der Nationalökonomie* (Stuttgart, 1835); Adolph Riedel, *Nationalökonomie oder Volkswirtschaft* (Berlin, 1838), and, above all, Wilhelm Roscher, *System der Volkswirthschaft*, 5 vols. (Stuttgart, 1854–94) ff.

56. Among the many noted German economists who accepted Hermann's theory of interest were Hans von Mangoldt, *Grundriss der Volkswirtschaftslehre* (Stuttgart, 1863), and Karl Knies, *Geld und Kredit*, 3 vols. (Berlin, 1873–79). In his critical analysis of the theories of interest (*Capital and Interest*, chap. 8, sect. 2), Böhm-Bawerk endeavored to show that, when strictly defined, capital is identical with the aggregate of its uses. He ascribed the fallacy involved in separating the "substance" of capital from the uses to which it is put to the transformation into a "reality" of a juridical fiction.

57. Hans von Mangoldt, *Die Lehre vom Unternehmergewinn* (Leipzig, 1855).

58. About the treatment of the wage problem by nineteenth-century German economists, see James W. Crook, *German Wage Theories* (New York, 1898).

59. About Mangoldt's presentation of the Ricardian theory of foreign trade, see Jacob Viner, *Studies in the Theory of International Trade* (New York, 1937), p. 458.

60. See J. Hoffman, *Weltwirtschaftliches Archiv* (1950), p. 29 ff. The literature on Thünen and his importance for economic reasoning is quite extensive. See E. Schneider, "Johann Heinrich von Thünen," trans. Anne von Bibra Sutton, *Econometrica* (January 1934).

61. Johann Heinrich von Thünen, *von Thünen's Isolabed Sbabe*, trans. Carla M. Wartenberg (London, 1966) esp. pp. 225–47.

62. Johann Heinrich von Thünen, *Der isolierte*

Staat in Besiehung auf Landwirtschaft und Na-tionalökonomie, 2 vols. (Hamburg, 1826; 1850–63).

63. Mounbifort Lonafield, *Lectures on Political Economy* (Dublin, 1834).

64. Bertil Ohlin, "Some Aspects of the Theory of Rent," in *Economic Essays in Honor of T. N. Carver* (Cambridge, 1935), p. 177.

65. For an extensive discussion of his problematic formula, see Crook, *German Wage Theories*, chap. 4.

66. Johann Karl Rodbertus, *Zur Erkenntnis un-srer staatswirtschaftlichen Zustände* (Neubranden-burg, 1842); *Sociale Briefe an von Kirchmann* (Berlin, 1850), trans. under the title *Overproduction and Crises* by Julie Franklin (London, 1898); *Das Kapital* (Berlin, 1884). The German literature on Rodbertus is very extensive. See, among many others, Heinrich Dietzel, *Karl Rodbertus* (Jena, 1886–88); Böhm-Bawerk, *Capital and Interest*, passim; Werner Halbach, *Carl Rodbertus* (Nürnberg, 1938).

67. Ideas of that kind were later elaborated by adherents of the so-called sociojuridical school. See Muriol, *Karl Rodbertus als Begründer der sozialrechtlichen Anschauungsweise* (1927).

68. Johann Karl Rodbertus, *Zur Beleuchtung der sozialen Frage* (Berlin, 1875), p. 71.

69. Idem, *Die Handelskrisen und die Hypo-thekennoth der Grundbesitzer* (Berlin, 1858).

70. Idem, *Overproduction and Crises* (London, 1898).

71. Karl Marlo, *Untersuchungen über die Organisation der Arbeit; oder, System der Weltökonomie*, 3 vols. (Kassel, 1850–59).

72. About some possible reasons for that lack of scientific interest and initiative, see Frank A. Fetter, "The Early History of Political Economy in the United States," *Proceedings of the American Philosophical Society* (1943), and Joseph H. Dorfman, *The Economic Mind in American Civilization*, 5 vols. (New York, 1946).

73. See J. B. Condliffe, *The Commerce of Nations* (New York, 1950), pp. 240, 244.

74. Daniel Raymond, *Thoughts on Political Economy* (Baltimore, 1820).

75. Raymond also advanced some arguments which were elaborated by Georg Friedrich List as discussed below, in chapter 14, "The German Historical Schools."

76. Carey, *Principles of Political Economy, The Past, the Present and the Future* (London, 1848), *Principles of Social Science*, 3 vols. (Philadelphia, 1858–59). About Carey's influence on Bastiat, see above.

77. About the various defects of Carey's theories of interest and profit, see Böhm-Bawerk, *Capital and Interest*, chap. 6, sect. 3.

78. Henry Charles Carey, *Financial Crises:*

Their Causes and Effect (Philadelphia, 1863). For some time Carey exercised considerable influence on American public opinion. In a letter written to Cairnes in 1864, J. S. Mill expressed his concern about this situation. See *Economica* (November 1943), p. 280.

79. Henry George, *Progress and Poverty* (Middleton, 1879). Although published in the last quarter of the nineteenth century, this book belongs to the Ricardian period. It ignored any changes in economic reasoning which had taken place after the appearance of J. S. Mill's *Principles*.

80. Henry George elaborated his economic theories in some subsequent works: *Social Problems* (Chicago, 1882), *The Science of Political Economy* (New York, 1897). For various similar proposals dealing with the imposition of taxes on land, see E. Whittaker, *A History of Economic Ideas* (London, 1940), p. 234.

81. The first occupants of such chairs were Charles F. Dunbar (1830–1900) at Harvard, who founded the *Quarterly Journal of Economics* in 1886, William Graham Sumner at Yale, and Francis A. Walker at Sheffield, the first president of the American Economic Association. Textbooks dealing with economics were published by Simon Newcomb (1835–1909) in 1885 and Arthur J. Hadley (1856–1930) in 1896.

82. Richard T. Ely propounded his views on the new school in an essay entitled *The Past and the Present of Political Economy* (Baltimore, 1884). See Jacob H. Hollander, ed., *Economic Essays in Honor of J. B. Clark* (New York, 1927), p. 2.

83. Between 1890 and 1902 Hawley published a series of articles on various aspects of the theory of distribution in the *Quarterly Journal of Economics*. His main works were *Capital and Population* (New York, 1882), and *Enterprise and the Productive Process* (New York, 1907). See Richard M. Davis, "Frederick B. Hawley's Income Theory," *Journal of Political Economy* (April 1953).

CHAPTER 14

1. Johann G. Fichte, *Ueber den Begriff der Wissenschaftslehre* (Weimar, 1794), trans. (1868); *Grundlage des Naturrechts* (Jena, 1796), trans. (1868).

2. Fichte's natural law philosophy originally had cosmopolitan features. He adopted a strongly nationalistic approach only later under the influence of the Napoleonic invasion of Europe.

3. Fichte and his successors were later hailed for having reestablished "the genuine universalistic conception of the higher solidarity of the state." See Othmar Spann, *The History of Economics*, trans. Eden Paul and Cedar Paul (New York, 1930), p. 64.

4. Johann G. Fichte, *Der geschlossene Handelsstaat* (Tübingen, 1800).

5. The dialectic aspects of Hegel's philosophy of history will be discussed in connection with the analysis of the Marxian doctrine.

6. Paramount among these philosophers were the historian Adam Ferguson, the Utilitarian Josiah Tucker, and the economist Adam Smith. See, among others, Friedrich A. Hayek, *Individualism and Economic Order* (London, 1949), p. 7.

7. One of the foremost German scholars who analyzed the spontaneous, unconscious developments in language, art, and religion was J. G. von Herder (*Ueber den Ursprung der Sprache* [Halle, 1771] and *Ideen zur Philosophie der Geschichte der Menschheit* [Leipzig, 1784–91]).

8. Adam Müller, *Elemente der Staatskunst* (Berlin, 1809). See also Jacob Baxa, *Adam Müller* (Jena, 1930).

9. Adam Müller, *Versuch einer neuen Theorie des Geldes* (Leipzig, 1816).

10. The leaders in that fight, Heeren Arnold (1760–1842), Rehberg, and Brandes, were members of the so-called School of Göttingen. See Vincenz John, *Geschichte der Statistik* (Stuttgart, 1884), 1: 129.

11. Edmund Burke, *Reflections on the Revolution in France* (London, 1792).

12. See Erich Rothacker, "Historismus," *Schmoller's Jahrbuch für Gesetzgebung, Verwaltung und Volkswirtschaft* (1938), p. 389.

13. Plato's theory of essences was motivated by the consideration that no change can be observed unless it is possible to determine certain "essential" elements which remain constant regardless of the change. See Karl Popper, "The Poverty of Historism," *Economica* (May 1944), p. 96.

14. Friedrich Karl von Savigny, *Vom Berf unserer Zeit für Gesetzgebung und rechtswissenschaft* (Heidelberg, 1814), *System des heutigen römischen Rechts* (Berlin, 1840–49).

15. See Carl Menger, *Untersuchungen über die Methode der Sozialwissenschaften* (Leipzig, 1883).

16. Georg Friedrich List, *Das nationale System der politischen Oekonomie* (Stuttgart, 1840), trans. Sampson S. Lloyd as *The National System of Political Economy* (London, 1885). See, among others, Arthur Sommer, *Friedrich List's System der politischen Oekonomie* (Jena, 1927).

17. List appears to have borrowed some criticisms of the laissez-faire doctrine from the American Daniel Raymond's book *Thoughts on Political Economy* (Baltimore, 1820).

18. Franz Eulenberg, *Aussenhandel und Aussenhandelspolitik* (Tübingen, 1929), p. 115.

19. See Schmoller, *Zur Literaturgeschichte der Staats und Sozialwissenschaften* (Leipzig, 1888).

20. Wilhelm Roscher, *Grundriss zu Vorlesungen über die Staatswissenschaft nach geschichtlicher Methode* (Göttingen, 1843).

21. Wilhelm Roscher, *System der Volkswirthschaft*, 5 vols. (Stuttgart, 1854–94), 1854 ff. Trans. in part J. J. Lalor (New York, 1878). Wilhelm Roscher, *Geschichte der Nationalökonomik in Deutschland* (Munich, 1874). Prior to Roscher a detailed survey of the economic literature had been published by K. Kautz, *Geschichtliche Entwicklung der Nationalökonomik under ihrer Literatur* (Vienna, 1860).

22. See Richard Schüller, *Die klassische Nationalökonomie und ihre Gegner* (Berlin, 1895).

23. Bruno Hildebrand, *Die Nationalökonomie der Gegenwart und Zukunft* (Frankfurt, 1848).

24. Karl Knies, *Die politische Oekonomie vom Standpunkte der geschichtlichen Methode* (Brunswick, 1853).

25. Karl Knies, *Geld und Kredit*, 3 vols. (Berlin, 1873–79).

26. Rothacker, "Historismus," p. 391.

27. Otto von Gierke, *Das deutsche Genossenschaftsrecht* (Berlin, 1868–1913).

28. Gustav Schmoller, "Justice in Political Economy," *Annals of the American Academy of Political and Social Sciences* (March 1894), p. 698.

29. Idem, *Zwanzig Jahre deutscher Politik, 1897–1917* (Munich, 1920), p. 204.

30. Idem, *Grundriss der Allgemeinen Volkswirtschaftslehre*, 2 vols. (Leipzig, 1900–1904), vol. 1.

31. Cited in Adolf Weber, *Einleitung in das Studium der Volkswirtschaftslehre* (1932), p. 29.

32. See Walter Eucken, "Wissenschaft im Stile Schmollers," *Weltwirtschaftliches Archiv* (November 1940), p. 471.

33. Sir Francis Galton, *Inquiries into Human Faculty and Its Development* (London, 1883), *Natural Inheritance* (London, 1889).

34. See W. Kromphardt, *Schmoller's Jahrbuch für Gesetzgebung, Verwaltung und Volkswirtschaft* (1938), p. 342.

35. Arthur Spiethoff, *Schmoller's Jahrbuch für Gesetzgebung, Verwaltung und Volkswirtschaft* (1938), p. 417. Schmoller's methodology was extensively discussed in a series of essays published in that periodical in honor of the hundredth anniversary of his birth.

36. Hans Ritschl, p. 256. The German expressions for the term *intuition* used above were *Einfühlung* and *Nacherleben*.

37. Schmoller, *Grundriss der Volkswirtschaftslehre*.

38. See W. Vleugels, *Schmoller's Jahrbuch für Gesetzgebung, Verwaltung und Volkswirtschaft* (1938), p. 427.

39. See Spiethoff, p. 404 ff.

40. See Spiethoff, 414; Vleugels, 421.

41. The most remarkable studies of this type were by Albert Schäffle, *Das gesellschaftliche System der menschlichen Wirtschaft* (Tübingen, 1867), and *Bau und Leben des sozialen Körpers* (Tübingen, 1875–78). Very significant was Schäffle's observation that "intuition" was needed to establish the balance of the "real economy."

42. Ferdinand Tönnies, *Gemeinschaft und Gesellschaft* (Leipzig, 1887).

43. It is interesting to note that the German term *Gemeinschaft* was originally meant to be a translation of the English term *partnership*, used by Burke in his *Reflections on the Revolution in France*. But F. Gentz, who coined the German term, gave it a romantic connotation. See O. Brunner's reference to an essay by E. Lerch, "Die alteuropäische ökonomik," *Zeitschrift für Nationalökonomie* (1950), p. 121.

44. Considerable divergences of views concerning the nature of the "national economy" and the "world economy" were reflected in the wide variety of definitions given for these concepts in the textbook of German economists. See the survey of such definitions made by Bernhard Harms, *Volkswirtschaft und Weltwirtschaft* (Jena, 1912).

45. Gustav Schmoller, M. Sering, and A. Wagner, *Handels und Machtopolitik* (Stuttgart, 1900).

46. These questions were, however, clearly stated in Albert Schäffle, *Die Quintessenz des Sozialismus* (Gotha, 1875).

47. Menger, *Untersuchungen über die Methode*.

48. In this connection Menger criticized the sociology of Auguste Comte, who had characterized social collectivities as "organisms." Comte's theoretical interpretation was incomparably more difficult than the analysis of "natural organisms." See Menger, *Untersuchungen über die Methode*, p. 157.

49. See Schmoller's article, "Zur Methodologie der Staats und Sozialwissenschaften" (1883); Menger retorted in an essay entitled "Die Irrtümer des Historismus" (1884). Schmoller's conviction that the principles of causality were not applicable to the analysis of social relationships was emphasized by Heinrich Dietzel, "Beitrag zur Methodologie," *Schmoller's Jahrbuch für Gesetzgebung, Verwaltung, und Volkswirtschaft* (1884). See also Schüller, *Die klassische Nationalökonomie*.

50. See Eucken, "Wissenschaft im Stile Schmollers," p. 496 ff., for a number of passages from Schmoller's writings which show very clearly how frequently and how thoroughly Schmoller misunderstood the leading ideas and the fundamental problems advanced by Menger and his followers.

51. Gustav Schmoller, *Grundfragen der Sozialpolitik und Volkswirtschaftslehre* (1897). See also Schmoller's article on political economy and its methods, in *Handwörterbuch der Staatswissenschaften* (1911). Limited application of deductive methods was recommended by various members of the historical school, such as Wilhelm Hasbach, *Jahrbuch für Nationalökonomie und Statistik* (1904), p. 289 and W. E. Biermann, *Staat und wirtschaft* (Berlin, 1904), p. 592.

52. See Hermann von Schullern-Schrattenhofen, *Die Theoretis cha Nationalökonomie Italiens* (Leipzig, 1891), section I.

53. About some logical aspects of the method of "intuitive understanding," and especially the application of "influence by analogy" from one historical period to another, see Popper, "The Poverty of Historism," p. 92.

54. See Georg Weippert, *Schmoller's Jahrbuch für Gesetzgebung, Verwaltung und Volkswirtschaft* (1938), p. 456.

55. Gustav Schmoller, *Ueber einige Grundfragen* (Leipzig, 1898), p. 280. In his textbook he emphasized the need to develop economics into a great "ethicopolitical" science, as opposed to the attempts to transform it into a "simple theory of exchange and market," a sort of business economics in defense of proprietary interests."

56. See Friedrich A. Hayek, "Scientism and the Study of Society, Part 2," *Economica* (February 1943), p. 45, and Popper, "The Poverty of Historism."

57. Adolf Held, *Zwei Bücher zur sozialen Geschichte von England* (Leipzig, 1881).

58. Wilhelm Hasbach, *Die allgemeinen philosophischen Grundlagen der von François Quesney und Adam Smith begrundeten politischen Oekonomic* (Leipzig, 1890).

59. Lujo Brentano, *Die klassische Nationalökonomie* (Leipzig, 1888). Brentano's attacks on Ricardian methods and his misinterpretations of the teachings of Adam Smith, J. B. Say, and David Ricardo were refuted by the Austrian economist Schüller in *Die klassische Nationalökonomie*.

60. Karl Diehl, *Sozialwissenschaftliche Erlauterungen zu Ricardo's Grundstzen* (Leipzig, 1908).

61. Götz Briefs, *Untersuchungen zur klassischen Nationalökonomie* (Jena, 1915).

62. Gustav Friedrich von Schönberg, *Handbuch der politischen Oekonomie* (Tübingen, 1896).

63. Karl Bücher, *Die Entstehung der Volkswirtschaft* (Tübingen, 1893), trans. S. Morley Wickett (New York, 1901).

64. See Alfons Dopsch, *Naturalwirtschaft und Geldwirtschaft* (Vienna, 1930). About objections raised especially against Bücher's conception of the medieval cities and their salient economic features, see the more recent studies of F. Rörig, H. Bechtel, and H. Jecht.

65. Schmoller, *Grundriss der Volkswirtschaftslehre* 2: 666. About Schmoller's analysis of stages,

see T. Mayer, *Zeitschrift für Staats und Volkswirtschaft* (1922). Harms, *Volkswirtschaft und Weltwirtschaft*, p. 89. He distinguished three stages: the "individual economy," the "national economy," and the "world economy."

66. For general discussions of the problem, see Johann Plenge, *Die Stammformen der vergleichenden Wirtschaftstheorie* (Essen, 1919); Waldemar Mitscherlich, *Die Wirtschaftsstufentheorie* (Leipzig, 1924); Gertrud Kalveram, *Die Theorien von den Wirtschaftsstufen* (Leipzig, 1933).

67. Edwin F. Gay, "The Tasks of Economic History," *Journal of Economic History* (1941).

68. See Iosif Kulischer, *Allgemeine Wirtschaftsgeschichte* (Munich, 1928); vol. 1; Walter Eucken, *The Foundations of Economics* (London, 1950), p. 70.

69. Eli Filip Heckscher, in *Economic Essays in Honor of Gustav Cassel* (London, 1933) and Sir John Clapham, in *The Encyclopedia of the Social Sciences*, ed. E.R.A. Seligman (New York, 1930), 5: 328.

70. See G. Albrecht, *Jahrbuch für Nationalökonomie und Statistik* (1942), and Brunner, "Die alteuropäische ökonomik," p. 134.

71. Eugen Böhm-Bawerk, "The Historical vs. the Deductive Method in Political Economy," *Annals of the American Academy of Political and Social Sciences* 1 (1890–91).

72. P. G. Frédéric Le Play, *Les Ouvriers européens* (Paris, 1855), *L'Organisation de la famille* (Paris, 1871), *L'Organisation du travail* (Paris, 1870).

73. Pierre Emile Levasseur, *Histoire des classes ouvrières en France* (Paris, 1859 and 1867); and Henri Sée, *Les Origines du capitalisme moderne* (1926).

74. Charles Seignobos, *La Méthode historique appliquée aux sciences sociales* (Paris, 1901); and Henri Hauser, *La Nouvelle Orientation économique* (Paris, 1924).

75. Charles Gide and Charles Rist, *Histoire des doctrines économiques* (Paris, 1909), trans. R. Richards as *A History of Economic Doctrines from the Times of the Physiocrats to the Present Day* (London, 1917).

76. Emile L. V. de Lavaleye, *De la propriété et des formes primitives* (1874).

77. Achille Loria, *La teoria del valore negli economisti Italiani* (Pisa, 1882), *La crisi del la scienza* (Turin, 1908).

78. Idem, *La sintesi economica* (Milan, 1909).

CHAPTER 15

1. See Theo Suranyi-Unger, *Economics in the Twentieth Century* (New York, 1931).

2. Rudolf Stammler, *Wirtschaft und Recht* (Leipzig, 1896).

3. Fritz Berolzheimer, *System der Rechts und Wirtschaftsphilosophie* (Munich, 1904–7); A periodical, *Archiv für Rechts und Wirtschaftsphilosophie*, founded in 1907, was designed to deal with the legal and political aspects of economics and to examine economic doctrines in the light of the philosophy of law.

4. Karl Diehl, *Die sozialrechtliche Richtung in der Nationalökonomie* (Jena, 1941).

5. Rudolf Stolzmann, *Die soziale Kategorie in der Volkswirtschaftslehre* (Berlin, 1896).

6. Wilhelm Dilthey, *Einleitung in die Geisteswissenschaften* (Leipzig, 1883).

7. Heinrich Rickert, *Kulturwissenschaft und Naturwissenschaft* (Freiburg, 1899), and *Die Grenzen der naturwissenschaftlichen Bergriffsbildung* (Tübingen, 1902).

8. That distinction had been anticipated in a similar way in Carl Menger's *Untersuchungen über die Methode der Sozialwissenschaften* (Leipzig, 1883). But Menger had insisted upon applying methods of the "nomothetic" sciences to economic analysis.

9. Rickert, *Grenzen*, p. 235.

10. See T. Parsons, *The Structure of Social Action* (New York, 1937), p. 478.

11. Werner Sombart, *Der moderne Kapitalismus*, 2 vols. (Leipzig, 1902); *Volkapitalismus*, 2 vols. (1916); *Frühkapitalismus*, 2 vols. (1917); *Hochkapitalismus*, 2 vols. (1927). For an English version of one of Sombart's books in which he presented his ideas in a popularized form, see *The Quintessence of Capitalism*, trans. M. Epstein (London, 1915).

12. Werner Sombart, *Die Juden und das Wirtschaftsleben* (Munich, 1911), trans. M. Epstein as *The Jews and Modern Capitalism* (London, 1913), pp. 2, 206.

13. Idem, *Ordnung des Wirtschaftlebens* (Leipzig, 1925).

14. That peculiarity was the object of repeated comments. See, for instance, Wesley C. Mitchell, "Sombart's Hochkapitalismus," *Quarterly Journal of Economics* (February 1929), p. 322.

15. About Sombart's definition of the "economic system" and his methodological ideas, see his article "Economic Theory and Economic History," *Economic History Review* (1929).

16. See, among others, Walter Eucken, *The Foundations of Economics* (London, 1950), p. 326; and the criticisms of Sombart's analysis of the original sources of capital accumulation and the initial organization of capitalist enterprises advanced by Jacob Strieder, *Studien zur Geschichte der Kapitalischen Organisationsformen* (Munich, 1925).

17. Max Weber discussed the methodological problems of sociology in a series of articles later collected in a volume entitled *Gesammelte Aufsätze zur*

Wissenschaftslehre (Tübingen, 1922). See Parsons, *The Structure of Social Action,* p. 580.

18. About Max Weber's methodology, see Bernhard Pfister, *Die Entwicklung zum Idealtypus* (Tübingen, 1928); A. von Schelting, *Max Weber's Wissenschaftslehre* (Tübingen, 1934); and Walter Eucken, *Die Grundlagen der Nationalökonomie* (Jena, 1940).

19. See Felix Kaufmann. "Was Kann die mathematische Methode in der Nationalökonomie leisten?," *Zeitschrift für Nationalökonomie* (1931), p. 773

20. Weber had elaborated these ideas in articles entitled "Ueber die Objektivität der soziologischen und sozialpolitischen Erkenntnis" and "Der Sinn der Wertfreiheit," later reproduced in *Gesammelte Aufsätze.*

21. Some years earlier, Werner Sombart had requested the establishment of the principle of "greatest productivity" as an autonomous ideal for the science of economics ("Ideale der Sozialpolitik," *Archiv für Sozialwissenschaft und Sozialpolitik* [1897]). At the 1909 meeting he seconded Max Weber's "principles of critical objectivity."

22. Lujo Brentano, "Die Werturteile in der Volkswirtschaftslehre," *Archiv für Sozialwissenschaft und Sozialpolitik* (1911); Julius Wolf, *Zeitschrift für Sozialwissenschaft* (1912); Adolf Weber, *Die Aufgaben der Volkswirtschaftslehre als Wissenschaft* (Tubingen, 1909); L. Pohle, *Die gegenwärtige Krisis* (Leipzig, 1911).

23. Andreas Voigt, *Zeitschrift für Sozialwissenschaft* (1912 and 1913); Richard Ehrenberg, *Gegen den Kathedersozialismus* (Berlin, 1909), and "Zur gegenwärtigen Krise in der Deutschen Wissenschaft," *Archiv für exakte Wirtschaftsforschung* (1912). For a more recent survey of the controversy, see Tullio Bagiotti, "Per una storia delle dottrine economiche," *Giornale degli economisti e annali de economia* (May 1954), p. 433.

24. Heinrich Herkner, *Schmoller's Jahrbuch für Gesetzgebung, Verwaltung und Volkswirtschaft* (1912).

25. Ianaz Jastrow, *Sein und Sollen* (Berlin, 1914).

26. E. Spranger, *Schmoller's Jahrbuch für Gesetzgebung, Verwaltung und Volkswirtschaft* (1914); Walter Köhler, *Die Objektivität* (1915); and Theodor Litt, *Erkenntnis und Leben* (Leipzig, 1923). See also V. Kraft, *Grundformen der wissenschaftlichen Methoden* (Vienna, 1925).

27. Albert Hesse, *Jahrbüch für Nationalökonomie und Statistik* (1912).

28. E. Schrödinger, *Nature and the Greeks* (Cambridge, 1954), p. 90.

29. The term *intuitional empiricism* has been suggested to denote this methodological attitude. See Parsons, *The Structure of Social Action,* p. 728.

30. The German literature on "social engineering" and related topics was very extensive and partly influenced by ideas propagated by the American "technocrats." See, among others, Max Weber, *Energetische Kulturtheorien* (1909); reprinted in *Gesammelte Aufsätze.* About a criticism of the economic views of the adherents of social energetics, see Friedrich A. Hayek, "Scientism and the Study of Society, Part 3," *Economica* (February 1944), p. 35.

31. Friedrich von Gottl-Ottlilienfeld, *Die Herrschaft des Wortes* (Jena, 1901), *Die Wirtschaftliche Dimension* (Jena, 1923). A collection of Gottl-Ottlilienfeld's methodological essays was published under the title *Wirtschaft als Leben* (Jena, 1925).

32. For an attempt to make Gottl-Ottlilienfeld's cryptic teachings at least somewhat intelligible, see Gottfried Haberler, "Wirtschaft als Leben: Kritische Bemerkungen zu Gottls methodologischen Schriften," *Zeitschrift für Nationalökonomie* (1930), p. 28 ff.

33. See Alfred Amonn, *Ricardo* (Jena, 1924), p. 6; Adolf Weber, *Einleitung in das Studium der Volkswirtschaftslehre* (1932), p. 19.

34. Wilhelm Lexis, *Naturwissenschaft und Sozialwissenschaft,* reprinted in *Abhandlungen zur Theorie der Bevölkerungs und Moralstatistik* (Jena, 1903).

35. Striving for originality has been regarded as a characteristic feature of the German mentality before the advent of the Hitler regime. The German educational system has been held responsible for that development. See Friedrich A. Hayek, *Individualism and Economic Order* (London, 1949), p. 26.

36. For a survey of the varying and partly conflicting views on productivity, see Karl Diehl, in Hans Mayer et al., eds., *Wirtschaftstheorie der Gegenwart,* 4 vols. (Vienna, 1927-32), 2:250.

37. Adolf Wagner, *Grundlegund der politischen Oekonomie* (Leipzig, 1892), p. 870.

38. Characteristic of that attitude was Karl Diehl's review of a number of textbooks in *Jahrbuch für Nationalökonomie und Statistik* (1902).

39. Robert Liefmann, *Ertrag und Einkommen* (Jena, 1907), *Grundsätze der Volkswirtschaftslehre* (Stuttgart, 1917-19).

40. Liefmann's theories were discussed and criticized by, among others, A. Amonn, J. B. Esslen, Franz Oppenheimer, Rudolf Stolzmann, Karl Diehl, Otto von Zwiedinek-Südenhorst, and W. Kromphardt.

41. Adolf Wagner, *Beiträge zur Lehre von den Banken* (Leipzig, 1857), *Die Geld und Credittheorie der Pell'schen Bankacte* (Vienna, 1862), *Sozialökonomische Theorie des Geldes und Geldwesens* (1909).

42. Nicholas Johannsen, *Der Kreislauf des Geldes und der Mechanismus des sozialen Lebens*

(Berlin, 1903). In his subsequent study *Die Steuer der Zukunft* (Berlin, 1913), Johannsen included a chapter in which he advanced the idea of a "permanent depression," anticipating the stagnation theorem of some Keynesian economists.

43. A noticeable theory of this type was developed by Otto Heyn, *Papierwahrung mit gold reserve für den Auslandsverkehr* (Berlin, 1894), *Irrtümer auf dem Gebiet des Geldwesens* (Berlin, 1900), J. Wolf, and Walter Hausman, *Der Goldwahn* (Berlin, 1911). *Das internationale Zahlungswesen* (1892).

44. About the treatment of the problems involved in the rapid but fluctuating increases of urban land rent, see Adolf Weber, in Mayer et al., eds., *Wirtschaftstheorie der Gegenwart*, 3: 236 ff.

45. See Michael Flürscheim, *Der einzige Rettungsweg* (Dresden, 1890); Theodor Hertzka, *Freiland* (Dresden, 1890) trans. Arthur Ransom (New York, 1891); Adolf Damaschke, *Bodenreform* (Berlin, 1903).

46. Heinrich Dietzel, *Kornzoll und Sozialreform* (Berlin, 1901). Paul Arndt, *Der Schutz der nationalen Arbeit* (Jena, 1902); and Karl Diehl, *Kornzoll und Sozialreform* (Jena, 1901).

47. For the analysis and the criticism of such theories, see chaps. 7 and 8 and the appendix of Eugen Böhm-Bawerk, *Geschichte und Kritik der Kapitalzinstheorien*, 3rd ed. (Innsbruck, 1914).

48. Julius Wolf, *Sozialismus und Kapitalistische gesellschaftsordnung* (Stuttgart, 1892); Karl Adler, *Kapitalzins und Preisbewegung* (Munich, 1913); Karl Diehl, *P. J. Proudhon: Seine Lehre und sein Leben* (Jena, 1888–96), vol. 2.

49. Albert Schäffle, *Das gesellschaftliches System der menschlichen Wirtschaft* (Tübingen, 1862); Karl Knies, *Der Kredit* (Berlin, 1876–79), vol. 2, chap. 2; Lujo Brentano, *Theorie der Bedürfnisse* (Munich, 1908); Henry Oswalt, *Vortrage über wirtschaftliche Grundbergriffe* (Jena, 1905); and "Theorie des Kapitalzinses," *Zeitschrift für Sozialwissenschaft* (1910).

50. Stolzmann, *Die soziale Kategorie*, and *Der Zweck in der Volkswirtschaft* (Berlin, 1909).

51. Wilhelm Lexis, *Jahrbuch für Nationalökonomie und Statistik* (1885). The theory of "surplus value" advanced by Lexis was much later elaborated by Hans Peter, *Grundprobleme der theoretischen Nationalökonomie* (Stuttgart, 1933–37), vol. 1.

52. Heinrich Dietzel, *Göttinger Gelehrte Azeigen* (1890), p. 930 ff.

53. See M. R. Weyermann, *Das Verhältnis der Privatwirtschaftslehre zur Nationalökonomie* (1913); Eugen Schmalenbach, ed., *Grundriss der Betriebswirtschaftslehre* (Leipzig, 1926); Areboe, *Allgemeine landwirtschaftliche Betriebslehre* (1917).

54. Ferdinand Lassalle, *Herr Bastiat-Schulze von Delitzsch* (Berlin, 1864).

55. C.F.H. Roesler, *Zur Kritik der Lehre vom Arbeitslohn* (Erlangen, 1861).

56. Lujo Brentano, "Die Lehre von den Lohnsteigerungen," *Jahrbuch für Nationalökonomie und Statistik* (1871); *Das Arbeitsverhältnis* (Leipzig, 1877).

57. See Hilde Oppenheimer, *Zur Lohntheorie der Gewerkvereine* (Berlin, 1917).

58. For a survey of these views, see Karl Masser, *Die volkswirtschaftliche Funktion hoher Löhne* (1927).

59. Eugen Böhm-Bawerk, "Macht oder ökonomisches Gesetz," *Zietschrift für Staats und Volkswirtschaft* (1914).

60. Joseph Alois Schumpeter, "Das Grundprinzip der Verteilungslehre," *Archiv für Sozialwissenschaft und Sozialpolitik* (1916–17). Later the problem was taken up again by Otto von Zwiedineck-Südenhorst, "Macht oder ökonomisches Gesetz," *Schmoller's Jahrbuch für Gesetzgebung, Verwaltung und Volkswirtschaft* (1925). He emphasized the elasticity of certain economic factors which would permit economic power to interfere with marginal situations. See also the survey of the conflicting views given by H. Honegger, "Der Machtgedanke und das Produktionsproblem," *Schmoller's Jahrbuch für Gesetzgebung, Verwaltung und Volkswirtschaft (1925).*

61. See Robert Liefmann, *Unternehmungen und ihre Zusammenschlüsse*, 2 vols. (Stuttgart, 1927–28), a new edition of a previous publication by the same author. See also a comprehensive review of the literature on cartels and other instruments of market control in A. Wolfers, "Das Kartellproblem in Lichte der Deutschen Kartelliteratur," *Schriften des Vereins für Sozialpolitik* (1931).

62. Adolf Wagner, *Vom Territorialstaat zur Weltmacht* (Berlin, 1900).

63. Idem, *Die Geld und Credittheorie*.

64. Wilhelm Lexis, "Ueberproduktion," in *Handwörterbuch der Staatswissenschaften* (Jena, 1904).

65. Heinrich Herkner, "Krisen," in *Handwörterbuch der Staatswissenschaften* (Jena, 1904).

66. Werner Sombart, *Die Störungen des Wirtschaftslebens: Schriften des Vereins für Sozialpolitik* (1904).

67. Arthur Spiethoff, *Beträge zur Analyse und Theorie der allgemeinen Wirtschaftskrisis* (Leipzig, 1905); "Krisen," in *Handwörterbuch der Staatswissenschaften*, 4th ed. (1923), trans. in *International Economic Papers*, 12 vols. (London, 1951–62), 2: 75.

68. Spiethoff acknowledged his dependence on Tugan-Baranowsky's ideas in an article published in 1902 in *Schmoller's Jahrbüch für Gesetzgebung, Verwaltung und Volkswirtschaft.*

69. See Gotfried Haberler, *Prosperity and Depression* (Geneva, 1936), p. 70.

70. Alfred Weber was a brother of the sociologist Max Weber. He is not to be confused with Adolf Weber, a distinguished teacher of economics and author of some textbooks which were widely used.

71. Wilhelm Roscher, *System der Volkswirthschaft*, 5 vols. (Stuttgart, 1854-94), (1881), vol. 3. Roscher advanced a considerable volume of empirical material to illustrate his propositions.

72. Schäffle, *Das gesellschaftliche System der menschlichen Wirtschaft*.

73. Wilhelm Launhardt, *Mathematische Begründung der Volkswirtschaftslehre* (Leipzig, 1885). Launhardt also published some instructive studies on the costs of operating railroads and the effects of changing costs on railroad rates.

74. Alfred Weber, *Uber den Standort der Industrien* (Tübingen, 1909), trans. Carl J. Friedrich (Chicago, 1929).

75. See A. Predöhl, ''Das Standortsproblem in der Wirtschaftstheorie,'' *Weltwirtschaftliches Archiv* 1 (1925); Tord Palander, *Beiträge zur Standortstheorie* (Uppsala, 1935).

76. See August Lösch, *The Economics of Location*, trans. William Waglom (New Haven, 1954), p. 29. Lösch admitted that, when correctly formulated, the problem of location did not yield unequivocal solutions.

77. Georg Friedrich Knapp, *Staatliche Theorie des Geldes* (Leipzig, 1905), trans. H. M. Lucas and James Bonar as *The State Theory of Money* (London, 1927).

78. See Ludwig von Mises, *Theorie des Geldes*, 2nd ed. (Leipzig, 1924), p. 246; and Robert Mossé, *La Monnaie* (Paris, 1950), p. 51.

79. Adherents of Knapp's monetary views, such as F. Bendixen, R. Dalberg, and K. Elster, failed to agree on the interpretation of the distinction drawn by Knapp between ''value'' and ''valuableness'' of money. See Howard S. Ellis, *German Monetary Theory, 1905-1933* (Cambridge, Mass., 1934).

80. Such ideas were elaborated by G. Schmidt, *Kredit und Zins* (Leipzig, 1910).

81. Georg Simmel, *Philosophe des Geldes* (Leipzig, 1900).

82. Friedrich Bendixen, *Das Wesen des Geldes* (Leipzig, 1908); *Geld und Kapital* (Leipzig, 1912).

83. Rudolf Dalberg, *Die Entthrønung des Goldes* (Stuttgart, 1916); Karl Elster, *Die Seele des Geldes* (Jena, 1920); Kurt Singer, *Das Geld als Zeichen* (Jena, 1920).

84. Mossé, *La Monnaie*, p. 29.

85. Arthur Nussbaum, *Money in the Law* (1925; Brooklyn, 1950).

86. Karl Helfferich, *Das Geld* (Leipzig, 1923), trans. Louis Infield (London, 1927), p. 568.

87. Karl Eugen Dühring, *Capital und Arbeit* (Berlin, 1865), *Cursus der National und Sozialökonomik* (Berlin, 1873); and *Kritische Geschichte der Nationalökonomie und des Sozialismus* (Berlin, 1871).

88. Michael Tugan-Baranowsky, *Soziale Theorie der Verteilung* (Berlin, 1913).

89. Franz Oppenheimer, *David Ricardo's Grundrententheorie* (Berlin, 1909). About the discussion of the distinction between personal and functional aspects of the distributive process, see Carl Landauer, *Grundprobleme der funktionellen Verteilung des wirtschaftlichen Wertes* (Jena, 1923), p. 54, and V. Zarnowitz, *Theorie der Einkommensverteilung* (Tübingen, 1951).

90. Oppenheimer presented his fully elaborated economic theories in *Theorie der Reinen und politischen Oekonomie* (Berlin, 1910), and later incorporated these theories into his sociological treatise *System der Soziologie* (Jena, 1924).

91. See the discussion between Oppenheimer and Schumpeter in *Archiv für Sozialwissenschaft* (1916, 1917, 1920).

92. Franz Oppenheimer, *Der Staat* (Frankfurt am Main, 1907).

93. Oppenheimer's theories were discussed and criticized by various German economists. See, for instance, Alfred Amonn, ''Oppenheimers Theorie der Reinen und Politischen Oekonomie,'' *Archiv für Sozialwissenschaft* (1928). For an analysis of Oppenheimer's economic principles, see Edward Heimann, *Social Research* (1944).

94. See A. Fossati, ''Achille Loria nella storio del pensiero economico italiano,'' *Giornale degli economisti e annali di economia* (September-October 1953).

95. Arturo Labriola, *La rendita fondiaria e la sua elisione naturale* (1880).

96. Jean Paul Alban de Villeneuve-Bargemont, *Economie politique chrétienne,* 3 vols. (Paris, 1834). About the French Catholic social doctrine, see René Gonnard, *Histoire des doctrines économiques,* 3 vols. (Paris, 1927), 3: 301.

97. P. G. Frédéric Le Play, *La Réforme sociale en France* (Paris, 1864), *La Constitution essentielle de l'humanité* (Tours, 1881).

98. Victor Brants, *Les Grandes lignes de l'économie politique* (Louvain, 1901).

99. Guiseppe Toniolo, *Trattato di economia sociale* (Florence, 1907-9).

100. Wilhelm E. von Ketteler, *Die Arbeiterfrage und das Christentum* (Mainz, 1864).

101. About the extensive literature devoted to that task, see, among others, Götz Briefs, ''Die wirtschaftlichen Ideen,'' *Festgabe für Lujo Brentano* 1 (1925), and Amintore Fanfani, *Catholicism, Protestantism and Capitalism* (London, 1935).

102. Heinrich Pesch, *Lehrbuch der Nationalökonomie*, 5 vols. (Freiburg, 1905-23). For a

critical discussion of Pesch's views, see Abraham Lincoln Harris, "The Scholastic Revival: The Economics of Heinrich Pesch," *Journal of Political Economy* (February 1946). For a defense of Pesch's moral approach to economics, see Richard E. Mulcahy, *The Economics of Heinrich Pesch* (New York, 1952).

103. Othmar Spann developed his epistemological ideas in his *Kategorienlehre* (Jena, 1924), and in *Tote und Lebendige Wissenschaft* (Jena, 1921). His main initial contributions to economics were *Wirtschaft und Gesellschaft* (Dresden, 1907) and *Fundament der Volkswirtschaftslehre* (Jena, 1918). His history of economic thought, which enjoyed a considerable number of editions, was translated into English under the title *The History of Economics* by Eden Paul and Cedar Paul (New York, 1930).

104. See Othmar Spann, *Theorie der Preisverschiebung* (Vienna, 1913); "Geichgewichtigkeit und Grensnutzen," *Jahrbüch für Nationalökonomie und Statistik* (1925).

105. A survey of the achievements which were due to Spann's social philosophy was later published in Walter Heinrich, ed., *Die Ganzheit in Philosophie und Wissenschaft* (Vienna, 1950).

106. See, among many others, Robert Liefmann, "Universalismus," *Weltwirtschaftliches Archiv* (1926), and a discussion between O. Conrad and Wilhelm Andreae in *Jahrbücher für Nationalökonomie und Statistik* (1936).

CHAPTER 16

1. The study of the intellectual and social conditions which have provided the background to that belief belongs to the primary tasks of the "sociology of knowledge."

2. G.W.F. Hegel, *Phaenomenologie des Geistes* (Bamberg, 1807); *Vorlesunger über die Philosophie der Geschichte* (Berlin, 1837), trans. J. Sibrea as *Lectures on the Philosophy of History* (New York, 1899).

3. Metaphysical conceptions of that kind were elaborated by Friedrich Engels in his polemics with the German Socialist Karl Eugen. Dühring, who emphasized the primacy of the political factor in shaping human history. See Friedrich Engels, *Herrn Eugen Dühring's Umwälzung der Wissenschaft* (Leipzig, 1878), trans. Emile Burns under the title *Anti-Dühring* (London, 1935). In the opening chapters of this treatise, Engels defended the proposition that, when force and matter are introduced into the analysis, "contradictions" are found at every turn, rendering necessary the application of dialectic methods.

4. Ludwig Feuerbach's main work was *Das Wesen des Christentums* (Leipzig, 1841), trans. Mar-

ian Evans as *The Essence of Christianity* (London, 1854).

5. See Charles Rist, "Karl Marx, Utopiste," *Revue d'économie politique* (1948), p. 21.

6. Friedrich Engels, *Ludwig Feuerbach und der Ausgang der klassischen deutsche Philosophie* (Berlin, 1886), trans. as *Ludwig Feuerbach and the Outcome of Classical German Philosophy* (New York, 1934).

7. See Georgi Plekhanov, *Fundamental Problems of Marxism,* trans. Eden Paul and Cedar Paul (London, 1929), p. 119. The original was published in 1908. Plekhanov is generally considered one of the most reliable interpreters of the Marxian methodology.

8. Convinced Marxists have protested against the view that a "teleological" conception of history was basic to Marxian dialectics. See, for instance, Nikolai I. Bukharin, et al., *Marxism and Modern Thought,* trans. Ralph Fox (New York, 1935), p. 37. There is no need to enter into a discussion of their tortuous interpretations of teleological terms used in pertinent passages of Marxian writings.

9. Karl Marx, *On the Critique of Political Economy* (Chicago, 1907), cited in M. M. Bober, *Karl Marx's Interpretation of History* (New York, 1965), pp. 4–5.

10. Karl Marx, *Das Kapital* (Hamburg, 1867), vol. 1; volumes 2 and 3 were edited by Engels in 1885 and 1894, after the death of the author, from partly unfinished manuscripts. See also Henryk Grossman, "Die Aenderung des unsprünglichen Aufbauplans," *Archiv für Geschichte des Sozialismus* (1929).

11. See especially Marx, *Misère de la philosophie,* chap. 2.

12. About some authors who had preceded Marx in a sort of materialistic interpretation of history, see Wilhelm Sulzbach, *Die Anfänge der materialistichen Geschichtsauffassung* (Freiburg, 1911).

13. See Karl Marx, *Zur Kritik des politischen Oekonomie* (Berlin, 1859), trans. N. I. Stone as *On the Critique of Political Economy.*

14. Engels, *Anti-Dühring.*

15. Ibid., p. 93.

16. About that controversy, see, among others, Charles Turgeon, "La Conception matérialiste," *Revue d'économie politique* (1911); and Bober, *Marx's Interpretation of History.*

17. See Joseph Alois Schumpeter, *History of Economic Analysis* (New York, 1954), pp. 786, 856–57; and Oskar Lange, *Political Economy: General Problems* (New York, 1963), chap. 2.

18. These letters were published in *Der sozialistische Akademiker* (October 1895).

19. Schumpeter, *History of Economic Analysis,* p. 438. See also Overton H. Taylor, "Schumpeter and Marx: Imperialism and Social Classes in the

Schumpeterian System," *Quarterly Journal of Economics* (November 1951).

20. See E.R.A. Seligman, *The Economic Interpretation of History* (New York, 1902). See also Melvin M. Knight in the introduction to the English edition of Henri Sée, *Economic Interpretation of History*, trans. Melvin M. Knight (New York, 1929).

21. See E. M. Winslow, *The Pattern of Imperialism* (New York, 1948), p. 42.

22. For a complete enumeration of the assumptions underlying that scheme, see Shigeto Tsuru, "Keynes versus Marx: The Methodology of Aggression," in Kenneth K. Kurihara, ed., *Post-Keynesian Economics* (New Brunswick, 1954), chap. 12, p. 340. It is beyond the scope of this study to discuss the thorny question of whether the device of a fictitious model of the economy as a starting point was compatible with the methods of dialectic materialism that were supposed to reveal the "real" functioning of the economy.

23. Vilfredo Pareto, *Les Systèmes socialistes*, 2 vols. (Paris, 1902–3); and Eugen Böhm-Bawerk, *Das Ende des Marx'schen Systems* (Berlin, 1896), trans. Alice M. MacDonald as *Karl Marx and the Close of His System* (London, 1898).

24. For a hopeless attempt to justify the Marxian treatment of this problem, see R. L. Meek, *Studies in the Labor Theory of Value* (London, 1956), p. 168.

25. See L. von Bortkiewicz, "Wertrechnung und Preisrechnung im Marxschen System," in *Archiv für Sozialwissenschaft und Sozialpolitik*, trans. J. Kahane as "Value and Price in the Marxian System," in *International Economic Papers*, 12 vols. (London, 1951–62), vol. 2.

26. The comprehensive results of these studies were published much later in *Theorien über den Mehrwert*, ed. Karl Kautsky, 3 vols. (Stuttgart, 1905–10).

27. See Frank H. Knight, *The Ethics of Competition* (London, 1935), p. 167.

28. About the question of whether the Marxian concept of variable capital was influenced by the Ricardian wage fund theory, see H. Gottlieb, "Marx's Mehrwert Concept and Theory of Pure Capitalism," *Review of Economic Studies* (1950), p. 172.

29. About the close association which Marx established between the existence of the "industrial reserve army" and the creation of surplus values, see Oskar Lange, "Marxian Economics and Modern Economic Theory," *Review of Economic Studies* (June 1935), p. 199.

30. See L. von Bortkiewicz's articles in *Archiv für Sozialwissenschaft und Sozialpolitik*.

31. See Paolo S. Labini, *Teoria e politica dello sviluppo economico* (Milan, 1954), p. 70 ff.

32. As expressed by Marx, the average rate of profit was determined by the "average rate of exploitation under the capitalist order."

33. Friedrich Engels and Karl Kautsky (1854–1938) strongly defended the validity of the Marxian reasoning, which was questioned in varying degrees by Vilfredo Pareto, Eugen Böhm-Bawerk, Karl Diehl, Werner Sombart, Eduard Bernstein, Achille Loria, Arturo Labriola, and Tomas Garrigue Masaryk (1850–1937). See especially the excellent critical analysis of the problems involved in that "riddle" by L. von Bortkiewicz, in *Archiv für Sozialwissenschaft und Sozialpolitik*.

34. See, for instance, Natalie Moszkowska, *Das Marx'sche System* (Berlin, 1929); Meek, *Labor Theory of Value*, pp. 186 and passim; and S. G. Strumlin, "The Time Factor in Capital Investment Projects," trans. R.F.D. Hutchings and S. Nedzynski in *International Economic Papers*, 12 vols. (London, 1951–62), 1:163.

35. See Tadeusz Dietrich, "Economic Accounting," trans. S. Nedzynski, in *International Economic Papers*, 12 vols. (London, 1951–62), 2:8.

36. Knut Wicksell qualified Engels's description of crises as a "piece of economic romanticism, not to say an adventure story." See Wicksell's article, "The Enigma of Business Cycles," written in 1907, trans. C. G. Uhr in *International Economic Papers*, 12 vols. (London, 1951–62), 3:61.

37. See Lange, "Marxian Economics," and John D. Wilson, "A Note on Marx and the Trade Cycle," *Review of Economic Studies* (February 1938).

38. "The superficiality of political economy," said Marx, "shows itself in the fact that such a symptom is looked upon as the cause of the industrial cycle" (see Bober, *Marx's Interpretation of History*, chap. 11).

39. About these aspects of the Marxian analysis of business fluctuations, see Erich Preiser, "Der Doppelbau der Marx'schen Krisentheorie," *Festgabe für Franz Oppenheimer* (1924).

40. For a good survey of the various aspects of the Marxian discussion of crisis, see Paul M. Sweezy, *The Theory of Capitalist Development* (New York, 1946). However, it is to be observed that, like various other American authors who have dealt with problems of Marxism, Sweezy practically ignored its dialectic features. Marxism deprived of dialectics is, of course, Hamlet without the prince of Denmark.

41. See also Joan Robinson, *An Essay on Marxian Economics* (London, 1942), chap. 10.

42. Lorenz von Stein, *Socialismus und Communismus des heutigen Frankreichs* (Leipzig, 1842).

43. Hence the violent objections raised by convinced Marxists to the establishment of economic categories that are valid for analytical purposes regardless of the specific structures of the various societies.

44. Friedrich Engels, *Der Ursprung der Familie, des Privateigentums und des Staates* (Hottingen-Zurich, 1884).

45. See, among many other publications, Bober, *Marx's Interpretation of History;* Lionel Robbins, *The Economic Bases of the Class Conflict* (London, 1939); and the proceedings of the American Economic Association in *American Economic Review* (May 1949), p. 16.

46. See also Vernon Venable, *Human Nature: The Marxian View* (New York, 1945).

47. Engels, *Anti-Dühring,* p. 310.

48. Richard H. Tawney, "The Study of Economic History," *Economica* (February 1933), p. 21.

49. Joseph Stalin, in *Bolshevik* (October 1952).

50. Characteristic of the impression that the Marxian doctrine made on a mind trained exclusively in hypothetical reasoning has been the judgment of John Maynard Keynes: "Marxian Socialism must always remain a portent to the historians of opinion—how a doctrine so illogical and so dull can have exercised so powerful and enduring an influence over the minds of men, and, through them, the events of history" (*The End of Laissez-Faire* [London, 1926], p. 34).

51. Paul M. Sweezy, "Declining Investment Opportunities," in Seymour Harris, ed., *The New Economics* (New York, 1947), p. 103.

52. See especially Joseph A. Schumpeter, *Capitalism, Socialism and Democracy* (New York, 1942).

CHAPTER 17

1. Eduard Bernstein, *Die Voraussetzungen des Sozialismus* (Stuttgart, 1899), trans. Edith C. Harvey as *Evolutionary Socialism* (New York, 1911).

2. That issue was raised by Eduard Bernstein and dealt with in Karl Kautsky's *Bernstein und das sozialdemokratische Program* (Stuttgart, 1899).

3. Karl Kautsky, *Agrarfrage* (Stuttgart, 1899).

4. See "Sozialismus und Kommunismus," in *Handworterbüch der Staatswissenschaften,* 4th ed. (Jena, 1923); and Werner Sombart, *Sozialismus und Soziale Bewegung* (Jena, 1905).

5. See Karl Renner, *Marxismus, Krieg und Internationale* (Stuttgart, 1917), Fritz Naphtali, *Wirtschaftsdemokratie* (Berlin, 1928).

6. See F. Borkenau, *Socialism National and International* (London, 1942).

7. Georges Sorel, *La Décomposition du Marxism* (Paris, 1908).

8. Idem, *Réflexions sur la violence* (Paris, 1909).

9. See Emile James, *Histoire des théories économiques* (Paris, 1950), p. 140. About the economic ideas and aspirations of the French socialist parties, see Gaëtan Pirou, *Les Doctrines économiques en France* (Paris, 1925).

10. Michael Tugan-Baranowsky was neither a Marxist nor a Revisionist, strictly speaking. He devel-

oped his leading ideas in *Theoretische Grundlagen des Marxismus* (Leipzig, 1905). His studies on the theory and history of commercial crises in England were first published in Russian in 1894, and appeared in a German translation in 1901.

11. Mentor Bouniatian elaborated on his theory in another treatise, *Les Crises économiques* (Paris, 1922).

12. Konrad Schmidt, "Zur Theorie der Handelskrisen und der Ueber production," *Sozialistische Monatshefte* (1901); and Louis B. Boudin, *The Theoretical System of Karl Marx* (Chicago, 1904).

13. Otto Bauer, *Die Nationalitatenfrage und die Sozialdemokratie* (Vienna, 1907).

14. Rudolf Hilferding, *Das Finanzkapital* (Vienna, 1910).

15. The tendency of large commercial banks to exercise a dominating influence on the policy of industrial enterprises was accentuated in Germany and Austria far more than in England or the United States. See Alfred Marshall, *Industry and Trade* (London, 1919), p. 566.

16. Nikolai Lenin, *Imperialism, the Highest Stage of Capitalism* (London, 1917).

17. About Hilferding's analysis, see, among others, J. Hashagen, "Marxismus und Imperialismus," *Jahrbüch für Nationalökonomie und Statistik* (1919); and Ludwig M. Lachmann, "Finance Capitalism?," *Economica* (May 1944).

18. Rosa Luxemburg, *Die Akkumulation des Kapitals* (Berlin, 1913).

19. For more recent comprehensive criticisms of the theory of "economic imperialism," see Hans Neisser, *Some International Aspects of the Business Cycle* (Philadelphia, 1936), appendix.

20. Otto Bauer, "Die Akkumulation des Kapitals," *Neue Zeit* (1913).

21. For these and other criticisms, see Paul M. Sweezy, *The Theory of Capitalist Development* (New York, 1946), p. 103.

22. Renner, *Marxismus, Kreig und Internationale.*

23. About possible connections between bolshevist thinking and prerevolutionary intellectual Russian trends and movements, see the extensive discussions in Ernest J. Simmons, ed., *Continuity and Change in Russian and Soviet Thought* (Cambridge, Mass., 1955).

24. See, among others, Rudolf Kjellén, *Die Grossmachte der Gegenwart,* 6th ed. (Leipzig, 1915), p. 164; and Robert F. Byrnes, "Pobedonostsev on the Instruments of Russian Government," in Simmons, ed., *Continuity and Change.*

25. The similarities between the logical backgrounds of Thomism and Marxism were emphasized by Jesuit scholars, such as Charles J. McFadden, in *The Philosophy of Communism* (New York, 1939).

26. That view had been clearly expressed by

Marx. See Solomon M. Schwarz, "Populism and Early Russian Marxism on Ways of Economic Development of Russia," in Simmons, ed., *Continuity and Change*, p. 47 ff.

27. Oliver H. Radkey, "Chernov and Agrarian Socialism before 1918," in Simmons, ed., *Continuity and Change*, p. 65.

28. See John D. Bergamini, "Stalin and the Collective Farm," in Simmons, ed., *Continuity and Change*, p. 219.

29. The independence and self-sufficient significance of the trade unions was defended by, among others, Peter Struve. See Thomas T. Hammond, "Leninist Authoritarianism before the Revolution," in Simmons, ed., *Continuity and Change*, pp. 154–55.

30. Ibid., p. 146.

31. Nikolai Lenin, *Materialism and Empiriocriticism* (Berlin, 1908). See Waldemar Gurian, "*Partiinost'* and Knowledge," in Simmons, ed., *Continuity and Change*, p. 303 ff.

32. Nikolai Lenin, *Imperialismus* (Zurich, 1916); idem, *Staat und Revolution* (Berlin, 1918), trans. as *The State and Revolution* (London, 1919).

33. See Adam Ulam, "Stalin and the Theory of Totalitarianism," in Simmons, ed., *Continuity and Change*, p. 159.

34. About the low level of prerevolutionary Russian reasoning, see Geroid T. Robinson, "Part IV Review," in Simmons, ed., *Continuity and Change*, p. 377.

CHAPTER 18

1. William Smart, *An Introduction to the Theory of Value* (London, 1891), p. 4.

2. Philip Henry Wicksteed, "The Scope and Method of Political Economy in Light of the 'Marginal' Theory of Value and of Distribution," *Economic Journal* (1914).

3. See L. M. Fraser, *Economic Thought and Language* (London, 1937), p. 80.

4. Joseph Alois Schumpeter, "The Nature and Necessity of a Price System," in Columbia University Commission, *Economic Reconstruction* (New York, 1934), p. 171.

5. Daniel Bernouilli developed his ideas on marginal utility in his essay "Specimen Theoriae Novae de Mensura Sortis," *Papers of the Imperial Academy of Sciences* 5 (1938): 175–92, trans. Louise Sommer as "Exposition of a New Theory on the Measurement of Risk," *Econometrica* (1954). In his analysis of the characteristics of games of chance, Bernouilli used interpersonal comparisons of marginal utilities. About the history of the marginal utility concept, see the instructive contribution of George J. Stigler, "The

Development of Utility Theory, Part 1," *Journal of Political Economy* (August 1950) and "The Development of Utility Theory, Part 2," *Journal of Political Economy* (October 1950).

6. See also *Pannonial Fragments*, in *Works of Jeremy Bentham* (Edinburgh, 1843), vol. 8.

7. About the influence of these psychological theories on the development of some general philosophical and logical aspects of the value problem, see Howard O. Eaton, *The Austrian Philosophy of Value* (Norman, Okla., 1930), p. 19 ff.

8. Hermann H. Gossen, *Die Entwicklung der Gesetze des menschlichen Verkehrs* (Brunswick, 1854).

9. This principle was subsequently reformulated to take account of the periodic recurrence of many wants in the spiritual and physical spheres.

10. See J. M. Clark, "Distribution," *Encyclopedia of the Social Sciences* 5 (1931).

11. Philip Henry Wicksteed, "Political Economy" (1914), in American Economic Association, *Readings in Price Theory* (Chicago, 1952).

12. The term *opportunity costs* was introduced into economic language by the American economist David I. Green ("Pain-Cost and Opportunity-Cost," *Quarterly Journal of Economics* [January 1894]). H. J. Davenport, *Value and Distribution* (Chicago, 1908), suggested the term *displacement cost*.

13. "The law of distribution," said Wicksteed, "is one, and is governed not by differences of nature in the factors, but by the identity of their differential effect" ("Political Economy").

14. "There is no occasion," said Wicksteed, "to define the economic motive or the psychology of the economic man, for economics study a type of relation, not a type of motive" ("Political Economy").

15. See Ross M. Robertson, "Jevons and His Precursors," *Econometrica* (July 1951), p. 234, and Oswald F. Boucke, *The Development of Economics, 1750–1900* (New York, 1921), p. 251.

16. William S. Jevons's *Principles of Science* (London, 1874) and *Elementary Lessons in Logic* (London, 1870) were widely used as textbooks.

17. See F. von Wieser, *Der Natürliche Werth* (Vienna, 1889), p. 13.

18. His procedure was criticized by Francis Ysidro Edgeworth, *Mathematical Psychics: An Essay on the Application of Mathematics to the Moral Sciences* (London, 1881), and Knut Wicksell, *Uber Wert, Kapital und Rente nach den Neueren Nationalökonomischen Theorien* (Jena, 1893).

19. Jevons, *Theory of Political Economy*.

20. Edgeworth, *Mathematical Psychics*. Edgeworth used the term *economical calculus* to denote mathematical methods of determining the ultimate object of economic behavior, namely, the maximization of utility.

21. Smart, *Theory of Value;* and Philip Henry Wicksteed, *An Essay on the Coordination of the Laws of Distribution* (London, 1894) and *The Common Sense of Political Economy* (London, 1910).

22. Léon Walras, *Eléments d'économie politique pure ou théorie de la richesse sociale* (Lausanne, 1874 and 1877). Walras continued his theoretical studies in his *Théorie mathématique de la richesse sociale* (Lausanne, 1883) and *Théorie de la monnaie* (Paris, 1886).

23. John R. Hicks, "Léon Walras," *Econometrica* (October 1934). See Friedrich A. Hayek, *Individualism and Economic Order* (London, 1949), p. 45.

24. See Umberto Ricci, "Pareto and Pure Economics," *Review of Economic Studies* (1933/34). See the quotation from an article on Pareto by G. Demaria in H. W. Spiegel, ed., *The Development of Economic Thought* (New York, 1952), p. 635.

25. See Oskar Lange, "Say's Law: A Restatement and Criticism," in Oskar Lange, Francis McIntyre, and Theodore O. Yntema, eds., *Studies in Mathematical Economics and Econometrics: In Memory of Henry Schultz* (Freeport, N.Y., 1942).

26. See Luigi Amoroso, "Discussion del sistema di equazioni che definiscono l'equilibrio del consumatore," *Annali di Economia* (1928).

27. Walras, *Eléments,* 10th lesson.

28. Francis Ysidro Edgeworth, *Papers Relating to Political Economy* (London, 1925), 2: 311.

29. About the question of how far Walras himself was aware of the logical necessity of recontracting, see Joseph Alois Schumpeter, *History of Economic Analysis* (New York, 1954), p. 1002. For a survey of the various aspects of "groping," see Don Patinkin, *Money, Interest and Prices* (Evanston, 1956), note B.

30. See Edgeworth, *Papers Relating to Political Economy,* 1:25. It is another question whether, as asserted by Schumpeter (*History of Economic Analysis,* p. 1049), the concept of that fictitious employer is of the utmost importance for the understanding of reality.

31. The change in the treatment of the coefficients of production was perhaps provided by Wicksteed's *Coordination of the Laws of Distribution.*

32. Alfred Marshall, *Principles of Economics,* 8th ed. (New York, 1950), p. 845.

33. Walras defended Gossen's view on the ownership of land in his essay "Théorie mathématique du prix de terres et de leur rachat par l'état" (1880), reprinted in Spiegel, ed., *Development of Economic Thought.*

34. See especially Kant's *Critique of Pure Reason,* trans. J.M.D. Meiklejohn (London, 1855). See also J. Dobretsberger, *Neue Beiträge zur Wissenschaftstheorie* (Vienna, 1949), p. 79 ff.

35. Carl Menger developed his theory in his main work, entitled *Grundsatze der Volkswirtschaftslehre* (Vienna, 1871).

36. Carl Menger, "Zur Theorie des Kapitals," *Jahrbüch für Nationalökonomie und Statistik* (1888).

37. Menger developed his monetary views in a comprehensive article entitled "Geld" (*Handwörterbuch der Staatswissenschaften* [1909]); he also contributed some important studies to the reform of the Austrian currency. See Friedrich A. Hayek, "Carl Menger," *Economica* (November 1934).

CHAPTER 19

1. J. B. Condliffe, *The Commerce of Nations* (New York, 1950), p. 359.

2. Henry Thomas Buckle, *History of Civilization in England,* 2 vols. (London, 1857–61).

3. W.E.H. Lecky, *History of the Rise and Influence of the Spirit of Rationalism in Europe* (London, 1865).

4. John R. Seeley, *The Expansion of England* (London, 1883).

5. John Elliott Cairnes, *The Character and Logical Method of Political Economy* (London, 1857).

6. Idem, *Some Leading Principles of Political Economy Newly Expanded* (London, 1874).

7. See Sydney G. Checklund, "Economic Opinion in England As Jevons Found It," *Manchester School* (May 1951), p. 164.

8. Henry Dunning MacLeod, *The Prnciples of Economic Philosophy,* 2 vols. (London, 1872–75).

9. Walter Bagehot, *Lombard Street* (London, 1873).

10. Idem, *Postulates of English Political Economy* (London, 1885), *Economic Studies* (London, 1880).

11. Henry Sidgwick, *The Principles of Political Economy* (London, 1883).

12. Idem, *The Methods of Ethics* (London, 1874).

13. See Ernest Barker, *Political Thought in England* (London, 1915), p. 76 and passim.

14. See John Dewey, *Liberalism and Social Action* (New York, 1935), p. 39.

15. T. E. Cliffe Leslie, *Essays on Political and Moral Philosophy* (Dublin, 1879). Other publications by Leslie were *Land Systems and Industrial Economy of Ireland, England and Continental Countries* (London, 1870) and *Essays in Political Economy* (Dublin, 1888).

16. Thorold Rogers, *The Economic Interpretation of History* (London, 1888).

17. Idem, *History of Agriculture and Prices in England, 1259–1793* (Oxford, 1866–87), and *Six Centuries of Work and Wages* (London, 1884).

18. In "The Perversion of Economic History," *Economic Journal* (September 1892), William Cun-

ningham criticized Rogers for "reading the past in the light of the modern doctrine."

19. Arnold Toynbee, *Lectures on the Industrial Revolution in England* (London, 1884).

20. John Kells Ingram, *The Present Position and Prospects of Political Economy* (Dublin, 1878).

21. Idem, *History of Political Economy* (Edinburgh, 1888).

22. William James Ashley, *An Introduction to English Economic History and Theory*, 2 vols. (London, 1888 and 1893).

23. Charles Darwin, *Origin of Species* (London, 1859). See Overton H. Taylor, "Economics and the Idea of Natural Laws," *Quarterly Journal of Economics* (November 1929), p. 9.

24. Herbert Spencer's *Synthetic Philosophy* was published in five volumes between 1862 and 1896.

25. About the "antiintellectualism" of Thomas Carlyle, James A. Froude (1818–1894), Charles Kingsley, and Thomas B. Macauley (1800–1859), see Walter E. Houghton, "Victorian Anti-Intellectualism," *Journal of the History of Ideas* (1952), p. 296.

26. Thomas Carlyle, *Past and Present* (New York, 1843), and *Latter-Day Pamphlets* (London, 1850).

27. John Ruskin, *Unto this Last* (London, 1862), *Munera Pulveris* (London, 1872), and *Time and Tide* (London, 1867).

28. Charles Kingsley, *Cheap Clothes and Nasty* (London, 1850).

29. William Morris, *News from Nowhere* (Boston, 1891).

30. See Edward R. Pease, *The History of the Fabian Society* (London, 1916); G.D.H. Cole, *Some Relations between Political and Economic Theory* (London, 1934); and Paul M. Sweezy, "Fabian Political Economy," *Journal of Political Economy* (June 1949), p. 243.

31. George Bernard Shaw, "Economics," in *Fabian Essays in Socialism*, no. 25 (London, 1889). A jubilee edition of the leading Fabian essays was published in London in 1948.

32. See Pease, *History of the Fabian Society*, p. 25.

33. Philip Henry Wicksteed published a criticism of Marx's *Kapital* in *Socialist Journal To-Day* (October 1884).

34. Sidney Webb and Beatrice Webb, *Industrial Democracy*, 2 vols. (London, 1897).

35. See Cole, *Political and Economic Theory*, p. 56.

36. See Maurice Dobb, *Political Economy and Capitalism* (London, 1937), p. 139.

37. Alfred Marshall, *Principles of Economics*, 8th ed. (New York, 1950). About the changes made in subsequent editions of that work, see Claude W.

Guillebaud, "The Evolution of Marshall's Principles of Economics," *Economic Journal* (December 1942).

38. Alfred Marshall, "The Social Possibilities of Economic Chivalry," *Economic Journal* (1907), quoted by John Maynard Keynes, *The End of Laissez-Faire* (London, 1926), p. 36.

39. See John Maynard Keynes, "The General Theory of Employment," *Quarterly Journal of Economics* (February 1937), p. 214.

40. See the analysis of Marshall's teachings in Paul Homan, *Contemporary Economic Thought* (New York, 1928), p. 201; and G. F. Shove, "The Place of Marshall's Principles in the Development of Economic Theory," *Economic Journal* 52 (December 1942): 308.

41. Claude W. Guillebaud, "Marshall's Principles of Economics in the Light of Contemporary Economic Thought," *Economica* (May 1952), p. 111.

42. Cunningham, "Perversion of Economic History."

43. Frank H. Knight, *Risk, Uncertainty and Profit* (Boston, 1921), p. 15.

44. See Guillebaud, "Marshall's Principles of Economics."

45. John Maynard Keynes, "The General Theory," in Seymour E. Harris, ed., *The New Economics* (New York, 1947), p. 184.

46. Alfred Marshall, *Industry and Trade* (London, 1919). It has been said that Marshall dreaded monopoly almost as much as he dreaded socialization (Shove, "Marshall's Principles in Economic Theory," p. 319).

47. Roy F. Harrod, "An Essay in Dynamic Theory," *Economic Journal* (March 1939), p. 296.

48. About Marshall's conception of general equilibrium analysis, see Lionel Robbins, "Schumpeter's History of Economic Analysis," *Quarterly Journal of Economics* (February 1955).

49. See Guillebaud, "Marshall's Principles of Economics," p. 155.

50. It has been observed that nowhere did Marshall clearly and completely determine the "other things" that he compounded with the *ceteris paribus* clause (see Frank H. Knight, "Statistik und Dynamic: Zur Frage der Mechanischen Analogie in den Wirtschaftswissenschaften," *Zeitschrift für Nationalökonomie* [1930], p. 1).

51. Shove, "Marshall's Principles in Economic Theory," p. 295.

52. Some interpreters of Marshall's principles have even argued that he did not draw anything of importance from the marginal utility doctrine (see ibid., p. 301; and John Maynard Keynes, *Essays in Biography* [London, 1933], p. 186). About Marshall's possible indebtedness to Jevons, Walras, Cournot, Dupuit, Jenkin, Thünen, and the Austrian

Marginalists, see Joseph Alois Schumpeter, *History of Economic Analysis* (New York, 1954), p. 839.

53. See George J. Stigler, "The Development of Utility Theory, Part 1," *Journal of Political Economy* (August 1950), p. 383.

54. See E. Cannan, p. 190; and Lionel Robbins, in the introduction to Philip Henry Wicksteed's *Common Sense of Political Economy* (London, 1933).

55. See Guillebaud, "Marshall's Principles of Economics."

56. George J. Stigler, *Production and Distribution Theories* (New York, 1941), p. 63.

57. See Nicholas Kaldor, "The Equilibrium of the Firm," *Economic Journal* (1934).

58. That change in terminology had been suggested by S. M. Macvane in "Analysis of Cost of Production," *Quarterly Journal of Economics* (July 1887).

59. Similar propositions had been advanced by the French engineer Dupuit and by the English engineer Henry C. Fleeming Jenkin (*Proceedings of the Royal Society of Edinburgh* [1871/72]).

60. See the discussion of the Marshallian surplus analysis in Hla Myint, chap. 9.

61. See Dionysus Lardner, *Railway Economy* (London, 1850), and Henry C. Fleeming Jenkin, *Graphic Representation of the Laws of Supply and Demand, and Their Application to Labor* (Edinburgh, 1870).

62. The term *operational time* was suggested by Redvers Opie ("Marshall's Time Analysis," *Economic Journal* [June 1931], p. 109) to characterize the nature of the time concept used in this connection.

63. See Stigler, *Production and Distribution Theories*, p. 81, about problems of "diseconomics," which Marshall neglected in his discussions.

64. These moralizing tendencies have been the object of repeated criticisms. See, for instance, Talcott Parsons, "Economics and Sociology: Marshall in Relation to the Thought of His Time," *Quarterly Journal of Economics* (February 1932).

65. The widely used *Principles of Political Economy*, published in three volumes between 1893 and 1901, by Joseph Shield Nicholson, was equally closely adjusted to the pattern established by John Stuart Mill. A Dutch textbook that enjoyed a good reputation among contemporary economists was Nikolas G. Pierson, *Leerbook der Staatshuishoudkunde*, written between 1884 and 1902, trans. A. A. Wotzel as *Principles of Economics* (London, 1902–12). It was almost entirely based on Ricardian economics.

66. In a presidential address delivered in 1939, Arthur Cecil Pigou, Marshall's successor at Cambridge, asserted that "the broader problems of economics being safe in Marshall's keeping, his disciples were content to attack narrow issues reasonable

within their compass" ("Presidential Address," *Economic Journal* [June 1939], p. 219).

67. Arthur Cecil Pigou, *Wealth and Welfare* (London, 1912). Later revised editions appeared under the title *The Economics of Welfare* (London, 1920, 1924).

68. See John R. Hicks, "Valuation of the Social Income," *Economica* (1940).

69. See Frank H. Knight, "The Ethics of Competition," *Quarterly Journal of Economics* (August 1923), and "Some Fallacies in the Interpretation of Social Costs," *Quarterly Journal of Economics* (August 1924).

70. John A. Hobson, *The Evolution of Modern Capitalism* (London, 1894), *The Economics of Distribution* (New York, 1900), *Work and Wealth* (New York, 1914), and *The Economics of Unemployment* (London 1922).

71. See Dobb, *Political Economy and Capitalism*, p. 148.

72. See Hobson's discussion with Lionel Robbins and E. F. Durbin, "Underconsumption: An Exposition and Reply," *Economica* (November 1933).

73. John A. Hobson, *Confessions of an Economic Heretic* (London, 1938), p. 168 ff.

74. John Maynard Keynes, *General Theory of Employment* (London, 1936), p. 371.

75. John A. Hobson's *Imperialism* (London, 1902) was suggested by the impression that the Boer War made on its author. For an able analysis of these aspects of Hobson's ideas, see E. M. Winslow, *The Pattern of Imperialism* (New York, 1948), chap. 5.

CHAPTER 20

1. Vilfredo Pareto, *Cours d'économie politique* (Paris, 1896–97); and *Manuale di Economia Politica* (Milan, 1906), French trans. Alfred Bonnet as *Manuel d'économie politique* (Paris, 1909).

2. The methodological aspects of the mechanical sciences were elaborated by the Austrian physicist Ernst Mach, in *Die Mechanik in ihrer Entwickelung* (Leipzig, 1883), and by the French mathematician Jules Henri Poincaré, in *La Science et l'hypothèse* (Paris, 1908).

3. That discussion was published in the *Giornale degli economisti e annali di economia* (1900 and 1901) and recently was reproduced in English in *International Economic Papers* 3 (New York, 1953).

4. Francis Ysidro Edgeworth, *Mathematical Psychics: An Essay on the Application of Mathematics to the Moral Sciences* (London, 1881).

5. See John Maynard Keynes, *Essays in Biography* (New York, 1951), p. 231. In order to describe the source of certain premises supplied by the theory of probabilities to economics and other sciences,

Edgeworth spoke even of "mathematical common-sense" ("Applications of Probabilities to Economics," *Economic Journal* [1910], p. 286).

6. The idea that the utility function is to a high degree interdeterminate had also been elaborated by Irving Fisher in *Mathematical Investigations in the Theory of Value and Prices* (New Haven, 1892).

7. The term *substitutive* has been used when the utility derived from one good can be derived from another—as is the case with bread and potatoes. Other goods, called *complementary*, have positively interdependent utilities in combination.

8. See George J. Stigler, "The Development of Utility Theory, Part 1," *Journal of Political Economy* (August 1950), p. 380.

9. See Hans Mayer et al., eds., *Wirtschaftstheorie der Gegenwart*, 4 vols. (Vienna, 1927–32), 2:216.

10. See Arthur Smithies, "The Boundaries of the Production Function," in *Explorations in Economics* (New York, 1936); and Joseph A. Schumpeter, "Vilfredo Pareto," *Quarterly Journal of Economics* (May 1949), p. 106.

11. See Giovanni Demaria, in H. W. Spiegel, ed., *Development of Economic Thought* (New York, 1952), p. 637.

12. See Pierre Bovens, *Les Applications mathématiques á l'économie politique* (Lausanne, 1912).

13. See, among others, Oskar Morgenstern, *Probleme der Wertlehre* (Munich and Leipzig, 1931), 1:28.

14. See the chapter on crises in the second volume of Pareto's *Cours d'économie politique*.

15. That proposition (see *Manuel d'économie politique*, chap. 6) was elaborated by Enrico Barone in an article entitled "Il ministro della produzione nello stato collettivista," trans. as "The Ministry of Production in the Collectivist State," in Friedrich A. Hayek, ed., *Collectivist Economic Planning* (London, 1935), appendix A.

16. See Hans Mayer, "Der Erkenntniswert der funktionellen Preistheorien," in Mayer et al., eds., *Wirtschaftstheorie der Gegenwart*, 2:183.

17. The theory of economic equilibrium has been compared to a magic castle, enchanting the mind but of little assistance in solving the housing problem (Umberto Ricci, "Pareto and Pure Economics," *Review of Economic Studies* [1933], p. 20).

18. About that controversy, see G. Masci, in Mayer et al., eds., *Wirtschaftstheorie der Gegenwart*, 1:76. For later criticisms of a similar type, see, among others, Leo Illy, *Das Gesetz des Grenznutzens* (Vienna, 1948); and A. Mahr, "Indifferenzkurven und Grenznutzenniveau," *Zeitschrift fur Nationalökonomie* (1954).

19. Constantino Bresciani-Turoni, *Giornale degli economisti e annali di economia* (1925).

20. See various articles published by Luigi Amoroso in the *Giornale degli economisti e annali di economia* in 1910, 1911, and 1912, and his *Lezioni di economia matematica* (Bologna, 1921). See also Enrico Barone, *Principi di economia politica* (Rome, 1908).

21. Pareto supplemented his economic studies mainly in two volumes: *Les Systèmes socialistes*, 2 vols. (Paris, 1902–3); and *Trattato di sociologia generale*, 2 vols. (Florence, 1916), trans. Andrew Bongiorno and Arthur Livingston as *Mind and Society* (New York, 1935).

22. About Pareto's relations to fascism, see G. H. Bosquet, *Vilfredo Pareto* (Paris, 1928).

23. About the possible application of Pareto's sociology to the analysis of complex social phenomena, such as imperfect competition, oligopoly, voluntary associations, etc., see G. Demaria, p. 630.

24. Friedrich von Wieser, *Uber den Ursprung und die Hauptgesetze des Wirtschaftlichen Wertes* (Vienna, 1884), *Der natürliche Werth* (Vienna, 1889).

25. See, for instance, Franz Cuhel, *Zur Lehre von den Bedurfnissen* (Innsbruck, 1907).

26. Rudolf Hilferding, *Böhm-Bawerk's Marx Kritik* (Vienna, 1904).

27. Nikolai I. Bukharin, *Die Politische Oekonomie des Rentners* (Berlin, 1926).

28. Friedrich von Wieser, *Theorie der gesellschaftlichen Wirtschaft* (Tübingen, 1914), trans. A. F. Hinrichs as *Social Economics* (New York, 1927). It is a moot question to what degree that analysis was affected by the use of organismic conceptions such as "social values."

29. One of the earliest studies dealing with the marginal utility aspects of economic and fiscal policies was Emil Sax, *Grundlegung der Staatswirtschaft* (Vienna, 1889).

30. Eugen Böhm-Bawerk, "The Ultimate Standard of Values," *Annals of the American Academy of Political and Social Science* (1894).

31. Idem, "Grundzunge einer Theorie der Wirtschaftlichen Guterwerts," *Jahrbücher fur Nationalökonomie und Statistik* (1886). See also R. Zuckerkandl, *Zur Theorie des Preises* (Leipzig, 1889).

32. One of the first authors to raise these objections was Rudolf Stolzmann, in *Die soziale Kategorie in der Volkswirtschaftslehre* (Berlin, 1896).

33. Knut Wicksell, *Geldzins und Guterpreise* (Jena, 1898).

34. Von Wieser, *Ursprung und Hauptgesetze*. Following a suggestion made in 1889 by the Italian Maffeo Pantaleoni, that definition has frequently been referred to as "von Wieser's law."

35. Philip Henry Wicksteed, *The Common Sense of Political Economy* (London, 1910).

36. H. J. Davenport, *Outlines of Economic Theory* (New York, 1896), p. 45. In his *Value and Distribution* (Chicago, 1908), p. 571, Davenport used the term *subjective worth* to denote the result of the "balancing of positive and negative desires." See also H. J. Davenport, "Cost and Its Significance," *American Economic Review* (1911).

37. For a discussion of the problems involved in the application of economic imputation, see Carl Landauer, *Grundprobleme der funktionellen Verteilung des Wirtschaftlichen Werts* (Jena, 1923). Landauer defined the theory of imputation as the value theory of complementary goods.

38. Von Wieser, *Der natürliche Wert*. For criticisms of the theory of "productive contributions," see Robert Liefmann, *Grundsätze der Volkswirtschaftslehre* (Stuttgart, 1917).

39. See C. Landauer, *Grundprobleme*, p. 127.

40. See Joseph Alois Schumpeter, "Zurechnungsproblem," *Zeitschrift für Staats und Volkswirtschaft* (1909), p. 103. See also George J. Stigler, *Production and Distribution Theories* (New York, 1941), p. 168 ff.

41. Eugen Böhm-Bawerk, *Positive Theorie des Kapitales*, 2nd ed. (1902), bk. 3, sect. 1, pt. 5.

42. Idem, "Macht oder ökonomisches Gesetz," *Zeitschrift für Staats und Volkswirtschaft* (1914), reprinted in *Gesammelte Schriften von Eugen von Böhm-Bawerk*, ed. F. X. Weiss (Vienna, 1924).

43. Eugen Böhm-Bawerk, *Geschichte und Kritik der Kapitalzinstheorien*, 3rd ed. (Innsbruck, 1914), trans. as *Capital and Interest* (Edinburgh, 1890).

44. Idem, *Positive Theorie des Kapitales*.

45. The logical validity of that argument has been questioned. See Joseph Alois Schumpeter, *History of Economic Analysis* (New York, 1954), p. 926.

46. For an analysis of Jevons's wage fund idea, see ibid., p. 902.

47. Thus, Frank H. Knight (*Risk, Uncertainty and Profit* [Boston, 1921], p. 130) argued that different individuals would give to their incomes the most varied forms of distribution over time, and that the disposition to spend or to save, to consume income in the present or to store up wealth, was much more influenced by other motives than by time preference in consumption. Another adversary of the idea of time preference was A. Mahr. See his discussion with R. van Genechten in *Zeitschrift für Nationalökonomie* (1932 and 1933).

48. L. von Bortkiewicz, "Der Kardinalfehler der Böhm-Bawerk'schen Zinstheorie," *Schmoller's Jahrbüch für Gesetzgebung, Verwaltung, und Volkswirtschaft* (1906).

49. See E. C. van Dorp, "Löhne und Kapitalzins," *Zeitschrift für Nationalökonomie* (1933).

50. Knut Wicksell's main publications were *Uber Wert, Kapital und Rente nach den Neueren Nationalökonomischen Theorien* (Jena, 1893); *Finanztheoretische Untersuchungen* (Jena, 1896); *Geldzins und Güterpreise;* and *Lectures on Political Economy*, trans. E. Classen 2 vols. (London, 1934–35), first published in Swedish in 1901 and 1906. Wicksell corrected various shortcomings of Böhm-Bawerk's presentation of the *agio* theory in his essay "Zur Zinstheorie," which he contributed to Mayer et al., eds., *Wirtschaftstheorie der Gegenwart*, vol. 3.

51. Wicksell, *Lectures*, 2: 205.

52. See Piero Sraffa, "Dr. Hayek on Money and Capital," *Economic Journal* (March 1932), p. 49; and Eric Lindahl, *Studies in the Theory of Money and Capital* (New York, 1939).

53. See Stigler, *Production and Distribution Theories*, p. 278.

54. Knut Wicksell, *Interest and Prices*, trans. R. F. Kahn, (London, 1936), p. xxvi. See Gunnar Myrdal, *Monetary Equilibrium*, trans. (London, 1939), p. 23.

55. Knut Wicksell, *Lectures*, 2: 160.

56. See Myrdal, *Monetary Equilibrium*, p. 37.

57. Wicksell, *Lectures*, 2: 190; *Interest and Prices*, chap. 9.

58. See also Knut Wicksell, "The Influence of Interest on Prices," *Economic Journal* (1907).

59. For a formulation of the Wicksellian system in mathematical terms, see R. Frisch, in Spiegel, ed., *Development of Economic Thought*, p. 653.

60. About the economic views of David Davidson, which were perceptibly influenced by Ricardo's *Principles of Political Economy and Taxation* (London, 1817), and the ideas of Rodbertus, see Eli Filip Heckscher, "David Davidson," trans. M. A. Michael, in *International Economic Papers*, 12 vols. (London, 1951–62), vol. 2.

61. See Carl G. Uhr, "Knut Wicksell," *American Economic Review* (December 1951), p. 857. See also an interesting article by Per Jacobson about a change in Wicksell's view concerning the general significance of the interest rate for the behavior of the economy (Schweizer, *Zeitschrift für Staats und Volkswirtschaft* [December 1952], p. 473). About the far-reaching acceptance of Davidson's principles, see Gottfried Haberler, *Prosperity and Depression* (Geneva, 1936), p. 33.

CHAPTER 21

1. See Francis Ysidro Edgeworth's articles in *Economic Journal* (June 1892); and S. M. Macvane, "Marginal Utility and Value," *Quarterly Journal of Economics* (April 1893).

2. Philip Henry Wicksteed, *The Common Sense*

of Political Economy (London, 1910), chap. 9. H. J. Davenport, *Value and Distribution* (Chicago, 1908).

3. Philip Henry Wicksteed, *An Essay on the Co-ordination of the Laws of Distribution* (London, 1894).

4. See George J. Stigler, *Production and Distribution Theories* (New York, 1941), p. 368 ff.

5. Knut Wicksell, *Vorlesungen über Nationalökonomie* (Jena, 1913), vol. 1, p. 187; and E. Schneider, "Bemerkungen zur Grenzproduktivitätslehre," *Zeitschrift für Nationalökonomie* (October 1933).

6. Wicksteed, *Common Sense*, p. 528.

7. In his interpretation of the "law of differential imputation," von Wieser arrived at a similar general application of the Ricardian rent principle. Another author who elaborated the idea that the principle of rent, when interpreted in accordance with the idea of marginal productivity, was applicable to all productive factors, was Joseph Alois Schumpeter, "Das Rentenprinzip in der Verteilungslehre," *Schmoller's Jahrbuch für Gesetzgebung, Verwaltung und Volkswirtschaft* (1907).

8. Stigler, *Production and Distribution Theories*, p. 67. The distinction between incremental and proportionate diminishing returns was frequently overlooked.

9. Schumpeter, "Das Rentenprinzip," p. 610.

10. Wicksell made frequent references to dynamic factors in his discussions of innovations and their effects on the increasing profitability of longterm investments. See Carl G. Uhr, "Knut Wicksell," *American Economic Review* (December 1951).

11. See also the discussion of the law of diminishing returns in Joseph Alois Schumpeter, *History of Economic Analysis* (New York, 1954), p. 588. The position assigned to that law in the various theories was obviously influenced to a considerable degree by methodological requirements.

12. H. J. Davenport, *The Economics of Enterprise* (New York, 1913), chap. 22.

13. L. M. Fraser, *Economic Thought and Language* (London, 1937), p. 203.

14. Schumpeter's "dynamic" theory of interest is discussed at other places in this work. That theory was only indirectly connected with the principles of marginalism.

15. John R. Hicks, *Value and Capital* (Oxford, 1939), p. 192.

16. Hence, the *agio* theory was occasionally qualified as a sort of productivity theory. See Marco Fanno, "Die reine Theorie des Geldmarktes," in Friedrich A. Hayek, ed., *Beiträge zur Geldtheorie* (Vienna, 1933), p. 15.

17. See Friedrich A. Hayek, "Utility Analysis and Interest," *Economic Journal* (March 1936), p. 59.

18. See Knut Wicksell, *Zeitschrift für Nationalökonomie* (1931), p. 244.

19. Irving Fisher, *The Rate of Interest* (New York, 1907). Fisher dedicated that book to the memory of John Rae, who had suggested an *agio* theory of interest in the first decades of the nineteenth century. See also Fisher's *Theory of Interest* (New York, 1930).

20. Simon Newcomb, *Principles of Political Economy* (New York, 1886).

21. Irving Fisher, "The Impatience Theory of Interest," *American Economic Review* (1912).

22. Idem, *Theory of Interest*, p. 42.

23. Frank A. Fetter, *Principles of Economics* (New York, 1904). See also idem, "Interest Theories New and Old," *American Economic Review* (March 1914).

24. See Fisher, *Rate of Interest;* L. von Bortkiewicz, "Der Kardinalfehler der Böhm-Bawerk'schen Zinstheorie," *Schmoller's Jahrbuch für Gesetzgebung, Verwaltung und Volkswirtschaft* (1906); and Knut Wicksell, "Zur Zinstheorie," in Hans Mayer et al., eds., *Wirtschaftstheorie der Gegenwart*, 4 vols. (Vienna, 1927–32), vol. 3.

25. See Friedrich von Wieser, *Social Economics*, trans. A. F. Hinrichs (New York, 1927), p. 248.

26. Albert Aftalion, "Les Trois Notions de la productivité," *Revue d'économie politique* (1911).

27. Thomas N. Carver, "The Place of Abstinence in the 'Theory of Interest,'" *Quarterly Journal of Economics* (October 1893); and Umberto Ricci, "La teoria dell'astinenza," *Giornale degli economisti e annali di economia* (1908).

28. About the meaning attached by Böhm-Bawerk to the term *capital*, see, among others, Edwin Cannan, *Review of Economic Theory* (London, 1929), p. 150; and Fritz Machlup, "Begriffliches und Terminologisches zur Kapitalstheorie," *Zeitschrift für Nationalökonomie* (1931), p. 633.

29. Irving Fisher, *The Nature of Capital and Income* (New York, 1906). These views were shared by other American economists, such as Frank A. Fetter, H. J. Davenport, H. R. Seager, and E.R.A. Seligman.

30. Eugen Böhm-Bawerk, "Capital and Interest Once More," *Quarterly Journal of Economics* (February 1907).

31. Karl Gustav Cassel, *The Nature and Necessity of Interest* (London, 1903); and *Theoretische Sozialokonomik* (Leipzig, 1918).

32. See Maurice Dobb, *Political Economy and Capitalism* (London, 1937), p. 275 ff.

33. See Thomas N. Carver, *The Distribution of Wealth* (New York, 1904), p. 259.

34. Such views were advanced by Adolphe Landry, *L'Utilité sociale de la propriété individuelle*

(Paris, 1901); Vilfredo Pareto, *Manuel d'économie politique*, trans. Alfred Bonnet (Paris, 1909); Otto Effertz, *Les Antagonismes économiques* (Paris, 1906); and Albert Aftalion, *Les Fondements du socialisme* (Paris, 1923).

35. Victor Mataja, *Der Unternehmergewinn* (Vienna, 1884); Rudolf Auspitz and Richard Lieben, *Untersuchungen über die theorie des Preises* (Leipzig, 1889); and Guido Sensini, *La teoria della rendita* (Rome, 1912).

36. Carver, *The Distribution of Wealth;* E.R.A. Seligman, *Principles of Economics* (New York, 1905); Frank A. Fetter, "The Passing of the Old Rent Concept," *Quarterly Journal of Economics* (May 1901), and "Relation between Rent and Interest," *Publications of the American Economic Association* (1904), p. 159. See also Richard T. Ely, "Land Economics," *Essays in Honor of J. B. Clark* (New York, 1927), p. 127.

37. See Schumpeter, "Das Rentenprinzip."

38. As Alfred Marshall said, "In a sense all rents are scarcity rents and all rents are differential rents" (*Principles of Economics,* 8th ed., appendix L). Marshall's "consumer's rents" need not be mentioned in this instance, since they were not connected with problems of distribution.

39. See Fraser, *Economic Thought and Language,* p. 309.

40. John B. Clark, *Essentials of Economic Theory* (New York, 1907), p. 159. That view was questioned by Ely, "Land Economics," p. 127. See also Carl R. Bye, *Developments and Issues in the Theory of Rent* (New York, 1940), p. 94.

41. Friedrich von Wieser, *Theorie der stadtischen Grundrente* (Vienna, 1909) and *Social Economics.* See also F. X. Weiss, "Die Grundrente," in Mayer et al., eds., *Wirtschaftstheorie der Gegenwart,* 3:228.

42. Frank W. Taussig, *Wages and Capital* (New York, 1896); "Outline of a Theory of Wages," *Proceedings of the American Economic Association* (April 1910).

43. Wicksteed, *Coordination of the Laws of Distribution.* That statement was violently denounced by some socialist authors as a defense of capitalism. In a pamphlet, Sidney J. Webb, *Problems of Modern Industry* (London, 1898), the Fabians had used a misleading version of the marginal productivity principle to demonstrate that wages were determined by the productivity of the workers employed under the worst conditions and that employers enjoyed a "buyer's rent."

44. *Scientific Management* (Boston, 1911).

45. Sir Arthur Salter, *Recovery* (New York, 1932), p. 17.

46. The functioning of London's international money market, as viewed by a highly educated banker, was expounded in George J. Goschen's widely read *Theory of Foreign Exchanges* (London, 1861). He regarded gold as a commodity and applied the mechanical approach to the movements of the monetary metals, especially to the analysis of the "gold points." He also gave a clear account of the discount rate as an instrument for attracting short-term foreign capital and exerting pressure on commodity prices. That process was similarly described by Walter Bagehot in *Lombard Street* (London, 1873).

47. Michel Chevalier, *La Monnaie* (Brussels, 1851); William Stanley Jevons, *A Serious Fall in the Value of Gold* (London, 1863); and "The Value of Gold," *Journal of the Statistical Society of London* 32 (1869).

48. Sir Robert Giffen, *Essays in Finance* (London, 1880). Giffen was a convinced advocate of the gold standard.

49. One of the most remarkable books on bimetallism was H. Gernuschi, *Mécanique de l'échange* (1865). See also Francis A. Walker, *International Bimetallism* (London, 1896).

50. See a review article by Wilhelm Lexis on publications dealing with monetary issues in *Jahrbuch für Nationalökonomie und Statistik* (1888). The proposition that the general fall in prices was not connected with the relative decline in gold production and the extension of the sphere of the gold standard was defended in the same periodical by Erwin Nasse.

51. That testimony was reproduced in Alfred Marshall, *Official Papers* (London, 1926).

52. Marshall published his views on monetary problems only much later, in *Money, Credit and Commerce* (London, 1923).

53. See Charles Rist, *History of Monetary and Credit Theory,* trans. Jane Degras (London, 1940), pp. 103, 357. "All currency devaluations represent a triumph for the state in a matter where its interests conflict with the interests of individuals or where the interests of certain groups conflict with those of other groups."

54. Silvio Gesell developed his ideas mainly in two books: *Die Verwirklichung des Rechtes auf den vollen Arbeitsvertrag* (Leipzig, 1906) and *Die neue Lehre von Geld und Zins* (Berlin, 1911). His *Die natürliche Wirtschaftsordnung* (1911) was translated into English in 1929 by Philip Pye as *The Natural Economic Order.* See Irving Fisher, *After Reflation, What?* (New York, 1933). See also John Maynard Keynes, *General Theory of Employment, Interest and Money* (London, 1936), p. 353.

55. See Carl Menger's article on money in *Handwörterbuch der Staatswissenschaften* (1911).

56. William Smart, *Introduction to the Theory of Value* (London, 1891), p. 45. Maffeo Pantaleoni considered the utility derived from its purely monetary functions a sufficient basis for the exchange value of

money (*Principi di economia pura* [Florence, 1889], p. 260 ff.).

57. William Stanley Jevons, *Money and the Mechanism of Exchange* (London, 1875). Jevons distinguished very clearly four different functions of money: as a medium of exchange, as a measure of value, as a standard of value, and as a store of value. He proposed to differentiate the instruments in accordance with these functions and recommended the establishment of a "tabular standard" for deferred payment. Jevons's recommendations were published posthumously in *Investigations in Currency and Finance*, ed. H. S. Foxwell (London, 1884), which also includes a contribution to the use of index numbers for the measurement of the value of the currency.

58. Walras modified his monetary theory perceptibly over the course of time, after the publication of his *Théorie de la monnaie* (Paris, 1886). He included a revised edition of *Théorie de la monnaie* in *Etudes d'économie politique appliquée* (Lausanne, 1898), and made corresponding adjustments in the last editions of his *Eléments d'économie politique pure ou théorie de la richesse sociale* (Lausanne, 1874, 1877).

59. Knut Wicksell, *Geldzins und Güterpreise* (Jena, 1898), p. 27; and L. von Bortkiewicz, "Der subjective Geldwert," *Schmoller's Jahrbuch für Gesetzgebung, Verwaltung und Volkswirtschaft* 44 (1920).

60. The Walrasian definition of the need to hold cash balances was discussed by John R. Hicks in "Gleichgewicht und Konjunktur," *Zeitschrift für Nationalökonomie* (June 1933), and by Arthur W. Marget in "The Monetary Aspects of the Walrasian System," *Journal of Political Economy* (April 1935). Marget observed that a need to hold cash balances would result not only from the uncertainty of future events but also from the lack of synchronization between the receipt of income and its expenditure.

61. Karl Schlesinger, *Theorie der Geld und Kreditwirtschaft* (Munich, 1914). See Arthur W. Marget, "Léon Walras and the Cash Balance Approach," *Journal of Political Economy* (1931), p. 594.

62. Friedrich von Wieser, "Uber die Messung der Veränderungen des Geldwerts," *Schriften des Vereins für Sozialpolitik* (1910).

63. See J. G. Koopmans, "Zum Problem des Neutralen Geldes," in Hayek, ed., *Beiträge zur Geldtheorie*, p. 221.

64. Another version of that "income theory" of money was advanced by Otto von Zwiedineck-Südenhorst, "Die Einkommensgestaltung als Geldwertbestimmungsgrund," *Schmoller's Jahrbuch für Gesetzgebung, Verwaltung und Volkswirtschaft* (1909).

65. Ludwig von Mises, *Theorie des Geldes und der Umlaufsmittel* (Munich, 1912), trans. H. E. Bateson as *The Theory of Money and Credit* (New York, 1934).

66. It has been shown in various anthropological studies that the origins of money were associated with the use of valuable commodities for religious rather than mercantile purposes. See Wilhelm Gerloff, *Die Entstehung des Geldes*, 3rd ed. (Frankfort, 1947).

67. John R. Hicks, "A Suggestion for Simplifying the Theory of Money," *Economica* (February 1935); B. M. Anderson, *The Value of Money* (New York, 1917), p. 103 ff; and Howard S. Ellis, *German Monetary Theory, 1905–1933* (Cambridge, Mass., 1934), p. 86.

68. Joseph A. Schumpeter, "Das Sozialprodukt und die Rechenpfennige," *Archiv für Sozialwissenschaft und Sozialpolitik* (1917).

69. That distinction was taken over by Alfred Amonn, *Objekt und Grundbegriffe der theoretischen Nationalökonomie* (Vienna, 1911), and subsequently by various Dutch authors, such as M. W. Holtrop and J. G. Koopmans.

70. Hence, price analysis was considered a foremost problem of monetary theory. See, for instance, Langford L. Price, *Money and Its Relation to Prices* (London, 1896); Edwin W. Kemmerer, *Money and Credit Instruments in Their Relation to General Prices* (New York, 1907); and James Laurence Laughlin, *Money and Prices* (New York, 1919). For a formulation of the "claim theory" in juridical terms, see Louis Baudin, *La Monnaie et la formation des prix* (Paris, 1936).

71. Gustav Cassel, *The Theory of Social Economy*, trans. Joseph M. McCabe (New York, 1924), pp. 359, 423. The manuscript of a German edition of that textbook was completed before the outbreak of the First World War, but was published in 1918.

72. See Don Patinkin, *Money, Interest and Prices* (Evanston, 1956), n. 2.

73. Such a version of the quantity theory of money was advanced by the American Francis A. Walker in "The Quantity Theory of Money," *Quarterly Journal of Economics* (1895). He believed that the general law of supply and demand could be applied to money, a view that was criticized by Wesley C. Mitchell in "The Quantity Theory of the Value of Money," *Journal of Political Economy* (March 1896), and by James Laurence Laughlin in "The Quantity Theory of Money," *Journal of Political Economy* (1924), p. 276. See also Frank W. Taussig, *Principles of Economics*, 3rd ed., 2 vols. (New York, 1925), vol. 1, who regarded the quantity theory as a special case of the general law of supply and demand without specifying the qualifications under which these concepts are applicable to the means of payment.

74. Schumpeter, "Das Sozialprodukt," p. 649. On Knapp's grouping of the monetary theories, see Ellis, *German Monetary Theory*, p. 4.

75. See Rist, *History of Monetary and Credit Theory*, p. 321.

76. That group included Dennis Holme Robertson (*Money* [London, 1921]); R. A. Lehfeldt (*Money* [London, 1926]), and R. G. Hawtrey (*Currency and Credit* [London, 1919]).

77. Karl Helfferich, *Das Geld* (Leipzig, 1923); Kurt Singer, *Das Geld als Zeichen* (Jena, 1920); and Robert Liefmann, *Geld und Gold* (Leipzig, 1910).

78. See Hugo Hegeland, *The Quantity Theory of Money* (Göteborg, 1951).

79. Irving Fisher, *The Purchasing Power of Money* (New York, 1911). For a scholarly history of previous mathematical expressions of the relationships between the volume of money and its velocity of circulation on the one hand and the volume of transactions on the other, see Arthur W. Marget, *The Theory of Prices*, 2 vols. (New York, 1938), vol. 1.

80. Newcomb, *Principles of Political Economy*.

81. See Gunnar Myrdal, "Der Gleichgewichtsbegriff als Instrument der geldtheoretischen Analyse," in Hayek, ed., *Beiträge zur Geldtheorie*, p. 372.

82. Fisher, *Purchasing Power of Money*, p. 150. See also James W. Angell, *The Behavior of Money: Exploratory Studies* (New York, 1936).

83. Irving Fisher, *Stabilizing the Dollar* (New York, 1920), and *The Money Illusion* (New York, 1928).

84. See Rist, *History of Monetary and Credit Theory*, p. 274.

85. Such a scheme was advanced by Sir Basil P. Blackett in *Planned Money* (London, 1932).

86. In his *Leerbook der Statshuishoudkunde* (Haarlem), the Dutch economist Nikolas G. Pierson examined the problems involved in such stabilization plans and elaborated the concept of sectional price levels.

87. In passing, reference may be made to some objections by adherents of the Ricardian cost of production theory of the value of money. See, for instance, Achille Loria, *Il valore della moneta* (Turin, 1891); and Thomas N. Carver, "The Value of the Money Unit," *Quarterly Journal of Economics* (1897).

88. Arguments of that kind were advanced by Laughlin, *Principles of Money*, and *Money and Prices*. Laughlin also questioned the validity of the concept of an abstract level of prices. A similar approach was adopted by Bertrand Nogaro, *La Monnaie et les phénomènes monétaires contemporains* (Paris, 1935).

89. Wesley C. Mitchell, *Business Cycles* (New York, 1927), p. 130.

90. The term *proportionality theory of money* was sometimes used to emphasize the correlation that had already attracted the attention of the Mercantilist Verri and had been mentioned in his *Meditazioni sulla economia politica* (Genoa, 1771). See Rist, *History of Monetary and Credit Theory*, p. 116. About the ques-

tion of how far the method of concomitant variations was applicable to the analysis of the relationship, see Ellis, *German Monetary Theory*, p. 139.

91. Anderson, *The Value of Money*, p. 137.

92. See Thomas Tooke, *An Inquiry into the Currency Principle* (London, 1844), chap. 8. That observation was termed the *Gibson Paradox* by Keynes (*Treatise on Money* [London, 1930], 2:198).

93. See Marget, *The Theory of Prices*, 1:64.

94. Knut Wicksell, *Lectures on Political Economy*, trans. E. Classen, 2 vols. (London, 1934–35), 2:143 ff.

95. Marshall, *Money, Credit and Commerce*, p. 48.

96. Arthur Cecil Pigou, "The Value of Money," *Quarterly Journal of Economics* (November 1917). See the analysis of the cash balance approach in Marget, *The Theory of Prices*, vol 1, chap. 15.

97. Thomas Tooke, *History of Prices*, 6 vols. (London, 1838–57), 6:637.

98. See Knut Wicksell, *Interest and Prices*, trans. R. F. Kahn (London, 1936), p. 44.

99. Von Wieser, "Uber die Messung der Varänderungen des Geldwerts."

100. Albert Aftalion, *Monnaie, prix et change* (Paris, 1927). See also Aftalion's contribution to Mayer et al, eds., *Wirtschaftstheorie der Gegenwart*, vol 2.

101. Ludwig von Mises, in Mayer et al, eds., *Wirtschaftstheorie der Gegenwart*, 2:312.

102. Schumpeter, "Das Socialprodukt."

103. See Marco Fanno, "Schumpeter et la vitesse de circulation de la monnaie," *Economie appliquée* (July–December 1950), p. 479, about the virtual identity of Schumpeter's notion of "efficiency of money" and Pigou's concept of "velocity of money."

104. As Fisher had done, Schumpeter ignored savings on the ground that the effect of savings made in an economic period could be considered offset by those that had occurred in the preceding periods and were available in the form of goods of production.

105. Hawtrey, *Currency and Credit*, p. 39 ff.

106. See Henry Dunning Macleod's contribution under "Credit," "Bank," and "Currency" in *Dictionary of Political Economy* (1863), and *The Theory and Practice of Banking*, 4th ed., 2 vols. (London, 1883–86).

107. Idem, *Theory and Practice of Banking*, 1:326. See, for instance, Laughlin, *Principles of Money*, and *Money and Prices*.

108. An exception was Hartley Withers, *The Meaning of Money* (New York, 1909). He called the deposit banks "banks of cheque issue," and ascribed to them the habit of "manufacturing" money.

109. Nicholas Johannsen, *Der Kreislauf des Geldes und Mechanismus des Soziallebens* (Berlin, 1903), and *A Neglected Point in Connection with*

Crises (New York, 1908). See K. Zimmerman, *Das Krisenproblem in der neueren ökonomischen Literatur* (Halberstadt, 1927), and T. W. Hutchison, *A Review of Economic Doctrines* (Oxford, 1953), p. 392.

110. See Laurence R. Klein, *The Keynesian Revolution* (New York, 1947), p. 143; H. W. Schmack, "Die Depressionstheorie bei N.A.L.J. Johannsen und J. M. Keynes," *Jahrbuch für Sozialwissenschaft und Sozialpolitik* (1951); Hugo Hegeland, *The Multiplier Theory* (Lund, 1954), p. 5 ff. Various objections were raised to the misleading assumptions made by Johannssen in his analysis of the effects of savings and the cumulative processes.

111. See Paul N. Rosenstein-Rodan, "Das Zeitmoment in der mathematischen Theorie des Wirtschaftlichen Gleichgewichts," *Zeitschrift für Nationalökonomie* (May 1929), p. 140.

112. As a young man, during a prolonged stay in Sydney, Australia, as assayer at the mint, Jevons had engaged in the study of meteorological problems. He published the first outline of his business cycle theory in 1862, then elaborated his ideas in 1875 and later in 1878 and 1879. For a list of authors who suggested definite relationships between periodical natural phenomena and changes in economic activity, see Ross M. Robertson, "Jevons and His Predecessors," *Econometrica* (July 1951), p. 247.

113. Alfred Marshall referred to crises and depressions in his *Economics of Industry* (London, 1879).

114. Jean Lescure, *Les Crises générales et périodiques de surproduction* (Bordeaux, 1906).

115. Albert Aftalion, *Les Crises périodiques de surproduction*, 2 vols. (Paris, 1913).

116. Among the economists who availed themselves of the acceleration principle during the period under review were C. F. Bickerdike ("A Non-Monetary Cause of Fluctuations in Employment," *Economic Journal* [September 1914]), Mentor Bouniatian (*Les Crises économiques* [Paris, 1922]), and John M. Clark ("Business Acceleration and the Law of Demand," *Journal of Political Economy* [March 1917]). The principle was later transformed into an effective instrument of dynamic economics.

117. Cassel, *Theory of Social Economy*, bk. 4, chap. 19.

118. Joseph Alois Schumpeter, *Theorie der wirtschaftlichen Entwickelung* (Leipzig, 1912), trans. Redvers Opie as *Theory of Economic Development* (Cambridge, Mass., 1934).

119. See Eugen Böhm-Bawerk, "Eine 'dynamische' Theorie des Kapitalzinses," *Zeitschrift für Staats und Volkswirtschaft* (1913), and Joseph Alois Schumpeter, "Eine 'dynamische' Theorie des Kapitalzinses: Eine Entgegnung," *Zeitschrift für Staats und Volkswirtschaft* (1913).

120. See E. Varga, "Schumpeter et le problème du risque," *Economie appliquée* (July 1950), p. 533.

121. About the influence of institutional changes on the behavior of the entrepreneurs, see Joseph Alois Schumpeter, *Business Cycles: A Theoretical, Historical, and Statistical Analysis of the Capitalist Process*, 2 vols. (New York, 1939), 1:11.

122. See Schumpeter, *Economic Development*, p. 127.

123. See Fritz Machlup, "Forced Individual Saving: An Exploration into Synonyms and Homonyms," *Review of Economics and Statistics* (February 1943), p. 27.

124. About the aspect of Schumpeter's theory that excluded the existence of regressive periods of business activity, see Pierre Dieterlein, "Schumpeter, analyste du profit," *Economie appliquée* (July 1950), p. 526.

125. See Arthur W. Marget, "The Monetary Aspects of the Schumpeterian System," *Review of Economics and Statistics* (May 1951), p. 112.

126. For discussions of Schumpeter's theory of interest, see Rudolf Streller, *Die Dynamik der theoretischen Nationalökonomie* (Tübingen, 1928); Lionel Robbins, "A Certain Ambiguity in the Conception of Static Equilibrium," *Economic Journal* (June 1930), p. 212; D. Warriner, "Schumpeter and the Conception of Static Equilibrium," *Economic Journal* (March 1931); and Gottfried Haberler, "Schumpeter's Theory of Interest," *Review of Economics and Statistics* (May 1951).

127. About various interpretations of the concept of "innovation" and the "clustering of innovations," see R. V. Clemence and F. S. Doddy, *The Schumpeterian System* (Cambridge, Mass., 1950).

128. Jan Tinbergen, "Schumpeter and Quantitative Research in Economics," *Review of Economics and Statistics* (May 1951), p. 109.

129. Böhm-Bawerk made that observation in 1896 in a review of Eugen von Bergmann, *Geschichte der nationalökonomischen Krisentheorien* (Stuttgart, 1895).

130. See Knut Wicksell, "The Enigma of Business Cycles," written in 1907 and reproduced in *International Economic Papers*, 12 vols (London, 1951–62), vol. 2. In his *Lectures*, Wicksell ascribed the origin of business cycles to the banks' failure to adjust loan rates to the spontaneous movements of natural rates.

131. Idem, *Lectures*, 1:214.

132. *Rate of Interest; The Purchasing Power of Money;* and *Theory of Interest*.

133. Fisher, *Theory of Interest*, p. 168. Broadly speaking, that concept corresponded approximately to Wicksell's "real" rate of interest.

134. Mises, *Theorie des Geldes und der Um-*

laufsmittel; Geldwertstabilisierung und Konjunktur-politik (Jena, 1928).

135. This reasoning was obviously based on the assumption of a capital market with high elasticity of expectations. About that question, see L. M. Lachmann, "The Role of Expectations in Economics As a Social Science," *Economica* (February 1943); and Ludwig von Mises, "Elastic Expectations and the Austrian Theory of the Trade Cycle," *Economica* (August 1943).

136. See Schumpeter, *History of Economic Analysis,* p. 1133.

CHAPTER 22

1. John Bates Clark, "The Philosophy of Value," *New Englander* (July 1881).

2. Clark developed his doctrine in three main works: *The Philosophy of Wealth* (Boston, 1886), *The Distribution of Wealth* (New York, 1899), and *Essentials of Economic Theory* (New York, 1907). See Paul T. Homan, *Contemporary Economic Thought* (New York, 1928).

3. John Maynard Clark, in H. W. Spiegel, ed., *Development of Economic Thought* (New York, 1952), p. 595.

4. See, for instance, E.R.A. Seligman, "Social Elements in the Theory of Value," *Quarterly Journal of Economics* (1901), and *Principles of Economics* (New York, 1905).

5. "It is final increments of wealth in commodities and not, as a rule, commodities in their entirety, that furnish those test measures of utility to which market values conform" (Clark, *Distribution of Wealth,* p. 219). That principle has sometimes been termed *Clark's law.*

6. The difference between the Ricardian conception of a more or less stationary state of the economy and the Clarkian construction of a rigid static equilibrium economy has been well analyzed by Lionel Robbins in "A Certain Ambiguity in the Conception of Static Equilibrium," *Economic Journal* (June 1930). See also Frank H. Knight, *Risk, Uncertainty, and Profit* (Boston, 1921), p. 143 note.

7. It has been observed on good grounds that the quantities referred to by the law of diminishing returns belonged to the sphere of physical production, whereas marginal utilities are psychological phenomena; two propositions dealing with heterogeneous variables hardly provided a sound basis for being combined in a single "economic law." See Joseph Alois Schumpeter, "Das Rentenprinzip in der Verteilungslehre," *Schmoller's Jahrbuch für Gesetzgebung, Verwaltung und Volkswirtschaft* (1907), p. 627.

8. See T. W. Hutchison, *A Review of Economic Doctrines* (Oxford, 1953), p. 259.

9. See George J. Stigler, *Production and Distribution Theories* (New York, 1941), p. 307.

10. Clark, *Essentials of Economic Theory,* p. 195.

11. See a criticism of Clark's profit theory in Knight, *Risk, Uncertainty and Profit,* chap. 2.

CHAPTER 23

1. Simon N. Patten, *The New Basis of Civilization* (New York, 1912). See Allan G. Gruchy, *Modern Economic Thought* (New York, 1947), p. 409.

2. The most important publications by Thorstein Veblen were *The Theory of the Leisure Class* (New York, 1899), *The Theory of Business Enterprise* (New York, 1904), *The Instinct of Workmanship* (New York, 1914), *The Place of Science in Modern Civilization* (New York, 1919), *Engineers and the Price System* (New York, 1921), and *Absentee Ownership and Business Enterprise in Recent Times* (New York, 1923). For a succinct analysis of Veblen's teachings, see Paul T. Homan, *Contemporary Economic Thought* (New York, 1928), p. 116.

3. Charles S. Peirce, *Collected Papers,* 8 vols. (Cambridge, Mass., 1931–58), 5: 258.

4. John Dewey, *Logic, the Theory of Inquiry* (New York, 1938), p. 8.

5. Veblen, *The Place of Science,* p. 65; see Dewey, *Logic,* p. 173.

6. That branch of psychology was developed in connection with the philosophy of pragmatism by William James in his works *Principles of Psychology* (New York, 1890) and *Pragmatism* (New York, 1907). Behaviorism was based on the principle that assertions concerning human attitudes can be derived only from the observation of human actions, since no direct knowledge of what takes place in another's mind is possible. In accordance with that view, psychological phenomena were excluded from the sphere of knowledge, and all human actions were regarded simply as relationships between stimuli and responses. Competent opinion was referred to for distinguishing desirable consequences of human behavior from those "harmful" to community interests. See also John B. Watson, *Behavior: An Introduction to Comparative Psychology* (New York, 1914).

7. See, among others, Karl L. Anderson, "The Unity of Veblen's Theoretical System," *Quarterly Journal of Economics* (August 1933), p. 604. Other equally ill-defined concepts that were frequently used by Veblen and his disciples to characterize the dynamic aspects of the economy were "process" and "going concern." See Gruchy, *Modern Economic Thought,* p. 52. Occasionally the misleading term *instrumentalism* has been suggested to denote Veblen's

way of thinking. See Clarence E. Ayres, *The Theory of Economic Progress* (Chapel Hill, 1944), p. 136.

8. Veblen defined "cultures" as complexes of "prevalent habits of thought with respect to particular relations and particular functions of the individual and the community" (*Theory of the Leisure Class,* p. 190).

9. In Veblen's economy, the beneficial effects of competition were only an incidental and very partial check on the various predatory methods of the pursuit of gain. See John M. Clark, *Preface to Social Economics* (New York, 1936), p. 20.

10. Veblen's grossly distorted picture of "business" was perhaps influenced by his judgment of the economic behavior of some leading nineteenth-century American industrialists and financiers. See R. L. Heilbronner, *The Worldly Philosophers* (New York, 1953), p. 226.

11. About the difficulties involved in interpreting Veblen's concept of "usefulness," see Gruchy, *Modern Economic Thought,* p. 105 ff.

12. See Wesley C. Mitchell, *Business Cycles* (Berkeley, 1927), p. 44.

13. See Veblen, *Engineers,* chap. 3.

14. It appears that most American economists who were between the ages of forty-five and seventy about the middle of this century had their train of thought seriously arrested by Veblen's work. See John S. Gambs, *Man, Money and Goods* (New York, 1952), p. 161. Outside the United States Veblen's writings were almost completely ignored.

15. The main theoretical works by John R. Commons were *Legal Foundations of Capitalism* (New York, 1924) and *Institutional Economics* (Madison, Wis., 1934). As a teacher at the University of Wisconsin, Commons exercised a remarkable influence on the development of labor legislation and "labor economics."

16. As defined by Commons, "pragmatic" economists were characterized by the endeavor to take account of the worth of their reasoning for understanding and guidance. See *Institutional Economics,* p. 102, and Gruchy, *Modern Economic Thought,* p. 155 ff.

17. Mitchell's *Lecture Notes on Types of Economic Theory* were published in an unauthorized edition in 1949. They are now published as *Types of Economic Theory: From Mercantilism to Institutionalism,* ed. Joseph Dorfman, 2 vols. (New York, 1967).

18. See Wesley C. Mitchell, "The Prospects of Economics," in R. G. Tugwell, ed., *The Trend of Economics* (New York, 1924), p. 11 ff.

19. Idem, "The Role of Money in Economic Theory," *American Economic Review* (March 1916). Mitchell's interest in the monetary aspects of the economy had been greatly stimulated by the lively discussion of the problems of the gold standard during

the 1890s, his formative years. Among his first studies was a *History of the Greenbacks* (Chicago, 1903).

20. Arthur F. Burns, *The Frontiers of Economic Knowledge* (Princeton, 1954), p. 75 and passim.

21. Edwin B. Wilson, "Measuring Business Cycles," *Quarterly Journal of Economics* (May 1950), p. 311 ff.

22. John M. Clark, "Wesley C. Mitchell's Contribution to the Theory of Business Cycles," in *Methods in Social Science* (Chicago, 1931), p. 662.

23. Mitchell published his first statistical investigation into economic fluctuations under the title *Business Cycles.*

24. Arthur F. Burns, "Wesley Mitchell and the National Bureau," *Annual Report of the National Bureau of Economic Research* (1949).

25. Mitchell, "The Role of Money." In *Business Cycles,* p. 87, Mitchell attached considerable importance to the effects of absentee ownership on the control of the management of large enterprises.

26. Mitchell's business cycle analysis was mainly responsible for making the American public conscious of the existence of the fluctuation in economic activity. (See Alvin H. Hansen, *Business Cycles and National Income* [New York, 1951], p. 395.) But his analysis did not prevent the belief in "lasting prosperity" from becoming widespread in the 1920s, so the nation was caught entirely unprepared by the crisis of 1929.

27. Mitchell, *Business Cycles.*

28. Idem, "Quantitative Analysis in Economic Theory," *American Economic Review,* supplement (March 1925).

29. Burns, "Mitchell and the National Bureau." See also Wesley C. Mitchell, in Arthur F. Burns, ed., *Wesley Clair Mitchell: The Economic Scientist* (New York, 1952), and also the contribution by Milton Friedman.

30. Arthur F. Burns and Wesley C. Mitchell, *Measuring Business Cycles* (New York, 1946). See Tjelling C. Koopmans, "Measurements without Theory," *Review of Economics and Statistics* (August 1947); and Lloyd A. Metzler, *Social Research* (September 1947).

31. See *Journal of Economic History,* supplement (December 1944), p. 66.

32. See, for instance, B. M. Anderson, Jr., *Social Value* (Boston, 1911).

33. E.R.A. Seligman, "Social Elements in the Theory of Value," *Quarterly Journal of Economics* (1900/1901).

34. See Friedrich von Wieser, *Social Economics,* trans. A. F. Hinrichs (New York, 1927); and Martha St. Braun, *Theorie der staatlichen Wirtschaftspolitik* (Leipzig, 1929).

35. Francis Ysidro Edgeworth, *Mathematical Psychics: An Essay on the Application of Mathematics to the Moral Sciences* (London, 1881).

36. But Wieser's claim that "common experience" was sufficient to demonstrate the validity of the marginal utility principle was questioned by a group of Austrian philosophers and psychologists (Christian von Ehrenfels, Alexius Meinong, and Oskar Kraus) who studied the general aspects of the value problem. See, among others, Howard O. Eaton, *The Austrian Philosophy of Value* (Norman, Okla., 1930).

37. The law of "subjective rationality" implied that the satisfaction of the least important wants was forgone in all cases in which the satisfaction of one of several wants was to be sacrificed.

38. For comprehensive discussions of the psychological foundation of the marginal utility principle and its application to economic analysis, see Hans Mayer, "Bedürfnis," in *Handwörterbuch der Staatswissenschaften*, 4th ed. (Jena, 1927); and Paul N. Rosenstein-Rodan, "Grenznutzen," in *Handwörterbuch der Staatswissenschaften*, 4th ed. (Jena, 1947).

39. John Neville Keynes, *Scope and Method of Political Economy* (London, 1891).

40. Philip Henry Wicksteed, *Common Sense of Political Economy* (London, 1910), p. 409.

41. H. J. Davenport, *Value and Distribution* (Chicago, 1908), p. 567, and *The Economics of Enterprise* (New York, 1913), p. 60.

42. Irving Fisher, *Elementary Principles of Economics* (New York, 1912), p. 282; and Frank H. Knight, "The Concept of Normal Price," *Quarterly Journal of Economics* (1917).

43. Frank A. Fetter, *Economics* (New York, 1915).

44. R. J. Bye, "Recent Developments of Economic Theory," in Tugwell, ed., *Trend of Economics;* and Gunnar Myrdal, *Das Politische Element in der Nationalökonomischen Doktrinbildung* (Berlin, 1932), trans. Paul Streeter as *The Political Element in the Development of Economic History* (London, 1953).

45. Jacob Viner, "The Utility Concept in Value Theory," *Journal of Political Economy* (1925), p. 376.

46. Davenport, *Value and Distribution*, p. 372.

47. Rudolf Auspitz and Richard Lieben, Untersuchungen über die Theorie des Preises (Leipzig, 1889).

48. Irving Fisher, *Mathematical Investigations in the Theory of Value and Prices* (New Haven, 1892–95).

49. Much later, Fisher made another attempt to subject marginal utilities to mathematical procedures ("A Statistical Method for Measuring 'Marginal Utility' and Testing the Justice of a Progressive Income Tax," in *Economic Essays in Honor of J. B. Clark* [New York, 1927]). He availed himself of the results of budgetary research and price statistics on the assumption that the wants of typical families were identical and that differences in the quantities consumed by families were exclusively due to differences in prices.

50. See Arthur Cecil Pigou, *Wealth and Welfare* (London, 1912).

51. See *Lectures on Political Economy*, trans. E. Classen, 2 vols. (London, 1934–35), 1:80 ff.

52. See Frank H. Knight, *Risk, Uncertainty and Profit* (Boston, 1921), p. 268.

53. See, for instance, Christian Cornélissen, *Théorie de la valeur* (Paris, 1903), and Oscar Engländer, *Bestimmungsgründe des Preises* (Reichenberg, 1921). Engländer's price theory was based on the assumption that prices of nonreproducible goods of consumption were determined only by subjective estimates, as distinct from the prices of goods produced by labor. Thus, he suggested analyzing separately prices determined by "objective" technical factors and prices influenced primarily by subjective factors. See also Oscar Engländer, *Theorie der Volkswirtschaft* (Vienna, 1929), vol 1.

54. Davenport, *The Economics of Enterprise,* p. 2; see also Knight, *Risk, Uncertainty and Profit,* p. 39, and idem, "A Suggestion for Simplifying the Statement of the General Theory of Prices," *Journal of Political Economy* (1928), p. 253.

55. See Alfred Amonn, "Der Stand der reinen Theorie," in M. J. Bonn and M. Palyi, eds., *Wirtschaftswissenschaft nach dem Krieg* (Munich, 1925), and Viner, "The Utility Concept in Value Theory." Adversaries of marginalism eagerly availed themselves of that failure to provide an explanation of the price system. The Socialist H. M. Hyndman spoke of "the final futility of final utility" (*The Economics of Socialism* [London, 1896]). Similar phrases were used equally by nonsocialist authors. See E. W. Downey, "The Futility of Marginal Utility," *Journal of Political Economy* (1910); Karl Diehl, "Von der Sterbenden Wertlehre," *Schmollers Jahrbuch für Gesetzgebung, Verwaltung und Volkswirtschaft* (1925). In France, Gruchy, in his *Cours d'économie politique,* suggested that marginal utility analysis was a key to many doors but that frequently there was nothing to be found behind the doors.

56. Joseph A. Schumpeter, *Ten Great Economists from Marx to Keynes* (New York, 1951), p. 126.

57. Idem, "Das Grundprinzip der Verteilungslehre," *Archiv für Sozialwissenschaft und Sozialpolitik* (1917).

58. These difficulties were emphasized by adversaries of the method of imputation, such as O. Conrad, *Die Lehre vom sujektiven Wert als Grundlage der Preistheorie* (Leipzig, 1912).

59. See L. M. Fraser, *Economic Thought and Language* (London, 1937), p. 100 ff.

60. J. M. Keynes, *Cambridge Economic Handbook*, introduction.

61. Eugen Slutsky, "Sulla teoria del bilancio

del consummatore," *Giornale degli economisti e annali di economia* (July 1915).

62. See Bernard F. Haley, "Value and Distribution," in Howard S. Ellis, ed., *A Survey of Contemporary Economics* (Philadelphia, 1948), p. 2.

63. Allyn Abbott Young emphasized that *value in exchange* and *price* were virtually identical terms, and suggested that the former expression be abandoned ("Some Limitations of the Value Concept," *Quarterly Journal of Economics* [May 1911]).

64. Karl Gustav Cassel, *The Nature and Necessity of Interest* (London, 1903); *Theoretische Sozialokonomie* (Leipzig, 1918), trans. Joseph McCabe as *The Theory of Political Economy* (1924); *On Quantitative Thinking in Economics* (Oxford, 1935).

65. Cassel defined "technical coefficients" as the amounts of the productive factors needed to produce the units of goods.

66. About the question of whether a normative element is implied in assumptions of that type, see Hans Mayer, ed., *Wirtschaftstheorie der Gegenwart* (Vienna, 1932), 2:230, and the comprehensive literature mentioned in that article.

67. See Alfred Amonn, "Cassels System der Theoretischon Nationalökonomie," *Archiv für Sozialwissenschaft und Sozialpolitik* 51 (1924): 358; and Lionel Robbins "Remarks on the Relationship between Economics and Psychology," *Manchester School* (1934), p. 98.

68. See also Kenneth J. Arrow and Gerard Debreu, "Existence of an Equilibrium for a Competitive Economy," *Econometrica* (July 1954), p. 287.

BOOK III

CHAPTER 24

1. See Albert Zimmerman, *Schmoller's Jahrbüch für Gesetzgebung, Verwaltung und Volkswirtschaft* (1938), p. 258.

2. See the observation in Adolf Weber, *Allgemeine Volkswirtschaftslehre*, 6th ed. (Berlin, 1953), p. 51.

3. Ludwig von Mises, *Probleme der Wertlehre*, 2 vols. (Munich, 1931, 1933); *Schriften des Vereins für Sozialpolitik* (Munich, 1931–33).

4. Othmar Spann's theory was sharply criticized by Julius Wyler, "Die Grenznutzenlehre und die Werttheorie Othmar Spanns," *Jahrbuch für Nationalökonomie und Statistik* 129 (1928).

5. About the development of German monetary views, see the excellent study by Howard S. Ellis, *German Monetary Theory, 1905–1933* (Cambridge, Mass., 1934).

6. Paramount among the writings which adopted that point of view were Karl Elster, *Die deutsche Not im Lichte der Währungstheorie* (Jena, 1921); Friedrich Bendixen, *Währungspolitik und Geldtheorie* (Munich, 1919); and Karl Helfferich, *Das Geld*, 4th ed. (Leipzig, 1919).

7. See L. Albert Hahn, *Geld und Kredit* (Tübingen, 1924), p. 119ff.

8. Karl Muhs, *Die Entthronung des Goldes* (Berlin, 1932); Hellmuth Weissmann, *Das Gold in Wirtschaft und Politik* (Leipzig, 1940). In Italy the abandonment of the gold standard was strongly advocated by Mario Alberti, *La guerra della moneta* (Como, 1937), vol. 1.

9. See also Wagemann's *Berühmte Denkfehler der Nationalökonomie* (Bern, 1951), chap. 4.

10. About the discussions of these and other "unsolved questions of monetary theory," see Melchior Palyi, "Ungelöste Fragen der Geldtheorie," *Die Wirtschaftwissenschaft nach dem Kriege* (Munich, 1925).

11. L. Albert Hahn, *Volkswirtschaftliche Theorie des Bankkredits* (Tübingen, 1920).

12. Walter Eucken, *Kritische Betrachtungen zum deutschen Geldproblem* (Jena, 1923); and Hans Neisser, *Der Tauschwert des Geldes* (Jena, 1928).

13. See Weber, *Allgemeine Volkswirtschaftslehre*, p. 235 ff.

14. See the contributions of these economists to Arthur Spiethoff, ed., *Der Stand und die nächste Zukunft der Konjunkturforschung* (Munich, 1933). This volume, published in commemoration of Spiethoff's sixtieth birthday, was a collection of over sixty short essays dealing with business cycle research, its achievements, and its prospects. Quite notable were the contributions of non-German scholars such as Albert Aftalion, Johan Akerman, R. G. Hawtrey, J. M. Keynes, and Gustavo Del Vecchio. A perusal of these essays provides a bird's-eye view of the bewildering variety of conflicting attitudes toward business cycle analysis.

15. Adolph Lowe, "Der Gegenwärtige Stand der Konjunkturforschung in Deutschland," *Die Wirtschaftswissenschaft nach dem Kriege: Festgabe für Lujo Brentano* (1925).

16. Ernst Wagemann, *Konjunkturlehre* (Berlin, 1928), trans. D. H. Blelloch as *Economic Rhythm: A Theory of Business Cycles* (New York, 1930); and idem. in *Cinq Conférences sur les méthodes dans les recherches économiques et sociales* (Paris, 1938), p. 32ff.

17. For a criticism of Wagemann's methods and especially of his organismic-biological interpretation

of the economy, see Hans Neisser, "Die Schichtung der Konjunkturtheorie," in Spiethoff, ed., *Stand und nächste Zukunft der Konjunkturforschung* (Munich, 1933), p. 121.

18. See, for instance, Emanuel H. Vogel, *Theorie des wirtschaftlichen Entwicklungsprozesses* (Vienna, 1917), and Rudolf Streller, *Die Dynamik der theoretischen Nationalökonomie* (Tübingen, 1928).

19. See, for instance, Erich Carell, *Sozialökonomische Theorie und Konjunkturproblem* (Munich, 1929).

20. Friedrich A. Lutz, *Das Konjunkturproblem in der Nationalökonomie* (Jena, 1932).

21. Rudolf Stucken, *Die Konjunkturen im Wirtschaftsleben* (Jena, 1932). The proposition that the fluctuations of the period of "late capitalism," especially the world-wide crisis of the thirties, had nothing in common with the cyclical movements of the period of "high capitalism" was also strongly emphasized by Werner Sombart, in Spiethoff, ed., *Stand und nächste Zukunft*, p. 277.

22. Hans Neisser, *Some International Aspects of the Business Cycle* (Philadelphia, 1936).

23. Adolph Lowe, in *Die Wirtschaftswissenschaft nach dem Kriege*, 2: 367.

24. W. C. Mitchell, *Business Cycles* (Berkeley, 1913), p. 59.

25. Adolph Lowe, "Wie ist Konjunkturtheorie überhaupt möglich?," *Weltwirtschaftliches Archiv* (October 1926).

26. Fritz Burchardt, "Entwicklungsgeschichte der monetären Konjunkturtheorien," *Weltwirtschaftliches Archiv* (July 1928).

27. Emil Lederer, "Konjunktur und Krisen," in *Grundriss der Sozialökonomik* 4 (1925). See also idem., "Der Zirkulationsprozess," *Archiv für Sozialwissenschaft und Sozialpolitik* (1926).

28. Erich Preiser, *Grundzüge der Konjunkturtheorie* (Tübingen, 1933).

29. *Schriften des Vereins für Sozialpolitik* 173 (1928/29).

30. Thus, the fundamental differences between the "world economy" and the "national economies" were looked for in structural divergencies. See Bernhard Harms, "Strukturwandlungen der Weltwirtschaft," and "Weltwirtschaftskonferenz," *Weltwirtschaftliches Archiv* (1927), pt. 1.

31. Wagemann, *Konjunkturlehre;* and M. R. Weyermann, *Die Konjunktur und ihre Beziehungen zur Wirtschaftsstruktur* (Jena, 1929).

32. H. Weigemann, "Ideen zu einer Theorie der Raumwirtschaft," *Weltwirtschaftliches Archiv* (1931), pt. 2. See also below, the section on "Location."

33. Ernst Wagemann, *Struktur und Rhythmus der Weltwirtschaft* (Berlin, 1931).

34. About the "neopagan" vocabulary of the German language, which was unparalleled in the West, see Eric Voegelin, "Extended Strategy," *Journal of Politics* (May 1940), p. 192.

35. Friedrich Naumann, *Mitteleuropa* (Berlin, 1915), trans. Christobel M. Meredith as *Central Europe* (London, 1916).

36. See, for instance, Karl Haushofer and K. Trempler, *Deutschlands Weg an der Zeitenwende* (Munich, 1932).

37. For an instructive survey of the conditions preparatory to these developments, see Felix Somary, *Wandlungen der Weltwirtschaft* (Tübingen, 1929).

38. Werner Sombart, *Zukunft des Kapitalismus* (Berlin, 1932).

39. E. Salin, "Von den Wandlungen der Weltwirtschaft," *Weltwirtschaftliches Archiv* (1932), pt. 1.

40. A. Sartorius von Waltershausen, *Der internationale Kapitalismus und die Krise* (Stuttgart, 1932), p. 93 ff. E. Burgdorfer, *Der Geburtenrückgang* (Berlin, 1929).

41. See, for instance, Werner Sombart, *Der moderne Kapitalismus*, 6th ed., 3 vols (Leipzig, 1902–28), vol. 3, Eduard Heimann, *Soziale Theorie des Kapitalismus* (Tübingen, 1929); P. Jostock, *Der Ausgang des Kapitalismus* (Munich, 1928); and Ferdinand Fried, *Das Ende des Kapitalismus* (Jena, 1931).

42. For these discussions, see, among others, L. Stephinger, "Methodik in der Volkswirtschaftslehre," *Schmoller's Jahrbuch für Gesetzgebung, Verwaltung und Volkswirtschaft* (1928); H. Wagenfuhr, "Theoretische und historische Volkswirtschaftslehre," *Schmoller's Jahrbuch für Gesetzgebung, Verwaltung und Volkswirtschaft* (1928); Louise Sommer, "Die Methode der exakten und historishen Nationalökonomie," *Schmoller's Jahrbuch für Gesetzgebung, Verwaltung und Volkswirtschaft* (1928).

43. Albert H. Hesse, *Gegenstand und Aufgabe der Nationalökonomie* (Berlin, 1926); Herbert Schack, "Das Geltungsproblem des sozialen Werturteils," *Jahrbuch für Nationalökonomie und Statistik* (1922); W. Weddigen, "Zur logischen Grundlegung der praktischen Wirtschaftswissenschaft," *Schmoller's Jahrbuch für Gesetzgebung, Verwaltung und Volkswirtschaft* (1928); and R. Wilbrandt, *Der Volkswirt als Berater der Volkswirtschaft* (Stuttgart, 1928); Georg Weippert, "Vom Werturteilsstreit zur politischen Theorie," *Weltwirtschaftliches Archiv* (1939).

44. See, among others, A. Pieper, *Kapitalismus und Sozialismus* (Munich, 1924); O. Schilling, *Katholische Sozialethik* (Munich, 1929); and Oswald von Nell Breuning, *Grundzüge der Börsenmoral* (Freiburg, 1928). The principles of economic morality

which had been laid down by Pope Leo XIII were reaffirmed and elaborated by the encyclical *Quadragesimo Anno* of Pope Pius XI in 1931.

45. See Georg Wunsch, *Evangelische Wirtschaftsethik* (Tübingen, 1927).

46. See Karl Dunkmann, *Der Kampf um Othmar Spann* (Leipzig, 1928), and Theo Suranyi-Unger, *Economics in the Twentieth Century* (New York, 1931), p. 32 and passim. Spann's theory of productivity was developed by Jacob Baxa, his concept of the corporative state by Wilhelm Andreae, his theory of money by F. Ottel, and his wage theory by F. A. Westphalen. E. H. Vogel published an economic textbook, *Lehr- und Handbuch der Volkswirtschaftlehre auf Grundlage einer sozialorganischen Leistungstheorie* (Stuttgart, 1944), based on the principles of a "social-organismic" theory of "performances." A symposium in honor of Spann's teachings was edited in 1950 by Walter Heinrich under the title *Die Ganzheit in Philosophie und Wissenschaft* (Vienna).

47. Friedrich von Gottl-Ottlilienfeld, *Wirtschaft als Leben* (Jena, 1925); idem, *Wirtschaft und Wissenschaft* (Jena, 1931); J. Back, *Die Entwicklung der reinen Oekonomie zur nationalokonomischen Wesenswissenschaft* (Jena, 1929); Erich Egner, *Blüte und Verfall der Wirtschaft* (Leipzig, 1935); and Georg Weippert, *Daseinsgestaltung* (Leipzig, 1938).

48. Werner Sombart, *Die drei Nationalökonomien* (Munich, 1930).

49. *Schmoller's Jahrbuch für Gesetzgebung, Verwaltung und Volkswirtschaft* (1931).

Sombart's book was hailed as a remarkable achievement by a considerable number of historically minded German economists. See *Schmoller's Jahrbuch für Gesetzgebung, Verwaltung und Volkswirtschaft* (1930), with contributions by E. Landmann, W. Mitscherlich, E. Salin, Herbert Schack, and K. Singer.

50. Arthur Spiethoff, "Die allgemeine Volkswirtschaftslehre als geschichtliche Theorie," *Schmoller's Jahrbuch für Gesetzgebung, Verwaltung und Volkswirtschaft* (1933); and idem, "Anschauliche und reine Theorie," in *Festgabe für Alfred Weber* (Heidelberg, 1948).

51. See also the introduction to Arthur Spiethoff, *Die wirtschaftlichen Wechsellagen* (1955). The intuitional background of that methodological approach is quite obvious.

52. The intuitive elements involved in grasping the "essential features" of a style were emphasized by E. Salin, "Hochkapitalismus," *Weltwirtschaftliches Archiv* (1927). In his *Geschichte der Volkswirtschaftslehre*, 4th ed. (Bonn, 1951), Salin undertook to survey the development of a synthesis of "intuitionist" and "rational" economic theories. In accordance with that approach he emphasized changes

in value orientation and methods which took place in the course of that development.

53. H. Mönch, "Das Wirtschaftliche und das Soziale als Lebendige Systemprinzipien," *Schmoller's Jahrbuch für Gesetzgebung, Verwaltung und Volkswirtschaft* (1937), p. 167.

54. Leopold von Wiese, "Wirtschaftstheorie und Wirtschaftssoziologie," *Schmoller's Jahrbuch für Gesetzgebung, Verwaltung und Volkswirtschaft* (1936).

55. See Boris Ischboldin, "Die Hauptrichtungen der Gegenwärtigen Französischen Wirtschaftssoziologie," *Schmoller's Jahrbuch für Gesetzgebung, Verwaltung und Volkswirtschaft* (1937), p. 535 ff. For a survey of the theoretical results of these discussions, see Hans Ritschl, *Theoretische Volkswirtschaftslehre* (Tübingen, 1947), vol. 1, chap. 4.

56. See Karl Popper, "The Poverty of Historism," *Economica* (August 1944). In that instructive article (which was published in book form in 1957), the author drew a distinction between two types of economic organization: "piecemeal engineering," based on methods of trial and error, and "holistic or utopian engineering," which starts from the conception of society as an integrated whole and is based on the belief that the true aims and ends of society can be determined by diagnosing the "needs of the time."

57. Friedrich A. Hayek, "Scientism and the Study of Society," *Economica* (February 1944), p. 37.

58. See, for instance, James T. Shotwell, *The Great Decision* (New York, 1944), p. 9.

59. See Walter Rathenau, *Von kommenden Dingen* (Berlin, 1917).

60. About these developments, see Karl Pribram, "Deutscher Nationalismus und deutscher Sozialismus," *Archiv für Sozialwissenschaft und Sozialpolitik* (1922).

61. *Schriften des Vereins für Sozialpolitik,* vol. 159.

62. The inevitable connection that existed between socialist planning and autarkic tendencies was recognized by Eduard Heimann, "Die Sozialisierung," *Archiv für Sozialwissenschaft und Sozialpolitik* (1919), p. 563 ff.

63. Walther Rathenau, *Die neue Wirtschaft* (Berlin, 1918).

64. That plan was prepared by R. Wissel, a trade union leader, and Wichard von Moellendorff, a collaborator of Rathenau. See R. Wissel, *Kritik und Aufbau* (1921), and Wichard von Moellendorff, *Konservativer Sozialismus* (Hamburg, 1932).

65. Fritz Naphtali, *Wirtschaftsdemokratie* (Berlin, 1928).

66. For a discussion of such views, see Karl

Kumpmann, *Kapitalismus und Sozialismus* (Essen, 1929).

67. Hendrik de Man, *Zur Psychologie des Sozialismus* (Jena, 1926).

68. Ludwig von Mises, *Die Gemeinwirtschaft* (Jena, 1922). See also Friedrich A. Hayek, ed., *Collectivist Economic Planning* (London, 1935), for a collection of essays dealing with these problems.

69. See, for instance, Carl Landauer, *Planwirtschaft und Verkehrswirtschaft* (Munich, 1931), and Walter Schiff, *Die Planwirtschaft* (Berlin, 1932).

70. See Robert Mossé, "The Theory of Planned Economy," *International Labour Review* (1937).

71. For a short history of guild socialism in England, see H. W. Laidler, *A History of Socialist Thought* (New York, 1933), p. 394 ff.

72. G.D.H. Cole, *Guild Socialism* (London, 1920).

73. Sidney Webb and Beatrice Webb, *A Constitution of the Socialist Commonwealth of Great Britain* (London, 1920).

74. Richard H. Tawney, *The Acquisitive Society* (London, 1924).

75. See also J. Ramsay Macdonald, *Socialism, Critical and Constructive* (Indianapolis, 1924).

76. The German so-called Cartel Decree issued during the inflation period in November 1923 was explicitly directed against the "abuse of economic power," but it in no way interfered with the commonly adopted methods of cartel policy.

77. See the various memoranda and studies on cartels, combines, and trusts published in *Reports and Proceedings of the World Economic Conference* (Geneva, 1927); and Ervin Hexner, *International Cartels* (Chapel Hill, 1945), chap. 7.

78. Karl Mannheim, *Diagnosis of Our Time* (New York, 1944).

CHAPTER 25

1. The philosophical background of the fascist doctrine was supplied by Giovanni Gentile, *Che cosa è il fascismo* (Florence, 1924).

2. Georges Sorel, *Réflexions sur la violence* (Paris, 1905).

3. The role of intuition as a kind of superrational insight into evolutionary processes was described by the philosopher Henri Bergson in *Introduction à la métaphysique* (Paris, 1903), trans. T. E. Hulme as *An Introduction to Metaphysics* (New York, 1912).

4. Carta del lavoro of 21 April 1927.

5. Wilhelm Röpke, "Fascist Economics," *Economia* (February 1935).

6. See Francesco Vito, in *Gli aggruppamenti di imprese nell' economia corporativa* (Milan, 1939), esp. pp. 28 ff.

7. The effects of the increasing rigidity of the economy were treated by, among others, G. Masci, *Alcuni aspetti odierni dell' organizzazione e delle transformazioni industriali* (Turin, 1934).

8. See the literature cited in Vito, *Gli aggruppamenti*, p. 29.

9. See Francesco Vito, *I sindicati industriali consorzii e gruppi* (Milan, 1939).

10. See the contribution of Franco Feroldi, in *Gli aggruppamenti*.

11. See Gino Arias, *Economia nazionale corporative* (Rome, 1929).

12. Such views were advanced by Lelo Gangemi, *Fascismo e Corporativismo* (1928), and Roberto Michels, *Economia vulgare, economia pura, economia politica*.

13. That attempt was made by Ugo Spirito, *La critica dell' economia liberale* (Milan, 1930), and answered by Umberto Ricci in a letter addressed to the *Nuovi Studi* in 1930.

14. Filippo Carli, *Teoria generale dell' economia politica nazionale* (Milan, 1931).

15. Guido Sensini, *Le equazioni del' equilibrio economico* (1932).

16. About the endeavors of various Italian economists to replace the prevailing mechanical construction of the economy and the reversible treatment of the variables of the equilibrium models by methods of "scientific historical dynamics," see Giovanni Demaria, "L'epistemologia Keynesiana," *Giornale degli economisti e annali de economia* (1952), p. 497.

17. The term *charismatic leader* was introduced by Max Weber, who analyzed the sociological aspects of leadership based on the belief in superhuman faculties ascribed to certain individuals. Other authors have emphasized the psychological features of that phenomenon.

18. Paul Lensch, *Drei Jahre Weltrevolution* (Berlin, 1917), p. 210 f.

19. Oswald Spengler, *Preussentum und Sozialismus* (Munich, 1919).

20. About these discussions, see Karl Pribram, "Deutscher Nationalismus und deutscher Sozialismus," *Archiv für Sozialwissenschaft und Sozialpolitik* (1922).

21. Friedrich Meinecke, *Weltbürgertum und Nationalstaat* (Munich, 1915), p. 5 ff. Similar ideas were emphasized by the Swedish author Rudolf Kjellén (*Der Staat als Lebensform* [Leipzig, 1917], p. 229), who attributed to the state the objective of promoting the well-being of the "nation."

22. Many national-socialist authors derived inspirations from a remote past. See, for instance, Alfred Rosenberg, *Der Mythus des zwanzigsten Jahrhunderts* (Munich, 1930).

23. Some apostles of the National-Socialist

creed refused to apply evolutionary concepts to historical developments. That was especially true of Arthur Moeller van den Bruck, author of *Das Dritte Reich* (Berlin, 1923).

24. See Fritz Nonnenbruch, *Die dynamische Wirtschaft* (Munich, 1936), p. 266.

25. About the political and administrative organization of Germany under the National-Socialist regime, see Franz Neumann, *Behemoth* (New York, 1942). Neumann's interpretation of National-Socialism, however, was misleading, as he applied to his analysis a sort of materialistic interpretation of history and held the "monopoly capitalism" of the German industry responsible for the ascendency of that movement.

26. G. Feder advanced that slogan and elaborated its essential aspects in *Nationalsozialistische Monatshefte* (1931). For an early critical discussion of these proposals, see Karl Wagner, *Jahrbuch für Nationalökonomie und Statistik* (1931).

27. Fritz Nonnenbruch, *Die dynamische Wirtschaft*, p. 198.

28. See Nicholas Kaldor, "The German War Economy," *Review of Economic Studies* (1945–46). For a critical discussion of the monetary and credit policy of the national socialist government, see A. Weber, *Allgemeine Volkswirtschaftslehre*, 6th ed. (Berlin, 1953), sect. 45.

29. See Friedrich von Gottl-Ottlilienfeld, *Wirtschaftspolitik und Theorie* (Berlin, 1939), and *Wirtschaft als Wissen, Tat und Wehr* (Berlin, 1940).

30. W. Zimmerman, *Schmoller's Jahrbuch für Gesetzgebung, Verwaltung und Volkwirtschaft* (1937), p. 362.

31. W. Vleugels, *Zur Gegenwartslage der deutschen Volkswirtschaftslehre* (Jena, 1939). Erich Carell, *Allgemeine Volkswirtschaftslehre* (Leipzig, 1939).

32. See Werner Sombart, *Deutscher Sozialismus* (Charlottenburg, 1934), trans. (1937). For an analysis of Sombart's glorification of National-Socialism, see A. L. Harris, "Sombart and German Socialism," *Journal of Political Economy* (December 1942).

33. Cited in Hermann Mönch, "Das Wirtschaftliche und das Soziale als lebendige Systemprinzipien," *Schmoller's Jahrbuch für Gesetzgebung, Verwaltung, und Volkswirtschaft* (1937), p. 163.

34. See Berhard Laum, "Methodenstreit oder Zusammenarbeit," *Schmoller's Jahrbuch für Gesetzgebung, Verwaltung und Volkswirtschaft* (1937), p. 257 ff.

35. Hans Jürgen Serephim, "Zur Theorie der Volksgebundenen Wirtschaftsgestalt der Gegenwart," *Schmoller's Jahrbuch für Gesetzgebung, Verwaltung und Volkswirtschaft* (1937), p. 56.

36. These studies were published in *Schmoller's Jahrbuch für Gesetzgebung, Verwaltung und Volkswirtschaft* (1938).

37. Walter Eucken, "Die Ueberwindung des Historismus," *Schmoller's Jahrbuch für Gesetzgebung, Verwaltung und Volkswirtschaft* (1938), p. 191. See also idem, "Wissenschaft im Stile Schmoller's," *Weltwirtschaftliches Archiv* (November 1940).

38. Eucken, "Wissenschaft."

39. F. Böhm, *Die Ordung der Wirtschaft* (Stuttgart, 1937).

40. Walter Eucken, *Die Grundlagen der Nationalökonomie* (Jena, 1940), trans. T. W. Hutchinson as *The Foundations of Economics: History and Theory in the Analysis of Economic Reality* (Chicago, 1950).

41. Serious objections were raised to Eucken's contention that he had arrived at his "pure forms" of economic order through observation of reality. This morphology was qualified as a series of "ideal types" of economic configurations. See Hans Ritschl, *Weltwirtschaftliches Archiv* (1950), 2: 235. Other criticisms were directed against Eucken's use of political and ethical postulates in his theoretical analysis. See Alan T. Peacock, *Weltwirtschaftliches Archiv* (1952), vol. 1.

42. In this connection, a peculiar version of neoliberalism was defended by Wilhelm Röpke (*Civitas Humana: Grundfragen der Gesellschafts- und Wirtschaftsreform* [Erlenbach-Zurich, 1944]), who recommended a "structural policy" designed to adjust the methods of production to the conditions of competitive small-scale enterprises.

CHAPTER 26

1. Oskar Morgenstern, *The Limits of Economics* (London, 1937), p. 21.

2. A German translation of that textbook, W. Gelesnoff, *Grundzüge der Volkswirtschaftslehre* (Leipzig, 1928), was edited by Eugen Altschul. See a review of it by M. M. Bober, "Academic Economics in Present Russia: Gelesnoff, Grundzüge," *Quarterly Journal of Economics* (1929).

3. Henryk Grossmann, *Das Akkumulations- und Zusammenbruchsgesetz des kapitalistischen Systems* (Leipzig, 1929).

4. About the absurdity of Grossmann's scheme, see Shigeto Tsuru, "Keynes versus Marx: The Methodology of Aggregates," in Kenneth K. Kurihara, ed., *Post-Keynesian Economics* (New Brunswick, 1954), p. 333.

5. Fritz Sternberg, *Der Imperialismus* (Berlin, 1926), and idem, *Der Imperialismus und seine Kritiker* (Berlin, 1929).

6. Idem, *Capitalism and Socialism on Trial* (New York, 1951).

7. See Karl Kautsky, *Labor Revolution,* trans. H. J. Stenning (New York, 1925).

8. Otto Bauer, *Der Weg Zum Sozialismus* (Vienna, 1919).

9. Eduard Heimann, *Mehrwert und Gemeinwirtschaft* (Berlin, 1922), and idem, *Soziale Theorie des Kapitalismus* (Tübingen, 1929).

CHAPTER 27

1. R. N. Carew Hunt, *The Theory and Practice of Communism* (New York, 1951), p. 34. At the beginning of the thirties, Nikolai I. Bukharin, then president of the Commission of the Soviet Academy of Sciences for the History of Knowledge, supplemented that problematic interpretation of the history of philosophical doctrines with the absurd statement that human practice corresponds to reality and that, consequently, a categorical contradiction was involved in the negation of objective reality (*Science at the Cross Roads: Papers Presented to the International Congress of the History of Science and Technology* [London, 1933]).

2. Tomas Garrigne Masaryk, *Sur le bolchévisme* (Geneva, 1921).

3. These ideas were elaborated by Lenin, *State and Revolution* (London, 1918), trans. (1926).

4. Edward H. Carr, *The Soviet Impact on the Western World* (New York, 1947).

5. As was stated in an often-quoted passage of *Das Kapital* (vol. 3), production would be brought under common control in the communist society, as a "law understood by the social minds."

6. R. L. Meek, *Studies in the Labor Theory of Value* (London, 1956), p. 264. See also three articles by A. Zauberman on "Economic Thought in the Soviet Union," *Review of Economic Studies* (1948–49 and 1949–50).

7. Lenin, *Die nächsten Aufgaben der Sowjetmacht* (Berlin, 1918).

8. About the much-discussed question of whether Marx adhered to the principle of labor-value as the basis of economic calculations in a communist society, see M. M. Bober, "Marx and Economic Calculation," *American Economic Review* (June 1946), p. 350 ff.

9. The glaring defeats of that tentative organization of the communist economy were analyzed by Boris Brützkus in a series of lectures published in 1921 (trans. Gilbert Gardiner as *Economic Planning in Soviet Russia* [London, 1935]).

10. The organization of the nationalized concerns was probably influenced by the proposals of two "bourgeois" authors: the German Walther Rathenau and the Russian Grienevetsky. See N. S. Timasheff, *The Great Retreat: The Growth and Decline of Communism in Russia* (New York, 1946), p. 120.

11. W. Gelesnoff, *Grundzüge der Volkswirtschaftslehre* (Leipzig, 1928).

12. Iosif Lapidus and Konstantin Ostrovitianov, *An Outline of Political Economy* (New York, 1929), cited in Meek, *Labor Theory of Value,* p. 267.

13. See *Blueprint for World Conquest* (Chicago, 1946).

14. Adam Ulan, "Stalin and the Theory of Totalitarianism," in Ernest J. Simmons, ed., *Continuity and Change in Russian and Soviet Thought* (Cambridge, Mass., 1955), p. 164.

15. *Science at the Cross Roads.*

16. Y. M. Uranovsky, "Marxism and Natural Science," in Nikolai I. Bukharin et al., *Marxism and Modern Thought,* trans. Ralph Fox (London, 1935), p. 154.

17. Bukharin et al., *Marxism and Modern Thought,* p. 28. See p. 21 for a list of abstruse dialectic laws of "being and becoming" advanced by Lenin and subsequently heatedly discussed by Bolshevist philosophers. About changing interpretations of Marxian dialectics, see John Somerville, *Soviet Philosophy* (New York, 1946).

18. Bukharin's proposals were published in 1926. See Alexander Erlich, "Stalin's Views on Soviet Economic Development," in Simmons, ed., *Continuity and Change,* p. 82.

19. C. E. Preobazhensky's book was *New Economics* (Moscow, 1926). See also E. M. Chossudowsky, "The Soviet Concept of Economic Equilibrium," *Review of Economic Studies* (1938–39).

20. A. Erlich, "Stalin's Views," p. 84 ff.

21. John D. Bergamini, "Stalin and the Collective Farm," in Simmons, ed., *Continuity and Change,* p. 225 ff.

22. Zauberman, "Economic Thought," p. 1.

23. Stalin's speech on 27 November 1929, reproduced in *Leninism* (London, 1933).

24. Walter W. Rostow, *The Dynamics of Soviet Society* (Cambridge, Mass., 1952), p. 87.

25. Alexander Gerschenkron, "The Problem of Economic Development in Russian Intellectual History of the Nineteenth Century," in Simmons, ed., *Continuity and Change,* p. 105.

26. A. Wishinsky, *The Law of the Soviet State,* trans. (New York, 1948). See also, among others, Julian Towster, "Vyshinsky's Concept of Collectivity," in Simmons, ed., *Continuity and Change,* p. 242.

27. Frederick C. Barghoorn, "Great Russian Messianism in Postwar Soviet Ideology," in Simmons, ed., *Continuity and Change,* p. 530 ff.

28. Timasheff, *Great Retreat,* p. 250.

29. Ernest Rubin, "The Rates of Soviet Economic Growth," *American Statistician* (June 1958). See also Henryk Grossman, "Some Current Trends in Soviet Capital Formation," in National Bureau of Economic Research, *Capital Formation and Economic Growth* (Princeton, 1955).

30. Gottfried Haberler, "Cycles in a Planned Economy," in *Conference on Business Cycles* (New York, 1951). About the difference between unemployment conditions in planned economics and those in capitalist countries, see Alfred R. Oxenfeldt and Ernest von den Haag, "Unemployment in Planned and Capitalist Economies," *Quarterly Journal of Economics* (February 1954); F. D. Holzman, "Unemployment in Planned and Capitalist Economies: Comment," *Quarterly Journal of Economics* (August 1955); and Alfred R. Oxenfeldt and Ernest von den Haag, "Reply," *Quarterly Journal of Economics* (August 1955).

31. Discussions in A. Bergson, ed., *Soviet Economic Growth* (Evanston, 1953). See also F. D. Holzman, "Financing Soviet Economic Development," in National Bureau of Economic Research, *Capital Formation and Economic Growth.*

32. Naum Jasny, *The Socialized Agriculture of the U.S.S.R.* (Stanford, 1949).

33. Ulam, "Stalin and Totalitarianism," p. 167.

34. Raya Dunayeskaya, "A New Revision of Marxian Economics," *American Economic Review* (September 1944), and, in the same issue, a discussion of the compatibility of Soviet economics with the principles of Marxism, idem, "Teaching of Economics in the Soviet Union," *American Economic Review* (September 1944).

35. Idem, "Teaching of Economics in the Soviet Union," p. 521.

36. Hunt, *Theory and Practice of Communism,* p. 27.

37. Carl Landauer, "From Marx to Menger," *American Economic Review* (June 1944), p. 340.

38. See, for instance, an article by the Polish economist Tadeusz Dietrich, "Economic Accounting," in *International Economic Papers,* 12 vols. (London, 1951–62), 2: 73, 81.

39. See the quotations from various Russian economic authors in Zauberman, "Economic Thought," p. 4.

40. Dietrich, "Economic Accounting."

41. S. G. Strumilin, "The Time Factor in Capital Investment Projects," trans. R.F.D. Hutchings and S. Nedzynski (1946), reproduced in *International Economic Papers,* 12 vols. (London, 1951–62), vol. 1.

42. Discussions of the Scientific Council of the Economic Institute of the Academy of Sciences held in Moscow at the end of 1948. See Fausto Pitigliani, in *Teoria politica dello viluppo economico* (Milan, 1954), p. 138.

43. Strumilin's study was published in 1932. See Zauberman, "Economic Thought," p. 113.

44. E. Rubin, "Soviet Economic Growth."

45. See Vsevolod Holubnychy, "Organization of Statistical Observation in the U.S.S.R.," *American Statistician* (June 1958).

46. Zauberman, "Economic Thought," p. 111.

47. D. Granick, *Management of the Industrial Firm in the U.S.S.R.* (New York, 1954).

48. Evsey D. Domar, *Essays in the Theory of Economic Growth* (New York, 1957), chap. 9.

49. Alexander Erlich, "Preobazhensky and the Economics of Soviet Industrialization," *Quarterly Journal of Economics* (February 1950).

50. For the following discussion, see Norman Kaplan, "Investment Alternatives in Soviet Economic Theory," *Journal of Political Economy* (April 1952), and Gregory Grossman, "Scarce Capital and Soviet Doctrine," *Quarterly Journal of Economics* (August 1953).

51. See the quotations in Grossman, "Scarce Capital," p. 313.

52. Zauberman, "Economic Thought," p. 7.

53. Dietrich, "Economic Accounting," p. 68.

54. See the instructive survey of such views in Kaplan, "Investment Alternatives," p. 142, and Grossman, "Scarce Capital," p. 328.

55. Strumilin, "Time Factor."

56. For an interpretation of that proposal, see M. H. Dobb, *On Economic Theory and Socialism* (London, 1955), p. 263.

57. About the use of profit calculations to determine the efficiency of individual plants, see Zauberman, "Economic Thought," p. 105.

58. Robert W. Campbell, "Accounting for Depreciation in the Soviet Economy," *Quarterly Journal of Economics* (November 1956).

59. V. S. Nemchinov, "Report on the Balance-Sheet Method in Economic Statistics" (Report to the Thirtieth Session of the International Statistical Institute, held in Stockholm in 1957).

60. Holubnychy, "Statistical Observation," p. 15.

61. Philip E. Moseley, "Part VI Review," in Simmons, ed., *Continuity and Change,* p. 553.

62. Nicolas Spulber, "Economic Thinking and Its Application and Methodology in Eastern Europe Outside of Soviet Russia," *American Economic Review* (May 1956), and his book *The Economics of Communist Eastern Europe* (New York, 1957).

63. Idem, "The Development of Industry," *Annals of the American Academy of Political and Social Science* (May 1958), p. 37.

64. Herbert Marcuse, "Dialectic and Logic since the War," in Simmons, ed., *Continuity and Change*, p. 352 ff.

65. Western influence found a characteristic expression in Georgii F. Aleksandrov, *A History of Western Philosophy*, trans. Hugh McLean, Jr. (New Haven, 1949). Zhdanov accused Aleksandrov of having failed to show that a completely new period in the "history of history" was initiated by Marx, that with Marx, philosophy had become an instrument of scientific investigation, a method penetrating all natural and social sciences. See Andrei A. Zhdanov, *Essays on Literature* (New York, 1950), p. 51, and Barghoon, "Great Russian Messianism," p. 345 ff.

66. Ernest J. Simmons, "Soviet Literature, 1950–1955," *Annals of the American Academy of Political and Social Science* (January 1956), p. 91.

67. Kermit E. McKenzie, "The Messianic Concept in the Third International, 1935–1939," in Simmons, ed., *Continuity and Change*, p. 517 ff.

68. Varga's studies were published in September 1946. See Evsey D. Domar, "The Varga Controversy," *American Economic Review* (March 1950), p. 132.

69. Zauberman, "Economic Thought," p. 197.

70. Stalin's declarations were published under the title *Economic Problems of Socialism in the U.S.S.R.* (Moscow, 1952).

71. Oskar Lange, "The Economic Laws of Socialist Society in the Light of Joseph Stalin's Last Work," trans. in *International Economic Papers*, 12 vols. (London, 1951–62), 4: 145.

72. For a critical summary of the content of the textbook, see Theo Suranyi-Unger, "Metamorphoses of the Soviet Textbook on Economics," *American Economic Review* (December 1956).

73. See the quotations from speeches by prime ministers of satellite countries in E. O. Stillman, "The Beginning of the Thaw, 1953–1955," *Annals of the American Academy of Political and Social Science* (May 1958), p. 12 ff.

74. A. Zauberman, "A Note on Soviet Capital Controversy," *Quarterly Journal of Economics* (August 1955), for discussions concerning the establishment of standards for measuring the efficiency of capital.

75. *American Economic Review* (May 1958).

76. *Economist*, 22 March 1958, p. 1010.

77. E. Ames, "Economic Policy in Eastern Europe from 1950 through 1956," *Annals of the American Academy of Political and Social Science* (May 1958), p. 34. At the same time considerable pressure developed for a greater scope of managerial decision making; see Oleg Hoeffding, "The Soviet Industrial Reorganization of 1957," *American Economic Review* (May 1959), p. 66.

78. Hoeffding, "Soviet Industrial Reorganization," p. 70.

79. *Economist*, 24 May 1958, p. 678.

CHAPTER 28

1. "The End of Laissez-Faire," title of a lecture delivered in 1924 at Oxford University and published in 1926. Reprinted in "Essays in Persuasion" (1931) in *The Collected Writings of John Maynard Keynes*, 25 vols., 9:272–94.

2. Ibid., p. 275.

3. Hubert O. Henderson, "The Price System," *Economic Journal* (December 1948).

4. The comprehensive symposium designed to survey the achievements of the Austrian doctrine was published in four volumes and entitled *Wirtschaftstheorie der Gegenwart* (Vienna, 1928–32).

5. Hans Mayer, "Der Erkenntniswert der funktionellen Preistheorien," in Hans Mayer et al., eds., *Wirtschaftstheorie der Gegenwart*, 4 vols. (Vienna, 1927–32), vol. 2. See also the articles by A. Mahr, Ewald Schams, and Bertrand Nogaro in *Neue Beiträge zur Wirtschaftstheorie* (Vienna, 1949), and K. P. Werner, "Die Bedeutung der Methode," *Zeitschrift für Nationalökonomie* (1952).

6. Hans Mayer, "Il concetto di equilibrio in teoria economica," cited in Werner, "Die Bedeutung der Methode," p. 548.

7. Paul N. Rosenstein-Rodan, "Das Zeitmoment in der mathematischen Theorie des wirtschaftlichen Gleichgewichts," *Zeitschrift für Nationalökonomie* (May 1929).

8. Ibid., and Oskar Morgenstern, "Das Zeitmoment in der Werttheorie," *Zeitschrift für Nationalökonomie* (1934).

9. Paul Sweezy, "Expectation and the Scope in Economics," *Review of Economic Studies* (June 1938).

10. Giovanni Demaria, in H. W. Spiegel, ed., *Development of Economic Thought* (New York, 1952), p. 637.

11. Vilfredo Pareto, *Manuel d'économie politique* (Paris, 1909), p. 172 ff. An excellent survey of the intricate problems involved in marginal utility analysis was supplied in the article "Grenznutzen," prepared by Paul N. Rosenstein-Rodan for the *Handwörterbuch der Staatswissenschaften*, 4th ed. (1927).

12. Felix Kaufmann, *Methodology of the Social Sciences* (New York, 1944), p. 224.

13. Henry Ludwell Moore, *Synthetic Economics* (1929), p. 23 ff.

14. Henry Schultz, *Statistical Laws of Demand and Supply* (Chicago, 1928), p. 26.

15. Oskar Lange, "Interdependenz der

Wirtschaftsgrössen und die Isolierungsmethode,'' *Zeitschrift für Nationalökonomie* (October 1932).

16. Benedetto Croce, "On the Economic Principle, II," *International Economic Papers* (1953), trans. from *Giornale degli economisti*, I (1901).

17. Oskar Morgenstern, "Vollkommene Voraussicht und wirtschaftliches gleichgewicht," *Zeitschrift für Nationalökonomie* (1935), p. 337. Other objections to the principle of perfect foresight were raised by Frank H. Knight, *Risks, Uncertainty and Profit* (Boston, 1921), p. 268.

18. Friedrich A. Hayek, "Scientism and the Study of Society," *Economica* (1937). See Léon H. Dupriez, "Du concept d'équilibre en économie politique," *Revue d'économie politique* (May 1948).

19. See Friedrich A. Hayek, "Economics and Knowledge" *Economica* (February 1937), p. 35 ff; idem, *Individualism and Economic Order* (London, 1949), p. 38.

20. Paul N. Rosenstein-Rodan, "The Coordination of the General Theories of Money and Price," *Economica* (August 1936).

21. Propositions of that type provided the background to Gunnar Myrdal's analysis of *The Political Element in the Development of Economic Theory*, trans. Paul Streeter (London, 1953); Swedish and German texts had been published in 1929.

22. Adolph Lowe, *Economics and Sociology* (London, 1935), p. 47. In his discussion of the *ceteris paribus* clause, Lowe pointed to the diversity of the natural, psychological, and institutional constants that, in the various economies, constitute the meta-economic framework of the individual economic transactions (p. 24).

23. Alfred Amonn, *Objekt und Grundbegriffe der theoretischen Nationalökonomie* (Vienna, 1911).

24. Richard Strigl, *Die Ökonomischen Kategorien und die Organisation der Wirtschaft* (Jena, 1923).

25. Lionel Robbins, *An Essay on the Nature and Significance of Economic Science* (London, 1932).

26. Idem, "Interpersonal Comparisons of Utility," *Economic Journal* (December 1938).

27. The conception of the economy as a system of exchange values was especially emphasized by Alfred Amonn in "Zu den methodologischen Grundproblemen," *Zeitschrift für Nationalökonomie* (1935), p. 616. A similar position was adopted by Gaëtan Pirou, *Introduction à l'étude de l'économie politique* (Paris, 1947).

28. Hans Mayer, *Zeitschrift für Staats und Volkswirtschaft*, N. F. 2, p. 5.

29. About the same time a similar idea was advanced by Felix Kaufmann, "On the Subject Matter and Method of Economic Science," *Economica* (November 1933).

30. Pirou, *L'Economie politique*.

31. See R. W. Souter, "The Nature and Significance of Economic Science in Recent Discussion," *Quarterly Journal of Economics* (May 1933), and idem, Prolegomena to Relativity, Economics (New York, 1933).

32. Roy F. Harrod, "Scope and Method of Economics," *Economic Journal* (September 1938). See also L. M. Fraser, "Economists and Their Critics," *Economic Journal* (June 1938), p. 196.

33. Presidential address on the "Economic Way of Thinking," *American Economic Review* (March 1950).

34. Robbins, *Nature and Significance of Economic Science*, p. 78.

35. Ludwig von Mises, *Grundprobleme der Nationalökonomie* (Jena, 1933), and Friedrich A. Hayek, "Scientism and the Study of Society," *Economica* (August 1942), p. 288.

36. Ludwig von Mises, *Human Action* (New York, 1949), p. 858.

37. Oskar Lange, "The Scope and Method of Economics," *Review of Economic Studies* (1945–46), p. 30.

38. T. W. Hutchison, *Significance and Basic Postulates of Economic Science* (London, 1938), p. 152 ff.

39. Frank H. Knight, "What Is Truth in Economics?," *Journal of Political Economics* (February 1940).

40. Ibid.

41. Idem, *The Ethics of Competition* (London, 1935), p. 41 ff. See also the discussion in Kenneth J. Arrow, *Social Choice and Individual Values* (New York, 1951), chap. 7.

42. Harrod, "Scope and Method of Economics." In his attempt to justify the empirical background of that principle, Lange ("Scope and Method of Economics," p. 30) drew a distinction between "private" and "social" rationality.

43. See also Andreas G. Papandreou, "Economics and the Social Sciences," *Economic Journal* (December 1950), p. 718.

44. That consequence was drawn by Hutchison, *Economic Science*, and by Kaufmann, "Economic Science."

45. Knight, "Truth in Economics."

46. Harro Bernardelli, *Die Grundlagen der ökonomischen Theorie* (Tübingen, 1933); and Hayek, "Scientism."

47. John R. Hicks, "A Suggestion for Simplifying the Theory of Money," *Economica* (February 1935), p. 3.

48. L. M. Fraser, *Economic Thought and Language* (London, 1937), p. 37; and Harrod "Scope and Method of Economics," p. 407. Harrod admitted the

validity of two common objections to the use of the deductive method: the impossibility of the "crucial experiment," and the difficulties involved in testing hypotheses by collected data of observation.

49. John M. Clark, *Preface to Social Economics* (New York, 1936), p. 206.

50. Kaufmann, "Economic Science," p. 392, and *Methodology of the Social Sciences*, chap. 16.

51. Milton Friedman, *Essays in Positive Economics* (Chicago, 1953), p. 3 ff. Friedman had developed these ideas in a critical analysis of Oskar Lange's study on "Price Flexibility and Employment," *American Economic Review* (September 1946).

52. A.C.L. Day, "The Taxonomic Approach," *American Economic Review* (March 1955), p. 69 ff.

53. Tjalling C. Koopmans, *Three Essays on the State of Economic Science* (New York, 1959).

54. Fritz Machlup, "Oligopolistic Indeterminacy," *Weltwirtschaftliches Archiv* (1952), p. 3.

55. Idem, "Verification in Economics," *Southern Economic Journal* (July 1955), p. 16.

56. Emile Grunberg, "Verifiability of Economic Laws," *Philosophy of Science* (October 1957). Grunberg spoke of "intended empirical laws" when talking of empirical laws which include the *ceteris paribus* clause and are, consequently, not disconfirmable. But he expected that the development of the behavioral sciences would permit the formulation of indirectly verifiable higher-level laws in behavioral terms from which the laws dealing with economic behavior could be deduced.

57. Kenneth E. Boulding, "Institutional Economics: A New Look at Institutionalism," *American Economic Review* (May 1957), p. 1.

58. Paul T. Homan, *Contemporary Economic Thought* (New York, 1928), p. 464.

59. Allan G. Gruchy, *Economic Journal* (December 1940), p. 842.

60. See Walton H. Hamilton, "The Institutional Approach to Economic Theory," *American Economic Review* (1919), supplement, p. 309, and the ensuing discussion.

61. R. G. Tugwell, ed. *The Trend of Economics* (New York, 1924).

62. Walton H. Hamilton, "Institution," in *Encyclopaedia of the Social Sciences* (New York, 1932), vol. 8.

63. The term *cultural lags,* as applied to such discrepancies in mutual adjustments of sociological factors, had been introduced into economics by Simon N. Patten.

64. See Paul T. Homan, "Appraisal of Institutional Economics," *American Economic Review* (March 1932), and the Round Table Conference, ibid., p. 105.

65. See Richard T. Bye, "Recent Developments

of Economic Theory," in Tugwell, ed., *Trend of Economics,* p. 291, and Albert Wolfe, "Functional Economics," in Tugwell, ed., *Trend of Economics,* p. 445 ff.

66. Tugwell elaborated his ideas in *Industry's Coming of Age* (New York, 1927). For a comprehensive analysis of Tugwell's views, see A. G. Gruchy, *Modern Economic Thought* (New York, 1947), p. 416 ff.

67. Sumner H. Slichter, "The Organization and Control of Economic Activity," in Tugwell, ed., *Trend of Economics,* p. 304 ff.

68. See Morris A. Copeland, "Communities of Economic Interest and the Price System," in Tugwell, ed., *Trend of Economics,* p. 109 ff.

69. In a later article, "Relations between States and Dynamics," contributed to Jacob H. Hollander, ed., *Economic Essays in Honor of J. B. Clark* (New York, 1927).

70. F. C. Mills, "On Measurement in Economics," in Tugwell, ed., *Trend of Economics,* p. 38.

71. Allyn Abbott Young, *Economic Problems, New and Old* (Boston, 1927), p. 242.

72. Mitchell's paper was entitled "Prospects of Economics."

73. Frank H. Knight, "Limitations of Scientific Methods in Economics," in S. A. Rice, ed., *Methods in the Social Sciences* (Chicago, 1931), p. 64.

74. John M. Clark, "Development in Economics," in Charles A. Ellwood et al., eds., *Recent Developments in the Social Sciences* (Philadelphia, 1927), p. 200 ff.

75. These attempts were later ridiculed by Robbins, who observed that the true precursor of "modern quantitative economics" was Sir Josiah Child, who endeavored to show that the concomitance of low interest rates and great riches was an indication that the latter were the result of the former (*Nature and Significance of Economic Science,* p. 114). About the attitude adopted by the Institutionalists toward economic theory, see the Round Table Conference, *American Economic Review* (March 1931).

76. Gruchy, *Modern Economic Thought,* p. 556. Adoption of the Keynesian theory of employment later led to the proposition that the "growth of the heritage of improvement was impeded by a feudally conditioned propensity to consume." That situation was to be remedied by altering the flow of income and by "planning" the realization of the social heritage. (See Clarence E. Ayres, "The Impact of the Great Depression on Economic Thinking," *American Economic Review* [May 1946], p. 123, and idem, *The Theory of Economic Progress* [Chapel Hill, 1944].)

77. Lev E. Dobriansky, *Veblenism* (Washington, D.C., 1957), p. 348.

78. Allan G. Gruchy, "A New Look at Institutionalism: A Discussion," *American Economic Review* (May 1957), p. 13. The participation of institutionalist economists in the official investigation of price and production policy organized by the Temporary National Economic Committees was quite conspicuous.

79. John M. Clark, *Social Control of Business,* 2nd ed. (New York, 1939), and idem, "Government and the Economy of the Future," *Journal of Political Economy* (1944), p. 815.

80. About the significance of institutionalist thought, see the discussion in Gruchy, *Modern Economic Thought,* pp. 593 ff, 622 ff.

81. See Kenneth H. Parsons, "A New Look at Institutionalism: Discussion," *American Economic Review* (May 1957), p. 23.

82. Outstanding examples of such studies were Walton H. Hamilton, "A Theory of the Rate of Wages," *Quarterly Journal of Economics* (August 1922), and Walton H. Hamilton and Stacy May, *The Control of Wages* (New York, 1923). See also John G. Gambs, *Beyond Supply and Demand* (New York, 1946).

83. See C. O. Hardy, "Liberalism in The Modern State: The Philosophy of Henry Simons," *Journal of Political Economy* (August 1948), p. 305.

84. Such an analysis of monopoly capitalism was the object of a remarkable study by A. Berle and Gardiner C. Means, *The Modern Corporation and Private Property* (New York, 1933).

85. Clarence E. Ayres, "The Co-ordinates of Institutionalism," *American Economic Review* (1951), p. 48.

86. Morris A. Copeland, "Institutional Economics and Model Analysis," *American Economic Review* (May 1951).

87. Clarence E. Ayres, "The Role of Technology in Economic Theory," *American Economic Review* (May 1953), p. 279 ff.

88. Allan G. Gruchy, "Issues in Methodology: Discussion," *American Economic Review* (May 1952), p. 69.

89. David Reisman and associates, *The Lonely Crowd* (New Haven, 1950).

90. Joseph J. Spengler, "Sociological Value Theory," *American Economic Review* (May 1953). See the sociological literature on the value problem cited in that article, especially Talcott Parsons and E. A. Shils, eds., *Towards a General Theory of Action* (Cambridge, 1951).

91. Jacques Rueff, *L'Ordre social* (Paris, 1945).

92. Ibid. See also Emile Mireaux, *Philosophie du libéralisme* (Paris, 1950), and Louis Baudin, *L'Aube d'un nouveau libéralisme* (Paris, 1953).

93. François Perroux, *La Valeur* (Paris, 1943), and *Le Néo-marginalisme* (Paris, 1941).

94. Bertrand Nogaro elaborated his methodological views mainly in two studies, *La Valeur logique des théories économiques* (Paris, 1947) and *La Méthode de l'économie politique* (Paris, 1950). The studies of Henri Denis (*La Valeur* [Paris, 1950], and *La Monnaie* [Paris, 1951]) were based on the Marxian proposition that economic problems are not determined by the relations of the individuals to the goods, but by social relationships.

95. Maurice Allais, *A la recherche d'une discipline économique,* part 1, *L'Economie pure* (Paris, 1943).

96. Maurice Fréchet, "Les Mathématiques dans les sciences humaines," *Conférence faite au Palais de la Découverte* (Paris, 1949).

97. Firmin Oulès, *L'école de Lausanne* (Paris, 1950).

98. See the list of authors cited by André Marchal, *La Pensée économique en France, depuis 1945* (Paris, 1953). See also Marchal, *Méthode scientifique et science économique* (Paris, 1955), 2: 12.

99. A comprehensive treatise by Gaetan Pirou was published in 5 volumes; a treatise by Bertrand Nogaro in 3 volumes. Treatises in two volumes were prepared by M. Antonelli, Jean Marchal, and Henri Guitton.

100. Gaëtan Pirou, *Les Théories de l'équilibre économique* (Paris, 1946).

101. Emile Dürkheim, *Les Règles de la méthode sociologique* (Paris, 1895).

102. Ibid.

103. About Dürkheim's sociology, see, among others, Talcott Parsons, *The Structure of Social Action* (New York, 1937).

104. François Simiand, *La Méthode positive en science économique* (Paris, 1912); *Statistique et expérience* (Paris, 1922).

105. François Simiand, *Le Salaire, évolution sociale et monnaie* (Paris, 1932), and *Inflation et stabilisation alternées* (Paris, 1934).

106. See Robert Marjolin, "Simiand's Theory of Economic Progress," *Review of Economic Studies* (June 1938).

107. See André Marchal, *L'Action ouvrière et la transformation du régime capitaliste,* reviewed by Paul Durand in *Revue d'économie politique* (January 1947), p. 110.

108. André Piatier, *L'Observation économique* (Paris, 1948), cited by Marchal, *La Pensée économique,* p. 173 ff. That excellent study has provided the main background for the following discussion.

109. Piatier, *L'Observation économique.*

110. P. L. Reynaud, *Economie politique et psychologique expérimentale* (Paris, 1946).

111. Jean Marchal, "Essai de révision de la théorie des prix à la lumière des progrès de la psychol-

ogie expérimentale,'' in *Neue Beiträge zur Wirtschaftstheorie* (Vienna, 1949).

112. See, for instance, Louis Baudin, "Irrationality in Economics," *Quarterly Journal of Economics* (November 1954).

113. See Marchal, *Méthode scientifique et science économique*, vol. 1; G. Lutfalla, "Sociologie économique et méthodologie," *Economie contemporaine* (1950); and Madeleine Apchie, "Economie politique et sociologie," *Revue des sciences économiques* (1951).

114. Pierre Dieterlen, *Les Normes économiques* (Thouars, 1943).

115. François Perroux, "Esquisse d'une théorie de l'économie dominante," *Economie appliquée* (1948); and idem, "Les Macrodécisions," *Economic appliquée* (1949).

116. François Perroux, "Les Trois Analyses de l'évolution," *Economie appliquée* (1950).

117. Jean Lhomme, "La Notion de structure sociale," *Revue des sciences économiques* (1949).

118. R. Goetz-Giray, "Inventaires sociaux et approche sociale," *Revue économique* (1951).

119. Henri Aujac, "Une Hypothèse de travail: L'Inflation," *Economie appliquée* (1950).

120. André Vincent, *La Conjoncture, science nouvelle* (Paris, 1943).

121. Henri Bartoli, *La Doctrine économique et sociale de K. Marx* (Paris, 1950). See Emile James, *Histoire de la pensée économique au XXe siècle* (Paris, 1955), p. 680.

122. C. Bettleheim, ed., *Economie politique et problèmes du travail* (Paris, 1949) and *Travaux des économistes de langue française* (Paris, 1950).

123. Pierre Bigo, *Marxisme et humanisme* (Paris, 1953).

124. Jean Fourastié, "Les Nouveaux Courants de la pensée économique (Economies, Sociétés, Civilisations)," *Annales d'économie politique* (1949); André L. A. Vincent, *Initiation à la conjoncture économique* (Paris, 1947); and Alfred Sauvy, *Le Pouvoir et l'opinion* (Paris, 1949).

125. Jean Marchal, "La Crise contemporaine de science économique," *Annales d'économie politique* (1950–51); and idem, "Approches et catégories à utiliser pour une théorie réaliste de la répartition," *Revue économique* (1953).

126. Marchal, *La Pensée économique*, introduction, p. 7.

CHAPTER 29

1. See Morris A. Copeland, "Determinants of Distribution of Income," *American Economic Review* (March 1947). William J. Fellner, "Significance and Limitations of Contemporary Distribution Theory," *American Economic Review* (May 1953), p. 484 ff.

2. See, among others, H. J. Davenport, *The Economics of Enterprise* (New York, 1913), p. 48 ff. The distinction between "limitational" and "compensatory" productive functions was connected with the fact that frequently several combinations of productive factors were so coordinated that each provided the same yield as the other. E. Schneider, "Bemerkungen zur Grenzproduktivitätslehre," *Zeitschrift für Nationalökonomie* (October 1933).

3. See L. M. Fraser, *Economic Thought and Language* (London, 1937), p. 352.

4. John M. Clark, *The Economics of Overhead Costs* (New York, 1923).

5. See Fritz Machlup, "On the Meaning of the Marginal Product," in *Explorations in Economics* (New York, 1936); Edward H. Chamberlin, "Monopolistic Competition and the Productivity Theory of Distribution," in *Explorations in Economics.*

6. Erich Preiser, "Grenzen der Grenzproduktivitätstheorie," *Schweizer Zeitschrift für Volkswirtschaft und Statistik* (February 1953); trans. as "Property and Power," in *International Economic Papers,* 12 vols. (London, 1951–62), vol. 2.

7. Frank H. Knight, *Risk, Uncertainty and Profit* (Boston, 1921), p. 124 ff. His discussion of four reasons commonly advanced for drawing a distinction between the services rendered by labor and those rendered by other productive agents was very characteristic.

8. Idem, "Capital and Interest," in American Economic Association, *Readings in the Theory of Income Distribution* (Philadelphia, 1949), reprinted from *Encyclopaedia Britannica* (1946).

9. Kenneth E. Boulding, "Professor Knight's Capital Theory: A Note in Reply," *Quarterly Journal of Economics* (May 1936), p. 325. Boulding sided with Hayek in defense of the definition of production as a physical process.

10. Knut Wicksell, *Lectures on Political Economy,* trans. E. Classen, 2 vols. (London, 1934–35), p. 154.

11. Friedrich A. Hayek, *Prices and Production* (London, 1931); "The Mythology of Capital," *Quarterly Journal of Economics* (February 1936).

12. Idem, *Pure Theory of Capital* (London, 1941), p. 409.

13. About the different interpretations of the period of production and certain ambiguities of the concept of "average period," see H.T.N. Caitskell, "Notes on the Theory of Production," *Zeitschrift für Nationalökonomie* (1936).

14. Frank H. Knight, "The Quantity of Capital," *Journal of Political Economy* (1936).

15. Irving Fisher, *The Theory of Interest* (New York, 1930). As distinct from Böhm-Bawerk, Fisher

failed to connect his theory with a general analysis of the functioning of the economic machinery.

16. Nicholas Kaldor, "Annual Survey of Economic Theory," *Econometrica* (April 1937); Frank H. Knight, "On the Theory of Capital," *Econometrica* (January 1938); Nicholas Kaldor, "The Theory of Capital," *Econometrica* (April 1938).

17. About various misunderstandings which were cleared up in the course of these discussions, see J. Fred Weston, "Some Perspectives on Capital Theory," *American Economic Review* (May 1951), p. 129.

18. About the difficulties involved in establishing the relationship between the rate of interest and the marginal productivity of "capital," as defined in various theories, see Lloyd A. Metzler, "The Rate of Interest and the Marginal Product of Capital," *Journal of Political Economy* (August 1950).

19. William J. Fellner and Howard S. Ellis, "Hicks and the Time-Period Controversy," *Journal of Political Economy* (1940), p. 574.

20. Knight, "Quantity of Capital," p. 637.

21. Idem, "Diminishing Returns for Investment," *Journal of Political Economy* (1944).

22. Oskar Lange, "The Place of Interest in the Theory of Production," *Review of Economic Studies* (1935-36); D. McCord Wright, "Prof. Knight on Limits to the Use of Capital," *Quarterly Journal of Economics* (1943-44); Evsey D. Domar, "The Problem of Capital Accumulation," *American Economic Review* (December 1948); Weston, "Capital Theory," and the literature cited in his article.

23. Arthur H. Leigh, "An Equilibrium Rate of Interest," *American Economic Review* (May 1951).

24. An attempt to show that both the productivity theory and the abstinence theory of interest are essential parts of a satisfactory explanation of interest was made by Thomas N. Carver, "A Synthetic Theory of Interest," *Quarterly Journal of Economics* (November 1954).

25. For a discussion of capitalization, credit, and discount in barter systems, see M. Bronfenbrenner, "The Role of Money," *Econometrica* (January 1948).

26. Schumpeter practically ignored speculative motives as incentives to the demand for capital.

27. For the following discussion, see H. M. Somers, "Monetary Policy," *Quarterly Journal of Economics* (1940-41), reprinted in *Readings in the Theory of Income Distribution,* no. 25 (1949).

28. Goran Nyblén, *The Problem of Summation in Economic Science* (Lund, 1951), chap. 5.

29. See John Maynard Keynes, *Treatise on Money* (London, 1930), 2: 198.

30. Nyblén, *Summation,* p. 165.

31. See also Albert Aftalion, *Les Fondements du socialisme* (Paris, 1923).

32. Joseph Alois Schumpeter, *Business Cycles: A Theoretical, Historical and Statistical Analysis of the Capitalist Process,* 2 vols. (New York, 1939), 1: 106.

33. H.B.S. Keirstead and D. H. Core, "A Dynamic Theory of Rents," *Canadian Journal of Economics* (May 1946).

34. Peter L. Bernstein, "Profit Theory," *Quarterly Journal of Economics* (August 1953).

35. Knight, *Risk, Uncertainty and Profit.* Much earlier a connection between risk and profit had been suggested (F. B. Bawley, *Enterprise and the Productive Process* [Boston, 1907]).

36. Knight, *Risk, Uncertainty and Profit,* p. 17. Such a statement can perhaps be interpreted as an expression of the view that the human mind tends to adjust its conception of outside events to equilibrium analysis.

37. See Jacob Marschak, "Lack of Confidence," *Social Research* (February 1941).

38. Knight, *Risk, Uncertainty and Profit,* p. 298. See also Joseph Alois Schumpeter, *History of Economic Analysis* (New York, 1954), p. 556.

39. C. O. Hardy, *Risk and Risk-Bearing* (Chicago, 1923). See Pierre Dieterlen, "Schumpeter, analyste du profit," *Economie appliquée* (July 1950), p. 499; and E. Varga, "Schumpeter et le problème du risque," *Economie appliquée* (July 1950).

40. Richard M. Davis, "The Current State of Profit Theory," *American Economic Review* (June 1952).

41. G.L.S. Shackle, *Uncertainty in Economics* (Cambridge, 1955), p. 93.

42. J. Fred Weston, "A Generalized Uncertainty Theory of Profit," *American Economic Review* (March 1950).

43. The usefulness of that distinction was questioned on the ground that *ex ante* anticipations are multivalued, and that, consequently, some selection from such anticipations must be made before the *ex post* profits can be identified even in theory, let alone in practice (Mary Jean Bowman, "Theories of Income Distribution: Where Do We Stand?," *Journal of Political Economy* [December 1948], p. 536).

44. John R. Hicks, "The Theory of Uncertainty and Profit," *Economica* (May 1931); George J. Stigler, *Production and Distribution Theories* (New York, 1941), p. 384 ff.

45. Robert Triffin, *Monopolistic Competition and General Equilibrium Theory* (Cambridge, Mass., 1940), chap. 5.

46. Fritz Machlup, "Competition, Pliopoly and Profit," *Economica* (February and May 1942); and R. G. Hawtrey, "Competition from Newcomers," *Economica* (August 1943), p. 220.

47. Evsey D. Domar, "The Theoretical Analysis of Economic Growth: An Econometric Ap-

proach," *American Economic Review* (May 1952), p. 492; Wright, "Prof. Knight," p. 499.

48. Jean Marchal, "The Construction of a New Theory of Profit," *American Economic Review* (September 1951). See also Jean Lhomme, "Le Profit et les structures sociales," *Review economique* (May 1952).

49. Bernstein, "Profit Theory."

50. See R. L. Hall and C. J. Hitch, "Price Theory and Business Behavior," *Oxford Economic Papers* (May 1939), and Richard A. Lester, "Shortcomings of Marginal Analysis for Wage-Employment Problems," *American Economic Review* (March 1946).

51. Shackle, *Uncertainty*, p. 90.

52. See E. Schneider, "Einführung in die Wirtschaftstheorie," *Weltwirtschaftliches Archiv* 1 (1954), and the discussion of his paper at the Uppsala meeting of the Econometric Society ("Report of The Uppsala Meeting, August 29–September 1, 1955," *Econometrica* [April 1955], p. 207).

53. B. F. Haley, "Value and Distribution," in Howard S. Ellis, ed., *Survey of Contemporary Economics* (Philadelphia, 1948), p. 47.

54. See the discussion of that problem in *American Economic Review* (May 1949).

55. Stephen Enke, "On Maximizing Profits," *American Economic Review* (September 1951); Kenneth J. Arrow, "Alternative Approaches to the Theory of Choice in Risk-Taking Situations," *Econometrica* (October 1951).

56. K. E. Boulding, "More Realistic Theories of the Firm," *American Economic Review* (May 1952), p. 41.

57. Jacques Rueff, "Les Variations du chômage en Angleterre," *Revue d'économie politique* (December 1925); idem, "L'Assurance-chômage, source du chômage permanent," *Revue d'économie politique* (1931); and idem, "Nouvelle Discussion sur le chômage," *Revue d'économie politique* (1951).

58. See the literature cited in Emile James, *Histoire de la pensée économique au XXe siècle* (Paris, 1955), p. 145.

59. Adolphe Landry, "Réflexions sur la théorie du salaire," *Revue d'économie politique* (1935); Maurice Dobb, *Wages* (London, 1933); Ferdinand Zeuthen, "Du monopole bilatéral," *Revue d'économie politique* (1933).

60. Arthur Cecil Pigou, "Real and Money Wages in Relation to Unemployment," *Economic Journal* (September 1937); idem, *The Economics of Welfare* (London, 1920).

61. John R. Hicks, *The Theory of Wages* (London, 1933).

62. See C. A. Verrijn Stuart, "Die Grundlage der Lohnbestimmung," *Zeitschrift für Staats und*

Volkswirtschaft (1922). Richard Strigl, *Angewandte Lohntheorie* (Leipzig, 1926).

63. An early attempt to verify statistically the Clarkian theory of marginal productivity, as applied to wages, was made by Henry Ludwell Moore, *Laws of Wages: An Essay in Statistical Economics* (New York, 1911).

64. Paul H. Douglas, *The Theory of Wages* (New York, 1934).

65. Pigou, *Economics of Welfare*, p. 554. Implied in Pigou's definition was the idea that absence of exploitation was a condition of optimum distribution of resources.

66. Joan Robinson, *The Economics of Imperfect Competition* (London, 1934), chap. 25.

67. C. F. Bloom, "A Reconsideration of the Theory of Exploitation," *Quarterly Journal of Economics* (May 1941).

68. The importance attached to their objections was questioned by Dennis Holme Robertson in a stimulating article entitled, "Wage Grumbles," published in 1931 and reprinted in *Readings in the Theory of Income Distribution* (1949), p. 221. Robertson regarded the statement that wages tended to measure the marginal productivity of labor as the most illuminating analytically and the most important practically for wage policy considerations.

69. Richard A. Lester, "Shortcomings of Marginal Analysis for Wage-Employment Problems," *American Economic Review* (1945).

70. See the controversies of Richard Lester versus F. Machlup, H. M. Oliver, and R. A. Gordon in *American Economic Review* (1946 to 1948); see also Haley, "Value and Distribution," p. 31.

71. That constancy did not obtain for Sweden. See Jan Tinbergen, *Revue de l'Institut International de Statistique* (1942), p. 39.

72. See M. Bronfenbrenner, "The Economics of Collective Bargaining," *Quarterly Journal of Economics* (August 1939); William J. Fellner, "Prices and Wages under Bilateral Monopoly," *Quarterly Journal of Economics* (August 1947); Paul H. Douglas, "Are There Laws of Production?," *American Economic Review* (1948).

73. See, among others, R. Ozance, "The Impact of Unions," *Quarterly Journal of Economics* (May 1959), and the literature surveyed in that article.

74. James Tobin, "Money Wage Rates and Employment," *New Economics*, I; John T. Dunlop, "The Movement of Real and Money Wage Rates," *Economic Journal* (September 1938); William J. Fellner, *Monetary Policy and Full Employment* (Berkeley, 1946), p. 94 ff. Statistical material for demonstrating a strong direct correlation between changes in money wages and changes in real wages was published by Lorie Tarshis in "Changes in Real and Money Wages," *Economic Journal* (March 1939).

75. John T. Dunlop, ed., *The Theory of Wage Determination: Proceedings of a Conference Held by the International Economic Association* (New York, 1957).

76. Emilio Zaccagnini, "Simultaneous Maxima in Pure Economics," in *International Economic Papers* 12 vols. (London, 1951–62), vol. 1.

77. As mentioned in another connection, it appears advisable to distinguish monopolies designed to restrict the exercise of free competition from monopolies operated under the influence of scholastic, organismic, or dialectic reasoning. Only monopolies of the first type will be referred to in this section.

78. Francis Ysidro Edgeworth, *Papers relating to Political Economy* (London, 1925), 1, p. 139.

79. About the "workability of imperfect competition" as understood by J. B. Clark and A. Marshall, see Shorey Paterson, "Antitrust and the Classic Model," *American Economic Review* (March 1957).

80. Piero Sraffa, "The Laws of Returns under Competitive Conditions," *Economic Journal* (1926), p. 535.

81. These developments were surveyed by John R. Hicks, "Annual Survey of Economic Theory," *Econometrica* (1935).

82. See, among others, A. J. Nichol, "Re-appraisal of Cournot's Theory of Duopoly Price," *Journal of Political Economy* (1934), p. 87 ff.

83. Bertrand's criticism was published in *Journal des Savants* (1883). Assumptions which render duopolistic situations "overdeterminate" because they attribute to the duopolists mutually incompatible objectives were discussed by Pareto. See also Pietro Tonelli, *Traité d'économie rationnelle* (Paris, 1927).

84. Francis Ysidro Edgeworth, *Mathematical Psychics: An Essay on the Application of Mathematics to The Moral Sciences* (London, 1881), p. 29.

85. Arthur Cecil Pigou, *Wealth and Welfare* (London, 1912).

86. A. Rowley, "Bilateral Monopoly," *Economic Journal* (1928).

87. Luigi Amoroso, *Lezioni di economia matematica* (Bologna, 1921); Knut Wicksell, in a review of Arthur Bowley's *Mathematical Groundwork of Economics* (London, 1924), *Archiv für Sozialwissenschaft und Sozialpolitik* (1927). Ferdinand Zeuthen, *Problems of Monopoly and Economic Warfare* (London, 1930). Edward H. Chamberlin, "Duopoly," *Quarterly Journal of Economics* (1929).

88. Harold Hotelling, "Stability in Competition," *Economic Journal* (1929). Hotelling's study dealt with the effects of the entry of a new firm into a market. But his assumptions were held to be not very realistic.

89. Bowley, *Mathematical Groundwork* (1924).

90. The various solutions of the duopoly problem were surveyed by Henrich von Stackelberg, "Sulla teoria del duopolio e del polipolio," *Rivista Italiana di Statistica* (June 1933). See also Roy F. Harrod, "The Equilibrium Duopoly," *Economic Journal* (June 1934), and Ragnar Frisch, "Monopoly-Polypoly," in *International Economic Papers,* 12 vols. (London, 1951–62), vol. 1.

91. E. Schneider, "Kostentheoretisches zum Monopolproblem," *Zeitschrift für Nationalökonomie* (1932), idem, *Reine Theorie der Monopolistischen Wirtschaftsformen* (Tübingen, 1932).

92. Zeuthen, *Problems of Monopoly.*

93. Hicks, *Theory of Wages,* chap. 7.

94. Vilfredo Pareto mentioned such cases in his *Manuel d'économie politique* (Paris, 1909) and discussed them from the point of view of price and profit analysis.

95. See Karl Pribram, "Die weltwirtschaftliche Lage im Spiegel des Schrifttums der Weltwirtschaftskonferenz," *Weltwirtschaftliches Archiv* (October 1927).

96. One of the first contributions to the analysis of the price policy of monopolistic organizations was an article of Karl Forchheimer, "Theoretisches zum unvollständigen Monopol," *Schmoller's Jahrbuch für Gesetzgebung, Verwaltung und Volkswirtschaft* (1908). It dealt mainly with the problem of price leadership.

97. Otto von Zwiedineck-Südenhorst, "Kritisches und Positives zur Preislehre," *Zeitschrift für die Gesamte Staatswissenschaft* (1909).

98. Heinrich von Stackelberg, *Marktform und Gleichgewicht* (Vienna, 1934). trans. (1952).

99. That scheme was later enlarged by Walter Eucken (*Die Grundlagen der Nationalökonomie* [Jena, 1940], p. 175 ff.), who arrived at twenty-five different market forms with additional subdivisions.

100. Clapham, "On Empty Economic Boxes," *Economic Journal* (1922).

101. Pigou, "Empty Economic Boxes: A Reply," *Economic Journal* (1922). Dennis Holme Robertson participated in the discussion with an article "Those Empty Boxes" (*Economic Journal* [1924]). He objected to the excessive use of "marginal cost" pricing and emphasized the need for a reformulation of the concept of competition.

102. Piero Sraffa, "Sulle relazioni fra costo e quantita prodotta," *Giornale di economisti e annali di economia* (1925), and idem, "Laws of Returns."

103. Sraffa, "Laws of Returns."

104. See Frank H. Knight, "Some Fallacies in the Interpretation of Social Costs," *Quarterly Journal of Economics* (August 1924), reprinted in Knight's *Ethics of Competition* (New York, 1935).

105. Lionel Robbins, "The Representative Firm," *Economic Journal* (September 1928). Sraffa participated with Robertson and G. F. Shove in a sym-

posium on "Increasing Returns and the Representative Firm," *Economic Journal* (March 1930). That symposium had been suggested by J. M. Keynes.

106. Roy F. Harrod, "The Law of Decreasing Costs," *Economic Journal* (1931).

107. Jacob Viner, "Cost Curves and Supply Curves," *Zeitschrift für Nationalökonomie* (1931). When that article was reproduced in R. V. Clemence, ed., *Readings in Economic Analysis* ([Cambridge, 1950], vol. 2), Viner added a note in which he extended his analysis to situations in which the total output of a commodity expands with ensuing contractions of the output of all other commodities considered in the aggregate. A similar problem was treated by Joan Robinson, "Rising Supply Price," *Economica*, new series (1941).

108. These discussions were surveyed by Jan Tinbergen in "Annual Survey of Significant Developments in General Economic Theory," *Econometrica* (January 1934). They were carried on by E. Schneider, E. Chamberlin, R. Frisch, and H. Hotelling.

109. Fritz Machlup, "Monopoly and Competition," *American Economic Review* (September 1937), p. 445. See also J. S. Bain, "Market Classification in Modern Price Theory," *Quarterly Journal of Economics* (August 1974).

110. Fritz Machlup suggested the term *pliopoly* to denote freedom of entry into a market, as distinct from *polypoly*, which refers to a large number of sellers ("Competition.")

111. Robinson, *Imperfect Competition* (London, 1934); Edward H. Chamberlin, *The Theory of Monopolistic Competition* (Cambridge, Mass., 1933).

112. The demand curve for a firm's output has conveniently been termed its *sales curve*. See Triffin, *Monopolistic Competition and General Equilibrium Theory*, Cambridge, Mass., 1940, p. 5.

113. See ibid., chap. 1, for a detailed comparison of the two theories.

114. The dissimilarities of the two theories have been especially emphasized by Edward H. Chamberlin. See his article "Monopolistic and Imperfect Competition," *Quarterly Journal of Economics* (August 1937); Nicholas Kaldor, "Professor Chamberlin on Monopolistic and Imperfect Competition," *Quarterly Journal of Economics* (1938); and Edward H. Chamberlin, "Reply," *Quarterly Journal of Economics* (1938).

115. The substitution of the equation of marginal cost and marginal revenue for the less general and "less elegant" equation of marginal cost and price was a significant contribution to equilibrium analysis. See Triffin, *Monopolistic Competition*, p. 5. About the relation between marginal cost curves and average cost curves, see Harrod, "Law of Decreasing Costs."

116. See Hicks, "Annual Survey." Nicholas

Kaldor, "Market Imperfection and Excess Capacity," *Economica* (February 1935), objected to the lack of realism involved in Chamberlin's assumptions. See also K. W. Rothchild, "Price Theory and Oligopoly," *Economic Journal* (1947).

117. Triffin, *Monopolistic Competition,* p. 78.

118. See also Kaldor, "Professor Chamberlin on Competition."

119. The usefulness of Chamberlin's concept of "perfect" competition was questioned by Roy F. Harrod, *Economic Essays* (London, 1952), p. 1976.

120. See Joan Robinson, "What Is Perfect Competition?," *Quarterly Journal of Economics* (November 1934), and the literature cited in that article.

121. See Chamberlin, "Monopolistic and Imperfect Competition," p. 577.

122. Triffin, *Monopolistic Competition,* p. 136.

123. Edward H. Chamberlin, "Product Heterogeneity and Public Policy," *American Economic Review* (May 1950), p. 87 ff.

124. Idem, *Theory of Monopolistic Competition,* p. 94; J. Cassels, "Excess Capacity," *Quarterly Journal of Economics* (1937); Edward H. Chamberlin, "Monopolistic Competition Revisited," *Economica* (November 1951).

125. That criterion had been suggested by Abba P. Lerner, "The Concept of Monopoly and the Measurement of Monopoly Power," *Review of Economic Studies* (June 1934).

126. Triffin, *Monopolistic Competition,* chap. 3. Nicholas Kaldor ("Professor Hayek and the Concertina Effect," *Economica* [November 1942], p. 410) favored the Marshallian conception of firms whose prices move together and exercise a joint influence on the sales of the individual firm.

127. See, for instance, Tibor Scitovsky, "Prices under Monopoly and Competition," *Journal of Political Economy* (October 1941), and the literature cited on p. 679 of that article. On balance, monopolistic prices were held to be less flexible than competitive prices.

128. See Michael Kalecki, *Essays in the Theory of Economic Fluctuations* (New York, 1939).

129. John M. Clark, "The Uses of Diversity," *American Economic Review* (May 1958); see also the literature cited in that paper. The range of economists who participated in these discussions was quite considerable. It included Robert Triffin, M. A. Copeland, Nicholas Kaldor, and R. F. Harrod.

130. Paul M. Sweezy, "Demand under Conditions of Oligopoly," *Journal of Political Economy* (1939); Abba P. Lerner and N. W. Singer, "Some Notes on Duopoly," *Journal of Political Economy* (April 1937); and George J. Stigler, "The Kinky Oligopoly Demand Curve and Rigid Prices," *Journal of Political Economy* (October 1947).

131. Roy F. Harrod, "The Theory of Imperfect Competition Revised," *Economic Essays* (1952) reprinted from *Quarterly Journal of Economics* (May 1934).

132. Hotelling made that assumption in his article "Stability in Competition."

133. Arthur Smithies, "Optimum Location in Spatial Competition," *Journal of Political Economy* (1941).

134. William J. Fellner, *Competition among the Few* (New York, 1949).

135. Theoretical problems involved in such situations were analyzed by Hans Brems, *Product Equilibrium under Monopolistic Competition* (Cambridge, Mass., 1951).

136. Chamberlin, "Monopolistic Competition Revisited." See also idem, *Towards a More General Theory of Value* (New York, 1957).

137. See also Robert Triffin, "Monopoly in Particular-Equilibrium and in General-Equilibrium Economics," *Econometrica* (April 1941), p. 122.

138. Edward S. Mason, "Various Views on the Monopoly Problem: Introduction," *Review of Economics and Statistics* (May 1949). For a survey of divergent views concerning the influence of oligopolies on the concentration of industries, see Willard D. Arant, "Competition of the Few," *Quarterly Journal of Economics* (August 1956).

139. E. G. Nourse, *Price Making in a Democracy* (Washington, D.C., 1944), p. 59. In his discussion of socially desirable price policies, Nourse objected to the "standard cost" principle of the accountant, the "inelastic demand curve" of the statistician, and the "high pressure salesmanship" of the advertising specialist; he recommended maintenance of a high and sustained economic activity through low price policy.

140. Friedrich A. Hayek, *Individualism and Economic Order* (Chicago, 1948), p. 94.

141. See John M. Clark, "Competition: Static Models and Dynamic Aspects," *American Economic Review,* supplement (May 1955). See the extensive discussion of the concepts of monopoly and competition in the same issue.

142. Hans Brems, "The Interdependence of Quality Variations," *Quarterly Journal of Economics* (May 1948); Lawrence Abbott, *Quality and Competition* (New York, 1955).

143. Machlup, "Competition, Pliopoly and Profit," *Economica* 1942.

144. Oskar Morgenstern, *The Limits of Economics* (London, 1937), p. 66.

145. See the discussion in Fritz Machlup, *Political Economy of Monopoly* (Baltimore, 1952), chap. 12.

146. Joe S. Bain, "The Profit Rate As a Measure of Monopoly Power," *Quarterly Journal of Economics* (February 1941).

147. See Clair Wilcox, *Competition and Monopoly in American Industry* (Washington, D.C., 1940).

148. Lerner, "Concept of Monopoly."

149. John T. Dunlop, "Price Flexibility and Degree of Monopoly," *Quarterly Journal of Economics* (August 1939).

150. See Kalecki, *Economic Fluctuations,* and *Theory of Economic Dynamics* (New York, 1944), chaps. 1 and 3. But various objections were raised to these procedures. See Davis, "Current State of Profit Theory," and Giovanni Demaria, "Sulla misura del grado di monopolio economico di una collecttivita nazionale," *Giornale degli economisti e annali di economia* (1949).

151. Triffin, *Monopolistic Competition,* p. 18.

152. Edward S. Mason, "Price and Production Policies of Large-Scale Enterprises," *American Economic Review* (March 1939), p. 64.

153. [See Karl Pribram, *Cartel Problems* (Washington, D.C.: Brookings Institution, 1935).—Ed.]

154. John Kenneth Galbraith, "Monopoly and the Concentration of Economic Powers," in Howard S. Ellis, ed., *A Survey of Contemporary Economics* (Philadelphia, 1948), p. 115.

155. For a summary of the principal findings of the Temporary National Economic Committee, see David Lynch, *The Concentration of Economic Power* (New York, 1946).

156. Galbraith, "Monopoly and Economic Powers," p. 124.

157. A. A. Berle and Gardiner C. Means, *The Modern Corporation and Private Property* (New York, 1937). Gardiner C. Means, *The Structure of the American Industry* (Washington, D.C., 1939).

158. E. S. Mason, "Price Inflexibility," *Review of Economics and Statistics* (May 1938); Donald H. Wallace, "Monopoly Prices and Depression," in *Explorations in Economics;* Scitovsky, "Prices under Monopoly and Competition."

159. Galbraith, "Monopoly and Economic Powers," p. 113.

160. See Arthur F. Burns, *The Decline of Competition* (New York, 1936); W. H. Nicholls, *Imperfect Competition within Agricultural Industries* (Ames, 1941); Donald H. Wallace, "Monopolistic Competition at Work," *Quarterly Journal of Economics* (1937–38); E. G. Nourse and H. B. Drury, *Industrial Price Policies and Economic Progress* (Washington, D.C., 1938).

161. James Burnham, *The Managerial Revolution* (London, 1942).

162. Joseph Alois Schumpeter, *Capitalism, Socialism and Democracy* (New York, 1942).

163. In an instructive table, Fritz Machlup confronted the "credits" ascribed by Schumpeter to monopolistic restrictions with "debits" as limited in

Wilcox, *Competition and Monopoly*, p. 16. See Machlup, *Political Economy of Monopoly*, p. 73.

164. See, for instance, C. O. Hardy's review of Schumpeter's book in "Schumpeter on Capitalism, Socialism, and Democracy," *Journal of Political Economy* (December 1945).

165. John Kenneth Galbraith, *American Capitalism: The Concept of Countervailing Power* (New York, 1952).

166. Walter Adams, "Competition, Monopoly and Power," *Quarterly Journal of Economics* (November 1953). See also the critical discussion of Galbraith's propositions in "Fundamental Characteristics of The American Economy: Degrees of Competition, of Monopoly, and of Countervailing Power; Theoretical Significance," *American Economic Review* (May 1954).

167. D. McCord Wright, *Economics of Distribution* (New York, 1946); idem, *Democracy and Progress* (New York, 1948).

168. For a survey of the proposals of eighteen authors, see Stephen H. Sosnick, "Critique of Concepts of Workable Competition," *Quarterly Journal of Economics* (August 1958).

169. John M. Clark, "Toward a Concept of Workable Competition," *American Economic Review* (January 1940). See also Joe S. Bain, "Workable Competition in Oligopoly," *American Economic Review* (May 1950), and Clark's "Competitive Hearings of Diversities in Costs and Demand Functions," *American Economic Review* (May 1958). About an attempt to determine for the United States the probable relationship between competitive or monopolistic organization and economic progress, see George J. Stigler, *The State of the Social Sciences* (Chicago, 1956), p. 274.

170. See M. Bronfenbrenner, "Contemporary Economics Resurveyed," *Journal of Political Economy* (1953).

171. See Rothchild, "Price Theory and Oligopoly." A similar idea had been advanced by E. G. Nourse, "The Meaning of Price Policy," *Quarterly Journal of Economics* (February 1941), p. 189.

172. Rigidity of prices as a policy dictated by security considerations was contrasted with price flexibility as required by a policy of profit maximization (Rothchild, "Price Theory and Oligopoly," p. 309). About price rigidity as an element of a long-range policy of profit maximization, see, however, Fritz Machlup, "Oligopolistic Indeterminacy," *Weltwirtschaftliches Archiv* (1952), p. 11.

173. See, among others, E. Böhler, "Die Konkurrenz als Organisationsprinzip der Wirtschaft," *Schweizerische Zeitschrift für Volkswirtschaft* (October 1950).

174. See the discussion between L. Miksch, who denied the existence of that tendency, and Hans Bayer, who asserted it, "Wirtschaftsentwicklung und Konjunkturstabilisierung," (*Weltwirtschaftliches Archiv* [1953]).

175. Tibor Scitovsky attempted to account for the difference in "Monopoly and Competition in Europe and America," *Quarterly Journal of Economics* (November 1955), p. 612.

176. Edward H. Chamberlin, ed., *Monopoly and Competition and Their Regulation: Papers and Proceedings* (London and New York, 1954).

CHAPTER 30

1. For a justification of the broad meaning attributed in this analysis to the term *economic planning*, see John E. Elliot, "Economic Planning Reconsidered," *Quarterly Journal of Economics* (February 1958).

2. Oskar Morgenstern, "Vollkommene Voraussicht und Wirtschaftliches Gleiengewich," *Zeitschrift für Nationalökonomie* (1935).

3. Knight, *Risk, Uncertainty and Profit*.

4. Nicholas Kaldor, "The Equilibrium of the Firm," *Economic Journal* (March 1934); E.A.G. Robinson, "The Problem of Management and the Size of the Firm," *Economic Journal* (1934); R. H. Coase, "The Nature of the Firm," *Economica* (1937).

5. Tibor Scitovsky, "A Note on Profit Maximization," *Review of Economic Studies* (1943). See also E. Nourse, *Price Making in a Democracy;* and Melvin W. Reder, "A Reconsideration of the Marginal Productivity Theory," *Journal of Political Economy* (October 1947).

6. J. R. Hicks, "Annual Survey"; and Benjamin Higgins, "Elements of Indeterminacy in the Theory of Non-Perfect Competition," *American Economic Review* (1939).

7. Hall and Hitch, "Price Theory and Business Behavior."

8. In order to account for differences in entrepreneurial aims, it was found advisable to distinguish between a firm's cost plan and its price plan. Giuseppe Ugo Papi, "Principles of Production Planning," in *International Economic Papers*, 12 vols. (London, 1951–62), vol. 2. Also, the discussion of the full cost principle in *Economic Journal* (December 1950 and June 1951).

9. W. H. Nicholls, "Social Biases," *Quarterly Journal of Economics* (November 1943).

10. Arthur H. Cole, "An Appraisal of Economic Change, Twentieth-Century Entrepreneurship in the United States and Economic Growth," *American Economic Review* (May 1954).

11. Kenneth E. Boulding, *A Reconstruction of Economics* (New York, 1950).

12. See the instructive survey made by Paul T. Homan, "Economic Planning: The Proposals and

The Literature,'' *Quarterly Journal of Economics* (November 1932).

13. Wallace B. Donham, *Business Looks at the Unforeseen* (New York, 1932).

14. George Soule, *A Planned Society* (New York, 1932).

15. C. A. Beard, ed., *America Faces the Future* (Boston, 1932).

16. Person, ''National and World Planning,'' *Annals of the American Academy of Political and Social Science* (July 1932).

17. Mordecai Ezekiel, *Jobs for All through Industrial Expansion* (New York, 1939). Ezekiel combined the establishment of production quotas for the key industries with measures of price control.

18. John H. G. Pierson, *Full Employment and Free Enterprise* (New Haven, 1947).

19. Alvin H. Hansen, *Economic Stabilization in an Unbalanced World* (New York, 1932).

20. Henry C. Simons, ''A Positive Program for Laissez Faire,'' *Journal of Political Economy* (February 1936); Irving Fisher, *100% Money* (New York, 1935).

21. B. S. Keirstead, ''American Capitalism, Where Are You Going?,'' *American Economic Review* (May 1950).

22. The article appeared in *Giornale degli economisti e annali di economia*. A translation was included in Fredrich A. Hayek, ed., *Collectivist Economic Planning* (London, 1935).

23. The approach to the problem was radically modified in an article by Herbert Zassenhaus (''Uber die ökonomische Theorie der Planwirtschaft,'' *Zeitschrift für Nationalökonomie* [1934]) in which political decisions made by the planning authorities were substituted for the freedom of choice granted to the members of the community in Barone's scheme. For a translation of the article, see ''Related Costs in Economics of Transport,'' *International Economic Papers*, 12 vols. (London, 1951–62), vol. 5.

24. See F. von Wieser, *Treatise on Social Economics*.

25. Ludwig von Mises, ''Die Wirtschaftsrechnung im sozialistischen Gemeinwesen,'' *Archiv für Sozialwissenschaft und Sozialpolitik* (1920), reproduced in Hayek, ed., *Collectivist Economic Planning*.

26. Hayek, *Individualism and Economic Order* (London, 1949), p. 34.

27. M. H. Dobb, *Capitalist Enterprise and Social Progress* (London, 1925); idem, ''Economic Theory and the Problems of a Socialist Economy,'' *Economic Journal* (December 1933). The question of how to deal in a planned economy with uncertainties played a considerable role in the ensuing discussion with Abba P. Lerner. See *Review of Economic Studies* (1934–35).

28. See also M. H. Dobb, *On Economic Theory and Socialism* (London, 1955).

29. E.F.M. Durbin, ''Economic Calculus in a Planned Economy,'' *Economic Journal* (December 1936).

30. Arthur Cecil Pigou, *Socialism versus Capitalism* (London, 1937).

31. *On the Economic Theory of Socialism,* with contributions by F. M. Taylor and Oskar Lange and an introduction by B. Lippincott (Minneapolis, 1938); H. D. Dickinson, ''The Economic Basis of Socialism,'' *Political Quarterly* (1930).

32. About ten years later, after he joined the Polish Communist party, Oskar Lange explained his approval of the Soviet economic organization with the argument that marginal analysis required much further elaboration to make it serviceable to purposes of economic planning (''The Practice of Economic Planning and The Optimum Allocation of Resources,'' *Econometrica,* supplement [July 1949], p. 166 ff).

33. H. D. Dickinson, ''Price Formation in a Socialist Economy,'' *Economic Journal* (1933). That scheme was criticized by M. H. Dobb, ''Economic Theory and the Problems of a Socialist Economy.''

34. Durbin, ''Economic Calculus in a Planned Economy.'' Lerner defended his proposals in *Economic Journal* (December 1936) and ''Statics and Dynamics in Socialist Economics,'' *Economic Journal* (1937), and in ''Theory and Practice in Socialist Economics,'' *Review of Economic Studies* (October 1938).

35. See J. Stafford, ''Optimal Utilization of National Resources,'' *Econometrica,* supplement (July 1949), p. 157.

36. The argument that in a collectivist economy much wasteful competition could be avoided through carefully coordinated large-scale investment schemes was discussed by Howard S. Ellis and William J. Fellner, ''External Economics and Diseconomics,'' *American Economic Review* (1943). An interesting attempt to connect the problem of planning efficient allocation of resources with the methods of linear programming was made by Tjalling C. Koopmans, ''Efficient Allocation of Resources,'' *Econometrica* (October 1951).

37. See Friedrich A. Hayek, ''Socialist Calculation,'' *Economica* (1940). See also F. J. Atkinson, ''Savings and Investment in a Socialist State,'' *Review of Economic Studies* (1947–48), p. 79.

38. Jacob Viner, *International Trade and Economic Development* (Oxford, 1953), p. 77.

39. For a criticism of theoretical mathematical or logical models of planned economics, see D. F. Bergum, ''Economic Planning and the Science of Economics,'' *American Economic Review* (June 1941).

40. Abba P. Lerner, *The Economics of Control* (New York, 1944).

41. Maurice Allais, "Le Problème de la planification dans une économie collectiviste," *Kyklos* (1947–48); idem, *Economie et intérêt* (Paris, 1947).

42. See, for instance, W. H. Hutt, *Plan for Reconstruction* (London, 1943).

43. See, for instance, Sir Oliver Franks, *Central Planning and Control: War and Peace* (London, 1947).

44. Mention may be made of Lionel Robbins, *The Economic Problems in Peace and War* (London, 1947); Roy F. Harrod, *Are These Hardships Necessary?* (London, 1947); John Jewkes, *Ordeal by Planning* (London, 1948); and James M. Meade, *Planning and the Price Mechanism* (London, 1948).

45. For an excellent survey of the problems of planning, as envisaged especially from the point of view of the English postwar economy, see Allen G. B. Fisher, *Economic Progress and Social Security* (London, 1945), chap. 13.

46. D. J. Dewey, "Occupational Choice in a Collectivist Economy," *Journal of Political Economy* (December 1948).

47. *Economist*, 17 January 1953. In the program of the British Labor party published in 1953 under the title "Challenge to Britain," additional nationalization of certain industries was recommended as a means of increasing exports.

48. *Economist*, 15 November 1958, p. 623.

49. C.A.R. Crossland, *The Future of Socialism* (London, 1956).

50. W. Weddingen, ed., *Untersuchungen zur sozialen Gestaltung der Wirtschaftsordnung* (Berlin, 1950).

51. Francis Ysidro Edgeworth, "The Pure Theory of Taxation," *Economic Journal* (1897).

52. Alfred Marshall, *Principles of Economics*, 8th ed. (New York, 1950), p. 130.

53. Pigou, *Economics of Welfare*.

54. For magnitudes of any kind to be measurable means that a unique and reciprocal correspondence, a one-to-one relation, can be established between the magnitudes in question and cardinal numbers (Arthur Cecil Pigou, "Some Aspects of Welfare Economics," *American Economic Review* [June 1951], p. 289).

55. Ragnar Frisch, *New Methods of Measuring Marginal Utility* (Tübingen, 1932).

56. Alexander Bilomovic, "Ein neurer Versuch der Bemmessung des Grenznutzens," *Zeitschrift für Nationalökonomie* (1933).

57. John R. Hicks and R.G.D. Allen, "A Reconsideration of the Theory of Value," *Economica* (February–March 1934); J. R. Hicks, *Value and Capital* (Oxford, 1939).

58. See Lionel Robbins, "Interpersonal Comparisons of Utility," *Economic Journal* (1938), p.

638, and Hla Myint, *Theories of Welfare Economics* (Cambridge, Mass., 1943), chap. 5.

59. Paul T. Homan, "Industrial Combination as Surveyed in Recent Literature," *Quarterly Journal of Economics* (February 1930), p. 355.

60. See Tibor Scitovsky, "The State of Welfare Economics," *American Economic Review* (June 1951), p. 305 ff.

61. See Pigou, "Welfare Economics."

62. Roy F. Harrod, "Scope and Method of Economics," *Economic Journal* (September 1938), p. 397.

63. Colin Clark, *Conditions of Economic Progress*, 2nd ed. (London, 1951), p. 16.

64. Frank H. Knight, "Realism and Relevance in the Theory of Demand," *Journal of Political Economy* (December 1944), p. 289 ff. Knight's views were shared by other authors, such as Dennis Holme Robertson, "A Revolutionist's Handbook," *Quarterly Journal of Economics* (February 1950), and "Utility and All That," *Manchester School Studies* (May 1951).

65. Marcus Fleming, "A Cardinal Concept of Welfare," *Quarterly Journal of Economics* (1952), p. 366.

66. The role played by moral principles in the various economic doctrines was analyzed by J. F. Flubacher, *The Concept of Ethics in the History of Economics* (New York, 1950).

67. John M. Clark, "Toward a Concept of Social Value," in his *Preface to Social Economics* (New York, 1936), p. 46.

68. The relationships among economics, morals, and jurisprudence were discussed between 1935 and 1937 in a series of contributions to the *Revue d'économie politique*. Among the contributors were the Italians F. Carli, G. del Vecchio, L. Einaudi, and Francisco Vito, and the Frenchmen G. Bousquet, F. Perroux, and G. Pigou. Del Vecchio considered it impossible to derive the definition of generally valid ends from theoretical knowledge, but expressed his belief in an absolutely valid ethical system based on "objective ends of life." Vito pointed to ethical precepts as an important element of means and ends relationships to be analyzed by the economist. See also Vito's contribution to *Neue Beiträge zur Wirtschaftstheorie* (Vienna, 1949), p. 67.

69. See George J. Stigler, "The New Welfare Economics," *American Economic Review* (1943), p. 355.

70. Pareto, *Manuel d'économie politique*, p. 354 ff. Enrico Barone, "Il ministro dalla produzione nello stato colletivista," *Giornale degli economisti e annali di economia* (1908), translated in Hayek, ed., *Collectivist Economic Planning*.

71. Kenneth E. Boulding, "Welfare Econom-

ics,'' in Howard S. Ellis, ed., *A Survey of Contemporary Economics* (Philadelphia, 1948), 2: 2.

72. Hicks and Allen, ''Theory of Value.''

73. See, among others, Kenneth E. Boulding, ''The Theory of the Firm,'' *American Economic Review* (December 1942) and his book, *Economic Analysis* (New York, 1948).

74. Paul A. Samuelson, ''A Note on the Pure Theory of Consumer's Behavior,'' *Economica* (February 1938). A similar suggestion was made by I.M.D. Little, *A Critique of Welfare Economics* (Oxford, 1950), p. 25.

75. Oskar Lange, ''The Foundations of Welfare Economics,'' *Econometrica* (July–October 1942).

76. Harold Hotelling, ''The General Welfare in Relation to the Problems of Taxation,'' *Econometrica* (July 1938).

77. John R. Hicks, ''The Foundations of Welfare Economics,'' *Economic Journal* (1939).

78. Little, *Welfare Economics*, p. 315 ff.

79. W. E. Armstrong, ''The Determinateness of the Utility Function,'' *Economic Journal* (1939).

80. Dennis Holme Robertson, *Utility and All That* (London, 1952), p. 26. See also Weber, ''Zur Problematik der neueren Welfare Economics,'' *Zeitschrift für Nationalökonomie* (1954), p. 499.

81. John M. Clark, ''Realism and Relevance,'' *Journal of Political Economy* (August 1946).

82. Nicholas Kaldor, ''Welfare Propositions of Economics and Interpersonal Comparison of Utility,'' *Economic Journal* (September 1939).

83. John R. Hicks, ''The Rehabilitation of Consumers' Surplus,'' *Review of Economic Studies* (February 1941).

84. Little, *Welfare Economics*, and Paul A. Samuelson, *Foundations of Economic Analysis* (Cambridge, Mass., 1947).

85. Tibor Scitovsky, ''Capital Accumulation, Employment and Price Rigidity,'' *Review of Economic Studies* (November 1941). See also idem, *Welfare and Competition* (Chicago, 1951), for a model of an efficient economy based on free competition. A modification of the efficiency criteria was suggested by Little, *Welfare Economics*. For a discussion of Little's proposals, see Kenneth J. Arrow, ''Little's Critique of Welfare Economics,'' *American Economic Review* (1951).

86. Kenneth J. Arrow, *Social Choice and Individual Values* (New York, 1951), p. 40.

87. Paul A. Samuelson, ''Welfare Economics and International Trade,'' *American Economic Review* (June 1938), and *Foundations of Economic Analysis;* Melvin W. Reder, *Studies in the Theory of Welfare Economics* (New York, 1947).

88. Lerner, *Economics of Control.*

89. Oskar Lange, ''Scope and Method of Economics,'' *Review of Economic Studies* (1945–46).

90. The validity of the theorem of ''marginal

cost pricing'' was questioned in prolonged discussions. See especially Nancy Ruggles, ''The Welfare Basis of the Marginal Cost Pricing Principle,'' *Review of Economic Studies* (1949), and idem, ''Recent Developments in the Theory of Marginal Cost Pricing,'' *Review of Economic Studies* (1950).

91. Melvin W. Reder, ''Welfare Economics,'' in Howard S. Ellis, ed., *A Survey of Contemporary Economics* (Philadelphia, 1948), 2: 35.

92. A. Bergson, ''A Reformulation of Certain Aspects of Welfare Economics,'' *Quarterly Journal of Economics* (February 1938). See also Samuelson, *Foundations of Economic Analysis*, p. 219.

93. See Little, *Welfare Economics*, p. 56, and P. Streeten, ''Economics and Value Judgments,'' *Quarterly Journal of Economics* (1950), p. 591 ff.

94. See Thorstein Veblen, *The Place of Science in Modern Civilization* (New York, 1919), p. 73; Clark, *Preface to Social Economics*, p. 92 ff. Knight, *Ethics of Competition*, p. 19.

95. That problem was discussed by Hla Myint, *Welfare Economics*, chap. 11; Reder, *Welfare Economics;* and Gerhard Tintner, ''Multiple Regression for Systems of Equations,'' *Econometrica* (January 1946), p. 69 ff.

96. K. W. Rothchild, ''The Meaning of Rationality,'' *Review of Economic Studies* (1946–47).

97. Arrow, *Social Choice and Individual Values.*

98. For comments on Arrow's procedures, see William J. Baumol, *Welfare Economics and the Theory of the State* (London, 1952); Jerome Rothenberg, ''Conditions for a Social Welfare Function,'' *Journal of Political Economy* (1953), p. 389; and J. M. Buchanan, ''Social Choice, Democracy, and Free Markets,'' *Journal of Political Economy* (1954), p. 114 ff. A. Bergson attempted to show that Arrow's theorem was relevant, under special conditions, to political theory, but had little or no bearing on welfare economics (''On The Concept of Social Welfare,'' *Quarterly Journal of Economics* [May 1954]).

99. Little, *Welfare Economics*. For similar judgments, see Boulding, ''Welfare Economics,'' and the comments of Melvin W. Reder and P. A. Samuelson, Ellis, ed., *Survey of Contemporary Economics*, and the discussions of the welfare theory in *Economie appliquée* (October–December 1952).

100. Jan Tinbergen, ''The Influence of Productivity on Economic Welfare,'' *Economic Journal* (1952).

101. Idem, ''Welfare Economics and Income Distribution,'' *American Economic Review* (May 1957), p. 490.

CHAPTER 31

1. Knut Wicksell, *Schmoller's Jahrbuch für Gesetzgebung, Verwaltung und Volkswirtschaft* (1928).

2. Paul N. Rosenstein-Rodan, "The Coordination of the General Theories of Money and Price," *Economica* (August 1936), p. 258.

3. R. G. Hawtrey, "Money and Index Numbers," *Journal of the Royal Statistical Society* (1930), reprinted in *Readings in Monetary Theory* (New York, 1951).

4. One of the most consistent advocates of the quantity theory of money was Karl Gustav Cassel, *Theoretische Socialökonomie* (Leipzig, 1918).

5. Henry H. Villard, "Monetary Theory," in Howard S. Ellis, ed., *A Survey of Contemporary Economics* (Philadelphia, 1949), p. 318.

6. L. Albert Hahn, *The Economics of Illusion* (New York, 1949), p. 114. See also Alfred Amonn, "Grundsätze der Finanzwissenschaft," *Schweizerische Zeitschrift für Volkswirtschaft* (December 1953).

7. James W. Angell, *The Behavior of Money: Exploratory Studies* (New York, 1936).

8. Dennis H. Robertson, *Money* (London, 1922).

9. See Villard, "Monetary Theory."

10. Arthur W. Marget, *The Theory of Prices* (New York, 1938), vol. 1.

11. John Maynard Keynes, *Treatise on Money* (London, 1930).

12. In the United SDates, the discussions and interpretations of the Keynesian equations greatly stimulated statistical research into the behavior of the various elements of the national income. See L. Currie, *The Supply and Control of Money in the United States* (Cambridge, Mass., 1934); and Angell, *Behavior of Money.*

13. See Friedrich A. Lutz, "The Outcome of the Saving Investment Discussion," *Quarterly Journal of Economics* (August 1938), p. 594.

14. See, for instance, Friedrich A. Hayek, "Reflections on the Pure Theory of Money of Mr. J. M. Keynes, Part I," *Economica* (August 1931) and ibid., part II (February 1932); John Maynard Keynes, "The Pure Theory of Money: A Reply to Dr. Hayek," *Economica* (November 1931); and Friedrich A. Hayek, "A Rejoinder to Mr. Keynes," *Economica* (November 1931).

15. Howard S. Ellis, "Some Fundamentals in the Theory of Velocity," *Annual Journal of Economics* (May 1938), p. 342.

16. See Joan Robinson, "The Concept of Hoarding," *Economic Journal* (June 1938); and Dennis Holme Robertson, "Mr. Keynes and Finance: A Note," *Economic Journal* (1938), and John Maynard Keynes, "Comment," *Economic Journal* (1938). About conflicting definitions of hoarding and dishoarding, see Gottfried Haberler, "Some Comments on Mr. Kahn's Review of Prosperity and Depression," *Economic Journal* (June 1938).

17. Marget, *Theory of Prices.*

18. See also Howard S. Ellis, *German Monetary Theory, 1905–1933* (Cambridge, Mass., 1934), p. 168 ff.; and Joseph Alois Schumpeter, *History of Economic Analysis* (New York, 1954), p. 1095 ff.

19. John R. Hicks, "A Suggestion for Simplifying the Theory of Money," *Economica* (February 1935).

20. For some comments on the Hicksian proposals, see Villard, "Monetary Theory," p. 237.

21. Joseph Alois Schumpeter, "Das Sozialprodukt und die Rechenpfennige," *Archiv für Sozialwissenschaft und Sozialpolitik* (1917); and Jacob Marschak, "Die Verkehrsgleichung," *Archiv für Sozialwissenschaft und Sozialpolitik* (1924).

22. See Rudolf Stucken, *Neue Beiträge zur Wirtschaftstheorie,* p. 303 ff.

23. See Ellis, *German Monetary Policy,* p. 132 ff.

24. Ibid., p. 184.

25. Gottfried Haberler, *Der Sinn der Indexzahlen* (Tübingen, 1927).

26. Hans Neisser, "Der Kreislauf des Geldes," *Weltwirtschaftliches Archiv* (1931); Marius Wilhelm Holtrop, "Die Umlaufsgeschwindigkeit des Geldes," in Friedrich A. Hayek, ed., *Beiträge zur Geldtheorie* (Vienna, 1933); and Jacob Marschak, "Vom Grössensystem der Volkwirtschaft," *Archiv für Sozialwissenschaft und Sozialpolitik* (1933).

27. Holtrop, "Umlaufsgeschwindigkeit"; Hans Neisser, *Der Tauschwert des Geldes* (Jena, 1928); Friedrich A. Hayek, *Prices and Production* (London, 1931); and Arthur W. Marget, "The Relation between the Velocity of Circulation of Money and the 'Velocity of Circulation of Goods,'" part 1, *Journal of Political Economy* (June 1932), and ibid., part 2, *Journal of Political Economy* (August 1932).

28. Friedrich A. Hayek, "Das Intertemporale Gleichgewichtssystem der Preise und die Bewegungen des Geldwertes," *Weltwirtschaftliches Archiv* (1928); idem, "Ueber neutrales Geld," *Zeitschrift für Nationalökonomie* (October 1933).

29. This view was advocated by Rudolf Streller, *Statik und Dynamik in der theoretischen Nationalökonomie* (Leipzig, 1926).

30. A similar proposal, though arrived at by different considerations, was made by James W. Angell, "Monetary Control and General Business Stabilization," in *Essays in Honor of Gustav Cassel* (London, 1967).

31. Hayek, *Prices and Production.*

32. Idem, "A Note on the Development of the Doctrine of 'Forced Savings,'" *Quarterly Journal of Economics* (November 1932).

33. Dennis Holme Robertson, "Some Notes on Mr. Keynes' General Theory of Employment," *Quarterly Journal of Economics* (1936). About various meanings attached to the concept of "forced savings," see Fritz Machlup, "Forced Individual Saving:

An Exploration into Synonyms and Homonyms," *Review of Economics and Statistics* (February 1943).

34. Gottfried Haberler, *Prosperity and Depression* (Geneva, 1936). About the effects of forced savings on the formulation of capital, see Richard Strigl, *Kapital und Production* (Vienna, 1934).

35. J. G. Koopmans, "Zum Problem des Neutralen Geldes," in Hayek, ed., *Beiträge zur Geldtheorie.*

36. See Arthur Cecil Pigou, "The Monetary Theory of the Trade Cycle," *Economic Journal* (June 1929); R. G. Hawtrey, "The Monetary Theory of the Trade Cycle," *Economic Journal* (December 1929); and Arthur Cecil Pigou, "Comment," *Economic Journal* (December 1929).

37. Rosenstein-Rodan, "Coordination of Money and Price."

38. See, among others, E. Gregory, *The Gold Standard* (London, 1924); R. G. Hawtrey, *The Gold Standard in Theory and Practice* (London, 1927); E. Kellenberger, "Die Rolls des Geldes," *Zeitschrift für Schweizerische Statistik* (1939); Albert Aftalion, *Monnaie, prix et change* (Paris, 1927); and Louis Baudin, *La Monnaie et la formation des prix,* 2nd ed. (Paris, 1947).

39. See the recommendations of the International Monetary Conference held in Genoa in 1922. See also Fritz Machlup, *Die Goldkernwährung* (Halberstadt, 1925); and Sir Arthur Salter, *Recovery* (London, 1933). About criticisms of the gold exchange standard, see Jacques Rueff, *Défense et illustration de l'étalon d'or* (1932).

40. See Joseph Alois Schumpeter, "Kreditkontrolle," *Archiv für Sozialwissenschaft und Sozialpolitik* (1925).

41. In two articles ("Zur Theorie des Geldmarktes zugleich eine Analyse des englischen Geldmarkts bei lreier Währung," *Weltwirtschaftliches Archiv* [1935]; and "Neue Goldwährung," *Weltwirtschaftliches Archiv* [1937]), Friedrich A. Lutz listed four "pillars" which had supported the observance of the gold standard: abstention from measures of active business cycle politics, abstention from "dynamic" measures of protectionism, maintenance of price flexibility, and mutual reliance on the observance of the standard.

42. John Maynard Keynes, *A Tract on Monetary Reform* (London, 1923).

43. Cassel elaborated his monetary views in League of Nations, *Interim Report of the Gold Delegation of the Financial Committee* (Geneva, 1930).

44. See the criticisms of Josiah T. Phinney, "Gold Production and the Price Level: The Cassel Three Per Cent Estimate," *Quarterly Journal of Economics* (August 1933); Bertrand Nogaro, *La Monnaie et les phénomènes monétaires contemporains* (Paris, 1935), p. 278 ff.; A. D. Gayer, *Monetary Policy and Economic Stabilization* (London, 1935); and C. O.

Hardy, *Is There Enough Gold?* (Washington, D.C., 1935). For a good survey of the entire discussion, see Michael A. Heilperin, *International Monetary Economics* (New York, 1935), chap. 3.

45. See Haberler, *Der Sinn der Indexzahlen;* idem, "Kaufkraft des Geldes," *Jahrbuch für Gesetzgebung, Verwaltung und Volkswirtschaft* (1932); Hawtrey, "Money and Index Numbers," p. 64.

46. Carl Synder, "A New Index of the General Price Level, from 1875," *Journal of the American Statistical Association* (June 1924).

47. See Nogaro, *La Monnaie.* Similar ideas were advanced by Basileios B. Damalas, *Monnaie et conjoncture* (Paris, 1946).

48. See Fred A. Bradford, "Some Aspects of the Stable Money Question," *Quarterly Journal of Economics* (August 1929).

49. Henry C. Simons, *Economic Policy for the Society* (Chicago, 1948).

50. Elaborate Commodity Reserve Schemes were advanced by Benjamin Graham, *Storage and Stability* (New York, 1937); idem, *World Commodities and World Currency* (New York, 1944); and Frank D. Graham, *Social Goals and Economic Institutions* (Princeton, 1942). See also Friedrich A. Hayek, "A Commodity Reserve Currency," *Economic Journal* (1943); M. K. Bennett and Associates, *International Commodity Stockpiling As an Economic Stabilizer* (Stanford, 1949); Lloyd W. Mints, *Monetary Policy for a Competitive Society* (New York, 1950); and Milton Friedman, *Essays in Positive Economics* (Chicago, 1953), p. 204 ff.

51. Carl Föhl, *Geldschöpfung und Wirtschaftskreislauf* (Munich, 1937).

52. See Emile James, *Histoire de la pensée économique au XXe siècle* (Paris, 1955), pp. 466.

53. Pierre Dieterlen, "Inflation primaire, inflation secondaire," *Revue économique* (January 1953).

54. Bert Hansen, *A Study in the Theory of Inflation* (London, 1951).

55. James S. Duesenberry, "The Mechanics of Inflation," *Economie Appliquée* (1950).

56. Henri Aujac, "Une Hypothèse de travail: L'Inflation," *Economie Appliquée* (1950).

57. James, *Histoire de la pensée économique,* p. 471.

CHAPTER 32

1. An attempt to clarify some fundamental problems involved in business forecasting and to determine the use of the consumption function for forecasting purposes was made by Elmer C. Gratt, *Business Cycles and Forecasting* (Chicago, 1940).

2. John R. Hicks, "Gleichgewicht und Konjunktur," *Zeitschrift für Nationalökonomie* (June 1933).

3. The list of authors who adopted that approach to business cycle analysis included the Austrians Friedrich A. Hayek, Gottfried Haberler, Fritz Machlup, Richard Strigl, and Oskar Morgenstern; the Germans Walter Eucken, Georg Halm, Wilhelm Ropke, and Adolph Weber; the Italians Constantino Bresciani-Turroni and Marco Fanno; and the Englishman Lionel Robbins. See Friedrich A. Hayek's untitled article in Arthur Spiethoff, ed., *Der Stand und die nächste Zukunft der Konjunkturforschung* (Munich, 1933), p. 110.

4. A. D. Knox, "The Acceleration Principle," *Economica* (August 1952), p. 271.

5. See Ragnar Frisch, "The Interrelation between Capital Production and Consumer-Taking," *Journal of Political Economy* (October 1931); John M. Clark, "Capital Production and Consumer-Taking: A Reply," *Journal of Political Economy* (December 1931); Frisch, "A Rejoinder," *Journal of Political Economy* (April 1932); Clark, "Capital Production and Consumer-Taking: A Further Word," *Journal of Political Economy* (October 1932); Frisch, "A Final Word," *Journal of Political Economy* (October 1932).

6. Simon Kuznets, "Relations between Capital Goods and Finished Goods," in *Economic Essays in Honor of W. C. Mitchell* (New York, 1935).

7. Gottfried Haberler, *Prosperity and Depression* (Geneva, 1939), p. 195.

8. Arthur F. Burns and Wesley C. Mitchell, *Measuring Business Cycles* (New York, 1946).

9. Ibid., p. 412.

10. Willard L. Thorp, *Business Annals* (New York, 1926).

11. Oskar Morgenstern, "International Vergleichende Konjunkturforschung," *Zeitschrift für die Gesamte Staatswissenschaft* (1927).

12. A. von Mühlenfels, "Internationale Konjunkturzusammenhänge," *Jahrbuch für Nationalökonomie und Statistik* (1929).

13. E. Döblin, "Internationale Konjunkturabhängigkeit," *Archiv für Sozialwissenschaft und Sozialpolitik* (1933). See also Hans Neisser, *Some International Aspects of the Business Cycle* (Philadelphia, 1936).

14. Howard S. Ellis, *German Monetary Theory, 1905–1933* (Cambridge, Mass., 1934), p. 307.

15. L. Albert Hahn, *Volkswirtschaftliche Theorie des Bankkredits* (Tübingen, 1920).

16. Much later, in the course of his attacks on the Keynesian theory of employment, Hahn disavowed his credit theory. See L. Albert Hahn, *The Economics of Illusion* (New York, 1949), p. 6.

17. R. G. Hawtrey, *Currency and Credit* (London, 1919).

18. Alfred Marshall, *Official Papers* (London, 1926), pp. 34–35, 267.

19. See R. G. Hawtrey, *Monetary Reconstruction* (London, 1923).

20. Idem, Hawtrey, *The Art of Central Banking* (London, 1932).

21. Idem, *The Gold Standard in Theory and Practice* (London, 1927).

22. John Maynard Keynes, *Treatise on Money* (London, 1930), p. 298.

23. John Maynard Keynes, Karl Pribram, and E. J. Phelan, *Unemployment As a World Problem, Harris Foundation Lectures* (Chicago, 1931).

24. Irving Fisher, *Booms and Depressions* (New York, 1933), and "The Debt-Deflation Theory of Great Depressions," *Econometrica* (October 1933).

25. See Reuben A. Kessel, "Inflation-Caused Wealth Redistribution: A Test of a Hypothesis," *American Economic Review* (March 1956), p. 128 ff.

26. Friedrich A. Hayek, *Geldtheorie und Konjunkturtheorie* (Vienna, 1929), trans. N. Kaldor and H. M. Croome as *Monetary Theory and the Trade Cycle* (New York, 1933); *Prices and Production* (London, 1931). Later Hayek elaborated and partly modified his theory in *Profits, Interest and Investment* (London, 1939) and *Pure Theory of Capital* (London, 1941). The same approach was adopted by Fritz Machlup, *Börsenkredit, Industriekredit und Kapitalbildung* (Vienna, 1931); Richard Strigl, *Kapital und Produktion* (Vienna, 1934); and Lionel Robbins, *The Great Depression* (London, 1934).

27. See also Eric Schiff, *Kapitalbildung und Kapitalaufzehrung im Konjunkturverlauf* (Vienna, 1933). The errors in bookkeeping procedures caused by the failure to take account of the changing value of the monetary unit provided the background for the business cycle theory of Fritz Schmidt, *Die Industriekonjunktur Ein Rechenfehler* (Berlin, 1927).

28. See Friedrich A. Hayek, "The Ricardo Effect," *Economica* (May 1942).

29. Idem, *Profits, Interest and Investment*.

30. See idem, "Capital and Industrial Fluctuations," *Econometrica* (April 1934).

31. See especially Strigl, *Kapital und Produktion*, and Robbins, *Great Depression*.

32. Wilhelm Röpke, *Crisis and Cycles*, trans. Vera C. Smith (London, 1936).

33. Hans Neisser, "Monetary Expansion and The Structure of Production," *Social Research* (November 1934); Haberler, *Prosperity and Depression*, p. 49.

34. Gunnar Myrdal, in Friedrich A. Hayek, ed., *Beiträge zur Geldtheorie* (1933), p. 348.

35. See the extensive criticism of Hayek's theory by Nicholas Kaldor, "Professor Hayek and the Concertina Effect," *Economica* (November 1942).

36. About the operation of the Ricardo effect, see William J. Baumol, "The Analogy between Producer and Consumer Equilibrium Analysis," *Economica* (February 1950), p. 76.

37. Neisser, "Monetary Expansion."

38. Jan Tinbergen, "Critical Remarks on Some Business Cycle Theories," *Econometrica* (April 1942).

39. Alec L. Macfie, *Theories of the Trade Cycle* (London, 1934), p. 75.

40. Percival W. Martin, *The Flaw in the Price System* (London, 1924), and *Unemployment and Purchasing Power* (London, 1929). Other publications which derived measures of business cycle policy from similar considerations were John R. Bellerby, *Control of Credit* (London, 1923); E.F.M. Durbin, *Purchasing Power and Trade Depression* (London, 1933).

41. William T. Foster and Waddill Catchings, *Money* (Boston, 1923), and *Profits* (Boston, 1925). Not less than 435 authors participated in a competition for prizes to be granted to the best critical refutations of the Foster-Catchings theory. The prize essays were published in 1927 by the Pollak Foundation.

42. Dennis Holme Robertson, *A Study of Industrial Fluctuation* (London, 1915), and *Banking Policy and the Price Level* (London, 1926); Arthur Cecil Pigou, *Industrial Fluctuations* (London, 1927).

43. William J. Fellner, "The Robertsonian Evolution," *American Economic Review* (June 1952).

44. Dennis Holme Robertson, *Essays in Monetary Theory* (London, 1940).

45. The reactions of the economy to changes in the material conditions of production were also emphasized in the business cycle theories of some Italian economists such as Ugo Papi and Constantino Bresciani-Turroni.

46. Frederick Lavington, *The Trade Cycle* (London, 1922).

47. Frank W. Taussig, *Principles of Economics*, 3rd ed., 2 vols. (New York, 1925).

48. William Beveridge, *Unemployment* (London, 1930).

49. Marco Fanno, "Cicli di Produzione," *Giornale degli economisti e annali di economia* (1931).

50. John M. Clark, *The Economics of Overhead Costs* (Chicago, 1923).

51. Idem, *Strategic Factors in Business Cycles* (New York, 1934).

52. Idem, *Economics of Planning Public Works* (Washington, D.C., 1935), and "Cumulative Effects of Changes in Aggregate Spending as Illustrated by Public Works," *American Economic Review* (March, 1935).

53. Kuznets, "Capital Goods and Finished Goods."

54. Idem, "Equilibrium Economics and Cycle Theory," *Quarterly Journal of Economics* (May 1930).

55. See Paul N. Rosenstein-Rodan, "Das Zeitmoment in der Mathematischen Theorie des Wirtschaftlichen Gleichgewichts," *Zeitschrift für Nationalökonomie* (May 1929).

56. R. W. Souter, "Equilibrium Economics and Business Cycle Theory," *Quarterly Journal of Economics* (1931).

57. Joseph Alois Schumpeter, *Business Cycles: A Theoretical, Historical, and Statistical Analysis of the Capitalist Process*, 2 vols. (New York, 1939).

58. Joseph Kitchin, "Cycles and Trends in Economic Factors," *Review of Economics and Statistics* (1924). See also William L. Crum, "Cycles of Rates on Commercial Paper," *Review of Economics and Statistics* (January 1923).

59. Simon Kuznets, "Schumpeter's Business Cycles," *American Economic Review* (June 1940).

60. See Jan Tinbergen, "Schumpeter and Quantitative Research in Economics," *Review of Economics and Statistics* (May 1951), p. 109.

61. See Oskar Lange's review in *Review of Economics and Statistics* (November 1941). Eugen Slutsky had advanced his model in a paper published in 1927 by the Conjuncture Institute of Moscow (for a translation, see "The Summation of Random Causes As the Source of Cyclic Processes," *Econometrica* [April 1937]).

62. For a criticism of Schumpeter's interpretations of the Kondratieff and Kitchin cycles, see, among others, Rendigs Fels, "The Theory of Business Cycles," *Quarterly Journal of Economics* (February 1952), and William J. Fellner, *Trends and Cycles in Economic Activity* (New York, 1956).

63. Haberler, *Prosperity and Depression*.

64. Oskar Morgenstern, *The Limits of Economics* (London, 1937), p. 89. Gerhard Tintner, *Prices in the Trade Cycle* (Vienna, 1935); Jan Tinbergen, "Die Preise im Konjunkturverlauf," *Zeitschrift für Nationalökonomie* (1936), p. 104.

65. This approach was adopted by Sumner H. Slichter, "The Period 1919–1936 in the United States: Its Significance for Business Cycle Theory," *Review of Economics and Statistics* (February 1937); Thomas Wilson, *Fluctuations in Income and Employment* (London, 1942); Robert A. Gordon, "Business Cycles in the Interwar Period: The 'Quantitative-Historical Approach,'" *American Economic Review* (May 1949); John H. Williams, "An Appraisal of Keynesian Economics," *American Economic Review* (May 1948), p. 11.

66. Kondratief's findings were summarized in "Die langen Wellen der Konjunktur," *Archiv für Sozialwissenschaft und Sozialpolitik* (1926) and "Die Preisdynamik der Industriellen und landwirtschaftlichen Waren," *Archiv für Sozialwissenschaft und Sozialpolitik* (1928). See also George Gary, "Kondratieff's Theory of Long Cycles," *Review of Economics and Statistics* (November 1943).

67. See Haberler, *Prosperity and Depression*, p. 176.

68. See, for instance, Léon H. Dupriez, *Philo-*

sophie des conjonctures économiques (Louvain, 1959).

69. François Simiand, *Les Fluctuations économiques à longue période* (Paris, 1932).

70. M. Saitzew, *Die Lange Welle der Arbeitslosigkeit* (Munich, 1932).

71. See T. McLintock Whitin, ed., *Theory of Inventory Management* (Princeton, 1953).

72. Arthur F. Burns, "Long Cycles in Residential Construction," in *Economic Essays in Honor of W. C. Mitchell;* Clarence D. Long, Jr., *Building Cycles and the Theory of Investment* (Princeton, 1940); J.B.D. Derksen, "Long Cycles in Residential Building," *Econometrica* (1940).

73. See *Monetary Policy and the Depression: A First Report on International Monetary Problems by a Group of the Royal Institute of International Affairs* (London, 1933), chap. 5.

74. See, for instance, the critical examination of antidepression measures in Alvin H. Hansen, *Economic Stabilization in an Unbalanced World* (New York, 1932), and idem, "The Maintenance of Purchasing Power," *Economic Essays in Honor of Gustav Cassel* (New York, 1933).

75. R. G. Hawtrey, *Trade and Credit* (London, 1928).

76. Karl Gustav Cassel, *Soziale Praxis,* 35, p. 1057 ff.

77. *International Labor Office Studies and Reports* C. 15 (1931).

78. See G. Bielschowsky, "Business Fluctuations and Public Works," *Quarterly Journal of Economics* (February 1930), p. 289 ff., and a well-reasoned study by Hans Richter, *Volkswirtschaftliche Theorie der öffentlichen Investitionen* (Munich, 1936).

CHAPTER 33

1. These discussions, which were published in the *Ekonomisk Tidskrift,* started in 1898 with an article in which David Davidson reviewed Wicksell's first great contribution to economic analysis, *Geldzins und Güterpreise* (Jena, 1898).

2. See Bertil Ohlin, "Some Notes on the Stockholm Theory of Savings and Investments," *Economic Journal* (June 1937), reprinted in *Readings in Business Cycle Theory* (Philadelphia, 1944). See also Gunnar Myrdal, *Value in Social Theory* (London, 1958), p. 249; André Marchal, *Revue d'économie politique* (January 1942); and Tord Palander, "On the Concepts and Methods of the Stockholm School," trans. R. S. Stedman, in *International Economic Papers,* 12 vols. (London, 1951–62), vol. 3.

3. In an article which Wicksell published in 1925 in *Ekonomisk Tidskrift,* he questioned the constancy of the velocity of circulation of money and

derived from these doubts strong arguments against the validity of the quantity theory. See Eric Lundberg, *Business Cycles and Economic Policy* (Cambridge, Mass., 1957), p. 156.

4. Myrdal stated that analysis in his doctoral dissertation, "Price Formation and Variability" (1927). He continued these studies in the essay "Der Gleichgewichtsbegriff als Instrument der geldtheoretischen Analyse," in Friedrich A. Hayek, ed., *Beiträge zur Geldlehre* trans. (Vienna, 1939).

5. In view of the existing variety of money and credit markets, Wicksell's disciples substituted the term *market rate* for the term *bank rate* in Hayek, ed., *Beiträge zur Geldtheorie,* p. 274.

6. These considerations were advanced as early as 1899 by D. Davidson. See Eli Filip Heckscher, "David Davidson," trans. M. A. Michael, in *International Economic Papers,* 12 vols. (London, 1951–62), 2: 132.

7. Eric Lindahl, *Studies in the Theory of Money and Capital* (New York, 1939). These studies included as part three an essay on "The Place of Capital in the Theory of Price."

8. A similar idea had been basic to the period analysis adopted by Dennis Holme Robertson in his *Banking Policy and the Price Level* (London, 1926).

9. Johan Åkerman's article, "Ekonomisk Kalkyl och Kausalanalys," *Ekonomisk Tidskrift* (1942), was reproduced as "Economic Plans and Causal Analysis," in *International Economic Papers,* 12 vols. (London, 1951–62), vol. 4.

10. For a broad analysis of the practical aspects of these problems, see Lundberg, *Business Cycles.*

11. See Ohlin, "Stockholm Theory," p. 93, and Lundberg, *Business Cycles,* p. 110 ff.

12. Lundberg, *Business Cycles,* p. 112 ff.

13. Lundberg, *Business Cycles,* p. 124.

14. Bertil Ohlin, *The Problem of Employment Stabilization* (New York, 1949), pp. 28, 76.

15. Eric Lundberg, *Studies in the Theory of Economic Expansion* (London, 1937).

16. In his study of the development of wages, Alf Johannsson conceived of the cyclical problem not primarily as a problem of prices and cost adjustments, but as a problem of mutual adjustments of quantitative relations between the successive stages of a productive process. See Lundberg, *Business Cycles,* p. 73.

17. That definition was used by Dag Hammarskjöld in his study dealing with the diffusion of economic fluctuations (*Konjunkturspridningen* [Stockholm, 1933]).

18. Lundberg, *Economic Expansion,* p. 243.

19. Idem, *Business Cycles,* p. 109.

20. Harold Dickson, *Weltwirtschaftliches Archiv* (1951), and Hans Brems, "Current Economic Thought in Europe: The Scandinavian Countries," *American Economic Review* (May 1956), p. 354.

21. Lundberg, *Business Cycles,* p. 160.

22. About the methods used by the Konjunkturinstitut for measuring the "inflationary gap," see ibid., p. 179 ff.

23. Eric Lindahl, "Swedish Experiences in Economic Planning," *American Economic Review* (May 1950), p. 11 ff.

CHAPTER 34

1. John Maynard Keynes, *The General Theory of Employment, Interest and Money* (New York, 1936).

2. Seymour E. Harris, "Ten Years After: What Remains of the *General Theory*," in Seymour E. Harris, ed., *The New Economics* (New York, 1947), p. 46. Harris was the editor of this collection of essays, which surveyed the influence of the Keynesian teachings on Anglo-American economics.

3. This qualification of Keynes's *General Theory* was proposed by John R. Hicks, "Mr. Keynes and the Classics," *Econometrica* (April 1937). See also Calvin B. Hoover, "Keynes and the Economic System," *Journal of Political Economy* (October 1948), p. 397; and D. McCord Wright, "The Future of Keynesian Economics," *American Economic Review* (June 1945), p. 295.

4. About the Keynesian interpretation of Say's Law, see, among others, Gary S. Becker and William J. Baumol, "The Classical Monetary Theory," *Economica* (November 1952).

5. Arthur Cecil Pigou, *Theory of Unemployment* (London, 1933). For discussions of Pigou's theory, see Edwin Cannan, "Demand for Labor," *Economic Journal* (1932); Pigou, "Real and Money Wage Rates in Relation to Unemployment," *Economic Journal* (September 1937); Hicks, "Keynes and the Classics"; Alvin H. Hansen, "Keynes on Economic Policy," in Harris, ed., *New Economics*, p. 200.

6. Keynes, *General Theory*, p. 32.

7. John Maynard Keynes, "The General Theory of Employment," *Quarterly Journal of Economics* (February 1937), reprinted in Harris, ed., *New Economics*, chap. 15.

8. Keynes, *General Theory*, p. 247.

9. Gottfried Haberler, "The Place of the General Theory of Employment, Interest, and Money in the History of Economic Thought," *Review of Economics and Statistics* (November 1946), p. 193; Wright, "Keynesian Economics"; Joseph Alois Schumpeter, "Keynes, the Economist," in Harris, ed., *New Economics*, chap. 9.

10. Joan Robinson, *The Rate of Interest* (London, 1952), p. 69.

11. Tjarden Creidanus, *The Development of Keynes' Economic Theories* (1939), p. 29.

12. Keynes, *General Theory*, p. 347. It would be tempting to analyze the changing attitudes toward saving and investment in the light of indifferences in prevailing patterns of thought. Conditions which were favorable to large-scale private investments were created only under the rule of nominalist thinking.

13. Ibid., p. 96.

14. Lloyd A. Metzler, "Keynes and the Theory of Business Cycles," in Harris, ed., *New Economics*, chap. 23, p. 438.

15. See also Armen A. Alchian, "The Rate of Interest," *American Economic Review* (December 1955), p. 938.

16. Keynes, *General Theory*, p. 293.

17. Chap. 20 of Keynes's *General Theory*, entitled "Notes on the Trade Cycle."

18. Karl Gustav Cassel, *Nature and Necessity of Interest* (London, 1903).

19. Roy F. Harrod, "Keynes, The Economist," in Harris, ed., *New Economics*, p. 69. See also Amedeo Gambino, "L'Offerta di moneta talone d'achilli dei modelli Keynesiani," *Giornale degli economisti e annali di economia* (July 1952), p. 415.

20. Harris, ed., *New Economics*, chap. 15, p. 187.

21. Keynes, *General Theory*, p. 307 ff.

22. Ibid., p. 31.

23. Ibid., p. 351 ff.

24. See ibid., chap. 23, p. 340.

25. R. F. Kahn, "The Relation of Home Investment to Employment," *Economic Journal* (June 1931).

26. For an analysis of the streams of thought which contributed to the formulation of the multiplier theorem, see G.L.S. Shackle, "A Survey of the Theory of the Multiplier," *Economic Journal* (June 1951).

27. See Hugo Hegeland, *The Multiplier Theory* (Lund, 1954), p. 26 ff.

28. For the mathematical aspects of the multiplier theorem, see R. M. Goodwin, "The Multiplier," in Harris, ed., *New Economics*, chap. 36.

29. Evsey D. Domar, *Essays in the Theory of Economic Growth* (New York, 1957), p. 6.

30. Joan Robinson, *An Essay on Marxian Economics* (London, 1942); Paul M. Sweezy, *The Theory of Capitalist Development* (New York, 1946).

31. Lawrence R. Klein, "Theory of Effective Demand," *Journal of Political Economy* (1947); J. Steindl, *Maturity and Stagnation in American Capitalism* (Oxford, 1952), chap. 14. See, however, Shigetu Tsuru, "Keynes Versus Marx: The Methodology of Aggregates," in Kenneth K. Kurihara, ed., *Post-Keynesian Economics* (New Brunswick, 1954), chap. 12.

32. Robinson, *Marxian Economics*, p. 74.

33. Keynes, *General Theory*, p. 379.

34. For a list of such passages where Keynes

expressed his belief in the free economic forces in the exercise of private initiative and individual responsibility, see Hansen, "Keynes on Economic Policy," p. 204.

CHAPTER 35

1. Roy F. Harrod, "Mr. Keynes and Traditional Theory," in Robert Leckachman, ed., *Keynes General Theory: Reports of Three Decades* (New York, 1963), p. 140.

2. Paul A. Samuelson, in Leckachman, ed., *Keynes General Theory,* p. 321.

3. For a critical discussion of this view, see Gottfried Haberler, *Prosperity and Depression* (Geneva, 1936), p. 270.

4. See Joan Robinson, *An Essay on Marxian Economics* (London, 1942), p. 74.

5. See, among others, John R. Hicks, "Mr. Keynes and the 'Classics,'" *Econometrica* (April 1937); Gary S. Becker and William J. Baumol, "The Classical Monetary Theory: The Outcome of the Discussion," *Economica* (November 1952); Joseph Alois Schumpeter, *History of Economic Analysis* (New York, 1954), p. 615 ff.; and Jacob Viner, "Mr. Keynes and the Causes of Unemployment," *Quarterly Journal of Economics* (November 1936). The Keynesian concept of hoarding was defended by Joan Robinson, "The Concept of Hoarding," *Economic Journal* (June 1938). About the question of whether in a highly developed economy full employment could be maintained only at the cost of a declining national dividend, see G. R. Holden, "Mr. Keynes' Consumption Function and the Time-Preference Postulate," *Quarterly Journal of Economics* (February 1938), and John M. Keynes, "Mr. Keynes' Consumption Function: Reply," *Quarterly Journal of Economics* (August 1938).

6. Bertil Ohlin, *The Problem of Employment and Stabilization* (New York, 1949), p. 144 ff; and Dennis Holme Robertson, *Essays in Monetary Theory* (London, 1940), p. 21.

7. See also Armen A. Alchian, "The Rate of Interest," *American Economic Review* (December 1955), p. 938.

8. Arthur Smithies, "Effective Demand and Employment," in Seymour E. Harris, ed., *The New Economics* (New York, 1942), chap. 39, p. 559.

9. See R. Ruggles, *National Income and Income Analysis* (New York, 1949).

10. See Abba P. Lerner, "Saving and Investment," *Quarterly Journal of Economics* (1937–38).

11. Friedrich A. Lutz, "The Outcome of the Saving-Investment Discussion," *Quarterly Journal of Economics* (August 1938); Bertil Ohlin, "Some Notes on the Stockholm Theory of Savings and Investments," *Economic Journal* (June 1937).

12. Haberler, *Prosperity and Depression,* chap. 8. For a discussion of the Keynesian identification of savings and investments, see also Lawrence R. Klein, *The Keynesian Revolution* (New York, 1947), p. 110.

13. See Dennis Holme Robertson, "Saving and Hoarding," *Economic Journal* (September 1933).

14. Ohlin, *Employment and Stabilization,* p. 144 ff.

15. The loan fund theory was defended by Bertil Ohlin, Dennis Holme Robertson, Gottfried Haberler, and others.

16. See Abba P. Lerner, "Alternative Formulations of the Theory of Interest," *Economic Journal* (June 1938); John R. Hicks, *Value and Capital* (Oxford, 1939), chap. 12; William J. Fellner and H. M. Somers, "Alternative Monetary Approaches to Interest Theory," *Review of Economics and Statistics* (February 1941).

17. See also D. McCord Wright, "The Future of Keynesian Economics," *American Economic Review* (June 1945), p. 292.

18. S. C. Tsiang, "Liquidity Preference and Loanable Funds Theories," *American Economic Review* (September 1956); see also Gardner Ackley, "Liquidity Preference and Loanable Funds Theories of Interest: Comment," *American Economic Review* (September 1957).

19. About the difference between the two conceptions, see Oskar Morgenstern, "Professor Hicks on Value and Capital," *Journal of Political Economy* (June 1941), p. 386, and Friedrich A. Lutz, "The Structure of Interest Rates," *Quarterly Journal of Economics* (November 1940).

20. See Gottfried Haberler, Claude Gruson, and Friedrich A. Lutz, "La Place de la théorie générale de l'emploi, de l'intérêt et de la monnaie dans l'histoire de la pensée economique," *Economie appliquée* (1948), and Emile James, *Histoire de la pensée économique au XXᵉ siècle* (Paris, 1955), p. 352. About the role played by the liquidity preference in the history of savings, see Eli Filip Heckscher, *Mercantilism* (London, 1955), 2: 348 ff.

21. Robinson, "Hoarding."

22. Robertson, *Monetary Theory,* p. 21 ff.

23. Viner, "Keynes and Unemployment."

24. John H. Williams, "An Appraisal of Keynesian Economics," *American Economic Review* (May 1948), p. 281.

25. Gardiner C. Means, "The American Economy in the Interwar Period: Discussion," *American Economic Review* (May 1946), p. 35.

26. Franco Modigliani, "Liquidity Preference, Interest and Money," *Econometrica* (January 1944); Klein, *Keynesian Revolution.*

27. Gottfried Haberler, "The General Theory," in Harris, ed., *New Economics,* p. 165.

28. Jacob Marschak and Helen Makower, "As-

sets, Prices and Monetary Theory," *Economica* (August 1938).

29. Simon Kuznets, "Relations between Capital Goods and Finished Goods," in *Economic Essays in Honor of W. C. Mitchell* (New York, 1935).

30. See Alvin H. Hansen, *Fiscal Policy and Business Cycles* (New York, 1941), and the bibliographical references cited in this book.

31. See Franco Modigliani and Ricard Brumberg, "Utility Analysis and the Consumption Function," in Kenneth K. Kurihara, ed., *Post-Keynesian Economics* (New Brunswick, 1954), chap. 15.

32. See Ohlin, "Stockholm Theory"; Henry H. Villard, *Deficit Spending and National Income* (New York, 1941); William J. Fellner, *Monetary Policies and Full Employment* (Berkeley, 1946); James S. Duesenberry, *Income, Savings and the Theory of Consumer Behavior* (Cambridge, Mass., 1949). See also G.L.S. Shackle, "A Survey of the Theory of the Multiplier," *Economic Journal* (June 1951); Trygve Haavelmo, "Methods of Measuring the Marginal Propensity to Consume," *Econometrica* (1947); and Jan Tinbergen, "Does Consumption Lag behind Income?," *Review of Economics and Statistics* (1942).

33. Arthur F. Burns, *The Instability of Consumer Spending*, Report of the National Bureau of Economic Research (New York, 1952).

34. Simon S. Kuznets, "Capital Formation, 1879–1938," *Studies in Economics and Industrial Relations* (Philadelphia, 1941).

35. Wright, "Keynesian Economics," p. 302.

36. Paul A. Samuelson, "Consumption Theory in Terms of Revealed Preference," *Econometrica* (November 1948).

37. Milton Friedman, *A Theory of Consumption Function* (Princeton, 1957).

38. Richard Schüller, "Keynes' Theorie der Nachfrage nach Arbeit," *Zeitschrift für Nationalökonomie* (1936).

39. Shackle, "Theory of the Multiplier," p. 250; and Hugo Hegeland, *The Multiplier Theory* (Lund, 1954), p. 63.

40. For a discussion of the effects of government spending published by the American National Association of Manufacturers, see P. A. Samuelson, ed., *Readings in Economics* (New York, 1952), p. 145.

41. See Arthur Smithies, "The Multiplier," *American Economic Review* (May 1948), p. 299 ff.

42. Various methods of establishing approximate numerical value for multipliers were examined by Richard and W. M. Stone in *Review of Economic Studies* (1938).

43. About these questions, see Fritz Machlup, *International Trade and the National Income Multiplier* (Philadelphia, 1943), p. 7 ff.

44. See the discussion of the multiplier problem in *American Economic Review* (May 1948), p. 306.

45. Gottfried Haberler, *Prosperity and Depression*, 3rd ed. (Geneva, 1941), p. 22 ff; Henry H. Villard, "Monetary Theory," in Howard S. Ellis, ed., *Survey of Contemporary Economics* (Philadelphia, 1949), p. 328.

46. Arthur Cecil Pigou, *Employment and Equilibrium* (London, 1941); Valentin F. Wagner, "Sparen und Vollbeschäftigung," *Zeitschrift für Nationalökonomie* (1954).

47. Robertson, *Essays in Monetary Theory*, p. 121.

48. The Keynesian interpretation of the position of the Ricardian economists was defended by Don Patinkin in a series of articles: "Relative Prices, Say's Law, and the Demand for Money," *Econometrica* (April 1948); "The Indeterminacy of Absolute Prices in Classical Economic Theory," *Econometrica* (January 1949); "Involuntary Unemployment and the Keynesian Supply Function," *American Economic Review* (September 1949); and "A Reconsideration of the General Equilibrium Theory of Money," *Review of Economic Studies* (1950).

49. For a discussion of these problems, see Arthur W. Marget, *The Theory of Prices* (New York, 1938), vol. 1, and Don Patinkin, "Keynesian Economics and the Quantity Theory," in Kurihara, ed., *Post-Keynesian Economics*, chap. 5.

50. See James R. Schlesinger, "After Twenty Years: The General Theory," *Quarterly Journal of Economics* (November 1956). See also Haberler, "General Theory," chap. 14, p. 167.

51. Wassily W. Leontief, "Postulates: Keynes' General Theory and the Classicists," in Harris, ed., *New Economics*, p. 233. See also Patinkin, "Involuntary Unemployment and the Keynesian Supply Function."

52. John Maynard Keynes, *General Theory of Employment, Interest and Money* (London, 1936), chap. 9. See also Lloyd A. Metzler, "Wealth, Savings and the Rate of Interest," *Journal of Political Economy* (April 1951).

53. Arthur Cecil Pigou, "The Classical Stationary State," *Economic Journal* (December 1953); idem, "Economic Progress in a Stable Environment," *Economica* (1947).

54. See Haberler, *Prosperity and Depression*, p. 403; idem, "The Pigou Effect Once More," *Journal of Political Economy* (June 1952); Alvin H. Hansen, "The Pigouvian Effect," *Journal of Political Economy* (December 1951).

55. Pigou, *Employment and Equilibrium*.

56. L. Albert Hahn, *The Economics of Illusion* (New York, 1949), p. 141.

57. Jacques Rueff, "The Fallacies of Lord Keynes' General Theory," *Quarterly Journal of Economics* (May 1947).

58. For a defense of the assumptions underlying

the Keynesian wage theorem, see James Tobin, "The Fallacies of Lord Keynes' General Theory: Comment," *Quarterly Journal of Economics* (November 1948). See also Gabriel Ardent, "A propos de la 'Théorie générale' de Lord Keynes," *Revue d'economie politique* (1947), p. 380.

59. The effects of changes in the monetary wage rate on the level of employment were discussed by James Tobin, "Money Wage Rates and Employment," in Harris, ed., *New Economics,* chap. 40; Smithies, "Effective Demand and Employment," chap. 39; Haberler, "General Theory," p. 167 ff.; and Lloyd G. Reynolds, "Wages in the Business Cycle," *American Economic Review* (May 1952), p. 86.

60. See Oskar Lange, *Price Flexibility and Employment* (Bloomington, 1944).

61. J. Shister, "Business Cycle Theory: Discussion," *American Economic Review* (May 1952), p. 105; see also Reynolds, "Wages in the Business Cycle," and the literature cited by the two economists.

62. John M. Clark, "Some Current Cleavages among Economists," *American Economic Review* (May 1947), p. 2.

63. Keynes, *General Theory,* pp. 308–9. See Schlesinger, "After Twenty Years," p. 584.

64. See Keynes, *General Theory,* chap. 16.

65. Joan Robinson, *Introduction to the Theory of Employment* (London, 1938). For a critical theoretical examination of the "New Economics of Spending," see Hans Neisser, *Econometrica* (July 1944).

66. Alvin H. Hansen, *Full Recovery or Stagnation* (New York, 1938); *Fiscal Policy and Business Cycles; Economic Policy and Full Employment* (New York, 1947); and *Business Cycles and National Income* (New York, 1951).

67. Hansen, *Fiscal Policy and Business Cycles,* p. 47. Another convinced adherent of the stagnation theorem was Paul M. Sweezy, "Secular Stagnation," in Seymour E. Harris, ed., *Postwar Economic Problems* (New York, 1943), and "Declining Investment Opportunities," in Harris, ed., *New Economics.* In Canada, the stagnation theory was elaborated by Benjamin Higgins. See his "Doctrine of Economic Maturity," *American Economic Review* (1946) and "The Concept of Secular Stagnation," *American Economic Review* (1950), and "The Modern Theory of Economic Fluctuations," in G. E. Hoover, ed., *Twentieth Century Economic Thought* (New York, 1950).

68. *Economic Program for the American Democracy* (New York, 1938).

69. See also Arthur Smithies, "Federal Budgeting and Fiscal Policy," in Ellis, ed., *Survey of Contemporary Economics.*

70. Michael Kalecki, *An Essay on the Theory of Business Cycle* (New York, 1933); *Theory of Economic Dynamics* (London, 1954).

71. See J. Steindl, *Maturity and Stagnation in American Capitalism* (Oxford, 1952).

72. See Robinson, *Marxian Economics.*

73. Keynes, *General Theory,* p. 378.

74. Sir William Beveridge, *Full Employment in a Free Society* (London, 1944).

75. Ibid., p. 252. A more fully elaborated system of planning organized on the lines suggested by Beveridge was proposed by Barbara Wooton, *Freedom under Planning* (Chapel Hill, 1945).

76. *The Economics of Full Employment,* Studies Prepared by the Oxford Institute of Statistics (Oxford, 1944).

77. William J. Fellner, "Employment Theory," in Ellis, ed., *Contemporary Economics,* 1: 88.

78. Dennis Holme Robertson, ed., *The Business Cycle in the Post-War World* (London, 1955), p. 9. See also Eric Lundberg, *Wages Policy under Full Employment,* trans. Ralph Turvey (London, 1952); and Lionel Robbins, *The Economist in the Twentieth Century* (London, 1954), p. 21.

79. *Economist,* 9 December 1950, p. 980, and 13 August 1951, p. 38. See also the article "The Uneasy Triangle," *Economist,* August 1952.

80. M. Bronfenbrenner, "Some Neglected Implications of Secular Inflation," in Kurihara, ed., *Post-Keynesian Economics,* chap. 2. See also Jacob Viner, "Full Employment at Whatever Cost," *Quarterly Journal of Economics* (August 1950).

81. Pigou, *Employment and Equilibrium;* idem, "Classical Stationary State"; Tibor Scitovsky, "Capital Accumulation, Employment and Price Rigidity," *Review of Economic Studies* (February 1941); Haberler, *Prosperity and Depression,* p. 491 ff. See also Lloyd Metzler, "Wealth, Savings and Interest"; and Gardner Ackley, "The Wealth-Saving Relationship," *Journal of Political Economy.* The Keynesian theorem concerning the effects of capital accumulation on the marginal efficiency of capital was defended by Joan Robinson, *The Accumulation of Capital* (London, 1956).

82. William J. Fellner, "The Technological Argument of the Stagflation Thesis," *Quarterly Journal of Economics* (August 1941), p. 642.

83. George Terborgh, *The Bogey of American Maturity* (Chicago, 1945). See also W. T. King, "Are We Suffering from Economic Maturity?," *Journal of Political Economy* (October 1939); Simon Kuznets, *Review of Economics and Statistics* (1942), p. 32 ff; Wright, "Keynesian Economics"; B. Graham, "Money as Pure Commodity," *American Economic Review* (May 1947), p. 387. Arthur F. Burns, *Economic Research and Keynesian Thinking* (New York, 1946); Howard S. Ellis, "Monetary Policy and Investment," *Readings in Business Cycle Theory* (1944); Melvin D. Brockie, "Population Growth and the Rate of Investment," *Southern Eco-*

nomic Journal (July 1950); George Garvy, "The Role of Dissaving in Economic Analysis," *Journal of Political Economy* (October 1948).

84. Simon Kuznets, *National Product since 1889* (New York, 1946).

85. Calvin B. Hoover, "Keynes and the Economic System," *Journal of Political Economy* (October 1948), p. 400.

86. D. McCord Wright, *The Economics of Distribution* (New York, 1947), *Democracy and Progress* (New York, 1948), and *Capitalism* (New York, 1951).

87. Erik Lundberg, *Business Cycles and Economic Policy* (Cambridge, Mass., 1957), p. 159. For a discussion of the experiences in Sweden during 1945–51 with full employment policies, see ibid., chaps. 10 and 11.

88. See James, *La pensée économique*, p. 355 f.

89. See André Marchal, *La Pensée économique en France, depuis 1945* (Paris, 1953), p. 37.

90. *Travaux du Congrès des Economistes de Langue Française* (Paris, 1951).

91. Henri Guitton, *Les Fluctuations économiques* (Paris, 1951).

92. See also Charles Rist, "La Théorie de maturité économique," *Révue d'économie politique* (1947).

93. For a critical discussion of mistaken objections by German economists to the Keynesian theory, see E. Schneider, *Jahrbuch für Nationalökonomie und Statistik* (May 1953), p. 94.

94. *Vollbeschäftigung, Inflation und Planwirtschaft*, ed. A. Hunold (Zurich, 1951).

95. See *American Economic Review* (May 1957).

96. See the papers of Dudley Dillard (p. 82), William J. Fellner (p. 69), and W. Salant (p. 91), in *American Economic Review* Proceedings (May 1957).

97. Tibor Scitovsky, ibid., p. 94. See also Harlan L. McCracken, *Keynesian Economics in the Stream of Thought* (Baton Rouge, 1961).

98. Ellis, *Contemporary Economics*.

CHAPTER 36

1. Evsey D. Domar, "The Theoretical Analysis of Economic Growth: An Econometric Approach," *American Economic Review* (May 1952), p. 479. About the assumptions and artificial abstractions which provided the background to the imaginary picture of a static competitive economy, see Frank H. Knight, *Risk, Uncertainty and Profit* (Boston, 1921), p. 76.

2. John Neville Keynes, *The Scope and Method of Political Economy* (London, 1891), p. 141.

3. Maffeo Pantaleoni, "Di alcuni fenomeni di dinamica economica," (Padua, 1909), reprinted in *Erotemi de economia* 2 (1925).

4. This assumption was questioned by Edward H. Chamberlin, *The Theory of Monopolistic Competition* (Cambridge, Mass., 1933), p. 6.

5. See Johan Akerman, "Dynamische Wertprobleme," *Zeitschrift für Nationalökonomie* (1931).

6. See Rudolf Streller, *Statik und Dynamik in der Theoretischen Nationalökonomie* (Leipzig, 1926). In his own analysis Streller used the time factor to differentiate the two concepts.

7. See M. R. Weyermann, *Die Konjunktur und ihre Beziehungen zur Wirtschaftsstruktur* (Jena, 1929).

8. Werner Sombart, *Die drei Nationalökonomien* (Munich, 1930), p. 187.

9. Alfred Amonn, *Grundzüge der Volkswirtschaftslehre* (Jena, 1926), p. 275. Ludwig von Mises, "Soziologie und Geschichte," *Archiv für Sozialwissenschaft und Sozialpolitik* (1929). Emma Schams, "Komparative Statik," *Zeitschrift für Nationalökonomie* (1931). See also Joseph Alois Schumpeter, *History of Economic Analysis* (New York, 1954), p. 965.

10. Enrico Barone, "Sul trattamento delle questioni dinamiche," *Giornale degli economisti e annali di economia* (November 1894).

11. See Joseph Alois Schumpeter's *Wesen und der Hauptinhalt der theoretischen nationalökonomie* (Leipzig, 1908), pt. 4.

12. Schams, "Komparative Statik." The use of the term *comparative statics* had been suggested by Franz Oppenheimer, *Wert und Kapitalprofit* (Jena, 1916).

13. Frank H. Knight, *The Ethics of Competition* (London, 1935), "Statics and Dynamics."

14. See idem, *Freedom and Reform* (New York, 1947).

15. Luigi Amoroso, "La meccanica economica," *Giornale degli economisti e annali di economia* (1924).

16. Abba P. Lerner, "Some Swedish Stepping Stones in Economic Theory," *Canadian Journal of Economics* (November 1940), p. 574 ff.

17. John M. Clark, "Relations between Statics and Dynamics," in Jacob H. Hollander, ed., *Economic Essays in Honor of J. B. Clark* (New York, 1927).

18. Simon Kuznets, "Static and Dynamic Economics," *American Economic Review* (1930).

19. Paul N. Rosenstein-Rodan, "The Role of Time in Economic Theory," *Economica* (1934).

20. The development of the dynamic approach was surveyed by Jan Tinbergen, "Ein Problem der Dynamik," *Zeitschrift für Nationalökonomie* (1932).

21. Dennis Holme Robertson, *Banking Policy and the Price Level* (London, 1926).

22. Tinbergen, "Ein Problem der Dynamik."

23. Roy F. Harrod, "Scope and Method of Economics," *Economic Journal* (September 1938).

24. Eventually Joseph Schumpeter joined the group; see his *Business Cycles: A Theoretical, Historical and Statistical Analysis of the Capitalist Process,* 2 vols. (New York, 1939).

25. For a defense of the methods of comparative statics, see Kenneth E. Boulding, "In Defense of Statics," *Quarterly Journal of Economics* (November 1955). Boulding argued that economic knowledge had been acquired largely through methods of comparative statics.

26. About problems connected with economic stability, see, among others, Ragnar Frisch, "On the Notion of Equilibrium and Disequilibrium," *Review of Economic Studies* (February 1936); Paul A. Samuelson, "The Stability of Equilibrium," *Econometrica* (April 1941), and "A Note on Alternative Regressions" (January 1942).

27. Ragnar Frisch developed the difference between static and dynamic analysis in "Equilibrium."

28. Paul A. Samuelson, "Dynamics, Statics and the Stationary State," *Review of Economics and Statistics* (February 1943).

29. William C. Hood, "Some Aspects of the Treatment of Time," *Canadian Journal of Economics and Political Science* (November 1948).

30. Michael Kalecki, *Theory of Economic Dynamics* (London, 1954).

31. This proposition was defended by Alvin H. Hansen, "Economic Progress and Declining Population Growth," *American Economic Review* (March 1939).

32. John H. Williams, "An Appraisal of Keynesian Economics," *American Economic Review* (May 1948); See also Bertil Ohlin, *The Problem of Employment Stabilization* (New York, 1949), p. 43.

33. G.L.S. Shackle, *Uncertainty in Economics* (Cambridge, 1955), p. 222.

34. Georges Lutfalla, "La Métastatique," *Econometrica* (July 1949), supplement, p. 283.

35. S. D. Merlin, *The Theory of Fluctuations in Contemporary Economic Thought* (New York, 1949), chap. 5.

36. See Lloyd A. Metzler, "Keynes and the Theory of Business Cycles," in Seymour E. Harris, ed., *The New Economics* (New York, 1947), chap. 33.

37. Roy F. Harrod, *Towards a Dynamic Economics* (London, 1948).

38. Previous references to this method of analysis had been made by N. Johannsson, Arthur Cecil Pigou, John M. Clark, and some Scandinavian authors. See Hugo Hegeland, *The Multiplier Theory* (Lund, 1954), pp. 14 ff.

39. Alvin H. Hansen, "Toward a Dynamic Theory of the Cycle," *American Economic Review* (May 1952), p. 77.

40. Fritz Machlup, "Period Analysis and Multiplier Theory," *Quarterly Journal of Economics* (1939). See also Gardner Ackley, "The Multiplier Time Period," *American Economic Review* (1951).

41. See Hegeland, *Multiplier Theory,* chap. 11 and p. 138.

42. See G.L.S. Shackle, "A Survey of the Theory of the Multiplier," *Economic Journal* (June 1951), p. 250.

43. For a discussion of the problem of how to determine the time lags that are relevant to the multiplier theory, see J. Tinbergen, "Does Consumption Lag behind Income?," *Review of Economics and Statistics* (1942); Lloyd A. Metzler, "Three Lags in the Circular Flow of Income," *Essays in Honor of A. Hansen* (1948).

44. R. M. Goodwin, "The Multiplier As Matrix," *Economic Journal* (1949). See J. S. Chipman, "Professor Goodwin's Matrix Multiplier," *Economic Journal* (December 1950); R. M. Goodwin, "Does the Matrix Multiplier Oscillate?," *Economic Journal* (December 1950); and A. G. Johnson, "The Matrix Multiplier," *Economic Journal* (1952).

45. See John R. Hicks, *A Contribution to the Theory of the Trade Cycle* (Oxford, 1950), p. 52.

46. A. D. Knox, "The Acceleration Principle," *Economica* (August 1952); R. S. Eckaus, "The Acceleration Principle Reconsidered," *Quarterly Journal of Economics* (1953); Hegeland, *Multiplier Theory,* chap. 12.

47. Arthur F. Burns, *The Frontiers of Economic Knowledge* (Princeton, 1954), p. 252.

48. Idem, "Hicks and the Real Cycle," *Journal of Political Economy* (1952), p. 7.

49. Gottfried Haberler, *Prosperity and Depression,* 3rd ed. (Geneva, 1941), p. 85 ff. In a discussion of "current research in business cycles," organized in 1948 by the American Economic Association, Haberler compared the acceleration principle with the body of a mouse in an advanced stage of decomposition ("Current Research in Business Cycles," *American Economic Review* [May 1949], p. 84).

50. See Hegeland, *Multiplier Theory,* p. 209. For objections to the analysis of the combined effects of the acceleration principle and growth of consumption, see A. D. Knox, "On the Theory of the Trade Cycle," *Economica* (August 1950).

51. Roy F. Harrod, *The Trade Cycle* (Oxford, 1936).

CHAPTER 37

1. Paul A. Samuelson, "Lord Keynes and the General Theory," *Econometrica* (July 1946).

2. Idem, "Interaction between the Multiplier Analysis and the Principle of Acceleration," *Review of Economics and Statistics* (May 1939).

3. Roy F. Harrod, "An Essay in Dynamic Theory," *Economic Journal* (March 1939).

4. Idem, *Towards a Dynamic Economics* (London, 1948); "Notes on the Trade Cycle Theory," *Economic Journal* (1951). See the extensive interpretations of Harrod's model of the economy by S. S. Alexander, "The Accelerator As a Generator of Economic Growth," *Quarterly Journal of Economics* (1949); idem, "Mr. Harrod's Dynamic Model," *Economic Journal* (December 1950).

5. For discussions of Harrod's theory, see John R. Hicks, "Mr. Harrod's Dynamic Theory," *Economica* (1949); Giovanni Demaria, "L'epistemologia Keynesiana," *Giornale degli economisti e annali di economia* (September 1952); Leland B. Yeager, "Some Questions about Growth Economics," *American Economic Review* (March 1954); F. W. Stolper, "Some Notes on Harrod's Dynamic Economics," *Schweizerische Zeitschrift für Volkswirtschaft und Statistik* (October 1952), p. 418.

6. T. C. Schelling, "Capital Growth and Equilibrium," *American Economic Review* (1947), p. 864.

7. Gottfried Haberler, in *Wirtschaftstheorie und Wirtschaftspolitik* (Bern, 1953), p. 234.

8. André Marchal, *Méthode scientifique et science économique* (Paris, 1955), p. 137.

9. See Frank E. Norton, Jr., "Capital Theory and Progressive Equilibrium," *American Economic Review* (May 1951), p. 146.

10. Joan Robinson, *The Rate of Interest and Other Essays* (New York, 1952).

11. Alvin H. Hansen, *Fiscal Policy and Business Cycle* (New York, 1941).

12. Ibid.

13. Benjamin Higgins, "The Modern Theory of Economic Fluctuations," in G. E. Hoover, ed., *Twentieth Century Economic Thought* (New York, 1950).

14. Evsey D. Domar, "Capital Expansion, Rate of Growth and Employment," *Econometrica* (1946); idem, "Expansion and Employment," *American Economic Review* (March 1947); idem, "The Problem of Capital Accumulation," *American Economic Review* (December 1948), republished in Domar's essays in *Theory of Economic Growth* (New York, 1957), chaps. 3–5.

15. For an adjustment of these considerations to the principles of monetary business cycle theories, see Lloyd A. Metzler, "Business Cycles and the Modern Theory of Employment," *American Economic Review* (June 1946).

16. See, among others, Ingvar Svennilson, *American Economic Review* (December 1958), p. 1007.

17. Evsey D. Domar, "Comment on Methodological Developments," in Howard S. Ellis, ed., *A Survey of Contemporary Economics* (Philadelphia, 1948), 2: 454.

18. Alvin H. Hansen, "Toward a Dynamic Theory of the Cycle," *American Economic Review* (May 1952), p. 74 ff.

19. Simon Kuznets, "Review of A. Hansen's Business Cycles," *American Economic Review* (December 1953).

20. John R. Hicks, *Value and Capital* (Oxford, 1939).

21. Paul A. Samuelson, "The Stability of Equilibrium," *Econometrica* (April 1941), and "The Relation between Hicksian Stability and True Dynamic Stability," (July–October 1944); see also Lloyd A. Metzler, "Stability of Multiple Markets," *Econometrica* (October 1945).

22. Especially Oskar Morgenstern, "Professor Hicks on Value and Capital," *Journal of Political Economy* (June 1941), p. 371.

23. John R. Hicks, *A Contribution to the Theory of the Trade Cycle* (Oxford, 1950).

24. For a discussion of the time sequences introduced by Hicks into the acceleration theory, see Hans Neisser, "Critical Notes on the Acceleration Principle," *Quarterly Journal of Economics* (May 1954).

25. Nicholas Kaldor, "Mr. Hicks on the Trade Cycle," *Economic Journal* (December 1951).

26. Samuelson, "Multiplier Analysis and Acceleration"; idem, "A Synthesis of the Principle of Acceleration and the Multiplier," *Journal of Political Economy* (1939).

27. Walter W. Rostow, "Notes on Mr. Hicks and History," *American Economic Review* (1951), p. 323.

28. G.L.S. Shackle, "A Survey of the Theory of the Multiplier," *Economic Journal* (June 1951).

29. Robert A. Gordon, "Discussion," *American Economic Review* (May 1952). Other authors who contributed to these discussions were William J. Baumol ("Notes on Some Dynamic Models," *Economic Journal* [1948]), and Harrod ("Notes on Trade Cycle Theory").

30. Arthur F. Burns, *The Frontiers of Economic Knowledge* (Princeton, 1959), pp. 238, 249.

31. S. C. Tsiang, "Accelerator, Theory of the Firm and the Business Cycle," *Quarterly Journal of Economics* (1951); A. D. Knox, "The Acceleration Principle," *Economica* (August 1952).

32. Lloyd A. Metzler, "Keynes and the Theory of Business Cycles," in Seymour E. Harris, ed., *The New Economics* (New York, 1947), p. 440.

33. Michael Kalecki, "Theory of the Business Cycle," *Review of Economic Studies* (1937), reproduced in idem, *Essays in the Theory of Economic Fluctuations* (New York, 1939). See also idem, *Theory of Economic Dynamics* (London, 1954).

34. About the strictly endogenous nature of the forces operating in that model, see Oskar Lange's review of Kalecki's *Theory of Economic Fluctuations,* in *Journal of Political Economy* (April 1941), p. 284.

35. Nicholas Kaldor, "A Model of the Trade Cycle," *Economic Journal* (1940).

36. R. M. Goodwin developed his model in "Econometrics in Business-Cycle Analysis," in Alvin H. Hansen, ed., *Business Cycles and National Income* (New York, 1951), and *The Business Cycle in the Post-War World* (London, 1955).

37. Kenneth K. Kurihara, "Distribution, Employment, and Secular Growth," in Kenneth K. Kurihara, ed., *Post-Keynesian Economics* (New Brunswick, 1954), p. 190.

38. Lloyd A. Metzler, "The Nature and Stability of Inventory Cycles," *Review of Economics and Statistics* (June 1941); idem, "Factors Governing the Length of Inventory Cycles," *Review of Economics and Statistics* (February 1947). See also Moses Abramovitz, *Inventories and Business Cycles* (New York, 1950).

39. Ragnar Nurkse, "The Cyclical Pattern of Inventory Investment," *Quarterly Journal of Economics* (August 1952).

40. Among others, Robert A. Gordon, "Stabilization Policy and the Study of Business Cycles," *American Economic Review* (May 1957), p. 122.

41. See the paper of John M. Clark, "Competition: Static Models and Dynamic Aspects," *American Economic Review* (May 1955), p. 451, and the discussion of this paper by Gardner Ackley, *American Economic Review* (May 1955) p. 487.

42. James W. Angell, *American Economic Review* (May 1949), p. 75.

43. Ibid., p. 85.

44. For the anticyclical behavior of savings, transfer of payments out of public funds, etc., see Albert G. Hart, *Money, Debt and Economic Activity* (New York, 1948), chap. 22.

45. For a discussion of the effects of short-run stabilizing measures, see Milton Friedman, *Essays in Positive Economics* (Chicago, 1953).

46. Arthur Smithies, "Economic Fluctuations and Growth," *Econometrica* (January 1957), p. 4.

47. See A.L.L. Wright, "The Rate of Interest in a Dynamic Model," *Quarterly Journal of Economics* (August 1958).

48. Guy H. Orcutt, "Microanalytic Models of the United States Economy: Need and Development," *American Economic Review* (May 1962), p. 236.

49. Emile James, *Histoire de la pensée économique au XXe siècle* (Paris, 1955), vol. 2, chap. 3, sect. 1.

50. Marchal, *Méthode scientifique,* vol. 2, p. 47.

51. Léon H. Dupriez, *Des mouvements économiques généraux,* 2 vols. (Louvain, 1947).

52. See the discussion of business cycle analysis in *Giornale degli economisti e annali di economia* (September 1952).

53. Giuseppe Ugo Papi, "Trend e Punti di Inversioni," *Giornale degli economisti e annali di economia* (September 1952).

54. See Marco Fanno's report, *Giornale degli economisti e annali di economia.* Fanno developed his ideas in *La Teoria delle fluttuazioni economiche* (Turin, 1947).

55. Gustavo del Vecchio, "La costruzione scientifica della dinamica economica," *Giornale degli economisti e annali di economia* (September 1952).

56. *Business Cycle in the Post-War World.*

57. For a discussion of the explanatory value of Goodwin's model, see the introduction to *Business Cycle in the Post-War World,* p. xi.

58. See Jacques Jacobus Polak, "The Repercussions of Economic Fluctuation in the United States on Other Parts of the World," *International Monetary Fund. Staff Papers* (August 1956), pp. 279–83.

59. For a discussion of the influence of the American trade unions on wage determination, see Clark Kerr, "Trade Unionism and Distributive Shares," *American Economic Review* (May 1954), pp. 279 ff.

CHAPTER 38

1. Charles F. Bastable, *The Theory of International Trade* (Dublin, 1887).

2. Francis Ysidro Edgeworth, "The Pure Theory of International Trade," *Economic Journal* (1894).

3. Richard Schuller, *Schutzoll und Freihandel* (Vienna, 1905). See also Gottfried Haberler, *The Theory of International Trade with Applications to Commercial Policy* (London, 1936), p. 187.

4. Alfred Marshall, *The Pure Theory of Foreign Trade* (1879); *Money, Credit, and Commerce* (London, 1923).

5. Mihail Manoilesco, *Théorie du protectionisme et de l'échange internationale* (Paris, 1929), trans. as *The Theory of Protection and International Trade* (London, 1931). See the review of that book by Jacob Viner in *Journal of Political Economy* (1932), p. 121 ff., and Gottfried Haberler, "Some Problems in the Pure Theory of International Trade," *Economic Journal* (June 1950).

6. Jacob Viner, *Studies in the Theory of International Trade* (New York, 1937), pp. 489 ff., 514.

7. Frank W. Taussig, *International Trade* (New York, 1928).

8. John H. Williams, *Argentine International Trade under Inconvertible Paper Money* (Cambridge, Mass., 1920); Jacob Viner, *Canada's Balance of International Indebtedness, 1900–1913: An Inductive Study in the Theory of International Trade* (Cambridge, Mass., 1924); and Harry D. White, *The French International Accounts, 1880–1913* (Cambridge, Mass., 1933).

9. James W. Angell, *Theory of International Prices* (Cambridge, Mass., 1926).

10. John H. Williams, "The Theory of International Trade Reconsidered," *Economic Journal* (1929).

11. Frank D. Graham, "International Values, Re-examined," *Quarterly Journal of Economics* (1923–24); idem, *The Theory of International Values* (Princeton, 1948).

12. See also Lloyd A. Metzler, "Graham's Theory of International Values," *American Economic Review* (June 1950).

13. T. O. Yntema, *A Mathematical Reformulation of the General Theory of Trade* (Chicago, 1932), and Jacob L. Mosak, *General Equilibrium Theory in International Trade* (Bloomington, 1944).

14. Folke Hilgerdt, *The Network of World Trade* (1942). See also Karl-Erik Hansson, "A General Theory of the System of Multilateral Trade," *American Economic Review* (March 1952). Hansson ascribed changes in multilateral patterns of trade to changes in factor proportions.

15. That proposition was advanced by Cassel in *Germany's Power of Resistance* (New York, 1916).

16. Karl Gustav Cassel, *The World's Monetary Problems* (London, 1921). See also idem, *Money and Foreign Exchange after 1914* (New York, 1923). Cassel's contention that his theory had been suggested by Ricardo was refuted by D. Davidson. See Eli Filip Heckscher, "David Davidson," trans. M. A. Michael, in *International Economic Papers,* 12 vols. (London, 1951–62), 2: 125.

17. See Viner, *International Trade,* p. 384.

18. About these discussions, see Michael A. Heilperin, *International Monetary Economics* (London, 1939), chap. 7.

19. See, among others, Ragnar Nurkse, *Internationale Kapitalbewegungen* (Vienna, 1935).

20. See Lloyd A. Metzler, "The Theory of International Trade," in Howard S. Ellis, ed., *A Survey of Contemporary Economics* (Philadelphia, 1948), 1: 225 ff.

21. Gottfried Haberler, *Der internationale Handel* (Berlin, 1933), trans. Alfred Stonier and Frederick Benham as *The Theory of International Trade with Applications to Commercial Policy.*

22. Gottfried Haberler, "Real Costs, Monetary Costs and Comparative Advantages," *UNESCO International Social Science Bulletin* (Spring 1951). See also Haberler, "Pure Theory of International Trade," and T. Balogh, "Welfare and Free Trade: A Reply," *Economic Journal* (March 1951).

23. Viner, *Theory of International Trade,* p. 532.

24. Subsequent studies in which the concept of indifference curves as applied to communities was used to analyze problems of international trade relationships were Wassily W. Leontief, "The Use of Indifference Curves in the Analysis of Foreign Trade," *Quarterly Journal of Economics* (May 1933); Abba P. Lerner, "Diagrammatical Representations," *Economica* (1934); and Tibor Scitovsky, "A Reconsideration of the Theory of Tariffs," *Review of Economic Studies* (1942). See also F. W. Stolper, "A Method of Constructing Community Indifference Curves," *Schweizerische Zeitschrift für Volkswirtschaft* (April 1950).

25. Bertil Ohlin reviewed Haberler's *Theory of International Trade,* in *Economic Journal* (September 1938), p. 498 ff.

26. Heckscher's investigations were published in Swedish in 1919. For an abridged translation, see "The Effect of Foreign Trade on the Distribution of Income," in *Readings in the Theory of International Trade* (Philadelphia, 1949), p. 272.

27. Bertil Ohlin, *Interregional and International Trade* (Cambridge, Mass., 1935).

28. Some objections were raised to Ohlin's assumption that the units of the various productive factors were homogeneous in quality. See Jacob Viner, *International Trade and Economic Development* (Oxford, 1953), p. 15, and Walter Isard, "The General Theory of Location," *Quarterly Journal of Economics* (November 1949), p. 503.

29. See Paul A. Samuelson, "International Trade and the Equilization of Factor Prices," *Economic Journal* (June 1943) and (June 1945); Abba P. Lerner, "Factor Prices and International Trade," *Economica* (February 1952).

30. Svend Laursen, "Production Functions and the Theory of International Trade," *American Economic Review* (September 1952).

31. F. W. Stolper and Paul A. Samuelson, "Protection and Real Wages," *Review of Economic Studies* (November 1941).

32. Viner, *International Trade,* and Walter W. Rostow, *The Process of Economic Growth* (New York, 1952), chap. 8.

33. John Maynard Keynes, "The German Transfer Problem," *Economic Journal* (March 1929); idem, "The Reparation Problem: A Discussion," *Economic Journal* (June 1929); and idem, "Views on the Transfer Problem: A Reply," *Economic Journal* (September 1929). Keynes ignored the income effects to which he later attached primary importance in his multiplier analysis. See Ragnar Nurkse, "Domestic and International Equilibrium," in Seymour E. Harris, ed., *The New Economics* (New York, 1947), p. 272.

34. Bertil Ohlin, "Transfer Difficulties, Real and Imagined," *Economic Journal* (June 1929); idem, "Transfer und Preisbewegung," *Zeitschrift für Nationalökonomie* (1930). Ohlin credited Knut Wicksell with having formulated the transfer problem as an

income problem in an article in *Quarterly Journal of Economics* (February 1918).

35. Gottfried Haberler, who surveyed the discussion of the reparation problems ("Wirtschaft als Leben: Kritische Bemerkungen zu Gottls Methodologischen Schriften," *Zeitschrift für Nationalökonomie* [1930], p. 547), arrived at the Solomonic conclusion that Keynes was right in theory but that his adversaries, mainly Ohlin and Jacques Rueff, were right in practice. Beginning with 1930, credit contractions exercised a heavy pressure on the prices of German products; exports were not perceptibly reduced, but imports experienced a heavy fall. The resulting substantial export surpluses provided the means for the transfer of reparations in 1930 and 1936.

36. August Lösch's article in *Jahrbuch für Nationalökonomie und Statistik* (1941).

37. Fritz Machlup. *International Trade and the National Income Multiplier* (1943).

38. See John H. Williams, *American Economic Review* (May 1957), p. 429.

39. John M. Keynes, "The End of the Gold Standard," in idem., *Essays in Persuasion* (1931), in *The Collected Writings of John Maynard Keynes* (London, 1972).

40. See R. F. Kahn, "The Relation of Home Investment to Employment," *Economic Journal* (June 1931), and J. Warming, "International Difficulties Arising out of the Financing of Public Works during Depression," *Economic Journal* (June 1932).

41. Joan Robinson, *Essays in the Theory of Employment* (Oxford, 1937), pt. 3. F. W. Paish, "Banking Policy and the Balance of International Payments," *Economica* (1936); Roy F. Harrod, *International Economics* (New York, 1948); Robinson, *Employment*.

42. See Metzler, "International Trade," p. 216.

43. Fritz Machlup, *International Trade and the National Income Multiplier* (Philadelphia, 1943).

44. Ragnar Nurkse, *Conditions of International Monetary Equilibrium* (Princeton, 1945); idem, "Domestic and International Equilibrium."

45. "Intersystem multipliers" of different kinds were studied by Oskar Lange, "The Multiplier Theory," *Econometrica* (1943).

46. About a "serial" interpretation of the multiplier theory, see Gottfried Haberler, "Comment," *American Economic Review* (December 1947), p. 898, and Haberler and J. J. Polak's joint statement, "A Restatement," *American Economic Review* (December 1947), p. 906.

47. See Metzler, "International Trade," p. 220 ff.

48. Abba P. Lerner, *The Economics of Control* (New York, 1944).

49. See appendix B, at the end of this chapter.

50. J. E. Meade, "The Balance of Payments," in *The Theory of International Economic Policy*, 2 vols. (London, 1951–55), vol. 1.

51. See Donald B. Marsh, "The Scope of the Theory of International Trade under Imperfect Competition," *Quarterly Journal of Economics* (1942); Gertrude Lovasy, "International Trade under Imperfect Competition," *Quarterly Journal of Economics* (1942).

52. Marsh, "International Trade under Imperfect Competition," p. 485.

53. See Paul A. Samuelson, "Welfare Economics and International Trade," *American Economic Review* (June 1938); F. Benham, "Terms of Trade," *Economica* (November 1940); Scitovsky, "Theory of Tariffs"; and Metzler, "International Trade."

54. Problems of that type were discussed by Nicholas Kaldor, Abba P. Lerner, Tibor Scitovsky, and J. E. Meade. See especially J. E. Meade, *A Geometry of International Trade* (London, 1952). The formulas advanced by these authors were criticized on the grounds that they were limited to the exchanges between two countries and predicated on the knowledge of elasticity of supply and demand. See I.M.D. Little, *A Critique of Welfare Economics* (Oxford, 1950), chap. 13.

55. Meade, *International Economic Policy*, vol. 2.

56. Jacob Viner, *International Economics* (Glencoe, Ill., 1951), introduction.

57. Gottfried Haberler, "The Relevance of Classical Theory under Modern Conditions," *American Economic Review* (May 1954), p. 545.

58. See Kenneth E. Boulding, "Defense and Opulence: The Ethics of International Economics," *American Economic Review* (May 1951), p. 210.

59. See the contribution of J. J. Polak in Dennis Holme Robertson, ed., *The Business Cycle in the Post-War World* (London, 1955), pp. 246 ff, 342 ff.

60. Viner, *International Trade*. For a list of arguments in favor of the free trade doctrine, see Haberler, *Theory of International Trade*, p. 551.

61. See Viner, *International Trade*, p. 4.

62. About international cartels, see Corwin D. Edwards, *Economic and Political Aspects of International Cartels* (Washington, D.C., 1944); Ervin Hexner, *International Cartels* (Chapel Hill, 1945).

63. U. S., Tariff Commission, *Foreign Trade and Exchange Control in Germany* (Washington, D.C., 1942); Howard S. Ellis, *Exchange Control in Central Europe* (Cambridge, Mass., 1941); *International Currency Experience*, League of Nations (Geneva, 1944).

64. Jacob Viner, *Trade Relations between Free Markets and Controlled Economies* (Geneva, 1943).

65. L. Bajugie, "L'Evolution de la théorie des coûts comparés," *Revue d'économie politique* (1947).

66. Jacob Viner, "International Relations between State Controlled Economies," *American Economic Review* (March 1944), supplement, M. L. Hoffman, "Problems of Trading between Planned Economies," *American Economic Review* (May 1951), p. 449.

67. Emile Despres and C. P. Kindleberger, "The Mechanism for Adjustment in International Payments," *American Economic Review* (May 1952), p. 332.

68. See Gottfried Haberler, in "Proceedings of a Round Table Discussion," *UNESCO International Social Science Bulletin* (1951). About the problems involved in promoting the European recovery, see the literature listed by P. T. Ellsworth, *The International Economy* (New York, 1950), p. 901 ff. About the attitude adopted toward the "dollar gap" in the reports of the United Nations, see R. F. Mikesell, "Economic Doctrines Reflected in U.N. Reports," *American Economic Review* (May 1954), p. 575. See also Herbert Furth, "The World Dollar Problem," *World Politics* (January 1959).

69. Some German authors elaborated Thünen's theory of the location of agricultural production. They showed that the sequence of the spatial order outlined by Thünen did not depend on the relative weight of the products nor on their value, but only on the yield per acre, expressed in weight. See Alfred Rühl, *Das Standortsproblem in der Landwirtschaftsgeographie* (Berlin, 1929).

70. Oscar Engländer, *Theorie des Güterverkehrs und der Frachtsätze* (Jena, 1924); idem, "Lahre vom Standort," *Zeitschrift für Staats und Volkswirtschaft* (1926).

71. A. Predöhl, "Das Standortsproblem in der Wirtschaftstheorie," *Weltwirtschaftliches Archiv* (1925).

72. For these criticisms, see Tord Palander, *Beiträge zur Standortstheorie* (Uppsala, 1935).

73. Hans Ritschl, "Reine und historische Dynamik der Erzeugungszweige," *Schmoller's Jahrbuch für Gesetzgebung, Verwaltung und Volkswirtschaft* (1927); idem, "Afgabe und Methode der Standortstheorie," *Weltwirtschaftliches Archiv* 1 (1941).

74. Palander, *Beiträge*.

75. These considerations were similar to those elaborated by E. H. Chamberlin in *The Theory of Monopolistic Competition* (Cambridge, Mass., 1933).

76. L. Miksch, "Zur Theorie des räumlichen Gleichgewichts," *Archiv für Sozialwissenschaft und Sozialpolitik* (1951). About some other German studies dealing with the location of industries and related spatial problems, see Adolf Weber, *Allgemeine Volkswirtschaftslehre*, 6th ed. (Berlin, 1953), p. 365–66.

77. Isard, "General Theory of Location"; "Distance and Inputs and the Space Economy," *Quarterly Journal of Economics* (1951); and *Location and Space Economy* (New York, 1956).

78. Walter Isard and M. J. Peck, "Location Theory and International and Interregional Trade Theory," *Quarterly Journal of Economics* (February 1954).

79. Ohlin, *Interregional and International Trade*.

80. In the United States researches into the location of various industries were undertaken by Edgar M. Hoover, *The Location of Economic Activity* (New York, 1948). Studies dealing with regional economic developments were made by D. Rutledge Vining, H. W. Odum, and others. See R. Vining, "The Region As a Concept in Business Cycle Analysis," *Econometrica* (July 1946).

81. August Lösch, *Die räumliche Ordnung der Wirtschaft* (Jena, 1940), trans. William Woglom as *The Economics of Location* (New Haven, 1954). The setting of the problem adopted by Lösch was strongly influenced by an analytical study of "central places" as the basic elements of "nodal regions," prepared by the geographer Walter Christaller, *Die zentralen Orte in Süddeutschland* (Jena, 1933). See Walter Isard, "Current Developments in Regional Analysis," *Weltwirtschaftliches Archiv* 2 (1952).

82. Robinson, *Employment*.

83. Arthur J. Brown, "Trade Balances and Exchange Stability," *Oxford Economic Papers* (April 1942). See Metzler, "International Trade," p. 230.

84. Frank D. Gresham, *Fundamentals of International Monetary Policy* (Princeton, 1943).

85. Joan Robinson, *Employment*.

86. Nurkse, *International Monetary Equilibrium;* idem, "Domestic and International Equilibrium."

87. The importance attached to the balance of payments was reflected in the periodical publication of these balances by the secretariat of the League of Nations and later by the International Monetary Fund. See Metzler, "International Trade," p. 220 ff.

88. See Gottfried Haberler, "Some Factors Affecting the Future of International Trade," written in 1945 and reprinted in *Readings in the Theory of International Trade* (Philadelphia, 1949), no. 23.

89. *Proposals for an International Clearing Union* (London, 1943), H. M. Stationary Office Cmd 6437.

90. Nurkse, *International Monetary Equilibrium*, p. 13.

91. Marcus Fleming, "Regional Organization of Trade and Payments," *American Economic Review* (May 1952), p. 354.

92. See Haberler, in "Round Table Discussion." About the "dollar gap" in the reports of the United Nations, see Mikesell, "Economic Doctrines," p. 575. See also Fürth, "World Dollar Problem."

93. About the problems involved in promoting

the European recovery, see the literature listed by Ellsworth, *International Economy*, p. 901 ff.

94. *The Work of the Organization for European Economic Cooperation*, Report of the Secretary General (April 1959), p. 30.

95. For a survey of the work of the conference, see, among others, *International Conciliation*, no. 55, issued by the Carnegie Endowment for International Peace (New York, 1954).

96. For a discussion of the various aspects of "liquidity," see Milton Gilbert, *Problems of the International Monetary System* (Princeton, 1966).

97. For the following discussion, see *International Payments Problem*, a symposium sponsored by the American Enterprise Institute (Washington, D.C., 1965). See also Fritz Machlup, *Pleas for Reform of the International Monetary System* (Princeton, 1968); Herbert Furth, in Federal Reserve Board of Chicago, *Business Conditions* (October 1964); *International Monetary Arrangements: The Problem of Choice* (Princeton, 1964). See also Pierre Paul Schweitzer, in *International Financial Survey* 4 December 1964, 5 February 1965, 20 May 1966; and reports on "Reserve Creation" and "The Balance of Payments Adjustment Process," *International Financial Survey*, 2 September and 9 September 1966.

98. See Friedrich A. Lutz, *The Problem of International Liquidity and the Multiple-Currency Standard* (Princeton, 1963).

99. Robert Triffin, *Gold and the Dollar Crisis* (New Haven, 1960). Triffin also elaborated his ideas in a great number of articles published in various journals.

100. Robert V. Rossa, *Monetary Reform for the World Economy* (New York, 1965).

CHAPTER 39

1. See among others, John M. Letiche, "Classical and Contemporary Theories of Growth," *American Economic Review* (May 1959), p. 487 ff.

2. For a discussion of Marshall's views on the organic and evolutionary aspects of the economy, and on economic and cultural progress, see Bruce Glassburner, "Alfred Marshall on Economic History," *Quarterly Journal of Economics* (November 1955).

3. Allyn Abbott Young, "Increasing Returns and Economic Progress," *Economic Journal* (December 1928).

4. See Gerald M. Meier and R. B. Baldwin, *Economic Development* (New York, 1957), p. 66.

5. For a survey of that literature, see René Gonnard, *Histoire des doctrines de la population* (Paris, 1923); J. Bonar, *Theories of Population from Raleigh to Arthur Young* (London, 1931); Joseph J. Spengler, "French Population Theory," *Journal of Political Economy* (1936).

6. Paul Mombert developed this "prosperity theory" in an essay which he contributed to the *Grundriss der Sozialökonomie* (1914), and later in a study entitled *Bevölkerungsentwicklung und Wirtschaftsgestaltung* (Leipzig, 1932).

7. See the instructive article by E. Ames, "A Theoretical and Statistical Dilemma," *Econometrica* (October 1948), p. 364.

8. See *Studies in Income and Wealth* and *Proceedings of the Conference on Research in Income and Wealth*, published by the National Bureau of Economic Research (New York).

9. A variety of factors were taken into account in Clarence E. Ayres, *The Theory of Economic Progress* (Chapel Hill, 1944); and H. G. Moulton, *Controlling Factors in Economic Development* (Washington, D.C., 1949).

10. Moses Abramowitz, "Economics of Growth," in Howard S. Ellis, ed., *A Survey of Contemporary Economics* (Philadelphia, 1952), vol. 2, chap. 4.

11. Giuseppe Ugo Papi, in *Teoria e politica dello sviluppo economico* (Milan, 1954).

12. Colin Clark, *Conditions of Economic Progress*, 2nd ed. (London, 1951).

13. François Perroux, *Theorie Générale du progrès économique*, 2 vols. (Paris, 1956–57).

14. See also Anatol Murad, "Net Investment and Industrial Progress," in Kenneth K. Kurihara, ed., *Post-Keynesian Economics* (New Brunswick, 1954), chap. 9, p. 231 ff.

15. Pierre Dieterlen, in "Travaux du congrès des économistes," p. 108. See also idem, *Au delà du capitalisme* (Paris, 1946).

16. See Evsey D. Domar, "Expansion and Employment," *American Economic Review* (March 1947) and idem, "The Problem of Capital Accumulation," *American Economic Review* (December 1948). See also Domar's article, "The Theoretical Analysis of Economic Growth: An Econometric Approach," *American Economic Review* (May 1952) and idem, *Essays in the Theory of Economic Growth* (New York, 1957).

17. About the use of the "average rate of productivity" for measuring the rate of economic growth, see William J. Fellner, "The Capital-Output Ratio in Dynamic Economics," in *Money, Trade and Economic Growth* (New York, 1951) and idem, "Capital Intensity and Economic Growth," *American Economic Review* (1952), p. 482.

18. James S. Duesenberry, *Income, Savings and the Theory of Consumer Behavior* (Cambridge, Mass., 1949). See also Ruth P. Mack, "Economics of Consumption," in Ellis, ed., *Contemporary Economics*, vol. 2, chap. 2, and "Trends in American Consumption and the Aspiration to Consume," *American Economic Review* (May 1956), p. 57 ff.

19. Leif Johnson, "Substitution vs. Fixed Pro-

duction Coefficients in the Theory of Economic Growth,'' *Econometrica* (April 1959).

20. Hans Brems, ''Constancy of the Proportionate Equilibrium Rate of Growth,'' *Review of Economics and Statistics* (February 1957); see also Robert Eisner, ''Depreciation Allowances, Replacement Requirements and Growth,'' *American Economic Review* (December 1952).

21. Daniel Hamberg, ''Full Capacity vs. Full Employment Growth,'' *Quarterly Journal of Economics* (August 1952) and ''Full Capacity vs. Full Employment Growth: Some Further Remarks,'' *Quarterly Journal of Economics* (November 1954); and Petrus J. Verdoorn, ''Complementarity and Long-Range Projections,'' *Econometrica* (October 1956).

22. Jan Tinbergen, *Weltwirtschaftliches Archiv* (1942); Trygve Haavelmo, *A Study in the Theory of Economic Evolution* (Amsterdam, 1954); and Robert Solow, ''A Contribution to the Theory of Economic Growth,'' *Quarterly Journal of Economics* (February 1956).

23. Leland B. Yeager, ''Some Questions about Growth Economics,'' *American Economic Review* (March 1954).

24. See the discussions of problems of economic growth in *American Economic Review* (May 1966).

25. Domar, *Economic Growth,* p. 31.

26. See Abbot Payson Usher, ''Technical Change and Capital Formation,'' in National Bureau of Economic Research, *Capital Formation and Economic Growth* (Princeton, 1955).

27. Franco Feroldi, ''La 'Neutralità' della invenzioni e la dinamica economica,'' *Giornale degli economisti e annali di economia* (1952). See also William J. Fellner, *Trends and Cycles in Economic Activity* (New York, 1956).

28. Fellner, *Trends and Cycles.*

29. Allen G. B. Fisher, ''The Economic Implications of Material Progress,'' *International Labour Review* (September 1933).

30. Idem, *Economic Progress and Social Security* (London, 1945).

31. Martin Wolfe, ''The Concept of Economic Sectors,'' *Quarterly Journal of Economics* (August 1955).

32. Colin Clark, *The Economics of 1960* (London, 1942).

33. About this distinction, see Wolfe, ''Economic Sectors.''

34. For a discussion of Clark's procedures, see Richard Stone, ''The Fortune Teller,'' *Economica* (February 1943), and Simon Kuznets, *Economic Change* (New York, 1953), p. 148 ff.

35. Jean Fourastié, *Esquisse d'une théorie générale de l'évolution économique contemporaine* (Paris, 1947); idem, *Le Grand Espoir du XXᵉ siècle* (Paris, 1949).

36. Walt W. Rostow, *The Process of Economic Growth* (New York, 1952); and idem, ''Trends in the Allocation of Resources in Secular Growth,'' in Léon H. Dupriez, ed., *Economic Progress,* Papers and Proceedings of the Round Table Conference held at Santa Margherita Ligure, Italy, in 1953 (Louvain, 1955).

37. James Baster, ''Economic Development,'' *Quarterly Journal of Economics* (November 1954), p. 588.

38. Benjamin Higgins, ''Incentives and Economic Growth: Discussion,'' *American Economic Review* (May 1960).

39. Walt W. Rostow, *The States of Economic Growth: A Non-Communist Manifesto* (Cambridge, Mass., 1960).

40. Dupriez, *Economic Progress.*

41. Walter W. Rostow, ed., *The Economics of Take-Off into Sustained Growth,* Proceedings of a conference held in 1960 of the International Economic Association (New York, 1963). See also Simon Kuznets, ''Notes on the Take-off,'' in *Economic Growth and Structure* (New York, 1965), p. 213 ff, and the discussion of Rostow's theory by Paul A. Baran, Goran Ohlin, and Rutledge Vining, ''The Problem of Achieving and Maintaining a High Rate of Economic Growth: A Historian's View,'' *American Economic Review* (May 1960).

42. Alexander K. Cairncross, ''Reflections on the Growth of Capital and Income,'' *Scottish Journal of Political Economy* (June 1955).

43. Ten general propositions concerning the relationship of capital formation to various economic factors were advanced by Moses Abramovitz in National Bureau of Economic Research, *Capital Formation and Economic Growth,* p. 658 ff.

44. Predöhl's evolutionary scheme was discussed by the German economist H. Griesch at the 1953 International Economic Conference. See H. Griesch, in Dupriez, ed., *Economic Progress.*

45. See Berthold F. Hoselitz, ''Entrepreneurship and Capital Formation in France and Britain since 1700,'' and Thomas C. Cochran, ''The Entrepreneur in American Capital Formation,'' in National Bureau of Economic Research, *Capital Formation and Growth,* about factors controlling the inducement to invest.

46. See the discussions in *American Economic Review* (May 1965).

47. About the effects of economic growth on changes in the distribution of income, see Simon Kuznets, ''Economic Growth and Income Inequality,'' *American Economic Review* (March 1955). About the changing role of savings in the process of capital formation and the determinants of the supply of savings, see idem, ''International Differences in Capital Formation and Financing,'' in National Bureau of Economic Research, *Capital Formation and Economic Growth.* About changes in the financial

structure of advanced countries, see R. W. Gold-smith, "Financial Structure and Economic Growth," in National Bureau of Economic Research, *Capital Formation and Economic Growth.* This list could easily be extended.

48. See Charles R. Whittlesey, "Relation of Money to Economic Growth," *American Economic Review* (May 1956), pp. 188 ff., and the ensuing discussion.

49. John Kenneth Galbraith, *The Affluent Society* (Boston, 1958).

50. Jacob Viner, *International Trade and Economic Development* (Oxford, 1953), chap. 6. See also Fritz Machlup, "Disputes, Paradoxes and Dilemmas," *Rivista internazionale di Scienze Economiche e Commerciali* (1957).

51. See *Economist,* 4 October 1958, p. 55.

52. See the discussions of the 1953 meeting of the American Economic Association, *American Economic Review* (May 1954).

53. See Theo Suranyi-Unger's comments, "Economic Doctrines Implied in U.N. Reports: Discussion," *American Economic Review* (May 1954), p. 607. For a carefully reasoned analysis of the problems involved in programming economic development, see Jan Tinbergen, *The Design of Development* (Baltimore, 1958).

54. Thus, between 1938 and the middle of this century per capita real income of Egypt and India does not appear to have increased; see E. M. Bernstein and I. G. Pate, "Inflation in Relation to Economic Development," *International Monetary Fund Staff Papers* (November 1952), p. 363. See also Gunnar Myrdal, *Rich Land and Poor Land* (New York, 1957), pp. 151 ff.

55. See Hla Myint, "An Interpretation of Economic Backwardness," *Oxford Economic Papers* (June 1954).

56. See two memoranda of the United Nations Secretariat entitled *Relative Prices of Exports and Imports of Underdeveloped Countries* (New York, 1949) and *Instability in Export Markets of Underdeveloped Countries* (New York, 1952).

57. Ragnar Nurkse, *Problems of Capital Formation in Underdeveloped Countries* (Oxford, 1953); Duesenberry, *Income, Savings and Consumer Behavior.*

58. That "theory" was suggested by R. T. Aleman in an article published in the *Archiv für Weltwirtschaftliches* 1 (1955). The report of the commission was published at Lake Success in 1950 under the title "Report of the Economic Development of Latin America and Its Principal Problems."

59. The findings of the commission were accepted at face value by various economists, such as Hans W. Singer, "The Distribution of Gains between Investing and Borrowing Countries," *American Economic Review* (May 1950), p. 478, and Gunnar Myr-

dal, *An International Economy* (New York, 1956), and *Economic Theory and Underdeveloped Regions* (New York, 1957).

60. Viner, *International Trade,* p. 43 ff. See also C. P. Kindleberger, *The Terms of Trade* (New York, 1956).

61. See Singer, "Distribution of Gains," and the discussion with A. N. McLeod, "Trade and Investment in Underdeveloped Areas: A Reply," *American Economic Review* (June 1951), p. 411 ff. John Adler, *American Economic Review* (June 1951), p. 588, and the discussion, p. 601.

62. *Measures of Financing Economic Developments in Underdeveloped Countries* (New York, 1949); Nurkse, *Capital Formation;* Federico Caffé, "Considerazione sulla formazione del capital," in *Teoria e politica.*

63. See Henry G. Aubrey, "The Role of the State in Economic Development," *American Economic Review* (May 1951), p. 271; Nurkse, *Capital Formation;* Vittorio Maramma, in *Teoria e politica,* p. 200 ff.

64. V. Maramma, "Reflessioni sullo sviluppo economico del paesi arestati," *Giornale degli economisti e annali di economia* (1952), p. 52.

65. For a condensed version of Hamilton's analysis, see his presidential address, "Prices and Progress," *Journal of Economic History* (1952). See also David Felix, "Profit, Inflation and Industrial Growth," *Quarterly Journal of Economics* (August 1956).

66. W. Arthur Lewis, *The Theory of Economic Growth* (London, 1955).

67. See the discussion of that problem in Bernstein and Patel, "Inflation."

68. Howard S. Ellis, "Relation of Money to Economic Growth: Discussion," *American Economic Review* (May 1956), p. 206.

69. About the question of how far consumption could be reduced in favor of capital formation, see Giacomo Della Porta, in *Teoria e politica,* p. 315 ff.

70. See, for instance, Sayre P. Schatz, "Inflation in Underdeveloped Areas," *American Economic Review* (September 1957).

71. See various reports of the Secretariat of the United Nations, the International Bank for Reconstruction and Development, the Food and Agricultural Administration, and the International Labour Organization. About the creation of supplementary institutions, see the report of the World Bank on the establishment of an International Finance Corporation (Washington, D.C., 1952), and the report on a special United Nations fund for economic development (New York, 1953).

72. Assistance schemes of that type were put into operation in accordance with the American so-called Point Four Program proposed by President Truman, the Colombo Plan of the British Common-

730 NOTES TO PAGES 559–62

wealth, the English Development and Welfare Act, and the American Alliance for Progress.

73. *Measures for the Development of Underdeveloped Countries* (1951). Another supplementary report dealt with the *National Income and Its Distribution in Underdeveloped Countries* (1951).

74. See S. H. Frankel, "United Nations Primer for Development," *Quarterly Journal of Economics* (August 1952), and the replies of W. Arthur Lewis, "United Nations Primer for Development: Comment," and Y. C. Koo, "United Nations Primer for Development: Further Comment," *Quarterly Journal of Economics* (May 1953). See also the observations of Walt W. Rostow, "A Historian's Perspective on Modern Economic Theory," *American Economic Review* (May 1952), p. 25.

75. See Fausto Clementi, "Commercio estero," in *Teoria e politica*, p. 450 ff. The importance of that factor was questioned by Celso Furtado, "Capital Formation and Economic Development," *Brazilian Economic Review* (September 1952), trans. J. Cairncross in *International Economic Papers*, 12 vols. (London, 1951–62), vol. 4.

76. An impressive catalogue of economic, political, and technological factors which have been responsible for frustrating the execution of development programs was prepared by Sam Hayes, Jr., "Personality and Culture Problems of Point IV," in Berthold F. Hoselitz, ed., *The Progress of Underdeveloped Areas* (Chicago, 1952).

77. E. S. Mason, *Promoting Economic Development* (Claremont, 1955).

78. Ragnar Nurkse in the discussion of the American Economic Association, *American Economic Review* (May 1959), p. 337.

79. Albert O. Hirschman, "Research on Economic Development: Discussion," *American Economic Review*.

80. Benjamin Higgins, "Economic Progress in Underdeveloped Countries: Discussion," *American Economic Review* (May 1959).

81. Paul N. Rosenstein-Rodan, "Problems of Industrialization of Eastern and Southeastern Europe," *Economic Journal* (June 1943).

82. For a discussion of the best methods of granting aid, see *American Economic Review* (May 1960) and the report of the World Bank and its affiliates.

83. Nurkse, *Capital Formation*; A. E. Kahn, "Investment Criteria in Development Programs," *Quarterly Journal of Economics* (February 1951). An attempt to apply the criterion of social marginal productivity to a number of empirical situations (Greece, Turkey, Portugal, Southern Italy) was made by Hollis B. Chenery, "The Application of Investment Criteria," *Quarterly Journal of Economics* (February 1953). See also the discussions of "Development Pol-

icy," *American Economic Review* (May 1950), p. 40 ff.

84. Nurkse, *Capital Formation*.

85. Marcus Fleming, "External Economics and the Doctrine of Balanced Growth," *Economic Journal* (June 1955).

86. Letiche, "Theories of Growth."

87. See J.R.T. Hughes, "Foreign Trade and Balanced Growth: The Historical Framework," and Goran Ohlin, "Balanced Economic Growth in History," submitted to the 1958 meeting of the American Economic Association, *American Economic Review* (May 1959), p. 330 ff.

88. Alexander Gerschenkron, "Economic Backwardness," in Berthold F. Hoselitz, ed., *The Progress of Underdeveloped Areas* (Chicago, 1952).

89. Walter Galenson and Harvey Leibenstein, "Investment Criteria, Productivity and Economic Development," *Quarterly Journal of Economics* (August 1955); Harvey Leibenstein, *Economic Backwardness and Economic Growth* (New York, 1957).

90. See Higgins in discussions of the American Economic Association, "Economic Progress in Underdeveloped Countries," p. 171; idem, *Economic Developments* (New York, 1957); Albert O. Hirschmann, *The Strategy of Economic Development* (New Haven, 1958); and François Perroux, *La Coexistence pacifique* (Paris, 1958).

91. Hirschmann, *The Strategy of Economic Development*, p. 79.

92. For a critical survey of these theories of "accelerated investment," see Howard S. Ellis, "Accelerated Investment As a Force in Economic Development," *Quarterly Journal of Economics* (November 1958).

93. G. S. Aubrey, "Investment Decisions in Underdeveloped Countries," in National Bureau of Economic Research, *Capital Formation and Economic Growth*, p. 397.

94. See Joseph S. Berliner, "Incentives and Economic Growth: Discussion," *American Economic Review* (May 1960).

95. S. H. Frankel, *The Economic Impact on Underdeveloped Societies* (Oxford, 1953). About the difficulties involved in applying especially the Keynesian categories to underdeveloped countries, see E. Stuart Kirby, "The Reception of Western Economics in the Orient," *Quarterly Journal of Economics* (August 1952), p. 414 ff. For a similar discussion in the light of the experiences in Turkey, see Osman Okyar, "La Théorie Keynésienne et l'économie sous-développée," *Economie appliquée* (1951), p. 106. For analyses of "economic thought" in the East and of the conflict between Western ways of thinking and the value systems prevailing in the East, see the discussions in *American Economic Review* (May 1956).

96. Haavelmo, *Economic Evolution*.

CHAPTER 40

1. Wesley C. Mitchell, *Business Cycles* (Berkeley, 1913); W. M. Persons, "Indices of Business Conditions," *Review of Economics and Statistics* 1 (January 1919).

2. Henry Ludwell Moore, *Economic Cycles* (New York, 1914), *Forecasting the Yield and the Price of Cotton* (New York, 1917), *Synthetic Economics* (New York, 1929).

3. Wassily W. Leontief, "Statistische Analyse von Angebot und Nachfrage," *Weltwirtschaftliches Archiv* (1929); Henry Schultz, *Statistical Laws of Demand and Supply* (Chicago, 1928); idem, *The Theory and Measurement of Demand* (Chicago, 1938).

4. Paul H. Douglas, *The Theory of Wages* (New York, 1934).

5. Charles F. Roos, "A Dynamic Theory of Economics," *Journal of Political Economy* (October 1927); idem, *Dynamic Economics* (Bloomington, Ind., 1934).

6. Oskar Lange, *Die Preisdispersion als Mittel zur Statistischen Messung Wirtschaftlicher Gleichgewichtsstörungen* (Leipzig, 1932).

7. The expression "cobweb theorem" was suggested by Nicholas Kaldor, "A Classificatory Note on the Determinateness of Equilibrium," *Review of Economic Studies* (February 1934).

8. Henry Schultz, "Der Sinn der statistischen Nachfragekurven," *Frankfurter Gesellschaft für Konjunkturforschung* 10 (1930); Jan Tinbergen, "Bestimmung und Deutung von Angebotskurven," *Zeitschrift für Nationalökonomie* (1930); Umberto Ricci, "Die synthetische Ökonomie von H. L. Moore," *Zeitschrift für Nationalökonomie* (1930). See Mordecai Ezekiel, "The Cobweb Theorem," *Quarterly Journal of Economics* (February 1938).

9. See also Jan Tinbergen, "Ein Schiffbauzyklus?," *Weltwirtschaftliches Archiv* (July 1930).

10. Ezekiel, "Cobweb Theorem," p. 279. About limits set to the applicability of the cobweb theorem, see F. G. Hooton, "Risk and the Cobweb Theorem," *Economic Journal* (March 1950).

11. Simon S. Kuznets, *National Income and Capital Formation* (New York, 1937).

12. Jan Tinbergen, *The Statistical Testing of Business Cycle Theories* (Geneva, 1939).

13. See also Jan Tinbergen, "Statistical Evidence on the Acceleration Principle," *Economica* (1938).

14. Idem, "Critical Remarks on Some Business Cycle Theories," *Econometrica* (April 1942); "Le Mécanisme des cycles," *Economie appliquée* (July 1949).

15. John Maynard Keynes, "The Statistical Testing of Business-Cycle Theories," *Economic Journal* (September 1939), p. 568 ff.

16. Jan Tinbergen, "On a Method of Statistical Business-Cycle Research: A Reply," *Economic Journal* (March 1940). See also Trygve Haavelmo, "Statistical Testing of Business-Cycle Theories," *Review of Economics and Statistics* (February 1943), p. 13 ff.

17. Trygve Haavelmo, "The Probability Approach in Econometrics," *Econometrica* (July 1944), supplement.

18. Cited in H. T. Davis, *The Theory of Econometrics* (Bloomington, Ind., 1941).

19. J. R. Hicks, *Economic Journal* (December 1942), p. 350.

20. Paul A. Samuelson, *Foundations of Economic Analysis* (Cambridge, Mass., 1947), p. 3.

21. Andreas G. Papandreou, *Economics As a Science* (Chicago, 1958), p. 7. For a study of the problems involved in ascertaining meaningful theorems, see Samuelson, *Foundations of Economic Analysis*. The principle of "operationalism" was developed by P. W. Bridgman, *The Logic of Modern Physics* (New York, 1927).

22. Cited in Gerhard Tintner, "Definitions of Econometrics," *Econometrica* (January 1953).

23. G. L. Shackle, *Uncertainty in Economics* (Cambridge, 1955), p. 233.

24. Tintner, "Definitions of Econometrics."

25. Wassily W. Leontief, "Econometrics," in Howard S. Ellis, ed., *A Survey of Contemporary Economics* (Philadelphia, 1948), vol. 1, p. 388.

26. Ragnar Frisch, "Propagation Problems and Impulse Problems in Dynamic Economics," in *Economic Essays in Honor of Gustav Cassel* (New York, 1933).

27. Idem, "On the Notion of Equilibrium and Disequilibrium," *Review of Economic Studies* (1935).

28. Fritz Machlup, *Essays on Economic Semantics* (Englewood Cliffs, N.J., 1963), p. 80.

29. Jan Tinbergen, "Suggestions on Quantitative Business Cycle Theories," *Econometrica* (1935). See also idem, "Schumpeter and Quantitative Research in Economics," *Review of Economics and Statistics* (May 1951), p. 1 ff.

30. Paul A. Samuelson, "Interaction between the Multiplier Analysis and the Principle of Acceleration," *Review of Economics and Statistics* (May 1939).

31. Jan Tinbergen, *Business Cycles in the United States of America, 1919–1932* (Geneva, 1939). This study formed the second part of a series published by the Economic Intelligence Service of the League of Nations under the title *Statistical Testing of Business Cycle Theories*.

32. Tjalling C. Koopmans, "The Econometric Approach to Business Fluctuations," *American Economic Review* (May 1949), p. 65 ff.

33. Lawrence R. Klein, *Economic Fluctuations in the United States, 1921–1941* (New York, 1950).

34. Lawrence R. Klein and A. Goldberger, *An Econometric Model of the United States, 1920–1952* (Amsterdam, 1955).

35. Jan Tinbergen, *The Dynamics of Business Cycles* (London, 1950); *On the Theory of Economic Policy* (Amsterdam, 1952); *Centralization and Decentralization in Economic Policy* (Amsterdam, 1954); *Economic Policy Principles and Design* (Amsterdam, 1956).

36. Haavelmo, "Probability Approach"; Tjalling C. Koopmans, "Statistical Estimations of Simultaneous Economic Relations," *Journal of American Statistical Association* (1945); idem, "Measurement without Theory," *Review of Economics and Statistics* (August 1947). For a survey of these techniques, see idem *Three Essays on the State of Economic Science* (New York, 1957), p. 197 ff.

37. Idem, "Identification Problems in Econometric Model Construction," *Econometrica* (April 1949); Leonid Hurwicz, "Generalization of the Concept of Identification," in Tjalling C. Koopmans, ed., *Statistical Inference in Dynamic Economic Models* (New York, 1950).

38. See also Jacob Marschak, "Statistical Inference in Economics," in Koopmans, ed., *Statistical Inference*.

39. Koopmans, *Three Essays*.

40. Wassily W. Leontief, "The State of Economic Science," *Review of Economics and Statistics* (May 1958).

41. See also the methodological controversy between Koopmans ("Measurement without Theory") and R. Vining ("Methodological Issues in Quantitative Economics," *Review of Economics and Statistics* [May 1949]).

42. See, among others, R. Ruggles, "Methodological Developments," in Ellis, ed., *Contemporary Economics,* vol. 2; D. Novick, "Mathematics, Logic, Quantity and Method" (with discussion by various economists) *Review of Economics and Statistics* (November 1954); and Maurice Allais, "Puissance et dangers de l'utilisation de l'outil mathématique en économique," *Econometrica* (January 1954), p. 58 ff.

43. Jacob Marschak, "Mathematics for Economists," *Review of Economics and Statistics* (November 1947).

44. Ruggles, "Methodological Developments."

45. John M. Clark, "Mathematical Economists and Others," *Econometrica* (April 1947); and George J. Stigler, *Five Lectures on Economic Problems* (London, 1949).

46. Joseph Alois Schumpeter, *Business Cycles: A Theoretical, Historical and Statistical Analysis of the Capitalist Process,* 2 vols. (New York, 1939), 1: 38.

47. See, among others, Robert A. Gordon, "The Quantitative Historical Approach," *Econometrica* (April 1949).

48. Koopmans, "Econometric Approach."

49. See a paper submitted by Herman O. A. Wold to the 1947 meeting of the Econometric Society, "Statistical Analysis of Economic Relationships," *Econometrica* (July 1949), supplement, p. 4 ff.

50. Dennis Holme Robertson, *Utility and All That* (London, 1952), p. 60.

51. Ragnar Frisch, "Opening Address of the Kiel Meeting," *Econometrica* (July 1956), p. 301.

52. Trygve Haavelmo, "Presidential Address," *Econometrica* (July 1958), p. 355.

53. For a critical discussion of the assumptions commonly made in econometric studies, see also S. Schoeffler, *The Failure of Economics* (Cambridge, Mass., 1955).

54. Papandreou, *Economics As a Science.*

55. Koopmans, *Three Essays.*

56. Erwin Kruh, "Econometric Models," *American Economic Review* (May 1965).

57. Trygve Haavelmo, "The Role of the Econometrician in the Advancement of Economic Theory," *Econometrica* (July 1958).

58. Carl Shoup, "Development and Use of National Income Data," in Ellis, ed., *Contemporary Economics,* vol. 1, chap. 8.

59. A first comprehensive study of this type was published by the board of governors of the Federal Reserve System, in *Flow of Funds in the United States, 1939–1953* (Washington, D.C., 1955).

60. Morris A. Copeland, *A Study of Moneyflows in the United States* (New York, 1952); Jan Tinbergen and Schouten, "National Income Accounts As a Means of Currency Analysis," trans. J. Kahane, in *International Economic Papers,* 12 vols. (London, 1951–62), vol. 5.

61. Claudio Segré, "Monetary Surveys and Monetary Analysis," *Quarterly Journal of Economics* (February 1958).

62. Gerhard Colm, "Economic Projections," *American Economic Review* (March 1958).

63. Eric Lindahl, "Swedish Experiences in Economic Planning," *American Economic Review* (May 1950).

64. See, for instance, C. Holt, "Linear Decision Rules for Economic Stabilization and Growth," *Quarterly Journal of Economics* (February 1962); H. Theil, *Optimal Decision Rules for Government and Industry* (Chicago, 1964).

65. Wassily W. Leontief, *The Structure of the American Economy* (New York, 1941, 2nd ed., 1951).

66. Wassily W. Leontief, "Recent Developments in the Study of Inter-Industrial Relationships," *American Economic Review* (May 1949).

67. Goran Nyblén, *The Problem of Summation in Economic Science* (Lund, 1951), pp. 22, 118, 240.

68. See "Proceedings of the American Economic Association," *American Economic Review* (May 1949). See also the proceedings of the 1952 session of the Conference on Income and Wealth organized by the National Bureau of Economic Research, *Input-Output Analysis: An Appraisal, Studies in Income and Wealth* (Princeton, 1955).

69. For instance, Koopmans, *Three Essays*, p. 191.

70. D. Hawkins, "Some Conditions for Macroeconomic Stability," *Econometrica* (October 1948).

71. R.G.D. Allen, "The Mathematical Foundation of Economic Theory," *Quarterly Journal of Economics* (1949); and George B. Dantzig and Marshall K. Wood, "Programming of Interdependent Activities," *Econometrica* (July–October 1949). See also Robert Dorfman, "Mathematical or Linear Programming," *American Economic Review* (December 1953); William J. Baumol, "Activity Analysis in One Lesson," *American Economic Review* (December 1958).

72. About the practical application of mathematical programming, see Robert Dorfman, *Application of Linear Programming to the Theory of the Firm* (Berkeley, 1951); Tjalling C. Koopmans, ed., *Activity Analysis of Production and Allocation* (New York, 1951). See also idem, *An Introduction to Linear Programming* (New York, 1953).

73. Koopmans, "Analysis of Production As an Efficient Combination of Activities," *Activity Analysis*, p. 33 ff, and Baumol, "Activity Analysis."

CHAPTER 41

1. Kenneth J. Arrow, "Utilities, Attitudes, Choices," *Econometrica* (January 1958).

2. Idem, "Alternative Approaches to the Theory of Choice in Risk-Taking Situations," *Econometrica* (October 1951), p. 406. For a critical discussion of the concept of "rational behavior," see G. Katona, "Rational Behavior and Economic Behavior," *Psychological Review* (September 1953).

3. Gerhard Tintner, "A Contribution to the Non-Static Theory of Choice," *Quarterly Journal of Economics* (February 1942), p. 278.

4. See Arrow, "Utilities, Attitudes, Choices" and idem, "Alternative Approaches."

5. See James S. Duesenberry, *Income, Savings and the Theory of Consumer Behavior* (Cambridge, Mass., 1949).

6. Johan Åckerman, "The Setting of the Central Problem," *Econometrica* (1963), and "Economic Plans and Causal Analysis," trans. by author in *International Economic Papers*, 12 vols. (London,

1951–62), vol. 4. Ackerman's main work was entitled "Ekonomisk Teori," *International Economics*, 2 vols. (1939 and 1944).

7. Frank H. Knight, *Risk, Uncertainty and Profit* (Boston, 1921).

8. See the analysis in Arrow, "Alternative Approaches."

9. Ibid., p. 409.

10. M. Shubik, "Information, Risk, Ignorance," *Quarterly Journal of Economics* (November 1954).

11. John Hicks, *Value and Capital* (Oxford, 1939); Nicholas Kaldor, "Speculation and Economic Stability," *Review of Economic Studies* (October 1939); M. Kalecki, *Theory of Economic Dynamics* (London, 1954); Friedrich A. Lutz, "The Structure of Interest Rates," *Quarterly Journal of Economics* (November 1940); Joan Robinson, *The Rate of Interest and Other Essays* (London, 1952).

12. See Holbrook Working, "The Investigation of Economic Expectations," *American Economic Review* (May 1949), p. 151 ff.

13. A considerable discussion was initiated by the "theory of normal backwardation" advanced by J. M. Keynes. See Nicholas Kaldor, J.C.R. Dow, and R. G. Hawtrey, "A Symposium on the Theory of the Futures Market," *Review of Economic Studies* (1939–40); Gerda Blau, "Some Aspects of the Theory of the Futures Market," *Review of Economic Studies* (1944–45).

14. Tintner, "Theory of Choice," p. 279.

15. Harold Hotelling, "The Statistical Method," *American Statistician* (December 1958).

16. Abraham Wald, *Statistical Decision Functions* (New York, 1950).

17. Jacob Marschak, "Rational Behavior, Uncertain Prospects and Measurable Utility," *Econometrica* (April 1950).

18. Such assumptions were made by Marschak, Hart, Tintner, and others. See, for example, Gerhard Tintner, "The Pure Theory of Production under Technological Risk and Uncertainty," *Econometrica* (1941). See also the discussion of Marschak's "Role of Liquidity under Complete and Incomplete Information," *American Economic Review* (May 1949).

19. Albert G. Hart, *Anticipations, Uncertainty and Dynamic Planning* (Chicago, 1940).

20. Milton Friedman and Leonard J. Savage, "Utility Analysis of Choices Involving Risk," *Journal of Political Economy* (August 1948). Idem, "The Expected Utility Hypothesis," *Journal of Political Economy* (December 1952).

21. Arrow, "Alternative Approaches."

22. Various axioms on the ordering of income functions were discussed by Arrow in "Alternative Approaches," p. 431.

23. Kenneth J. Arrow, "Statistics and Economic Policy," *Econometrica* (October 1957).

24. See the discussion in *American Economic Review* (May 1949), p. 197.

25. Nicholas Georgescu Roegen, "Choice, Expectations and Measurability," *Quarterly Journal of Economics* (November 1954). An extensive literature about this controversy is listed in this article.

26. Richard M. Goodwin, "Liquidity and Uncertainty: Discussion," *American Economic Review* (May 1949), p. 200.

27. G. L. Shackle, *Expectations in Economics* (Cambridge, 1949); idem, *Uncertainty in Economics* (Cambridge, 1955).

28. Arrow, "Alternative Approaches," p. 415.

29. Maurice Allais, *Fondement d'une théorie positive des choix* (Paris, 1955).

30. Maurice Fréchet, "Sur la distinction entre les probabilités rationnelles et irrationnelles," *Econometrica* (July 1955). See the literature cited in this article.

31. D. van Dantzig, "Sur quelques questions de la théorie mathématique du choix pondéré," referred to in *Econometrica* (January–April 1963), p. 281.

32. See *19th Annual Report (1950–51)* of the Cowles Commission for Research in Economics (Chicago, 1951), p. 8.

33. John von Neumann and Oskar Morgenstern, *Theory of Games and Economic Behavior* (Princeton, 1944).

34. Oskar Morgenstern, "Limits to the Use of Mathematics in Economics," in James C. Charlesworth, ed., *Mathematics and the Social Sciences* (Philadelphia, 1963), p. 18.

35. See Oskar Morgenstern, "Oligopoly, Monopolistic Competition, and the Theory of Games," *American Economic Review* (May 1948).

36. R. H. Strotz, "Cardinal Utility," *American Economic Review* (May 1953).

37. Ferdinand Zeuthen, "Science and Welfare in Economic Policy," *Quarterly Journal of Economics* (November 1959); Ragnar Frisch, "Dynamic Utility," *Econometrica* (July 1964).

38. Leonid Hurwicz, "What Happened to the Theory of Games?," *American Economic Review* (May 1953).

39. See also Marschak, "Rational Behavior."

40. Thomas Schelling, *The Strategy of Conflict* (Cambridge, 1960).

41. Leonid Hurwicz, "Mathematics in Economics," in Charlesworth, ed., *Mathematics and the Social Sciences.*

42. For a short survey of such studies, see H. A. Simon, "Theories of Decision-Making in Economics and Behavioral Science," *American Economic Review* (June 1959).

43. S. Siegel and L. E. Fouraker, *Bargaining and Group Decision Making Experiment in Bilateral Monopoly* (New York, 1960).

NOTES TO APPENDIXES

APPENDIX A

1. See Karl Pribram *Conflicting Patterns of Thought* (Washington, D.C., 1949).

2. Considerations of space do not permit a discussion of the methods of reasoning which are coordinated to that pattern. The author intends to supplement the present short outline by a comprehensive history of economic reasoning.

3. The role played by the equilibrium concept in the social and moral philosophies of the seventeenth and eighteenth centuries deserves careful examination.

4. *Statistics,* in the modern sense of the term, developed after the Scholastic distinction between essential and accidental attributes of the things had lost importance. Thus the freedom was gained to group things and events in accordance with any characteristics. A similar logical process led to the introduction of insurance as applied to a great variety of risks.

5. It may be mentioned that John Law's value concept, as distinct from John Locke's concept, was tinged with important "subjective" elements.

6. American economists and sociologists who were not familiar with the methods of dialectic reasoning substituted for the rigid concept of "materialistic" interpretation of history the loose concept of "economic interpretation." Adjusted to the nominalistic pattern of thought, the latter concept simply implied the search for causal relationships between specific historical events and the interests of specific economically powerful groups.

7. Among various absurd statements which Marx requested his followers to believe was the contention that in a "classless" society the laws of dialectics would cease to operate and men would acquire full "freedom" in relation to nature.

8. In Central Europe the capital of Austria, Vienna, was practically the only place where hypothetical reasoning had secured a firm foothold.

9. Although fairly obvious, it is frequently overlooked that the use of fictions is incompatible with all methods of reasoning which are based on the belief in the identity of the rules of reason and the rules governing the behavior of the outside events.

10. For reasons of space it is considered sufficient to indicate briefly Marshall's position in the history of economic reasoning, without entering into a closer analysis of his well-known doctrine.

11. It is an open question whether the Darwinian concept of evolution had a teleological connotation. Although that concept had been suggested by the Malthusian theory of population, it was hardly ever used in economic analysis.

12. More recent developments of that reasoning will be summarized in a second article.

APPENDIX B

1. See Karl Pribram, *Conflicting Patterns of Thought* (Washington, 1949).

APPENDIX C

1. K. J. Arrow, "Mathematical Models," in *The Policy Sciences* (1951), Chapter 8, p. 135.

2. About a number of meanings attached by economists to the terms *structure* and *structural change*, see an interesting article by F. Machlup in *Zeitschrift für Nationalökonomie* (1958). This analysis could be supplemented by grouping the various meanings according to the patterns of thought used in applying them.

Works by Karl Pribram

This list of works does not include minor articles, minor contributions to conferences, or any papers or monographs written for internal use by government or other offices.

BOOKS

Geschichte der österreichischen Gewerbepolitik von 1740 bis 1798 (History of Austria's Commercial Policy for Trades and Manufacturing, from 1740 to 1798). Based on the original documents. Leipzig, 1907. 614 pp.

Die Entstehung der individualistischen Sozialphilosophie (The Origins of the Individualistic Social Philosophy). Leipzig, 1912. 102 pp.

Die Probleme der Internationalen Sozialpolitik (The Problems of International Social Policy). Vol. 3., pt. 3, *Zeitfragen aus dem Gebiete der Soziologie (Topical Questions in the Field of Sociology).* Leipzig, 1927. 196 pp.

Cartel Problems: An Analysis of Collective Monopolies in Europe with American Application. Washington, D.C.: Institute of Economics of the Brookings Institution, 1935.

Conflicting Patterns of Thought. Public Affairs Press. Washington, D.C., 1949. 176 pp.

John Maynard Keynes, Karl Pribram, and E. J. Phelan. "World Unemployment and Its Problems." In *Unemployment as a World Problem* (Lectures of the Harris Foundation, 1931), edited by Quincy Wright. Chicago: University of Chicago Press, 1931.

ARTICLES, ESSAYS, AND REVIEWS

History of Social Philosophy and of Economic Reasoning

"Die Idee des Gleichgewichts in der alteren nationaloekonomischen Theorie" (The Equilibrium Concept in Older Economic Theory). *Zeitschrift für Volkswirtschaft, Sozialpolitik und Verwaltung* (1908): 28 pp.

"Der Individualismus in der neueren Rechtsphilosophie" (Individualism in the Recent Philosophy of Law). *Festschrift für Franz Klein Manzsche k.u.k. Hof-und Universitäts-Buchhandlung* (Vienna), 1914. 43 pp.

"Preisbildung und Recht" (Price Formation and the Law). *Oesterreichische Zeitschrift für Strafrecht* 7 (1916): 39 pp.

"Freiheit oder Zwang im Wirtschaftsleben der Zukunft" (Freedom or Coercion in the Economic Life of the Future). *Oesterreichische Eisenbahnzeitung* (November 1916): 14 pp.

"Sozialisierung und wirtschaftliche Individualrechte" (Socialization and Economic Rights of Individuals). *Oesterreichischer Volkswirt* (1916?): 14 pp.

"Erkenntniskritische Betrachtungen zum Streit Über

die Landerautonomie in Oesterreich" (Reflections of a Legal, Constitutional, and Philosophical
Nature on the Autonomy Struggle of the Austrian
Provinces). *Zeitschrift für öffentliches Recht* 1
(1917): 40 pp.

"Die Weltanschauungen der Völker und ihre Politik"
(The Philosophies of Nations and Their Politics).
Archiv für Sozialwissenschaft und Sozialpolitik
44, no. 1 (1917): 36 pp.

> This article, together with the 1912 book
> *Origin of the Individualistic Social Philoso-*
> *phy*, had a decisive and long-lasting influ-
> ence on the intellectual discussion of these
> problems in the early part of the century and
> is still quoted today.

"Deutscher Nationalismus und Deutscher Sozialismus" (German Nationalism and German Socialism). *Archiv für Sozialwissenschaft und*
Sozialpolitik 49, no. 2 (1922): 78 pp.

"Zur Klassifizierung der soziologischen Theorien"
(On Classifying Sociological Theories). *Kölner*
Vierteljahrshefte für Soziologie 5, no. 3 (1925?):
7 pp.

"Les Caractères Essentiels de la Démocratie" (The
Essential Characteristics of Democracy). *Revue*
de Genève (1926): 14 pp.

"Nominalismus und Bergriffsrealismus in der Nationalökonomie" (Nominalism and Realism in
the Scholastic Sense, Applied to Economics).
Schmollers Jahrbuch 55 (1931): 42 pp.

"Die vier Begriffe der Weltwirtschaft und ihre Problematik" (The Four Concepts of World Economy
and Their Problems). In *Festschrift für Werner*
Sombart. Munich: Duncker and Humblot, 1933.
30 pp.

"Prolegomena to a History of Economic Reasoning."
Quarterly Journal of Economics 65, no. 1 (February 1951): 37 pp.

"Patterns of Economic Reasoning." *American Eco-*
nomic Review, 43, no. 2 (May 1953): 15 pp.

Review of *The Psychology of Economics* by Walter
Weisskopf, *American Economic Review* (September 1956): 674–76.

Review of *Economic Fictions—A Critique of Subjec-*
tivistic Economic Theory by Paul K. Crosser,
American Economic Review (1958): 440–42.

Economics and Business Cycle Problems

"Das erste österreichische Patentgesetz vom 16. Janner
1810. Ein Beitrag zur Geschichte der österreichischen Gewerbepolitik" (The First Austrian
Patent Law of 16 January 1810. A Contribution to
the History of Austrian Commercial Policy for
Trades and Manufacturing). *Oesterreichisches*
Patentblatt (1910), nos. 2 and 3. Reprint. Manzsche k.u.k. Hof Verlagsund- und Universitäts-
Buchhandlung (1910): 49 pp.

"Über die Beziehungen zwischen der Handelspolitik
und der auswärtigen Politik" (On the Relations
between Trade Policy and Foreign Policy).
Zeitschrift für Volkswirtschaft, Sozialpolitik und
Verwaltung 25 (1916).

"Die weltwirtschaftliche Lage im Spiegel des Schrift-
tums der Weltwirtschaftskonferenz (Mai 1927)"
(The International Economic Situation, as Re-
flected in the Literature of the World Economic
Conference of May 1927). *Weltwirtschaftliches*
Archiv. Institut für Weltwirtschaft (University of
Kiel) 26 (October 1927): 133 pp.

"Konjunkturbeobachtung" (Observation of the Business
Cycle). *Zeitschrift für Schweizer Statistik und Vol-*
kswirtschaft 64 (1928).

"Internationale Wirtschaftspolitik und Internationale
Sozialpolitik. Ihre Wurzeln und Anschauungsformen" (International Economic Policy and International Social Policy: Their Roots and Their
Various Implications). Public inaugural address

on taking over the chair for economics at the
University of Frankfort. *Oeffentliche Antritts-*
vorlesung am (14 Novmber 1928). Frankfurter
Universitätsreden, Frankfurt am Main: Verlag
Englert and Schlosser, 1928. 16pp.

"Die städtische Grundrente im Konjunkturverlauf"
(The Urban Groundrent in the Course of the Business Cycle). *Frankfurter Gesellschaft für Kon-*
junkturforschung. Bonn (1930).

Encyclopaedia of the Social Sciences, s. v. "Christian
Jacob Kraus," "Heinrich Rau," "Sartorius von
Waltershausen," 1933.

"Equilibrium Concept and Business Cycle Statistics."
Twenty-second Session of the International Statistical Institute in London. The Hague, 1934.

"Controlled Competition and the Organization of
American Industry." *Quarterly Journal of Eco-*
nomics 49 (May 1935): 22 pp.

"How to Ascertain the Definition of Some Notions
Which Are Fundamental to Business Cycle Anal-
ysis." Twenty-third Session of the International
Statistical Institute in Athens. The Hague, 1936.

"The Notion of 'Economic System' Underlying
Business Cycle Analysis." *Review of Economic*
Statistics (May 1937): 16 columns.

"Gleichgewichtsvorstellungen in der Konjunkturtheorie" (Equilibrium Concepts in Business Cycle Theory). *Zeitschrift für Nationalökonomie*
(Vienna) 8, no. 2 (1937): 16 pp.

"Cartel Problems: A Rejoinder to a Review of Pribram's Book of That Title." *Journal of Political Economy* 45, no. 1 (February 1937): 3 pp.

"Some Dynamic Aspects of the Urban Groundrent: I. Europe, II. United States." Cowles Commission for Research in Economics, Report of the Fifth Annual Conference on Economics and Statistics, held at Colorado Springs, Colo., 3–28 July 1939. 6 pp.

"Residual, Differential, and Absolute Groundrents and Their Cyclical Fluctuations." *Econometrica* (January 1940): 16 pp.

"Rearmament and a More Flexible Tariff Structure for the United States." *American Economic Review* 42, no. 3 (June 1952): 11 pp.

Social Policy, Employment, and Labor Problems

"Der Lohnschutz des gewerblichen Arbeiters nach österreichischem Recht" (Wage Protection for the Industrial Worker According to Austrian Law). Vienna, 1904.

"Die Sozialpolitik im neuen Oesterreich" (The Social Policy in the New Austria). *Archiv für Sozialwissenschaft und Sozialpolitik* 48, no. 3 (1921): 65 pp.

"Die Vereinheitlichung der Sozialversicheiung" (The Unification of Social Insurance). *Internationale Rundschau der Arbeit* (Geneva) 3 (March 1925): 18 pp.

> Also published in English, *The International Labour Review*, International Labour Office, and in French, *Revue Internationale du Travail*.

"Die Wandlungen des Begriffs der Sozialpolitik" (Changing Concepts in Defining Social Policy). *Die Wirtschaftswissenschaft nach dem Kriege (Economic Science after the War)*. In *Festschrift für Lujo Brentano*, 1924. Munich: Duncker and Humblot, 1925. 42 pp.

"Die Sozialpolitik als theoretische Disziplin" (Social Policy as a Theoretical Discipline). *Archiv für Sozialwissenschaft und Sozialpolitik* 55 (1926): 52 pp.

"Problemi Internazionali delle Assicurazioni Sociali" (International Problems of Social Insurance). *Cassa Nazionale per le Assicurazioni Sociali*. Rome, 1926. Vol. 2. 18 pp.

"Die englische Gewerkschafsbewegung der Kriegs— und Nachkriegszeit" (The English Trade Union Movement in the War and Postwar Period). Review of *Early Socialist Days*, by W. Stephen Sanders, *Archiv für Geschichte des Sozialismus und der Arbeiterbewegung* 13 (1927/1928): 315–20.

"Die Verteilung der finanziellen Lasten in der Sozialversicherung" (The Distribution of the Financial Burden of Social Insurance). *Beiträge zur Finanzwissenschaft* (Tübingen) 1 (March 1928): 19 pp.

"Die Deutungen der Sozialpolitik" (Definitions of Social Policy). *Schmollers Jahrbuch (für Gesetzgebung, Verwaltung, und Volkswirtschaft im Deutschen Reich)* 56, no. 2 (1932): 33 pp.

"Das Problem der Verantwortlichkeit in der Sozialpolitik" (The Problem of Responsibility in Social Policy). In *Festschrift für Carl Gründberg*, edited by C. L. Hirschfeld. Leipzig, 1932. 12 pp.

"Einigungs- und Zwangssysteme im Schlichtungswesen" (Systems of Mediation and Compulsion in Labor Arbitration). *Schriften des Vereins für Sozialpolitik* 179 (1932): 40 pp.

Encyclopaedia of the Social Sciences, s.v. "Unemployment," 1933.

Encyclopaedia of the Social Sciences, s.v. "Trade Unions in Eastern Europe," 1933.

"A Unified Program for the Unemployed." *American Economic Review* (Suppl.). 25, no. 1 (March 1935).

"European Experience with Social Insurance." *Plan Age* (April 1935).

"Some Causes of Economic Distress and Their Social Significance." National Conference of Social Work. Atlantic City, N.J., 1936.

"Some Economic and Social Problems in Health Insurance: Social Security in the United States." *Social Security in the United States* (1936): 12 pp.

"Social 'Insurance' in Europe and Social 'Security' in the United States. A Comparative Analysis." *International Labor Review* (Geneva) (December 1937). (Also published in French and German. The German version was published in two parts, February and March 1938.) Approx. 32 pp.

"The Functions of Reserves in Old Age Benefit Plans." *Quarterly Journal of Economics* (August 1938): 25 pp.

"Labor Dispute Disqualification in Unemployment Compensation." *Monthly Labor Review* (January 1941).

"Employment Stabilization through Pay Roll Taxation." *Quarterly Journal of Economics* (November 1942).

"The Future of the International Labor Organization."
    Foreign Affairs (October 1942): 10 pp.
"Observations on the Influence of Philosophical Prin-
    ciples on Social Organization." International In-

stitute of Sociology. Papers and Proceedings on
the Nineteenth International Congress of Sociology. Mexico City. 31 August–6 September 1960.
Vol. 2. 10 pp.

Housing and Urban Development

Please refer to two articles on the urban groundrent
listed under "Economics and Business Cycle Problems": "Die städtische Grundrente im Konjunkturverlauf," 1930, and "Residual, Differential, and Absolute Groundrents and Their Cyclical Fluctuations,"
1940.
"Wohngrösse und Mietzinshöhe in den Hauszinss-
    teuerpflichtigen Orten Oesterreichs" (Apartment
    Sizes and Rent Costs in Localities in Austria with
    Taxes on Their Rental Building). *Statistische
    Monatsschrift* 17 (November 1912). Reprint.
    Brünn, 1912. 43 pp. Tables.
"Probleme des Städtebaues im Lichte der
    Wirtschaftspolitik" (Problems of Urban Develop-
    ment in the Light of Economic Policy).
    *Schmollers Jahrbuch (für Gesetzgebung, Ver-
    waltung, und Volkswirtschaft)*, n.s. 41 (1917): 14
    pp.
"Die Finanzierung des Wohnungsbaues im den Länd-

ern mit Mietzinsbeschränkung" (The Financing
of Housing Construction in Countries with Rent-
Control). *Internationale Rundschau der Arbeit
Genf* (Geneva) (November/December 1928): 30
pp.

> Also published in English, *The International
> Labour Review,* International Labour Office,
> and in French, *Revue International du
> Travail.*

"Die volkswirtschaftlichen Probleme der Deutschen
    Wohnungswirtschaft" (The Economic Problems of
    the German Housing Policy). *Schriften des Ver-
    eins für Sozialpolitik* 177 (1930): 112 pp.
Encyclopaedia of the Social Sciences, s.v. "European
    Housing," 1932.
"Housing Policy and the Defense Program." *Ameri-
    can Economic Review* 31, no. 4 (December 1941):
    6 pp.

Statistics

"Die Statistik als Wissenschaft in Oesterreich im 19.
    Jahrhundert, nebst einem Abriss einer Allge-
    meinen Geschichte der Statistik" (Statistics as
    Science in Austria in the Nineteenth Century, In-
    cluding a Synopsis of the General History of Sta-
    tistics). *Statistische Monatsschrift* 18 (August/
    September 1913). Reprint. Brünn, 1913. 79 pp.
"Der Wert des landwirtschaftlichen Grundbesitzes in
    Ungarn und Oesterreich" (The Value of Agri-
    cultural Real Estate Holdings in Hungary and
    Austria). *Statistische Monatsschrift* 20 (1915).
    Reprint. Brünn, 1915. Tables.
"Die Entwicklung der Lebensmittelpreise in Oester-
    reich in den Kriegsjahren 1914 und 1915" (The
    Development of Food Prices in Austria during the
    War Years, 1914–1915). *Statistische Mon-
    atsschrift Neue Folge* 21 (February/March 1916).
    Reprint. Brunn, 1916. 51 pp. Tables, graphs.
"Der Mehlverbrauch der Bevölkerung Oesterreichs in
    der Friedenszeit." (The Consumption of Flour in
    Peacetime by the Population of Austria). *Statis-
    tische Monatsschrift* 21 (December 1916). Re-
    print. Brünn, 1916. 21 pp. Tables.
"Zur Entwicklung der Lebensmittelpreise in der
    Kriegszeit" (On the Development of Food Prices
    in Wartime). *Archiv für Sozialwissenschaft und*

Sozialpolitik 43, no. 3 (1917). (*Krieg und
    Wirtschaft*, no. 6): (May 1917). 34 pp. Tables.
"Note sur les Nombres Indices du Coût de la Vie"
    (Remark on the Index Figures of Living Costs).
    Bulletin de l'Institut Internationale de Statistique
    (The Hague) 21 (1924).
"Das International Arbeitsamt und die international
    vergleichende Statistik" (International Labour Of-
    fice [ILO] and International Comparative Statis-
    tics). *Deutsches Statistisches Zentralblatt*, nos.
    5/6 and 7/8 (1925): 9 columns.
"Probleme der Internationalen Arbeitsstatistik"
    (Problems of International Labor Statistics),
    Kieler Vorträge, no. 14. Institut für Welt-
    wirtschaft. Universitat Kiel (Lectures at the In-
    stitute for International Economics, University of
    Kiel, Germany). Geneva, 1925, 16 pp.
"The Scope of Labour Statistics." *International La-
    bour Review* (Geneva) 14, no. 4 (October 1926).

> Also published in French, *Revue Interna-
> tionale du Travail,* and in German, *Interna-
> tionale Rundschau der Arbeit.*

*Handwörterbuch der Arbeitswissenschaft (Encyclo-
    paedia of Labor Science)*, s.v. "Internationale Ar-
    beitsstatistik, Grundbegriffe und Verfahren" (In-

ternational Labor Statistics, Basic Concepts and Methods), 1926 or early 1927.

"Die Zukunft des Internationalen Statistischen Instituts" (The Future of the International Statistical Institute). *Allgemeines Statistisches Archiv*. Verlag Gustav Fischer (Geneva) 18 (1929): 10 pp.

"Rapport sur l'Uniformisation Internationale des Statistiques de l'Habitation Urbaine" (Report on the International Uniformization of Urban Housing Statistics). *Bulletin de l'Institut International de Statistique* 24 (1930).

"European Experience and New Deal Statistics." *Journal of the American Statistical Association* 30 (March 1935): 6 pp.

Index

Abelard, Pierre, 21
Absolute monarchy, 35
Abstraction concept, 5
Acceleration principle, 477, 483, 484, 486, 520–27
Achenwall, Gottfried, 93
Acquisitive principle, 39
Addresses to the German Nation (Fichte), 210
Adler, Max, 270
Aeterni Patria, 241
Affluent Society, The (Galbraith), 556–57
Aftalion, Albert, 328, 345, 512
Agio theory of interest, 319–22, 326–28; adoption of, 327–28
Agriculture: law of diminishing returns of, 85, 88, 119, 154, 174; Physiocratic theory of, 110; *Tableau économique*, 104–6; of USSR, 397–99, 401, 409–10, 412
Åkerman, Johan, 493, 574
Albertus Magnus, 4, 14
Alchemy, 53, 90
Alembert, Jean d', 102
Alexander of Hales, 11, 16
Alexandrists, 33
Allais, Maurice, 460
Allen, R.G.D., 462
Allgemeine Geldlehre (Wagemann), 375
Alternative costs principle, 316
Althusius, Johannes, 61
Ambrosius, bishop of Milan, 10
American Economic Association, 230
Ami des hommes, L' (Mirabeau), 107
Amonn, Alfred, 420
Amoroso, Luigi, 287, 444, 517
Anderson, James, 154
Angell, James W., 468

Annuities, usury prohibition and, 19, 25, 53
Anti-Bullionists, 163
Antonius of Florence, Saint, 24, 25
Aquinas, Saint Thomas, 4; *Summa Theologica*, 4. *See also* Thomistic economics
Arabian philosophy, 21
Argenson, Marc René de Voyer D', 99
Aristotelianism, 4–20; Renaissance and, 32–33
Aristotle, 4
Arrow, Kenneth J., 466
Asgill, John, 74
Ashley, William James, 295
Associationism, 124, 142, 144, 166, 171, 434
Ateliers nationaux, 199
Augustine, Saint, 10, 16
Aujac, Henri, 475
Auspitz, Rudolf, 304
Austria: industrial planning in, 96; Marxism in, 267, 270; socialism in, 382
Austrian Cameralists, 91–93
Austrian economics, 298, 372; business cycle theory, 480–82; capital theory, 436; income analysis, 470–73; marginalism methodology, 418–23; marginal utility analysis, 231, 279, 314–19, 363; monetary theory, 335–36, 470–73; neoscholastic economics, 241, 243–44; price theory, 342; production theory, 437; profit theory, 329–30; static vs. dynamic analysis, 516; value theory, 373–74; wage theory, 331–32
Averroës, 4
Averroism, 33

Back, Joseph, 379
Bacon, Francis, 35; *Novum Organum*, 56
Bacon, Roger, 21, 33

Baconian economics, prolegomenon, 587–91

Baconian mercantilism, 37, 55–78

Baden-Durlach, Karl Friedrich von, 114

Baden School, 225

Bagehot, Walter, 293

Bailey, Samuel, 176–77

Balance of industry concept, 77, 78, 84, 85, 96

Balance of payments, 67. *See also* International trade

Balance of trade: Baconian mercantilism on, 70; in eighteenth century, 84, 98–99; equivalence principle and, 45–47; in the fifteenth and sixteenth centuries, 45–49; Italian mercantilism on, 87; refined mercantilism on, 81; species transactions and, 46–49. *See also* International trade

Balkans, 59

Bank Bill (1819), 162

Bank Charter Act (1844), 187–88

Bank of England, 74

Banking, 81; business cycle theory and, 343–44, 348, 350, 351, 476–81; monopoly, 271; reserve policy, 474

Banking School, 187–88

Bank notes, 26, 338; issue of, 334; and metallic reserves, 73

Barbon, Nicholas, 71, 73, 74, 77

Barone, Enrico, 457, 459, 463–65

Barth, Paul, 251

Barton, John, 152

Bastable, Charles F., 531

Bastiat, Claude Frédéric, 193

Baudeaux, Nicholas, 107

Baudin, Louis, 193

Baudrillart, Henri, 191

Bauer, Otto, 270, 272, 394, 395

Bazard, Saint-Amand, 198

Bebel, August, 216

Beccaria, Marchese di, 86; *Dei delitti e delle pene,* 86; *Elementi di economia pubblica,* 86

Becher, Johann Joachim, 91–92; *Physica subterranea,* 90; *Politische Discurs . . . ,* 92

Becher's principle, 92

Behavior analysis: in decision making, 573–76, 578; rationality factor, 621–23

Behaviorism, 423–26

Belgium: historism in, 223; neoscholastic economics in, 241

Bellamy, Edward, *Looking Backward,* 208

Belloni, Girolamo, 99

Belloni, Marchese Dirolamo, 87

Bendixen, Friedrich, 239

Benedict XIV, pope, 55

Benevolence, 121

Bentham, Jeremy: analytic methods of, 141–42; on government function, 143; marginal utility analysis of, 279; on natural law, 141; utilitarianism of, 141, 143

Benthamite economics, 139–46, 166–67; population theory, 153–54; prolegomenon, 591–94

Bergson, Abram, 466

Bergson, Henri, 269

Berkeley, George, 122

Bernardelli, Hano, 423

Bernard of Clairvaux, 21

Bernardino of Siena, 25

Bernoulli, Daniel, 279

Bernstein, Edward, 268

Bernstein, P. L., 441

Bernstein Plan, 549

Berolzheimer, Fritz, 224

Beveridge, Sir William, 510

Biblical precepts: on private property, 11; on usury, 17

Bickerdike, C. F., 477

Biel, Gabriel, 25

Bills of exchange, 26–27

Bimetalism, 333–34

Blackstone, Sir William, 141

Blanc, Louis, 199

Blanqui, Jérôme A., 190

Block, Maurice, 193

Bodin, Jean, 35, 44–45, 52; *Reply to the Paradoxes of M. de Malestroit,* 45

Böhm, F., 391

Böhm-Bawerk, Eugen: business cycle theory, 349; capital interest theory, 319–23, 326–28; capital theory, 329; economic theory, 235; interest theory, 116, 118; marginal utility analysis, 315–16, 318; productivity theory, 319–22; on time factor, 176; wage theory, 321

Boisguillebert, Sieur de, 97–98

Bolshevism, 272–75; Lenin and, 273–75; revolution and, 397–98

Bolshevist economics, 396–413; capitalist categories in, 402; depreciation in, 405; dynamic equilibrium principle of, 399, 401; interest on capital in, 404–5; labor cost theory of value of, 402, 404; law of value of, 401; Marxist profit theory of, 259

Bonar, James, 327, 585

Boniface VIII, *Unam Sanctam,* 7

Bonnet, V., 192

Bookkeeping, 26, 46

Bortkiewicz, L. von, 255, 258

Bosanquet, Bernard, 294

Bossuet, Jacques Bénigne, 51

Botero, Giovanni, 34, 76

Bottomry, 19

Boudin, Louis B., 270

Bougeois, Léon, 243

Bouniatian, Mentor, 270

Bowley, Arthur, *Mathematical Groundwork of Economics,* 444–45

Brants, Victor, 241

Bray, John Francis, 178

Brentano, Lujo, 221

Bresciani-Turoni, Constantino, 512

Brief Observations concerning Trade . . . (Child), 67

Brinkmann, Carl G. von, 375

British economics: balance of trade concept, 45–49; empiricism, 55–57; equilibrium principle, 304; historism in, 223–24; marginal utility analysis, 285, 363; Marxism and, 267; value theory, 277–78

British Empire, intellectual background of, 292

Bücher, Karl, 222

Bukharin, N. I., 397–99

Bullionism, 37, 43, 46–48, 70

Bullion Report, 162–63, 185, 186

Burchardt, Fritz, 377

Burckhardt, Jakob, 32

Buridan, Jean, 23–24

Burke, Edmund, 134, 211

Burnham, James, 452

Burns, Arthur, 477

Business barometers, 476

Business cycle paradox, 563

Business cycle theory, 85–86, 189, 195, 475–88; acceleration principle, 345, 477; approaches to, 528; in Austrian economics, 480–82; bank credit and, 476–81; banking policy and, 348, 350, 351; capital efficiency and, 526–27; contagion of confidence in, 483–84; deceleration principle, 481; disequilibrating forces, 525; disproportionality theories, 345–49; double-system monetary theory, 480–82; downturn factor, 486; dynamic models, 522–29; econometric analysis, 563–72; economic maturity theory, 509, 510; economic policy and, 487–88; endogenous vs. exogenous theories, 351; entrepreneurial factor, 485; in French economics, 432; in German economics, 375–78; impulse principle, 484; industrial fluctuations and, 483–84; interest rate and, 477–81; international aspects of, 478; investment and, 477; investment / consumption disproportion and, 482, 484; Keynesian, 479–80, 502; in marginal economics, 343–51; Marxist, 261–62; mechanical models of, 525–28; methodological assumptions of, 475–78; monetary equilibrium, and, 479; monetary theory and, 478–82; movement types, 485–87; neural money and, 480–81; nonmonetary, 482–87; overinvestment factor, 480, 486; post–World War I, 415; psychological factor, 483–84, 486; public works in, 488; Ricardian, 344; savings in, 482; statistical analysis of, 192; sunspot, 344; underconsumption, 377; United States economy and, 528

Business economics, 234

Cairnes, John Elliott, 170, 292–93

Calvin, John, 54

Calvinism, 39–40, 89

Cambridge School: cash balance approach, 341–42; monetary theory, 468, 469; welfare economics, 462

Cameralism, 38, 89–96; in fiscal administration, 90–93; in Germany, 201; university chairs in, 93

Campanella, Tommaso, 61

Campbell, Robert W., 405

Cannan, Edwin, 335

Canon law, 7–10, 28

Cantillon, Richard, 111; *Essai sur la nature du commerce en général,* 79–81; on foreign trade, 80–81; monetary theory, 80–81; population theory, 81; price theory, 80–81; value theory, 79–80

Capital accumulation: Malthus on, 168; Marx on, 258, 270–71; Ricardo on, 168; savings and, 83

Capitalism: bolshevist definition of, 403; breakdown theory, 259–62, 271–72, 394, 407, 410; church doctrine, 35; dialectic conception, 253–59; imperialism and, 308; Judaism and, 226; money supply and, 42; nominalism and, 40; origins of, 38–42; reasoning principles, 42; risk factor, 40; Soviet view of, 408, 410; "the spirit of capitalism," 38–42

Capitalism's own law of population, 257

Capital theory, 155; in Austrian economics, 436; in French economics, 192–93; in German economics, 202; in marginal economics, 319–24, 326–29; marginal efficiency concept, 499–502, 505; Marx on, 249, 253–62; post-Thomistic, 26; productivity in, 118; in Ricardian economics, 158–61; Smith on, 126, 131; terminology, 131; in United States, 207; utilitarian, 158–61

Carell, Erich, 376

Carey, Henry Charles, 193, 207

Carl, Ernst Ludwig, 98

Carli, Giovanni Rinaldo, 87

Carlyle, Thomas, 296

Cartels, 41, 384, 386, 388, 395, 451

Cartesian economics, 57–58, 97–114; prolegomenon, 587–91

Carver, Thomas N., 328

Cary, John, 78

Cash balance approach, 71, 341–43, 467–70, 479

Cassel, Karl Gustav: business cycle theory, 346; economic analysis, 366–67; equation of change, 340; monetary theory, 337; purchasing power parity theory, 533–34; *Social Economics,* 372

Cassirer, Ernst, 32

Catchings, Waddill, 482

Categorical imperative, 201

Catholicism, 4, 6–7; on capitalism, 35; neoscholastic economics and, 241–44

Ceteris paribus clause, 172, 174, 341, 420, 426

Chalmers, Thomas, 189

Chamberlin, Edward H., 436, 447–50

Chartered companies, 41
Checks and balances concept, 101
Cherbuliez, Antoine E., 190
Chernov, Viktor Mikhailovich, 273
Chesterton, Gilbert K., 384
Chevalier, Michel, 190
Child, Sir Josiah, 55; *Brief Observations concerning Trade . . .* , 67
Choice theory, 572–76
Chrysostem, Saint, 10, 16
Circulating capital, 155
Circulation of the elites, 313
Claphman, Sir John, 306, 446
Clark, Colin, 554
Clark, John Bates, 352–55; capital theory, 329; *Distribution of Wealth,* 353; marginal economics of, 352–55; *Philosophy of Wealth,* 352; production theory, 322; profit theory, 439; static vs. dynamic analysis, 515–16; wage theory, 442
Clark, John M., 423, 426, 427, 436, 484, 517
Clarke, William, 297
Class concept, 628–29
Class struggle, 217; Lenin on, 273; Marx on, 262–67; revolutionary aspects of, 264
Closed Commercial State, The (Fichte), 210
Cobweb theories, 563
Cognition, 57
Cohen, Hermann, 224
Cohn, G., 219
Coke, Roger, 58
Colbert, Jean Baptiste, 36, 38, 51
Colbertism, 36, 38, 41, 49–52, 97–98. *See also* Mercantilism
Cole, G.D.H., 384
Collective bargaining, 442, 443
Collectivism, 274, 457–60
Colm, G., 374
Colquhoun, Patrick, 178
Comintern, 407–8
Commercial enterprise, 26; fiduciary money and, 74–76
Commodity, in Marxian analysis, 253–56
Commodity reserve concept, 474
Commons, John R., 359–60, 427
Communism: as international movement, 407–8; primitive, 10–11
Communist International, 397
Communist Manifesto (Marx), 249, 263
Communist society, 102
Commutative justice, 14–17, 45, 106
Compensation theory, 152
Competition, 443–54; equilibrium analysis and, 443–44; freedom of, 126, 133–34; in German economics, 235; Smith on, 126, 133–34; uncontrolled, 92; workable, 453. *See also* Monopoly

Complementary concept, 282, 290, 309–10, 317
Composite reserve unit, 549
Comte, Auguste, 195–96
Condillac, Etienne Bonnot de, 101, 119
Conrad, O., 367
Conring, Herman, 93
Conscience, collective, 431
Conservatism, historism and, 213
Consumers' rent, 303
Consumer surplus concept, 195, 465
Consumption function, 498–501, 504, 506, 507, 511
Consumption theory, 97; in German economics, 205
Cooper, Anthony Ashley, 121
Cooperatives, Fourierism and, 198–99
Coquelin, Charles, *Du crédit et des banques,* 191–92
Corn bounty, 154
Corn laws, 44
Corporative state, 211, 244, 313, 386
Cossa, Luigi, 220
Cost analysis, 435–36
Cost of production theory, 79–80
Cost theory: alternative costs principle, 316–17; comparative costs principle, 164–65; marginal utility analysis, 364
Council for Economic Mutual Assistance (1949), 406
Council of Trent, 35
Countervailing power principle, 453
Courcelle-Seneuil, Jean Gustav, 190
Cournot, Antoine Augustin, 194–95, 444–45
Craig, John, 177
Credit expansion, 75–76
Crédit mobilier, 198
Credit theory, 81; in French economics, 191–92; in Marxism, 260; in Ricardian economics, 161–64; in Saint-Simonianism, 198; in utilitarianism, 161–64; in utopian schemes, 199–200. *See also* Interest *entries*
Crises (economic), 188–89; in French economics, 192; in German economics, 235–36; in Marxism, 260–62; in revisionist theory, 269–70. *See also* Business cycle theory; Depression
Critique of Practical Reason (Kant), 201, 209
Critique of Pure Reason (Kant), 209
Croce, Benedetto, 309, 419
Culpeper, Sir Thomas, 55, 72
Cumberland, Richard, 121
Cunningham, William, 36
Cunow, H., 251
Currency: circulation velocity of, 82, 88; managed, 75
Currency depreciation, 52, 82, 89; international trade and, 533, 538; price and, 45

Currency School, 186–88
Custodi, Pietro, 193

Dahmen, Eric, 555
Daire, Eugene, 98
Damaschke, Adolf, 233
Dantzig, D. van, 576
Darwinism, 295–96
Davanzati, Bernardo, 44, 52
Davenant, Charles, 65–66; *Essay . . . upon the Balance of Trade,* 66
Davenport, H. J., 317
Davidson, D., 324
Deceleration principle, 481
Decision making: behavior analysis, 573–76, 578; choice theory, 572–76; economic aggregates in, 574; expectations in, 573, 574; expected utility hypothesis, 575; game theory, 576–79; general possibility theorem, 575; indifference analysis in, 573; multipersonal choice, 576; non-probabilistic uncertainty in, 577; objectivity vs. subjectivity in, 574–75; preference analysis, 573; probability analysis, 574–76; probability vs. credibility in, 575; risk factor, 574; theory, 572–79
Decline of the West (Spengler), 387
Deductive reasoning, 56–58, 65, 123, 161, 171–72, 175, 200, 220–21, 309, 416
Deficit spending, 509–10
Defoe, Daniel, 78
Dei delitti e delle pene (Beccaria), 86
Deism, 101
De jura belli ac pacis (Grotius), 60
De la recherche de la vérité (Malebranche), 103
Della economia nazionale (Ortes), 87
Della moneta (Galiani), 115
De l'ordre social (Le Trosne), 108
Demand, 497; inelastic, 66; in Marshallian economics, 366. *See also* Supply and demand
Demaria, Giovanni, 512
Demographic analysis, 65, 76–78, 81. *See also* Population theory
Depression: of 1930s, 416, 418, 427; public works and, 168. *See also* Crises
DeQuincey, Thomas, 169
Derivations concept, 313
De Santis, Marc Antonio, 49
Descartes, René, *Discourse on Methods,* 57
Desirability concept, 363
De Soto, Domingo, 29
Destutt de Tracy, A.L.C., 190
Determinism, 112, 197
Developing countries: economic growth in, 557–62; international trade and, 547, 550
Development concept, 626–27
De Vití de Marco, Antonio, 512
Dewey, John, 356

Dialectic economics, 245–75, 393–413; interpretation changes, 407–13; philosophical background, 245–50; prolegomenon, 596–98; social theory, 246–50
Dialectic materialism, 249–53, 265, 371, 407
Dialectic methods, 245–50, 393–95; in capitalism analysis, 253–59; of Proudhon, 199; terminology, 265, 266
Dickinson, Henry, 459
Dictatorship, USSR, 400
Dictatorship of the proletariat, 396
Diderot, Denis, 102
Diehl, Karl, 222, 224
Dieterlen, Pierre, 432–33
Dilthey, Wilhelm, 225
Dimensions concept, 230
Discourse of the Common Weal of this Realm of England, 44, 61
Discourse on Methods (Descartes), 57
Discourse upon Trade (North), 67
Displacement cost principle, 317
Disproportionality theories, 345–49, 394
Distribution of Wealth (Clark), 353
Distribution theory, 435–43; in German economics, 233, 240; in marginal utility analysis, 324–32; in Marshallian economics, 300–301; personal vs. functional aspects of, 435; in Ricardian economics, 145–46, 154–61, 174; Smith on, 126, 129–31, 154–55; in utilitarianism, 154–61
Distributive justice, 11, 106
Distributive process, 81
Disutility concept, 128, 284, 364
Divine law, 8
Divine right, 35
Dobb, Maurice H., 458
Domar, Evsey D., 523
Domestic workshops, 41
Domination theory, 433
Dominicans, 23, 27–30, 33, 54
Douglass, Paul H., 442, 482, 497
Drei Nationalökonomien, Die (Sombart), 379–80
Du crédit et des banques (Coquelin), 191–92
Duesenberry, James S., 475
Dühring, Karl Eugen, *. . . Nationalökonomie und der Sozialismus,* 239–40
Dumoulin, Charles, 54
Dunoyer, Charles, 192
Duns Scotus, John, 11, 14–16, 18, 20–21, 28
Duopoly, 444–45; pricing theory, 316
Du Pont de Nemours, Pierre Samuel, 103, 107–9, 113; *Physiocratie . . . ,* 108
Dupriez, Léon, 527
Dupuit, A.J.E.J., 195
Dupuit, Jules, 279
Durbin, E.F.M., 458
Dürkheim, Emile, 429, 431

Dutot, Charles, 98
Dynamic analysis: in Keynesian economics, 521–23; mechanical approach, 525–28; methodology, 515–21; models, 521–29; sociopolitical factor, 525–26; time factor, 515–16
Dynamic equilibrium principle, 399, 401

Eastern Europe, industry nationalization in, 406–7
East India Company, 41, 67
Eck, Johannes, 53
Eclecticism, 373
Econometrica, 565
Econometrics, 562–72; business cycle models, 566–67, 570; definitions of, 565–66; input-output analysis, 571; methodology, 568–69; model construction and, 566; statistical technique, 567–68; testing controversy, 565
Econometric Society, 565
Economic analysis: dynamic, 515–29; dynamic vs. static, 515–19; patterns of, 610–21; quantitative aspect of, 234
Economic calculus, 363
Economic categories, 231
Economic cycle. *See* Business cycle theory
Economic determinism, 250–51, 272–73
Economic development: ''spirit'' categories, 226–27; stages of, 214–15, 217, 222, 226
Economic freedom, 109–10. *See also* Laissez-faire
Economic growth: accelerated investment and, 561; aid factor, 561; balanced, 560; capital formation and, 555–56; determinants, 551–52; in developing countries, 557–62; fixed social capital and, 560; industrialization and, 556; in industrialized countries, 550–57; inflationary measures and, 558–59; in Latin American, 558; marginal social productivity and, 560; measurement of, 551, 552; models, 552–53; national income and, 551; peripheral economy theory, 558; resource allocation and, 558–59; sector concept, 554–55; stagnation theorem and, 551, 552; technology and, 553; theories, 553–56, 560–62; transition to maturity, 555; in United States, 556–57; in USSR, 403, 404; warranted rate of, 522
Economic history, 222–24
Economic imperialism, 205, 272, 394
Economic institutions, post-Thomistic development, 25–27. *See also specific institutions*
Economic interpretation of history, 252
Economic man, 172–73
Economic maturity theory, 509, 510
Economic planning, 454–61; assumptions of, 454–55; marginalism in, 454–55; monopoly in, 456; New Deal, 456; organismic economics and, 381–87, 389; profit maximization in, 455–56; under socialism, 457–60; in USSR, 397, 399–407; welfare economics and, 465

Economic sociology, 380, 431–32
Edgeworth, Francis Ysidro, 309–10, 444, 445
Egalitarianism, 428
Egner, Erich, 379
Ehrenberg, Richard, 229
Eichhorn, Karl F. von, 213
Einarsen, J., 327
Einaudi, Luigi, 134
Élan vital, 269
Elementi del commercio (Verri), 86
Elementi di economia pubblica (Beccaria), 86
Elitism, 313, 386, 388
Elizabethan poor laws, 76
Ellis, H. S., 417
Ely, Richard T., 208
Eminent domain, 11
Empiricism, 35, 55–57, 61, 63, 65–68, 123, 422–24
Employment theory: international trade and, 537, 538; Keynesian, 497–503, 507–8; multiplier concept, 501–2, 507; Stockholm school, 492–94. *See also* Full employment
Enclosure movement, 41, 44, 76
Encyclicals, 241
Encyclopedists, 100–102
Enfantin, Barthélemy Prosper, 198
Engels, Friedrich, 247, 251, 400; on class struggle, 262–63
England: capitalism development in, 40–41; mid-sixteenth-century economy of, 44; ''royal letters patent of monopoly,'' 41. *See also* British *entries*
Engländer, Oscar, 542
English Renaissance, 35–36
Engrossing, 14
Enlightenment, 100–102
Enquiry concerning Human Understanding (Hume), 122
Entrepreneurship, 81, 191, 440–42; in business cycle theory, 485
Euality of opportunity, 198
Equation of change, 339–45
Equation of exchange, 468, 470
Equilibrium principle, 56–57, 87, 88, 96, 98, 101, 107, 133, 172, 421, 612–14; dynamic analysis, 494–95; in English economics, 304; in marginal economics, 278, 279, 281, 282, 284, 286–88; in Marshallian economics, 299, 303–5; prolegomenon, 605–8; in Ricardian economics, 144–45
Equivalence principle, 12, 17, 23, 24, 68, 110, 118, 119; balance of trade and, 45–47
Espèce de ce bénéfice, 195
Essai sur la nature du commerce en général (Cantillon), 79–81
Essai politique sur le commerce (Melon), 98
Essay . . . upon the Balance of Trade (Davenant), 66

Essay concerning Human Understanding (Locke), 63

Essay on Population (Malthus), 153

Essays on Philosophical Subjects (Smith), 132

Essays on Some Unsettled Questions of Political Economy (Mill), 183–84

Esthetical issues, 296

Ethical issues, 64, 121, 296, 305

Études d'économie appliquée (Walras), 289

Eucken, Walter, 391

European Common Market, 99

European Economic Community, 547

European Monetary Agreement, 547

European Payments Union, 546, 547

Evolutionary processes, 217, 218, 222, 626–27

Evolutionary theory, 295

Exchange, 27; control of, 47

Exchange rates, 544–46, 548–49

Exchange relations: in Ricardian economics, 146–50; subjective vs. objective, 336–37

Expectations concept, 86, 327, 472–73; in decision making, 573, 574; in Keynesian theory, 499–500

Exports. *See* International trade

Fabian socialism, 268, 297–98

Fable of the Bees, The (Mandeville), 120–21

Factor price equalization law, 535–36

Fairs, 27, 28

Fanno, Marco, 484

Fascism, 196, 244, 371; economics of, 385–87; Pareto and, 313

Fechner, Gustav, 279

Felicific calculus, 141, 142

Fellner, William J., 450

Ferguson, Adam, 124

Ferrara, Francesco, 193

Fetter, Frank K., 327–28

Feudalism, 9–10; disintegration of, 20; national wealth concept and, 43. *See also* Medieval economics

Feuerbach, Ludwig, *Das Wesen des Christentums,* 247

Fichte, Johann G., 388; *Addresses to the German Nation,* 210; *The Closed Commercial State,* 210

Fiduciary money, 73–76, 98, 338; commercial enterprise and, 74–76

Final degree of utility, 284

First International, 216

Fiscalists, 91

Fisher, Allen G. B., 554

Fisher, Irving: business cycle theory, 350, 480; capital theory, 329; equation of change, 339–42, 468, 470; interest theory, 327; *Mathematical Investigations,* 310; monetary theory, 339–42; price theory, 364

Five-Year Plans (USSR), 399–406, 409

Fleming, Marcus, 463

Flürscheim, M., 233

Föhl, Carl, 474

Forbonnais, François de, 98–99, 113

Foreign trade. *See* International trade

Forestalling, 14, 92

Foster, William T., 482

Foundations of Leninism (Stalin), 397

Fourastié, Jean, 554

Fourier, François Marie Charles, 198–99

France: capitalism development in, 41; Cartesian philosophy in, 57–58; Colbertism in, 49–52, 97–99; communist party in, 434; economic activity regulation in, 51, 97–99; Gallicanism in, 51; industrial development in, 50–51; philosophical disputes, 99–103; price stabilization policy of, 474–75; seventeenth-century economics of, 49–51

Franciscans, 23, 54

Francisco di Vitoria, 43

Francis of Assisi, Saint, 11

Fraser, L. M., 326, 435

Freedom concept, 618–19

Free enterprise, 151

Free trade, 86, 109, 531, 532, 540; political influence, 67–68; Smith on, 131. *See also* International trade

French economics: analytic methods, 194–96; credit theory, 191–92; on dynamic models, 527; historism in, 223; Keynesian theory and, 511–12; liberal theory, 190–93; marginal utility analysis, 362; marketing theory, 191; Marxist, 267, 269; methodological principles, 429–34; neoscholastic, 241; profit theory, 441; socialist theory, 196–200; textbooks on, 434; university chairs, 223; utopian theory, 198–200; value theory, 148–49, 278

Friedman, Milton, 424, 506

Frisch, Ragnar, 462, 566

Fructification theory of interest, 118

Fugger, Mark, 53

Fullarton, John, 187

Full employment: Beveridge on, 510; Keynesian theory, 497–501, 503, 508, 511, 512; Oxford economists on, 510

Furstliche Schatz- und Rent Kammer (Schröder), 90

Further Considerations concerning Raising the Value of Money (Locke), 69

Future uncertainty principle, 65

Galbraith, John Kenneth, 453; *The Affluent Society,* 556–57

Galiani, Fernando, 113, 115–17; *Della monete,* 115

Gallicanism, 51

Galton, Sir Francis, 217

Game theory, 576–79; essential vs. nonessential games, 577; minimax principle, 577–78

Garnier, Joseph, 190
Gassend, Pierre, 57
Gaunt, John, *Natural and Political Investigations . . .* , 65
Gazette du Commerce, 99
Gec, Joshua, 78
Gelesnoff, W., 394
General Agreement on Tariffs and Trade (GATT), 547
Generalized utility functions, 364
General Theory of Employment, Interest and Money, The (Keynes), 496–503; interpretations, 503–9
Genovesi, Antonio, 86; *Lezioni di commercio . . .* , 86
Gentz, Friedrich, 212
George, Henry, 207
Gerhard, Johan, 54
German economics: business cycle theory, 375–78; Cameralism and, 201; capital theory, 202; competition in, 235; consumption theory, 205; crisis analysis, 235–36; distribution theory, 233, 240; gold standard in, 232–33, 238; historicoethical school, 215–19; historism in, 212–15; interest theory, 233; international trade in, 203, 218–19, 235, 540; Keynesian, 512; labor theory, 205; marginal productivity theory, 204; Marxism in, 267–69; monetary theory, 237–39, 274–75; neoscholasticism, 241–43; organismic theory, 224–42; price theory, 202, 232; production theory, 236–37; profit theory, 233–34; rent theory, 202, 204; Ricardian theory, 203–6; Smith's influence on, 200–206; social collectivities in, 218; social psychology in, 217–18; textbooks on, 372–73, 375; university chairs, 372–73; value theory, 201–2, 373–74; wage theory, 202–3, 205–6, 234–35
German Social Democratic party, 267, 269
German Social Democratic Worker's party, 234
Germany: fiscal administration of, 90–93; geopolitics of, 378, 389; idealistic philosophy of, 209–12; inflation in, 239, 374–75; intellectual concepts in, 89–90; labor movement in, 216; liberal socialists in, 239–41; Marxism in, 373; nationalism in, 210, 213–19, 235–36, 372, 378; National Socialism in, 372–73, 378, 379, 382, 387–91; political policy / organismic reasoning relation in, 371; price stabilization policy of, 474; Protestant theology in, 58–59; racism in, 388, 389; reparations payments to, 536; Romanticism in, 211–12; socialism in, 206, 219, 234; social philosophy of, 209–12; trade unions in, 268
Gerschenkron, Alexander, 560
Gerson, Jean de, 24
Gervaise, Isaac, 70
Gesell, Silvio, 335

Gide, Charles, 223
Godwin, William, 153
Gold standard, 163, 238, 333–35, 473–74; business cycle and, 488; in German economics, 232–33, 238; international trade and, 536–37, 544–49; Ricardian economics and, 185–87
Good / evil concept, 64
Goodwin, R. M., 525, 526
Gossen, Hermann H., 279–80
Gottl-Ottlilienfeld, Friedrich von, 230, 373, 379, 390
Gournay, Jacques Vincent de, 99
Graham, Frank D., 533
Graslin, Jean L., 113
Gray, John, 178
Graziani, A., 258
Great Britain: economic planning in, 460–61; industrial development in, 40–41; industry nationalization in, 460–61; socialism in, 384
Green, David I., 282
Gresham's law, 24
Gross, G., 329
Grossman, Henryk, 394
Grossman-Doerth, H., 391
Grotius, Hugo, 61; *De jure belli ac pacis,* 60
Group mind, 431
Grünberg, C., 223
Grundsätze der Polizey, Handlung und Finanz (Sonnenfels), 96
Guilds, 50, 109; monopoly and, 41
Guitton, Henri, 512
Gumplowicz, L., 240

Haavelmo, Trygve, 565, 570
Haberler, Gottfried, 471, 486, 534–35, 539
Hahn, L. Albert, 375, 478–79
Haller, Carl Ludwig von, *Restoration of the Political Science,* 212
Hamberg, Daniel, 553
Hamilton, Alexander, *Report on the Subject of Manufactures,* 206
Hamilton, Count, 327
Hansen, Bert, 475
Hansen, Alvin, 509, 522–23
Happiness maximization principle, 122; in marginal utility analysis, 280, 283; utilitarianism and, 141; wealth and, 142–43
Harms, Bernhard, 222
Harris, Joseph, 84
Harrod, Roy F., 421, 503, 518, 522
Hart, Albert G., 575
Hartley, David, 283
Harvard Business Barometer, 476
Hasbash, Wilhelm, 221
Hawley, F. B., 208
Hawtrey, Ralph G., 343, 441, 479

Hayek, Friedrich A., 420; on *agio* theory, 327; business cycle theory, 480–82; capital theory, 436; monetary theory, 471–72
Heckscher, Eli Filip, 36, 42, 535
Heckscher-Ohlin law of factor price equalization, 535–36
Hegel, G.W.F., 210–11, 246
Hegelian dialectics, 246–47
Heilperin, Michelangelo, 548
Heimann, Edward, *Social Theory of Capitalism,* 395
Held, Adolf, 216
Helfferich, Karl, 239
Helvétius, Claude Adrien, 101; *De l'esprit,* 141
Henry IV, French king, 50
Herkner, Heinrich, 229, 236
Hermann, F.B.W. von, 180, 202
Herrenschwand, Jean, 114
Hertzka, Theodor, 233
Hesse, Albert, 229
Hicks, John R.: business cycle theory, 524–25; dynamic model, 523–25; monetary theory, 470; wage theory, 442
Higgins, Benjamin, 523
Hildebrand, Bruno, 215
Hilferding, Rudolf, 270–71
Historical materialism, 407
Historical research, 100–101
Historicoethical school, 215–19; methodological issues, 219–24
Historism, 294–96; in Belgium, 223; decline of, 372–85; in England, 223–24; in France, 223; in Germany, 212–15; in Italy, 223–24; methodological problems, 379
History: economic interpretation of, 252; materialistic interpretation of, 250–53
Hitler, Adolf, 387
Hitze, Franz, 241
Hoarding, 468
Hobbes, Thomas, *Leviathan,* 62
Hobson, John A., 274, 307–8
Hodgkin, Thomas, 178
Holy Roman Empire, 7
Hooker, Richard, 36
Horner, Francis, 162
Hornigk, Philipp W. von, 91, 92; *Oesterreich . . . ,* 92
Hotelling, Harold, 444, 464
Hufeland, Gottlieb, 202
Hugo, Gustav F., 213
Human behavior, 61
Humanism, 32, 33, 36, 60
Human law, 8
Human rights, 10
Hume, David, 82–83, 122–24, 163–64, 359; *Enquiry concerning Human Understanding,* 122; monetary theory, 82–83; *Political*

Discourses, 82; price theory, 82; trade theory, 82, 83
Hutcheson, Francis, 121–22, 141
Hutchison, T.W., 422
Hyndman H. M., 267, 297
Hypothetical economics, 123, 415–88; prolegomenon, 598–603

Idealism, 294; in German philosophy, 209–12
Ideal types, 227–28
Il Principe (Machiavelli), 34
Imperialism: capitalist, 308; economic, 205, 272, 394; Lenin on, 274
Imports. *See* International trade
Imputation concept, 291, 317–18
Income tax, 97
Income theory, 81, 97, 470–73; circular flow, 105–7; in marginal economics, 326; Pareto's law, 312; Physiocrat, 105–7; *Tableau économique,* 104–7
Income velocity concept, 468–69
Indifference curves, 310, 311, 463–65
Indifference ratios, 365
Indifference theory, 64–65
Individualism, 7, 39
Inductive reasoning, 66, 171–72, 220–21, 416, 430
Industrial democracy, 269
Industrialization: economic growth and, 550–57; wage rates and, 83, 84
Industry location, 236–37
Industry nationalization, 460–61; in Eastern Europe, 406–7
Inflation: economic growth and, 558–59; in Germany, 374–75; gold standard and, 473–74; monetary metals and, 42; money supply and, 28, 29; price stabilization policy and, 473–75
Ingram, John Kells, 294
Input-output analysis, 571
Instincts, 124
Institutionalism, 357–62, 424–29
Insurance contracts, 27
Intellect concept, 63–64
Interest on capital theory, 404–5
Interest prohibition, 110–11. *See also* Usury
Interest rate, 81; business cycle and, 477–81; commercial development and, 83; factors determining, 55; fixed, 54–55, 72, 73, 110, 116; monetary vs. real (natural), 489–91; money supply and, 73
Interest theory, 68–73, 118; "abstinence," 326, 328, 438; *agio,* 319–22, 326–28; of capital, 319–24, 326–29; *ex ante,* 438; fructification, 118; in German economics, 233; impatience, 437; Keynesian, 498–501, 504, 505; land rent analogy, 72, 73; liquidity preference, 438, 439; loanable fund, 439; macroeconomic interpreta-

Interest theory (*cont.*)

tion, 321; marginal productivity, 436, 439; Marshallian, 302, 305; monetary, 438–39; nonmonetary, 438, 439; productivity, 326, 328; Ricardian, 158–61; risk factor, 116; time factor, 327; time preference, 439; utilitarian, 158–61

International Monetary Fund, 545–46, 548, 549

International trade, 67–68, 80–83, 531–50; assumptions of, 531; balance of payments disequilibria and, 546; balancing process of, 531–33, 537–39, 544–45; bilateral agreements and, 540–41; capital concentration and, 271; capitalism and, 26; capital transfers in, 536; commercial rivalry in, 83; comparative cost theory, 164–65; cost factor, 531–35; currency depreciation and, 533, 538; developing countries and, 547, 550; disruptions in, 533; employment theory and, 537, 538; economic policy and, 539–42; exchange rates and, 544–46, 548–49; export theory and, 46; fairs and, 28; foreign policy and, 46; in German economics, 203, 218–19, 235, 540; gold standard and, 530–37, 544–49; Heckscher-Ohlin law of factor equalization on, 535–36; labor factor, 77–78; liberalization of, 140; location factor and, 542–44; low cost principle, 542; marginal propensity to import and, 537; market monopoly and, 271; monetary metals and, 531, 533, 536–37; monetary policy and, 332–33, 544–50; multilateral agreements and, 541; multiplier principle and, 537–38; national interests and, 43; national wealth and, 46; post–World War II, 544–50; product substitution curve, 534–35; purchasing power parity theory, 533–34; restrictions, 538–41; Ricardian theory, 164–66; self-sufficiency and, 92; Smith on, 131; spatial factor, 542–44; USSR, 541; utilitarian theory, 164–66

"Intrinsic virtue," 71

Introductory Lectures on Political Economy (Whately), 179

Intuitional economics, prolegomenon, 594–96

Intuitive reasoning, 221, 222, 225–27, 231

Investment: business cycle and, 477; economic growth and, 561; induced vs. autonomous, 520–21. *See also* Savings theory

Investment function, 498, 499, 504, 507

Investment multiplier concept, 501–2

"Invisible hand" concept, 132

Iron law of wages, 234

Isolated exchange theory, 316

Italian city-states, 32; economic institutions, 25–27

Italian economics: balance of trade concept, 49; chairs of political economy, 86; on dynamic models, 527; historism in, 223–24; liberal theory, 193; marginal utility analysis, 362; mercantilism, 86–88; neoscholasticism in, 241

Italian fascism, 385–87

Italian Renaissance, 32–34

Italian socialism, 240–41

Italian universities, 32–33

James Emile, 432

James, William, 356

Janssen, Sir Theodore, 78

Jaurès, Jean, 269

Jenkin, Henry C. Fleeming, 185

Jennings, Richard, *The Natural Elements of Political Economy*, 283

Jesuits, 28–30

Jevons, William Stanley: on business cycle, 344; marginal utility analysis, 280, 283–85; *The Theory of Political Economy*, 283

Jews: in capitalism development, 39, 226; usury and, 18

Johannsen, Nicholas, 344

Joplin, Thomas, 187

Journal d'agriculture, du commerce et des finances, 99

Journal oeconomique, 99

Juglar, Clement, 192

Juglar cycles, 485–87

Jus civile, 8

Jus gentium, 8–9, 11, 14

Justi, Johann Heinrich Gottlob von, 95; *Natur und Wesen der Staaten . . .* , 95

Just price, 24–25, 106; Dominican concept, 28–29; Jesuit concept, 28; Thomistic concept, 12, 14–16

Just wage, 15, 204–5

Kahn, R. F., 501, 502

Kaldor, Nicholas: business cycle theory, 525–26; capital theory, 437; on welfare economics, 465

Kalecki, Michael, 525, 526

Kant, Immanuel: *Critique of Practical Reason*, 201, 209; *Critique of Pure Reason*, 209; influence of, 224–25

Kapital, Das (Marx), 249, 254–58, 260–66

Katallactics, 172, 173

Kaufmann, Felix, 424

Kautsky, Karl, 270

Keirstead, H.B.S., 457

Ketteler, Wilhelm E. von, 241

Keynes, J. N., 363

Keynes, John Maynard, 417–18; critical views of, 507–8; *The General Theory of Employment, Interest and Money*, 496–509; on laissez-faire, 417–18; Malthus-Ricardo comparison, 168–69; *Treatise on Money*, 469–70, 479–80

Keynes effect, 508

Keynesian economics, 428; antinomies, 519; business cycle theory, 479–80, 502; criticism of, 510–12; on demand factor, 497; dynamic models, 521–23; economy model, 498–99; employment theory, 497–503, 507–8; evaluation, 513–15; in France, 511–12; in Germany, 512; I + C = Y, 498–99; interest theory, 438–39, 498, 500, 501, 504, 505; international trade theory, 537, 538; interpretations, 503–9; Marxism and, 502–3; monetary theory, 469–70, 472; on money supply, 498, 501, 504, 507; on monopoly, 452; multiplier principle, 501–2, 507, 519–21; profit expectations in, 499–500; psychological factors, 498, 506; savings in, 499, 500, 502, 505; savings / investment relation, 500; in United States, 511, 512; wage theory, 497, 501, 507–9; wage unit, 498

Khatchaturov, T. S., 412

Khrushchev, Nikita S., 412

King, Gregory, 66

King's estimate, 66

Kingsley, Charles, 296

Kitchin cycles, 485, 487

Klein, Lawrence R., 567

Kleinwächter, K., 329

Knapp, Georg Friedrich: "chartel" theory, 375; monetary theory, 237–39, 336, 374, 375

Knies, Karl, 215

Knight, Frank H.: capital theory, 436–38; on decision making, 574; marginal productivity analysis, 436–37; on methodology, 422–23; profit theory, 440; on social costs, 306–7; on static vs. dynamic analysis, 516–17

Knight, M., 252

Knowledge concept, 63–64

Kondratieff, N. D., 485, 486–87

Kondratieff cycles, 485, 486–87

Koopmans, Tjalling C., 567–69

Koopmans, J. G., 424

Krapotkin, Prince Pëtr A., 200

Kritische Geschichte der Nationökonomie und des Sozialismus (Dühring), 240

Kromphardt, W., 373

Kurihara, Kenneth K., 526

Kuznets, Simon, 484, 517

Labor: domestic vs. foreign, 77–78; as international movement, 78; productive vs. nonproductive, 128; productivity of, 76–78. See also Wage entries

Labor cost theory of value, 14–15, 68, 69, 72, 128, 131, 147–50, 205, 285; in bolshevism, 402, 404; in Marxism, 254–59; in Ricardian economics, 176–79, 185

Labor exploitation, 442

Labor movement: in Germany, 216; in Marxism, 274

Labor theory: cost / foreign enterprise relation and, 83, 84; on division of labor, 126; in German economics, 205; quantitative, 76; Smith on, 126, 128; Thomistic concept of, 14–15

Labriola, Arturo, 240–41

Lafargue, Paul, 258

Laffemas, Barthelemy de, 50

Lag concept, 517–19, 524, 525

Laissez-faire, 66–67, 99, 352, 416–18

Land: net product and, 105–6; quantitative theory of, 76

Land banks, 74

Land rent, 130, 297

Landry, Adolphe, 327

Lange, Oskar, 422

Langenstein, Heinrich von, 24

Langton, W., 189

Lardner, Dionysius, 185

Lassalle, Ferdinand, 234

Latin America, economic growth, 558

Lauderdale, Lord, 149, 160

Launhardt, Wilhelm, 237, 542

Laurentius de Rodulphis, 26, 27

Lausanne School, 308, 314, 372, 374, 418, 430, 457

Laveleye, Emile de, 223

Laverge, de, 333

Lavington, Frederick, 483

Law, John, 98; Money and Trade, 74–76

Law concept, 619–21

Law of differential imputation, 318

Law of diminishing returns, 85, 88, 89, 119, 154, 174; in marginal productivity analysis, 325–26

Law of diminishing utility, 280

Law of markets (Say), 151, 168, 191

Law of motivation, 363, 423

Law of reflux, 187

Law of subjective rationality, 363

Laws of life, 363

Lectures on Political Economy (Wicksell), 322

Lederer, Emil, 377, 382

Lehfeldt, Robert A., 487

Leibniz, Gottfried Wilhelm, 93–94

Lenin, Vladimir Ilyich (Nikolai), 271, 396; bolshevism and, 273–75; The New Tasks of the Soviets, 39

Leo XIII, pope, 241

Leontief, L. A., 402

Leontief, Wassily W., 568, 571

Le Play, P. G. Frédéric, 223

Lerner, Abba P., 451, 459

Leroy-Beaulieu, Pierre Paul, 193

Lescure, Jean, 345

Leslie, T. E. Cliffe, 294

Lessines, Aegidius, 12

Levasseur, Pierre Emile, 223

"Levellers," 61

Leviathan (Hobbes), 62

Lewis, Arthur, 449

Lexis, Wilhelm, 219, 258

Lezioni di commercio . . . (Genovesi), 86

Lhomme, Jean, 433

Liberalism, 98, 99, 140; in France, 190–93; in Italy, 193

Liberal socialism, 239–41
Lieben, Richard, 304
Liebknecht, William, 216
Liefmann, Robert, 232, 373
Life insurance, 27
Limited companies, 40
Lindahl, Eric, 492
Liquidity preference, 498, 500, 504–6
List, Friedrich, 213–14
Literary economists, 308
Litt, Theodor, 229
Little, I.M.D., 465
Lloyd, William F., 177
Loans: contracts, 53. *See also* Interest entries;
    Usury
Location factor, 542–44
Locke, John: *Essay concerning Human Under-
    standing,* 63; *Further Considerations concern-
    ing Raising the Value of Money,* 69; interest
    theory, 72–73; monetary theory, 69; on money
    circulation velocity, 71; *Some . . . Conse-
    quences of the Lowering of Interest . . . ,* 69;
    Two Treatises on Government, 64, 68; value
    theory, 68
Longfield, Mountifort, 177, 204, 278
Long Parliament, 41
Looking Backward (Bellamy), 208
Loria, Archille, 223–24
Lösch, August, 536
Lotz, D.F.E., 202
Lowe, Adolph, 376–78
Lugo, Juan de, 28
Lundberg, Eric, 494–95, 528
Luther, Martin, 58–59, 89
Lutheranism, 89
Lutz, Friedrich, 376
Luxemburg, Rosa, 271
Luxuries, 83

Mably, Gabriel Bonnet de, 102, 113
Macfarlane, Charles W., 328
Machiavelli, Niccolo, *Il Principe,* 34
Machlup, Fritz, 424, 443, 520
MacKenroth, G., 374
Macleod, Henry Dunning, 343
Macmillan Report (1931), 271
Macvane, S. M., 328
Maine, Sir Henry, 294
Maitland, F. H., 294
Malebranche, Nicolas de, *De la recherche de la
    vérité,* 103
Malenkov, Georgi M., 411
Malthus, Thomas Robert: on capital accumulation,
    168; *Essay on Population,* 153; on law of
    diminishing returns, 154; productivity theory,
    160; supply and demand theory, 167–68; the-
    oretical analysis, 167–69; theory of gluts, 168;
    wage theory, 156–57

Malthusian law, 88
Malynes, Gerard, 47, 55
Man, Hendrik de, 383
Man (mankind) concept, 7
Manchester Statistical Society, 189
Mandeville, Bernard, *The Fable of the Bees,*
    120–21
Mangoldt, Hans von, 202, 203
Mannheim, Karl, 266
Manoilesco, Mihail, 532
Marburg School, 224–25
Marchal, André, 434
Marchal, Jean, 434, 441
Marget, Arthur, 469–70
Marginalism: in Austrian economics, 231; busi-
    ness cycle theory, 343–51; capital interest theo-
    ry, 319–24; 326–29; capital theory, 329; in
    economic planning, 454–55; equilibrium princi-
    ple in, 278, 279, 281, 282, 286–88; income
    theory, 326; in Marshallian theory, 303; meth-
    odology, 417–24; monetary aspects, 332–43;
    profit theory, 329–30; rent theory, 330–31; in
    United States, 352–55; utilitarian version,
    283–85; wage theory, 331–32; welfare econom-
    ics, 306–8
Marginal private net product, 306
Marginal productivity analysis, 325–26, 435–43;
    in German economics, 204; law of diminishing
    returns and, 325–26
Marginal revenue product, 436
Marginal social net product, 306
Marginal social productivity, 560
Marginal utility analysis, 115, 195, 232, 372–74,
    461–62; approaches to, 279; in Austrian eco-
    nomics, 314–19, 363; in British economics,
    363; criticism, 362–67, 421–22; distribution
    theory and, 324–32; final degree of utility in,
    284; in French economics, 362; in Italian eco-
    nomics, 362; mathematical formulations,
    279–81, 283–89, 308–13; methodological is-
    sues, 282–84; psychological approach, 279–81,
    289–91, 314–19; roots of, 277–83; terminol-
    ogy, 278; time factor, 320–22; in United States,
    362–64; in utilitarianism, 279
Marginal utility function, 316
Marginal utility schools, 277–91
Mariana, Juan de, 51
Market control, 445–50; national / international
    aspects, 451. *See also* Duopoly; Monopoly;
    Oligopoly
Marlo, Karl. *See* Winkelblech, Karl Georg
Marschak, Jacob, 565
Marshall, Alfred: on entrepreneurship, 302; on
    equation of exchange, 341; ethical principles,
    305; interest theory, 302, 305, 328; on interna-
    tional trade, 532; monetary theory, 334; *Princi-
    ples of Economics,* 298–306; profit theory, 302,
    329, 330; rent theory, 303; surplus concept,

303; wage theory, 302–3; welfare economics, 305–8, 461

Marshallian economics: demand theory, 366; distribution theory, 300–301; equilibrium principle, 299, 303–5; on market control, 446–50; methodology, 298–301, 363; production theory, 304–5

Martin, P. W., 482

Martineau, Henriette, 417

Marx, Karl, 247–50, 396; business cycle analysis, 261–62; on capital accumulation, 258; capitalism breakdown theory, 259–62, 271–72; capital theory, 253–62; on class struggle, 262–69; commodity concept, 253–56; *Communist Manifesto*, 249, 263; credit theory, 260; *Das Kapital*, 249, 254–58, 260–66; ideology of, 251–52, 266; on labor cost theory of value, 254–59; *Misère de la philosphie*, 248; monetary theory, 256, on Physiocrats, 112; production theory, 251–53; profit theory, 257–59, 261; on Ricardian economics, 248–49, 253–58; "surplus value" theory, 255–56; value theory, 254–59

Marxism, 245–67; bolshevist theory, 272–75; economic planning, 395; in France, 434; in Germany, 373; Keynesian theory and, 502–3; marginal economics and, 314–15; monetary theory, 335, 374, 375; orthodox, 270–72; philosophical background of, 245–50; political front in, 274; revisionist movement in, 267–70, 410; revolutionary aspects of, 395; in Western Europe, 393–95

Marxist-Leninist-Stalinist doctrine, 400

Mataja, Victor, 329

Materialism, 247, 249

Mathematical analysis, 416–19; Baconian mercantilism, 56–57, 64–66; Cartesian economics, 104, 106, 108; cobweb theorem, 563; definition of, 308; in French economics, 194–95, 430; functional price theories, 418; Galiani theory, 115; Hume theory, 122; marginal utility analysis, 279–89, 308–13; Ricardian economics, 185. *See also* Econometrics

Mathematical Groundwork of Economics (Bowley), 444–45

Mathematical Investigations (Fisher), 310

Matter concept, 247

Maurice, J.F.D., 296

Mauss, M., 431

Mauvillon, Jakob, 114

Maximization principle, 614–16; for Happiness, 122; in Ricardian economics, 173; Smith on, 133

Mayer, Hans, 418

McCulloch, John R., 150, 266

Meade, J. E., 538

Means, Gardiner C., 427

Mechanism doctrine, 82–83, 87, 115

Medieval economics, 6, 9–10; profit principle, 15–17; Thomistic reasoning disintegration and, 20–30; usury concept, 18–20. *See also* Feudalism

Meditazioni sull' economia politica (Verri), 86

Melanchthon, Philipp S., 58, 59

Melon, Jean François, *Essai politique sur le commerce*, 98

Menger, Carl: 199–200; Austrian economics and, 291; business cycle theory, 349; distribution theory, 291; marginal utility analysis, 280–81; 289–91; monetary theory, 291, 335; production theories, 291; on want satisfaction, 290

Mensheviki, 273–74

Mercado, Thomas de, 29

Mercantilism, 36–38, 42–45, 84–86, 125; Baconian, 37, 55–78; Colbertism and, 49; in Italy, 86–88; refined, 37–38; Smith on, 126–27; theoretical refinement of, 79–88

Merchant Adventurers, 41

Mercier de La Rivière, Comte de, 107, 109

Metaeconomic concepts, 621–31

Metallists, 164

Metzler, Lloyd A., 526

Microeconomics, 416

Mikoyan, A. J., 412

Miksch, Leonhard, 543

Mill, James, 163

Mill, John Stuart: on capital investment, 183; on competition vs. monopoly, 173; on crises, 189; distribution theory, 174; economic man concept, 172–73; economic theory, 181–85; *Essays on Some Unsettled Questions of Political Economy*, 183–84; on hypothetical assumptions, 174; on international trade, 184; *On Liberty*, 173; monetary theory, 188; *Principles of Political Economy*, 180, 181, 183, 185; on Ricardian economics, 171–73, 182–85; on social reform, 184–85; on static vs. dynamic analysis, 515; on wage fund theory, 183

Mills, F. C., 426

Mills, John, 189

Minimax principle, 577–78

Mirabeau, Marquis de, 36, 107–8; *L'Ami des hommes*, 107; *Philosophie rurele*, 108; *Theorie de l'impôt*, 108

Misère de la philosophie (Marx), 248

Mises, Ludwig von, 337, 350, 374, 383, 422, 458

Misselden, Edward, 47–48

"Mississippi scheme," 75, 98

Mitchell, Wesley C., 360–62, 426; busines cycle theory, 361, 477–78; social psychology, 360; statistical investigation, 361–62

Molina, Luis, 28

Molinari, Gustave de, 193

Mombert, Paul, 551

Monetary metals, 28–29, 42; foreign policy and, 45–46; inflation and, 42; international move-

Monetary metals (*cont.*)
ment of, 46–49, 67, 70, 81, 83; international
trade and, 531, 533, 536–37; national wealth
and, 43, 44, 46, 50–51, 84, 85, 92; ratio: value
relation of, 71; in Ricardian economics, 166.
See also Gold standard

Monetary policy: business cycle and, 487-88; international trade and, 332-33

Monetary theory, 52–55, 68–73, 467–75; in Austrian economics, 335–36, 470–73; balance
sheet vs. income accounts, 470; business cycle
and, 476–82; cash balance approach, 467–70;
claim concept, 337, 338; circulation velocity
and, 71, 80, 81, 88, 471; commodity (cost of
production) concept, 75, 87, 163, 338; Dominican concept, 29; economic evils and, 44; equations, 467–70; exchange value differentiation,
44, 467; fiduciary money problems, 73–76; in
German economics, 237–39, 374–75; income
concept, 338, 470–73; in international trade,
544–50; intrinsic value, 80; intrinsic value vs.
declared value concept, 43, 44, 71–72; Jesuit
concept, 29, 30; in marginal economics,
315–16, 332–43; Marxist, 256, 374, 375; metallic content / value relation, 71, 72; Neoscholastic, 43; of neutral money, 471–73;
nominalistic, 238; post-Thomistic, 23–25; price
theory and, 467–68; quantity concept, 70, 72,
82, 163, 338–43; quantity equations, 467–70;
quantity / price relation, 45; Ricardian
economics, 161–64, 185–89; "state" concept,
237–39, 338; Stockholm School, 495–96;
supply and demand and, 29; Thomistic concept,
13–14; in utilitarianism, 161–64

Money and Trade (Law), 74–76
Money changing, 17, 26–27
Money efficiency, 470
Money supply, 69, 70; capitalism and, 42; deficit
spending and, 509–10; fiduciary money and,
74–75; inflation and, 28, 29; interest rate and,
73; international price mechanism and, 70; Keynesian theory of, 498, 501, 504, 507; price
theory and, 52, 82, 89–90

Monopoly, 14, 67, 92, 109, 385–87, 395,
443–54; bilateral, 445; collective, 445; degree
measurement, 450–51; degree of resistance concept, 445; in economic planning, 456; of guilds,
41; in Ricardian economics, 173–74; trading
company, 41. *See also* Competition

Monopoly capitalism, 407
Montanari, Geminiano, 71
Montchrétien, Antoine de, 35; *Traicté de
l'oeconomie politique,* 50–51
Montesquieu, Charles de, 100–101
Moral calculus, 363
Moral philosophy, 121–22; neoscholastic econom-
ics, 241–42; Smith and, 125–26
More, Thomas, *Utopia,* 60

Morelly, André, 102
Morgenstern, Oskar, 373, 478; *Theory of Games*
(with Neumann), 576–78
Morris, William, 297
Mosse, Robert, 432
Müller, Adam, 211–12
Multiplier principle, 344, 501–2, 507, 519–27; in
international trade, 537–38
Mun, Thomas, 48–49
Mussolini, Benito, 385–86
Myrdal, Gunnar, 490–91
Mysticism, 59

Narodniki, 273
Nasse, Erwin, 216
National Bureau of Economic Research, 361
Nationalism, 372; in Germany, 213–19; organismic reasoning and, 372
National Socialism, 265, 372, 378, 379; economic
theory, 387–91
National states, 35; supremacy / fixed wealth rela-
tion, 35
National wealth, 110; agricultural production and,
106; feudalism and, 43; fixed magni-
tude / national supremacy and, 35; international
trade and, 43, 46; monetary metals and, 43, 44,
46, 50–51, 84, 85, 92; "natural" vs. "artifi-
cial," 77
Natorp, Paul, 224
Natural and Political Investigations . . . (Gaunt),
65
Natural Elements of Political Economy, The (Jen-
nings), 283
Natural law, 8, 9, 11, 34, 43, 59–65, 89, 90,
100–104, 112
Natural rights, 64
Natural theology, 6
Natur und Wesen der Staaten . . . (Justi), 95
Necker, Jacques, 113
Negotiable paper, 26
Neisser, Hans, 375, 376
Nemchinov, V. S., 406
Neokantianism, 224–25
Neomarginalism, 430
Neoplantonism, 4, 5, 32
Neoscholastics, 43, 44, 241–44
Netherlands: capitalist development in, 41; re-
ligious tolerance / trading policies relation in,
58; Renaissance in, 36
Net product (*produit net*) distribution, 105–7
Neumann, John von, *Theory of Games* (with Mor-
genstern), 576–78
Neutral money concept, 471–73; business cycle
theory and, 480–81
Newcomb, Simon, 339
New Deal, 360, 456
New Economic Policy (USSR), 397
New economics, 489–529

Newmarch, William, 175–76
New Tasks of the Soviets, The (Lenin), 397
Newton, Isaac, *Principles of Natural Philosophy*, 56
Nider, Johannes, 24
Nietzsche, Friedrich, 391
Nogaro, Bertrand, 430
Nominalism, 7, 20–23, 34, 36, 37, 40, 49, 63, 64, 79, 122, 309
Noncompeting groups concept, 293
Normative concepts, 224–25
North, Sir Dudley, 66, 70, 73; *Discourse upon Trade*, 67
Nourse, E. G., 450
Novarro, Martin di Azpilcueta, 29
Novum Organum (Bacon), 56
Numéraire, 287
Nurkse, Ragnar, 526

Obrecht, Georg, 91
Ockhamism, 33
Oesterreich . . . (Hornigk), 92
Ohlin, Bertil, 535–36
Oligopoly, 445, 450, 451, 453
On Liberty (Mill), 173
Ophélimité élémentaire, 284
Oppenheimer, Franz, 240, 273–74
Opportunity costs principle, 204, 282
Ordre naturel . . . , L' (Rivière), 108
Oresme, Nicole, 24
Organic composition of capital, 257, 272
Organismic economics, 209–44, 371–91; economic planning and, 381–87, 389; in Germany, 224–42; theoretical analysis, 230–35
Ortes, Giammaria, *Della economia nazionale*, 87
Osse, Melchior von, 91
Ostrovitianov, K. V., 408
Oswalt, H., 233
Oulès, Firmin, 430
Oversaving theory, 307–8
Overstone, Baron Samuel Jones Loyd, 188
Owen, Robert, 178–79
Oxford economists, 510

Palander, Tord, 490
Paley, William, 417
Palmer, J. Horsley, 186–87
Palmer's rule, 186–87
Pantaleoni, Maffeo, 515, 531
Paper money, 73–75, 98
Papi, Giuseppi Ugo, 527
Paracelsus, 59
Paradox of value, 13,127, 277
Paretian models, 430
Pareto, Vilfredo, 308–13, 386, 387, 419; decision-making theory, 573; sociological theory, 312–13; welfare economics, 463–65
Pareto's law, 312
Partnerships, 26

Patten, Simon N., 355–56
Pauperism, 76
Pawnbroking, 54
Peel's Resumption Bill (1819), 185
Peirce, Charles S., 356
Pereire brothers, 198
Period analysis multiplier, 519–20
Periodicals, 99, 107
Peripheral economies theory, 558
Perroux, François, 430, 433, 511
Pesch, Heinrich, 242
Petrarch, Francesco, 33
Petty, Sir William: on circulation velocity, 71; interest theory, 72; *Political Anatomy of Ireland*, 65; *Political Arithmetick*, 65; *Treatise of Taxes and Contributions*, 65, 71; value theory, 68–69; *Verbum Sapienti*, 71
Phalanges concept, 199
Philanglus, 76
Philippovich, Eugen, 230–31
Philosophie rurale (Mirabeau), 108
Philosophy of Wealth (Clark), 352
Physical productivity concept, 106
Physica subterranea (Becher), 90
Physiocratie . . . (Du Pont de Nemours), 108
Physiocrats, 81, 103–14; doctrine disintegration, 113–14; international trade theory, 113; philosophical background, 103–4; political organization, 108–9; rent theory, 157; Smith on, 127, socioeconomic doctrine, 107–12; *Tableau économique*, 104–7; utilitarianism and, 111–12
Piatier, André, 432
Pierson, Nicholas G., 327
Pigou, Arthur C., 306; business cycle theory, 483; on socialist planning, 458; wage theory, 442, 508; welfare economics, 462
Pigou effect, 508
Pirou, Gaëtan, 431
Place, Francis, 183
Plan Monnet, 433
Plato, 17
Pleasure / pain concept, 64, 142–43
Plekhanov, Georgi, 264, 267
Pohle, L., 229
Pollexfen, John, 76
Political Anatomy of Ireland (Petty), 65
Political Arithmetick (Petty), 65
Political Discourses (Hume), 82
Politische Discurs . . . (Becher), 92
Population theory, 76–78, 81, 85, 88, 92, 97; of Malthus, 153–54; in Ricardian economics, 152–54; of Smith, 152; in utilitarianism, 152–54
Positivism, 195, 198
Pothier, Robert Joseph, 110
Potter, William, 71, 74
Pragmatism, 355–60, 425
Prebisch, Raul, 547

Precious metals. *See* Monetary metals
Predöhl, Andreas, 367, 542
Preference analysis, 573
Preference curves, 463–65
Preiser, Erich, 436
Preobazhensky, C. E., 397
Price stabilization policy, 473–75
Price theory, 52, 68–73; in Austrian economics, 342; circulation velocity and, 88; currency debasement and, 45; expectations in, 472–73; functional, 418; in German economics, 202, 232; income approach, 342–43; inelastic demand and, 66; marginal utility analysis, 364–65; mathematical formulations, 87; monetary theory and, 467–68; money supply and, 52, 70, 82, 89–90; post-Thomistic, 24–25; quantitative relationships, 71; Ricardian economics, 150–51; Smith on, 150; supply and demand and, 85, 87; value / cost relation, 80; value theory and, 52, 373. *See also* Just price
Prince-Smith, John, 203
Principles of Economics (Marshall), 298–306
Principles of Natural Philosophy (Newton), 56
Principles of Political Economy (J. S. Mill), 181, 183, 185, 189
Private property: opposition to, 100, 102; Thomistic concept of, 10–12
Probability analysis, 27, 66; in decision making, 574–76
Problems of Planning in the U.S.S.R. (Strumilin), 403, 405
Producer associations, 199
Production factors, 76
Production theory: in Austrian economics, 437; factor price equalization, 535–36; in German economics, 236–37; marginal utility analysis, 365; in Marshallian economics, 304–5; Marxian, 251–53; opportunity costs principle, 282; in Ricardian economics, 145
Productive contribution concept, 317–18
Productivity, 118, 160; labor supply factor, 76–78; maximization, 197–98; in organismic economics, 231–32; in Ricardian economics, 159; technology and, 77
Product substitution curves, 534
Profit concept, 155, 159
Profit maximization, 63, 442, 455–56
Profit motive, 26, 27, 39, 44, 109, 115–16
Profit theory, 439–42; in Austrian economics, 329–30; bolshevist view of, 409; *ex ante* vs. *ex post*, 441; in French economics, 441; in German economics, 233–34; in marginal economics, 329–30; Marxist, 257–59, 261; in Ricardian economics, 158–61; of Smith, 130–31, 159; utilitarianism, 158–61
Projet d'une dixme royale (Vauban), 97
Prolegomenon, 585–609; Baconian economics, 587–91; Benthamite economics, 591–94; Carte-
sian economics, 587–91; dialectic economics, 596–98; equilibrium concept, 605–8; hypothetical reasoning refinement, 598–603; intuitional economics, 594–96; Ricardian economics, 591–94, 603–4
Proletariat, 273–74; dialectic materialism and, 265
Propensity to consume, 498–501, 504, 506, 507, 511
Propensity to import, 537
Propensity to invest, 498, 499, 504, 507
Protectionism, 67–68, 78, 83, 538–41; in United States, 206–7. *See also* Mercantilism
Protestantism, 53, 54, 89–90
Proudhon, Pierre J., 199–200
Psychological factor, 432; in business cycle theory, 483–84, 486; in Keynesian theory, 498, 506; in marginal utility analysis, 279–81, 289–91, 314–19
Psychological marginalism, 363–66
Psychological motivation, 61, 62
Psychological nominalism, 122
Public administration: cameralism concept, 90–96; in Germany, 91
Public interest, self-interest and, 120–21, 124
Public loans, 25
Public works, 168, 488, 493
Pufendorf, Samuel von, 60, 90
Purchasing power, 470–71; parity theory, 533–34

Quantitative analysis, 361
Quantity equations, in monetary theory, 467–70
Quesnay, François, 103–7, 109–11, 262; Cantillon influence, 111; *Tableau économique*, 104–7
Quod Apostolici Muneris, 241

Racism, in Germany, 388, 389
Rae, John, 176
Ramée, Pierre La, 33
Ranke, Leopold von, 213, 217
Rareté, 284, 286
Rathenau, Walther, 382
Rationalism, 58, 298
Rationality factor, 62, 63, 454–55, 621–23
Rau, Karl Heinrich, 201
Raymond, Daniel, 206
Read, Samuel, 177
Realists, 309
Reality concept, 7
Reasoning: deductive, 56–58, 65, 123, 161, 171–72, 175, 200, 220–21, 309, 416; inductive, 66, 171–72, 220–21, 416, 430; intuitive, 221, 222, 225–27, 231
Reformation, 36, 39, 53–54
Registration period concept, 492
Regrating, 14
Relief policy, 76

Religious issues, 296. *See also specific dogmas and orders*
Renaissance, 32–38
Renner, Karl, 270
Rent concept, 155
Rent theory, 440; in German economics, 202, 204; in marginal economics, 330–31; Marshallian, 303; Physiocratic, 157; in Ricardian economics, 157–58; of Smith, 130, 157
Reparations payments, 536
Reply to the Paradoxes of M. de Malestroit (Bodin), 45
Report of a Parliamentary Committee on Monetary Conditions in Ireland (1804), 163
Report on the Subject of Manufactures (Hamilton), 206
Rerum Novarum, 241
Residues concept, 312–13
Resource allocation: economic growth and, 558–59; in welfare economics, 306–7
Restoration of the Political Sciences (Haller), 212
Restriction Act (1797), 162
Revolutionary movements, 217; class struggle and, 264; revisionist, 267
Revolutionary socialism, 271. *See also* Bolshevism
Revolutionary theory: in bolshevism, 397–98; Marx on, 249; in Saint-Simonianism, 198
Reynaud, P. L., 432
Ricardian economics, 146–66; analytical shortcomings, 175–76; assumptions, 489; British imperialism and, 292–98; business cycle theory, 344; capital theory, 158–61, 168; credit theory, 161–64; distribution theory, 145–46, 154–61, 174; equilibrium principle, 144–45; exchange relations, 146–50; four postulates, 171; in Germany, 203–6; gold standard and, 185–87; interest theory, 158–61; international trade theory, 164–66; labor cost theory of value, 176–79, 185; Marx on, 248–49, 253–58; mathematical analysis, 185; maximization principle, 173; methodology, 143–46, 169–75, 293–98; modifications, 179–89; monetary theory, 161–64, 166, 185–89, 338; on monopoly, 173–74; moral factor, 170; political factor, 169–70; population factor, 152–54; price theory, 150–51; production factors, 145; productivity concept, 159; profit theory, 158–61; prolegomenon, 591–94, 603–4; rent theory, 157–58; savings theory, 159; on technology, 152; theoretical analysis, 166–89; in United States, 206–8; utilitarian criticism, 175–79; value theory, 146–50; wage theory; 156–57. *See also* Marshallian economics
Ricardian socialists, 177–79
Ricardo, David: criticism of, 169; utilitarianism of, 143–46
Ricardo effect, 481

Ricca-Salerno, Guisseppe, 327
Ricci, Umberto, 563
Richard of Middletown, 15
Rickert, Heinrich, 225
Risk factor, 34; in business cycle theory, 509, 510; in capitalism theory, 40; in contracts, 19; in decision making, 574; vs. uncertainties, 440
Rist, Charles, 223
Ritschl, Hans, 542
Rivière, Mercier de la, *L'Ordre naturel,* 108, 111
Robbins, Lionel, 420–22
Robertson, Dennis Holme, 468, 483
Robinson, E.A.G., 528
Robinson, Joan, 442, 447–48, 522
Roche-Agussol, M., 362
Rodbertus, Johann Karl, 203, 205–6
Rogers, Thorold, 294
Roll, Eric, 36
Romagnosi, Giovanni D., 193
Roman law, 389
Romanticism, 211–12
Roos, Charles F., 563
Roosa currency plan, 549
Roscellinus de Compiegne, 21
Roscher, Wilhelm, 214–15
Rosenstein-Rodan, Paul N., 472–73, 517
Rossi, Pellegrino, 190
Rostow, Walt W., 554–55; *The Stages of Economic Growth,* 555
Rothaker, Erich, 390
Roundabout production concept, 437
Rousseau, Jean Jacques, 102
Royal letters patent of monopoly, 41
Rueff, Jacques, 429–30, 442
Ruskin, John, 296
Russia. *See* Union of Soviet Socialist Republics
Russian revolution, 275, 396; Proudhon influence, 200

Sacra doctrine (supernatural theology), 6
St. Petersburg paradox, 279
Saint-Simon, Comte de, Claude Henri de Rouvroy, 197–98
Saitzew, Manuel, 487
Salamanca, University of, 27–30
Samuelson, Paul A.: dynamic model, 522; on Keynesian theory, 521–22; "revealed preference" theorem, 506; static vs. dynamic analysis, 518
Saumaise, Claude de, 55
Sauvy, Alfred, 434
Savage, Leonard J., 575
Savigny, Friedrich K. von, 213
Savings theory, 307–8; business cycle and, 344, 482; capital accumulation in, 83; forced, 472; investment relation, 307, 491, 492, 494, 500–502, 509; Keynesian, 499, 500, 502, 505; in Ricardian economics, 159

Sax, Emil, 320

Say, Jean Baptiste: distribution theory, 155, 160; influence, 190–91; law of markets, 151, 168, 191; monetary theory, 162; *Traité d'économie politique,* 135; value theory, 148–49

Say, Leon, 193

Scaccia, Sigismondo, 43–44

Scarcity concept, 195

Scaruffi, Gasparo, 44

Schäffle, A., 233

Schanz, G., 222

Scheel, H. von, 216

Schelle, Gustave, 193

Schelling, F.W.J. von, 210

Schlesinger, Karl, 336

Schlettwein, Johann August, 114

Schmidt, Konrad, 258, 270

Schmoller, Gustav, 36, 216–23, 372

Schneider, Erich, 450

Scholasticism, 3–20, 45–47, 53, 54, 56–59. *See also* Thomistic economics

Schonberg, G., 222

School of Salamanca, 27–30

Schroder, Wilhelm von, 90–93; *Furstliche Schatz- und Rent Kammer,* 90

Schüller, Richard, 532

Schulze-Gävernitz, Gerhard von, 222

Schumpeter, Joseph, 423–24; business cycle theory, 346–49, 484–85; economic theory, 235; interest theory, 438; on materialistic interpretation of history, 252; monetary theory, 337, 470; price theory, 342–43; profit theory, 440; socioeconomic analysis, 452

Scientific method, 21–23, 56, 123

Scitovsky, Tibor, 465

Scrittori Classici Italiani di economia politica, 193

Scrope, Georg Julius Poulett, 153, 177

Seager, H. R., 328

Seckendorff, Veit Ludwig von, 91

Security factor, 62

Sée, Henri, 223

Seeley, John R., 292

Seignobos, Charles, 223

Self-interest principle, 61–62, 65, 86, 120–21, 124–26; Smith on, 132–34

Self-regulating mechanisms, 66, 67, 79–83

Seligman, E.R.A., 251, 252

Senior, Nassau William: economic theory, 179–81; on hypothetical assumptions, 174; on law of diminishing returns, 174; on political factor, 170; population theory, 153; Ricardian economics postulates, 171

Sensini, Guido, 330

Sensualists, 100, 101

Separation of powers concept, 101

Serra, Antonio, 44, 49

Shackle, G. L., 576

Shaw, George Bernard, 297

Shove, G. F., 447

Sidgwick, Henry, 293

Simiand, François, 431–32

Simmel, Georg, 238

Single tax principle, 112, 207–8

Sismondi, J.C.L. Simonde de, 196–97

Slavery, 11–12

Slichter, Sumner H., 426, 457

Slutsky, Eugen, 366, 485

Small, Albion W., 91

Smith, Adam: American influence of, 206–8; capital theory, 126, 131; on competition, 126, 133–34; distribution theory, 126, 129–31, 154–55; *Essays on Philosophical Subjects,* 132; free trade theory, 131; German followers of, 200–206; on government regulation, 133–34; influence of, 190–208; labor theory, 126, 128; on maximization principle, 133; on mercantilism, 36, 126–27; monetary theory, 131, 161; on monopoly, 133; moral philosophy, 125–26; on motivation, 125; natural order concept, 132–34; on Physiocrats, 114, 127; population theory, 152; price theory, 150; profit theory, 130–31, 159; rent theory, 130, 157; on self-interest, 132–34; on taxation, 127; *Theory of Moral Sentiments,* 125; value theory, 127–29, 147–49; wage theory, 129–30; on want satisfaction, 133; *Wealth of Nations,* 126–35, 139, 140

Snyder, Carl, 474

Social class, 9, 433

Social collectivities concept, 7–10, 218

Social contract, 34–35, 61, 62, 98, 102

Social costs, 307

Social credit scheme, 482

Social Democratic parties, 373, 393, 395

Social Economics (Cassel), 372

Social energetics, 230

Social evolution, 295

Socialism: in Austria, 382; in England, 384; in Germany, 219, 234, 239–41, 372–73, 382; in Italy, 240–41; marginal economics in, 311; monetary theory, 335; post–World War I, 382

Socialist movements, 192, 296–97

Socialist planning, 457–60

Socialists of the chair, 206, 229

Socialist theory: in France, 196–200; in Germany, 206; in United States, 208

Socialization, Commission for (1919), 383

Socialization of production, 382–84

Social order, 124

Social productivity, marginal, 560

Social Theory of Capitalism (Heimann), 395

Social values concept, 362–63

Sociological approach, 62–65, 209–12, 217–18, 227–28, 360, 428–34, 452

Solidarism, 242–43

Sombart, Werner, 39, 226, 378, 379; *Die drei Nationalökonomien*, 379–80

Some . . . Consequences of the Lowering of Interest . . . (Locke), 69

Sonnenfels, Joseph von, 95; *Grundsätze der Polizey, Handlung und Finanz*, 96

Sorel, Georges, 269, 385–86

Soto, Domingo de, 29

Spain: clericalism in, 58; monetary metals from New World, 28–29; seventeenth-century economics in, 51–52; Thomistic economics, 27–30

Spann, Uthmar, 7, 211, 379

Spence, Thomas, 169

Spencer, Herbert, 217, 295–96

Spengler, Oswald, *Decline of the West*, 387

Spiethoff, Arthur, 217, 380

Spranger, E., 229

Sraffa, Piero, 446–47

Stachle, Hans, 373

Stackelberg, Heinrich von, 445–46

Stages of Economic Growth, The (Rostow), 555

Stagnation theorem, 509–12, 523, 551, 552

Stalin, Joseph, *Foundations of Leninism*, 397; politico-economic strategy, 398–402, 408–11

Stammler, Rudolf, 224

State socialism, 199, 269

Static analysis, 515–19; comparative, 518

Statistics, 65–66, 176, 426; administrative, 93. *See also* Mathematical analysis

Stein, Lorenz von, 247, 262

Sternberg, Fritz, 394

Steuart, Sir James, 84–85; on law of diminishing returns, 154; monetary theory, 84; population theory, 85; price theory, 85

Stigler, George, 450

Stirner, Max, 248

Stockholm School, 489–96; employment theory, 493–94; monetary theory, 495–96

Stolzmann, Rudolf, 225

Strigl, Richard, 420

Strumilin, S. G., *Problems of Planning in the U.S.S.R.*, 403, 405

Struve, Petr, 410

Suarez, Francisco, 43

Subjective value, 281, 316

Substance concept, 5–6

Substitutive goods, 310, 318

Sully, Duke of, 50

Summa Theologica (Aquinas), 4

Summa totius logicae (William of Ockham), 21–22

Sunspot theory, 344

Supply and demand: price theory and, 85, wage theory and, 130

Surplus concept, 303

Surplus value theory, 255–56

Suslov, M. A., 412

Sweezy, Paul, 266

Syndicalism, 269, 386

System concept, 623–26

Tableau économique, 104–7

Tabula rasa, 63

Tariffs, 538–41

Tautscher, A., 244

Taussig, Frank William, 532–33

Tawney, Richard H., 264

Taxation, 97; single tax principle, 111, 112, 207–8; Smith on, 127

Taylor, Frederick W., 332

Technocrats, 230

Technology: economic growth and, 553; productivity and, 77; Ricardian economics and, 152; utilitarianism and, 152

Temple, Sir William, 77

Temporary National Economic Committee (1941), 271

Terms of trade concept, 532

Tertullian, 10

Textile industry, "putting out" system, 41

Théorie de l'impôt (Mirabeau), 108

Theory of gluts (Malthus), 168

Theory of Moral Sentiments (Smith), 125

Theory of Political Economy, The (Jevons), 283

Theory of specific causation, 69

Thomistic economics, 3–20; disintegration, 20–30; just price concept, 12, 14–16; labor in, 14–15; money concept, 13–14; private property concept, 10–12; on slavery, 11–12; social collectivities concept, 7–10; in Spain, 27–30; on unlawful profit, 15–17; on usury, 17–20; value concept, 12–14

Thomistic philosophy, 33

Thompson, William, 178

Thornton, Henry, 162

Thorp, Willard L., 478

Thünen, Johann Heinrich von, 203–5, 278

Time factor, 80, 176, 416, 418–19, 616–18; in dynamic analysis, 515–18; in interest theory, 327; in marginal utility analysis, 320–22; Stockholm School on, 489, 490, 492, 494, 495

Tinbergen, Jan, 466–67; business cycle models, 566–67; econometric theory, 563–65; static vs. dynamic analysis, 518

"To each according to his capacity, . . .", 198

Tomski, Mikhail, 398

Toniolo, Guiseppe, 241

Tönnies, Ferdinand, 218

Tooke, Thomas, 187; price theory, 342; on Ricardian economics, 175

Torrens, Robert, 157, 164

Totalitarian economics, 385–91

Toynebee, Arnold, 294

Trade, fiduciary money and, 74–76. *See also* Balance of trade; International trade
Trading companies, 41, 47, 48, 67, 68
Traicté de l'oeconomie politique (Le Montchrétien), 50
Traité d'économie politique (Say), 135
Treatise on Money (Keynes), 469–70, 479–80
Treatise on Social Economics (Wieser), 318, 457–58
Treatise of Taxes and Contributions (Petty), 65, 71
Triffin, Robert, 441
Triffin plan, 549
Troeltsch, Ernst, 225
Trosne, Guillaume François Le, 107, 109, 113; *De l'ordre social,* 108
Trotsky, Leon, 273, 274, 397–98
Trusts, 384, 386, 388, 451
Tucker, Josiah, 84
Tugan-Baranowsky, Michael, 269–70, 345
Tugwell, R. G., 425–26
Turgot, Anne Robert Jacques, 110–11; capital theory, 118; interest theory, 118; on law of diminishing returns, 119, 154; productivity theory, 118; value theory, 117–18
Two Treatises on Government (Locke), 64, 68

Unam Sanctam (Boniface VIII), 7
Underconsumption, 377; in Marxism, 272
Underdeveloped countries. *See* Developing countries
Unearned income theory, 297
Unearned increments, 112
Union of Soviet Socialist Republics, 59, 371; administrative statistics, 403, 405–6; agriculture in, 397–99, 401, 409–10, 412; bolshevist movement in, 273–75; business cycle theory of, 485–87; capital investment policy of, 411–12; cost accounting in, 405; cultural controls in, 407; dictatorship interpretation of, 400; economic criticism of, 410–11; economic growth in, 403, 404; economic planning in, 397, 399–407; economic teaching in, 401–2; economic textbooks in, 408–11; Five-Year Plans of, 399–406, 409; foreign policy of, 397; industrial management of, 403–4; international trade of, 541; Marxist influence in, 267; New Economic Policy of, 397; post-Stalinist reforms in, 412; Soviet block economy and, 406–7
Unions, 268. *See also* Labor *entries*
United States: balance of payments and, 545–46; capital theory in, 207; econometric models, 566–67, 570; economic growth in, 556–57; economic planning in, 456–57; Keynesian theory in, 511, 512; marginal economics in, 352–55, 362–64; market control in, 451; pragmatism in, 355–58; price stabilization policy of,

474; protectionist policy of, 206–7; Ricardian economics in, 206–8; Smith influence in, 206–8; socialist theory, 208; stagnation theorem in, 511; university chairs of economics, 208; as welfare state, 360; worldwide business fluctuations and, 528
Universal economy (wealth), 43
Universalism, 5, 7, 243
Ustariz, Geronimo, 51
Usury: Dominican concept, 28, 29; Jesuit concept, 30; post-Thomistic theory, 25; prohibitions, 17–20, 53–55, 158; Thomistic concept, 17–20
Utilitarianism, 39, 59–65, 86–88, 111–12, 115, 120–35, 363; of Jeremy Bentham, 141–43; capital theory, 158–61; credit theory, 161–64; distribution theory, 154–61; general methodology, 139–43; interest theory, 158–61; international trade theory, 164–65; marginal economics and, 279, 283–85; methodological issues, 169–74; monetary theory, 161–64; population factor, 152–54; profit theory, 158–61; Ricardian economics and, 143–46, 175–79; technology and, 152
Utility theory, 461–66
Utopia (More), 60–61
Utopian theory, 60, 192–200

Valla, Lorenzo, 33
Valor impositus, 72
Value judgments, 228–30
Value paradox, 13
Value theory, 68–73, 629–31; in Austrian economics, 373–74; in British economics, 277–78; cost of production and, 128; disutility factor, 128; exchange / individual valuations relations, 281–82; in French economics, 278; in German economics, 201–2, 373–74; individual valuation, 119, 120, 281–82; intrinsic value in, 72; land-labor input and, 79–80; marginalism, 373; Marxist, 254–59; Physiocratic, 106; post-Thomistic, 23–25; price theory and, 52, 373; Ricardian economics, 146–50; Smith on, 127–29, 147–49; subjective value concept, 115–20; substance concept, 122; surplus value in, 112; Thomistic doctrine, 12–14; want / scarcity relation, 71, 72; welfare economics and, 463, 464, 466. *See also* Labor cost theory of value
Vanderlint, Jacob, 70
Varge, E., 408
Variations theory, 421
Vauban, Marquis de, *Projet d'une dixme royale,* 97
Vaughan, Rice, 53
Veblen, Thorstein Bunde, 39, 271, 356–58, 425–28; influence, 358–62
Vecchio, Gustavo del, 527

Velocity of goods circulation concept, 470
Velocity of money circulation concept, 71, 80, 81, 88, 471
Verbum Sapienti (Petty), 71
Verein für Sozialpolitik: business cycle debate, 377–78; socialization debate, 392; value theory debate, 373–74
Verri, Pietro, 86; *Elementi del commercio,* 86; *Meditazioni sull' economia politica,* 86
Vico, Giovanni Battista, 116
Victorian Age, 292–98
Villeneuve-Bargemont, Jean Paul Alban de, 241
Vincent, A., 434
Viner, Jacob, 532, 539
Vishinsky, Andrej, 400
Vleugels, W., 374
Vogelsang, K. von, 241
Voigt, Andreas, 229
Volkgeist, 210–11
Voltaire, 101

Wagemann, Ernst, 376, 378; *Allgemeine Geldlehre,* 375
Wage rates: foreign enterprise development and, 83, 84; incentives and, 78; international comparison of, 78
Wage theory, 442–43; in Austrian economics, 331–32; in German economics, 202–3, 205–6, 234–35; imputation principle, 318; in marginal economics, 331–32; marginal productivity analysis and, 442–43; price theory and, 78; residual, 130; in Ricardian economics, 156–57, 178–79; Smith on, 129–30; supply and demand, 130; wage fund, 130, 183, 322. *See also* Just wage
Wagner, Adolf, 242
Wald, Abraham, 567
Walker, Francis A., 353
Wallace, Robert, 84, 153
Walras, Auguste, 195
Walras, Leon, 192, 280–81; cash balance approach, 341; *Études d'économie appliquée,* 289; marginal utility analysis, 280–81, 285–89; monetary theory, 335–36; price-cost equation, 325
Walrasian economics, 430, 459–60
Walras's law, 286
Want, randomness of, 62
Want satisfaction, 39, 64, 115, 280; in marginal utility analysis, 309–11; optimum collective, 211–12; Smith on, 133
Ware, Norman J., 112
"War of all against all," 62, 63
Warville, Jacques Pierre Brissot de, 102
Wealth of Nations (Smith), 126–35, 139, 140; evaluation of, 134–35; influence of, 134–35; structure of, 126–27

Webb, Beatrice, 298
Webb, Sydney, 298
Weber, Adolf, 373
Weber, Alfred, 542
Weber, Ernst H., 279
Weber, Max, 39, 227–29
Weippert, Georg, 379
Welfare economics, 306–8, 461–67; economic planning and, 465; efficiency analysis in, 464, 465; indifference curves and, 463–65; preference curves and, 463–65; value theory and, 463, 464, 466
Welfare state, 95, 96, 363; United States as, 360
Wesen des Christentums, Das (Feuerbach), 247
West, Edward, 154, 157
Westergaard, Harold L., 327
Whately, Richard, 172; . . . *Political Economy,* 179
Wheatley, George, 531
Whewell, William, 185
Whitlesley, Charles R., 548
Wicksell, Knut, 316; on *agio* theory, 327; business cycle theory, 349–50; capital interest theory, 322–24; cash balance approach, 341; economy model, 489–92; on equilibrium conditions, 490–91; on exhaustion problem, 325; influence of, 415; *Lectures on Political Economy,* 322; monetary theory, 323–24, 337; on monetary vs. real (natural) interest rate, 489–91; price theory, 323–24; savings / investment relation, 491, 492; unemployment theory, 492–93
Wicksteed, Philip Henry, 281, 317; laws of life, 363; marginal productivity analysis, 325–26
Wieser, Friedrich von, 284, 314–18, 423; alternative costs principle, 316–17; interest theory, 328; monetary theory, 336; *Treatise on Social Economics,* 318, 457–58
Wieser's law, 317
Wilbrandt, R., 382
Will, concept of, 34
William of Ockham, *Summa totius logicae,* 21–22
Williams, John H., 533
Wilson, James, 189
Wilson, Thomas, 54
Windelband, W., 225
Windelblech, Karl Georg, 206
Wirth, Max, 203
Wirtschaftstheorie der Gegenwart, 418
Wold, Herman O. R., 569
Wolf, J., 258
Wolfe, Martin, 554
Wolff, Christian von, 93, 94
Wolowski, Louis, 190
Work ethic, 121; Scholastic vs. Calvinistic, 39
World Bank, 547

World War I: economic planning, 381; German
    inflation, 239; postwar economics, 371, 393,
    415, 417, 425, 429
World War II: economic planning, 460–61; inter-
    national trade and, 544–50; postwar economics,
    371–72, 551
Worswick, G.D.N., 510
Wright, D. McCord, 438
Wunderlich, Frieda, 232

Yntema, I. D., 533
Young, Allyn Abbott, 360, 550
Yugoslavia, 407

Zeisl, H., 374
Zeitgeist, 246
Zeuthen, Ferdinand, 444
Zhdanov, Andrei, 407–8
Zwiedineck-Südenhorst, Otto von, 445

ABOUT THE AUTHOR

KARL PRIBRAM held important positions in the Austrian government before and during the First World War and concurrently lectured at the University of Vienna. He served as chief of research with the International Labour Office in Geneva in the 1920s. Thereafter, he was professor of economic sciences at the University of Frankfurt am Main. He joined the staff of the Brookings Institution in Washington, D.C., in 1934. Later he moved to the newly founded Social Security Board and after a few years accepted a position with the U.S. Tariff Commission. During most of that time he also taught economics at the graduate school of the American University. His comprehensive program of social legislation, written for the new Republic of Austria after the First World War, served as a model for similar laws in other nations. He was the author of a number of books and scores of articles in several languages in European and American journals. Among his works are *Cartel Problems, Conflicting Patterns of Thought,* and *Unemployment as a World Problem.*